CONSTITUTIONAL LAW

Custom Textbook Series for Hillsborough Community College

Criminal Justice Undergraduate Studies Program

Taken From:
Constitutional Values: Governmental Powers and Individual Freedoms,
by Daniel E. Hall and John P. Feldmeier

Criminal Procedure: Constitution and Society, Fifth Edition
by Marvin Zalman

Learning Solutions

New York Boston San Francisco
London Toronto Sydney Tokyo Singapore Madrid
Mexico City Munich Paris Cape Town Hong Kong Montreal

Cover Art: Courtesy of Hillsborough Community College

Taken from:

Constitutional Values: Governmental Powers and Individual Freedoms
by Daniel E. Hall and John P. Feldmeier
Copyright © 2009 by Pearson Education, Inc.
Published by Prentice Hall
Upper Saddle River, New Jersey 07458

Criminal Procedure: Constitution and Society, Fifth Edition
by Marvin Zalman
Copyright © 2008, 2005, 2002 by Pearson Education, Inc.
Published by Prentice Hall

This special edition published in cooperation with Pearson Learning Solutions.

All trademarks, service marks, registered trademarks, and registered service marks are the property of their respective owners and are used herein for identification purposes only.

Printed in the United States of America

4 5 6 7 8 9 10 V092 16 15 14 13 12 11

2009340102

WH

www.pearsonhighered.com

ISBN 10: 0-558-47215-X
ISBN 13: 978-0-558-47215-3

CONTENTS

Taken from:
Constitutional Values: Governmental Powers and Individual Freedoms
by Daniel E. Hall and John P. Feldmeier

Taken from:
Criminal Procedure: Constitution and Society, Fifth Edition
by Marvin Zalman

CHAPTER 1

The Meaning of Criminal Procedure   2

CHAPTER 4

Arrest and Stop under the Fourth Amendment   186

CHAPTER 7

Interrogation and the Law of Confessions   374

1 History of the Constitution

An assembly of demi-gods.

Thomas Jefferson, commenting on the delegates to the Constitutional Convention

1.1 CONSTITUTIONS AND RULE OF LAW

This book is concerned with constitutional law. But what exactly is a constitution? *Ballentine's Legal Dictionary* defines *constitution* as "[t]he system of fundamental principles by which a nation . . . is governed. A nation's constitution may be written or unwritten." In short, a constitution is fundamental law. In terms of a hierarchy, a constitution sits at the apex and all forms of law below it (statutes, ordinances, regulations, executive orders) must conform to it. Constitutional law is the foundation upon which government is built and other laws are created. Hence, an understanding of constitutional law is imperative in any law-related endeavor.

The influence of the United States Constitution is much broader than commonly realized. For example, the daily actions of police officers are guided by many constitutional provisions, such as the Fourth Amendment (prohibition of unreasonable searches and seizures). Attorneys, process servers, and legal assistants must contend with constitutional law in nearly every case. As examples, the due process guarantees of the Fifth and Fourteenth Amendments regulate service of process (especially on out-of-state defendants), the full faith and credit clause provides the law for enforcing foreign judgments, and many clients present cases that arise directly under the Constitution.

A constitution may be written or unwritten. The United States has a written constitution, whereas England has an unwritten one. In England, the rights of citizens are secured through the common law, customs, and several Acts of Parliament. There is no single constitutional document. Some commentators argue that England does not have a constitution, because Parliament is free to abolish all the rights enjoyed by the people. Others contend that these rights are so much a part of English society that they are secure against parliamentary intrusion. Today, most nations have written constitutions. The Constitution of the United States is the oldest written constitution in the world.

This book examines the law of the United States Constitution. Important historical and social influences are discussed, as are institutions (e.g., the United States Supreme Court), constitutional methodology, and case law. American constitutional law is commonly divided into two fields of study: one focusing on governmental authorities and structures and another examining civil liberties. This text addresses both, as well as the values that underpin the Constitution.

In terms of development, legal systems and nations are often characterized as either adhering to rule of law or not. Rule of law is achieved in a legal system if the following elements are present:

1. There is fundamental law
2. that limits the authority of government and
3. is enforceable by citizens.[2]

The United States operates under rule of law because there is fundamental law (federal and state constitutions) that is enforceable by citizens in the courts through judicial review.

To understand why the framers chose the particular governmental architecture they did, a brief historical context must be drawn.

YOUR CONSTITUTIONAL VALUES

In each of the following chapters, you will find a special feature entitled *Your Constitutional Values*. In this feature you will find examples of constitutional conflicts that did not make it to the Supreme Court of the United States for resolution. These case studies illustrate that constitutional law occurs at all levels and in all branches of government. Consistent with the adage that "all politics is local," These case studies illustrate that constitutional conflicts occur with relative frequency in communities all around the nation.

As your read *Your Constitutional Values*, consider the following:

1. What values are in conflict?
2. What is the state of the law? Does precedent adequately consider all the values at stake? If not, how can you distinguish this case from the existing precedent?
3. Has this or a similar case occurred in your community or state?

1.2 ARTICLES OF CONFEDERATION

After the colonists arrived in what is now known as the United States, they established colonies. The original thirteen states were established from the geographical boundaries of these colonies. Although the states were largely autonomous and self-governing, they remained, ultimately, governed by England. Each state's governmental structure and relationship with England varied, but all shared common grievances with their mother country that led to the war for independence. Their declaration of independence was issued in 1776. Independence was won in 1781.

Even before independence was declared, the states had established a body to meet and address issues of national concern, the Continental Congress. The Continental Congress first met in Philadelphia on September 5, 1774. It operated from this date until 1781. This organization, though national in representation, did not have the authority* to make binding laws. Its authority was primarily limited to raising an army and conducting diplomacy.

By the time the Declaration of Independence was adopted, there had been discussions in the Continental Congress concerning the adoption of a constitution to formally recognize a confederacy of the thirteen colonies. On June 7, 1776, Richard Henry Lee, a delegate to the Congress from Virginia, introduced a resolution that declared the "United Colonies" to be "free and independent states, that they are absolved from all allegiance to the British Crown, and that all political connection between them and the State of Great Britain is, and ought to be, totally dissolved." Additionally, the resolution called for the development of a plan of confederation to be submitted to the states.[1] The resolution was adopted on July 2, 1776, and incorporated into the Declaration of Independence, which was largely drafted by Thomas Jefferson, on July 4, 1776.

It was not until 1781 that the colonies adopted the Articles of Confederation and Perpetual Union, the first constitution of the United States. Under the Articles, the Continental Congress was disbanded and replaced by the Confederation Congress. Although the new Congress had more authority than its predecessor, the states continued to be the most powerful political entities. It was proclaimed in the Articles that "[e]ach state retains its sovereignty, freedom and independence, and every power, jurisdiction and right, which is not expressly delegated to the united states, in Congress assembled." Politically, the United States was a loose union of independent and sovereign states and members of the Congress were little more than ambassadors representing their respective states. As expressly stated in the Articles, the states entered into a "firm league of friendship."[3]

Not many years passed before this league proved unworkable. The states were distant from one another. In an age without modern travel and technological means to disseminate information, this was problematic. Compounding the problem, they were distant in more ways than miles; they differed in history, culture, and politics. The result was parochialism, localism, and an interest in empowering the states rather than the national government. In the end, the states proved to be too independent and powerful; the national government too dependent and powerless.

Under the Articles of Confederation, the national government was responsible for negotiating treaties with foreign governments. That authority, however, was thwarted by the authority of the states to tax imports and exports, regardless of any treaties negotiated by the national government. Although the national government had the authority to declare war, it had no authority to establish a standing army. If it declared war, it could enlist volunteers, but lacked the power of conscription. It could request the assistance of state militias, but the states could refuse. Even more, funding for war efforts came from the states.[4]

Also, each state could prohibit the export and import of goods. The consequence was inconsistent and often competing commercial laws between the states. For the same reasons, foreign governments and merchants were discouraged from trading with the United States.

Jealousies between the states led to factionalism. Nine of the thirteen states had their own navies. Territorial disputes, as well as disputes over the authority to control the nation's waterways, plagued the nation.[5] Many of the states were engaged in economic war with one another and there were concerns that civil war would destroy the union.

The national government was clearly financially subservient to the states. Specifically, it did not have the authority to raise revenues directly from its citizens. The Articles provided that the states were to make contributions to the national treasury. However, the contributions were to be raised by action of each state and the national government lacked the authority to compel a state to contribute. As a result, the national government suffered financial difficulties because many of the states were regularly in arrears in their payments. As a result, the national government itself could not pay debts it owed to foreigners and citizens.

Governmental structure under the Articles was also confused. There was no independent executive. The president of the Congress served as the nation's highest executive officer, but the role of the president was not clearly understood and confusion between legislative and executive authority resulted. Many executive responsibilities were performed by legislative committees rather than the president—a practice that proved to be ineffective.

There was no national judiciary, except that the Congress selected four judges to hear cases in the territory northwest of the Ohio River and a Court of Capture heard appeals from the state courts in admiralty cases.[6] Otherwise, there was no national court to bring the national perspective to litigation or to develop a uniform national jurisprudence.

The private sector was also affected. Inflation was high and the laws governing commerce differed from state to state. Inconsistent and often competing laws regulating interstate commerce impeded economic development. Again, the national government was virtually powerless to remedy the nation's ills. Lack of confidence in the future of the nation resulted in little investment and a significant decrease in the value of land.

In 1786, the nation's economic problems provoked a group of radical farmers in Massachusetts, led by Daniel Shays, to rebel against local government. The rebels, angered by the poor state of the economy, the imprisonment of small farmers who could not pay their debts, and court-ordered land forfeitures, took control of a number of courts and prevented them from operating. There was no national authority to defeat the rebellion and initially many local authorities were reluctant to become involved. Eventually, **Shays' Rebellion** was quelled by a privately financed (merchants and creditors), state-legislature-authorized militia, but it was further proof that the nation's problems needed to be addressed.

The inadequacies of the Articles became critical. James Madison stated that the "insufficiency of present confederation [threatened the] preservation of the union." He continued, "we may indeed with propriety be said to have reached almost the last stage of national humiliation. There is scarcely anything that can wound the pride or degrade the character of an independent nation which we do not experience."[7] Madison was speaking for many. The mood of the nation was one for change in order to save the union. The proponents of change recognized the problem to be the weakness of the national government. However, the colonists had also learned a lesson about unchecked centralized power while under British rule: it can be unfair and arbitrary.

These two experiences—the excesses of British power and the inadequacies of the Confederation—resulted in a reserved and cautious attitude in favor of strengthening the national government. Some people, notably George Washington, Alexander Hamilton, James Madison, John Marshall, and John Hancock, favored a strong national government and thus are known as **federalists.** There were also people who opposed the creation of a strong national government. This group, known as the **antifederalists,** had among its ranks Thomas Jefferson, Luther Martin, George Mason, and Patrick Henry.

Shays' Rebellion
Daniel Shays, a veteran of the American Revolutionary War, and a group of fellow farmers rebelled in protest of economic conditions. This incident was cited by many as justification for abandoning the Articles of Confederation, the theory being that a stronger national government could provide better economic conditions and that a national military would be most effective in defeating rebellions.

federalist
(1) A person who supports a strong, centralized government. (2) A political party that advocates a strong, centralized government.

antifederalist
(1) A person who opposes establishment of a strong, centralized government in favor of local control. (2) A party that opposes establishment of a strong, centralized government in favor of local control.

A newspaper commentary on the shortcomings of the Articles of Confederation.
Brian Lies

1.3 PHILADELPHIA CONVENTION

The prevailing attitude was that a stronger national government could provide economic and political stability for the young nation. For several years the Congress had called for an increase in national authority to cure the nation's ills. James Madison zealously fought for a constitutional convention. The highly respected George Washington bitterly complained of the impotence of the national government. But the states were reluctant to give up any power, and this caused delay. Finally, there came a chance to mend the nation's problems.

1.3(a) The Delegates and Their Mandate

In 1786, a group of prominent Americans met in Annapolis, Maryland, to discuss interstate commerce issues. The meeting had been urged by the Virginia state legislature and was supported by many politicians from other states. However, little occurred, as only five states were represented. One important product did result from this meeting, however. Alexander Hamilton submitted, and the body approved, a recommendation to the Continental Congress that a convention be held to examine the problems of the nation and its constitution. The Continental Congress approved such a meeting.

The congressional resolution approving of the convention read, in part, "Resolved that . . . on the second Monday in May next a Convention of delegates who shall have been appointed by the several states be held at Philadelphia for the sole and express purpose of revising the Articles of Confederation." There was no mandate to the delegates to create a new constitution. Even more, they were representatives of the states and, arguably, not the people. In spite of this, they chose to act as representatives of the people. Consequently, they chose to begin the new constitution with "We the People," rather than the suggested "We the States."

Philadelphia was an appropriate location for such an auspicious gathering. Philadelphia was where the first Continental Congress met, where George Washington was appointed Commander of the Continental Army by the Second Continental Congress, and where two important documents—the Declaration of Independence and the Articles of Confederation—had been signed. Philadelphia would add the new constitution to its impressive list.

In total, seventy-four delegates were selected to attend the convention (see Figure 1-1), although only fifty-five actually attended. The reasons for not attending varied—some

Connecticut Oliver Ellsworth Roger Sherman William Samuel Johnson	Nathaniel Gorham Rufus King Caleb Strong	**Pennsylvania** Benjamin Franklin George Clymer Thomas Fitzsimons
Delaware Richard Bassett Jacob Broom Johnson Dikinson George Read Gunning Bedford, Jr.	**New Hampshire** John Langdon Nicholas Gilman **New Jersey** David Brearley Jonathan Dayton William Churchill Houston William Livingston William Paterson	Jared Ingersoll Thomas Mifflin Gouverneur Morris Robert Morris James Wilson **Rhode Island** None
Georgia Abraham Baldwin William Houston William Pierce William Few		**South Carolina** Charles Pinckney Charles Cotesworth Pinckney Pierce Butler John Rutledge
Maryland Daniel Carroll Daniel of St. Thomas Jenifer James McHenry Luther Martin John Francis Mercer	**New York** Alexander Hamilton John Lansing, Jr. Robert Yates **North Carolina** William Blount William Richardson Davie Alexander Martin Richard Dobbs Spaight Hugh Williamson	**Virginia** George Washington James Madison George Mason Edmund Randolph John Blair James McClurg George Wythe
Massachusetts Elbridge Gerry		

FIGURE1-1

The states' delegates to the Constitutional Convention of 1787

**S
I
D
E
B
A
R**

WHERE WAS THOMAS JEFFERSON?

Although it is commonly believed that Thomas Jefferson attended the Constitutional Convention, he did not. Where was the author of the Declaration of Independence and future president during such an important gathering? He was in France, serving in the nation's diplomatic corps. Mr. Jefferson had great respect for the delegates, however. When he learned the identities of the membership, he commented that it was "[a]n assembly of demi-gods."

personal, others political. Patrick Henry rejected his appointment because he "smelt a rat."[8] He correctly foresaw what the convention would produce: not a revision of the Articles, but a whole new constitution, creating a whole new government. Later, during the ratification debates in the states, he would prove to be a vocal and vehement opponent of the new constitution.

The delegates who attended were the who's-who of colonial life. They were among the most respected men of politics, law, and business. It is said that Thomas Jefferson, who was in Paris during the convention, remarked that it was "an assembly of demi-gods," when he learned who the delegates were.

Of the attending delegates, one-half were college graduates, most were attorneys, and all were part of America's political or economic aristocracy.[9] Eight were foreign-born and eighteen had worked or studied abroad. Some were obviously influenced by what they had learned from the political experiences of other peoples in other nations. A few delegates were clergymen, but this did not affect the secular atmosphere of the convention.[10]

The convention was scheduled to open on May 14, 1787. Because of the absence of a quorum, though, the proceedings did not begin until May 25th. They continued until September 17 with only two breaks, two days to celebrate Independence Day and another work-related, ten-day recess.

Of the thirteen states, all but one were represented at the convention. Rhode Island refused to send delegates. Two matters were immediately considered and agreed upon. First, with little discussion, George Washington was selected to chair the convention. Second, the delegates decided that what was to transpire was to remain secret until the final document was completed. Although there were small leaks during the convention, the rule was generally complied with by the members.

The absence of information from the delegates led to speculation and rumor about what was transpiring inside the hall. So wild was one rumor, to the effect that the delegates were considering a monarchy, that they issued a statement on August 15 to the contrary. Interestingly, there were a few delegates who supported the establishment of some form of monarchy. Alexander Hamilton, for example, proposed an "elective monarchy." Under this system, the president would have been elected for life, as would the Senate. Hamilton advocated for an English-like government, equating the House of Representatives to England's House of Commons, the Senate to the House of Lords, and the president to the Crown. Edmund Randolph admitted to preferring the English system, but he also recognized that the people of the United States would never accept such a government.[11] Hamilton and Randolph's feelings did not represent those of most of the delegates. As a whole, they were faithful to republican (representative democratic, if you will) principles and were mindful not to place too much authority in any one person's or group's hands.

1.3(b) The Debates

Details of what transpired at the convention are not known. An official journal was kept and provides some insights. More thorough than the convention journal are the notes of James Madison, who was so diligent in his record keeping that he never left the convention for more than an hour. In total, his notes occupy three volumes. These items, as well as the personal notes and correspondence of all the delegates, give us an idea of what the delegates debated during that hot summer of 1787.

Independence Hall, Philadelphia, Pennsylvania.
Getty Images, Inc.-Taxi

On the second day of the convention, Edmund Randolph, governor of Virginia, presented the Virginia Plan, which was in large measure the work of James Madison. Although the Virginia Plan was not the only proposal presented to the convention,[12] it was to be the most influential. The Virginia Plan, or Virginia Resolves, set the tone for the convention and controlled the issues that would be considered. Many of the plan's initial concepts were made a part of the Constitution, in whole or in part. Although the Virginia Plan claimed to be a revision of the Articles of Confederation, it was clear to the delegates that it was more: it was a proposal to replace the existing confederation with a strong, centralized, and supreme national government. The convention took up the plan resolve by resolve. Some of the issues debated at the convention are discussed here.

The nature of the national legislature, Congress, was of particular importance to the delegates. What would be each state's representation in the new Congress? How would its members be selected? What powers would it possess? These are all issues that were considered, debated, and resolved by the delegates.

General Pinckney objected at this point and reminded the delegates that they were only authorized to revise the Articles of Confederation, not to replace them. Later, Edmund Randolph commented, "when the salvation of the Republic is at stake . . . it would be treason to our trust not to propose what we find necessary."

The Virginia Plan called for a separation of powers: legislative, executive, and judicial. Madison, Hamilton, and other delegates were influenced by the theories of John Locke and Charles de Montesquieu, who had written extensively about the importance of dividing the functions and powers of government to preserve liberty. As stated by Madison, "The accumulation of all powers, legislative, executive, and judiciary, in the same hands may justly be pronounced the very definition of tyranny."[13] There was little discussion about the concept, as it was generally accepted. Additionally, all agreed, as evidenced by the final product, that few decisions should be made by one branch alone. The branches should check one another to maintain a balance of power.

As for a national legislature, the Virginia Plan provided for a bicameral Congress. There appears to have been little disagreement with this idea. However, the remaining questions were not so easily answered. Concerning each state's representation, the plan called for state representation to be based upon each state's number of free people or, in the alternative, based upon each state's contribution to the national treasury. The small states opposed the proposal, as they were accustomed to being treated as equals under the Articles of Confederation. The smaller states were convinced that the larger would always have their will, unless all were equals in Congress. They particularly feared the West, which represented potentially large and wealthy states in the future. Roger Sherman commented, "The smaller states will never agree to the plan on any other principle than an equality of suffrage in this branch." The larger states objected to equal representation, contending that this would devalue the franchise of their citizens.

Ultimately, an agreement known as the "Great Compromise" was reached. Representation in the lower house, the House of Representatives, would be based on population (the number of free persons, excluding Indians that were not taxed, and three-fifths of others); representation in the upper house, the Senate, was to be equal. Initially, the delegates agreed that each state would be entitled to one representative to the Senate, but later this was changed, with no debate, to two. Included in this compromise was the resolution of another troubling issue: whether slaves were to be part of the equation for deciding representation. Because the delegates had decided, after debate, that the national government's taxes were to be based upon the same equation, the issue was doubly important.

This issue divided the delegates. Philosophically, the division was geographic, North versus South over whether slavery should be permitted. But the delegates did not seriously debate this issue. However, the division over whether to count slaves for the purpose of representation and taxation transcended the North/South divide. The South would pay more in taxes if slaves were counted. At the same time, the added numbers could increase its representation. Some of the southern delegates contended that southern white citizens would never accept being placed on a one-to-one basis with slaves.

Northern delegates were also split. Some contended that because slaves were property, they should not be included. Others insisted that all people should be included in the census. The two sides compromised and allowed three-fifths of slaves to be counted in determining both taxation and representation. The drafters of the Constitution were careful not to use the term *slave*, referring to "other persons" instead.

**COMPARING THE ARTICLES OF CONFEDERATION
TO THE CONSTITUTION OF THE UNITED STATES**

Articles	*Constitution*
States are supreme	National government is supreme
Source of authority was states	Source of authority is people
Unicameral legislature	Bicameral legislature
No judiciary	Supreme Court and lower courts as Congress may establish
No independent executive	Independent executive
Limited authority to regulate interstate commerce	Broad authority to regulate interstate commerce
No authority to draft soliders	Conscription
No authority to issue paper money	May issue paper money
No authority to tax directly	May tax directly
Could not compel states to respect treaties	Authority to make treaties that are binding upon states

The number of representatives was thus set, but how were they to be selected? This proved to be another hotly debated issue. Delegates such as Elbridge Gerry and Roger Sherman believed that the people could not be trusted to choose their own representatives. To them, the people were an uninformed mass, subject to being "duped" by unscrupulous, charismatic politicians. They proposed that the state legislatures be empowered to appoint the representatives.

George Mason wanted the power to rest with the states, not because he distrusted the people, but because he was a states' rights advocate. "Whatever power may be necessary for the national government, a certain portion must necessarily be left in the states . . . . The state legislatures also sought to have some means of defending themselves against encroachments of the national government . . . . And what better means can we provide than to make them a constituent part of the national establishment." John Dickinson felt similarly. He contended that direct election would result in the total annihilation of the states as political entities.

Others believed that the people should directly elect their representatives. This issue was central to the convention. Were they creating a government of the states, or of the people? George Mason and James Madison were proponents of the direct election of at least one chamber of Congress. Mason pointed out that under the Articles of Confederation, the national government represented the states, which then represented the people. He contended that the states should not stand between the people and the national government, as the states' interests are sometimes at odds with the people's. Oliver Ellsworth warned that the "people will not readily subscribe to the national constitution if it should subject them to be disfranchised." The decision went to the heart of how to define this new democratic republic.

The delegates were influenced by writings of John Locke, Charles de Montesquieu, and Thomas Hobbes. Natural-law theory was a part of the delegates' collective political ideology. If the authority to create a constitution emanates from the people, some delegates wondered how the people could be disenfranchised. Again, a compromise was reached. The members of the House of Representatives would be elected directly; senators were to be selected by the state legislatures. This method for selecting senators remained until the adoption of the Seventeenth Amendment in 1913, which provided for direct election.

The delegates also tackled the issue of qualifications to vote. There was discussion of limiting the right to vote to landowners. There were concerns that the less wealthy would sell their votes. This idea was defeated and the franchise was extended to all free men.

There was little debate over the powers that should be possessed by Congress. These were spelled out in the first article of the Constitution. The framers intended for the national government to be a limited government. Said another way, the national government possesses no authority that is not specifically granted through the Constitution. However, in the enumeration of its powers, Congress was granted the authority to regulate interstate commerce and to make all laws "necessary and proper" for enforcing its other enumerated powers. These clauses, matched with social, political, and technological changes, have proven instrumental to the growth of the national government and are concomitantly responsible for decreasing the authority of the states.

Another thorny issue for the delegates was the Virginia Plan's resolve that provided the national congress with veto power over state laws. The original proposal allowed the legislative veto of state laws that were in conflict with the national constitution. Later in the convention, this was extended to all laws that Congress found improper. Madison supported the idea, as did Pinckney. They contended that it was an effective and necessary means of keeping the states from encroaching upon the national sphere. There were strong objections. Elbridge Gerry argued that through such power, the national government could "enslave the states." It was suggested that the new constitution could enumerate the instances when Congress could exercise the power, but that idea was rejected, as was the entire proposal. The legislative veto was dead. Madison was not happy, but was consoled by the fact that the judiciary would apparently have the authority to protect the national government from the excesses of the states.

What were the framers' thoughts on the executive branch? Under the Virginia Plan, the executive power would have rested in one person, who was to be limited to one term and selected by Congress. George Mason thought there should be three coequal executives. It was decided, with little debate, that executive authority should reside with one person. Nevertheless, the framers feared a monarchy and were careful not to create one. The title *President* was chosen over other more regal titles, such as *His Highness,* to avoid the appearance of monarchy.

One of the hardest decisions for the delegates to reach was the method of selecting the president. For the same reasons discussed earlier in regard to selecting members of Congress, direct election was not seriously considered. It was proposed that Congress make the selection. However, there was general agreement that this would place too much authority with the legislature and create too much executive dependence on the legislature. Others wanted greater state involvement in the process. Perhaps the state legislatures should select the highest executive? Most agreed that this process would be too political and too regional, likely resulting in each state supporting one of its own. There was intense debate over the issue. The result was the electoral college. Under the electoral college system, each state has a number of electors equal to the total number of national Congress members (members of the House and Senate) it possesses. These persons constitute the electoral college. The president is selected by this electoral college. Alexander Hamilton said of this system:

> It was desirable that the sense of the people should operate in the choice of the person to whom so important a trust was to be confided. This end will be answered by committing the right of making it, not to any preestablished body, but to men chosen by the people for the special purpose, and at the particular conjuncture.
>
> It was equally desirable that the immediate election should be made by men most capable of analyzing the qualities adapted to the station and acting under circumstances favorable to deliberation, and to a judicious combination of all the reasons and inducements which were proper to govern their choice. A small number of persons, selected by their fellow citizens from the general mass, will be most likely to possess the information and discernment requisite to so complicated an investigation.[14]

The delegates agreed that, in the event of a tie in the electoral college, the House of Representatives would choose between the candidates. The Senate was originally considered, but the delegates felt that they had already significantly empowered the Senate and that, in the interest of balance, this responsibility should be placed with the House of Representatives.

In regard to presidential responsibilities, the delegates agreed that the president should be the commander-in-chief of the military, negotiate and make treaties, and nominate the cabinet members, members of the national judiciary, and other government officials, with the advice and consent of the Senate. They also decided to give the president the power to veto legislation, but checked that power by providing that Congress could override the veto with a two-thirds vote. Edmund Randolph believed that the total grant of authority to the president was excessive and characterized it as the "fetus of monarchy."

The final issue to be discussed concerning the executive also concerns the judiciary. It was proposed that a council be established comprising the president and a number of the justices of the Supreme Court to review acts of Congress for constitutionality. Under the proposal, acts contrary to the Constitution could be declared void or revised by the council. Gerry opposed the measure because he believed it to be superfluous, as the judiciary has the power to nullify laws contrary to the Constitution. James Madison agreed, "A law violating a constitution established by the people themselves . . . would be considered by judges as null and void." Rufus King also opposed the council. He contended that because it was the responsibility of the courts to review laws before them, and nullify those repugnant to the Constitution, it would be an improper mixing of functions to have judges participate in revising or voiding laws with the executive. Still another voice was heard in this vein. Luther Martin stated, "[A]s to the Constitutionality of laws, that point will come before the judges in their proper official character. In this character they have a negative on the laws." The measure was defeated, but the president was given the veto power, subject to override.

Interestingly, the delegates did not specifically mention, in the Constitution, the power of the judiciary to declare the acts of its coordinate branches or the states unconstitutional. However, the Supreme Court has determined that such a power is implicit in the judicial function. (This issue is discussed again in Chapter 3.)

Another issue the delegates debated was the role the national judiciary should play in the new United States. Some contended that they should create a system of national courts through the new constitution. Others feared, however, that if they created national courts, state courts would be displaced and divested of their authority. The compromise agreement was that the Supreme Court of the United States would be created by the new constitution along with "inferior Courts as the Congress may from time to time ordain and establish." Without a system of lower national courts, many delegates feared that national laws would go unenforced. To remedy this problem, the delegates included a provision in the new constitution requiring state courts to enforce national laws. This is embodied in Article VI, and reads, in relevant part:

> This Constitution, and the Laws of the United States which shall be made in Pursuance thereof: and all Treaties made, or which shall be made, under the Authority of the United States, shall be the supreme Law of the Land; and the Judges in every State shall be bound thereby, any Thing in the Constitution of any State to the Contrary notwithstanding.

This compromise satisfied the delegates who wanted to control the size of the national government and also assured that national laws would be enforced. Congress exercised its power to create inferior national courts when it enacted the Judiciary Act of 1798, which established thirteen district and three circuit courts.

There was little debate concerning the jurisdiction of the national judiciary by the delegates. This issue is examined more closely in Chapters 3 and 4.

1.3(c) Individual Rights and Slavery

To many people, there were two glaring problems with the Constitution. First, it did not explicitly set out individual rights. Second, it did not address slavery.

First, it must be pointed out that the delegates did not totally ignore issues of individual liberty. The Constitution does contain a number of provisions intended to protect civil rights. For example, Article I, Section 9 provides for writs of **habeas corpus.** Section 10 prohibits Congress from passing any **bills of attainder** or **ex post facto laws.** Article III, Section 3, provides that no person shall be convicted of treason except upon the testimony of two witnesses to the same act or upon a confession in open court.

In spite of this, the first ten amendments, commonly known as the Bill of Rights, were added to assure that the government would not encroach upon civil liberties. At the Constitutional Convention, George Mason argued for the inclusion of a bill of rights, and Elbridge Gerry moved for such a bill to be included in the Constitution. Alexander Hamilton saw no need to include a bill of rights, because the government lacked the authority to encroach upon an individual's liberty: "Why declare that things shall not be done, which there is no power to do."

Hamilton did not foresee the significant change that would come to the United States. Industrialization, a huge growth in population, and a specialization of functions have led to increased interdependence among people. Today, few persons live so remotely that their activities do not affect others, and few supply their own food, clothes, and other necessities. Contemporary life in the United States involves continuous and frequent contact with other people. As human contact increases, so do conflicts and, accordingly, rules to regulate conduct. We look to government to establish and enforce most of these rules. To protect ourselves from an overzealous government, which we have entrusted with an ever-increasing amount of authority, we need a Bill of Rights.

Hamilton's view prevailed. The delegates decided not to include a bill of rights in the original document because they simply did not believe the government had the authority to legislate in the areas a bill of rights would cover. After the convention voted ten to zero to exclude it, Gerry moved that the freedom of the press should at least be included. For the same reason—that the delegates did not believe the government had the authority to regulate the press—this motion was also defeated. There was no bill of rights in the original Constitution.

Nevertheless, the absence of a bill of rights was troubling to the nation. A few states, such as New York and Virginia, attached to their resolutions of approval of the Constitution proposals to amend the new constitution to add a bill of rights. In total, over 200 amendments to the constitution were discussed in the state ratifying conventions.[15] It was a popular idea, and only three years after the Constitution was ratified, the Bill of Rights was ratified.

Slavery was a divisive issue. The issue arose in the context discussed previously: taxation and representation. It was at that juncture that many delegates voiced their objections to slavery.

habeas corpus
Latin term for "you have the body." A writ whose purpose is to obtain immediate relief from illegal imprisonment by having the "body" (that is, the prisoner) delivered from custody and brought before that court. A writ of habeas corpus is a means for attacking the constitutionality of the statute under which, or the proceedings in which, the original conviction was obtained. There are numerous writs of habeas corpus, each applicable in different procedural circumstances. The full name of the ordinary writ of habeas corpus is *habeas corpus ad subjiciendum.*

bill of attainder
A legislative act that inflicts capital punishment upon named persons without a judicial trial. Congress and the state legislatures are prohibited from issuing bills of attainder by the Constitution.

ex post facto law
A law making a person criminally liable for an act that was not criminal at the time it was committed. The Constitution prohibits both Congress and the states from enacting such laws.

**S
I
D
E
B
A
R**

CONSTITUTION DAY

Does your college or university celebrate Constitution Day? If it receives financial support from the federal government, it must.

In 2004, Senator Robert Byrd attacked an amendment to the Omnibus Spending Bill that recognized September 17th, the day the Constitution was signed, as Constitution Day and Citizenship Day. The law requires all educational institutions who receive federal support to provide constitutional education on that day. Schools and colleges around the nation have embraced the day, many offering programming and events beyond the day, e.g., Constitution Week.

Luther Martin asserted that the slave trade was "inconsistent with the principles of the revolution and dishonorable to the American character to have such a feature in the Constitution."

The issue of slavery also arose in the context of the importation of slaves. Under the new constitution, this was an area under national jurisdiction, but many delegates representing the southern states did not want the national government to interfere with the importation of slaves. Again, some delegates who were opposed to slavery believed that the document should include a provision prohibiting the importation of slaves into the United States. George Mason, himself a slave owner, opposed slavery and wanted to include such a provision in the new constitution.

There were also delegates who opposed slave traffic but believed that the constitution should not prohibit it. Roger Sherman was in this group. He thought the states were moving toward abolition and that this movement should be permitted to run its course. Charles Pinckney warned that South Carolina would not accept any constitution that forbade the importation of slaves. He voiced what all the delegates feared: factionalism. They did not want to include a provision so repugnant to any particular region that ratification would be jeopardized. Benjamin Franklin, president of the Pennsylvania Society for the Abolition of Slavery, refused to present a petition from the group to the convention, fearing that it would drive an irreparable wedge between the states.

A compromise was reached. First, as discussed earlier, three-fifths of slaves were included in the initial determination of representation and taxation. As to the importation of slaves, the delegates agreed that Congress could not prohibit the importation of slaves until 1808 and capped the tax on each slave at $10. On January 1, 1808, Congress prohibited the importation of slaves. This did not, however, end slavery. It took a civil war to accomplish that goal.

1.3(d) Women and the Franchise

Women were not extended the right to vote by the new constitution. In fact, it appears that there was no discussion of the issue at the Constitutional Convention. Women were not excluded entirely from political processes during this period, however. For example, the New Jersey Constitution of 1776 extended the vote to women who owned property (African Americans were also allowed to vote). This was changed, however, in 1807 when the New Jersey Constitution was amended to restrict suffrage to "men."[16]

The women's suffrage movement can be traced back to Abigail Adams, wife of President John Adams. Later, feminists such as Elizabeth Cady Stanton and Susan B. Anthony led the women's suffrage movement that resulted in the Nineteenth Amendment (1920), which extended the right to vote to women.

1.4 RATIFICATION

James Madison, Alexander Hamilton, Gouverneur Morris, and Rufus King were responsible for drafting the Constitution. A local clerk was hired to actually pen the document. It took him forty hours to write the 4,400 words on a four-page parchment made of either calf or lamb skin. He was paid $30 for this task.

The signing occurred on September 17, 1787. Thirty-nine delegates signed. Three delegates, George Mason, Edmund Randolph, and Elbridge Gerry, refused to sign. Edmund Randolph was the delegate who introduced the Virginia Plan from which the Constitution was constructed. He, like Mason and Gerry, was concerned that too much power had been vested in

RATIFICATION OF THE CONSTITUTION

Article VII of the Constitution of the United States reads, in part, "The Ratification of the Conventions of nine States, shall be sufficient for the Establishment of this Constitution between the States so ratifying the Same." The delegates had decided that ratification would occur through conventions to be conducted in each state. Further, it took nine states' approval before the Constitution could be ratified, and then only among the ratifying states. It took two and a half years, but eventually all thirteen states accepted the Constitution. The order of state approval was as follows:

December 7, 1787	Delaware
December 15, 1787	Pennsylvania
December 18, 1787	New Jersey
January 2, 1788	Georgia
January 4, 1788	Connecticut
February 6, 1788	Massachusetts
April 26, 1788	Maryland
May 23, 1788	South Carolina
June 21, 1788	New Hampshire
June 25, 1788	Virginia
July 26, 1788	New York
November 21, 1789	North Carolina
May 29, 1790	Rhode Island

Rhode Island remained obstinate. Congress voted to sever the new nation's commercial relations with Rhode Island, which helped push that state to approval. Finally, on May 29, 1790, Rhode Island gave its approval. The nation was united under the Constitution.

the national government. Later, however, during the Virginia Ratification Convention, Randolph supported the Constitution to avoid dividing the nation. [17] Mason and Gerry, in contrast, later opposed the Constitution in their state conventions. Mason commented that he would rather cut off his hand than see the Constitution ratified.

The delegates transmitted a copy to the Congress, where it was received on September 20, 1787. Richard Henry Lee opposed sending the Constitution on to the states for ratification, and there was discussion of sending it on with objections. The Congress decided to do neither. Instead, it was transmitted to the states without any comment whatsoever.

The delegates had debated the method of ratification. Special conventions won out over state legislatures. Further, they decided that it should take only nine states to ratify the document, rather than the total of thirteen, and that ratification would be effective only among the ratifying states. All thirteen states would have at least one ratification convention. The state conventions were limited to ratifying or rejecting the document; no revisions or conditional ratifications were allowed. The conventions began in November 1787 and ended in May 1790.

During this period, numerous articles were published in magazines and newspapers, pamphlets were distributed, and speeches were made, arguing the pros and cons of the new constitution. The most influential writings were those of James Madison, Alexander Hamilton, and John Jay, who published a series of eighty-five articles under the pseudonym *Publius*. Today, we know these as the *Federalist Papers*. Through these articles, these men made forceful arguments in support of the Constitution. The antifederalists had their outlet as well. Another series of articles, entitled the *Federal Farmer*, was published in opposition to ratification.

During the debates in the state conventions, three common objections were made to the Constitution. First, it was missing a bill of rights. Second, it emasculated the sovereignty of the states. Third, the delegates had exceeded their authority in replacing the Articles of Confederation. Delegates Luther Martin, Elbridge Gerry, and George Mason passionately opposed ratification.

Delaware was the first state to approve the Constitution, doing so on December 7, 1787. New Hampshire approved on June 21, 1788. It was the critical ninth state to approve, so the Constitution was then ratified and the Articles of Confederation superseded, and a new government could be formed. During the formation of the new government, the state conventions continued. By February 4, 1789, every state but Rhode Island had joined the Union, and the nation's first electoral college had selected George Washington the first president under the Constitution. In April of that year, Congress had its first meeting. John Jay was selected as the nation's first chief justice during 1789.

1.5 AMENDMENTS

The framers of the Constitution lived in an era when changes to government came either by edicts of kings or by revolution. They desired to have a more fair and civil method. At the same time, they did not want to empower Congress to amend the Constitution. After all, the Constitution is fundamental law, intended to restrict the power of government in many instances.

The framers devised two methods to amend the Constitution. They are found in Article V. The first method is initiated by Congress. With a two-thirds vote in both houses, Congress may propose an amendment to the states. In the alternative, two-thirds of the state legislatures may call for a convention to make proposals. Congressional initiation is the only method of proposal that has been used to date.

A proposal is then ratified either by the legislatures of three-fourths of the states or conventions in three-fourths of the states. Congress designates the ratification method. Thomas Jefferson believed that this process realized the dream of providing for bloodless change by the people. He said

> [h]appily for us, that when we find our constitutions defective and insufficient to secure
> the happiness of our people, we can assemble with all the coolness of philosophers, and
> set them to rights, while every other nation on earth must have recourse to arms to amend
> or to restore their constitutions.[18]

Although the states were only given two alternatives in regard to the Constitution (adoption or rejection), many states attached lists of proposed amendments to their adoption resolutions anyway. A few states, such as Virginia and New York, called for a bill of rights. Eight states called for an amendment protecting the sovereignty of the states. To satisfy these concerns, it was agreed that a bill would be added immediately after the original Constitution was ratified. James Madison initially suggested a single general statement affirming that the source of all governmental power is derived from the people. This was rejected and he eventually composed a bill of seventeen amendments. After House of Representative and Senate revisions, twelve rights remained. Ten of the twelve were ratified on November 3, 1791. They have become known as the Bill of Rights. The Bill of Rights include protections of individual rights and liberties and a provision intended to preserve the integrity of state sovereignty. The two provisions that were not ratified concerned the number of representatives in the lower house and compensation for members of Congress. See Chapter 9 for a more thorough discussion of this topic.

Today, there are a total of twenty-seven amendments. Ratification of the twenty-seventh amendment, which provides that changes in the compensation of members of Congress shall not be implemented until there has been an intervening election of the House of Representatives, traveled an interesting road. It was one of the two amendments proposed by Madison that was not ratified as part of the original Bill of Rights. Ratification restarted in 1978. Ultimately, it was ratified in 1992, two hundred and one years after it was proposed.[19] The ratifying state, Michigan, did not exist at the time the amendment was proposed. Although the number of amendments is relatively small, the number of proposals to amend the Constitution that have been submitted is staggering. By 2004, the number of proposals introduced in Congress to amend the Constitution exceeded 11,000.[20] You will learn more about the amendments, with an emphasis on the rights protected by them, in the second part of this book.

1.6 VALUES, POLITICS, AND CONSTITUTIONAL LAW

The remainder of this book examines how the Constitution has been applied and interpreted. Examining the decisions of the courts of the United States, particularly of the United States Supreme Court is the most common method of learning this subject. Be aware, however, that the judiciary does not exist in a vacuum. Its coequal branches (president and Congress) must interpret the Constitution, apply its principles, and, in certain ways, influence the judiciary's interaction with and interpretation of the Constitution.

For example, administrative agencies are largely responsible for the administration of government in this nation. They are the front line of government. To function, administrative agencies must interpret the law, often before any court has had an opportunity to address objections to that law. In some cases, a party may obtain pre-enforcement judicial review of a law, and in such instances the agency's role is diminished. When pre-enforcement review is not sought or is unavailable, the agency's role becomes more significant. In instances when a law is valid as written, but the agency's method of enforcement is questionable, the agency's role is again emphasized.

The perceived constitutionality of a bill may also affect legislative decision making. A bill that is seen as unconstitutional may not make it out of committee. Individual legislators may oppose proposed legislation that seems unconstitutional. This is not always the case, however. For political reasons, legislators may support a bill known to be unconstitutional. For example, the Supreme Court invalidated a Texas statute that protected the United States flag from desecration by a political protester in the 1989 case of *Texas v. Johnson*.[21] The Court reasoned that the protester's right to political expression under the First Amendment outweighed Texas's interest in protecting the integrity of the flag. One year later, the Congress enacted similar legislation, even though it clearly contradicted the Supreme Court's ruling in *Texas v. Johnson*. For that reason, the new law was quickly invalidated as well.

Also, Congress possesses considerable authority over the jurisdiction of the federal courts. Political concerns could, therefore, cause legislators to limit the jurisdiction of the judiciary over certain issues.

Many of the petitions filed with the Supreme Court are filed by the United States, by the solicitor general of the United States. Such filings are examined with special care by the Court when it determines whether to hear the appeals. The executive branch therefore influences the Court by its partial control over the issues presented to the Court.

Although the Court is generally insulated from politics, it is generally believed that politics and public opinion play at least a minor role in influencing the Court's decision making. Because the Court has no method of enforcing its orders, it relies on the executive branch. This unenforceability, some contend, keeps the Court's decisions within the bounds of reason—that is, within a range the public will tolerate and the executive will enforce.

Politics also play a role in the selection of Article III judges. Supreme Court justices and judges of federal district and appellate courts are selected by the political branches of government—the president nominates and the Senate must confirm. In recent years, the process has been criticized as being too political, focusing on the political and ideological beliefs of nominees rather than on other qualifications, such as education, employment experience, prior judicial experience, intellectual ability, and the like. The confirmation hearings of Robert Bork (nominated by President Reagan and rejected by the Senate) and Clarence Thomas (nominated by President Bush and confirmed by the Senate) are used to illustrate this point.

Once appointed, an Article III judge maintains his or her position until one of three occurrences: retirement, death, or impeachment. The power to impeach a judge rests with Congress. Congress may impeach for high crimes and misdemeanors. This is, therefore, another limitation upon the judiciary by an external force. Congress has been true to the purpose of impeachment and has not used the power to achieve political objectives.

When possible, this book recognizes and refers to political or social influences, as well as to other actors that influence constitutional law. In any event, however, it is the judiciary that is charged with interpreting the law; the Supreme Court of the United States has the final word on what the Constitution means. For that reason, this book focuses on the decisions of that Court. To fully understand a decision of the Court, one must grasp the history and facts that gave rise to the case; the law itself, including any policy considerations, as expressed in the Court's decisions; the political and social atmosphere surrounding the opinion; and the composition of the Court. Also significant are the values that underpin decisions. Constitutional decisions often reinforce the Court's conception of what our democratic republic should look like and, occasionally, reflect other values of individual justices.

1.7 JUDICIAL ERAS

There have been several significant "eras" in the history of the Supreme Court. These eras are marked by particular ideologies that were dominant on the Court. These often, but not always, coincide with chief justice terms. The respective powers of the national and state governments are the primary point of reference for the periods discussed in the rest of this chapter.

1.7(a) Early Court

Even though the Constitution was intended to greater centralize governmental authority, state authority, especially judicial authority, was much greater in 1789 than it is now. As a result, the status of the Supreme Court was uncertain for many years. The early years of the Court were characterized by resignations for other positions that today would be less desirable. John Jay, one of three authors of the *Federalist Papers* and the Nation's first Chief Justice, assumed office in 1789 and resigned in 1795 to run for governor of New York. John Rutledge was also nominated by President Washington and confirmed in 1789 but he never appeared for duty. He resigned in 1791 and was later nominated to replace John Jay as chief justice. He began serving immediately but ultimately was not confirmed by the Senate. Oliver Ellsworth (1796–1800) followed John Rutledge as Chief Justice. There were few significant decisions rendered in the early years of the Court. One exception is *Chisholm v. Georgia,* 2 v.s. 419 (1793) which held that States may be liable in federal court. The decision was so unpopular that it led to the adoption of the Eleventh Amendment in 1795. The Court began to establish itself as an important legal institution during the tenure of Chief Justice John Marshall.

1.7(b) Marshall Court

John Marshall was chief justice of the United States from 1801 to 1836. John Marshall, nominated by President John Adams, was a strong nationalist (federalist). Marshall had been President Adams's secretary of state. Adams lost his re-election bid to an antifederalist, Thomas Jefferson. In an effort to continue to influence government, Adams, with the support of a lame-duck federalist Congress, made a number of appointments of federalists to vacant judicial positions. Marshall was one of these appointees.

The Marshall Court is known for establishing the supremacy of the national government over the state governments. A number of important decisions were handed down by the Marshall Court, including *Marbury v. Madison,* 5 U.S. (1 Cranch) 137 (1803); *McCulloch v. Maryland,* 17 U.S. (4 Wheat) 316 (1819); and *Martin v. Hunter's Lessee,* 14 U.S. (1 Wheat) 304 (1816). (These decisions are discussed in Chapter 3.) In *McCulloch,* Marshall addressed the power of Congress; this decision is discussed further in Chapter 4. *Hunter's Lessee* concerned the division of authority between the national government and state governments and is the subject of more thorough examination in Chapter 7. The theme of *Marbury v. Madison* was different. In that case, the power of **judicial review** was established. Judicial review is the authority of the judiciary, as the final interpreter of the law, to declare the acts of the other coordinate branches unconstitutional. *Marbury v. Madison* and judicial review are discussed fully in Chapter 3.

1.7(c) Taney Court

Roger Taney replaced John Marshall as chief justice of the United States in 1836. Between 1836 and 1843, four other justices were appointed: Philip Barbour, John Catron, John McKinley, and Peter Daniel. McKinley and Daniel filled two new seats, expanding the number of justices on the Court to nine. Eight other justices would join the Court during Taney's tenure as chief justice, which did not end until 1865.

During this era, the Court's philosophy changed from strongly nationalist to one favoring states' rights. The Taney Court was not activist; that is, it was not aggressive in reversing the decisions of the Marshall Court. The Court did favor states' rights, however, when new issues were raised concerning the balance of power between the national and state governments.

The Taney Court is best known for *Dred Scott v. Sandford,* 60 U.S. (19 How.) 393 (1856). In that decision, the Supreme Court held that slaves were property and possessed

judicial review
The power of the judiciary, as the final interpreter of the law, to declare an act of a coordinate governmental branch of state unconstitutional. The power is not expressly stated in the Constitution, but the Supreme Court announced that the judiciary possesses this power in *Marbury v. Madison,* 5 U.S. (1 Cranch) 137 (1803).

no rights or privileges under the Constitution. Further, for the second time in history, the first being *Marbury v. Madison,* the Court relied upon judicial review to invalidate a statute. In *Dred Scott,* the Court held a federal statute that conferred rights upon slaves unconstitutional. In short, the Court concluded that slavery was an issue of local, not national, concern.

1.7(d) Reconstruction Era

Salmon P. Chase became chief justice in 1865 and remained in that position until 1874. The Civil War had ended and the nation was rebuilding. The South had been defeated and slavery abolished. Most significant, the war proved that the states were not independent members of a league, but parts of a larger, more powerful nation. The nation's political identity changed as a result of the war. People began to identify more closely with their national citizenship and less with their state affiliations. The consequence was a strengthening of the national government and a concomitant weakening of the state governments.

During this period, the so-called reconstruction amendments were adopted. The Thirteenth Amendment, ratified in 1865, forbids slavery. The Fourteenth Amendment, ratified in 1868, has four sections, but the first is the most significant, as it provides that every state shall extend to all persons due process and equal protection of the law. The Fourteenth Amendment extends to Congress the power to enact legislation to enforce its mandates. Congress did that through the Civil Rights Acts, found at 42 U.S.C. §1981, 1982, and 1983. The Fifteenth Amendment, ratified in 1870, assures the franchise to persons of all color and race.

The Thirteenth and Fourteenth Amendments were not ratified under the most favorable of circumstances. The southern states were coerced into ratification. In fact, most of the southern states initially rejected the Fourteenth Amendment and acquiesced only after Congress enacted a reconstruction act that denied each state representation in Congress until it ratified the amendment. Such coercion would not be acceptable today, but the methods used by the national government in coercing the states into ratifying the reconstruction amendments have to be considered in light of the circumstances of the day.

It would be decades before the full force of these amendments would be realized. However, the reconstruction period marks an important point in constitutional history. Today, the reconstruction amendments and statutes are applied often and with significant effect on state actions. For example, the Fourteenth Amendment and federal discrimination statutes forbid state governments from discriminating against individuals on the account of race, religion, or gender when hiring employees or providing benefits to citizens.

1.7(e) Pre–New Deal Era

Salmon Chase was followed by Morrison Waite (1874–1888), Melville Fuller (1888–1910), Edward White (1910–1921), and William Taft (1921–1930) as Chief Justices. Again, the Court's philosophy changed during the tenure of these men, at least regarding federalism issues. During this period, the Fourteenth Amendment was used to limit the power of the states to regulate intrastate commerce. For example, in *Lochner v. New York,* 198 U.S. 45 (1905), the Court invalidated a state statute that set maximum working hours for bakers. The Court found the statute to be an unwarranted burden upon the right to contract, a liberty interest protected by the Fourteenth Amendment.

The authority of the federal government to regulate interstate commerce was also limited during this period, often for Tenth Amendment reasons (the federal government was encroaching upon the domain of the states).

Ironically, while the Court was using the Fourteenth Amendment to protect economic interests, it did not concomitantly protect the rights of black citizens, the primary goal of the amendment. The case that established the "separate but equal" doctrine, *Plessy v. Ferguson,* 163 U.S. 537 (1896), was rendered during this period. Not until 1954, when *Brown v. Board of Education,* 381 U.S. 479 (1954) was decided, was the separate but equal doctrine overturned as violative of the Fourteenth Amendment.

1.7(f) New Deal Era

The next significant judicial era occurred during the Great Depression. President Franklin D. Roosevelt was elected with a popular mandate to correct the nation's serious economic crisis. Roosevelt's New Deal plan included significant federal government involvement in economic matters. A number of programs were created with the intention of stimulating the economy. Additionally, national governmental regulation of commercial activities increased during the New Deal.

Early in Roosevelt's administration, the Court rendered a number of unpopular decisions invalidating some of the New Deal legislation. In 1935, the Court held the National Industrial Recovery Act unconstitutional in *Panama Refining Co. v. Ryan,* 293 U.S. 388 (1935), as it found that Congress had made an unlawful delegation of legislative authority to the president (violating separation of powers principles). There were other decisions unfavorable to President Roosevelt: *Schechter Poultry Corp. v. United States,* 295 U.S. 495 (1935); *Railroad Retirement Board v. Alton Railroad,* 295 U.S. 330 (1935); and *United States v. Butler,* 297 U.S. 1 (1936). (This line of cases is more fully discussed in Chapters 5 and 7.) In short, they stood for the principle of a limited national government, one whose authority to regulate interstate commerce is limited by the right of individual contract and by federalism principles. These cases asserted the importance of separation of powers, substantive due process, and limitations on the authority that may be delegated by Congress to administrative agencies.

These decisions angered President Roosevelt, who reacted with the famous "court-packing" plan. In an effort to "pack" the Court with justices sympathetic to his objectives, President Roosevelt proposed that for every justice over Seventy years of age, an additional justice be appointed. At the time the suggestion was made, there were six justices over age seventy on the Court. He contended that the additional justices were needed to meet the Court's heavy burden. Congress saw the proposal for what it was—an attempt to control the Court by President Roosevelt—and ultimately it was defeated. Also contributing to the defeat were two decisions issued by the Court upholding New Deal legislation. The decisions represented a change in direction from the court. Justice Roberts, the swing vote on the divided Court, is credited with saving the nine-member court by changing his vote, favoring federal authority in commerce cases. This has become commonly known as the *switch in time that saved nine.* Roosevelt's court-packing scheme presented one of the most serious threats to the integrity and independence of the Court in its history.

As it turned out, Roosevelt did not need the court-packing scheme to gain the ideological sympathy of the Court. Recall that six justices were over the age of seventy when he made his proposal. As might be expected, a number left the Court during the New Deal era. By 1941, Roosevelt had nominated seven new justices, all of whom were confirmed.

The new membership on the Court transformed its attitude and approach to substantive due process and federalism. Beginning in 1938, and continuing thereafter, the Court consistently upheld New Deal legislation.

1.7(g) Warren Court

In 1953, Earl Warren, a nominee of President Eisenhower, became the new chief justice. Warren presided over a Court that is best known for its decisions protecting individual rights (civil liberties). Three other justices were prominent during this time for their "liberal" philosophies: William Douglas, William Brennan, and Hugo Black. In 1967, two years before the end of Warren's tenure, another liberal justice, Thurgood Marshall, was added to the Court.

Much constitutional law was established during the Warren Court era. Included in this Court's decisions are: the invalidation of the separate but equal doctrine of *Plessy,* in *Brown v. Board of Education;* the finding that privacy is protected by the Constitution, in *Griswold v. Connecticut,* 381 U.S. 479 (1965); the establishment of much of the First Amendment free speech law used today; and enhanced protection of the rights of persons accused of crimes, including *Katz v. United States,* 389 U.S. 347 (1967) (Fourth Amendment protects reasonable expectations of privacy), *United States v. Wade,* 338 U.S. 218 (1967) (right to counsel at pretrial [postarrest or charge] identifications), and *Miranda v. Arizona,* 384 U.S. 436 (1966) (right to counsel during interrogations), to name only a few.

1.7(h) Burger Court

Warren Burger was nominated by President Richard M. Nixon to follow Earl Warren as chief justice in 1969. President Nixon appointed three other justices, Harry Blackmun, Lewis Powell, and William Rehnquist, who were either conservative or moderate, to replace three more liberal members of the Warren Court, Earl Warren, Abe Fortas, and Hugo Black.

Although the Burger Court was more conservative than the Warren Court, it was not activist in its approach. Few decisions of the Warren Court were reversed; in fact, the early years of the Burger Court continued in the Warren Court tradition, emphasizing the preservation of civil liberties. However, just as the Burger Court did not proactively pursue a conservative agenda, it did not continue the liberal activism of the Warren Court. Rather, on the whole, the Court maintained the status quo, neither disturbing precedent nor engaging in social engineering.

This is not to say that the Burger Court did not issue important decisions. Important precedents concerning the freedom of speech, the rights of racial minorities, and the rights of women were established during the Burger era. For example, the Burger Court decided *Roe v. Wade,* 410 U.S. 113 (1973), wherein the Court determined that the right to privacy protects a woman's right to elect abortion in some situations. The Burger Court was also responsible for ordering President Nixon to hand over tape recordings of Oval Office conversations that related to the Watergate affair, in *Nixon v. United States,* 418 U.S. 683 (1974), *reh'g denied,* 433 U.S. 916 (1977). It was during the Burger era that the first woman joined the Court. Justice Sandra Day O'Connor was nominated by President Reagan and confirmed by the Senate in 1981.

1.7(i) Rehnquist Court

William Rehnquist was appointed associate justice of the Supreme Court in 1972 and he succeeded Warren Burger as chief justice in 1986. Between 1988 and 1991, Associate Justices Lewis Powell, Jr., William Brennan, Jr., and Thurgood Marshall retired. Their replacements, Justices Anthony Kennedy, David Souter, and Clarence Thomas were all more conservative than the justices they replaced. Accordingly, the Court had a more conservative leaning during the Rehnquist tenure than during the Warren and Burger eras. This was particularly true for issues concerning economic and states' rights.

Some of the important federalism cases decided during Rehnquist's term are *United States v. Lopez,* 115 S. Ct. 1624 (1995) and Morrison v. United States, 529 U.S. 598 (2000), both limiting Congress's power over interstate commerce. In *United States Term Limits v. Thornton,* 115 S. Ct. 1842 (1996), the Court invalidated state-imposed term limits on United States Congress members, and *Bush v. Gore*, 531 U.S. 98 (2000) brought closure to the closest presidential election in history. Another important decision was *Casey v. Planned Parenthood,* 112 S. Ct. 2791 (1992), wherein the Court reaffirmed the basic holding of the Burger Court decision in *Roe v. Wade;* namely, that women have a privacy right to elect abortions in some situations. However, the Rehnquist Court invalidated the trimester analysis established in *Roe* in favor of another test. Justice Rehnquist died in office in 2005.

1.7(j) Roberts Court

John G. Roberts was nominated by President George W. Bush to replace Associate Justice Sandra O'Connor. During the pendency of his nomination, Chief Justice Rehnquist died and President Bush nominated Roberts to succeed Chief Justice Rehnquist. He was confirmed as Justice Rehnquist's successor in 2005. The direction his leadership will take the Court remains to be seen.

Some of the most significant cases of recent years are discussed throughout this book, and from those cases certain common themes may be discovered. See Appendix E for a chronological chart of the members of the Supreme Court.

1.8 SUMMARY

Under the Articles of Confederation, the nation was fragmented and the national government was too weak to effectively deal with the challenges facing our young nation. The framers gathered in Philadelphia to revise the Articles of Confederation. Understanding that their task was greater than this, the delegates chose to abolish the Articles of Confederation and to write a new constitution. They knew that presenting a new constitution would be controversial. To preserve the integrity of the process, they agreed to keep their proceedings secret until the final document was completed.

They created a new governmental structure in the new constitution. The national government would be stronger, but it was limited to the authorities directly given it by the people through the Constitution. Although they intended to strengthen the federal government, they were careful to preserve local governmental authority. The concern about excessive federal authority was so great that the principle of dual sovereignty, or concurrent federal and state authority, was reinforced through the Tenth Amendment only two years after the Constitution was enacted. Thus, powers that appeared inherently national were delegated to the national government, such as foreign relations and war. In addition, control over interstate, foreign, and Indian commerce was assigned to Congress. Everyday matters, such as intrastate commerce, crime, and social concerns, were left to the states.

The first state to accept the new constitution was Delaware. The delegates decided that ratification would occur when the ninth state ratified. This happened in New Hampshire on June 21, 1788. The last of the thirteen states to ratify was Rhode Island, which did so on May 29, 1790. The Bill of Rights was added to the Constitution one year later.

The framers were successful in establishing a stronger national government and are credited with saving the Union from economic disaster and civil war. For reasons that will be more fully discussed later in this book, the federal government has continually grown in size and authority under this Constitution. Whether the federal government has become too large and powerful is the subject of continual discussion. Federalism, or the division of governmental powers among the federal and state governments, is the subject of Chapters 2 and 8.

REVIEW QUESTIONS

1. What were the names of the national legislative bodies before and during the period of the Articles of Confederation and Perpetual Union?
2. Distinguish federalists from antifederalists. State the basic philosophical differences between the two.
3. Identify two of the weaknesses of the Articles of Confederation that contributed to the need for a new constitution.
4. What was the mandate of the delegates to the Philadelphia convention?
5. Name the only one of the original thirteen colonies that was not represented at the Philadelphia convention.
6. Edmund Randolph introduced a plan, largely written by James Madison, that became the working document at the Philadelphia convention. What is the common name of this plan?
7. The delegates considered empowering the Congress with the authority to invalidate state laws. The idea was rejected. Madison, a proponent of the idea, was disappointed, but was consoled by what fact?
8. The delegates agreed to strengthen the national (federal) government but maintain considerable state powers. Describe the relationship between the federal government and state governments as envisioned by the framers.
9. What were the terms of the Great Compromise?
10. Why did Alexander Hamilton oppose including a bill of rights in the original Constitution?

ASSIGNMENTS

1. Do you believe that a bicameral legislature is necessary today? Explain your answer.
2. Amending the Constitution is a difficult process, at least when compared to creating legislation. The framers intended this. Why?

NOTES

*A note about the use of the terms *power* and *authority*. The authors prefer the use of *authority*, using that term to describe the legitimate use of power. However, separation of powers, war powers, police powers, and other uses of the constitutional nomenclature exist and are used herein.

1. A. McLaughlin, *A Constitutional History of the United States* 99–100 (D. Appleton-Century 1935).
2. Documents preceding the Constitution, such as the Declaration of Independence, have no legal authority.
3. Articles of Confederation of Perpetual Union, art. III.
4. Thomas and Thomas, *The War-Making Powers of the President* 3–4 (SMU Press 1982).
5. Catherine Bowen, *Miracle at Philadelphia* 9 (Little, Brown, & Co. 1966).
6. *Judges of the United States,* 2d ed. (Bicentennial Committee of the Judicial Conference of the United States 1983).
7. The Federalist No. 15.
8. George Anastaplo, *The Constitution of 1787* (Johns Hopkins University Press 1989).
9. For a comprehensive discussion of the delegates' respective wealth and how their personal economic interests may have been a factor in their decision making at the convention, see Charles Beard's *Economic Interpretation of the Constitution* (1913) and Forrest McDonald's *We The People: The Economic Origins of the Constitution* (Transaction Publishers 1992).
10. William Peters, *A More Perfect Union* 25 (Crown Publishers 1982).
11. Neil MacNeil, "The First Congress, A Republic If You Can Keep It," 1 *Constitution* 5–6 (No. 3 1989).
12. The other significant proposal was introduced by William Paterson. His plan became known as the New Jersey Plan and was in most respects the antithesis of the Virginia Plan. It called for continuing the Articles of Confederation with revision. Notable differences between the two plans include: the Virginia Plan saw the Constitution's authority emanating from the people, whereas the New Jersey Plan continued to view the national government as representing the states; the Virginia Plan provided for a bicameral Congress, the New Jersey Plan for a unicameral Congress; the Virginia Plan gave the national government wide-sweeping jurisdiction, whereas the New Jersey Plan severely limited the jurisdiction of the national government.
13. The Federalist No. 47.
14. The Federalist No. 68.
15. "The Fourth Amendment," *The Bill of Rights and Beyond.* Bicentennial Calendar (Commission on the Bicentennial of the Constitution 1991).
16. Sara M. Shumer, "Ratifying the Constitution." In *New Jersey,* Gillespie et al., eds. (1989), 76–77.
17. *The Creation of the Constitution* 58. Opposing Viewpoints Series (Greenhaven Press 1995).
18. Letter to C.W.F. Dumas, September 1787, cited in Richard Bernstein, *Amending America* 222 (Random House 1993).
19. It was originally the second amendment. The other unenacted amendment provided for an increase in the membership of the House of Representatives as the nation's population increased. It has never been enacted.
20. See U.S. Senate document http://www.senate.gov/reference/resources/pdf/proposedamend. pdf#search='number%20of%20amendments%20constitution%20introduced%20congress and Richard B. Bernstein, *Amending America: If We Love the Constitution So Much, Why Do We Keep on Trying to Change It?* xii (Random House 1993).
21. 491 U.S. 397 (1989).

2 Dividing Governmental Power

> The accumulation of all power, legislative, executive and judiciary in the same hands, whether hereditary, self-appointed, or elective, may justly be pronounced the very definition of tyranny.
>
> *James Madison[1]*

2.1 FEDERALISM

The men who met in Philadelphia during the hot summer of 1787 firmly believed that a new government would have to be formed to solve the nation's many problems. Under the Articles of Confederation, the nation's first constitution, the nation floundered. Economic and political instability were generally attributed to the weakness of the national government. Therefore, a new, stronger, national government was established.

The framers were concerned, however, with the centralization of power. Too much power residing in any one person or group could lead to tyranny. The belief that absolute power corrupts absolutely predominated the political philosophy of the framers.

Also, the framers were protective of state sovereignty. They wanted a stronger national government, but not to the point of obliterating the states. Three important concepts were included in the Constitution to prevent both the centralization of power and the death of state sovereignty: federalism, separation of powers, and checks and balances. This chapter introduces those concepts. Chapters 3 through 6 expand the discussion to include particular cases in which the concepts have been raised and applied.

The Constitution recognizes two forms of government: the national (federal) government and the government of the states. The division of governmental power between the federal and state governments is called **federalism**. Federalism represents a vertical division of power.

The Constitution specifically enumerates the powers of the federal government. Articles I, II, and III set forth the powers of the national Congress, president, and judiciary. The powers of the states are not specifically enumerated, for the most part. The absence of an enumeration of state powers concerned state rights advocates. The Tenth Amendment was included in the Bill of Rights to appease these concerns. That amendment reads, "The powers not delegated to the United States by the Constitution, nor prohibited by it to the States, are reserved to the States respectively, or to the people."

Federalism
(1) Pertaining to a system of government that is federal in nature.
(2) The system by which the states of the United States relate to each other and to the federal government.

James Madison said, of the balance of powers between the national government and the states, that:

> The powers delegated by the proposed Constitution to the federal government are few and defined. Those which are to remain in the State governments are numerous and indefinite. The former will be exercised principally on external objects, such as war, peace, negotiation, and foreign commerce; with which last the power of taxation will, for the most part, be connected. The powers reserved to the several States will extend to all the objects which, in the ordinary course of affairs, concern the lives, liberties, and properties of people, and the internal order, improvement, and prosperity of the State.[2]

Several other clauses of the Constitution are critical to understanding federalism in the United States. First, Articles I, II, and III enumerate the powers of the national government by defining its three branches. Article I, section 8, for instance, lists the various powers of Congress. There are many, including, for example, the power to coin and borrow money, establish a post office, establish and maintain military forces, promote the arts and sciences, and create immigration laws. Article I, section 8, clause 18 is known as the **necessary and proper clause**. That clause provides that Congress shall have the power to "make all Laws which shall be necessary and proper for carrying into execution the foregoing Powers, and all other Powers vested by this Constitution in the Government of the United States, or in any Department or Officer thereof." The "foregoing Powers" referred to in the clause are the enumerated powers of Congress, the president, and the judiciary. This clause, as discussed in Chapter 5, has been used to increase federal jurisdiction.

The **commerce clause**, also found in Article I, section 8, at clause 3, states that Congress has the power to regulate foreign and interstate commerce. Like the necessary and proper clause, the commerce clause has been used to expand the realm of the national government.

Article VI contains another important provision, the **supremacy clause**. The relevant part of Article VI provides that "This Constitution, and the Laws of the United States which shall be made in Pursuance thereof; and all Treaties made, or which shall be made, under the Authority of the United States, shall be the supreme Law of the Land; and the Judges in every State shall be bound thereby, any Thing in the Constitution or Laws of any State to the Contrary notwithstanding." In other words, any state or local law that conflicts with the Constitution or a treaty of the United States is invalid. Also, any state or local law that conflicts with any national law, when the policy area is exclusively national, is invalid.

Finally, the Civil War Amendments—Amendments Thirteen, Fourteen, and Fifteen—contributed to an increase in federal power. The Fourteenth Amendment, for example, adopted in 1868, increased the authority of the national government as against the states in regard to civil liberties. A post–Civil War amendment, it protects due process and equal protection rights of all persons in the United States. The amendment further provides that Congress "shall have power to enforce, by appropriate legislation, the provisions of this article." Legislation enacted to enforce this and the other Civil War Amendments limits the authority of the states.

2.1(a) Dual, Hierarchical, and Cooperative Federalism

The balancing of national and state powers has not been an easy task. How exactly is the Tenth Amendment to be construed—as a limitation upon the national authority, or as a truism? How far does Congress's power over interstate commerce extend? What is necessary and proper?

Different theories have been developed concerning the nature of the federal–state relationship. One theory is that the federal government and state governments are coequal sovereigns. This is known as **dual federalism**. Under this approach, the Tenth Amendment is read broadly and the supremacy, necessary and proper, and commerce clauses are read narrowly. Only if the national government clearly has jurisdiction are its laws supreme over the states. Further, the Tenth Amendment is construed as establishing a particular sphere of state power; that is, it is considered an independent source of states' rights. As a result, there is a large group

necessary and proper clause
Article I of the Constitution grants to Congress the power to make all laws "necessary and proper" for carrying out its constitutional responsibilities. The Supreme Court has long interpreted this provision to mean that Congress has the right not only to enact laws that are absolutely indispensable, but any laws that are reasonably related to effectuating the powers expressly granted to it by the Constitution.

commerce clause
The clause in Article I, Section 8, of the Constitution that gives Congress the power to regulate commerce between the states and between the United States and foreign countries. Federal statutes that regulate business and labor are based upon this power.

supremacy clause
The provision in Article VI of the Constitution that "this Constitution and the laws of the United States . . . shall be the supreme law of the land, and the judges in every state shall be bound thereby."

dual federalism
The theory that the national government and the state governments are coequal sovereigns. The national government is supreme only when its jurisdiction is explicitly granted by the Constitution.

COMPARING THE ARTICLES OF CONFEDERATION TO THE CONSTITUTION OF THE UNITED STATES

Articles	Constitution
States are supreme	National government is supreme
Source of authority was states	Source of authority is people
Unicameral legislature	Bicameral legislature
No judiciary	Supreme Court and lower courts as Congress may establish
No independent executive	Independent executive
Limited authority to regulate interstate commerce	Broad authority to regulate interstate commerce
No authority to draft soldiers	Conscription
No authority to issue paper money	May issue paper money
No authority to tax directly	May tax directly
Could not compel states to respect treaties	Authority to make treaties that are binding upon states

THE FIRST PRESIDENT OF THE UNITED STATES AND THE FIRST CONSTITUTION OF THE UNITED STATES

S I D E B A R

Who was the first President of the United States? Most people would say that George Washington was the first president. However, this is a matter of perspective.

The first national government maintained by the colonists was that under the Continental Congress. On September 5, 1774, Peyton Randolph was the first man elected president of that body; thus, he could be considered the first president of the United States.

John Hanson is another possible first president. He was the first president elected under the Articles of Confederation, although he had little authority in this position.

Finally, the third possible first president is George Washington, the first person elected president under the current Constitution of the United States.

The current Constitution is not this nation's first. The Articles of Confederation and Perpetual Union, commonly known as the Articles, were adopted in 1781. In most people's eyes, this was the nation's first constitution. However, the colonists operated under British rule prior to winning independence. Although the British do not have a single document expounding their fundamental law, they do have a body of law that, when taken together, constitutes the British "Constitution." During this period, the colonists were subject to and received the benefits of the British Constitution. Arguably, then, the nation's first fundamental law was that of England.

Finally, it has been asserted that the fundamental laws of the several Native American nations represent the true first constitutions of this land.

of exclusive state powers, a smaller group of exclusive federal powers, and few, if any, concurrently held powers. This approach predominated until the early twentieth century.

Another theory, **hierarchical federalism**, asserts that the national government is supreme in the scheme. Using this approach, the supremacy, necessary and proper, and commerce clauses are read expansively, whereas the Tenth Amendment is interpreted as not creating any specific state powers. Dual federalists, alternatively, view the Tenth Amendment as an independent source of states' rights. It is seen as establishing a state domain upon which the national government may not encroach. Under the hierarchical federalism approach, the Tenth Amendment is viewed as a truism, a negative statement of state power. No domain is staked out; rather, the states are left with whatever the national government cannot lawfully regulate. In addition, there is a large area over which the federal and state governments exercise concurrent jurisdiction, albeit with federal law reigning supreme. Intrastate commercial ventures that affect interstate commerce are examples.

hierarchical federalism
The theory that the national government is supreme to the state governments. The powers of the national government are read broadly and the Tenth Amendment is read as not granting any specific powers to the states.

preemption doctrine
Doctrine that state laws that interfere with federal laws are invalid pursuant to the supremacy clause.

dormant commerce clause doctrine
The idea that state laws that unduly burden interstate commerce, even if the subject is unregulated by the national government, are invalid under federalism principles, because the regulation of interstate and foreign commerce belongs exclusively to the federal government.

intergovernmental immunity doctrine
The doctrine that both the states and the national government possess some immunity from the regulation of the other under federalism principles. Generally, the federal government enjoys greater immunity than do the states.

A third model, which is less authority focused and more relationally focused, is cooperative federalism. A characteristic of cooperative federalism is increased interaction between the states and national government (and local forms of government) in an effort to effectively regulate and administer law and programs. The War on Drugs waged during the Reagan and George H. W. Bush administrations and the War on Terror waged during the George W. Bush administration are examples of cooperative federalism, as federal law-enforcement agencies worked more closely with their counterpart state agencies, including sharing and coordinating resources, all toward policy objectives that were identical or substantially similar.

This aspect of cooperative federalism is a product of the political branches, the executive and legislative. The judiciary has little to do with the cooperative aspect because it does not engage in creation or development of programs and therefore does not interact with state authorities in the administration of those programs. The judiciary usually becomes involved when there is a dispute over jurisdiction; accordingly, it is normally concerned with defining the relative powers of the national and state governments.

The judiciary has had to deal with federalism issues in three contexts, and through its decisions in these contexts, it has advanced the supremacy of national power. First, under the **preemption doctrine**, state laws are invalidated if they interfere or conflict with national legislation. For example, the federal government has preempted state regulation of aviation. Thus, a state cannot enact airline safety regulations, because the federal government has completely regulated the area.

Second, state laws that interfere with interstate commerce, even if largely unregulated by the federal government, are invalidated. This is known as the **dormant commerce clause doctrine**. Pursuant to this doctrine, laws that discriminate against out-of-state market participants have been invalidated. Hence, a state law that prohibited the sale of milk produced outside New York at a lower price than milk produced within the state was held unconstitutional.[4]

Third, through the **intergovernmental immunity doctrine**, the national government possesses greater immunity from state regulation than the states do from federal regulation. That is, the federal government has greater authority to impose obligations upon the states than vice versa. Accordingly, federal overtime and wage laws apply against the states, but similar state laws do not protect federal employees. These three doctrines are discussed more fully in Chapter 7.

Which theory has been applied in the United States? Both the dual and hierarchical models have been applied by the Court cyclically. As discussed in Chapter 1, the Marshall Court was strongly nationalist. It operated under a hierarchical federalism approach. The same was true of the post–Civil War and late New Deal Courts. It was also true of the Burger Court in its late years.

The Taney Court, Pre–New Deal Court, and the early Burger Court followed the dual federalism approach. Notice that the Burger Court is split between the two theories. This is because the Court issued two opinions, only seven years apart, reaching opposite conclusions concerning the allocation of power between the national and state governments.[5]

In many respects, it is easy to understand why the federal government would today possess broader authority than during the framers' time. At the time the Constitution was created, most commercial activities occurred locally. Industries were small and affected their local areas only. Travel and mobility were much more limited than today. National communication was minimal. People's social lives did not stretch far beyond their local communities.

Today, industries are large and have the ability to significantly affect not only other states, but also the nation and even the world. Through cyberspace and other forms of high-tech communication, nearly all persons are connected. Travel is no longer a local matter. Long-distance air, land, and sea carriers have become commonplace, as have immigration and emigration. These changes have caused an increase in the federal government's sphere. In some instances, the need for uniformity of law has caused the federal government to become involved. In others, the impetus has been the lack of resources of the states. In still others, social, technological, or political change has converted what was once a traditional state issue into a national one.

ILLEGAL IMMIGRATION: FEDERAL, STATE, OR LOCAL AUTHORITY?

Article I, Section 8 of the United States Constitution delegates the authority to "establish a uniform rule of naturalization" to the Congress of the United States. This provision, in combination with many other provisions delegating foreign affairs powers to the United States, makes it clear that immigration and naturalization are largely federal policy issues. And indeed, the United States has regulated immigration since the early days of the Constitution, beginning with the Alien Act of 1798. Today, the most significant legislation regulating the field is the Immigration and Naturalization Act of 1952, with several subsequent amendments. This law generally regulates who may enter the United States, for how long, and under what conditions. Many other federal laws exist, such as the Alien Registration Act of 1940, the Immigration Reform and Control Act of 1986, Immigration Act of 1990, Patriot Act, and Enhanced Border Security and Visa Entry Reform Act, which, when taken in aggregate, amount to near federal preemption of immigration.

Although immigration is nearly preempted, many state and local governments are confronting challenges that are a consequence of immigration. Immigrants impact state and local resources, as well as political and social life. Accordingly, there is an ongoing tug-of-war between federal and state control of immigration related issues that have a local dimension. For example, may a state make aliens ineligible for welfare, education, or other benefits? May a state or local government impose registration requirements or impose conditions upon their residence? Generally, if the federal government has regulated the area, local law is invalid, even if not directly contradictory. For example, a state law that imposed registration and fingerprinting requirements beyond what federal law required was stricken down in *Hines v. Davidowitz*, 312 U.S. 52 (1941). On the other hand, the inherent authority (police power) of local authorities to arrest aliens for criminal violations is not seriously questioned. Whether a local authority may retain custody for purposes of trial against the wishes of the United States, which may want to begin deportation proceedings, is a more difficult constitutional question. While it is generally understood that state and local officers may make arrests while enforcing federal criminal laws, whether local officials may make arrests to enforce federal administrative and civil laws is not as clear.

In recent years, the immigration of illegal Mexicans into the United States has been controversial. By the early years of the 2000s, at least ten million illegal immigrants, most of whom were Mexican, resided in the United States. For many years, the impact these individuals had was most acutely felt by border states. By the late 1990s, many midwestern communities, who were home to large numbers of Mexican immigrants, were impacted as well.

Many people were of the opinion that the federal government should do more to control the influx of illegal Mexicans and that it could do more to locate and deport them after entry. As the impact of these individuals on localities grew, so did local reaction. An example is what transpired in Butler County, Ohio in the first decade of the new century. Like many regions in the Midwest, Butler County had experienced a large influx of illegal immigrants. According to the sheriff of Butler County, Richard Jones, the county spent over $1 million in one year housing over 900 illegal aliens who were accused of criminal violations.

Concerned that the federal government was not adequately responding to illegal immigration, Sheriff Jones sent President Bush a letter imploring him to act. He also sent the United States Bureau of Immigration and Customs Enforcement (ICE) a bill for the costs associated with housing the illegal immigrants. The bill was not paid. Sheriff Jones also advocates the use of local police to identify and seize suspected illegal immigrants. Sheriff Jones found an ally in a local state representative, who proposed that legislation be enacted allowing illegal immigrants, who have been lawfully stopped by police for an unrelated traffic or other violation, to be charged with trespassing. Whether the state has the authority to make and enforce such a law is an interesting unanswered constitutional question. It is unlikely that this particular case will find itself before the Supreme Court because, at least at the time of this writing, the federal government and Butler County have begun to discuss how they can better coordinate and cooperate in immigration enforcement this a good example of cooperative federalism. Concerning the relative authorities of the state/local authorities as opposed to federal authorities, what constitutional values are implicated? Precedent aside, how would you weigh these conflicting interests?

Exclusive National Powers
Coining money
Foreign diplomacy
Making treaties
Regulating interstate and foreign commerce
Establishing a post office
Taxing imports and exports
Regulating naturalization of citizenship
Regulating immigration and emigration
Establishing bankruptcy law

Exclusive State Powers
Providing for the health and welfare of
   state citizens
General police and fire protection
Licensing most professions
Providing education, Regulate domestic relations

Concurrently Held Powers
Taxing citizens
Chartering banks
Constructing roads
Borrowing money
Eminent domain
Punishing crime

Powers Denied to Both
Ex post facto laws
Bills of attainder
Other encroachments upon civil rights
   protected by the Constitution

FIGURE 2-1
Comparing state and federal powers

Finally, note that examples of cooperative federalism can be found during periods where dual and hierarchical federalism are dominant. Need, finances, and whether dual or hierarchical federalism are dominant all influence the extent to which states of the federal government cooperate.

2.1(b) State and National Powers Compared

Some powers are held exclusively by the national government, others are held exclusively by the states, and some are held concurrently (see Figure 2-1). Then there are some actions that neither may take, because of rights retained by the people.

The powers of the national government are set out in the Constitution. Many of these are found in Article I, which enumerates the powers of Congress. Examples of exclusive national powers are coining money, declaring war, conducting foreign diplomacy, making treaties, regulating interstate and international commerce, establishing a post office, taxing imports and exports, regulating naturalization of citizenship, and establishing bankruptcy law.

Article II, which establishes the national executive, grants to the president of the United States the responsibility of conducting foreign diplomacy and negotiating treaties. Treaties must be ratified by the Senate, however. The states are forbidden from engaging in diplomacy and entering into agreements with other nations.

Although the sovereignty of the states has diminished since the Constitution was created, certain areas remain within the exclusive domain of the states. Regulating for the health and welfare of citizens and regulating domestic affairs are within the state sphere.[6] Providing police and fire protection is another matter within a state's control. These functions make up what is generally referred to as the **police power**. The licensing of professions, such as physicians, plumbers, electricians, and attorneys, is regulated by the states. Education has also been a traditional state function. Just as the national government has the exclusive authority to regulate interstate and foreign commerce, the states possess the exclusive authority to regulate intrastate commerce.

Finally, some powers are held concurrently. The power to tax citizens, charter banks and corporations, and build roads are examples.

If the authority over a policy area has been delegated to the federal or state governments, the delegatee is generally permitted to engage in regulation of any type—civil, administrative, or criminal. Frequently, the result is an overlapping of administrative functions, as well as civil and criminal laws. For example, the United States Department of Transportation has overlapping jurisdiction with state agencies charged with highway administration. Also, robbery of a federally insured or chartered bank is a violation of both state and federal criminal law. The state in which the robbery occurred has jurisdiction pursuant to its general police powers, and the federal government has jurisdiction by virtue of its charter or insurance coverage.

Finally, civil rights, or rights of the people, are a limitation upon the authority of both the states and the national government. Some of these rights are found in the original Constitution. For example, Article I forbids Congress from enacting ex post facto laws and bills of attainder. The Bill of Rights also protects a number of civil rights, such as freedom from self-incrimination, freedom of the press, freedom of assembly, and freedom from cruel and unusual punishment. The rights specifically mentioned in the Constitution are not intended to be exclusive. The Tenth Amendment, often referred to as the *state rights amendment*, also reserves powers to the people. Further, the Ninth Amendment reserves rights not mentioned in the Constitution exclusively to the people. It states, "The enumeration in the Constitution, of certain rights, shall not be construed to deny or disparage others retained by the people." To date, the Supreme Court has not read this amendment as solely reserving any particular right. Although it has cited it as supporting rights founded largely upon another right, e.g., due process.

Be aware, however, that the Supreme Court has determined that the Bill of Rights was intended to be a limitation upon the national government, not the states. Support for this decision can be found in the reaction to James Madison's proposed Bill of Rights. He proposed seventeen rights which were eventually consolidated and winnowed to twelve, from which the ten we know today were ratified. One that was rejected provided that states may not "violate the equal right of conscience, freedom of the press, or trial by jury in criminal cases."

This changed, however, as a result of the post–Civil War Amendments (Amendments 13–15). Specifically, the Court has determined that the Fourteenth Amendment's due process clause "incorporates" most of the amendments. Any amendment incorporated applies against the states. Nearly every amendment has been incorporated, and therefore the Bill of Rights limits the authority of the states as well as the national government.[7] See Chapter 5 for a thorough discussion of **incorporation**. See Chapters 5 and 9 for more thorough discussions of incorporation.

The debate over the balancing of federal and state authorities continues today. Proponents of "states' rights" claim that the national government, through all three of its branches, has emasculated state sovereignty. The national government has extended its authority in two primary ways. First, the sphere of the national government's jurisdiction has widened considerably, through a liberal reading of the Constitution's delegation of authority to the national government (i.e., commerce and necessary and proper clauses) and a narrow interpretation of the Tenth Amendment. This has already been mentioned and is the subject of further discussion in Chapter 5.

Second, if the national government wants to effectuate a policy objective that falls within the exclusive (or concurrent) jurisdiction of the states, it may impose its will on the states through economic coercion. It does this by attaching conditions to subsidies, grants, and appropriations made to the states. For example, to further the national government's policy of racial integration at public events, one condition placed on money awarded to states is that it may not be used to fund segregated functions. The fifty-five-mile-per-hour speed limit is another example. The regulation of state and local highways is outside the direct regulation of the

police power
The power of government to make and enforce laws and regulations necessary to maintain and enhance the public welfare and to prevent individuals from violating the rights of others.

incorporation
The Bill of Rights was intended to be applied only against the national government. However, the Supreme Court determined that most of the rights contained therein were "incorporated" by the due process clause of the Fourteenth Amendment. A right is *incorporated* if it is fundamental and necessary to an ordered liberty. Once incorporated, the right applies against the states.

national government. When the federal government wanted to impose a nationwide fifty-five-mile-per-hour speed limit, it accomplished that aim by threatening to withhold funding from states that did not adopt the fifty-five-mile-per-hour limit. The federal government similarly coerced the states to come into compliance with federal clean air laws by threatening to withhold federal highway funds.[8]

Various presidents have attempted to address states' rights concerns, such as Presidents Nixon and Ford, who advocated a "new federalism," whereby the federal government would place fewer conditions on the use of federal subsidies. President Carter implemented rules requiring federal administrative officers to work directly with state officials to accomplish policy objectives. President Carter's approach, as you have learned, is a form of *shared and cooperative federalism.* President Reagan advocated states' rights, claiming that authority should be returned to the states; however, little authority was actually transferred during his administration.

As we have seen, the political branches of government are not alone in struggling with the complexity of federalism. The Supreme Court has wavered between dual and hierarchical federalism, with its approach being dependent upon the ideology of its members.

Undoubtedly, the debate over the allocation of authorities between the states and national government will continue as an inherent feature of a federalist system like that of the United States. The vacillation between dual and hierarchical federalism will also continue, as a result of political, social, and economic factors. At times when national or international concerns consume the nation's attention and conscience, such as war and economic crisis, hierarchical federalism will predominate. During periods when there are no pressing national problems, dual federalism is more likely to predominate.

2.2 SEPARATION OF POWERS

Under the Articles of Confederation, there was no national judiciary. Also, there was no independent executive, as the president was a member of, and selected by, the Congress. The framers were heavily influenced by the theories of philosophers James Harrington, John Locke, and Charles de Montesquieu."[9] These men advanced the theory that, to avoid tyranny, a separation or division of governmental authority must exist. To the framers, the need for a separation of powers was more than a theory. They had had experience with a centralized authority, the English Crown, and had found it arbitrary and unjust. Concerning the centralization of powers, James Madison stated that "[t]he accumulation of all power legislative, executive and judiciary in the same hands, whether hereditary, self-appointed, or elective, may justly be pronounced the very definition of tyranny."[10]

Although the phrase "separation of powers" does not appear in the Constitution, the framers employed its architecture in their design of the new government. Hence, there is a horizontal division of governmental authority, just as there is a vertical division (federalism) (see Figure 2-2).

SEPARATION OF POWERS			
	Executive	*Legislative*	*Judicial*
United States	*President* ■ Second-level executive officials	*Congress* ■ Senate ■ House	*Federal courts* ■ Article III ■ Supreme Court ■ Appeals courts ■ Trial courts
States	*Governor* ■ Second-level officials	*State legislatures* ■ Typically bicameral	*State courts (Non-Article III)* ■ Highest court ■ Intermediate appeal ■ Trial

(Left vertical label spanning both rows: **FEDERALISM**)

FIGURE 2-2
Dividing governmental power

Horizontally, the national government's authorities are divided among three branches, the legislative, executive, and judicial. This division is found in the first three articles of the Constitution. Article I establishes Congress and sets forth its authorities. Congress is comprised of two chambers, the House of Representatives and the Senate. Article II establishes the presidency and also sets forth the authorities of the executive. Article III establishes the Supreme Court and such inferior courts as Congress may establish and sets forth the authorities of the judiciary. Indeed, Congress has exercised the authority to create lower judicial tribunals on several occasions. Today, there are three levels of federal courts. The trial level courts are called *district courts*. Appeals are taken to the courts of appeals, which are divided into thirteen circuits. Finally, the Supreme Court sits at the apex of the judiciary. In addition, there are a few specialty courts in the federal system. See Figure 2-3, which diagrams the federal court structure.

The authority and responsibilities of the three branches are not equally well defined by the Constitution. Congress's authority is the best defined, with the president's and the judiciary's falling second and third, respectively.

Congress is responsible for making the nation's laws; the president is responsible for administering and enforcing the nation's laws, conducting foreign affairs, and negotiating treaties, and is the commander-in-chief of the military; the judiciary is responsible for administering justice, resolving disputes, and interpreting the law. Today, the judiciary also plays a role in preserving the balance of powers and protecting civil liberties.

As a general proposition, one branch may not exercise the functions of any other coordinate branches. However, no one function is vested entirely in one branch. The framers went one step further in preventing abuse—they incorporated a system of checks and balances.

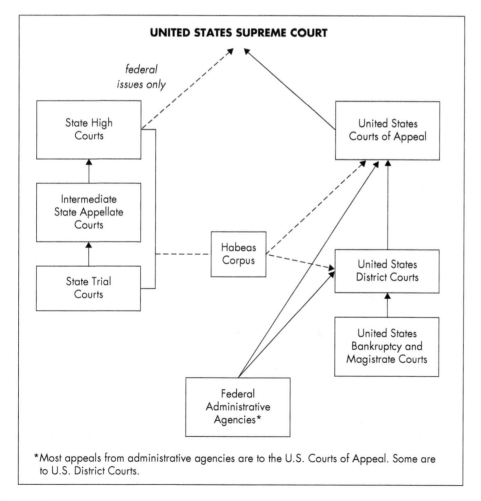

FIGURE 2-3

Courts and appellate procedure

2.3 CHECKS AND BALANCES

Although the framers intended to separate the three governmental branches, they did not intend for the branches to be "wholly unconnected with each other."[11] The branches do come into contact with one another on occasion. For example, executive officials and judges may testify at congressional hearings concerning their functions and needs. The president, justices of the Supreme Court, and the entire Congress assemble for the president's State of the Union address. The branches also come into contact (albeit often indirect contact) as a result of the many checks and balances found in the Constitution.

Through checks and balances, the framers prevented one branch from possessing absolute authority over any particular function. Rather, the functions delegated to one branch are "checked" by, or shared with, another branch. This provides balance to the system by keeping each branch accountable to its coordinate branches. Several checks can be found in the Constitution (see Figure 2-4). Some scholars argue that the systems of checks and balances is so robust that there is no genuine "separation of powers."

Congress is responsible for making the law. It is checked in this function by the president, who may veto legislation. The president is then checked by Congress, which can override a veto with a two-thirds majority. Also, Congress enacts laws, but it depends on the president to enforce them. The judiciary also checks Congress. Legislation that conflicts with the Constitution may be declared void by the courts.

The president conducts foreign affairs and negotiates treaties. Congress, the Senate in particular, must ratify treaties. The president is the commander-in-chief of the military, but Congress possesses significant authority over the military as well. It is charged with making rules regulating the military and is responsible for declaring war. The president has been delegated the authority to nominate federal judges and other governmental officers, but the appointments are final only after Senate confirmation. As a check on both the president and the judiciary, Congress holds the authority of impeachment. Finally, through judicial review, the judiciary checks the president's actions for constitutionality.

The judiciary is also checked. Article III judges are nominated by the president and the Senate must approve the nominations. Congress has the authority to remove cases from the appellate jurisdiction of the Supreme Court and, presumably, could limit the jurisdiction of lower courts. Also, because the courts inferior to the Supreme Court were created by Congress, they may be abolished by Congress. As previously mentioned, judges may be removed through impeachment by Congress. The states and Congress (the people) check the constitutional pronouncements of the Court through the amendment process.

Therefore, no branch is completely independent in the performance of its functions. Because of these checks, interbranch cooperation, especially between Congress and the president, is increased and the potential for unlawful, unethical, and unreasonable governmental behavior is decreased.

Another method of checking government is through the varying methods of selecting governmental officials. This authority is diffused—that is, no one entity is responsible for

Authority	Checked By
President negotiates treaties	Senate ratification
President nominates judges and officers	Senate confirmation
Congress enacts laws	Presidential approval and judicial review
Presidential veto	Congressional override
President is commander-in-chief of the military	Congress declares war and creates rules regulating the military
Courts exercise judicial review	Impeachment by Congress and constitutional amendment process
Elected officials are not responsive to public	People, through the vote

FIGURE 2-4
Examples of checks and balances

choosing the representatives of the people. Even within Congress, for example, two methods of selection were incorporated by the original framers: members of the House of Representatives were elected directly by the people, and senators were chosen by state legislatures. The method of selecting senators by the states did not change until the Seventeenth Amendment was adopted in 1913. Today, members of both houses are selected by direct election.

The president is elected by the electoral college, a small group of people chosen at the state level nationwide. Federal judges are nominated by the president and must be confirmed by the Senate. Other federal officials, such as diplomats and cabinet officials, must undergo the same process.

Federalism, separation of powers, and checks and balances are all intended to prevent tyranny and the usurpation of state sovereignty. In the following five chapters, these issues are examined more closely. In Chapters 3, 4, 5, and 6, the authorities of the national legislative, executive, and judicial branches are discussed. Chapter 7 discusses a particular separation of powers problem, that of delegations to administrative agencies. The authorities of the states as opposed to the national government are explored in greater detail in Chapter 8. The remainder of the text is devoted to the rights of the people.

2.4 FORMS OF STATE AND FEDERAL LAW

The division of governmental authority into state and federal levels and between branches at each level creates a complex system within which there are many forms of law, from many sources, at many levels.

Of course, the fundamental law of the nation, and the subject of this text, is the United States Constitution. Each state also has a constitution. The United States Constitution is the highest form of law. The United States Constitution recognizes, inherently through its structural provisions and explicitly in the Ninth and Tenth Amendments, that certain authorities belong to the states. Accordingly, state constitutions are the highest form of law for state law subjects. Similarly, the highest court of each state is the final arbiter of state law, not the Supreme Court of the United States. When in conflict, state law falls to federal law under the Supremacy Clause of Article VI, and the Supreme Court of the United States is the final interpreter of federal law.

As you will learn in a later chapter, the Constitution assigns the authority to make federal law to the United States Congress. The laws enacted by this body are known as public laws or statutes. These laws are organized by subject matter into the United States Code. Each state also has a legislature that makes law. Many lawmaking bodies also exist at the local level, such as city councils, county councils, and school boards. Local laws are generally known as ordinances.

Although largely an enforcement officer, the president, as well as his gubernatorial counterparts, has limited lawmaking authority. The common vehicle for presidential lawmaking is the executive order. If legitimate, an executive order has the authority of a statute. The president has the authority make law in those subject areas that are inherently executive or where Congress has appropriately delegated the authority to the president. Orders managing the operations of government are examples of the former because as the chief executive, the president is responsible for managing the daily operations of government. Many examples of congressional delegations of authority enabling presidents to issue executive orders can be found and will be discussed later in this text. Other executive tools exist through which "law" is sometimes made, such as military orders and presidential proclamations. Statute requires that all executive orders be published in the *Federal Register,* a United States government publication of new regulations, executive orders and proclamations, notices by government agencies of impending action, and other documents required to be published by government agencies.

Administrative rulemaking is another form of law. Congress often empowers administrative agencies to create rules, also known as regulations, to enforce their mandates. When properly created, administrative rules have the authority of legislation. In most cases, the authority to make rules must be delegated from the legislative authority. Administrative regulations are always subordinate to legislation. Today, there are more administrative rules than statutes. By the 1990's, the Code of Federal Regulations, where all federal rules can be found, exceeded 135,000 pages. State agencies have, in varying degrees, similar authority to make regulations.

At the state level and to a lesser extent, the federal level, the common law continues to be an important source of law. The common law, which is of English heritage, has a judicial origin. Before Parliament existed in England, judges developed legal principles to guide their decision making. These legal principles generally followed the customs and practices of the time. For political and prudential reasons, the doctrine of *stare decisis et non quieta movera* (Latin for "stand by precedents and do not disturb settled points") was developed in early English courts. This doctrine requires that all lower courts adhere to the law announced by a superior court when the facts of the present case are identical or nearly identical to the facts of the earlier case. The application of this doctrine over time had the effect of homogenizing the law. Said another way, the law began to be common to all. The colonists who founded the United States brought the English common law with them. Today, Congress and the state legislatures, and administrative agencies as described earlier, are the primary source of new laws. The common law continues to fill in the gaps where legislatures have not spoken and it continues to be important in understanding and defining existing law. Of course, any common law principle that is contrary to the Constitution of the United States, or a state constitution if a state common law principle, is invalid. For example, ancient courts would often declare an act to be criminal, and therefore create a precedent of the act's criminality, on a case-by-case basis. So, there had to be a first case where a court declared murder to be a crime. Now that we have legislatures, some courts have found that the creation of common law crimes violates the due process clause's guarantee of notice of which acts are criminal. This idea is expressed in the Latin phrase *nulla poena sine lege*, meaning "there shall be no crime if there is no statute."

Finally, judicial decisions interpreting the Constitution and statutes are another form of law. A perennial debate exists over whether this is lawmaking or simply interpretation. For some people, departures from precedent by the Supreme Court amount to lawmaking. For others, interpretation is a natural process and the limits on this authority, such as the ability to amend a constitution or statute that is being interpreted, keep it from being pure lawmaking.

2.5 SUMMARY

Even though the framers wanted to increase the national government's authority from its weak position under the Articles of Confederation, they did not want to centralize all governmental authority into one hand or into a small number of hands. Instead, they controlled authority through structure. First, they created a federation. Second, they further divided federal authority into three departments or branches. These authority divisions are not absolute, however. The federal and state governments often share jurisdiction and the three branches of the federal government check each other. These additional features of the United States government are intended to protect the people against tyranny.

The precise relationship between the federal and state governments is continually being redefined. The social, economic, and political circumstances of each case determine the legal outcome of any jurisdictional conflicts. The Supreme Court has vacillated between the dual and hierarchical federalism perspectives since the Constitution was enacted. There is no question, however, that the federal government has experienced enormous growth and increases in authority during the past two hundred years. Some of this can be attributed to population growth and the globalization of economic, travel, political, and social aspects of the world. Other factors, such as internal politics, have also contributed to the current federal scheme. As you will learn later there has been a shift on the Supreme Court in recent years favoring limited federal authority and reinforcing state authority. Whether this will continue with the Robert's court remains to be seen.

REVIEW QUESTIONS

1. Define federalism and separation of powers.
2. Why did the framers separate governmental authority?
3. List two authorities held exclusively by the federal government, two held exclusively by the state governments, and two concurrently held.
4. Identify two checks and balances provided for in the Constitution.
5. Briefly describe the functions of each of the three branches of government.

ASSIGNMENTS

1. Compare and contrast dual and hierarchical federalism. Which do you believe the framers intended? Should the framers' intent matter today? Explain your answers.
2. Congress enacts the following statute:

   Section One TRAFFIC LAWS: FTPA; exclusive national jurisdiction

   The Federal Traffic Police Administration is hereby established. It shall have jurisdiction over all traffic offenses defined by federal law. The federal government shall be the source of all traffic laws and law enforcement on all roads, paved and unpaved, in the United States.

   Section Two TRAFFIC LAWS: FTT; Trials

   A system of Federal Traffic Tribunals is hereby established. The FTT shall be located within the Department of Justice. The FTT shall have exclusive jurisdiction over every traffic violation charge in the United States. The judges of the tribunal shall be appointed by the Attorney General and may be removed by the Attorney General without cause.

   Under further provisions, all traffic offenses are characterized as criminal and punishment varies from small fines to several years in prison (e.g., vehicular manslaughter, ten years).

   Is this statute constitutional? Explain fully.

NOTES

1. The Federalist No. 47.
2. The Federalist No. 45.
3. Essay published in the *New York Journal* on October 18, 1787, taken from *The Creation of the Constitution* 109–111. Opposing Viewpoints Series (Greenhaven Press 1995).
4. *Baldwin v. G.A.F. Seelig, Inc.*, 294 U.S. 511 (1935).
5. The two cases are *National League of Cities v. Usery*, 426 U.S. 833 (1976), and *San Antonio Independent School District v. Rodriguez*, 411 U.S. 1 (1973).
6. See *Elk Grove Unified School District v. Newdow*, 542 U.S. 1 (2004) in Chapter 4.
7. The amendments that have not been incorporated are the right to a jury trial in civil cases (Seventh Amendment), the right to grand jury indictment (Fifth Amendment), and the right to have a twelve-person jury (Sixth Amendment and case law).
8. For a discussion of this topic, see William Klein, "Pressure or Compulsion? Federal Highway Fund Sanctions of the Clean Air Act Amendments of 1990," 26 *Rutgers L.J.* 855 (1995).
9. See James Harrington, *Oceana* (1656), John Locke, *Civil Government* (1690), and Charles de Montesquieu, *Spirit of the Laws* (1748).
10. The Federalist No. 47.
11. The Federalist No. 48.

9 The Bill of Rights

9.1 WHY DO WE HAVE A BILL OF RIGHTS?

The first ten amendments to the Constitution are referred to as the **Bill of Rights**. These provisions, although considered a fundamental and inseparable part of the modern-day Constitution, were not included in the document when it was originally ratified in 1789.[2] In fact, some of the constitutional framers deemed such a supplemental list of rights to be unnecessary for, and perhaps even harmful to, protecting individual rights and liberties. Those who opposed a bill of rights asserted that if rights were specifically enumerated, they might be viewed as an exhaustive list of liberties, thereby leaving unprotected all other freedoms not specifically mentioned.[3] **James Madison**, the chief architect of the Bill of Rights, initially stated that the document was "unnecessary, because it was evident that the general government had no power but what was given it [by the Constitution]" and "dangerous, because an enumeration which is not complete is not safe." By omitting a bill of rights, some framers argued that citizens could always claim, in the face of governmental intrusion, that because citizens did not specifically limit the nature and extent of their freedoms, they reserved the right to do what they pleased.

But still other constitutional sponsors maintained that a bill of rights was necessary to preserve the blessings of liberty against governmental infringement. During the Constitutional Convention, George Mason, a delegate from Virginia, urged the delegates to adopt a bill of rights, claiming that such a document "would give great quiet to the people; and with the aid of the state declarations, a bill might be prepared in a few hours." Mason, along with delegates Charles Pinckney and Elbridge Gerry of Massachusetts, and Edmund Randolph of Virginia, further believed that without a bill of rights, the powers vested in Congress under the proposed Articles eventually would lead to "monarchy or a tyrannical aristocracy." The efforts to include a bill of rights, however, were unsuccessful at the Constitutional Convention, and the Articles of the Constitution were adopted as an insulated document and sent to the states for ratification.

It was not until the ratification proceedings that the movement to include a bill of rights ultimately became successful. During the states' ratification debates, many delegates reintroduced objections to ratifying the proposed Constitution without the inclusion of a bill of rights. In Virginia, Patrick Henry questioned why the Constitution

---

[A] bill of rights is what the people are entitled to against every government on earth, general or particular, and what no just government should refuse, or rest on inference.

*Thomas Jefferson,
Letter to
James Madison,
December 20, 1987[1]*

Bill of Rights
The first ten amendments to the Constitution, which were written in 1789 and ratified in 1791, contain the primary civil liberties protected under the Constitution.

James Madison
A "founding father" of the Constitution and the chief architect of the Bill of Rights.

lacked specific protections for individual rights when the Declaration of Independence itself went to so much trouble to chronicle the "unalienable rights" of individuals and to assert protection for these rights against governmental interference. Henry asserted that without the inclusion of a bill of rights, the proposed Articles were inconsistent with the values and claims set forth in the nation's founding document.

Beyond the principled arguments surrounding the debate, the failure to include a bill of rights within the Constitution presented serious strategic problems for the framers seeking the document's ratification. Although many constitutional proponents believed that it was possible that the Constitution would be ratified by the requisite nine states even without including a bill of rights, some believed that Virginia, New York, and Massachusetts—three of the largest states at the time—were likely to vote against the new Constitution without some guarantee that a bill of rights would be added. And given the size of these states, some framers believed that any constitution implemented without their approval stood little chance of succeeding in the long term. Accordingly, in an effort to secure the approval of these states and others, James Madison, who had opposed the inclusion of a bill of rights during the Constitutional Convention, along with other members of the Constitutional Convention, agreed to propose a bill of rights to the First Congress after the Constitution was ratified. This concession, along with other promotional efforts, ultimately secured unanimous ratification of the Constitution by the then-thirteen states.

The First Congress was convened in March 1789. During this time, James Madison began to draft proposals for the new bill of rights, which were to be submitted for congressional consideration and approval and then to the states for ratification. In September 1789, after Madison had drafted a list of suggested amendments, Congress approved twelve amendments to the Constitution. The first of these amendments altered the manner by which seats in the House of Representatives were apportioned and, through a comparatively complex formula, sought to preserve the total number of House members as the nation grew. The second amendment barred congressional salaries from being effectuated prior to the following House election. However, during state ratification proceedings between November 1789 and December 1791, these two amendments were not approved by a sufficient number (eleven) of these states,[4] thereby leaving the remaining ten amendments as the adopted bill of rights. As a result, the amendment approved by Congress as the third amendment became the first amendment; the fourth amendment became the second amendment; and so forth. These ten provisions reflect the Bill of Rights as we know the document today. (See Figure 9-1.)

Since the ratification of the Bill of Rights on December 15, 1791, seventeen additional amendments have been added to the Constitution. Some of these amendments address the manner in which governmental institutions fulfill their duties and exercise their powers. For example, the Seventeenth Amendment provides for the popular election of United States senators; the Twenty-second Amendment places term limits on presidents; and the Twenty-seventh Amendment imposes restrictions on congressional pay raises. Other amendments are designed to secure additional rights and liberties for individuals. For example, the Thirteenth Amendment bars slavery and involuntary servitude; the Fourteenth Amendment entitles individuals to equal

---

S I D E B A R

PRESIDENTS AND JUSTICES AS LAWYERS

Given the nature of the government service and its relationship to the law, lawyers have historically been attracted to elected office. As of 2008, twenty-five of the forty-three presidents of the United States had been attorneys. John Adams was the first. William J. Clinton was the most recent. There were many accomplished attorneys between the two, including Abraham Lincoln and Martin Van Buren.

Eight actually appeared before the Supreme Court of the United States. John Adams was the first. He appeared on several occasions, including his famous post-presidency appearance in the Amistad case, which was later popularized by a film of that name. James Polk, Abraham Lincoln, James Garfield, Benjamin Harrison, Grover Cleveland, William Howard Taft, and Richard Nixon were the other seven.

Interestingly, Justices appointed to the Supreme Court do not have to be lawyers. But since 1957, the Court has been an all-lawyer bench. The last non-lawyer Justice was Stanley Reed, who had received substantial legal training and education, but had never become a lawyer.

See Norman Gross, AMERICA'S LAWYER-PRESIDENTS: FROM LAW OFFICE TO OVAL OFFICE, 14 SUM Experience 4 (2004).

First Amendment
Bars government from passing laws respecting an establishment of religion
Bars government from prohibiting the free exercise of religion
Bars government from abridging the freedom of speech
Bars government from abridging the freedom of the press
Bars government from abridging the right to peacefully assemble
Bars government from abridging the right to petition government for redress of grievances

Second Amendment
Bars government from infringing on the right to bear arms

Third Amendment
In peacetime, bars government from quartering soldiers in homes without an owner's consent
During war, allows troops to be quartered in a manner prescribed by law

Fourth Amendment
Bars government from violating the right against unreasonable searches and seizures
Requires probable cause, oath or affirmation, and particularity for the issuance of warrants

Fifth Amendment
Requires grand jury indictment for charges of capital or infamous charges
Bars government from trying a person twice for the same offense (double jeopardy)
Bars government from compelling persons to testify against themselves in criminal cases
Bars government from depriving persons life, liberty, or property without due process of law
Bars government from taking private property for public use without just compensation

Sixth Amendment
Provides accused persons with the right to a speedy, public, and jury trial in criminal cases
Provides accused persons with the right to be notified of the criminal charges against them
Provides accused persons with the right to confront witnesses against them
Provides accused persons with the right to compel witnesses to appear on their behalf
Provides accused persons with the right to the assistance of legal counsel in criminal cases

Seventh Amendment
Provides the right to a jury trial in civil cases involving disputes valued over twenty dollars
Provides common law rules to be used when federal courts review common law suits

Eighth Amendment
Bars government from imposing excessive bail or fines
Bars government from inflicting cruel and unusual punishment

Ninth Amendment
Provides that the Constitution's enumeration of specific rights should not be interpreted to deny other rights retained by the people

Tenth Amendment
Provides that all powers not given to the United States or taken from the states by the Constitution are reserved to the States or to the people

FIGURE 9-1
Textual contents of the Bill of Rights

protection and due process in state proceedings; and the Nineteenth Amendment gives women the right to vote. But even with these additional amendments, the Bill of Rights is still regarded as the primary document for protecting individual rights and liberties against governmental interference.

9.2 WHERE DO RIGHTS COME FROM?

One of the major questions debated by constitutional scholars is the source of individual rights. Some claim that these rights are created by the Constitution, and that without the existence of this document, the enumerated rights therein would not exist. Others claim that people have individual rights by virtue of their birth and that these rights are not dependent upon any formal written document. In other words, some scholars view the Constitution as simply reaffirming and otherwise acknowledging rights that are vested in individuals independently from the document.

Upon reading the Constitution, one of the first things you may notice is the difference in the language between the Articles of the Constitution and the Bill of Rights. Generally, the powers held by the three branches of government under the Articles of the Constitution are treated as grants or investments of authority. For example, Article I provides that "All legislative

social compact
A term used to describe the Constitution as a contract between two primary parties—the people and the government—wherein the people have given their consent to political institutions to be their sovereign governing authority, granting to them certain powers of structure, process, and support, and in exchange, the government has agreed to provide the people with certain levels of protection and sustenance.

compact theory
A theory of individual liberties that considers liberties to be the product of a negotiated contract. Under this approach, rights are derived from an agreement or compact between the individuals being protected and those individuals or institutions providing the protection. Through negotiation, individuals and institutions receive rights, powers, and protections by virtue of compact or constitution.

natural rights theory
A theory of individual liberties that maintains that liberties are the result of the "laws of nature." This theory recognizes life itself as the source of certain individual rights, which exist independent of any constitution or contract. Natural rights theory insists that the rights enumerated in the Bill of Rights are natural, inherent, and unalienable to individuals.

Powers herein *granted* shall be *vested* in a Congress of the United States"; Article II states that "The executive Power shall be *vested* in a President"; And Article III says that "The judicial Power of the United States, shall be *vested* in one Supreme Court, and in such inferior Courts as the Congress may from time to time ordain and establish." The use of the terms "granted" and "vested" in these provisions, along with the phrase "We the People . . . do ordain and establish this Constitution for the United States of America," found in the Preamble, suggests that the enumerated governmental powers found in the Constitution initially were not held by the government prior to the formation of the document, but instead, were held by "the People" who ultimately chose to delegate these authorities to three governmental institutions.

The Preamble and Articles reflect a **social compact** or contract between two primary parties—the people and the government. Under this contract, the people have given their consent to political institutions to be their sovereign governing authority, granting to them certain powers of structure, process, and support. And in exchange, the government has agreed to provide the people with certain levels of protection and sustenance. This "agreement" provides that the parties' relationship may be changed under Article V's amendment procedure, depending upon the needs and desires of the parties. In other words, the duties and powers of the government are not inherent or unalienable; rather, they are dependent upon the continued consent of the governed and can be removed or altered at any time through constitutional amendment.[5]

Treating individuals rights as the product of a negotiated contract is known as the **compact theory** of individual rights. Under this approach, rights are derived from an agreement or compact between the individuals being protected and those individuals or institutions providing the protection. Through negotiation, individuals and institutions receive rights, powers, and protections by virtue of compact or constitution. Under this theory, people have rights to the freedom of speech, religion, and assembly because the Bill of Rights provides for these rights and secures them against governmental interference, and without these contractual (constitutional) provisions, these rights would not exist.[6]

Others assert that individuals have rights within the "laws of nature," and thus certain liberties regardless of whether any social compact is formed. This approach is called the **natural rights theory** of individual rights—a belief that some rights are vested in individuals by the "laws of nature" at the time of birth. This theory recognizes life itself as the source of certain individual rights, which exist independent of any constitution or contract. Natural rights theory insists that the rights enumerated in the Bill of Rights are natural, inherent, and unalienable to individuals.[7] Natural rights theory maintains there are certain fundamental privileges that are afforded individuals simply as human beings and that are universal in application. As evidence of this theory, some point to the language of the Declaration of Independence, which cites to the "laws of nature" and provides that "all men . . . are endowed by their Creator with certain unalienable Rights." These provisions suggest that rights, while not always recognized or protected by governments, nevertheless are naturally vested in all persons at birth and held by virtue of their humanity until death.

Natural rights theorists also point to the language used in the Bill of Rights to support their theory. Unlike the words used in the Articles of the Constitution, the Bill of Rights does not speak in terms of *vesting, granting,* or *establishing* rights of speech, religion, press, and so on to the people. Instead, the document references the enumerated rights and freedoms as if they already existed, independent of the Constitution, and suggests that the Bill of Rights was drafted in order to ensure that these preexisting rights are protected by the government. For example, the First Amendment does not state that individuals are *vested* with the freedom of speech, freedom of the press, or right to peaceably assemble; rather, it provides that the government may not *abridge* these rights and freedoms. Similarly, the Fourth Amendment does not say that the people are *granted* the right to be secure in their persons, houses, papers, and effects, but instead, it provides protection of this right against unreasonable searches and seizures. Natural rights theorists maintain that this language suggests that the Bill of Rights protects all persons, regardless of their citizenship, against governmental interference.

The difference between compact theory and natural rights theory is much more than an academic debate. The nature and source of rights in the Bill of Rights have real and potentially enormous consequences, particularly during times of war, international conflict, and domestic disputes involving a person's nationality. Consider, for example, situations where

Sher Singh, left, appears with his attorney,
Mark B. Laroche, in Providence District Court in
Providence, R.I., Wednesday, Oct. 10, 2001.
AP Wide World Photos

the United States acts outside of its geographic jurisdiction against individuals who are not
U.S. citizens. Under compact theory, foreign individuals likely would be considered to have
few, if any, rights under the Bill of Rights to assert against the government's actions because
they are not U.S. citizens, and thus they are not parties to the contract of the Constitution. But
if rights are regarded as natural and universal, as natural rights theory suggests, then, in the
face of action by the United States, foreign nationals would possess rights by virtue of their
birth and regardless of their citizenship.

UNITED STATES v. VERDUGO-URQUIDEZ
494 U.S. 259 (1990)

CHIEF JUSTICE REHNQUIST delivered the opinion of the
Court.

The question presented by this case is whether the Fourth
Amendment applies to the search and seizure by United States
agents of property that is owned by a nonresident alien and
located in a foreign country. We hold that it does not.

Respondent Rene Martin Verdugo-Urquidez is a citizen
and resident of Mexico. He is believed by the United States
Drug Enforcement Agency (DEA) to be one of the leaders of a
large and violent organization in Mexico that smuggles narcotics into the United States. Based on a complaint charging
respondent with various narcotics-related offenses, the Government obtained a warrant for his arrest on August 3, 1985. In

January 1986, Mexican police officers, after discussions with
United States marshals, apprehended Verdugo-Urquidez in
Mexico and transported him to the United States Border Patrol
station in Calexico, California. There, United States marshals
arrested respondent and eventually moved him to a correctional
center in San Diego, California, where he remains incarcerated
pending trial.

Following respondent's arrest, Terry Bowen, a DEA agent
assigned to the Calexico DEA office, decided to arrange for
searches of Verdugo-Urquidez's Mexican residences located in
Mexicali and San Felipe . . . Thereafter, DEA agents working in
concert with officers of the [Mexican Federal Judicial Police]
searched respondent's properties in Mexicali and San Felipe and

seized certain documents. In particular, the search of the Mexicali residence uncovered a tally sheet, which the Government believes reflects the quantities of marijuana smuggled by Verdugo-Urquidez into the United States. . . .

The Fourth Amendment provides:

> "The right of the people to be secure in their persons, houses, papers, and effects, against unreasonable searches and seizures, shall not be violated, and no Warrants shall issue, but upon probable cause, supported by Oath or affirmation, and particularly describing the place to be searched, and the persons or things to be seized."

That text, by contrast with the Fifth and Sixth Amendments, extends its reach only to "the people." Contrary to the suggestion of amici curiae that the Framers used this phrase "simply to avoid [an] awkward rhetorical redundancy," "the people" seems to have been a term of art employed in select parts of the Constitution. The Preamble declares that the Constitution is ordained and established by "the people of the United States." The Second Amendment protects "the right of the people to keep and bear Arms," and the Ninth and Tenth Amendments provide that certain rights and powers are retained by and reserved to "the people." While this textual exegesis is by no means conclusive, it suggests that "the people" protected by the Fourth Amendment, and by the First and Second Amendments, and to whom rights and powers are reserved in the Ninth and Tenth Amendments, refers to a class of persons who are part of a national community or who have otherwise developed sufficient connection with this country to be considered part of that community. The language of these Amendments contrasts with the words "person" and "accused" used in the Fifth and Sixth Amendments regulating procedure in criminal cases.

What we know of the history of the drafting of the Fourth Amendment also suggests that its purpose was to restrict searches and seizures which might be conducted by the United States in domestic matters. The Framers originally decided not to include a provision like the Fourth Amendment, because they believed the National Government lacked power to conduct searches and seizures. Many disputed the original view that the Federal Government possessed only narrow delegated powers over domestic affairs, however, and ultimately felt an Amendment prohibiting unreasonable searches and seizures was necessary. Madison, for example, argued that "there is a clause granting to Congress the power to make all laws which shall be necessary and proper for carrying into execution all of the powers vested in the Government of the United States," and that general warrants might be considered "necessary" for the purpose of collecting revenue. The driving force behind the adoption of the Amendment, as suggested by Madison's advocacy, was widespread hostility among the former colonists to the issuance of writs of assistance empowering revenue officers to search suspected places for smuggled goods, and general search warrants permitting the search of private houses, often to uncover papers that might be used to convict persons of libel. The available historical data show, therefore, that the purpose of the Fourth Amendment was to protect the people of the United

States against arbitrary action by their own Government; it was never suggested that the provision was intended to restrain the actions of the Federal Government against aliens outside of the United States territory. . . .

For better or for worse, we live in a world of nation-states in which our Government must be able to "functio[n] effectively in the company of sovereign nations." . . . Some who violate our laws may live outside our borders under a regime quite different from that which obtains in this country. Situations threatening to important American interests may arise halfway around the globe, situations which in the view of the political branches of our Government require an American response with armed force. If there are to be restrictions on searches and seizures which occur incident to such American action, they must be imposed by the political branches through diplomatic understanding, treaty, or legislation.

The judgment of the Court of Appeals is accordingly Reversed.

. . .

JUSTICE BRENNAN, with whom JUSTICE MARSHALL joins, dissenting.

Today the Court holds that although foreign nationals must abide by our laws even when in their own countries, our Government need not abide by the Fourth Amendment when it investigates them for violations of our laws. I respectfully dissent. We investigate, prosecute, and punish them. We have recognized this fundamental principle of mutuality since the time of the Framers.

In drafting both the Constitution and the Bill of Rights, the Framers strove to create a form of Government decidedly different from their British heritage. Whereas the British Parliament was unconstrained, the Framers intended to create a Government of limited powers. The colonists considered the British Government dangerously omnipotent. After all, the British declaration of rights had been enacted not by the people, but by Parliament. Americans vehemently attacked the notion that rights were matters of "'favor and grace,'" given to the people from the Government.

Thus, the Framers of the Bill of Rights did not purport to "create" rights. Rather, they designed the Bill of Rights to prohibit our Government from infringing rights and liberties presumed to be pre-existing. See e. g., U.S. Const., Amdt. 9 ("The enumeration in the Constitution of certain rights, shall not be construed to deny or disparage others retained by the people"). The Fourth Amendment, for example, does not create a new right of security against unreasonable searches and seizures. It states that "[t]he right of the people to be secure in their persons, houses, papers, and effects, against unreasonable searches and seizures, shall not be violated . . . ." The focus of the Fourth Amendment is on what the Government can and cannot do, and how it may act, not on against whom these actions may be taken. Bestowing rights and delineating protected groups would have been inconsistent with the Drafters' fundamental conception of a Bill of Rights as a limitation on the Government's conduct with respect to all whom it seeks to govern. It is thus extremely unlikely that the Framers intended the narrow construction of the term "the people" presented today by the majority.

Consider the Supreme Court's opinion in *United States v. Verdugo-Urquidez*,[8] which addresses the issue of whether the Fourth Amendment's protections against unreasonable searches and seizures apply to foreign citizens who are arrested and whose homes are searched by American agents in other countries. Notice that one of the primary disagreements between the majority and dissenting opinions involves a debate between compact theory and natural rights theory. Notice as well the potential implications of this opinion for the United States' "War on Terror," which includes establishing internment camps at places like Guantanamo Bay, Cuba, and holding foreign nationals as "enemy combatants" without charging them with any criminal offense.

9.3 TO WHOM DOES THE BILL OF RIGHTS APPLY?

One of the most frequently misunderstood areas of constitutional law involves the question of who must comply with the Bill of Rights. Specifically, students often ask why state and local governments have to comply with the Bill of Rights when the First Amendment begins by stating that "*Congress* shall make no law. . . ." The short answer to this question is that, even though the Bill of Rights only mentions Congress, state and local governments also must comply with most provisions of the Bill of Rights because these provisions have been made applicable to these levels of government through the Fourteenth Amendment due process clause. This, however, has not always been the case.

Initially, the Bill of Rights was interpreted and applied as placing limitations only on the federal government. For example, the Supreme Court held in *Barron v. The Mayor and City of Baltimore* (1833)[9], that the Fifth Amendment's provision regarding governmental takings of private property for public use and without just compensation was "a limitation on the exercise of power by the government of the United States, and is not applicable to the legislation of the States . . . ." In *Barron*, a wharf owner sued the mayor and city of Baltimore, claiming that the city deprived him of his property by completing harbor projects that reduced the access to and profitability of his wharf. Barron claimed that the Fifth Amendment should apply to limit state and local government conduct as well as that of the national government. The Supreme Court, however, disagreed, stating, "[h]ad the framers of [the] amendments intended them to be limitations on the powers of the State governments they would have imitated the framers of the original Constitution, and have expressed that intention." As a result, the Court made it clear that the Bill of Rights was "intended solely as a limitation on the exercise of power by the government of the United States, and [was] not applicable to legislation of the states."

The limited application and scope of the Bill of Rights eventually changed following the ratification of the **Fourteenth Amendment** to the Constitution. In the aftermath of the Civil War, Congress passed and the states ratified the Fourteenth Amendment, which includes a **due process clause** that specifically applies to the states.[10] Section 1 of the Fourteenth Amendment provides, in relevant part, "nor shall any State deprive any person of life, liberty, or property, without due process of law . . . ." The 1868 ratification of the due process clause, and other provisions within the Fourteenth Amendment, provided an explicit mandate to the states regarding civil liberties, a mandate that was not found in the original Bill of Rights. With the Fourteenth Amendment in place, the states are now required to protect liberty, as well as life and property, under mandate of the federal constitution.

It is important to note that the Constitution does not specifically mention local governments. But when the Constitution refers to "any state" or "the states," including such references in the Fourteenth Amendment, by implication, this reference includes local governments, such as counties, cities, townships, villages, and so on. The reason is that these smaller units of government are regarded essentially as agents or creatures of their respective state governments.[11] In other words, the reasoning is that because local governments are created by and largely regulated by the states, they should be subject to many of the constitutional duties imposed on the states. As a result, the Fourteenth Amendment's mandate that no state shall deprive a person of life, liberty, or property without due process of law also applies to local governments.

But even with the due process clause in place in 1868, it was not clear that the Bill of Rights would apply to state and local governments. The due process clause provided only that states must not deny life, liberty, or property without due process of law; it did not

Fourteenth Amendment
An amendment ratified in 1868 that contains a due process clause and equal protection clause that applies to the states. The ratification of the Fourteenth Amendment provided explicit mandates to the states regarding civil liberties, mandates not found in the original Bill of Rights. Under this amendment, the states are required to protect liberty, as well as life and property, under mandate of the federal constitution.

due process clause
A provision found in the Fifth and Fourteenth Amendments, that government cannot deprive individuals of life, liberty, or property without due process of law.

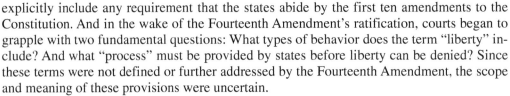

The Figurative Effect of the Incorporation Doctrine on the Fourteenth Amendment Due Process Clause

"[N]or shall any State deprive any person of life, liberty or property, without due process of law."[1]

[1]For more information on what "life, liberty, or property" includes and what "due process" means, please see and apply selected portions of the above-referenced Bill of Rights.

FIGURE 9-2

incorporation doctrine
A legal theory that maintains that the Bill of Rights (or at least portions thereof) should be incorporated through the Fourteenth Amendment due process clause and made applicable to the states.

explicitly include any requirement that the states abide by the first ten amendments to the Constitution. And in the wake of the Fourteenth Amendment's ratification, courts began to grapple with two fundamental questions: What types of behavior does the term "liberty" include? And what "process" must be provided by states before liberty can be denied? Since these terms were not defined or further addressed by the Fourteenth Amendment, the scope and meaning of these provisions were uncertain.

In addressing the effect of the due process clause in civil liberties cases, the Supreme Court was frequently urged to apply the constitutional standards established for protecting liberties under the Bill of Rights to resolve such disputes involving the states. Under this approach, if a state was accused of infringing upon an individual's liberty of speech, in violation of the Fourteenth Amendment due process clause, the Court would simply apply the standards traditionally used for addressing similar cases under the First Amendment. This approach is known as the **incorporation doctrine** because it maintains, to varying degrees (see following discussion), that the provisions of the Bill of Rights ought to be applied to the states by "incorporating" them through the due process clause. This doctrine maintains that when the Court considers whether a state is violating the due process clause, there is essentially a footnote to the clause effectively stating, "please see the above-referenced provisions in the Bill of Rights." (Illustrated in Figure 9-2.) In essence, the incorporation doctrine maintains that courts do not need to "reinvent the wheel" when it comes to interpreting the due process clause of the Fourteenth Amendment. Under this doctrine, if a constitutional standard under the First Amendment is good enough to resolve free speech cases involving the federal government, it should be good enough for those disputes involving state governments as well (See Figure 9-2).

HURTADO v. CALIFORNIA
110 U.S. 516 (1884)

On February 20, 1882, the state of California charged Joseph Hurtado with murdering Jose Antonio Stuardo. The state's charge against Hurtado did not come by way of grand jury indictment, but rather, through an information filed by the prosecutor. Following trial on the charge, a jury found Hurtado guilty of murder and he was later sentenced to death by the trial court. In his appeal, Hurtado asserts that his conviction should be reversed because his murder charge was not issued by a grand jury as required by the Fifth Amendment to the United States Constitution.

MATTHEWS, J. delivers the opinion of the Court.

It is claimed on behalf of the prisoner that the conviction and sentence are void, on the ground that they are repugnant to that clause of the fourteenth article of amendment to the constitution of the United States, which is in these words: "Nor shall any state deprive any person of life, liberty, or property without due process of law." The proposition of law we are asked to affirm is that an indictment or presentment by a grand jury, as known to the common law of England, is essential to that "due process of law," when

applied to prosecutions for felonies, which is secured and guarantied by this provision of the constitution of the United States, and which accordingly it is forbidden to the states, respectively, to dispense with in the administration of criminal law . . .

We are to construe this phrase in the fourteenth amendment by the *usus loquendi* of the constitution itself. The same words are contained in the fifth amendment. That article makes specific and express provision for perpetuating the institution of the grand jury, so far as relates to prosecutions for the more aggravated crimes under the laws of the United States. It declares that "no person shall be held to answer for a capital or otherwise infamous crime, unless on a presentment or indictment of a grand jury, except in cases arising in the land or naval forces, or in the militia when in actual service in time of war or public danger; nor shall any person be subject for the same offense to be twice put in jeopardy of life or limb; nor shall he be compelled in any criminal case to be a witness against himself." It then immediately adds: "nor be deprived of life, liberty, or property without due process of law." According to a recognized canon of interpretation, especially applicable to formal and solemn instruments of constitutional law, we are forbidden to assume, without clear reason to the contrary, that any part of this most important amendment is superfluous. The natural and obvious inference is that, in the sense of the constitution, "due process of law" was not meant or intended to include, *ex vi termini*, the institution and procedure of a grand jury in any case. The conclusion is equally irresistible, that when the same phrase was employed in the fourteenth amendment to restrain the action of the states, it was used in the same sense and with no greater extent; and that if in the adoption of that amendment it had been part of its purpose to perpetuate the institution of the grand jury in all the states, it would have embodied, as did the fifth amendment, express declarations to that effect. Due process of law in the latter refers to that law of the land which derives its authority from the legislative powers conferred upon congress by the constitution of the United States, exercised within the limits therein prescribed, and interpreted according to the principles of the common law. In the fourteenth amendment, by parity of reason, it refers to that law of the land in each state which derives its authority from the inherent and reserved powers of the state, exerted within the limits of those fundamental principles of liberty and justice which lie at the base of all our civil and political institutions, and the greatest security for which resides in the right of the people to make their own laws, and alter them at their pleasure. "The fourteenth amendment," as was said by Mr. Justice BRADLEY in *Missouri v. Lewis*, 101 U.S. 22–31, "does not profess to secure to all persons in the United States the benefit of the same laws and the same remedies. Great diversities in these respects may exist in two states separated only by an imaginary line. On one side of this line there may be a right of trial by jury, and on the other side no such right. Each state prescribes its own modes of judicial proceeding." . . .

Tried by these principles, we are unable to say that the substitution for a presentment or indictment by a grand jury of the proceeding by information after examination and commitment by a magistrate, certifying to the probable guilt of the defendant, with the right on his part to the aid of counsel, and to the cross-examination of the witnesses produced for the prosecution, is not due process of law. It is, as we have seen, an ancient proceeding at common law, which might include every case of an offense of less grade than a felony, except misprision of treason; and in

every circumstance of its administration, as authorized by the statute of California, it carefully considers and guards the substantial interest of the prisoner. It is merely a preliminary proceeding, and can result in no final judgment, except as the consequence of a regular judicial trial, conducted precisely as in cases of indictments. . . .

For these reasons, finding no error therein, the judgment of the supreme court of California is affirmed.

HARLAN, J., dissenting.

"Due process of law," within the meaning of the national constitution, does not import one thing with reference to the powers of the states and another with reference to the powers of the general government. If particular proceedings, conducted under the authority of the general government, and involving life, are prohibited because not constituting that due process of law required by the fifth amendment of the constitution of the United States, similar proceedings, conducted under the authority of a state, must be deemed illegal, as not being due process of law within the meaning of the fourteenth amendment. The words "due process of law," in the latter amendment, must receive the same interpretation they had at the common law from which they were derived, and which was given to them at the formation of the general government. . . .

It seems to me that too much stress is put upon the fact that the framers of the constitution made express provision for the security of those rights which at common law were protected by the requirement of due process of law, and, in addition, declared, generally, that no person shall "be deprived of life, liberty, or property without due process of law." The rights, for the security of which these express provisions were made, were of a character so essential to the safety of the people that it was deemed wise to avoid the possibility that congress, in regulating the processes of law, would impair or destroy them. Hence, their specific enumeration in the earlier amendments of the constitution, in connection with the general requirement of due process of law, the latter itself being broad enough to cover every right of life, liberty, or property secured by the settled usages and modes of proceedings existing under the common and statute law of England at the time our government was founded. . . .

PALKO v. STATE OF CONNECTICUT
302 U.S. 319 (1937)

The state of Connecticut charged Frank Jacob Palko with the murder of two police officers in 1935. Following a trial, Palko was convicted of second-degree murder and sentenced to life imprisonment. The state, however, sought to appeal Palko's conviction and sentence, seeking to retry Palko for first-degree murder and obtain a death sentence. Applying a Connecticut statute that allowed prosecutors to appeal criminal convictions in certain cases, Connecticut's supreme court of appeals agreed with the state, reversed Palko's conviction, and ordered a new trial. After a second trial, Palko was convicted of first-degree murder and sentenced to death. Palko appealed his conviction, asserting

that the Fifth Amendment protection against double jeopardy applied to the states and barred his second trial.

Mr. Justice CARDOZO delivered the opinion of the Court.

The argument for appellant is that whatever is forbidden by the Fifth Amendment is forbidden by the Fourteenth also. The Fifth Amendment, which is not directed to the States, but solely to the federal government, creates immunity from double jeopardy. No person shall be "subject for the same offense to be twice put in jeopardy of life or limb." The Fourteenth Amendment ordains, "nor shall any State deprive any person of life, liberty, or property, without due process of law." To retry a defendant, though under one indictment and only one, subjects him, it is said, to double jeopardy in violation of the Fifth Amendment, if the prosecution is one on behalf of the United States. From this the consequence is said to follow that there is a denial of life or liberty without due process of law, if the prosecution is one on behalf of the people of a state. . . .

We have said that in appellant's view the Fourteenth Amendment is to be taken as embodying the prohibitions of the Fifth. His thesis is even broader. Whatever would be a violation of the original bill of rights (Amendments 1 to 8) if done by the federal government is now equally unlawful by force of the Fourteenth Amendment if done by a state. There is no such general rule.

The Fifth Amendment provides, among other things, that no person shall be held to answer for a capital or otherwise infamous crime unless on presentment or indictment of a grand jury. This court has held that, in prosecutions by a state, presentment or indictment by a grand jury may give way to informations at the instance of a public officer. *Hurtado v. California*, 110 U.S. 516, 4 S.Ct. 111, 292. The Fifth Amendment provides also that no person shall be compelled in any criminal case to be a witness against himself. This court has said that, in prosecutions by a state, the exemption will fail if the state elects to end it. The Sixth Amendment calls for a jury trial in criminal cases and the Seventh for a jury trial in civil cases at common law where the value in controversy shall exceed $20. This court has ruled that consistently with those amendments trial by jury may be modified by a state or abolished altogether. . . .

On the other hand, the due process clause of the Fourteenth Amendment may make it unlawful for a state to abridge by its statutes the freedom of speech which the First Amendment safeguards against encroachment by the Congress, or the free exercise of religion, or the right of peaceable assembly, without which speech would be unduly trammeled, or the right of one accused of crime to the benefit of counsel. In these and other situations immunities that are valid as against the federal government by force of the specific pledges of particular amendments have been found to be implicit in the concept of ordered liberty, and thus, through the Fourteenth Amendment, become valid as against the states.

The line of division may seem to be wavering and broken if there is a hasty catalogue of the cases on the one side and the other. Reflection and analysis will induce a different view. There emerges the perception of a rationalizing principle which gives to discrete instances a proper order and coherence. The right to trial by jury and the immunity from prosecution except as the result of an indictment may have value and importance. Even so, they are not of the very essence of a scheme of ordered liberty. To abolish them is not to violate a "principle of justice so rooted in the traditions and conscience of our people as to be ranked as fundamental." Few would be so narrow or provincial as to maintain that a fair and enlightened system of justice would be impossible without them. What is true of jury trials and indictments is true also, as the cases show, of the immunity from compulsory self-incrimination. *Twining v. New Jersey* [211 U.S. 78 (1908)]. This too might be lost, and justice still be done. . . .

We reach a different plane of social and moral values when we pass to the privileges and immunities that have been taken over from the earlier articles of the Federal Bill of Rights and brought within the Fourteenth Amendment by a process of absorption. These in their origin were effective against the federal government alone. If the Fourteenth Amendment has absorbed them, the process of absorption has had its source in the belief that neither liberty nor justice would exist if they were sacrificed. This is true, for illustration, of freedom of thought and speech. Of that freedom one may say that it is the matrix, the indispensable condition, of nearly every other form of freedom. . . .

Our survey of the cases serves, we think, to justify the statement that the dividing line between them, if not unfaltering throughout its course, has been true for the most part to a unifying principle. On which side of the line the case made out by the appellant has appropriate location must be the next inquiry and the final one. Is that kind of double jeopardy to which the statute has subjected him a hardship so acute and shocking that our policy will not endure it? Does it violate those "fundamental principles of liberty and justice which lie at the base of all our civil and political institutions"? The answer surely must be "no." What the answer would have to be if the state were permitted after a trial free from error to try the accused over again or to bring another case against him, we have no occasion to consider. We deal with the statute before us and no other. The state is not attempting to wear the accused out by a multitude of cases with accumulated trials. It asks no more than this, that the case against him shall go on until there shall be a trial free from the corrosion of substantial legal error. This is not cruelty at all, nor even vexation in any immoderate degree. . . .

The judgment is affirmed.

Mr. Justice BUTLER dissents.

The incorporation doctrine, however, was not immediately accepted by the Court. Instead, throughout the rest of the nineteenth century and early part of the twentieth century, the Court generally relied upon its holding in *Barron v. The Mayor and City of Baltimore* to conclude that the Bill of Rights did not apply to the states.[12] For example, in *Hurtado v. California* (1884),[13] the Court refused to apply the Fifth Amendment's guarantee of a grand jury indictment in all capital cases to the states. The Court reasoned that the Fourteenth Amendment's due process clause was not intended to include the Fifth Amendment's indictment provision. Similarly, in *Palko v. Connecticut* (1937),[14] the Court refused to apply the Fifth Amendment's guarantee against double jeopardy to the states, reasoning that such a right was not so "implicit in the concept of ordered liberty" to be included among the liberties protected by the Fourteenth Amendment's due process clause. And in *Adamson v. California* (1947),[15] the Court used similar logic to reject the

Incorporated or Nonincorporated?	
1st Amendment:	Totally incorporated.
2nd Amendment:	Not officially incorporated by the Supreme Court (Court rejected incorporation in 1876).
3rd Amendment:	Not officially incorporated by the Supreme Court decision (2nd Circuit Court of Appeals found to be incorporated).
4th Amendment:	Totally incorporated.
5th Amendment:	Incorporated except for provision guaranteeing criminal prosecution only on a grand jury indictment.
6th Amendment:	Totally incorporated.
7th Amendment:	Not officially incorporated.
8th Amendment:	Provision against "cruel and unusual punishments" has been incorporated, but provisions regarding "excessive fines" and "excessive bail" have not been officially incorporated.

FIGURE 9-3

incorporation of the Fifth Amendment's protection against self-incrimination in a California case where the prosecutor criticized a criminal defendant for not testifying in his own defense.

Gradually, however, the Court changed its course and began to incorporate select provisions of the Bill of Rights through the Fourteenth Amendment's due process clause, thereby making these provisions applicable to the states. For example, in *Benyton v. Maryland* (1969),[16] the Court reversed its decision in *Palko,* and found that the Fifth Amendment right against double jeopardy should be incorporated through the due process clause. And in *Malloy v. Hogan*, 378 U.S. 1 (1964),[17] the Court likewise rejected its holding in *Adamson,* finding that the states must abide by the Fifth Amendment's protection against self-incrimination. Note, however, that the Court has not reversed its holding in *Hurtado* to make the grand jury indictment provision of the Fifth Amendment applicable to the states.

Between 1896 and 1972, the Court used the Fourteenth Amendment's due process clause to incrementally incorporate nearly all of the provisions of the Bill of Rights. And today, only five provisions remain unincorporated. (See Figure 9-3.) Officially, the Court has not incorporated the Second Amendment right to bear arms, the Third Amendment right against quartering troops in a person's house, the Fifth Amendment right to indictment by grand jury, the Seventh Amendment right to jury trial in civil cases, and the Eighth Amendment right against excessive fines and bail. However, many states have their own constitutional protections for these and other liberties.[18]

The Court's rationale for incorporating the Bill of Rights through the Fourteenth Amendment has varied. Some members of the Court have maintained that the Fourteenth Amendment requires that all of the provisions of the Bill of Rights be incorporated because they are the same liberties referenced in the due process clause. This approach is called the **total incorporation doctrine**. Others maintain that only select portions of the Bill of Rights, which are deemed to involve "preferred freedoms" or rights "implicit in the concept of ordered liberty," should be applied to the states. This approach is referred to as the **select incorporation doctrine**. Either way, the reality today is that most of the provisions found in the Bill of Rights apply to state and local governments through the due process clause of the Fourteenth Amendment. And so when asked why the states are required to avoid the establishment of religion, even though the First Amendment explicitly says that "Congress shall make no law respecting an establishment of religion," the answer is that, despite its facially restrictive language, the First Amendment has been incorporated and made applicable to the states through the Fourteenth Amendment due process clause.

total incorporation doctrine
A theory held by some jurists and legal scholars maintaining that the Fourteenth Amendment requires that all of the provisions of the Bill of Rights to be incorporated and applied to the states.

select incorporation doctrine
A theory held by some jurists and legal scholars that maintains that only select portions of the Bill of Rights, which are deemed to involve "preferred freedoms" or rights "implicit in the concept of ordered liberty," should be incorporated through the due process clause and made applicable to the states.

9.4 WHAT RIGHTS ARE PROTECTED?

Some people may be tempted to read the Bill of Rights in much the same manner as they would read the Articles of the Constitution—as an exhaustive and restrictive list of provisions that are not to be added to or modified without formal amendment. But there are reasons to be

YOUR CONSTITUTIONAL VALUES

SHOULD THE SECOND AMENDMENT APPLY TO STATE AND LOCAL AUTHORITIES?

Unlike most provisions of the Bill of Rights, the Supreme Court has not held that the Second Amendment is applicable to the states through the Fourteenth Amendment. In *United States v. Cruikshank*, 92 U.S.542 (1876), the Court found that "[t]he second amendment declares that [the right to bear arms] shall not be infringed; but this . . . means no more than that it shall not be infringed by Congress." Likewise, in *Presser v. Illinois,* 116 U.S. 252 (1886), the Court held that a prohibition on unlicensed armed marches "do[es] not infringe the right of the people to keep and bear arms." And in *United States v. Miller*, 307 U.S. 174 (1939), the Court concluded that the Second and Fourth Amendments did not directly apply to the states, citing *Barron v. Baltimore* (1833).

Consider the following case and opinion to assess whether you believe that the "nonincorporation" of the Second Amendment should continue.

NORDYKE v. KING, 229 F.3d 1266, 1267 (9th Cir. 2000)

In 1991, Russell and Sallie Nordyke began promoting gun shows at the Alameda County Fairgrounds, which was located on public property in Alameda County, California. These shows included gun exhibitors selling antique firearms, modern firearms, ammunition, and memorabilia. However, in August 1999, Alameda County passed an ordinance making illegal the possession of firearms on county property. Specifically, the ordinance stated, "Every person who brings onto or possesses on county property a firearm, loaded or unloaded, or ammunition for a firearm is guilty of a misdemeanor." If applied to the Nordykes, the law would forbid the presence of firearms at their gun shows held at the Fairgrounds.

The Nordykes attempted to stop the ordinance from being applied to them by bringing suit against the county in the United States District Court for the Northern District of California. The Nordykes made several arguments, including the claim that the ordinance violated the Second Amendment. But the district court rejected their request for a restraining order against the county. On appeal, the Ninth Circuit upheld the district court's order, finding, among other things, that the Second Amendment protected a collective right by the state to form a well-regulated militia, not an individual right for persons to hold guns. The court, however, did not address squarely whether the Second Amendment should be incorporated through the Fourteenth Amendment. But in a footnote within his concurring opinion, Circuit Judge Ronald Gould addressed the issue:

> We have held that the Second Amendment is not incorporated and does not apply to the states. *Fresno Rifle and Pistol Club, Inc. v. Van de Kamp*, 965 F.2d 723 (9th Cir. 1992). If *Fresno* controls, then the Second Amendment cannot be considered to apply to state and local regulation. . . . .

Based on your constitutional values, what do you think? Should the Second Amendment be incorporated through the Fourteenth Amendment and applied to state and local governments? What is the constitutional basis for your judgment?

In late 2007, the Supreme Court granted review in *District of Columbia v. Heller*, Case No. 07-290, a Second Amendment case out of the District of Columbia. Although the case does not involve a state or local government, and thus, may not address incorporation issues, the Court's decision nonetheless may shed some light on the scope and nature of the right to bear arms.

Fundamental Rights Not Specifically Listed in the Bill of Rights But Deemed Protected by the Constitution
Right to privacy—*Griswold v. Connecticut* (1965)
Right to travel—*Shapiro v. Thompson* (1969)
Right to an abortion—*Roe v. Wade* (1973)
Freedom of association—*NAACP v. Alabama* (1958)
Right to marriage—*Zablocki v. Redhail* (1978)

FIGURE 9-4
Other fundamental liberties

Inclusio unis est exclusio alterius
A Latin maxim used as a principle in drafting some documents, meaning "the inclusion of one item is the exclusion of all others." Under this theory, the framers maintained that they could limit the scope and power of government by enumerating or listing the government's specific powers in the Constitution, and that such documentation, by implication, would curtail any subsequent argument that the government had powers beyond those listed in the Constitution.

penumbras
A penumbra is a lunar shadow. Justice Douglas used this term as a metaphor in *Griswold v. Connecticut* (1965) to describe an individual's right to privacy under the Constitution. According to Douglas, even though privacy is not specifically enumerated in the Bill of Rights, there are certain penumbras or shadows cast by the First, Third, Fourth, Fifth, and Ninth Amendments that reflect that a right to privacy is protected by the Constitution.

cautious about equating the drafting strategies employed to write the Articles of the Constitution with those used to write the Bill of Rights.

The Articles were designed to be a document that limited government, with the powers and duties delegated to the newly formed government designed to be exhaustive and exclusive. Note, for example, Article I, section 8, which provides an itemized (although, in some cases, vaguely worded) list of the powers vested in Congress—the power to regulate commerce, to coin money, to declare war, to establish post offices, and so on. The purpose of providing this detailed list was to ensure limited government, thereby making it known that if Congress was not constitutionally vested with a particular power, it was barred from exercising it. This drafting technique is captured in the Latin maxim "***inclusio unis est exclusio alterius***," which means the inclusion of one item is the exclusion of all others. Under this theory, the framers maintained that they could limit the scope and power of government by enumerating or listing the government's specific powers in the constitution, and that such documentation, by implication, would curtail any subsequent argument that the government had powers beyond those listed in the constitution. So essentially, the framers theorized that if they went to the trouble of delegating specific powers to the three branches of government, all other forms of power not specifically mentioned would be excluded. Indeed, the Tenth Amendment reinforces this principle by providing that those powers not given to the federal government are reserved to the states or to the people.

This drafting strategy of limiting items by omitting them from the Constitution, however, does not apply to the rights contained in the Bill of Rights. In contrast to their desire to limit the authority of the federal government, many of the framers wanted to ensure that the Bill of Rights was not viewed as an exhaustive list of rights held by individuals. In other words, the framers did not seek to apply the doctrine of "*inclusio unis est exclusio alterius*" to the Bill of Rights. Instead, the Ninth Amendment makes it clear that, although certain rights are specifically enumerated in the first eight amendments, other rights, which are not explicitly listed, may be protected against governmental interference as well. This drafting technique later opened the door for the Supreme Court to conclude that the freedom to marry, the right to travel, the right to privacy, and other rights, which are not specifically mentioned in the Bill of Rights, are nonetheless fundamental rights protected by the Constitution. (See Figure 9-4.)

For example, notice how the Supreme Court used the Ninth Amendment, in conjunction with other Amendments, in *Griswold v. Connecticut* (1965)[19] to conclude that the Constitution protects an individual's right to privacy even though such a right is not specifically enumerated in the document. Specifically, the opinion of Justice William Douglas found that there are certain **penumbras** or shadows cast by the First, Third, Fourth, and Fifth Amendments that reflect that a right to privacy, although not explicitly enumerated, is nonetheless protected by the Constitution.

GRISWOLD v. CONNECTICUT
381 U.S. 479 (1965)

MR. JUSTICE DOUGLAS delivered the opinion of the Court.

Appellant Griswold is Executive Director of the Planned Parenthood League of Connecticut. Appellant Buxton is a licensed physician and a professor at the Yale Medical School who served as Medical Director for the League at its Center in New Haven—a center open and operating from November 1 to November 10, 1961, when appellants were arrested.

They gave information, instruction, and medical advice to married persons as to the means of preventing conception. They examined the wife and prescribed the best contraceptive device or material for her use. Fees were usually charged, although some couples were serviced free.

The statutes whose constitutionality is involved in this appeal are 53-32 and 54-196 of the General Statutes of Connecticut. The former provides:

> "Any person who uses any drug, medicinal article or instrument for the purpose of preventing conception shall be fined not less than fifty dollars or imprisoned not less than sixty days nor more than one year or be both fined and imprisoned."

Section 54-196 provides:

> "Any person who assists, abets, counsels, causes, hires or commands another to commit any offense may be prosecuted and punished as if he were the principal offender."

The appellants were found guilty as accessories and fined $100 each, against the claim that the accessory statute as so applied violated the Fourteenth Amendment. . . .

Coming to the merits, we are met with a wide range of questions that implicate the Due Process Clause of the Fourteenth Amendment. . . . We do not sit as a super-legislature to determine the wisdom, need, and propriety of laws that touch economic problems, business affairs, or social conditions. This law, however, operates directly on an intimate relation of husband and wife and their physician's role in one aspect of that relation.

The association of people is not mentioned in the Constitution nor in the Bill of Rights. The right to educate a child in a school of the parents' choice—whether public or private or parochial—is also not mentioned. Nor is the right to study any particular subject or any foreign language. Yet the First Amendment has been construed to include certain of those rights. . . .

[Our] cases suggest that specific guarantees in the Bill of Rights have penumbras, formed by emanations from those guarantees that help give them life and substance. Various guarantees create zones of privacy. The right of association contained in the penumbra of the First Amendment is one, as we have seen. The Third Amendment in its prohibition against the quartering of soldiers "in any house" in time of peace without the consent of the owner is another facet of that privacy. The Fourth Amendment explicitly affirms the "right of the people to be secure in their persons, houses, papers, and effects, against unreasonable searches and seizures." The Fifth Amendment in its Self-Incrimination Clause enables the citizen to create a zone of privacy which government may not force him to surrender to his detriment. The Ninth Amendment provides: "The enumeration in the Constitution, of certain rights, shall not be construed to deny or disparage others retained by the people." . . .

The present case, then, concerns a relationship lying within the zone of privacy created by several fundamental constitutional guarantees. And it concerns a law which, in forbidding the use of contraceptives rather than regulating their manufacture or sale,

seeks to achieve its goals by means having a maximum destructive impact upon that relationship. Such a law cannot stand in light of the familiar principle, so often applied by this Court, that a "governmental purpose to control or prevent activities constitutionally subject to state regulation may not be achieved by means which sweep unnecessarily broadly and thereby invade the area of protected freedoms." Would we allow the police to search the sacred precincts of marital bedrooms for telltale signs of the use of contraceptives? The very idea is repulsive to the notions of privacy surrounding the marriage relationship. . . .

Reversed.

MR. JUSTICE GOLDBERG, whom THE CHIEF JUSTICE and MR. JUSTICE BRENNAN join, concurring.

The Ninth Amendment reads, "The enumeration in the Constitution, of certain rights, shall not be construed to deny or disparage others retained by the people." The Amendment is almost entirely the work of James Madison. It was introduced in Congress by him and passed the House and Senate with little or no debate and virtually no change in language. It was proffered to quiet expressed fears that a bill of specifically enumerated rights could not be sufficiently broad to cover all essential rights and that the specific mention of certain rights would be interpreted as a denial that others were protected. . . .

In sum, I believe that the right of privacy in the marital relation is fundamental and basic—a personal right "retained by the people" within the meaning of the Ninth Amendment. Connecticut cannot constitutionally abridge this fundamental right, which is protected by the Fourteenth Amendment from infringement by the States. I agree with the Court that petitioners' convictions must therefore be reversed.

MR. JUSTICE HARLAN, concurring in the judgment.

In my view, the proper constitutional inquiry in this case is whether this Connecticut statute infringes the Due Process Clause of the Fourteenth Amendment because the enactment violates basic values "implicit in the concept of ordered liberty," . . . The Due Process Clause of the Fourteenth Amendment stands, in my opinion, on its own bottom.

MR. JUSTICE WHITE, concurring in the judgment.

In my view this Connecticut law as applied to married couples deprives them of "liberty" without due process of law, as that concept is used in the Fourteenth Amendment. I therefore concur in the judgment of the Court reversing these convictions under Connecticut's aiding and abetting statute.

MR. JUSTICE BLACK, with whom MR. JUSTICE STEWART joins, dissenting. . . .

The Court talks about a constitutional "right of privacy" as though there is some constitutional provision or provisions forbidding any law ever to be passed which might abridge the "privacy" of individuals. But there is not. . . .

9.5 WHAT DOES THE BILL OF RIGHTS REQUIRE OF THE GOVERNMENT?

Finally, it should be noted that the Bill of Rights and the due process clause of the Fourteenth Amendment are generally written in negative language. For example, the First Amendment begins by stating "Congress shall make *no* law respecting an establishment of religion." The

Fourth Amendment provides, in part, that "The right of the people to be secure . . . against unreasonable searches and seizures shall *not* be violated." And the Fourteenth Amendment provides, "*nor* shall any state *deprive* any person life, liberty, or property without due process of law." Each of these provisions essentially tells the government what *not* to do—do not make a law respecting the establishment of religion; do not violate the right against unreasonable searches and seizures; and do not deny a person due process. But these provisions do not tell the government what it must affirmatively do, if anything, regarding civil liberties. In other words, generally speaking, the government's obligation with respect to individual rights is formed in the negative (don't interfere with certain rights) as opposed to the affirmative (government must promote and advance individual rights).

Consistent with the facial language of the Bill of Rights and due process clause, the Supreme Court generally has refrained from imposing any affirmative obligations on the government when it comes to the Bill of Rights and due process clause. As Chief Justice Rehnquist explained in *DeShaney v. Winnebago County Department of Social Services* (1989):[20]

> [N]othing in the language of the Due Process Clause itself requires the State to protect the life, liberty, and property of its citizens against invasion by private actors. The Clause is phrased as a limitation on the State's power to act, not as a guarantee of certain minimal levels of safety and security. It forbids the State itself to deprive individuals of life, liberty, or property without "due process of law," but its language cannot fairly be extended to impose an affirmative obligation

---

Compare Sections 25, 26, and 27 of the Republic of South Africa's Bill of Rights as adopted on 8 May 1996 and amended on 11 October 1996 by the Constitutional Assembly.

Property

25. (1) No one may be deprived of property except in terms of law of general application, and no law may permit arbitrary deprivation of property.

    (2) Property may be expropriated only in terms of law of general application
        a. for a public purpose or in the public interest; and
        b. subject to compensation, the amount of which and the time and manner of payment of which have either been agreed to by those affected or decided or approved by a court.

    . . .

    (5) The state must take reasonable legislative and other measures, within its available resources, to foster conditions which enable citizens to gain access to land on an equitable basis. . . .

    (6) A person or community whose tenure of land is legally insecure as a result of past racially discriminatory laws or practices is entitled, to the extent provided by an Act of Parliament, either to tenure which is legally secure or to comparable redress.

    (9) Parliament must enact the legislation referred to in subsection (6).

. . .

Housing

26. (1) Everyone has the right to have access to adequate housing.

    (2) The state must take reasonable legislative and other measures, within its available resources, to achieve the progressive realisation of this right.

    (3) No one may be evicted from their home, or have their home demolished, without an order of court made after considering all the relevant circumstances. No legislation may permit arbitrary evictions.

Health care, food, water, and social security

27. (1) Everyone has the right to have access to
        a. health care services, including reproductive health care;
        b. sufficient food and water; and
        c. social security, including, if they are unable to support themselves and their dependants, appropriate social assistance.

    (2) The state must take reasonable legislative and other measures, within its available resources, to achieve the progressive realisation of each of these rights.

    (3) No one may be refused emergency medical treatment.

FIGURE 9-5
The Bill of Rights in context

on the State to ensure that those interests do not come to harm through other means. Nor does history support such an expansive reading of the constitutional text. Like its counterpart in the Fifth Amendment, the Due Process Clause of the Fourteenth Amendment was intended to prevent government "from abusing [its] power, or employing it as an instrument of oppression[.]" Its purpose was to protect the people from the State, not to ensure that the State protected them from each other. The Framers were content to leave the extent of governmental obligation in the latter area to the democratic political processes.

Consistent with these principles, our cases have recognized that the Due Process Clauses generally confer no affirmative right to governmental aid, even where such aid may be necessary to secure life, liberty, or property interests of which the government itself may not deprive the individual. . . .

Under this reasoning, the Bill of Rights is regarded as a document that protects several explicit and implied liberties held by individuals, but that does not impose any affirmative obligations upon government to promote or advance these liberties. The government fulfills its constitutional duty simply by refraining from interfering with these liberties. Compare, however, the Bill of Rights adopted by the Republic of South Africa (see Figure 9-5), where, with respect to some enumerated liberties—property, housing, and health care, and so on—the government has an affirmative constitutional duty to promote civil liberties through legislative and other means.

9.5 SUMMARY

The Bill of Rights consists of the first ten amendments to the Constitution. They are regarded as safeguards to individual liberties, protecting such interests as the freedom of speech, freedom of religion, the right against unreasonable searches and seizures, and the right to be free from cruel and unusual punishment. The Bill of Rights was drafted in 1789, after the ratification of the Articles of the Constitution, fulfilling a promise made to those who were concerned that the Articles themselves did not do enough to guard against governmental encroachment of personal liberties.

For some, the freedoms contained in the Bill of Rights are natural rights, which are vested in all individuals as a matter of birthright. For others, these freedoms are not inherently given, but rather, negotiated for under the terms of the Constitution. Either way, the Bill of Rights provides important limitations on governmental authority in the face of individual liberties.

Initially, the Bill of Rights was applied only to the federal government, not to state or local governments. But following the ratification of the Fourteenth Amendment, the Court began to slowly incorporate or apply most of the rights contained in the Bill of Rights to the states, using the due process clause as the method for such incorporation. Today, all but five provisions of the Bill of Rights have been applied to the states.

Although the Bill of Rights contains several enumerated rights, the Court also has held that the document protects a number of additional rights as well. These rights include the right to privacy, marriage, travel, and association. Some members of the Court have justified the addition of these rights by referencing the Ninth Amendment, which makes it clear that the enumeration of certain rights within the Bill of Rights was not intended to exclude other rights of the people that still must be protected against governmental intrusion.

The Bill of Rights generally gives the government a number of negative instructions—do not interfere with the freedom of speech, do not engage in unreasonable searches and seizure, and so on. And while we hold these freedoms to be essential to the success and survival of our constitutional democracy, note that the government is under no obligation to promote or advance the freedom of speech or the right to privacy. The Bill of Rights simply tells the government not to interfere with these and other liberties.

REVIEW QUESTIONS

1. How does the Bill of Rights differ from the Articles of the Constitution?
2. Why was the Bill of Rights added to the Constitution?

3. Explain the difference between the compact theory and natural rights theory of civil liberties.

4. What was James Madison's role in drafting the Bill of Rights?

5. Why do state and local governments have to comply with most of the provisions in the Bill of Rights when the document begins with "Congress shall make no law"?

6. Explain how most of the liberties found in the Bill of Rights are incorporated through the Fourteenth Amendment due process clause.

7. What rights are protected under the Bill of Rights even though they are not specifically listed in the document?

8. Where does the right to privacy come from?

9. What purpose does the Ninth Amendment serve?

10. What affirmative obligations are imposed on the government under the Bill of Rights?

ASSIGNMENTS

1. Identify the rights given to criminally accused persons under the Bill of Rights. Do you think these rights should be applied to individuals whom the federal government has identified as "enemy combatants" or illegal aliens? Give your reasons for offering or not offering these rights.

2. Compare the Bill of Rights found in the United States Constitution to the Bill of Rights in the Republic of South Africa's Constitution. What features of South Africa's Bill of Rights do you find compelling? Would you recommend any changes to the United States Bill of Rights based on your review of South Africa's Bill of Rights?

NOTES

1. Thomas Jefferson, *The Papers of Thomas Jefferson*, Vol. 14, ed. Julian Boyd (Princeton, NJ: Princeton University Press 1950), p. 440.

2. Technically, the Articles of the Constitution were ratified on June 21, 1788, when New Hampshire became the ninth state to approve the document. Under Article VII of the new Constitution, only nine of the thirteen states were required to ratify the document to make it effective.

3. This theory is reflected in a Latin maxim that frequently governs legal disputes over contracts: "*inclusio unis est exclusio alterious*," which means "the inclusion of one is the exclusion of all others." Under this theory, if parties to a contract go to the trouble of enumerating a list of specific items to be covered by the agreement, by inference, the inclusion of these specific items bars any additional items from being covered after the contract is finalized.

4. The original Second Amendment affecting congressional pay raises was later adopted and ratified on May 7, 1992, as the Twenty-Seventh Amendment.

5. The Declaration of Independence provides that in order to secure unalienable rights, "governments are instituted among men, deriving their just powers from the consent of the governed."

6. Alan Dershowitz, *Rights from Wrongs: The Origins of Human Rights in the Experience of Injustice* (Basic Books 2004).

7. Louis Henkin, "Rights: Here and There," 81 *Columbia Law Review* 1582 (1981).

8. 494 U.S. 259 (1990).

9. 32 U.S. 243 (1833).

10. Note that the Fifth Amendment contains a due process clause as well. But this clause has been interpreted to apply to the federal government. See *Bolling v. Sharpe*, 347 U.S. 497 (1954).

11. See Ted Gurr and Desmond King, *The State and the City* (The University of Chicago Press: Chicago 1987).

12. In 1896 and 1897, the Court did incorporate the Fifth Amendment's guarantee to just compensation for the government's taking of private property. See *Missouri Pacific Railway Co. v. Nebraska*, 164 U.S. 403 (1896); *Chicago, Burlington & Quincy Railway Co. v. Chicago*, 166 U.S. 226 (1897).

13. 110 U.S. 516 (1884).

14. 302 U.S. 319 (1937).
15. 332 U.S. 46 (1947).
16. 395 U.S. 784 (1969).
17. 378 U.S. 1 (1964).
18. See Robert Dowlut, "Federal and State Constitutional Guarantees to Arms," 15 *U. Dayton L. Rev.* 1–89 (1989).
19. 391 U.S. 145 (1965).
20. 489 U.S. 189 (1989).

10 The Freedom of Expression

> The right to think is the beginning of freedom, and speech must be protected from the government because speech is the beginning of thought.
>
> *Justice Anthony Kennedy[1]*

OUTLINE

10.1 THE VALUES SERVED BY THE FREEDOM OF EXPRESSION

The First Amendment provides that "Congress shall make no law respecting an establishment of religion, or prohibiting the free exercise thereof; or abridging the freedom of speech, or of the press; or the right of the people peaceably to assemble, and to petition the Government for a redress of grievances." Within this provision, the Constitution offers protection for a number of different freedoms. The first two—the right to be free from the establishment of religion and the right to be free to exercise religion—will be covered in Chapter 11. The remaining freedoms of speech, press, assembly, and petition, while conceptually and fundamentally distinct from one another, all promote at least three common values: (1) the idea that governmental power can be limited by allowing individuals to critique and otherwise scrutinize their public officials and policies, (2) the notion that a democratic government functions best when conflicting interests are allowed to compete in an open marketplace, and (3) the belief that individual expression is a necessary condition for human health.

With regard to the first value, it is clear from the ratification proceedings surrounding the Articles of the Constitution that the First Amendment was designed to install additional checks and balances on governmental power. As discussed in Chapter 9, many of those debating the proposed Constitution were concerned that it gave the new government too much authority and that additional measures were necessary to further guard against tyranny. To accommodate these concerns, the framers added a bill of rights following the ratification of the Constitution. And so just as the

Several thousand protestors march down Fifth Avenue from the First United Methodist Church in downtown Seattle to protest the World Trade Organization (WTO) conference being held at the Washington State Convention Center in Seattle November 29. Officials
Corbis/Bettmann

factions
Individual or isolated interests that can destroy or substantially impair government if they are allowed to override the common good. According to James Madison in *Federalist No. 10*, the only way to address factions in a democratic society was to allow them to exist, but to manage them, so that one interest did not rise to dominate the rest. To that end, Madison believed that the Constitution would allow factions to be pitted against one another, thereby allowing them to be managed in a marketplace of competition.

marketplace of ideas
A phrase used in some free speech cases to describe the type of environment the First Amendment fosters for individuals to sell, purchase, and evaluate different ideas through speech. The idea is that if individual ideas are allowed to compete against one another through open exchange, using speech, assembly, press, and petition, society will be in a better position to manage and balance the diversity of "products" (ideas) being offered.

Articles of the Constitution sought to limit the power of the new government by separating its powers and by providing oversight authorities to each branch over the other branches, the First Amendment similarly provides legal mechanisms for scrutinizing and otherwise limiting governmental authority. Whether publicly protesting a piece of legislation, publishing a news article against a president's decision, gathering together for a common cause, or organizing a group demonstration to achieve greater legal protections, the First Amendment provides methods for individuals to interact with and to regulate governmental activity. As the Supreme Court has observed, "speech concerning public affairs . . . is the essence of self-government."[2]

And in reality, there are plenty of examples where these methods have been successful in limiting or directing governmental authority. In the 1950s, organized efforts by the National Association for the Advancement of Colored People led to the Supreme Court striking down school segregation. In the 1960s, public speeches and rallies led by Martin Luther King convinced Congress to pass legislation banning certain forms of discrimination. In the early 1970s, news stories written by Carl Bernstein and Bob Woodward of *The Washington Post* led to the resignation of President Richard Nixon and the criminal prosecution of several members of the president's staff. And in 2002, a voter initiative by California citizens resulted in Governor Gray Davis being removed from office and replaced by Arnold Schwarzenegger. In each instance, an individual or group of individuals exercised their First Amendment freedoms to effectuate or change the power of government.

In addition to impacting public policy, the freedom of expression is also valued because it promotes peace and stability among diverse groups of people. In lobbying for the ratification of the Constitution, James Madison spoke in *Federalist No.10* of the impact of **factions** upon government. Factions are individual or isolated interests that can destroy or substantially impair government if they are allowed to override the common good. Accordingly to Madison, there are two ways to deal with factions—eliminate them or manage them. For Madison, the first option was not realistic because it would result in a totalitarian government suppressing and otherwise quashing individual interests. As a result, Madison felt that the only way to address factions in a democratic society was to allow them to exist, but to manage them, so that one interest did not rise to dominate the rest. To that end, Madison believed that the Constitution would allow factions to be pitted against one another, thereby allowing them to be managed in a marketplace of competition.

Consistent with Madison's recommended treatment of factions, courts frequently have adopted the notion that the First Amendment fosters a **marketplace of ideas** for individuals to sell, purchase, and evaluate different concepts, thereby allowing individual factions to check one another. Through open exchange, based on speech, assembly, press, and petition, it is believed society will be in a better position to manage and balance the diversity of "products" (ideas) being offered.[3] In an often-quoted dissenting opinion, Justice Oliver Wendell Holmes supported this marketplace theory, stating, "When men have realized that time has upset many fighting faiths, they may come to believe even more than they believe the very foundations of their own conduct that the ultimate good desired is better reached by free trade in ideas—that the best test of truth is the power of the thought to get itself accepted in the competition of the market, and that truth is the only ground upon which their wishes safely can be carried out."[4]

Finally, the freedom of expression is also valued because it offers individuals an outlet for personal thoughts and creativity. Regardless of the practical benefits to government, it is believed that the First Amendment's protections provide individuals with a means for expressing themselves, thereby providing a healthy method of developing and releasing emotions and ideas. Rather than forcing individuals to bottle up their thoughts and beliefs, as is the case with more totalitarian governments, the First Amendment generally gives individuals the opportunity to release their innermost ideas and beliefs in public discourse. Of course, that often means that unpopular views and ideas will enter the public arena. For example, in some contexts, protesters will be allowed to burn a United States flag,[5] Neo-Nazis will be permitted to march down Main Street,[6] and the KKK will be given a permit to erect a cross on the public square.[7] But such public expression of unpopular views is generally preferred to the suppression of ideas, which, if allowed to fester behind closed doors with no available outlet, may lead to far more destructive behavior. In other words, the expression of thought is generally viewed as being beneficial to human development. As Justice Anthony Kennedy stated, "[t]he right to think is the beginning of freedom, and speech must be protected from the government because speech is the beginning of thought."[8]

YOUR CONSTITUTIONAL VALUES

CAN A PERSON BE PROSECUTED FOR PRIVATELY EXPRESSING CRIMINAL THOUGHTS?

In 1998, Brian J. Dalton was charged with ten counts of pandering obscenity involving a minor and twenty counts of pandering sexually oriented material involving a minor in an Ohio state court. Dalton eventually pled guilty to five counts of pandering obscenity involving a minor and five counts of pandering sexually oriented material involving a minor. The trial court sentenced Dalton to eighteen months in prison.

After serving almost four months of his prison term, Dalton was granted judicial release and placed on probation for three years. However, shortly thereafter, Dalton was arrested for lack of participation in his sex-offender-treatment program, a violation of his probation. After his arrest, Dalton's mother contacted Scott Merrick, Dalton's probation officer. She told Merrick that she had visited Dalton's apartment and was concerned about some items she had discovered there. She asked Merrick to come to the apartment and remove those items.

That same day, Merrick and another probation officer met Dalton's mother at Dalton's apartment. When they arrived, she had already placed several items on Dalton's bed, including Dalton's personal, handwritten journal. Merrick took all of the items back to the probation department, where he began to read Dalton's journal. The journal depicted Dalton's personal fantasies of the violent torture and rape of a number of purely fictitious children. After reading Dalton's journal, Merrick contacted a detective from the Columbus Police Sexual Abuse Squad, who came to the probation department and took the journal.

Authorities later charged Dalton with two counts of pandering obscenity involving a minor. Both charges were based solely upon Dalton's personal journal discovered in his apartment. The trial court appointed an attorney to represent Dalton. In July 2001, Dalton entered a guilty plea to one count of pandering obscenity involving a minor in exchange for the dismissal of the other count of the indictment. The trial court accepted appellant's guilty plea and sentenced him to seven years in prison. In addition, the court found that Dalton violated the terms of his probation, and ordered him to serve the remainder of his original prison term consecutive to the seven-year prison term.

In August 2001, Dalton filed a motion to withdraw his guilty plea, asserting that, under the First Amendment, he should not have been charged with two counts of pandering obscenity based on his personal thoughts in his journal. The trial court, however, denied Dalton's motion.

Based on your constitutional values, do you think Dalton's expression was protected by the First Amendment? What impact does the Court's decision in *Ashcroft v. Free Speech Coalition* (2002) (see below), have on your decision?

To see how the court of appeals decided this case, go to *State v. Dalton*, 153 Ohio App.3d 286, 2003-Ohio-3813.

10.2 THE SCOPE AND SUBSTANCE OF THE FIRST AMENDMENT

First Amendment provisions protecting expression generally are not read or applied literally. The phrase "Congress shall make no law . . . abridging the freedom of speech, or of the press; or the right of the people peaceably to assemble, and to petition the Government for a redress of grievances" does not merely apply to Congress; nor does it simply apply to laws or legislation; nor does it provide absolute protection for all forms of speech, press, assembly, petition, and association. Instead, through judicial interpretation, the text of the First Amendment has been interpreted to apply to other bodies and layers of government; to extend to more governmental activity than just legislation; and to impose certain limits on individual expression.

As discussed in Chapter 9, the Supreme Court gradually has incorporated most of the provisions within the Bill of Rights, thereby making them applicable to the states. This is true for all rights of expression protected by the First Amendment. In 1927, the Supreme Court formally incorporated the freedom of speech through the Fourteenth Amendment and applied it to the states in *Fiske v. Kansas*,[9] although the Supreme Court had suggested in 1920 and 1925 that the states were obligated to protect this freedom.[10] In 1931, the Court incorporated the freedom of the press in *Near v. Minnesota*.[11] Six years later, in *DeJonge v. Oregon*,[12] the Court incorporated the freedom of assembly, an incorporation that has been interpreted to include the freedom to petition the government for redress of grievances. And in 1958, the Court decided *NAACP v. Alabama*,[13] concluding that the First Amendment implicitly included another freedom—the freedom of association—and made this right applicable to the states. Consequently, governments at all levels—federal, state, and local—are required to protect the freedom of expression, in its various forms, as required by the First Amendment.

Similarly, the First Amendment's protections extend to more than just laws passed by legislatures. In addition to legislation, the First Amendment also applies to executive, judicial, and administrative conduct that interferes with such freedoms. And so, for example, the First Amendment has been applied to presidential attempts to restrict the dissemination of information,[14] to judicial orders that restrict the press from public courtrooms,[15] and to administrative actions that try to curb "indecent" language on radio and television.[16]

Finally, it is important to appreciate that the First Amendment protections of expression are not absolute. Despite the seemingly unequivocal wording of the amendment, the rights of speech, press, assembly, petition, and association have been interpreted to have certain limitations. The most common statement offered to illustrate this point is the claim that individuals do not have the right to falsely shout "fire!" in a crowded theatre.[17] The idea behind this is that, although this situation involves a person's speech, it also involves the safety of others, and there are times when a second value, such as human safety or national security, is going to trump or otherwise limit the value of speech. This "trumping" may also occur when a newspaper publishes false information, individuals threaten bodily harm to public officials, or people assemble or associate in a conspiracy to commit a crime. In each case, a competing value—a person's reputation, individual health, or public safety—likely will be deemed to outweigh the individual's interest in self-expression.

As discussed in the next section, the Supreme Court frequently adopts balancing tests or doctrines to resolve controversies over free expression. These balancing tests are designed not only to assist in resolving the immediate controversy before the Court, but to provide other courts and litigants in future cases with some guidelines or standards for interpreting First Amendment protections. One may think of these balancing tests as scales used to weigh the value of expression against other competing values (national security, public safety, equality, etc.). In visualizing these tests as scales, there are two important considerations. First, has the Court "calibrated" the scale (balancing test) in advance of the "weigh-in" to favor one side over the other? In other words, has the Court presumed certain forms of expression to be constitutionally protected, thereby requiring the government to produce a very heavy (compelling) interest on the other side of the scale before the Court will find the right of expression to be unprotected? And second, how compelling (heavy) are the interests placed on each side of the scale? Appreciate the fact that the weighing of competing interests on each side of the scale involves certain value judgments to be made by those doing the weighing. As the Court has stated, "[i]t is pertinent to the decision before us to consider where on the scales of values we have in the past placed the type of speech now claiming constitutional immunity."[18]

10.3 BASIC APPROACHES TO FREEDOM OF SPEECH

One of the first questions that must be addressed when discussing the freedom of speech is the nature and scope of speech itself. Obviously, the First Amendment includes speech that involves verbal communication. But what about other types of human activity, such as electronic messaging, visual images, art, music, movies, signs, symbols, and dancing? These forms and activities, on the surface, are not pure forms of speech because they do not necessarily involve a person speaking verbally. At the same time, each has the potential for communicating ideas in a manner similar to that offered by verbal speech. Consistent with the latter observation, the Supreme Court often has treated nonverbal expression as "speech," as long as it communicates or expresses an idea that can readily be received and understood by others. Promoting the notion that the First Amendment should promote and protect a "marketplace of ideas," the Court has treated such things as books, movies, photographs, electronic texts and images, messages on clothing, flag burning, flag saluting, commercial advertising, and dancing as forms of speech.[19]

There are times, however, when an individual's conduct will be viewed as just that—conduct—with very little or no communicative value. As a result, in examining the government's regulation of speech, the first issue that must be addressed is whether the government is regulating the expression of ideas (speech) or harmful behavior (conduct). In most cases, such an examination will involve contextual analysis and value judgments. If the case involves speech, the government likely will have to satisfy a more rigorous standard or balancing test. But if the case involves conduct, the government generally will be allowed more discretion in regulating the targeted activity, and in most cases, the government's actions will be permitted if they are reasonably related to a legitimate governmental interest. Read the Court's decision in *Texas v. Johnson* (1989) to see how the Court has considered this initial question regarding the difference between speech and conduct.

TEXAS v. JOHNSON
491 U.S. 397 (1989)

During the 1984 Republican National Convention in Dallas, Texas, Gregory Johnson participated in a political demonstration to protest the policies of the Reagan administration and some Dallas-based corporations. After a march through the city streets, Johnson burned an American flag while protesters chanted. No one was physically injured or threatened with injury, although several witnesses were seriously offended by the flag burning. Johnson was convicted of desecration of a venerated object in violation of a Texas statute, and a state court of appeals affirmed. However, the Texas Court of Criminal Appeals reversed, holding that the state, consistent with the First Amendment, could not punish Johnson for burning the flag in these circumstances. The state appealed that decision to the Supreme Court.

JUSTICE BRENNAN delivered the opinion of the Court.

Johnson was convicted of flag desecration for burning the flag rather than for uttering insulting words. This fact somewhat complicates our consideration of his conviction under the First Amendment. We must first determine whether Johnson's burning of the flag constituted expressive conduct, permitting him to invoke the First Amendment in challenging his conviction. If his conduct was expressive, we next decide whether the State's regulation is related to the suppression of free expression. See, e.g., *United States v. O'Brien*, 391 U.S. 367, 377 (1968). If the State's regulation is not related to expression, then the less stringent standard we announced in *United States v. O'Brien* for regulations of noncommunicative conduct controls. If it is, then we are outside of O'Brien's test, and we must ask whether this interest justifies Johnson's conviction under a more demanding standard. A third possibility is that the State's asserted interest is simply not implicated on these facts, and in that event the interest drops out of the picture . . .

The First Amendment literally forbids the abridgment only of "speech," but we have long recognized that its protection does not end at the spoken or written word. While we have rejected "the view that an apparently limitless variety of conduct can be labeled 'speech' whenever the person engaging in the conduct intends thereby to express an idea," we have acknowledged that conduct may be "sufficiently imbued with elements of communication to fall within the scope of the First and Fourteenth Amendments[.]"

In deciding whether particular conduct possesses sufficient communicative elements to bring the First Amendment into play, we have asked whether "[a]n intent to convey a particularized message was present, and [whether] the likelihood was great that the message would be understood by those who viewed it." . . .

The State of Texas conceded for purposes of its oral argument in this case that Johnson's conduct was expressive conduct . . . Johnson burned an American flag as part—indeed, as the culmination—of a political demonstration that coincided with the convening of the Republican Party and its renomination of Ronald Reagan for President. The expressive, overtly political nature of this conduct was both intentional and overwhelmingly apparent. At his trial, Johnson explained his reasons for burning the flag as follows: "The American Flag was burned as Ronald Reagan was being renominated as President. And a more powerful statement of symbolic speech, whether you agree with it or not, couldn't have been made at that time. It's quite a just position [juxtaposition]. We had new patriotism and no patriotism." In these circumstances, Johnson's burning of the flag was conduct "sufficiently imbued with elements of communication," to implicate the First Amendment.

The government generally has a freer hand in restricting expressive conduct than it has in restricting the written or spoken word. It may not, however, proscribe particular conduct because it has expressive elements. . . . It is, in short, not simply the verbal or nonverbal nature of the expression, but the governmental interest at stake, that helps to determine whether a restriction on that expression is valid.

Thus, although we have recognized that where "'speech' and 'nonspeech' elements are combined in the same course of conduct, a sufficiently important governmental interest in regulating the nonspeech element can justify incidental limitations on First Amendment freedoms," we have limited the applicability of *O'Brien's* relatively lenient standard to those cases in which "the governmental interest is unrelated to the suppression of free expression." . . .

In order to decide whether *O'Brien's* test applies here, therefore, we must decide whether Texas has asserted an interest in support of Johnson's conviction that is unrelated to the suppression of expression. If we find that an interest asserted by the State is simply not implicated on the facts before us, we need not ask whether *O'Brien's* test applies. The State offers two separate interests to justify this conviction: preventing breaches of the peace and preserving the flag as a symbol of nationhood and national unity. We hold that the first interest is not implicated on this record and that the second is related to the suppression of expression.

Texas claims that its interest in preventing breaches of the peace justifies Johnson's conviction for flag desecration. However, no disturbance of the peace actually occurred or threatened to occur because of Johnson's burning of the flag. Although the State stresses the disruptive behavior of the protestors during their march toward City Hall, it admits that "no actual breach of the peace occurred at the time of the flagburning or in response to the flagburning." . . .

The State also asserts an interest in preserving the flag as a symbol of nationhood and national unity. . . . We are equally persuaded that this interest is related to expression in the case of Johnson's burning of the flag. The State, apparently, is concerned that such conduct will lead people to believe either that the flag does not stand for nationhood and national unity, but instead reflects other, less positive concepts, or that the concepts reflected in the flag do not in fact exist, that is, that we do not enjoy unity as a Nation. . . . We are thus outside of O'Brien's test altogether.

It remains to consider whether the State's interest in preserving the flag as a symbol of nationhood and national unity justifies Johnson's conviction. . . .

Whether Johnson's treatment of the flag violated Texas law thus depended on the likely communicative impact of his expressive conduct. Our decision in *Boos v. Barry*, [485 U.S. 312 (1988)], tells us that this restriction on Johnson's expression is content based. In *Boos*, we considered the constitutionality of a law prohibiting "the display of any sign within 500 feet of a foreign embassy if that sign tends to bring that foreign government into 'public odium' or 'public disrepute.'" Rejecting the argument that the law was content neutral because it was justified by "our international law obligation to shield diplomats from speech that offends their dignity," we held that "[t]he emotive impact of speech on its audience is not a 'secondary effect'" unrelated to the content of the expression itself.

According to the principles announced in *Boos*, Johnson's political expression was restricted because of the content of the message he conveyed. We must therefore subject the State's asserted interest in preserving the special symbolic character of the flag to "the most exacting scrutiny." . . .

The State's argument is not that it has an interest simply in maintaining the flag as a symbol of something, no matter what it symbolizes; indeed, if that were the State's position, it would be difficult to see how that interest is endangered by highly symbolic conduct such as Johnson's. Rather, the State's claim is that it has an interest in preserving the flag as a symbol of nationhood and national unity, a symbol with a determinate range of meanings. According to Texas, if one physically treats the flag in a way that would tend to cast doubt on either the idea that nationhood and national unity are the flag's referents or that national unity actually exists, the message conveyed thereby is a harmful one and therefore may be prohibited.

If there is a bedrock principle underlying the First Amendment, it is that the government may not prohibit the expression of an idea simply because society finds the idea itself offensive or disagreeable. . . .

In short, nothing in our precedents suggests that a State may foster its own view of the flag by prohibiting expressive conduct relating to it. . . .

It is not the State's ends, but its means, to which we object. It cannot be gainsaid that there is a special place reserved for the flag in this Nation, and thus we do not doubt that the government has a legitimate interest in making efforts to "preserv[e] the national flag as an unalloyed symbol of our country." . . .

The way to preserve the flag's special role is not to punish those who feel differently about these matters. It is to persuade them that they are wrong. . . .

The judgment of the Texas Court of Criminal Appeals is therefore

Affirmed.

JUSTICE KENNEDY, concurring.

With all respect to [the dissenters], I do not believe the Constitution gives us the right to rule as the dissenting Members of the Court urge, however painful this judgment is to announce. Though symbols often are what we ourselves make of them, the flag is constant in expressing beliefs Americans share, beliefs in law and peace and that freedom which sustains the human spirit. The case here today forces recognition of the costs to which those beliefs commit us. It is poignant but fundamental that the flag protects those who hold it in contempt. . . .

CHIEF JUSTICE REHNQUIST, with whom JUSTICE WHITE and JUSTICE O'CONNOR join, dissenting.

The American flag, then, throughout more than 200 years of our history, has come to be the visible symbol embodying our Nation. It does not represent the views of any particular political party, and it does not represent any particular political philosophy. The flag is not simply another "idea" or "point of view" competing for recognition in the marketplace of ideas. Millions and millions of Americans regard it with an almost mystical reverence regardless of what sort of social, political, or philosophical beliefs they may have. I cannot agree that the First Amendment invalidates the Act of Congress, and the laws of 48 of the 50 States, which make criminal the public burning of the flag. . . .

JUSTICE STEVENS, dissenting.

The Court is . . . quite wrong in blandly asserting that respondent "was prosecuted for his expression of dissatisfaction with the policies of this country, expression situated at the core of our First Amendment values." Respondent was prosecuted because of the method he chose to express his dissatisfaction with those policies. Had he chosen to spray-paint—or perhaps convey with a motion picture projector—his message of dissatisfaction on the facade of the Lincoln Memorial, there would be no question about the power of the Government to prohibit his means of expression. The prohibition would be supported by the legitimate interest in preserving the quality of an important national asset. Though the asset at stake in this case is intangible, given its unique value, the same interest supports a prohibition on the desecration of the American flag.

June 28, 1989: Gregory Johnson is shown. He is the man around whom the flag burning controversy began because he burned the American flag.

Corbis/Bettmann

clear and present danger test
A theory adopted by the Supreme Court in the early twentieth century as a means to interpret and apply the free speech clause of the First Amendment. Under this theory, Justice Holmes provided that "[t]he question in every case is whether the words used are used in such circumstances and are of such a nature as to create a clear and present danger that they will bring about the substantive evils that Congress has a right to prevent. It is a question of proximity and degree."

The fact that a case involves a person's speech does not necessarily mean that it will be protected under the First Amendment. Assuming that the government is attempting to regulate speech, as opposed to conduct, the next question that must be addressed is to what extent government can regulate such speech. As we have discussed, the freedom of speech is not absolute. And in balancing the interests of speech against competing governmental interests, there has been an evolution of balancing tests created and modified by the Supreme Court.

In the early twentieth century, as the Court began to address matters under the free speech clause, the Court initially adopted the **clear and present danger test.** This test was crafted in a unanimous opinion written by Justice Oliver Wendell Holmes in *Schenck v. United States* (1919)[20] (see below). In *Schenck*, the defendant was charged with attempts to cause insubordination in the military and obstruction of enlistment during World War I. Schenck was the secretary of the Socialist Party and had distributed pamphlets urging resistance to the draft, denouncing conscription, and challenging the motives of those supporting U.S. involvement in the war. Schenck asserted that his actions were protected under the First Amendment. But Justice Holmes rejected this claim, stating, "[t]he question in every case is whether the words used are used in such circumstances and are of such a nature as to create a clear and present danger that they will bring about the substantive evils that Congress has a right to prevent. It is a question of proximity and degree." This standard became known as the clear and present danger test and served as the initial prototype for balancing interests under the free speech clause. Read the Court's opinion in *Schenck* to appreciate the contextual analysis used by the Court in adopting this initial test.

SCHENCK v. UNITED STATES
249 U.S. 47 (1919)

Schenck held the position of Secretary within the Socialist Party, as organized in the United States. In this position, he was responsible for printing and distributing leaflets that urged men to oppose and resist the military draft during World War I. Based on these actions, federal authorities arrested and tried Schenck under the Espionage Act of 1917, which was enacted in the wake of the so-called "Red scare"—the fear of Communist invasion. After his conviction, Schenck challenged the constitutionality of the Espionage Act before the Supreme Court.

Mr. Justice HOLMES delivered the opinion of the Court.

This is an indictment in three counts. The first charges a conspiracy to violate the Espionage Act of June 15, 1917, by causing and attempting to cause insubordination in the military and naval forces of the United States, and to obstruct the recruiting and enlistment service of the United States, when the United States was at war with the German Empire, to-wit, that the defendant wilfully conspired to have printed and circulated to men who had been called and accepted for military service under the Act of May 18, 1917, a document set forth and alleged to be calculated to cause such insubordination and obstruction. The count alleges overt acts in pursuance of the conspiracy, ending in the distribution of the document set forth. The second count alleges a conspiracy to commit an offense against the United States, to-wit, to use the mails for the transmission of matter declared to be non-mailable by title 12, 2, of the Act of June 15, 1917, to-wit, the above mentioned document, with an averment of the same overt acts. The third count charges an unlawful use of the mails for the transmission of the same matter and otherwise as above. The defendants were found guilty on all the counts. They set up the First Amendment to the Constitution forbidding Congress to make any law abridging the freedom of speech, or of the press, and bringing the case here on that ground have argued some other points also of which we must dispose.

The document in question upon its first printed side recited the first section of the Thirteenth Amendment, said that the idea embodied in it was violated by the conscription act and that a conscript is little better than a convict. In impassioned language it intimated that conscription was despotism in its worst form and a monstrous wrong against humanity in the interest of Wall Street's chosen few. It said, "Do not submit to intimidation," but in form at least confined itself to peaceful measures such as a petition for the repeal of the act. The other and later printed side of the sheet was headed "Assert Your Rights." It stated reasons for alleging that any one violated the Constitution when he refused to recognize "your right to assert your opposition to the draft," and went on, "If you do not assert and support your rights, you are helping to deny or disparage rights which it is the solemn duty of all citizens and residents of the United States to retain." It described the arguments on the other side as coming from cunning politicians and a mercenary capitalist press, and even silent consent to the conscription law as helping to support an infamous conspiracy. It denied the power to send our citizens away to foreign shores to shoot up the people of other lands, and added that words could not express the condemnation such cold-blooded ruthlessness deserves, &c., &c., winding up, "You must do your share to maintain, support and uphold the rights of the people of this country." Of course the document would not have been sent unless it had been intended to have some effect, and we do not see what effect it could be expected to have upon persons subject to the draft except to influence them to obstruct the carrying of it out. The defendants do not deny that the jury might find against them on this point.

But it is said, suppose that that was the tendency of this circular, it is protected by the First Amendment to the Constitution. Two of the strongest expressions are said to be quoted respectively from well-known public men. It well may be that the prohibition of laws abridging the freedom of speech is not confined to previous restraints, although to prevent them may have been the main purpose.... We admit that in many places and in ordinary times the defendants in saying all that was said in the circular would have been within their constitutional rights. But the character of every act depends upon the circumstances in which it is done. The most stringent protection of free speech would not protect a man in falsely shouting fire in a theatre and causing a panic. It does not even protect a man from an injunction against uttering words that may have all the effect of force. The question in every case is whether the words used are used in such circumstances and are of such a nature as to create a clear and present danger that they will bring about the substantive evils that Congress has a right to prevent. It is a question of proximity and degree. When a nation is at war many things that might be said in time of peace are such a hindrance to its effort that their utterance will not be endured so long as men fight and that no Court could regard them as protected by any constitutional right. It seems to be admitted that if an actual obstruction of the recruiting service were proved, liability for words that produced that effect might be enforced. The statute of 1917 in section 4 punishes conspiracies to obstruct as well as actual obstruction. If the act, (speaking, or circulating a paper,) its tendency and the intent with which it is done are the same, we perceive no ground for saying that success alone warrants making the act a crime....

Judgments affirmed.

Six years after *Schenck*, a majority of the Court rejected the clear and present test in *Gitlow v. New York* (1925).[21] In Gitlow, the defendant, who was a socialist, published a pamphlet called *Left Wing Manifesto*, which predicted the inevitability of a proletarian revolution in the United States. In a 7–2 opinion, the Court upheld the federal Advocacy of Criminal Anarchy, which barred advocating the overthrow of the government, as it was used against Gitlow. In upholding Gitlow's conviction, the Court declined to apply the clear and present danger test, and instead concluded that the government could restrict speech if the "natural tendency and probable effect [of the speech] was to bring about the substantive evil which the legislative body might prevent." This standard is known as the **bad tendency test** because it allowed the government to predetermine and ban types of speech that may have a *tendency* to bring about harm, regardless of whether the speech, in actuality, poses a clear and present danger. Essentially, under this standard, the Court concluded that the government need not wait to protect itself until the danger of speech is clear and present.

Later, the Court resurrected and modified the clear and present danger test in *Dennis v. United States* (1951),[22] a case in which a member of the Communist Party was convicted under the federal Smith Act for knowingly conspiring to teach and advocate overthrow of government. In upholding Dennis's conviction, the Court found validity in a standard offered by Judge Learned Hand, a federal circuit court judge who earlier had ruled upon the case. Under Judge Hand's approach, the Court asked "whether the gravity of the 'evil,' discounted by its improbability, justifies such invasion of free speech as is necessary to avoid the danger." Under this **probability test**, the likelihood that the speech will succeed in bringing about the identified harm is considered in addition to the traditional factors of whether the speech is advocating a clear and present danger.

The final standard in the Court's evolution of free speech doctrines is known as the ***Brandenburg* test**. In *Brandenburg v. Ohio* (1969)[23] (see below), the Court reviewed the conviction of a Klu Klux Klan leader under an Ohio law barring a person from advocating violence or terrorism. Brandenburg was convicted based on a speech in which he claimed that if the government did not stop suppressing the white majority, "there might have to be revengenance [*sic*] taken." In reversing Brandenburg's conviction, the Court adopted what is regarded as the modern-day approach to free speech cases, concluding that before the government may suppress or punish speech, the speech must be "directed to inciting or producing imminent lawless action and . . . likely to incite or produce such action." Notice how the Court incorporated a value from the clear and present danger test (adopting an imminent or present requirement) with a value from the probability test (likelihood or probability of success). Read the opinion in *Brandenburg* to assess how the Court decided upon its current balancing test and how it applied this test to reverse Brandenburg's conviction.

bad tendency test
Another test used by the Court to interpret and apply the free speech clause, which allows government to predetermine and ban types of speech that may have a *tendency* to bring about harm, regardless of whether the speech, in actuality, poses a clear and present danger.

probability test
A third approach to the free speech clause adopted by some members of the Court in the mid-twentieth century. This test asks "whether the gravity of the 'evil,' discounted by its improbability, justifies such invasion of free speech as is necessary to avoid the danger."

***Brandenburg* test**
The current standard used by the Court in many free speech cases. Under this test adopted in *Brandenburg v. Ohio* (1969), the government may not suppress speech unless the speech is "directed to inciting or producing imminent lawless action and . . . likely to incite or produce such action."

BRANDENBURG v. OHIO
395 U.S. 444 (1969)

PER CURIAM.

[Charles Brandenburg], a leader of a Ku Klux Klan group, was convicted under the Ohio Criminal Syndicalism statute for "advocat[ing] . . . the duty, necessity, or propriety of crime, sabotage, violence, or unlawful methods of terrorism as a means of accomplishing industrial or political reform" and for "voluntarily assembl[ing] with any society, group, or assemblage of persons formed to teach or advocate the doctrines of criminal syndicalism." Ohio Rev. Code Ann. 2923.13. He was fined $1,000 and sentenced to one to 10 years' imprisonment. The appellant challenged the constitutionality of the criminal syndicalism statute under the First and Fourteenth Amendments to the United States Constitution, but the intermediate appellate court of Ohio affirmed his conviction without opinion. The Supreme Court of Ohio dismissed his appeal. . . . We reverse.

The record shows that a man, identified at trial as the appellant, telephoned an announcer-reporter on the staff of a Cincinnati television station and invited him to come to a Ku Klux Klan "rally" to be held at a farm in Hamilton County. With the cooperation of the organizers, the reporter and a cameraman attended the meeting and filmed the events. Portions of the films were later broadcast on the local station and on a national network.

The prosecution's case rested on the films and on testimony identifying the appellant as the person who communicated with the reporter and who spoke at the rally. The State also introduced into evidence several articles appearing in the film, including a pistol, a rifle, a shotgun, ammunition, a Bible, and a red hood worn by the speaker in the films.

One film showed 12 hooded figures, some of whom carried firearms. They were gathered around a large wooden cross, which they burned. No one was present other than the participants and the newsmen who made the film. Most of the words uttered during the scene were incomprehensible when the film was projected, but scattered phrases could be understood that were derogatory of Negroes and, in one instance, of Jews. Another scene on the same film showed the appellant, in Klan regalia, making a speech. The speech, in full, was as follows:

> "This is an organizers' meeting. We have had quite a few members here today which are—we have hundreds, hundreds of members throughout the State of Ohio. I can quote from a newspaper clipping from the Columbus, Ohio Dispatch, five weeks ago Sunday morning. The Klan has more members in the State of Ohio than does any other organization. We're not a revengent organization, but if our President, our Congress, our Supreme Court, continues to suppress the white, Caucasian race, it's possible that there might have to be some revengeance taken.
>
> "We are marching on Congress July the Fourth, four hundred thousand strong. From there we are dividing into two groups, one group to march on St. Augustine, Florida, the other group to march into Mississippi. Thank you."

The second film showed six hooded figures one of whom, later identified as the appellant, repeated a speech very similar to that recorded on the first film. The reference to the possibility of "revengeance" was omittted, and one sentence was added: "Personally, I believe the nigger should be returned to Africa, the Jew returned to Israel." Though some of the figures in the films carried weapons, the speaker did not. . . .

[The Court's] decisions have fashioned the principle that the constitutional guarantees of free speech and free press do not permit a State to forbid or proscribe advocacy of the use of force or of law violation except where such advocacy is directed to inciting or producing imminent lawless action and is likely to incite or produce such action. As we said in *Noto v. United States*, 367 U.S. 290, 297–298 (1961), "the mere abstract teaching . . . of the moral propriety or even moral necessity for a resort to force and violence, is not the same as preparing a group for violent action and steeling it to such action." A statute which fails to draw this distinction impermissibly intrudes upon the freedoms guaranteed by the First and Fourteenth Amendments. It sweeps within its condemnation speech which our Constitution has immunized from governmental control.

Measured by this test, Ohio's Criminal Syndicalism Act cannot be sustained. The Act punishes persons who "advocate or teach the duty, necessity, or propriety" of violence "as a means of accomplishing industrial or political reform"; or who publish or circulate or display any book or paper containing such advocacy; or who "justify" the commission of violent acts "with intent to exemplify, spread or advocate the propriety of the doctrines of criminal syndicalism"; or who "voluntarily assemble" with a group formed "to teach or advocate the doctrines of criminal syndicalism." Neither the indictment nor the trial judge's instructions to the jury in any way refined the statute's bald definition of the crime in terms of mere advocacy not distinguished from incitement to imminent lawless action.

Accordingly, we are here confronted with a statute which, by its own words and as applied, purports to punish mere advocacy and to forbid, on pain of criminal punishment, assembly with others merely to advocate the described type of action. Such a statute falls within the condemnation of the First and Fourteenth Amendments. . . .

Reversed.

MR. JUSTICE BLACK, concurring.

I agree with the views expressed by MR. JUSTICE DOUGLAS in his concurring opinion in this case that the "clear and present danger" doctrine should have no place in the interpretation of the First Amendment. . . .

MR. JUSTICE DOUGLAS, concurring.

10.4   FREEDOM OF SPEECH: THE REST OF THE STORY

While the *Brandenburg* standard is applied in many free speech cases, there are other situations where this test is insufficient. And in those cases, there may be other terms and tests that are important to evaluating the level of First Amendment protection. These items are outlined individually below. At the end of this discussion, a framework of questions is provided to help organize the individual terms and tests and to demonstrate how they can be used together to assess future free speech cases.

10.4(a)   Content versus Conduct

As discussed earlier, one of the first considerations in free speech cases is whether the government is directly targeting the content of speech or whether it is trying to regulate conduct and, in so doing, is imposing a restriction on speech. For example, a law that bans signs critical of the government would be a policy directly aimed at curbing speech.[24] But a law that punishes disorderly conduct, if applied to a person screaming profanities at 2:00 A.M. in a neighborhood, would be an example of a conduct-focused law that affects speech. Typically, government will be given greater discretion to enforce laws that are focused on conduct, even if they slightly or indirectly impact speech, than to enforce laws that specifically target speech.

Pay particular attention to the concept of **symbolic speech**, which is nonverbal communication that is akin to pure speech. At first glance, a person using symbols (signs, flags, arm bands, or other tangible items) or conduct (hand gestures, burning objects, or other behavior) may appear not to be speech. But the Court has cautioned that such nonverbal expression will receive First Amendment protection to the extent that it conveys a message capable of being received and understood by others.[25]

10.4(b)   Vagueness and Overbreadth

The vagueness and overbreadth doctrines are also critical to free speech analysis. The **vagueness doctrine** essentially maintains that the government cannot impose standards that the average person is not likely to understand. Consistent with the constitutional requirement that government provide due process of law (see Chapter 12), the Court requires governmental standards to be sufficiently clear and defined so that individuals can understand what is being prohibited. For example, a law that bans "indecent" communications on the Internet would be viewed as a vague standard for regulating speech because the term *indecent*, without a more precise definition, is not a readily and commonly understood term. Under these circumstances, it would be very difficult for individuals to conform their speech to meet this standard.[26] Such attempts to apply vague standards in regulating speech are generally deemed unconstitutional.

The **overbreadth doctrine** is also grounded in notions of due process, and generally provides that the government cannot regulate or prohibit more speech than is necessary to address the identified harm. For example, although the government may prohibit depictions of child pornography (see discussion below), it may not ban all forms of expression that "appear to be" child pornography because such a ban is likely to capture expression that does not include depictions of actual children.[27] Under the overbreadth doctrine, the Court essentially asks whether the government's restriction on speech is properly tailored to address the harm the government is seeking to prevent. But in cases where the government bans large amounts of protected speech in an effort to stop harmful speech, known as "burning the house down to roast the pig," such restrictions on speech will be deemed overly broad and therefore unconstitutional.

10.4(c)   Ban versus Regulation

Another consideration is the type of action taken by the government in restricting speech. Is it attempting to impose a complete **ban on speech** ("thou shall never criticize the government")? Or is it trying to impose a **time, place, and manner regulation** of speech (you must get a permit for a parade and it can only be held between 9:00 A.M. and 7:00 P.M.)? A ban on speech prohibits expression at all times and in all places, whereas a regulation of speech allows expression in certain given contexts.[28] In most cases, governmental bans on speech will be scrutinized more rigorously under the First Amendment than reasonable time, place, and manner regulations of

symbolic speech
Nonverbal communication that is akin to pure speech, including symbols (signs, flags, arm bands, or other tangible items) or conduct (hand gestures, burning objects, or other behavior). This nonverbal expression may receive First Amendment protection to the extent that it conveys a message capable of being received and understood by others.

vagueness doctrine
A constitutional theory of due process that maintains that the government cannot impose legal standards that the average person cannot or is not likely to understand. Attempts to apply vague standards in regulating speech are generally deemed unconstitutional.

overbreadth doctrine
A constitutional theory of due process that generally provides that the government cannot regulate or prohibit more speech than is necessary to address the identified harm. Under this doctrine, the Court essentially asks whether the government's restriction on speech is properly tailored to address the harm the government is seeking to prevent.

ban on speech
A governmental policy barring a particular form of expression at any time or place or in any manner.

time, place, and manner regulation
A government restriction on speech that restricts speech but allows the expression in certain given contexts.

strict scrutiny test
A legal standard requiring the government to prove that its policy is necessary (or narrowly tailored) to promote a compelling governmental interest. This test imposes the strictest burden upon government in its attempt to regulate speech.

speech. In fact, in most cases where the government is seeking to impose a complete and direct ban on speech, the government will have to prove that its actions are necessary to promote a compelling governmental interest. This standard is known as the **strict scrutiny test** because it imposes the strictest burden upon government in its attempt to regulate speech.

Read the decision in *Republican Party of Minnesota v. White* (2002) to see how the Court determines whether to apply the strict scrutiny test and how the test actually works. Notice that even when members of the Court agree on the constitutional standard to be applied in a given case, they may not agree on the result it yields.

REPUBLICAN PARTY OF MINNESOTA v. WHITE
536 U.S. 765 (2002)

Justice Scalia delivered the opinion of the Court.

The question presented in this case is whether the First Amendment permits the Minnesota Supreme Court to prohibit candidates for judicial election in that State from announcing their views on disputed legal and political issues.

Since Minnesota's admission to the Union in 1858, the State's Constitution has provided for the selection of all state judges by popular election. Since 1912, those elections have been nonpartisan. Since 1974, they have been subject to a legal restriction which states that a "candidate for a judicial office, including an incumbent judge," shall not "announce his or her views on disputed legal or political issues." This prohibition . . . is known as the "announce clause." Incumbent judges who violate it are subject to discipline, including removal, censure, civil penalties, and suspension without pay. Lawyers who run for judicial office also must comply with the announce clause. Those who violate it are subject to, inter alia, disbarment, suspension, and probation.

In 1996, one of the petitioners, Gregory Wersal, ran for associate justice of the Minnesota Supreme Court. In the course of the campaign, he distributed literature criticizing several Minnesota Supreme Court decisions on issues such as crime, welfare, and abortion. A complaint against Wersal challenging, among other things, the propriety of this literature was filed with the Office of Lawyers Professional Responsibility. . . . The Lawyers Board dismissed the complaint; with regard to the charges that his campaign materials violated the announce clause, it expressed doubt whether the clause could constitutionally be enforced. Nonetheless, fearing that further ethical complaints would jeopardize his ability to practice law, Wersal withdrew from the election. In 1998, Wersal ran again for the same office. Early in that race, he sought an advisory opinion from the Lawyers Board with regard to whether it planned to enforce the announce clause. The Lawyers Board responded equivocally, stating that, although it had significant doubts about the constitutionality of the provision, it was unable to answer his question because he had not submitted a list of the announcements he wished to make.

Shortly thereafter, Wersal filed this lawsuit in Federal District Court against respondents, seeking, *inter alia*, a declaration that the announce clause violates the First Amendment and an injunction against its enforcement. Wersal alleged that he was forced to refrain from announcing his views on disputed issues during the 1998 campaign, to the point where he declined response to questions put to him by the press and public, out of concern that he might run afoul of the announce clause. . . .

As the Court of Appeals recognized, the announce clause both prohibits speech on the basis of its content and burdens a

category of speech that is "at the core of our First Amendment freedoms"—speech about the qualifications of candidates for public office. The Court of Appeals concluded that the proper test to be applied to determine the constitutionality of such a restriction is what our cases have called strict scrutiny, the parties do not dispute that this is correct. Under the strict-scrutiny test, respondents have the burden to prove that the announce clause is (1) narrowly tailored, to serve (2) a compelling state interest. In order for respondents to show that the announce clause is narrowly tailored, they must demonstrate that it does not "unnecessarily circumscrib[e] protected expression."

We think it plain that the announce clause is not narrowly tailored to serve impartiality (or the appearance of impartiality). . . . Indeed, the clause is barely tailored to serve that interest at all, inasmuch as it does not restrict speech for or against particular parties, but rather speech for or against particular issues. To be sure, when a case arises that turns on a legal issue on which the judge (as a candidate) had taken a particular stand, the party taking the opposite stand is likely to lose. But not because of any bias against that party, or favoritism toward the other party. Any party taking that position is just as likely to lose. The judge is applying the law (as he sees it) evenhandedly. . . .

The short of the matter is this: In Minnesota, a candidate for judicial office may not say "I think it is constitutional for the legislature to prohibit same-sex marriages." He may say the very same thing, however, up until the very day before he declares himself a candidate, and may say it repeatedly (until litigation is pending) after he is elected. As a means of pursuing the objective of open-mindedness that respondents now articulate, the announce clause is so woefully underinclusive as to render belief in that purpose a challenge to the credulous. . . .

Moreover, the notion that the special context of electioneering justifies an abridgment of the right to speak out on disputed issues sets our First Amendment jurisprudence on its head. "[D]ebate on the qualifications of candidates" is "at the core of our electoral process and of the First Amendment freedoms," not at the edges. "The role that elected officials play in our society makes it all the more imperative that they be allowed freely to express themselves on matters of current public importance." "It is simply not the function of government to select which issues are worth discussing or debating in the course of a political campaign." We have never allowed the government to prohibit candidates from communicating relevant information to voters during an election. . . .

The Minnesota Supreme Court's canon of judicial conduct prohibiting candidates for judicial election from announcing their views on disputed legal and political issues violates the

First Amendment. Accordingly, we reverse the grant of summary judgment to respondents and remand the case for proceedings consistent with this opinion.

It is so ordered.

Justice O'Connor & Justice Kennedy concurring.

Justice Stevens, with whom Justice Souter, Justice Ginsburg, and Justice Breyer join, dissenting.

The disposition of this case on the flawed premise that the criteria for the election to judicial office should mirror the rules applicable to political elections is profoundly misguided. I therefore respectfully dissent.

Justice Ginsburg, with whom Justice Stevens, Justice Souter, and Justice Breyer join, dissenting.

Prohibiting a judicial candidate from pledging or promising certain results if elected directly promotes the State's interest in preserving public faith in the bench. When a candidate makes such a promise during a campaign, the public will no doubt perceive that she is doing so in the hope of garnering votes. And the public will in turn likely conclude that when the candidate decides an issue in accord with that promise, she does so at least in part to discharge her undertaking to the voters in the previous election and to prevent voter abandonment in the next. The perception of that unseemly quid pro quo—a judicial candidate's promises on issues in return for the electorate's votes at the polls—inevitably diminishes the public's faith in the ability of judges to administer the law without regard to personal or political self-interest. . . .

10.4(d) Public Versus Nonpublic Forum

A frequent distinction made in free speech cases is that between public forums and non-public forums. Generally, the Court has described **public forums** as properties historically associated with the exercise of First Amendment rights. This would include such places as public sidewalks, parks, and cartilages outside courthouses and statehouses.[29] Conversely, **nonpublic forums** are regarded as those places that are not historically associated with the exercise of First Amendment rights. Such locations may include military bases, jails, and certain interior portions of public buildings.[30] In most cases, the government will be given greater leeway to regulate speech in nonpublic forums than in public forums.[31]

public forums
Properties historically associated with the exercise of First Amendment rights, including public sidewalks, parks, and cartilages outside courthouses and statehouses.

10.4(e) Content and Viewpoint Neutrality

The concepts of content neutrality and viewpoint neutrality are also important in many free speech controversies. **Content neutrality** (also known as subject-matter neutrality) means that the government, in attempting to regulate speech, is not discriminating against speech based on its content or subject matter. For example, a law that punishes "unruly behavior" takes no position on the content of speech that might result in a violation of this standard. However, a governmental action that prohibits public displays regarding war, either pro or con, would be an example of a content-based regulation of speech because it targets a specific subject matter for regulation.

Viewpoint neutrality means that the government does not favor one side or another within a given subject matter of speech. For example, a government ban on abortion-related demonstrations, while content based, would be viewpoint neutral. But if the government were to ban antiabortion protests, while allowing pro-choice demonstrations, such an approach would not be viewpoint neutral.

There are times when the Court will require the government to have content-neutral laws in place before it will be allowed to regulate speech. Such is often the case when the government attempts to regulate speech within a traditional public forum. In other instances, such as where the government attempts to regulate speech within a nonpublic forum, viewpoint neutrality will suffice.[32]

nonpublic forums
Places that are not historically associated with the exercise of First Amendment rights. Such locations may include military bases, jails, and certain interior portions of public buildings.

content neutrality
Also known as subject-matter neutrality, this term means that the government, in attempting to regulate speech, is not discriminating against speech based on its content or subject matter.

viewpoint neutrality
A term used to require the government not to favor one side or another within a given subject matter of speech.

10.4(f) Types of Speech

A final, although substantial, consideration is the nature and type of speech being regulated by the government. The Court has often noted that certain forms of speech are less protected or unprotected under the First Amendment. The Court has identified forms of expression, such as fighting words, defamation, obscenity, child pornography, and commercial speech, as types of speech that are somewhat removed from the pure political speech that, according to the Court, the First Amendment was designed to protect. Accordingly, the Court has drafted specialized balancing tests or doctrines to apply when these forms of expression are being regulated.

In the area of sexual expression, there is a fundamental constitutional distinction that is made between obscenity, pornography, vulgarity, and profanity. The Court has ruled that obscene materials generally are undeserving of any First Amendment protection. As the Court

obscenity
A form of unprotected sexual expression. As the Court defined the term in *Miller v. California* (1973), obscenity is a specific type of sexual expression that: (1) taken as a whole, appeals to a prurient (unhealthy) interest in sex; (2) portrays sexual conduct in a patently offensive way; and (3) taken as a whole, lacks serious literary, artistic, political, or scientific value.

pornography
Materials that depict sexual expression, which may or may not meet the *Miller* standards of obscenity.

vulgarity
Expression, which is sometimes sexual in nature, that is regarded as highly crude and offensive.

profanity
Words, which often include slang references to sexual activity, that are viewed as highly offensive and impolite, but may still be afforded constitutional protection, as long as they do not fall into another category of unprotected speech, such as fighting words.

child pornography
Materials that depict actual children (persons under the age of eighteen) engaged in sexual conduct.

defined the term in *Miller v. California* (1973),[33] **obscenity** is a specific type of sexual expression that: (1) taken as a whole, appeals to a prurient (unhealthy) interest in sex; (2) portrays sexual conduct in a patently offensive way; and (3) taken as a whole, lacks serious literary, artistic, political, or scientific value. If a work meets each of these three standards, government may regulate, ban, or prosecute such materials. Interestingly, however, the Court has ruled that government may not punish the mere private possession of obscene materials by an individual.[34] As a result, obscenity prosecutions are mostly limited to the sale, distribution, or transmission of obscene materials.

While obscenity is categorized as a form of unprotected expression, **pornography** (materials that depict sexual expression but fall short of meeting the *Miller* standards), **vulgarity** (expression, which is sometimes sexual in nature, that is regarded as highly crude and offensive), and **profanity** (words, which often include slang references to sexual activity, that are viewed as highly offensive and impolite) are still afforded constitutional protection, as long as they do not fall into another category of unprotected speech, such as fighting words or child pornography (see following discussion).

Child pornography is another category of unprotected speech. Regardless of whether the expression meets *Miller's* obscenity standards, government may ban, regulate, or prosecute materials that depict actual children (persons under the age of eighteen) engaged in sexual conduct. And unlike obscene materials, government may also ban the mere possession of child pornography. The Court deemed this category of expression unprotected in *New York v. Ferber* (1982)[35] because this form of pornography has the potential to harm real children during the production of the materials and after they are distributed. Note, however, that in *Ashcroft v. Free Speech Coalition* (2002), the Court ruled that the unprotected category of child pornography is limited to those materials in which a real child, as opposed to a computer-generated or fictional child, is depicted.[36]

Read the majority opinion by Justice Kennedy in *Ashcroft v. Free Speech Coalition* to understand the unprotected status of child pornography and the constitutional difficulties that the government often faces when it attempts to regulate sexual expression in cyberspace. Also, pay particular attention to the Court's treatment of the overbreadth doctrine as it is applied to the government's attempt to expand the definition of child pornography.

S I D E B A R

"MOVIE DAY" AT THE SUPREME COURT

From the late 1950s through the early 1970s, the Supreme Court decided several cases involving the constitution and allegedly-obscene materials. These cases included *Roth v. United States* and *Alberts v. California*, 354 U.S. 476 (1957), *Ginzburg v. United States*, 383 U.S. 463 (1966), *Miller v. California*, 413 U.S. 15 (1973), and *Paris Adult Theatre I v. Slaton*, 413 U.S. 49 (1973). In these and many other cases, the underlying materials at issue were pornographic films. Given this context, the members of the Court often saw it necessary to watch the films in order to determine whether they depicted obscenity or constitutionally-protected sexual expression. Such viewings it is reported occurred in the basement of the Supreme Court building where the Justices and their law clerks would gather to watch the movies.

One notable exception was Justice Hugo Black, who purportedly refused to attend the movie shows because he did not believe that watching such films would change his mind about the constitutional protection that should be afforded the films. Regarded as an "absolutist" in the area of free speech, Black regularly found governmental regulations of adult films to be unconstitutional. For Black, when the First Amendment said, "Congress shall make no law . . . abridging the freedom of speech," the phrase "no law" should be interpreted and applied strictly and absolutely.

On a more humorous note, it is reported that, during "movie days," Justice Thurgood Marshall, who served on the bench from 1967 to 1991, would sit in the front row of the Court's "theater" and crack jokes about many of the scenes being depicted. It is also reported that Justice John Marshall Harlan, who was a Justice from 1955 to 1971 and who suffered from near blindness due to extreme cataracts, had to rely upon Court colleagues to orally describe for him the visual events on the screen.

Sources: The Brethren, Bob Woodward and Scott Armstrong, Simon & Schuster (1979); Joyce Murdoch and Deb Price, *Courting Justice: Gay Men and Lesbians v. the Supreme Court*, Basic Books (2001).

ASHCROFT v. FREE SPEECH COALITION
535 U.S. 234 (2002)

Justice Kennedy delivered the opinion of the Court.

We consider in this case whether the Child Pornography Prevention Act of 1996 (CPPA) abridges the freedom of speech. The CPPA extends the federal prohibition against child pornography to sexually explicit images that appear to depict minors but were produced without using any real children. The statute prohibits, in specific circumstances, possessing or distributing these images, which may be created by using adults who look like minors or by using computer imaging. The new technology, according to Congress, makes it possible to create realistic images of children who do not exist.

By prohibiting child pornography that does not depict an actual child, the statute goes beyond *New York v. Ferber*, 458 U.S. 747 (1982), which distinguished child pornography from other sexually explicit speech because of the State's interest in protecting the children exploited by the production process. As a general rule, pornography can be banned only if obscene, but under *Ferber*, pornography showing minors can be proscribed whether or not the images are obscene under the definition set forth in *Miller v. California*, 413 U.S. 15 (1973). *Ferber* recognized that "[t]he *Miller* standard, like all general definitions of what may be banned as obscene, does not reflect the State's particular and more compelling interest in prosecuting those who promote the sexual exploitation of children." . . .

The principal question to be resolved, then, is whether the CPPA is constitutional where it proscribes a significant universe of speech that is neither obscene under *Miller* nor child pornography under *Ferber*. . . .

As a general principle, the First Amendment bars the government from dictating what we see or read or speak or hear. The freedom of speech has its limits; it does not embrace certain categories of speech, including defamation, incitement, obscenity, and pornography produced with real children. While these categories may be prohibited without violating the First Amendment, none of them includes the speech prohibited by the CPPA. . . .

As we have noted, the CPPA is much more than a supplement to the existing federal prohibition on obscenity. Under *Miller v. California*, 413 U.S. 15 (1973), the Government must prove that the work, taken as a whole, appeals to the prurient interest, is patently offensive in light of community standards, and lacks serious literary, artistic, political, or scientific value. The CPPA, however, extends to images that appear to depict a minor engaging in sexually explicit activity without regard to the Miller requirements. The materials need not appeal to the prurient interest. Any depiction of sexually explicit activity, no matter how it is presented, is proscribed. The CPPA applies to a picture in a psychology manual, as well as a movie depicting the horrors of sexual abuse. It is not necessary, moreover, that the image be patently offensive. Pictures of what appear to be 17-year-olds engaging in sexually explicit activity do not in every case contravene community standards.

The CPPA prohibits speech despite its serious literary, artistic, political, or scientific value. The statute proscribes the visual depiction of an idea—that of teenagers engaging in sexual activity—that is a fact of modern society and has been a theme in art and literature throughout the ages. Under the CPPA, images are prohibited so long as the persons appear to be under 18 years of age. This is higher than the legal age for marriage in many States, as well as the age at which persons may consent to sexual relations. It is, of course, undeniable that some youths engage in sexual activity before the legal age, either on their own inclination or because they are victims of sexual abuse.

Both themes—teenage sexual activity and the sexual abuse of children—have inspired countless literary works. William Shakespeare created the most famous pair of teenage lovers, one of whom is just 13 years of age. *See* Romeo and Juliet, act I, sc. 2, l. 9 ("She hath not seen the change of fourteen years"). In the drama, Shakespeare portrays the relationship as something splendid and innocent, but not juvenile. The work has inspired no less than 40 motion pictures, some of which suggest that the teenagers consummated their relationship. Shakespeare may not have written sexually explicit scenes for the Elizabethan audience, but were modern directors to adopt a less conventional approach, that fact alone would not compel the conclusion that the work was obscene.

Contemporary movies pursue similar themes. Last year's Academy Awards featured the movie, *Traffic*, which was nominated for Best Picture. The film portrays a teenager, identified as a 16-year-old, who becomes addicted to drugs. The viewer sees the degradation of her addiction, which in the end leads her to a filthy room to trade sex for drugs. The year before, *American Beauty* won the Academy Award for Best Picture. In the course of the movie, a teenage girl engages in sexual relations with her teenage boyfriend, and another yields herself to the gratification of a middle-aged man. The film also contains a scene where, although the movie audience understands the act is not taking place, one character believes he is watching a teenage boy performing a sexual act on an older man.

Ferber upheld a prohibition on the distribution and sale of child pornography, as well as its production, because these acts were "intrinsically related" to the sexual abuse of children in two ways. First, as a permanent record of a child's abuse, the continued circulation itself would harm the child who had participated. Like a defamatory statement, each new publication of the speech would cause new injury to the child's reputation and emotional well-being. Second, because the traffic in child pornography was an economic motive for its production, the State had an interest in closing the distribution network. "The most expeditious if not the only practical method of law enforcement may be to dry up the market for this material by imposing severe criminal penalties on persons selling, advertising, or otherwise promoting the product." Under either rationale, the speech had what the Court in effect held was a proximate link to the crime from which it came. . . .

In contrast to the speech in *Ferber*, speech that itself is the record of sexual abuse, the CPPA prohibits speech that records no crime and creates no victims by its production. Virtual child pornography is not "intrinsically related" to the sexual abuse of children, as were the materials in *Ferber*. While the Government asserts that the images can lead to actual instances of child abuse, the causal link is contingent and indirect. The harm does not necessarily follow from the speech, but depends upon some unquantified potential for subsequent criminal acts. . . .

The CPPA, for reasons we have explored, is inconsistent with *Miller* and finds no support in *Ferber*. The Government seeks to justify its prohibitions in other ways. It argues that the CPPA is necessary because pedophiles may use virtual child pornography to seduce children. There are many things innocent in themselves, however, such as cartoons, video games, and candy, that might be used for immoral purposes, yet we would not expect those to be prohibited because they can be misused. The Government, of course, may punish adults who provide unsuitable materials to children, and it may enforce criminal penalties for unlawful solicitation. The precedents establish, however, that speech within the rights of adults to hear may not be silenced completely in an attempt to shield children from it. In *Butler v. Michigan*, 352 U.S. 380, 381 (1957), the Court invalidated a statute prohibiting distribution of an indecent publication because of its tendency to "incite minors to violent or depraved or immoral acts." A unanimous Court agreed upon the important First Amendment principle that the State could not "reduce the adult population . . . to reading only what is fit for children." . . .

The Government submits further that virtual child pornography whets the appetites of pedophiles and encourages them to engage in illegal conduct. This rationale cannot sustain the provision in question. The mere tendency of speech to encourage unlawful acts is not a sufficient reason for banning it. The government "cannot constitutionally premise legislation on the desirability of controlling a person's private thoughts." . . . First Amendment freedoms are most in danger when the government seeks to control thought or to justify its laws for that impermissible end. The right to think is the beginning of freedom, and speech must be protected from the government because speech is the beginning of thought.

The Government next argues that its objective of eliminating the market for pornography produced using real children necessitates a prohibition on virtual images as well. Virtual images, the Government contends, are indistinguishable from real ones; they are part of the same market and are often exchanged. In this way, it is said, virtual images promote the trafficking in works produced through the exploitation of real children. The hypothesis is somewhat implausible. If virtual images were identical to illegal child pornography, the illegal images would be driven from the market by the indistinguishable substitutes. Few pornographers would risk prosecution by abusing real children if fictional, computerized images would suffice. . . .

Finally, the Government says that the possibility of producing images by using computer imaging makes it very difficult for it to prosecute those who produce pornography by using real children. Experts, we are told, may have difficulty in saying whether the pictures were made by using real children or by using computer imaging. The necessary solution, the argument runs, is to prohibit both kinds of images. The argument, in essence, is that protected speech may be banned as a means to ban unprotected speech. This analysis turns the First Amendment upside down.

The Government may not suppress lawful speech as the means to suppress unlawful speech. Protected speech does not become unprotected merely because it resembles the latter. The Constitution requires the reverse. . . .

In sum, [the CPPA] covers materials beyond the categories recognized in *Ferber* and *Miller*, and the reasons the Government offers in support of limiting the freedom of speech have no justification in our precedents or in the law of the First Amendment. The provision abridges the freedom to engage in a substantial amount of lawful speech. For this reason, it is overbroad and unconstitutional . . . .

For the reasons we have set forth, the prohibitions of [the CPPA] are overbroad and unconstitutional. Having reached this conclusion, we need not address respondents' further contention that the provisions are unconstitutional because of vague statutory language.

The judgment of the Court of Appeals is affirmed.

It is so ordered.

Justice Thomas, concurring in the judgment.

Chief Justice Rehnquist, with whom Justice Scalia joins in part, dissenting.

I agree with Part II of Justice O'Connor's opinion concurring in the judgment in part and dissenting in part. Congress has a compelling interest in ensuring the ability to enforce prohibitions of actual child pornography, and we should defer to its findings that rapidly advancing technology soon will make it all but impossible to do so.

I also agree with Justice O'Connor that serious First Amendment concerns would arise were the Government ever to prosecute someone for simple distribution or possession of a film with literary or artistic value, such as "Traffic" or "American Beauty." I write separately, however, because the Child Pornography Prevention Act of 1996 (CPPA), 18 U. S. C. §2251 *et seq.,* need not be construed to reach such materials.

We normally do not strike down a statute on First Amendment grounds "when a limiting instruction has been or could be placed on the challenged statute." This case should be treated no differently.

Justice O'Connor, with whom The Chief Justice and Justice Scalia join as to Part II, concurring in the judgment in part and dissenting in part.

Although in my view the CPPA's ban on youthful-adult pornography appears to violate the First Amendment, the ban on virtual-child pornography does not. It is true that both bans are authorized by the same text: The statute's definition of child pornography to include depictions that "appea[r] to be" of children in sexually explicit poses. 18 U.S.C. §2256(8)(B). Invalidating a statute due to overbreadth, however, is an extreme remedy, one that should be employed "sparingly and only as a last resort." We have observed that "[i]t is not the usual judicial practice, . . . nor do we consider it generally desirable, to proceed to an overbreadth issue unnecessarily."

Heeding this caution, I would strike the "appears to be" provision only insofar as it is applied to the subset of cases involving youthful-adult pornography. . . .

Another category of unprotected speech is **fighting words**, which are forms of expression that "by their very utterance inflict injury or tend to incite an immediate breach of the peace."[37] Consistent with the balancing test established in *Brandenburg v. Ohio* (1969) (see earlier discussion), the Court has ruled that fighting words "are no essential part of any exposition of ideas, and are of such slight social value as a step to truth that any benefit that may be derived from them is clearly outweighed by the social interests in law and order."[38]

YOUR CONSTITUTIONAL VALUES

CAN A PERSON BE ARRESTED FOR USING PROFANITIES TOWARD A POLICE OFFICER?

On April 9, 1997, Officer Alan J. Oaks responded to an unknown problem at the residence of Richard Lowery in Chillicothe, Ohio. When Officer Oaks arrived at Lowery's home, Lowery approached the officer, pointing his finger at him and yelling, "You motherfuckers better do something." Officer Oaks told Lowery to lower his voice and to stop using profane language. Officer Oaks told Lowery to explain why the officer had been called to his residence. Lowery responded, "Fuck you, you motherfuckers never do anything." Officer Oaks noticed some children outside riding their bicycles and some neighbors outside of their homes. Officer Oaks again warned Lowery to stop using profane language. Lowery responded, "Fuck you."

Officer Oaks then arrested Lowery for violating Chillicothe Revised Ordinance 509.08(a), which provides, "No person, being in or upon any street, avenue, sidewalk, alley, bridge or public place, or being in a situation to be seen or observed from any street, avenue, alley, bridge or public place, shall commit or perpetrate or assist in the commission or perpetration of any lewd, indecent, obscene, filthy or lascivious act, gesture, movement or behavior, or shall utter or use any profane, indecent or obscene language."

On July 1, 1997, a trial court found Lowery guilty of using indecent or profane language in violation of Chillicothe Revised Ordinance 509.08. The trial court ordered Lowery to pay a $ 25.00 fine. Lowery appealed the verdict, claiming that that the United States and Ohio Constitutions' freedom of speech provisions prohibit punishment for his statements because his language did not constitute "fighting words." The city, however, claimed that Lowery's language constituted "fighting words" and that the trial court correctly found appellant guilty of using indecent or profane language.

Based on your Constitutional values, what do you think? Was Lowery's speech protected? Or did it constitute "fighting words"?

To see how an Ohio court of appeals decided this case, go to *City of Chillicothe v. Lowery*, Case No. 97 CA 2331, 1998 Ohio App. LEXIS 3336.

fighting words
A category of unprotected speech that "by their very utterance inflict injury or tend to incite an immediate breach of the peace."

offensive speech
Expression that is likely to cause the sensibilities of others to be offended.

hate speech
Expression that is directly aimed at insulting, derogating, or intimidating a particular class of individuals, often based on race, sex, religion, or ethnicity.

defamation
A form of unprotected speech that involves a false statement that causes injury to another.

slander
A form of defamation that involves published verbal communications that are false and cause injury.

libel
A form of defamation that involves published written communications that are false and cause injury.

Two categories of speech that are often discussed along with fighting words are offensive speech and hate speech. **Offensive speech** is expression that is likely to cause the sensibilities of others to be offended. For example, calling a person unflattering names or revealing embarrassing information that may result in the person being offended. **Hate speech** may overlap many forms of offensive speech, but generally is regarded as expression that is directly aimed at insulting, derogating, or intimidating a particular class of individuals, often based on race, sex, religion, or ethnicity. By itself, offensive speech or speech that expresses hateful attitudes is constitutionally protected.[39] But if such expression (1) leads to a direct and immediate breach of the peace consistent with the *Brandenburg* or "fighting words" doctrine, (2) is defamatory (see following discussion), or (3) involves a significant amount of harmful conduct, which the government is permitted to regulate, such expression may become constitutionally unprotected. Appreciate how the dividing line between protected and unprotected offensive/hate speech often depends on the context in which the speech is being offered. For example, burning an American flag during political protest will likely be deemed protected expression, while offering the same message on the lawn of a VFW Hall may be found to be unprotected fighting words. Similarly, writing an opinion piece for a newspaper that contains racist ideas will likely be protected, while creating a hostile environment in your work setting through the use of racist jokes or other messages will likely be treated as unprotected.

An additional category of unprotected speech is **defamation**, which is a false statement that causes injury to another. There are two primary forms of defamation—**slander** (verbal communications that are false and cause injury) and **libel** (written communications that are false and cause injury). In order for expression to be defamatory, and thus, unprotected: (1) it must be a statement of fact (George sells drugs), as opposed to a statement of opinion (I think Suzie dresses provocatively); (2) it must be false and capable of being proven as such; (3) it must cause injury to another (damage of reputation, loss of job, emotional distress, etc.); and (4) if the person harmed by the statement is a **public figure** (a person with particular notoriety in the community, which includes, but is not limited to, public officials), the statement must be offered with **malice** (knowledge of the statement's falsity or reckless disregard as to its falsity).[40]

Commercial speech is also a category of underprotected speech for which the Court uses a specialized balancing test. Beginning with the proposition that commercial speech—expression offered to promote the sale of a commodity—should not receive less constitutional protection than political speech,[41] the Court has adopted a four-part approach to assess regulations of commercial speech. This approach is often referred to as the ***Central Hudson* test** because it was offered in *Central Hudson Gas & Electric Corp. v. Public Service Comm. of New York* (1980).[42] First, the Court considers whether the speech concerns a lawful activity and whether it is truthful and not misleading. Commercial speech that promotes unlawful activity (illegal narcotic sales) or that is false or misleading has the potential to harm the public, and therefore is regarded as unprotected speech. Second, the Court asks whether there is a substantial governmental interest in regulating the speech. Notice that this standard is less rigorous for the government than the "compelling" interest test, which must be met when attempting to regulate many forms of political speech.[43] Third, the Court evaluates whether the government's regulation directly advances its substantial interest. Essentially, the Court wants to know whether there is a direct fit between the government's regulation and its claimed interest. And finally, the Court considers whether the government's regulation is overbroad. Consistent with the overbreadth doctrine (discussed earlier), the Court requires that the government target no more expression than is necessary to satisfy its substantial interest.

10.4(g) Assessing Governmental Limitations on Speech

In the end, there are several concepts and doctrines that can be important to resolving free speech controversies. The challenge is knowing which terms and tests apply in a given dispute and understanding how they should be used. And while there is no mathematical formula or computer program for analyzing free speech controversies, there is a basic framework that can be applied. Within this framework, there are four basic considerations: (1) What is the government seeking to regulate—speech or conduct? (2) What standards are being used to regulate speech—are they clear, well defined, and sufficiently limited? (3) What is the scope of the government's action—a complete ban on speech or a more limited time, place, and manner restriction? (4) How much constitutional protection is traditionally afforded the type of speech being targeted—fully protected (political speech), somewhat protected (commercial speech), or unprotected (obscenity, fighting words, child pornography, etc.)? Of course, within each of these four basic questions, there can be several additional questions and concepts that might need to be considered as well. And in the end, even after all of the relevant terms and tests are sufficiently identified and understood in a given case, the ultimate resolution of the case may come down to how a person interprets these standards and applies them to a particular set of facts.

Review the framework of analysis offered below to see how the various concepts and balancing tests outlined in section 10.4 can be organized and applied in free speech disputes.

Review the chart in Figure 10-1 to see how the concepts and balancing tests used in free speech jurisprudence relate to one another.

10.5 SPEECH AND POLITICAL CAMPAIGNS

During the last several decades, there has been a general recognition that campaign fundraising and spending has gotten out of control and that the large amounts of money flowing in and out of campaigns is damaging the overall electoral process. According to the Federal Election Commission (FEC), candidates running for Congress during the 2004 general election raised $985.4 million and spent $911.8 million. This was a 20% increase in fundraising and an 18% increase in spending over the 2002 general election. And during the 2004 presidential campaign, the candidates and the national conventions generated more than $1 billion, which was a 56% increase over similar activity during the 2000 campaign. More

public figure
A person with particular notoriety in the community, including, but not limited to, public officials.

malice
A legal standard in defamation cases involving public figures requiring the speech to be made with knowledge of the statement's falsity or reckless disregard as to its falsity.

commercial speech
Expression offered to promote the sale of a commodity or service.

***Central Hudson* test**
Constitutional standard for commercial speech adopted by the Court in *Central Hudson Gas & Electric Corp. v. Public Service Comm. of New York* (1980). This test considers whether (1) the speech concerns a lawful activity and is truthful and not misleading, (2) there is a substantial governmental interest in regulating the speech, (3) the government's regulation directly advances its substantial interest, and (4) there is a direct fit between the government's regulation and its claimed interest.

A Framework For Free Speech Analysis

I. What is being regulated, the content of speech or conduct?
   A. If purely conduct, proceed with rational basis test (is regulation reasonably related to a legitimate governmental purpose?).
   B. If speech, go to the next step.

II. Do the government's standards for regulating/banning speech:
   A. Rely upon unduly vague terms or concepts (vagueness doctrine); or
   B. Impose overly broad restrictions on speech (overbreadth doctrine)?
   C. If so, the government's actions are unconstitutional.
   D. If not, proceed to next step.

III. Is the government seeking to regulate speech (impose reasonable time, place, and manner restrictions) or ban speech (remove it entirely)?
   A. If ban, is the speech at issue unprotected *per se*?
      1. Categories of unprotected speech (apply relevant test for each)
         (a) clear and present danger of imminent lawlessness (*Brandenburg* test)
         (b) obscene (*Miller* test)
         (c) fighting words (*Chaplinsky* and *Brandenburg*)
         (d) defamation (*New York Times Co. v. Sullivan*)
         (e) false or deceptive commercial speech (*Central Hudson* test)
         (f) child pornography (*New York v. Ferber* and *Ashcroft v. Free Speech Coalition*)
      2. If speech is unprotected, ban is valid as long as reasonable.
      3. If ban is of protected speech, apply strict scrutiny test (is ban necessary to promote a compelling governmental interest?).
   B. If time, place, and manner regulation, does it involve a public forum (property historically associated with exercise of First Amendment rights—streets, sidewalks, parks) or a nonpublic forum (property not traditionally associated with exercise of First Amendment rights—military bases, schools, jails)?
      1. If regulation targets certain categories of speech (obscene, fighting words, defamation, commercial speech, child pornography), apply test appropriate for that category.
      2. If regulation involves a public forum, all of the following criteria must be met by the government:
         (a) regulation must be content neutral (not discriminate based on the subject of speech)
         (b) regulation must be narrowly tailored (not burden any more speech than necessary) to serve a significant governmental interest (traffic safety, orderly crowd, personal privacy)
         (c) regulation must leave open alternative channels of communication (allow other means of expressing oneself)
      3. If regulation involves a nonpublic forum, the following criteria must be met by the government
         (a) action must be viewpoint neutral (does not discriminate against sides of issue)
         (b) action must be reasonably related to a legitimate governmental purpose

FIGURE10-1

Free speech: putting it all together

---

critically, a large majority of campaign contributions came from a relatively few number of donors. For example, FEC records for the 2006 congressional election show that only 0.27% of eligible voters made financial contributions of $200 or more to a candidate, but that these donations represented 82% of individual contributions received by primary candidates.

For years, Congress and other governmental authorities have tried to limit the harmful effects of money on elections by seeking to limit campaign contributions, expenditures, and other related facets of campaigns. These measures are called **campaign finance reform laws** because they seek to change the way campaigns are run and funded. The basic challenge to these efforts, however, has come by way of the first amendment, which the Supreme Court generally has interpreted as providing certain levels of constitutional protection to campaign contributions and expenditures as forms of political speech. By treating the transfer of money in and around political campaigns as a form of political speech, the Court has imposed certain parameters on the types of regulations government can impose on campaign finance.

Campaign finance reform laws
Legislation that seeks to change the way campaigns are run and funded. Often challenged as unconstitutional restrictions on political speech.

Federal Election Campaign Act
Passed in 1971 and amended in 1974, this was the first major effort to control campaign finances at the federal level. The law included measures limiting the amount of money that could be donated and spent during federal campaigns. The Supreme Court reviewed this law in Buckley v. Valeo (1976) and upheld the contributions limitations, but struck down most of the limits on campaign spending.

Bipartisan Campaign Reform Act of 2002 (BCRA)
Also known as the McCain-Feingold Act, this law sought to address some of the gaps that candidates, parties, and donors had exposed under the Federal Election Campaign Act of 1971. This law bans the use of soft money in federal elections and limits issue ads during periods immediately preceding elections. The Supreme Court upheld most of BCRA's provisions in McConnell v. Federal Elections Commission (2003).

Soft money
Money that is not given directly by a donor to a campaign and that is not offered for the purpose of influencing a federal election. Soft money includes individual contributions to political parties for purposes of influencing state or local elections. The Bipartisan Campaign Reform Act of 2002 imposed substantial restrictions on the acceptance and use of this money in federal elections.

The first major effort to control campaign finances at the federal level came in 1971, when Congress passed the **Federal Election Campaign Act.** This law, as amended in 1974, sought to control the flow of money in federal elections by imposing (1) a $1000 contribution limit upon individuals and groups and a $5000 limit on political action committees per candidate in an election, with an annual limitation of $25,000 imposed on individual donors; (2) a $1000 expenditure limitation on individuals or groups seeking to spend money for a clearly identified candidate, (3) a personal contribution limitation for candidates and their relatives, (4) an overall expenditure limitation on candidates, and (5) record keeping requirements for political committees in order to track and make public contributions and expenditures. Some elected officials objected to these regulations and challenged them in court, asserting among other things that the limitations imposed an unconstitutional restriction on political speech and the freedom of association. This effort quickly reached the Supreme Court.

In 1976, an incredibly divided Court issued its opinion in *Buckley v. Valeo* (1976),[44] wherein the Court upheld, among other things, the individual contribution limitations and the reporting provisions within the federal law. But the Court struck down the limitations on campaign expenditures, independent expenditures by individuals and groups, and expenditures by candidates from their personal funds. In a *per curiam* opinion, the Court rejected the notion that campaign contributions and expenditures were simply forms of conduct that could be broadly regulated by the government. Instead, the Court concluded that the contribution and expenditure limitations "implicate[d] fundamental First Amendment interests," including political speech and the freedom of association. The Court, however, also recognized Congress's interest in eliminating abuse and corruption in federal elections. In balancing the government's interest against the identified First Amendment concerns, the Court ruled that the contribution limitations did not unduly interfere with First Amendment rights of candidates, campaigns, and donors, but that the expenditure limitations were "significantly more severe" on the freedoms of expression and association.

The next major effort to enact campaign finance reform at the federal level occurred in 2002, when Congress passed the **Bipartisan Campaign Reform Act of 2002** (BCRA). This law is also known as the McCain-Feingold Act, a term reflecting the names of the two primary Senators, John McCain and Russ Feindgold, who sponsored the law. BCRA was written in an effort to address some of the gaps that candidates, parties, and donors had exposed under the Federal Election Campaign Act (FECA). Two particular problems identified by BCRA were so-called "soft money" contributions and "issue advocacy." **Soft money** refers to money that is not given directly by a donor to a campaign and that is not offered for the purpose of influencing a federal election. Soft money includes individual contributions to political parties for purposes of influencing state or local elections. Before BCRA, these contributions were largely unregulated under FECA and national parties could solicit and receive these monies from state and local parties without restriction and use it to promote candidates for federal office. Proponents of BCRA viewed soft money as a way around the direct contribution (hard money) limitations imposed by FECA.

Issue advocacy is a form of electoral communication that mentions a candidate by name in association with a particular issue or cause, but stops short of actually urging the public to vote for or against the identified candidate. For example, an advertisement may address a proposed law regarding abortion and then urge viewers or listeners to "call Congressman Smith and tell him to vote against the law." This ad would not expressly state to vote for or against Congressman Smith, but the tenor and tone of the ad would offer strong overtones of support or opposition. BCRA proponents viewed issue ads as a way of getting around FECA, which limited the expenditure of funds for "communications that expressly advocate the election or defeat of a clearly identifiable candidate."

To address these and other issues, BCRA imposed several new limitations on campaign financing. Among these restrictions was a limitation on the spending of soft money by national political parties, officeholders, and candidates, and a ban on the use of general funds by corporations and unions for issue ads and other forms of "electioneering communications" within thirty days of a primary election and sixty days of a general election. The law also sought to stop individuals from making additional campaign contributions in the names of their children by barring persons under the age of seventeen from making political contributions.

In 2003, a divided Supreme Court upheld BCRA's restrictions on soft money and issue advocacy, but found the age restriction on donors to be unconstitutional. In *McConnell v. Federal Election Commission* (2003),[45] the Court essentially reaffirmed the basic tenets of *Buckley v. Valeo*, by recognizing the First Amendment value of campaign contributions but by also acknowledging the compelling interest of the government in ensuring uncorrupted elections at the federal level. The *McConnell* decision, however, may not be the end of the Court's review of BCRA. In 2006, the Court ruled in *Wisconsin Right to Life, Inc. v. Federal Election Commission* (2006)[46] that it did not intend to prohibit additional "as applied" challenges to the law that might be brought by parties asserting particular first amendment interests not addressed in *McConnell*.

10.6 FREEDOM OF ASSOCIATION

The First Amendment's textual reference to "the right of the people to peaceably assemble, and to petition the Government for a redress of grievances" offers a constitutional foundation for a right that is not explicitly mentioned in the Bill of Rights—the **freedom of association**. Essentially, this freedom includes the right of individuals to gather together and express themselves collectively. In many ways, this right is considered to be the plural version of the First Amendment's freedom of speech. Just as the freedom of speech generally is regarded as protecting an individual's right of expression (see previous discussion), the freedom of association is viewed as protecting the right of collective expression. And, despite any specific constitutional mention, this freedom nonetheless is deemed to be a fundamental right under the First Amendment. In fact, early in the nation's history, American observer and political philosopher Alexis de Tocqueville asserted, "The most natural privilege of a man next to the right of acting for himself, is that of combining his exertions with those of his fellow creatures and of acting in common with them. The right of association therefore appears to be as almost inalienable in its nature as the right of personal liberty. No legislator can attack it without impairing the foundations of society."[47]

The Supreme Court officially acknowledged the fundamental nature of the freedom of association in *NAACP v. Alabama* (1958),[48] a case in which Alabama's attorney general sought to acquire the membership lists of the NAACP. In response, the NAACP argued that providing the state's attorney general with the names of its members would likely lead to harassment, discrimination, and violence against its members. Moreover, because this case occurred during the age of segregation and legal discrimination, the group also believed that the disclosure of the list might lead to a chilling of speech and participation among its members. In a unanimous opinion, the Court sided with the NAACP, holding that the state's efforts violated the freedom of association that was held by the members of the NAACP. The Court connected this freedom to both the due process clause and the right to the freedom of speech, stating, "[i]t is beyond debate that freedom to engage in association for the advancement of beliefs and ideas is an inseparable aspect of the 'liberty' assured by the Due Process Clause of the Fourteenth Amendment, which embraces the freedom of speech. . . ."[49] The fact that the Court tied the freedom of association to the freedom of expression has been a critical factor in deciding other cases involving this asserted right.

The freedom of association has been addressed in a number of different contexts. The right has been asserted in other cases where government sought the membership lists of organizations,[50] cases involving the firing or mistreatment of employees based on their political-party affiliations or political views,[51] and cases where private organizations have sought to exclude members based on race, sex, or sexual orientation.[52] Oftentimes, in balancing the private group's constitutional right to associate against the government's interest in law enforcement, the central question is: to what extent will the government's application of the law interfere with or undermine the expression of the private organization? In cases where the governmental action interferes with the primary message of the group, the right of association is more likely to be protected. But where the government's regulation does not substantially undermine the primary message of the group, the law will be upheld.

In 2000, the Supreme Court relied upon the freedom of association to uphold the right of the Boy Scouts of America to expel a scoutmaster because he was gay. In *Boy Scouts of America v. Dale* (see following), the Court held that New Jersey could not enforce a state public

Issue advocacy
A form of electoral communication that mentions a candidate by name in association with a particular issue or cause, but stops short of actually urging the public to vote for or against the identified candidate. The Bipartisan Campaign Reform Act of 2002 imposed substantial restrictions on the use of issue ads by unions and corporations during certain periods before federal elections.

freedom of association
The First Amendment right of individuals to gather together and express themselves collectively.

accommodations law, which barred discrimination based on sexual orientation, against the Boy Scouts for their removal of James Dale, a troop leader. In a 5-4 ruling, the Court found that the state law infringed upon the organization's right to the freedom of association. Read the Court's opinion below and observe how the Boy Scouts' purported message (or lack thereof) regarding homosexuality lies at the heart of both the majority and dissenting opinions. Read the Court's opinion in *Boy Scouts of America v. Dale* (2000) and observe how the group's message (or lack thereof) lies at the heart of both the majority and dissenting opinions.

BOY SCOUTS OF AMERICA v. DALE
530 U.S. 640 (2000)

Chief Justice Rehnquist delivered the opinion of the Court.

Petitioners are the Boy Scouts of America and the Monmouth Council, a division of the Boy Scouts of America (collectively, Boy Scouts). The Boy Scouts is a private, not-for-profit organization engaged in instilling its system of values in young people. The Boy Scouts asserts that homosexual conduct is inconsistent with the values it seeks to instill. Respondent is James Dale, a former Eagle Scout whose adult membership in the Boy Scouts was revoked when the Boy Scouts learned that he is an avowed homosexual and gay rights activist. The New Jersey Supreme Court held that New Jersey's public accommodations law requires that the Boy Scouts admit Dale. This case presents the question whether applying New Jersey's public accommodations law in this way violates the Boy Scouts' First Amendment right of expressive association. We hold that it does.

In *Roberts v. United States Jaycees*, 468 U. S. 609, 622 (1984), we observed that "implicit in the right to engage in activities protected by the First Amendment" is "a corresponding right to associate with others in pursuit of a wide variety of political, social, economic, educational, religious, and cultural ends." This right is crucial in preventing the majority from imposing its views on groups that would rather express other, perhaps unpopular, ideas. . . . Forcing a group to accept certain members may impair the ability of the group to express those views, and only those views, that it intends to express. Thus, "[f]reedom of association . . . plainly presupposes a freedom not to associate."

To determine whether a group is protected by the First Amendment's expressive associational right, we must determine whether the group engages in "expressive association." The First Amendment's protection of expressive association is not reserved for advocacy groups. But to come within its ambit, a group must engage in some form of expression, whether it be public or private.

Because this is a First Amendment case where the ultimate conclusions of law are virtually inseparable from findings of fact, we are obligated to independently review the factual record to ensure that the state court's judgment does not unlawfully intrude on free expression. The record reveals the following. The Boy Scouts is a private, nonprofit organization. According to its mission statement:

> "It is the mission of the Boy Scouts of America to serve others by helping to instill values in young people and, in other ways, to prepare them to make ethical choices over their lifetime in achieving their full potential.

"The values we strive to instill are based on those found in the Scout Oath and Law." . . .

Thus, the general mission of the Boy Scouts is clear: "[T]o instill values in young people." The Boy Scouts seeks to instill these values by having its adult leaders spend time with the youth members, instructing and engaging them in activities like camping, archery, and fishing. During the time spent with the youth members, the scoutmasters and assistant scoutmasters inculcate them with the Boy Scouts' values—both expressly and by example. It seems indisputable that an association that seeks to transmit such a system of values engages in expressive activity.

Given that the Boy Scouts engages in expressive activity, we must determine whether the forced inclusion of Dale as an assistant scoutmaster would significantly affect the Boy Scouts' ability to advocate public or private viewpoints. This inquiry necessarily requires us first to explore, to a limited extent, the nature of the Boy Scouts' view of homosexuality.

The values the Boy Scouts seeks to instill are "based on" those listed in the Scout Oath and Law. The Boy Scouts explains that the Scout Oath and Law provide "a positive moral code for living; they are a list of 'do's' rather than 'don'ts.'" The Boy Scouts asserts that homosexual conduct is inconsistent with the values embodied in the Scout Oath and Law, particularly with the values represented by the terms "morally straight" and "clean."

The Boy Scouts asserts that it "teach[es] that homosexual conduct is not morally straight," and that it does "not want to promote homosexual conduct as a legitimate form of behavior." We accept the Boy Scouts' assertion. We need not inquire further to determine the nature of the Boy Scouts' expression with respect to homosexuality. . . .

We must then determine whether Dale's presence as an assistant scoutmaster would significantly burden the Boy Scouts' desire to not "promote homosexual conduct as a legitimate form of behavior." As we give deference to an association's assertions regarding the nature of its expression, we must also give deference to an association's view of what would impair its expression. That is not to say that an expressive association can erect a shield against antidiscrimination laws simply by asserting that mere acceptance of a member from a particular group would impair its message. But here Dale, by his own admission, is one of a group of gay Scouts who have "become leaders in their community and are open and honest about their sexual orientation." Dale was the copresident of a gay and lesbian organization at college and remains a gay rights activist. Dale's presence in the Boy Scouts would, at the very least, force the organization to send a message, both to the youth members and the world, that the Boy Scouts accepts homosexual conduct as a legitimate form of behavior.

Hurley [*v. Irish-American Gay, Lesbian, and Bisexual Group of Boston*, 515 U.S. 557 (1995)] is illustrative on this point. There we considered whether the application of Massachusetts' public accommodations law to require the organizers of a private St. Patrick's Day parade to include among the marchers an Irish-American gay, lesbian, and bisexual group, GLIB, violated the parade organizers' First Amendment rights. We noted that the parade organizers did not wish to exclude the GLIB members because of their sexual orientations, but because they wanted to march behind a GLIB banner. . . .

Here, we have found that the Boy Scouts believes that homosexual conduct is inconsistent with the values it seeks to instill in its youth members; it will not "promote homosexual conduct as a legitimate form of behavior." As the presence of GLIB in Boston's St. Patrick's Day parade would have interfered with the parade organizers' choice not to propound a particular point of view, the presence of Dale as an assistant scoutmaster would just as surely interfere with the Boy Scout's choice not to propound a point of view contrary to its beliefs. . . .

Having determined that the Boy Scouts is an expressive association and that the forced inclusion of Dale would significantly affect its expression, we inquire whether the application of New Jersey's public accommodations law to require that the Boy Scouts accept Dale as an assistant scoutmaster runs afoul of the Scouts' freedom of expressive association. We conclude that it does.

The judgment of the New Jersey Supreme Court is reversed, and the cause remanded for further proceedings not inconsistent with this opinion . . . .

Justice Stevens, with whom Justice Souter, Justice Ginsburg and Justice Breyer join, dissenting.

The majority holds that New Jersey's law violates BSA's right to associate and its right to free speech. But that law does not "impos[e] any serious burdens" on BSA's "collective effort on behalf of [its] shared goals," *Roberts v. United States Jaycees*, 468 U.S. 609, 622, 626-627 (1984), nor does it force BSA to communicate any message that it does not wish to endorse. New Jersey's law, therefore, abridges no constitutional right of the Boy Scouts. . . .

In light of BSA's self-proclaimed ecumenism, furthermore, it is even more difficult to discern any shared goals or common moral stance on homosexuality. Insofar as religious matters are concerned, BSA's bylaws state that it is "absolutely nonsectarian

in its attitude toward . . . religious training." "The BSA does not define what constitutes duty to God or the practice of religion. This is the responsibility of parents and religious leaders." In fact, many diverse religious organizations sponsor local Boy Scout troops. Because a number of religious groups do not view homosexuality as immoral or wrong and reject discrimination against homosexuals, it is exceedingly difficult to believe that BSA nonetheless adopts a single particular religious or moral philosophy when it comes to sexual orientation. This is especially so in light of the fact that Scouts are advised to seek guidance on sexual matters from their religious leaders (and Scoutmasters are told to refer Scouts to them); BSA surely is aware that some religions do not teach that homosexuality is wrong. . . .

The evidence before this Court makes it exceptionally clear that BSA has, at most, simply adopted an exclusionary membership policy and has no shared goal of disapproving of homosexuality. BSA's mission statement and federal charter say nothing on the matter; its official membership policy is silent; its Scout Oath and Law—and accompanying definitions—are devoid of any view on the topic; its guidance for Scouts and Scoutmasters on sexuality declare that such matters are "not construed to be Scouting's proper area," but are the province of a Scout's parents and pastor; and BSA's posture respecting religion tolerates a wide variety of views on the issue of homosexuality. Moreover, there is simply no evidence that BSA otherwise teaches anything in this area, or that it instructs Scouts on matters involving homosexuality in ways not conveyed in the Boy Scout or Scoutmaster Handbooks. In short, Boy Scouts of America is simply silent on homosexuality. There is no shared goal or collective effort to foster a belief about homosexuality at all—let alone one that is significantly burdened by admitting homosexuals. . . .

Furthermore, it is not likely that BSA would be understood to send any message, either to Scouts or to the world, simply by admitting someone as a member. Over the years, BSA has generously welcomed over 87 million young Americans into its ranks. In 1992 over one million adults were active BSA members. The notion that an organization of that size and enormous prestige implicitly endorses the views that each of those adults may express in a non-Scouting context is simply mind boggling. . . .

If we would guide by the light of reason, we must let our minds be bold. I respectfully dissent.

10.7 FREEDOM OF THE PRESS

Just like the freedoms of speech and association, the **freedom of the press** is grounded in the value of protecting and promoting expression. As the Supreme Court has observed, "[t]he freedom of speech and of the press guaranteed by the Constitution embraces at least the liberty to discuss publicly and truthfully all matters of public concern without previous restraint or fear of subsequent punishment."[53] But the First Amendment's textual inclusion of the freedom of the press leaves several practical questions about this freedom unanswered—questions that are inevitably addressed through the balancing of constitutional values.

For example, what types of people and organizations are included in the category "the press"? Does it include just newspapers? What about radio, television, and Internet messages? Are Internet blogs considered part of the press? What about entertainment programs? Each of these questions presents, as Justice White put it, "practical and conceptual difficulties of a high order."[54] The Court has addressed press freedoms in terms of newspapers,[55] television stations,[56] and radio reporters.[57] But this treatment largely has left the constitutional status of numerous other informational outlets unresolved. In many cases, the Court simply

freedom of the press
The First Amendment right guaranteeing some level of protection for press-based expression.

has avoided labeling certain entities as "press" or "nonpress," by concentrating its rulings on the more general right to the freedom of speech. Essentially, the Court has approached many of these controversies from the standpoint that regardless of the press or nonpress status of the claimants, at the very least, they have First Amendment interests to speech.[58]

The Court's treatment of certain cases involving purported members of the press as simply free speech controversies raises another question regarding the freedom of the press, namely, given the First Amendment's specific reference to this right, should the press receive special constitutional status and protection beyond that afforded other individuals under the freedom of speech provision? For some members of the Court, the press should be treated as a unique class deserving of special constitutional protection. For example, Justice Stewart referred to the press as the "fourth institution" of government and urged his colleagues to appreciate the fact that it was "the only organized private business that is given explicit constitutional protection."[59] But for other members of the Court, members of the press are to be afforded no greater constitutional status than that given to the ordinary citizen.

In many cases, the latter approach has ruled the day. For example, in 2005, *New York Times* reporter Judy Miller spent twelve weeks in jail for refusing to testify before a federal grand jury that was investigating purported leaks of confidential information by the Bush administration. Miller had argued, among other things, that the First Amendment protected her from revealing the confidential sources of her news information, but lower federal courts rejected this argument, finding that the First Amendment afforded Miller no special protection to withhold her testimony, and the Supreme Court declined to accept her appeal.[60] Still in other cases, the protection of the press is enhanced by state laws, many of which afford journalists with special privileges, including so-called **reporter shield laws**, which prevent reporters from being compelled to reveal their confidential news sources. In these jurisdictions, legislative and judicial efforts have attempted to fill the constitutional void by protecting and enhancing the status of the press.[61]

A final item that must be addressed with constitutional questions about press is how the Court should go about balancing competing interests against this constitutional freedom. There are three basic forms of constitutional controversy that can occur between the press and the government. First, there are times when the government tries to prevent the press from disclosing information to third parties, such as the publication or transmission of sensitive or objectionable information. Second, there are times when the government attempts to stop the press from accessing information, such as when the government refuses to provide public documents or attempts to close public meetings or trials. And finally, there are times when the government seeks to acquire information from the press, such as when a prosecutor subpoenas a reporter for testimony during a criminal proceeding. In each of these instances, a balancing test is applied to determine whether the government's interest in blocking or obtaining information outweighs the values associated with a free press.

In cases where the government seeks to stop the press from disseminating information, the doctrine of **prior restraint** is highly important. Under this doctrine, there is a strong constitutional presumption against government restraining the press prior to its publication of information. As a result, the government generally will be required to demonstrate a compelling and immediate interest in restraining the press before it will be allowed to override the First Amendment. In many cases, the government has failed in this attempt, such as in *New York Times v. United States* (1971).[62] In that case, the government sought to restrain *The New York Times* and *Washington Post* from further publishing the so-called Pentagon Papers, which contained government studies related to the Vietnam War. The Court rejected the government's efforts, finding that any request for a prior restraint on press "bears a heavy presumption against its constitutional validity" and that the government had not met this heavy burden.

In cases where the government attempts to block access to information by the press, the First Amendment interests of the press are often balanced against other competing constitutional rights and powers. For example, where the press seeks to cover certain high-profile judicial proceedings, the courts must weigh the right of the defendant to receive a fair trial, as protected by the Sixth Amendment, against the right of a free press.[63] And where the press tries to compel the disclosure of government documents, the interests of national

reporter shield laws
State laws that prevent reporters from being compelled to reveal their confidential news sources.

prior restraint
An attempt by government to prevent or restrain expression, including press publication, before it is uttered.

YOUR CONSTITUTIONAL VALUES

SHOULD BOOK AUTHORS BE PROTECTED FROM DISCLOSING CONFIDENTIAL INFORMATION?

In 1997, Doris Angleton, the wife of Texas millionaire Robert Angleton, was found shot to death in Houston, Texas. Purportedly, she was killed just as she was about to file for divorce from her husband. The state of Texas charged her husband, Robert, with murder, asserting that he hired his brother, Roger Angleton, to kill Doris.

As news of Doris's death came to light, an aspiring writer, Vanessa Leggett, set out to investigate the case with the intention of writing a book. Leggett had worked as a private investigator and police instructor in Texas, but sought to begin a writing career. And so during the four years after Doris Angleton's death, Leggett investigated Doris's death by performing and taping interviews with several witnesses, including Roger Angleton, who was being held in a county jail pending trial. In February 1998, Roger committed suicide in his jail cell, but left a note indicating that his brother, Robert, was not responsible for Doris's death.

State investigators subpoenaed Leggett to testify before a grand jury, but she refused. Later, she agreed to provide prosecutors with some of the tapes she had made of her interviews, tapes that purportedly were incriminating to Robert Angleton. The state, however, did not use the tapes in its trial against Robert nor did it call Leggett as a witness, and in 1998, Angleton was acquitted of murder by a state jury.

Shortly thereafter, a federal grand jury began to investigate Angleton's actions under federal law and sought Leggett's information through a subpoena. Leggett testified before the federal grand jury in December 2000 under the condition that she not be forced to reveal her confidential sources. But in June 2001, federal prosecutors subpoenaed Leggett again to the grand jury, only this time they wanted materials that would ostensibly reveal her sources.

This time, Leggett refused to comply with the subpoena and filed a motion to have it quashed based, in part, on the First Amendment claim that she was protected from testifying under the freedom of the press. But the federal district court rejected Leggett's motion and ordered her to testify. Ultimately, in July 2001, after again refusing to testify, Leggett was held in contempt of court and placed in jail. Leggett's appeal to the Fifth Circuit Court of Appeals was denied. The appeals court acknowledged that Leggett was "an aspiring freelance writer," but did not address her First Amendment objections. The Supreme Court declined to accept her case.

Leggett was eventually released in January 2002, after having spent 168 days in jail, which is believed to be the longest time served by an American journalist for a contempt citation.

Using your constitutional values, how would you address this matter? Should Leggett be included as a member of "the press" under the First Amendment? Should Leggett have been constitutionally protected from testifying before the federal grand jury?

For more information, go to Sue Ellison, "Vanessa Leggett: Defying Court Subpoenas in the Name of the First Amendment," *Montana Journalism Review*, Vol. 31 (Summer 2002).

security and executive authority, which are often rooted, among other sources, in Article II of the Constitution, must be balanced against the public's right to know.[64]

Finally, where newspapers or reporters have sought special protection against governmental or third-party requests for information, typically the interest of the press in maintaining the confidentiality of news sources is pitted against the public's general interest in pursuing criminal investigations or the right to a fair trial.[65] And, in the modern era, absent legislative or judicial measures enacted to shield the press, this is where the constitutional protections of the press appear to be at their lowest ebb.

10.8 SUMMARY

The First Amendment contains a number of provisions that protect values associated with the freedom of expression. The explicitly referenced freedoms of speech, press, assembly, and the right to petition the government of redress of grievances, as well as the implicit freedom of association, are all based upon the belief that human expression is valuable to a democratic society. Such protections allow citizens to check and otherwise supervise their government; they allow competing individual interests or factions to check one another to prevent monopolies of interest; and they encourage human health by allowing individuals to release thoughts and feelings.

The freedoms of expression have all been incorporated through the Fourteenth Amendment due process clause and made applicable to state and local governments. Moreover, these freedoms protect individuals against unconstitutional restrictions by any and all forms of government—legislative, executive, judicial, and administrative. These freedoms, however, are not absolute. Rather, the values of speech, press, assembly, redress of grievances, and association are balanced against other competing interests, such as national security, human safety, or other civil liberties. And through the use of various balancing tests, the Supreme Court weighs these competing interests against the values of expression to determine the appropriate constitutional standard for protecting First Amendment liberties.

The balancing test used to judge freedom of speech controversies has evolved over time. Beginning with the clear and present danger test adopted in 1919, the Court has gradually modified its approach to free speech cases, which has included brief periods where it used the bad tendency test and then the probability test. Currently, the Court uses the *Brandenburg* test, which provides that government may regulate or restrict speech when the speech is directed at inciting imminent lawless action and is likely to incite such action. This basic test, however, is only one consideration in free speech cases. Other questions must also be considered, including: (1) whether the government is attempting to regulate speech or conduct, (2) whether the government's policy is vague or overly broad, (3) whether the government's action toward speech is a ban or a regulation, (4) whether the regulation applies to a public or nonpublic forum, and (5) whether the type of speech being regulated is regarded as constitutionally unprotected or underprotected, such as obscenity, fighting words, defamation, child pornography, or commercial speech.

The freedom of speech poses particular challenges when trying to regulate some of the abuses in political campaigns and elections. For years, policymakers have recognized the abuses of excessive money in campaigns and elections and have sought to regulate such abuses. But the Court has viewed financial campaign contributions to be a form of political speech. Nevertheless, the Court generally has regarded Congress's interest in preventing campaign abuse to be substantial and has upheld reasonable efforts to limit campaign contributions and certain forms of electioneering, including so-called soft money and advocacy advertisements. However, the Court has refused to uphold limitations on the amount of money that can be spent by individual political campaigns.

The freedom of association includes the right of individuals to gather together and express themselves collectively. Despite any specific mention of this right in the First Amendment, the Court has found it to be implicitly protected and essential to protecting rights of expression. This right, however, often conflicts with other governmental interests, such as law enforcement and measures protecting equality, where the government is seeking to regulate the behavior of private groups. In these cases, the central question for the Court in balancing the two competing values is to what extent the government's actions would interfere with the primary message of the group.

The freedom of the press is also associated with the value of free expression consistent with the belief that the Constitution protects the liberty to discuss publicly and truthfully all matters of public concern. This provision, however, presents some practical problems. For example, what individuals should be included as members of "the press"? And should the press be given special protections for its expression above and beyond those given to individuals under the freedom of speech? Finally, in cases where the freedom of press is asserted, the Court often must balance competing governmental interests, such as national security, criminal investigation, and executive privilege, against this First Amendment liberty.

REVIEW QUESTIONS

1. Name the different types of expression protected by the First Amendment.
2. In what ways is the freedom of expression valuable to a constitutional democracy?
3. Discuss why the First Amendment has not been applied in a literal fashion to bar all forms of governmental interference with self-expression, regardless of the circumstances.
4. How has the balancing test used to resolve free speech cases evolved over time? What is the current standard for such cases?
5. Explain and discuss the relevance of the distinction between content and conduct when it comes to resolving free speech controversies.
6. How do the terms *vagueness, overbreadth, public forum, nonpublic forum, ban*, and *regulation* relate to free speech jurisprudence?
7. What is the constitutional difference between obscenity, pornography, profanity, and vulgarity?
8. Identify and discuss the constitutional standard for addressing governmental regulations of commercial speech.
9. What is the "fighting words" doctrine?
10. Describe the terms "soft money" and advocacy advertisements. What has Congress done to regulate these items and how has the Supreme Court viewed these legislative efforts?
11. Why is the freedom of association protected if it is not specifically mentioned in the First Amendment? What balancing test is used to weigh the freedom of association?
12. What practical problems are presented by the First Amendment's freedom of the press?

ASSIGNMENTS

1. Obtain a copy of your school's code of conduct for students. Are there any provisions addressing the rights of students to demonstrate or protest? How do these standards measure up to the constitutional parameters requirement of the First Amendment? Apply the chart in Figure 10-1 to your school's policy.
2. Contact some members of your local police force, perhaps even members of your school's law-enforcement department. Ask them how they handle matters involving people using profanities in public or offering offensive gestures with their hands. Compare these responses to the standards required by the First Amendment.
3. Obtain a copy of the USA PATRIOT Act—the federal law passed shortly after September 11, 2001—and review the provisions that restrict certain record keepers from discussing governmental searches of private records, such as those from a library, academic records, or medical information. Discuss whether these restrictions are constitutional under the First Amendment.
4. Contact some editors or reporters from your local newspaper. Ask them whether their paper has a policy regarding confidential new sources. Assess how these journalists would handle a government subpoena for their testimony regarding a confidential source. Then discuss whether their approach would survive constitutional scrutiny under the First Amendment.

NOTES

1. *Ashcroft v. Free Speech Coalition*, 535 U.S. 234 (2002).
2. *Garrison v. Louisiana*, 379 U.S. 64 (1964).
3. Douglas M. Fraleigh and Joseph S. Tuman, *Freedom of Speech in the Marketplace of Ideas* (Bedford/St. Martin's 1996).
4. *Abrams v. United States*, 250 U.S. 616, 630 (1919), dissenting opinion.
5. *Texas v. Johnson*, 491 U.S. 397 (1989); *United States v. Eichmann*, 496 U.S. 310 (1990).

6. *Smith v. Collin*, 439 U.S. 916 (1978) (denying petition for writ of certiorari).

7. *Capitol Square Review Bd. v. Pinette*, 515 US 753 (1995).

8. *Ashcroft v. Free Speech Coalition*, 535 U.S. 234 (2002).

9. 274 U.S. 380 (1927).

10. See *Gitlow v. New York*, 268 U.S. 652 (1925) and *Gilbert v. Minnesota*, 254 U.S. 325 (1920) (both offering dicta suggesting that the First Amendment speech clause should be applied to the states).

11. 283 U.S. 697 (1931).

12. 299 U.S. 353 (1937).

13. 357 U.S. 449 (1958).

14. *New York Times Company v. United States*, 403 U.S. 670 (1971).

15. *Globe Newspaper Company v. Superior Court for the County of Norfolk*, 457 U.S. 596 (1982).

16. *Federal Communications Commission v. Pacifica Foundation*, 438 U.S. 726 (1978).

17. See *Schenck v. United States*, 249 U.S. 47 (1919), where Justice Holmes uses this example to justify certain governmental limitations on speech.

18. *Dennis v. United States*, 341 U.S. 494 (1951).

19. See *Kingsley International Corp. v. Regents of Univ. of New York*, 360 U.S. 684 (1959) (books and movies, including *Lady Chatterley's Lover*); *Reno v. ACLU*, 521 U.S. 844 (1997) (Internet communications); A *Book Named "John Cleland's Memoirs of a Woman of Pleasure" v. Massachusetts*, 383 U.S. 413 (1966) (book); *Schad v. Borough of Mt. Ephraim*, 452 U.S. 61 (1981) (nude dancing); *Cohen v. California*, 403 U.S. 15 (1971) (clothing messages); *West Virginia Bd. of Education v. Barnette*, 319 U.S. 624 (1943) (flag saluting); *Texas v. Johnson*, 491 US 397 (1989) (flag burning); *44 Liquormart, Inc. v. Rhode Island*, 517 U.S. 484 (1996) (commercial advertising).

20. 249 U.S. 47 (1919).

21. 268 U.S. 652 (1925).

22. 341 U.S. 494 (1951).

23. 395 U.S. 444 (1969).

24. See *Boos v. Barry*, 485 U.S. 312 (1988) (striking down a law prohibiting "the display of any sign within 500 feet of a foreign embassy if that sign tends to bring that foreign government into 'public odium' or 'public disrepute'").

25. See *Wooley v. Maynard*, 430 U.S. 705 (1977) (license plate messages); *Tinker v. Des Moines Independent Community School District*, 393 U.S. 503 (1969) (wearing armbands to protest war).

26. *Reno v. American Civil Liberties Union*, 521 U.S. 844 (1997) (striking down Communications Decency Act of 1996, which, among other things, banned indecent Internet transmissions).

27. *Ashcroft v. Free Speech Coalition*, 535 U.S. 234 (2002) (striking down portions of the Child Pornography Prevention Act of 1996 because the phrases "appears to be" a minor and "conveys the impression" that a minor is depicted were unduly overbroad).

28. See *Renton v. Playtime Theatres, Inc.*, 475 U.S. 41 (1986) (upholding zoning ordinance keeping adult movie theaters out of residential neighborhoods, but allowing them to operate in other areas).

29. See *Hague v. CIO*, 307 U.S. 496 (1937) (public streets and meeting halls); *Edwards v. South Carolina*, 371 U.S. 229 (1963) (steps of state capitol building).

30. See *Greer v. Spock*, 424 U.S. 828 (1976) (military bases); *Adderly v. Florida*, 385 U.S. 39 (1966) (area surrounding jails).

31. See *Forsyth County v. The Nationalist Movement*, 505 U.S. 123 (1992) (striking down ordinance imposing a fee of up to $1000 per day for parades).

32. See *Rosenberger v. The Rector and Visitors of the University of Virginia*, 515 U.S. 819 (1995) (5–4 ruling upholding the right for a student religious publication to receive funding from public university, wherein justice disagreed over the neutrality of the university's funding policy).

33. 413 U.S. 15 (1973).

34. *Stanley v. Georgia*, 394 U.S. 561 (1969).

35. 458 U.S. 747 (1982).

36. 535 U.S. 234 (2002).

37. *Chaplinsky v. New Hampshire*, 315 U.S. 568 (1942).

38. *Id.*

39. See *Cohen v. California*, 403 U.S. 15 (1971) (upholding the right of a man to wear a jacket bearing the phrase "Fuck the Draft," while in a courthouse, because there was no immediate threat of breaching the peace); *R.A.V. v. City of St. Paul*, 505 U.S. 377 (1992) (striking down a sentencing law that allowed courts to enhance a defendant's punishment based on the message offered by his speech).

40. See *The New York Times Co. v. Sullivan*, 376 U.S. 254 (1964) (rejecting the defamation claim of an elected city official [a public figure] based on a lack of evidence that he was harmed and because the state's defamation statute did not address the requirement of malice).

41. See *Valentine v. Chrestensen*, 316 U.S. 52 (1942) (unanimously finding that there was no "restraint on the government as respects purely commercial advertising.").

42. 447 U.S. 557 (1980).

43. Note that some members of the current Court, Justices Scalia and Thomas, have expressed the view that regulations of commercial speech should be made to satisfy the full rigors of the strict scrutiny analysis, not the less-strict standard of *Central Hudson*. See *Lorillard Tobacco Co. v. Reilly*, 533 U.S. 525 (2001).

44. 424 U.S. 1 (1976).

45. 540 U.S. 93 (2003).

46. 546 U.S. ___ (2006).

47. Alexis de Tocqueville, *Democracy in America*, Vol. 2, ed. Phillips Bradley (New York: Vintage Books 1954), p. 196.

48. 357 U.S. 449 (1958).

49. *Id.*

50. See *Communist Party v. Subversive Activities Control Board*, 367 U.S. 1 (1961) (requiring members of "subversive" organizations to register with control board); *Bryant v. Zimmerman*, 278 U.S. 63 (1928) (upholding New York law requiring KKK to submit membership lists); *Gibson v. Florida Legislative Investigation Committee*, 372 U.S. 539 (1963) (requiring government to show immediate and substantial interest for membership information).

51. *United States v. Harris*, 347 U.S. 612 (1954); *U.S. Civil Service Comm. v. National Assoc. of Letter Carriers*, 413 U.S. 548 (1973) (both upholding federal laws barring civil servants from participating in political campaigns); *Elrod v. Burns*, 427 U.S. 347 (1976); *Branti v. Finkel*, 445 U.S. 507 (1980); *Rutan v. Republican Party of Illinois*, 497 U.S. 62 (1990) (all striking down patronage-based or political-expression-based firings).

52. *Roberts v. United States Jaycees*, 468 U.S. 609 (1984) (upholding a Minnesota human rights law and requiring organization to admit women); *City of Dallas v. Stanglin*, 490 U.S. 1591 (1989) (upholding law barring sex-based discrimination and requiring club to admit women); *Hurley v. Irish-American Gay, Lesbian, and Bisexual Group of Boston*, 515 U.S. 557 (1995) (rejecting the application of Massachusetts public accommodation law to organizers of a St. Patrick's Day parade).

53. *Thornhill v. Alabama*, 310 U.S. 88 (1940).

54. *Branzburg v. Hayes*, 408 U.S. 665 (1972).

55. See *New York Times Co. v. United States*, 403 U.S. 670 (1971) (rejecting the Nixon administration's attempt to stop the *New York Times* from publishing "the Pentagon Papers").

56. *Branzburg v. Hayes, In re Pappas, and United States v. Caldwell*, 408 U.S. 665 (1972) (addressing the freedom of the press as it applies to television and newspaper reporters subpoenaed before a grand jury).

57. *Houchins v. KQED, Inc.*, 438 U.S. 1 (1978) (addressing press freedoms as applied to a radio reporter seeking access to interview state prisoners).

58. See *Simon & Schuster, Inc. v. Members of the New York State Crime Victims Bd.*, 502 U.S. 105 (1991) (the Court struck down New York's "Son-of-Sam" law barring criminals from profiting from stories about their crimes because it imposed "a financial burden on speakers because of the content of their speech."); *Denver Area Educational Telecommunications Consortium, Inc. v. F.C.C.*, 518 U.S. 727 (1996) (striking down portions of the federal Cable Television Consumer Protection and Competition Act because they violated principles of free speech).

59. Potter Stewart, "Or of the Press," 26 *Hastings Law Journal* 631 (1975); see also, *Branzburg v. Hayes, In re Pappas, and United States v. Caldwell*, 408 U.S. 665 (1972) (Stewart dissenting).

60. *In re Special Counsel Investigation*, Misc. No. 04-407, http://www.dcd.uscourts.gov/04ms407.pdf; files.findlaw.com/news.findlaw.com_/nytimes/docs/plame/_inregjmiller21505opn.

61. See, for example, Ohio Revised Code sections 2739.04 and 2739.12; Oklahoma Statute, Title 12, section 2506; Nevada Revised Statute, section 49.275.

62. 403 U.S. 670 (1971).

63. See *Sheppard v. Maxwell*, 385 U.S. 333 (1966) (overturning a conviction due to unfair publicity during trial); *Nebraska Press Association v. Stuart*, 427 U.S. 539 (1976) (rejecting a court-imposed gag order on the press).

64. *Cheney v. United States District Court for the District of Columbia*, 124 S. Ct. 2576 (2004) (rejecting efforts to obtain information about the vice-president's meetings with energy-related executives).

65. *Branzburg v. Hayes, In re Pappas, and United States v. Caldwell*, 408 U.S. 665 (1972) (rejecting request for constitutional-based reporter's privilege); *Cohen v. Cowles Media Co.*, 501 U.S. 663 (1991) (refusing constitutional protection for a newspaper against civil suits brought by a confidential news source).

GLOSSARY

accommodationist approach An interpretation of the religion clauses that maintains that it is appropriate for government to accommodate or otherwise assist religious interests or organizations.

adequate and independent state grounds doctrine Federal judicial review of a state decision in a case that included both state and federal claims will not occur if the lower court's decision rested upon adequate and independent state law.

advisory opinion A judicial interpretation of a legal question requested by the legislative or executive branch of government. Typically, courts prefer not to give advisory opinions and federal courts are generally prohibited from rendering advisory opinions.

affectation doctrine Rule that provides Congress with authority to regulate intrastate activities that affect interstate commerce. Even though individual activity may not affect interstate commerce, the total effect of all individuals who engage in the activity may affect interstate commerce and provide Congress with the jurisdiction to regulate the activity.

affidavit A written statement made under oath typically completed by a police officer when seeking a search warrant.

affirmative action Any policy that seeks to promote greater opportunities for individuals of an identifiable group, whose members have been previously excluded from or who are currently underrepresented in particular educational, employment, or social settings, using *proactive* (affirmative) measures, as opposed to more punitive methods (criminal laws, civil rights legislation, etc.).

Age Discrimination in Employment Act (ADEA) Passed in 1967, this form of civil rights legislation bars employers from using age to disadvantage employees between the ages of forty and seventy.

alienage A person's status as a non-U.S. citizen. Viewed as a suspect classification in some cases, but in others where an important governmental function is being performed, is treated as a nonsupsect form of discrimination.

amnesty An act of the government granting a pardon for a past crime. Amnesty is rarely exercised in favor of individuals, but is usually applied to a group or class of persons who are accountable for crimes for which they have not yet been convicted.

antifederalist (1) A person who opposes establishment of a strong, centralized government in favor of local control. (2) A party that opposes establishment of a strong, centralized government in favor of local control.

appellate jurisdiction The authority of one court to review the proceedings of another court or of an administrative agency.

arrest A governmental seizure of an individual, whereby a person is apprehended by a public official and taken into custody for purposes of criminal process.

assistance of counsel provision Sixth Amendment clause providing that the accused has the right to have counsel (an attorney) assist in defending against the criminal charges.

automobile exception Another exception to the warrant requirement that allows police to search a vehicle without a warrant if they have probable cause to believe that the vehicle or part thereof contains evidence of criminality.

avoidance The Supreme Court's practice of avoiding constitutional issues by deciding cases upon nonconstitutional grounds.

bad tendency test Another test used by the Court to interpret and apply the free speech clause, which allows government to predetermine and ban types of speech that may have a *tendency* to bring about harm, regardless of whether the speech, in actuality, poses a clear and present danger.

ban on speech A governmental policy barring a particular form of expression at any time, place, or manner.

bicameral Two-chambered, referring to the customary division of a legislature into two houses (a Senate and a House of Representatives).

bill A proposed law, presented to the legislature for enactment; that is, a legislative bill.

bill of attainder A legislative act that inflicts capital punishment upon named persons without a judicial trial. Congress and the state legislatures are prohibited from issuing bills of attainder by the Constitution.

Bill of Rights The first ten amendments to the Constitution, which were written in 1789 and ratified in 1791, contain the primary civil liberties protected under the Constitution.

Blockburger test A legal standard created by the Supreme Court under the double jeopardy clause that provides that two or more criminal charges are not the same offense if each charge requires proof of an additional criminal element (another form of intent or an additional act).

***Brady* Rule** A legal standard adopted by the Court that requires the prosecution to provide exculpatory evidence within the possession of the government to the defendant.

***Brandenburg* test** The current standard used by the Court in many free speech cases. Under this test adopted in *Brandenburg v. Ohio* (1969), the government may not suppress speech unless the speech is "directed to inciting or producing imminent lawless action and . . . likely to incite or produce such action."

canons of construction and interpretation A set of judicially created rules that govern the interpretation of written law, such as statutes, regulations, and constitutions.

capable of repetition yet evading review An exception to the mootness doctrine, which provides that if an alleged harm may be repeated, but by its nature cannot be judicially determined in the normal legal process, that harm may become the basis of jurisdiction.

capital offense An offense punishable by death.

***Central Hudson* test** Constitutional standard for commercial speech adopted by the Court in *Central Hudson Gas & Electric Corp. v. Public Service Comm. of New York* (1980). This test considers whether (1) the speech concerns a lawful activity and is truthful and not misleading, (2) there is a substantial governmental interest in regulating the speech, (3) the government's regulation directly advances its substantial interest, and (4) there is a direct fit between the government's regulation and its claimed interest.

child pornography Materials that depict actual children (persons under the age of eighteen) engaged in sexual conduct.

civil rights legislation Laws designed to prohibit government and nongovernment agents from discriminating.

class action An action brought by one or several plaintiffs on behalf of a class of persons. A class action may be appropriate when there has been injury to so many people that their voluntarily and unanimously joining in a lawsuit is improbable and impracticable. In such a situation, injured parties who wish to do so may, with the court's permission, sue on behalf of all. A class action is sometimes referred to as a *representative action*.

clear and present danger test A theory adopted by the Supreme Court in the early twentieth century as a means to interpret and apply the free speech clause of the First Amendment. Under this theory, Justice Holmes provided that "[t]he question in every case is whether the words used are used in such circumstances and are of such a nature as to create a clear and present danger that they will bring about the substantive evils that Congress has a right to prevent. It is a question of proximity and degree."

code (1) The published statutes of a jurisdiction, arranged in systematic form. (2) A portion of the statutes of a jurisdiction, especially the statutes relating to a particular subject.

codification (1) The process of arranging laws in a systematic form covering the entire law of a jurisdiction or a particular area of the law; the process of creating a code. (2) The process of turning a common law rule into a statute.

coercion test A third legal standard used to evaluate establishment clause cases. This test essentially asks whether the government is acting in a manner that may have a coercive effect on individuals to support or participate in a particular religion.

collateral consequences An exception to the mootness doctrine, which provides for jurisdiction in cases in which the primary issue is moot, but secondary *collateral* issues remain.

commerce clause The clause in Article I, section 8, of the Constitution that gives Congress the power to regulate commerce between the states and between the United States and foreign countries. Federal statutes that regulate business and labor are based upon this power.

commercial speech Expression offered to promote the sale of a commodity or service.

commutation of sentence The substitution of a less severe punishment for a more severe punishment.

compact theory A theory of individual liberties that considers liberties to be the product of a negotiated contract. Under this approach, rights are derived from an agreement or compact between the individuals being protected and those individuals or institutions providing the protection. Through negotiation, individuals and institutions receive rights, powers, and protections by virtue of compact or constitution.

compelling governmental interest test or **strict scrutiny** A constitutional litmus test that weighs the government's interest in advancing a particular policy against the free exercise interests of the individual. In order for the government's interest to outweigh the individual's, the government must prove that its interest is *necessary* to promote a *compelling* governmental interest. This standard is also used to assess other constitutional rights, including some free speech issues (see Chapter 10), fundamental freedoms (see Chapter 12), and some matters of equal protection (see Chapter 13).

compulsory process clause Sixth Amendment clause that allows defendants to compel witnesses to appear on their behalf.

confrontation clause Sixth Amendment provision that provides the accused with the right to confront (generally interpreted as to view and cross-examine) any witnesses providing testimony against them.

consent searches An exception to the Fourth Amendment warrant requirement that allows police to perform searches with the permission or consent of a person who has actual or apparent authority over the property being searched.

content neutrality Also known as subject-matter neutrality, this term means that the government, in attempting to regulate speech, is not discriminating against speech based on its content or subject matter.

contract clause A provision in Article I, section 10 of the Constitution that provides that states cannot impair the obligations of contracts.

Cooley doctrine Named for the case in which it was announced, *Cooley v. Board of Wardens*, 53 U.S. 299 (1851); provides that if a subject of interstate commerce is national in character, then regulation of that subject is exclusively federal.

cooperative federalism The theory that the national government is supreme to the state governments. The powers of the national government are read broadly and the Tenth Amendment is read as not granting any specific powers to the states.

Corrections Day Part of Congress's schedule; occurs twice a month. A time specially set aside for legislation intended to amend or repeal administrative rules.

countermajoritarian institution Because its members are not elected by the people, are not accountable to the people, and are not required to consider public opinion in their decision making, the Supreme Court is considered by most to be a countermajoritarian institution. This does not mean, however, that the Court has historically been countermajoritarian in its decision making.

court of general jurisdiction Generally, another term for trial court; that is, a court having jurisdiction to try all classes of civil and criminal cases except those that can be heard only by a court of limited jurisdiction.

court of limited jurisdiction A court whose jurisdiction is limited to civil cases of a certain type or that involve a limited amount of money, or whose jurisdiction in criminal cases is confined to petty offenses and preliminary hearings. A court of limited jurisdiction is sometimes called a *court of special jurisdiction.*

court-packing plan A phrase used to describe President Franklin Roosevelt's proposal in early 1937 to enlarge the Supreme Court by six members in order to ensure that his New Deal plan would be found constitutional. This proposal never became reality because the Court ultimately began approving social and economic legislation passed by Congress and state governments, thereby eliminating the perceived need to enlarge the Court.

cruel and unusual punishment clause Eighth Amendment provision that provides that government may not inflict cruel and unusual punishment upon individuals.

custodial requirement A standard requirement before a person will have a constitutional right against self-incrimination. In some cases, custody is determined based on whether a person's ability to move is restricted in a substantial manner. In other cases, custody is based on whether a reasonable person (not the actual suspect) placed in similar circumstances would feel free to leave the presence of police.

de facto **segregation** Segregation created based on factors (social, economic, etc.) not directly linked to law or public policy.

de jure **segregation** Segregation established or formally reinforced by law or policy.

de novo Anew; over again; a second time.

deadly force The application of potentially deadly techniques by police in an effort to apprehend or stop individuals. The use of deadly force to seize or stop individuals is unreasonable under the Fourth Amendment unless the officer has probable cause to believe that the person presents a substantial threat of death or serious physical harm to the officer or other persons.

death penalty or **capital punishment** The imposition of death as criminal punishment. Since 1976, the Court has ruled that the death penalty does not inherently violate the Eighth Amendment.

declaratory judgment (declaratory relief) A judgment that specifies the rights of the parties but orders no relief. Nonetheless, it is a binding judgment and the appropriate remedy for the determination of an actionable dispute when the plaintiff is in doubt as to his or her legal rights.

defamation A form of unprotected speech that involves a false statement that causes injury to another.

delegation of powers The transfer of power from the president to an administrative agency.

dictum (obiter dictum) Expressions or comments in a court opinion that are not necessary to support the decision made by the court; they are not binding authority and have no value as precedent. If nothing else can be found on point, an advocate may wish to attempt to persuade by citing cases that contain dicta.

distinguish To explain why a particular case is not precedent or authority with respect to the matter in controversy.

distinguishing on the facts Choosing not to apply a rule from a previous case because its facts differ from the case sub judice.

diversity jurisdiction The jurisdiction of a federal court arising from diversity of citizenship, when the jurisdictional amount has been met.

diversity of citizenship A ground for invoking the original jurisdiction of a federal district court, the basis of jurisdiction being the existence of a controversy between citizens of different states.

dormant commerce clause Judicial doctrine providing that even if federal power to regulate interstate and international commerce is not exercised, state power to regulate these areas is sometimes precluded.

dormant commerce clause doctrine The idea that state laws that unduly burden interstate commerce, even if the subject is unregulated by the national government, are invalid under federalism principles, because the regulation of interstate and foreign commerce belongs exclusively to the federal government.

double jeopardy clause Fifth Amendment provision that provides that government may not punish a person twice for the same offense.

dual federalism The theory that the national government and the state governments are coequal sovereigns. The national government is supreme only when its jurisdiction is explicitly granted by the Constitution.

dual sovereignty An approach to constitutional interpretation that requires state judges to apply both the federal and state constitutions simultaneously.

dual sovereignty doctrine A legal theory associated with the double jeopardy clause that provides that federal and state governments may try a person for the same act just as two or more states may try a person for the same act because they are separate sovereigns.

due process clause A provision found in the Fifth and Fourteenth Amendments, which states that government cannot deprive individuals of life, liberty, or property without due process of law. This clause requires, among other things, that government treat individuals fairly during the criminal process, which may include such protections as the right to a fair trial, the right to be free from outrageous conduct by prosecutors or judges, the right to a full and fair appeal of a conviction, and the right to humane conditions of confinement. The Sixth Amendment provides several standards for the criminal process. As contained in the Fourteenth Amendment, this clause prevents the states from denying persons life, liberty, or property without due process of law. Found in section 1 of the Fourteenth Amendment, this clause provides, "nor shall any State deprive any person of life, liberty, or property, without due process of law." The Supreme Court has interpreted this clause as making most of the provisions within the Bill of Rights applicable to the states.

effective assistance of counsel The more specific standard used to assess the right to counsel under the Sixth Amendment. To prove a violation of the right to counsel a defendant must show two fundamental things: (1) the attorney's representation fell below objective standards of reasonableness (it was deficient), and (2) there is a reasonable probability that the outcome of the criminal proceedings would have been different but for counsel's deficient performance.

electoral college The body empowered by the Constitution to elect the president and vice-president of the United States, composed of presidential electors chosen by the voters at each presidential election. In practice, however, the electoral college votes in accordance with the popular vote.

eminent domain The process of government obtaining private property from individuals for public use under the Fifth Amendment. See also the *takings clause*.

en banc French for "on the bench." A court, particularly an appellate court, with all the judges sitting together (sitting en banc) in a case.

enabling act (enabling legislation) (1) A statute that grants new powers or authority to persons or corporations. (2) A statute that gives the government the power to enforce other legislation or that carries out a provision of a constitution. The term also applies to a clause in a statute granting the government the power to enforce or carry out that statute. Such a provision is called an enabling clause.

endorsement test Another legal standard used to assess establishment clause issues. Under this standard, the Court essentially collapses the first two questions of the *Lemon* test (the secular purpose and primary effect requirements) by asking the more general question of whether the government's activity conveys a message of endorsement or disapproval of religion.

Enforcement Clause Found in section 5 of the Fourteenth Amendment, this provision allows Congress to pass legislation to enforce the other clauses contained within the amendment, including equal protection and due process. This provision serves as the constitutional basis for many forms of federal civil rights legislation.

equal protection clause Precludes the states from denying persons equal protection of the law.

equality The third primary value promoted by the Constitution, chiefly by the due process and equal protection clauses, which involves the standard that similarly situated persons ought to be treated similarly.

establishment clause The first provision of the First Amendment, which provides that "Congress shall make no law respecting an establishment of religion." This clause generally regulates the extent to which government can participate in, assist, or otherwise further religious activity or organizations.

ex post facto law A law making a person criminally liable for an act that was not criminal at the time it was committed. The Constitution prohibits both Congress and the states from enacting such laws.

excessive bail provision Eighth Amendment clause stating that the amount of bail, which is the collateral imposed by a court as a condition for pretrial release of the defendant, cannot be excessive.

excessive fines provision Eighth Amendment clause providing that a fine, which is a postconviction punishment in the form of monetary payment, cannot be excessive.

exclusionary rule A judicially created remedy for violations of the Fourth, Fifth, or Sixth Amendments, which excludes unconstitutionally obtained evidence from a criminal trial.

exculpatory evidence Materials or information that might lead to a defendant's exoneration.

executive agency An agency whose head serves at the pleasure of the president.

executive agreement An agreement with a foreign government, made by the president acting within his or her executive powers.

executive order An order issued by the chief executive officer of government, whether national, state, or local.

executory Not yet fully performed, completed, fulfilled, or carried out; to be performed, either wholly or in part; not yet executed.

exigent circumstances exception An exception to the Fourth Amendment warrant requirement that allows officers to conduct warrantless searches where there is a need to apprehend a dangerous person or prevent an imminent and serious threat to the police or public.

factions Individual or isolated interests that can destroy or substantially impair government if they are allowed to override the common good. According to James Madison in *Federalist No. 10*, the only way to address factions in a democratic society was to allow them to exist, but to manage them, so that one interest did not rise to dominate the rest. To that end, Madison believed that the new constitution would allow factions to be pitted against one another, thereby allowing them to be managed in a marketplace of competition.

federal jurisdiction The jurisdiction of the federal courts. Such jurisdiction is based upon the judicial powers granted by Article III of the Constitution and by federal statutes.

Federal Register An official publication, printed daily, containing regulations and proposed regulations issued by administrative agencies, as well as other rulemaking and other official business of the executive branch of government. All regulations are ultimately published in the Code of Federal Regulations.

federalism A governmental structure in which two or more levels of government operate concurrently with jurisdiction over the same citizens, and in which each governmental entity has some autonomy over specific policy areas. This is opposed to a *unitary system,* where there is one centralized government; and a *confederation,* where two or more governments combine to create a confederation government that has no direct authority over the citizens of each of its members.

federalist (1) A person who supports a strong, centralized government. (2) A political party that advocates a strong, centralized government.

felony Generally defined to mean a crime for which the punishment may include a year or more of incarceration.

Fifteenth Amendment Ratified in 1870, this amendment states that government cannot deny persons the right to vote based on race, color, or previous servitude.

fighting words A category of unprotected speech that "by their very utterance inflict injury or tend to incite an immediate breach of the peace."

formal rulemaking A process used by administrative agencies to create rules and regulations. The Administrative Procedure Act provides that formal rulemaking is required only when mandated by statute. Otherwise, informal rulemaking may be used by an agency. Formal rulemaking involves formal hearings and is more expensive and time-consuming than informal rulemaking. This process is also known as *rulemaking on the record.*

Fourteenth Amendment The ratification of the Fourteenth Amendment provided explicit mandates to the states regarding civil liberties, mandates not found in the original Bill of Rights. Under this amendment, the states are required to protect liberty, as well as life and property, under mandate of the federal constitution. Ratified in 1868, this amendment provides for several things, but primarily it provides the privileges or immunities clause, the due process clause for states, and the equal protection clause for states. This amendment was designed to promote equality and fairness in the aftermath of the Civil War and abolition of slavery.

free exercise clause The second provision of the First Amendment, which provides that "Congress shall make no law . . . prohibiting the free exercise [of religion] thereof."). This clause addresses the extent to which government can interfere with an individual's religious practices.

freedom of association The First Amendment right of individuals to gather together and express themselves collectively.

freedom of the press The First Amendment right guaranteeing some level of protection for press-based expression.

frisk To pat the outer clothing of an individual.

fruit of the poisonous tree doctrine A doctrine that extends the exclusionary rule to all evidence obtained as the result of the initial piece of unconstitutionally obtained evidence.

full faith and credit A reference to the requirement of Article IV of the Constitution that each state give "full faith and credit" to the "public acts, records, and judicial proceedings" of every other state. This means that a state's judicial acts must be given the same effect by the courts of all other states as they receive at home.

fundamental right A constitutional right of the highest order and one to which utmost constitutional protection is applied, including strict scrutiny protection.

gerrymandering Manipulating the boundary lines of a political district to give an unfair advantage to one political party or to dilute the political strength of voters of a particular race, color, or national origin.

good faith exception or *Leon* rule An exception to the valid warrant requirement that holds that an invalid warrant, which appears on its face to be valid, will not automatically result in an unconstitutional search if the officer executing the warrant reasonably relied on the facial validity of the warrant.

governmental conduct Action that is performed by police officers and their agents performing work that is funded or facilitated by public resources.

grand jury indictment A formal charge by a group of citizens sitting as a jury who have reviewed the evidence and decided that there is sufficient cause to charge a person with a criminal offense.

grand jury provision Fifth Amendment clause that requires government to obtain a grand jury indictment in order to charge someone with a capital offense or felony.

habeas corpus Latin for "you have the body." A writ whose purpose is to obtain immediate relief from illegal imprisonment by having the "body" (that is, the prisoner) delivered from custody and brought before the court. A writ of habeas corpus is a means for attacking the constitutionality of the statute under which, or the proceedings in which, the original conviction was obtained. There are numerous writs of habeas corpus, each applicable in different procedural circumstances. The full name of the ordinary writ of habeas corpus is *habeas corpus ad subjiciendum.*

harmless error An error made during trial that ostensibly does not change the outcome of the case.

hate speech Expression that is directly aimed at insulting, derogating, or intimidating a particular class of individuals, often based on race, sex, religion, or ethnicity.

history of discrimination One of the three criteria used to determine whether a form of discrimination will be deemed suspect under the due process clause. This involves a retrospective examination of whether and to what extent the characteristic has been unjustifiably mistreated in the United States.

hot-pursuit rule A form of the exigent circumstances exception to the warrant requirement that allows police to enter places without a warrant where they are pursuing a fleeing felon, where evidence may be destroyed or evaporated, where contaminated food or narcotics present immediate danger, and where an ongoing crisis poses a threat to public safety.

hung jury A jury that cannot reach a decision after sufficient deliberations.

immutable characteristic Another factor used to determine whether a form of discrimination will be deemed suspect under the equal protection clause. An immutable characterisic is an attribute of a person that is not readily changeable. A person's race, sex, and eye color are considered immutable characteristics because they cannot be easily changed.

impeachment The constitutional process by which high elected officers of the United States, including the president, may be removed from office. The accusation (articles of impeachment) is made by the House of Representatives and tried by the Senate, which sits as an impeachment court. Under the Constitution, the grounds for impeachment are "treason, bribery, or other high crimes and misdemeanors."

"implicit in the concept of ordered liberty" A phrase frequently offered by the Court as the standard for assessing whether a particular human activity will be included as a "liberty interest" under the due process clauses.

important governmental functions A legal standard development by the Court that allows government to discriminate against aliens when the position or function for which the alien seeks an opportunity involves an important government function, including jobs as police officers, public school teachers, and probation officers.

inclusio unis est exclusio alterius A Latin maxim used as a principle in drafting some documents, meaning "the inclusion of one item is the exclusion of all others." Under this theory, the framers maintained that they could limit the scope and power of government by enumerating or listing the government's specific powers in the Constitution, and that such documentation, by implication, would curtail any subsequent argument that the government had powers beyond those listed in the Constitution.

incorporation The Bill of Rights was intended to be applied only against the national government. However, the Supreme Court determined that most of the rights contained therein were "incorporated" by the due process clause of the Fourteenth Amendment. A right is *incorporated* if it is fundamental and necessary to an ordered liberty. Once incorporated, the right applies against the states.

incorporation doctrine A legal theory that maintains that the Bill of Rights (or at least portions thereof) should be incorporated through the Fourteenth Amendment due process clause and made applicable to the states.

independent agency An agency whose head may be terminated by the president only for good cause.

independent counsel Under federal statute, counsel who may be specially appointed to investigate and prosecute high government officials for crimes committed in office.

independent source rule An exception to the exclusionary rule that will not exclude evidence if police can show that it was obtained by a source that is separate or independent from the originally tainted method.

indigency A person's status as lacking wealth, which the Court has treated as a nonsuspect classification for equal protection purposes.

inevitable discovery rule Another exception to the exclusionary rule that allows illegally obtained evidence or the fruit derived therefrom to be admitted if the government can show that the evidence eventually would have been discovered through proper means.

informal rulemaking A process used by administrative agencies to create rules and regulations. The Administrative Procedure Act provides that agencies may use this procedure unless formal rulemaking is required by statute. Informal rulemaking is less costly and less time-consuming than its formal counterpart. This process is also known as *notice-and-comment rulemaking.*

information clause Sixth Amendment clause that requires government to notify defendants of the nature and cause of the criminal charges.

intelligible principle test The test used to determine if Congress has provided an agency with sufficient guidance in the performance of a delegated duty.

intergovernmental immunity doctrine The doctrine that both the states and the national government possess some immunity from the regulation of the other federalism principles. Generally, the federal government enjoys greater immunity than do the states.

intermediate scrutiny test A constitutional standard used in cases involving a semisuspect form of discrimination that requires the government to show that its semisuspect form of discrimination is substantially related to an important governmental interest.

interrogation Efforts, including questions, by police designed to obtain incriminating information.

interstitial An approach to constitutional interpretation that requires state judges to apply the federal Constitution before turning to their state's constitution.

intervening circumstances rule Another exception to the exclusionary rule that allows evidence to be admitted if new circumstances or events break the causal link between the illegal actions of the police and the ill-gotten evidence.

investigatory detention An officer's relatively brief stop of an individual for purposes of conducting a reasonable investigation of possible criminal activity. In these situations, an officer must have reasonable suspicion that the person being stopped is involved in criminal activity.

James Madison A "founding father" of the Constitution and the chief architect of the Bill of Rights.

joint resolution A resolution passed by both houses of a bicameral legislature and eligible to become a law if signed by the chief executive or passed over the chief executive's veto.

judicial activism (1) Use of judicial decisions to engage in social engineering. (2) A judicial philosophy that gives little deference to precedent and therefore commonly results in the abrogation of prior decisions.

judicial neutrality and detachment Fourth Amendment standard required for the person issuing a search warrant that generally requires the judicial authority to be free of conflicts of interest in evaluating the request for the warrant or its execution and sufficiently objective (neutral) regarding the persons or matters involved in the search warrant.

judicial review The power of the judiciary, as the final interpreter of the law, to declare an act of a coordinate governmental branch or state unconstitutional. The power is not expressly stated in the Constitution, but the Supreme Court announced that the judiciary possesses this power in *Marbury v. Madison,* 5 U.S. (1 Cranch) 137 (1803).

jurisdiction A term used in several senses: (1) In a general sense, the right of a court to adjudicate lawsuits of a certain kind. (2) In a specific sense, the right of a court to determine a particular case; in other words, the power of the court over the subject matter of, or the property involved in, the case at bar. (3) In a geographical sense, the power of a court to hear cases only within a specific territorial area.

jury trial clause Sixth Amendment provision that individuals have a right to have their criminal cases decided by an impartial jury (as opposed to a judge) within the jurisdiction where the crime was allegedly committed.

justiciability doctrine Rules that limit the authority of federal courts to hear cases, such as ripeness, mootness, political question, and standing.

laissez-faire era A phrase used to describe the nature of the Supreme Court during the latter part of the nineteenth and early part of the twentieth centuries. Also referred to as the *Lochner* era, this period is marked by the Court's frequent rejection of government regulations of business and the work setting.

legislative veto An act of a legislature invalidating executive action in a particular instance. Generally, legislative vetos are unconstitutional. Once power is delegated by Congress to the president, it is generally prohibited from interfering with the president's enforcement.

***Lemon* test** Legal standard developed by the Court in *Lemon v. Kurtzman* (1971) to evaluate establishment clause cases. Under this test, the challenged government action must meet three guidelines: (1) it must have a secular (nonreligious) purpose, (2) its primary effect must neither advance nor inhibit religion, and (3) it must not foster an excessive entanglement with religion and government.

libel A form of defamation that involves published written communications that are false and cause injury.

liberty One of the three primary values promoted by the Constitution, particularly the Bill of Rights, which involves the ability to act and think without government interference.

liberty of contract A liberty interest under the Fourteenth Amendment due process clause as determined by the Court during the latter part of the nineteenth and early part of the twentieth centuries (the laissez-faire era of the Court). The Court deemed this liberty interest to offer a constitutional right to engage in contractual relations without governmental interference.

line item veto The right of a governor under most state constitutions to veto individual appropriations in an appropriation act rather than being compelled either to veto the act as a whole or to sign it into law. The president of the United States does not have a line item veto.

literalism An approach to interpreting the Constitution that focuses on the literal meanings of its words, rather than on other factors, such as the original intent of the framers. There are two forms of literalism, historical and contemporary. *Historical literalism* defines terms in the context of when the particular provision being considered was ratified. *Contemporary literalism* uses contemporary definitions.

living will A legal document in which a person provides instructions for medical treatment (or the lack thereof) in cases where the person becomes incapacitated.

majoritarian process A third consideration in determining whether a form of discrimination is suspect in nature. This essentially involves a prediction about the future—namely, whether, without sufficient constitutional protection, it is likely that democratic processes (such as legislative action, electoral results, influence of public opinion, etc.) will continue to allow the identified characteristic to be used as a basis for discrimination.

malice A legal standard in defamation cases involving public figures requiring the speech to be made with knowledge of the statement's falsity or reckless disregard as to its falsity.

manifest necessity A compelling need to stop the trial prior to a verdict being reached.

marketplace of ideas A phrase used in some free speech cases to describe the type of environment the First Amendment fosters for individuals to sell, purchase, and evaluate different ideas through speech. The idea is that, if individual ideas are allowed to compete against one another through open exchange, using speech, assembly, press, and petition, society will be in a better position to manage and balance the diversity of "products" (ideas) being offered.

marking up The detailed revision of a bill by a legislative committee.

minimum contacts test A doctrine under which a state court is permitted to acquire personal jurisdiction over a nonresident, although he or she is not personally served with process within the state, if he or she has had such a substantial connection with that state that due process is not offended by the court's exercise of jurisdiction over him or her.

***Miranda* warnings** Information the police must provide to suspects before a custodial interrogation, which includes notice that (1) they have the right to remain silent; (2) anything they say can and will be used against them in court; (3) they have the right to the presence of an attorney; and (4) if they cannot afford an attorney, one will be provided for them.

mistrial The termination of a trial prior to a verdict.

modernism An approach to interpreting the Constitution that allows courts to consider changes in social, economic, and political forces.

natural law A term referring to the concept that there exists, independent of manmade law, a law laid down (depending upon one's beliefs) by God or by nature, which human society must observe in order to be happy and at peace.

natural right A right existing under natural law, independent of manmade law.

natural rights theory A theory of individual liberties that maintains that liberties are the result of the "laws of nature."

This theory recognizes life itself as the source of certain individual rights, which exist independent of any constitution or contract. Natural rights theory insists that the rights enumerated in the Bill of Rights are natural, inherent, and unalienable to individuals.

necessary and proper clause Article I of the Constitution grants to Congress the power to make all laws "necessary and proper" for carrying out its constitutional responsibilities. The Supreme Court has long interpreted this provision to mean that Congress has the right not only to enact laws that are absolutely indispensable, but any laws that are reasonably related to effectuating the powers expressly granted to it by the Constitution.

neutrality test An approach to free exercise cases adopted in *Employment Division v. Smith* (1990) that maintains that governmental policies that are neutral in form and generally applied will be deemed constitutional, regardless of their adverse impact on certain religious practices.

Nineteenth Amendment Ratified in 1920, this amendment guarantees voting rights regardless of a person's sex, thereby essentially affording women the right to vote.

Ninth Amendment A constitutional amendment providing that "[t]he enumeration of certain rights in the bill of rights, shall not be construed to deny or disparage others retained by the people." This amendment suggests that beyond those listed in the First through Eighth Amendments, there are other unenumerated rights that individuals retain that are to be protected against governmental intrusion.

nonpublic forums Places that are not historically associated with the exercise of First Amendment rights. Such locations may include military bases, jails, and certain interior portions of public buildings.

nonsuspect classification Forms of discrimination that are not suspicious under the Constitution and thus require only minimal judicial scrutiny. This includes discrimination based on a person's wealth, age, alienage (in some cases), sexual orientation, and discrimination depriving individuals of education, welfare, or housing.

obscenity A form of unprotected sexual expression. As the Court defined the term in *Miller v. California* (1973), obscenity is a specific type of sexual expression that: (1) taken as a whole, appeals to a prurient (unhealthy) interest in sex; (2) portrays sexual conduct in a patently offensive way; and (3) taken as a whole, lacks serious literary, artistic, political, or scientific value.

offensive speech Expression that is likely to cause the sensibilities of others to be offended.

original intent An approach to interpreting the Constitution that uses historical analysis to assess what the authors of the Constitution meant or intended by a particular term or provision, including the term "liberty" within the due process clauses. This view maintains that judicial interpretation of the Constitution should be based on the words of the Constitution itself and the framers' "original intent," not on a contemporary understanding of the Constitution in the context of current realities. Adherents of this doctrine are sometimes referred to as *strict constructionists*.

original jurisdiction The jurisdiction of a trial court, as distinguished from the jurisdiction of an appellate court.

original understanding An approach to interpreting the Constitution that is similar to original intent, except it seeks to determine what the legal culture understood (as opposed to intended) under the provision when it was originally written.

origination clause Found in Article I, section 7, clause 1, of the United States Constitution, requires all revenue-raising bills to originate in the House of Representatives.

overbreadth doctrine A constitutional theory of due process that generally provides that the government cannot regulate or prohibit more speech than is necessary to address the identified harm. Under this doctrine, the Court essentially asks whether the government's restriction on speech is properly tailored to address the harm the government is seeking to prevent.

pardon An act of grace by the chief executive of the government, relieving a person of the legal consequences of a crime of which he or she has been convicted. A pardon erases the conviction.

parens patriae Latin for "the parent of the country."

particularity requirement Fourth Amendment standard for warrants that requires the judicial authority issuing a warrant to be sufficiently precise in writing the warrant so as to avoid a general or overreaching search by the executing officer.

pendent jurisdiction The rule that even though there is no diversity of citizenship, a federal court has the right to exercise jurisdiction over a state matter if it arises out of the same transaction as a matter already before the federal court.

penumbras A penumbra is a lunar shadow. Justice Douglas used this term as a metaphor in *Griswold v. Connecticut* (1965) to describe an individual's right to privacy under the Constitution. According to Douglas, even though privacy is not specifically enumerated in the Bill of Rights, there are certain penumbras or shadows cast by the First, Third, Fourth, Fifth, and Ninth Amendments that reflect that a right to privacy is protected by the Constitution.

plain-feel exception Allows officers performing stop and frisks to seize nonweapon forms of contraband (drugs, drug paraphernalia, etc.) that the officer reasonably detects as a part of a properly executed pat-down.

plain-meaning rule The rule that in interpreting a statute whose meaning is unclear, the courts will look to the "plain meaning" of its language to determine legislative intent. The plain-meaning rule is in opposition to the majority view of statutory interpretation, which takes legislative history into account.

plain view doctrine Another exception to the Fourth Amendment warrant requirement that allows police to search and seize items if they are lawfully in a location where they plainly see evidence of criminal activity.

plenary Full; complete.

pocket veto The veto of a congressional bill by the president by retaining it until Congress is no longer in session, neither signing nor vetoing it. The effect of such inaction is to nullify the legislation without affirmatively vetoing it. The pocket veto is also available to governors under some state constitutions.

police power (1) The power of government to make and enforce laws and regulations necessary to maintain and enhance the public welfare and to prevent individuals from violating the rights of others. (2) The sovereignty of each of the states of the United States that is not surrendered to the federal government under the Constitution.

political question A nonjudicial issue. The political question doctrine states that under the Constitution, certain questions belong to the nonjudicial branches of the federal government to resolve.

pornography Materials that depict sexual expression, which may or may not meet the *Miller* standards of obscenity.

prayer Portion of a bill in equity or a petition that asks for equitable relief and specifies the relief sought.

preemption The doctrine that once Congress has enacted legislation in a given field, a state may not enact a law inconsistent with the federal statute. A similar doctrine also governs the relationship between the state government and local government.

pretext principle A law that is enacted by Congress supposedly under one of its enumerated powers, when the law's true purpose is to regulate a subject belonging to the states, is invalid. Today, the affectation doctrine has made the pretext principle of little significance.

primacy An approach to constitutional interpretation that requires state judges to apply their state's constitution before turning to the federal Constitution.

prior restraint An attempt by government to prevent or restrain expression, including press publication, before it is uttered.

privileges or immunities clause Prohibits states from denying persons the privileges or immunities of American citizenship.

probability test A third approach to the free speech clause adopted by some members of the Court in the mid-twentieth century. This test asks "whether the gravity of the 'evil,' discounted by its improbability, justifies such invasion of free speech as is necessary to avoid the danger."

probable cause A legal standard requiring the officer to have sufficient and trustworthy information to reasonably believe that a person has committed a crime.

procedural due process One dimension of the due process clause as contained in the Fifth and Fourteenth Amendments. It requires government to treat persons fairly while it attempts to interfere with their liberty interests. Put another way, procedural due process concerns *how* the government processes and safeguards individuals and their claims.

profanity Words, which often include slang references to sexual activity, that are viewed as highly offensive and impolite, but may still be afforded constitutional protection, as long as they do not fall into another category of unprotected speech, such as fighting words.

proportionality A theory of equality based on the notion that resources and opportunities ought to be allocated based upon individual circumstances.

proportionality doctrine A legal doctrine under the cruel and unusual punishment clause that requires criminal punishment to be proportional to the crime committed.

pseudonym A fictitious name. A plaintiff may sometimes be permitted to file a case using a fictitious name, if the plaintiff has a legitimate interest in protecting his or her privacy, such as when the facts of the case are embarrassing or the plaintiff's life may be threatened.

public figure A person with particular notoriety in the community, including, but not limited to, public officials.

public forum Properties historically associated with the exercise of First Amendment rights, including public sidewalks, parks, and cartilages outside courthouses and statehouses.

public rights doctrine Rule providing that if a claim is public in nature and not private, Congress may delegate its adjudication to a non-Article III tribunal.

public safety exception An exception to the *Miranda* requirement that has allowed police, in at least one instance, to question a suspect in custody without supplying the requisite warnings when the questions were designed to address an imminent matter of public safety.

public trial provision Sixth Amendment clause that states that individuals are entitled to a public trial.

quasi-judicial A term applied to the adjudicatory functions of an administrative agency, that is, taking evidence and making findings of fact and findings of law.

quasi-legislative A term applied to the legislative functions of an administrative agency, such as rulemaking.

rational basis test A constitutional standard used to review cases involving a nonsuspect form of discrimination that requires the government to show that its nonsuspect distinction is rationally related to a legitimate governmental interest.

reasonable expectation of privacy A legal standard used by the Court to assess Fourth Amendment rights against unreasonable searches and seizures. Under this standard, the Court asks whether the individual had a reasonable expectation that a particular activity or location would be kept private.

reasonable suspicion A less rigorous legal standard than probable cause, which generally requires an officer to have articulable facts that would lead a reasonable person to suspect that criminal activity is afoot.

reasonableness A legal standard that attempts to assess what a reasonable person would believe or do under the circumstances.

Religious Freedom Restoration Act (RFRA) A law passed by Congress in 1993 that sought to reinstate the strict scrutiny standard for free exercise cases. The RFRA bars government from substantially burdening an individual's exercise of religion, even if such burden stems from a neutral and generally applicable law, unless the government can demonstrate that the burden (1) furthers a compelling governmental interest, and (2) is the least restrictive means of furthering such interest.

Religious Land Use and Institutionalized Persons Act of 2000 (RLUIPA) Another law passed by Congress that attempted to reinstate the strict scrutiny standard in free exercise clause cases. The RLUIPA reinstates strict scrutiny analysis in two types of cases: (1) those involving land-use regulation, and (2) those involving religious exercise by institutionalized persons.

remand The return of a case by an appellate court to the trial court for further proceedings, for a new trial, or for entry of judgment in accordance with an order of the appellate court.

removal of case The transfer of a case from a state court to a federal court.

reporter shield laws State laws that prevent reporters from being compelled to reveal their confidential news sources.

reprieve The postponement of the carrying out of a sentence. A reprieve is not a commutation of sentence; it is merely a delay.

right to a fair trial A general term used to describe a variety of fairness-based rights during a criminal trial, including the right to a speedy and public trial by an impartial jury and the right to due process.

right to privacy Defined in a number of different ways, including the "right to be left alone"; the "freedom of personal choice in matters of marriage and family life"; and the "right to be secure in persons, houses, papers, and effects." The Court formally recognizes this right as a fundamental right of individuals, despite the fact that it is not specifically mentioned by the Constitution.

rule of four An internal rule of the Supreme Court, which provides that a case will be reviewed by the Court if four justices wish it to be reviewed.

sameness A theory of equality based on the notion that each person should be given the same amount and type of resources and opportunities regardless of individual circumstances.

search and seizure clause Fourth Amendment provision that precludes government from engaging in unreasonable searches and seizures of persons, houses, papers, and effects.

search incident to a lawful arrest An exception to the Fourth Amendment warrant requirement that allows police to search an arrestee during a valid arrest of a person.

search warrant Written authorization from a court to perform a search that is supported by probable cause.

security A primary value promoted by the Constitution that seeks stability, safety, and reliable structures.

segregation A tool used to discriminate whereby individuals are separated based on a particular attribute—race, sex, and so on.

seizure of a person Occurs when a law-enforcement officer uses force or the threat of force to detain a person, thereby causing the person to reasonably believe that he or she cannot freely leave the presence of the official.

select incorporation doctrine A theory held by some jurists and legal scholars that maintains that only select portions of the Bill of Rights, which are deemed to involve "preferred freedoms" or rights "implicit in the concept of ordered liberty," should be incorporated through the due process clause and made applicable to the states.

selective prosecution The process of selecting a person for criminal charge based on a prohibited criterion, such as race, sex, or ethnicity.

self-incrimination provision Fifth Amendment clause stating that within a criminal case, persons cannot be forced to provide testimony against themselves.

self-executing Self-acting; going into effect without need of further action.

semi-suspect classification A type of distinction or discrimination that is partially or somewhat suspicious under the Constitution and that deserves heightened, though not the highest, form of judicial scrutiny. This includes sex-based (male v. female) discrimination and distinctions based on whether a person's parents were married when the person was born.

separate but equal doctrine A legal theory promulgated in *Plessy v. Ferguson* (1896) holding that as long as government provides individuals with relatively the same amount of resources or services, it may segregate individuals based on race without denying them equal protection. This theory was rejected by the Court in *Brown v. Board of Education* (1954).

separationist approach A view of the religion clauses that generally asserts that government should remain strictly separate or removed from religious activity. Under this approach, it is asserted that government should not aid, fund, or otherwise assist religious organizations or individual religious activity.

serious offense An offense for which a defendant could receive more than six months of imprisonment.

severability rule A rule of interpretation that allows a court to remove unconstitutional portions from a law and leave the remainder intact.

Shays' Rebellion Daniel Shays, a veteran of the American Revolutionary War, and a group of fellow farmers rebelled in protest of economic conditions. This incident was cited by many as justification for abandoning the Articles of Confederation, the theory being that a stronger national government could provide better economic conditions and that a national military would be most effective in defeating rebellions.

slander A form of defamation that involves published verbal communications that are false and cause injury.

sobriety checkpoints A police procedure that involves the stopping of vehicles at a fixed checkpoint without any particularized suspicion in order to detect drunk driving.

social compact A term used to describe the Constitution as a contract between two primary parties—the people and the government wherein the people have given their consent to political institutions to be their sovereign governing authority, granting to them certain powers of structure, process, and support, and in exchange, the government has agreed to provide the people with certain levels of protection and sustenance.

sovereign immunity The principle that the government specifically, the United States or any state of the United States— is immune from suit except when it consents to be sued.

special master A person appointed by the court to assist with certain judicial functions in a specific case.

speedy trial provision Sixth Amendment clause that provides individuals with a right to a speedy trial.

standing The legal capacity to bring and to maintain a lawsuit. A person is without standing to sue unless some interest of his or hers has been adversely affected or unless he or she has been injured by the defendant. The term "standing to sue" is often shortened simply to "standing."

stare decisis Latin for "standing by the decision." Stare decisis is the doctrine that judicial decisions stand as precedents for cases arising in the future. It is a fundamental policy of our law that, except in unusual circumstances, a court's determination on a point of law will be followed by courts of the same or lower rank in later cases presenting the same legal issue, even though different parties are involved and many years have elapsed.

state action requirement An essential element to any due process or equal protection claim that requires sufficient government action—federal, state, or local—to be involved.

status crimes Also known as personal characteristic offenses, these are attempts to punish individuals based on their reputation or propensity for certain behavior and are generally prohibited as cruel and unusual punishment.

statute A law enacted by a legislature; an act.

stop and frisk exception An exception to the Fourth Amendment warrant requirement that allows officers who are conducting a brief investigation of a person based on reasonable suspicion to conduct a warrantless "pat-down" of the person's outer clothing in order to ensure that the person is not armed or dangerous.

stop and identify laws Laws in some jurisdictions that require individuals to provide their identity to the investigating officer during the stop.

strict constructionist An approach to interpreting the Constitution that strictly construes the explicit words of the Constitution to determine whether a particular right is protected. This approach generally leads to the conclusion that there is no independent right of privacy.

strict scrutiny test A legal standard requiring the government to prove that its policy is necessary (or narrowly tailored) to promote a compelling governmental interest. This test imposes the strictest burden upon government in its attempt to justify policies infringing fundamental rights.

sub judice Before the court for consideration and determination.

substantive due process A second dimension of the due process clause that concerns the type or substance of behavior that is included as a "liberty" under the due process clause. The primary question under this dimension of the due process clause is *what* activities does "liberty" include?

supremacy clause The provision in Article VI of the Constitution that "this Constitution and the laws of the United States . . . shall be the supreme law of the land, and the judges in every state shall be bound thereby."

suspect classification A type of distinction or discrimination that is highly questionable and that deserves the highest form of judicial scrutiny. Governmental distinctions based on race and alienage (in some cases) have been deemed "suspect" forms of discrimination.

symbolic speech Nonverbal communication that is akin to pure speech, including symbols (signs, flags, arm bands, or other tangible items) or conduct (hand gestures, burning objects, or other behavior). This nonverbal expression may receive First Amendment protection to the extent that it conveys a message capable of being received and understood by others.

takings clause A provision found in the Fifth Amendment that states that government cannot take private property for public use without just compensation. Also known as the *eminent domain provision*.

***Terry* stop** Also known as a "stop and frisk," this can be conducted during an investigatory stop where the officer has reasonable suspicion that the person is armed, thereby allowing the police to frisk an individual.

the switch in time that saved nine A phrase used to describe the change in the Court's approach to economic and social legislation, chiefly marked by the Court's opinion in *West Coast Hotel v. Parrish* (1937), where the Court upheld a Washington State minimum-wage law. The difference or "switch" in the case was the vote of Justice Owen Roberts, who previously had voted to strike down New Deal policies under the doctrine of liberty of contract. In *West Coast Hotel*, however, Roberts switched sides and voted to uphold the Washington law. This change not only negated any New Deal–related motive for Roosevelt's court-packing plan (which Congress never adopted), it also ushered in a new era of jurisprudence regarding economic liberty under the due process clause.

Thirteenth Amendment Ratified in 1865, this amendment bans "involuntary servitude" (slavery) within the United States.

three-strikes-and-you're-out laws Statutes in some states that impose life sentences for repeat (usually third) offenses, regardless of the seriousness of the offense.

time, place, and manner regulation A government restriction on speech that allows the expression in certain given contexts.

total incorporation doctrine A theory held by some jurists and legal scholars that maintains that the Fourteenth Amendment requires that all of the provisions of the Bill of Rights be incorporated and applied to the states.

totality of the circumstances A legal standard used to review arrests and seizures of persons and property to determine whether probable cause or reasonable suspicion exists. Under this standard, the overall context of the detention or seizure is reviewed, including what actions and words the officer used, the location of the detention, and the length of the stop.

Twenty-Fourth Amendment Ratified in 1964, this amendment prohibits poll taxes or other taxes, which had been employed in some jurisdictions as a means of preventing blacks from voting.

Twenty-Sixth Amendment Ratified in 1971, this amendment ensures that persons eighteen years and older would be entitled to vote.

undue burden   A legal standard used to review restrictions on abortion for their constitutionality. Under this standard, restrictions may not place an undue burden on a woman's right to choose an abortion.

use immunity   A guarantee given to a person that if he or she testifies against others, his or her testimony will not be used against him or her if he or she is prosecuted for involvement in the crime.

vagueness doctrine   A constitutional theory of due process that maintains that the government cannot impose legal standards that the average person cannot or is not likely to understand. Attempts to apply vague standards in regulating speech are generally deemed unconstitutional.

viewpoint neutrality   A term used to require the government not to favor one side or another within a given subject matter of speech.

voluntary cessation of illegal acts   An exception to the mootness doctrine, which provides that if an alleged harm has been ceased in order to avoid review, and there is a reasonable likelihood that the harm will reoccur or be recommenced, then the case may be heard.

vulgarity   Expression, which is sometimes sexual in nature, that is regarded as highly crude and offensive.

warrant provision   Fourth Amendment provision that requires government to demonstrate probable cause before a warrant will be issued by a judge.

***Younger* doctrine**   The doctrine, drawn from *Younger v. Harris*, that federal courts will abstain in most cases from interfering with state court proceedings, even if federal constitutional issues are present. Except in extreme cases, federal review of federal constitutional issues must wait until appeal or habeas corpus review.

INDEX

Taken from:

Criminal Procedure: Constitution and Society

Fifth Edition

by Marvin Zalman

1 The Meaning of Criminal Procedure

CHAPTER OUTLINE

ORDER AND LIBERTY
  Two Models of Criminal
    Justice
  Order and Liberty in a Time of
    Terror
  The Dangers of Injustice
THE CONTEXT OF CRIMINAL
  PROCEDURE
  The Criminal Justice System
  The Court System
  Law
  Federalism
  Political Theory
  History
  Politics
  Race and Racism

  Judicial Biography
  Human Rights
  Law and Society
INCORPORATION OF THE BILL
  OF RIGHTS
  Before the Civil War
  The Growth of Federal Judicial
    Power
  The *Dred Scott* Case and the
    Fourteenth Amendment
  The Anti-incorporation Cases,
    1884–1908
  The Adoption of the Due Process
    Approach
  The Incorporation of First
    Amendment Civil Liberties

  Resistance to Incorporation
    and Growing Support,
    1937–1959
  The Due Process Revolution
  The Counterrevolution
APPENDIX TO CHAPTER 1: HOW TO
  READ AND BRIEF CASES
  Notes on Legal Precedent
  The Components of an Opinion
  Briefing a Case
JUSTICES OF THE SUPREME COURT:
  THE PRECURSOR JUSTICES
  John M. Harlan I
  Oliver Wendell Holmes Jr.
  Louis Dembitz Brandeis
  Benjamin Nathan Cardozo

KEY TERMS

adequate and independent state
  grounds
affirm
brief
Burger Court
case law
certiorari, writ of
checks and balances
common law
constitutionalism
court of general jurisdiction
court of limited jurisdiction
Crime Control Model
dictum
due process approach
Due Process Model
ex post facto law
federalism

fundamental rights test
habeas corpus, writ of
hierarchy of constitutional rights
holding
human rights
incorporation doctrine
incorporation plus
judicial craftsmanship
judicial restraint
judicial review
jurisdiction
law
legal reasoning
liberty
opinion
order
overrule
precedent

private law
procedural law
public law
Rehnquist Court
remand
remedial law
reverse
rule application
rule making
Rule of Law
selective incorporation
"shocks the conscience" test
stare decisis
substantive law
Supremacy Clause
total incorporation
Warren Court

The Constitution of the United States was ordained, it is true, by descendants of Englishmen, who inherited the traditions of English law and history; but it was made for an undefined and expanding future, and for a people gathered and to be gathered from many nations and of many tongues.

—Justice Stanley Matthews, *Hurtado v. California,*
110 U.S. 516, 530–31 (1884)

ORDER AND LIBERTY

Criminal procedure is the branch of American constitutional law concerned with the state's power to maintain an orderly society and the rights of citizens and residents to live in freedom from undue government interference with their liberty. It is based on the U.S. Constitution, which went into effect in 1789, and several later amendments. Most important for the study of criminal procedure are the Fourth, Fifth, Sixth, and Eighth amendments—ratified in 1791 in the Bill of Rights—and the Fourteenth Amendment, ratified shortly after the Civil War in 1868. Equally important are the decisions of the U.S. Supreme Court interpreting the constitutional text. For the most part, the study of constitutional criminal procedure is the study of the Supreme Court's **opinions.**

Criminal procedure is vitally important in the criminal justice curriculum because it deals directly with the tension between **order** and **liberty,** which is involved in every area of criminal justice practice. The machinery of criminal justice—police, prosecution, courts, and corrections—is the formal means by which order is maintained in our society. The system employs two million people and is authorized to use awesome powers against individuals and companies. These include the power to arrest and detain people; to break into homes and offices; to search purses, backpacks, and computer files; and to put people through a bewildering and expensive court process. If the process results in a criminal conviction, the state is authorized to execute, imprison, or fine defendants and to control the lives of offenders placed on probation and parole in ways not consistent with individual liberty.

The need for this system of enormous powers is obvious. Levels of crime are high in the United States.[1] Every year, violent crime takes the lives and destroys the safety of tens of thousands of people, while property and white-collar crimes deprive millions more of their wealth and their sense of security. Without effective means of crime control, the lives of many more would be at risk, undermining the normal functioning of society. Widespread riots have become rare in the United States, and real anarchy has never been a feature of American life. The daily killings and sectarian violence in Iraq since the United States-led invasion in 2003 gives Americans a glimpse into societal breakdown and the effects of virtually total lawlessness.[2] A society without order does not enjoy liberty—it endures license.

The obverse is the repressive "order" of tyranny. The dictatorship of former Iraqi president Saddam Hussein benefited some classes of society at the expense of a brutal repression that killed hundreds of thousands. The former regime "apparently killed its citizens on a huge scale, both systematically and indiscriminately. Human rights groups . . . estimate that nearly 300,000 Iraqis are missing and were probably executed. Tens of thousands more, according to Iraqi opposition groups, may have been imprisoned and tortured, their lives warped forever by what they saw and experienced."[3] Nothing close to this characterizes abuses that do, unfortunately, occur in the American criminal justice system. Every society, however, must continuously curb the dangers of corruption, abuse of power, and excessive use of force that inevitably arise when criminal justice powers are placed in the hands of human beings.

What is required, in short, is a balance between the order of legitimate state power and the liberty from state control that is the cherished right of all Americans. Nowhere is this balance more important and more difficult to achieve than in the criminal justice process. The law of criminal procedure is essential for maintaining ordered liberty.

Two Models of Criminal Justice

A classic exposition of the order–liberty tension in the context of constitutional criminal procedure is Herbert Packer's "two models of the criminal process"[4] Rather than using the terminology of political theory—"liberty" and "order"—Packer examined the competing values that underlie our constitutional order through two models. A model, like a map, is an abstraction of reality that allows us to better understand the practices and rules of criminal procedure. Packer calls these the **Due Process Model** and the **Crime Control Model.** He warns that one is not "good" and the other "bad"; both models embrace constitutional values that are necessary to the kind of society in which we wish to live.

Even though people tend to identify more with one model than the other, they share many values in common. Police and prosecutors, who tend to favor the crime control model, support many constitutional protections, including the rule that a person can only be prosecuted for violating a law that is "on the books." Suppose police could arrest someone for "bad" behavior that is not a violation of law, and the legislature could later pass a law criminalizing those "bad" acts, allowing the state to prosecute a person for behavior that violated no law when committed. This situation violates the constitutional prohibition against **expost facto laws;** neither the state nor the federal governments may do this (U.S. Const. art. I.§, § 9 ¶ 3, and § 10 ¶ 1). Police officers might wish for the ability to arrest people for "bad" behavior, but on reflection, they will realize that a state that gave them such powers would be a dictatorship in which they themselves would not be safe.

Another value shared by proponents of both models is that police and prosecutors have a duty to enforce the criminal law; in other words, they cannot ignore violations of the law. A third shared understanding, according to Packer, "is the assumption that there are *limits to the powers of government* to investigate and apprehend persons suspected of committing crimes." Finally, there is a shared belief "that the alleged criminal is not merely an object to be acted upon, but an independent entity" who deserves his or her day in court and may demand a trial and other procedural safeguards. This last assumption of the adversary system is central to the Due Process Model and is de-emphasized but not entirely eliminated by the Crime Control Model.

Packer notes that the Crime Control Model emphasizes that "the *repression of criminal conduct* is by far the most important function to be performed by the criminal process" because public safety is essential to personal freedom. To be effective, the criminal justice system must efficiently process those who have been lawfully apprehended. There is a premium on speed and finality. Speed "depends on informality and uniformity" (for example, plea bargaining); "*finality* depends on minimizing the occasional challenge" (for example, limiting the right to appeal). The administrative and routine functioning of criminal justice is stressed, almost viewing the system as a conveyor belt. An attitude of supporters of the Crime Control Model is a "presumption of guilt"—an assumption that police and prosecutors are accurate in their decisions to arrest and apprehend prosecute suspects. Because of this confidence that the investigative process has identified the right person, the remaining steps in the process can be relatively perfunctory, and any restrictions on the investigative stages are to be resisted.

"If the Crime Control Model resembles an assembly line," Packer says, "the Due Process Model looks very much like an obstacle course." Although it values the repression of crime, it does not assume that police fact-finding is accurate. Indeed, it assumes that the criminal justice system is prone to error. Because of this, there is an "insistence on *formal, adjudicative, adversary* fact-finding processes in which the factual case against the accused is publicly heard by an impartial tribunal and is evaluated only after the accused has had a full opportunity to discredit the case against him." Even after a full trial, the fear of an erroneous conviction generates a desire for many avenues of appeal. "The demand for finality is thus very low in the Due Process Model," Packer says. This model demands the "prevention and *elimination of mistakes* to the extent possible; the Crime Control Model accepts the probability of mistakes up to the level at which they interfere with the goal of repressing crime." For the Due Process Model, the "aim of the process is at least as much to protect the factually innocent as it is to convict the factually guilty." The Due Process Model is highly suspicious of those who wield power and is ideologically driven by the "primacy of the individual and the complementary concept of limitation on official power. The Due Process Model insists on legal guilt, whereas the Crime Control Model stresses factual guilt. The concept of legal guilt pervades the formal legal and trial process; no matter how "factually" guilty a person is, there can be no conviction and punishment unless a court has **jurisdiction,** unless the prosecution occurs within the period of the statute of limitations, and unless the offender is lawfully responsible (for example, not insane). At this point, the "quixotic" presumption of innocence rises to the fore. The presumption of innocence is *not* the opposite of the presumption of guilt, but is a normative principle that insists that the defendant be treated as if he or she were innocent, no matter how apparent the factual guilt. To this end, the prosecutor must prove a case beyond a reasonable doubt, and the jury verdict must be unanimous. The equality of treatment of all suspects is an important attribute of the Due Process Model attribute. Finally, it includes the strong belief that serious procedural errors invalidate convictions. This last point is the one over which many of the most bitter disputes in constitutional criminal procedure have arisen.

Order and Liberty in a Time of Terror

Five years after the September 11, 2001, terrorist attacks on the United States by radical jihadists that took almost three thousand lives, the "war on terror" has polarized the nation and has put the tension between order and liberty into sharp relief. The immediate response to 9/11 was a military campaign authorized by Congress that wrested Afghanistan from Taliban control and suppressed the al Qaeda movement, which was responsible for 9/11 and earlier attacks against U.S. interests, including the 1993 World Trade Center bombing. The military action in Afghanistan was followed by two major campaigns, one domestic and the other foreign.

The domestic campaign involves defensive homeland security measures, including increased airport security and an important new focus on terrorism investigation and prosecution. The other campaign was the ill-conceived war in Iraq. During the war's fourth year, the administration of President George W. Bush has admitted that Iraq was not formerly a sponsor of Islamist terrorism. The lack of plans for controlling the country after a swift but superficial military victory led to unrest, continuing insurgency, and fears of civil war and the rise of a radical Islamist state.[5] The war in Iraq is beyond the scope of this text, except insofar as it has generated important Supreme Court rulings on issues of liberty and justice.

The war metaphor for the anti-terror campaign, according to one expert, actually makes it more difficult to think of and act on effective counterterrorism strategies.[6] For the purposes of this book, it is useful to contrast the "war model" and "criminal model" metaphors as paradigms for action taken by the government in responding to real and perceived threats. The criminal model has emerged painstakingly over centuries of English and American constitutional history. It is grounded in the concept of due process, as stated in Magna Carta of 1215: "No freeman shall be captured or imprisoned or disseised [deprived of his property] or outlawed or exiled or in any way destroyed, nor will we go against him or send against him, except by the lawful judgment of his peers by the law of the land."[7] It is a model of constitutional balance and holds that government can act only against those who have already committed acts that have been defined as crimes. It holds that the criminal justice apparatus must act under the law and under such constitutional guarantees as search warrants, the privilege against self-incrimination, and trial rights. The criminal model gives people the liberty to be free of state spying or constraint until they have given others sound suspicion to believe they have violated the law. The chief goals of the criminal model are retribution for and deterrence of criminal behavior.

When a country goes to war, this all changes. The goal of the war model is prevention.[8] Under this "new 'paradigm of prevention' . . . prosecutors [have used] every tool at their disposal to investigate, observe and detain potential terrorists before they strike."[9] In time of war, civil liberties are curtailed. The press is more circumspect; military censorship is necessary; certain areas are off limits; freedom of movement is curtailed; and intelligence agencies are given a freer hand to probe civilian secrets.

Two risks to civil liberties arise out of war situations: (1) the risk that emergency powers concentrated in the hands of government agents will be misused and (2) the risk that when the emergency ends, liberties formerly enjoyed will be permanently eroded. A brief survey of American history indicates that virtually every war has been accompanied not only by necessary restrictions on individual freedoms but on overreactions, often hysterical, that have unnecessarily curtailed the liberty of Americans. Here are several examples:

- The undeclared naval war by Britain and France on the fledgling United States in the 1790s led the Federalist-controlled Congress to pass the Alien and Sedition Laws, which clearly violated the First Amendment. Prosecutions under the law, which was soon repealed, were politically motivated.[10]
- President Abraham Lincoln suspended the writ of habeas corpus in thousands of cases during the Civil War. Although historians have granted the necessity and even the restraint of these acts, the Supreme Court repudiated this unilateral presidential power after the war ended.[11]
- A World War I sedition law made criticism of the military draft a crime. Sedition prosecutions stifled free speech. In reaction, the American Civil Liberties Union (ACLU) was formed, and in a series of landmark cases, the Supreme Court strengthened First Amendment freedoms, limiting the ability of government to stifle unpopular political expression.[12]
- In the turmoil following World War I, a fear of Bolsheviks, a deadly Wall Street bombing, and assassination threats led to the "Palmer raids" in which thousands of people around the country, mostly leftist or pro-labor, were rounded up for interrogation and deportation. The raids were organized by J. Edgar Hoover, who was then a special assistant to Attorney General A. Mitchell Palmer.[13]
- More than a hundred thousand Japanese-Americans were interned for the duration of World War II in a tragic overreaction to the Japanese attack on Pearl Harbor. Their internment was upheld by the Supreme Court.[14]
- Also during World War II, President Franklin D. Roosevelt authorized wiretapping and eavesdropping for the protection of national security, a necessary expansion of power that led to later abuses that were curbed by the Foreign Intelligence Surveillance Act (FISA).[15]
- During the Korean War, President Harry S. Truman nationalized the steel industry in order to break a strike that threatened war production. The Supreme Court swiftly ruled that this was an unconstitutional extension of the president's war powers.[16]
- The longest and most severe threat to civil liberty was the rise of the "national security state" for at least half of the twentieth century in an effort to thwart the real threats of fascism, Nazism, and expansionist Soviet communism under Stalin. Fascism and the Axis Powers were defeated both by military victories in World War II and by postwar assistance that painstakingly built democratic regimes in Japan, Germany, and Italy. The long struggle to contain communist global expansion warped American politics and justice in the 1950s with political trials, loyalty oaths, and communist witch hunts (which missed the real Soviet spies). Artists were blacklisted, local police departments formed "red squads" for snooping on citizens, CIA operatives spied on Americans within the country, and the FBI wiretapped Martin Luther King Jr. and other civil rights leaders—all of which led to a climate of political fear in which the FBI equated a belief in racial equality or other liberal opinions with support for communism.[17]
- The protests against the Vietnam War in the 1960s and early 1970s produced repressive political crimes and political trials (such as the Anti-Riot Act of 1968 and the infamous Chicago 7 trial of anti-war activists). This carried over into the wiretapping abuses of the Nixon administration and led to the president's resignation under threat of impeachment.[18]

After these emergency periods passed, repressive laws were typically repealed or declared unconstitutional, and curbs were placed on excessive law enforcement behavior.

The current crisis has generated vituperative politics. The administration and its supporters paint those who oppose the Iraq War as appeasers and perhaps traitors in a continuing and possibly decades-long "war on terror."[19] This conflates the reaction to the ongoing sectarian violence in Iraq to the larger issue of a complex international jihad movement without any central organization.[20] The terror bombings in Madrid, Bali, and London in recent years have not been planned by any central al Qaeda organization, which according to counterterrorism experts is smaller than it was before 9/11, but by diffuse groups infused with the Islamist jihadist ideology, which is far removed from mainstream Islam.

If, as *The 9/11 Commission Report*[21] makes clear, the jihadist enemies of modern, secular states in the global economy are grounded in extremist views of Islam and in social and economic malaise, it would seem that classic counterinsurgency tactics that rely heavily on police techniques of monitoring, infiltration, interdiction, and prosecution, along with the judicious use of the military and material support for civilians not involved in terrorism, is the way to successfully counter terrorism.[22] It is, after all, patient, meticulous police work in Britain and elsewhere that identified and thwarted the 2006 plot by a small group of criminal terrorists to destroy airliners with explosives disguised as carry-on liquids.[23] The understanding that law enforcement is a key to fighting terrorism is reflected in the Anti-Terrorism Advisory Councils. These councils, involving federal, state, and local governments and the private sector, were set up by the Justice Department to coordinate antiterrorism training and action.[24] The bulk of their activity focuses on police and prosecution.

An extended discussion of operational topics is not the subject matter of criminal procedure. However, many events that have occurred in the "war on terror" have addressed central questions of constitutional criminal procedure. The Supreme Court has spoken forcefully in support of the rule of law in response to administration actions that have sought to extend executive power to unprecedented levels. Indeed, a guest scholar at the prestigious, middle-of-the road Brookings Institution has labeled administration efforts as "an *extralegal* terrorism war."[25] Acknowledging the government's ongoing need for "spying at home, detaining terror suspects, and conducting tough interrogations," this author criticizes the Bush administration for not "making proper legal provisions for those practices."

Subsequent chapters in this text will briefly examine facets of criminal procedure in a time of terror. In Chapter 3, a discussion of "sneak and peek" warrants, legislatively authorized by the USA PATRIOT Act, is integrated into the larger section on search warrants. Chapter 4 includes a description of how panic can lead to mistaken arrests. In Chapter 10, a statistical analysis of federal antiterror prosecutions, as an additional "Law in Society" section, strongly indicates that the prosecution of serious terror cases has been burdened by an unusually large number of weak cases.

The Dangers of Injustice

Every case reaching the Supreme Court involves not only questions of law, state power, and the individual's political relationship to the state, but also questions of justice and injustice. The student should not forget, while grappling with concepts and cases, that each case involves a fight for justice. This is not to say that every defendant has a good case; it would be unwise to romanticize defendants. As Justice Felix Frankfurter said, "It is a fair summary of history to say that the safeguards of liberty have frequently been forged in controversies involving not very nice people."[26] On the other hand, several famous defendants, like the Scottsboro boys and Earl Clarence Gideon and Dr. Sam Sheppard, were innocent of the crimes for which they were convicted.[27] It is important to keep in mind that rights are fundamental and must be available to everyone, not just reserved for "actually innocent" defendants.

Every chapter in this book details abuses of power and errors in the justice system. Many of the "Law in Society" sections focus on the negative—on errors, abuses, and even crimes committed by criminal justice officials. It goes without saying that most police officers, prosecutors, defense attorneys, and judges act competently and professionally; they often perform their work courageously or selflessly. Nevertheless, the burden of constitutional criminal procedure is to unflinchingly confront the negligent and malignant aspects of criminal justice.

Because the text focuses on rules of criminal procedure that concern police practices, it devotes a fair amount of space to police-generated abuses that undermine defendants' constitutional rights. (Other significant problems, like police brutality, raise few constitutional issues.) Police perjury, for example, can destroy a defendant's Fourth Amendment and other rights. When police play end-run games around the *Miranda* rules, they in effect overrule the Supreme Court's decisions. Overzealous police officers have unintentionally gulled some defendants into giving false confessions. Errors or falsehoods in search warrant affidavits undermine the privacy and security of citizens. Sloppy police work has made worse the underlying problems of mistaken eyewitness identification, leading to the conviction of innocent people. The blue wall of silence makes it even more difficult to ensure professionalism and lawful behavior in criminal justice practice.

Other actors outside police agencies must act properly to ensure that the criminal justice system lives up to its constitutional ideals. Prosecutorial misconduct occurs with regularity and can negate the very rationale of the adversary system. The same effect is produced by inadequate, poorly prepared, and overworked defense lawyers. The history of American justice is replete with trials that were mockeries, with judges unable or unwilling to conduct the proceedings to guarantee fairness.[28] All judges have to remain vigilant to ensure evenhanded trials.

Mechanisms to correct injustice in the justice system include appeals in criminal cases and civil lawsuits against criminal justice officials. Judges, however, have total immunity against civil suits for acts performed in the course of their duty, and prosecutors have qualified immunity. Police officers are most likely to face the challenge of civil lawsuits. Incompetent and unjust acts by a minority of criminal justice practitioners have opened the door wider to appeals and civil lawsuits against all officers. In the last analysis, competent and honest police officers, lawyers, and judges should be as eager to eradicate injustice as are defendants.

A lesson of the long struggle to ensure **Rule of Law** and a civilized justice system is the need to treat suspects and defendants fairly. An unfair or incompetent system leads to the conviction of the innocent. The conviction of "actually innocent" people has been a concern of the common law since the middle ages, as reflected in the maxim, "Better ten guilty go free than one innocent convicted." The maxim is supported by the high level of evidence needed to convict: proof beyond a reasonable doubt. The large number of wrongful convictions revealed since DNA testing became feasible in the early 1990s brings home the inadequacies of criminal procedure law to prevent injustice.

The Innocence Project has confirmed 189 DNA exonerations as of January 2007.[29] At least 340 innocent prisoners were exonerated between 1988 and 2003, and it is plausible that thousands are wrongly convicted each year.[30] The causes for wrongful convictions include mistaken eyewitness identification and poor lineup procedures, police "tunnel vision" on the first suspect, interrogation methods that elicit false confessions, pressure for convictions in high-profile cases, jailhouse snitches who lie to get favorable treatment, overzealous prosecutors, incompetent or dishonest forensic investigators, "junk science" (e.g., hair evidence), incompetent defense lawyers, and legal and constitutional rules that act as roadblocks to the truth.[31]

The world of criminal justice is just beginning to absorb the complex of problems that produce wrongful convictions. Late in 2004, Congress passed the Innocence Protection Act, which increased compensation for wrongly convicted federal prisoners and provided funds for post-conviction DNA testing.[32] Although growing concerns about wrongful conviction involve the entire criminal justice system, they also focus on several special concerns of criminal procedure. This text pays special attention to wrongful conviction in the chapters on the right to counsel (Chapter 6), interrogations and confessions (Chapter 7), identification and lineups (Chapter 8), the pretrial process (Chapter 10), and the trial process (Chapter 11).

THE CONTEXT OF CRIMINAL PROCEDURE

Criminal procedure is not a "closed system" of Supreme Court cases and statutes cut off from the larger society. Because criminal procedure relates to criminal justice, the student must have basic knowledge about the criminal justice system. As a branch of constitutional law, the study of criminal procedure requires a basic understanding of American history, values, and society, including an appreciation of race relations. Knowledge of these subjects helps the student understand why the cases are important and what impact they are likely to have on criminal justice practice and American society. In addition, an academic grounding in English and American constitutional history, political theory, and human rights enhances an understanding of criminal procedure. Since it cannot be assumed that students are grounded in all of these subjects, this section briefly reviews areas of basic knowledge that are important to understanding criminal procedure.

The Criminal Justice System

The criminal justice system consists mostly of government agencies, although some private citizens play important roles, including jurors, bail bondsmen, and private defense lawyers. The major criminal justice agencies—police, prosecution, and corrections—are parts of the executive branch of government. The judicial branch of government, which adjudicates civil and criminal cases, ensures fair procedures. Legislatures also play a central role by enacting criminal law, prescribing sentencing guidelines and structures, and setting budgets for the primary agencies of criminal justice.

Understanding criminal justice practices allows a better appreciation of criminal procedure. For example, knowing that police officers have a good deal of discretion and often are not closely supervised by their superiors helps us understand how some facts get into court. The sociology of police behavior on the job is useful in understanding the limits of legal rules in shaping police behavior.

Criminal procedure law covers six major stages of criminal justice practice by police, prosecutors, defense attorneys, trial judges, and appellate courts. These are (1) police investigation, interrogation, search, and arrest; (2) the pretrial process, including the decision to grant bail, grand jury operations, preliminary examination of the charges, and pretrial motions; (3) formal charging by the prosecutor; (4) adjudication—the determination of guilt or innocence by a jury or a bench trial or by the plea negotiation process; (5) sentencing—imposing punishment on the convicted, a judicial decision in which probation officers, prosecutors, defense attorneys, and sometimes victims play roles; and (6) appellate review by higher courts.[33] This book concentrates on the first stage of the criminal process—police activities that touch on individuals' rights and liberties—and also includes information on the pretrial process, charging, and adjudication. Sentencing and correctional law, including prisoners' rights, are distinct areas of law that are not covered in this text. The last stage of the criminal process, appellate review, is where most of the constitutional rights of suspects are formed. This text does not discuss highly technical appellate issues but emphasizes the substance of Supreme Court cases that shape constitutional criminal procedure.

The Court System

In the American constitutional framework, courts of law constitute a separate branch of government. They exist not only to decide legal disputes but also to provide **checks and balances** against the risk that the "political branches" of government—the executive and legislative branches—will violate the rights of individuals for improper political or corrupt purposes.

Courts are hierarchical; that is, they are ranked by authority into trial and appellate courts. The basic function of trial courts is **rule application**—deciding individual cases in accord with the law. Trial courts decide issues of fact and resolve issues of law that apply to a case. They also encourage pleas in criminal cases. Many states have different levels of trial courts. Lower-tier courts are **courts of limited jurisdiction** (often called "district" or "municipal courts"). They decide misdemeanor cases and oversee the pretrial stages of felony cases. Felony cases are decided in **courts of general jurisdiction** (called "superior courts" in most states, but also known as "circuit" or "district courts"). Trial judges can oversee juries, which decide issues of fact under rules of law and evidence specified by the judge. Juries, incidentally, are not part of the judicial branch but are "the people." If a jury trial is waived, a judge sits as the trier of facts and law.

Appellate courts are "above" (or "superior to") trial courts in the court hierarchy. The basic function of appellate courts is **rule making**—that is, making law (legal precedents) by a process of legal interpretation. Every state—and the United States—has a supreme court, which are the final arbiters of issues of law that may be appealed by losing parties in civil lawsuits or criminal cases. Most states and the United States also have established intermediate courts of appeal, which became necessary as the volume of legal appeals grew too large to be handled by supreme courts. Issues of fact are typically not appealable. This text concentrates on constitutional rule making by the U.S. Supreme Court.

A basic knowledge of the terminology and process of appellate courts is helpful for understanding criminal procedure. A party who loses a case in the trial court may have a right to appeal or may have to seek permission from the courts to appeal. In either case, the party has to initiate an appeal by asserting that his or her legal rights were violated during the trial. The violation may have been based on an incorrect application or interpretation of the substantive law in the case, an error involving the law of evidence, or as is often the case in criminal procedure, a violation of rights committed by the police. Parties in appellate proceedings cannot (with rare exceptions) argue that the facts were incorrectly decided. This rule is based on the idea that juries or trial judges who actually saw witnesses testify are in a better position than appellate judges to decide what happened. Appellate courts assume that the facts decided during the trial are the facts of the case. Unlike trials, in which witnesses are sworn in and testify, appellate courts decide cases based only on legal arguments presented by the lawyers. The arguments are presented in formal written essays called **briefs** and may also be presented in relatively short oral arguments before the court.

> The appeal begins when the party losing the case in the trial court, the "appellant," files a notice of appeal, usually a month or two after the trial court decision. Then within a few months the appellant files the trial court record in the appellate court. The record, often bulky, consists of the papers filed in the trial court along with a transcript of the trial testimony. Next the appellant and the opposing party, the "appellee," file briefs that argue for their respective positions. The briefs are usually followed by short oral presentations to the judge. Finally, the judges decide the case and issue a written opinion.[34]

Appeals to the U.S. Supreme Court are discretionary; the Supreme Court hears only those cases that it wishes to decide. The appellate process in the Supreme Court is taken under a writ with a Latin title that goes back to English procedure: a **writ of certiorari.** Appellants in Supreme Court cases are known as "petitioners," and appellees are called "respondents."

Appellate courts issue very specific decisions in an appeal, in reference to the decision in the last court from which an appeal was taken. For example, before a case reaches the U.S. Supreme Court, there may have been a trial verdict, an appeal in the state court of appeals, a decision of the state supreme court, a decision by a federal district court on a federal **writ of habeas corpus,** followed by a decision by a federal court of appeals.

In such a case, the Supreme Court will **affirm** or **reverse** the decision of the federal court of appeals—the court just "below" the Supreme Court. If the appeal involves several legal issues, the Supreme Court may affirm in part and reverse in part. The Supreme Court usually does not apply its decision directly to the parties. Instead, it usually **remands** the case, sending it back to the lower court to handle the details of applying its decision. An appellate court can **overrule** its own prior precedent when it finds that its prior decision was incorrect, was unsound, or has become obsolete, and can replace it with a different ruling.

Although the Supreme Court's decision (e.g., "Judgment below affirmed") is exceedingly terse, the important part of the case is the Court's opinion, which is usually a lengthy essay written for the benefit of lawyers and judges in a formal style, which purports to explain the reasons behind the Court's decision. We study these opinions to understand the Court's reasoning.

Law

There are several "sources" or types of law, and they exist in a hierarchical order. A statute or a court's decision is typically referred to as "law," but is also called a "source of law" to convey the idea that law is not only the words of the rule issued by the state but the result of those words, or their effects, that are enforced by the government. As commonly understood, **law** is a body of written rules issued by a legitimate government authority and designed to guide and control the action of individuals and institutions. In the United States, there are different forms of law, each of which the government can enforce. The most important forms of law are (1) statutes or legislation and (2) rules created by appellate courts, called **case law** or **common law** (explained further in the section on history). Both legislation and case law are legitimate sources of law that government officials can enforce. The Constitution of the United States and the state constitutions are a special kind of statute. The U.S. Constitution was ratified not by an ordinary session of the legislature, but by a special ratifying convention, and so it represents the will of the people. Other forms of law include executive orders of the president or state governors, the regulations of administrative agencies, ordinances passed by local units of government, and court rules detailing court procedures.

These sources of law stand in a hierarchical relationship that depends on the relative authority of the agency issuing the law. Let's begin with case law. Our legal system inherited the English common law tradition that courts are part of the governing structure and that the rules of **precedent** that constitute case law are rules of law binding on everyone who is subject to the state's authority. Earlier in England, judges were high officials of the king and spoke for him. However, in the American republican form of government, the people are sovereign and delegate their sovereign power to their elected representatives. Because of this, legislation duly passed by a majority of the legislature under its established rules, and signed by the president or a state governor, is a "higher" form of law than case law. Legislation derives legitimacy from a source that more directly represents the sovereign people. Consequently, a legislature can modify or abolish common law precedent. For example, many legislatures passed no-fault insurance laws that replaced common law rules establishing liability for people who negligently caused injuries. In the United States, virtually all states have replaced older "common law crimes" with crimes specifically defined by legislation.

Constitutional case law is an exception to the ability of a legislature to revise case law. The U.S. Constitution was ratified by "the people of the United States" and cannot be changed by ordinary legislation. Its text can be formally amended only by procedures specified in Article V—by a proposed amendment passed by two-thirds of the House of Representatives and two-thirds of the Senate (or by a convention called by two-thirds of the state legislatures) and ratified by three-fourths of the state legislatures. Direct constitutional amendments are rare; only twenty-seven have been ratified.

In addition, the meaning of the Constitution's words is determined by Supreme Court decisions. Thousands of specific rules of constitutional law—created by the Supreme Court—are deemed to be part of the Constitution and therefore cannot be overruled by legislation. For example, in 1968 Congress passed a law supposedly overruling *Miranda v. Arizona* (1966), which requires that suspects be informed of their constitutional, Fifth Amendment right to silence. (Any confessions they make under custodial interrogation before being apprised of their right to silence will not be admissible in a court.) In 2000, the Supreme Court ruled that law unconstitutional: "We hold that *Miranda,* being a constitutional decision of this Court, may not be in effect overruled by an Act of Congress, and we decline to overrule *Miranda* ourselves" (*Dickerson v. U.S.,* 2000). It is obvious, then, that the Supreme Court has enormous power to determine the meaning and content of constitutional law and thus to impose rules of conduct on police, prosecutors, judges, and other officials. In a real sense, the Constitution's meaning is amended as the Supreme Court's constitutional doctrines evolve.

The law is classified in other ways. For example, **private law** concerns private disputes and rights between private individuals, groups, and corporations, while **public law** involves government power and arises from disputes between government departments or between private people or groups and government agencies. Law is also classified by its specific subject matter. Private law covers contracts, property, torts (the law of injuries), commercial law, copyright, sports law, civil procedure, and the like. Public law includes constitutional law, administrative law, tax law, substantive criminal law, and criminal procedure.

Law is also classified by three functions. **Substantive law** establishes and defines rights, powers, and obligations. Major areas of substantive private law, for example, establish contractual obligations, property rights, and the freedom from intentional or negligent harm. Substantive criminal law defines crimes such as homicide and theft and defenses such as insanity. **Procedural law** prescribes methods of enforcing substantive rights that are breached and includes rules of jurisdiction, the serving of legal process (e.g., a summons), and rules that guide the conduct of a trial. **Remedial law** determines the actual benefits or "remedies" obtained by a successful party to a lawsuit. Civil remedies include (1) legal remedies or money damages to compensate loss and may include punitive damages and (2) equitable remedies (i.e., injunctions or specific performance to rectify a violation of rights). Criminal law "remedies" are the lawful punishments that may be inflicted on convicted criminals.[35]

An attempt to classify constitutional criminal procedure produces a surprise. It is, first, an important branch of public law because it regulates the relationship between the individual and the state. Its subject matter is that of constitutional rights, including the right to trial (U.S. Const. art. III; amend. VI), protection against unlawful arrest and search and seizure (U.S. Const. amend. IV), the privilege against self-incrimination (U.S. Const. amend. V), and others. By its title, criminal procedure would also appear to be procedural law. However, this is not so simple a matter. On the one hand, some criminal procedure rules, especially those created by statute and court rule, are true procedural rules that facilitate the prosecution of a criminal case. On the other hand, most rules of constitutional criminal procedure created by the Supreme Court grant rights and protections to suspects and defendants in accord with the purpose of constitutional provisions and in reaction to unfair violations by police, prosecutors, and judges. Criminal procedure can therefore also be classified as substantive law.

The substantive nature of criminal procedure rights raises the question of what remedies exist for violations of these rights. Under some circumstances, individuals can bring civil suits against state officers and win money damages for violations of their rights.

An important attribute of criminal procedure has been the creation of exclusionary rules by the courts. Such rules disallow the use of illegally obtained evidence. The Fourth Amendment exclusionary rule, an important and controversial topic, is the subject of Chapter 2.

Federalism

A police officer makes a lawful arrest. Under which law does the officer operate? In a unitary nation like France or England, the arrest is made under the nation's laws. The United States, however, is a federated nation (as are Canada, Germany, and Mexico) with a national government and state governments. An officer making a lawful arrest in Augusta, Maine, must therefore comply with both Maine law and applicable U.S. law.

This complicated arrangement is the result of **federalism**—the legal and power relationship between the national government and the state governments. Federalism is a very important topic in American criminal procedure because up until the mid-twentieth century, state and local criminal justice officials were guided exclusively by state law. In the twentieth century, the Supreme Court began to apply the Bill of Rights to state officials, and this movement created modern constitutional criminal procedure. The story of how this happened and its effects are detailed later in this chapter in the section on the **incorporation doctrine.** This section provides a brief foundation for understanding "incorporation."

The Constitution's Framers understood that some level of friction (as well as cooperation) would exist between the national and state governments and between the states. They provided rules in the Constitution to create a nation in which the limited sovereignty of the states would be respected but in which the federal government would have certain exclusive powers. Foreign affairs and the war-making power are examples of exclusive federal authority.[36] The Constitution also established numerous rules to ensure a unified nation rather than competing states. These include a federally controlled postal system, federal oversight of interstate and foreign commerce, the prohibition of a state's giving favorable treatment to its own citizens over the residents of other states, the requirement that states appropriately apply the laws or court judgments of another state ("full faith and credit"), the extradition of felons to the state from which the person fled, federal control over territories, and the like.[37] Finally, the Constitution requires federal and state governments to adhere to a political philosophy of liberal republicanism. The preamble to the Constitution emphasizes that one of the six purposes of American government is to "secure the Blessings of Liberty to ourselves and our Posterity." The national government guarantees to every state a "republican form of government"—in Abraham Lincoln's words, a "government of the people, by the people, for the people."[38] The states and the federal government are prohibited from passing ex post facto laws or bills of attainder that could undermine political liberty; nor may they create "titles of Nobility" that could create a class of Americans other than citizens.[39]

To understand how federalism works in the criminal procedure context, we must consider the topics of jurisdiction, the Supremacy Clause, the special role of the U.S. Supreme Court, and adequate and independent state grounds. Each state is a limited sovereign within the national framework. Each has a constitution that establishes a "republican form of government." The structures of state governments are quite similar, including a chief executive or governor, a legislature, and a state court system with a supreme court and trial courts. With some small variations, the legal systems of each state are comparable and parallel to the federal legal system. Each state legislature makes laws for the benefit of its people, and each has its own bill of rights to guarantee the rights of its citizens and residents.

American federalism recognizes areas of exclusive federal control, areas of exclusive state action, and many areas where both federal and state laws and executive branch agencies can work together. For example, in the last forty years Congress has passed federal criminal laws that overlap substantially with state criminal laws, allowing either federal or state law enforcement agencies to investigate and either federal or state courts to try cases under their respective laws.[40]

Jurisdiction. Jurisdiction is both the lawful authority of a government to exercise its powers in its territory and the authority of a court to decide cases brought before it. States are not administrative arms or subdivisions of the national government, but they do come under the Constitution's jurisdiction in specific ways.[41] Every government officer, state and federal, swears to uphold the U.S. Constitution.[42] Despite this, the federal government, which was established by the Constitution, is formally a government of limited powers. In the legislative realm, state legislatures have *plenary,* or general, powers to pass laws for the good of their residents, whereas the U.S. Congress can only pass laws on topics listed in Article I, section 8 of the Constitution.

Courts can decide cases only if they have lawful jurisdiction to do so. State courts derive their jurisdiction from state constitutions and statutes, and federal court jurisdiction is conferred by the U.S. Constitution and by congressional statutes. The Constitution and federal statutes grant jurisdiction to the Supreme Court and to any federal courts created by Congress only over federal questions—specifically, issues of law that arise under the U.S. Constitution, federal legislation, or treaties made by the United States and a foreign nation. As a result, the Supreme Court can review almost all decisions of lower federal courts.[43] On the other hand, the Supreme Court has no jurisdiction over matters of state law. Cases based exclusively on provisions of state constitutions, state legislation, or rules of state common law can be decided only by the courts of the state. The U.S. Supreme Court can review a case from the highest tribunal of a state only if it concerns a federal question.

In constitutional criminal procedure, a federal question arises in a state court when a criminal defendant claims that an action taken by a local or state officer or court violated a right protected by the Fourteenth Amendment or elements of the Bill of Rights that have been applied to the states. Under the Fourteenth Amendment, "No State shall . . . deprive any person of life, liberty, or property, without due process of law." The discussion of the incorporation doctrine below will explain how the interpretation of this provision allowed federal courts to impose the Bill of Rights on local and state officers and courts in criminal appeals. Federal issues can arise out of state criminal justice and be appealed to the U.S. Supreme Court where state residents file civil suits in federal court against municipalities or local or state officers (but not against the state government), claiming that the local officers violated their constitutional rights. This is authorized by a civil rights law (42 U.S.C. § 1983) passed in 1871 under the authority of the Fourteenth Amendment.

The Supremacy Clause.   State judges can decide issues under the U.S. Constitution when defendants claim that their federal constitutional rights have been infringed by state officers in state proceedings. When a state court interprets the U.S. Constitution, the state judge's ruling can be appealed to a federal court. It is logical that the final determination of the meaning of the Constitution be vested in the Supreme Court. This understanding is confirmed by the **Supremacy Clause** of the Constitution.

Article III of the U.S. Constitution (the "judicial article"), which confers jurisdiction on the Supreme Court, does not directly give that Court the jurisdiction to hear federal questions that arise in state courts. Nevertheless, this power was asserted by the Supreme Court in the early Republic and is inherent in the Supremacy Clause

THE SUPREMACY CLAUSE

This Constitution, and the Laws of the United States which shall be made in Pursuance thereof; and all Treaties made, or which shall be made, under the Authority of the United States, shall be the supreme Law of the Land; and the Judges in every State shall be bound thereby, any Thing in the Constitution or Laws of any State to the Contrary notwithstanding.

Source: U.S. Constitution, Article VI, paragraph 2.

(Article VI, paragraph 2).[44] The clause says that where an issue of law applies to both the federal and the state governments, federal law and the interpretation of the federal courts control. The Supremacy Clause ensures that the United States will be a united nation, for if every state could decide the meaning of the U.S. Constitution in its own way, constitutional law would not be uniform.

The Special Role of the Supreme Court.

We are used to thinking of constitutional interpretation as "belonging" to the courts. Nevertheless, the president and Congress often justify their actions by citing the Constitution. The courts, however, have final say about the meaning of the Constitution. A state supreme court is the final authority on the meaning of a state constitution, and the U.S. Supreme Court has the last say on the meaning of the U.S. Constitution, giving it great power in shaping criminal procedure.

From the beginning of the Republic, the Framers believed that courts play an essential role in protecting individual liberty. In a speech to the House of Representatives in 1789 proposing the Bill of Rights, James Madison said that by placing rights "into the constitution, independent tribunals of justice will consider themselves in a peculiar manner the guardians of those rights; they will be an impenetrable bulwark against every assumption of power in the legislative or executive; they will be naturally led to resist every encroachment upon rights expressly stipulated for in the constitution by the declaration of rights."[45]

Adequate and Independent State Grounds.

In the mid-twentieth century, the Supreme Court decided that the Bill of Rights applied to the states through the appellation of the Due Process Clause of the Fourteenth Amendment. (See "The Incorporation of the Bill of Rights" later in this chapter.) For the most part, the Constitution was applied equally to state and federal law enforcement and courts. After 1972, the U.S. Supreme Court began to water down individual rights and rule more favorably toward the prosecution, while some state supreme courts ruled in favor of defendants on the same issue, creating potential conflicts.

In the American system of judicial federalism, a state court cannot deprive a defendant of rights granted by decisions of the U.S. Supreme Court. The reason is that the Fourteenth Amendment declares, "No State shall . . . deprive any person of life, liberty, or property, without due process of law." This provision gives the U.S. Supreme Court jurisdiction to rule over state cases that involve deprivations of life, liberty, or property. It would violate a person's federal rights for a state court to ignore a federal decision granting these rights. This is known as the "federal constitutional floor."

Nevertheless, because the United States is a federation and states are quasi-sovereign, state law operates independently of federal jurisdiction as long as no federal issue arises. Therefore, a state court can decide that state defendants are entitled to more or greater rights than granted by federal courts, as long as the decision is made exclusively under the state's constitution. The U.S. Supreme Court said that each state has the "sovereign right to adopt in its own Constitution individual liberties more expansive than those conferred by the Federal Constitution" (*Prune Yard Shopping Center v. Robins,* 1980). This is known as the "state constitutional ceiling."

There are several reasons why a state supreme court might interpret its constitution differently from the U. S. Supreme Court's interpretation of a Bill of Rights provision. The wording of a state's constitution might grant greater or different individual freedoms or might put them in positive rather than negative form. A state's constitutional history might show that its Framers intended to award greater liberties, or early state legislation might have more broadly defined the meaning of rights later written into a state bill of rights. Local traditions might lead to heightened definitions of state rights, or distinctive local popular attitudes might lead a state supreme court to interpret a state constitutional provision as more favorable to liberty.[46]

If a case involving an issue of constitutional criminal procedure comes to the U.S. Supreme Court from a state court, and the state court's decision grants greater rights than does federal doctrine, the Supreme Court has to decide whether the state decision was based on an interpretation of the state constitution or the U.S. Constitution. Because of the style in which judicial opinions are written, this is not always easy. To clarify the matter, the Supreme Court ruled in *Michigan v. Long* (1983) that it will not disturb a state court ruling if it is based on **adequate and independent state grounds.** The Court said that a state court could guarantee that its ruling would be based on these grounds if it included a "plain statement" in its opinion that federal cases are discussed in the state opinion only for the purpose of guidance and not as the basis of the state court's decision. In the opinion of many, the *Long* ruling created a wedge that allows prosecutors an opportunity to have a conservative U.S. Supreme Court overturn more liberal state court opinions and "reflects the Supreme Court's animosity to expansion of individual rights."[47] In *Arizona v. Evans* (1995), Justice Ruth Bader Ginsburg, joined by Justice John Paul Stevens, forcefully attacked the *Long* doctrine because experience had shown that the "plain statement" rule was not working and that it "interferes prematurely with state-court endeavors to explore different solutions to new problems facing modern society."

Political Theory

Law is not a self-referential "closed system" of rules. To be fully understood and to be legitimate, law must rest on fundamental beliefs held by the people. For example, criminal laws against murder, rape, robbery, and arson are uncontested because of the powerful underlying value that we place on life, personal autonomy, and the safe enjoyment of the home. On the other hand, laws criminalizing the recreational use of marijuana are controversial because they pit the fears of negative health effects and flouting the law against beliefs in personal autonomy in acts that do not directly harm others.

Similarly, criminal procedure law—and the rights it ensures—draws full meaning and importance from its underlying political theories and values. Individual *liberty* is the central American political philosophy.[48] It was deemed an "unalienable right" in the Declaration of Independence (1776). The Preamble to the Constitution (1789) declares that a basic purpose of government is to "secure the Blessings of Liberty to ourselves and our Posterity." To operate effectively, however, law enforcement officers must deprive people of liberty. The Framers' study of history taught them that rulers had used the state's monopoly of force to unjustly deprive people of liberty, thus leading to tyranny. Because "policing is a metaphor for state power [and] the capacity to use force is the defining characteristic of the police,"[49] the criminal justice system both protects and threatens the basis of American political life.

Many rules of criminal procedure are designed to ensure that the individual's liberty will not be violated without good cause. Most importantly, any exercise of power by executive branch officers that interferes with liberty is subject to review by the judicial branch. Searches of persons and places, including electronic eavesdropping, have to be authorized by judicial warrants, although some exceptions exist. Arrested suspects have to be brought before a magistrate within forty-eight hours to ensure that the police had probable cause for arrest. Illegal detention may be questioned by a court under a writ of habeas corpus. People who are charged with crimes are presumed to be innocent and are, for the most part, entitled to bail.

The Fourth Amendment's warrant requirement also supports the value of personal *privacy.* The Supreme Court was strongly criticized in 1928 when it held that wiretapping is not a search and does not violate Fourth Amendment rights (*Olmstead v. United States,* 1928).[50] Such an obvious invasion of privacy did not sit well with the American ethos. In 1968, Congress passed a law saying that all forms of electronic eavesdropping presumably violate Fourth Amendment rights. The law created a complex system for authorization and judicial warrants to ensure that electronic eavesdropping for legitimate law enforcement purposes was supported by probable cause.[51] Thereafter, Congress passed many laws designed to ensure liberty of personal records, in bank records and the like, but exceptions were created by the USA PATRIOT Act.[52] The most troubling are "sneak and peek" warrants that allow officers to enter private premises surreptitiously and remain for lengthy periods of time without notifying the homeowner. Such warrants have been authorized many times since 2001, and many are now used not for investigating suspected terrorists, but for investigating ordinary crimes.[53] In these troubled times, the balance of privacy and security is a critical issue.

Equality is another hard-won political value in American life that is supported by criminal procedure rules.[54] One of the most important is the rule that a criminal trial or a guilty plea is not valid unless a defendant is represented by a competent lawyer; if a person is too poor to afford a lawyer, the state must provide one (*Gideon v. Wainwright,* 1963). Depending on the circumstances, the state may also have to pay for an expert witness (*Ake v. Oklahoma,* 1985). These rules reflect the value of equal treatment before the law, which demands that both rich and poor have a fair trial. Other basic rules are that the defendant must be "confronted with the witnesses against him" and be allowed to subpoena favorable witnesses (Sixth Amendment). Earlier in English history, defendants did not have these rights in cases where the Crown was directly concerned, especially in treason trials. These hard-fought rights reflect the value that the state does not have legally superior standing in court but is equal to the defense.

Political philosophies such as liberty, privacy, and equality, dearly held in the United States and other western democracies, rest on two essential legal and political institutions: **constitutionalism** and the Rule of Law. Broadly speaking, a nation's constitution is its rules and stable arrangements for the exercise of government power. Constitutionalism is essentially the ideal that government balances the interests of all its members and is not "captured" by and used for the benefit of one faction. It has roots in Roman ideals of a state's political structure:[55] "For more than two thousand years there has been a remarkably wide and stable consensus that government ought to be carried on within publicly known and enforceable restraints."[56] The modern concept of constitutionalism includes two ideas: limited government and the Rule of Law—"that governments exist only to serve specified ends and properly function only according to specified rules."[57] Constitutionalism implies balanced government and is antithetical to absolutism or tyranny.

The Rule of Law is neither a rule nor a law, but instead a concept of political and legal theory that holds that the government and its officers are not above the law and that the government conducts its business in accord with established legal norms and procedures. In enforcing the law, the government may not exceed its legal authority. The Rule of Law stands in contrast to arbitrary rule and applies to all branches of government. The president, for example, may be subjected to a civil lawsuit while in office (*United States v. Nixon,* 1974; *Clinton v. Jones,* 1997). Legislation is declared void by courts if found to be unconstitutional, and Supreme Court justices' constitutional rulings can be reversed only by constitutional amendment or by a later Court that interprets the Constitution differently.[58]

Constitutional criminal procedure advances constitutionalism and the Rule of Law primarily when the courts prevent governmental abuses of power. Every trial conducted under due process is an example of the need for the government to attorn to the judicial branch in enforcing the law; today, the government routinely operates under the law. Civil lawsuits against police officers also manifest the Rule of Law. In our democracy, abuses by law enforcement can also be checked by legislative action and by chief executives. A good example was an executive order by President George W. Bush banning racial profiling in federal law enforcement, with certain exceptions for terrorism investigations.[59] The constitutional ban on ex post facto laws is a classic example of the Rule of Law because conviction under a retroactive law is conviction under no law at all. The same is true for vague laws (*Papachristou v. City of Jacksonville,* 1972).[60]

The courts, as guardians of constitutional liberties, play a central role in maintaining the Rule of Law and constitutionalism. But the courts cannot maintain freedom if the people are not willing to fight for their rights. To a significant degree, the Rule of Law lies in "supporting institutions, procedures, and values."[61] Traditions of liberty, real political competition between the party in power and the "loyal opposition," a spirit of tolerance, the existence of interest groups who will fight vigorously in the political realm to enforce their rights, the absence of an oligarchy (an extremely lopsided distribution of wealth), a measure of political and economic stability, a vigorous political press, a literate and aware citizenry—all play a role in maintaining the Rule of Law. In this kind of society, courts can more effectively ensure that the Rule of Law continues.

History

In several places, this text refers to English and American legal, constitutional, and political history. Legal history is more than an aid to understanding constitutional law—it is an integral part of the reasoning process used by constitutional lawyers to argue cases and by judges to justify their opinions. For example, in *Printz v. United States* (1997), the Supreme Court declared unconstitutional a section of the federal Brady Handgun Violence Prevention Act, which requires local law enforcement officers to participate in background checks of prospective handgun purchasers. Justice Antonin Scalia noted that the decision would turn in large part on the Court's exploration of legal history: "Because there is no constitutional text speaking to this precise question, the answer to the [sheriff's] challenge must be sought in historical understanding and practice, in the structure of the Constitution, and in the jurisprudence of this Court."

The historical references in the text are not included for ornamentation but to provide information essential to understanding the Court's decision. A few definitions and basic points are included here to clarify the text. References in the text to "the common law" can be confusing because the term is used as a synonym for "case law" or "judge-made law" and is also used to describe the long period in English history, from the twelfth century to the eighteenth century, when the bulk of English law was developed by the courts rather than by statutes of Parliament. The term also refers to the body of law developed in this period.

Many of the great rights essential to American freedom and enshrined in the Constitution were products of the English common law period. The concept of *due process* has its roots in the provision of Magna Carta (1215) that no free man would be deprived of life, property, or liberty but according to the law of the land. The mode of *trial by jury* emerged at that time and was the hallmark of the common law justice system. The *writ of habeas corpus,* which is protected by the Constitution, emerged in the fifteenth century. The *privilege against self-incrimination* became a standard of individual rights during the seventeenth century, a period of civil war that led to the victory of Parliament and the development of the constitutional monarchy. The use of *judicial warrants* to justify entry into homes to search for stolen goods is an English practice that became solidified into a constitutional principle at the time of the American Revolution. The colonists praised these "British liberties," and when the original thirteen colonies declared their independence, each adopted the common law of England as their model.

Additional protections that make a jury trial fair were rooted in common law developments: the right to subpoena witnesses, the right to be notified of charges, the rule against double jeopardy, the right to be confronted with accusing witnesses, the right to an impartial and local jury, and the right to have trials open to the public. The independence of the courts is critical to individual liberty. The Constitution gives federal judges life tenure and does not allow their pay to be cut specifically to ensure that judges would not be subservient to the legislative or executive branches. This concept was first developed by English statute in 1702, after the autocratic monarchy had been replaced with a balanced, constitutional system of government. Only the right to counsel in criminal cases came to be seen as essential to fair trials in America before being universally adopted in England.[62]

The creation of the Constitution in 1789 and the Bill of Rights in 1791 reflected the dominant concern of the governing class in the early Republic for the survival of the United States as a nation. The premise of those who framed, ratified, and implemented these foundational documents was that only a united nation with a strong government would survive against external rivals and internal jealousies. A strong government was created, but it was restrained by deliberately fashioned checks and balances and constitutional guarantees of liberty. These ensure that elected officials would not misuse their power. It is not an accident that the Constitution protects a free political culture by placing limits on the state's criminal justice apparatus.

The Civil War (1861–1865) was as much a constitutional as a national crisis. In the Reconstruction period following the war, the Constitution was reframed, in Lincoln's words, to shape a "new nation" that was not only "conceived in Liberty" but also "dedicated to the proposition that all men are created equal."[63] The three "Reconstruction Amendments" did this by abolishing slavery, establishing national citizenship, and guaranteeing the vote to former slaves in the Thirteenth (1865), Fourteenth (1868), and Fifteenth (1870) amendments, respectively. Section 1 of the Fourteenth Amendment is discussed frequently in the text and is a foundation of modern criminal procedure. Under it, "All persons born or naturalized in the United States, and subject to the jurisdiction thereof, are citizens of the United States and of the State wherein they reside." This overruled the Supreme Court's decision in the *Dred Scott* case (1857) that barred persons of African ancestry from obtaining U.S. citizenship. The next sentence extended three rights to citizens as against the states: the "privileges or immunities of citizens," due process, and "the equal protection of the laws." Over the next century, the Fourteenth Amendment's Due Process Clause became the vehicle used by the Supreme Court to ensure that basic liberties were extended to state residents or citizens. Note the terms of the clause: "nor shall any State deprive any person of life, liberty, or property, without due process of law." If a state deprives a citizen or resident of "due process," that person has recourse to the federal courts for protection. The process by which this occurred is fleshed out later in this chapter.

Politics

Constitutional law cannot be entirely separated from politics. Politics is often defined as a contest for "who gets what." Political goals include not only political office and tangible benefits (e.g., appropriations, contracts, favorable tax laws) but symbolic and ideological "goods" as well. The most acrimonious debates in recent American history over things like school prayer, abortion, gay rights, the war on drugs, and gun control are concerned not with tangible gains, but with complex symbols that uphold popular values. There are examples in the text that link criminal procedure and politics, including information about the appointment of justices in their biographical sketches.

From the beginning of the Republic, political calculations have been intertwined with constitutional law and the Constitution. The Constitutional Convention in 1787 did not include a bill of rights in its draft and was soundly criticized for this by "anti-federalists" who argued for the defeat of the Constitution in state-ratifying conventions in 1787 and 1788. The antifederalists had a number of motives for opposing the Constitution, but they found it convenient to use the lack of a bill of rights as a rallying point.[64]

The Fourteenth Amendment (1868) is the essential foundation for applying the Bill of Rights to the states under the incorporation doctrine. The post–Civil War Congress that framed that amendment was motivated both by high principles and by the intense and convoluted politics of Reconstruction.[65] The Supreme Court, which grappled with the question of incorporation or "nationalizing" the Bill of Rights from the 1880s to the 1960s, was not immune from consideration of the effect of such rulings on federalism and the political outcry that would result from imposing federal limitations on the local administration of justice.[66]

Beginning with the 1964 presidential election campaign, crime and criminal justice have become major national political issues. In the 1968 election campaign, candidate Richard Nixon politicized constitutional criminal procedure. He accused the U.S. Supreme Court and its famous 1966 *Miranda* ruling as being responsible for increasing crime rates and for the visible lawlessness of rioting by disaffected African Americans in inner cities and antiwar demonstrations by students on college campuses. Nixon accused the Supreme Court of having "gone too far in weakening the peace forces as against the criminal forces in this country."[67]

As president, Nixon appointed justices who were expected to take a "hard line" on criminal justice issues. Since 1970, Republican presidents have appointed twelve Supreme Court justices, and Democratic presidents have appointed only two. These appointees have generally favored the crime control model of criminal justice. Not every Supreme Court case raises major political issues, but this branch of constitutional law is often fraught with partisanship. It is impossible to entirely eliminate political considerations and influences from constitutional law. In this text, reference is frequently made to the general trend by which criminal procedure doctrines shifted from a "conservative," state-interests phase before 1960 to a "liberal" phase under the **Warren Court** (1953–1969), then back to a more conservative phase under the **Burger Court** (1969–1986) and the **Rehnquist Court** (1986–2005). Keep in mind that characterizing an era, a Court, or a justice as "conservative" or "liberal" is always a matter of generalization. This overly simplified historic pattern (conservative to liberal to conservative) is traced in subsequent chapters in the development of search and seizure, the right to counsel, confessions, and lineups. Keeping these historic shifts in mind will help the student understand the otherwise bewildering twists and turns in constitutional criminal procedure.

Race and Racism

The link between criminal procedure and the long and troubled history and politics of the search for civil rights by African Americans, subjects that seem unrelated, deserves special mention. The foundation of modern criminal procedure—the Fourteenth Amendment—was ratified in 1868 as part of the post–Civil War Reconstruction to guarantee basic civil and political rights for freedmen.[68] The promise of equality faded and died in the late nineteenth century with the rise of "Jim Crow" segregation, economic oppression, and the political exclusion of African Americans.[69] This oppression was enforced by the criminal justice system in the South, which tolerated vigilantism and Ku Klux Klan terrorism. Violent opposition to the civil rights movement in the 1950s and 1960s made it clear to the Supreme Court that the racial equality required by the Constitution and epitomized by *Brown v. Board of Education* (1954) was threatened by a "lawless" criminal justice system.[70]

This understanding links three of the great themes, or "agenda items," of the Warren Court. In a lecture delivered six years after he retired from the Supreme Court, Arthur J. Goldberg outlined these themes:

> To me, the major accomplishments of the Court during the fifteen years in which Earl Warren was Chief Justice were a translation of our society's proclaimed belief in racial equality into some measure of legal reality, the beginning of a profound change in the mechanics of our political democracy and the revolution in criminal justice, both state and federal.[71]

It is easy to read criminal procedure cases and miss the link between racial segregation, the misapportionment of legislative districts, and the violation of defendant's rights in criminal cases. The cases themselves often avoid explicitly mentioning the fact that the defendant is African American (as in *Terry v. Ohio,* 1968). In addition, legal segregation is now a relic of the past, and legislative apportionment issues are more complex today.

The extension of formal rights, however, has not ended the troubling mix of skewed criminal justice policies and racial inequality. In the decades since the civil rights revolution and the Warren Court era, advances for large numbers of African Americans and other minorities have been matched with the stubborn perpetuation of low-paying employment, weak schools, inadequate social services, and substantial disenfranchisement of poor inner-city minorities. Much has changed since the days when legal segregation, overt racism, and terroristic law enforcement kept minorities from the polls.[72] Nevertheless, sober arguments have been made that the "war on drugs" has been responsible for the incarceration of disproportionate numbers of minorities and that this, in turn, has critically undermined the voting power of African American communities.[73] The intertwining of race, crime, and the law is beyond the scope of this text,[74] but it forms an important historic and contemporary context for criminal procedure.

Judicial Biography

This text includes biographical sketches of most Supreme Court justices who served since the beginning of the twentieth century to demonstrate that law is a human product. Supreme Court decisions are not the mechanical application of preexisting legal rules to fact patterns. Every Supreme Court decision concerns important issues of legal or constitutional policy that influence the policies and behaviors of the two million people who operate the criminal justice system.

The reality of judicial policy making is complicated because Supreme Court justices carefully consider every case they decide to review, and their decisions are not perfectly predictable. On the other hand, most justices develop patterns of decisions that allow them to be classified. In criminal procedure, some justices are associated with the Crime Control Model and are called "conservative" justices. Others more in tune with the Due Process Model are labeled "liberal" justices. Justices whose decisions do not fall consistently on one side or the other are called "moderate" or "swing" justices. This spectrum is filled out by identifying some justices as "moderate conservatives" or "moderate liberals."[75] The Appendix to this text includes a table titled "Summary Information about Selected Supreme Court Justices" that lists the positions of individual justices.

In general, liberal justices tend to decide in favor of defendants and tend to support the individual's liberty over the power of the state. Conservative justices tend to decide in favor of the prosecution and thus lean toward the state's authority over individuals. Nevertheless, all of the justices appreciate the need to maintain an effective criminal justice system with proactive policing and vigorous prosecution. Likewise, each justice adheres to the values of individual liberties and rights specified in the Constitution. In short, the justices struggle with the tension between liberty and order that lies at the heart of constitutional criminal procedure. The fact that they often differ about the results of specific cases reflects the tendency of people to differ ideologically.

Judicial biography is important because the justices' predilections are the result of their total experiences: their early socialization, education, and professional experience and the formation of their philosophies about public issues. In addition, some justices are especially influential because of the quality of their judicial opinions. **Judicial craftsmanship** is displayed in opinions that express a wealth of legal scholarship, a depth of judicial wisdom, and an ability to reach readers through powerful or memorable phrases. One aspect of judicial craftsmanship is the ability to write an opinion that gives clear guidance to judges, lawyers, government officers, and individuals who rely on the Court's rulings. Well-crafted opinions have the greatest potential to shape the body of law and to leave a lasting legal legacy.

Finally, justices have differed in their views toward *judicial activism* and *judicial restraint*. Conservative justices who opposed the application of the Bill of Rights to the states in the 1960s accused the liberal justices of violating judicial restraint and "making law." Today, many conservative decisions are quite "activist." In reality, the Supreme Court cannot help but "make law," however it decides a case.

Human Rights

Although this text focuses on U.S. law, it is worth noting that the constitutional liberties of American criminal procedure are **human rights** under international law. Human rights law grew rapidly after the horrors of World War II and the disclosures of Nazi crimes during the Nuremberg War Crimes Trials.[76] A landmark development in establishing human rights as an essential concern of legitimate governments was the adoption of the Universal Declaration of Human Rights (UDHR) in 1948 by the United Nations.[77]

Rights are claims created by law and enforced by courts. Human rights are a special class of rights held by a person simply by virtue of being human. They are moral rights of the highest order, grounded in the equal moral dignity of each person, that can and should be made legally binding in national, regional, or international law.[78] With this in mind, it is noteworthy that many of the rights of constitutional criminal procedure are specified as human rights under the UDHR.[79]

These include such provisions of the Sixth Amendment as the rights to a speedy and public trial, to subpoena and examine witnesses, and to a lawyer. Due process rights such as notice of charges, the presumption of innocence, and the right to be present at one's trial are also counted as human rights. An independent and impartial judge is a human right, an element of justice enshrined in the lifetime tenure provision of Article III of the U.S. Constitution.

The UDHR lists other criminal procedure rights that are essential to a civilized society. For example, Article 5 states that "No one shall be subjected to torture or to cruel, inhuman or degrading treatment or punishment," which is borrowed from and elaborates on the Eighth Amendment prohibition on cruel and unusual punishment. Article 9 states that "no one shall be subjected to arbitrary arrest, detention or exile," a right that is in essence part of the Fourth Amendment. One right not included as a human right is trial by jury, which is unique to the common law system and is not typically used in other civilized nations.[80]

While it is gratifying to know that many American constitutional rights are recognized as human rights by the world community, this text is not the place to cover the growth of human rights in international charters, the development of regional and international courts of justice, or the difficulties in enforcing human rights around the globe.[81] These rights appeal to a sense of justice that transcends local cultures. They are central to other rights because democratic politics and human dignity cannot exist when a government's police power can crush all opposition. A criminal justice system that adheres to human rights principles of criminal procedure ensures a democratic form of government bound by restraint and decency, which, in turn, helps ensure its legitimacy.[82] In this light, it is a matter of concern that the Bush administration has condoned torture in the campaign against terrorism, a matter briefly discussed in Chapter 7.

Law and Society

This text focuses primarily on the legal content and analysis of criminal procedure, but placing it in a "law and society" context helps students better understand the legal rules. Each subsequent chapter concludes with a section exploring the relationship between law and contemporary society. These "Law in Society" sections examine social forces that changed legal doctrines (e.g., concerns over domestic violence), social science findings that illuminate weaknesses in legal doctrine (e.g., research on the exclusionary rule), or the fairness of the actual practice of criminal justice personnel in light of the ideals of constitutional criminal procedure (e.g., racial profiling, prosecutorial misconduct, and police perjury).

The "Law in Society" sections that highlight abuses of constitutional rights do not mean that such abuses are the norm and are not meant to condemn the entire criminal justice system. The great majority of police officers, prosecutors, defense attorneys, and judges act professionally, competently, and within the law. Complacency, however, is never a wise attitude when considering liberties, and abuses in the system must be studied if they are to be corrected. Lon Fuller, in his classic study of the Rule of Law, notes that the greatest way in which law fails is by a lack of congruence between the law as written and the law as practiced.[83] It is too much to expect perfection; but too great a gap between professed constitutional liberties and actual practice will breed cynicism and demoralization and may bring about the collapse of our system, as Justice Louis Brandeis warned in his 1928 dissent in *Olmstead v. United States.* (See the biographical sketch of Justice Brandeis for the quotation.)

INCORPORATION OF THE BILL OF RIGHTS

Under the incorporation doctrine, most rights in the Bill of Rights apply not only to the federal government but to state legislatures, courts, and executive branch officers, including local police officers. (References to "state" officials in this text includes state and local officers, as distinguished from federal officers.) The term *incorporation* indicates that the mechanism by which specific Bill of Rights provisions (e.g., the Fourth Amendment) apply to state officers is by application of the provision through the Due Process Clause of the Fourteenth Amendment. To use an awkward metaphor, it is as if the Due Process Clause were a "container" into which Bill of Rights provisions are poured.

At the outset of the Republic, under the government structure established by the Constitution, the Bill of Rights was held to *not* apply to the states. When the Fourteenth Amendment was ratified in 1868, some proponents in Congress believed that establishing the "dual citizenship" of Americans (as state and U.S. citizens) meant that the Bill of Rights would protect citizens against unconstitutional actions by local and state officials. This, however, did not occur and indeed was resisted by the Supreme Court for a century. When most of the criminal procedure provisions of the Bill of Rights were finally incorporated in the 1960s by the liberal Warren Court, its decisions generated an intense political debate. This debate, part of a larger contest over the meaning of the Constitution in such areas as abortion, affirmative action, flag burning and free speech, voting rights, property rights, and the like, polarized constitutional law to a greater extent than had been the case since the days of the struggle over the constitutionality of President Franklin D. Roosevelt's New Deal legislation in the 1930s. After 1972, the composition of the Court became far more conservative. Although the Burger and Rehnquist courts did not dismantle incorporation, they did whittle down the extent to which provisions of the Bill of Rights protect individuals in a host of rulings that are the main subject of this text.

This section explores the process by which the Supreme Court resisted incorporation. The major reason for resistance was the tug of federalism—the belief that the federal courts should not interfere in state matters. When incorporation occurred in the 1960s, it indicated that the nation had become more unified about the rights of its citizens, a result that was set in motion by the Civil War and its legal and constitutional outcome. It is worth noting that the full context of criminal procedure, reviewed in the previous section, came into play in the process of incorporation.[84]

Before the Civil War

Before the Civil War, the Supreme Court held that the Bill of Rights applied only to the federal government and not to the states, despite the fact that the Constitution itself does apply to the states. Article I, section 10, for example, prohibits the states from many actions. Nevertheless, in Chief Justice John Marshall's last constitutional opinion, *Barron v. Baltimore* (1833), the Supreme Court held that the Bill of Rights did not apply to the states. Barron's waterfront land was taken by Baltimore for public use. He felt Maryland did not pay him enough money and sued in federal court, arguing that the state violated his right to just compensation under the Fifth Amendment. The Supreme Court rejected his claim, saying that Barron simply had no case in the federal courts under the Bill of Rights, primarily because the Framers had intended the Bill of Rights to restrict only the federal government, not state or local governments:

> The Constitution was ordained and established by the people of the United States for themselves, for their government, and not for the Government of the individual States. Each State established a Constitution for itself, and, in that Constitution, provided such limitations and restrictions on the powers of its particular government as its judgment dictated. (*Barron v. Baltimore,* 1833)

Although not all Americans accepted the *Barron* ruling, it was the law of the land, and there was no way to change it without amending the Constitution.[85]

The Growth of Federal Judicial Power

At the founding of the nation, most observers—and even some Supreme Court justices—felt that the Supreme Court would play a small role in the governing of the nation. Under the Court's third chief justice, John Marshall, the Court became a powerful institution. Because the Court *is* a powerful institution, its modern rulings on criminal procedure, including the incorporation of rights, the right to counsel, confessions, search and seizure, and other topics, help to shape our national policy on fundamental rights.

The Court's authority rests on three major powers that, while not explicitly conferred in the text of the Constitution, are implicit in constitutional history and were confirmed in authoritative decisions authored by Chief Justice Marshall. The first is the power of **judicial review**—that is, the power to declare acts of Congress unconstitutional when they conflict with the Court's interpretation of the Constitution. This power was asserted in *Marbury v. Madison* (1803):

> Certainly all those who have framed written constitutions contemplate them as forming the fundamental and paramount law of the nation, and consequently the theory of every such government must be, that an act of the legislature, repugnant to the Constitution, is void. . . .
>
> It is emphatically the province and duty of the judicial department to say what the law is. Those who apply the rule to particular cases, must of necessity expound and interpret that rule. If two laws conflict with each other, the courts must decide on the operation of each. . . . (*Marbury v. Madison,* 1803)

Marbury continues to be controversial, but there is no questioning the judicial review power of the U.S. Supreme Court.[86]

The Court's second great power is its ability to declare a state ruling, statute, or constitutional provision void because it conflicts with the U.S. Constitution. This may seem axiomatic under the Supremacy Clause (U.S. Const. art. VI, cl. 2). Nevertheless, the Court's power was directly challenged by the Supreme Court of Virginia at a time when the large states were very powerful and the reach of the federal government's authority was not entirely spelled out. In *Fletcher v. Peck* (1810), the Court ruled a state law unconstitutional because it conflicted with the Contract Clause (U.S. Const. art. I, § 10), which prohibits a state from "impairing the Obligation of Contracts." *Fletcher*'s constitutional significance lay in Marshall's opinion, which

> declared categorically that the states could not be viewed as a single, unconnected sovereign power, on whom no other restrictions are imposed than those found in its own constitution. On the contrary, it is a member of the Union, and "that Union has a constitution the supremacy of which all acknowledge, and which imposes limits to the legislatures of the several states, which none claim a right to pass."[87]

The third great power of the Supreme Court is to take jurisdiction over any state case that interprets federal law, including the Constitution, whether in a civil or in a criminal case, so as to have the final say. The Virginia Supreme Court again tried to shield its rulings over the application of federal laws in Virginia from federal Supreme Court review. In *Martin v. Hunter's Lessee* (1816) and *Cohens v. Virginia* (1821), the U.S. Supreme Court held that the Virginia Supreme Court could not hold federal civil and criminal statutes unconstitutional.

Together, these cases helped establish the United States as a "real country" and not a loose federation of fully sovereign states. They confirmed the Supreme Court's authority as the final arbiter of cases arising under the Constitution. They made state governments and state courts responsible to act under the Constitution to uphold national law. Under Chief Justice Marshall, the Court became a legitimate wielder of power because "the Justices were able to elevate their decisions above the plane of partisan politics, to transform political issues into legal ones, and thereby to increase the political power of the Court."[88] This power, established in the early Republic, allowed the Court to play a central role in the fight to apply the Bill of Rights to the states a century and a half later.

The *Dred Scott* Case and the Fourteenth Amendment

The infamous *Dred Scott* case, *Scott v. Sandford* (1857), ruled that the "Missouri Compromise" of 1820, which drew an East-West line between free states to the north and slave states to the south, was unconstitutional. In the course of its ruling, it also held that whether or not a state granted freedom and even state citizenship to Americans of African descent, such persons could not be U.S. citizens. This case inflamed political passions and probably hastened the Civil War. The ruling, part of the nation's constitutional law, could not be eradicated by simple legislation. The Thirteenth Amendment (1866), abolishing slavery, did not entirely clarify the civil status of ex-slaves; they were "free," but were they citizens invested with political as well as social and economic rights? The first sentence of the Fourteenth Amendment was designed to overrule *Scott v. Sandford:* "All persons born or naturalized in the United States and subject to the jurisdiction thereof, are citizens of the United States and of the State wherein they reside."

Having established national citizenship in all state citizens, the Fourteenth Amendment went on to confer three rights that national citizens could assert against the states: "the privileges or immunities of citizens of the United States," due process of law, and the "equal protection of the laws." These were vague and open-ended provisions. Did the Framers intend the amendment to "incorporate" the Bill of Rights into the privileges of national citizenship and overrule *Barron v. Baltimore* (1833), as the first sentence of the amendment had overturned *Dred Scott* (1857)? Statements by the amendment's leading proponents, Representative John A. Bingham and Senator Jacob M. Howard, made in the House and Senate during the debate concerning the Fourteenth Amendment, supported this intent. Nevertheless, for a century this interpretation was refused.[89] An early sign in the opposite direction, however, was found in the *Slaughterhouse Cases* (1873). By declaring that common employment like butchering is not a privilege and immunity of federal citizenship and thus beyond the protection of federal courts, the Supreme Court permanently made the Privileges or Immunities Clause a dead letter.[90] Could the Bill of Rights be applied to the states through the Due Process Clause?

The Anti-incorporation Cases, 1884–1908

The *Slaughterhouse Cases* aborted the idea that the Privileges or Immunities Clause would be used to inaugurate **total incorporation** of the Bill of Rights. In a series of criminal appeals brought before the Supreme Court from state convictions, lawyers argued that specific provisions of the Bill of Rights of the U.S. Constitution should be held to apply to the states under the Due Process Clause of the Fourteenth Amendment. The Supreme Court consistently refused to adopt this position in each of these cases from 1884 to 1908, with one exception.

In these cases, Justice John M. Harlan was the lone voice whose dissents consistently argued for the application of the Bill of Rights to the states. He contributed to the debate by ending the focus on the Framers' original intent and asserting the idea that due process was a fundamental right whose lineage went back to Magna Carta (1215). He argued that a state could not pretend to have a civilized system of government under constitutional requirements if it were allowed to violate the fundamental due process rights of its citizens.

In *Hurtado v. California* (1884), the first of these cases, a defendant convicted of murder argued that the use of a prosecutor's information to indict him, instead of a grand jury's decision to indict, as required in federal prosecutions under the Fifth Amendment, was unconstitutional. The majority of justices held that using an information to bring formal charges against the defendant did not violate his Fourteenth Amendment due process rights. Justice Harlan's dissenting opinion reviewed centuries of common law history to argue that common law institutions, including the grand jury, were essential to the political rights cherished by Americans. The majority opinion agreed with this concept as a general matter but concluded that the grand jury was not a guarantee of liberty and therefore not a component of due process. Note the language used by the majority:

> In the Fourteenth Amendment, by parity of reason, it refers to that law of the land in each State, which derives its authority from the inherent and reserved powers of the State, exerted *within the limits of those fundamental principles of liberty and justice which lie at the base of all our civil and political institutions.* . . . (*Hurtado* at 121, emphasis added)

This phrasing in effect adopted what came to be called the **fundamental rights test,** which became the ultimate criterion of incorporation and gained clarity as it was applied in specific cases. It meant, in theory, that the Supreme Court would not uphold any state procedure of criminal justice. Laws or government practices that are blatantly arbitrary or discriminatory would violate due process, even though established by the democratic process, for they would constitute the "despotism of the many, of the majority."[91] To the *Hurtado* majority, an information issued by an elected prosecutor was not unfair and did not undermine "fundamental principles of liberty and justice which lie at the base of all our civil and political institutions." In short, the grand jury is not a "fundamental" right. This is still the law.

Following *Hurtado,* the Court refused to incorporate a variety of other rights, finding that none of them were fundamental rights essential to the civil and political liberty of Americans. One case held that a state eight-person felony jury did not violate due process although federal felony juries had to be composed of twelve, the traditional common law number, under Article III and the Sixth Amendment (*Maxwell v. Dow,* 1900). The last major nonincorporation case of this era, *Twining v. New Jersey* (1908), held that the Fifth Amendment privilege against self-incrimination was not incorporated into the Fourteenth Amendment. The state trial judge informed members of the jury that when deciding guilt or innocence they could take into consideration a defendant's refusal to testify in his own behalf. In federal courts, an instruction like this from a judge violated a defendant's Fifth Amendment absolute right to remain silent at trial. Although jurors are likely to wonder why the defendant did not take the stand, they are instructed that the defendant has an absolute right to not testify under the Fifth Amendment. But if the judge adds that they can still take the defendant's silence into account, the jury will be prone to take such statement as a green light to presume that the defendant has something to hide.

The only case that came close to an incorporation was *Chicago, Burlington and Quincy Railroad Company v. Chicago* (1897). The Court ruled that compensation paid by Illinois for some land taken from a railroad company for street improvements was inadequate and a violation of federal due process standards under the Fourteenth Amendment.

This case did not mention or overrule *Barron v. Baltimore* (1833). Holding that the Due Process Clause required the states to grant just compensation, the Court seemed to "incorporate" the Fifth Amendment's Just Compensation Clause. A double standard clearly applied. Property rights were deemed so fundamental to the American polity that state violations of the Just Compensation Clause violated the constitutional rights of property owners. Liberty rights, however, were not offended by state rules of criminal procedure that afforded criminal defendants fewer protections than did federal rules under the Bill of Rights.

Federalism was an underlying reason for the reluctance to apply the Bill of Rights to the states. The Court made clear it was protecting states' rights, warning that incorporation "diminishes the authority of the State, so necessary to the perpetuity of our dual form of government, and changes its relation to its people and to the Union" (*Twining*, p. 92). Perhaps the Court also feared that the federal judiciary, few in number and hampered by the jurisdictional limits of the time, did not have the capacity to enforce civil rights on recalcitrant states. In the final analysis, it was just too big a change in the federal–state relationship for the majority of Supreme Court justices to accept.

Nevertheless, the language and reasoning of the cases denying incorporation opened the door to "selective" incorporation in the 1960s by accepting Justice Harlan's fundamental-rights analysis. If a later Court viewed provisions of the Bill of Rights as fundamental, the state would be obligated to abide by them and by the Supreme Court's interpretation of these rights.

The next two steps in the story of incorporation helped pave the way, although neither step directly involved incorporation. These steps were the adoption of the due process approach and the incorporation of First Amendment rights.

The Adoption of the Due Process Approach

In this text, the **due process approach** is defined as a ruling by the U.S. Supreme Court that an action of a state criminal justice officer violates the Due Process Clause of the Fourteenth Amendment but does not violate a specific provision of the Bill of Rights, even if there is a parallel between the action held unconstitutional under due process and a specific Bill of Rights provision.

In 1923, the Supreme Court held, for the first time in a criminal appeal from a state, that state court procedures violated a defendant's Fourteenth Amendment due process rights. Five African Americans were sentenced to death after a murder trial that, although perfect in form, was dominated by a bloodthirsty Arkansas lynch mob just outside the courthouse, screaming for death (*Moore v. Dempsey,* 1923).[92] A similar case had come before the Court in 1915, the notorious *Leo Frank* case in which an Atlanta mob's anti-Semitic chants and threats of lynching (later carried out) could be heard by the jury.[93] The Supreme Court in *Frank v. Mangum* (1915) held that a state prisoner could not use a federal writ of habeas corpus to challenge "mere errors" in his trial. Justice Oliver Wendell Holmes Jr. strenuously dissented in *Frank,* arguing, "Mob law does not become due process of law by securing the assent of a terrorized jury. We are not speaking of mere disorder, or mere irregularities in procedure, but of a case where the processes of justice are actually subverted." Despite the hideous injustices surrounding Leo Frank's trial, the majority of the Court could see no violation of due process.

In the next eight years, four members of the Court retired and were replaced, setting the stage for a different decision. Justice Holmes, now writing for the Court's majority, held that federal habeas corpus applied:

> It certainly is true that mere mistakes of law in the course of a trial are not to be corrected in that way. But if the case is that the whole proceeding is a mask—that counsel, jury and judge were swept to the fatal end by an irresistible wave of public passion, and that the State Courts failed to correct the wrong—neither perfection in the machinery for correction nor the possibility that the trial court and counsel saw no other way of avoiding an immediate outbreak of the mob can prevent this Court from securing to the petitioners their constitutional rights. (*Moore v. Dempsey,* p. 91)

The effect of *Moore v. Dempsey* was that a federal district judge could upset the verdict of a local jury, which had been upheld by a state supreme court, if the federal judge found that the conviction violated the defendant's Fourteenth Amendment right to not be deprived of life, liberty, or property without due process of law. This was a revolutionary change in practice and in judicial attitude, even if it fit the text and logic of the Fourteenth Amendment. *Moore v. Dempsey* breached the wall of federal judicial noninterference in state criminal justice. In the next fifteen years, the Court would slowly begin to use this newfound authority to correct gross injustices in a handful of significant cases, typically featuring appalling examples of racism.

The first was *Powell v. Alabama* (1932), the notorious "Scottsboro Case." The Court held that due process was violated because the defendants were not allowed time to prepare a defense and, under the circumstances, were not afforded lawyers. The Scottsboro defendants were retried, found guilty, and on further appeal, the Supreme Court held that their trial was unfair because African Americans were systematically excluded from Alabama grand juries (*Norris v. Alabama,* 1935). In 1936, the Court ruled that a confession obtained by torture violated due process (*Brown v. Mississippi,* 1936). This trickle of cases became a stream in the 1940s and a river by the 1950s. The Court had, by that time, given state criminal justice a place on its annual dockets. Without the increased attention to criminal cases on the Court's growing civil rights agenda, it is unlikely that the Court would have eventually incorporated the criminal provisions of the Bill of Rights.

The Incorporation of First Amendment Civil Liberties

Before the Court again considered incorporating criminal procedure provisions in the Bill of Rights, a momentous shift occurred in American constitutional liberties. By the 1930s, the Supreme Court, for the first time, struck down state laws that violated First Amendment rights by reading them into the Fourteenth Amendment, despite the amendment's text which began, "Congress shall make no law . . ." The free speech cases arose out of (1) state "criminal syndicalism" prosecutions for advocating violence against the government, designed to suppress left-wing political parties, and (2) World War I–era laws making it criminal to advocate resistance to the military draft.

In dictum in *Gitlow v. New York* (1925), Justice Edward T. Sanford assumed that "freedom of speech and of the press . . . are among the fundamental personal rights and liberties, protected by the Due Process Clause of the Fourteenth Amendment from impairment by the States." In *Fiske v. Kansas* (1927), the Court overturned the conviction of a person who simply carried a radical labor manifesto on his person, stating that the Kansas Criminal Syndicalism Law infringed on due process but without mentioning First Amendment free speech. Finally, *Stromberg v. California* (1931) overturned a California law making it a crime to display a red flag as an emblem of opposition to organized government. Chief Justice Charles Evans Hughes's opinion ruled that First Amendment free speech was "embraced by" Fourteenth Amendment liberty; the state law therefore violated the First and the Fourteenth amendments. *Near v. Minnesota* (1931) followed, in which the Court struck down a state law that allowed a judge, acting without a jury, to stop publication of a newspaper article deemed "malicious, scandalous, and defamatory." *Near* prohibited censorship and "prior restraint" of publications and explicitly stated that the freedom of press is included in Fourteenth Amendment due process and that prior restraint strikes at the core of the First Amendment. And in January 1937, a unanimous Court ruled in *DeJonge v. Oregon* that making it a crime to participate in a peaceful political rally violated the First Amendment right of peaceful assembly via the Due Process Clause. Together, these cases clearly "incorporated" First Amendment rights.

In the First Amendment cases, the Court applied the fundamental rights test that the Court had developed during the nonincorporation era. On the next occasion in which the Court faced challenges to a state criminal prosecution under the Fifth or Sixth Amendment, the constitutional landscape was vastly different. The Court had incorporated several provisions of the First Amendment. Did the incorporation of First Amendment rights (with the free exercise of religion to soon follow) mean that the Court would be obliged to incorporate rights into the criminal procedure amendments as well?

Resistance to Incorporation and Growing Support, 1937–1959

The great weight of the anti-incorporation precedent in criminal cases still had a hold on the Court. In 1937, an important eight-to-one decision by Justice Benjamin Nathan Cardozo in *Palko v. Connecticut* held that the double jeopardy clause of the Fifth Amendment was not a fundamental right and therefore was not incorporated into Fourteenth Amendment due process. The defendant had been convicted once for the murder of a police officer during a robbery and sentenced to life imprisonment. Under existing state law, the prosecution appealed on the ground of trial errors. On retrial, Palko was again found guilty and sentenced to death. He argued to the Supreme Court that a retrial after an appeal by the prosecutor violated the double jeopardy guarantee. Because the first jury had implicitly acquitted him of first-degree murder, he argued that the retrial on that charge was double jeopardy.[94] The Court held that the Fifth Amendment double jeopardy guarantee did not apply against the states, despite the fact that a federal prosecution would violate double jeopardy on the facts of this case.

Why were First Amendment rights incorporated but not Fifth Amendment rights? Justice Cardozo drew a distinction between fundamental rights and formal rights. Freedoms of speech and press were "so rooted in the traditions and conscience of our people as to be ranked as fundamental" and thus included in due process liberty, he wrote. Criminal procedure rights were merely "formal" and not a part of due process liberty. To be fundamental, a right had to be essential to justice and to the American system of political liberty. The First Amendment cases blocked the operation of state laws out of the "belief that neither liberty nor justice would exist if [these rights] were sacrificed. . . . This is true, for illustration, of freedom of thought, and speech. Of that freedom one may say that it is the matrix, the indispensable condition, of nearly every other form of freedom" (*Palko v. Connecticut*, pp. 326–27).

First Amendment rights are fundamental, then, because political freedom rests on the free exchange of political ideas and the ability of citizens to address the government in protest. On the other hand, to Cardozo the criminal procedure provisions in the Bill of Rights were not "of the very essence of a scheme of ordered liberty." He indicated that many democracies had criminal procedure rules that did not afford procedures such as trial by jury, and that Palko's case was not the same as the state trying him many times to get a conviction. The *Palko* doctrine held sway for a quarter of a century before the Court began to incorporate most of the criminal procedure rights in the Bill of Rights into the Fourteenth Amendment Due Process Clause.

Justice Hugo Black's dissenting opinion in *Adamson v. California* (1947) marked a turning point that eventually led to incorporation. The case dealt with the same issue as *Twining v. New Jersey* (1908)—that is, whether a judge's comment on a defendant's failure to testify violated his Fifth Amendment rights as incorporated by the Due Process Clause. Again the Court held that it did not. A defendant in Adamson's position, with a prior criminal record, faced a dilemma: If he testified, the prosecutor could bring out the existence of prior convictions to impeach his testimony. If he did not testify, the prosecutor could not introduce his prior convictions. If Adamson had been tried in federal court, the judge would not have been allowed to comment. Applying the Bill of Rights to the states would make the administration of justice in the United States more uniform and would afford greater constitutional protection to individuals.

The majority opinion essentially rested upon precedent. Justice Felix Frankfurter wrote a strong concurring opinion. He was a political liberal but also a judicial conservative and a supporter of **judicial restraint;** his concurrence made him the champion of the Court's anti-incorporation faction. He challenged Justice Black's "total incorporation" idea by stressing that the Court could employ the due process approach to overturn atrocious state action. Justice Black's opinion, based on solid research, powerfully supported the position that the original intent of the Framers of the Fourteenth Amendment was to incorporate the Bill of Rights. This argument placed incorporation of the Bill of Rights on the "constitutional agenda," as three other liberal justices, Justices William O. Douglas, Frank Murphy, and Wiley Blount Rutledge, agreed that the Bill of Rights should be incorporated. With four votes in favor, the chance that incorporation would become the law of the land was in reach of realization.

Justice Black, as much a "constitutional fundamentalist" as a liberal, argued for "total incorporation" in his *Adamson* dissent. There are at least two problems with a Supreme Court decision in one case to apply all of the twenty-six provisions of the Bill of Rights to the states via the Fourteenth Amendment. The first is that no case can come before the Court raising such an issue. A defendant's case gets to the Court by arguing that a *specific* right has been violated. Second, a case that incorporates a provision of the Bill of Rights involves an intense study of the history and jurisprudence of the right and of its impact on criminal justice practice. To do this for each of the twenty-six rights embedded in the first eight amendments is simply beyond the Court's capacity and would violate norms of the judicial process.

Instead, the incorporation process proposed in these cases, and that indeed occurred in the 1960s, was **selective incorporation,** the decision in a single case that a *specific* right in the Bill of Rights is included in the concept of Fourteenth Amendment due process "liberty" because the particular right is fundamental to the system of "ordered liberty." Any infringement by a state undermines "those fundamental principles of liberty and justice which lie at the base of all our civil and political institutions" (*Twining v. New Jersey,* 1908).

The next incorporation case demonstrated the cleavages between Justice Black and his more liberal colleagues. Police officers in *Wolf v. Colorado* (1949) entered a doctor's office without a warrant and seized patient files. In a federal prosecution, this blatant violation of the Fourth Amendment would have invoked the exclusionary rule, established in 1914 in *Weeks v. United States,* to exclude the use of these records at trial. The issue was whether the exclusionary rule applied to the states. (This issue is covered in greater depth in Chapter 2.)

The majority held, under the *Palko* standard, that it did not. In an adroit majority opinion, Justice Cardozo held that the substance of the Fourth Amendment is a fundamental right and therefore incorporated into the Due Process Clause. However, the exclusionary rule was characterized as a remedy, and the Court declined to incorporate it. Justice Black, the champion of incorporation, concurred. As a "constitutional fundamentalist," he was stymied by the fact that the text of the Fourth Amendment does not include the exclusionary rule, and therefore it could not be applied to the states as a constitutional rule. He believed, however, that the exclusionary rule was appropriately applied to the federal courts under the Supreme Court's supervisory authority. Justices Murphy, Rutledge, and Douglas dissented; they believed that exclusion was the only real "remedy" because the police virtually never lost civil suits brought against them in state courts: A right without a remedy is not a true right.

A further division between Justice Black and the rest of the Court was seen in his growing and partial opposition to the due process approach. Justices who opposed incorporation took the position that the due process approach, initiated with *Moore v. Dempsey* (1923) and which had been used more frequently in cases examining confessions taken by local police officers, was sufficient to protect the rights of Americans against the excesses of state and local criminal justice officers. The three liberal justices who followed Justice Black's incorporation lead (Justices Douglas, Murphy, and Rutledge) nevertheless went beyond total incorporation to espouse **incorporation plus—** that is, incorporation of the Bill of Rights plus the due process approach where appropriate. Justice Black opposed the due process approach because he saw the use of discretionary power by the justices as a harbinger of judicial tyranny and a violation of the limited constitutional powers of judges to decide cases. His position was designed not only to limit state and local government, but also to limit the discretion of federal judges.

Justice Murphy, in a separate dissenting opinion in *Adamson,* stated, "Occasions may arise where a proceeding falls so far short of conforming to fundamental standards of procedure as to warrant constitutional condemnation in terms of a lack of due process despite the absence of a specific provision in the Bill of Rights."

The Court next applied the due process approach in a case that created the **"shocks the conscience" test.** In *Rochin v. California* (1952), police broke into the home of a suspected drug seller, invaded his bedroom, scuffled with him after seeing him swallow pills, and dragged him off to a hospital where he was forced to swallow an emetic to vomit up evidence. Justice Frankfurter, writing for the Court, threw out the evidence by relying on a subjective Fourteenth Amendment due process standard: "[T]he proceedings by which this conviction was obtained do more than offend some fastidious squeamishness or private sentimentalism about combating crime too energetically. This is action that shocks the conscience." These police activities "are methods too close to the rack and the screw to permit of constitutional differentiation." The phrase "shocks the conscience" created a label for the Court's due process rule in search and seizure cases: the "shocks the conscience" test. Justice Black concurred but argued instead that such acts compelled a defendant to be a witness against himself, suggesting that the Fifth Amendment prohibition against self-incrimination, which should be incorporated, applied to tangible as well as to testimonial evidence.

The *Rochin* test was criticized as too vague. What shocked the conscience of appellate judges was too capricious a standard to give guidance to police officers or trial judges. It gave the Court sweeping power to inject its likes and dislikes into the Constitution. This criticism was borne out by *Irvine v. California* (1954). Some justices were clearly shocked by FBI electronic eavesdropping of the bedroom of a married suspect for over a month. Justice Frankfurter characterized it as "repulsive." Still, the majority upheld the introduction of the wiretap evidence, did not incorporate the Fourth Amendment exclusionary rule, and limited *Rochin* to acts of physical violence.

The Court signaled its growing concern with civil liberties in search and seizure by overturning the "silver platter" doctrine in *Elkins v. United States* (1960). State police officers obtained evidence of crime by means of an illegal search and seizure of the defendant's home. The evidence was suppressed by a state court. Afterward, the state officers left the evidence (illegal telephone wiretapping equipment) in the safe-deposit box of a local bank, where federal agents obtained it and used the evidence as the basis of a federal prosecution. The Supreme Court held that the federal exclusionary rule applied even though the federal officers did not directly engage in the illegal search and seizure. This practice undermined state efforts to exclude illegally seized evidence by encouraging federal officers "tacitly to encourage state officers in the disregard of constitutionally protected freedom." Justice Potter Stewart's majority opinion was quite favorable to the exclusionary rule, signaling the coming era of incorporation.

The Due Process Revolution

By 1962, the Supreme Court's membership had changed to include five pro-incorporation liberals: Justices Black and Douglas (Roosevelt appointees), Chief Justice Earl Warren and Justice William Brennan (Eisenhower appointees), and Justice Arthur Goldberg, appointed in 1962 by President John F. Kennedy. But even before this shift, the Court opened the floodgate of incorporation cases with *Mapp v. Ohio* (1961) (reviewed in the next chapter), which held that the Fourth Amendment exclusionary rule applied to eliminate illegally seized evidence from state as well as federal trials.

After *Mapp,* virtually every year during the 1960s brought the incorporation of an additional Bill of Rights provision into Fourteenth Amendment due process. (See Table 1–1.) The Eighth Amendment Cruel and Unusual Punishment Clause was applied to the states in 1962. A state law criminalized narcotics addiction, but the Court viewed addiction as a disease and held in *Robinson v. California* (1962) that the conviction and punishment of a person for a status such as a disease were constitutionally forbidden cruel and unusual punishment. *Robinson* opened the door for the Supreme Court to consider state death penalty

TABLE 1–1	Rights Enumerated in Amendments I–VIII of the Bill of Rights		
RIGHTS ENUMERATED		**SELECTIVE INCORPORATION**	
	Date	Case	
Amendment I			
Establishment of religion	1947	*Everson v. Board of Education*	
Free exercise of religion	1940	*Cantwell v. Connecticut*	
Freedom of speech	1925	*Gitlow v. New York*	
	1927	*Fiske v. Kansas*	
	1931	*Stromberg v. California*	
Freedom of press	1931	*Near v. Minnesota*	
Freedom to peaceably assemble	1937	*DeJong v. Oregon*	
Amendment II			
Militia/right to bear arms	NI	[*Presser v. Illinois,* 1886]	
Amendment III			
No quartering soldiers	NI		
Amendment IV			
No unreasonable search and seizure	1949	*Wolf v. Colorado* (basic right)	
	1961	*Mapp v. Ohio* (exclusionary rule)	
Amendment V			
Grand jury	NI	[*Hurtado v. California,* 1884]	
No double jeopardy	1969	*Benton v. Maryland*	
Due process	NI		
No self-incrimination	1964	*Malloy v. Hogan*	
Just compensation for taking private property	1897	*Chicago, Burlington & Quincy Railroad Co. v. Chicago*	
Amendment VI			
Speedy trial	1967	*Klopfer v. North Carolina*	
Public trial	1948	*In re Oliver*	
Impartial jury	1966	*Parker v. Gladden*	
Jury trial	1968	*Duncan v. Louisiana*	
Vicinage and venue	NI	[implied in due process]	
Notice	NI	[implied in due process]	
Confrontation	1965	*Pointer v. Texas*	
Compulsory process	1967	*Washington v. Texas*	
Counsel	1963	*Gideon v. Wainwright*	
Amendment VII			
Jury trial in civil case	NI	[*Walker v. Sauvinet,* 1875]	
Amendment VIII			
No excessive bail	[implied]	[*Schilb v. Kuebel,* 1971]	
No excessive fine	NI		
No cruel or unusual punishment	1962	*Robinson v. California*	

NI, not incorporated.

cases in *Furman v. Georgia* (1972) and *Gregg v. Georgia* (1976). In 1962, however, *Robinson* did not attract much popular attention.

The next incorporation case, *Gideon v. Wainwright* (1963), was widely publicized and quite popular. It incorporated the right to counsel in an opinion authored by Justice

Black, who had argued for its incorporation in a dissent twenty-one years earlier. Over half the states provided counsel for indigent defendants by 1963. The decision appealed to the American sense of fair play: Once a defendant is haled into court, he should have the same basic "equipment" to fight his fight as does the prosecutor. Congress acted to ensure that counsel would be available for indigents in federal cases, and many local bar associations and courts willingly developed systems to provide counsel. There were no dissents in *Gideon,* although some justices argued that the decision should be based on the due process approach rather than incorporation.

The right against self-incrimination, the point of contention in *Twining v. New Jersey* (1908) and *Adamson v. California* (1947), was incorporated and *Twining* was overruled in 1964 in *Malloy v. Hogan* and *Murphy v. Waterfront Commission of New York Harbor. Malloy* was a five-to-four decision bringing the Fifth Amendment right against self-incrimination into the Fourteenth Amendment by allowing a witness to refuse to answer questions before a state investigatory body under the Fifth Amendment. *Murphy* unanimously held that a state witness was protected from self-incrimination in federal courts and a federal witness was protected from self-incrimination in state courts. The specific issue in *Adamson* (1947)—whether a judge could comment on a defendant's failure to testify in a state trial—was in effect overruled in *Griffin v. California* (1965).

Other cases incorporating Bill of Rights provisions came in quick succession: *Pointer v. Texas* (1965)—Sixth Amendment Confrontation Clause; *Parker v. Gladden* (1966)—Sixth Amendment right to an impartial jury; *Washington v. Texas* (1967)—Sixth Amendment right to subpoena witnesses under the Compulsory Process Clause; *Klopfer v. North Carolina* (1967)—Sixth Amendment right to a speedy trial; and *Benton v. Maryland* (1969)—Fifth Amendment protection against double jeopardy, overruling *Palko v. Connecticut* (1937).

The Court incorporated the Sixth Amendment right to trial by jury in *Duncan v. Louisiana* (1968). Was a jury trial required for a crime carrying a maximum penalty of two years' imprisonment? To answer this, Justice Byron White analyzed the trend of the incorporation cases and concluded that the standard of what constituted a fundamental right, worthy of incorporation into the Due Process Clause and made applicable against the state, had shifted considerably since the 1937 *Palko* case:

> Earlier the Court can be seen as having asked, when inquiring into whether some particular procedural safeguard was required of a State, if a civilized system could be imagined that would not accord the particular protection. . . . The recent cases, on the other hand, have proceeded upon the valid assumption that state criminal processes are not imaginary and theoretical schemes but *actual systems bearing virtually every characteristic of the common-law system* that has been developing contemporaneously in England and this country. The question thus is whether given *this kind of system* a particular procedure is fundamental—whether, that is, a procedure is necessary to an Anglo-American regime of ordered liberty. (*Duncan v. Louisiana,* 1968, emphasis added)

By the late 1960s, it appeared that the effect of incorporation rulings was to make state rules of constitutional criminal procedure identical to the federal rules. However, several important decisions made it clear that this was not always the case. The basic reason is that the Court did not hold that the Bill of Rights applied *directly* to the states.[95] To this extent, *Barron v. Baltimore* (1833) still had a residual effect. Incorporation meant that a state procedure that came within the general scope of a Bill of Rights provision but did not afford rights that had been granted to federal defendants under the specific provision was held to violate the Due Process Clause of the Fourteenth Amendment. The ruling then applied the interpretation that had been applied to federal defendants. But the intermediate step of incorporation—going *through* the Fourteenth Amendment—gave the Court some "wiggle room" in a few cases decided after 1970 to hold that the precise impact of the federal rule would not apply to the states.

The Sixth Amendment, for example, guarantees federal defendants a jury trial in all crimes. The Court, nevertheless, upheld state laws that eliminated jury trials for crimes punishable by six months or less of imprisonment, calling them "petty crimes." In *Baldwin v.*

New York (1970), the Court drew the line of "petty crimes" at six months and struck down a New York law that allowed the crowded New York court system to deprive defendants of a jury trial for crimes carrying penalties of up to one year of imprisonment. In a case decided the same day, *Williams v. Florida* (1970), federal and state standards for rights diverged for the first time. The Supreme Court held that the common law twelve-person jury was not constitutionally mandated by the Sixth Amendment, upholding a state felony conviction by a six-person jury.

Justice Harlan, who opposed the incorporation doctrine, noted that flexibility could have been introduced into constitutional criminal procedure by adhering to the due process case-by-case approach of *Palko, Adamson,* and *Rochin.* Now, he argued, rights guaranteed to federal defendants were being diluted in order to impose Bill of Rights protections on the states. The Court was softening the clear meaning and requirements of the Bill of Rights in federal cases.

The Court continued this trend in jury cases. State felony convictions based on less than unanimous jury verdicts were upheld in *Johnson v. Louisiana* (1972) and *Apodaca v. Oregon* (1972), creating the risk that plurality juries would be far less deliberative than unanimous juries. The Court may have felt that it went far enough with these jury cases, and in *Ballew v. Georgia* (1978), it held that a five-person jury violated the constitutional guarantee of a jury.

At present, a few rights in the First through Eighth amendments have not been incorporated into the Fourteenth Amendment. These include indictment by grand jury, no excessive bail, jury trial in civil cases, the quartering of soldiers, and the right to bear arms as part of a militia. Reflecting on the rights excluded as a result of the selective incorporation approach, a leading commentator suggests that "perhaps it is just as well that they remain unincorporated."[96]

The due process revolution nationalized criminal justice by opening the door to federal court intervention of local and state agencies and courts, making criminal procedure somewhat more uniform. The due process revolution was in sync with the Warren Court's other major agenda items: eradicating legal racial segregation, providing "one person, one vote," and protecting First Amendment rights. Together, all of these advances were designed to ensure the equal participation of all citizens in the political life of the nation. The due process revolution and the other parts of the Court's agenda generated enormous antagonism toward the Supreme Court and its liberal chief justice, Earl Warren, on the part of conservative politicians and many in law enforcement. Since 1970, the Supreme Court, with a more conservative membership under Chief Justices Warren Burger and William Rehnquist, and now Chief Justice John Roberts, has limited the expansion of pro-defendant criminal procedure rights but has not overruled incorporation. Most Americans, while having mixed views of defendants' rights, nevertheless have come to accept the nationalization of the Bill of Rights.

The Counterrevolution

With historic regularity, revolutions produce counterrevolutions. The Warren Court had severe political critics, and a reaction to its rulings began in the early 1970s. Between 1969 and 1996, twelve new justices were appointed to the Court, four by President Richard M. Nixon, one by President Gerald R. Ford, three by President Ronald Reagan, two by President George H. W. Bush, and two by President Bill Clinton. The appointment of ten new justices by conservative Republicans and two by a "new," or middle-of-the-road, Democrat definitely swung the ideological makeup of the Court to the right. This section provides an overview of the shift from liberal to more-or-less conservative rulings in the period since the due process revolution. This overview is a prelude to most of the cases analyzed in this text.

The Counterrevolution That Wasn't: The Burger Court (1969–1986). President Nixon's appointment of four justices led many to believe that the selective incorporation of the Bill of Rights would be overturned.[97] These fears were abetted by Chief Justice Burger's attack on the *Miranda* doctrine and the

Mapp exclusionary rule in his early cases.[98] The Burger Court did not, however, execute a reactionary return to the preincorporation era. Instead, it held the line against the expansion of rights. "In place of the expected counterrevolution, the Burger Court waged a prolonged and rather bloody campaign of guerilla warfare. It typically left the facade of Warren Court decisions standing while it attacked these decisions from the sides and underneath."[99] For example, the *Miranda* rule stands after more than thirty years of conservative criticism, but a "public safety" exception allows prewarning questions (*New York v. Quarles,* 1984), and a defendant may subsequently be questioned after having exercised *Miranda* rights by requesting the right to remain silent (*Michigan v. Mosley,* 1975). And although the *Mapp v. Ohio* (1961) exclusionary rule was not overruled, an exception was created that allowed the introduction of evidence based on a defective search warrant if the officer relied on it in "good faith" (*United States v. Leon,* 1984).

The Burger Court was not uniformly pro-prosecution and did extend defendants' rights on several occasions. For example, it established a warrant requirement for entry of a house to make a felony arrest (*Payton v. New York,* 1980), and it declared random automobile stops to check driver licenses to be a Fourth Amendment violation (*Delaware v. Prouse,* 1979).

One measure of the success of a Supreme Court's "agenda" over the period of a chief justice's tenure is whether the Court provides a coherent conceptual foundation for its decisions. In general, scholars have found the Burger Court to be lacking a coherent set of guiding principles by which decisions can be measured. Professor Charles Whitebread, examining the lack of doctrinal consistency, has suggested five ways in which the Burger Court approached criminal procedure cases that account for its generally conservative rulings, while not going to the point of rolling back the Warren Court's Bill of Rights incorporation revolution.

First, the Court emphasized the Crime Control Model of the criminal process and was "eager to accommodate what it perceived as legitimate needs of effective law enforcement" rather than taking an evenhanded approach.[100] Second, the Court established a **hierarchy of constitutional rights.** The Sixth Amendment rights concerned with the integrity of the trial and the truth-finding process are protected more strictly than are Fifth Amendment self-incrimination issues, which in turn are given more protection than Fourth Amendment rights concerning search and seizure. Third, this hierarchy is connected with a concern for the factual guilt or innocence of the party whose case is before the Supreme Court. Whitebread believes that this concern distorted the Supreme Court's overriding duty to develop sound and principled general rules for the guidance of the entire court system.

A fourth aspect of the Court's approach was a "jurisprudential preference for case-by-case analysis rather than announcing its decisions in criminal cases in rules."[101] Whitebread sees this as the most dangerous characteristic of the Court's approach. This attribute fails to give lower courts and police clear-cut rules by which to guide their actions. Whitebread correctly predicted a spate of future cases generated by a need to determine how the narrow distinctions established by the Court are to be applied in specific instances. Fifth, the Court fostered the "new federalism" that partially closed the door to federal courts for state defendants, thus transferring significant power over criminal procedure to the state courts. For example, the Court applied a cost-benefit analysis in *Stone v. Powell* (1976) and ruled that Fourth Amendment claims, once raised and decided in state courts, could not be heard again on federal habeas corpus when the state provided a full and fair hearing. The narrowing of federal habeas corpus jurisdiction reversed a hallmark of the Warren Court: opening the door of the federal courts to state defendants in *Fay v. Noia* (1963). The reimposition of procedural barriers indicated an attitude of wishing to return to an era when federal protection of constitutional rights was minimal.

The Counterrevolution That Was: The Rehnquist Court (1986–2005).

It now seems clear that with a few exceptions, the Supreme Court from the mid-1980s to the present has taken a far more conservative stance than the Burger Court. Mary Weddington and W. Richard Janikowski write about the "counter-revolution that is."[102]

The counterrevolution can be seen in search and seizure decisions. Although a few Rehnquist Court rulings have upheld traditional Fourth Amendment rights, these have had little practical effect on law enforcement. For example, the Court ruled that the common law "knock and announce" procedure is required by the Fourth Amendment. This ruling has little practical effect, for the "Amendment's flexible requirement of reasonableness should not be read to mandate a rigid rule of announcement that ignores countervailing law enforcement interests" (*Wilson v. Arkansas,* 1995). On the other hand, rulings that acknowledge drug courier profiles as a basis to stop individuals (*United States v. Sokolow,* 1989), that authorize "bus sweeps" for drugs (*Florida v. Bostick,* 1991), that allow searches based on anonymous telephone tips (*Alabama v. White,* 1990), that uphold the "protective sweep" of homes during an arrest (*Maryland v. Buie,* 1990), that permit "plain feel" pat-downs (*Minnesota v. Dickerson,* 1993), that license electronic eavesdropping without minimization procedures (*United States v. Ojeda Rios,* 1990), that sanction arrests in violation of international law (*United States v. Alvarez-Machain,* 1992), that treat a police chase as not being a "search and seizure" (*California v. Hodari D.,* 1991), and that favor full searches of containers in automobiles without warrants (*California v. Acevedo,* 1991) have all substantially unshackled police from serious Fourth Amendment limitations. Many see this diminution of rights as giving political support to an uncontrolled war on drugs and as condoning modern racism.

As for the highly controversial law of confessions, John Decker writes, "The Burger and Rehnquist Courts have more recently reflected a degree of apparent discomfort with the principles of *Miranda,* for the great majority of the opinions interpreting *Miranda* decided since the Warren Court period have not vigorously followed its lead."[103] For example, the use of undercover agents in a jail setting is allowed. While *Miranda* on its face prohibits custodial interrogation without Fifth Amendment warnings, the Court held that because a jailed suspect who speaks to an officer posing as a fellow inmate is not compelled, no warnings need be given (*Illinois v. Perkins,* 1990). The Court has also supported an aggressive campaign by federal prosecutors to disallow effective opposing defense attorneys (*Wheat v. United States,* 1988), claiming there would be a conflict of interest, and has allowed money paid to defense attorneys by drug defendants to be forfeited (*United States v. Monsanto,* 1989; *Caplin & Drysdale v. United States,* 1989).

More telling than specific conservative rulings is the Rehnquist Court's tampering with underlying doctrines. In *Arizona v. Fulminante* (1991), a majority overturned a long-standing precedent and ruled that a coerced confession could be deemed "harmless error." Thus if police coerce a confession and a court, in error, allows such a constitutionally invalid confession to be heard by a jury, a conviction based on the coerced confession can be upheld. The Court was explicit in directing that the central purpose of a trial is to decide questions of guilt or innocence; the introduction of unconstitutional evidence is of lesser importance. Perhaps the most dramatic example of the Rehnquist Court as an activist-conservative Court, interested more in achieving the "right" result than in upholding basic principles, is *Payne v. Tennessee* (1991), which allowed victim impact statements at death penalty hearings. What has shocked commentators is that *Payne* overruled two precedents that were only four years old and that Chief Justice Rehnquist openly stated that precedent is not important where earlier cases were decided by close votes (*Booth v. Maryland,* 1987; *South Carolina v. Gathers,* 1989). He believed "that **stare decisis** 'is not an inexorable command' but instead a 'principle of policy.' . . . *Stare decisis* principles are at their weakest point in 'constitutional cases,' he said, because correction through legislative initiative is virtually impossible."[104] He went on to say that precedent is more important in property and contract rights than in procedural and evidentiary cases. Justice Thurgood Marshall, dissenting, noted that under the majority's theory, the Court's rulings cannot be considered "impersonal reasoned judgements" and that "[p]ower, not reason, is the new currency of this Court's decisionmaking." This was a polite way of saying that the majority opinion was lawless.

Finally, the Rehnquist Court has extended the work of the Burger Court in closing the door to federal and collateral appeals. *Brecht v. Abrahamson* (1993) made it more difficult for defendants to challenge errors on habeas corpus review of constitutional error than on direct appeal. Justice Rehnquist "explained that the beyond-reasonable-doubt standard had become too costly for the government."[105] These decisions display a Court that has become hostile to the claims of defendants. What is curious, and even brilliant, is that the Court has shifted virtually every rule and underlying doctrine in favor of the state while at the same time maintaining the facade of the essential right. Thus the *Mapp* exclusionary rule exists and the *Miranda* warnings are still required, but these general rules are shot through with exceptions.

SUMMARY

Criminal procedure is a branch of constitutional law that pits public safety against the guarantee of liberty. This tension is resolved by the U.S. Supreme Court, which balances the need for public order against the need for liberty. The poles of the tension between order and liberty are also represented by the Crime Control Model, which stresses finality, and the Due Process Model, which stresses the overriding need to avoid miscarriages of justice. These orientations influence the direction of the Court's decisions.

Knowledge of the context of criminal procedure provides a better understanding of the subject than can be gleaned only by reading Supreme Court decisions. The context includes the criminal justice system. The Supreme Court helps to make rules for the criminal justice system and for the people who enforce the rules. As a human process, the way criminal justice works in practice does not always accord with the dictates of the law.

The context of criminal procedure includes an understanding of the law and legal rules as the creation of different bodies and people, including legislatures, courts, and chief executives, who are organized hierarchically according to legitimate legal and constitutional authority. Statutes or actions of executive officers are illegal if they conflict with rules of constitutional law. Substantive law creates rights and obligations; procedural law directs officers, lawyers, and judges about how to proceed in carrying out their functions; and remedial law determines what benefits or remedies can be won by parties who prevail in lawsuits. Criminal procedure is procedural law in that it guides the conduct of criminal justice personnel, but at the same time constitutional criminal procedure is substantive law because it creates constitutional rights of suspects and defendants.

The jurisdiction and hierarchy of the courts are a central aspect of criminal procedure. Appellate courts resolve issues of law; they do not retry the facts of a case. The U.S. Supreme Court decides only federal issues, but when it does, its rulings under the Constitution are superior to federal legislation and to state law (including state constitutions). State high courts can decide criminal procedure issues exclusively under their own state constitutions.

When they base decisions on adequate and independent state grounds, state supreme courts can grant parties a greater level of individual rights than granted by the U.S. Supreme Court under the federal Constitution.

Other contextual aspects of criminal procedure that are found in the text include history, politics, judicial biography, and human rights. The context of political theory indicates that underlying ideas such as liberty and equality give meaning to the rules of criminal procedure. They are reflected in the everyday working of criminal procedure.

The incorporation doctrine is the idea that the Bill of Rights applies as a limitation on state law and state and local officers. Before the Civil War, the Supreme Court ruled that the Bill of Rights applied only to the federal government. Under the Due Process Clause of the Fourteenth Amendment, a state cannot infringe upon the rights of a person, who is both a state and a federal citizen, to due process and equal protection. Congress and the federal courts have the power to enforce the Fourteenth Amendment. During the century after 1868, the argument was made that specific provisions of the Bill of Rights are also guarantees of due process. The Court accepted this concept in the 1960s, and in that decade incorporated most of the criminal procedure rights in the Bill of Rights, thus requiring that states abide by those rights.

The federal courts, in addition to finding that a state law or practice violated a right inherent in the Bill of Rights, may also find that a state practice violated Fourteenth Amendment due process if such a practice is fundamentally unfair, as determined by examining all of the facts and circumstances of the case.

Since the due process revolution of the 1960s, the Supreme Court has become quite conservative in its criminal procedure rulings. The Burger Court (1969–1986), in accord with the temper of the times that combined political conservatism with individualism, maintained the incorporation of rights but limited the expansion of most rights and created several exceptions. The Rehnquist Court (1986–2005) accelerated this trend.

FURTHER READING

Context

Benjamin N. Cardozo, *The Nature of the Judicial Process* (New Haven: Yale University Press, 1921).

Charles Rembar, *The Law of the Land: The Evolution of Our Legal System* (New York: Touchstone, 1981).

Bernard Schwartz, *A History of the Supreme Court* (New York: Oxford University Press, 1993).

Incorporation

Akhil Reed Amar, *The Constitution and Criminal Procedure: First Principles* (New Haven: Yale University Press, 1997).

Michael Kent Curtis, *No State Shall Abridge: The Fourteenth Amendment and the Bill of Rights* (Durham: University of North Carolina Press, 1986).

Leonard W. Levy, *Original Intent and the Framers' Constitution* (New York: Macmillan, 1988).

USEFUL WEB SITES

U.S. Supreme Court

http://www.supremecourtus.gov/

Includes PDF versions of the latest cases and information about the Supreme Court and individual justices.

Cornell Law School, Legal Information Institute (LII)

http://www.law.cornell.edu/

Another source of Supreme Court opinions. For a useful document, click on "Introduction to Basic Legal Citation."

ENDNOTES

1. U.S. Bureau of Justice Statistics, "Criminal Victimization, Summary Findings," http://www.ojp.usdoj.gov/bjs/cvictgen.htm (accessed June 23, 2006). In 2004, U.S. residents age twelve or older experienced approximately 24 million crimes, according to findings from the National Crime Victimization Survey: 18.6 million were property crimes, and 5.2 million were crimes of violence.

2. Patrick E. Tyler, "After the War: Disorder; Across Iraq, the Dark Shadow of Hussein Still Looms Large," *New York Times,* June 22, 2003; and Michael Moss and David Rohde, "Misjudgments Marred U.S. Plans for Iraqi Police," *New York Times,* May 21, 2006.

3. Susan Sachs, "After the War: Mass Executions; A Grim Graveyard Window on Hussein's Iraq," *New York Times,* June 1, 2003.

4. Herbert L. Packer, *The Limits of the Criminal Sanction* (Stanford, Calif: Stanford University Press, 1968).

5. Thomas E. Ricks, *Fiasco: The American Military Adventure in Iraq* (New York: Penguin, 2006); and Larry Diamond, *Squandered Victory: The American Occupation and the Bungled Effort to Bring Democracy to Iraq* (New York: Times Books, 2006).

6. Philip B. Heyman, *Terrorism, Freedom, and Security: Winning without War* (Cambridge, Mass.: MIT Press, 2003).

7. Magna Carta, art. 39, in C. Stephenson and F. G. Marcham, *Sources of Constitutional History* (New York: Harper and Row, 1937), 121.

8. See George C. Harris, "Book Review: Terrorism and the Constitution: Sacrificing Civil Liberties in the Name of National Security," *Cornell International Law Journal* 36 (2003): 135–50 (review of David Cole and James X. Dempsey, *Terrorism and the Constitution: Sacrificing Civil Liberties in the Name of National Security,* 2nd ed. [New York: New Press, 2002]).

9. Mark Hamblett, "Terrorism Cases Put Judges Front and Center in Terror Cases," *New York Law Journal,* July 7, 2003, 1.

10. David McCullough, *John Adams* (New York: Simon and Schuster, 2001); and James F. Simon, *What Kind of Nation? Thomas Jefferson, John Marshall, and the Epic Struggle to Create a United States* (New York: Simon and Schuster, 2002).

11. Mark E. Neely Jr., *The Fate of Liberty: Abraham Lincoln and Civil Liberties* (New York: Oxford University Press, 1991).

12. Richard Pollenberg, *Fighting Faiths: The Abrams Case, the Supreme Court, and Free Speech* (New York: Viking, 1987).

13. Roberta Strauss Feuerlicht, *America's Reign of Terror: World War I, the Red Scare, and the Palmer Raids* (New York: Random House, 1971).

14. Peter H. Irons, *Justice at War* (New York: Oxford University Press, 1983); and *Korematsu v. United States* (1944).

15. Victor S. Navasky, *Kennedy Justice* (New York: Atheneum, 1971).

16. Alan F. Westin, *The Anatomy of a Constitutional Law Case: Youngstown Sheet and Tube Co. v. Sawyer: The Steel Seizure Decision* (New York: Macmillan, 1958).

17. Stanley I. Kutler, *The American Inquisition: Justice and Injustice in the Cold War* (New York: Hill and Wang, 1982); Frank Donner, *Protectors of Privilege: Red Squads and Police Repression in Urban America* (Berkeley: University of California Press, 1990); David Wise, *The American Police State* (New York: Random House, 1976); and James MacGregor Burns and Stewart Burns, *A People's Charter: The Pursuit of Rights in America* (New York: Alfred Knopf, 1991).

18. M. Zalman, "The Federal Anti-Riot Act and Political Crime: The Need for Criminal Law Theory," *Villanova Law Review* 20 (1975): 897–937; and Stanley I. Kutler, *The Wars of Watergate* (New York: Knopf, 1990).

19. H. D. S. Greenwood, "The Reality in Iraq," *Boston Globe,* September 12, 2006.

20. Scott Shane, "Terrorism Experts Say Focus on Al Qaeda Misses a Broader Threat," *New York Times,* August 13, 2006.

21. National Commission on Terrorist Attacks upon the United States, *The 9/11 Commission Report,* authorized ed. (New York: Norton, n.d.), 48–53.

22. Ricks, *Fiasco,* 250–51, 264–67, 418–21.

23. McClatchy-Tribune News Service, editorials on failed terror plot: *Monitor* (McAllen, Texas), August 11, 2006; Alan Cowell and Dexter Filkins, "Terror Plot Foiled; Airports Quickly Clamp Down," *New York Times,* August 11, 2006.

24. The Department of Justice's Terrorism Task Forces: Evaluation and Inspections Report I-2005-007 (Office of the Inspector General, June 2005), http://www.usdoj.gov/oig/reports/plus/e0507/index.htm (accessed September 17, 2006).

25. Jonathan Rauch, "Comment: Unwinding Bush," *The Atlantic,* October 2006 (emphasis added).

26. *United States v. Rabinowitz,* 339 U.S. 56, 69 (1950) (Frankfurter, J., dissenting).

27. James Goodman, *Stories of Scottsboro* (New York: Pantheon, 1994); Anthony Lewis, *Gideon's Trumpet* (New York: Vintage Books, 1964); and James Neff, *The Wrong Man: The Final Verdict on the Dr. Sam Sheppard Murder Case* (New York: Random House, 2001).

28. Paul Averich, *The Haymarket Tragedy* (Princeton, N.J.: Princeton University Press, 1984); and Felix Frankfurter, *The Case of Sacco and Vanzetti* (Boston: Little, Brown, 1927).

29. The Innocence Project, http://www.innocenceproject.org/ (accessed January 11, 2007).

30. Samuel R. Gross et al., "Exonerations in the United States, 1989 through 2003," *Journal of Criminal Law and Criminology* 95 (2005): 523–60.

31. Jim Dwyer, Barry Scheck, and Peter Neufeld, *Actual Innocence* (New York: New American Library, 2003); and *Arizona v. Youngblood* (1988).

32. Michael E. Kleinert, "Note: Improving the Quality of Justice: The Innocence Protection Act of 2004 Ensures Post-conviction DNA Testing, Better Legal Representation, and Increased Compensation for the Wrongfully Imprisoned," *Brandeis Law Journal* 44 (2006): 491–508.

33. Barton L. Ingraham, *The Structure of Criminal Procedure: Laws and Practice of France, the Soviet Union, China, and the United States* (New York: Greenwood Press, 1987), 22–25.

34. Bureau of Justice Statistics, *The Growth of Appeals, 1973–83 Trends* (Washington, D.C.: Bureau of Justice Statistics, 1985).

35. Stanley Kinyon, *Introduction to Law Study and Law Examination in a Nutshell* (St. Paul: West, 1971), 8–17.

36. Congress has power to make war (art. I, § 8, cl. 8), raise an army and maintain a navy (art. I, § 8, cl. 9 and 10), punish piracy on the high seas (art. I, § 8, cl. 10), and organize militias, allowing some state authority (art. I, § 8, cl. 16). The president is commander in chief of the armed forces (art. II, § 2, cl. 1).

37. Postal (art. I, § 8, cl. 7); commerce (art. I, § 8, cl. 3); equal privileges and immunities (art. IV, § 2, cl. 1); full faith and credit (art. IV, § 1); extradition (art. IV, § 2, cl. 2); and territories (art. IV, § 3, cl. 2). No new state can be carved out of an existing state or by combining states without the consent of both state legislatures and Congress (art. IV, § 3, cl. 1).

38. U.S. Const. art. IV, § 4 (republican form of government); and Abraham Lincoln, *The Gettysburg Address* (1863) (Hay Draft), Library of Congress Web site: http://www.loc.gov/exhibits/gadd/gatr2.html (accessed August 3, 2003).

39. U.S. Const. art. I, § 9, cl. 3 and 8; § 10, cl. 1.

40. John S. Baker Jr., "State Police Powers and the Federalization of Local Crime," *Temple Law Review* 72 (1999): 673–713.

41. The original thirteen states agreed to be bound by relevant portions of the Constitution, and new states may be admitted to the Union only under art. IV, § 3, and under laws passed under the authority of that section. In *Printz v. U.S.* (1997), the Supreme Court held that Congress could not require local sheriffs to enforce the background check portions of the Brady Handgun Violence Prevention Act and the portion of the Brady Bill requiring such action was held to be unconstitutional.

42. U.S. Const. art. VI, cl. 3.

43. A federal court can hear state law issues under Article III's diversity jurisdiction (the parties reside in

different states) or under "pendent jurisdiction" in which the court hears a case with federal and state issues. Federal courts decide the state law issues in accord with state precedents. The Supreme Court has no jurisdiction to decide a case based exclusively on state grounds, so it cannot take appeals in such cases from lower federal courts.

44. Bernard Schwartz, *A History of the Supreme Court* (New York: Oxford University Press, 1993), 43–45.

45. Helen E. Veit, Kenneth R. Bowling, and Charlene Bangs Bickford, eds., *Creating the Bill of Rights: The Documentary Record from the First Federal Congress* (Baltimore: Johns Hopkins University Press, 1991), 83–84.

46. See the opinion of New Jersey Supreme Court Justice Handler in *State v. Hunt* (1982).

47. Kermit L. Hall, ed., *The Oxford Companion to the Supreme Court of the United States* (New York: Oxford University Press, 1992), 545.

48. Michael Kammen, *Spheres of Liberty: Changing Perceptions of Liberty in American Culture* (Madison: University of Wisconsin Press, 1986).

49. Candace McCoy, "The Cop's World: Modern Policing and the Difficulty of Legitimizing the Use of Force," *Human Rights Quarterly* 8 (1986): 270–93.

50. Walter F. Murphy, *Wiretapping on Trial: A Case Study in the Judicial Process* (New York: Random House, 1967).

51. Yale Kamisar et al., *Modern Criminal Procedure,* 10th ed. (St. Paul: West Group, 2002), 348–87.

52. Patricia Mell, "Big Brother at the Door: Balancing National Security with Privacy under the USA PATRIOT Act," *Denver University Law Review* 80 (2002): 374–427.

53. Nathan H. Seltzer, "Still Sneaking and Peeking," *Criminal Law Bulletin* 42 (2006): 289–307.

54. J. R. Pole, *The Pursuit of Equality in American History* (Berkeley: University of California Press, 1978).

55. For a readable account of Rome's greatest exponent of constitutionalism and the decline of that ideal, see Anthony Everitt, *Cicero: The Life and Times of Rome's Greatest Politician* (New York: Random House, 2003).

56. Glenn Tinder, *Political Thinking: The Perennial Questions,* 4th ed. (Boston: Little, Brown, 1986), 117.

57. Gordon J. Schochet, "Constitutionalism, Liberalism, and the Study of Politics," in J. Roland Pennock and John W. Chapman, eds., *Constitutionalism* (New York: New York University Press, 1979), 1.

58. Compare Raoul Berger, *Government by Judiciary* (Cambridge, Mass.: Harvard University Press, 1977), with R. Dworkin, "Political Judges and the Rule of Law," in *A Matter of Principle* (Cambridge, Mass.: Harvard University Press, 1985), 9–32.

59. Eric Lichtblau, "Bush Issues Racial Profiling Ban but Exempts Security Inquiries," *New York Times,* June 18, 2003.

60. Marvin Zalman et al., "Michigan's Assisted Suicide Three Ring Circus," *Ohio Northern University Law Review* 23 (1997): 863–968.

61. Jerome Hall, *General Principles of Criminal Law,* 2nd ed. (Indianapolis: Bobbs-Merrill, 1961), 27.

62. Charles Rembar, *The Law of the Land: The Evolution of Our Legal System* (New York: Touchstone, 1981).

63. Abraham Lincoln, Gettysburg Address (Hay Draft), Library of Congress Web site: http://www.loc.gov/exhibits/gadd/gatr2.html (accessed August 3, 2003).

64. Leonard W. Levy, *Original Intent and the Framers' Constitution* (New York: Macmillan, 1988), 137–73.

65. Eric Foner, *Reconstruction: America's Unfinished Revolution, 1863–1877* (New York: Harper and Row, 1988), 251–61.

66. Michael Kent Curtis, *No State Shall Abridge: The Fourteenth Amendment and the Bill of Rights* (Durham, N.C.: Duke University Press, 1986).

67. Fred P. Graham, *The Due Process Revolution: The Warren Court's Impact on Criminal Law* (New York: Hayden, 1970), 15. Also see Louis M. Kohlmeier Jr., *"God Save This Honorable Court!"* (New York: Charles Scribner's Sons, 1972), 79; and Willard M. Oliver, *The Law and Order Presidency* (Upper Saddle River, N.J.: Prentice-Hall, 2003), 70–76.

68. Earl M. Maltz, *Civil Rights, The Constitution, and Congress, 1863–1869* (Lawrence: University of Kansas Press, 1990); and William E. Nelson, *The Fourteenth Amendment: From Political Principle to Judicial Doctrine* (Cambridge, Mass.: Harvard University Press, 1998).

69. August Meier and Elliott Rudwick, *From Plantation to Ghetto,* 3rd ed. (New York: Hill and Wang, 1976).

70. Richard Kluger, *Simple Justice* (New York: Andre Deutsch, 1977), 748–78.

71. Arthur J. Goldberg, *Equal Justice: The Warren Era of the Supreme Court* (New York: Farrar, Straus, and Giroux, 1971), 5–6.

72. Richard C. Cortner, *A Mob Intent on Death: The NAACP and the Arkansas Riot Case* (Middletown, Conn.: Wesleyan University Press, 1988); and James Goodman, *Stories of Scottsboro* (New York: Pantheon, 1994).

73. Michael Tonry, *Malign Neglect—Race, Crime and Punishment in America* (New York: Oxford University Press, 1995); and Jamie Fellner and Marc Mauer, *Losing the Vote: The Impact of Felony Disenfranchisement Laws in the United States* (Washington, D.C. and New York: Sentencing Project; Human Rights Watch, 1998).

74. The story has been ably told by Randall Kennedy, *Race, Crime and the Law* (New York: Pantheon, 1997).

75. Marvin Zalman and Elsa Shartsis, "A Roadblock Too Far? Justice O'Connor's Left Turn on the Fourth," *Journal of Contemporary Criminal Justice* 19 (2003): 182–204.

76. Ann Tusa and John Tusa, *The Nuremberg Trials* (New York: McGraw-Hill, 1983); and Telford Taylor, *The Anatomy of the Nuremberg Trials* (Boston: Little, Brown, 1992).

77. Mary Ann Glendon, *A World Made New: Eleanor Roosevelt and the Universal Declaration of Human Rights* (New York: Random House, 2001).

78. Jack Donnelly, *Universal Human Rights in Theory and Practice* (Ithaca, N.Y.: Cornell University Press, 1989), 9–14; and John Humphrey, *No Distant Millennium: The International Law of Human Rights* (Paris: UNESCO, 1989), 20–21.

79. One author simply uses "human rights" as a term for constitutional rights: Michael J. Perry, *The Constitution, The Courts, and Human Rights* (New Haven, Conn.: Yale University Press, 1982).

80. See Richard J. Terrill, *World Criminal Justice Systems: A Survey,* 5th ed. (Cincinnati: Anderson, 2003); and Bron McKillop, "Anatomy of a French Murder Case," *American Journal of Comparative Law* 45 (1997): 527–83. Some nations use juries, but they do not have the same power of juries in the United States to render verdicts without the direct supervision and vote of judges. For recent exceptions, see Stephen C. Thaman, "Europe's New Jury Systems: The Cases of Spain and Russia," *Law and Contemporary Problems* 62 (1999): 233–59.

81. See M. Cherif Bassiouni, ed., *The Protection of Human Rights in the Administration of Criminal Justice: A Compendium of United Nations Norms and Standards* (Irvington-on-Hudson, N.Y.: Transnational, 1994). Reports such as Amnesty International, *Amnesty International Report 2006: The State of the World's Human Rights* (2006), information on the status of human rights at a given point in time.

82. "Of course, procedural justice must contribute to the common goal of all governments, which is to further the freedom of each member of society and to secure the liberty of all. . . . Thus, criminal investigations and proceedings full of blind revenge and abhorrent to the spirit of the law are detested in western democratic societies." Wilfried Bottke, "'Rule of Law' or 'Due Process' as a Common Feature of Criminal Process in Western Democratic Societies," *University of Pittsburgh Law Review* 51 (1990): 419–61, 439.

83. Lon Fuller, *The Morality of Law,* rev. ed. (New Haven, Conn.: Yale University Press, 1969).

84. For a readable review of the scholarship on incorporation, see Henry J. Abraham, *Freedom and the Court: Civil Rights and Civil Liberties in the United States,* 4th ed. (New York: Oxford University Press, 1982), 28–91.

85. Akhil Reed Amar, *The Bill of Rights: Creation and Reconstruction* (New Haven, Conn.: Yale University Press, 1998), 145–62 (discussing the existence of "contrarians" who believed that the Bill of Rights should apply to state and local government).

86. See Robert Lowry Clinton, *Marbury v. Madison and Judicial Review* (Lawrence: University of Kansas Press, 1989); Wallace Mendelson, *Supreme Court Statecraft: The Rule of Law and Men* (Ames: Iowa State University Press, 1985), 207–62; and Raoul Berger, *Congress v. the Supreme Court* (New York: Bantam, 1969).

87. Bernard Schwartz, *A History of the Supreme Court* (New York: Oxford University Press, 1993), 43, citing *Fletcher v. Peck* at 136.

88. G. Edward White, *The Marshall Court and Cultural Change,* abridged ed. (New York: Oxford University Press, 1991), 197.

89. Michael Kent Curtis, *No State Shall Abridge: The Fourteenth Amendment and the Bill of Rights* (Durham, N.C.: Duke University Press, 1986), 129: The "weight of the evidence from the Thirty-ninth Congress supports the conclusion that the Fourteenth Amendment was designed to require the states to respect all guarantees of the Bill of Rights." See also Amar, *The Bill of Rights.*

90. David A. J. Richards, *Conscience and the Constitution: History, Theory, and Law of the Reconstruction Amendments* (Princeton, N.J.: Princeton University Press, 1993), makes a convincing argument for the idea of total incorporation based on the Privileges or Immunities Clause.

91. For an excellent history of the case, see Richard C. Cortner, *The Supreme Court and the Second Bill of Rights: The Fourteenth Amendment and the Nationalization of Civil Liberties* (Madison: University of Wisconsin Press, 1981), 12–24.

92. Cortner, *A Mob Intent on Death.*

93. Leonard Dinnerstein, *The Leo Frank Case* (University of Georgia Press, 1987); and Liva Baker, *The Justice from Beacon Hill* (New York: HarperCollins, 1991).

94. Cortner, *The Supreme Court and the Second Bill of Rights,* 126–39.

95. For an argument that such a theory is feasible, see Amar, *The Bill of Rights.*

96. Abraham, *Freedom and the Court,* 90.

97. See, for example, Leonard Levy, *Against the Law: The Nixon Court and Criminal Justice* (New York: Harper & Row, 1974).

98. *Bivens v. Six Unknown Named Agents* (1971); *Harris v. New York* (1971); and see M. Braswell and J. Scheb II, "Conservative Pragmatism versus Liberal Principles: Warren E. Burger on the Suppression of Evidence, 1956–86," *Creighton Law Review* 20 (1987): 789–831.

99. Albert Alschuler, "Failed Pragmatism: Reflections on the Burger Court," *Harvard Law Review* 100 (1987): 1436–56, 1442.

100. C. Whitebread, "The Burger Court's Counter-revolution in Criminal Procedure: The Recent Criminal Decisions of the United States Supreme Court," *Washburn Law Journal* 24 (1985): 471–98.

101. Whitebread, "The Burger Court's Counter-revolution," 472.

102. Mary Margaret Weddington and W. Richard Janikowski, "The Rehnquist Court: The Counter-revolution That Wasn't. Part II: The Counter-revolution That Is," *Criminal Justice Review* 21, no. 2 (1997): 231–50.

103. John F. Decker, *Revolution to the Right: Criminal Procedure Jurisprudence during the Burger-Rehnquist Court Era* (New York: Garland, 1992), 65.

104. Decker, *Revolution,* 112.

105. Weddington and Janikowski, "The Counter-revolution That Is."

Appendix to Chapter 1: How to Read and Brief Cases

Reading and understanding Supreme Court opinions is a necessary skill in a constitutional law course. A Supreme Court case is likely to include concurring and dissenting opinions, authored by individual justices, as well as the Court's majority opinion, authored by one justice who speaks for the other justices who join the majority. The opinions are not written in hypertechnical language and so can be understood with a bit of practice. The challenge for beginning students is grasping the formal and polished usage in Supreme Court opinions, sorting out the major components of the opinion, and understanding the decision and, more importantly, the reasoning by which the Court arrived at the decision. In this book, the cases presented in the Case and Comments are accompanied by side comments that act like color commentary in a sports broadcast. The comments help readers by defining technical terms, highlighting conflicts between the justices, noting interesting reasoning strategies, and asking questions about values inherent in the case. The **legal reasoning** of Supreme Court opinions is embedded in a system of precedent.

NOTES ON LEGAL PRECEDENT

An appellate decision is precedent—a rule of case law (the holding) that binds lower courts within the court's jurisdiction (e.g., the state for a state supreme court, or the circuit for a federal Court of Appeals, or the nation for the U.S. Supreme Court). A lower court decision that does not follow precedent can be reversed on appeal. Precedent is also called "authority." A supreme court will generally follow its own precedent. American law, however, is dynamic, and many Supreme Court cases overrule prior precedent. For example, the landmark case of *Gideon v. Wainwright* (1963), which held that a defendant has a right to counsel in all state felony trials, at state expense if necessary, overruled the prior precedent of *Betts v. Brady* (1942), which had stood for two decades (see Chapter 6). The overruling of prior precedent is infrequent and tends to produce policy discussions in the Court's opinions.

A more subtle process of modifying earlier case decisions is by *distinguishing* the earlier precedent. Distinguishing prior precedent requires knowing the difference between a court's **holding** and its decision. A decision is the simple rule issued by the Court. It includes the ruling as to whether the decision of the court below is affirmed or reversed, indicating which party "won" the case. The decision, or the judgment of the Court, includes the specific legal rule for which the case stands. The Court's holding is more complex. The holding is the essential legal principle that is derived from a full reading of the Court's opinion, which is based on the facts that are essential to the Court's decision.

The result of every case can be reduced to an abstract statement of a legal principle. Unfortunately, the usage to describe this is not precise. It might be called the "rule" or the "principle" or the "decision" or the "holding" of a case. But for purposes of briefing a case, the holding is the principle attached to the facts of the case.

When a court decides a case and writes an opinion, this does not fix the meaning of its rule for all time. A later case can widen or narrow the impact of a prior precedent by the way in which it follows or distinguishes the prior case. Take, for example, the decision in *Rochin v. California* (1952) that the use of evidence obtained by the police from Rochin, by entering his home without a warrant and by taking him to a hospital where he was subjected to "stomach pumping" that forced him to vomit up swallowed drugs, "shocked the conscience" and therefore violated due process. Two years later, in *Irvine v. California* (1954), the Court ruled that evidence of conversations obtained by placing a listening device in the bedroom of a married couple for twenty days did not "shock the conscience." The evidence was admitted. *Irvine* did not follow the *Rochin* decision (i.e., it was not bound by *Rochin*) because it distinguished that case on its facts, even though the *Irvine* majority excoriated the police action: "Few police measures have come to our attention that more flagrantly, deliberately, and persistently violated the fundamental principle declared by the Fourth Amendment as a restriction on the Federal Government." Nevertheless, the exclusionary rule did not apply to states at that time, under *Wolf v. Colorado* (1949). Justice Frankfurter, the author of the *Rochin* opinion, felt that the police did shock the conscience and that the evidence should be excluded under the Due Process Clause. The majority of the Court, however, disagreed and distinguished the earlier case:

> An effort is made, however, to bring this case under the sway of *Rochin v. California*. That case involved, among other things, an illegal search of the defendant's person. But it also presented an element totally lacking here—coercion . . . , applied by a physical assault upon his person to compel submission to the use of a stomach pump. This was the feature which led to a result in *Rochin* contrary to that in *Wolf*. Although *Rochin* raised the search-and-seizure question, this Court studiously avoided it and never once mentioned the *Wolf* case. Obviously, it thought that illegal search and seizure alone did not call for reversal. However obnoxious are the facts in the case before us, they do not involve coercion, violence or brutality to the person, but rather a trespass to property, plus eavesdropping. (*Irvine v. California*, 1954, Jackson, J. for the majority)

The Court could have expanded the *Rochin* rule to include, in the category of searches that shocked the conscience, those not involving physical coercion that undermined intimate privacy, but it did not.

A supreme court might modify an earlier precedent because its composition has changed and the new judges have different policy perspectives. This has clearly been the case in the realm of constitutional criminal procedure, as the U.S. Supreme Court's policy orientation shifted from conservative before the 1960s, to liberal in that decade, and back to conservative again in the following years. The process of distinguishing precedent requires great legal skill, and how well it is done is a mark of a judge's craftsmanship. Lower courts can also distinguish precedent laid down by higher courts, and in this way they help influence the development of legal doctrines.

THE COMPONENTS OF AN OPINION

Turn to *Mapp v. Ohio*, found in Chapter 2 on page 68. The first line gives the title of the case. The *v.* stands for "versus": The appeal is an adversary contest or fight between two parties seeking victory. The battle is conducted with words and with legal ideas. Mapp is the *petitioner*—the party that lost the case in the court from which the case was appealed. The state of Ohio is the *respondent*—the party that is responding to the petitioner. In state appellate cases, the terms *appellant* and *appellee* may be used instead.

The citation is in next line. It tells readers where they can find the original printed source of the excerpted case: volume 367 of the United States Reports (the official reporter published by the U.S. Government Printing Office), beginning at page 643; volume 81 of the Supreme Court Reports (published by the West Group) at page 1684 (published by the West Group, St. Paul); or volume 6 of the United States Reports, Lawyer's Edition, Second Series (published by the Lexis Corporation), beginning at page 1081. Next, the name of the justice who wrote the majority opinion appears. This opinion is usually the majority opinion, but on rare occasions where a clear majority cannot be mustered, it is the plurality opinion. Not every opinion is authored. *Per curiam* opinions are issued by the Court without indicating an author. Most *per curiam* opinions are brief, straightforward opinions in relatively minor cases. The name of the justice is followed by the body of the majority opinion, followed by concurring and dissenting opinions, listed in order of the seniority of the justices. The majority opinion ends with a line indicating the decision (e.g., "Reversed and Remanded").

The opinion is the essay written by the justice explaining the decision; it includes the holding and the reasons given by the Court for its decision. The reasoning process of an opinion may be complex or simple, eloquent or plain, convincing or vapid, based on narrow legal precedent or on grand principles. Some opinions of Supreme Court justices are classics of American political rhetoric. A majority opinion is not the author's lone effort but has been agreed to by the justices who "sign on" to it. Often, the opinion's reasoning is a matter of compromise, as each of the justices who votes for it makes suggestions as to the proper legal basis for the decision. A statement in the opinion that is not necessary for the decision or the holding is called **dictum** (or *obiter dictum*). Dicta, which can be several paragraphs in length, do not have weight as precedent.

An appellate case may include more than the court's opinion. In addition, some judges may author "concurring" opinions, in which they join the decision or "judgment" of the court but do so for different reasons. A justice who disagrees with the decision "dissents." A dissenting judge need not explain the dissent in a separate opinion, but it is now typical for dissenting justices of the U.S. Supreme Court to do so. Throughout American constitutional history, many doctrines of constitutional law have been overruled by later courts. When this has happened, the later Court often looks to a dissenting opinion in an earlier case. Thus a dissenting justice writes for the future, in the hope that in a later era his dissenting view will be adopted.

BRIEFING A CASE

A Supreme Court opinion includes some or all of the following elements:

- The prior history of the case in the lower courts.
- The facts of the case.
- The legal/constitutional issue or issues that the Court is called on to decide.
- The statute or administrative rule that is relevant to the case.
- Prior precedent.
- The "holding," or legal rule in the case as applied to the case facts.
- The reasoning that is essential to the resolution of the case.
- Other nonessential information, known as *obiter dictum.*
- The decision or judgment (e.g., reversed, affirmed, remanded).

Justices need not write these parts of the opinion in any particular order or fashion, although they are usually presented in the order listed.

Students should make notes (called **briefs**) of each case to help etch the case in memory and to provide a study aid. It is advised that you read the entire case once without taking notes, though underlining or highlighting may be helpful. After this first reading, write the title, the page number in the text, the year of the decision, the justice who authored the opinion, and enough of the prior history of the case so it is clear how the case got to the Court. This mechanical information is not the essence of the case and should be kept short.

There is no one way to brief a case—just use the method that works best for you. Use abbreviations and short phrases, as long as you will be able to understand them later when studying for a test. Once you have successfully thought through the case and understand the opinion, complete the process by writing out—*in your own words*—the most important parts of the case: the decision, the facts essential for the holding, the legal issue, the essence of the reasoning used to resolve the issues, and the holding. The Supreme Court sometimes explicitly states the issue; at other times, one has to read the entire case carefully to understand the actual issue. Once you have read the case through one time, you will know which party won the case and will have an idea of the issue and how it was resolved.

Stating the legal issue or issues in the case with precision is the key to fully comprehending the Court's reasoning. The Court often announces the issue, but at times it is only a formal issue and not the real issue. In a sense, you have to understand the entire case to accurately ascertain the issue. If you think the Court's statement of the issue is accurate, do not copy it; instead, restate it in your own words.

The Court's reasoning, which it uses to resolve the issue, may include analyses of relevant statutes or prior decisions (precedent) and appeals to history, logic, and social policy. For example, in some criminal procedure cases, the justices will to some degree argue that the convenience of the police in enforcing the law is a factor in the decision. In cases arising from state courts, the Court will often raise the issue of federalism. It can be difficult to determine which parts of the opinion contain essential reasoning and which contain statements that are not essential.

The holding of the case is a concise statement of the decision and the facts on which the decision was based. The holding is different from an abstract rule of law and from the decision. The holding is especially important because the precedent of a case is based on the holding rather than on an abstract statement of the law. The concept of the holding is related to the role of courts, for it prevents appellate courts from usurping the legislative function. A court's primary function is to decide cases, and legal rules are formulated in the context of the case's specific facts. Since only the holding is precedent, courts cannot (or should not) issue broad rules that go beyond the facts of the case. In this way, case law builds incrementally, one case after another, based on unfolding experience. A legal doctrine is ascertained by following a "line" of case holdings on an issue. Learning how to trace the development of case law into doctrines is an important legal skill. Appellate courts often try to clarify a ruling by explicitly stating in a case, "We hold . . ." Look for this when reading cases. The holding is more comprehensive than the decision of a case, but it is important to know who won. Students sometimes get so involved in the reasoning of the Court that they forget the outcome. It is useful to indicate "who won" the case in your brief.

Your brief is a practical thing. It should not be longer than a page or two. When preparing for tests, writing a brief once is a more efficient use of your time than rereading a case multiple times, as long as the brief is the product of your thinking about and understanding the case.

JUSTICES OF THE SUPREME COURT

The Precursor Justices:
Harlan I, Holmes, Brandeis, and Cardozo

The "precursor" justices of the U.S. Supreme Court include some of the greatest who have sat on the Court. They occupied seats on the Court from 1877 (Harlan) to 1939 (Brandeis) and for the most part decided cases in areas other than criminal procedure. However, each did make an important contribution to constitutional criminal procedure, especially in framing positions concerning the incorporation of the criminal justice provisions of the Bill of Rights into the Due Process Clause of the Fourteenth Amendment.

Justice John Marshall Harlan I forcefully advocated the total incorporation of the Bill of Rights into the Fourteenth Amendment, thereby anticipating the revival of this doctrine by Justice Hugo Black and its eventual adoption, albeit in its "selective" form, during the 1960s. Justices Oliver Wendell Holmes Jr. and Louis Brandeis contributed to incorporation indirectly. First, they championed First Amendment freedom of speech as fundamental to American democracy. At first dissenting against the violation of free speech by state laws, they ultimately convinced the other justices that state laws that violate free speech are unconstitutional. This amounted to the incorporation of key provisions of the First Amendment and so "breached the wall" of the nonincorporation position. This foundation for incorporation was blocked by Justice Benjamin Cardozo, who built an intellectually strong argument against incorporation in the *Palko* (1938) case. That is, he defined First Amendment rights as fundamental and therefore as a part of due process. Fourth, Fifth, and Sixth amendment rights, however, were defined as "formal" and not worthy of incorporation.

A profound principle of federalism, with enormous practical implications, was at play. Incorporation would undoubtedly bring the federal courts into the running of state criminal justice, and from the creation of the Republic criminal justice had been left entirely to the states. On this point, incorporation was also assisted by an important ruling, *Moore v. Dempsey* (1923) championed by Justice Holmes. It held that a fundamentally unfair state trial violated the Due Process Clause of the Fourteenth Amendment, which prohibits any state from depriving a person of life, liberty, or property without due process of law. Thus, well before the incorporation doctrine became a matter of constitutional law in the 1960s, the door to federal court interference into state criminal justice had been opened.

Collection of the Supreme Court of the United States. Photographer: Mathew Brady.

John M. Harlan I

Kentucky, 1833–1911

Republican

Appointed by Rutherford B. Hayes

Years of Service: 1877–1911

Life and Career.   Harlan was the son of a prominent Kentucky attorney and of a slaveholding family. An 1850 graduate of Centre College, he studied law in his father's office. After admission to the bar in 1853, he practiced law and was politically active. During the Civil War, he fought on the Union side. In 1864, he was elected attorney general of Kentucky as a Democrat and opposed the Thirteenth Amendment. He later underwent an extreme change of views, becoming a radical Republican and an ardent supporter of African American civil rights.

Harlan ran unsuccessfully for Kentucky governor in 1871 and 1875. At the 1876 Republican nominating convention, he swung the Kentucky delegation to Rutherford B. Hayes and was rewarded with a nomination to the Supreme Court the following year.

Contribution to Criminal Procedure. Harlan's great contribution to criminal procedure was to champion the incorporation of the Bill of Rights into the Fourteenth Amendment in order to make the federally guaranteed rights apply against state and local officers. He never succeeded in convincing the Court to incorporate any right other than the Just Compensation Clause of the Fifth Amendment, but his efforts paved the way for the due process revolution of the 1960s.

The importance of Harlan's dissents in *Hurtado v. California* (1884), *Twining v. New Jersey* (1908), and other cases concerning the rights of state criminal defendants under the Fifth, Sixth, and Eighth amendments was not simply that he championed incorporation. As a "great dissenter," his forceful opinions required the majority to formulate reasoned arguments in response to his position that the post–Civil War Reconstruction amendments fundamentally changed the nature of American federalism. To his mind, these rights were essential to citizenship. The majority opinions in these cases were forced to agree that if a state were to violate the fundamental rights of a citizen, this would violate due process. Although the Court at that time did not view the criminal procedure rights as fundamental, a later Supreme Court used the "fundamental rights" formulation to selectively incorporate most of the Bill of Rights.

Signature Opinion. Dissenting opinion in *Hurtado v. California* (1884). Harlan argued that the grand jury provision of the Fifth Amendment was violated by charging a person with a felony by a prosecutor's information rather than a grand jury indictment.

Assessment. In economic matters, Harlan opposed state economic regulations and favored laissez-faire pro-capitalist doctrines; on the other hand, he was a nationalist and so supported federal regulation, such as the Sherman Anti-Trust Act, against great economic concentration. He is best known for his lone dissent in *Plessy v. Furguson* (1896), arguing against the "separate but equal" interpretation of the Equal Protection Clause that upheld the state segregation laws. Harlan, arguing that the very intent of the law was to perpetuate inequality, castigated the majority for joining Louisiana in a charade. He wrote that "there is in this country no superior, dominant, ruling class of citizens. There is no caste here. Our Constitution is color-blind, and neither knows nor tolerates classes among citizens. . . . The destinies of the two races, in this country, are indissolubly linked together, and the interests of both require that the common government of all shall not permit the seeds of race hate to be planted under the sanction of the law." The Great Dissenter discerned with more accuracy than his brethren the true nature of the American polity and its ideals.

Further Reading

Tinsley E. Yarbrough, *Judicial Enigma: The First Harlan* (New York: Oxford University Press, 1995).

Oliver Wendell Holmes Jr.

Massachusetts, 1841–1935

Republican

Appointed by Theodore Roosevelt

Years of Service: 1902–1932

Collection of the Supreme Court of the United States. Photographer: Harris and Ewing.

Life and Career. Holmes was born in Boston to an established "Boston Brahmin" family, but not one of great wealth. His father was a professor of medicine at Harvard and a famous essayist. Holmes attended Harvard College in 1857. His family was devoted to the Union cause, and Holmes entered military service soon after the Civil War broke out. He was seriously wounded three times during his three years of service. He rose to the rank of captain and mustered out in the summer of 1864. His war experiences led him to see life as a struggle.

His great ambition was to become famous through his philosophical writings, but he entered the law in order to make a living. Nevertheless, while practicing law he pursued legal scholarship, editing the *American Law Review* and studying the old English cases of the common law. This resulted in a series of lectures and a book,

The Common Law (1881), a seminal work of legal scholarship that did indeed make him famous. The book delved into the tangled web of old cases and demonstrated that there were coherent utilitarian reasons for seemingly irrational rules of law. The magisterial opening phrase of *The Common Law* sounded the theme of the pathbreaking philosophy of legal realism: "The life of the law has not been logic; it has been experience. The felt necessities of the time, the prevalent moral and political theories, intuitions of public policy, avowed or unconscious, even the prejudices which judges share with their fellow men, have a good deal more to do than the syllogism in determining the rules by which men should be governed."

After a brief appointment to the Harvard law faculty, he accepted an appointment to the Massachusetts Supreme Judicial Court (1883–1902), on which he served with distinction before his appointment to the U.S. Supreme Court.

Contribution to Criminal Procedure.   The Supreme Court heard few criminal procedure cases in his era, and so Holmes had little opportunity to write extensively on these issues. He took a conservative stance in an early Eighth Amendment case, viewing the "cruel or unusual punishment" clause as static; he advanced modern Fourth Amendment law in the *Weeks* (1914) and *Silverthorne* (1920) cases by voting for and writing in favor of the exclusionary rule. His adherence to the Rule of Law was displayed in his dissent in the *Olmstead* (1928) wiretapping case. Although not as eloquent as Brandeis who also dissented in that case, he stated bluntly that the government should not be above the law, even at some cost to public safety. "We have to choose, and for my part I think it is a less evil that some criminals should escape than that the government should play an ignoble part."

Signature Opinion.   *Moore v. Dempsey* (1923). This was a monumentally important case. In *Frank v. Mangum* (1915), Holmes had failed to convince the Court that a sham trial violates due process. When the Court's composition changed, Holmes's views became law. The importance of *Moore* was that the Supreme Court for the first time reversed a state criminal decision as a violation of due process. This opened the door to federal court intrusion into state criminal procedure, making criminal justice more civilized and uniform throughout the nation.

Assessment.   Holmes was one of the great Supreme Court justices, perhaps second only to Chief Justice John Marshall (1801–1835). He also stands as one of the greatest shapers of the English and American common law in its eight hundred-year history.

Holmes's accomplishments on the Supreme Court include (along with Brandeis) the creation of modern First Amendment law enshrining free speech as a foundation of democracy, for free government is not possible unless all ideas are allowed to compete in the "marketplace of ideas."

Further Reading

Liva Baker, *The Justice from Beacon Hill: The Life and Times of Oliver Wendell Holmes* (New York: HarperCollins, 1991).

Collection of the Supreme Court of the United States. Photographer: Harris and Ewing.

Louis Dembitz Brandeis

Massachusetts, 1856–1941

Republican

Appointed by Woodrow Wilson

Years of Service: 1916–1939

Life and Career.   Brandeis was born in Louisville, Kentucky, to a German Jewish family that sided with the Union during the Civil War. He entered Harvard Law School shortly before his nineteenth birthday, supported himself as a tutor, earned the highest grades, and spent a third year at Harvard as an instructor and graduate student. Attracted by Boston's liberal and intellectual atmosphere, he entered law practice there with his classmate Samuel Warren. They built a thriving practice representing midsize businesses.

Brandeis developed a tremendous reputation as a thorough attorney whose success was built on a deep study of the law.

Brandeis became wealthy practicing law, but he gave it up to represent the interests of laborers struggling for economic security and protection of health and safety on the job. As an unpaid mediator and attorney in labor disputes, he became a renowned defender of workers' rights in the early twentieth century. In his victory before the conservative Supreme Court in *Muller v. Oregon* (1908), which upheld a state law limiting the working hours of female laundry employees, Brandeis used an innovative written argument (or "brief") consisting of ninety-six pages of social, economic, and health facts about the damaging effects of long working hours and only ten pages with the usual legal arguments. Since that time, this form of presentation has been known as a "Brandeis brief."

As a leading progressive who opposed monopolies, he drew the animosity of the propertied classes but also became a key adviser to President Woodrow Wilson, who nominated him to the Supreme Court. He was appointed after a long and acrimonious confirmation debate in the Senate based mainly on his "radicalism" but also supported to some degree by anti-Semitism.

Contribution to Criminal Procedure.   Brandeis supported the federal exclusionary rule and the extension of federal due process against the states in important cases like *Moore v. Dempsey* (1923), *Powell v. Alabama* (1932)—counsel, and *Brown v. Mississippi* (1936)—confessions.

Signature Opinion.   Dissent in *Olmstead v. United States* (1928). Federal agents violated a state criminal law against wiretapping. The issue was whether this was a search and seizure and, if so, whether the illegally seized wiretap evidence should be excluded. Brandeis's dissent is a classic statement of the Rule of Law:

> Decency, security, and liberty alike demand that government officials shall be subjected to the same rules of conduct that are commands to the citizen. In a government of laws, existence of the government will be imperiled if it fails to observe the law scrupulously. Our government is the potent, the omnipresent teacher. For good or for ill, it teaches the whole people by its example. Crime is contagious. If the government becomes a lawbreaker, it breeds contempt for law; it invites every man to become a law unto himself; it invites anarchy. To declare that in the administration of the criminal law the end justifies the means—to declare that the government may commit crimes in order to secure the conviction of a private criminal—would bring terrible retribution. Against that pernicious doctrine this court should resolutely set its face.

Assessment.   The dissents of Brandeis and Holmes in First Amendment cases ultimately persuaded the Court to hold that free speech and free press rights were so fundamental that the states could not abridge them. This incorporation of First Amendment rights helped open the door to the later incorporation of criminal procedure rights. His work in this and many other areas ranks him as one of the greatest justices.

Further Reading

Philippa Strum, *Louis D. Brandeis: Justice for the People* (New York: Schocken, 1984).

Collection of the Supreme Court of the United States. Photographer: Harris and Ewing.

Benjamin Nathan Cardozo

New York, 1870–1938

Democrat

Appointed by Herbert Hoover

Years of Service: 1932–1938

Life and Career.   Cardozo, born into a distinguished New York family of Sephardic Jews who emigrated to America in the mid-eighteenth century, was a brilliant student and a noted lawyer, in practice with his older brother for twenty years. Despite his personality (described as gentle, courteous, lonely, ascetic, and saintly) and his apparent lack of political involvement, his reputation as a practitioner led to a judicial appointment to New York's highest court, the Court of Appeals, on which he served from 1913 to 1932.

Cardozo's outstanding reputation as a person and a judge led to an unparalleled national clamor for his appointment as the most worthy replacement for Justice Holmes. Thus, despite the facts that he was nominally of the wrong political party, that two justices from New York (Harlan Fiske Stone and Charles Evans Hughes) already sat on the Court, and that a Jewish justice (Brandeis) occupied another seat, President Hoover named Cardozo to the Court.

Contribution to Criminal Procedure. Cardozo was a conservative judge in criminal matters and had opposed the exclusionary rule as a judge on the New York Court of Appeals.

Signature Opinion. *Palko v. Connecticut* (1938). The Supreme Court had from 1925 to 1933 incorporated several First Amendment rights; it seemed likely that the Court would next incorporate criminal procedure rights. Palko, found guilty of murder and sentenced to prison, was retried after the prosecutor appealed under state law, was again found guilty, and was sentenced to death. He argued that this second conviction violated the Fifth Amendment Double Jeopardy Clause, which should apply to the states via due process. Cardozo's majority opinion held that the Connecticut law did not violate due process or incorporate the Double Jeopardy Clause. This was achieved by distinguishing between "fundamental" First Amendment rights and "formal" Fifth Amendment rights:

> The line of division may seem to be wavering and broken if there is a hasty catalogue of the cases on the one side and the other. Reflection and analysis will induce a different view. There emerges the perception of a rationalizing principle which gives to discrete instances a proper order and coherence. The right to trial by jury and the immunity from prosecution except as the result of an indictment may have value and importance. Even so, they are not of the very essence of a scheme of ordered liberty. To abolish them is not to violate a 'principle of justice so rooted in the traditions and conscience of our people as to be ranked as fundamental.' . . .
>
> We reach a different plane of social and moral values when we pass to the privileges and immunities that have been taken over from the earlier articles of the Federal Bill of Rights and brought within the Fourteenth Amendment by a process of absorption. These in their origin were effective against the federal government alone. If the Fourteenth Amendment has absorbed them, the process of absorption has had its source in the belief that neither liberty nor justice would exist if they were sacrificed. . . . This is true, for illustration, of freedom of thought and speech. Of that freedom one may say that it is the matrix, the indispensable condition, of nearly every form of freedom.

The conservative *Palko* rationale retarded the advance of the incorporation doctrine for another quarter century.

Assessment. Cardozo's reputation as a great common law judge is based mainly on his work on the New York Court of Appeals. His opinions were masterpieces of judicial craft that precisely analyzed basic principles of law; his decisions were neither immobilized by precedent nor excessively experimental. His fame was enhanced by his lectures and books (especially *The Nature of the Judicial Function,* 1921), which dissected the work of the appellate judge with such penetrating candor as to add a new chapter to the philosophy of judicial realism. His Supreme Court opinions were marked by total mastery over the subject matter at hand, a graceful and fluid writing style, and a penetrating intelligence. On the Court for only five and a half terms, he mainly supported the New Deal in economic cases and had a mixed record in civil rights cases.

Further Reading

Andrew L. Kaufman, *Cardozo* (Cambridge, Mass.: Harvard University Press, 1998).

2

The Fourth Amendment and the Exclusionary Rule

CHAPTER OUTLINE

KEY TERMS

This guarantee of protection against unreasonable searches and seizures extends to the innocent and guilty alike. It marks the right of privacy as one of the unique values of our civilization and, with few exceptions, stays the hands of the police unless they have a search warrant issued by a magistrate on probable cause supported by oath or affirmation.

—Justice William O. Douglas, *McDonald v. United States,*
335 U.S. 451, 453 (1948)

A GOVERNMENT OF LAWS

In *Marbury v. Madison* (1803), Chief Justice John Marshall wrote, "The government of the United States has been emphatically termed a government of laws, and not of men. It will certainly cease to deserve this high appellation, if the laws furnish no remedy for the violation of a vested legal right." The **exclusionary rule** holds that evidence seized illegally by government officers cannot be introduced by the prosecution in a criminal trial to prove the defendant's guilt. This "remedy" for constitutional violations is controversial because it is not found in the text of the Fourth Amendment and because it actually enforces the rights of typically despised suspects and defendants. It became a firm part of constitutional law in 1914 via the Court's interpretation of the Fourth Amendment (*Weeks v. United States*). At first, it applied only to federal law enforcement because the Bill of Rights was not incorporated in that era. (See Chapter 1.)

The rule's history and controversy, reviewed in this chapter, range from constitutional theory to its impact on routine police and court action in search and seizure cases. There was little controversy surrounding the rule until the Court applied it to the states in 1961 (*Mapp v. Ohio*). The rule then became an affront to proponents of the Crime Control Model. (See Chapter 1.) Attacking the rule was a political strategy used by conservative presidents to denigrate any liberal decisions of the Supreme Court. When the balance of ideological control on the Supreme Court tipped to the conservative side in 1972, the Court began a campaign that eroded the exclusionary rule's status as a constitutional rule. The rule still exists, but it has been shot through with legal exceptions. A relentless series of Supreme Court cases, for example, has given police such extensive powers to stop, question, and search people outside the home as to undermine the idea that police cannot stop a citizen without just cause.[1] At the same time, many local courts have condoned widespread police perjury, which effectively undermines Fourth Amendment protections. (See the "Law in Society" section in Chapter 3).

Chapters 2 through 5 explore Fourth Amendment search and seizure law. The historic developments that shaped search and seizure law began with the common law ideal of the privacy of the home, which solidified into a British legal rule protecting home privacy against government invasion shortly before the framing of the U.S. Constitution (1787). Next, the Constitution's Framers guaranteed this right in the Bill of Rights (1791). At the beginning of the twentieth century, the Supreme Court developed the remedial exclusionary rule to ensure that evidence seized in violation of the Fourth Amendment's requirements would not be used in federal court to convict a person. The next major historic development in Fourth Amendment doctrine was the extension of the federal exclusionary rule to the states via the process of incorporation in *Mapp v. Ohio* (1961). Another historic doctrinal change occurred in the 1960s when the Court sought to replace the property-rights (trespass) theory of Fourth Amendment protections with the **expectation of privacy** doctrine announced in *Katz v. United States* (1967). (See Chapter 3.) During the Burger Court era, the exclusionary rule was "demoted" in status from a constitutional rule to a rule designed only to deter police illegality.

The shifts in doctrine discussed in this chapter are a case study of incorporation and the tug of federalism. They display the importance of history and politics in the development of doctrines, show the tension between liberal and conservative understandings of the law, demonstrate the power of the justices to mold rules to fit their view of proper policy, and show that constitutional law cannot be understood apart from its role in society.

THE COMMON LAW BACKGROUND

The old English saying that "a man's home is his castle" expresses a universal desire for privacy. Until 1600, English law protected against private but not government intrusion. "By 1760, however, public opinion had inverted the relative importance that it assigned to these considerations. Promiscuous searches by the *government* were now recognized as more onerous than undesired visits by private persons."[2] This change was rooted in altered social conditions and political thought, especially the emergence of the English constitutional monarchy in the eighteenth century.

Two important legal cases of the 1760s that influenced the development of the Fourth Amendment reflected this new thinking. The first, known as Paxton's Case or the Writs of Assistance Case, arose in colonial Massachusetts and was decided in 1761. The second, the Wilkes cases, was a series of civil lawsuits arising out of the political persecution of John Wilkes, a critic of King George III. These cases confirmed the hatred of "general warrants" in the colonies and the new Republic and led to the Fourth Amendment prohibition on "unreasonable searches and seizures."

Up to 1760, most English search warrants were general warrants. A **general warrant** could be issued by a judicial or nonjudicial government official who did not personally have to be aware of probable cause for a search. "Promiscuously broad warrants allowed officers to search wherever they wanted and to seize whatever they wanted, with few exceptions."[3] General warrants were described as "a sort of legal pass key to all doors that places everyone's privacy at the capricious mercy of its holder."[4] Criticism of general warrants began in the mid-seventeenth century, and public opinion came to favor specific warrants specifying the place to be searched and the items to be seized.[5] Nevertheless, most British warrants continued to be of the general kind.

A **writ of assistance** was a type of general warrant authorizing a crown official "to command the assistance" of a peace officer or a nearby person to execute the writ. The writ allowed a search for a specific purpose and was executed in the daytime. Writs of assistance were used by British officers in the colonies to enforce unpopular customs laws and were enormously unpopular. Customs officers with writs of assistance could enter warehouses and even homes to search for goods that were imported without paying the customs taxes and to collect unpaid duties. Crown impressment gangs used writs of assistance to invade private homes and public places like taverns "to kidnap able bodied men for service in the royal navy."[6] Once issued, the writ lasted for the life of the sovereign, plus six months.

After the death of George II, a customs officer in Massachusetts petitioned for a new writ of assistance. In February 1761, sixty-three leading Boston merchants challenged the legality of the application, presenting their case in the colony's high court. James Otis, a leading attorney, represented the merchants and offered a learned and passionate argument: The law authorizing the writs of assistance "is against the fundamental principles of English law" and is therefore unconstitutional and void. John Adams, a young attorney and future president of the United States, was deeply impressed by Otis's argument. In 1776, as a delegate to the Continental Congress and as a signer of the Declaration of Independence, Adams reflected that the movement for American independence began with the dispute over the writs of assistance. The Boston merchants lost their case; nevertheless, the writs continued to be unpopular and were not well enforced because of hostile attacks on revenue collectors. To generate revenue, England passed the Townshend Act (1767), authorizing high courts in each colony to issue writs of assistance to customs officers. The local Massachusetts grievance became a major source of friction between the colonies and the mother country.[7]

The Wilkes cases, argued in England, were a resounding political defeat of general warrants. They arose in 1763 after John Wilkes (1725–1797), a British agitator, journalist, and member of Parliament, published issue 45 of the *North Briton,* a newsletter sharply critical of George III and his government. The king and Parliament tried to stifle his political attacks by charging him with seditious libel, a serious political crime. An English secretary of state issued a general warrant to officers to search for the newsletter and other writings. "Crown agents enforcing the warrants had unfettered discretion to search, seize, and arrest anyone as they pleased. They ransacked printer's shops and houses, and arrested forty-nine persons, including Wilkes, his printer, publisher, and bookseller. The officers seized his private papers for incriminating evidence after a thorough search; thousands of pages and scores of books belonging to persons associated with him were also seized."[8]

The case was a major political controversy on both sides of the Atlantic Ocean. "In the colonies, 'Wilkes and Liberty' became a slogan that patriot leaders exploited in the service of American causes."[9] Wilkes and his colleagues fought back in the courts in a series of civil lawsuits charging that the general searches were illegal. The courts upheld Wilkes and his allies. In general, the cases found that the searches were not authorized by law, were excessive, and that officers of the crown could be sued. "[T]he government paid a total of about 100,000 pounds in costs and judgments," an enormous sum at the time.[10]

In the most important of these cases, ***Entick v. Carrington*** (1765),[11] Lord Camden, chief justice of the Court of Common Pleas, demolished every argument put forth by the government to support the legality of the warrants. He ruled that general warrants were not authorized by act of Parliament or by case law; that general warrants to search for papers were not like specific search warrants for stolen goods; and although the government had issued such warrants since the Glorious Revolution of 1688, that fact does not make the warrants legal "simply through long usage" or the previous silence of the courts. The court firmly rejected the blatantly political argument that the needs of the state took precedence over individual rights: "Political policy is not an argument in a court of law."[12] Lord Camden stressed that the case was of constitutional importance—it upheld the liberal "social contract" political theory, which stressed that a primary function of government is to protect the property of individuals.

Thus, just prior to the era in which American state and federal governments wrote new constitutions (1776–1791), the common law had evolved to a point where general warrants were so disfavored as to be declared illegal in some cases. A person who had been arrested under a general warrant and whose home and other property had been invaded and searched by government agents could now sue executive officers who authorized general search warrants and agents who executed the warrants, and they could recover substantial **damages** if the arrests and searches were illegal.

In sum, the common law rule—which was to have enormous influence on the development of the exclusionary rule in the United States—was that searches of private property by government officers without a warrant or based on defective warrants (such as general warrants) were illegal. The only remedy known to the common law to redress such illegality was a civil lawsuit for money damages against the officers who took part. There was no common law rule excluding the use of illegally seized evidence from a criminal trial.

THE FOURTH AMENDMENT'S STRUCTURE

The new state constitutions ratified between 1776 and 1787, when the U.S. Constitution was drafted, included prohibitions against general warrants.[13] In the first Congress, Representative James Madison included such a provision in his draft of the Bill of Rights. His draft drew heavily on the Massachusetts provision, written by John Adams, which used the novel phrase "unreasonable search and seizure." The provision that became the Fourth Amendment was ratified in 1791:

> The right of the people to be secure in their persons, houses, papers, and effects, against unreasonable searches and seizures, shall not be violated, and no Warrants shall issue, but upon probable cause, supported by Oath or affirmation, and particularly describing the place to be searched, and the persons or things to be seized. (U.S. Const. amend. IV)

The Fourth Amendment did not simply outlaw "general warrants" in specific terms, although that was its motivation. The modern interpretation, stated in many cases, is that the amendment contains two clauses: the **Reasonableness Clause** and the **Warrant Clause.** Under this construction, the ultimate test of constitutionality of any search and seizure is whether it is reasonable. Not all searches have to be authorized by a judicial warrant. If a search or arrest warrant is required, then it must meet the **particularity requirements** stated in the Warrant Clause.

Conservative and liberal justices and scholars strongly disagree about the relative importance of the Warrant Clause. Conservative jurists apply a **general-reasonableness construction** that established a **balancing test** to determine if search and seizures are proper without a warrant; this comes close to saying that search warrants are not actually required by the Fourth Amendment. This construction has gained ground in recent decades and allows the Court to give police greater leeway to search and seize without prior judicial authorization.

The more traditional **warrant-preference construction,** favored by liberal jurists, holds that warrantless searches and seizures are presumptively unreasonable. A narrow group of search warrant exceptions known as common law are allowed under this construction: entries in hot pursuit, the search of mobile vehicles, and a "search incident to arrest" (the search of a person who has just been arrested). All modern legal thinkers, whether favoring the general-reasonableness approach or the warrant-preference approach, agree on the two-clause understanding of the Fourth Amendment.[14] Indeed, until the recent findings of historians, it was generally believed that the Framers intended this two-clause construction.[15] More recent studies lead to the conclusion that the original intent of the Fourth Amendment's Framers and ratifiers was to prevent Congress from authorizing general warrants and to ban judges from issuing them—nothing more.[16] This interpretation threatens the more conservative view but is unlikely to overthrow the established two-clause interpretation.

This seemingly arcane historical debate offers a lesson on how contemporary realities, forgotten centuries later, influence constitutional interpretation. The idea that the Fourth Amendment has two discrete clauses, not easily inferred from its obscure text, is a modern invention. Pressing needs of modern law enforcement to allow a variety of warrantless arrests are so great that modern commentators have "read back" the two-clause understanding of the Fourth Amendment into their perceptions of the intent of the Framers. It seems inconceivable today that the Framers were not concerned with warrantless searches of police officers. Yet, as Professor Thomas Y. Davies notes, there were no police officers in 1791—at least not in the modern sense. Constables were few, were viewed as untrustworthy, and had no discretion to make warrantless arrests or probable cause searches in the late colonial era or at the time of the framing.[17] Like any citizen, a constable could lawfully arrest or search only if the person to be arrested did in fact commit the crime or if **contraband** was actually found. If the constable acted on suspicion or probable cause and was wrong, the constable could be sued for false imprisonment or **trespass.** Paradoxically, misconduct by an officer was seen not as official misconduct, but as personal misconduct. As a result, the government never committed a wrongful arrest or search, and officers who made arrests or conducted searches almost always did so under the authorization of a warrant. "[F]raming-era common law never permitted a warrantless officer to justify an arrest or search according to any standard as loose or flexible as 'reasonableness.' "[18] There was, consequently, no proactive policing at this time.

The needs of modern society eroded the original understanding and its tight rein on official discretion. The Supreme Court began to erect modern Fourth Amendment law in the late nineteenth and early twentieth centuries, recognizing police discretion but with the exclusionary rule at its center. Organized police departments are so actively involved in performing warrantless arrests, stops, and searches that any Court that took Fourth Amendment values seriously would inevitably attempt to provide reasonable controls. Virtually none of the hundreds of Supreme Court Fourth Amendment cases deal with issues of general warrants. Indeed, the Supreme Court seems to have authorized, even required, general warrants for administrative searches (e.g., *Camara v. Municipal Court,* 1967).

The historical debate is relevant because the Supreme Court (or at least some of its justices) purports to base its jurisdiction and the legitimacy of its decisions on being true to "the intent of the Framers." If the justices are mistaken regarding the intent of the Fourth Amendment, the body of law they have created may be in question. Worse still, the Framers' intent that constables have absolutely no authority to act "reasonably" when interfering with a person's liberty or privacy, and must instead be strictly controlled by judicial warrant, threatens the constitutionality of modern law enforcement.

Much depends on the philosophy of judging held by members of the Court. In major cases, most justices have been guided by societal needs and have not been distracted by recent historical interpretation.[19] Justices Antonin Scalia and Clarence Thomas claim that their decisions are guided by the original intent of the Framers and therefore are most likely to be swayed by Davies's "authentic" reading of the Fourth Amendment; this, however, would conflict with their conservative crime control policy orientation.

Two points are important for the student. First, some changes to Fourth Amendment doctrines may occur if the "authentic" understanding of the amendment is accepted, making it important to understand the underlying reasons for doctrines rather than simply memorizing the rules. Second, however, the large body of constitutional law is kept fairly stable by the operation of stare decisis, and it is unlikely that there will be a wholesale revolution in Fourth Amendment law. For that reason, the text presents the standard two-clause understanding of Fourth Amendment law, based primarily on the analysis of Supreme Court decisions.

DEVELOPMENT OF THE EXCLUSIONARY RULE, 1886–1921

There was no exclusionary rule at common law, and the Fourth Amendment's text does not explicitly state that illegally seized evidence must be excluded. Nevertheless, the Supreme Court established the rule by constitutional interpretation, as it has done in many other areas. Few Fourth Amendment cases were decided by the Supreme Court in the nineteenth and early twentieth centuries, but these cases were sensitive to the Fourth Amendment's civil liberty values. *Ex Parte Jackson* (1878), for example, stated in dictum that postal authorities could not open sealed letters sent through the mails without a warrant. Although in the major case of ***Boyd v. United States*** (1886) the Supreme Court did suppress the use of evidence obtained illegally by federal customs authorities, it did not establish a clear Fourth Amendment exclusionary rule.

Boyd was an odd case. There was no actual search and seizure; instead, a subpoena was issued to E. A. Boyd & Co. to turn over an invoice on cases of imported glass to determine whether proper customs taxes had been paid. Boyd challenged the subpoena, which he said would create a presumption that import duties had not been paid if he did not present the invoice. The Supreme Court agreed with Boyd, holding that the order to produce the invoice and the law authorizing the order were unconstitutional and void under the Fourth Amendment and the Fifth Amendment privilege against self-incrimination. The opinion, infused with constitutional history, created an expansive definition of a search and seizure that favored the individual over the state:

> The principles laid down in [*Entick v. Carrington*] affect the very essence of constitutional liberty and security. They reach farther than the concrete form of the case then before the court, with its adventitious circumstances; they apply to all invasions on the part of the government and its employés of the sanctity of a man's home and the privacies of life. It is not the breaking of his doors, and the rummaging of his drawers, that constitutes the essence of the offence; but it is the invasion of his indefeasible right of personal security, personal liberty and private property, where that right has never been forfeited by his conviction of some public offence,—it is the invasion of this sacred right which underlies and constitutes the

essence of Lord Camden's judgment. Breaking into a house and opening boxes and drawers are circumstances of aggravation; but any forcible and compulsory extortion of a man's own testimony or of his private papers to be used as evidence to convict him of crime or to forfeit his goods, is within the condemnation of that judgment. In this regard the Fourth and Fifth Amendments run almost into each other. (*Boyd v. United States*, 1886)

By ruling that a subpoena was the equivalent of a search and by conflating the Fourth Amendment with the Fifth Amendment's right against self-incrimination, the Court avoided establishing a clear-cut exclusionary rule that applied to search and seizures generally. Virtually none of *Boyd*'s expansive Fifth Amendment rules, by the way, are operative today (e.g., a subpoena is not a search[20]). *Boyd* is important, however, as a precursor to the Fourth Amendment exclusionary rule.

The Supreme Court moved hesitantly toward this rule. It affirmed the traditional rule in *Adams v. New York* (1904), saying that "courts do not stop to inquire as to the means by which the evidence was obtained." This holding, that illegally seized evidence may be admitted in evidence in criminal trial, while apparently maintaining that the exclusionary ruling in *Boyd* was good law, meant that the Court still felt that exclusion should be limited to cases in which some self-incrimination element was present.

This changed radically in **Weeks v. United States** (1914), which adopted a straightforward Fourth Amendment exclusionary rule not tied to the Fifth Amendment privilege against self-incrimination. Fremont Weeks was arrested by local police without a warrant at his place of work; at the same time, a U.S. marshal entered Weeks's home without a warrant and "carried away certain letters and envelopes found in the drawer of a chiffonier." Weeks's demand for the return of incriminating papers before trial was denied. He was convicted in federal court for using the mails to transport lottery tickets. The Supreme Court held that all evidence seized without warrant was in violation of the Fourth Amendment and had to be returned; it could not be used against the defendant to prove his guilt. Its language was expansive and protective of individual privacy:

> The effect of the Fourth Amendment is to put the courts of the United States and Federal officials, in the exercise of their power and authority, under limitations and restraints as to the exercise of such power and authority, and to forever secure the people, their persons, houses, papers and effects against all unreasonable searches and seizures under the guise of law. This protection reaches all alike, whether accused of crime or not, and the duty of giving to it force and effect is obligatory upon all entrusted under our Federal system with the enforcement of the laws. The tendency of those who execute the criminal laws of the country to obtain conviction by means of unlawful seizures and enforced confessions, . . . should find no sanction in the judgments of the courts which are charged at all times with the support of the Constitution and to which people of all conditions have a right to appeal for the maintenance of such fundamental rights. (*Weeks v. United States*, 1914)

The exclusionary rule was limited to federal law enforcement only. *Weeks* firmly tied the remedy of exclusion to the constitutional right, making it a part of the Constitution. A deterrence rationale was also hinted at: "If letters and private documents can . . . be seized and held and used in evidence against a citizen accused of an offense [as in this case], the protection of the Fourth Amendment declaring his right to be secure against such searches and seizures is of no value, and, so far as those thus placed are concerned, might as well be stricken from the Constitution."

The constitutional basis of the exclusionary rule was confirmed and strengthened in Justice Oliver Wendell Holmes's opinion in **Silverthorne Lumber Co. v. United States** (1920). Frederick W. Silverthorne and his father were indicted for a federal crime and arrested at home while federal agents entered their business offices without a warrant and took business documents. The district court agreed with the defendants' contention that their Fourth Amendment rights were violated and, on their demand, ordered the documents returned. Before complying, the government photographed the documents and used these copies to get a subpoena for the originals. Silverthorne refused to comply with the subpoena. The district court found that the documents had originally been seized illegally but nevertheless ordered Silverthorne to comply with the subpoena. Silverthorne refused, the company was fined, and he was ordered jailed until he turned over the original documents.

The Supreme Court reversed the lower court's judgment. In Holmes's words, to allow the government to seize evidence in violation of the Fourth Amendment, and then use the knowledge gained by that wrong to obtain the evidence "legally," "reduces the Fourth Amendment to a form of words." Therefore, "[t]he essence of a provision forbidding the acquisition of evidence in a certain way is that not merely evidence so acquired shall not be used before the Court but that it shall not be used at all." This is the crux of one exclusionary rule theory that will be addressed later in this text: The government cannot profit from its illegal action. As Professor William Heffernan notes, this "no use" rule was fully rights-based and went further than the present scope of the exclusionary rule, which allows illegally obtained evidence to be used to impeach a lying witness, in civil deportation cases, as a basis for framing grand jury questions, and in other areas.[21]

Holmes added an important exception to the exclusionary rule: "Of course this does not mean that the facts thus obtained become sacred and inaccessible. If knowledge of them is gained from an independent source they may be proved like any others, but the knowledge gained by the Government's own wrong cannot be used by it in the way proposed." These rules later became known as the **"fruits of the poisonous tree" doctrine** and the "independent source exception." The rationale is that government violation of a defendant's Fourth Amendment rights does not lead to a windfall in the guise of the dismissal of the case. The government can use other evidence to convict, if that evidence is obtained by legal means.

Gouled v. United States (1921) filled out the law on the development of the exclusionary rule. It first held that the Fourth Amendment is as much violated by a "fraudulent" entry into a home or business office as by a forcible entry. In this case, a government investigator who happened to know Gouled, a fraud suspect, pretended to make a friendly call on Gouled at his business office. While Gouled was out of the room, the investigator furtively took incriminating papers. The Court ruled that the admission of these papers violated the Fifth Amendment privilege against self-incrimination, thus continuing to conflate the Fourth and Fifth amendments when papers that communicated a person's state of mind were in question.

In this case, search warrants were issued to seize papers that were not the direct fruits of crime but were only evidence of Gouled's fraudulent conspiracy. The Court made a common law rule, known as the "mere evidence rule," part of the Fourth Amendment exclusionary rule by holding that these papers could not be admitted into evidence. The theory was that property that was not itself a part of the crime (as opposed to items like stolen goods, the document on which a fraud was based, weapons, or burglar's tools used to commit a crime) could not be seized. This rule shows that the Court saw the rights protected by the Fourth Amendment as essentially resting on the idea of trespass to property rights. The Court eventually dropped this rule in *Warden v. Hayden* (1967), one of a series of cases that shifted the conceptual basis of the Fourth Amendment from a property to a functional basis.

State Action Doctrine

A central purpose of the Constitution is to protect persons from excessive action by government officers that threaten individual liberties and the Rule of Law. (See "Political Theory" in Chapter 1.) As a result, the exclusionary rule applies only to evidence illegally seized by the government. When a private party turns over evidence to a prosecutor, courts follow the common law rule that they will not ask about the source of relevant evidence, even if the person committed a civil trespass or a burglary to obtain the incriminating evidence (*Burdeau v. McDowell,* 1921). In legal terms, the Fourth Amendment applies only when there is state action. State action exists when a private person acts as a proxy for or at the direction of the police; evidence illegally seized by a private person acting as a proxy is not admissible.

The initial seizure by a private party does not mean that a police agent can proceed without obtaining a warrant. When a private individual turns suspicious items over to police, they may subject the items to only minimal investigation before requesting a search warrant. In *Walter v. United States* (1980), a box with pornographic videos was mistakenly sent to a company, which turned it over to the FBI. Without obtaining a warrant, agents screened the films to determine their content. This screening was held to be state action, and the evidence was inadmissible because it constituted an investigation into an area of privacy. The labels on the outside of the film boxes raised probable cause of the films' content, and further search had to be authorized by a warrant. To the contrary, in *United States v. Jacobsen* (1984), Federal Express employees opened a suspiciously wrapped package, discovered white powder, and turned it over to federal Drug Enforcement Administration (DEA) agents. The agents chemically "field tested" the powder and found it to be cocaine. The action by the FedEx employees raised no issue because it was conducted by private individuals with no police support. The warrantless examination by DEA agents was proper because it was not a significant expansion of the earlier private search; thus this evidence was admissible.

The state action doctrine means that any search conducted by a government officer, not just by police officers acting for law enforcement purposes, falls under the protection of the Fourth Amendment. Searches by public school teachers, public hospital supervisors, probation officers, municipal building inspectors, Occupational Safety and Health Administration (OSHA) inspectors, federal mine-safety investigators, municipal fire department investigators, and customs agents must adhere to Fourth Amendment rules. Illegal searches by these personnel require the exclusion of evidence. This branch of search and seizure law, under which lesser standards for a valid search have been created for government personnel other than law enforcement officers, will be reviewed in Chapter 5.

Private Security Personnel.

Is a detention or search by a private security agent considered to be state action? The issue arises in federal civil lawsuits (under 42 U.S.C. § 1983, discussed later in this chapter), alleging that security personnel have violated a person's civil rights while acting "under color of state law." The Supreme Court has not decided this issue (*Flagg Bros. v. Brooks,* 1978). Lower federal courts have ruled that private police are state actors "when the state delegates a public function to a private entity."[22]

Privately employed railroad policemen who brutally beat vagrant trespassers and private security personnel at a Chicago hospital who detained a person were held liable under the federal civil rights lawsuit as "state actors." The reason is that legislation gave them the powers of regular police officers. They were known as "special police officers," were licensed by the city, underwent background checks, wore "suitable badges" issued by the superintendent of police, and conformed to police officer regulations.[23]

On the other hand, security guards at a private mall who exercised no "police powers" were held not to be state actors.[24] Similarly, a private security guard hired by a Chicago public housing agency who shot a person in the groin was not a state actor. The housing authority did have a private police force with police powers, but this guard was a contract person and not part of the private police force. Although the guard was in uniform and armed, he was assigned specifically to guard lobbies and had no authority to act outside the lobby of the assigned building.

In another case, a grandmother was arrested by security guards in a Detroit casino for taking a token worth five cents from the tray of an abandoned slot machine. She was banned from the casino and was not allowed to physically contact her friends with whom she was spending the day. In a federal civil suit against the casino, the federal district court held that the security personnel in this case acted under "the color of state law." Under Michigan law, an employer may either maintain private security guards in order to protect its property or may employ private security police. The casino's licensed private security police officer had to meet state training requirements and, when working on the employer's property, had the same authority to arrest a person without a warrant as a municipal police officer. Private guards, on the contrary, would not come under state action because they only had the same right as private business owners to protect their property and so could temporarily detain an individual clearly stealing something.[25] In this case, the officers detained the grandmother, displayed handcuffs, photographed her, obtained personal information, including her Social Security number, and ordered her banned from the casino for six months.

These cases show that some private guards were held to exercise state authority and to be subject to constitutional rules if state powers were specifically conferred by law and if the functions exercised by the security personnel are as expansive, within spatial limits, as those exercised by police officers. The enormous growth of the private security industry has led some commentators to question the general rule that arrests and searches by private security agents are not state action. They would extend the Fourth Amendment exclusionary rule to unreasonable searches and seizures committed by private security personnel.[26] For others, the issue is not clear-cut, and the state action doctrine is a poor way of ascertaining the liability of security personnel. Meanwhile, the issue has become more urgent with the expansion of the private police role in protecting the nation against terrorism.[27]

"Fruits of the Poisonous Tree" Doctrine

Silverthorne v. United States (1920) added a necessary corollary to the exclusionary rule: Evidence derived from knowledge obtained by an illegal search and seizure is not admissible. Were such **derivative evidence** admissible, police officers could violate Fourth Amendment rights with impunity and then, after the original evidence is excluded, use information gained from the illegality to get a "legal" search warrant.

The derivative evidence rule reflects the axiom that under the Fourth Amendment, justification for searches must be provided *prior to* the search. Retroactive justification turns the amendment into a sham. An example is the *per curiam* decision of **Smith v. Ohio** (1990).[28] Two plainclothes police officers, without a warrant and without probable cause or reasonable suspicion, stopped Smith exiting a convenience store carrying a brown paper grocery bag marked with the store's logo. The officers identified themselves, and Smith put the sack on the hood of his car. Smith did not answer a question about the bag's content and tried to push an officer's hand away as he opened the bag. Drug paraphernalia was found and became the basis of an arrest and conviction, which the Supreme Court later reversed. The search was not justified on any Fourth Amendment ground. There was no basis for a self-protective stop under *Terry v. Ohio* (1967), the property was not abandoned, and there was no search incident to arrest—indeed, in *Smith,* the arrest occurred after the search. The obvious point is that the police simply cannot search whatever they choose and then make a "legal" arrest or seizure if their hunch or baseless action turns up contraband. If they could, the Fourth Amendment would be worthless. The exclusionary rule thus is essential.

The "fruits of the poisonous tree" metaphor for the derivative evidence rule was penned by Justice Felix Frankfurter in *Nardone v. United States* (1939): What is excluded is not only the illegally seized evidence (the "poisonous tree"), but also other evidence *derived from* the illegally seized evidence (the "fruits"). Allowing the use of derivative evidence would create a rule "inconsistent with ethical standards and destructive of personal liberty." The Court in *Nardone* excluded not only the exact words overheard in a wiretap that violated a federal statute but also any information derived from the overheard conversations.

Silverthorne and *Nardone* recognize, however, that the exclusionary rule, including the exclusion of derivative evidence, is not a windfall to the defendant—it does not lead to an automatic dismissal of charges or to a prohibition on the use of other, properly obtained, evidence. The Supreme Court has recognized three exceptions to the derivative evidence exclusion: (1) evidence obtained from an **independent source,** (2) **inevitable discovery,** and (3) **attenuation.** One case noted that the inevitable discovery exception is an extrapolation of the independent source exception (*Murray v. United States,* 1988).

Independent Source.

The Supreme Court has allowed illegally seized evidence when the evidence was obtained in a constitutional manner that was entirely unconnected to the illegality—that is, from an independent source. In **Segura v. United States** (1984), a group of police officers illegally entered Segura's apartment and saw incriminating evidence in plain view. A search warrant was later obtained based on information developed before the illegal entry took place. The Supreme Court excluded the evidence in plain view during the illegal search but allowed use of evidence obtained under the search warrant because it was independent of the illegal entry. In **Murray v. United States** (1988), police illegally entered a warehouse and saw suspicious bales believed to contain marijuana. This illegal entry was not mentioned in an affidavit for a search warrant. Nevertheless, the Court allowed the use of evidence obtained under the warrant because it was lawfully issued on the basis of other competent evidence.

Inevitable Discovery.

Illegally seized evidence is admissible if it was inevitably discovered independently of the unconstitutional action. *Brewer v. Williams* (1977, known as *Williams I*) held that evidence of a murdered girl's body was excluded because it was discovered based on an unconstitutional interrogation (a so-called Christian burial speech; see Chapter 7). On retrial, Williams's confession was excluded, but the location of the dead girl's body was introduced into evidence. In **Nix v. Williams** (1984, known as *Williams II*), the Supreme Court held that this evidence was properly introduced because a search party was within two and a half miles of the body when it was found. Members of the search party were instructed to look into culverts (where the body was placed) and would have covered the area where the body was located. Thus the body would inevitably have been found, whether or not the defendant divulged its location to the police. The motivations of the police who improperly took the confession were irrelevant.

Attenuation.

Evidence derived from an illegal or unconstitutional source is admissible when, for some reason, the link between the initial illegality and the evidence sought to be introduced has become so weak or tenuous that the "fruits" have become "untainted." In *Nardone,* Justice Frankfurter wrote: "Sophisticated argument may prove a causal connection between information obtained through illicit wiretapping and the Government's proof. As a matter of good sense, however, such connection may have become so attenuated as to dissipate the taint."

Wong Sun v. United States (1963) explicates the attenuation doctrine. Six or seven narcotics officers illegally entered the San Francisco apartment of James Wah Toy behind his laundry shop at 6 A.M., looking for drugs. They rousted the inhabitants and questioned Toy. No drugs were found, but Toy named some people whom the agents questioned about drug dealing, including Wong Sun. The Supreme Court excluded from evidence an incriminating statement made by Toy as well as confessions and drugs obtained from a person questioned immediately after the raid on Toy's apartment because this evidence was the "tainted" fruits of the illegal entry into Toy's apartment. Wong Sun was arrested but then released; a few days later, he returned voluntarily and made an incriminating statement. The Court held that this voluntary statement was admissible because the connection between the arrest and the statement had "become so attenuated as to dissipate the taint." The test for determining whether attenuation exists is this: "whether, granting establishment of the primary illegality, the evidence to which instant objection is made has been come at by exploitation of that illegality or instead by means sufficiently distinguishable to be purged of the primary taint."

Attenuation issues arise when a "proper" confession is made after an illegal arrest. The fact that *Miranda* warnings are given does not automatically break the link between the illegal arrest and a resulting confession, nor does the passage of two hours between the illegal arrest and the confession attenuate the illegality (*Brown v. Illinois,* 1975). To make *Miranda* warnings a "cure-all" for illegal police action would encourage illegal arrests and would dilute the effectiveness of the *Miranda* exclusionary rule. Likewise, a six-hour delay between an illegal arrest and a confession, followed by a ten-minute meeting between the defendant and friends, did not attenuate the initial illegality despite three *Miranda* warnings (*Taylor v. Alabama,* 1982).

On the contrary, a confession was allowed into evidence in **New York v. Harris** (1990). Police illegally arrested Harris at his home without a warrant, read *Miranda* warnings, and obtained a confession in the house. Taken to the police station, Harris again was read his rights, signed a waiver form, and confessed. The first confession was suppressed as the fruit of an illegal police action: entry into the home without a warrant when no exigency existed (*Payton v. New York,* 1980). But the Court held the station house confession to be admissible. The Court ruled that Harris was legally in custody because an illegal arrest does not deprive the court of jurisdiction to try the suspect. Therefore "the statement, while *the product* of an arrest and being in custody, was *not the fruit* of the fact that the arrest was made in the house rather than somewhere else" (*New York v. Harris,* emphasis added). The Court did not apply attenuation analysis but rather saw the case as a straightforward example of evidence not being the "fruit," or actual result of a prior illegal police action. The 5–4 decision in *Harris* may be explained by the hostility of the majority toward the exclusionary rule. The majority, however, distinguished the facts of *Harris* from those of *Brown* and *Taylor* because in *Harris,* the police had probable cause to arrest the defendant, unlike the earlier cases. The opinion said that excluding the first confession vindicated the rule that made in-home arrests without a warrant unconstitutional, but as for allowing the second confession, "it does not follow from the emphasis on the exclusionary rule's deterrent value that 'anything which deters illegal searches is thereby commanded by the Fourth Amendment'" (*New York v. Harris,* 1990).

Determining whether the original illegality has become attenuated is not found by applying mechanical rules, but depends on whether, considering the totality of the circumstances, the questioned evidence in the case would have been discovered had not the original violation taken place. If the subsequent evidence is considered to be independent of the original "tainted" search and seizure, then it can be used against the defendant in a court of law. Thus attenuation depends on specific case facts. In **United States v. Ceccolini** (1978), a police officer, without any design to investigate gambling, discovered betting slips in the defendant's flower shop by improperly looking into an envelope with cash sticking out located behind the customer counter. Before a federal grand jury, Ceccolini denied that gambling occurred in his place of business, but he was convicted of perjury after an employee testified about illegal gambling at his shop. The Court of Appeals, ruling that the employee's statement was the fruit of the officer's original unconstitutional search, excluded the testimony. The Supreme Court reversed, finding that the link between the search and the witness's testimony had become so attenuated that the testimony could no longer be considered to be caused by the officer's unconstitutional act. The Court relied on a variety of facts: Federal officials previously had the shop under suspicion and observation; several months passed between the officer's telling the FBI about the slips and the initial questioning of the employee; the witness was in no way coerced or induced to testify, but did so for honorable motives; the betting slips were not used in the questioning of the witness; and the officer had no intent to investigate gambling. In this case, the Court also felt that the deterrent effect on police misconduct of excluding the evidence would be very limited.

THE FEDERALIZATION OF THE EXCLUSIONARY RULE, 1949–1963

The Movement to Incorporate

Shortly after *Adamson v. California* (1947), the Court considered incorporating the Fourth Amendment and its exclusionary rule into the Fourteenth Amendment, making them applicable to the states. (See Chapter 1.) In **Wolf v. Colorado** (1949), authorities in Denver received "definite information" that Dr. Wolf had performed an abortion. Sheriff's deputies under the district attorney's instruction "went to the office of Wolf without a warrant and took him into custody and there they took possession of . . . his day books of 1944 and 1943 up to the time of the arrest. They were records of patients who consulted him professionally." The records were introduced in evidence and used to convict Dr. Wolf, who received a twelve- to eighteen-month prison sentence. The Colorado Supreme Court held the evidence admissible, although the search was illegal.[29] Had this been a federal search, it would have violated the Fourth Amendment, and the evidence would have been ruled inadmissible under the *Weeks* exclusionary rule. The Fourth Amendment, however, did not bind local or state police and courts at that time. The U.S. Supreme Court held, in an opinion by Justice Frankfurter, that (1) the Fourth Amendment *is* "incorporated" but (2) the exclusionary rule is *not* "incorporated." That is, "in a prosecution in a State court for a State crime the Fourteenth Amendment does not forbid the admission of evidence obtained by an unreasonable search and seizure" (*Wolf v. Colorado,* 1949). As to the first holding, Justice Frankfurter dismissed the idea of "total incorporation" as one that had consistently been rejected by the Supreme Court in many cases. Turning to "selective incorporation" under the Due Process Clause, he wrote:

> Due process of law thus conveys neither formal nor fixed nor narrow requirements. It is the compendious expression for all those rights which the courts must enforce because they are basic to our free society. But basic rights do not become petrified as of any one time, even though, as a matter of human experience, some may not too rhetorically be called eternal verities. It is of the very nature of a free society to advance in its standards of what is deemed reasonable and right. Representing as it does a living principle, due process is not confined within a permanent catalogue of what may at a given time be deemed the limits or the essentials of fundamental rights.
>
> The security of one's privacy against arbitrary intrusion by the police—which is at the core of the Fourth Amendment—is basic to a free society. It is therefore implicit in "the concept of ordered liberty" and as such enforceable against the States through the Due Process Clause. The knock at the door, whether by day or by night, as a prelude to a search, without authority of law but solely on the authority of the police, did not need the commentary of recent history to be condemned as inconsistent with the conception of human rights enshrined in the history and the basic constitutional documents of English-speaking peoples.
>
> Accordingly, we have no hesitation in saying that were a State affirmatively to sanction such police incursion into privacy it would run counter to the guaranty of the Fourteenth Amendment. (*Wolf v. Colorado,* 1949)

This elegant language, interspersed among paragraphs that disparage the incorporation doctrine, incorporates the substance of the Fourth Amendment; that is, it forbids the states from creating rules that violate the Fourth Amendment. However, the Court's majority refused to impose the exclusionary rule on the states via incorporation:

> But the ways of enforcing such a basic right raise questions of a different order. How such arbitrary conduct should be checked, what remedies against it should be afforded, the means by which the right should be made effective, are all questions that are not to be so dogmatically answered as to preclude the varying solutions which spring from an allowable range of judgment on issues not susceptible of quantitative solution.
>
> In *Weeks v. United States,* this Court held that in a federal prosecution the Fourth Amendment barred the use of evidence secured through an illegal search and seizure. This ruling

was made for the first time in 1914. It was not derived from the explicit requirements of the Fourth Amendment; it was not based on legislation expressing Congressional policy in the enforcement of the Constitution. The decision was a matter of judicial implication. Since then it has been frequently applied and we stoutly adhere to it. But the immediate question is whether the basic right to protection against arbitrary intrusion by the police demands the exclusion of logically relevant evidence obtained by an unreasonable search and seizure because, in a federal prosecution for a federal crime, it would be excluded. As a matter of inherent reason, one would suppose this to be an issue as to which men with complete devotion to the protection of the right of privacy might give different answers. When we find that in fact most of the English-speaking world does not regard as vital to such protection the exclusion of evidence thus obtained, we must hesitate to treat this remedy as an essential ingredient of the right. The contrariety of views of the States is particularly impressive in view of the careful reconsideration which they have given the problem in the light of the *Weeks* decision. (*Wolf v. Colorado,* 1949)

Justice Frankfurter emphasized that the basic Fourth Amendment right, now applicable against state as well as federal encroachment, was protected by the "remedies" of civil lawsuits in all states, whether or not they had adopted their own exclusionary rules. As of 1949, sixteen states had adopted the *Weeks* exclusionary doctrine as a matter of local law, while thirty-one had rejected it.

Justice Black, the leading proponent of incorporation, nevertheless joined the majority because he felt that "the federal exclusionary rule is not a command of the Fourth Amendment but is a judicially created rule of evidence which Congress might negate"—that is, it is not a constitutional requirement. He managed to combine judicial activism with **originalism**—a seemingly incongruous combination. He believed that the Fourteenth Amendment incorporated the Fourth Amendment and supported the *Weeks* exclusionary rule as it applied to federal law enforcement, but because the Fourth Amendment text did not specify an exclusionary rule, he saw it as not extending to the states. This seemed inconsistent, and his position in *Wolf* would later create an anomaly in *Mapp v. Ohio* (1961).

Three liberal justices, William O. Douglas, Frank Murphy, and Wiley Rutledge, dissented in *Wolf,* arguing for incorporating the exclusionary rule. They argued that civil lawsuits and criminal prosecutions against police and prosecutors are virtually never successful, especially if the person claiming an unconstitutional search has a criminal record. For all practical purposes, without exclusion the Fourth Amendment was a right without a remedy. Justice Murphy noted that police are carefully trained in the law of search and seizure in states with the exclusionary rule, whereas the subject was virtually ignored in states without it. "The conclusion is inescapable that but one remedy exists to deter violations of the search and seizure clause. That is the rule which excludes illegally obtained evidence" (*Wolf v. Colorado,* 1949).

Three years after *Wolf,* the Supreme Court in **Rochin v. California** (1952) did suppress evidence obtained in a state search and seizure, not via *Weeks*'s Fourth Amendment exclusionary rule, but under the more flexible due process rule of the Fourteenth Amendment. Los Angeles police officers, believing that Rochin was dealing drugs, invaded his home without a warrant, went up the stairs, and forced open a door to his bedroom.

Inside they found [Rochin] sitting partly dressed on the side of the bed, upon which his wife was lying. On a "night stand" beside the bed the deputies spied two capsules. When asked "Whose stuff is this?" Rochin seized the capsules and put them in his mouth. A struggle ensued, in the course of which the three officers "jumped upon him" and attempted to extract the capsules. The force they applied proved unavailing against Rochin's resistance. He was handcuffed and taken to a hospital. At the direction of one of the officers a doctor forced an emetic solution through a tube into Rochin's stomach against his will. This "stomach pumping" produced vomiting. In the vomited matter were found two capsules which proved to contain morphine. (*Rochin v. California,* 1952)

The justices unanimously agreed that the evidence obtained by this outrageous police action was inadmissible, but for different reasons. Justice Frankfurter's majority opinion avoided the *Weeks* automatic exclusionary rule by a rule excluding evidence where the totality of the circumstances "shocked the conscience" of the appellate court. To him, the "shocks the conscience" test was an objective standard that would guide lower courts.

Justice Douglas concurred in the decision but strongly disagreed with the "shocks the conscience" test. As with any due process test that rests on the "totality of the circumstances," the application of the rule could differ from one judge to another. As he saw it, unlike the "unequivocal, definite and workable rule of evidence" of the *Weeks* exclusionary rule, the rule fashioned in *Rochin* "turn[s] not on the Constitution but on the idiosyncrasies of the judges who sit here" (*Rochin v. California,* 1952).

Justice Douglas's criticism was proven true in ***Irvine v. California*** (1954). Local police, suspecting Irvine of illegal bookmaking, secretly entered his home and, without a judicial search warrant, wired the house for sound, including the bedroom. The police listened in on the private conversations of Irvine and his wife for weeks and testified to what they heard at Irvine's trial. The evidence was used to convict Irvine. Justice Robert Jackson's majority opinion stated, "Few police measures have come to our attention that more flagrantly, deliberately, and persistently violated the fundamental principle declared by the Fourth Amendment" (*Irvine v. California,* 1954). The Supreme Court, nevertheless, upheld the use of the evidence. The *Weeks* exclusionary rule did not apply to the states, and the majority refused to apply the *Rochin* "shocks the conscience" test because the facts of *Rochin* included the element of coercion not found in the *Irvine* case. This was too much for Justice Frankfurter, who dissented on the grounds that *Rochin* did apply, arguing fruitlessly that "a State cannot resort to methods that offend civilized standards of decency and fairness." The subjectivity of the "shocks the conscience" test was exposed when the majority in *Irvine* did not find such a flagrant violation of Fourth Amendment privacy to "shock the conscience." In a spirited dissent, Justice Douglas called again for incorporating the exclusionary rule, saying, "The search and seizure conducted in this case smack of the police state, not the free America the Bill of Rights envisaged."

As the 1950s wore on, more states adopted the exclusionary rule by court action, most notably the California Supreme Court.[30] The tide in favor of reversing *Weeks* was "halting but seemingly inexorable."[31] A harbinger was ***Elkins v. United States*** (1960). Soon after *Weeks* (1914), the **"silver platter" doctrine,** an end-run around the exclusionary rule, arose. If state or local police seized evidence of a federal crime by an illegal search and seizure, the evidence was admissible in a federal trial as long as the federal officers did not participate in the illegal search. This, of course, put a premium on "pious perjury," or winking at the truth.

The Supreme Court signaled its unhappiness with this in ***Rea v. United States*** (1956). The Court exercised its supervisory authority to enjoin a federal narcotics agent, who illegally seized marijuana that was excluded from a federal prosecution, from testifying about the marijuana in a state prosecution. This eliminated a federal-to-state "silver platter" delivery of tainted evidence.

In *Elkins v. United States* (1960), the Supreme Court put an end to the state-to-federal transfer of illegally seized evidence. Justice Potter Stewart, writing for the majority in a five-to-four decision, noted that the basis of the "silver platter" doctrine was eroded once *Wolf v. Colorado* (1949) held that substantive Fourth Amendment rights applied against the states. The four dissenting justices complained that the Court was interfering with states' rights. In reply, Justice Stewart wrote, "The very essence of a healthy federalism depends upon the avoidance of needless conflict between federal and state courts." Thus, in states with state exclusionary rules, the "silver platter" doctrine undermined state policy. *Elkins* was decided not on constitutional grounds but on "the Court's supervisory power over the administration of criminal justice in the federal courts." Justice Stewart's strong defense of the exclusionary rule foreshadowed the decision in *Mapp v. Ohio* (1961).

Incorporating the Exclusionary Rule

The due process revolution of the 1960s, which incorporated a host of rights (see Chapter 1), was initiated by *Mapp v. Ohio* (1961). Although the movement is associated with a five-justice majority of the Warren Court in the 1960s, the *Mapp* opinion was authored by Justice Tom Clark, who more often than not voted for the state.

Read Case and Comments: *Mapp v. Ohio*

Mapp v. Ohio

367 U.S. 643, 81 S.Ct. 1684, 6 L.Ed.2d 1081 (1961)

MR. JUSTICE CLARK delivered the opinion of the Court.

[Cleveland police officers went to Mrs. Mapp's home on a tip that a suspected gambler involved in a bombing was residing there. She refused to let them enter without a warrant. The police broke in after a three-hour wait. There was a scuffle for a piece of paper that the police waved, but no warrant was ever produced. Mrs. Mapp and her daughter were handcuffed and confined to a bedroom while the police ransacked the house (looking into all rooms and into her personal papers and photograph albums). The police found obscene books in a trunk in the basement belonging to a roomer who was no longer living in the house. At trial, the alleged warrant was never produced. Mrs. Mapp was convicted for possession of obscene books seized during a search of her home. [a] The Ohio courts acknowledged that the books and pictures were "unlawfully seized during an unlawful search of [her] home, * * *" but still allowed the evidence to be used, relying on *Wolf v. Colorado*.]

I

Seventy-five years ago, in *Boyd v. United States* (1886), considering the Fourth and Fifth Amendments as running "almost into each other," on the facts before it, this Court held that the doctrines of those Amendments [b]

> "apply to all invasions on the part of the government and its employés of the sanctity of a man's home and the privacies of life. * * * "

The Court noted that

> "constitutional provisions for the security of person and property should be liberally construed. . . . It is the duty of courts to be watchful for the constitutional rights of the citizen, and against any stealthy encroachments thereon."

* * * Concluding, the Court specifically referred to the use of the evidence there seized as "unconstitutional." Less than 30 years after *Boyd,* this Court, in *Weeks v. United States* (1914), stated that

> "the Fourth Amendment . . . put the courts of the United States and Federal officials, in the exercise of their power and authority, under limitations and restraints." * * *

Specifically dealing with the use of the evidence unconstitutionally seized, the Court concluded:

> "If letters and private documents can thus be seized and held and used in evidence against a citizen accused of an offense, the protection of the Fourth Amendment declaring his right to be secure against such searches and seizures is of no value, and, so far as those thus placed are concerned, might as well be stricken from the Constitution." * * *

Finally, the Court in that case clearly stated that use of the seized evidence involved "a denial of the constitutional rights of the accused." . . . Thus, in the year 1914, in the *Weeks* case, this Court "for the first time" held that "in a federal prosecution the Fourth Amendment barred the use of evidence secured through an illegal search and seizure." * * *

[a] This case was appealed to the Supreme Court primarily on First Amendment (free speech) grounds. The Fourth Amendment issue was added perfunctorily. The dissent accused the majority of "reaching out" to settle an issue that was not fully briefed.

[b] Justice Clark begins by quoting the *Boyd* view that exclusion depends on the Fourth and Fifth amendments operating together, rather than on the idea that *Weeks* created an exclusionary rule based exclusively on the Fourth Amendment. This might seem odd, but in fact it is a necessary tactic to gain a majority for the decision. What is his motive for this reasoning?

There are in the cases of this Court some passing references to the *Weeks* rule as being one of evidence. But the plain and unequivocal language of *Weeks*—and its later paraphrase in *Wolf*—to the effect that the *Weeks* rule is of constitutional origin, remains entirely undisturbed. * * * **[c]**

II

[In *Wolf v. Colorado* (1949), the Court first considered the applicability of the Fourth Amendment against the states, and] after declaring that the "security of one's privacy against arbitrary intrusion by the police" is "implicit in 'the concept of ordered liberty' and as such enforceable against the States through the Due Process Clause," * * * and announcing that it "stoutly adhere[d]" to the *Weeks* decision, [nevertheless] the Court decided that the *Weeks* exclusionary rule would not then be imposed upon the States as "an essential ingredient of the right." * * *

[Since 1949, a majority of the states have adopted the exclusionary rule and federal courts no longer allow into evidence items that were illegally seized by state officers.]

It, therefore, plainly appears that the factual considerations supporting the failure of the *Wolf* Court to include the *Weeks* exclusionary rule when it recognized the enforceability of the right to privacy against the States in 1949, while not basically relevant to the constitutional consideration, could not, in any analysis, now be deemed controlling.

III

* * * Today we once again examine *Wolf*'s constitutional documentation of the right to privacy free from unreasonable state intrusion, and, after its dozen years on our books, are led by it to close the only courtroom door remaining open to evidence secured by official lawlessness in flagrant abuse of that basic right, reserved to all persons as a specific guarantee against that very same unlawful conduct. We hold that all evidence obtained by searches and seizures in violation of the Constitution is, by that same authority, inadmissible in a state court.

IV

Since the Fourth Amendment's right of privacy has been declared enforceable against the States through the Due Process Clause of the Fourteenth, it is enforceable against them by the same sanction of exclusion as is used against the Federal Government. * * * **[d]** In short, the admission of the new constitutional right by *Wolf* could not consistently tolerate denial of its most important constitutional privilege, namely, the exclusion of the evidence which an accused had been forced to give by reason of the unlawful seizure. To hold otherwise is to grant the right but in reality to withhold its privilege and enjoyment. * * *

V

Moreover, our holding that the exclusionary rule is an essential part of both the Fourth and Fourteenth Amendments is not only the logical dictate of prior cases, but it also makes very good sense. There is no war between the Constitution and common sense. Presently, a federal prosecutor may make no use of evidence illegally seized, but a State's attorney across the street may, although he supposedly is operating under the enforceable prohibitions of the same Amendment. **[e]** Thus the State, by admitting evidence unlawfully seized, serves to encourage disobedience to the Federal Constitution which it is bound to uphold. * * * "[The] very essence of a healthy federalism depends upon the avoidance of needless conflict between state and federal courts." * * * **[f]**

(continued)

[c] Is saying that a rule is "of constitutional origin" the same as saying that it is "a constitutional rule"? In *Mapp*, the Court rejected *Wolf*'s theory of the exclusionary rule, following changes of national politics and judicial policy. The change is traced in the next section.

[d] The "same sanction" phrase is important to the incorporation doctrine. It requires an identical interpretation of the U.S. Constitution in cases coming from state and federal courts. While this fits the idea that as the "supreme law of the land" the Constitution should be identical in state and federal cases, this strict view did not hold up in future cases.

[e] This refers not to the "silver platter" doctrine, eliminated in *Elkins v. United States* (1960), but to the incongruity of uneven enforcement of constitutional rights.

[f] It appears that even with the elimination of the "silver platter" doctrine, Justice Clark feared that allowing different search and seizure rules would cause tension between state and federal officers.

Federal–state cooperation in the solution of crime under constitutional standards will be promoted, if only by recognition of their now mutual obligation to respect the same fundamental criteria in their approaches. "However much in a particular case insistence upon such rules may appear as a technicality that inures to the benefit of a guilty person, the history of the criminal law proves that tolerance of shortcut methods in law enforcement impairs its enduring effectiveness." * * * Denying shortcuts to only one of two cooperating law enforcement agencies tends naturally to breed legitimate suspicion of "working arrangements" whose results are equally tainted. * * *

There are those who say, as did JUSTICE (then Judge) CARDOZO, that under our constitutional exclusionary doctrine "[the] criminal is to go free because the constable has blundered." * * * In some cases this will undoubtedly be the result. **[g]** But, * * * "there is another consideration—the imperative of judicial integrity." The criminal goes free, if he must, but it is the law that sets him free. Nothing can destroy a government more quickly than its failure to observe its own laws, or worse, its disregard of the charter of its own existence. * * *

The ignoble shortcut to conviction left open to the State tends to destroy the entire system of constitutional restraints on which the liberties of the people rest. * * * [W]e can no longer permit that right to remain an empty promise. * * * *Reversed and remanded.*

[g] The arguments in favor of and opposed to the exclusionary rule, and the various theories of the exclusionary rule, are considered later in this chapter.

MR. JUSTICE BLACK, concurring.

[JUSTICE BLACK noted that in *Wolf,* he stated that "the federal exclusionary rule is not a command of the Fourth Amendment but is a judicially created rule of evidence which Congress might negate."]

* * *

I am still not persuaded that the Fourth Amendment, standing alone, would be enough to bar the introduction into evidence against an accused of papers and effects seized from him in violation of its commands. **[h]** For the Fourth Amendment does not itself contain any provision expressly precluding the use of such evidence, and I am extremely doubtful that such a provision could properly be inferred from nothing more than the basic command against unreasonable searches and seizures. Reflection on the problem, however, in the light of cases coming before the Court since *Wolf,* has led me to conclude that when the Fourth Amendment's ban against unreasonable searches and seizures is considered together with the Fifth Amendment's ban against compelled self-incrimination, a constitutional basis emerges which not only justifies but actually requires the exclusionary rule. * * *

[h] Justice Black's vote in favor of the exclusionary rule is the crucial fifth majority vote. His rationale makes it clear why Justice Clark's argument included *Boyd*'s theory that the Fourth and Fifth amendments operate in conjunction to exclude evidence. It is worth noting that the Fifth Amendment basis of the exclusionary rule, while still alluded to, had become obsolete by the 1960s, as the search and seizure exclusionary rule was treated exclusively as a Fourth Amendment issue.

[JUSTICE DOUGLAS concurred, expanding on the facts of the case and emphasizing the inability of any method other than exclusion to deter police illegalities.]

[JUSTICE STEWART expressed no opinion on the search and seizure issue; he would have reversed the conviction on First Amendment grounds.]

MR. JUSTICE HARLAN, whom MR. JUSTICE FRANKFURTER and MR. JUSTICE WHITTAKER join, dissenting.

In overruling the *Wolf* case the Court, in my opinion, has forgotten the sense of judicial restraint which, with due regard for *stare decisis,* is one element that should enter into deciding whether a past decision of this Court should be overruled. **[i]** Apart from that I also believe that the *Wolf* rule represents sounder Constitutional doctrine than the new rule which now replaces it. * * *

[i] Justices differ in their adherence to precedent or stare decisis. Justice Harlan was a strong believer in restraint, or a reluctance to change established rules. Judicial restraint was seen as an attribute of judicial "conservatism." However, many justices who today advance a conservative policy agenda are "activist" in changing the law to suit their policy views.

II

Essential to the majority's argument against *Wolf* is the proposition that the [exclusionary] rule of *Weeks* * * * derives not from the "supervisory power" of this Court over the federal judicial system, but from Constitutional requirement. This is so because no one, I suppose, would suggest that this Court possesses any general supervisory power over the state courts. **[j]** Although I entertain considerable doubt as to the soundness of this foundational proposition * * * I shall assume, for present purposes, that the *Weeks* rule "is of constitutional origin."

At the heart of the majority's opinion in this case is the following syllogism: (1) the rule excluding in federal criminal trials evidence which is the product of an illegal search and seizure is "part and parcel" of the Fourth Amendment; (2) *Wolf* held that the "privacy" assured against federal action by the Fourth Amendment is also protected against state action by the Fourteenth Amendment; and (3) it is therefore "logically and constitutionally necessary" that the *Weeks* exclusionary rule should also be enforced against the States.

This reasoning ultimately rests on the unsound premise that because *Wolf* carried into the States, as part of "the concept of ordered liberty" embodied in the Fourteenth Amendment, the principle of "privacy" underlying the *Fourth Amendment,* * * * it must follow that whatever configurations of the Fourth Amendment have been developed in the particularizing federal precedents are likewise to be deemed a part of "ordered liberty," and as such are enforceable against the States. For me, this does not follow at all. **[k]**

It cannot be too much emphasized that what was recognized in *Wolf* was not that the Fourth Amendment *as such* is enforceable against the States as a facet of due process, * * * but the principle of privacy "which is at the core of the Fourth Amendment." * * * It would not be proper to expect or impose any precise equivalence, either as regards the scope of the right or the means of its implementation, between the requirements of the Fourth and Fourteenth Amendments. For the Fourth, unlike what was said in *Wolf* of the Fourteenth, does not state a general principle only; it is a particular command, having its setting in a pre-existing legal context on which both interpreting decisions and enabling statutes must at least build.

* * * Since there is not the slightest suggestion that Ohio's policy is "affirmatively to sanction * * * police incursion into privacy" * * * what the Court is now doing is to impose upon the States not only federal substantive standards of "search and seizure" but also the basic federal remedy for violation of those standards. For I think it entirely clear that the *Weeks* exclusionary rule is but a remedy which, by penalizing past official misconduct, is aimed at deterring such conduct in the future. **[l]**

I would not impose upon the States this federal exclusionary remedy. The reasons given by the majority for now suddenly turning its back on *Wolf* seem to me notably unconvincing.

[JUSTICE HARLAN then gave several reasons for not extending the exclusionary rule to the states: (1) that many states have voluntarily adopted the exclusionary rule does not determine a constitutional question; (2) "the preservation of a proper balance between state and federal responsibility in the administration of criminal justice" constitutionally forbids the federal courts from developing solutions for perceived problems of state law enforcement; (3) procedural symmetry between the federal system and the states is not required by the Constitution; and (4) the purported analogy between the exclusion of involuntary confessions under the Fourteenth Amendment and search and seizure cases is spurious.]

[j] Look up "supervisory authority" in the Glossary. Why doesn't the Supreme Court have supervisory authority over state courts and state law enforcement?

[k] What follows is the nonincorporation view that had been part of Fourteenth Amendment jurisprudence since *Hurtado v. California* (1884). Justice Harlan's strenuous dissent is indeed a cry for stare decisis, for the majority decision in *Mapp* was genuinely revolutionary, by overturning the theory of the relationship between the Bill of Rights and the Fourteenth Amendment.

[l] A dissent is always a call to the future. As the personnel of the Supreme Court changed and the Court adopted a more activist–conservative stance, Justice Harlan's view of the nature of the exclusionary rule has become the accepted view of the Court. (See "History and Theories of the Exclusionary Rule" later in this chapter.)

Two years after *Mapp,* in ***Ker v. California*** (1963), the Court fully "federalized" the exclusionary rule, saying that the "standard of reasonableness is the same under the Fourth and Fourteenth Amendments." Essentially, state courts would have to abide by the U.S. Supreme Court's exclusionary rule interpretations. The Court noted that it had no supervisory authority over the states, only the jurisdiction to interpret the Constitution. The majority opinion said that *Mapp* "implied no total obliteration of state laws relating to arrests and searches in favor of federal law. *Mapp* sounded no death knell for our federalism." On the other hand, "Findings of reasonableness, of course, are respected only insofar as consistent with federal constitutional guarantees." In practice, this meant that state search and seizure law had to conform to minimum constitutional standards as determined by the Supreme Court, but under the adequate and independent state grounds concept, a state could expand a suspect's rights in a search and seizure case. (See Chapter 1.)

In 1965, the Supreme Court held, in ***Linkletter v. Walker,*** that the exclusionary rule was not retroactive to state cases decided prior to *Mapp;* its effect was prospective only. Applying the Court's pragmatic approach to determining if a constitutional rule should be applied retroactively, the seven-to-two majority opinion stated that "*Mapp* had as its prime purpose the enforcement of the Fourth Amendment through the inclusion of the exclusionary rule within its rights. This, it was found, was the *only effective deterrent to lawless police action.* Indeed, all of the cases since *Wolf* requiring the exclusion of illegal evidence have been based on the necessity for an effective *deterrent* to illegal police action. . . . We cannot say that this purpose would be advanced by making the rule retrospective" (*Linkletter v. Walker,* 1965, emphasis added). At the time of this decision, the majority probably felt that the exclusionary rule was relatively secure. But these words in the *Linkletter* case became highly significant in the 1970s, when the theory of the exclusionary rule was reconsidered by a more conservative Court with a view to eliminating or weakening the rule.

The Warren Court's positive approach to the exclusionary rule was underscored by applying it to the civil forfeiture of an automobile that state liquor control officers stopped and searched because it was "low in the rear, quite low." Upon inspection, the officers found thirty-one cases of liquor. In ***One 1958 Plymouth Sedan v. Pennsylvania*** (1965), the Court agreed with the state trial judge's finding that the stop was made without probable cause. In applying the exclusionary rule, the Court noted that forfeitures are quasi-criminal procedures in which the penalty is often more onerous than a criminal sentence.

The exclusionary rule was subjected to judicial and political criticism during the remaining years of the Warren Court (to 1969). In fact, liberal Warren Court decisions regarding criminal suspects became a major issue in the 1968 presidential campaign. After his election, President Richard M. Nixon sought to nominate justices who would reverse these decisions. (See Chapter 1.) Within a decade of *Mapp,* a "counterattack" to erode the exclusionary rule was begun by a Supreme Court that had become more conservative.

UNDERMINING THE EXCLUSIONARY RULE

After 1972, the Court's new conservative majority had a guarded, if not outrightly hostile, attitude toward the exclusionary rule. Chief Justice Warren Burger, dissenting in *Bivens v. Six Unknown Agents* (1971), called for its overruling and stated that the only foundation for the rule was the deterrence of police illegality. The Court has never overruled the exclusionary rule, but it has limited its application since 1974. ***United States v. Calandra*** (1974) was the first case to limit the exclusionary rule. A six-justice majority held that a grand jury question could be based on information obtained from an unconstitutional search resulting from a defective search warrant. Justice Lewis Powell's majority opinion set the foundation for the Court's later exclusionary rule decisions. These reasons upended the constitutional foundation of the exclusionary rule established in *Weeks* and *Mapp*.

The heart of the majority's reasoning in *Calandra* is that the "purpose of the exclusionary rule is not to redress the injury to the privacy of the search victim. . . . Instead, the rule's prime purpose is to *deter future unlawful police conduct* and thereby effectuate the guarantee of the Fourth Amendment against unreasonable searches and seizures" (*United States v. Calandra*, 1974, emphasis added). The logic of this reasoning is that the government has already "ruptured [the] privacy of the victims' homes and effects, [which] cannot be restored. Reparation comes too late" (*Calandra*, quoting *Linkletter v. Walker*, 1965). An important consequence is that in deciding how and when to apply the exclusionary rule, the Court has to balance the needs of law enforcement against individual rights. The Court emphasized that grand juries have broad powers to investigate crimes that are necessary to effective law enforcement. Applying the exclusionary rule to grand jury proceedings would turn them into protracted "preliminary trials" while adding little deterrence to police. Illegally seized evidence could still not be admitted at trial.

Justice William Brennan, dissenting, held a very different view of the exclusionary rule. Although deterrence was one reason for the exclusionary rule, the Court's primary goal was "to fashion an enforcement tool to give content and meaning to the Fourth Amendment's guarantees" (*Calandra*, 1974, Brennan, J., dissenting). A "vital function of the rule [is] to insure that the judiciary avoid even the slightest appearance of sanctioning illegal government conduct," he wrote. Otherwise, judges become "accomplices in the willful disobedience of a Constitution they are sworn to uphold" and undermine popular trust in the government (*Calandra*, quoting *Elkins v. United States*, 1960).

In ***Stone v. Powell*** (1976), the Supreme Court held that challenges to illegal searches from state courts under federal habeas corpus were no longer allowed if state courts already provided a full and fair opportunity to litigate a Fourth Amendment claim. Justice Powell stressed that the exclusionary rule was a judicially created means of enforcing Fourth Amendment rights by deterring police misconduct, rather than a right itself. He denied that the rule was based on "the imperative of judicial integrity." He criticized the rule, noting that it "deflects the truthfinding process and often frees the guilty." The Burger and Rehnquist courts, by not limiting federal habeas corpus review of other constitutional guarantees, has created a hierarchy of constitutional rights, with Fourth Amendment rights held in lower esteem than Fifth or Sixth amendment rights.

Chief Justice Burger, who had earlier called for overruling the exclusionary rule, came to accept it but in a weakened form. He stated that "the exclusionary rule has been operative long enough to demonstrate its flaws. The time has come to modify its reach, even if it is retained for a small and limited category of cases" (*Stone v. Powell*, 1976, concurring). A majority of the Court may have felt constrained by stare decisis and uneasy with dismantling an important protection of a fundamental constitutional right. Chief Justice Burger thus shifted toward limiting the exclusionary rule rather than eliminating it.[32]

Calandra and *Stone* set the foundation of constitutional reasoning on which the Court weakened the exclusionary rule. It held, in a series of cases, that the exclusionary rule does not apply to various procedures. These include the Internal Revenue Service in a civil tax proceeding (***United States v. Janis***, 1976) and Immigration and Naturalization Service deportation hearings (***I.N.S. v. Lopez-Mendoza***, 1984). These rulings undercut the viability of *One 1958 Plymouth Sedan*, although that decision was never overruled. The Court also declined to apply the exclusionary rule to parole revocation in ***Pennsylvania Board of Probation and Parole v. Scott*** (1998). Parole officers, without a warrant, entered the home of a parolee whom they believed possessed weapons in violation of parole conditions. The state courts ruled that the warrantless search of a parolee's home violated the Fourth Amendment because "illegal searches would be undeterred when officers know that the subjects of their searches are parolees and that illegally obtained evidence can be introduced at parole hearings." The Supreme Court reversed the lower court in an opinion by Justice Clarence Thomas that referred to the exclusionary rule as a "grudgingly taken medicant" (*Scott*, 1998). He reviewed the Court's approach to the exclusionary rule in cases since *Calandra* and noted that the rule now applies only in criminal trials, and even there with some exceptions. Justice John Paul Stevens, writing for four dissenting justices in *Scott,* endorsed the view made by Justice Stewart in a journal article: The "rule *is* constitutionally required, not as a 'right' explicitly incorporated in the fourth amendment's prohibitions, but as a remedy necessary to ensure that those prohibitions are observed in fact."[33] Justice David Souter, in dissent, noted that parole revocation proceedings often serve the same function as criminal trials.

The Supreme Court also held that illegally obtained evidence can be used to impeach the credibility of a defendant who testifies—that is, to show that the defendant's testimony is contradicted by the illegally seized evidence. This exception to the exclusionary rule was first recognized in **Walder v. United States** (1954), where a prosecutor was allowed to introduce heroin seized in an illegal search to undermine the credibility of the defendant's testimony that he never possessed drugs. An impeachment exception has also been recognized in confessions law (*Harris v. New York,* 1971; *Oregon v. Hass,* 1975; see Chapter 7). In **United States v. Havens** (1980), the Supreme Court allowed the introduction of illegally seized drugs that were found in Havens's specially constructed T-shirt, when on proper cross-examination Havens denied any connection to the shirt, which was designed to conceal drugs. The decision was based on the importance of getting at the truth in criminal trials and not allowing a constitutional shield to be "perverted into a license to use perjury."

The Supreme Court drew the line to this exception in **James v. Illinois** (1990). In this case, the defendant was arrested without probable cause. During this illegal detention, he made a statement indicating that he tried to change his appearance on the day after a killing. The statement itself was inadmissible under the exclusionary rule. A defense witness testified that James's appearance was the same after the killing as before, although several prosecution witnesses testified that his appearance had changed. The prosecutor then introduced James's illegally obtained statement to impeach the defense witness. The Supreme Court ruled that this was improper. The impeachment exception to the exclusionary rule is limited to the defendant's testimony and not that of other witnesses. The Court reasoned that a witness will be more constrained by the risk of a perjury conviction than a defendant. Allowing the impeachment exception to expand to witnesses would give the prosecutor leverage to discourage honest defense witnesses from telling the truth. Thus the majority in *James* felt that expanding the impeachment exception would not clearly advance the truth-seeking value of a trial. In an opinion that bucked the trend of cases undermining the exclusionary rule, the *James* opinion reasserted that the exclusionary rule was essential to giving Fourth Amendment protections real effectiveness. Expanding the exception "would significantly weaken the exclusionary rule's deterrent effect on police misconduct."

The phenomenon of a line of cases weakening a major ruling is familiar in constitutional law. The Court often speaks of a rule having been "eroded" by a series of inconsistent cases, often preceding the overruling of the precedent. Although this has not happened to the *Weeks–Mapp* exclusionary rule, the law as it now stands has been permanently weakened. Most recently, the Court ruled in **Hudson v. Michigan** (2006) that evidence seized in a drug raid on a house was admissible after police, although armed with a warrant, did not obey the constitutionally required "knock and announce" rule (discussed in Chapter 3). Michigan courts found that waiting only three to five seconds before entering a home before executing a warrant to search for drugs and guns violated the Fourth Amendment, a finding not disputed by the Supreme Court. Justice Scalia's majority opinion stated that a Fourth Amendment violation is a necessary but not a sufficient reason for exclusion. He reasoned that the "knock and announce" rule protected such values as the lives, safety, and dignity of inhabitants and the protection of property, but not the "interest in preventing the government from seeing or taking evidence described in a warrant." Since the warrant was properly issued, this opinion attached the reasoning of the "fruits of the poisonous tree" cases and argued that since the government could have lawfully obtained the drug evidence, the exclusionary rule did not apply. The majority also said that even if it were true that "without suppression there will be no deterrence of knock-and-announce violations at all," it would make no difference because there are "many forms of police misconduct that are similarly 'undeterred'" where civil lawsuits are available. Justice Stephen Breyer, writing for four dissenting justices, said that because the Supreme Court has ruled that the "knock and announce" rule is part of the Fourth Amendment (*Wilson v. Arkansas,* 1995), a search made in violation of the rule is unreasonable and illegal. The exclusionary rule therefore applies as a matter of "elementary logic." There are many reported cases of "knock and announce" violations and no cases showing that victims of such government misconduct "have collected more than nominal damages" in civil suits. "The upshot is that the need for deterrence—the critical factor driving this Court's Fourth Amendment cases for close to a century—argues with at least comparable strength for evidentiary exclusion here." He further argued that relying on the reasoning from the derivative evidence (fruits of the poisonous tree) cases were misplaced. Even if evidence was seized improperly, the government cannot avoid suppression of evidence by showing that it *could have* been properly seized.

The next two sections on the good faith exceptions and on the doctrine of standing analyze the further weakening of the exclusionary rule.

Good Faith Exceptions

The Supreme Court's strongest attack on the exclusionary rule allowed illegally seized evidence to be introduced into the trial to prove the defendant's guilt, unlike *Calandra* and similar cases that allowed tainted evidence only in peripheral proceedings. The "good faith exception" theory reasoned that allowing tainted evidence in the "case in chief" would not undermine the exclusionary rule's deterrent effect. These cases consolidated the Court's view that the rule is "only" a judicially created remedy designed to deter police from violating Fourth Amendment rights while modifying the original theory of the exclusionary rule.

The good faith exception in *United States v. Leon* (1984) was presaged by **Michigan v. DeFillippo** (1979). Evidence was allowed of illegal drugs, obtained in a search incident to an arrest made in good faith reliance on a local ordinance allowing police to demand personal identification of a reasonably stopped person, even though on appeal state courts held the ordinance to be unconstitutional. The stage was set for a major reassessment and limitation of the exclusionary rule.

Read Case and Comments: *United States v. Leon*

Leon was followed by **Illinois v. Krull** (1987), which held that the exclusionary rule does not apply where the police violate a person's rights in good faith reliance on a statute. Chicago police officers, under an Illinois regulatory statute, searched cars and records of an automobile wrecking yard without a search warrant. The statute was declared unconstitutional by a federal court. On appeal, the Supreme Court, applying the reasoning of *Leon,* found that because similar regulatory search schemes had been held constitutional in the past, the officers relied on the law in good faith. Justice Sandra Day O'Connor wrote the dissent in this five-to-four decision, joined by Justices William Brennan, Thurgood Marshall, and John Paul Stevens. Noting that the Fourth Amendment was originally designed to constrain the legislature, she minced no words: "Legislatures have, upon occasion, failed to adhere to the requirements of the Fourth Amendment." She argued that a legislature could be deterred by applying the exclusionary rule in a case like this one. "Providing legislatures a grace period during which the police may freely perform unreasonable searches in order to convict those who might otherwise escape provides a positive incentive to promulgate unconstitutional laws." Justice O'Connor's experience as a leader of the Arizona Senate provided the insight that legislators sometimes intentionally pass laws for political gain that violate individual rights.

In **Massachusetts v. Sheppard** (1984), a companion case to *Leon,* a police officer filed a homicide search warrant affidavit on a form for controlled substances searches because it was Sunday, the courts were closed, and the officer could not find the proper form. Although the officer and the magistrate modified the form, the search warrant

United States v. Leon

468 U.S. 897, 104 S.Ct. 3405, 82 L.Ed.2d 677 (1984)

JUSTICE WHITE delivered the opinion of the Court.

This case presents the question whether the Fourth Amendment exclusionary rule should be modified so as not to bar the use in the prosecution's case in chief of evidence obtained by officers acting in reasonable reliance on a search warrant issued by a detached and neutral magistrate but ultimately found to be unsupported by probable cause. **[a]** To resolve this question, we must consider once again the tension between the sometimes competing goals of, on the one hand, deterring official misconduct and removing inducements to unreasonable invasions of privacy and, on the other, establishing procedures under which criminal defendants are "acquitted or convicted on the basis of all the evidence which exposes the truth." * * *

I

[Local police obtained a "facially valid" search warrant from a state judge based on information from a confidential informant "of unproven reliability." A stakeout revealed suspected drug dealing at a house, and a car parked outside belonged to Leon, a previously convicted drug dealer. A search warrant affidavit was prepared by an experienced drug enforcement officer and reviewed by several assistant prosecutors. A warrant was issued by a state judge. The warrant was executed, and drugs were found. On this evidence, Leon and others were indicted in a federal district court for drug dealing. They moved to suppress evidence and challenged the constitutionality of the search warrant. The federal judge overturned the warrant—the informant's reliability was not established and probable cause of drug sales was not independently established. (This rule is covered in Chapter 3 under "Probable Cause" and the Fourth Amendment.) The court stated that the case was a close one and that the officers acted on the warrant in the good faith belief that it was based on probable cause, even though probable cause was not established. The federal court of appeals upheld the district court. The case is decided on the understanding that the search warrant was not valid under the Fourth Amendment and that, in effect, the search violated Leon's Fourth Amendment rights.]

We have concluded that, in the Fourth Amendment context, the exclusionary rule can be modified somewhat without jeopardizing its ability to perform its intended functions. **[b]** Accordingly, we reverse the judgment of the Court of Appeals.

II

Language in opinions of this Court * * * has sometimes implied that the exclusionary rule is a necessary corollary of the Fourth Amendment, * * * [or] the conjunction of the Fourth and Fifth Amendments. [*Mapp v. Ohio*] **[c]** * * * These implications need not detain us long. The Fifth Amendment theory has not withstood critical analysis or the test of time, * * * and the Fourth Amendment "has never been interpreted to proscribe the introduction of illegally seized evidence in all proceedings or against all persons." * * *

A

The Fourth Amendment contains no provision expressly precluding the use of evidence obtained in violation of its commands, and * * * the use of [unlawfully seized evidence] "work[s] no new Fourth Amendment wrong." * * * The wrong condemned by the Amendment is "fully accomplished" by the unlawful search or seizure itself, * * * and the exclusionary rule is neither intended nor able to "cure the invasion of the defendant's rights which he has already suffered." The rule thus operates as "a judicially created remedy

[a] Justice White states the issue and establishes a "judicial methodology"—the "balancing test"—to resolve the issue. The choice assists in producing the desired outcome. Is anything left out of the "competing goals"?

[b] This conclusion is analogous to a structural engineer deciding to construct a bridge without using materials that maximize safety. Does this kind of cost/benefit analysis have a place in civil rights law?

[c] Justice White dismisses the *Mapp* holding that the exclusionary rule is a *constitutional* rule—by his phrasing. The Fifth Amendment theory, used in *Mapp* to gain Justice Black's vote, linked the Fourth Amendment to a clear-cut exclusionary rule in the Fifth Amendment. By relying on post-*Mapp* cases, Justice White, a long-standing critic of *Mapp,* is now able to use precedents he helped create to weaken its effect.

designed to safeguard Fourth Amendment rights generally through its deterrent effect, rather than a personal constitutional right of the party aggrieved." * * *

Whether the exclusionary sanction is appropriately imposed in a particular case is "an issue separate from the question whether the Fourth Amendment rights of the party seeking to invoke the rule were violated by police conduct." * * * **[d]** Only the former question is currently before us, and it must be resolved by weighing the costs and benefits of preventing the use in the prosecution's case-in-chief of inherently trustworthy tangible evidence obtained in reliance on a search warrant issued by a detached and neutral magistrate that ultimately is found to be defective.

The substantial social costs exacted by the exclusionary rule for the vindication of Fourth Amendment rights have long been a source of concern. **[e]** * * * "[U]nbending application of the exclusionary sanction to enforce ideals of governmental rectitude would impede unacceptably the truth-finding functions of judge and jury."* * * Particularly when law enforcement officers have acted in objective good faith or their transgressions have been minor, the magnitude of the benefit conferred on such guilty defendants offends basic concepts of the criminal justice system. * * * Indiscriminate application of the exclusionary rule, therefore, may well "generat[e] disrespect for the law and administration of justice." * * * Accordingly, "[a]s with any remedial device, the application of the rule has been restricted to those areas where its remedial objectives are thought most efficaciously served." * * *

B

[This section reviews cases in which the Court has "demoted" the exclusionary rule, including *Stone v. Powell* (1976); *United States v. Calandra* (1974); and *United States v. Janis* (1976), the attenuation cases, the impeachment cases, and the retroactivity cases.] **[f]**

III

A

* * *

* * * To the extent that proponents of exclusion rely on its behavioral effects on judges and magistrates, * * * their reliance is misplaced. **[g]** First, the exclusionary rule is designed to deter police misconduct rather than to punish the errors of judges and magistrates. Second, there exists no evidence suggesting that judges and magistrates are inclined to ignore or subvert the Fourth Amendment or that lawlessness among these actors requires application of the extreme sanction of exclusion.

* * *

[M]ost important, we discern no basis, and are offered none, for believing that exclusion of evidence seized pursuant to a warrant will have a significant deterrent effect on the issuing judge or magistrate. **[h]** * * * [A]s neutral judicial officers, they have no stake in the outcome of particular criminal prosecutions. * * * Imposition of the exclusionary sanction is not necessary meaningfully to inform judicial officers of their errors. * * *

B

If exclusion of evidence obtained pursuant to a subsequently invalidated warrant is to have any deterrent effect, therefore, it must alter the behavior of individual law enforcement officers or the policies of their departments. One could argue that applying the exclusionary

[d] In criminal law, a crime definition is incomplete without the penalty provision—the public's remedy is part of the right. Is the Fourth Amendment a true right without a remedy? Is the exclusionary rule a true remedy? (See "History and Theories of the Exclusionary Rule" in this chapter.)

[e] The exclusionary rule is "put on the defensive," stressing its costs, limits, and status as a "mere" remedy. The social costs of the exclusionary rule are still open to debate. Note how the "imperative of judicial integrity" of liberal justices becomes the "ideal of governmental rectitude" to conservative justices; the phrases convey different meanings.

[f] The text has reviewed these cases, showing the exclusionary rule's erosion. Precedent is "ammunition" used by the justice to get the desired result.

[g] The Bill of Rights protects individual rights against violations by all branches of government. Excluding judges from the exclusionary rule means that it is not viewed as a constitutional right.

[h] Judges have immunity from lawsuit for errors made on the bench but are subject to reversal on appeal to correct their errors and deter them from not following precedent. Are not magistrates concerned if their warrants are overturned as illegal?

(continued)

77

[i] Does Justice White select his assumptions? He brushes aside the educative function of the law—the idea that over time the exclusionary rule will educate police officers to follow the amendment. (See the "Law in Society" section on the effects of the exclusionary rule.)

rule in cases where the police failed to demonstrate probable cause in the warrant application deters future inadequate presentations or "magistrate shopping" and thus promotes the ends of the Fourth Amendment. Suppressing evidence obtained pursuant to a technically defective warrant supported by probable cause also might encourage officers to scrutinize more closely the form of the warrant and to point out suspected judicial errors. **[i]** We find such arguments speculative and conclude that suppression of evidence obtained pursuant to a warrant should be ordered only on a case-by-case basis and only in those unusual cases in which exclusion will further the purposes of the exclusionary rule.

We have frequently questioned whether the exclusionary rule can have any deterrent effect when the offending officers acted in the objectively reasonable belief that their conduct did not violate the Fourth Amendment. "No empirical researcher, proponent or opponent of the rule, has yet been able to establish with any assurance whether the rule has a deterrent effect. * * *" But even assuming that the rule effectively deters some police misconduct and provides incentives for the law enforcement profession as a whole to conduct itself in accord with the Fourth Amendment, it cannot be expected, and should not be applied, to deter objectively reasonable law enforcement activity.

* * *

[j] What does Justice White imply by "no police illegality"? Leon's Fourth Amendment rights *have* been violated. If the officer is not civilly liable and there is no exclusion, what is the value of Leon's rights?

This is particularly true, we believe, when an officer acting with objective good faith has obtained a search warrant from a judge or magistrate and acted within its scope. In most such cases, there is no police illegality and thus nothing to deter. * * * **[j]**

C

* * *

Suppression * * * remains an appropriate remedy if the magistrate or judge in issuing a warrant was misled by information in an affidavit that the affiant knew was false or would have known was false except for his reckless disregard of the truth. * * * The exception we recognize today will also not apply in cases where the issuing magistrate wholly abandoned his judicial role. * * * Nor would an officer manifest objective good faith in relying on a warrant based on an affidavit "so lacking in indicia of probable cause as to render official belief in its existence entirely unreasonable." * * * Finally, depending on the circumstances of the particular case, a warrant may be so facially deficient—*i.e.*, in failing to particularize the place to be searched or the things to be seized—that the executing officers cannot reasonably presume it to be valid. * * * **[k]**

[k] The good faith reliance-on-the-warrant exception is not a blank check to the police. Four exceptions to the exception are set out where the exclusionary rule applies. This cautions police to get warrants where possible. Would it not be simpler for the Court to issue a bright line rule requiring warrants?

* * *

JUSTICE BLACKMUN, concurring.

* * *

[l] Justice Blackmun's concurrence says that the Court may reverse its rule in *Leon* if the police misuse it with pretext searches. Isn't the Court supposed to establish firm rules of law? Is he just being honest about the flexibility of constitutional law?

* * * [T]he Court has narrowed the scope of the exclusionary rule because of an empirical judgment that the rule has little appreciable effect in cases where officers act in objectively reasonable reliance on search warrants. * * * **[l]**

What must be stressed, however, is that any empirical judgment about the effect of the exclusionary rule in a particular class of cases necessarily is a provisional one. By their very nature, the assumptions on which we proceed today cannot be cast in stone. To the contrary, they now will be tested in the real world of state and federal law enforcement, and this Court will attend to the results. If it should emerge from experience that, contrary to our expectations, the good-faith exception to the exclusionary rule results in a material change in police compliance with the Fourth Amendment, we shall have to reconsider what we have undertaken here. The logic of a decision that rests on untested predictions about police conduct demands no less.

* * *

JUSTICE BRENNAN, with whom JUSTICE MARSHALL joins, dissenting.

Ten years ago in *United States v. Calandra,* 414 U.S. 338 (1974), I expressed the fear that the Court's decision "may signal that a majority of my colleagues have positioned themselves to reopen the door [to evidence secured by official lawlessness] still further and abandon altogether the exclusionary rule in search-and-seizure cases" (dissenting opinion). **[m]** Since then, in case after case, I have witnessed the Court's gradual but determined strangulation of the rule. It now appears that the Court's victory over the Fourth Amendment is complete. * * *

[m] This strong language may be discounted as a tactic, but it *is* a way of reaching beyond the majority to stir a wider audience and future generations in the hope that a different Court might overturn this decision.

* * *

The majority ignores the fundamental constitutional importance of what is at stake here. * * * [W]hat the Framers understood [in 1791] remains true today—that the task of combating crime and convicting the guilty will in every era seem of such critical and pressing concern that we may be lured by the temptations of expediency into forsaking our commitment to protecting individual liberty and privacy. It was for that very reason that the Framers of the Bill of Rights insisted that law enforcement efforts be permanently and unambiguously restricted in order to preserve personal freedoms. * * * **[n]** [T]he sometimes unpopular task of ensuring that the government's enforcement efforts remain within the strict boundaries fixed by the Fourth Amendment was entrusted to the courts. * * * If those independent tribunals lose their resolve, however, as the Court has done today, and give way to the seductive call of expediency, the vital guarantees of the Fourth Amendment are reduced to nothing more than a "form of words." * * *

[n] Justice Brennan accuses the majority of "selling out" the constitutional rights of citizens because fear of crime was a popular political issue to the presidents who appointed them. Do you agree?

I

* * *

A

[JUSTICE BRENNAN restated the majority argument here: The exclusionary rule is a mere judicial remedy designed to deter police illegality; the constitutional wrong is complete when the police invade a person's constitutionally protected privacy; and thus there is no constitutional violation if unconstitutionally seized evidence is admitted into evidence.]

Such a reading appears plausible, because * * * The Fourth Amendment makes no express provision for the exclusion of evidence secured in violation of its commands. * * * [M]any of the Constitution's most vital imperatives are stated in general terms and the task of giving meaning to these precepts is therefore left to subsequent judicial decisionmaking in the context of concrete cases. **[o]** The nature of our Constitution, as CHIEF JUSTICE MARSHALL long ago explained, "requires that only its great outlines should be marked, its important objects designated, and the minor ingredients which compose those objects be deduced from the nature of the objects themselves." * * *

[o] This point might better apply to a more open-textured right such as "due process" than to the more narrowly focused Fourth Amendment.

A more direct answer may be supplied by recognizing that the Amendment, like other provisions of the Bill of Rights, restrains the power of the government as a whole; it does not specify only a particular agency and exempt all others. The judiciary is responsible, no less than the executive, for ensuring that constitutional rights are respected.

(continued)

[p] Do you agree that the line between Fourth Amendment rights and the exclusionary rule is artificial—that is, that the two should be inseparable? All legal doctrine involves line drawing. Do you think Justice Brennan provides a better rationale for the exclusionary rule as a constitutional right?

* * * Once that connection between the evidence-gathering role of the police and the evidence-admitting function of the courts is acknowledged, the plausibility of the Court's interpretation becomes more suspect. * * * The Amendment therefore must be read to condemn not only the initial unconstitutional invasion of privacy—which is done, after all, for the purpose of securing evidence—but also the subsequent use of any evidence so obtained.

The Court evades this principle by drawing an artificial line between the constitutional rights and responsibilities that are engaged by actions of the police and those that are engaged when a defendant appears before the courts. [p] According to the Court, the substantive protections of the Fourth Amendment are wholly exhausted at the moment when police unlawfully invade an individual's privacy and thus no substantive force remains to those protections at the time of trial when the government seeks to use evidence obtained by the police.

I submit that such a crabbed reading of the Fourth Amendment * * * rests ultimately on an impoverished understanding of judicial responsibility in our constitutional scheme. For my part, "[t]he right of the people to be secure in their persons, houses, papers, and effects, against unreasonable searches and seizures" comprises a personal right to exclude all evidence secured by means of unreasonable searches and seizures. The right to be free from the initial invasion of privacy and the right of exclusion are coordinate components of the central embracing right to be free from unreasonable searches and seizures.

* * *

B

* * *

* * * [T]he Court since *Calandra* has gradually pressed the deterrence rationale for the rule back to center stage. * * * [JUSTICE BRENNAN then reviewed the cost-benefit analysis utilized by the majority.] * * *

* * * To the extent empirical data are available regarding the general costs and benefits of the exclusionary rule, it has shown, on the one hand, as the Court acknowledges today, that the costs are not as substantial as critics have asserted in the past, * * * and, on the other hand, that while the exclusionary rule may well have certain deterrent effects, it is extremely difficult to determine with any degree of precision whether the incidence of unlawful conduct by police is now lower than it was prior to *Mapp*. * * * The Court has sought to turn this uncertainty to its advantage by casting the burden of proof upon proponents of the rule. * * *

[q] This is a strong point. Should basic rights depend on measured effectiveness? If so, could a tyrant fail to uphold rights and then demand that they be abolished because they don't "work." Does this critique properly apply to a "remedy"?

* * * [B]y basing the rule solely on the deterrence rationale, the Court has robbed the rule of legitimacy. A doctrine that is explained as if it were an empirical proposition but for which there is only limited empirical support is both inherently unstable and an easy mark for critics. [q] The extent of this Court's fidelity to Fourth Amendment requirements, however, should not turn on such statistical uncertainties. * * * Rather than seeking to give effect to the liberties secured by the Fourth Amendment through guesswork about deterrence, the Court should restore to its proper place the principle framed 70 years ago in *Weeks* that an individual whose privacy has been invaded in violation of the Fourth Amendment has a right grounded in that Amendment to prevent the government from subsequently making use of any evidence so obtained.

* * *

erroneously authorized a search for controlled substances and did not incorporate the affidavit. (See Chapter 3.) The officers executing the warrant searched Sheppard's residence for items listed in the affidavit but not in the warrant. Incriminating evidence was found and entered into the trial. The Supreme Court held that the police objectively relied in good faith on a defective warrant. In this instance, the good faith reliance exception avoided an unreasonable conclusion. Indeed, Justice Stevens, who concurred in the decision, felt that the warrant and affidavit were quite specific and that the magistrate and the police officers were fully aware of their contents. Thus he believed there was no Fourth Amendment defect and that the majority manufactured one in order to expand the good faith exception.

Arizona v. Evans (1995) is more disturbing. Evans was stopped by a Phoenix police officer for driving the wrong way on a one-way street. A computer check indicated an outstanding misdemeanor warrant; he was arrested, and marijuana was discovered. However, the arrest warrant against Evans had, in actuality, been quashed seventeen days prior to his arrest. An error in the court clerk's office resulted in the information not being conveyed to the sheriff's office to remove the arrest notation from the law enforcement computer database. The Arizona Supreme Court excluded the evidence because there was no basis for the arrest and the "application of the exclusionary rule would 'hopefully serve to improve the efficiency of those who keep records in our criminal justice system.'"

The state appealed, and the Supreme Court reversed. Chief Justice William Rehnquist, writing for the Court, held that the exclusionary rule did not apply. The Court noted that the rule is designed to deter unconstitutional police activity, and not errors made by judges or personnel in judicial bureaucracies. It reasoned that there is no reason to believe that the exclusionary rule will deter errors by court clerks. Unlike police who are "zealous" in their desire to "get" suspects, court clerks "have no stake in the outcome of particular criminal prosecutions."

This reasoning seems as wrongheaded as the application of the exclusionary rule in *Sheppard*. Justice O'Connor apparently recognized this in her concurring opinion, which expressed concern that widespread computer errors might undermine individual rights. Justice Stevens dissented on the grounds that the Fourth Amendment's text and history have the more majestic goal of protecting individual privacy and liberty from encroachment from any part of the government. *Arizona v. Evans* (1995) shows that rights can be lost from the negligent maintenance of modern technology as they can from more direct state action.

It is extremely important to note that there is no free-floating "good-faith exception" that allows police officers to enter homes or other areas in which people have an expectation of privacy because they reasonably feel they have probable cause. The Supreme Court has not approved an exclusionary rule exception for using illegally obtained evidence based on a police officer's good faith observations leading to a warrantless stop, arrest, or search. Each good faith exception is tied to the officer's reliance on the decision of a magistrate, a statute, or official records. According to Professors Charles Whitebread and Christopher Slobogin, the Court has deliberately avoided the issue of a general good faith exception.[34] There may indeed be instances when police arrest or search without probable cause but do so in objective good faith. Nevertheless, the inherent human subjectivity that tends to make every person a "biased judge" about his or her own actions would make such an exception a more risky proposition for individual rights than allowing the use of unconstitutional evidence obtained by the officer's good faith reliance on the judgment of the legislature or a judge. It seems that allowing officers to dispense with warrants on their own evaluation would tend to weaken if not destroy the Warrant Clause and seriously damage Fourth Amendment protections.

The Supreme Court has reminded police officers that they are personally liable in lawsuits to those whose houses they enter if they rely on obviously defective search warrants. *Groh v. Ramirez* (2004) held, in a five-to-four decision, that a search warrant that did not list any of the items to be seized is plainly unconstitutional. Joseph Ramirez was not prosecuted after a search of his ranch, and he sued Special Agent Jeff Groh, of the Bureau of Alcohol, Tobacco and Firearms (ATF), for violating his Fourth Amendment rights. The Supreme Court ruled that Agent Groh could not claim qualified immunity from the lawsuit because it was clear to a reasonably competent officer that his conduct was unreasonable. The Court, in *Groh,* quoted *Leon:* "[D]epending on the circumstances of the particular case, a warrant may be so facially deficient—*i.e.,* in failing to particularize the place to be searched or the things to be seized—that the executing officers cannot reasonably presume it to be valid." A law enforcement officer is not absolved from personal responsibility to read a warrant carefully and be sure it is constitutional on its face before executing it merely because a magistrate has issued the warrant. (The case is discussed in Chapter 3.)

Standing

To have "**standing** to sue," a party must have a real stake in a legal controversy to bring a lawsuit. In federal cases, standing is predicated on Article III of the Constitution, which confers jurisdiction on federal courts only in "cases or controversies." A "stranger" to a controversy, who does not have a real legal claim, is not allowed to file a case or to pursue an issue in a court case. As applied to Fourth Amendment issues, the standing rule weakens the exclusionary rule because it prevents defendants from challenging the legality by which the evidence is obtained unless they have standing.

The search and seizure standing doctrine grew out of the older concept that Fourth Amendment rights are based on property interests: One had to have some level of property interest to assert a claim against an alleged illegal search and seizure. Standing was at first limited to owners, renters, or others with a legal connection to a place, like a hotel guest. House guests did not have standing. Suspects charged with possessory crimes (e.g., drugs) or crimes where possessing an item proved guilt (e.g., burglar's tools) had standing only by claiming possession of the seized item, which was an admission of guilt.

Jones v. United States (1960) eased standing rules. Police entered an apartment with a warrant, discovered drugs inside, and charged Jones with possession. Jones did not rent the apartment, but the owner gave him a key to the place and allowed him to sleep there and keep some clothing there. The Supreme Court held that a defendant who is "legitimately on the premises" and has some connection to the place has standing to raise a Fourth Amendment challenge. Jones, therefore, did not have to assert ownership of the drugs to claim that the search warrant was unconstitutional. In *Jones,* the Court rejected technical property law classifications as the basis of standing.

The *Jones* opinion used broad language that suggested the **target theory** of standing: that anyone charged with a crime based on evidence obtained in a search and seizure (except burglars or trespassers) could challenge the legality of the seizure. The Court, however, rejected the target theory and retained the standing requirement in *Alderman v. United States* (1969). *Alderman* held that "Fourth Amendment rights are personal rights which, like some other constitutional rights, may not be vicariously asserted." In *Alderman,* conversations made by co-defendants that did not include Alderman were picked up by electronic eavesdropping. The Court ruled that Alderman's Fourth Amendment right to privacy was not violated by eavesdropping on the conversations of others.

The Court has continued to uphold standing and the specific rule of *Jones.* In fact, a person without a key has standing to challenge an apartment entry as long as there is enough of a connection to create an expectation of privacy. *Minnesota v. Olson* (1990) affirmed a state court ruling that held that a defendant who was an overnight guest had standing to challenge the introduction of evidence taken from the apartment. Olson had indefinite permission to stay and had the right to allow or deny visitors entry. "To hold that an overnight guest has a legitimate expectation of privacy in his host's home merely recognizes the everyday expectations of privacy that we all share. . . . From the overnight guest's perspective, he seeks shelter precisely because it provides him with privacy, a place where he and his possessions will not be disturbed by anyone but his host and those his host allows inside" (*Minnesota v. Olson,* 1990).

Business occupants of an apartment, to the contrary, generally do not have standing. In **Minnesota v. Carter** (1998), police entered an apartment on a tip that illicit drug business was being conducted there and found two men bagging cocaine. They were from out of town and "had come to the apartment for the sole purpose of packaging the cocaine. [They] had never been to the apartment before and were only in the apartment for approximately 2 1/2 hours. In return for the use of the apartment, [they] had given [the renter] one-eighth of an ounce of the cocaine." On these facts, the Court held that the defendants had no standing to challenge the constitutionality of the police search. The majority noted that the apartment was not the dealers' home and that they had less connection to the apartment than an employee has in his or her private office. The Court characterized the facts of this case as "between" the expectation of privacy of the apartment dweller in *Olson* and a case where someone who is "legitimately on the premises" has no standing. Factors that negated standing included "the purely commercial nature of the transaction engaged in here, the relatively short period of time on the premises, and the lack of any previous connection between respondents and the householder" (*Minnesota v. Carter,* 1998). Justice Ruth Bader Ginsburg dissented, arguing that the decision undermines the security of short-term guests and that anyone whom a homeowner or renter invites "into her home to share in a common endeavor, whether it be for conversation, to engage in leisure activities, or for business purposes licit or illicit, . . . should share his host's shelter against unreasonable searches and seizures."

These holdings reflect the impact of *Katz v. United States,* which created the "expectation of privacy" doctrine in 1967. (See Chapter 3.) The idea that a person, under *Katz,* has a subjective and objective expectation of privacy in a premises where a search took place would tend to expand Fourth Amendment standing. The Supreme Court, however, has not applied *Katz* consistently, as seen in **Rakas v. Illinois** (1978). A police officer on a routine patrol stopped an automobile fitting the description of a getaway car used in a robbery and ordered the four occupants to exit. Two officers searched the vehicle's interior and found a box of rifle shells in the locked glove compartment and a sawed-off rifle under the front passenger seat. The woman who owned the car was the driver. This issue was whether Rakas, as a passenger, had standing to claim that the automobile search was unconstitutional in a prosecution in which the shells and rifle were entered into evidence against him. Rakas did not claim ownership or possession of the gun and shells. He argued that he had standing because he was legitimately in the car.

The Supreme Court, refusing to expand the *Jones* rule, and even narrowing it, held that Rakas did not have standing. Justice Rehnquist, writing for a five-justice majority, said that the concept of standing added little to the analysis of the case. The real issue was whether the search violated the defendant's personal Fourth Amendment rights, which had to be determined by examining the facts of the case. The *Rakas* majority stated that the phrase "legitimately on the premises" is too broad and would extend standing too far. Instead, a court must examine the defendant's connection with the premises. A casual visitor to an apartment, for example, has no standing to challenge a search, while an overnight guest does have standing. By analogy, the Court ruled that a passenger in a car does not have enough of a connection to challenge the seizure of a weapon that he claimed not to own.

Justice Byron White dissented. He felt that *Katz*'s "expectation of privacy" doctrine clarified the focus of Fourth Amendment analysis as being on the defendant's privacy right, uncoupled from ownership. Because Rakas was legitimately in the car, he had as much a privacy interest against an improper police search as did the driver. The flaw in the majority opinion was that "[t]he distinctions the Court would draw are based on relationships between private parties, but the Fourth Amendment is concerned with the relationship of one of those parties to the government" (*Rakas v. Illinois,* 1978, White, J., dissenting). The dissent noted that "the ruling today undercuts the force of the exclusionary rule in the one area in which its use is most certainly justified—the deterrence of bad-faith violations of the Fourth Amendment." The *Rakas* holding tempts police to engage in questionable automobile searches in which there is a passenger, in the hope that the passenger would not have standing to challenge an illegal search.

The extremes to which police may go when unconstrained by the exclusionary rule is seen in **United States v. Payner** (1980). Jack Payner was convicted of income tax fraud on the basis of information illegally seized from the briefcase of Michael Wolstencroft, the vice president of a Bahamian bank. Richard Jaffe, an Internal Revenue Service (IRS) special agent, hired Norman Casper, a private investigator, to study the bank. Casper struck up a friendship with Wolstencroft and introduced him to Sybol Kennedy, also a private investigator. On a business trip to Miami, Wolstencroft went to Kennedy's apartment, and the two went out to dinner. Wolstencroft left his briefcase in the apartment. Using a key supplied by Kennedy, Casper delivered the briefcase to Jaffe, who had four hundred bank documents photographed. A "lookout" observed Kennedy and Wolstencroft at dinner to ensure that the "briefcase caper" would not be discovered. Because the seizure violated only Wolstencroft's privacy, Payner had no standing to attack the legality of the seizure, even though the evidence was used against him.

Justice Powell, in his majority opinion, wrote, "No court should condone the unconstitutional and possibly criminal behavior of those who planned and executed this 'briefcase caper'" (*United States v. Payner,* 1980). The majority nevertheless upheld the use of the evidence, noting that the Court had to weigh the benefits of the exclusionary rule "against the considerable harm that would flow from indiscriminate application of an exclusionary rule." Justice Marshall, dissenting, commented that the Court's "holding effectively turns the standing rules created by this Court for assertions of Fourth Amendment violations into a sword to be used by the Government to permit it deliberately to invade one person's Fourth Amendment rights in order to obtain evidence against another person." The reason for this observation was that the lower courts found that the IRS "affirmatively counsel[ed] its agents that the Fourth Amendment standing limitation permits them to purposefully conduct an unconstitutional search and seizure of one individual in order to obtain evidence against third parties, who are the real targets of the governmental intrusion, and that the IRS agents in this case acted, and will act in the future, according to that counsel."

Heffernan points out that the Supreme Court's restrictive standing rule is in conflict with its theory that the only purpose of the exclusionary rule is to deter police illegality. If the Court were more serious about deterrence, it would allow a broader scope for challenging possibly illegal searches.[35] It seems unmistakable that the Burger and Rehnquist courts' restrictive standing doctrine is tied to their distaste for the exclusionary rule, a distaste that continues into the Roberts Court (*Hudson v. Michigan,* 2006).

ALTERNATIVE REMEDIES FOR FOURTH AMENDMENT VIOLATIONS

This section and the next examine the exclusionary rule through the perspective of the law of remedies. A substantive legal rule, whether in civil or criminal law, has no real effect without a remedy. People sue other people to get relief or recompense for legal wrongs they have suffered. A criminal statute that does not include a penalty is not a valid criminal law. The death of a defendant after a criminal conviction but before sentencing extinguishes the conviction.[36] The necessity of legal remedies is embedded in the Constitution. *Marbury v. Madison* (1803), the foundation of federal judicial power, stated

> The very essence of civil liberty certainly consists in the right of every individual to claim the protection of the laws, whenever he receives an injury.

> * * *

> The government of the United States has been emphatically termed a government of laws, and not of men. It will certainly cease to deserve this high appellation if the laws furnish no remedy for the violation of a vested right.

"According to *Marbury*'s ideal," asserts Professor Cornelia Pillard, "legal rights are not mere precatory or aspirational statements, but remediable claims, redressable in courts, for violations of law."[37] Legal remedies reflect the legitimacy of the government's constitutional promise to do justice (U.S. Const., preamble). To be blunt, constitutional rights become meaningless platitudes unless officers and the state are held accountable and are made to pay if and when their acts trample on the rights of individuals.

The basic question here is, What remedies are available when the government violates a person's constitutional rights? Is the exclusionary rule a valid or even a real remedy? The exclusionary rule is a point of furious contention in criminal procedure. The debate has proceeded on two tracks. A utilitarian track focuses on the effectiveness of the exclusionary rule as a deterrent to unconstitutional police action in comparison to other remedies and considers empirical questions as to the "costs" of the exclusionary rule (which are discussed in the "Law in Society" section in this chapter). The other track involves philosophical questions about the meaning of legal remedies, the status of the exclusionary rule as a constitutional doctrine, whether the rule is constitutionally required, and the extent to which the rule can be manipulated (topics discussed further in "Debating the Exclusionary Rule" later in this chapter). These debates have been played out in the Supreme Court's cases, and as was seen, the Court has provided shifting and inconsistent justifications for or about the rule in *Boyd, Weeks, Elkins, Mapp, Calandra, Leon,* and other cases. Although the Court's conservative majority has espoused the deterrence theory since *Calandra,* the Court's more liberal justices believe that this approach is flawed.

A major argument in favor of incorporating the exclusionary rule in *Wolf* (1949) and *Mapp* (1961) was that other means of gaining police compliance were not effective. Because of changed legal and social conditions in the last half century, it appears that civil lawsuits and administrative measures have a better chance of modifying police behavior. In *Hudson v. Michigan* (2006), Justice Scalia gave the "increasing professionalism of police forces, including a new emphasis on internal police discipline" as a reason to deny the application of the exclusionary rule to violations of the Fourth Amendment "knock and announce" rule. The issue is not whether there ought to be remedies for Fourth Amendment violations, but whether the exclusionary rule ought to be part of the remedial panoply.

There is no doubt that federal and state civil lawsuits against police and municipalities for money damages, injunctions against police action for widespread Fourth Amendment violations, and criminal prosecution of police officers who egregiously violate rights are true remedies. It is also undisputed as a matter of law that a variety of administrative measures, discussed below, which may be the most effective means of ensuring compliance with the Fourth Amendment, are not traditionally considered legal remedies. There has been jurisprudential debate as to whether the exclusionary rule is a "true" remedy, a question related to the Supreme Court's past flirtation with eliminating the rule.

A Theory of Remedies

Exclusionary rule opponents argue that it is not a legal remedy at all. In answer to the critics and as a prelude to the concluding sections, consider Heffernan's analysis. Unlike most commentators who discuss remedies as a unitary concept, Heffernan demonstrates that there are three types and goals of remedies. *First-party remedies* aim at **reparation,** to restore the injured party to the position he or she occupied before the injury occurred. *Second-party remedies* have the goal of **disgorgement,** to place the wrongdoer in no better position than the one he or she occupied prior to the wrongful conduct. *Third-party remedies* aim at deterring future wrongdoing, to the benefit of the general public—that is, "plac[ing] the public in a better position than it would be in if deterrence were not undertaken."[38] In practice, these types and goals of remedies may overlap in a single case and may be mutually supportive or at odds with one another. All three rationales have been used by the Supreme Court to support the exclusionary rule.

The Fourth Amendment protects three distinct rights—liberty, property, and privacy—not just privacy alone. It is true, as conservative justices have said, that once a suspect's privacy rights have been breached by a wrongful search and seizure, it is irreversible. The privacy violation by an illegal search and seizure "is *fully accomplished* by the original search" (*United States v. Calandra,* 1974, opinion of Powell, J., emphasis added). In this view, the only true remedy for a completed violation of privacy rights is reparation, a first-party remedy, via a civil lawsuit for money damages against the officer. However, if the state exploits the privacy violation by also violating a defendant's property or liberty interests, these are ongoing violations that can be repaired by returning the property or freeing the defendant. When the various interests protected by the Fourth Amendment, especially liberty, are considered, the exclusionary rule can be considered as much a true legal remedy as a lawsuit for money. While the invasion of privacy may have been "fully accomplished" at the time police illegally entered a premises, the invasion of the suspect's liberty interests continue during the prosecution, and the exclusionary rule provides a familiar remedy that courts are competent to administer.

The reparation remedy of monetary damages does not exhaust the range of available remedies. Note, by analogy, that a person harmed by a convicted criminal can sue the criminal in a civil suit. Nor does the existence of civil actions against police for Fourth Amendment violations undermine the legitimacy of the additional remedial goals of disgorgement and deterrence. In civil lawsuits for **injunctions** or specific performance, for example, disgorgement may be ordered where possible to prevent one who violated a person's rights from benefiting from the wrong. In the section "Debating the Exclusionary Rule," we return to this idea to demonstrate that a disgorgement theory of the exclusionary rule is not only plausible, but is embedded in the Fourth Amendment. Also by way of example, punitive damages may be paid to an injured party above what is needed to compensate for actual losses, specifically to deter the wrongdoer from doing the acts in the future—that is, to protect the public. Although the Supreme Court now rests the exclusionary rule solely on the deterrence rationale, it has so hedged in the rule that it is reasonable to ask whether the Supreme Court is "soft" on civil liberties.

Civil Lawsuits for Money Damages

The king's officers who invaded the homes of John Wilkes and his associates in the 1760s were sued in English common law courts, found liable for trespass, and ordered to pay substantial sums for violating the rights of British subjects. The colonials challenging writs of assistance were, in effect, seeking injunctions to prevent the Crown from issuing general search warrants. When the Bill of Rights was ratified, the Framers likely assumed that violations of privacy by the government would lead to lawsuits, which in turn would embarrass the government into preventing further abuses. As dissenting justices in *Wolf v. Colorado* and the majority in *Mapp v. Ohio* noted, however, police officers were almost never held responsible for violating individuals' Fourth Amendment rights. *Mapp* was predicated in part on the belief that *Weeks'* exclusionary rule was the best way of deterring police breach of rights. More recently, exclusionary rule critics have argued that alternate remedies are preferable.

Section 1983 Suits: State Officers in Federal Courts. Most civil rights lawsuits against municipal police officers are conducted in federal court under the Civil Rights Act of 1871, which is found in Title 42 *United States Code,* section 1983, and consequently are commonly known as **Section 1983 suits.** This right of action in federal courts against state and local officers was created by Congress after the Civil War, under the authority of the Fourteenth Amendment, in order to counteract Ku Klux Klan terrorism against African Americans. Such a lawsuit is based on a violation of a person's federal statutory or constitutional rights by someone "acting under the color of state law" or custom.

The law was not much used for a century. After the Supreme Court held in ***Monroe v. Pape*** (1961) that a Section 1983 claim could be based on a Fourth Amendment violation, thousands of Section 1983 suits proliferated. In *Monroe,* Chicago police officers entered the plaintiff's home at night without a warrant, rousted his family, and arrested and detained the plaintiff for ten hours without probable cause before releasing him. The history and wording of Section 1983 prevent lawsuits against state governments. In 1978, the Court reexamined the statute's history and extended Section 1983 lawsuits to cases against municipal governments, making them more attractive to plaintiffs; such suits are limited to situations in which the officer acted pursuant to a municipal policy.[39]

A study of hundreds of Section 1983 appeals decided between 1989 and 1993 found that 58 percent were for excessive force, false arrest, and illegal search and seizure. Plaintiffs suing the police won 24 percent of the illegal search and seizure cases. The police prevailed in 44 percent of these cases, and in 32 percent, the case was remanded for further findings. This study indicated that this form of civil lawsuit is not rare, that plaintiffs who sue law enforcement for rights violations have an opportunity to gain redress, but that a strong legal and factual case is needed to prevail.[40]

Bivens Suits: Federal Officers in Federal Courts.

In ***Bivens v. Six Unknown Named Agents*** (1971), the Supreme Court held for the first time that there is a federal constitutional **tort** remedy for violations of constitutional rights by federal agents. Prior to that time, a person whose only remedy was a civil suit had to pursue a doubly anomalous suit against such officers under state common law torts. The Civil Rights Act of 1871 (creating Section 1983 suits) applied only against local officers.

Webster Bivens was arrested at home by federal narcotics agents who searched his Brooklyn apartment "from stem to stern" and was strip-searched at booking. He was never prosecuted, so exclusion of evidence was a meaningless remedy. Because it was unlikely that he would again be arrested, an injunction suit made no sense. This made a civil lawsuit for money damages the only logical remedy for the wrongs done to him. His suit for damages based on an illegal arrest and search and seizure, however, was thrown out of federal court because no such cause of action existed in federal law. If Bivens sued in state court, the federal government might have tried to remove the case to federal court, where it would be dismissed on jurisdictional grounds. So Bivens appealed this catch-22 to the U.S. Supreme Court, urging the creation of a federal tort remedy.

The Supreme Court agreed with Bivens, saying that the fundamental rule that there must be a legal remedy for every legal wrong outweighed the doctrine of **sovereign immunity** that had previously blocked a federal constitutional tort. The Court noted that the constitutional interests in a federal suit were more serious than a trespass suit under state law, especially after *Katz v. United States* (1967) created the "expectation of privacy" doctrine, wherein the Fourth Amendment was held to be based on constitutional interests and not simply on property rights that are vindicated by the law of civil trespass. These federal lawsuits are known as ***Bivens*** **suits.**

State Common Law Tort Suits.

A person alleging that an arrest or a search occurred without probable cause can sue the offending police officer for an intentional tort such as false imprisonment or trespass. Private lawsuits against government units or agents were at one time blocked by the common law doctrine of sovereign immunity that was inherited from England. States have lifted sovereign immunity in part, but actual rules differ in different states. In a Florida case, for example, a sheriff's deputy gratuitously beat a suspect in handcuffs during a booking procedure, and the injured person sued the deputy and the Volusia County Sheriff's Department. Under Florida law, the deputy could be held liable for a civil battery if he acted within the scope of his employment. The department could be liable only if the deputy's acts exceeded the scope of his employment. Florida law was structured so that either the agency could be held liable or the deputy, but not both.[41]

State Constitutional Torts: State Officers in State Court.

In addition to shoehorning a constitutional violation into the shape of a common law tort, some state supreme courts, following the federal example, have established distinct state constitutional torts: a direct cause of action for damages for violation of a state constitutional right against a government or individual defendants. Unlike a state common law tort, which is designed to vindicate personal interests, a constitutional tort "reinforces the moral accountability of the state and vindicates the reliance interest of the people; . . . [it] holds the government responsible as an agent of the people."[42]

By 1998, twenty-one states had recognized an implied cause of action for state constitutional violations. Three additional states had indicated that they would do so under certain narrow circumstances. A private cause of action has been recognized in a twenty-fifth state by federal courts, and four states have enacted statutes that authorize causes of action for violation of state constitutional rights. Seven states have specifically rejected state constitutional causes of action.[43] For example, the New York Court of Appeals, that state's highest court, established a constitutional tort based on a violation of the New York constitution's search and seizure clause. In that case, state police and local law enforcement officials embarked on a five-day "street sweep" in which every nonwhite male found in and around the city of Oneonta was stopped and interrogated for a reported crime.[44]

In addition to these standard avenues of redress, lawyers may seek other remedies that exist in state or federal common law. A startling example, in a ruling by a Reagan-appointed federal trial judge, allowed the Los Angeles Police Department to be sued in August 2000 under the RICO (Racketeer Influenced and Corrupt Organizations) Act for the notorious Ramparts Division scandal. The scandal involved many police officers systematically arresting at least one hundred innocent people, planting incriminating evidence on them, giving perjured testimony, improperly using immigration officials in making arrests, and physically assaulting people without cause. The RICO law was first established to attack organized crime families but has been extended to other organizations that use illegal means to further their goals and interfere with interstate commerce. The benefit to the plaintiffs in the suit is that the RICO statute of limitations is ten years, and it allows triple damages. The potential damages to Los Angeles were put at $100 million.[45] Plaintiffs have not been successful in these cases, however, because a private RICO suit requires a showing of injury to business or property.[46]

Injunctions

Injunctions are not common remedies for Fourth Amendment violations. An injunction is a judicial order that either (1) commands a defendant to perform a particular act, (2) prohibits specified activity, or (3) orders a defendant to cease wrongful activity. Injunctions may be granted by a court where plaintiffs can prove that rights violations are persistent and repeated and that an injunction is the only effective remedy. Injunctions are enforced by the judicial power of **contempt of court,** which can include fines or jail for disobedience.

A prohibitory injunction was issued by a lower federal court and upheld on appeal by the Fourth Circuit in *Lankford v. Gelston* (1966) against a local police department that had been conducting a "dragnet" type search. Police officers searching for the killers of fellow police officers had, over a three-week period, entered three hundred houses based on anonymous tips and without legal justification. Because there were no arrests, the exclusionary rule could not be used to deter the officers; police activity was flagrant and persistent. Under these circumstances, the injunction was justified.[47]

The Supreme Court, however, has struck down federal injunctions against local police departments. In **Rizzo v. Goode** (1976), the Court reversed a federal injunction against the Philadelphia Police Department's cumbersome procedural process for investigating citizens' complaints about the use of excessive force. The Court reasoned that complainants had failed to demonstrate that the existing policy resulted in routine and persistent patterns of excessive force and civil rights violations. It did so despite the fact that the District Court heard a "staggering amount of evidence, including 250 witnesses over a 21-day period" who testified to widespread police abuses.[48] In *Los Angeles v. Lyons* (1983), the Court also struck down an injunction against the Los Angeles Police Department that prohibited the use of chokeholds, which were not specifically prohibited or authorized by departmental regulations. "At the time *Lyons* was decided, the chokehold had caused the deaths of over a dozen persons; by 1991, twenty-seven people had died as a result of this restraint technique. The Court dismissed the suit, holding that in order to have standing to sue for an injunction, the plaintiff must show that he is likely to be a future victim of that same technique."[49] These cases demonstrate that the Supreme Court believes it is unwise for federal courts to become involved in close judicial supervision of police department administration. Samuel Walker notes that this is odd in light of the Court's expansion of judicial oversight of prisons at that time.[50] It is noteworthy that effective federal oversight is now occurring under congressionally authorized pattern and practices lawsuits (discussed below).

Criminal Prosecution

State Prosecutions.   Criminal prosecutions of police officers for acts committed in the line of duty are rare and are limited to egregious cases, typically involving the death of a suspect.[51] It is difficult to obtain such a conviction if the defense attorney convinces the jury that the officer acted reasonably to enforce the law or if the victim suffered little or no personal injury. A notable example was the acquittal in February 2000 of four New York City Street Crime Unit police officers of the murder of Amadou Diallo, an African immigrant who was shot nineteen times as he reached for his wallet. The late James Fyfe, an expert who more often testified against police, concluded that the facts showed that the officers, who believed Diallo had a gun, had acted properly. A juror said the prosecution had not proved that the officers acted criminally.[52]

The past decade and a half was rife with notorious prosecutions of police officers, including the trial and first acquittal of Los Angeles police officers for beating Rodney King, a speeding motorist—a beating that was videotaped and played to a national audience.[53] In Detroit, police officers were convicted and imprisoned for the beating death of Malice Green.[54] Three white suburban Pittsburgh police officers were acquitted of manslaughter in the asphyxiation death of an African American motorist, Jonny Gammage.[55] In 2005, a New York City police officer who shot an immigrant during a warehouse chase was found guilty of criminally negligent homicide by a judge after a jury deadlocked on more serious charges. It was the first conviction of an on-duty New York officer for killing a civilian in a chokehold since a 1998 civil rights conviction.[56]

These sporadic prosecutions are a proper response to specific cases but have no impact on systemic errors or abuse unless they spark reforms. In the aftermath of the Louima case, which involved the sexual brutalization of Haitian immigrant Abner Louima by New York City police officers, for example, the city bowed to pressure and agreed to federal monitoring of the way in which officers accused of abuse are investigated and disciplined.[57]

Federal Prosecutions of Local Police Officers.   A federal civil rights law originally enacted in 1866 authorizes federal prosecution of local officers who, acting under color of local law or custom, deprive a person of rights under the Constitution (18 U.S.C. § 242). The Supreme Court has held that a conviction requires an intent to deprive a person of a specific constitutional right.[58] In recent decades, federal prosecutors have become more active in investigating and prosecuting crimes by local police. Federal civil rights prosecutions have included several high-profile cases, such as the second trial of the police officers involved in the Rodney King beating and the trial of officers involved in the brutalization of Haitian immigrant Abner Louima. If the sexual torture inflicted on

Louima was perpetrated by a private person, all bystanders would justly be horrified. But the additional concern in a civil rights violation was captured by the words of the federal judge who sentenced the police officer to thirty years' imprisonment: "Short of intentional murder, one cannot imagine a more barbarous misuse of power than Volpe's."[59] Misuse of power undermines trust in the government, makes people—especially the poor and dispossessed—skeptical of protection by the criminal justice system, and leads to the suspicion that honest police officers are actual or potential rights violators.

Administrative Measures

Ideally, violations of constitutional rights should rarely, if ever, occur. External legal sanction, such as the exclusionary rule or civil suits, may control police behavior to some extent, but they are reactions to past violations. They encourage future compliance through punishment, which has had limited effectiveness. (See the "Law in Society" section in this chapter.) Police officers are most likely to obey constitutional mandates like the Fourth Amendment when support and rewards for doing so come from within their departments. William Bratton, the innovative former New York City police commissioner, made obedience to the Constitution a key goal for the NYPD.[60] Nonjudicial and administrative methods, therefore, are essential to encourage police to adhere to the Rule of Law.

Many methods have been suggested for making police officers more understanding of the people they police and more mindful of their rights: community policing, civilian review boards,[61] police ombudsman programs,[62] accreditation of police departments,[63] civilianizing many roles in police departments,[64] tightening rules on the use of lethal force,[65] cultural diversity and sensitivity training,[66] higher standards for police recruits,[67] training in Asian martial arts,[68] and similar improvements. Better academy and in-service training in constitutional law is important. Slobogin has proposed replacing the exclusionary rule with a legal–administrative procedure in which a judge would hear defendants' complaints of privacy violations. If the judge found that a violation had occurred, he or she would require the officer personally to pay liquidated damages of between one to five percent of the officer's salary unless the violation was in good faith, in which case the police department would be financially responsible. In addition, class actions and injunctions would be available remedies.[69] This proposal may prove less than fully effective because the qualified immunity doctrine would protect officers from liability where it is not apparent that a suspect's rights have been violated. A more promising alternative approach was enacted by Congress: the pattern and practice review.

Pattern and Practice Review.

A federal law passed as part of the Violent Crime Control and Law Enforcement Act of 1994 has brought the weight of the Department of Justice (DOJ) to bear on finding nonjudicial solutions to police violations of constitutional rights. Title 42 U.S.C. § 14141 prohibits governmental authorities from engaging in a "pattern or practice of conduct by law enforcement officials" that deprives persons of constitutional rights. When the attorney general has reasonable cause to believe that a violation has occurred, the Justice Department is authorized to sue for equitable and declaratory relief "to eliminate the pattern or practice." DOJ monitoring is not triggered by isolated incidents of unlawful acts but by conditions where unlawful acts have virtually become "standard operating procedure." The law is an attempt to find a better way to respond to situations like the Rodney King beating than civil and criminal cases aimed at specific officers.

In 1999, two police departments (Pittsburgh, Pennsylvania, and Steubenville, Ohio) entered pattern and practice consent decrees for excessive force, improper searches and seizures, and false arrest. Since that beginning, other major departments, including Cincinnati, Detroit, Los Angeles, and the New Jersey State Police, were investigated and have entered into monitoring processes designed to improve critical police performance.[70] "By 2004, the Department of Justice had reached settlements with 19 law enforcement agencies, either through consent decrees, memoranda of understanding, or settlement letters."[71]

The principal provisions of Section 14141 settlements impose requirements in the areas of police "training, the receipt and investigation of referrals and complaints concerning improper police behavior; and the development and maintenance of an early warning system." Although enforcement of Section 14141 is in its earliest stages, this "new remedy for police misconduct" seems to offer a substantial improvement over traditional tort remedies.[72] According to leading police scholar Samuel Walker, **pattern and practice suits** are an important part of a new thinking in policing that focuses on organizational and management problems as causes of police misconduct and that offers new organizational strategies to improve policing. Walker points out that while these approaches hold great promise for reducing police misconduct, they face considerable obstacles and are not yet the norm in policing.[73]

Although some have argued that the remedies and administrative measures described in this section can replace the exclusionary rule, a safer course suggests that the entire spectrum of remedies is necessary to ensure that police comply with fundamental constitutional law and values.

DEBATING THE EXCLUSIONARY RULE

History and Theories of the Exclusionary Rule

The Supreme Court developed the exclusionary rule from 1886 to 1984 in a series of cases from *Boyd* to *Leon,* with different justifications offered in different cases. Some of the older theories were either discarded entirely or have limited sway. As a result of these competing theories, Fourth Amendment law is not entirely coherent. Although the Court has not recently threatened to abolish the exclusionary rule, the open hostility to the rule by the Court's conservative majority leads to more and more exceptions that give the rule a "Swiss cheese" quality (*Pennsylvania Board of Probation and Parole v. Scott,* 1998; *Hudson v. Michigan,* 2006).

Fifth Amendment Theory. The strange case of *Boyd v. United States* (1886) excluded evidence on the theory that the "Fourth and Fifth Amendments run almost into each other." The Fourth Amendment exclusionary rule has been criticized because the amendment does not explicitly include a rule of exclusion, while the Fifth Amendment *is* an exclusionary rule. (Saying that "no person shall be compelled in any criminal case to be a witness against himself" means that compelled evidence is inadmissible.) Several cases relied on the *Boyd* Fourth + Fifth formula (*Gouled v. United States,* 1921), and Justice Black's crucial fifth vote in *Mapp* was based on this theory. It made some sense because in many early exclusionary rule cases, including *Weeks,* letters or documents were seized. Nevertheless, the Court discarded the theory in *Andresen v. Maryland* (1976), which held that business records could be seized under a warrant. In *Leon* (1984), Justice White buried the Fifth Amendment theory, stating that it "has not withstood critical analysis or the test of time."[74] The idea that a search compels the disclosure of evidence would make searches impossible, because "the Fifth Amendment excludes all compelled testimony, whether or not it was obtained by police who had probable cause."[75] This could not have been contemplated by the Fourth Amendment's Framers.

Property Theory. *Weeks* (1914), *Silverthorne* (1920), and other cases seemed to rest on the idea that a defendant has a greater property right over evidence illegally seized than the state does. Several inconsistencies undermine the **property theory.** A successful defendant, for example, will not have contraband returned, even if the evidence is suppressed.[76] Under existing forfeiture laws, all sorts of "innocent" items used in the commission of a crime may be forfeited. In theory, the "expectation of privacy" doctrine of *Katz v. United States* (1967) abolished the property basis of Fourth Amendment jurisprudence. By making nontangible information "seized" by electronic eavesdropping the subject of the Fourth Amendment, property was displaced, if not eliminated, as a theoretical basis of the exclusionary rule. The *Katz* philosophy was confirmed and strengthened by *Warden v. Hayden* (1967), which abolished the "mere evidence" rule. After *Warden*, police could lawfully seize any property relevant to a criminal investigation, not just contraband, loot, or instruments used to commit the crime, and they could hold it until the case was completed. The *Katz* doctrine balances law enforcement needs against individual privacy and property rights. As will be seen later in this text, however, the Court in some cases has implicitly relied on the value of property, especially private homes, in applying the rule.

The Imperative of Judicial Integrity/Rule of Law. In *Weeks* (1914) and *Mapp* (1961), the Court justified the rule as one required by the Constitution and applicable to federal and (later) state legislatures, executive agencies (i.e., the police), and courts. In *Elkins v. United States* (1960), which banned the "silver platter" doctrine, Justice Potter Stewart reasoned that by incorporating the Fourth Amendment's ban on illegal search and seizures into the Fourteenth Amendment Due Process Clause, *Wolf v. Colorado* (1949) undermined its ruling that the exclusionary rule did not apply to the states. It is true that the exclusionary rule rested in part on deterring police illegality. "But there is another consideration—the imperative of judicial integrity" (*Elkins*, 1960). The courts undermine the Rule of Law if they allow illegally seized evidence to be admitted. There are several nonutilitarian aspects to this rationale. First, it enables "the judiciary to avoid the taint of partnership in official lawlessness," no small matter in a branch of government destined by the founders to be the guardian of civil rights and liberties (*Calandra*, 1974, Brennan, J., dissenting). Second, it is an "enforcement tool [that] give[s] content and meaning to the Fourth Amendment's guarantees" (ibid.). In other words, it serves a similar function as the penalty portion of a criminal statute, that by prescribing a sanction for wrongful conduct, gives moral substance to the rule whatever its effectiveness. The imperative also assures "the people—all potential victims of unlawful government conduct—that the government would not profit from its lawless behavior" (ibid.). This is the disgorgement rationale, discussed below. To the extent that the imperative of judicial integrity is an ethical basis for the rule, it implies that courts must never allow evidence seized in violation of the Constitution to be used. As Justice Holmes wrote in *Silverthorne* (1920), "The essence of a provision forbidding the acquisition of evidence in a certain way is that not merely evidence so acquired shall not be used before the Court but that it shall not be used at all."

Deterrence Theory. The cases that developed the exclusionary rule, *Weeks* (1914) and *Mapp* (1961), did not rest entirely on nonconsequentialist theories of constitutional imperatives, but also on the idea that the exclusion of evidence would deter the government from violating constitutional rights. The current Supreme Court has taken this rationale and made it the only basis for the exclusionary rule. This approach was first declared in *Calandra* (1974) and has been applied in subsequent cases, most notably in *Leon* (1984). Where deterrence is thought minimal, the rule does not apply.[77] Because deterrence is a utilitarian rationale, its legitimacy turns largely on whether it is effective, a subject of debate that is the focus of the "Law in Society" section in this chapter.

Is the Exclusionary Rule Constitutionally Required?

The *Calandra–Leon* thesis seems to say that the rule is not required. First, the rule is not explicitly mentioned in the Fourth Amendment's language. This should not be a problem because the Court has created so many constitutional doctrines not explicitly stated in the constitutional text as to lead scholars to discuss "constitutional common law."[78] It is only a concern because justices recite this reason even while enforcing the exclusionary rule.

Next, because the Fourth Amendment's purpose is said to be preventing unreasonable government intrusions into the privacy of one's person, house, papers, or effects, and the invasion of privacy is fully accomplished by the original search without probable cause, excluding evidence cannot repair that loss. Connected to this, the *Calandra–Leon* thesis says that the use of illegally seized evidence causes no new Fourth Amendment wrong but is only a derivative use of the product of past unlawful search and seizure. The "fully accomplished" argument is answered by the thesis, discussed in the previous section, that the Fourth Amendment protects several values (liberty, privacy, and property) and thus exclusion of evidence obtained during the violation of a person's privacy also protects liberty and property rights.

To Slobogin, exceptions to the rule, even when the *Weeks* doctrine was in force (e.g., *Walder v. U.S.,* 1954), plus the ruling that *Mapp* was not retroactive (*Linkletter v. Walker,* 1965), mean that it is not an absolute constitutional right and is not "appropriate as a remedy in the typical case."[79] The Supreme Court, however, has made it quite clear that a constitutional rule may have exceptions (*Dickerson v. U.S.,* 2000; see Chapter 7). Also, the nonretroactivity of *Mapp* (1961) was based in part on the fact that the states' reliance on *Wolff* (1949) between 1949 and 1961 "would have required the wholesale release of innumerable convicted prisoners, few of whom could have been successfully retried" and that to do so would not further "the administration of justice and the integrity of the judicial process" (*United States v. Calandra,* Brennan, J., dissenting).

Nevertheless, the Court did create and extend the exclusionary rule in *Weeks* and *Mapp* and did base it in part on deterrence. Furthermore, the Court continues to apply the rule and impose it on the states. Although the Court's majority "has been strangely silent as to its authority for the exclusionary rule in state courts," it is clear that this authority must come from the Fourth Amendment and not from the Court's supervisory power, which extends only to federal cases.[80] This has to be true even if the Court says that the rule "is not derived from the Constitution but rather is merely a judicially created remedy that continues to exist solely for its alleged deterrent effect"[81] because the Court's decision is what ultimately counts as law, and the Court has no power to simply create a rule without some foundation in its statutory or constitutional jurisdiction. The rule may be based on its deterrent purpose, but it is still grounded in the Fourth Amendment. This level of incoherence and dissonance between the Court's language and its actions was not anticipated in a report issued by the Justice Department during the Reagan administration, which forthrightly urged the Court to abolish the exclusionary rule because cases since *Mapp* emphasized the "non-constitutional status of the rule."[82] This is an example of the occasional need in interpreting case law to look beyond the words in opinions to fathom what the law has to mean.

The constitutional basis of the exclusionary rule can be logically confirmed by considering one additional theory, based on the second-part remedy of disgorgement: the status quo ante theory.

Status Quo Ante Theory.
The exclusionary rule returns the parties to where they would have been had the Constitution been followed. This is a commonsense and ethical rationale. It also explains the inevitable discovery exception to the "fruits of the poisonous tree" doctrine: Because the police would have legally obtained the evidence in any event, they should not be placed in a difficult position because an unconstitutional search occurred. Slobogin claims that the theory is inadequate because it does not result in the return of contraband, but this is no answer to the underlying logic that this would not have been an issue if the Constitution had been obeyed. His objection that the rule cannot restore the "ruptured privacy" of the person subjected to an illegal search and seizure misses the multiple values protected by the amendment. Slobogin also objects that the status quo ante does not allow introduction of evidence where the police could have

lawfully obtained the evidence; this is specious because it is always possible to conjure up some way in which police might have properly obtained evidence—such reasoning makes any compliance rule impossible.[83] In any event, the Supreme Court has allowed exceptions to the exclusionary rule where police would have properly obtained evidence under the "fruits of the poisonous tree" doctrine.

The *per curiam* case of *Smith v. Ohio* (1990), enforcing the rule against retrospective justification, was discussed earlier in the section on the "fruits of the poisonous tree" doctrine. The rule is simplicity itself. Police cannot search without any legal justification or otherwise commit illegal search and seizures and then argue that the search is proper if they find incriminating evidence. The Fourth Amendment, which protects individual privacy, liberty, and property, requires that government officers have justification before they search or seize. This rule is so basic that it is rarely discussed, but it embodies all of the justifications of the exclusionary rule: deterrence, status quo ante, and judicial integrity.

According to Heffernan, the internal logic of the Fourth Amendment against retroactive justification requires the "remedy" of exclusion even if the Framers did not consider exclusion, because without the exclusionary rule the amendment "collapses on itself."[84] The government cannot insist on holding on to illegally seized evidence in order to determine if it discloses incriminating information, for that would allow seizures before probable cause is obtained. "Absent exclusion, all personal property is held on a probationary basis: government agents can seize personal property at will, inspect it, and return it only if it is found not to provide evidence of a crime."[85] The internal logic of the Fourth Amendment cannot allow this kind of retroactive legitimation. If the exclusionary rule were totally eliminated, police could choose to violate Fourth Amendment rights in specific cases they deem important and be willing to pay the price in a tort action if it came to that. Thus Heffernan believes that Justice Holmes and the Court had it right in *Silverthorne* (1920). Whatever the Framers thought about exclusion as a remedy, the Court in *Weeks* and *Silverthorne* intuited that the exclusionary principle "emerges from an analysis of the internal logic of the Amendment itself."[86] This is so even if exclusion does not repair the violation of first-party privacy interests and extracts a heavy cost to the public whose third-party interest in deterrence is offset by an interest in convicting the guilty. Nevertheless, the liberty-protecting function of the Constitution coalesces with and is required by the second-party remedy of disgorgement via exclusion that is required by the logic of the Fourth Amendment.

If this is correct and the exclusionary rule is required by the Fourth Amendment, the situation still is that the Court has riddled the exclusionary rule with exceptions. The dissonance in the Court's language hinting that the exclusionary rule is not based on the Constitution when it continued to apply it to the states (which would violate the Constitution if the Court's words were taken at face value) and the many exceptions to the rule appear to be driven in part by the distaste for Warren Court rulings that has been part of the ideology of American conservatism since the administration of Richard Nixon. The dislike of the exclusionary rule is closely linked to the crime control approach in that the exclusionary rule logically suppresses relevant evidence of a suspect's guilt. In the worst-case scenario, it may allow a dangerous criminal go free because of a "technical violation." As Justice (then Judge) Cardozo, put it, "The criminal is to go free because the constable has blundered."[87] Of course, the rule may also apply when police officers ride roughshod over the rights of nondangerous petty criminals, like low-level drug users and sellers.[88] The effect of the Fourth Amendment exclusionary rule contrasts with Fifth and Sixth amendment exclusionary rules that suppress confessions or lead to dismissals for lack of effective counsel, because those errors might lead to the conviction of innocent defendants.

The dislike of the exclusionary rule is also connected to the belief that the exclusionary rule is a completely ineffective deterrent to police illegality. This argument seems logical because (1) the impact of exclusion is directly felt by the prosecutor rather than the officer, (2) police know and count on the fact that the rule is rarely applied, (3) judges are reluctant to find a Fourth Amendment violation when they know that evidence points to guilt (hindsight biasing),[89] (4) negative sanctioning for improper searches occurs indirectly via prosecutors' complaints to police administrators, which are relayed down the chain of command, and (5) negative sanctioning for illegal searches is offset by the praise and recognition that officers receive for making good arrests.[90] The "costs" and the deterrent effect are empirical questions that will be reviewed in the "Law in Society" section in this chapter.

Another argument against the exclusionary rule is that it encourages police perjury. Very few rogue police officers manufacture or plant evidence on innocent suspects, but many officers "shade the truth" when testifying in court, especially in possession cases. (See the "Law in Society" section in Chapter 3.) Not only is this a negative consequence for a sense of fairness in the courts, but police know that they can reduce the effectiveness of the exclusionary rule by their own success in undermining it.[91]

The result of these negative views is a situation where the Court views the "cost" of the exclusionary rule as worth paying by excluding evidence from the "case in chief" where it is likely to have the greatest deterrent effect. To the contrary, the Court has held that the exclusionary rule need not be imposed where it will have limited effect, such as impeachment, grand jury questions, civil cases, deportation, and parole revocation cases. It can be disregarded even in the trial to prove guilt where the officer reasonably and in good faith relied on the Fourth Amendment judgment of another official, such as a magistrate or the legislature, because it will have limited deterrent effect.[92] A leading law school textbook declares that "despite the Supreme Court's recent inroads, the exclusionary rule still operates to exclude most illegally obtained evidence from the guilt adjudication stage."[93]

DOMESTIC SPYING IN A TIME OF TERROR

The Supreme Court brought electronic eavesdropping under Fourth Amendment control in the 1960s (*Katz v. United States,* 1967; see Chapter 3). A 1968 comprehensive electronic eavesdropping law, known as "Title III," established elaborate procedures and required high levels of evidence before federal officers could obtain eavesdropping warrants.[94] The law was later extended to more advanced forms of communication.[95] A Title III provision excluded from the warrant requirement national security eavesdropping conducted under the president's authority. Evidence of abuses of domestic spying, authorized at the highest levels of government, came to light during the 1970s, including electronic spying on anti–Vietnam War protesters and civil rights activists. The Supreme Court held in *United States v. United States District Court* (1972) that the Title III warrant exemption did not apply to the electronic eavesdropping of citizens in criminal cases. The president was still permitted to spy on foreign embassies and agents, however, without a warrant.

After the Watergate crisis, a 1975 Senate report criticized the use of national security eavesdropping by the Nixon administration to spy on its political opponents. This led to the passage of the Foreign Intelligence Surveillance Act (FISA) in 1978. The president now had to apply to a special Foreign Intelligence Surveillance Court (FISC), consisting of seven sitting federal judges, for an electronic surveillance warrant to obtain foreign intelligence information. The act was expanded in 1994 to cover physical searches.[96] Between 1979 and 2001, there were 14,036 applications for FISA surveillances or searches, and all but one of these requests were granted.[97] Only four applications were modified before being issued.

The 2001 USA PATRIOT Act expanded the number of FISC judges to eleven and significantly changed FISA's language. Previously, FISA authorized warrants only when foreign intelligence was "the purpose" of the investigation. It was amended to allow authorizations when foreign intelligence information was "a significant purpose of the surveillance." A "foreign power" includes "a group engaged in international terrorism or activities in preparation therefor."[98] The language change from "the purpose" to "a significant purpose" eliminated a practice, known as "the wall," that prevented cooperation between the Justice Department (e.g., the FBI), which was responsible for domestic investigations, and intelligence agencies (especially the CIA), which conducted foreign investigations. Because of the low evidentiary standard for obtaining a FISA warrant, there was a desire to prevent the kind of misuse of foreign intelligence eavesdropping that had occurred under the Nixon administration.

After the September 11, 2001, terrorist attacks on the United States, it came to light that FBI field agents had sought help from the CIA to investigate Zacarias Moussaoui, believed to be the twentieth 9/11 hijacker. FBI officials saw this as a breach of protocol and before September 11 had rejected a request from the Minneapolis field office to seek a warrant to search Moussaoui's computer.[99] In light of the FBI's demonstrated weaknesses in antiterrorism, greater cooperation was certainly called for. Whether it should include using FISA warrants only for preventive purposes in the "war on terrorism," and not for prosecution, was answered by the courts and Congress.

After passage of the USA PATRIOT Act, the FISC attempted to preserve "the wall" by adding a condition to a warrant that "law enforcement officials shall not make recommendations to intelligence officials concerning the initiation, operation, continuation or expansion of FISA searches or surveillances." The FISC decision may have been stimulated by the fact that the FBI misstated or omitted material facts in at least seventy-five cases and sought to share intelligence material freely with criminal investigators.[100] The FISC decision was nevertheless reversed in the only appeal taken from a FISC decision to the Foreign Intelligence Surveillance Court of Review. It noted that the FISC "apparently believes it can approve applications for electronic surveillance only if the government's objective is *not* primarily directed toward criminal prosecution of the foreign agents for their foreign intelligence activity."[101] This, however, was not supported by the text of FISA or the USA PATRIOT Act or the intent of Congress. Separating counterterrorism entirely from prosecution made no sense because "the definition of foreign intelligence information includes evidence of crimes such as espionage, sabotage or terrorism" and "arresting and prosecuting terrorist agents of, or spies for, a foreign power may well be the best technique to prevent them from successfully continuing their terrorist or espionage activity."[102]

Although the end of "the wall" between the FBI and the CIA raises legitimate concerns about "law enforcement officials . . . [conducting] illegitimate and indiscriminate wiretapping on individuals without the threshold requirements mandated by the Fourth Amendment," such abuses are less likely in a reorganized FBI that has counterterrorism units in each district.[103] More importantly, the transnational and decentralized nature of adherents of Islamist ideologies makes the cooperation of domestic and foreign counterterrorism agencies necessary.

In late 2005, the *New York Times* reported that since 2002, under a secret presidential order, the National Security Agency (NSA), without court orders, monitored hundreds if not thousands of telephone calls and international e-mails where one party was not in the United States and the other was. The reason given for bypassing the FISC was that the FISC procedure was occasionally deemed too cumbersome and could impede the need for immediate eavesdropping. However, FISA allows for emergency eavesdropping under "extraordinary circumstances," as long as the government submits a warrant application within seventy-two hours. The NSA still submits FISC applications for calls being monitored for terror-related matters that are made within the United States.[104]

The NSA's warrantless eavesdropping, however, seems less concerned with listening in on specific individuals suspected of terrorism-related crimes and more attuned to a new concept of monitoring calls and messages known as "data mining." This technique relies on the assistance of telecommunication companies that give the NSA access to switches, located in the United States, that act as gateways to the borders between U.S. and international communications networks.[105] The actual number of communications swept up in these programs is not known, but a former AT&T employee disclosed, in a pending lawsuit seeking damages on behalf of AT&T customers, that the numbers may be very large.[106] According to James Bamford, a surveillance expert,

> Rather than monitoring a dozen or so people for months at a time, as had been the practice, the decision was made to begin secretly eavesdropping on hundreds, perhaps thousands, of people for just a few days or a week at a time in order to determine who posed potential threats.
>
> Those deemed innocent would quickly be eliminated from the watch list, while those thought suspicious would be submitted to the FISA court for a warrant.
>
> In essence, N.S.A. seemed to be on a classic fishing expedition, precisely the type of abuse the FISA court was put in place to stop.[107]

Data mining, combined with the NSA's "broad analytical searches" and actual eaves-dropping, is defended by Bush administration insiders as "an essential part of detecting and preventing terror attacks."[108] "President Bush characterized the eavesdropping program as a 'vital tool' against terrorism; Vice President Dick Cheney said it has saved 'thousands of lives.'"[109] To the contrary, however, the FBI has complained that virtually all of the "steady stream of telephone numbers, e-mail addresses and names" sent to them by the NSA just after the 9/11 attacks, which later grew to a flood and required "hundreds of agents to check out thousands of tips a month," led to dead ends or to innocent Americans.[110]

The data-mining story led to a year of heated politics. The president went on the air two days after the story broke to defend warrantless eavesdropping. The administration was angry at concerned officials who spoke anonymously to the press, and it initiated action to investigate the leaks for possible criminal violations. Top government leaders publicly defended the program, and the administration engaged in several media blitzes to support domestic spying, including a highly publicized visit by President Bush to the pre-viously off-limits NSA headquarters. Congress held hearings to investigate the program, and at one point Senate Intelligence Committee Chairman Pat Roberts, a Republican from Kansas, publicly supported FISC warrants. Lawsuits initiated by the American Civil Liberties Union and the Center for Constitutional Rights have resulted in a Detroit federal judge declaring the program unconstitutional; the New York case is pending. These cases will be appealed. By midyear 2006, the administration proposed to allow the Foreign Intelligence Surveillance Court of Review to determine the constitutionality of its warrant-less snooping. The administration, seeking to shift public debate toward national security and away from the Iraq War, worked to secure an antiterror program bill. At the end of 2006, the Senate Judiciary Committee approved three contradictory proposals. One would allow the FISA court to determine the constitutionality of the secret domestic spying program, another would authorize warrantless secret spying, and a third would affirm the 1978 FISA as the "exclusive" means of obtaining domestic electronic eavesdropping data against suspected terrorists (i.e., requiring warrants).[111]

Most significant for understanding the tension between security and liberty are the administration's legal arguments used to support secret spying on Americans. On its face, President Bush's secret order authorizing the NSA to spy on Americans without a judicial warrant seems to be a clear violation of FISA, which requires a warrant if even one party to the conversation is a "United States person." This would violate the president's duty under Article II to "take Care that the Laws be faithfully executed" (U.S. Const. art. II, § 3). The government argument, set forth in a letter to Congress, is based on (1) the president's inherent powers as commander in chief in a time of war and (2) the one-sentence congressional Authorization to Use Military Force (AUMF) to go to war in Afghanistan against al Qaeda and other terrorist organizations and persons responsible for the 9/11 attacks.[112]

A finely balanced analysis by the Congressional Research Service found that the arguments against the administration's position were far stronger than those in support. In *Youngstown Sheet and Tube v. Sawyer* (1952), the "Steel Seizure Case," the Supreme Court declared President Harry S. Truman's executive order seizing steel plants during the Korean War to be unconstitutional. *Youngstown Sheet and Tube* put definite limits on the president's wartime powers, especially where the president's actions are "incompatible with the expressed or implied will of Congress" (*Steel Seizure Case,* Jackson, J., concurring). When FISA was passed, the Title III provision that excluded national security eavesdropping conducted under the president's authority was eliminated and replaced by FISA. Congress intended to make the FISA procedure the only way in which the government could engage in national security eavesdropping of Americans on American soil. This militates against President Bush's position. In favor of his position, there is a statement by the Foreign Intelligence Review Court in *In re Sealed Case* (2002) that "takes for granted" the president's authority to conduct foreign intelligence eavesdropping.

As for the argument that electronic eavesdropping is the equivalent of the "force" allowed by the AUMF's authorization to "use all necessary and appropriate force against" nations, organizations, or persons that "planned, authorized, committed, or aided" in the 9/11 attacks, the president's lawyers argue that *Hamdi v. Rumsfeld* (2004) included the detention of "enemy combatants" captured in Afghanistan within the meaning of force.

> However, the Court appears to have relied on a more limited interpretation of the scope of the AUMF than that which the Administration had asserted in its briefs, and, declaring that a "state of war is not a blank check for the President when it comes to the rights of the Nation's citizens," the Court clarified that notwithstanding the authorization, such detainees have some due process rights under the U.S. Constitution.[113]

The administration position rests on two debatable assumptions: that electronic eavesdropping "is an essential aspect of the use of military force in the same way that the capture of enemy combatants on the battlefield is a necessary incident to the conduct of military operations," and that the "battlefield" in the war on terrorism extends beyond the area of traditional military operations to include U.S. territory.[114] These assumptions appear to go far beyond the intent of Congress in passing the AUMF. Congress certainly intended the military in Afghanistan to gather intelligence in the pursuit of the "conventional aspect of the conflict" even if it spread beyond the borders of Afghanistan. Only Justice Thomas, however, agreed with the administration's argument in *Hamdi* that the indefinite confinement of "enemy combatants" was an equivalent of battlefield intelligence. At the very least, the president's assumption that "the United States is under actual and continuing enemy attack, and the President has the authority to conduct electronic surveillance in the same way the armed forces gather intelligence about the military operations of enemy forces, even if no actual combat is taking place . . . may be seen as being overly broad."[115] The Congressional Research Service memorandum concludes,

> From the foregoing analysis, it appears unlikely that a court would hold that Congress has expressly or impliedly authorized the NSA electronic surveillance operations here under discussion, and it would likewise appear that, to the extent that those surveillances fall within the definition of "electronic surveillance" within the meaning of FISA or any activity regulated under Title III, Congress intended to cover the entire field with these statutes.[116]

Observers have noted that the arguments generated by administration lawyers are part of a longer range objective of reversing the limits placed on the presidency in the 1970s and restoring what has been called the "imperial presidency" by Defense Secretary Donald Rumsfeld and Vice President Richard Cheney, who were high executive branch officials in the Nixon and Ford administrations.[117] Shifts in the relative power of the various branches of government are a continuing theme in American politics, but the lesson of the warrantless eavesdropping episode is that the thrust for power may unnecessarily trample on the kind of constitutional balance that the United States fights for in its struggle against terrorism.

LAW IN SOCIETY

COSTS AND BENEFITS OF THE EXCLUSIONARY RULE

Since 1974, the Supreme Court has confronted two empirical issues concerning the exclusionary rule: its deterrent effect and its costs in lost convictions. Both issues have been used in arguments for and against the rule, such that studies and findings have been examined with partisan intensity. In the course of examining these empirical questions, the Supreme Court has used and, on occasion, misused social science data. This section reviews some of the findings on these sensitive issues.

To understand human behavior, social scientists first attempt to measure behavior accurately, systematically, and with quantitative precision to the greatest extent possible. Statistical tests are applied to data to determine the extent to which the collected data (a sample) reflect actual behavior (the universe). These rigorous attempts to quantify knowledge contrast with the human tendency to generalize—that is, to make overly broad conclusions about human behavior based on a small number of personal experiences or on the basis of a few secondhand stories.

The Deterrent Effect of the Exclusionary Rule

United States v. Calandra (1974) "adopted the view that the primary rationale for the federal exclusionary rule is the factual premise that suppression of illegally seized evidence will deter the police from conducting illegal searches."[118] Only a few studies of the exclusionary rule had been published by 1974. The most prominent, by Dallin Oaks, appeared to show that the exclusionary rule had no effect on police behavior in several cities.[119] Oaks's data did not conclusively show whether the exclusionary rule deterred police misconduct. Rather, his stated personal opinion was that the rule failed to deter and should be abolished. According to Thomas Davies, "the Oaks study has probably established something of a record for being widely cited as empirical support for a finding it did not really claim to make."[120]

Proponents of the exclusionary rule were fearful that the Supreme Court would use a finding of no deterrence to abolish the rule. For example, in his *Bivens* dissent, Chief Justice Burger stated: "If an effective alternative remedy is available, concern for official observance of the law does not require adherence to the exclusionary rule." This would be especially troublesome if the Court made constitutional law based on flawed research. Indeed, Oaks's research conclusion, if not his data, was flawed in that he believed the exclusionary rule failed simply because Fourth Amendment violations continued to occur after the *Mapp* decision. This was a conceptual failure: The more

appropriate question was whether the number and rates of such violations increased, decreased, or remained level after *Mapp*. Oaks failed to make these comparisons.[121]

In *United States v. Janis* (1976), a careful and exhaustive review of the deterrence research in Justice Harry Blackmun's majority opinion finally put to bed the deterrence issue. The issue in *Janis* was whether the exclusionary rule would be extended to federal IRS civil tax assessment hearings to exclude illegally seized evidence. A strong finding about the deterrent effect could sway the Court to extend the rule or to abolish it. Justice Blackmun's honest review of the research literature concluded that there is no conclusive evidence that the rule has or does not have a deterrent effect: "The final conclusion is clear. No empirical researcher, proponent or opponent of the rule, has yet been able to establish with any assurance whether the rule has a deterrent effect even in the situations in which it is now applied" (*Janis,* fn. 22). The way in which the Court applied this equivocal and correct empirical conclusion is interesting. Justice Blackmun said that even if the exclusionary rule has a strong deterrent effect, "the additional marginal deterrence provided" by extending the rule to federal civil tax proceedings "surely does not outweigh the *cost to society* of extending the rule to that situation" (*Janis,* pp. 453–54, emphasis added). The majority in *Janis* clearly did not want to extend the exclusionary rule, and so its analysis had a "heads I win, tails you lose" quality, switching the focus of inquiry from deterrence to the costs of the exclusionary rule.

Nevertheless, the Court's conclusion in *Janis* in regard to the empirical research is supported by Davies's most thorough review of the issue.[122] The problem is not so much that of poor research designs, but of the special difficulty of defining and studying legal deterrence. According to Davies, "It is quite unlikely that there will be any rigorous measurement of the rule's specific deterrent effect in terms of how often illegal searches have been prevented."[123] This problem arose partly because the research community paid little attention to the exclusionary rule when criminal justice research made it clear that the rule was a minor factor in the total disposition of cases. Thus studies on the effectiveness of deterrence and on its "costs" were left to policy-relevant studies that framed the issue narrowly.[124]

The Educative Effect of the Exclusionary Rule

Another empirical question is whether the exclusionary rule has had a broad educative effect. Proponents have not been able to establish this by rigorous empirical research, but there is some anecdotal evidence suggesting that because of the rule, police are now trained in the law, police and prosecutors seriously discuss search and seizure rules, and the police community generally takes the Fourth Amendment more seriously than it did before *Mapp*.[125] A study comparing drug, weapons, and gambling arrests in nineteen cities before and after *Mapp* appears to indicate that *Mapp* had a decided effect in six cities, an intermediate effect in three cities, and no effect in ten cities.[126] This suggests that *"Mapp*'s impact largely has been mediated by differentials in attitudes and styles among police and civic leaders. . . . [T]he police are likely to behave differently in a city where the chief almost openly encourages evasion of a Supreme Court decision than in one where the chief insists on obedience."[127]

This is supported by the observational study of police by law professor Richard Uviller, who noted that honest police officers bring to their work an "innate sense of limits" that prevails "over the broad license allowed by law" in many situations.[128] Too often the "legal focus" portrays police as overly aggressive, overly zealous, and guided only by a crime control mentality. Uviller's closely observed police officers displayed common sense, decency, and a real desire to operate within the limits of the law, even if they are not always precisely correct about the operative rules. This perspective suggests that over the long run, police behavior actually will become more law-abiding. One may also speculate that as Court decisions become more favorable to the police, it will be easier for officers to obey the rules of constitutional criminal procedure. A more cynical possibility may be that successful evasion of the exclusionary rule is a factor in police acquiescence to the rule. All these factors may be at play simultaneously. In any event, to bring police behavior into line with constitutional norms requires practical training for police officers. Where the law does place limits on what the police may do, departments are well advised to include some training into the reasons for these limits.

Costs of the Exclusionary Rule

The Court, in its anti–exclusionary rule mood, tended to emphasize the costs of lost convictions in broad terms. Justice White's concurrence in *Illinois v. Gates* (1983) is an example of the poor review of social science studies. For example, White's broad conclusion—"We will never know how many guilty defendants go free as a result of the rule's operation"[129]—is wrong. To make matters worse, he quoted a misleading National Institute of Justice (NIJ) study that reported that "prosecutors rejected approximately 30 percent of all felony drug arrests because of search and seizure problems."[130] As we shall see, this was a gross exaggeration of the costs of the exclusionary rule.

Unlike deterrence, which is inherently difficult to measure, lost cases can be more precisely measured.

Because the total number of arrests and the number of cases dismissed owing to search and seizure errors can be obtained from prosecution and court records, the proportion of "lost cases" can be calculated. Several research studies are in general agreement that the "costs" of the exclusionary rule are not great. In almost all instances, the percentage of cases dropped because of search and seizure problems is less than 1 percent:

1. *Forst, Lucianovic, and Cox* (1977). In Washington, D.C., prosecutors rejected 168 out of 17,534 arrests (1 percent) for all kinds of due process problems, including search and seizure violations.[131]

2. *Brosi* (1979). Prosecutors declined to issue complaints for all types of due process errors in 1 percent of the cases in Washington, D.C.; 2 percent in Cobb County, Georgia; 2 percent in Salt Lake City; 4 percent in Los Angeles; and 9 percent in New Orleans.[132]

3. *Forst et al.* (1977 and 1982). Due process violations led to dismissals in less than 1 percent of arrests in six cities, 2 percent in Los Angeles, and 6 percent in New Orleans.[133]

4. *General Accounting Office* (1979). Prosecutors declined to accept 46 percent of all cases; 6.6 percent of the declined cases were rejected for legal violations overall, and 0.4 percent of all cases were declined because of illegal searches.[134]

5. *Nardulli* (1983). A review of 7,500 cases in nine counties in three states found that motions to suppress physical evidence were filed in fewer than 5 percent of the cases and were successful in 0.69 percent of the cases, and motions to suppress illegal confessions or identifications were filed in 2 percent of the cases and were successful in 4 percent of these. Some defendants were convicted even after the evidence was suppressed. In the entire sample, 46 out of 7,500 cases were lost (less than 0.6 percent) because of the three exclusionary rules combined.[135]

6. *Feeney et al.* (1983). Nine out of 885 nonconvictions (1 percent) were lost due to illegal searches; since about half of the arrests resulted in nonconvictions, 0.5 percent of the cases in Jacksonville and San Diego were lost because of the exclusionary rule.[136]

7. *Uchida and Bynum* (1991). In seven cities, 1.4 percent of all defendants (19 out of 1,355) in cases based on search warrants were granted motions to suppress.[137]

Despite the virtually unanimous conclusion that about 1 percent or less of cases are lost because of the rule, Justice White claimed in *Gates* that 30 percent of the cases were lost due to excluded evidence. He based this on a federal study of California case processing and repeated the figure put forward in the solicitor general's brief. Davies notes that the NIJ study was seriously flawed and that the 30 percent figure is grossly misleading. First, the NIJ study showed that 4.8 percent of all rejected felony cases are lost because of search and seizure problems. This in no way indicates the cost of the exclusionary rule; it instead shows that among those cases *that prosecutors rejected*, 4.8 percent were lost due to the exclusionary rule. This is meaningless because the percentage calculated in this way can change dramatically depending on changes in the other reasons for dismissals. When the NIJ data of lost cases are calculated against a base figure of total arrests, those lost due to the exclusionary rule drop to about 0.8 percent, more in line with the other studies. As for the 30 percent figure, it was drawn from a sample of 150 drug cases from two local prosecutors' offices in Los Angeles, which was not at all representative: As Davies indicates, between 1978 and 1982, California prosecutors rejected 2.4 percent of felony drug arrests because of illegal searches.

Further, the studies show that the number of cases rejected on Fourth Amendment grounds in serious violent felonies is lower, about 0.2 percent of all arrests, and somewhat higher for drug offenses. Davies makes the point that many such rejected arrests in drug cases may not be those of carefully planned raids, but rather are arrests on suspicion where drugs are found and the probable cause basis is very weak to begin with. Thus, unlike the inconclusive result of the exclusionary rule's deterrent effect, research findings of its costs firmly show that fewer than 1 percent of arrests are lost because of the exclusionary rule. In half of these lost cases, convictions are still obtained because of other evidence.

Do these findings mean that the costs are low? This is a normative issue. The figures show that the exclusionary rule is not subverting law enforcement efforts. Yet its effect may still be unacceptably high to some. "Indeed, some critics have taken the position that *even one lost arrest* is an excessive cost."[138] Thus when Justice White had to confront this new evidence, he stated that "the small percentages with which [the researchers] deal mask a large absolute number of felons who are released because the cases against them were based in part on illegal searches or seizures" (*United States v. Leon,* 1984, fn. 6). Of course, in a country with a population of 300 million, virtually any small percentage will generate large numbers. I would tend to agree with Uchida and Bynum "that the exclusionary rule, though seldom invoked, serves as an incentive for many police officers to follow the limits imposed by the Fourth Amendment as defined in their jurisdictions."[139] Thus the exclusionary rule debate presents an interesting case history of the use and misuse of social science data in the judicial decision-making process.

The Effectiveness of Tort Remedies

Another aspect of the exclusionary rule debate is the effectiveness of tort suits against the police. The evidence is generally that they do not provide strong control over police misbehavior, including police brutality. Empirical studies of *Bivens* suits, for example, disclose that they virtually never lead to findings of police officer liability.

Government figures reflect that out of approximately 12,000 *Bivens* claims filed between 1971 and 1985, *Bivens* plaintiffs actually obtained a judgment that was not reversed on appeal in only four cases. While similar figures have not been systematically kept since 1985, recoveries from both settlements and litigated judgments continue to be extraordinarily rare. According to one estimate, plaintiffs obtain a judgment awarding them damages in a fraction of 1 percent of *Bivens* cases and obtain a monetary settlement in less than 1 percent of such cases. The low rate of successful claims indicates that, notwithstanding *Bivens,* federal constitutional violations are almost never remedied by damages. The low success rate of these claims also reflects that the courts are processing a tremendous amount of *Bivens* litigation. When analyzed by traditional measures of a claim's "success"—whether damages were obtained through settlement or court order—*Bivens* litigation is fruitless and wasteful because it does not provide the remedies contemplated by the decision, and it burdens litigants and the judicial system.[140]

While recovery in other kinds of tort cases against the police does exist, such recovery is hard to obtain, and monetary claims are low. In a study based on telephone interviews with civil rights attorneys in southern California, a variety of reasons were given for the lack of success:[141]

- Civil rights attorneys are unwilling to take weak cases.
- Witnesses with past criminal records are not credible to jurors.
- Police have a qualified immunity defense for acts done in good faith.
- Municipalities provide the costs of defense and pay for any settlement in cases won by plaintiffs.
- It is more difficult for plaintiffs to discover facts in the hands of defendants in these cases compared to other civil litigation.
- Defendants can tie up plaintiffs, who tend to have limited resources, with interlocutory appeals in Section 1983 suits.
- The "blue curtain" of silence makes police witnesses very reluctant to testify.
- Police perjury is rampant. (See the "Law in Society" section in Chapter 3.)
- Jurors almost always believe the police.

As a result, the likely deterrent effect of lawsuits on police brutality is very low. Commissions on police brutality report that many cases of abuse are committed by officers who are repeat offenders, indicating that departments do a poor job of sanctioning officers with a history of excessive violence. Many cities in the last decade have paid millions of dollars in tort damages for police brutality, and the numbers do not appear to have substantially diminished. Although there seems to be a slight, growing public interest in police brutality currently, there is virtually no political pressure for police departments to abide by the Constitution.[142] As Professor Bradley Canon noted in his study of police departments that follow warrant procedure, much depends on the attitudes of the police chief. "The chief and higher-ranking supervisors establish the tone and culture within a police department. If the upper ranks do not enforce violations of department policy, there will be no curb on officers' misconduct out on the street."[143]

Chiefs who are concerned with the legal conduct of their officers can affect policy and action by the selection of field training officers, by their own disciplinary decisions, by the emphasis given to legal issues in academy and in-service training, and by having records of tort cases become part of an officer's file and be taken into account in promotions.[144] All such measures should not lead to demoralization or overdeterrence that causes police officers to shy away from performing their difficult jobs effectively. But there are examples, such as William Bratton's tenure as New York City police commissioner, demonstrating that, to paraphrase Justice Tom Clark, there is no war between effective policing and law-abiding policing.

SUMMARY

The structure and content of search and seizure law are the product of history. English common law came to protect the privacy of one's home against government invasion shortly before the framing of the Constitution (1787) in the *Writs of Assistance* case and the *Wilkes* cases. They held that general warrants are illegal and that a victim of a general warrant could sue the government for damages.

The Fourth Amendment was intended to eliminate the government's use of general search warrants. In the founding era, police had no power to conduct warrantless arrests or searches based on probable cause; a warrant was required. Nevertheless, modern constitutional interpretation authorizes warrantless arrests and searches upon probable cause under the general-reasonableness construction of the Fourth Amendment. The warrant-preference construction holds that warrants are required except in hot pursuit, vehicle searches, and search incident to arrest.

The Fourth Amendment exclusionary rule states that illegally seized evidence may not be introduced into evidence in a trial. It was established in *Weeks v. United States* (1914) and *Silverthorne Lumber Co. v. United States* (1920). The rule was based on the Constitution and stated that illegally seized evidence shall not be used at all. The rule applies only to government officers, not to illegal searches by private individuals. Evidence derived from illegally seized materials cannot be introduced into evidence ("fruits of the poisonous tree" doctrine). However, illegally obtained evidence of a crime may be introduced if it is obtained from an independent source, by inevitable discovery, or because the link between the primary illegality and the evidence seized has become attenuated.

The Supreme Court incorporated the exclusionary rule (extended it to the states) in *Mapp v. Ohio* (1961) after having refused to do so in *Wolf v. Colorado* (1949) and *Rochin v. California* (1952). In the latter case, the Court excluded evidence that was seized by methods that "shocked the conscience." This was a due process, "totality of the circumstances" test, and criticism of its subjectivity was a factor in the *Mapp* decision. The basis of *Mapp* was that the exclusionary rule is required by the Fourth Amendment and that exclusion is the best deterrent of police misbehavior.

After *Mapp,* a more conservative Supreme Court eroded the exclusionary rule. It upheld the use of illegally seized evidence as a basis of a grand jury question in *United States v. Calandra* (1974), which modified the theoretical basis of the exclusionary rule. It became viewed as a judicially created remedy designed to safeguard Fourth Amendment rights generally through its deterrent effect on future unlawful police conduct, rather than a personal constitutional right of the aggrieved party. This concept was expanded by *United States v. Leon* (1984), which allowed the introduction of illegally seized evidence for the proof of guilt where the evidence was obtained by police officers in the "good faith" reliance on a statute or search warrant. It also held that the exclusionary rule does not apply to unconstitutional acts committed by the judiciary. A ruling that evidence is admissible where police execute a search without complying with the knock and announce rule, a constitutional requirement, exemplifies the Court's distaste for the exclusionary rule (*Hudson v. Michigan,* 2006).

To challenge evidence taken in violation of the Fourth Amendment, a party must have standing—that is, the party must have suffered a personal invasion of privacy rights rather than suffered harm because of the invasion of the privacy rights of another person. In *Rakas v. Illinois* (1978), the Court held that a passenger of an automobile does not have such a personal right. A personal interest to raise a Fourth Amendment challenge does not depend on the defendant's strict property right but in his or her level of interest in a place; thus overnight guests in an apartment have standing, but guests invited into an apartment for business purposes do not have standing.

Aside from the exclusionary rule, individuals whose Fourth Amendment rights have been violated have other potential sources of relief. These include lawsuits against the police officer or the department. The different types of tort lawsuits include state common law tort suits, state constitutional torts wherein state officers are sued in state courts, Section 1983 civil rights suits against state and local officers and municipalities (but not state governments) in federal courts, and *Bivens* suits against federal officers in federal courts. For violations that are likely to persist against specific individuals, injunctions that prohibit the illegal police activity from recurring are available, but the Supreme Court generally disfavors injunctions. Federal and state criminal prosecutions may also be brought against police officers, but they are typically reserved for the most egregious violations involving unnecessary violence. Police departments can improve their record of abiding by the law by adopting better recruitment, training, and supervision procedures and by other administrative measures. Congress passed 42 U.S.C. § 14141 in 1994, allowing the Department of Justice to bring suits against police departments to correct violations by means such as improved hiring, training, and complaint procedures where a pattern or practice of conduct by law enforcement officials that deprives people of constitutional rights has been proven.

The exclusionary rule remains controversial. Arguments against it include these: It is not a true remedy against the offending officer; it suppresses relevant evidence of crime and thus thwarts the truth-finding goal of the criminal trial; it has little or no deterrent effect; it leads to police perjury; and it undermines the authority of the states to fashion their own rules of criminal procedure.

Fourth Amendment law has been confused because there are overlapping and conflicting theories of the exclusionary rule. These include the idea that the rule is required by the Constitution; that it is only a judicially created rule designed to deter police from violating individuals' rights; that it is based on the Fifth Amendment privilege against self-incrimination; that it is based on property rights; that it is based on returning the parties to their original position; that, once breached, privacy rights can never be repaired; and that violations of privacy interests involve property or liberty violations that should be repaired under a theory of disgorgement. Each of these theories has at least one weakness. Thus there is some level of policy choice open to jurists in deciding how to justify the exclusionary rule. The most philosophically coherent view is that the exclusionary rule is a Fourth Amendment requirement; otherwise, the government could justify illegal searches retroactively, subject only to tort remedies, which causes the amendment to collapse.

LEGAL PUZZLES

How Have Courts Decided These Cases?

State Action or Private Action?

2–1. A computer hacker ("Hacker") in Turkey sent an untraceable e-mail to the Montgomery (Alabama) Police Department (MPD), saying that he discovered evidence of child sexual abuse on a computer in Montgomery; he said that the victimizer "is a doctor or a paramedic." The anonymous hacker attached an electronic image file of a white male sexually abusing a young white female approximately five years old. MPD officers replied by e-mail, asking Hacker for more information. He sent additional images of sexual abuse. Hacker identified a man named Steiger as the molester and provided identifying information, including Steiger's Internet service account information and, after an additional request, the Internet Protocol ("IP") address (a unique address assigned to a particular computer connected to the Internet). An investigator corroborated identifying information about Steiger. Based on this information, investigators prepared a search warrant affidavit without mentioning that the source of the information was a hacker. A search of Steiger's home produced incriminating evidence that was used to convict him.

Were the hacker's actions the behavior of a private person or state action?

Held.   Private action. The evidence was admissible.

A private person's search does not implicate the Fourth Amendment unless he acts as a government instrument or agent. A private person is considered an agent of the government when (1) the government knew of and acquiesced in the intrusive conduct, and (2) the private actor's purpose was to assist law enforcement efforts rather than to further his own ends. The probable cause for the search warrant was based on the information provided in the anonymous source's first and second e-mails, together with the investigator's description of her personal corroboration of that information. The information in those two e-mails was limited to that which the source had acquired before making any contact with the MPD. Even assuming that the MPD tacitly encouraged further nonconsensual searches, the information relied on in support of the warrant—graphic images showing Steiger sexually abusing a young child and identifying information regarding Steiger that the agent corroborated—more than sufficed to establish probable cause.

United States v. Steiger, 318 F.3d 1039 (11th Cir. 2003)

Probable Cause; Good Faith Reliance

2–2. On September 15, 2000, Officer Doughty swore to an affidavit for a search warrant, the magistrate issued the warrant, and Officer Doughty executed it. The affidavit's "material facts constituting probable cause" for the search read as follows:

> On March 17, 2000, . . . Tolentito and . . . Velasco were shot to death with 9 millimeter rounds. . . . An individual incarcerated in the Northampton County Jail has become a suspect in the offense in that he has made incriminating statements to at least three persons. An intimate friend of the suspect has informed the undersigned that the suspect informed the intimate friend that he had traded a pistol to an individual named as "Cowboy" for marijuana, "Cowboy" being known to her as residing at the place to be searched. The undersigned has personal knowledge that "Cowboy" is Delio Anzualda.

The affidavit described the "thing to be searched for" as a "9 millimeter pistol and/or ammunition" and the place to be searched as Anzualda's family home.

While searching Anzualda's home, Doughty and his fellow officers found several items that they suspected were stolen. They also discovered cocaine and related paraphernalia, marijuana, and several firearms. However, a pistol was not among the items seized.

Was the warrant supported by probable cause? Did the officer rely in good faith on the warrant?

Holding available from instructor.

Standing

2–3. Greenville, South Carolina, detectives, investigating a crack cocaine ring, obtained a warrant to search the apartment of Curtis and Laura Sibert for cocaine. Victor Missouri was in the apartment at the time of the search, standing near a quantity of crack cocaine. He was arrested and charged with trafficking in crack cocaine. He seeks to challenge the search; the lead detective admitted that he lied in the affidavit issued in support of the search warrant. South Carolina claims that Missouri has no standing to challenge the evidence because he has no reasonable expectation of privacy in the Siberts' apartment.

Missouri and Curtis Sibert have been close friends for many years. On occasion, Curtis gave Missouri a key to the Siberts' apartment, allowing Missouri to come and go as he pleased. Even though Missouri lived only a few miles away, he would stay at the Siberts' apartment whenever he wanted to "get away." Missouri testified that the apartment was a place of comfort and solace for him and that he felt a sense of privacy there. At the time of the arrest, Missouri's key ring contained two car keys and a key to his own apartment, but he was in the Siberts' apartment for at least seven hours.

Does Missouri have standing to challenge the search?

Holding available from instructor.

Basis for a *Bivens* Action?

2–4. Mueller was a DEA agent, and Gallina was the Special Agent in charge of the Detroit DEA office. In 1997, Gallina supposedly issued a letter to a firearm manufacturer authorizing Mueller to buy an otherwise unobtainable firearm. In 2000, the DEA's Office of Professional Responsibility (OPR) investigated whether Mueller lawfully obtained the firearm. Gallina, no longer in charge of the Detroit office, was interviewed by the OPR and said he did not review, sign, or authorize the 1997 letter. Partly on the basis of Gallina's statement, the OPR obtained a search warrant, searched Mueller's home and DEA office, and seized items. Mueller was then questioned by the OPR and federal tax authorities. In November 2000, the Department of Justice dropped the matter against Mueller. Mueller sued Gallina under *Bivens v. Six Unknown Agents* (1971), claiming that Gallina's lie caused a violation of Mueller's Fourth Amendment right to be free from unreasonable search and seizures.

Assuming that Mueller correctly alleged that Gallina lied to the OPR, does Mueller have a valid cause of action under *Bivens*?

Holding available from instructor.

FURTHER READING

Richard C. Cortner, *The Supreme Court and the Second Bill of Rights: The Fourteenth Amendment and the Nationalization of Civil Liberties* (Madison: University of Wisconsin Press, 1981).

J. David Hirschel, *Fourth Amendment Rights* (Lexington, Mass.: Lexington Books, 1979).

H. Richard Uviller, *The Tilted Playing Field: Is Criminal Justice Unfair?* (New Haven, Conn.: Yale University Press, 1999).

USEFUL WEB SITE

National Criminal Justice Reference Service

http://www.ncjrs.gov/index.html

Essential information for everyone interested in criminal justice. Includes reports from the National Institute of Justice, the Bureau of Justice Statistics, and the Office of Juvenile Justice and Delinquency Prevention. Links for courts, crime, justice, law enforcement, and other topics.

ENDNOTES

1. Marvin Zalman, "Fleeing from the Fourth Amendment," *Criminal Law Bulletin* 36, no. 2 (2000): 129–47.

2. William J. Cuddihy, "The Fourth Amendment: Origins and Meaning, 602–1791" (unpublished doctoral dissertation, Claremont Graduate School, 1990), c.

3. Leonard W. Levy, *Original Intent and the Framers' Constitution* (New York: Macmillan, 1988), 224.

4. Cuddihy, "Fourth Amendment," cii.

5. Cuddihy, "Fourth Amendment," 200–34.

6. Levy, *Original Intent,* 226.

7. Levy, *Original Intent,* 222–29; and Catherine Drinker Bowen, *John Adams and the American Revolution* (New York: Grosset and Dunlap, 1950), 208–19. See also Cuddihy, "Fourth Amendment," 757–825; and M. H. Smith, *The Writs of Assistance Case* (Berkeley: University of California Press, 1978).

8. Levy, *Original Intent,* 229.

9. Levy, *Original Intent,* 230.

10. Levy, *Original Intent,* 231.

11. 95 Eng. Rep. 807. See C. Stephenson and F. Marcham, *Sources of English Constitutional History* (New York: Harper, 1937), 705–10.

12. C. R. Lovell, *English Constitutional and Legal History* (New York: Oxford University Press, 1962), 454.

13. Cuddihy, "Fourth Amendment," 1231–1358; and Thomas Y. Davies, "Recovering the Original Fourth Amendment," *Michigan Law Review* 98, no. 3 (1999): 547–750 , 668–93.

14. Davies, "Recovering the Original Fourth Amendment," 557–60.

15. Akhil Reed Amar, *The Constitution and Criminal Procedure: First Principles* (New Haven, Conn.: Yale University Press, 1997), 1–45. Professor Amar's scholarship is refuted in detail by Professor Davies, "Recovering the Original Fourth Amendment."

16. Gerard V. Bradley, "The Constitutional Theory of the Fourth Amendment," *DePaul Law Review* 38, no. 4 (1989): 817–72; and Davies, "Recovering the Original Fourth Amendment."

17. Davies, "Recovering the Original Fourth Amendment," 577.

18. Davies, "Recovering the Original Fourth Amendment," 578, 620–29, 632–34, 660–64.

19. *Planned Parenthood v. Casey* (1992); and *Dickerson v. United States* (2000).

20. *Hale v. Henkel* (1906); *Fisher v. United States* (1976); and *Andresen v. Maryland* (1976).

21. William C. Heffernan, "Foreword: The Fourth Amendment Exclusionary Rule as a Constitutional Remedy," *Georgetown Law Journal* 88, no. 5 (2000): 799–878, 812.

22. *Payton v. Rush,* 184 F.3d 623, 628 (7th Cir. 1999).

23. *Payton v Rush,* 184 F.3d at 624; *United States v. Hoffman,* 498 F.2d 879, 881-82 (7th Cir. 1974).

24. *Payton v. Rush,* 184 F.3d at 628, citing district court cases.

25. *Romanski v. Detroit Entertainment, L.L.C.,* 265 F. Supp.2d 835 (E.D. Mich. 2003).

26. John M. Burkoff, "Not So Private Searches and the Constitution," *Cornell Law Review* 66 (1981): 627; and Lynn M. Gagel, "Comment: Stealthy Encroachments upon the Fourth Amendment: Constitutional Constraints and Their Applicability to the Long Arm of Ohio's Private Security Forces," *University of Cincinnati Law Review* 63 (1995): 1807–50.

27. David A. Sklansky, "The Private Police," *UCLA Law Review* 46 (1999): 1165–1287; and Elizabeth E. Joh, "Conceptualizing the Private Police," *Utah Law Review* (2005): 573–617.

28. The case was brought to my attention by Heffernan, "Foreword," 838–40.

29. *Wolf v. People,* 117 Colo. 279, 187 P.2d 926 (1947).

30. *People v. Cahan,* 44 Cal.2d 434, 282 P.2d 905 (1955).

31. *Elkins v. United States* (1960), 218.

32. Justice Burger's thinking is examined in M. Braswell and J. Scheb II, "Conservative Pragmatism versus Liberal Principles: Warren E. Burger on the Suppression of Evidence, 1956–86," *Creighton Law Review* 20 (1987): 789–831.

33. Potter Stewart, "The Road to *Mapp v. Ohio* and Beyond: The Origins, Development and Future of the Exclusionary Rule in Search-and-Seizure Cases," *Columbia Law Review* 83 (1983): 1365–1404, 1389.

34. Charles H. Whitebread and Christopher Slobogin, *Criminal Procedure: An Analysis of Cases and Concepts,* 4th ed. (New York: Foundation Press, 2000), 33–34.

35. Heffernan, "Foreword," 859.

36. Simon Romero, "A Verdict Interrupted," *New York Times,* July 6, 2006 (reporting that the death of former Enron chief Kenneth Lay before sentencing for his fraud conviction would complicate the government's plan to forfeit his property based on the conviction).

37. Cornelia T. L. Pillard, "Taking Fiction Seriously: The Strange Results of Public Officials' Individual Liability under *Bivens,*" *Georgetown Law Journal* 88 (1999): 65–105, 69.

38. Heffernan, "Foreword," 806.

39. *Monell v. Department of Social Services* (1978). Cities have "deeper pockets" than individual officers do.

40. Kathryn Scarborough and Craig Hemmens, "Section 1983 Suits against Law Enforcement in the Circuit Courts of Appeal," *Thomas Jefferson Law Review* 21 (1999): 1–21.

41. *McGhee v. Volusia County,* 679 So.2d 729 (Fla. 1996).

42. T. Hunter Jefferson, "Note: Constitutional Wrongs and Common Law Principles: The Case for the Recognition of State Constitutional Tort Actions against State Governments," *Vanderbilt Law Review* 50 (1997): 1525–76, 1549–50.

43. Gail Donoghue and Jonathan I. Edelstein, "Life after *Brown:* The Future of State Constitutional Tort Actions in New York," *New York Law School Law Review* 42 (1998): 447–556, 447, n. 2.

44. *Brown v. New York,* 89 N.Y.2d 172, 674 N.E.2d 1129, 652 N.Y.S.2d 223, 75 A.L.R. 5th 769 (1996).

45. Henry Weinstein, "Judge OKs Use of Racketeering Law in Rampart Suits; Scandal: LAPD Can Be Sued as a Criminal Enterprise, He Rules. The Decision Could Triple the City's Financial Liability for Mistreatment of Citizens, Experts Say," *Los Angeles Times,* August 29, 2000, A1; and David Rosenzweig, "L.A. Seeks to Appeal Racketeering Ruling; Rampart: The City Asks Judge's Permission to Challenge His Decision That the LAPD Can Be Sued under RICO Law," *Los Angeles Times,* August 31, 2000, B3.

46. *Diaz v. Gates,* 354 F.3d 1169 (9th Cir. 2004).

47. *Lankford v. Gelston,* 364 F.2d 197 (4th Cir. 1966).

48. Samuel Walker, *The New World of Police Accountability* (Thousand Oaks, Calif.: Sage, 2005), 34 (internal quotation marks ignored).

49. Alison L. Patton, "Note: The Endless Cycle of Abuse: Why 42 U.S.C. § 1983 Is Ineffective in Deterring Police Brutality," *Hastings Law Journal* 44 (1993): 753–808, 766–67.

50. Walker, *The New World of Police Accountability,* 34.

51. P. Applebome and R. Suro, "Texas Slaying: A Tale of Two Counties," *New York Times,* May 11, 1990. In 1990, a local jury in Tyler, Texas, convicted three white police officers of the killing of Loyal Garner Jr., an African American man with no prior criminal history, while he was held in jail for alleged drunk driving.

52. Jan Hoffman, "Police Reformer Draws on His Experience," *New York Times,* February 24, 2000; Somini Sengupta, "The Diallo Case: The Jurors; 2 Jurors Defend Diallo Acquittal," *New York Times,* February 27, 2000; and Winnie Hu, "The Diallo Case: The Deliberations; When Case Was Weighed, Prosecution Was Wanting, Juror Says," *New York Times,* February 28, 2000.

53. M. Zalman and M. Gates, "Rethinking Venue in Light of the 'Rodney King' Case: An Interest Analysis," *Cleveland State Law Review* 41, no. 2 (1993): 215–77.

54. J. Wilson, "Ex-Cops Get Prison, Budzyn, Nevers Are Remorseful over Death," *Detroit Free Press,* October 13, 1993.

55. Robyn Meredith, "Jurors Acquit White Officer in the Death of Black Driver," *New York Times,* November 14, 1996.

56. Anemona Hartocollis, "Officer Guilty of Negligence in '03 Killing," *New York Times,* October 22, 2005.

57. William K. Rashbaum, "A Reversal on Oversight of the Police," *New York Times,* July 7, 2000.

58. *United States v. Screws* (1945).

59. Joseph P. Fried, "Volpe Sentenced to a 30-Year Term in Louima Torture," *New York Times,* December 14, 1999.

60. William Bratton and Peter Knobler, *Turnaround: How America's Top Cop Reversed the Crime Epidemic* (New York: Random House, 1998), 241–44.

61. Samuel Walker, *Police Accountability: The Role of Citizen Oversight* (Belmont, CA: Wadsworth, 2001).

62. Suggested in Whitebread and Slobogin, *Criminal Procedure,* 65.

63. Jerome H. Skolnick and James J. Fyfe, *Above the Law: Police and the Excessive Use of Force* (New York: Free Press, 1993), 243–45.

64. Skolnick and Fyfe, *Above the Law,* 255–57.

65. D. Johnston, "Reno Tightening Rules on Use of Lethal Force by Federal Agents," *New York Times,* October 18, 1995.

66. M. Newman, "Training for Trust; A Course for Police Recruits Examines How They Judge and Are Judged," *Pittsburgh Post-Gazette,* April 10, 1996.

67. Editorial, "Higher Standards for Police Recruits," *New York Times,* November 28, 1995.

68. J. McKinnon, "Police Add Japanese Martial Art to Skills," *Pittsburgh Post-Gazette,* January 23, 1996.

69. Christopher Slobogin, "Why Liberals Should Chuck the Exclusionary Rule," *University of Illinois Law Review* 1999 (1999): 363–446, 405–6.

70. M. L. Elrick and Ben Schmitt, "U.S. Plans to Oversee Detroit Cops; Costly Changes May Be Required," *Detroit Free Press,* June 11, 2003; David Shepardson and Darren A. Nichols, "Detroit Cop Reform Launched; Federal Watchdog Takes Over Today, Says Five-Year Oversight Plan Will Top $6 Million," *Detroit News,* July 23, 2003; and Eugene Kim, "Note: Vindicating Civil Rights under 42 U.S.C. 14141: Guidance from Procedures in Complex Litigation," *Hastings Constitutional Law Quarterly* 29 (2002): 767–805.

71. Walker, *The New World of Police Accountability,* 33.

72. Debra Livingston, "Police Reform and the Department of Justice: An Essay on Accountability," *Buffalo Criminal Law Review* 2 (1999): 815–57.

73. Walker, *The New World of Police Accountability,* 171–94.

74. See Slobogin, "Why Liberals Should Chuck the Exclusionary Rule," 425–27.

75. Slobogin, "Why Liberals Should Chuck the Exclusionary Rule," 427.

76. Federal Rules of Criminal Procedure 41(e). Heffernan notes that several lower courts in the 1920s did return contraband, but the issue never reached the Supreme Court ("Foreword," 813).

77. Slobogin, "Why Liberals Should Chuck the Exclusionary Rule," citing *U.S. v. Havens* (1980) and *U.S. v. Janis* (1976).

78. Henry P. Monaghan, "Foreword: Constitutional Common Law," *Harvard Law Review* 89 (1975): 1–45 (arguing that Congress should have the right to revise such Supreme Court doctrines, although *Dickerson v. U.S.* [2000] makes it clear that in criminal procedure, constitutional common law is superior to legislation). (See Chapter 7.)

79. Slobogin, "Why Liberals Should Chuck the Exclusionary Rule," 435–36.

80. Lawrence Crocker, "Can the Exclusionary Rule Be Saved?" *Journal of Criminal Law and Criminology* 84 (1993): 310–51, 329. Crocker provides a refined explanation of why *U.S. v. Payner* (1980) necessarily implied a Fourth Amendment basis for the exclusionary rule, despite the fact that Justice Scalia suggested that *Weeks* (1914) was an exercise of the Court's supervisory authority in *United States v. Williams* (1992); see Crocker, 328–31.

81. Slobogin, "Why Liberals Should Chuck the Exclusionary Rule," 424.

82. Office of Legal Policy, "Report to the Attorney General on the Search and Seizure Exclusionary Rule" (1986), *University of Michigan Journal of Law Reform* 22 (1989): 573–659, 652.

83. Slobogin, "Why Liberals Should Chuck the Exclusionary Rule," 430–33.

84. Heffernan, "Foreword," 832–40, 848–60, quote at 840.

85. Heffernan, "Foreword," 837.

86. Heffernan, "Foreword," 838.

87. *People v. Defore,* 242 N.Y. 13, 21, 150 N.E. 585, 587 (1926).

88. Nate Blakeslee, *Tulia: Race, Cocaine, and Corruption in a Small Texas Town* (New York: Pubic Affairs, 2005).

89. Slobogin, "Why Liberals Should Chuck the Exclusionary Rule," 372–76.

90. Slobogin, "Why Liberals Should Chuck the Exclusionary Rule," 378–79.

91. Slobogin, "Why Liberals Should Chuck the Exclusionary Rule," 376, n. 40.

92. Heffernan, "Foreword," 826.

93. Whitebread and Slobogin, *Criminal Procedure,* 47.

94. 18 U.S.C. 2510–2521. The act was title III of the Omnibus Crime Control and Safe Streets Act of 1968.

95. Gina M. Stevens and Charles Doyle, *Privacy: Wiretapping and Electronic Eavesdropping* (New York: Novinka, 2002).

96. Gerald H. Robinson, "We're Listening! Electronic Eavesdropping, FISA, and the Secret Court," *Willamette Law Review* 36 (2000): 51–81.

97. Michael P. O'Connor and Celia Rumann, "Emergency and Anti-terrorist Power: Going, Going, Gone: Sealing the Fate of the Fourth Amendment," *Fordham International Law Journal* 26 (2003): 1234–64, 1240–41.

98. 50 U.S.C. 1801, 1804.

99. James Risen and David Johnston, "F.B.I. Report Found Agency Not Ready to Counter Terror," *New York Times,* June 1, 2002; and David Johnston and Don Van Natta Jr., "Wary of Risk, Slow to Adapt, F.B.I. Stumbles in Terror War," *New York Times,* June 2, 2002.

100. Philip Shenon, "Secret Court Says F.B.I. Aides Misled Judges in 75 Cases," *New York Times,* August 23, 2002.

101. *In re: Sealed Case,* 310 F.3d 717, 721 (U.S. FISCR 2002).

102. *In re: Sealed Case,* 310 F.3d at 723, 724.

103. David Hardin, "Note: The Fuss over Two Small Words: The Unconstitutionality of the USA PATRIOT Act Amendments to FISA under the Fourth Amendment," *George Washington Law Review* 71 (2003): 291–345.

104. James Risen and Eric Lichtblau, "Bush Lets U.S. Spy on Callers without Courts," *New York Times,* December 16, 2005.

105. Eric Lichtblau and James Risen, "Spy Agency Mined Vast Data Trove, Officials Report," *New York Times,* December 24, 2005.

106. "AT&T and Domestic Spying," *New York Times,* April 17, 2006.

107. James Bamford, "The Agency That Could Be Big Brother," *New York Times,* December 25, 2005.

108. Eric Lichtblau, "Officials Want to Expand Review of Domestic Spying," *New York Times,* December 25, 2005.

109. Lowell Bergman et al., "Spy Agency Data after Sept. 11 Led F.B.I. to Dead Ends," *New York Times,* January 17, 2006.

110. Bergman et al., "Spy Agency Data."

111. Based on *New York Times* articles appearing on December 18, 19, 21, and 28, 2005; January 17, 24, and 26, 2006; February 7 and 18, 2006; July 14, 2006; August 18, 2006; and September 6 and 14, 2006.

112. Elizabeth B. Bazan and Jennifer K. Elsea, "Memorandum: Presidential Authority to Conduct Warrantless Electronic Surveillance to Gather Foreign Intelligence Information" (Congressional Research Service, January 5, 2006), http://www.fas.org/sgp/crs/intel/m010506.pdf (accessed January 13, 2007); and Eric Lichtblau and Adam Liptak, "Bush and His Senior Aides Press on in Legal Defense for Wiretapping Program," *New York Times,* January 28, 2006.

113. Bazan and Elsea, *Presidential Authority,* 33–34.

114. Bazan and Elsea, *Presidential Authority,* 34.

115. Bazan and Elsea, *Presidential Authority,* 37.

116. Bazan and Elsea, *Presidential Authority,* 44.

117. Scott Shane, "Behind Power, One Principle," *New York Times,* December 17, 2005.

118. Thomas Davies, "A Hard Look at What We Know (and Still Need to Learn) about the 'Costs' of the Exclusionary Rule: The NIJ Study and Other Studies of 'Lost' Arrests," *American Bar Foundation Research Journal* 1983 (1983): 611–90, 626.

119. Dallin Oaks, "Studying the Exclusionary Rule in Search and Seizure," *University of Chicago Law Review* 37 (1970): 665.

120. Davies, "A Hard Look," 628.

121. This criticism is raised by Donald Horowitz, who is generally not an advocate of an activist judiciary. See D. Horowitz, *The Courts and Social Policy* (Washington, D.C.: Brookings Institution, 1977), 224–25.

122. Davies, "A Hard Look."

123. Davies, "A Hard Look," 619.

124. For example, D. Oaks, "Studying the Exclusionary Rule in Search and Seizure," *University of Chicago Law Review* 37 (1970): 665; and J. Spiotto, "Search and Seizure: An Empirical Study of the Exclusionary Rule and Its Alternatives," *Journal of Legal Studies* 2 (1973): 243. These were sharply criticized by Davies, "A Hard Look," 627–28.

125. Davies, "A Hard Look," 630.

126. Bradley C. Canon, "Testing the Effectiveness of Civil Liberties Policies at the State and Federal Levels: The Case of the Exclusionary Rule," *American Politics Quarterly* 5, no. 1 (1977): 57–82.

127. Canon, "Testing the Effectiveness," 71.

128. H. R. Uviller, *Tempered Zeal* (Chicago: Contemporary Books, 1988), 131.

129. *Illinois v. Gates* (1983), 257.

130. National Institute of Justice, *The Effects of the Exclusionary Rule: A Study in California* (Washington, D.C.: U.S. Dept. of Justice, 1982).

131. B. Forst, J. Lucianovic, and S. Cox, *What Happens after Arrest: A Court Perspective of Police Operations in the District of Columbia* (Washington, D.C.: U.S. Dept. of Justice, Law Enforcement Assistance Administration, 1977).

132. K. Brosi, *A Cross City Comparison of Felony Case Processing* (Washington, D.C.: U.S. Dept. of Justice, Law Enforcement Assistance Administration, 1979).

133. B. Forst et al., *Arrest Convictability as a Measure of Police Performance* (Washington, D.C.: U.S. Dept. of Justice, National Institute of Justice, 1982).

134. Report of the Comptroller General of the United States, *Impact of the Exclusionary Rule on Federal Criminal Prosecutions* (Washington, D.C.: U.S. General Accounting Office, 1979).

135. P. Nardulli, "The Societal Cost of the Exclusionary Rule: An Empirical Assessment," *American Bar Foundation Research Journal* 1983 (1983): 585–609.

136. F. Feeney, F. Dill, and A. Weir, *Arrests without Conviction: How Often They Occur and Why* (Washington, D.C.: U.S. Dept. of Justice, National Institute of Justice, 1983).

137. Craig D. Uchida and Timothy S. Bynum, "Search Warrants, Motions to Suppress and 'Lost Cases': The Effects of the Exclusionary Rule in Seven Jurisdictions," *Journal of Criminal Law and Criminology* 81, no. 4 (1991): 1034–66.

138. Davies, "A Hard Look," 679 (emphasis in original).

139. Uchida and Bynum, 1065, quoting from R. Van Duizend, L. Sutton, and C. Carter, *The Search Warrant Process: Preconceptions, Perceptions, and Practices* (National Center for State Courts, 1985), 106.

140. Pillard, "Taking Fiction Seriously," 65–105, 69, 66 (footnotes excluded).

141. Patton, "The Endless Cycle," 753–808, 755–67. See John L. Burris, *Black vs. Blue* (New York: St. Martin's Press, 1999).

142. Patton, "The Endless Cycle," 767–79.

143. Canon, "Testing the Effectiveenss,"

144. Patton, "The Endless Cycle," 780–90, drawing heavily on the Christopher Commission Report, issued after the Los Angeles riots following the Rodney King beating case.

JUSTICES OF THE SUPREME COURT

The Adversaries: Black and Frankfurter

It is ironic that two New Deal liberals appointed by President Franklin Roosevelt came to be bitter foes on the Supreme Court. For many years, Justices Hugo Black and Felix Frankfurter clashed over vital issues, including the incorporation of the Bill of Rights, the extent to which speech could be regulated by the government, and whether the Supreme Court should intervene to equalize the voting representation of electoral districts. In the 1940s and 1950s, Justice Frankfurter usually had the upper hand as the intellectual leader of the conservative wing of the Court. But over time, Black's dogged pursuit of a more liberal agenda bore fruit, preventing Frankfurter from imposing his views on the entire Court.

Both justices championed democracy, yet each took a different approach to modern government and the Court's role in it. Their disagreements, based on deeply held philosophies of judging, became a matter of personal antagonism. On the question of incorporation, Justice Black was motivated by a strong belief that the Supreme Court must adhere as closely as possible to the strict meaning of the Constitution and should not use the Due Process Clause to insert its notion of what is "reasonable" into constitutional law. He recalled that a conservative Supreme Court had done this very thing prior to the New Deal, and he understood that unfettered power allowed courts to be as unjust as the legislative or executive branches. Out of this emerged the idea that the Supreme Court had to apply the Bill of Rights totally and literally to the states. Justice Frankfurter, although a great proponent of the philosophy of judicial restraint, came to opposite conclusions. He believed not only that the justices ought to fill out the contours of the Due Process Clause in order to achieve fundamental fairness in criminal procedure, but also that the Fourteenth Amendment was not intended to incorporate the Bill of Rights.

Hugo LaFayette Black

Collection of the Supreme Court of the United States. Photographer: Harris and Ewing.

Alabama, 1886–1971

Democrat

Appointed by Franklin Delano Roosevelt

Years of Service: 1937–1971

Life and Career.   The son of a country storekeeper, Black received a law degree from the University of Alabama. He practiced law in Birmingham, representing poor people, white and black, in civil cases against large corporations and in criminal matters. He also served terms as a district attorney and as a city judge, where he tried to mitigate the harsh treatment of poor people. Active in politics, he was elected to the U.S. Senate in 1926 as a populist. He was a key supporter of President Roosevelt's New Deal program, backed the "court packing" legislation to increase the size of the Supreme Court, and was Roosevelt's first choice to fill a vacancy on the Court.

Contribution to Criminal Procedure.   Justice Black was the chief architect of modern constitutional criminal procedure. His foremost contribution was to champion the incorporation doctrine, picking up the mantle of the first Justice Harlan and ultimately getting the Court to agree in the 1960s that the criminal provisions of the Bill of Rights should apply to the states as a matter of Fourteenth Amendment due process. He also wrote powerful opinions against coerced confessions and took the lead in formulating the doctrine that an attorney was an absolute requirement in all criminal cases.

Signature Opinion. *Gideon v. Wainwright* (1963). In 1942, Justice Black dissented in *Betts v. Brady,* which held that a state felony trial in which an indigent had to defend himself or herself was fair under the Due Process Clause. He strongly believed that a fair trial is impossible without a defense attorney and that if a person cannot afford a lawyer, the government must provide one without cost. Prior to *Betts,* he wrote the majority opinion in *Johnson v. Zerbst* (1938), which held that in a federal felony prosecution, the assistance of counsel is essential unless the defendant knowingly and intelligently waives counsel. His persistence in pursuing this goal succeeded in *Gideon,* where the Court incorporated the Sixth Amendment right to counsel into the Fourteenth Amendment, thus requiring the states to provide counsel for indigent defendants.

Assessment.   Justice Black is widely recognized as one of the greatest justices, an intellectual leader of the Warren Court, and the single greatest influence on the development of modern constitutional criminal procedure. In other constitutional areas, he led the Court, along with Justice Douglas, toward an "absolutist" vision of First Amendment free speech, and he spearheaded the move to require states to reapportion voting districts to equalize the voting power of voters in different districts.

Although many of the positions he supported defined a "liberal" policy agenda, he was not as liberal in judicial philosophy as were other Roosevelt appointees, such as Justices Douglas, Murphy, and Rutledge. Rather, his judicial philosophy may be better described as "strict constructionist" or "constitutional fundamentalist." He believed that the Court should strictly adhere to the terms of the Constitution, which he tended to define rather narrowly.

Thus even in the incorporation area, he maintained an independent stance. He did not vote for the incorporation of the Fourth Amendment exclusionary rule in *Wolf v. Colorado* (1949) because the rule was not stated explicitly in the Constitution. He later developed the perspective that the exclusionary rule could be incorporated only if it were seen as also protecting Fifth Amendment values against self-incrimination.

Further Reading

Gerald T. Dunne, *Hugo Black and the Judicial Revolution* (New York: Simon and Schuster, 1977).

Collection of the Supreme Court of the United States. Photographer: Pach Brothers Studio.

Felix Frankfurter

Massachusetts, 1882–1965

Independent

Appointed by Franklin Delano Roosevelt

Years of Service: 1939–1962

Life and Career.   Frankfurter emigrated to America with his family from Vienna at the age of twelve and grew up in the Lower East Side Jewish ghetto in New York City. He graduated from the City College of New York and attended Harvard Law School, becoming editor of the *Harvard Law Review* on the basis of his top grades. After graduating in 1906, he worked in a large law firm for a while but soon chose a public service career. As a protégé of Henry L. Stimson, a leading Progressive, he went to Washington in 1911 when Stimson became secretary of war, forming an intellectual circle of young lawyers who befriended Justice Holmes.

In 1914, Frankfurter was appointed to the Harvard Law School faculty, a position he held until his appointment to the Court. During his tenure, he became a nationally known liberal activist who served as a labor mediator during World War I, attended the Paris Peace Conference in 1919, represented Zionist interests, cofounded the American Civil Liberties Union, contributed to the *New Republic* magazine, spoke out for the convicted anarchists Sacco and Vanzetti, and provided free counsel for the National

Consumers' League. His coauthored book, *The Labor Injunction,* attacked the federal courts for stifling the labor movement. He was the codirector in 1921 of the groundbreaking Cleveland Crime Survey, a multidisciplinary social scientific study of the administration of justice. He appeared frequently before the Supreme Court on behalf of unions and other progressive causes.

As a Harvard professor, he developed a following among his students as a result of his passion for academic excellence and his zeal for public service. He had a close rapport with several Supreme Court justices and selected law clerks from among his students for Justices Oliver Wendell Holmes and Louis Brandeis. During the New Deal, he became an important adviser to President Roosevelt and placed many of his former students in important administrative and policy-shaping positions, thus enhancing his influence.

Contribution to Criminal Procedure.   Justice Frankfurter's liberal policy temperament clashed with his philosophy of judicial restraint. As a result, his positions in criminal procedure were inconsistent but must generally be counted as conservative. For example, he staunchly opposed the total incorporation of the Bill of Rights championed by Justice Black and favored by the liberal wing of the Court; he voted for the rule that a judge's comment on a defendant's silence does not undermine the privilege against self-incrimination; he opposed the extension of the right to counsel to all defendants in state cases; and he characterized the Fourth Amendment exclusionary rule as a mere remedy and not a constitutional rule. Nevertheless, he was sharply critical of abuses of power by the police, and when interpreting the flexible Due Process Clause, he ruled in favor of defendants in cases involving coerced confessions and search and seizures that "shocked the conscience." In the entrapment area, he favored the objective test.

Signature Opinion.   *Rochin v. California* (1952). The "stomach pump" case perfectly expressed Justice Frankfurter's judicial philosophy of restraint and respect for the authority of the states, except where the actions of local police or state courts have so grossly violated a person's right to fair treatment that a judge could exercise judgment to deem the actions as violations of due process. In these instances, Frankfurter's standard was that due process is violated where police action "shocks the conscience." He trusted the wisdom of courts to determine what shocks the conscience, and he somehow believed that such judgment would be objective and not simply private notions of what is acceptable. Justices Black and Douglas dissented in *Rochin,* arguing that this vague standard gave judges too much power.

Assessment.   Justice Frankfurter was a giant of American constitutional law as a scholar, a public servant, and a justice. He was expected to be a leading liberal on the Court, but his judicial philosophy of restraint overcame his liberal instincts. As the Court's agenda swung from economic issues to civil liberties, he failed to sense the direction of the country and the Court's special role as a guardian of liberty. Thus he adopted cramped positions in many free speech cases and ruled against finding that seriously imbalanced state electoral districts violated the Equal Protection Clause. In supporting the school desegregation case, Frankfurter played a leading liberal role, but thereafter he took a more cautious approach than did other justices. His conservative views were generally repudiated by the liberal Warren Court, although some of his rulings, including the "shocks the conscience" test, have been relied on by today's far more conservative Court.

Further Reading

Melvin I. Urofsky, *Felix Frankfurter: Judicial Restraint and Individual Liberties* (Boston: Twayne, 1991).

3 Essential Fourth Amendment Doctrines

CHAPTER OUTLINE

KEY TERMS

anticipatory warrant

beeper

consent search

constitutionally protected area

controlled delivery

curtilage

enhancement device

exigency

ex parte

industrial curtilage

inventory and return

"knock and announce" rule

magistrate

media ride-along

neutral and detached magistrate

no-knock warrant

open fields

plain feel rule

plain view

plurality opinion

probable cause

reasonable suspicion

secret informant

"sneak and peek" warrant

telephonic warrant

thermal imaging

two-pronged test

undercover agent

These [Fourth Amendment rights], I protest, are not mere second-class rights but belong in the catalog of indispensable freedoms. Among deprivations of rights, none is so effective in cowing a population, crushing the spirit of the individual and putting terror in every heart. Uncontrolled search and seizure is one of the first and most effective weapons in the arsenal of every arbitrary government. And one need only briefly to have dwelt and worked among a people possessed of many admirable qualities but deprived of these rights to know that the human personality deteriorates and dignity and self-reliance disappear where homes, persons and possessions are subject at any hour to unheralded search and seizure by the police.

—Justice Robert Jackson, dissenting in *Brinegar v. United States,*
338 U.S. 160, 180–81 (1949)

This chapter presents five basic areas of Fourth Amendment law: (1) the search warrant, (2) the "expectation of privacy" doctrine, (3) probable cause, (4) the plain view doctrine, and (5) consent searches. Although most searches are warrantless, the Fourth Amendment presumes that judicial search warrants are essential for preserving its protections. The "expectation of privacy" doctrine, established in 1967, is now the theoretical backbone of Fourth Amendment analysis. **Probable cause,** the level of evidence required by the Constitution before government agents can invade individual privacy, is the required basis for arrests and searches and seizures. Plain view is a concept that helps us understand when the Fourth Amendment applies and when it does not. Individuals may voluntarily waive their Fourth Amendment protections, and the consent doctrine is thus a highly practical aspect of police work, for it eliminates the need for police to follow Fourth Amendment strictures.

THE SEARCH WARRANT

Search Warrant Values: A Neutral and Detached Magistrate

A prime function of the Constitution is to protect individuals' liberty and rights from excessive government and law enforcement control. Requiring *executive branch* officers to get permission from *judicial* officers, via search warrants, is a principal method of keeping the government under control.

> The presence of a search warrant serves a high function. Absent some grave emergency, the Fourth Amendment has interposed a **magistrate** between the citizen and the police. This was done not to shield criminals nor to make the home a safe haven for illegal activities. It was done so that an objective mind might weigh the need to invade that privacy in order to enforce the law. The right of privacy was deemed too precious to entrust to the discretion of those whose job is the detection of crime and the arrest of criminals. (*McDonald v. United States,* 1948)

These values are embodied in the Fourth Amendment's traditional "warrant-preference construction" (see Chapter 2), under which search and seizures are presumed unreasonable unless authorized by a judicial warrant, except for a few well-established exceptions.

The Supreme Court has expressed a preference for search warrants and has encouraged police use of warrants by easing strict probable cause requirements for warrants in close cases. The issue in *United States v. Ventresca* (1965), for example, was whether hearsay was sufficient to establish probable cause and support a warrant to search a house for an illegal liquor distillery.

The Court made clear it would lean in favor of upholding searches in *close cases,* where warrants are obtained: "A grudging or negative attitude by reviewing courts toward warrants will tend to discourage police officers from submitting their evidence to a judicial officer before acting." Of course, this does not mean that a magistrate must automatically grant a warrant simply on request (*Ventresca*).

Three factors support the search warrant preference: the long history of warrant use, the Fourth Amendment's text, and the values that underlie the amendment. The values protected are highly prized by Americans: personal autonomy, privacy, security, and freedom. The amendment's policy is to protect these values via procedures that place the decision whether to invade a person's liberties for law enforcement purposes in the hands of judges. The rationale was best expressed by Justice Robert Jackson:

> The point of the Fourth Amendment, which often is not grasped by zealous officers, is not that it denies law enforcement the support of the usual inferences which reasonable men draw from evidence. Its protection consists in requiring that those inferences be drawn by a **neutral and detached magistrate** instead of being judged by the officer engaged in the

often competitive enterprise of ferreting out crime. Any assumption that evidence sufficient to support a magistrate's disinterested determination to issue a search warrant will justify the officers in making a search without a warrant would reduce the Amendment to a nullity and leave the people's homes secure only in the discretion of police officers. (***Johnson v. United States,*** 1948)

In *Johnson,* an experienced federal narcotics officer standing in a hotel corridor smelled burning opium coming from a closed hotel room. He demanded entry and found one person in the room in possession of opium. The Court noted, "At the time entry was demanded the officers were possessed of evidence which a magistrate might have found to be probable cause for issuing a search warrant." The evidence was nevertheless excluded because the officer invaded Anne Johnson's room without first submitting his evidence to the judgment of a judicial officer.

Judges are not given priority in ascertaining probable cause because of any belief of greater intelligence or expertise than police officers, or simply because warrant use is traditional. The policy is wrapped up in Justice Jackson's memorable phrase "a neutral and detached magistrate." The point is that the magistrate is part of the judicial branch, *detached* from "the government" (i.e., the executive branch) and therefore not part of the apparatus that seeks to prosecute the suspect. Further, the judge is *neutral* in the case. The officer is a partisan who is "engaged in the often competitive enterprise of ferreting out crime." Because the officer is a partisan, he or she is prone to judge a case in his or her own favor and thus find that probable cause exists. This does not mean that the officer is dishonest; but human nature is such that a partisan almost always sees things his or her way. The judge is formally neutral—an arbiter between the police and prosecution on the one side, and the defendant on the other. It is because the magistrate is neutral that he or she is more likely to exercise balanced judgment.

The Supreme Court has decided several revealing cases that determined whether the actions of magistrates or other government officers rose to the standards of a "neutral and detached magistrate." In ***Coolidge v. New Hampshire*** (1971), the state attorney general, an executive branch officer, personally took charge of a murder investigation. An archaic statute made him a justice of the peace, and as such, he issued a search warrant to himself! Over the dissents of three justices, who viewed this action as "harmless error," the Supreme Court ruled that it violated the fundamental Fourth Amendment premise that warrants must issue from a neutral and detached magistrate. Although the statute called the attorney general a "justice of the peace," in fact he was not a "detached" judicial officer but was the chief investigator and prosecutor in the case.

Shadwick v. City of Tampa (1972) shows that a formal title is less important than the actual situation of the officer issuing a warrant. Here, law and practice allowed a municipal court clerk to issue arrest warrants for municipal ordinance violations. This was upheld because the clerk met two tests: (1) he was capable of determining whether probable cause existed as to ordinance violations, such as impaired driving or breach of the peace, and (2) he was neutral and detached—he was not under the authority of the prosecutor or police but worked in the judicial branch, subject to the supervision of the municipal court judge. Thus, under limited circumstances, a valid warrant can be issued by a person who is not a lawyer or a judge.

A magistrate is *not* neutral or detached if he receives a fee, even a small one, for each warrant that is issued, instead of a salary. In ***Connally v. Georgia*** (1977), the magistrate received five dollars for each search warrant issued but nothing if a warrant was denied. The possibility of personal, financial gain is sufficient to violate a suspect's due process and Fourth Amendment rights, whatever the magistrate's subjective disposition. In addition, a magistrate's actions can cause the loss of neutrality in a specific case. This occurred in ***Lo-Ji Sales, Inc. v. New York*** (1979). An overly helpful town justice, rather than simply issuing a search warrant for the seizure of films from an adult bookstore, joined police officers and prosecutors on a six-hour raid of the store, determining at the scene whether there was probable cause to seize various materials. In determining that the warrant was improper, a unanimous Court said, "The Town Justice did not manifest that neutrality and detachment demanded of a judicial officer when presented with a warrant application for a search and seizure." This loss of "detachment" was not, according to the Court, a matter of subjective intent but was inferred from the objective fact that the town justice "allowed himself to become a member, if not the leader, of the search party which was essentially a police operation." Yet despite the objective nature of the rule, it is easy to imagine that a judge who works too closely with the prosecutors will subjectively come to see himself as a member of the "prosecution team" rather than as a neutral and detached magistrate in a subjective sense.

The neutral and detached magistrate principle led the Supreme Court to invalidate a portion of the 1968 electronic eavesdropping law that allowed the president of the United States to authorize electronic eavesdropping for a "national security" purpose without a warrant (***United States v. United States District Court,*** 1972). The Court ruled that even if the president was exempt from the particular procedural requirements of the rest of the electronic eavesdropping statute, he was still required to seek "judicial approval prior to initiation of a search or surveillance" under the Fourth Amendment. The Court reasoned that dangers to free speech and political liberty are of great concern in national security cases to entrust exclusively to the executive branch, and that national security would not be compromised by requiring the president to seek prior judicial approval for electronic eavesdropping. Since 1978, under the Foreign Intelligence Surveillance Act (FISA), warrants for electronic eavesdropping for national security purposes are issued by a special court drawn for each case from among sitting federal judges.[1] This formerly obscure function has moved to center stage since the September 11, 2001, terror attack. It is discussed below.

There are costs to the warrant process. Obtaining a search warrant from a judge is less efficient than allowing police to decide for themselves to enter a home on their assessment of probable cause. This may add a cost to public safety—a cost that the Framers felt was necessary to maintain liberty, exhibiting a consciousness of the due process model. Skeptics question whether the warrant practice, in fact, adds that much protection. In high publicity cases, public pressure can cause a magistrate to blunder. This happened when Judge Kathleen Kennedy-Powell ruled that Los Angeles Police detectives Mark Fuhrman and Philip Vannatter were justified in vaulting over the wall of O. J. Simpson's estate in the early morning hours of June 13, 1994, without a search warrant because they claimed that they feared for his safety.[2] This was a patently weak reason because ex-husbands are typically prime suspects in spouse killings, and Fuhrman had been called to the Simpson residence earlier to investigate a wife beating. As lawyer–novelist Scott Turow noted, "If veteran police detectives did not arrive at the gate of Mr. Simpson's home thinking he might have committed these murders, then they should have been fired."[3] Ironically, Judge Kennedy-Powell's case-saving ruling backfired. When Fuhrman's perjurious, racist statements later came out, the jury might have also questioned his truthfulness about the entry and search of Simpson's home and grounds.

To add to the skepticism, there is some concern that magistrates tend to rubber-stamp warrant requests. Despite all this, the late Professor Richard Uviller, after observing police for a year, reflected on the value of search warrants:

> It's easy to say that the whole routine is a sham: magistrates are not actually neutral or detached but just as closely associated with the prosecution as the cops; they don't really read the affidavits, many of those exercising the authority would not know the difference between probable cause and potato chips, much less the complexities of the law regarding the reliability of third-party informants who supply the hearsay on which the cop's belief may be founded.
>
> However much truth there may be in such assertions, it has always seemed to me that the real values of the search warrant procedure are: (1) It makes the officer pause in his pursuit and reflect on whether he has a good reason to go into someone's private space; (2) it requires him to make a record of his reasons, recording what he knows about the case before he makes the move; and (3) his recorded reasons stand immutably for review by a knowledgeable judge

after the fact, at trial, and again on appeal, if the search is challenged. In the enforced hesitation, recorded articulation, and prospect of true review, the objectives of the Fourth Amendment are well served.[4]

These comments remind us that the warrant procedure still requires police and prosecutors to fairly evaluate the facts and make their own probable cause decisions before applying for a warrant.

Obtaining a Search Warrant

The Fourth Amendment states that "no Warrants shall issue, but upon probable cause, supported by Oath or affirmation." To obtain a search warrant, law enforcement officers must (1) *present a written affidavit* to a magistrate requesting that a warrant be issued (see the example), (2) *swear under oath* that the information in the affidavit is truthful, and (3) convince the magistrate that the information they have sworn to *establishes probable cause* to believe that the warrant is justified. The magistrate should question the officer requesting the warrant about the circumstances of the case and must be personally satisfied that the evidence constitutes probable cause. The oath signifies that the officer takes responsibility for the facts alleged.[5]

The affidavit, or sworn statement, is presented to the court at an ***ex parte*** hearing—that is, a hearing with only one party present. Such a procedure would normally violate due process but is allowed out of necessity and is hemmed in with other safeguards, such as the **inventory and return,** which requires the officer to report on the execution of the warrant. The magistrate usually questions only the affiant but may require additional witnesses to testify before being satisfied that there is sufficient evidence to issue a warrant. The law enforcement agency applying for a warrant should keep all evidence and records of its application; if the warrant is challenged, the loss of such information would weigh heavily against the agency. Also, if a jurisdiction allows the agency to make a new warrant application to a different magistrate if an initial request is turned down, then the evidence submitted in the first application must be submitted in the second application.

The *classes of evidence* that may be searched and seized under a warrant are spelled out in the Federal Rules of Criminal Procedure: "A warrant may be issued for any of the following (1) *evidence* of a crime; (2) *contraband,* fruits of crime, or other items illegally possessed; (3) *property* designed for use, intended for use, or used in committing a crime; or (4) a *person* to be arrested or a person who is unlawfully restrained." (F.R.C.P. Rule 41(c), 2006, emphasis added).

The typical affidavit and warrant for a search need not be lengthy; they are often only one or two pages long. It is essential that the affidavit provide sufficient information to establish probable cause and that the warrant give clear directions to the executing officers. In some jurisdictions, a warrant is issued without attaching the affidavit; in others, the warrant incorporates the affidavit. This is the practice in Detroit, Michigan, which supplied the sample warrant and affidavit (with names and identifying information changed) as an example of what is required to establish probable cause.

Telephonic Warrants.   With laptop computers in police cars and officers armed with smart phones and personal digital assistants (PDAs), it is now possible for officers to obtain search warrants from the field in less than an hour, regardless of the distance from the crime site to the courthouse.[6] California first enacted legislation to allow **telephonic warrants** in 1970, and nineteen states and the federal government now authorize oral search warrants.[7]

Under F.R.C.P. Rule 41(d)(3), a federal magistrate may issue a warrant "based on information communicated by telephone or other appropriate means, including facsimile transmission." The officer requesting the warrant is placed under oath and a record of the conversation providing the warrant information is made, signed by the magistrate, and filed with the court clerk.

EXAMPLE OF A WARRANT AND AFFIDAVIT

STATE OF MICHIGAN

SEARCH WARRANT AND AFFIDAVIT
County of Wayne

TO THE SHERIFF OR ANY PEACE OFFICER OF SAID COUNTY: Wayne; Police Officer Phillip Melon.

Affiant, having subscribed and sworn to an affidavit for a Search Warrant, and I having under oath examined affiant, am satisfied that probable cause exists.

THEREFORE, IN THE NAME OF THE PEOPLE OF THE STATE OF MICHIGAN, I command that you search the following described place:

18793 Colorado, a one story brick building, bearing the name O'Grady's Collision, located in the City of Detroit, County of Wayne, State of Michigan, and to seize, secure, tabulate and make return according to law the following property and things:

1. A 1984 Chevrolet Nova, Blue, VIN#1FABPO758EW236587, bearing license plate #241-LUS
2. Any stolen vehicles or parts of stolen vehicles
3. Any and all other vehicles belonging to Stephen Switzerland and Warren Switzerland
4. Any repair orders, estimates or other paperwork relating to the repair of vehicles.

The following facts are sworn to by affiant in support of the issuance of this Warrant:

Affiant is a member of the Detroit Police Department, assigned to the Commercial Auto Theft Section. Affiant on January 19, 1988 and January 20, 1988 executed search warrants on this location and seized a stolen vehicle, a 1984 Chevrolet, 241-LUS. Affiant while conducting an investigation in regards to this stolen vehicle discovered that the vehicle had been falsely reported stolen in order to collect the insurance monies from Mackinac Insurance Company. On March 24, 1988, a warrant for Attempted OMUFP 0/100 (Obtaining Money under False Pretenses over $100) was obtained against Irwin Schmidlopp (Owner of the 1984 Chevrolet Nova) and for Stephen Switzerland (Owner of O'Grady's Collision). During the investigation it was discovered that persons would obtain insurance through the Mackinac Agency for vehicles that they did not own and then a claim would be submitted to the insurance company and an adjuster would arrive at O'Grady's Collision (an unlicensed motor vehicle repair facility). The insurance company would then issue a check to O'Grady's Collision and the insured party for the repair of this vehicle. One vehicle, a 1985 Oldsmobile, was repaired at least three times by O'Grady's listing three different owners when in fact, none of these alleged owners ever owned the vehicle or got into an accident with this 1985 Oldsmobile. All three checks were co-issued to O'Grady's Collision and all three checks, totaling about $15,000.00, were cashed by Stephen Switzerland through his account at First of America. Affiant on March 29, 1988, observed the 1984 Chevrolet, belonging to defendant, Irwin Schmidlopp, still inside this location. Affiant believes that estimates and bills and receipts will be found inside this location to show further schemes and frauds committed by these suspects to defraud the insurance companies.

Phillip Melon
Affiant

Subscribed and sworn to before me and issued under my hand this **30**th day of
March, 19**88**

Approved:
John Carter

Assistant Prosecuting Attorney

P91234

Jane Ellis

Judge of 36th District Court,
Wayne County, Michigan, and a Magistrate

It appears that little use is made of telephonic warrants in the United States. "While law enforcement eagerly uses the latest technology to catch criminals, it rarely uses that technology to comply with the command of the Constitution requiring search warrants."[8] Detective Mark Fuhrman stated on cross-examination in the notorious O. J. Simpson trial that he never used telephonic warrants.[9] Failure to use telephonic warrants is especially serious because widespread use of the subjective exigent circumstances exception "is arguably the greatest threat to the continued viability of the warrant requirement"[10] Although a few courts in the 1980s excluded searches because police did not seek telephonic warrants, few do so today. Police will have no incentive to use telephonic warrants until defense attorneys press this issue in appropriate cases.

Particularity

The Fourth Amendment requires that a warrant "particularly describ[e] the place to be searched, and the persons or things to be seized." This is a substantive and not merely a formal rule. An officer making an affidavit, for example, must investigate and accurately describe the place to be searched in addition to providing a street number, because a mistake might render a search illegal. Police, planing a drug raid at a house located at the corner of Short and Adkinson Streets, incorrectly listed the place as "325 Adkinson Street" on the warrant when in fact it was 325 Short Street. The affidavit, however, described the house as a single residence with silver siding and red trim on the south side of the street. Despite the street number error, the search was held to be valid because the description met the particularity requirement. The "test for determining the sufficiency of the description of the place to be searched is whether [it] is described with sufficient particularity as to enable the executing officer to locate and identify the premises with reasonable effort, and whether there is any reasonable probability that another premise might be mistakenly searched."[11]

The Supreme Court confirmed that "reasonable" mistakes in a warrant do not violate the Fourth Amendment. In ***Maryland v. Garrison*** (1987), police obtained "a warrant to search the person of Lawrence McWebb and 'the premises known as 2036 Park Avenue third floor Apartment.'" Diligent police investigation did not reveal that there was another apartment on the third floor. When executing the warrant, police officers encountered McWebb downstairs and required him to walk up to the third floor. He opened the only apartment door, which led to a vestibule. Garrison was standing there, and doors to both Garrison's and McWebb's apartments were open. The police did not know at that time that there were two apartments. They entered Garrison's apartment and seized drugs in plain view. As soon as they were told that it was not McWebb's apartment, they left. Because the police could not have reasonably known that there were two apartments on the third floor, the Supreme Court ruled that their mistake did not invalidate an otherwise valid warrant and the seizure of drugs in Garrison's apartment. "[S]ufficient probability, not certainty, is the touchstone of reasonableness under the Fourth Amendment."

The goal of the "things to be seized" particularity requirement is that "nothing is left to the discretion of the officer executing the warrant" (*Marron v. United States,* 1927). Nonetheless, reasonable latitude is allowed. If police investigation shows that heroin is being sold from a particular location, the warrant can specify that police search for and seize "a quantity of drugs." It is important that the police investigate the situation to the greatest extent feasible and make a good faith effort to know in advance what is likely to be discovered in the place to be searched. The plain view doctrine (discussed later in this chapter) necessarily creates an expansion of what items the police may lawfully seize from a premises. Executing a valid search warrant is one of the ways in which police are legitimately in a premises; once legitimately in a place, they may seize all contraband in plain view, even if it is unrelated to the object of the search warrant.

In ***Groh v. Ramirez*** (2004), "a concerned citizen informed [Bureau of Alcohol, Tobacco and Firearms (ATF) agent Groh] that on a number of visits to [the Ramirez] ranch the visitor had seen a large stock of weaponry, including an automatic rifle, grenades, a grenade launcher, and a rocket launcher." Agent Groh prepared and signed a warrant application to search for "any automatic firearms or parts to automatic weapons, destructive devices to include but not limited to grenades, grenade launchers, rocket launchers, and any and all receipts pertaining to the purchase or manufacture of automatic weapons or explosive devices or launchers." The application was supported by a detailed affidavit and a warrant form that Agent Groh filled out. A federal magistrate signed the warrant, even though it completely "failed to identify any of the items that [Groh] intended to seize." In the place on the form "that called for a description of the 'person or property' to be seized, [Groh] typed a description of respondents' two-story blue house rather than the alleged stockpile of firearms." When he executed the warrant, only Mrs. Ramirez was home. Agent Groh apparently told her that he was looking for "an explosive device in a box."

The Supreme Court held that by failing to particularly describe the things to be seized, the warrant violated the Fourth Amendment. Despite the absence of *any* description of the things to be seized, the warrant would have been found constitutional if a detailed affidavit were attached or if it cross-referenced a supporting application or affidavit that accompanied the warrant. The fact that the magistrate *believed* there was probable cause to support the warrant does not cure this defect. Groh argued that the search itself was reasonable, and because of this, the warrant's defect should be overlooked. The Court rejected this: "Even though [Groh] acted with restraint in conducting the search, 'the inescapable fact is that this restraint was imposed by the agents themselves, not by a judicial officer.'" (*Groh v. Ramirez,* 2004, citing *Katz v. United States,* 1967). Groh also argued that he "orally described" what he was searching for to Mrs. Ramirez , thus giving her actual notice. But the Supreme Court ruled that her version, that the agents were looking for explosives in a box, had to be believed. The problem with police officers' giving verbal descriptions of what they are authorized to take from a person whose house is being entered, is that the descriptions will tend to become open-ended, leaving the householder no basis to argue that a search may be going too far. Searches based on verbal descriptions in effect become general searches.

The Intersection of the First, Fourth, and Fifth Amendments

Defendants in some cases have argued that the search and seizure of documents had violated not only the Fourth Amendment but also the First and the Fifth amendments. Searches that tread on the First Amendment are closely scrutinized because free speech is a highly valued liberty. In **Stanford v. Texas** (1965), a warrant authorized police to search Stanford's San Antonio home to seize "books, records, pamphlets, cards, receipts, lists, memoranda, pictures, recordings and other written instruments concerning the . . . operations of the Communist Party of Texas." In actions eerily reminiscent of *Entick v. Carrington* (1765), officers spent almost five hours in Stanford's home, taking more than a thousand books from his small business and his personal library, including books written by "Karl Marx, Jean Paul Sartre, Theodore Draper, Fidel Castro, Earl Browder, Pope John XXIII, and MR. JUSTICE HUGO L. BLACK." Many of Stanford's private documents and papers, "including his marriage certificate, his personal insurance policies, his household bills and receipts, and files of his personal correspondence," were seized. Ironically, no "records of the Communist Party" or any "party lists and dues payments" were found. This was a general warrant. It violated the Fourth and Fourteenth amendments. When the things to be seized are books "and the basis of their seizure is the ideas which they contain," the First Amendment is implicated and particularity must "be accorded the most scrupulous exactitude." Noting the historic continuity between this case and the earliest days of the American republic, Justice Potter Stewart concluded by stating that "the Fourth and Fourteenth amendments guarantee to John Stanford that no official of the State shall ransack his home and seize his books and papers under the unbridled authority of a general warrant—no less than the law 200 years ago shielded John Entick from the messengers of the King."

A search warrant supported by probable cause was issued in **Andresen v. Maryland** (1976) for the seizure of business records and employees' notes in Andresen's law office related to a real estate fraud that he was alleged to have committed. Andresen challenged the introduction of these records on the ground that "the seizure of these business records, and their admission into evidence at his trial, compelled [him] to testify against himself in violation of the Fifth Amendment." The trend of modern cases is that the Fifth Amendment does not protect business records; the state does not violate a person's privilege against self-incrimination by obtaining business records by subpoena. A search warrant did not require Andresen to do or say anything and so had no element of self-incrimination. Papers could be seized like any other property as long as there was probable cause that the papers were contraband or evidence of crime. Neither the seizure of the papers nor their introduction into evidence at a trial violated the Fifth Amendment.

In *Zurcher v. Stanford Daily* (1978), a violent demonstration led to assaults on police officers. The police could not identify most perpetrators but knew that photographs of the incident were taken by the student-run *Stanford Daily* newspaper. The police obtained and executed a warrant to seize photographs of the demonstration in order to identify the assailants. A civil suit was brought to challenge the use of the search warrant. The *Stanford Daily* argued that the police had to use a subpoena *duces tecum* instead of a warrant because it sought evidence from a third party and not from the suspect, and because the First Amendment Free Press Clause requires a process that allows a newspaper to voluntarily turn over the relevant documents to prevent the police from rummaging through all of the newspaper's files.

The Court dismissed both arguments. As to the first, the "third-party" search issue, the Court held that the "critical element in a reasonable search is not that the owner of the property is suspected of crime but that there is reasonable cause to believe that the specific 'things' to be searched for and seized are located on the property to which entry is sought." The state's interest in enforcing the criminal law and recovering evidence is the same whether the evidence is in the premises of the suspect or a third person. As to the second point, allowing a third party the option and the time to decide whether to obey a subpoena would make criminal investigations more cumbersome and could undermine effective prosecution in many cases.

The arguments for requiring the police to proceed via a subpoena when searching a newspaper office were based on these concerns: that searches would disrupt the timely publication of the news, that confidential sources would dry up, that reporters would not record and preserve their recollections for future use, that news processing and dissemination would be chilled by the fear that searches would disclose editorial deliberations, and that the press would resort to self-censorship to conceal information of potential interest to the police. The Court discounted these fears as speculative and indicated that if abuses arose, they could be dealt with in later cases. The warrant in this case was narrowly tailored to specific kinds of items that would not implicate confidential sources or interfere with editorial decisions. The Court declined to "reinterpret the Amendment to impose a general constitutional barrier against warrants to search newspaper premises."

Justice Stewart, joined by Justice Thurgood Marshall, dissented on the grounds that "police searches of newspaper offices burden the freedom of the press." Barring exigencies, "a subpoena would afford the newspaper itself an opportunity to locate whatever material might be requested and produce it." Unlike the majority's dismissal of the newspaper's arguments, Justice Stewart cited cases of intrusive police searches of news offices and felt that the ransacking of news offices, the drying up of information sources, and "unannounced police searches of newspaper offices will significantly burden the constitutionally protected function of the press to gather news and report it to the public."

Anticipatory Warrants and Controlled Deliveries

Courts since the 1980s have issued **anticipatory warrants** to police, typically involving **controlled deliveries** of contraband. This useful law enforcement tool was recognized by the Federal Rules of Criminal Procedure in 1991.[12] The Supreme Court upheld the constitutionality of anticipatory search warrants in *United States v. Grubbs* (2006). Grubbs purchased a child pornography videotape from a Web site run by an undercover postal inspector. In such cases, there may be additional child pornography on the premises. Postal inspectors applied for a warrant to search Grubbs's house; the affidavit stated that the warrant would not be executed until a person received the package and physically took it into the home. This "triggering condition" was not stated in the search warrant, which did include a description of the house and of the items to be seized. The warrant issued; two days later, the videotape was delivered. Grubbs's wife signed for it and took the unopened package into the house. Grubbs was detained as he left the house, and the search commenced. He was given a copy of the warrant, but not the affidavit, a half hour into the search. Grubbs argued that the search violated the Particularity Clause because the warrant did not include the triggering condition.

The Court unanimously held that anticipatory warrants are constitutional. "An anticipatory warrant is a warrant based upon an affidavit showing probable cause that at some future time (but not presently) certain evidence of crime will be located at a specified place" (*Grubbs,* 2006, internal quote marks deleted).

> Most anticipatory warrants subject their execution to some condition precedent other than the mere passage of time—a so-called "triggering condition." . . . If the government were to execute an anticipatory warrant before the triggering condition occurred, there would be no reason to believe the item described in the warrant could be found at the searched location; by definition, the triggering condition which establishes probable cause has not yet been satisfied when the warrant is issued. (*United States v. Grubbs,* 2006)

The Court noted that in a sense all search warrants are "anticipatory" because a warrant requires "the magistrate to determine (1) that it is *now probable* that (2) contraband, evidence of a crime, or a fugitive *will be* on the described premises (3) when the warrant is executed" (*United States v. Grubbs*). An anticipatory warrant complies with the Fourth Amendment when the magistrate is given probable cause to believe that the triggering condition will occur and that if the triggering condition occurs "there is a fair probability that contraband or evidence of a crime will be found in a particular place" (*United States v. Grubbs*).

As for Grubbs's specific challenge, the Court noted that the Fourth Amendment does not require a warrant to include information about the method or conditions of execution; it only requires the warrant to state the particular place to be searched and the persons or things to be seized. The Court also did not credit Grubbs's argument that a warrant has to be presented to the homeowner before the search commences. A concurrence by Justice David Souter noted that the failure of an anticipatory warrant to state the triggering condition can lead to unconstitutional searches when the warrant is executed by an officer who did not write the affidavit. He also noted that the issue of whether an owner has a right to demand to see a copy of the warrant before "making way for the police" was not settled by the case.

Anticipatory warrants encourage the use of search warrants over warrantless searches based on exigent circumstances, especially in drug-related crimes.[13] Controlled deliveries in drug cases often arise when police become aware that illicit drugs are in transit. Police then *delay* the movement of the goods long enough to obtain a warrant and follow the package to its destination. Probable cause is established by a reasonable seizure made by customs or mail officials establishing that the goods are contraband. At that point, law enforcement agents will have probable cause to arrest the recipient of the package and to search the package.

This, however, does not give agents probable cause to search the place to which the suspected package was delivered because it is not certain that other contraband is in the place.[14] Therefore, the scope of the search following the controlled delivery depends on the extent of the information that the police have *before* they initiate the search. To be sure that officers do not write affidavits for anticipatory searches that are subterfuges for officers to enter and to "create" plain view, "affidavits in support of such warrants should demonstrate probable cause to believe additional evidence is on the premises and should specify the nature of that additional evidence."[15]

When the final destination of the contraband is not previously known, it may be impossible to meet the Fourth Amendment requirement that the place to be searched be particularly described. In that case, several courts have stated that the police should have as little discretion in determining the place, or the "ultimate location," as possible.[16]

Controlled deliveries create extra hazards of unconstitutional searches. Therefore, police who request and magistrates who issue anticipatory warrants have to be especially careful about (1) the basis for probable cause, (2) the degree of certainty that a seizable item will be delivered to a specified location, (3) the specificity of the place to be searched, and (4) the appropriate scope of the warrant.[17]

Challenging a Search Warrant Affidavit

Police officers who lie on search warrant affidavits, or glide around the truth, subvert the integrity of the warrant system. In *Franks v. Delaware* (1978), the Court held (7–2) that a defendant is entitled to a hearing to challenge a warrant if he can show that police injected lies into an affidavit. Two detectives swore in an affidavit that they contacted Jerome Franks's coworkers about relevant evidence of an alleged rape and "did have personal conversation with both these people." After the warrant was executed, the defense attorney requested a hearing in order to call Franks's coworkers to testify that they never spoke personally to the detectives and that "although they might have talked to another police officer, any information given by them to that officer was 'somewhat different' from what was recited in the affidavit." The Delaware courts, under the established rule at that time, denied the hearing. The U.S. Supreme Court reversed.

Franks v. Delaware requires that a defendant first make a substantial preliminary showing that the police made a false statement on the search warrant affidavit, either knowingly and intentionally or with reckless disregard for the truth. If this can be shown, then the Fourth Amendment requires a hearing. At the hearing, the defendant must establish falsehoods by a preponderance of the evidence. If the defendant prevails, the magistrate then sets aside the false statements and decides whether probable cause still exists to support the warrant. If not, the warrant is voided, and the fruits of the search are excluded to the same extent as if probable cause was lacking on the face of the affidavit. This exacting standard precludes frequent challenges to affidavits.

Several arguments were raised against *ever* allowing a hearing to challenge an affidavit, including the weak ones that police are deterred from lying by swearing an oath and by the fear of perjury prosecutions. It was also argued that allowing a post-warrant challenge somehow diminished the authority of the magistrate who issued the warrant and that the magistrate could screen out lies on affidavits at the *ex parte* warrant application. This makes little sense as a magistrate does not have the means to expose perjury in a brief and often perfunctory *ex parte* session to review the affidavit. A more substantial objection was that an additional hearing was collateral to the truth, wasted time and resources, and weakened finality. Against this, Justice Harry Blackmun noted that the need to make a preliminary showing would prevent frivolous challenges, and such hearings do not undermine the truth-finding aspects of the criminal case. The dissenters were upset that this provided an area where the exclusionary rule would operate, but the majority believed that the exclusionary rule should be applied to evidence obtained by means of police perjury and that a "flat ban on impeachment of veracity could denude the probable-cause requirement of all real meaning" (*Franks v. Delaware*, 1978).

Executing a Search Warrant: Knock and Announce

Search warrants can become stale. If not executed quickly, the probable cause that supported the warrant may disappear if the evidence is moved, destroyed, or loses its character as contraband. Therefore, F.R.C.P. Rule 41(e)(2)(A) states: "The warrant must command the officer to execute the warrant within a specified time no longer than 10 days." Similar rules exist in every state. Because nighttime searches create a greater intrusion on privacy and raise the risk of greater violence born of confusion, the federal rules specify: "The warrant must command the officer to execute the warrant during the daytime, unless the judge for good cause expressly authorizes execution at another time" (F.R.C.P. 41(e)(2)(B)). Some states leave the decision of whether to conduct nighttime searches to the discretion of law enforcement officers.

The common law rule that officers must announce their presence before entering and state that they have a warrant—the **"knock and announce" rule**—is designed to (1) reduce the potential for violent confrontations, (2) protect individual privacy by minimizing the chance of forced entry into the dwelling of the wrong person, and (3) prevent a physical invasion of privacy by giving the occupant time to voluntarily admit the officers.[18] However, when officers have reason to believe, based on specific facts, that prior announcement of entry would produce immediate violence or an attempt to destroy all the evidence, they may dispense with the announcement.[19] Although this is a well-litigated area, the Supreme Court only recently decided the constitutional status of the knock and announce rule.

Petitioner Sharlene Wilson, in ***Wilson v. Arkansas*** (1995), made a series of narcotics sales to a police informant at the home that she shared with Bryson Jacobs. At one sale, Wilson produced a semiautomatic pistol, waved it in the informant's face, and threatened to kill her if she turned out to be working for the police. Based on information supplied by the informant, police obtained a warrant, which included a knock-and-announce provision, to search the house and to arrest Wilson and Jacobs. The affidavits stated that Jacobs had previously been convicted of arson and firebombing.

> The search was conducted later that afternoon. Police officers found the main door to petitioner's home open. While opening an unlocked screen door and entering the residence, they identified themselves as police officers and stated that they had a warrant. Once inside the home, the officers seized marijuana, methamphetamine, valium, narcotics paraphernalia, a gun, and ammunition. They also found petitioner in the bathroom, flushing marijuana down the toilet. Petitioner and Jacobs were arrested and charged with delivery of marijuana, delivery of methamphetamine, possession of drug paraphernalia, and possession of marijuana. (*Wilson v. Arkansas,* 1995)

The Arkansas Supreme Court upheld the search and seizure and specifically found that the Fourth Amendment does not include a rule that police must knock and announce. A unanimous U.S. Supreme Court reversed that decision.

Because there is no "knock and announce" rule in the Fourth Amendment's text, it can be argued that it is not a constitutional rule. The opinion of "originalist" Justice Clarence Thomas took a different tack: "In evaluating the scope of this right, we have looked to the traditional protections against unreasonable searches and seizures afforded by the common law at the time of the framing." The Court, that is, will engraft a rule onto the Fourth Amendment so long as it existed in English common law prior to the adoption of the Constitution. This was justified by arguing that the general-reasonableness construction of the Fourth Amendment (see Chapter 2) requires that searches be reasonable, and what was reasonable to the Framers is determined by knowing late-eighteenth-century common law rules. Also significant was the fact that most new states, shortly after July 4, 1776, passed "reception" statutes making the English common law the law of the state up until independence. Justice Thomas cited a noted seventeenth-century case, *Semayne's Case* (1603), and several prominent English commentators to establish that "[a]t the time of the framing, the common law of search and seizure recognized a law enforcement officer's authority to break open the doors of a dwelling, but generally indicated that he first ought to announce his presence and authority." Furthermore, the "common-law knock-and-announce principle was woven quickly into the fabric of early American law." In all, the Court's opinion surmised that the Framers thought that the "knock and announce" rule was part of the "reasonableness" analysis of the Fourth Amendment.

The Court did not pass on the constitutionality of the actual search in this case. It did note that exceptions to the "knock and announce" rule existed under various circumstances:

- A threat of physical violence exists.
- A suspect escapes from an officer and retreats to his dwelling.

- A demand to open the door is refused.
- There is reason to believe that evidence would likely be destroyed if advance notice were given.

The case was remanded to the Arkansas courts to determine if any exception existed to uphold the search and seizure in this case.

Indeed, *Wilson v. Arkansas* does not create an impediment to unannounced entry when justified by an exception. The Supreme Court has insisted, nevertheless, that the circumstances allowing a constitutional unannounced search must be justified in each case. In *Richards v. Wisconsin* (1997), the magistrate denied a police request for a **no-knock warrant** and issued a regular warrant. Police tried to enter the hotel room of a suspected drug dealer with a ruse, but when Richards saw a uniformed officer, he slammed the door shut. The officers waited two or three seconds and then broke in the door. Richards was caught trying to escape through the window, and cash and cocaine hidden in the room were seized. Although the police did not comply with the "knock and announce" requirement, the trial court allowed the introduction of the evidence under the specific facts of the case, emphasizing the easily disposable nature of the drugs as justifying their decision to identify themselves as they crossed the threshold instead of announcing their presence before seeking entry. The Wisconsin Supreme Court, affirming, held that when police officers execute a warrant to search for drugs, the circumstances automatically raise exigent circumstances. This in effect held that police *never* have to knock and announce in a drug case. The U.S. Supreme Court unanimously reversed. A blanket no-knock exception has two flaws: (1) some drug search warrants might be executed at a house where the occupants, at the time of the search, were not involved in the drug trade; and (2) such an exception would soon negate the rule, because it would be extended to all other crimes. The *Richards* Court specified *reasonable suspicion*—a very low standard—as the evidentiary standard to support the no-knock warrant exception.

In *United States v. Ramirez* (1998), the Court confirmed that police officers are not held to a higher standard than "reasonable suspicion" when the execution of a no-knock warrant results in damage to property. A reliable confidential informant told federal agents that a dangerous prisoner, who escaped from an Oregon county jail where he was held while testifying in a case, was hiding in the home of Hernan Ramirez. A "no-knock" warrant was obtained to search Ramirez's home for the prisoner.

> In the early morning of November 5, approximately 45 officers gathered to execute the warrant. The officers set up a portable loud speaker system and began announcing that they had a search warrant. Simultaneously, they broke a single window in the garage and pointed a gun through the opening, hoping thereby to dissuade any of the occupants from rushing to the weapons the officers believed might be in the garage.

Ramirez, awakened by this, thought his house was being burglarized and took his pistol and fired it into the garage ceiling. He dropped the gun when he realized the besiegers were police officers. Ramirez was indicted for being a felon in possession of firearms. The federal district court granted his motion to suppress evidence regarding the weapon possession; it found that the Fourth Amendment had been violated because there were "insufficient exigent circumstances" to justify the police officer's destruction of property in their execution of the warrant. The Ninth Circuit Court of Appeals affirmed, holding that property destruction accompanying a no-knock entry required more than a "mild" **exigency.**

The Supreme Court unanimously reversed. It held that there is not a higher standard for a no-knock entry when property damage occurs as part of the entry. While noting that excessive property damage created during an entry could amount to a Fourth Amendment violation, the breaking of a single pane of glass in this case was reasonable.

The standard by which to evaluate the constitutionality of the delay between announcing police presence and breaking into a home was established in *United States v. Banks* (2003).

The Supreme Court unanimously announced that the test is whether the entry is reasonable under all of the facts and circumstances of the case. In the *Banks* case, the police executed a warrant to search for cocaine during the daytime, when people are up and about. They loudly announced their presence. Under these circumstances, the Court ruled that it was reasonable to force open the door after waiting for fifteen to twenty seconds with no answer. The test was not the time it would take a person to get to the door, but the time a person needed to destroy contraband. A "prudent dealer" was likely to keep cocaine "near a commode or kitchen sink" and would have the opportunity to get rid of the illegal drugs within a short period of time. "Police seeking a stolen piano may be able to spend more time to make sure they really need the battering ram" (*United States v. Banks,* 2003).

As discussed in Chapter 2, the Supreme Court held (5–4) in ***Hudson v. Michigan*** (2006) that violations of the "knock and announce" rule, which are violations of the Fourth Amendment, do not result in excluding the evidence seized. In reaching this conclusion, the majority offered several comments about the "knock and announce" rule that diminished its stature. The rule has many exigency exceptions that are put into operation if the police or magistrate merely have reasonable suspicion of their existence. Further, the rule is somewhat vague, depending on the facts and circumstances of the situation to determine whether the delay between announcing police presence and forced entry was reasonable. To cap it off, while the "knock and announce" rule is designed to protect "life and limb," property, and elements of privacy and dignity, "[w]hat the knock-and-announce rule has never protected . . . is one's interest in preventing the government from seeing or taking evidence described in a warrant. Since the interests that *were* violated in this case have nothing to do with the seizure of the evidence, the exclusionary rule is inapplicable" (*Hudson v. Michigan,* 2006). The majority and the dissenters differed as to whether eliminating exclusionary rule protection will undermine the rule. The effects of *Hudson* remain to be seen, although with no effective remedy it is logical to believe that the "knock and announce" rule will not be followed in the most typical kinds of drug busts.

Searches in a Time of Terror: Inventory and Delayed Notice; "Sneak and Peek" Warrants

Federal rules require that a copy of the search warrant be given to the property owner or left at the premises after execution (F.R.C.P. Rule 41(f)(3)). An officer present at the search must prepare and verify a detailed written inventory of the property seized in the presence of another (F.R.C.P. Rule 41(f)(2)). The officer must return the warrant and the inventory to the judge who issued the warrant, and the judge in turn must give a copy of the inventory to the person from whom the property was taken and to the warrant's applicant (F.R.C.P. Rule 41(f)(4)). These practices ensure the regularity of the search warrant process, provide notice to suspects that the state has intruded on their privacy, and protects police officers from charges of theft.

A significant exception to the rule of immediate notice is the relatively novel "sneak and peek" or "covert-entry" warrant. Beginning in 1984, federal agents in a few drug cases requested warrants to enter a premises, observe the premises and perhaps take photographs, and leave the premises undisturbed. The few federal appeals courts that decided cases where **"sneak and peek" warrants** were issued have held that covert entry under a warrant is a search and that information gained about the area of privacy is a seizure. The courts held that "sneak and peek" warrants violated the Federal Rules of Criminal Procedure, which required immediate notice, but did not necessarily violate the Fourth Amendment. The 1968 federal wiretap law, for example, was held to allow covert entry into places without immediate notice in *Dalia v. United States* (1979), which ruled that the Fourth Amendment or Title III did not require a separate warrant to authorize a covert entry to install the listening device. Covert entries are constitutional as long as they are made pursuant to a warrant. The cases make it clear that to be constitutional, "sneak and peek" warrants have to provide notice of the entry to the defendants within a reasonable time, which usually means within a week.[20]

Legislative authorization for "sneak and peek" warrants in all cases, not just terrorism investigations, was established by the USA PATRIOT Act in 2001. The law now allows delay in the notice of a warrant execution if the issuing court finds that immediate notification may have adverse results such as endangering the life or physical safety of an individual, flight from prosecution, destruction or tampering with evidence, intimidation of potential witnesses, or something else that seriously jeopardizes an investigation or unduly delays a trial. Notice of the search can also be delayed if the warrant prohibits the seizure of any tangible property. A "sneak and peek" warrant must provide "notice within a reasonable period not to exceed 30 days after the date of its execution, or on a later date certain if the facts of the case justify a longer period of delay" (18 U.S.C. §§ 3103a, 2705).[21]

Author Robert Duncan, who favors surreptitious or covert-entry warrants as necessary law enforcement tools in a dangerous age, nevertheless is concerned that the new law is too broad and has suggested modifications. First, requesting agents should provide more information than is needed for an ordinary search warrant, similar to that required for electronic eavesdropping warrants (e.g., showing that other law enforcement techniques have failed to provide needed information). The time limit for notice should be reduced to seven days, and there should be limits on the number of times extensions can be requested. Finally, covert-entry warrants should be limited to crimes that involve "well-planned, well-organized, and in-depth criminal behavior," including terrorism, racketeering, and gang-related activity.[22]

Notice—in other words, formally alerting individuals that the government will or has acted against their interests—is a fundamental part of the due process "timely notice and fair hearing" formula, stretching back in our law to Magna Carta (1215). Secret arrest, secret search, secret interrogation, secret trial, and secret detention are the very definition of lawless government. Being able to spy on someone's constitutionally protected private areas should raise profound concerns about "Big Brother" government.[23] One innovation that has allowed greater intrusion with delayed notice has been electronic eavesdropping. There is no disagreement that electronic eavesdropping is a necessary law enforcement tool in serious conspiracy, white-collar crime, organized crime, bribery, and terrorism cases. But the 1968 electronic eavesdropping law (and subsequent additions) has been carefully hedged in with a massive number of checks to ensure that this potentially coercive tool will not be abused by government officials for partisan or corrupt purposes.

The problem, five years after the 9/11 attacks, is that the public and even members of Congress may be kept in the dark by the administration about the scope of "sneak and peek" warrants. According to the *Los Angeles Times,* "FBI agents are [using] 'sneak and peek' warrants on a wider scale, entering hundreds of homes clandestinely to gather intelligence and copy files and computer drives . . . without notification. And they have conducted surveillance on antiwar, religious, civil rights and environmental groups, including Greenpeace and the American-Arab Anti-Discrimination Committee."[24] This politicized use of the government's law enforcement powers is reminiscent of the Watergate abuses that brought down the Nixon administration in the 1970s.[25] In a time of war, ordinary political differences become magnified, and opponents come to be seen as traitors. Prosecutions in such times of crisis can be motivated by these deep emotions, even if the actual charges are not for treason.[26]

Even if fears about the politicized use of "sneak and peek" warrants are exaggerated, a highly intrusive law enforcement technique has been slipped into the law with virtually no discussion—and it can be used in ordinary criminal investigations, not just terror-related cases.[27] The "sneak and peek" provision was in the Justice Department's grab bag of desired powers, just waiting for the right opportunity to be enacted.[28] Another concern is that state and local law enforcement authorities are likely to lobby for such powers, and the potential exists for "sneak and peek" searches to become a regular feature of investigations of low-level drug possession and other crimes that occur with regularity.

Deadly Errors

The importance of police honesty and accuracy in the search warrant process cannot be overstated. In September 1999, four Denver SWAT officers were sent to execute a no-knock warrant at 3738 High Street, a two-story home. It was the wrong house. While executing the warrant, the officers who broke in killed forty-five-year-old Mexican migrant laborer Ismael Mena, father of nine, who raised a gun as the police entered his bedroom. Officer Joseph Bini, who swore out the affidavit, however, was charged with perjury for "'unlawfully and knowingly' lying on a search warrant affidavit." He swore in his affidavit that "he *personally* observed an informant make his or her way on foot to the house" at 3738 High Street. Based on his affidavit, an assistant district attorney and a county judge signed off on the warrant. In fact, the drug deal took place at 3742 High Street, a single-story home. Bini dropped the informant off four blocks from the house. The district attorney believed "[the informant] attempted to determine the address by counting the houses down the alley and up the front on this particular block. He apparently miscounted the houses and wrote the address down wrong."

As a result, a man died, Denver paid Mena's family $400,000 to settle legal claims, and the police chief was fired. Officer Bini pleaded guilty to misdemeanor charges, and the SWAT team was officially exonerated in the shooting after a close examination of their responses. Denver adopted several reforms: Police have only three days instead of ten days to serve no-knock warrants, more training is provided, and experienced police supervisors evaluate and approve no-knock raids. Denver's mayor said that "the public can expect to see a decrease in the number of no-knock raids" as a result of the tighter guidelines. But it took an unnecessary death to achieve that result.[29] Unfortunately, the overuse of paramilitary police raids by SWAT teams in America, estimated at forty thousand per year, has led to many cases like that of Ismael Mena.[30]

REVOLUTIONIZING THE FOURTH AMENDMENT

For many years, Fourth Amendment law was tied to property concepts, especially the idea that a search and seizure involved a physical trespass onto a person's **constitutionally protected area.** This concept was based on traditional practice and on the Fourth Amendment's words, protecting "persons, houses, papers, and effects" from unreasonable search and seizure. This thinking created problems when in *Olmstead v. United States* (1928), the Supreme Court held that wiretapping did not constitute a search and seizure. This decision withdrew constitutional protection from a vital area of privacy and caused many to realize that the Fourth Amendment protected vital interests and not simply property. The Court finally overruled *Olmstead* in 1967, but to do so it had to establish an entirely new "expectation of privacy" doctrine because protecting intangible privacy rights was not compatible with the older "constitutionally protected area" doctrine.

Modernizing Search and Seizure Law

In 1967 and 1968, the Supreme Court "revolutionized" Fourth Amendment law in four cases that upset established doctrines and opened the door for a more flexible mode of search and seizure interpretation. The first of these cases, *Katz v. United States* (1967), was the centerpiece of this revolution. It broke the law of search and seizure away from its traditional mooring in property law. In its stead, issues were now to be decided more explicitly on balancing of the interests deemed central to the Fourth Amendment: the need for effective law enforcement versus the protection of privacy and liberty rooted in the expectation of privacy.

Katz was followed by **Warden v. Hayden** (1967), the second case in this series, which abolished the "mere evidence" rule of *Gouled v. United States* (1921). (See Chapter 2.) *Gouled* held that only the fruits of a crime, contraband, or the instrumentality used to commit the crime could be seized by police. So-called *mere evidence* that did not fit these categories could not be seized by police to be used in evidence. In *Warden v. Hayden,* police seized clothing that could be used to identify an alleged robber during a lawful search of Hayden's house. The Supreme Court held that seizing the clothing was proper, and it could be held by the state for the duration of the prosecution to be used as evidence that a man wearing similar clothing was the perpetrator. The mere evidence rule (1) did not serve a defendant's legitimate privacy interest; (2) was based on outmoded property concepts; and (3) hampered the legitimate law enforcement interests of the state. The new rule better balanced the competing interests.

Next came **Camara v. Municipal Court** (1967) and its companion case, *See v. City of Seattle* (1967), which appeared to expand Fourth Amendment rights of individuals by requiring a warrant for administrative searches that did not directly enforce the criminal law. Under a 1959 case, *Frank v. Maryland,* the Supreme Court held that the search of a house or a business place, conducted by an *administrative officer* for the purpose of enforcing administrative regulations rather than the state's penal code, was simply not a search protected by the Fourth Amendment. In *Camara,* the Court rethought the issue and held that the Fourth Amendment text applied to an intrusion by any government officer into "areas" protected by the expectation of privacy. Entry by health, fire, or housing inspectors, for purposes of enforcing regulations, were now covered by the Fourth Amendment.

This, however, created a dilemma. Most administrative inspection programs are based not on particularized probable cause of a safety hazard in a particular home or business, but on bureaucratic assessments that houses or businesses in an entire neighborhood should be entered and inspected. Requiring a municipality to get particularized probable cause for each house in the neighborhood would be too burdensome, and the inspection program would fail. The Court solved the problem by authorizing less-specific administrative warrants based on general area inspections. Information about such general conditions as the age of buildings in a subdivision or statistical information about the number of fires in a neighborhood would support such warrants. Probable cause was "defined down," so to speak. This solution created a new and more flexible way of thinking about the Fourth Amendment. *Camara* thus opened the door to the general-reasonableness construction of the Fourth Amendment. (See Chapter 2.) The Court reasoned that the Fourth Amendment text does not absolutely require search warrants, and at minimum requires that all search and seizures be reasonable. Under this newer, flexible reasoning, the Supreme Court upheld general or "area" warrants, the very thing that the generation of 1776 found abominable. This relaxed mode of interpretation was later used to allow greater government intrusion into areas of privacy by non-law enforcement officers under the special needs doctrine. (See Chapter 5.)

The last case in this series, **Terry v. Ohio** (1968), for the first time in American constitutional history, upheld temporary but forcible stops of individuals even though the police officer did not have probable cause to believe that the person committed a crime, the only evidentiary standard found in the Fourth Amendment's text. A state deprivation of liberty could now be based on a lesser standard of evidence that came to be known as **reasonable suspicion.** (*Terry* is covered in Chapter 5.) The decision in *Terry* depended on the new mode of Fourth Amendment reasoning: balancing of interests between the state and the individual, flexibility, and reliance on the Reasonableness Clause.

These four revolutionary decisions were not inherently liberal or conservative. Two of them, *Warden* and *Terry,* explicitly expanded the state's powers, while *Katz* and *Camara* formally expanded the rights of individuals. In their larger effects, the cases were "liberal" in that they brought a larger measure of police work under constitutional oversight, but they were "conservative" in permitting a flexible approach that made it easier for the Court to water down traditional Fourth Amendment standards. It is ironic that the liberal Warren Court laid a foundation for flexible interpretation—an approach that was resisted by relatively "conservative" justices like John M. Harlan II. The flexible approach was then adapted by the politically conservative Burger and Rehnquist Courts to expand the powers of the state against the individual.

Creating the "Expectation of Privacy" Doctrine

This section takes a closer look at the decision and reasoning in *Katz v. United States* (1967). Modern conditions generate problems that require novel legal thinking. Electronic communication by telegraph, telephone, and wireless communication—unknown to the Framers in 1791—led to invasions of privacy by police that did not have the appearance of a traditional search and seizure, with the police pounding at the door and physically searching the home. In 1928, the Supreme Court thus ruled in *Olmstead v. United States,* by a five-to-four decision, that wiretapping did *not* constitute a search because there was no physical trespass into the house and no tangible evidence was taken. This ruling was deeply disturbing because wiretapping and electronic eavesdropping by the government are an obvious intrusion into the lives and privacy of individuals, and privacy is at the core of the Fourth Amendment. A powerful dissent by Justice Louis Brandeis reflected the decision's unpopularity. (See the biographical sketch of Brandeis following Chapter 1.) A federal statute soon placed some controls on telephone wiretapping.[31] The federal law, incidentally, did not cover "bugging"—electronic eavesdropping by means of a wireless listening device—which was not as well known and not then seen as being within the purview of the federal government's jurisdiction over interstate communications.[32]

Over the next few years, the Court grappled with the question of electronic eavesdropping. The application of traditional, property-based Fourth Amendment concepts produced weirdly inconsistent results. *Goldman v. United States* (1942), for example, held that placing an electronic listening device against a wall of a house was not a trespass and therefore, under *Olmstead,* was not a search and seizure under the Fourth Amendment. Evidence so obtained could be used against the defendant. Dissatisfied with the notion of leaving individuals open to government spying, the Court in *Silverman v. United States* (1961) held that when a microphone was driven into a wall, rather than placed up against it, there was a physical trespass and it was thus a search and seizure subject to the rules of the Fourth Amendment. In this case, the evidence seized by the eavesdropping was not admissible. These contradictory decisions were inherently unstable. The Supreme Court, nevertheless, was not eager to clear up this doctrinal mess.

The Court was chiefly concerned that a case squarely holding electronic eavesdropping to be a search and seizure within the purview of the Fourth Amendment could entirely outlaw bugging and wiretapping. The reason is that a bug or wiretap is an inherently general search that picks up all conversations, of nonsuspected people who happen to call or be in the place being bugged, as well as the suspect. It was difficult to see how a warrant for an electronic eavesdropping device could ever square with the Fourth Amendment's particularity requirement. The justices in the 1940s and 1950s included former prosecutors, senators, and attorneys general who were familiar with how government worked. They knew that electronic eavesdropping was a useful law enforcement tool and that it was often impossible to obtain evidence of organized crime, white-collar crime, and government fraud and bribery without bugs and taps. On the other hand, they were well versed in the dangers of unchecked government electronic spying. As became later known to the general public, the FBI under its long-time director J. Edgar Hoover, often with the compliance of presidents, spied on members of Congress and a significant number of citizens. At least one Supreme Court justice believed that he was the subject of FBI taps.[33] The dilemma confronting the Court, seemingly insoluble until the late 1960s, was how to allow but to tame electronic eavesdropping.

The answer to this dilemma emerged in the 1960s. Under established doctrine, no statutory or Fourth Amendment rights (including the expectation of privacy) are violated when a person's voice is secretly recorded while voluntarily talking to an interceptor. A person who says things in a conversation to another lives with the risk that the false friend will reveal any confidences to others, including the authorities (*Hoffa v. United States,* 1966; *Lewis v. United States,* 1966). This is the case even if the false friend is speaking on a telephone and a police officer is listening on an extension line (*Rathbun v. United States,* 1957) or secretly wearing a listening device (*On Lee v. United States,* 1952; *Lopez v. United States,* 1963). In short, a law enforcement officer or agent need not obtain a judicial warrant to "wear a wire."[34] Despite this firm rule, to be on the safe side government investigators in **Osborn v. United States** (1966) had Vick, a private cooperating undercover agent, make a written statement under oath that he had been hired by Osborn, an attorney, to bribe a juror in a prosecution of national labor leader James R. Hoffa. The statement was taken to two federal district judges who authorized Vick to wear an electronic recorder when next speaking to Osborn about the bribery. This practice was upheld by the Court in *Osborn,* although not made mandatory. The following year, in *Katz,* the Supreme Court praised the practice of seeking a warrant for a narrow and precise electronic search—for capturing a conversation that would not draw in innocent speakers.

Shortly before deciding *Katz,* the Supreme Court struck down New York's electronic eavesdropping law as too broad in **Berger v. New York** (1967). Objectionable features of the New York law included the fact that it "lays down no requirement for particularity in the warrant as to what specific crime has been or is being committed," that a warrant is granted for sixty days of uninterrupted listening, that the statute failed to describe the conversations sought with specific particularity, that once incriminating conversations were recorded the eavesdropping did not have to cease, that extensions of the initial sixty-day listening period could be obtained without new reasons, and that no return was required, so that a person who was tapped or bugged would not know of it. *Osborn* and *Berger* were the extreme ends of electronic eavesdropping—one extremely precise and narrow, and the other overly broad.

The facts in *Katz* were simple. Federal agents suspected that Charles Katz, a "bookie," was transmitting betting information across state lines by telephone in violation of federal law. Katz was observed making calls from the same telephone booth at about the same time every day in Los Angeles. For a week, FBI agents placed a microphone on the top of the telephone booth and activated it only when Katz used the booth to make calls, recording incriminating conversations. Katz appealed his conviction on the ground that the electronic eavesdropping violated his Fourth Amendment rights. The government argued that this case was the same as *Goldman* in that no physical intrusion into a constitutionally protected area, and so no Fourth Amendment violation, had occurred.

The Supreme Court overruled *Olmstead* and *Goldman* and replaced the concept that the Fourth Amendment applies in "constitutionally protected areas" with a memorable phrase in Justice Potter Stewart's majority opinion: "For *the Fourth Amendment protects people, not places.* What a person knowingly exposes to the public, even in his own home or office, is not a subject of Fourth Amendment protection. But what he seeks to preserve as private, even in an area accessible to the public, may be constitutionally protected" (*Katz v. United States,* 1967, emphasis added). It did not matter that Katz was visible to the eye in the phone booth.

> But what he sought to exclude when he entered the booth was not the intruding eye—it was the uninvited ear. He did not shed his right to do so simply because he made his calls from a place where he might be seen. . . . One who occupies it, shuts the door behind him, and pays the toll that permits him to place a call is surely entitled to assume that the words he utters into the mouthpiece will not be broadcast to the world. To read the Constitution more narrowly is to ignore the vital role that the public telephone has come to play in private communication. (*Katz,* 1967)

The Court made it clear that property interests do not determine the scope of Fourth Amendment protections. It held that "[t]he Government's activities in electronically listening to and recording the petitioner's words violated the privacy upon which he justifiably relied while using the telephone booth and thus constituted a "search and seizure" within the meaning of the Fourth Amendment" (*Katz,* 1967).

The government's search and seizure of Katz's conversations violated the Fourth Amendment because the agents did not seek a warrant. The Court took special pains to note that the search was very narrow in that it seemed to be based on probable cause and was conducted in such a way as to obtain only Katz's words at a time and place likely to involve his suspected criminal activity. The Court noted that a magistrate probably could have issued a warrant. Nevertheless, the warrant is of great importance, the Court said, and the failure to obtain one rendered the search unconstitutional.

The Katz doctrine is a product not only of the majority opinion but of that decision plus the heart of Justice Harlan's concurrence. "My understanding of the rule that has emerged from prior decisions is that there is a twofold requirement, first that a person have exhibited an actual (subjective) expectation of privacy and, second, that the expectation be one that society is prepared to recognize as 'reasonable'" (*Katz v. United States,* 1967, Harlan, J., concurring). This **two-pronged test** means that there is a *subjective* (personal) and an *objective* (societal) component of the expectation of privacy. The objective component prevents defendants from making outlandish or unacceptable claims of Fourth Amendment privacy.

Justice Hugo Black was the lone dissenter. He argued that although electronics were unknown in 1791, eavesdropping was a familiar practice, and the Framers could have protected private conversations if they so wished. He instead adhered to the notion of *Olmstead,* that the Fourth Amendment indeed did refer to and protect the seizure of tangible items. By this narrow adherence to the words of the Fourth Amendment, Justice Black solidified his standing as a "constitutional fundamentalist" rather than a "judicial liberal."

Applying the "Expectation of Privacy" Doctrine

Despite the new mode of expectation of privacy Fourth Amendment analysis introduced by *Katz,* the Supreme Court continues to decide some cases under the "constitutionally protected area" idea, which affords greater protection to the home than other places. In Fourth Amendment standing cases, for example, the Court has resisted the logic of *Katz.* Justice Byron White, dissenting in *Rakas v. Illinois* (1978), noted that

> [t]he Court today holds that the Fourth Amendment protects property, not people, and specifically that a legitimate occupant of an automobile may not invoke the exclusionary rule and challenge a search of that vehicle unless he happens to own or have a possessory interest in it. . . . The majority's conclusion has no support in the Court's controlling decisions, in the logic of the Fourth Amendment, or in common sense.

In such cases. the conservative Court seems to be motivated more to limit suspects' rights than to create a coherent body of Fourth Amendment law. One might almost say that the *Katz* doctrine is used by the Court to resolve Fourth Amendment issues except when it does not.

Expectation of Privacy in One's Body.
Obtaining physical evidence from within a person's body raises Fourth Amendment questions that are answered by examining the severity of the intrusion and the law enforcement interests. Factors include the risk to a person's safety or health in the procedure, the extent of control used on the body, and the effect on the suspect's dignity. Forced surgery to remove a bullet lodged in a robbery suspect was held to violate his Fourth Amendment rights because the expectation of privacy in one's bodily integrity is great (***Winston v. Lee,*** 1985). On the other hand, taking blood in a medical setting to determine a driver's blood alcohol level after a fatal accident has been upheld as constitutional: It presents virtually no health risk and is so routine as to involve minimal interference with Fourth Amendment dignity interests (***Schmerber v. California,*** 1966). Lower courts have also perceived a greater privacy interest in bodily integrity in cases involving body cavity searches and strip searches. (See Chapter 4.)

A person's observable physical characteristics, such as one's facial description, voice, or handwriting, are not "seized" if someone testifies to them at a trial or if a person's description is taken by police in an investigation (***Holt v. United States,*** 1910;

United States v. Dionisio, 1973; *United States v. Mara,* 1973). Requiring a person to participate in a lineup does not violate that person's Fourth or Fifth amendment rights (*United States v. Wade,* 1967).

The Supreme Court has held that urine collection and testing to ascertain the presence of drugs in a person's body intrudes upon expectations of privacy that society has long recognized as reasonable. "There are few activities in our society more personal or private than the passing of urine. Most people describe it by euphemisms if they talk about it at all. It is a function traditionally performed without public observation; indeed, its performance in public is generally prohibited by law as well as social custom." The Court noted that the expectation of privacy is not only rooted in the traditional dictates of modesty but also in the fact that the chemical analysis of urine, like that of blood, can reveal a host of medical facts about a person. Although urine testing by state agencies in order to detect drugs or alcohol is protected by the Fourth Amendment, the collection is allowed under certain conditions (***Skinner v. Railway Labor Executives' Association,*** 1989). (See Chapter 5.) In contrast, private business is not restricted in this practice by the Fourth Amendment because there is no state action.

Maintaining Property Interests after Katz.

The Fourth Amendment continues to protect property interests. In ***Soldal v. Cook County*** (1992), a mobile home park evicted Soldal and his mobile home from its property and utilities. The park's owner requested that sheriff's deputies stand by in the event that the eviction might lead to violence. The park's employees, not acting in accordance with local statutes, pushed Soldal's trailer into a road, causing major property damage. There was no invasion of Soldal's privacy, because the employees never entered Soldal's trailer—but his property was damaged. The officers did not physically assist in the eviction, but the Supreme Court held that their presence established state action. (See Chapter 2.) Soldal sued the sheriff's department under 42 U.S.C. §1983, claiming that his Fourth Amendment rights were violated. The government argued that without a *Katz*-like violation of privacy rights, there was no Fourth Amendment wrong. This argument was firmly rejected: *Katz* protects both privacy and property rights. According to Justice White, although there was no search, there was a seizure—a "meaningful interference with an individual's possessory interests in that property." Because "[w]hat matters is the intrusion on the people's security from governmental interference," this case fell within the Fourth Amendment, allowing Soldal's lawsuit to go forward.

Expectation of Privacy in Dwellings.

"At the risk of belaboring the obvious, private residences are places in which the individual normally expects privacy free of governmental intrusion not authorized by a warrant, and that expectation is plainly one that society is prepared to recognize as justifiable." (*United States v. Karo,* 1984, p. 714). The Supreme Court often leans in favor of a defendant's home rights for this reason. In *Payton v. New York* (1980) (see Chapter 4), for example, the Court ruled that an arrest warrant must be obtained in order to forcibly enter a home to arrest a person. The "physical entry of the home is the chief evil against which the wording of the Fourth Amendment is directed" (*Payton,* citing *United States v. United States District Court,* 1972). The protection of the home applies to apartments, offices, garages, and temporary dwellings, such as hotel rooms. This has been confirmed in cases where the Court has denied landlords and hotel keepers the right to consent to police searches of tenants' rooms (*Chapman v. California,* 1967; *Stoner v. California,* 1964). The protection of home privacy was a key reason for the Court's modification of the hot pursuit doctrine to disallow warrantless home entry for relatively minor offenses (*Welsh v. Wisconsin,* 1984; see Chapter 5).

Even a conservative Court has scrupulously upheld the Fourth Amendment protections of the warrant and probable cause when the core area of the home is involved. A person has no expectation of privacy in his or her public movements, and thus no warrant was required when police placed an electronic **beeper** in a drum containing chloroform to monitor a suspected drug manufacturer route along public streets (*U.S. v. Knotts,* 1983). On the other hand, a suspect's Fourth Amendment rights were violated when, without a warrant, agents used a beeper to trace the movement of a drum *inside* the suspect's home. "The beeper tells the agent that a particular article is actually located at a particular time in the private residence and is in the possession of the person or persons whose residence is being watched. Even if visual surveillance has revealed that the article to which the beeper is attached has entered the house, the later monitoring not only verifies the officers' observations but also establishes that the article remains on the premises" (*United States v. Karo,* 1984).

There is no Fourth Amendment protection of real estate as such, called **open fields** in *Hester v. United States* (1924) and *Oliver v. United States* (1984). The Supreme Court has taken the common law concept of the **curtilage**—the area immediately surrounding a house—and has given it constitutional protection (*Oliver v. United States* 1984; *United States, v. Dunn,* 1987). Still, the Court has strained to not apply the curtilage idea to police observations of backyards from low-flying fixed-wing airplanes and helicopters (*California v. Ciraolo,* 1986; *Florida v. Riley,* 1989).

Persons under Correctional Jurisdiction.

The one dwelling not clothed with Fourth Amendment protection is a prison cell, no matter how strong a prisoner's subjective sense of privacy in it. A "prison shares none of the attributes of privacy of a home." Although prisoners retain constitutional rights that do not conflict with legitimate prison objectives (rights such as freedom of religion and protection from cruel and unusual punishment), "society is not prepared to recognize as legitimate any subjective expectation of privacy that a prisoner might have in his prison cell; . . . the Fourth Amendment proscription against unreasonable searches and seizures does not apply within the confines of the prison cell." As a result, prison authorities are allowed under the Constitution to make random shakedown searches of prisoners' cells. There are limits to the practice if it is intended only to harass prisoners (**Hudson v. Palmer,** 1984).

Similarly, the Court, over a strong dissent, allowed a probation officer to enter a probationer's home without a warrant and on less than probable cause (**Griffin v. Wisconsin,** 1987). The Court said that a "probationer's home, like anyone else's, is protected by the Fourth Amendment's requirement that searches be 'reasonable.'" On the other hand, in Wisconsin all probationers came under a regulation that permits any probation officer to search a probationer's home without a warrant as long as his supervisor approves and as long as there are "reasonable grounds" to believe that contraband is present. The Supreme Court upheld the regulation on the ground that probation supervision is a "special need beyond the normal need for law enforcement"—a Fourth Amendment doctrine that permits warrantless searches on less than probable cause. (See Chapter 5.) *Griffin* implied that a probationer's status imposes a lower expectation of privacy at home than that of an unconvicted person. It was the last case in this group based on the special needs doctrine, which upholds standardless searches that are not designed to promote law enforcement.

Probationers' home privacy rights were further diminished in **United States v. Knights** (2001). A California probationer signed a probation order acknowledging as a condition of probation that he would "submit his . . . person, property, place of residence, vehicle, personal effects, to search at anytime, with or without a search warrant, warrant of arrest or reasonable cause by any probation officer or law enforcement officer." Knights's apartment was searched by a police officer who investigated an arson and had reasonable suspicion but not probable cause that evidence of the crime was in the apartment. The officer did not obtain a search warrant because he knew of Knights's probation condition. Incriminating evidence was found in a search of Knights's home and was used to convict him of a new crime. Knights argued that a warrantless search was permissible only for the special needs purpose of enforcing probation regulations and not for the investigation of new crimes. In rejecting this position, the Court noted that "'the very assumption of the institution of probation' is that the probationer 'is more likely than the ordinary citizen to violate the law.'"

The major difference between the privacy expectation in a prison cell and in a probationer's home is the level of cause required before probation or police officers can enter without a warrant. A few years before *Knights,* the Supreme Court held, in **Pennsylvania Board of Probation and Parole v. Scott** (1998), that the exclusionary rule does not apply to exclude evidence from a parole revocation hearing, where a parole officer illegally entered the home that a parolee shared with his mother, without consent, a warrant, or authorization "by any state statutory or regulatory framework ensuring the reasonableness of searches by parole officers." This clearly implies that a parolee has a lesser expectation in the privacy in a home than a free citizen does, although the Supreme Court did not analyze the case under *Katz.*

In a six-to-three decision, the Court held in **Samson v. California** (2006) that a state can, by statute, obliterate virtually all of the Fourth Amendment rights of a parolee. Donald Samson was walking down the street with a woman and a child. A police officer who knew that Samson was a parolee verified that there were no outstanding warrants against him. The officer nevertheless searched Samson and found drugs. A California law, probably the only one like it in the United States, required a parolee to consent to warrantless and standardless searches at any time. The majority found the condition to be reasonable and upheld the search because a parolee's status is essentially like that of a prisoner and because of the high recidivism rates of California parolees.

Media Ride-alongs.
Wilson v. Layne (1999) held it to be "a violation of the Fourth Amendment for police to bring members of the media or other third parties into a home during the execution of a warrant when the presence of the third parties in the home was not in aid of the execution of the warrant." A proper arrest warrant, supported by probable cause, was issued to U.S. Marshals to enter a Rockville, Maryland, home to arrest Dominic Wilson, a dangerous fugitive. Unbeknownst to the police, it was the home of Wilson's parents. The arrest warrant was executed at 6:45 A.M., much to the surprise of Wilson's parents. After discovering that Dominic was not at the house, the arrest team departed. The team "was accompanied by a reporter and a photographer from the *Washington Post,* who had been invited by the Marshals to accompany them on their mission as part of a Marshal's Service ride-along policy." The photographer took numerous photographs but published none. The reporters did, however, observe a scuffle and the handcuffing of Mr. Wilson, who was wearing briefs. They did not assist in executing the warrant. The Wilsons brought a civil lawsuit for money damages against the Marshal's Service for violating their Fourth Amendment right of privacy by bringing reporters into their home.

The government tried to justify the **media ride-along** by arguing that (1) media presence promotes accurate reporting and crime fighting, (2) the presence of third parties minimizes police abuses and protects the suspects, and (3) the police should be allowed to determine whether these law enforcement interests are advanced by the ride-along. The Court was unpersuaded by these reasons. These factors, even if reasonable, promote general interests and are not sufficient to overcome the specific constitutional right held by the Wilsons.

The Court did not refer to *Katz* or to the expectation of privacy in *Wilson;* instead, it emphasized "the importance of the right of residential privacy at the core of the Fourth Amendment," a "centuries-old principle of respect for the privacy of the home." Beyond this, the Court did not reason except to say, "Were such generalized 'law enforcement objectives' themselves sufficient to trump the Fourth Amendment, the protections guaranteed by that Amendment's text would be significantly watered down." *Wilson* shows a trend of recent cases that emphasize the expectation of privacy in the home but do not apply the *Katz* doctrine to the fullest extent in other areas of law enforcement.

Expectation of Privacy in Automobiles.

There is a lesser expectation of privacy in an automobile than in a home (*California v. Carney*, 1985). The Supreme Court has found that at common law, mobile vehicles could be stopped without a warrant and has generally extended this exception into the Fourth Amendment "automobile exception" (*Carroll v. United States*, 1925). Yet the Court has applied the "expectation of privacy" doctrine to the stopping of automobiles by law enforcement officers, on the ground that stopping an automobile is a seizure that can cause annoyance or fright. A warrantless stop of a vehicle, therefore, must be justified by reasonable suspicion or probable cause of a traffic violation or crime (*United States v. Brignoni-Ponce*, 1975; *Delaware v. Prouse*, 1979). To the contrary, a stop at a fixed checkpoint does not produce the same level of anxiety as being stopped by a roving patrol, and so the expectation of privacy is less and the stop need not be justified by particularized suspicion (*United States v. Martinez-Fuerte*, 1976; *Michigan Department of State Police v. Sitz*, 1990).

Expectation of Privacy in Property and Effects.

In *United States v. Chadwick* (1977), the Supreme Court held that a footlocker is protected by a subjective and objective expectation of privacy. Police had probable cause to believe that a footlocker contained marijuana, had arrested its possessor, and had the luggage in custody. Opening the footlocker violated Chadwick's Fourth Amendment rights, and the evidence was suppressed. The police should have sought a search warrant from a magistrate. The Court has further extended the expectation of privacy to soft baggage that was squeezed by a Border Patrol agent. A bus traveling from California to Arkansas stopped at a Border Patrol checkpoint in Texas, and the agent boarded the bus to check the immigration status of its passengers. After reaching the back of the bus, having satisfied himself that the passengers were lawfully in the United States, the agent began walking toward the front. Along the way, he squeezed the soft luggage that passengers had placed in the overhead storage space above the seats. He squeezed a green canvas bag belonging to passenger Steven Dewayne Bond and noticed that it contained a "brick-like" object later identified as methamphetamine. The Supreme Court held that this physical examination was a search. Bond exhibited an actual expectation of privacy by using an opaque bag and placing that bag directly above his seat. The agent's manipulation of the bag went beyond that tolerated by society:

> When a bus passenger places a bag in an overhead bin, he expects that other passengers or bus employees may move it for one reason or another. Thus, a bus passenger clearly expects that his bag may be handled. He does not expect that other passengers or bus employees will, as a matter of course, feel the bag in an exploratory manner. But this is exactly what the agent did here. We therefore hold that the agent's physical manipulation of petitioner's bag violated the Fourth Amendment. (***Bond v. United States***, 2000)

On the other hand, the Court has come close to stating that a person has no expectation of privacy in the odor of drugs emanating from a piece of luggage in a public area if detected by a trained drug-sniffing canine (*United States v. Place*, 1983). There is no expectation of privacy in abandoned property such as trash left in opaque plastic bags at the curb. It may be seized and searched without a warrant. The general public does not believe that a person expects trash to be kept private because the bags can be opened by children playing, by animals, or by scavengers (***California v. Greenwood***, 1988). The same result occurs under the older property theory: Once people abandon property, they lose all control over it.

Expectation of Privacy in Business Records and Commercial Property.

The Court has held that by depositing money in banks, people expose financial information in bank records to strangers such as bank employees and thus lose an expectation of privacy. As a result, Congress may require that large cash or other transactions be reported to federal agencies without showing particularized suspicion. One's banking records can be subpoenaed by the government under the Bank Secrecy Act (*California Bankers Association v. Schultz,* 1974; *United States v. Miller,* 1976).

The Court has held that business records are not protected by the Fifth Amendment privilege against compelled self-incrimination and thus are subject to seizure under the Fourth Amendment with a proper search warrant (*Andresen v. Maryland,* 1976). Business premises, however, are protected by the Fourth Amendment (*Hale v. Henkel,* 1906; *See v. City of Seattle,* 1967). If commercial property such as a retail store is open to the public, a police agent may enter the premises and observe or purchase suspected items, and such an entry and purchase is not a search and seizure (*Maryland v. Macon,* 1985). Although warrants are required for commercial health or safety inspections under the *Camara–See* doctrine, they require a lesser standard of evidence than the traditional probable cause standard (*Marshall v. Barlow's, Inc.,* 1978). Some commercial properties are subject to warrantless inspections, although retaining expectations of privacy, because of the nature of the business or the special risks that the business creates (e.g., mining). (*Donovan v. Dewey,* 1981).

Undercover Agents and the Fourth Amendment

In **Gouled v. United States** (1921), Army investigators sent a "secret agent" into Gouled's office, not by means of a trespass or burglary, but by false pretenses. The Court held that a physical seizure of papers in these circumstances violated Gouled's Fourth Amendment rights. The question not answered was whether gaining entry by false pretenses invalidated the use of statements made in confidence by the suspect to the **undercover agent.** The Supreme Court resolved the issue in two cases decided on the same day in 1966. There is no Fourth Amendment right of privacy against "inviting" a person who is a secret government agent into the home.

Lewis v. United States (1966) dealt with the common situation of a narcotics agent being invited into a home to conclude an illicit drug transaction after having misrepresented his intentions. The Fourth Amendment was not violated because Lewis had converted his home "into a commercial center to which outsiders are invited for purposes of transacting unlawful business." Whether one applies the older property theory or the *Katz* "expectation of privacy" concept of Fourth Amendment rights, there is no constitutional violation in this scenario. The Court warned that entry gained by invitation did not give the undercover investigator the right to conduct a general search of the premises. In *Lewis,* the Court also expressed its concern for the practical needs of law enforcement:

> Were we to hold the deceptions of the agent in this case constitutionally prohibited, we would come near to a rule that the use of undercover agents in any manner is virtually unconstitutional *per se*. Such a rule would, for example, severely hamper the Government in ferreting out those organized criminal activities that are characterized by covert dealings with victims who either cannot or do not protest. A prime example is provided by the narcotics traffic. (*Lewis v. United States,* footnote omitted)

In **Hoffa v. United States** (1966), national Teamsters Union president James Hoffa was convicted of bribing jurors in an earlier trial. Evidence of the jury tampering was offered by Edward Partin, a Teamsters Union official who was in trouble with the law and who was present in Hoffa's hotel apartment during the earlier trial. He had assisted Hoffa while simultaneously reporting on the jury tampering to federal agents. Partin went to Hoffa's apartment as a government agent; in return for his spying, state and federal criminal charges against him were dropped, and Partin's wife was paid $1,200 out of government funds. Hoffa argued that Partin's entry into the apartment violated his Fourth Amendment right to privacy and was an illegal "search" for verbal evidence. The Court agreed that Hoffa had a Fourth Amendment right to privacy in the hotel apartment and that entry could have been made both by a trespass and, as in *Gouled,* by trickery. What Hoffa relied on was the protection offered by the place. Thus if Partin had opened a desk drawer or a filing cabinet and had stolen incriminating evidence, this would have intruded into Hoffa's constitutionally protected area. The same result would occur by applying the *Katz* expectation of privacy analysis. However,

> [i]t is obvious that [Hoffa] was not relying on the security of his hotel suite when he made the incriminating statements to Partin or in Partin's presence. Partin did not enter the suite by force or by stealth. He was not a surreptitious eavesdropper. Partin was in the suite by invitation, and every conversation which he heard was either directed to him or knowingly carried on in his presence. The petitioner, in a word, was not relying on the security of the hotel room; he was relying upon his misplaced confidence that Partin would not reveal his wrongdoing. . . .
> Neither this Court nor any member of it has ever expressed the view that the Fourth Amendment protects a wrongdoer's misplaced belief that a person to whom he voluntarily confides his wrongdoing will not reveal it. (*Hoffa v. United States,* 1966)

The Fourth Amendment does not protect a person against false friends.

A related question is whether there is any Fourth Amendment protection when a "false friend" wears a concealed microphone on his body to transmit and/or record incriminating conversations. The Supreme Court has consistently ruled that this practice is not prohibited by the Fourth Amendment. When a person "invites" an undercover agent to speak with him voluntarily, the effect of the recording device is to improve the accuracy of the agent's testimony against the defendant. The Court has so held, both before and after *Katz,* and the federal electronic eavesdropping law has confirmed this rule as a matter of federal law.[35]

PROBABLE CAUSE AND THE FOURTH AMENDMENT

The Fourth Amendment states that warrants must be issued on probable cause, a standard that is the evidentiary touchstone of all Fourth Amendment action, including arrests, warrantless searches, and both search and arrest warrants. Until *Terry v. Ohio* (1968), a forcible police interference with liberty, property, or privacy on less than probable cause violated the Fourth Amendment. *Terry's* flexible interpretation, first applied to field interrogation, introduced the lower evidentiary standard of reasonable suspicion. This section explores the meaning and contours of probable cause.

The Concept of Evidence Sufficiency

Liberty is a fundamental precept of American political life. This means that a person's liberty interests—freedom of movement, privacy, and property—must not be stopped or interfered with by the government unless the government can first show a need to interfere that is justified by law. In Fourth Amendment terms, a police officer must have evidence to support a stop, arrest, or search *before* the search takes place. The best way for a police agent to do this is to obtain a warrant. If a warrantless stop, arrest, or search is challenged, the officer must convince a court that he or she had a sufficient level of evidence to lawfully interfere with the defendant's liberty interests. In other areas where the criminal justice or legal process interferes with liberty, different levels of evidence sufficiency are required. The concept of evidence sufficiency is therefore a latent part of due process and helps to ensure fundamental fairness.

Defining Probable Cause

Probable cause, defined as "known facts that could lead a reasonably prudent person to draw conclusions about unknown facts," is a standard of evidence that triggers and justifies government interference with liberty. It is also referred to as "reasonable cause." Because the evidence standard of stops under *Terry v. Ohio* is commonly known as "reasonable suspicion," it is important to use these technical terms precisely. *Evidence* is any kind of proof offered to establish the existence of a fact. Evidence may be (a) the testimony of a witness as to what was heard, seen, smelled, tasted, or felt; or (b) physical items such as documents, drugs, or weapons. Physical evidence is sometimes called "real evidence."

Probable cause is one of several standards of evidence that trigger and justify intrusive governmental action. Table 3–1 displays a hierarchy of evidentiary standards. These standards pertain to the sufficiency or weight of evidence rather than to its admissibility. In general, the greater the impact of a legal action on an individual, the more stringent is the evidentiary standard.

Probable cause is the evidentiary standard for a wide variety of police and legal decisions in the pretrial criminal process: arrest, search and seizure, a magistrate's authorizing a charge after an initial hearing, a magistrate's bind-over decision after a preliminary hearing, and the formal charging of a criminal defendant by a prosecutor's information or by an indictment by a grand jury's voting a "true bill" against a suspect. (In some states, the grand jury or bind-over decision might be subjected to the slightly more rigorous "prima facie case" standard.) Probable cause to arrest a person consists of facts that would lead a

TABLE 3–1 Standards of Evidence Sufficiency

STANDARD	MEANING	LEGAL CONSEQUENCE
Proof beyond a reasonable doubt	No actual and substantial doubt must be present; not a vague apprehension or imaginary doubt; not absolute certainty	Conviction of guilt in a criminal trial
Clear and convincing evidence	Higher than a preponderance of evidence; need not be conclusive	Hold a person without bail under preventive detention; involuntary civil commitment; establish civil fraud; prove a gift
Preponderance of the evidence	Evidence reasonably tending to prove the essential facts in a case; the greater weight of the evidence	Verdict for the plaintiff in a civil litigation
Prima facie case	Evidence good and sufficient on its face to prove a fact or group of facts	Evidence that makes out the plaintiff's or prosecutor's case at trial and is strong enough to prevent a directed verdict for the defendant; in some jurisdictions, a prima facie case is required as the basis for indictment instead of probable cause
Substantial evidence on the whole record	Such evidence that a reasonable mind might accept as adequate to support a conclusion	Judicial review upholding administrative agency action
Probable cause	Known facts that would lead a reasonably prudent person to draw a conclusion about unknown facts	Lawful arrest; reasonable search and seizure; judicial determination to hold a suspect after an initial inquiry; bind-over by magistrate after preliminary examination; prosecutor's information; indictment after grand jury deliberations
Reasonable suspicion	Facts that would lead an experienced police officer to believe that a crime has been, is, or is about to be committed	Stop, pat-down search of outer clothing, and brief questioning of a person
None or "mere" suspicion	Whimsy; randomness; mere suspicion	Observation and surveillance of a person by police or government agent that do not amount to harassment or otherwise unduly interfere with the reasonable expectation of privacy

prudent person to believe that a crime has been committed and that the suspect has committed it. Probable cause to search a place and seize evidence consists of facts that would lead a prudent person to believe that "seizable" items (i.e., contraband, the fruits of a crime, instrumentalities used to commit a crime, or evidence of criminality) are or soon will be located at a particular place.

There is a fine line between probable cause and reasonable suspicion. *Terry* (1967) did not use the term "reasonable suspicion" but upheld a temporary "stop"—a lesser intrusion than an arrest—where an officer believed that "criminal activity is afoot" based on articulable facts, taken together with logical inferences from those facts. A mere hunch does not support reasonable suspicion. (Reasonable suspicion will be explored at greater length in Chapter 4.)

Probable cause is not only a lower "weight" of evidence than that needed for civil or criminal verdicts, but it also relies on less stringent rules guiding the admissibility of evidence. Thus probable cause may be established on the basis of hearsay evidence; it is up to the magistrate to weigh the hearsay to determine whether it is plausible and genuine on the one hand, or farfetched or even fabricated on the other.

Probable Cause Based on Informers' Tips

An officer/affiant seeking a search warrant swears to the magistrate that the information presented is true. Where the officer affirms that he or she saw things or smelled odors (common in drug cases) that would lead a prudent person to believe that contraband is located at a specific place, the magistrate can directly question the officer to be sure of the accuracy of the evidence. Likewise, information given to an officer or magistrate by a victim of a crime is usually considered to be honest and accurate.

However, much criminal activity—including bribery by government officials, white-collar crime, organized crime, and illicit drug trading—is conducted in secret. Officers or blameless victims cannot get access to the criminal behavior. Often, the only way for law enforcement agencies to detect and prosecute such crimes is by using undercover agents to infiltrate the worlds of drug trafficking, organized crime, and white-collar crime. These **secret informants** are themselves often involved in criminal activity. Professors Robert Reinertsen and Robert Bronson note, "Informants are generally unsavory types, engaged in marginal activities that involve betrayal of others. Nonetheless, despite their negative image, informants play such a large and important role in law enforcement efforts that they cannot be ignored."[36] The common terms "snitch," "fink," and "stool pigeon" attest to the negative image and reality of informants. They rarely aid the police out of altruistic motives. More likely, they are being paid, given a promise of prosecutorial leniency, or even rewarded with illicit drugs.

Law enforcement agencies are caught in a dilemma. Knowing the risk of receiving unreliable information when using criminal informants, agencies establish policies regarding informants' recruitment, control, and payment. The proper use of informants depends in large measure on the honesty and mature judgment of the law enforcement officers who control them and good management practices.[37]

Despite internal law enforcement controls, informants have an incentive to lie and have sent many innocent people to prison.[38] The question facing the judicial system is whether it can take steps to ensure that the threat to justice from lying informants is minimized. One solution would be to have the police bring informers before the magistrate so that instead of accepting hearsay, the magistrate can examine the informant personally. The Supreme Court refused to take this path. In **Rovario v. United States** (1957), the Court held that the identity of an informant must be made available at the trial, but prior to trial, law enforcement agencies are allowed to keep the identity of informants secret. (See the biographical sketch of Justice Harold Burton following Chapter 4.) There is a legitimate fear that bringing the informant to the courthouse and having the identity made known to judges and other court personnel would undermine the integrity and success of investigations. It is also not the role of the judicial branch to exercise administrative oversight of the executive branch.

Still, magistrates play an important role in screening out fabrications by informants. When magistrates receive affidavits for search warrants based on information supplied by unnamed informants, they have good reason to be cautious and to examine the affidavit with special care. The Court has, indeed, confirmed this notion by establishing an exclusionary rule: Evidence seized on the basis of a search warrant or a warrant affidavit that does not adequately state the facts that constitute probable cause and explain the source of its information violates the probable cause requirement of the Fourth Amendment and is inadmissible.

In *Nathanson v. United States* (1933), the Court excluded liquor seized from a private home based on a warrant that "went upon a mere affirmation of suspicion and belief without any statement of adequate supporting facts." A magistrate cannot "properly issue a warrant to search a private dwelling unless he can find probable cause therefor from facts or circumstances presented to him under oath or affirmation. Mere affirmance of belief or suspicion is not enough." Another way of stating the rule of *Nathanson* is that a magistrate cannot issue a warrant on the mere say-so of the officer.

Nathanson was supported in *Aguilar v. Texas* (1964). The search warrant application from police officers simply stated that "[a]ffiants have received reliable information from a credible person and do believe" that drugs are located in Aguilar's home. Here, the hearsay basis of the officers' suspicions were more clearly stated than in *Nathanson*. The Court reaffirmed that "an affidavit may be based on hearsay information and need not reflect the direct personal observations of the affiant." Nevertheless, "the magistrate must be informed of some of the *underlying circumstances* from which the informant concluded that the narcotics were where he claimed they were, and some of the underlying circumstances from which the officer concluded that the informant, whose identity need not be disclosed, was '*credible*' or his information '*reliable*.'" (*Aguilar v. Texas,* emphasis added). Again, the Supreme Court ruled that a magistrate's warrant is fatally flawed under the Fourth Amendment if the magistrate simply takes the police officer's word that an informant is reliable or credible and that the contraband is where the officer says it is. This rule is a necessary corollary to the "detached and neutral magistrate" doctrine. If a warrant is issued simply on an officer's say-so, the magistrate becomes a rubber stamp for the executive branch and fails to uphold his or her duty under the Constitution.

Justice Harlan, a conservative jurist, concurred in *Aguilar.* Justice Tom Clark's dissent, joined by Justices Black and Stewart, argued that the officers' statement that they "received reliable information from a credible person" was sufficient to provide probable cause.

The rule of *Aguilar* was confirmed and strengthened in *Spinelli v. United States* (1969). William Spinelli was being investigated by the FBI for bookmaking in St. Louis. A search warrant was obtained to enter an apartment for evidence of an illegal gambling establishment. The affidavit, when reduced to its essential information, contained four facts: (1) that for four of the five days he was followed, Spinelli crossed into Missouri from Illinois at about noon, went to the same apartment house at about 4:00 P.M., and was seen to enter a particular apartment; (2) that there were two telephones in the apartment listed under another's name; (3) that Spinelli had a reputation as a bookmaker and gambler among law enforcement agents, including the affiant; and (4) that a "confidential reliable informant" told the FBI agent that Spinelli was operating a gambling operation with the telephones in the apartment. Evidence seized in the apartment was used to convict Spinelli of interstate travel in aid of racketeering, specifically, of illegal bookmaking.

Justice Harlan wrote the majority opinion holding that this affidavit did not provide probable cause and that the evidence seized had to be excluded. He quickly tossed out the first three items in the affidavit as essentially not supportive of probable cause. There is simply no reason why traveling from one city to another every day would lead anyone to suspect the traveler of being a bookie. The existence of two telephones in the apartment, described as a "petty luxury," was also not deemed at all suspicious.

The third item, Spinelli's reputation, was dismissed: "[T]he allegation that Spinelli was 'known' to the affiant and to other federal and local law enforcement officers as a gambler is but a bald and unilluminating assertion of suspicion that is entitled to no weight in appraising the magistrate's decision." Justice Harlan cited *Nathanson* for this point, although *Nathanson* does not discuss reputation evidence. Reputation evidence is hearsay, and hearsay is proper evidence in a search warrant affidavit. It would appear that the Court, almost instinctively, understood that hearsay about an individual can be entirely baseless and scurrilous and indeed could even be manufactured by the government. Although it may be useful as a starting point for investigation, the reliance on a person's reputation as a matter of Fourth Amendment law could lead to gross injustices.

This, then, left the statement about the "confidential reliable informant" as the sole basis for the warrant. The prosecution argued that the innocent facts in the affidavit corroborated the informant's tip, "thereby entitling it to more weight." The Court disagreed, saying that "the *'totality of circumstances'* approach . . . paints with too broad a brush." Instead of a "totality" approach, Justice Harlan, refining the elements of the *Aguilar* case, provided "a more precise analysis" by which the affidavit's statements regarding a secret informant had to stand on its own. He stated the rules of *Aguilar* that could be reduced to two tests:

> [W]e first consider the weight to be given the informer's tip when it is considered apart from the rest of the affidavit. It is clear that a Commissioner could not credit it without abdicating his constitutional function. Though the affiant swore that his confidant was "reliable," he offered the magistrate no reason in support of this conclusion. Perhaps even more important is the fact that *Aguilar*'s other test has not been satisfied. The tip does not contain a sufficient statement of the underlying circumstances from which the informer concluded that Spinelli was running a bookmaking operation. We are not told how the FBI's source received his information—it is not alleged that the informant personally observed Spinelli at work or that he had ever placed a bet with him. Moreover, if the informant came by the information indirectly, he did not explain why his sources were reliable. . . . In the absence of a statement detailing the manner in which the information was gathered, it is especially important that the tip describe the accused's criminal activity in sufficient detail that the magistrate may know that he is relying on something more substantial than a casual rumor circulating in the underworld or an accusation based merely on an individual's general reputation. (*Spinelli v. United States,* 1969)

The *Aguilar–Spinelli* two-pronged test to obtaining a warrant based on an informer's hearsay includes (1) a veracity, or truthfulness, prong—showing that the informant is truthful because he was used successfully in the past or because the tip is so strong that it is inherently believable; and (2) a basis-of-knowledge prong—showing that the facts were obtained by the informant in a manner that is sufficiently reliable to establish probable cause. The facts that support the prongs must be strong enough to convince the magistrate making an independent determination that the informant had a real basis for knowing about the criminal activity. The facts would also give the magistrate a basis for ascertaining whether they support probable cause.

The dissenters in *Spinelli,* Justices Black and Fortas and Stewart, felt that the four elements found wanting by the majority constituted probable cause. Justice Abe Fortas referred to the length of the affidavit to indicate that it was not simply conclusory. But he did not adequately respond to Justice Harlan's analysis that cut through the lengthy verbiage of the affidavit to reduce it to its essential elements. Justice White concurred in the holding of *Spinelli,* but he expressed concern that it did not fully comport with that of *Draper v. United States* (1959), on which the Court relied.

Justice Harlan, in *Spinelli,* demonstrated how a magistrate should critically evaluate information presented in an affidavit by drawing on the 1959 case of ***Draper v. United States.***

In that case, a paid informer named Hereford told Bureau of Narcotics agents that Draper would travel from Chicago to Denver on a train on one of two days with three ounces of heroin. Hereford precisely described what Draper looked like and told the agents that Draper would be carrying "a tan zipper bag," that he habitually "walked real fast," and that he would be wearing a light-colored raincoat, brown slacks, and black shoes. Agents waited at the incoming trains from Chicago in the Denver station and saw a man fitting the exact description given by Hereford. The man, who turned out to be Draper, was found to be carrying heroin and was arrested. The Supreme Court held that the agents had probable cause to arrest and search Draper, based on the hearsay description of the informant, Hereford. Although Hereford did not provide information to show how he obtained his information about Draper, the "basis of knowledge" prong of the *Aguilar-Spinelli* rule was inferred. The Supreme Court upheld the seizure and search in *Draper* because the highly detailed facts were verified by the agent (except for the possession of heroin) before making the arrest. *Draper,* therefore, stands for the proposition that the police can strengthen any weaknesses in the information provided by the informant by gathering corroborating information.

Conservative Revisions

A task of the Supreme Court, to lay down clear rules for the guidance of lower court judges and government officers, seems to have been fulfilled in *Spinelli* when the Court clarified a line of informers' tip decisions, beginning with *Nathanson v. United States* (1933), with relatively clear procedural guides for resolving probable cause issues. *Spinelli* exemplified the Warren Court's penchant for establishing structured rules. This changed with the advent of the Burger Court, as conservative activism replaced liberal activism.

Professor Charles Whitebread described the five elements of the Burger Court's criminal procedure jurisprudence (see Chapter 1):[39]

- A crime control orientation.
- A hierarchy of constitutional values, with Sixth Amendment trial rights on a higher plane than Fourth Amendment rights.
- A preference for case-by-case analysis rather than establishing general rules.
- A tendency to uphold the prosecution side if the Court believes in the defendant's factual guilt.
- The denial of federal jurisdiction from state cases.

These tendencies were clearly at work in *Illinois v. Gates,* which upset the *Aguilar-Spinelli* rule after fourteen years during which there was little criticism of the two-pronged test.

Read Case and Comments: *Illinois v. Gates*

It is interesting that the nine justices in *Illinois v. Gates* came up with four different analyses of whether the facts established probable cause:

1. The majority (Chief Justice Warren Burger and Justices William Rehnquist, Harry Blackmun, Lewis Powell, and Sandra Day O'Connor) found probable cause to exist under the new totality-of-the-circumstances test.
2. Justice White, concurring, found that probable cause existed under the *Aguilar-Spinelli* two-pronged test.
3. Justices William Brennan and Thurgood Marshall, dissenting, found that the anonymous letter plus the corroboration did not amount to probable cause under either test.
4. Justice John Paul Stevens, dissenting, found no probable cause because at the time when the magistrate issued the warrant, he did not know that the Gateses had driven twenty-two hours nonstop from West Palm Beach to Bloomingdale, a suspicious activity in light of the anonymous letter. The anonymous letter predicted that Sue Gates would fly back to Illinois while Lance drove. This discrepancy undermined probable cause because (1) the couple's willingness to leave their house unattended suggested that it did not contain drugs, and (2) their activity was not as unusual as if they had left separately.

Illinois v. Gates

462 U.S. 213, 103 S.Ct. 2317, 76 L.Ed.2d 527 (1983)

JUSTICE REHNQUIST delivered the opinion of the Court.

Respondents Lance and Susan Gates were indicted for violation of state drug laws after police officers, executing a search warrant, discovered marihuana and other contraband in their automobile and home. * * * The Illinois Supreme Court * * * held that the affidavit submitted in support of the State's application for a warrant to search the Gateses' property was inadequate under this Court's decisions in *Aguilar v. Texas,* 378 U.S. 108 (1964) and *Spinelli v. United States* [this volume] (1969).

We granted certiorari to consider the application of the Fourth Amendment to a magistrate's issuance of a search warrant on the basis of a partially corroborated anonymous informant's tip. * * *

* * *

II

* * * On May 3, 1978, the Bloomingdale Police Department received by mail an anonymous handwritten letter which read as follows: **[a]**

> "This letter is to inform you that you have a couple in your town who strictly make their living on selling drugs. They are Sue and Lance Gates, they live on Greenway, off Bloomingdale Rd. in the condominiums. Most of their buys are done in Florida. Sue his wife drives their car to Florida, where she leaves it to be loaded up with drugs, then Lance flys [*sic*] down and drives it back. Sue flys back after she drops the car off in Florida. May 3 she is driving down there again and Lance will be flying down in a few days to drive it back. At the time Lance drives the car back he has the trunk loaded with over $100,000.00 in drugs. Presently they have over $100,000.00 worth of drugs in their basement.
>
> "They brag about the fact they never have to work, and make their entire living on pushers.
>
> "I guarantee if you watch them carefully you will make a big catch. They are friends with some big drugs dealers, who visit their house often.
>
> "Lance & Susan Gates
> "Greenway
> "in Condominiums"

The letter was referred by the Chief of Police * * * to Detective Mader, who decided to pursue the tip. Mader learned * * * that an Illinois driver's license had been issued to one Lance Gates, residing at a stated address in Bloomingdale. He contacted a confidential informant, whose examination of certain financial records revealed a more recent address for the Gateses, and he also learned from a police officer assigned to O'Hare Airport that "L. Gates" had made a reservation on Eastern Airlines Flight 245 to West Palm Beach, Fla., scheduled to depart from Chicago on May 5 at 4:15 P.M.

Mader then made arrangements with an agent of the Drug Enforcement Administration for surveillance of the May 5 Eastern Airlines flight. The agent later reported to Mader that Gates had boarded the flight, and that federal agents in Florida had observed him arrive in West Palm Beach and take a taxi to the nearby Holiday Inn. They also reported that Gates went to a room registered to one Susan Gates and that, at 7 o'clock A.M. the next morning, Gates and an unidentified woman left the motel in a Mercury bearing Illinois license plates and drove northbound on an interstate highway frequently used by travelers to the Chicago area. In addition, the DEA agent informed Mader that the license plate number

[a] What motivates such an anonymous letter? Motives like envy or revenge could enhance its reliability; on the other hand, a false, incriminating letter could be written as a prank or as a means to harass someone. The police and the magistrate did not rely exclusively on the letter to initiate the search.

on the Mercury was registered to a Hornet station wagon owned by Gates. The agent also advised Mader that the driving time between West Palm Beach and Bloomingdale was approximately 22 to 24 hours. **[b]**

Mader signed an affidavit setting forth the foregoing facts, and submitted it to a judge of the Circuit Court of Du Page County, together with a copy of the anonymous letter. The judge of that court thereupon issued a search warrant for the Gateses' residence and for their automobile. The judge, in deciding to issue the warrant, could have determined that the *modus operandi* of the Gateses had been substantially corroborated. As the anonymous letter predicted, Lance Gates had flown from Chicago to West Palm Beach late in the afternoon of May 5th, had checked into a hotel room registered in the name of his wife, and, at 7 o'clock A.M. the following morning, had headed north, accompanied by an unidentified woman, out of West Palm Beach on an interstate highway used by travelers from South Florida to Chicago in an automobile bearing a license plate issued to him. **[c]**

At 5:15 A.M. on March 7, only 36 hours after he had flown out of Chicago, Lance Gates, and his wife, returned to their home in Bloomingdale, driving the car in which they had left West Palm Beach some 22 hours earlier. The Bloomingdale police were awaiting them, searched the trunk of the Mercury, and uncovered approximately 350 pounds of marihuana. A search of the Gateses' home revealed marihuana, weapons, and other contraband. * * *

The Illinois Supreme Court concluded—and we are inclined to agree—that, standing alone, the anonymous letter * * * would not provide the basis for a magistrate's determination that there was probable cause to believe contraband would be found in the Gateses' car and home. **[d]** The letter provides virtually nothing from which one might conclude that its author is either honest or his information reliable; likewise, the letter gives absolutely no indication of the basis for the writer's predictions regarding the Gateses' criminal activities. Something more was required.

* * *

[The evidence was suppressed by the Illinois courts. They all held that probable cause was not made out under the *Aguilar-Spinelli* test.]

* * * The Illinois Supreme Court, like some others, apparently understood *Spinelli* as requiring that the anonymous letter satisfy each of two independent requirements before it could be relied on. * * * According to this view, the letter, as supplemented by Mader's affidavit, first had to adequately reveal the "basis of knowledge" of the letterwriter—the particular means by which he came by the information given in his report. Second, it had to provide facts sufficiently establishing either the "veracity" of the affiant's informant, or, alternatively, the "reliability" of the informant's report in this particular case.

The Illinois court * * * found that the test had not been satisfied. First, the "veracity" prong was not satisfied because, "[t]here was simply no basis [for] conclud[ing] that the anonymous person [who wrote the letter to the Bloomingdale Police Department] was credible." * * * The court indicated that corroboration by police of details contained in the letter might never satisfy the "veracity" prong, and in any event, could not do so if, as in the present case, only "innocent" details are corroborated. * * * **[e]** In addition, the letter gave no indication of the basis of its writer's knowledge of the Gateses' activities: [it] * * * failed to provide sufficient detail to permit such an inference. Thus, it concluded that no showing of probable cause had been made.

We agree with the Illinois Supreme Court that an informant's "veracity," "reliability," and "basis of knowledge" are all highly relevant in determining the value of his report. We do not agree, however, that these elements should be understood as entirely separate and independent requirements to be rigidly exacted in every case, which the opinion of the Supreme Court of Illinois would imply. Rather, as detailed below, they should be

(*continued*)

[b] Can you think of any legitimate explanations for this travel plan? Is the couple's travel consistent only with a criminal conspiracy? If there is a legitimate explanation, does it negate probable cause to search?

[c] Are the level and type of specificity in the letter similar to, or different from, that given by Hereford in *Draper*? Although the travel plans stated in the letter were mostly corroborated, does that dissolve doubts about the fact that Officer Mader had no idea who wrote the letter?

[d] The Court is wary of information from anonymous tips—yet it does not close the door on the use of such information.

[e] Did the close match between the couple's travels and the letter establish the veracity of the anonymous letter writer? If so, was it veracity regarding the couple's travel patterns or veracity as to their drug dealing?

understood simply as closely intertwined issues that may usefully illuminate the common-sense, practical question whether there is "probable cause" to believe that contraband or evidence is located in a particular place.

III

[f] "Totality of the circumstances" was proposed to the Court by the government in *Spinelli* but rejected by the Court at that time. What factors caused the Court to shift gears?

This totality-of-the-circumstances approach is far more consistent with our prior treatment of probable cause than is any rigid demand that specific "tests" be satisfied by every informant's tip. **[f]** Perhaps the central teaching of our decisions bearing on the probable-cause standard is that it is a "practical, nontechnical conception." * * * "In dealing with probable cause, * * * as the very name implies, we deal with probabilities. These are not technical; they are the factual and practical considerations of everyday life on which reasonable and prudent men, not legal technicians, act." * * *

* * * [P]robable cause is a fluid concept—turning on the assessment of probabilities in particular factual contexts—not readily, or even usefully, reduced to a neat set of legal rules. * * * "Informants' tips, like all other clues and evidence coming to a policeman on the scene, may vary greatly in their value and reliability." Rigid legal rules are ill-suited to an area of such diversity. "One simple rule will not cover every situation." * * *

[g] Justice Harlan, a noted conservative, said in *Spinelli* that a weakness in one prong should not be made up in another: Even a "reliable" informant may, at times, obtain information from a weak hearsay source.

Moreover, the two-pronged test directs analysis into two largely independent channels—the informant's "veracity" or "reliability" and his "basis of knowledge." **[g]** There are persuasive arguments against according these two elements such independent status. Instead, they are better understood as relevant considerations in the totality-of-the-circumstances analysis that traditionally has guided probable-cause determinations: a deficiency in one may be compensated for, in determining the overall reliability of a tip, by a strong showing as to the other, or by some other indicia of reliability. * * *

[Justice Rehnquist suggests that an unusually reliable informant should be believed when on occasion he fails to state the basis of knowledge regarding a prediction of crime.] * * *

* * *

[h] This analysis is belied by a recent article that shows that police agencies prefer the two-prong rule, reviewed at the conclusion of this case. Is Justice Rehnquist setting his sights too low regarding the mental capabilities of lay magistrates and police officers?

We also have recognized that affidavits "are normally drafted by nonlawyers in the midst and haste of a criminal investigation. Technical requirements of elaborate specificity once exacted under common law pleadings have no proper place in this area." * * * Likewise, search and arrest warrants long have been issued by persons who are neither lawyers nor judges, and who certainly do not remain abreast of each judicial refinement of the nature of "probable cause." * * * **[h]** The rigorous inquiry into the *Spinelli* prongs and the complex superstructure of evidentiary and analytical rules that some have seen implicit in our *Spinelli* decision, cannot be reconciled with the fact that many warrants are—quite properly,—issued on the basis of nontechnical, common-sense judgments of laymen applying a standard less demanding than those used in more formal legal proceedings. Likewise, given the informal, often hurried context in which it must be applied, the "built-in subtleties," * * * of the "two-pronged test" are particularly unlikely to assist magistrates in determining probable cause.

* * *

[i] Is this a "constitutional" reason or a "policy" reason? Can such a division be neatly made? Does this seem result oriented?

[Justice Rehnquist urged that courts not review the facts of magistrates' probable cause decisions but pay them great deference. He also argued that if courts continue to scrutinize affidavits according to the two-prong test, police will stop using warrants and will turn more to warrantless searches.]

Finally, the direction taken by decisions following *Spinelli* poorly serves "[t]he most basic function of any government": "to provide for the security of the individual and of his property." * * * **[i]** If, as the Illinois Supreme Court apparently thought, that test must be rigorously applied in every case, anonymous tips would be of greatly diminished value in police work. * * *

* * * [W]e conclude that it is wiser to abandon the "two-pronged test" established by our decisions in *Aguilar* and *Spinelli*. In its place we reaffirm the totality-of-the-circumstances analysis that traditionally has informed probable-cause determinations. * * *

* * *

JUSTICE BRENNAN's dissent also suggests that "[w]ords such as 'practical,' 'nontechnical,' and 'common sense,' as used in the Court's opinion, are but code words for an overly permissive attitude towards police practices in derogation of the rights secured by the Fourth Amendment." * * * **[j]** [N]o one doubts that "under our Constitution only measures consistent with the Fourth Amendment may be employed by government to cure [the horrors of drug trafficking];" * * * but this agreement does not advance the inquiry as to which measures are, and which measures are not, consistent with the Fourth Amendment. "Fidelity" to the commands of the Constitution suggests balanced judgment rather than exhortation. The highest "fidelity" is not achieved by the judge who instinctively goes furthest in upholding even the most bizarre claim of individual constitutional rights, any more than it is achieved by a judge who instinctively goes furthest in accepting the most restrictive claims of governmental authorities. The task of this Court, as of other courts, is to "hold the balance true," and we think we have done that in this case.

IV

Our decisions applying the totality-of-the-circumstances analysis outlined above have consistently recognized the value of corroboration of details of an informant's tip by independent police work. * * *

* * *

The showing of probable cause in the present case was * * * compelling. * * * **[k]** Even standing alone, the facts obtained through the independent investigation of Mader and the DEA at least suggested that the Gateses were involved in drug trafficking. In addition to being a popular vacation site, Florida is well known as a source of narcotics and other illegal drugs. * * * Lance Gates' flight to Palm Beach, his brief, overnight stay in a motel, and apparent immediate return north to Chicago in the family car, conveniently awaiting him in West Palm Beach, is as suggestive of a prearranged drug run, as it is of an ordinary vacation trip.

In addition, the judge could rely on the anonymous letter, which had been corroborated in major part by Mader's efforts. * * *

Finally, the anonymous letter contained a range of details relating not just to easily obtained facts and conditions existing at the time of the tip, but to future actions of third parties ordinarily not easily predicted. The letterwriter's accurate information as to the travel plans of each of the Gateses was of a character likely obtained only from the Gateses themselves, or from someone familiar with their not entirely ordinary travel plans. If the informant had access to accurate information of this type a magistrate could properly conclude that it was not unlikely that he also had access to reliable information of the Gateses' alleged illegal activities. Of course, the Gateses' travel plans might have been learned from a talkative neighbor or travel agent; under the "two-pronged test" developed from *Spinelli,* the character of the details in the anonymous letter might well not permit a sufficiently clear inference regarding the letterwriter's "basis of knowledge." But, as discussed previously, * * * probable cause does not demand the certainty we associate with formal trials. It is enough that there was a fair probability that the writer of the anonymous

[j] Justice Brennan, a result-oriented liberal, argues in his dissent that Justice Rehnquist's opinion is result oriented. In reply, Justice Rehnquist makes the valid point that different justices (and different people) genuinely view constitutional rules differently.

[k] Do you agree with Justice Rehnquist that this evidence is "compelling," or is it a close call? When deciding to intrude into a person's home and car, should magistrates lean toward restraint? If the warrant were not issued in this case, how much additional investigation would the Bloomingdale Police Department have to do after the couple's return to make a stronger case for probable cause? Given the Court's allowance of a corroborated anonymous letter as the basis of probable cause, does this create a risk that a dishonest police officer will be tempted to have an "anonymous" letter submitted in a hard-to-crack case?

(continued)

letter had obtained his entire story either from the Gateses or someone they trusted. And corroboration of major portions of the letter's predictions provides just this probability. It is apparent, therefore, that the judge issuing the warrant had a "substantial basis for * * * conclud[ing]" that probable cause to search the Gateses' home and car existed. The judgment of the Supreme Court of Illinois therefore must be

Reversed.

JUSTICE BRENNAN, with whom JUSTICE MARSHALL joins, dissenting.

* * *

I

* * *

[I] What sort of fact would verify the basis of knowledge in an anonymous tip? Perhaps a verifiable reference to criminal activity that would not be known to an average person? If it would be impossible for a magistrate to rely on an anonymous tip, would the proper law enforcement response be to get additional corroboration in order to establish independent probable cause?

Until today the Court has never squarely addressed the application of the *Aguilar* and *Spinelli* standards to tips from anonymous informants. Both *Aguilar* and *Spinelli* dealt with tips from informants known at least to the police. * * * And surely there is even more reason to subject anonymous informants' tips to the tests established by *Aguilar* and *Spinelli.* By definition nothing is known about an anonymous informant's identity, honesty, or reliability. * * *

To suggest that anonymous informants' tips are subject to the tests established by *Aguilar* and *Spinelli* is not to suggest that they can never provide a basis for a finding of probable cause. **[I]** It is conceivable that police corroboration of the details of the tip might establish the reliability of the informant under *Aguilar*'s veracity prong, as refined in *Spinelli,* and that the details in the tip might be sufficient to qualify under the "self-verifying detail" test established by *Spinelli* as a means of satisfying *Aguilar*'s basis of knowledge prong. The *Aguilar* and *Spinelli* tests must be applied to anonymous informants' tips, however, if we are to continue to ensure that findings of probable cause, and attendant intrusions, are based on information provided by an honest or credible person who has acquired the information in a reliable way. * * *

II

* * *

* * * But of particular concern to all Americans must be that the Court gives virtually no consideration to the value of insuring that findings of probable cause are based on information that a magistrate can reasonably say has been obtained in a reliable way by an honest or credible person. I share JUSTICE WHITE's fear that the Court's rejection of *Aguilar* and *Spinelli* and its adoption of a new totality-of-the-circumstances test, * * * "may foretell an evisceration of the probable-cause standard. * * *" * * *

Gates is a constitutionally important decision that significantly shifted the criminal procedure balance in favor of the state, a result that has been criticized by some legal commentators.[40] An interesting study published in 2000, examining the practices of six Atlanta-area police academies, shows that the departments train their officers in the *Aguilar-Spinelli* two-pronged test rather than the open-ended *Gates* totality test. Two reasons were given by the training officers: (1) they felt that prosecutors and courts were likely to demand adherence to the two-pronged or a similar test, and (2) "almost all of the instructors stated that they did not believe a majority of their recruits could master the intricacies of an open-ended standard such as the *Gates* standard."[41] This is contrary to the main reason given by Justice Rehnquist for the majority opinion, and it is not the first time that police practice did not agree with legal speculation.

PLAIN VIEW AND RELATED DOCTRINES

Plain view is a useful doctrine for police officers. It allows seizures of evidence without a warrant when the police are already lawfully in a place or have made a lawful search. This section also examines the related "open fields" doctrine and the use of enhancement devices.

Plain View

The simple idea that a police officer can seize contraband lying about in a public place is so obvious that it has rarely been litigated. In **Cardwell v. Lewis** (1974), the Court articulated the principle that there is no Fourth Amendment privacy interest in material or possessions that are exposed to public scrutiny. In this case, a car owned by a murder suspect was in a public parking lot; the police scraped a bit of paint from a fender to be used as evidence. The court found no constitutional violation: "[W]here probable cause exists, a warrantless examination of the exterior of a car is not unreasonable under the Fourth and Fourteenth Amendments."

It is a different matter for police to seize material from inside a place that is protected by the Fourth Amendment. Professors Whitebread and Slobogin assert, correctly, that a police officer who saw marijuana through a house window while standing on a sidewalk could not enter and seize the evidence, although in a factual sense it was in "plain view."[42] As the Supreme Court stated in *Agnello v. United States* (1925): "Belief, however well-founded, that an article sought is concealed in a dwelling house furnishes no justification for a search of that place without a warrant." In such a case, the officer would have to obtain a warrant to enter lawfully.

Prior Justified Search.   The basic rules of plain view were established in **Coolidge v. New Hampshire** (1971). In that case, Justice Stewart, writing for a plurality, made clear the ancillary, or "piggy-back," nature of the doctrine:

> What the "plain view" cases have in common is that the police officer in each of them had a *prior justification* for an intrusion. . . . The doctrine serves to supplement the prior justification— whether it be a warrant for another object, hot pursuit, search incident to lawful arrest, or some other legitimate reason for being present unconnected with a search directed against the accused—and permits the warrantless seizure. (*Coolidge v. New Hampshire,* p. 466, emphasis added)

Under *Katz,* a plain view seizure of property is justified on the ground that there is no reasonable expectation of privacy in items that are contraband or the clear evidence of crime; police have a legitimate interest, not blocked by the Fourth Amendment, to take such items.

Nevertheless, it must be stressed that the first rule of plain view is that there must be a lawful intrusion. In *Coolidge,* Justice Stewart noted,

But it is important to keep in mind that, in the vast majority of cases, *any* evidence seized by the police will be in plain view, at least at the moment of seizure. The problem with the "plain view" doctrine has been to identify the circumstances in which plain view has legal significance rather than being simply the normal concomitant of any search, legal or illegal. (*Coolidge v. New Hampshire,* 1971, emphasis in original)

Police cannot "create" plain view by taking advantage of an illegal search. Justice Stewart put it this way: "[P]lain view alone is never enough to justify the warrantless seizure of evidence." It would destroy Fourth Amendment protections to allow the police to search at will, or without a warrant where a warrant is otherwise required, and to rationalize a seizure because an unearthed item is seen to be contraband or evidence of criminality.

Immediately Apparent.

Coolidge established a second rule of plain view—the "immediately apparent" rule. The police in *Coolidge* conducted a warrantless search of an automobile suspected to contain fiber evidence and sought to justify it because the car itself was "in plain view." The car was obviously in plain view, but the vacuumed microscopic particles certainly were not. Justice Stewart said, "Of course, the extension of the original justification is legitimate only when it is *immediately apparent* to the police that they have evidence before them; the 'plain view' doctrine may not be used to extend a general exploratory search from one object to another until something incriminating at last emerges." The rule that the evidence in plain view must be immediately apparent as contraband is another way of saying that probable cause must exist to secure the evidence at the moment of seizure.

As with all probable cause decisions, absolute certainty is not required. For example, in *Texas v. Brown* (1983), a police officer looked into an automobile at night with a flashlight at a routine traffic license checkpoint and saw an opaque, green party balloon knotted about one-half inch from the tip. The Supreme Court ruled that he had probable cause to believe that the balloon contained illegal drugs because it was known that this was a common way for drug dealers to carry their wares. The Court thus allows the police some leeway for making an inference in determining whether it was immediately apparent that drugs were in the car.

Read Case and Comments: *Arizona v. Hicks*

Plain Feel.

Plain view is not limited to matters viewed by eyesight, but applies to evidence known to any of the senses. In **Minnesota v. Dickerson** (1993), police lawfully stopped Dickerson outside a known drug house when his overall behavior created a reasonable suspicion that he carried drugs. An officer, following the rule of *Terry* (1968), patted down the outside of Dickerson's jacket to check for weapons. He testified, "I felt a lump, a small lump, in the front pocket. I examined it with my fingers and it slid and it felt to be a lump of crack cocaine in cellophane." The officer then retrieved a small plastic bag with crack cocaine from Dickerson's pocket.

Dickerson raised two plain view issues. First, must the police visually observe an item for it to be in plain view? The Court answered that plain "view" applies to any seizable item apparent to any of the senses:

> To this Court there is no distinction as to which sensory perception the officer uses to conclude that the material is contraband. An experienced officer may rely upon his sense of smell in DWI stops or in recognizing the smell of burning marijuana in an automobile. The sound of a shotgun being racked would clearly support certain reactions by an officer. The sense of touch, grounded in experience and training, is as reliable as perceptions drawn from other senses. "Plain feel," therefore, is no different than plain view and will equally support the seizure here. (*Minnesota v. Dickerson,* 1993, quoting trial judge)

Two arguments to the contrary were raised by the Minnesota Supreme Court to reject the so-called **plain feel rule:** (1) that the sense of touch is inherently less immediate and less reliable than the sense of sight and (2) that the sense of touch is far more intrusive into personal privacy. The U.S. Supreme Court, noting that the facts in *Terry* (1968) allowed the sense of touch to be used for pat-down searches, disagreed.

The *Dickerson* case required the resolution of a second issue: whether what the officer felt was *immediately apparent* as crack cocaine. Justice White's close examination of the facts led to the conclusion that the officer "overstepped the bounds" of the limited search authorized by *Terry* because he continued to explore Dickerson's outer pocket after determining that it contained no weapon. The *Terry* rule overlapped with the immediacy/probable cause rule: "If . . . the police lack probable cause to believe that an object in plain view is contraband without conducting some further search of the object— *i.e.,* if 'its incriminating character [is not] "immediately apparent," ' . . . the plain-view doctrine cannot justify its seizure."[43] Here, because the officer had to slide the object in the pocket around, it was not immediately apparent as contraband and was not admissible as evidence in a trial.

Inadvertence.

Coolidge stated a third plain view rule, that the officer must come across incriminating evidence inadvertently. This rule, supported by a plurality of four justices and not a majority in *Coolidge,* was overturned by the Court in **Horton v. California** (1990). Justice Stewart, in *Coolidge,* thought that without the rule of inadvertence police could simply dispense with a search warrant whenever they had reason to believe that contraband was located in a premises. This, of course, is not the case. But *Horton*'s facts made it reasonable to dispense with the inadvertency rule.

Justice Stevens, writing for the majority in *Horton,* stated that the inadvertency requirement served no purpose in protecting individual rights and could frustrate legitimate searches. The police had probable cause to believe that Horton committed a robbery and that he had the stolen property (three specifically described rings) and weapons (an Uzi machine gun, a .38-caliber revolver, and a stun gun) in his home. The warrant affidavit mentioned both the robbery proceeds and the weapons, but the magistrate's warrant mentioned only the stolen property. When executing the warrant, an officer saw and seized the weapons but did not find the stolen property. Because the officer had prior knowledge of the weapons, they were not seized inadvertently. Horton argued that the evidence should be suppressed under the *Coolidge* plurality rule. The Supreme Court disagreed.

The majority concluded that the rule adds nothing to protect an individual's right to privacy. First, an officer's anticipation that evidence would be present does not harm the defendant's rights as long as the officer is legitimately on the premises. Second, the inadvertency requirement itself does not prevent a search from becoming a general search or prevent a particular warrant from becoming a general warrant. If the police go beyond the terms of a valid warrant or exceed the limits of a warrantless search, the evidence will be inadmissible as a violation of the Fourth Amendment particularity requirement. A second protection is not needed. On the other hand, if a search is within the scope of a warrant, the Court reasoned that the individual's privacy has already been legitimately invaded and that no additional right against seizure is needed other than the "immediately apparent" requirement.

Justice Brennan, joined by Justice Marshall, dissented in *Horton*. He argued that an officer who fails to mention an item known to be in a place in an affidavit, and then seizes it anyway, violates the Fourth Amendment. He was also concerned that the lack of an inadvertency requirement for plain view would lead to a larger number of pretext searches. He cited several state cases where this had happened, while admitting that the entry in *Horton* did not seem to be a pretext to seize the guns. Given the fact that the Court has since ruled that a pretextual auto stop is not unconstitutional as long as an officer has a valid basis to search or make an arrest, this argument takes on greater urgency.[44]

Arizona v. Hicks

480 U.S. 321, 107 S.Ct. 1149, 94 L.Ed.2d 347 (1987)

Justice SCALIA delivered the opinion of the Court.

In *Coolidge v. New Hampshire* (1971), we said that in certain circumstances a warrantless seizure by police of an item that comes within plain view during their lawful search of a private area may be reasonable under the Fourth Amendment. * * * [The issue] in the present case [is] whether this "plain view" doctrine may be invoked when the police have less than probable cause to believe that the item in question is evidence of a crime or is contraband.

I

[Police entered an apartment without a warrant to search for a person who shot a bullet through the floor, injuring a man in the apartment below.] **[a]** They found and seized three weapons, including a sawed-off rifle. * * *

One of the policemen, Officer Nelson, noticed two sets of expensive stereo components, which seemed out of place in the squalid and otherwise ill-appointed four room apartment. Suspecting that they were stolen, he read and recorded their serial numbers—moving some of the components, including a Bang and Olufsen turntable, in order to do so—which he then reported by phone to his headquarters. On being advised that the turntable had been taken in an armed robbery, he seized it immediately. It was later determined that some of the other serial numbers matched those on other stereo equipment taken in the same armed robbery, and a warrant was obtained and executed to seize that equipment as well. Respondent was subsequently indicted for the robbery.

[On a suppression motion, the state trial court and court of appeals held that the view of the serial numbers was an additional search unrelated to the exigency of the search for the shooter. These holdings implied rejection of the idea that the actions were justified by the plain view doctrine. The evidence was suppressed, and the state appealed.]

II

* * * We agree that the mere recording of the serial numbers did not constitute a seizure. * * * In and of itself * * * it did not "meaningfully interfere" with respondent's possessory interest in either the serial number or the equipment, and therefore did not amount to a seizure. * * *

Officer Nelson's moving of the equipment, however, did constitute a "search" separate and apart from the search for the shooter, victims, and weapons that was the lawful objective of his entry into the apartment. Merely inspecting those parts of the turntable that came into view during the latter search would not have constituted an independent search, because it would have produced no additional invasion of respondent's privacy interest. **[b]** But taking action, unrelated to the objectives of the authorized intrusion, which exposed to view concealed portions of the apartment or its contents, did produce a new invasion of respondent's privacy unjustified by the exigent circumstance that validated the entry. This is why * * * the "distinction between 'looking' at a suspicious object in plain view and 'moving' it even a few inches" is much more than trivial for purposes of the Fourth Amendment. It matters not that the search uncovered nothing of any great personal value to the respondent—serial numbers rather than (what might conceivably have been hidden behind or under the equipment) letters or photographs. A search is a search, even if it happens to disclose nothing but the bottom of a turntable.

[a] The three standard exigency exceptions to the warrant requirement are hot pursuit, automobile search, and search incident to arrest. The fact that the Court upheld the entry in *Hicks* means that a general exigency category exists, based on reasonableness.

[b] This paragraph implies that the plain view rule simply recognizes common-sense reality. If Officer Nelson saw obvious contraband—e.g., drugs—sitting on a table in the apartment, it would be silly to hold that the officer could not act on that information. On the other hand, allowing Officer Nelson, lawfully in the apartment for the limited purpose of looking for the shooter, to expand that search into another, could provide incentives for pretext searches of homes.

III

The remaining question is whether the search was "reasonable" under the Fourth Amendment.

* * * [W]e reject, at the outset, the * * * position * * * that because the officers' action directed to the stereo equipment was unrelated to the justification for their entry into respondent's apartment, it was *ipso facto* unreasonable. **[c]** That lack of relationship *always* exists with regard to action validated under the "plain view" doctrine; where action is taken for the purpose of justifying entry, invocation of the doctrine is superfluous. * * *

We turn, then, to application of the doctrine to the facts of this case. "It is well established that under certain circumstances the police may *seize* evidence in plain view without a warrant," *Coolidge v. New Hampshire* * * * (**plurality opinion**) (emphasis added). Those circumstances include situations "[w]here the initial intrusion that brings the police within plain view of such [evidence] is supported . . . by one of the recognized exceptions to the warrant requirement. * * * It would be absurd to say that an object could lawfully be seized and taken from the premises, but could not be moved for closer examination." It is clear, therefore, that the search here was valid if the "plain view" doctrine would have sustained a seizure of the equipment.

There is no doubt it would have done so if Officer Nelson had probable cause to believe that the equipment was stolen. **[d]** The State conceded, however, that he had only a "reasonable suspicion," by which it means something less than probable cause. * * *

We now hold that probable cause is required. To say otherwise would be to cut the "plain view" doctrine loose from its theoretical and practical moorings. The theory of that doctrine consists of extending to nonpublic places such as the home, where searches and seizures without a warrant are presumptively unreasonable, the police's longstanding authority to make warrantless seizures in public places of such objects as weapons and contraband. And the practical justification for that extension is the desirability of sparing police, whose viewing of the object in the course of a lawful search is as legitimate as it would have been in a public place, the inconvenience and the risk—to themselves or to preservation of the evidence—of going to obtain a warrant. **[e]** Dispensing with the need for a warrant is worlds apart from permitting a lesser standard of *cause* for the seizure than a warrant would require, *i.e.,* the standard of probable cause. No reason is apparent why an object should routinely be seizable on lesser grounds, during an unrelated search and seizure, than would have been needed to obtain a warrant for that same object if it had been known to be on the premises.

We do not say, of course, that a seizure can never be justified on less than probable cause. **[f]** We have held that it can—where, for example, the seizure is minimally intrusive and operational necessities render it the only practicable means of detecting certain types of crime. See, *e.g., United States v. Cortez (1981)* (investigative detention of vehicle suspected to be transporting illegal aliens);* * * *United States v. Place, (1983)* (dictum) (seizure of suspected drug dealer's luggage at airport to permit exposure to specially trained dog). No special operational necessities are relied on here, however—but rather the mere fact that the items in question came lawfully within the officer's plain view. That alone cannot supplant the requirement of probable cause.

The same considerations preclude us from holding that, even though probable cause would have been necessary for a *seizure,* the *search* of objects in plain view that occurred here could be sustained on lesser grounds. A dwelling-place search, no less than a dwelling-place seizure, requires probable cause, and there is no reason in theory or practicality why application of the "plain view" doctrine would supplant that requirement. * * * **[g]** [T]o treat searches more liberally would especially erode the plurality's warning in *Coolidge* that "the 'plain view' doctrine may not be used to extend a general exploratory

(continued)

[c] The defendant argued that the police could seize only items in plain view that related to the shooting; such an argument would destroy the practical value of the plain view doctrine and would not adhere to its logic. Note that both the defense and the prosecution make extreme arguments to the Court in this case.

[d] Why should the turntable be in "plain view" if Officer Nelson had probable cause to believe it was stolen but not if he had reasonable suspicion?

[e] The *practical* justification for the plain view rule is couched in terms of assisting police. The theoretical justification is not discussed in depth. Does the rule have practical justification that benefits the defendant?

[f] The examples in this paragraph are applications of the *Terry* "stop and frisk" doctrine. This simply does not apply to the facts of *Hicks.*

[g] To the dissent, lifting the stereo is not a search but a "cursory inspection." But the majority fears that to allow police to rummage in a home beyond their lawful purpose, to *create* plain view, opens a theoretical rift in the plain view doctrine that can have negative, practical consequences.

search from one object to another until something incriminating at last emerges." * * * In short, whether legal authority to move the equipment could be found only as an inevitable concomitant of the authority to seize it, or also as a consequence of some independent power to search certain objects in plain view, probable cause to believe the equipment was stolen was required. **[h]**

[h] Is Justice Scalia's opinion "conservative" or "liberal"?

* * *

For the reasons stated, the judgment of the Court of Appeals of Arizona is *Affirmed.*

JUSTICE O'CONNOR, with whom THE CHIEF JUSTICE and JUSTICE POWELL join, dissenting.

The Court today gives the right answer to the wrong question. The Court asks whether the police must have probable cause before either seizing an object in plain view or conducting a full-blown search of that object, and concludes that they must. I agree. In my view, however, this case presents a different question: whether police must have probable cause before conducting a cursory inspection of an item in plain view. **[i]** Because I conclude that such an inspection is reasonable if the police are aware of facts or circumstances that justify a reasonable suspicion that the item is evidence of a crime, I would reverse the judgment of the Arizona Court of Appeals, and therefore dissent.

[i] Justice O'Connor seeks to create a new rule: a "cursory inspection" plain view seizure.

[A *Coolidge* requirement is that for evidence to be within the "plain view" exception,] it must be "immediately apparent" to the police that the items they observe may be evidence of a crime, contraband, or otherwise subject to seizure.

* * *

The purpose of the "immediately apparent" requirement is to prevent "general exploratory rummaging in a person's belongings." If an officer could indiscriminately search every item in plain view, a search justified by a limited purpose—such as exigent circumstances—could be used to eviscerate the protections of the Fourth Amendment. * * *

* * *

[j] Do you think that a "cursory examination" doctrine based on reasonable suspicion would prevent police from engaging in "exploratory rummaging"? If this rule existed, do you think that Officer Nelson would have limited his exploration only to moving the turntable?

* * * When a police officer makes a cursory inspection of a suspicious item in plain view in order to determine whether it is indeed evidence of a crime, there is no "exploratory rummaging." Only those items that the police officer "reasonably suspects" as evidence of a crime may be inspected, and perhaps more importantly, the scope of such an inspection is quite limited. **[j]** In short, if police officers have a reasonable, articulable suspicion that an object they come across during the course of a lawful search is evidence of crime, in my view they may make a cursory examination of the object to verify their suspicion. If the officers wish to go beyond such a cursory examination of the object, however, they must have probable cause. This distinction between a full-blown search and seizure of an item and a mere inspection of the item * * * [is] based on their relative intrusiveness. * * *

* * *

Curtilage and Open Fields

The Fourth Amendment protects the privacy, liberty, and property interests of "persons, houses, papers, and effects, against unreasonable searches and seizures." Does Fourth Amendment protection extend to landed property? The answer depends on the location of the land in relation to a house. As a general rule, what is referred to as "open fields" in Fourth Amendment law does not come under the protection of the amendment, whereas areas close to the house—known as the curtilage—are protected. As a result, police do not need a warrant to go onto open fields, and any contraband found there may be seized in plain view. In other words, a government intrusion in an open field in not a "search" in the constitutional sense.

Curtilage.   In *Oliver v. United States* (1984), the Supreme Court noted that "[a]t common law, the curtilage is the area to which extends the intimate activity associated with the 'sanctity of a man's home and the privacies of life,' . . . and therefore has been considered part of the home itself for Fourth Amendment purposes. Thus, courts have extended Fourth Amendment protection to the curtilage; and they have defined the curtilage, as did the common law, by reference to the factors that determine whether an individual reasonably may expect that an area immediately adjacent to the home will remain private."

More precisely, the curtilage included the area under the eaves of the main house; small structures near the main house such as a shed, smokehouse, or garage; and the area around a house. The yard of a typical suburban home is a curtilage; the wall around O. J. Simpson's Brentwood estate (the scene of one of the most notorious police investigations of the twentieth century) described its curtilage, and before Detective Mark Fuhrman could enter he should have had a search warrant or a valid warrant exception.

In *United States v. Dunn* (1987), Drug Enforcement Administration (DEA) agents, without a warrant, went onto Dunn's land to see if they could detect evidence of illegal amphetamine manufacture. Dunn's house was a half mile from a public road on a 198-acre ranch that was completely encircled by a perimeter fence. Two barns were located about fifty yards from the residence. The property contained several interior fences, constructed mainly of posts and multiple strands of barbed wire. The house and a small greenhouse were surrounded by a fence. One barn was enclosed by a wooden fence. The DEA agents crossed the perimeter fence and one interior fence. Standing approximately midway between the residence and the barns, they smelled what was believed to be the odor of phenylacetic acid coming from the direction of the barns. They then crossed another barbed wire fence and a wooden fence to get to the large barn. They walked under the barn's overhang and, using a flashlight, peered into the barn. "They observed what the DEA agent thought to be a phenylacetone laboratory. The officers did not enter the barn. At this point the officers departed from respondent's property." A warrant was issued on the basis of facts obtained by police observations of the barn (*United States v. Dunn,* 1987).

The Court ruled that the barn was not within the curtilage and that the police officers violated no Fourth Amendment expectation of privacy when they went up to the barn and observed an illegal drug factory inside.

Open Fields.   "Conversely, the common law implies, as we reaffirm today, that no expectation of privacy legitimately attaches to open fields" (*Oliver v. United States,* 1984). The rule was first stated tersely by Justice Oliver Wendell Holmes Jr. in *Hester v. United States* (1924): The "special protection accorded by the Fourth Amendment to the people in their 'persons, houses, papers, and effects,' is not extended to the open fields. The distinction between the latter and the house is as old as the common law." After *Katz,* the question arose as to whether this distinction still stood under a modernized, nonproperty interpretation of the Fourth Amendment, or whether expectation of privacy analysis would extend Fourth Amendment protection to so-called open fields.

Oliver v. United States (1984) was two consolidated cases. The essential facts were that police officers, without warrants or consent, went into the lands owned by defendants and discovered marijuana patches. The privately owned fields were posted with "No Trespassing" signs. One site was highly secluded, over a mile from the defendant's house, and a gate to the fields was locked. To reach the other site, officers had to walk a path between the defendant's house and a neighbor's house. In one case, the lower court upheld the search; in the other, the evidence was suppressed.

Justice Powell's majority opinion provided several reasons for upholding the "open fields" rule. First, the explicit language of the Fourth Amendment "is not extended to the open fields." Second, open fields are not "effects" within the meaning of the Fourth Amendment. Significantly, a first draft of the Fourth Amendment included a protection of "other property" along with persons, houses, and papers. The change in wording confirms the idea that "effects" refers to personal property. Third, the majority felt there was no expectation of privacy in open fields that society is prepared to recognize as reasonable—in other words, *Katz* had not changed the "open fields" rule. Open land is put to uses, such as the cultivation of crops, that are not the kinds of intimate activities that occur in homes and have historically called for strong privacy protection.

Fourth, "as a practical matter these lands usually are accessible to the public and the police in ways that a home, an office, or commercial structure would not be." Rural land may be fenced and posted with "No Trespassing" signs, but these do not effectively keep hikers or hunters off the land. They certainly do not provide the same kind of psychological barrier that apartment and house doors and windows provide. Also, "the public and police lawfully may survey lands from the air." Fifth, the common law distinction between open fields and the curtilage supports the idea that the Framers did not intend to extend Fourth Amendment protection to open fields. Sixth, a defendant's property interest, such as ownership or leaseholding, that is violated by police committing a trespass to land, no longer decides the case under *Katz*. "The existence of a property right is but one element in determining whether expectations of privacy are legitimate."

The Court also provided practical reasons for supporting the "open fields" doctrine. An argument was made that in each case where police trespass on real estate and discover contraband, the courts should conduct a factual inquiry to discover whether the land and its uses come within the "open fields" rule. The Court rejected this. Under a case-by-case approach, "police officers would have to guess before every search whether landowners had erected fences sufficiently high, posted a sufficient number of warning signs, or located contraband in an area sufficiently secluded to establish a right of privacy. The lawfulness of a search would turn on '[a] highly sophisticated set of rules, qualified by all sorts of ifs, ands, and buts and requiring the drawing of subtle nuances and hairline distinctions. . . . '" A bright-line rule better serves law enforcement and ensures that constitutional rights will uniformly be enforced.

Justice Marshall, joined by Justices Brennan and Stevens, wrote a spirited dissent. He felt, first, that provisions that "identify a fundamental human liberty" should "be shielded forever from government intrusion" and so should be interpreted in an expansive manner "to lend them meanings that ensure that the liberties the Framers sought to protect are not undermined by the changing activities of government officials." Next, he argued that if, as the majority believed, the Fourth Amendment offered no protection to real property, then the protection extended to the curtilage is inconsistent. Again, the objective expectation of privacy is seen in laws that allow the prosecution of trespassers. Posting and fencing are clear ways in which owners announce their expectation of privacy, and they are understood by all. Finally, the dissent disagreed with the majority that the uses to which property owners put lands are not the sort of activities that society deems worthy of privacy:

> The uses to which a place is put are highly relevant to the assessment of a privacy interest asserted therein. . . . If, in light of our shared sensibilities, those activities are of a kind in which people should be able to engage without fear of intrusion by private persons or government

officials, we extend the protection of the Fourth Amendment to the space in question, even in the absence of any entitlement derived from positive law. . . .

> Privately owned woods and fields that are not exposed to public view regularly are employed in a variety of ways that society acknowledges deserve privacy. Many landowners like to take solitary walks on their property, confident that they will not be confronted in their rambles by strangers or policemen. Others conduct agricultural businesses on their property. Some landowners use their secluded spaces to meet lovers, others to gather together with fellow worshippers, still others to engage in sustained creative endeavor. Private land is sometimes used as a refuge for wildlife, where flora and fauna are protected from human intervention of any kind. Our respect for the freedom of landowners to use their posted "open fields" in ways such as these partially explains the seriousness with which the positive law regards deliberate invasions of such spaces, . . . and substantially reinforces the landowners' contention that their expectations of privacy are "reasonable." (*Oliver v. United States*)

The curtilage concept expands the Fourth Amendment definition of a house to a certain "reasonable" amount of land around a house. This gives the constitutional protections of the Fourth Amendment some "breathing room" and prevents the "open fields" exception from allowing police to tightly surround a house or creep up to windows to peer in or eavesdrop.

Airspace

If the curtilage is open to view, police may observe it from a public vantage point such as a road. What they may not do is physically invade the curtilage itself to encroach on the zone of privacy that one expects to have around a dwelling. In several cases that the Framers surely could not have contemplated, the Supreme Court considered the extent to which the curtilage protection applied to airspace above premises.

The *Katz* doctrine provided no protection against the warrantless aerial surveillance by police of a backyard where marijuana was growing. The Court in ***California v. Ciraolo*** (1986) upheld the police action, saying that the defendant's expectation of privacy in his backyard was not one that society was prepared to honor. The owner had surrounded the backyard, which also contained a swimming pool, with a six-foot outer fence and a ten-foot inner fence. Police could not observe the backyard to confirm an anonymous tip that marijuana was growing in Ciraolo's backyard, so they hired a private airplane and buzzed the suburban backyard to gather visual evidence with the naked eye from about one thousand feet. The Court reasoned that the yard was *exposed to the public* because it was subject to the gaze of passengers in commercial airplane overflights. In effect, the search was held to be within the "open fields" category. Justice Powell, in a stinging dissent, accused the Court of failing to uphold its role as a guardian of rights by allowing a "stealthy encroachment" on rights by the remote intrusion of commercial overflights. He noted that the curtilage was entitled to similar protections as a home and that the use of a private airplane to peer down into Ciraolo's backyard, pool and all, was similar to the use of listening devices by law enforcement officers.

On the same day, the Court, in ***Dow Chemical v. United States*** (1986), upheld an aerial search of two thousand acres of commercial property by an airplane equipped with a sophisticated camera that could magnify its pictures to detect pipes a half-inch thick from twelve hundred feet. Even if the government officers could not, under the Fourth Amendment, physically go onto the commercial complex, the warrantless overflight was held not to be a search and seizure. Thus, *Dow Chemical* upheld the concept of an **industrial curtilage** but, as in *Ciraolo,* held that it did not protect property from aerial surveillance while using ordinary camera resolution.

The Court continued this approach in ***Florida v. Riley*** (1989). A four-justice plurality upheld the surveillance of a partially covered greenhouse in a residential backyard from a helicopter hovering four hundred feet above the ground. Justice White reasoned that this flight did not violate any law or regulation, and any member of the public with a helicopter could have legally hovered above Riley's property and observed the contents of the greenhouse. This reasoning was not satisfactory to Justice O'Connor, who concurred only in the judgment. She thought that the Court relied too heavily on police compliance with Federal Aviation Administration (FAA) regulations and suggested that if lower overflights were sufficiently rare, even if they were in FAA compliance, in such a case, the householder would have a reasonable expectation of privacy. Justice Brennan dissented (joined by Justices Marshall and Stevens), arguing that by not taking into account the difficulty and lengths to which the police must go in making an "open fields" aerial search, the Court was ignoring the "the very essence of *Katz.*"

In these cases, areas that are within the curtilage and nominally protected by the Fourth Amendment were, in fact, opened up to warrantless police surveillance under reasoning that stretched the traditional categories of open fields and narrowed the protection of the curtilage. The fact that conservative justices such as Lewis Powell and Sandra Day O'Connor were bothered by the decisions shows the malleability of constitutional concepts and suggests the extent to which the Court's decisions are influenced by result-oriented jurisprudence.

Enhancement Devices

Is an item in plain view if it is detected, or its contraband nature is disclosed, by the use of an **enhancement device?** Logically, if the police have to resort to technology to determine whether evidence is incriminating, then it is not immediately apparent as such. If so, a judicial warrant based on probable cause is required to use the technology. This logic seemed to be at work in *Coolidge v. New Hampshire* (1971), where evidence obtained by the warrantless vacuuming of a car for fiber evidence was deemed inadmissible. Similarly, in *Katz* and other surreptitious electronic eavesdropping cases, private conversations that are obtained via enhancement devices that amplify the aural sense are protected by the Fourth Amendment. Such information is within the individual's zone of constitutionally protected privacy.

The Supreme Court's cases on the use of "beepers" provide a baseline of analysis. Beepers are radio transmitters, usually battery-operated, that emit periodic signals. They allow agents to trace the movement of an object in which the beeper is surreptitiously placed. As noted previously, the Court ruled that there is no constitutional impediment to the government's using beepers to enhance the senses (e.g., visual observation) if the device does not infringe on an expectation of privacy. In *United States v. Knotts* (1983), agents placed a beeper in a five-gallon can of chloroform and tracked its movement in an automobile driven on public streets. A person has no reasonable expectation of privacy in his movements from one place to another, and so the use of the beeper was held not to constitute a search. In *United States v. Karo* (1984), however, the Court ruled that detecting motion with the use of beepers inside a person's house equated to a search and required a prior warrant. The beeper was the equivalent of an agent secretly entering a house to verify that a drum of ether is inside, a clear Fourth Amendment violation. Justice White expressed the policy that "[i]ndiscriminate monitoring of property that has been withdrawn from public view would present far too serious a threat to privacy interests in the home to escape entirely some sort of Fourth Amendment oversight." For this kind of in-house tracking to be constitutional, a warrant must be obtained.

Some uses of enhancement devices pose no constitutional problems. In *Texas v. Brown* (1983), the Court said that it was "beyond dispute" that an officer "shining his flashlight to illuminate the interior of [a] car trenched upon no right secured . . . by the Fourth Amendment." Citing *United States v. Lee* (1927), the Court also found no constitutional objection to "the use of a marine glass or a field glass. It is not prohibited by the Constitution." Flashlights and field glasses are in such common use that allowing their use may be explained by the fact that they are common devices used everyday in ordinary situations. However, the Court has also found no Fourth Amendment impediment to more high-tech devices. In *Dow Chemical* (1986), the Court upheld a warrantless aerial surveillance of a two-thousand-acre chemical manufacturing facility, heavily secured against entry on the ground but partially exposed to visual observation from the air, by agents of the Environmental Protection Agency, to check emissions from the facility's power plant. The "EPA employed a commercial aerial photographer, using a standard floor-mounted, precision aerial-mapping camera, to take photographs of the facility from altitudes of 12,000, 3,000, and 1,200 feet." In upholding this level of surveillance as not protected by the Fourth Amendment, the Court noted, "The photographs at issue in this case are essentially like those commonly used in mapmaking. Any person with an airplane and an aerial camera could readily duplicate them." With the end of the Cold War, "spy satellites" are now commercially available and have been used by "mining companies, mapmakers, geologists, city planners, ecologists, farmers, hydrologists, road makers, journalists, land managers, disaster-relief officials and others seeking to monitor the planet's changing face. The global market in such imagery is expected to reach as high as $5 billion by 2004."[45] The implications are that there are virtually no limits to aerial surveillance by the police for law enforcement purposes.[46]

The Supreme Court has recently acted to exert some judicial control over the use of **thermal imaging** and has attempted to establish rules to guide the use of advanced information-gathering technology.

Read Case and Comments: Kyllo v. United States

CONSENT SEARCHES

"The consent-based procedure is the bread and butter of the criminal justice system."[47] While precise figures are impossible to determine, "there is no dispute that [consent] searches affect tens of thousands, if not hundreds of thousands of people every year."[48] In one city, an estimated 92 percent of searches were **consent searches.**[49] Most consent searches occur in the course of traffic enforcement and automobile stops, and they play a significant role in racial profiling.[50] (See the "Law in Society" section in Chapter 5.) "Moreover, even if there is probable cause to search, obtaining a warrant may be time consuming or inconvenient. 'A consent search allows an officer to bypass paperwork and the need to locate a magistrate who can issue a warrant.'"[51] To an astonishing degree, criminal suspects plead guilty, confess to crime, allow police into their homes, and meekly submit to arrests rather than go to jury trial, stay mum, refuse to allow police entry without a warrant, and forcibly resist arrest. In these scenarios, suspects give up their constitutional rights to trial, self-incrimination, and privacy, which are guaranteed by the Sixth, Fifth, and Fourth amendments. Defendants are allowed to give up these rights under certain conditions, although other fundamental rights, like prohibitions on cruel and unusual punishment or slavery or the guaranty of due process, cannot be voluntarily set aside.

Police favor consent searches and stops because they eliminate questions about a suspect's constitutional rights. "[B]ecause consent searches require no degree of suspicion on the officer's part, they allow an officer to pursue inarticulable hunches in detecting crime."[52] A person may have an absolute constitutional right to refuse to stop or to open the door to his or her home or automobile trunk when requested to do so by a police officer. But if the person consents, it matters not that the officer had no reasonable suspicion to stop or no warrant to enter. Once voluntarily allowed in, the officer is lawfully in the premises; if contraband happens to be observed in plain view, it may be seized and the possessor arrested for possession. "[A] search authorized by consent is *wholly* valid."[53]

Voluntariness Requirement

The basic requirement of a valid consent search is that consent must be given voluntarily. A consent search obtained by threats or force will be voided by the courts. The test of voluntariness is the totality of circumstances. Courts routinely apply the "totality of the

Kyllo v. United States

533 U.S. 27, 121 S. Ct. 2038, 150 L. Ed. 2d 94 (2001)

[a] After reading the entire case, do you think that the case and its rule apply only to thermal-imaging technology or to all sense-enhancing technology?

JUSTICE SCALIA delivered the opinion of the Court.

This case presents the question whether the use of a thermal-imaging device aimed at a private home from a public street to detect relative amounts of heat within the home constitutes a "search" within the meaning of the Fourth Amendment. **[a]**

I

[U.S. Department of Interior Agent Elliott suspected] that marijuana was being grown in the home belonging to * * * Danny Kyllo, part of a triplex * * * in Florence, Oregon. Indoor marijuana growth typically requires high-intensity lamps. In order to determine whether an amount of heat was emanating from petitioner's home consistent with the use of such lamps, at 3:20 A.M., * * * Agent Elliott and Dan Haas used an Agema Thermovision 210 thermal imager to scan the triplex. Thermal imagers detect infrared radiation, which virtually all objects emit but which is not visible to the naked eye. The imager converts radiation into images based on relative warmth—black is cool, white is hot, shades of gray connote relative differences; in that respect, it operates somewhat like a video camera showing heat images. The scan of Kyllo's home took only a few minutes and was performed from the passenger seat of Agent Elliott's vehicle across the street from the front of the house and also from the street in back of the house. The scan showed that the roof over the garage and a side wall of petitioner's home were relatively hot compared to the rest of the home and substantially warmer than neighboring homes in the triplex. Agent Elliott concluded that petitioner was using halide lights to grow marijuana in his house, which indeed he was. Based on tips from informants, utility bills, and the thermal imaging, a Federal Magistrate Judge issued a warrant authorizing a search of petitioner's home, and the agents found an indoor growing operation involving more than 100 plants. * * *

[Kyllo was indicted and pled conditionally guilty. On appeal, the Court of Appeals upheld the conviction: Kyllo had shown no subjective expectation of privacy because he had made no attempt to conceal the heat escaping from his home, and even if he had, there was no objectively reasonable expectation of privacy because the imager "did not expose any intimate details of Kyllo's life," only "amorphous 'hot spots' on the roof and exterior wall."]

II

[b] Does Agent Elliott's thermal scan fit your idea of a search? Do you think what constitutes a search can be determined by an "objective" test, or should the definition of a search depend on the policy issues and values involved?

[c] Would it make sense to require a search warrant every time investigators "stake out" a house to see who enters and leaves?

* * * With few exceptions, the question whether a warrantless search of a home is reasonable and hence constitutional must be answered no. * * *

On the other hand, the antecedent question of whether or not a Fourth Amendment "search" has occurred is not so simple under our precedent. **[b]** The permissibility of ordinary visual surveillance of a home used to be clear because, well into the 20th century, our Fourth Amendment jurisprudence was tied to common-law trespass. * * * Visual surveillance was unquestionably lawful. . . . As we observed * * * "the Fourth Amendment protection of the home has never been extended to require law enforcement officers to shield their eyes when passing by a home on public thoroughfares." **[c]**

* * * [W]e have held that visual observation is no "search" at all. * * * In assessing when a search is not a search, we have applied somewhat in reverse the principle first enunciated in *Katz* (1967). * * *

The present case involves officers on a public street engaged in more than naked-eye surveillance of a home. We have previously reserved judgment as to how much technological enhancement of ordinary perception from such a vantage point, if any, is too much.

While we upheld enhanced aerial photography of an industrial complex in *Dow Chemical,* we noted that we found "it important that this is *not* an area immediately adjacent to a private home, where privacy expectations are most heightened." * * *

III

It would be foolish to contend that the degree of privacy secured to citizens by the Fourth Amendment has been entirely unaffected by the advance of technology. For example, * * * the technology enabling human flight has exposed to public view (and hence, we have said, to official observation) uncovered portions of the house and its curtilage that once were private. * * * The question we confront today is what limits there are upon this power of technology to shrink the realm of guaranteed privacy.

* * * While it may be difficult to refine *Katz* when the search of areas such as telephone booths, automobiles, or even the curtilage and uncovered portions of residences are at issue, in the case of the search of the interior of homes—the prototypical and hence most commonly litigated area of protected privacy—there is a ready criterion, with roots deep in the common law, of the minimal expectation of privacy that *exists,* and that is acknowledged to be *reasonable.* To withdraw protection of this minimum expectation would be to permit police technology to erode the privacy guaranteed by the Fourth Amendment. We think that obtaining by sense-enhancing technology any information regarding the interior of the home that could not otherwise have been obtained without physical "intrusion into a constitutionally protected area," * * * constitutes a search—at least where (as here) the technology in question is not in general public use. **[d]** This assures preservation of that degree of privacy against government that existed when the Fourth Amendment was adopted. **[e]** On the basis of this criterion, the information obtained by the thermal imager in this case was the product of a search.

The Government maintains, however, that the thermal imaging must be upheld because it detected "only heat radiating from the external surface of the house." * * * The dissent makes this its leading point, contending that there is a fundamental difference between what it calls "off-the-wall" observations and "through-the-wall surveillance." But just as a thermal imager captures only heat emanating from a house, so also a powerful directional microphone picks up only sound emanating from a house—and a satellite capable of scanning from many miles away would pick up only visible light emanating from a house. We rejected such a mechanical interpretation of the Fourth Amendment in *Katz,* where the eavesdropping device picked up only sound waves that reached the exterior of the phone booth. **[f]** Reversing that approach would leave the homeowner at the mercy of advancing technology—including imaging technology that could discern all human activity in the home. While the technology used in the present case was relatively crude, the rule we adopt must take account of more sophisticated systems that are already in use or in development. **[g]** The dissent's reliance on the distinction between "off-the-wall" and "through-the-wall" observation is entirely incompatible with the dissent's belief * * * that thermal-imaging observations of the intimate details of a home are impermissible. The most sophisticated thermal-imaging devices continue to measure heat "off-the-wall" rather than "through-the-wall"; the dissent's disapproval of those more sophisticated thermal-imaging devices * * * is an acknowledgment that there is no substance to this distinction. As for the dissent's extraordinary assertion that anything learned through "an inference" cannot be a search, * * * that would validate even the "through-the-wall" technologies that the dissent purports to disapprove. Surely the dissent does not believe that the through-the-wall radar or ultrasound technology produces an 8-by-10 Kodak glossy that needs no analysis (*i.e.,* the making of inferences). And, of course, the novel proposition that inference insulates a search is blatantly contrary to *United States v. Karo,*

(continued)

[d] Notice that the definition of a search has two parts. What are they? Also notice that the sentence preceding Justice Scalia's definition of a search is a statement of policy—a concern that a different definition could erode in-home protections.

[e] Notice this reference to the expectations of Congress and the states in 1791. As in Justice Thomas's *Wilson v. Arkansas* (1995) opinion, Justice Scalia, the other originalist on the Court, feels that the legitimacy of a ruling depends on whether it squares with the purported intent of the Framers and their common law environment.

[f] This statement seems to answer the question raised in Comment [a]: The Court always deals in questions of constitutional policy and has to consider the consequences of its decisions.

[g] One consequence, as Justice Scalia states, is to attempt to foresee a future when highly intrusive technology would allow easy observation into the privacy of houses and apartments. In a footnote, the opinion said, "The ability to 'see' through walls and other opaque barriers is a clear, and scientifically feasible, goal of law enforcement research and development."

(1984), where the police "inferred" from the activation of a beeper that a certain can of ether was in the home. The police activity was held to be a search, and the search was held unlawful.

The Government also contends that the thermal imaging was constitutional because it did not "detect private activities occurring in private areas." * * * It points out that in *Dow Chemical* we observed that the enhanced aerial photography did not reveal any "intimate details." * * * *Dow Chemical,* however, involved enhanced aerial photography of an industrial complex, which does not share the Fourth Amendment sanctity of the home. The Fourth Amendment's protection of the home has never been tied to measurement of the quality or quantity of information obtained. In *Silverman,* for example, we made clear that any physical invasion of the structure of the home, "by even a fraction of an inch," was too much, * * * and there is certainly no exception to the warrant requirement for the officer who barely cracks open the front door and sees nothing but the nonintimate rug on the vestibule floor. **[h]** In the home, our cases show, *all* details are intimate details, because the entire area is held safe from prying government eyes. Thus, in *Karo,* the only thing detected was a can of ether in the home; and in *Arizona v. Hicks,* (1987), the only thing detected by a physical search that went beyond what officers lawfully present could observe in "plain view" was the registration number of a phonograph turntable. These were intimate details because they were details of the home, just as was the detail of how warm—or even how relatively warm—Kyllo was heating his residence.

[It would be extremely difficult, if not impossible, to determine what is an "intimate detail" and what is a "nonintimate detail" in a house. Even if a rule could make out this distinction, police would not know in advance if the search with a thermal imager or other high-tech device would disclose an intimate or nonintimate detail.]

Where, as here, the Government uses a device that is not in general public use, to explore details of the home that would previously have been unknowable without physical intrusion, the surveillance is a "search" and is presumptively unreasonable without a warrant.

Since we hold the Thermovision imaging to have been an unlawful search, it will remain for the District Court to determine whether, without the evidence it provided, the search warrant issued in this case was supported by probable cause—and if not, whether there is any other basis for supporting admission of the evidence that the search pursuant to the warrant produced.

* * *

The judgment of the Court of Appeals is reversed; the case is remanded for further proceedings consistent with this opinion.

It is so ordered.

JUSTICE STEVENS, with whom THE CHIEF JUSTICE, JUSTICE O'CONNOR, and JUSTICE KENNEDY join, dissenting.

* * *

I

* * * [S]earches and seizures of property in plain view are presumptively reasonable. * * * Whether that property is residential or commercial, the basic principle is the same: "'What a person knowingly exposes to the public, even in his own home or office, is not a subject of Fourth Amendment protection.'" That is the principle implicated here.

While the Court "takes the long view" and decides this case based largely on the potential of yet-to-be-developed technology that might allow "through-the-wall surveillance," * * * this case involves nothing more than off-the-wall surveillance by law enforcement officers to gather information exposed to the general public from the outside of petitioner's home. **[i]** All that the infrared camera did in this case was passively measure

[h] Is this distinction between business premises and a home sound? What if a person operates a business out of a home office? For purposes of a search, is this a home or a business? Similarly, is a fully mobile home, such as a recreational vehicle, a home, or a vehicle?

[i] Was the heat emanating from Kyllo's house in *plain* view if it took a heat sensor to detect it?

heat emitted from the exterior surfaces of petitioner's home; all that those measurements showed were relative differences in emission levels, vaguely indicating that some areas of the roof and outside walls were warmer than others. As still images from the infrared scans show, * * * no details regarding the interior of petitioner's home were revealed. Unlike an x-ray scan, or other possible "through-the-wall" techniques, the detection of infrared radiation emanating from the home did not accomplish "an unauthorized physical penetration into the premises," * * * nor did it "obtain information that it could not have obtained by observation from outside the curtilage of the house." ***

Indeed, the ordinary use of the senses might enable a neighbor or passerby to notice the heat emanating from a building, particularly if it is vented, as was the case here. Additionally, any member of the public might notice that one part of a house is warmer than another part or a nearby building if, for example, rainwater evaporates or snow melts at different rates across its surfaces. * * * [j]

[j] Is this the same as thermal imaging by a government agent?

Thus, the notion that heat emissions from the outside of a dwelling is a private matter implicating the protections of the Fourth Amendment (the text of which guarantees the right of people "to be secure *in* their . . . houses" against unreasonable searches and seizures [emphasis added]) is not only unprecedented but also quite difficult to take seriously. Heat waves, like aromas that are generated in a kitchen, or in a laboratory or opium den, enter the public domain if and when they leave a building. A subjective expectation that they would remain private is not only implausible but also surely not "one that society is prepared to recognize as 'reasonable.'" * * *

* * * In my judgment, monitoring such emissions with "sense-enhancing technology," * * * and drawing useful conclusions from such monitoring, is an entirely reasonable public service.

On the other hand, the countervailing privacy interest is at best trivial. After all, homes generally are insulated to keep heat in, rather than to prevent the detection of heat going out, and it does not seem to me that society will suffer from a rule requiring the rare homeowner who both intends to engage in uncommon activities that produce extraordinary amounts of heat, and wishes to conceal that production from outsiders, to make sure that the surrounding area is well insulated. * * * The interest in concealing the heat escaping from one's house pales in significance to "the chief evil against which the wording of the Fourth Amendment is directed," the "physical entry of the home," * * * and it is hard to believe that it is an interest the Framers sought to protect in our Constitution.

Since what was involved in this case was nothing more than drawing inferences from off-the-wall surveillance, rather than any "through-the-wall" surveillance, the officers' conduct did not amount to a search and was perfectly reasonable.

II

[The application of the Court's holding to technology that is "not in general public use" means that as intrusive technology becomes commonplace, it will allow searches of private areas to be held constitutional. The dissent noted that over ten thousand thermal-sensing units had been manufactured and could be purchased by anyone. Another criticism is that the holding was limited to privacy only in the home; if new technology has the effect of getting information that otherwise could be obtained only by having an officer enter a place, under the expectation of privacy doctrine, it should apply to commercial places as well as to homes.]

* * *

I respectfully dissent.

circumstances" rule to determine whether an arrested person voluntarily consented to a search of a car or house and the like. A consent obtained within a few minutes of a routine arrest, for example, will be upheld, while an arrest made by four officers with guns drawn will negate the voluntariness of a consent to search.[54] This seems incongruous because an arrested person is by definition in custody of the police and forcibly detained. The incongruity is reflected in the holding in *Schneckloth v. Bustamonte* (1973), the Supreme Court's primary consent search decision, which defines voluntary consent as when the "subject of a search is *not in custody*" (emphasis added). Courts nevertheless continue to uphold most consents to search given by suspects under arrest.[55]

The burden of proof is on the government to prove consent: "When a prosecutor seeks to rely upon consent to justify the lawfulness of a search, he has the burden of proving that the consent was, in fact, freely and voluntarily given. This burden cannot be discharged by showing no more than acquiescence to a claim of lawful authority" (*Bumper v. North Carolina,* 1968). The following cases help to define voluntariness by example.

In *Amos v. United States* (1921), two federal "revenuers" looking for untaxed whiskey came to Amos's house without a warrant. He was not there, and his wife opened the door. They told her "that they were revenue officers and had come to search the premises 'for violations of the revenue law'; that thereupon the woman opened the store and the witnesses entered, and in a barrel of peas found a bottle containing not quite a half-pint of illicitly distilled whisky, which they called 'blockade whisky.'" A unanimous Court summarily dismissed the contention that the officers were let in voluntarily because they demanded entry under government authority. A similar case is *Bumper v. North Carolina* (1968). Bumper, an at-large murder suspect, "lived with his grandmother, Mrs. Hattie Leath, a 66-year-old Negro widow, in a house located in a rural area at the end of an isolated mile-long dirt road." Four officers came to the house and told Mrs. Leath that they had a search warrant. In response, she allowed them to search the house, and they discovered a weapon. It was later determined that there never was a search warrant. The Supreme Court held that Mrs. Leath, who did not appear from her testimony to have been at all intimidated, nevertheless did not give valid consent to the warrantless search:

> A search conducted in reliance upon a warrant cannot later be justified on the basis of consent if it turns out that the warrant was invalid. The result can be no different when it turns out that the State does not even attempt to rely upon the validity of the warrant, or fails to show that there was, in fact, any warrant at all.
>
> When a law enforcement officer claims authority to search a home under a warrant, he announces in effect that the occupant has no right to resist the search. The situation is instinct with coercion—albeit colorably lawful coercion. Where there is coercion there cannot be consent.
>
> We hold that Mrs. Leath did not consent to the search, and that it was constitutional error to admit the rifle in evidence against the petitioner. (*Bumper v. North Carolina,* 1968)

Officers who falsely claim to have a warrant or who demand entry as if the law required it are acting under color of law, and *Amos* and *Bumper* deem such action to be legal coercion. But it is not coercion for a police officer to ask a person, in a nonthreatening manner, if he or she may enter a home, search a car, or view a backpack and the like. If a person agrees, she has voluntarily relinquished her Fourth Amendment right to privacy. It does not matter whether the officer believes that the person is a suspect.

Despite these earlier cases, "it was not until 1973, in *Schneckloth v. Bustamonte* that the Supreme Court clearly articulated the requirements for a voluntary consent search consistent with the Fourth Amendment."[56] In *Schneckloth,* the Supreme Court found that the following scenario resulted in a voluntary consent to search the trunk of an automobile:

> While on routine patrol in Sunnyvale, California, at approximately 2:40 in the morning, Police Officer James Rand stopped an automobile when he observed that one headlight and its license plate light were burned out. Six men were in the vehicle. Joe Alcala and the respondent, Robert Bustamonte, were in the front seat with Joe Gonzales, the driver. Three older men

were seated in the rear. When, in response to the policeman's question, Gonzales could not produce a driver's license, Officer Rand asked if any of the other five had any evidence of identification. Only Alcala produced a license, and he explained that the car was his brother's. After the six occupants had stepped out of the car at the officer's request and after two additional policemen had arrived, Officer Rand asked Alcala if he could search the car. Alcala replied, "Sure, go ahead." Prior to the search no one was threatened with arrest and, according to Officer Rand's uncontradicted testimony, it "was all very congenial at this time." Gonzales testified that Alcala actually helped in the search of the car, by opening the trunk and glove compartment. In Gonzales' words: "The police officer asked Joe [Alcala], he goes, 'Does the trunk open?' And Joe said, 'Yes.' He went to the car and got the keys and opened up the trunk." Wadded up under the left rear seat, the police officers found three checks that had previously been stolen from a car wash. (*Schneckloth v. Bustamonte,* 1973)

The six-to-three majority decided that Alcala's consent was voluntary and the checks were admissible. Justice Stewart stated in his opinion for the majority that the "precise question in this case, then, is what must the prosecution prove to demonstrate that a consent was 'voluntarily' given." The issue included the subsidiary question of whether the police have to inform those from whom they request consent to search that they have a constitutional right to refuse, where police do not have probable cause or reasonable suspicion to force a search. This specific issue is discussed in the next section. In coming to its conclusion, the Court noted that the atmosphere surrounding the search was said to be "congenial," there had been no discussion of any crime, and Gonzales said that Alcala even tried to aid in the search.

As for the general issue of voluntariness, Justice Stewart turned to confessions law and the more than thirty Supreme Court cases that explored the voluntariness of confessions under the "facts and circumstances" test of the Fourteenth Amendment Due Process Clause. (See Chapter 7.) He concluded that there is no formula to determine whether a consent is voluntary. On the one hand, even a person subjected to torture retains some level of choice in deciding whether to talk, while on the other it can be said that consent is never voluntary because a person would never give up her rights "in the absence of official action of some kind." As a result, the Court was guided, as to sorting out voluntary from involuntary confessions, by "the complex of values implicated in police questioning of a suspect." In other words, the Supreme Court has balanced the need of law enforcement to question suspects against a "set of values reflecting society's deeply felt belief that the criminal law cannot be used as an instrument of unfairness." The Supreme Court accommodated these competing interests in the confessions cases by looking to a number of circumstances: the suspect's age, education, and intelligence; the length of detention; the repeated and prolonged nature of the questioning; and the use of physical punishment. The decision in each case depended on an evaluation of a number of factors. In sum, the issue of "whether a consent to a search was in fact 'voluntary' or was the product of duress or coercion, express or implied, is a question of fact to be determined from the totality of all the circumstances."

Professor Marcy Strauss suggests that the voluntariness test "is so vague that it provides little guidance to courts, litigants or police officers."[57] Moreover, although *Schenckloth* emphasized subjective factors about the suspect's understanding of events, "lower courts may ignore or short-change subjective factors of the suspect because judges may believe that *Schneckloth* has been overturned sub silentio, or, at a minimum, may be confused about the appropriate standard to apply. Recent Supreme Court decisions . . . seem to be moving the law away from subjective considerations and towards an objective standard."[58] These decisions include the third-party consent cases and **United States v. Mendenhall** (1980), discussed below. Thus if the voluntariness of consent is determined exclusively by objective factors of police behavior (e.g., whether the officer brandished a gun), determining whether the will of the suspect was in fact overborne will disappear as a test.

Chapter 4 presents many cases in which the validity of a personal search turns on whether the person was arrested, temporarily stopped on the basis of reasonable suspicion, or gave consent. *United States v. Mendenhall* (1980) demonstrates the difficulty of determining consent and the use of an objective standard for a seizure. The defendant, Sylvia Mendenhall, deplaned at the Detroit Metropolitan Airport. She was observed by two DEA agents, who thought her conduct appeared to be "characteristic of persons unlawfully carrying narcotics." They approached Mendenhall, identified themselves as federal agents, and asked to see her identification and airline ticket. The name on her driver's license, Sylvia Mendenhall, and that on the ticket, Annette Ford, did not match. When asked why, she replied that she "just felt like using that name." One agent then specifically identified himself as a narcotics agent, and Mendenhall "became quite shaken, extremely nervous. She had a hard time speaking." She was then asked if she would accompany the agents to offices just fifty feet away. Once there, she was asked if she would allow a search of her person and handbag. She was told she had the right to decline if she desired. She responded, "Go ahead." A female police officer conducting the search asked Mendenhall if she consented to the search; she replied that she did. Heroin was found in her undergarments, and she was arrested and convicted. The District Court concluded that Mendenhall had consented to the search.

Two justices, Stewart and Rehnquist, believed that Mendenhall had consented to the initial stop. Justice Stewart's plurality opinion reasoned that not every police–citizen encounter is a seizure of the person requiring reasonable suspicion or probable cause to be lawful. The test that distinguishes between a consent stop and a seizure is whether, in view of all the facts and circumstances, a reasonable person would believe that he or she is not free to leave; "a person is 'seized' only when, by means of physical force or show of authority, his freedom of movement is restrained." The plurality opinion therefore concluded that Mendenhall could have walked away from the agents at any point. No grabbing or touching occurred. The agents were not in uniform, and no weapons were displayed. The initial encounter occurred in public. They asked, but did not demand, to see her identification. The consequences of this objective test will be discussed in the next section.

Three justices (Burger, Powell, and Blackmun) felt that the initial stop was a seizure but that it was constitutional because the officers had reasonable suspicion to believe that Mendenhall was a drug courier. These five justices agreed that she had consented to going to the office and to the search of her person—that is, that there was no arrest until the heroin was found. Four dissenting justices (White, Brennan, Marshall, and Stevens) concluded, to the contrary, that Mendenhall was seized without reasonable suspicion and subject to an unconstitutional arrest and that the search was unconstitutional. Although the legality of airport drug stops has been clarified by the Court's acceptance of drug courier profiles as constituting reasonable suspicion, *Mendenhall* demonstrates the difficulty of sorting out the facts that constitute consent.

Knowledge of One's Rights

A major issue in *Schenckloth v. Bustamonte* (1973) was whether consent is possible when a defendant has no knowledge that he or she has a right to refuse a police request to search. The court of appeals had held that "a consent was a waiver of a person's Fourth and Fourteenth Amendment rights, and that the State was under an obligation to demonstrate, not only that the consent had been uncoerced, but that it had been given with an understanding that it could be freely and effectively withheld. Consent could not be found, the court held, solely from the absence of coercion and a verbal expression of assent. Since the District Court had not determined that Alcala had *known* that his consent could have been withheld and that he could have refused to have his vehicle searched, the Court of Appeals vacated the order denying the writ and remanded the case for further proceedings." In reversing the decision, the Supreme Court held that the police are under no obligation to inform those from whom they seek consent to search that they have a constitutional right to refuse.

One reason for this decision was the fear that police, without probable cause or reasonable suspicion, would have no other way of getting evidence. "In situations where the police have some evidence of illicit activity, but lack probable cause to arrest or search, a search authorized by a valid consent may be the only means of obtaining important and reliable evidence" (*Schneckloth,* 1973). The Court did not define "some evidence," so the police could be requesting to search based only on a hunch or perhaps on categorical information (e.g., the person is a white male). Another reason is that a consent search could clear an innocent person of suspicion and stop the police from applying for a warrant where they have probable cause (but are in error) that contraband is in a house or office. A further reason is that it may be difficult to prove the person's subjective understanding of his rights, and after a consent search any defendant "could effectively frustrate the introduction into evidence of the fruits of that search by simply failing to testify that he in fact knew he could refuse to consent" (*Schneckloth,* 1973).

Borrowing from the Fifth and Sixth amendment *Miranda* and right-to-counsel cases, where a defendant must be informed of his or her rights, Bustamonte had argued that there is a Fourth Amendment obligation on the police to inform a person that he has a right to refuse consent. The Court rejected this contention. A Fourth Amendment consent is not the same as a waiver of the rights to silence or an attorney under the Fifth or Sixth amendments. Waivers are valid only if made knowingly, and to ensure knowledge, suspects or defendants must be informed of these rights before giving them up. Waivers are "applied only to those rights which the Constitution guarantees to a criminal defendant in order to preserve a fair trial. . . . The requirement of a 'knowing' and 'intelligent' waiver was articulated in a case involving the validity of a defendant's decision to forgo a right constitutionally guaranteed to protect a fair trial and the reliability of the truth-determining process" (*Schneckloth,* 1973). In other words, violations of the privilege against self-incrimination or right to counsel might result in the conviction of an innocent person. "The protections of the Fourth Amendment are of a wholly different order, and have nothing whatever to do with promoting the fair ascertainment of truth at a criminal trial" (*Schneckloth,* 1973). Consents to search that result in the seizure of evidence of crime provide good evidence that would not otherwise be obtained. This analysis clearly indicates that the Court's majority believed that Fourth Amendment rights are not as important as other elements in the Bill of Rights. In addition, the Court found that it "would be unrealistic to expect that in the informal, unstructured context of a consent search, a policeman, upon pain of tainting the evidence obtained, could make the detailed type of examination" that occurs in courthouses when informing a defendant of his or her right to counsel. Similar considerations precluded extending the reasoning of *Miranda v. Arizona* (1966) to consent situations. The impracticality of obtaining written consents to search is a reasonable argument, although the extension of modern technology makes it less so, and many police departments utilize written consent-to-search forms. The Court did say that the suspect's knowledge and whether he or she was informed of the right to refuse consent are factors in assessing voluntariness.

In a brief dissent, Justice Brennan wrote: "It wholly escapes me how our citizens can meaningfully be said to have waived something as precious as a constitutional guarantee without ever being aware of its existence. In my view, the Court's conclusion is supported neither by 'linguistics,' nor by 'epistemology,' nor, indeed, by 'common sense'" (*Schneckloth v. Bustamonte,* 1973, Brennan, J., dissenting). A more elaborate dissent by Justice Marshall offered a different basis for accepting the validity of consent searches. He felt that the Court was mistaken to rely on the confessions cases because consent cases do not deal with the "coercion" present in confessions cases. Rather than extolling consent, as does the majority, Justice Marshall noted that police have weaker interests when they lacked probable cause, suggesting that the Court ought not encourage police to seek consents. He then put the basis of consent on a different footing: "Thus, consent searches are permitted, not because such an exception to the requirements of probable cause and warrant is essential to proper law enforcement, but because we permit our citizens to choose whether or not they wish to exercise their constitutional rights" (*Schneckloth v. Bustamonte,* 1973, Marshall, J., dissenting). In this view, consent is a freedom to give up a constitutional right and as such should be narrowly construed. This disagrees sharply with Justice Stewart's view that consent is a law enforcement tool that courts should broadly construe and support.

Indeed, Justice Marshall was sharply critical of the majority: "[W]hen the Court speaks of practicality, what it really is talking of is the continued ability of the police to capitalize on the ignorance of citizens so as to accomplish by subterfuge what they could not achieve by relying only on the knowing relinquishment of constitutional rights" (*Schneckloth v. Bustamonte,* 1973). But more than ignorance may be at work in consent searches. Quoting from the Ninth Circuit opinion, Justice Marshall concluded that "under many circumstances a reasonable person might read an officer's 'May I' as the courteous expression of a demand backed by force of law." This alludes to what Strauss calls the "fiction of consent"—the observation supported by substantial scholarship and common sense "that most people would not feel free to deny a request by a police officer," a position that some judges agree with.[59] Mendenhall, after all, was told that she had a right to not be searched, but she agreed anyway (*United States v. Mendenhall,* 1980).

To the extent that this is true, it suggests that the *Schneckloth* consent rules significantly weaken Fourth Amendment protections. Potential solutions include (1) partially overruling *Schneckloth* to require police to inform people that they have a constitutional right to refuse a search when asking for consent, a position that only three states have followed;[60] (2) requiring that police have reasonable suspicion before requesting consent, a rule that has been imposed on New Jersey state troopers in a consent decree following a major racial profiling case;[61] (3) creating a rule allowing racial minorities to raise cultural arguments to the effect that in view of the history of racially biased police action, the subjective attitude of blacks and Hispanics is to see most police requests for consent as coercive—a rule that Strauss believes would be difficult for courts to apply and would raise claims that the system is unfair in allowing this "strange form of affirmative action";[62] or (4) overruling *Schneckloth* and abolishing the consent exception to searches based on evidence, a position supported by Strauss.[63]

The *Schneckloth* approach was confirmed in ***Ohio v. Robinette*** (1996). A police officer stopped a motorist, Robinette, for speeding and issued a warning but did not tell him that he was "free to go," as was then required under a controversial Ohio Supreme Court decision.[64] In answer to the officer's question, Robinette said he was not carrying any contraband. The officer then asked if he could search the car, Robinette consented, and the officer uncovered contraband. The Supreme Court found that the search was constitutional because Robinette consented voluntarily and that the officer did not have to inform him that he was "free to go." After the U.S. Supreme Court's decision, the Ohio Supreme Court rescinded its 1995 decision that required police to warn motorists that in effect they did not have to allow a police search without individualized suspicion, finding that the added warning was not required under the state constitution.[65] An empirical study of written and verbal warnings issued by the Ohio Highway Patrol (OHP) during the year and a half that the Ohio Supreme Court required "*Robinette* warnings" shows that the number and rate of requests for consent by OHP officers increased during the period that they had to issue *Robinette* warnings, a finding that appears to allay the fears underlying *Schneckloth* that consent warnings would undermine law enforcement effectiveness.[66]

Third-Party Consent

When two or more people share a room or common area, one person may voluntarily consent to a police search of the common area. Evidence found that incriminates the other party may be admitted in evidence. The prosecution need only show by a preponderance of the evidence that the person who gave consent had authority to do so, based on her or his relationship to the property.

In the leading case on third-party consent searches, **United States v. Matlock** (1974), police searched the bedroom of a house, with the consent of Gayle Graff, who was living with Matlock. Evidence of a bank robbery was found and admitted to prove guilt. The fact that the couple was not married was irrelevant for Fourth Amendment purposes to negate consent. The authority of a third party to consent to the search depends not on property law concepts or on rules of evidence that apply in a trial, "but rests rather on mutual use of the property by persons generally having joint access or control for most purposes, so that it is reasonable to recognize that any of the coinhabitants has the right to permit the inspection in his own right and that the others have assumed the risk that one of their number might permit the common area to be searched" (*United States v. Matlock,* 1974). Similarly, a roommate who shares a duffel bag may consent to its search (*Frazier v. Cupp,* 1969).

In contrast to *Matlock,* the Court held in **Stoner v. California** (1964) that a hotel clerk did not have authority to consent to a police search of a guest's room. The Court said, "It is important to bear in mind that it was the petitioner's constitutional right which was at stake here, and not the night clerk's or the hotel's." Although *Stoner* was decided before the "expectation of privacy" principle of *Katz* (1967) was enunciated, as a rule of thumb it seems that only those with an expectation of privacy over an area may consent to a search. *Stoner* was preceded by *Chapman v. California* (1967), which held that a landlord may not give consent to a police search into a tenant's apartment or house, even though the landlord has a general right of entry for normal inspection purposes.

Matlock and *Stoner* were clarified, extended, and harmonized in **Illinois v. Rodriguez** (1990). Police were given consent to enter a house by a person who, in reality, did not possess common authority over the premises; however, the police reasonably believed that she had common authority and possession of the place. The Court held that the entry was reasonable under the Fourth Amendment. Gail Fisher complained to Chicago police that Edward Rodriguez had beaten her. The police accompanied Fisher from her mother's apartment to Rodriguez's apartment, where she let them in with a key that she had. On the drive to Rodriguez's apartment, she referred to his apartment as "our" place. The officers did not know that she had moved out a month earlier, had removed her clothing, did not invite friends there, was never in the house when Rodriguez was not there, did not contribute to the rent, and did not have her name on the lease.

Instead of characterizing the issue as a valid waiver of Fourth Amendment rights, the proper question is "whether the right to be free of *unreasonable* searches has been *violated.*" The Court noted that in making probable cause decisions, police and magistrates do not violate Fourth Amendment rights if they make reasonable mistakes. By analogy, a reasonable mistake in a consent case does not violate the individual's Fourth Amendment rights. Thus, *Illinois v. Rodriguez* answers a question left open by *Matlock* and extends the authority of police to enter a place under third-party consent. The Court differentiated *Stoner,* which is still good law, by indicating that the case does not mean that apparent authority can never be the basis for a third-party search, only that the police must have a reasonable basis to believe that a third party has authority over a place. Ordinarily, motel personnel do not have general authority to enter a guest's room outside of normal cleaning and maintenance functions. On the other hand, when a woman with a key to an apartment claims that her boyfriend beat her, there is no reason why the police should not believe that she lives in the apartment. Justice Marshall dissented in *Rodriguez* (joined by Justices Brennan and Stevens), urging the theory that because entry into a home without a warrant is presumptively unreasonable, police cannot dispense with the rights of a person where that person has not limited his expectation of privacy by sharing his home with another. Under this analysis, the reasonableness of the police officers' action is irrelevant. He stressed that the police should have obtained a warrant in this situation and that the warrant requirement should not be dropped to prevent inconvenience to police officers.

In **Georgia v. Randolph** (2006), Scott and Janet Randolph had separated; she moved out and took their son. She returned to the marital residence a few months later, but after a domestic dispute with Scott called police saying that he took their son. When the police arrived, Janet told them that Scott used cocaine. Scott returned shortly, having taken his son to a neighbor's. He denied cocaine use and accused Janet of abusing drugs and alcohol. After the police went with Janet to retrieve the son, she said that Scott had drugs in the house. At the door to the house, the officer asked for consent to enter. Scott flatly refused, but Janet gave consent. Janet led the officer to Scott's bedroom, where he saw a straw with a powdery residue, which was seized. Under a warrant, police later found more evidence of drug use. Scott was convicted of cocaine possession. The Georgia appellate courts reversed the conviction on the grounds that "the consent to conduct a warrantless search of a residence given by one occupant is not valid in the face of the refusal of another occupant who is physically present at the scene to permit a warrantless search" (*Georgia v. Randolph,* 2006, quoting the Georgia Supreme Court).

The U.S. Supreme Court affirmed the decision (5–3). The reasoning of Justice Souter's majority opinion was based on the idea that widely shared social expectations, a source outside the Fourth Amendment, should be used to interpret the amendment's Reasonableness Clause and the expectation of privacy. Widely shared social expectations made it reasonable for police to enter the Matlock residence when a person who obviously belonged there came to the door and voluntarily let the police in to look around. Likewise, a tenant or motel occupant does not expect that a landlord or motel clerk would have implied permission to allow others to enter the occupant's apartment or room. Therefore, "a caller standing at the door of shared premises would have no confidence that one occupant's invitation was a sufficiently good reason to enter when a fellow tenant stood there saying, 'stay out.' Without some *very good reason,* no sensible person would go inside under those conditions" (*Georgia v. Randolph,* 2006, emphasis added). In coming to this conclusion, the majority placed the "centuries-old principle of respect for the privacy of the home" above law enforcement convenience needs. "Disputed permission is . . . no match for this central value of the Fourth Amendment" (*Georgia v. Randolph,* 2006). The police could have obtained a warrant and could have prevented the residents from destroying any property while waiting for the warrant (*Illinois v. McArthur,* 2001). The majority noted that its decision was in accord with the preference for search warrants (*United States v. Ventresca,* 1965). The majority opinion took special pains to make it clear that its decision did not prevent police from entering a premises for the very good reason that an occupant made a complaint about domestic violence, which was not a factor in this case. The majority also made it clear that the police have no responsibility to search for another occupant who might object to the consent to enter (as long as they do not deliberately remove a potentially objecting occupant from the entrance). The Court acknowledged the contingent nature of the holding, depending as it does on the fortuitous circumstance of a consenting and an objecting occupant standing at the entrance to the premises.

Chief Justice John Roberts dissented. He pointed out that a number of differing social situations could give rise to different social expectations about entering where two occupants differ, as where the entering person is a close friend or relative, or where the premises of the "feuding roommates" is a single room or a spacious house; or where there are more than two occupants and a majority invite a guest in. The dissent's basic reasoning is that the Fourth Amendment protects privacy, and when the privacy of an area is shared, the occupant assumes the risk that the privacy will be breached by the other occupant. Finally, the dissent raised an alarm that the decision would be an impediment to entry in domestic violence cases.

Scope of Consent

Dade County police officer, Frank Trujillo, overheard . . . Enio Jimeno, arranging what appeared to be a drug transaction over a public telephone. Believing that Jimeno might be involved in illegal drug trafficking, Officer Trujillo followed his car. The officer . . . pulled Jimeno over to the side of the road in order to issue him a traffic citation [for making an illegal turn]. Officer Trujillo told Jimeno that he had been stopped for committing a traffic infraction. The officer went on to say that he had reason to believe that Jimeno was carrying narcotics in his car, and asked permission to search the car. He explained that Jimeno did not have to consent to a search of the car. Jimeno stated that he had nothing to hide and gave Trujillo permission to search the automobile. After Jimeno's spouse, respondent Luz Jimeno, stepped out of the car, Officer Trujillo went to the passenger side, opened the door, and saw a folded, brown paper bag on the floorboard. The officer picked up the bag, opened it, and found a kilogram of cocaine inside.

> The Jimenos were charged with possession with intent to distribute cocaine in violation of Florida law. (***Florida v. Jimeno,*** 1991, pp. 249–50)

The Florida Supreme Court ruled that the officer had to receive specific consent to open the container. The U.S. Supreme Court reversed, holding that under the Fourth Amendment the scope of a consent search depends on whether the search was reasonable. In this case, the search was reasonable because, according to Chief Justice Rehnquist, the "scope of a search is generally defined by its expressed object." Jimeno "did not place any explicit limitation on the scope of the search," and a "reasonable person may be expected to know that narcotics are generally carried in some form of a container." He stressed that Jimeno could have limited the scope of the search, and he concluded with the policy expressed in *Schneckloth* that "[t]he community has a real interest in encouraging consent, for the resulting search may yield necessary evidence for the solution and prosecution of crime."

Justice Marshall dissented, joined by Justice Stevens. He noted that under the Court's precedent, there is a lesser expectation of privacy in cars, but a heightened expectation of privacy in the content of closed containers. These "distinct privacy expectations . . . do not merge when the individual uses his car to transport the container." Also, the way in which "reasonableness" is used by the majority could lead to absurd or unacceptable results. After all, if "a reasonable person may be expected to know that drug couriers frequently store their contraband on their persons or in their body cavities," then consent to search a car could lead to a body-cavity search. He argued that Jimeno, in fact, did not consent to a search of the paper bag and the Court should interpret rights expansively and should interpret limitation of rights (such as consent) narrowly.

LAW IN SOCIETY

POLICE PERJURY AND THE FOURTH AMENDMENT

A decade ago, police perjury was "the dirty little secret of our criminal justice system."[67] Now it is common knowledge, thanks in large part to the exposed perjury of Detective Mark Fuhrman in the O. J. Simpson murder trial.[68] A law professor reports that his students frequently interrupt classroom hypotheticals involving illegal police conduct with questions like "What if the police just lie about what happened?"[69] And this, indeed, is the critical point. People in all walks of life, from presidents on down, have been known to lie; and it is necessary for society to prosecute business fraud, for professional organizations to investigate and sanction falsehoods by their members, and so forth. "What distinguishes police officers is their unique power—to use force, to summarily deprive a citizen of freedom, to even use deadly force, if necessary—and their commensurately unique responsibilities—to be the living embodiment of the 'law' in our communities, as applied

fairly to every member."[70] If police officers routinely commit perjury about the legality of arrests or searches and routinely get away with it, then the true result is not a personal benefit (a good arrest record) or even a misguided belief that this enhances public safety—it effectively destroys the basic constitutional rights of every person who is subject to such illegal action and threatens the rights of the rest of us (including cops) who have not yet been framed by police lies. This kind of perjury occurs most frequently in drug enforcement.

It is important to begin with Professor Morgan Cloud's observation that it's not true that "all police officers lie under oath, or that most officers lie, or that even some officers lie all the time."[71] An insightful article by Professor Andrew McClurg notes a profound paradox: "Most police officers are honorable, moral persons," yet "many of these same police officers lie in the course of their official duties." Any resolution of the problem of police perjury requires understanding the pressures that proliferate police perjury.

The kind of police perjury most likely to undermine Fourth Amendment rights occurs when (1) a police officer thinks that a defendant was in possession of contraband or incriminating evidence, (2) the officer obtained the evidence by an unconstitutional act, and (3) in a suppression hearing the officer "embellishes" the truth by testifying so as to make it appear as if the stop, arrest, or search was performed in a constitutional manner. "Routine" perjury is a greater threat to rights than more outrageous action, such as planting evidence on innocent individuals or "booming" (illegally breaking into homes without a warrant or pretense of legality),[72] because most cops, being honorable, draw the line at such over-the-top behavior. But they will "shade" the truth if they view constitutional rights as "mere technicalities"—as impediments to effective law enforcement. Professor Richard Uviller, who spent a year observing a New York Police Department street crimes unit, notes that like most people, "cops were raised with a strong sense of justice, and they naturally apply it when the occasion arises."[73]

Scholars who have studied this issue believe that routine perjury in regard to the seizure of incriminating evidence began as a result of the federalization of the exclusionary rule in *Mapp v. Ohio* (1961). A frequently cited 1971 article by Irving Younger, a former prosecutor and judge, noted that before *Mapp,* police easily testified to making illegal stops and finding contraband—"This had the ring of truth." After *Mapp,* judges suppressed evidence obtained in this way. Police officers then discovered "that if the defendant drops the narcotics on the ground, after which the policeman arrests him, then the search is reasonable and the evidence is admissible." Hence "dropsy" testimony increased enormously.[74] Younger's observations were substantiated by a before–after empirical study of police testimony in misdemeanor narcotics arrests showing that the percent of arrests where narcotics were "hidden on the body" dropped from about 25 percent of all arrests to about 5 percent, while "dropsy" cases, which accounted for about 10 to 15 percent of arrests before *Mapp,* increased to 41 percent for narcotics officers.[75]

"Routine" perjury is close to impossible for defense lawyers, prosecutors, or judges to detect because it is so simple:

> Lying about search and seizure matters "was part of everyday police work" according to a former New York City police officer interviewed for an article announcing that cops in New York must now go to school to learn to tell the truth. The Mollen Commission cataloged a "litany" of manufactured search and seizure tales uncovered by its investigation:
>
> > For example, when officers unlawfully stop and search a vehicle because they believe it contains drugs or guns, officers will falsely claim in police reports and under oath that the car ran a red light (or committed some other traffic violation) and that they subsequently saw contraband in the car in plain view. To conceal an unlawful search of an individual who officers believe is carrying drugs or a gun, they will falsely assert that they saw a bulge in the person's pocket or saw drugs and money changing hands. To justify unlawfully entering an apartment where officers believe narcotics or cash can be found, they pretend to have information from an unidentified civilian informant or claim they saw the drugs in plain view after responding to the premises on a radio run. To arrest people they suspect are guilty of dealing drugs, they falsely assert that the defendants had drugs in their possession when, in fact, the drugs were found elsewhere where the officers had no lawful right to be.[76]

A Harvard Law School conference held shortly after the verdict in the O. J. Simpson case concluded: "There are no national studies or statistics on police perjury, and there is considerable disagreement on how widespread the problem is."[77] Nevertheless, a great deal of anecdotal evidence from police commissions and others indicates that police perjury is widespread.[78] A study of 26 Chicago narcotics detectives asked them: "In your experience, do police officers ever shade the facts a little (or a lot) to establish probable cause when there may not have been probable cause in fact?" Sixteen officers responded "yes," and five responded "no."[79] Of course, the actual number is unknown because "[b]y their very nature, successful lies will remain undetected, and we would expect a perjurer to attempt to conceal his crime."[80] Former Kansas City and San Jose police chief and Hoover Institution research fellow Joseph D. McNamara estimated "that hundreds of thousands of law-enforcement officers commit felony perjury every year testifying about drug arrests." He based this estimate on the fact that about one million drug arrests a year are for possession, not selling, and that hundreds of thousands of police swear under oath that the drugs were in plain view or that the defendant gave consent to a search. "This may happen occasionally but it defies belief that so many drug users are careless enough to leave illegal drugs where the police can see them or so dumb as to give cops consent to search them when they possess drugs."[81]

"Routine" perjury has serious consequences. First, there is the danger that police fabrication will lead to the charging or conviction of innocent people. In some cases, the police have convinced themselves, against the evidence, that the victim of their lies was guilty. Well-known cases include Richard Jewell, suspected of bombing Olympic Park at the 1996 Atlanta Olympics, and Rolando Cruz, who was on death row in Illinois, but there are many others.[82]

Second, the frequent commission of "pious perjury" creates an enabling atmosphere that allows a minority of "rogue cops" to go over the top by planting evidence on innocent people or booming. There is no way of knowing whether such abuses are widespread. Commission reports and the anecdotes of police and lawyers do not indicate that such practices are routine. Nevertheless, when such cases do occur, they are reported, and quite a few have appeared in the last decade:

- In Philadelphia's 39th District scandal, six "rogue cops" planted evidence on many innocent people, including a grandmother who pestered them with questions when they came looking for her grandson and spent two years in prison for her verbal challenges. The city paid out at least seven million dollars, and fourteen hundred cases were reviewed.[83]
- In the mid–1990's NYPD 30th Precinct scandal, wrongful arrests and booming were connected to police participation in illegal drug sales.[84]
- Five New York State Troopers were convicted of faking fingerprint evidence in thirty cases. In one case, they lifted fingerprints from a corpse and planned to plant the evidence on anyone charged with the crime.[85]
- In Hartford, Connecticut, police officers committed perjury to cover up a police ring that systematically shook down drug dealers.[86]
- Eufrasio G. Cortez, a California narcotics Officer of the Year, was convicted after he admitted that he stole a half million dollars from drug busts, committed perjury thirty times, beat suspects on twenty occasions, and used false statements in search warrants one hundred times over his fifteen-year police career.[87]

Third, the practice cannot be kept hidden and eventually leads to a loss of public confidence in the police. As a result, jurors become skeptical of police testimony, which undermines fair prosecutions; minorities become less willing to call the police for protection; and the public is less interested in law enforcement as a career.[88]

Fourth, the practice undermines the morale and diminishes the sense of pride felt by honest officers.[89] When police lie to cover their corruption, the professional self-esteem of honest cops is injured. Uviller noted in honest cops "a sense of betrayal by the corrupt members who have demeaned the job and made it harder for the rest to convince the public of their probity."[90]

Fifth, the practice leads to corrupt police work, including the use of drugs by undercover officers who then lie to the jury about such practices. East Texas police officer and FBI undercover agent Kim Wozencraft admitted routinely planting evidence, using drugs with suspects, and lying about it in court. She was convicted of perjury, served time, and later resumed her life as a novelist and editor of *Prison Life* magazine.[91]

Sixth, police perjury forces honest cops into the risky role of becoming whistle-blowers and suffering the consequences, or joining the "blue wall of silence" and tolerating the corruption around them. Officer Michael McEvoy of the Arlington Heights, Illinois, Police Department "blew the whistle" on a case of police perjury and would have been fired by his chief, but the Arlington Heights Board of Fire and Police Commissioners reinstated McEvoy when his account was substantiated by a third officer.[92] It is not implausible to believe that a number of whistle-blowers were not as lucky as McEvoy.

Seventh, the practice drives a wedge between judges who occasionally suppress evidence and police who become angry at judges who do not accept their lies. Judge Joseph Q. Koletsky of Hartford, Connecticut, threw out evidence of a crime after the testimony of arresting police officers was clearly contradicted by physical evidence. Detectives told a plausible story of stopping a suspect next to his truck. He was arrested because he reached behind himself, establishing the basis for an arrest and a search incident to arrest during which cocaine was supposedly found. However, spilled powder cocaine in the cab of the truck supported the defendant's testimony that the officers simply drew guns and arrested him, illegally, in his truck. After the evidence was suppressed, the detectives insisted that they did the right thing. "It's a bad decision, but what can you do?" Officer Murzin said. "Some people live in the real world and some people don't."[93] In the "real world," people with power can lie and get away with it.

In a more famous case, federal judge Harold Baer suppressed evidence in a New York City drug bust. A former member of the Mollen Commission on Police Corruption, he had expressed skepticism of the police in his decision. After media coverage, it quickly became a national issue during the 1996 presidential campaign. In an unusual move, the judge ordered a second hearing, heard more testimony, and decided that the search and seizure had been lawful.[94]

Finally, and most important, police perjury diminishes liberty and undermines the constitutional order. In addition to the growing subcultural belief that the Constitution is an impediment to be overcome, judicial acceptance of police perjury undermines the very rationale given for the exclusionary rule: deterrence of police illegality.

An important reason why police perjury is pervasive is that it is in large measure condoned by the courts. According to Alan Dershowitz, "[a] judge in Detroit after listening on one day to more than a dozen 'dropsy' cases . . . chastised the police for not being more 'creative,' but nonetheless accepted their testimony."[95] Cloud gives five reasons why judges accept police perjury:

1. It can be difficult to determine if a witness is lying.
2. Judges dislike the exclusionary rule.
3. Judges cynically believe that "most defendants in the criminal justice system are guilty," and "even if they are innocent of these specific crimes, [they] are guilty of something." Therefore "it is not too disturbing that evidence will not be suppressed."

4. Judges assume that criminal defendants will commit perjury and so distrust the testimony of suspects.

5. "Judges simply do not like to call other government officials liars—especially those who appear regularly in court. It is distasteful; it is indelicate; it is bad manners."[96]

To this list McClurg adds that "judges do not want to generate adverse publicity that portrays them as being 'soft on crime.'" Elected judges, in particular, "are afraid of jeopardizing their chances of reelection."[97]

Numerous proposals have been made to deal with this issue, and many involve modifying legal rules and procedures:

- Eliminating the exclusionary rule.
- Eliminating the exclusionary rule for violent crimes but not for crimes like drug possession.
- Expanding the use of judicial warrants to all nonexigent searches and seizures while narrowing the exigency exception.
- Admitting polygraphs of witnesses in suppression hearings.
- Making probable cause more flexible to allow common-sense judgments.
- Permitting impeachment of police testimony through proof of bias and motive to lie and by allowing evidence of the prevalence of the blue wall of silence.
- Allowing judges to order discovery and allow cross-examination where there is an initial showing of police perjury in a suppression hearing.[98]

Some of these proposals are implausible, but some may have a limited impact on police perjury. Institutional changes have been proposed. Jerome Skolnick and James Fyfe propose major changes in police departments and a move toward community policing as a way to ameliorate the problem.[99] McClurg believes that "[w]e cannot rely with confidence on external actors or institutions to control police lying" and that "[p]olice lying will be substantially reduced only when more police officers come to view it as an unacceptable practice."[100] He believes that police perjury is so pervasive because of the contradiction between the fact that most police officers are moral persons and that many will commit "routine" perjury, which causes cognitive dissonance. To reduce the tension, the officers rationalize their behavior by coming to believe that lying is moral behavior.[101] To deal effectively with police perjury, he proposed a system of police academy training and on-the-street mentoring to show that the "end justifies the means" reasoning that supports perjury is shortsighted and injurious. He suggests fortifying the initial decency that rookies bring to the academy before it becomes hardened into cynicism.[102] The details of this interesting proposal are beyond the scope of this section. Clearly, though, it can work only if the head of the law enforcement agency and the political leadership of the municipality support it.

To sum up, "routine" police perjury is pervasive, and it seriously threatens the existence of Fourth Amendment rights. As noted in Chapter 1, the most important aspect of the rule of law is "congruence." The practices of the government must be congruent with the law as written. The glorious promises of procedural justice enshrined in the Bill of Rights can quickly become hollow and breed a terrible cynicism against government and law if they are routinely ignored. Such cynicism is widespread, and it is vital that judges and especially the police take rights seriously.

SUMMARY

The Supreme Court has expressed a preference for the search warrant over warrantless searches. The most important reason is that a warrant places the judgment of a detached and neutral judicial officer between the police and the citizen in deciding whether probable cause exists to effect a search. A judicial officer who receives fees from warrants issued or who becomes too closely attached to the police search effort is not a neutral and detached magistrate. To obtain a search warrant, an officer must present a written affidavit to a magistrate and swear to the truth of the facts in an *ex parte* hearing that purports to show probable cause. If authorized by statute, a warrant can be obtained by telephone. The place to be searched must be precisely described, but a reasonable mistake in describing the place will not make the search illegal. Search warrants for materials protected by the First Amendment must describe the materials exactly. Statutes allow anticipatory warrants that authorize police to seize evidence from places that do not contain the contraband at the time the warrant is issued, but reasonably expect the contraband to be delivered to the location. Anticipatory search warrants are constitutional.

A defendant can obtain a hearing to challenge an executed search warrant in cases where he or she can make out a preliminary showing that the officer who made out the warrant intentionally lied about material facts or made statements in the warrant with reckless disregard for the truth. Search warrants must be executed within ten days of issuance. The Fourth Amendment requires that police officers knock and announce their presence when executing a warrant; the "knock and announce" element can be set aside by a magistrate in a no-knock warrant where potential danger to officers or loss of evidence is likely if the police knock and announce. However, a blanket no-knock policy violates the Fourth Amendment. Evidence seized during searches in which violations of the knock and announce rule occurred are admissible; that is, the exclusionary rule does not apply. After a warrant is executed, the officer must specify each item seized on an inventory and return, and a copy must be presented to the person whose premises were searched.

In the 1960s, search and seizure law was modernized by creating the "expectation of privacy" doctrine under *Katz v. United States,* eliminating the mere evidence rule, and utilizing the general-reasonableness construction of the Fourth Amendment to weaken the particularity requirement to support administrative search warrants and to authorize investigative stops on less than probable cause, as in *Terry* (1968). Together, these changes made Fourth Amendment interpretation more flexible. The "expectation of privacy" doctrine holds that the Fourth Amendment protects that which a person seeks to keep private and that which society is prepared to recognize as reasonable. The "expectation of privacy" doctrine brought electronic eavesdropping by the government within the parameters of the Fourth Amendment. Property interests are still protected by the Fourth Amendment, but the Court looks to the subjective and objective expectation of privacy balanced against the needs of effective law enforcement. The expectations given the greatest weight are those of the privacy of the home and bodily integrity. Under *Camara v. Municipal Court* (1967), a nonpolice government employee who seeks to enter a home without the consent of the owner to enforce an administrative ordinance must have a judicial warrant; such a warrant, however, need not have all the characteristics of a criminal search warrant and, indeed, in some ways resembles a general warrant. The Fourth Amendment does not prohibit the use of undercover agents who are invited into homes and private areas under false pretense. Such an agent cannot conduct a general search of the premises but can testify as to any criminal activity that occurs in his or her presence.

Eavesdropping warrants are easier to obtain under the Foreign Intelligence Surveillance Act than under normal warrant procedures. A change of the law under the USA PATRIOT Act allows the CIA and FBI to trade information more easily but also allows such warrants to be used for ordinary law enforcement purposes as well as against terrorism, raising threats to civil liberties.

Probable cause is defined as known facts that could lead a reasonably prudent person to draw conclusions about unknown facts. It is a standard of evidence

sufficiency that allows a law enforcement official to arrest a person, obtain a warrant, or perform a warrantless search. Probable cause may be based on hearsay. When the hearsay is provided by a secret informant, the Supreme Court has required magistrates to examine the affidavits carefully. Under the older *Aguilar-Spinelli* two-pronged test, the magistrate had to be convinced that the officer's affidavit supplied credible information about the informant's veracity and his or her basis of knowledge. The Court in *Illinois v. Gates* (1983) replaced the two-pronged test with a "totality of the circumstances" test, which it applied to an anonymous tip so that a deficiency in one prong can be compensated for by a strong showing as to the other or by some other indicia of reliability in determining the overall reliability of a tip.

The plain view doctrine allows the seizure of contraband when a police officer who makes the seizure is lawfully in the place (by a warrant or by virtue of being in a public place) and the illegal nature of the thing seized is immediately apparent. The "immediately apparent" rule is, in effect, a rule of probable cause. A police officer cannot create plain view by illegally entering a premises or by manipulating evidence beyond that authorized by the purpose of the officer's mandate. A plain view seizure can be based on any of the senses, not only on sight. Open fields are not protected by the Fourth Amendment; evidence seized by officers who trespass on open land is admissible. The curtilage, the area and buildings immediately surrounding a house, is protected by the Fourth Amendment to the extent that the expectation of privacy in the area is secured. Airplane and helicopter flyovers may lawfully obtain evidence of what is visible in a curtilage, even if fenced, because commercial overflights have eliminated the expectation of privacy from the air. Ordinary devices, such as flashlights and field glasses, that enhance the senses do not undermine the "immediately apparent" rule. The use, without a warrant, of an enhancement device such as a beeper or a thermal imager that detects movement within a home and suggests criminal activity violates the Fourth Amendment. A warrant must be obtained for enhancement devices that are not in general public use.

A person may consent to relinquish to a law enforcement officer his or her Fourth Amendment right to privacy. An officer who seeks consent to search need have no reasonable suspicion or probable cause to do so. An officer need not inform a person, when requesting consent to search, that he or she has a constitutional right to refuse. Facts and circumstances of a consent encounter must show that the consent was voluntary. The burden of proof is on the government to show voluntariness. Entry under the pretense of having a search warrant negates consent. A person who shares a common area with another may give consent to the police to search, as may a person who reasonably appears to share a place. Landlords or hotel keepers cannot give consent for a criminal search. Police may rely on consent given by a person who reasonably appears to have shared control over an area even if, in fact, the person has no authority or control over the area. Consent to search an area, such as a car, gives police the right to open containers located in the area. When two people have apparent authority over a place and one gives police permission to enter but the other does not, the police have not received valid consent and must obtain a warrant to lawfully enter the premises.

LEGAL PUZZLES

HOW HAVE COURTS DECIDED THESE CASES?

Was It a Search?

3–1.   James Rabb was followed, while driving, by drug officers acting on an unverified tip. He was stopped for making an improper lane change. He was observed making furtive hand movements in the car. As he exited his vehicle, officers observed a book and video on cultivating cannabis. Rabb was nervous; he was read his rights and did not answer questions about having a marijuana-cultivation operation in his house. A drug dog alerted on the car, cannabis was found, and Rabb was arrested. The officers, without obtaining a warrant, brought the drug dog to the exterior of Rabb's house, where it alerted again. The house was searched, and a cannabis-growing operation was found. There was no indicia of a marijuana-growing operation, such as covered windows, high pedestrian traffic, or higher than normal use of electricity.

Was the dog sniff outside the house a search requiring a warrant?

Held: Yes. The trial judge's suppression of evidence was upheld.

Whether a dog sniff at the exterior of a house is a search under the Fourth Amendment depends on whether it violates a constitutionally protected reasonable expectation of privacy. Protecting the privacy of a home is at the core of the Fourth Amendment's protections. *Kyllo v. United States* (2001) controls this case. It held that "obtaining by sense-enhancing technology any information regarding the interior of the home that could not otherwise have been obtained without physical 'intrusion into a constitutionally protected area,' constitutes a search." The smell of marijuana was an *intimate detail* of Rabb's house, as was the relative warmth of Kyllo's house. "Therefore, until the United States Supreme Court indicates otherwise, we are bound to conclude that the use of a dog sniff to detect contraband at a house does not pass constitutional muster." Although *Kyllo* involved advanced technology, the use of a trained dog is not a mere improvement of officers' sense of smell, as ordinary eyeglasses improve vision, but is a significant enhancement accomplished by a different, and far superior, sensory instrument. The use of such a technique by law enforcement, without a warrant, constitutes an illegal search.

State v. Rabb, 881 So. 2d 587 (Fla. App. 2004).

Neutral and Detached Magistrate

3–2.   Two warrants to search for drugs and weapons were issued and signed by Ohio County Trial Commissioner Michelle Madison. Madison, not a lawyer, had been sworn in a few weeks before issuing the warrants by her sister-in-law, District Judge Renona C. Browning, to fill a vacancy. Judge Browning received permission for the temporary appointment from the chief justice of the Ohio Supreme Court. Madison was an employee of the Ohio County Detention Center. Her title was Chief Lieutenant Deputy Jailer, but her duties were those of an administrative assistant and included jail budgeting, bookkeeping, purchasing, billing, correspondence, and the like. Unlike the county's deputy jailers, Madison did not carry a weapon, nor did she wear a badge or a uniform. She never arrested anyone, did not participate in the ongoing training required of deputy jailers, and was not on the regular rotation of duties for monitoring prisoners. Madison did serve at the pleasure of a law enforcement agent, as the Ohio County Jailer had hired and could fire her. Suspects arrested under warrants issued by the trial commissioner could be required to pay jail fees.

Was Madison a "neutral and detached magistrate"?

Holding available from instructor.

Plain Feel

3–3.   Jermain Howard was on probation for cocaine trafficking. His driver's license was revoked as a condition of probation. At a meeting, Wiant, his probation officer, said he saw Howard behind the wheel of a car at a shopping mall and warned him against driving. After the meeting, Wiant followed Howard into the parking lot and saw him place a key in the driver's side door. No one else appeared to be coming to drive the car. Wiant and a supervisor told

Howard to stop. Howard complied. Because it was evening and dark out and many people were roaming around the streets, Wiant decided to frisk Howard for weapons before questioning him. The court decided that this stop and frisk was proper.

During the pat-down, Wiant felt a lump in Howard's pocket. He testified that the lump felt like a wad of folded paper money and not a weapon. Wiant removed the cash from Howard's pocket and counted $361 in Howard's presence. Wiant knew that Howard was unemployed. Howard said he received the cash from his girlfriend to pay the bill at her child's day care service. Wiant called her and received an inconsistent story. Thinking that the cash came from drug dealing, Wiant searched the car and found a gun.

Was the seizure of the money from Howard's pocket proper under the plain feel doctrine?

Holding available from instructor.

Curtilage

3–4. Officers responded to a shots-fired call at a residential street corner at approximately 6:20 A.M. One of the suspects was described as a black male wearing a blue Nike coat. The first officer on the scene saw Zhivargo Jenkins peeking out from the corner of the house at 833 Brewer Street. When the officer called Jenkins over, Jenkins ran across the front of the house and between two cars parked in the yard, bent down beside one of the cars, an inoperative red Chevrolet Lumina, and made a throwing motion. Jenkins then ran, stopped, and surrendered. The officers searched under the Lumina and found a stolen 9mm handgun, hollow-point ammunition, and a plastic bag containing 3.6 grams of crack rocks. They arrested Jenkins. The front yard of 833 Brewer Street was unfenced, the backyard was fenced and guarded by a dog, and the Lumina was seven to eight feet from the house.

Was the area searched within the curtilage of the house?

Holding available from instructor.

Consent

3–5. Narcotics Officer Odell followed Kimberly's car and stopped her at 12:15 A.M. after she made a turn from a left-turn lane without using her turn signals. A registration check indicated that the license plate was registered to a different vehicle. Odell asked for and Kimberly gave consent to search the car, which took about ten minutes. Odell discovered a seed and a flake of marijuana on the driver's side floorboard. Odell told Kimberly that he would not charge her for the marijuana. He determined that she and her boyfriend were staying at a motel a quarter of a mile away and asked for permission to search her room. She consented and drove her car to the motel. Officer Odell found personal amounts of marijuana and crack cocaine in the room.

Was Kimberly's consent to search her motel room voluntary?

Holding available from instructor.

FURTHER READING

Craig M. Bradley, *The Failure of the Criminal Procedure Revolution* (Philadelphia: University of Pennsylvania Press, 1993).

Fred P. Graham, *The Due Process Revolution: The Warren Court's Impact on the Criminal Law* (New York: Hayden, 1970).

Barbara J. Shapiro, *"Beyond Reasonable Doubt" and "Probable Cause": Historical Perspectives on the Anglo-American Law of Evidence* (Berkeley: University of California Press, 1991).

USEFUL WEB SITES

Police Foundation

http://www.policefoundation.org/

Includes a research-based publication and links to Internet sites on diverse topics, including domestic violence policing and racial profiling.

Police Executive Research Forum (PERF)

http://www.policeforum.org/

Publications on many issues related to criminal procedure, such as the police use of force. Free document library includes a variety of topics, such as policing and terrorism. PERF members lead large police agencies.

ENDNOTES

1. Jeremy D. Mayer, "9–11 and the Secret FISA Court: From Watchdog to Lapdog?" *Case Western Reserve Journal of International Law* 34 (2002): 249–52; and J. Christopher Champion, "Special Project Note: The Revamped FISA; Striking a Better Balance between the Government's Need to Protect Itself and the 4th Amendment," *Vanderbilt Law Review* 58 (2005): 1671–703.

2. B. Drummond Ayres Jr., "The Simpson Case: The Law; For Judge, a Case Where Circumstances Outweigh Safeguards," *New York Times,* July 8, 1994.

3. Scott Turow, "Policing the Police: The D.A.'s Job," in Jeffrey Abramson, ed., *Postmortem: The O.J. Simpson Case* (New York: Basic Books, 1996), 190.

4. H. R. Uviller, *Tempered Zeal* (Chicago: Contemporary Books, 1988), 125–26.

5. Commentary to *Federal Rules of Criminal Procedure,* 1987–88, Educational Edition (St. Paul: West, 1987), 129, quoting *United States ex rel., Pugh v. Pate,* 401 F.2d 6 (7th Cir. 1968).

6. Justin H. Smith, "Press One for Warrant: Reinventing the Fourth Amendment's Search Warrant Requirement through Electronic Procedures," *Vanderbilt Law Review* 55 (2002): 1591–696, 1595; and Walter Gerash, "Next Two Days Critical for Simpson Hearing," *Rocky Mountain News,* July 6, 1994. (In Colorado, telephonic warrants were obtained in an hour and a half.)

7. John Henry Hingson III, "Telephonic and Electronic Search Warrants: A Fine Tonic for an Ailing Fourth Amendment—Part One," *Champion* 29 (September/October 2005): 38.

8. Hingson, "Telephonic and Electronic Search Warrants."

9. P. Pringle, "Officer Explains Search of Simpson's Property: Police Say They Saw Blood, Feared a Life at Stake," *Dallas Morning News,* July 6, 1994; and S. Estrich, "Who's on Trial, O.J. or Cops?" *USA Today,* September 22, 1994.

10. Smith, "Press One," 1604.

11. *Lyons v. Robinson,* 783 F.2d 737 (8th Cir. 1985), citing *U.S. v. Gitcho,* 601 F.2d 369, 371 (8th Cir. 1979).

12. James A. Adams, "Anticipatory Search Warrants: Constitutionality, Requirements, and Scope," *Kentucky Law Journal* 79 (1991): 681–733, 695.

13. Adams, "Anticipatory Search Warrants," 705–6, n. 67.

14. Adams, "Anticipatory Search Warrants," 698–99.

15. Adams, "Anticipatory Search Warrants," 720–21.

16. Adams, "Anticipatory Search Warrants," 715, 727–29.

17. Adams, "Anticipatory Search Warrants," 709–10.

18. *United States v. Ruminer,* 786 F.2d 381 (10th Cir. 1986).

19. *Ker v. California* (1963).

20. Robert M. Duncan Jr., "Surreptitious Search Warrants and the USA PATRIOT Act: 'Thinking Outside the Box but Within the Constitution,' or a Violation of Fourth Amendment Protections?" *New York City Law Review* 7 (2004): 1–38, 6–24.

21. Duncan, "Surreptitious Search Warrants," 24–28.

22. Duncan, "Surreptitious Search Warrants," 32–35.

23. George Orwell, *1984: A Novel* (New York: Harcourt and Brace, 1983).

24. Josh Meyer, "Five Years After; Hidden Depths to U.S. Monitoring," *Los Angeles Times,* September 11, 2006.

25. Stanley I. Kutler, *The Wars of Watergate* (New York: Alfred A. Knopf, 1990), 222–26.

26. M. Zalman, "The Federal Anti-Riot Act and Political Crime: The Need for Criminal Law Theory," *Villanova Law Review* 20 (1975): 897–937.

27. Michelle Mittelstadt, "Patriot Act Available against Many Types of Criminals," *Dallas Morning News,* September 8, 2003.

28. Bob Barr, "Patriot Act Games: It Can Happen Here," *The American Spectator* (August–September 2003).

29. Information from the *Denver Post,* February 4, 2000, July 18, 2000; and the *Denver Rocky Mountain News,* February 5, 2000, February 6, 2000, March 14, 2000, June 28, 2000; and Police Crimes.com, http://flyservers.com/members5/policecrime.com/killed/co_police.html (accessed July 14, 2006).

30. Radley Balko, *Overkill: The Rise of Paramilitary Police Raids in America* (Cato Institute, 2006), available at http://www.cato.org/pub_display.php?pub_id=6476 (accessed August 30, 2006).

31. *Federal Communications Act of 1934,* § 605.

32. Walter F. Murphy, *Wiretapping on Trial: A Case Study in the Judicial Process* (New York: Random House, 1965).

33. Bruce Allen Murphy, *Wild Bill: The Legend and Life of William O. Douglas* (New York: Random House, 2003).

34. This rule is expertly criticized by Donald L. Doernberg, "'Can You Hear Me Now?': Expectations of Privacy, False Friends, and the Perils of Speaking under the Supreme Court's Fourth Amendment Jurisprudence," *Indiana Law Review* 39 (2006): 253–308.

35. *On Lee v. United States* (1952); *Lopez v. United States* (1963); *United States v. White* (1971) (plurality opinion); and 18 U.S.C. § 2511 (2) (c) and (d).

36. Robert R. Reinertsen and Robert J. Bronson, "Informant Is a Dirty Word," in James N. Gilbert, ed., *Criminal Investigation: Essays and Cases* (Columbus, OH: Merrill, 1990), 99–103.

37. Reinertsen and Bronson, "Informant," 99.

38. "Snitches" have been implicated in many cases of wrongful conviction. See Clifford Zimmerman, "From the Jailhouse to the Courthouse: The Role of Informants in Wrongful Convictions," in Saundra D. Westervelt and John A. Humphrey, eds., *Wrongly Convicted: Perspectives of Failed Justice* (New Brunswick, N.J.: Rutgers University Press, 2001), 55–76.

39. C. Whitebread, "The Burger Court's Counter-revolution in Criminal Procedure: The Recent Criminal Decisions of the United States Supreme Court," *Washburn Law Journal* 24 (1985): 471–98.

40. See Wayne R. LaFave, "Fourth Amendment Vagaries (of Improbable Cause, Imperceptible Plain View, Notorious Privacy, and Balancing Askew)," *Journal of Criminal Law and Criminology* 74 (1983): 1171–224.

41. Corey Fleming Hirokawa, "Making the 'Law of the Land' the Law on the Street: How Police Academies Teach Evolving Fourth Amendment Law," *Emory Law Journal* 49, no. 1 (2000) : 295–334, 319–20.

42. Charles H. Whitebread and Christopher Slobogin, *Criminal Procedure: An Analysis of Cases and Concepts,* 4th ed. (New York: Foundation Press, 2000), 225.

43. *Dickerson v. Minnesota* (1993).

44. *Whren v. United States* (1996). See Chapter 4.

45. William J. Broad, "Ideas and Trends: We're Ready for Our Close-ups Now," *New York Times,* January 16, 2000, Sec. 4, p. 4.

46. The Joint Operations Command Center, operational in Washington, D.C., since September 11, 2001, and shared by the Metropolitan Police Department, the FBI, the Secret Service, the State Department, and the Defense Intelligence Agency, quickly allowed writer Matthew Brzezinski to view on a screen the lawn furniture and plantings in his backyard in a Washington, D.C., neighborhood. "Theoretically, with a few clicks of the mouse the system could also link up with thousands of closed-circuit cameras in shopping malls, department stores and office buildings, and is programmed to handle live feeds from up to six helicopters simultaneously." Matthew Brzezinski, "Fortress America," *New York Times Magazine,* February 23, 2003, Sec. 6, p. 38.

47. F. J. Remington et al., *Criminal Justice Administration, Materials and Cases,* 1st ed. (Indianapolis: Bobbs-Merrill, 1969), 32.

48. Marcy Strauss, "Reconstructing Consent," *Journal of Criminal Law and Criminology* 92 (2001): 211–72, 214.

49. Paul Sutton, "The Fourth Amendment in Action: An Empirical View of the Search Warrant Process," *Criminal Law Bulletin* 22 (1986): 405, 415.

50. Illya Lichtenberg, "Police Discretion and Traffic Enforcement: A Government of Men?" *Cleveland State Law Review* 50 (2002): 425–53.

51. Strauss, "Reconstructing Consent," 211–72, 259, quoting David S. Kaplan and Lisa Dixon, "Coerced Waiver and Coerced Consent," *Denver University Law Review* 74 (1997): 941–56, 948.

52. Kaplan and Dixon, "Coerced Waiver," 948.

53. *Schneckloth v. Bustamonte* (1973), 222 (emphasis added).

54. *United States v. Santiago,* 428 F.3d 699 (7th Cir. 2005); and *Reasor v. State,* 988 S.W.2d 877 (Tex. App., 4th Dist. 1999).

55. L. A. Bradshaw, "Validity of Consent to Search Given by One in Custody of Officers," *American Law Reports,* 3rd series 9 (1966, updated 2005): 858.

56. Strauss, "Reconstructing Consent," 216.

57. Strauss, "Reconstructing Consent," 221.

58. Strauss, "Reconstructing Consent," 229.

59. Strauss, "Reconstructing Consent," 236–44; *State v. Johnson,* 346 A.2d 66, 68 (N.J. 1975); and *Commonwealth v. Cleckley,* 738 A.2d 427, 434 (Pa. 1999) (Nigro, J., dissenting).

60. *Cleckley,* 738 A2d 427, 432 listed decisions of the supreme courts of Mississippi, New Jersey, and Hawaii as requiring individuals to be informed of their right to refuse a search.

61. Strauss, "Reconstructing Consent," 265, n. 194, referencing Consent Decree, *United States v. State of New Jersey,* C.A. No. 99-5970 (D.N.J. 1999), and other cases.

62. Strauss, "Reconstructing Consent," 256–58.

63. Strauss, "Reconstructing Consent," 258–71.

64. Ilya Lichtenberg, "The Impact of a Verbal Warning on Police Consent Search Practices," *Journal of Criminal Justice,* 32 (2004): 85–87.

65. Lichtenberg, "The Impact of a Verbal Warning"; and *State v. Robinette,* 80 Ohio St.3d 234, 685 N.E. 2d 762 (1997).

66. Lichtenberg, "The Impact of a Verbal Warning."

67. Morgan Cloud, "The Dirty Little Secret," *Emory Law Journal* 43 (1994): 1311–49, 1311.

68. Scott Turow, "Simpson Prosecutors Pay for Their Blunders," *New York Times,* October 4, 1995; *Larry King Live,* 9:00 P.M. ET, CNN, August 28, 1995, transcript no. 1524-2, "Will O.J. Testify?" (guests: Alan Dershowitz, Simpson defense attorney; and Bill Hodes, professor of law, Indiana University); David Margolick, "Forget O. J.— The Question Becomes: Is Fuhrman the Question?" *New York Times,* September 10, 1995; Carl Rowan, "Fuhrman Tips the Scale at Simpson Trial," *Chicago Sun-Times,* September 10, 1995; and Charles L. Lindner, "The Simpson Trial: When You Can't See the Forest for the Leaf," *Los Angeles Times,* September 3, 1995.

69. Andrew J. McClurg, "Good Cop, Bad Cop: Using Cognitive Dissonance Theory to Reduce Police Lying," *University of California at Davis Law Review* 32 (1999): 389–453, 398.

70. David N. Dorfman, "Proving the Lie: Litigating Police Credibility," *American Journal of Criminal Law* 26 (1999): 462–503.

71. Cloud, "The Dirty Little Secret," 1313, footnote omitted.

72. George James, "Officer Admits Illegal Apartment Entries," *New York Times,* January 10, 1996, B6. The officer claimed that the precinct's most senior officers raided and searched a building without first obtaining a warrant, and "[i]t was kind of implied that this was what they wanted." This account was hotly denied by Commissioner Bratton, who claimed that it was not corroborated: Barbara Ross and Wendell Jamieson, "Bratton Slams Dirty 30 Sgt.," *New York Daily News,* January 12, 1996.

73. Uviller, *Tempered Zeal,* 158.

74. Irving Younger, "The Perjury Routine," *The Nation,* 1967, 596–97, cited in Cloud, "The Dirty Little Secret,"

1317; as a judge, he noted the problem in *People v. McMurtry,* 314 N.Y.S.2d 194 (Crim. Ct. 1970).

75. Sarah Barlow, "Patterns of Arrests for Misdemeanor Narcotics Possession: Manhattan Police Practices, 1960–62," *Criminal Law Bulletin* 4 (1968): 549–81. See Paul Chevigny, "Comment," *Criminal Law Bulletin* 4 (1968): 581.

76. McClurg, "Good Cop, Bad Cop," 398–99, footnotes omitted.

77. Sarah Terry, "Experts Try to Pin Down Extent of Police Misconduct," *New York Times,* November 19, 1995.

78. See Joseph D. Grano, "A Dilemma for Defense Counsel: *Spinelli-Harris* Search Warrants and the Possibility of Police Perjury," *University of Illinois Law Forum* (1971): 405, 409, cited in Cloud, "The Dirty Little Secret," 1312, n. 4. Other legal commentators cited in Cloud include Alan Dershowitz, *The Best Defense,* xxi–xxii (1982); and "Police Perjury in Narcotics 'Dropsy' Cases: A New Credibility Gap," *Georgetown Law Journal* 60 (1971): 507. Professors Cloud, McClurg, "Good Cop, Bad Cop," 396–404, and Dorfman, "Proving the Lie," 460–62, review all these materials, and they all believe that these kinds of practices are routine.

79. Myron W. Orfield Jr., "The Exclusionary Rule and Deterrence: An Empirical Study of Chicago Narcotics Officers," *University of Chicago Law Review* 54 (1987): 1016–69, 1050–51.

80. Cloud, "The Dirty Little Secret," 1313, footnote omitted.

81. Joseph D. McNamara, "Law Enforcement: Has the Drug War Created an Officer Liars' Club?" *Los Angeles Times,* February 11, 1996.

82. McClurg, "Good Cop, Bad Cop," 417–19; and Daniel Jeffreys, "Last Hope on Death Row: Call McCloskey; He Gave up a Lucrative Career in Business to Help People Wrongly Imprisoned. He Has Saved Four Lives: So Far," *Independent,* January 3, 1996.

83. Don Terry, "Philadelphia Shaken by Criminal Police Officers," *New York Times,* August 28, 1995; and Barbara Whitaker, "Philadelphia Still Reeling from Police Scandal: Officials Review More Than 1,400 Arrests Made by Six Officers Charged with Theft, Framing Suspects," *Dallas Morning News,* September 3, 1995.

84. "Officer Is Acquitted in Theft and Perjury," *New York Times,* January 26, 1996. (Earlier, Officer John Arena had been cleared by a federal jury in Manhattan; *New York Times,* January 5, 1996.) Seth Faison, "In Plea Deal, Officer Agrees to Give Details of Corruption," *New York Times,*

May 24, 1994; and James, "Officer Admits Illegal Apartment Entries."

85. "Ex-Trooper Admits a Plot to Falsify Fingerprints," *New York Times,* December 29, 1995; and "Prosecutor Tries to Make Trooper Talk on Tampering," *New York Times,* January 4, 1996.

86. Lynne Tuohy, "Grand Juror Details Police Abuse of Power; 6 Arrests Made, More Expected; Police Corruption Probe Leads to Six Arrests in Hartford," *Hartford Courant,* December 2, 1993; and "Police Arrested in Corruption Probe; State Trooper, Hartford Officer in Custody after 9-Month Inquiry," *Hartford Courant,* December 1, 1993.

87. Victor Merina, "Officers Marked Sobel for Death, Jury Told; Trial: Ex-deputy Says He and Colleagues Wanted to Eliminate the Sheriff's Sergeant When They Learned He Secretly Cooperated with Prosecutors," *Los Angeles Times,* March 21, 1992.

88. Joe Sexton, "Jurors Question Honesty of Police," *New York Times,* September 25, 1995, B3.; and McClurg, "Good Cop, Bad Cop," 419–23.

89. Uviller, *Tempered Zeal,* 115.

90. Uviller, *Tempered Zeal,* 12–13.

91. Keith Kachtick, "Rush to Justice," *Texas Monthly,* January 1996, 56.

92. Marco Buscaglia, "Board Clears Officer of Misconduct Charges," *Chicago Tribune,* January 5, 1996.

93. Matthew Kauffman, "Judge Doubts City Officers' Account of Arrest," *Hartford Courant,* February 6, 1996.

94. Dorfman, "Proving the Lie," 471, n. 73; and McClurg, "Good Cop, Bad Cop," 406–11.

95. Alan Dershowitz, "Police Tampering: How Often, Where," *Buffalo News,* February 21, 1995.

96. Cloud, "The Dirty Little Secret," 1321–24, footnotes omitted.

97. McClurg, "Good Cop, Bad Cop," 405.

98. The many sources of these proposals are found in Dorfman, "Proving the Lie." The last proposal is Dorfman's.

99. Jerome K. Skolnick and James J. Fyfe, *Above the Law: Police and the Excessive Use of Force* (New York: Free Press, 1993).

100. McClurg, "Good Cop, Bad Cop," 410.

101. McClurg, "Good Cop, Bad Cop," 412–15, 424–29.

102. McClurg, "Good Cop, Bad Cop," 412–13, 428–53.

JUSTICES OF THE SUPREME COURT

Roosevelt's Liberals: Douglas, Murphy, Jackson, and Rutledge

Franklin Roosevelt appointed no justices during his first term in office and yet ended up appointing more justices (nine) than any president except George Washington, thanks in large part to his unprecedented four terms in office. Roosevelt's primary goal was to name individuals who would support New Deal legislation on economic and labor issues. For a half century, a conservative Supreme Court had, on behalf of the wealthy, more or less restricted the ability of the Democratic branches of government to pass legislation to improve working conditions and to benefit workers, farmers, and the lower middle class.

The ascendancy of the Roosevelt administration during the great economic crisis of the 1930s finally led to a liberalization of the bench. As the Supreme Court reduced its role in passing on the wisdom of economic legislation, a new wave of civil rights cases began to press forward for hearing. The civil liberties cases of the 1940s and 1950s included freedom of speech, freedom of the press, religious freedom, freedom of conscience regarding loyalty issues, and criminal procedure. It was not a foregone conclusion that justices who were liberal on economic matters would also be liberal on civil rights and criminal procedure questions. Four of Roosevelt's appointees—Justices Hugo Black, William O. Douglas, Frank Murphy, and Wiley B. Rutledge—were "liberal" in favoring the incorporation of the Bill of Rights into the Fourteenth Amendment. They tended to vote for criminal defendants and, when joined by Justices Felix Frankfurter and Robert H. Jackson, placed limits on local police officers whose actions were found to have violated the Due Process Clause of the Fourteenth Amendment.

Justices Douglas, Rutledge, and Jackson have been ranked as "near great" and Justice Murphy as average by a poll of scholars, but Murphy's originality in criminal procedure stands as a real contribution to criminal jurisprudence, as it defined the actual position taken during the due process revolution of the 1960s.

Collection of the Supreme Court of the United States. Photographer: Harris and Ewing.

William O. Douglas

Connecticut, 1898–1980

Democrat

Appointed by Franklin Delano Roosevelt

Years of Service: 1939–1975

Life and Career.   Douglas grew up in relative poverty in Yakima, Washington; he was six years old when his father, a Presbyterian missionary, died. He entered Whitman College in 1916 and taught school for a few years before entering law school. He graduated second in his class at Columbia Law School, practiced briefly at a Wall Street law firm, and then taught at Columbia and Yale law schools, gaining recognition as an expert in financial law and as a proponent of the pragmatic jurisprudence of legal realism.

Douglas joined President Roosevelt's New Deal administration in 1934 to work on the Securities and Exchange Commission (SEC), a new watchdog agency designed to regulate the stock market. He became a member of the SEC in 1936 and its chairman in 1937. First known as antibusiness, Douglas built bridges to the business world and tried to stimulate internal reform in the stock exchange to minimize governmental intrusion. He became an adviser to the president and was Roosevelt's fourth nominee to the Court at the young age of forty. Intensely ambitious, Douglas was seen as a potential presidential candidate before President Roosevelt ran for a third term, and he was a leading candidate for the vice presidential post in 1940 and 1944 after he had been appointed to the Supreme Court.

A restless man and a hard worker, he traveled to all parts of the world, authored thirty-two books (many were travelogues), was a frequent speaker on issues of foreign policy, and was a staunch environmentalist long before the environment was a popular issue. When not traveling, he spent his summers hiking and camping in Washington State. He was married four times and divorced three times, indicating a somewhat chaotic personal life.

Contribution to Criminal Procedure.   Despite his enormous output of cases, Justice Douglas wrote relatively few criminal procedure opinions. In his early years on the Court, he was tentative in taking a consistent liberal position; in fact, he wrote a 1944 opinion holding that an arrest in a public place involving public property was not entitled to the same protection as a search of the home, a decision severely criticized by Justice Frankfurter. Nevertheless, he became a very liberal justice and consistently voted for the "incorporation plus" doctrine. His solid liberal vote on criminal issues under five chief justices was a critical element in the due process revolution.

Signature Opinion.   *Griffin v. California* (1965). In this case, the Court held that a state judge could not tell a jury that although a defendant had a right to remain silent, the jury could take the defendant's failure to deny or explain facts in the case into consideration in determining whether the facts were true. The Court held that the federal rule against such comment was based on the Fifth Amendment privilege against self-incrimination and that it therefore applied to the states via the Due Process Clause of the Fourteenth Amendment. "For comment on the refusal to testify is a remnant of the 'inquisitorial system of criminal justice,' which the Fifth Amendment outlaws. It is a penalty imposed by courts for exercising a constitutional privilege."

Assessment.   Justice Douglas served longer than any other justice: thirty-six years. He was steeped in the philosophy of legal realism, which holds that a judge's policy preferences are the prime determiner of the judge's decisions. His outspoken activism made him one of the most controversial justices. He was a hard worker; he wrote a large number of opinions (many on antitrust and economic issues), but he wrote them very quickly. Despite his acknowledged brilliance, his opinions did not always spell out the doctrinal foundation of his decisions. His *Douglas v. California* (1963) opinion, holding that a defendant has a right to counsel on first appeal, did not clarify whether the decision rested on due process or equal protection.

In addition to his contributions to the law of business regulation, Justice Douglas helped to advance an absolutist concept of free speech with his dissent in *Dennis v. United States* (1951), arguing against the conviction of Communist Party leaders for advocating the violent overthrow of the government. His dissent became the law in the 1970s. He wrote, "Free speech has occupied an exalted position because of the high service it has given our society. Its protection is essential to the very existence of a democracy." His *Griswold v. Connecticut* (1965) contraception law opinion established the right of privacy, based on values inherent in the First, Fourth, and Fifth amendments. *Griswold* laid the foundation for the *Roe v. Wade* (1973) abortion rights ruling.

Further Reading.

Bruce Allen Murphy, *Wild Bill: The Legend and Life of William O. Douglas* (New York: Random House, 2003).

Frank Murphy

Collection of the Supreme Court of the United States. Photographer: Pach Brothers Studio.

Michigan, 1890–1949

Democrat

Appointed by Franklin Delano Roosevelt

Years of Service: 1940–1949

Life and Career.   Murphy, a native of Michigan, obtained his undergraduate and law degrees from the University of Michigan. He had an extensive public career prior to his appointment to the Court. He served as an army officer in World War I; a federal assistant prosecutor; a judge of the Detroit Recorder's Court; mayor of Detroit from 1930 to 1933, when he gained national fame for innovative attempts to ease the burden of the Great Depression; governor-general of the Philippines from 1933 to 1937, on a presidential appointment; governor of Michigan from 1937 to 1939, during which time he refused to order the violent suppression of automobile workers' sit-down strikes; and attorney general of the United States from 1939 to 1940, when he established the civil rights division. His vigor and compassion made him a leading political figure and even a potential presidential candidate despite the fact that he was Catholic, a handicap at that time.

Contribution to Criminal Procedure.   In criminal procedure cases, Justice Murphy voted in favor of the defendant's right to counsel in every case; wrote a majority opinion that struck down the systematic exclusion of day laborers from juries; and dissented in cases that allowed the government to wiretap and electronically eavesdrop without a warrant. With one exception, he sided with the defendant in coerced confessions cases.

Signature Opinion.   Dissent in *Adamson v. California* (1947). The majority held that the Fifth Amendment is not incorporated into the Fourteenth Amendment. Justice Black dissented, arguing for total incorporation. Justice Murphy's dissent best anticipated the due process revolution of the 1960s by establishing the "incorporation plus" concept, which supported both the incorporation of the Bill of Rights into the Fourteenth Amendment *and* the independent use of the Due Process Clause to strike down unfair government action. "Occasions may arise where a proceeding falls so far short of conforming to fundamental standards of procedure as to warrant constitutional condemnation in terms of a lack of due process despite the absence of a specific provision in the Bill of Rights."

Assessment.   Justice Murphy was, with Justices Douglas and Rutledge, one of the most liberal justices on the Court in the 1940s. He dissented in the case upholding the removal of Japanese Americans from their homes to relocation centers during World War II. He wrote many pro-worker opinions in the field of labor law. He consistently favored the expansion of First Amendment rights, opposed racial segregation, favored gender equality, and generally supported the underdog.

Murphy was not a great legal stylist or a profound legal thinker and has been rated an average justice by scholars. He probably delegated more drafting to his law clerks than other justices did. However, he brought to the Court his extensive experience in public life and "a great heart attuned to the cries of the weak and suffering." His unwavering commitment to civil liberties strengthened the "solid minority" of criminal procedure liberals in the Stone and Vinson courts and helped pave the way to the due process revolution.

Further Reading.

J. Woodford Howard Jr., *Mr. Justice Murphy: A Political Biography* (Princeton, N.J.: Princeton University Press, 1968).

Collection of the Supreme
Court of the United States.
Photographer: Harris
and Ewing.

Robert H. Jackson

New York, 1892–1954

Democrat

Appointed by Franklin Delano Roosevelt

Years of Service: 1941–1954

Life and Career.   Robert Jackson developed a reputation as the most skillful government litigator in Washington, D.C., in the heady days of the New Deal. Yet his formal educational background consisted only of high school and a year at Albany Law School. He trained for the law as an apprentice in a law office and opened his own practice in Jamestown, New York, in 1913. Over the next twenty years, he developed a prosperous practice and became a respected attorney in his region.

Treasury Secretary Henry Morgenthau persuaded Jackson to join the New Deal administration in 1934 as general counsel for the Bureau of Internal Revenue. His reputation soared by winning complex cases for the government. He was appointed assistant attorney general in charge of the Antitrust Division in 1936 and argued ten cases for the government before the Supreme Court. He won the important case upholding the Social Security Act on broad grounds that made the laws easier to administer. He supported President Roosevelt's "court-packing" plan. He became solicitor general in 1938, where he "showed a remarkable insight into both basic governmental policy and the tactics of advocacy." His service as attorney general from January 1940 to mid-1941 was marked more by careful legal advice than by administrative innovations. His most brilliant achievement was his Attorney General's Opinion justifying President Roosevelt's controversial "lend-lease" program in the dark days before America's entry into World War II, whereby fifty over-age destroyers were transferred to the British navy in return for military bases in Bermuda.

Contribution to Criminal Procedure.   Justice Jackson generally joined Justice Frankfurter in opposing incorporation. His votes were mixed; in some Fourth Amendment cases, he was quite critical of abusive police work, but he was not as consistently liberal as Justices Black, Douglas, Murphy, and Rutledge. He believed in judicial restraint and was a strong proponent of federalism. Thus, in state confessions cases he often voted to uphold the confession under the Due Process Clause, especially where a very serious crime was charged, unless the police action made it perfectly clear that the confession was obtained involuntarily.

Signature Opinion.   *Johnson v. United States* (1948). Police standing outside a hotel room smelled opium and entered without a warrant. In holding that this was a violation of the Fourth Amendment, Justice Jackson issued the classic statement about the value of a search warrant: "The point of the Fourth Amendment, which often is not grasped by zealous officers, is not that it denies law enforcement the support of the usual inferences which reasonable men draw from evidence. Its protection consists in requiring that those inferences be drawn by a neutral and detached magistrate instead of being judged by the officer engaged in the often competitive enterprise of ferreting out crime."

Assessment.   Justice Jackson generally was liberal on civil rights issues, writing the decisive compulsory flag-salute opinion (holding that requiring schoolchildren to salute the flag violated First Amendment rights). In substantive criminal law, he wrote a ringing affirmation of the common law principle that the government cannot create a legislative definition of a serious crime, such as theft, without the element of criminal intent (*mens rea*).

He was a great stylist, and many of his opinions are filled with engaging and quotable passages. He was interested in the improvement of criminal justice and chaired the American Bar Association's special committee on the administration of criminal justice. He interrupted his service as a justice for over a year after World War II to serve as the chief American prosecutor at the Nuremberg War Crimes trials of the top Nazi leaders. In this role, he made an abiding contribution to international law and the development of human rights.

Further Reading.

Glendon Schubert, ed., *Dispassionate Justice: A Synthesis of the Judicial Opinions of Robert H. Jackson* (Indianapolis: Bobbs-Merrill, 1969).

Collection of the Supreme Court of the United States. Photographer: Harris and Ewing.

Wiley B. Rutledge

Iowa, 1894–1949

Democrat

Appointed by Franklin Delano Roosevelt

Years of Service: 1943–1949

Life and Career.   Rutledge was the son of a fundamentalist Baptist minister who preached in Kentucky, Tennessee, and North Carolina. A biographer notes that "although in later life he became a Unitarian, his father's fervor was reflected in his zeal for justice and right." He graduated from the University of Wisconsin in 1914, taught school for a few years, and nearly died from tuberculosis. Following his recovery, he received his LL.B. degree from the University of Colorado in 1922. After two years of law practice in Boulder, he became a law professor and then dean of the University of Iowa College of Law in the 1930s. He developed a reputation as an inspiring teacher and civic activist.

Moved by the plight of the poor and unemployed during the Great Depression, he spoke out publicly against the Supreme Court's rulings that struck down New Deal legislation. As one of the few academics to support President Roosevelt's "court-packing" scheme in 1937—a stance that led several Iowa state legislators to threaten to withhold law school salaries in reprisal—Rutledge came to the attention of the Roosevelt administration. He was appointed to the U.S. Court of Appeals for Washington, D.C., in 1939 and served for four years before his nomination to the Supreme Court.

Contribution to Criminal Procedure.   Rutledge joined Justice Black in supporting incorporation of the Bill of Rights in *Adamson* (1947), helping to make incorporation a respectable, if controversial, position. Indeed, he joined the more liberal "incorporation plus" position with Justices Murphy and Douglas.

Signature Opinion.   *Brinegar v. United States* (1949). Writing for the majority in upholding an automobile search of a bootlegger, Justice Rutledge stated the classical definition of probable cause that has been oft-repeated by the Court: "In dealing with probable cause, however, as the very name implies, we deal with probabilities. These are not technical; they are the factual and practical considerations of everyday life on which reasonable and prudent men, not legal technicians, act. . . . Requiring more would unduly hamper law enforcement. To allow less would be to leave law-abiding citizens at the mercy of the officers' whim or caprice."

Assessment.   Justice Rutledge's tenure on the Court was marked by a fierce dedication to the principles of liberty. His most famous opinion, a dissent in the *Yamashita* (1946) case, acknowledged the authority of the United States to try the former Japanese commander of the Philippines, who was accused of authorizing or allowing atrocities by his troops, but he dissented bitterly that the proceeding was characterized by none of the hallmarks of due process. He agreed with the Court in another case that a naturalized citizen could not have his citizenship revoked merely because he had belonged to the Communist Party at the time of his naturalization.

Further Reading.

Landon G. Rockwell, "Justice Rutledge on Civil Liberties," *Yale Law Journal* 59 (1949): pp. 27–59.

4 Arrest and Stop under the Fourth Amendment

CHAPTER OUTLINE

KEY TERMS

arrest
arrest warrant
body cavity search
booking
brevity requirement
bright-line rule
citizen's arrest
companion case
custodial arrest
custody
drug courier profile
false arrest
field interrogation
"fleeing felon" rule

frisk
illegal arrest
in personam jurisdiction
in-presence rule
internal passport
inventory search
investigative stop
least intrusive means
merchant's privilege
mistaken arrest
police officer expertise
pretext search
protective sweep
public duty doctrine

reasonable force
roadblock
scope of a search incident to arrest
search incident to arrest
seizure of the person
sobriety checklane
source city
stop
stop and frisk
strip search
sui generis
Terry stop
vagrancy statute

Because the strongest advocates of Fourth Amendment rights are frequently criminals, it is easy to forget that our interpretations of such rights apply to the innocent and the guilty alike.

—Justice Thurgood Marshall, *United States v. Sokolow,* 490 U.S. 1, 11 (1989)

ARREST IN A TIME OF TERROR

In the weeks and months following 9/11, federal agents rounded up twelve hundred people, keeping their identity secret and detaining some for months. "Except for 93 individuals facing criminal charges, virtually none of the detainees has been identified publicly, and the locations where they are held also remain secret."[1] Most of the arrests were based on the alien or illegal alien status of detainees, so that the strict rules of arrest under probable cause did not apply. In June 2003, the Department of Justice (DOJ) Office of the Inspector General (OIG) issued a report critical of many of these arrests and the conditions of detention. For example, "The FBI in New York City made little attempt to distinguish between aliens who were subjects of the FBI terrorism investigation . . . and those encountered coincidentally. . . . [E]ven in the chaotic aftermath of the September 11 attacks, the FBI should have expended more effort attempting to distinguish between aliens who it actually suspected of having a connection to terrorism from those aliens who, while possibly guilty of violating federal immigration law, had no connection to terrorism but simply were encountered in connection with" a lead.[2] The DOJ admitted that it sought every legal way to detain suspects in the immediate aftermath of the attack. "But the inspector general's report found that some lawyers in the department raised concerns about the legality of the tactics, only to be overridden by senior officials."[3] As evidence that the DOJ cast "too wide a net," none of the 762 immigrants of the twelve hundred arrestees were charged as terrorists, although most were deported. A "communications blackout" and limits on phone calls to one per week kept families of the detainees in the dark about their whereabouts. Some were not notified of charges against them for over a month, although pre-9/11 Immigration and Naturalization Service (INS) rules required notice within twenty-four hours.[4]

Although aliens can be detained without probable cause, no good purpose is served by using law enforcement resources on flimsy cases. Some arrests were based on mere rumors. "Some illegal immigrants were picked up at random traffic stops, others because of anonymous tips that they were Muslims with erratic schedules, officials said. . . . A Muslim man, for instance, was arrested when an acquaintance wrote to officials that the man had made 'anti-American statements.' The statements 'were very general and did not involve threats of violence or suggest any direct connection to terrorism,' the report found, but the man had overstayed his visa and was held."[5] The arrests did not follow standard procedures for arrests of aliens before 9/11. On September 17, 2001, Chief INS Administrative Judge Michael Creppy issued an order closing all postarrest hearings of "special interest" cases to the public; deleting case identification from court calendars posted outside courtrooms where hearings were held; and restricting the means of contacting lawyers. (The government does not provide counsel for INS deportation hearings.) Professor Stephen Schulhofer has criticized these postarrest procedures for "the strict conditions of *secrecy* that surround the program, the *length* of detentions, and the absence of any *judicial review* at key stages.[6]

An egregious case was the arrest of Dr. Al Bader al-Hazmi, a Saudi citizen, on September 12, 2001, in his San Antonio town house.[7] Dr. al-Hazmi, thirty-one years old, "a wisp of a man with soulful eyes and an almost unsettling serenity," was living in the United States with his wife and young daughters while in radiology residency at the University of Texas Health Science Center. FBI agents came to his home because the passenger list of the flight that crashed into the Pentagon included Nawaf and Salem Alhazmi (an alternate spelling of the doctor's name). Dr. al-Hazmi told the agents that "Al-Hazmi is common like the Smith name in Saudi Arabia." The doctor said he would not answer questions without seeing a lawyer. The agents searched his home for six hours, allowing al-Hazmi to make a call after five hours. He called a lawyer for Saudi Aramco, the oil company that sponsored his medical residency. Knowing of his good character, the lawyer told him not to worry. Nevertheless, al-Hazmi was arrested and taken from his home in his nightshirt. No word was heard from him for about a week, and he was not informed of any charges.

There was no suspicious background evidence whatsoever against Dr. al-Hazmi. After a night in a holding cell with illegal aliens from Mexico, he spent a second night in solitary confinement in the county jail. The next day, he was flown to New York in a plane that stopped in Minneapolis to pick up the genuine 9/11 suspect, Zacarias Moussaoui. After seven days in custody in Manhattan, he was again transferred, shackled, to a prison in Brooklyn. He finally saw a court-appointed lawyer on his seventh day of confinement in New York. On the tenth day, he met with a lawyer hired by the Saudi consulate.

On his twelfth day of confinement, he was able to explain away a variety of facts that appeared suspicious to the investigators: that al-Hazmi is a common name; that it was common for Saudis to obtain American visas in Jiddah; that the $10,000 he wired from Saudi Arabia to another Saudi doctor in Texas was for him to buy furniture and a car when he moved to America; that recent trips to Boston and Washington were to attend medical courses; that five plane tickets to California that he had purchased on Travelocity for "people with Saudi names" were for him, his wife, and his three children to accompany him to a medical conference; and that two calls that he had received in the last couple of years from a bin Laden were from an Abdullah bin Laden who directed the Northern Virginia office of a world assembly of Muslim youth. An FBI spokesman said that this was not cleared up when the FBI agents first came to Dr. al-Hazmi's home because "as soon as he lawyered up, we couldn't ask him to clear up our questions, and then the system took over and he was off to New York." This is not entirely convincing, for had he been allowed better access to a lawyer on the day he was arrested, he and his family would have been spared a good deal of trauma, and the United States would have not wasted valuable investigation resources on an innocent man.

The post-9/11 "sweeps" were aimed at aliens, who have lesser rights against arrest for immigration purposes. This episode is an example of the kinds of excesses that can occur when a generalized panic sweeps through a community. Unfortunately, even domestic law enforcement today, having nothing to do with terrorism, is not immune from the pressures and panics that can sweep up scores, if not hundreds, of innocent persons into dragnets.[8] And what is worse, while the "sweeps" in the immediate aftermath of the 9/11 attacks can be understood, if not justified, by the immediate reaction to the terror attacks, evidence of terror-related cases dismissed by prosecutors through 2006 seems to indicate that law enforcement officers continue to overreact in many cases.

OVERVIEW OF THE LAW OF PERSONAL DETENTION

Even a routine **arrest**—physically detaining a person—is a drastic event. For some people being arrested, even justifiably, the arrest is psychologically traumatic. For the police officer, a routine detention may quickly escalate into a life-threatening episode, although firearms are not used in 99.8 percent of all arrests. Only 5.1 percent of arrests involve the use or display of weapons of any type. Indeed, in 84 percent of all arrests, police use no tactics at all—the arrestees simply submit.[9] Nevertheless, all seizures of people are, by law, forcible detentions in that they are not consensual.

Arrests and Investigative Stops

A police detention of a person can be *lawful* or *illegal*. Because liberty has priority in American political theory and constitutional law, all detentions by government officers must be justified by legal standards. In the past, the only dividing line between lawful or unlawful detention was whether probable cause existed to make an arrest. In **Henry v. United States** (1959), FBI agents suspected two men of interstate thefts of whiskey based on a vague tip by their employer. The agents watched the men loading a few boxes into a car during the daytime, followed them for a short period, and stopped the car. "The agents searched the car, placed the cartons (which bore the name 'Admiral' and were addressed to an out-of-state company) in their car, took the merchandise and [the men] to their office and held them for about two hours when the agents learned that the cartons contained stolen radios. They then placed the men under formal arrest." The Supreme Court reversed the conviction and ruled that an arrest took place when the car was stopped. At that point, the two men were forcibly detained (although they offered no resistance). The Court ruled that the agents did not have probable cause, making the arrest illegal.

Terry v. Ohio (1968) modified the old rule. There is now a lesser type of detention known as a **stop** or **investigative stop** that is predicated on a lesser standard of evidence, which is typically called "reasonable suspicion." Under the Fourth Amendment, both arrests and stops are "seizures." Seizures are lawful if justified by probable cause or reasonable suspicion, but a detention or seizure is illegal if police act on hunches or arbitrarily.

There is no seizure, however, in consensual encounters, where a person voluntarily agrees to talk to officers or to allow his or her belongings to be searched. As discussed in Chapter 3, no evidentiary standard is necessary for consent searches. The same is true when officers simply observe or follow people in public places. Both scenarios, important to police work, "intrude[] upon no constitutionally protected interest" (*United States v. Mendenhall*, 1980).

The legality of arrests, stops, and consensual encounters explored in this chapter has been developed both in criminal cases that test the admissibility of evidence seized after seizures of people and in civil lawsuits against the police for wrongful arrests seeking money damages. A few distinctions and definitions provide useful guideposts:

- When *arrested*, a person is in the **custody** of the police and loses his or her freedom; the person may be taken to a police station for booking and jailed during the pretrial process; the arrest is executed for the purpose of initiating a criminal prosecution. In contrast, a *stop* confers limited powers allowing an officer to temporarily detain a person; its purpose is to give the officer a short time to question the detainee to determine whether suspicious circumstances are criminal or innocent, and not to initiate a criminal prosecution.

- An arrested person may be thoroughly searched for weapons and for incriminating evidence. A person held briefly under a *Terry* **stop** may be subjected only to a brief pat-down of outer clothing to determine whether he or she is armed.

- If a person is properly stopped based on reasonable suspicion, but the personal search becomes too intrusive or the person is held for too long a time, the officer has overstepped the bounds and has, unlawfully, turned the stop into an arrest. Likewise, a consensual encounter may escalate into an investigative stop or an arrest if the encounter becomes coercive. It then becomes a Fourth Amendment seizure, justified only by the requisite level of evidence.

The Supreme Court can create new legal categories to meet the needs of an ordered society, and it did so in *Terry v. Ohio* (1968) with the investigative stop, which brought police practices within the scope of judicial control. The Court believed that the investigative stop function ("field interrogation" in police lingo) is necessary to police work and, when conducted properly, balances law enforcement needs with individual liberty. The Court has also considered other kinds of detention that only partially fit the arrest and stop categories and has, up to a point, made special rules to deal with them. Two examples are detentions for investigative purposes and detention while executing a search warrant.

Detention to Investigate

Physical personal characteristics—such as fingerprints, a voiceprint (*United States v. Dionisio,* 1973), or a handwriting sample (*United States v. Mara,* 1973)—are not protected by the expectation of privacy. They may be rightfully "obtained" or identified during an investigation when a defendant is lawfully in custody. A person in custody can therefore be required to appear at a lineup and cannot hide his face during a trial. In Fourth Amendment terms, observing a defendant's face is not a seizure.

However, may police detain a person for investigation purposes without probable cause or reasonable suspicion? The Supreme Court twice held that detaining suspects to fingerprint them violated the Fourth Amendment but held open the possibility that a one-time detention for fingerprinting might be lawful in some circumstances. In ***Davis v. Mississippi*** (1969), police rounded up twenty-five African American teenagers to collect fingerprint samples, attempting to match those found at the scene of a crime. These mass arrests, justified only by a witness's statement that the offender was black, were not authorized by a judicial warrant. The detentions did not focus on a specific group of people on whom some suspicion fell and involved a second fingerprinting session and interrogations. This violated the Fourth Amendment. Yet the Court, in dictum, stated that a brief detention for fingerprinting may be reasonable because (1) fingerprinting does not intrude into a person's thoughts or belongings, (2) fingerprints can be obtained briefly during normal business hours and need be taken only once, and (3) fingerprints are an inherently reliable means of identification. In ***Hayes v. Florida*** (1985), a majority of the Court, again in dictum, suggested that fingerprinting at the crime scene might be permissible. In this case, however, the Court found that fingerprinting at the station house was impermissible because the defendant was forcibly taken to the station house without probable cause.

The Court categorically stated that the police have no authority to detain people at will and take them to the police station—without probable cause, reasonable suspicion, or consent—to investigate a crime. In ***Dunaway v. New York*** (1979), an informant told Rochester police that Dunaway was involved in a murder and robbery. Without gaining any more evidence, the detective in charge ordered officers to "pick up" Dunaway and "bring him in" for questioning. At that point, the police did not have sufficient evidence to obtain an arrest warrant. Dunaway was not told that he was under arrest, but he would have been restrained if he had attempted to leave. He made incriminating statements during the interrogation and was later convicted of murder. The Court reversed and refused to extend the *Terry* principle; if police have reasonable suspicion against a person, they can briefly detain and question him where he is found, but they cannot take him into custody. Dunaway was unlawfully arrested without probable cause.

In ***Kaupp v. Texas*** (2003), the Supreme Court said that the evidence in this case "points to arrest even more starkly than the facts in *Dunaway v. New York* (1979)." Although Robert Kaupp, age seventeen, was suspected of involvement in a murder, he passed a polygraph examination, and a magistrate refused to issue an arrest warrant. Detectives nevertheless went to his house at 3 A.M. on a January morning, were let in by his father, and woke him with a flashlight. Told "we need to go and talk," Robert said, "Okay." The Court ruled that this was not consent but "a mere submission to a claim of lawful authority."

Kaupp was then handcuffed. Shoeless and dressed only in boxer shorts and a T-shirt, he was taken to the station house, where he made incriminating statements during an interview after being read *Miranda* warnings. The Supreme Court held that Kaupp was seized and arrested without probable cause. Because the arrest was illegal, the confession was excluded as the "fruits of the poisonous tree" under *Brown v. Illinois*. (See Chapter 2.)

Detention and Search during the Execution of a Search Warrant

In ***Michigan v. Summers*** (1981), Detroit police officers executed a valid search warrant of a house for narcotics. They encountered Summers, the owner, walking down the front steps, asked his assistance in entering the house, and detained him during the search. He was arrested after police discovered narcotics in the basement. A search incident to the arrest revealed an envelope with heroin in Summers's pocket. Although the police did not have probable cause to believe that Summers was carrying drugs before the arrest, the seizure was nevertheless upheld. The Supreme Court concluded that there was reasonable suspicion for the initial stop; the arrest and search were justified by finding drugs in his house.

Summers is general authority for a categorical rule that police may detain home-owners or others present in a place while executing a search warrant. The individual's significant right to liberty is outweighed by law enforcement needs. Giving police routine "command of the situation" reduces the likelihood of harm to the officers and residents that may be caused by sudden violence or frantic efforts to conceal or destroy evidence. Detaining a resident facilitates the orderly completion of the search with minimal damage to property because the owner can open locked doors and cabinets. Detention in the person's own home also avoids the public stigma and inconvenience of being taken to the police station. Further, there is a legitimate law enforcement interest in preventing the flight of a person if incriminating evidence is found. The length of the detention, however, is limited to the time it takes to search the house.

In contrast to the *Summers* rule, which categorically allows police to detain people while executing a warrant, **Muehler v. Mena** (2005) held that police may handcuff a resident detained during a search if it is reasonable to do so. A federal jury found that police violated Iris Mena's Fourth Amendment rights by handcuffing her arms behind her back for two to three hours while conducting a search of her house. The jury awarded her $60,000 in compensatory and punitive damages. Police in Simi Valley, California, investigating a gang-related drive-by shooting, obtained a warrant to search Mena's house because a particular gang member, Romero, rented a room there. The warrant authorized a "broad search" of the house and premises for the gang member, deadly weapons, and evidence of gang membership. Supposedly because of the danger, a SWAT team of eighteen officers executed the search, although a simultaneous search of the home of Romero's mother, who had cooperated with the police in the past, did not use a SWAT team. Romero was found and arrested at his mother's house.

The search of Mena's property was executed at 7 A.M. She was alone in the house. Three others who lived in trailers on her property, along with Mena, were detained in a garage, handcuffed, for three hours. "To get to the garage, Iris, who was still in her bedclothes, was forced to walk barefoot through the pouring rain. . . . Although she requested [the police] to remove the handcuffs, they refused to do so. For the duration of the search, two officers guarded Iris and the other three detainees. A .22 caliber handgun, ammunition, and gang-related paraphernalia were found in Romero's bedroom, and other gang-related paraphernalia was found in the living room. Officers found nothing of significance in Iris' bedroom" (*Muehler v. Mena*, 2005, Stevens, J., concurring).

In light of the dangers involved, the use of force to effectuate this search—in the form of handcuffs—was reasonable. Chief Justice William Rehnquist, for the majority, noted that the use of handcuffs was more intrusive than the detention in the garage, and he wrote that here "the governmental interests outweigh the marginal intrusion" (*Muehler v. Mena*, 2005). Further, the Court held that the length of detention was reasonable. "The duration of a detention can, of course, affect the balance of interests. . . . However, the 2 to 3-hour detention in handcuffs in this case does not outweigh the government's continuing safety interests. . . . [T]his case involved the detention of four detainees by two officers during a search of a gang house for dangerous weapons" (*Muehler v. Mena*, 2005).

Justice Anthony Kennedy concurred "to help ensure that police handcuffing during searches becomes neither routine nor unduly prolonged" (*Muehler v. Mena*, 2005, Kennedy, J., concurring). Justice John Paul Stevens, writing for three other concurring justices, felt that the Court of Appeals made mistakes and that it was proper to remand the case "to consider whether the evidence supports Iris Mena's contention that she was held longer than the search actually lasted" (*Muehler v. Mena*, 2005, Stevens, J., concurring). The case stands for the proposition that handcuffing people present during the execution of a search warrant may be reasonable if the circumstances are fraught with danger. Five justices believed that the handcuffing in this case was objectively reasonable, and four concurring justices seemed to believe that the jury was justified in finding that the extent of the handcuffing was excessive.

Summers did not create a rule that allows police to automatically search anyone present in a premises during the execution of a warrant. In **Ybarra v. Illinois** (1979), police had a valid warrant to search a bar and a bartender for drugs, but not to search the patrons. Police entered the bar and announced to a dozen patrons that they would all be frisked for weapons. Ybarra, a bar patron, was searched. A cigarette pack was retrieved from his pants pocket, and heroin was found inside. The Supreme Court overturned Ybarra's conviction. There was no probable cause to search Ybarra or any of the patrons. Simply because Ybarra was a patron in a bar where drugs were sold was no indication that he participated in purchases. "[A] person's mere propinquity to others independently suspected of criminal activity does not, without more, give rise to probable cause to search that person." The patrons' passive behavior when the raid was announced gave rise to no facts amounting to a reasonable suspicion that they were armed and presently dangerous.

The Supreme Court in **Illinois v. McArthur** (2001) ruled that, where reasonable, police can prevent a householder from entering his or her home while awaiting the arrival of a search warrant. Officers accompanied Tera McArthur to the trailer where she lived with her husband, Charles, to keep the peace while she removed her belongings. The police stayed outside. After Tera removed her belongings, she told the officers that "Chuck had dope in there" and that she had seen Chuck "slide some dope underneath the couch." Charles refused to consent to a search of the trailer. He was then prevented from reentering his home without an officer present for about two hours in the afternoon until one of the officers had obtained a search warrant. A search turned up marijuana, and Charles was charged with misdemeanors. The Illinois courts suppressed the evidence.

The Supreme Court held that the police acted reasonably under the Fourth Amendment. The search and seizure, and the temporary removal of Charles McArthur from his home, were constitutional. There was *probable cause* (the police positively assessed Tera's reliability) and an *exigency* (a good chance that if left alone, Charles would destroy the marijuana). The Court reasoned that the police "made reasonable efforts to reconcile their law enforcement needs with the demands of personal privacy" and "imposed a significantly less restrictive restraint, preventing McArthur only from entering the trailer unaccompanied" rather than searching without a warrant. The restriction on McArthur's freedom to enter his home was for a limited and reasonable period of time. Justice Stevens, dissenting, argued that the balance should be struck in favor of liberty where the offense was a minor one, relying on the rule of *Welsh v. Wisconsin.* (See Chapter 5.) "[S]ome offenses may be so minor as to make it unreasonable for police to undertake searches that would be constitutionally permissible if graver offenses were suspected."

ARREST

Arrest and Police Discretion

Fourth Amendment cases examine arrest from the defendant's perspective to ensure that police act within the law; there is no Fourth Amendment issue if police do not arrest. Police discretion to *not* arrest is widely acknowledged and may be wise in cases involving minor offenses or juveniles. From the victim's perspective, however, is there an enforceable legal right to police protection? These issues arise in civil tort suits against police officers and their agencies by injured parties. The general rule—the **public duty doctrine**—is that a law enforcement officer's "specific duty to preserve the peace is one which the officer owes to the public generally, and not to particular individuals, and that the breach of such duty accordingly creates no liability on the part of the officer to an individual who was damaged by the lawbreaker's conduct."[10] A different rule could open police departments to lawsuits by all assault victims, or at least those who could plausibly argue that the police were in a position to protect them.

The public duty doctrine has been modified in states that have mandated arrest in domestic violence cases. (See the "Law in Society" section in this chapter.) Several state cases held that domestic violence mandatory arrest statutes imposed obligations on police officers to arrest those who violated domestic protection orders. The Supreme Court faced the issue of whether such mandatory state laws created a property right in a victim when police fail to enforce a protection order in *Town of Castle Rock v. Gonzales* (2005). Jessica Gonzales's restraining order against her estranged husband was violated when he picked up their three daughters (ages ten, nine, and seven) about 5:30 one afternoon while they were playing in their yard. Jessica went to the Castle Rock, Colorado, police station or called the police station at 7:30 P.M., 8:30 P.M., 10:10 P.M., 12:10 A.M., and 12:50 A.M., asking the police to look for her husband and children. She informed them of the restraining order and its violation. At 8:30 P.M., she notified the police that her husband had taken the children to an amusement park in Denver. At each contact, the police refused to act and told Jessica to call later. At 3:20 A.M., the husband was killed in a shoot-out at the police station. The three children were found in the car, shot to death by Jessica's husband.

A 1994 Colorado statute was designed to correct the type of inaction that Jessica Gonzales faced. The law stated that a peace officer "*shall* use every reasonable means" to enforce a protection order; when an officer has probable cause that the "restrained person" violated the protection order, the officer "*shall* arrest, or, if an arrest would be impractical under the circumstances, seek an arrest warrant against the restrained person." Despite the statute's mandatory language and the clear intent of the legislature that police officers should not ignore restraining order violations, the Supreme Court held that the police inaction did not violate Gonzales's due process rights under the Fourteenth Amendment.

In past cases, the Supreme Court held that where state law created a "property interest" in tangible and intangible rights, those substantive rights are protected by procedural due process. These state-created property interests included welfare benefits, disability benefits, public education, utility services, and government employment. Arbitrary termination or failure to supply such benefits was held to violate the Due Process Clause. In *Castle Rock,* seven justices held that Colorado did not create a personal entitlement to the enforcement of restraining orders. Justice Antonin Scalia, whose judicial philosophy includes "textualism" as well as an "originalism," authored the opinion:

> The procedural component of the Due Process Clause does not protect everything that might be described as a "benefit": To have a property interest in a benefit, a person clearly must have more than an abstract need or desire and more than a unilateral expectation of it. He must, instead, have a legitimate claim of entitlement to it. (*Castle Rock v. Gonzales,* 2005, internal quotations omitted)

In effect, the majority said that the mandatory language in Colorado's law and on Ms. Gonzales's protection order did not change the common law public duty doctrine. Several reasons were given. First, despite the law's mandatory language, "a well established tradition of police discretion has long coexisted with apparently mandatory arrest statutes." Next, the statute "does not specify the precise means of enforcement" when the restrained person is not present: The statute's command that police seek an arrest warrant if an arrest is impractical was deemed vague, undermining the special duty that overrides the public duty doctrine. An entitlement guaranteed by procedural due process cannot be vague. Enforcement of the protection order was deemed to be an indirect rather than a direct benefit to Jessica Gonzales. Calling a property interest in the enforcement of restraining orders "vague and novel," the Court concluded that its creation cannot simply go without saying.

Justice Stevens, joined by Justice Ruth Bader Ginsburg, dissented. He refuted every argument that the majority put forward regarding the nature of the Colorado protection order. The majority superficially examined general arrest laws with mandatory provisions and did not properly account for the difference between such laws and domestic violence mandatory arrest laws. Colorado has joined other states in responding to a crisis in the underenforcement of domestic violence laws and protection orders. The fact that police had an option to get an arrest warrant when immediate arrest was impractical did not make the law vague. The "crucial point is that, under the statute, the police were *required* to provide enforcement; *they lacked the discretion* to do nothing" (*Castle Rock v. Gonzales,* 2005, Stevens, J., dissenting; emphasis in original). Justice Stevens also argued that the majority undermined proper federalism by not giving due weight to the clear language of the state law and the intent of the state legislature. More important, the majority refused to send the case to the Colorado courts, in a procedure known as "certification," to allow state courts to determine whether the statute created a property interest. This means that no language used by a state legislature can ever create a § 1983 property interest in enforcing protection orders that is federally enforceable without the Supreme Court's approval.

Consequences of Arrest

A person seized by police officers is in their custody. The lawful "purpose of an arrest at common law . . . was 'only to compel an appearance in court'" (*Albright v. Oliver,* 1994, Ginsburg, J., concurring). The judicial process will put the arrested person through various "screens" (initial appearance, preliminary hearing, grand jury) to determine whether to charge the person with a crime and to adjudicate guilt. Because of this goal, there is a belief that a "real" arrest does not occur until *administrative formalities* occur at the police station, including fingerprinting, identification, and a criminal history check. The colorful phrase—**booking** the suspect—indicates the bureaucratic process of filling out forms and entering the arrest in computer files to begin court processing.

Legally, these formalities are not the essence of arrest. Arrest occurs at the moment a police officer significantly interferes with a person's liberty and takes him or her into custody. The lawfulness of an arrest is determined by what happens at the moment of the seizure. Custody means that a suspect loses his or her freedom of movement and most rights of personal privacy. A major consequence of arrest is that the person is subject to a "search incident to arrest" (discussed later in this chapter). The search incident to arrest is a major exception to the Fourth Amendment warrant requirement.

Arrested people have no right to prevent police officers from observing their movements and activities. In **Washington v. Chrisman** (1982), the Court announced a clear rule: "[I]t is not 'unreasonable' for a police officer, as a matter of routine, to monitor the movements of an arrested person, as his judgment dictates, following an arrest. The officer's need to ensure his own safety—as well as the integrity of the arrest—is compelling." In this case, a campus police officer arrested an apparently underage student for possessing a bottle of gin. The officer followed the student into his dormitory room as he retrieved his identification. While standing outside the door, the officer saw what appeared to be marijuana seeds and a pipe lying on a desk. The officer entered the room, confirmed that the seeds were marijuana and determined that the pipe smelled of marijuana. The Court ruled that the officer had a right to follow the arrested student into the room—without a warrant—to maintain secure custody; any motivation the officer had for observing the room in addition to keeping the arrested person under custody was irrelevant. Because the contraband was in plain view and the officer was lawfully in the room, the marijuana was lawfully seized.

The Supreme Court held in **Atwater v. City of Lago Vista** (2001) that an officer can take a person into custody for an offense punishable with only a minor fine. Gail Atwater, an established resident of Lago Vista, Texas, was driving at about 15 miles per hour with her two young children (ages three and five) in the front seat. None were wearing seatbelts. Driving without a seatbelt is a misdemeanor in Texas punishable with a fine of $25 for the first offense and $50 for the second offense. She was pulled over by Officer Bart Turek. The children began to scream; Ms. Atwater asked Officer Turek to lower his voice because he was scaring the children. The officer jabbed his finger in her face and said, "You're going to jail." She asked if her children could be brought to a neighbor's house, but Turek told her that the children would also be brought to the police station. Neighborhood children saw these events, an adult neighbor was called, and Ms. Atwater had her neighbor take her children. "With the children gone, Officer Turek handcuffed Ms. Atwater with her hands behind her back, placed her in the police car, and drove her to the police station. Ironically, Turek did not secure Atwater in a seat belt for the drive." At "the local police station, . . . booking officers had her remove her shoes, jewelry, and eyeglasses, and empty her pockets. Officers took Atwater's 'mug shot' and placed her, alone, in a jail cell for about one hour, after which she was taken before a magistrate and released on $310 bond." She later pleaded no contest to the misdemeanor and paid the $50 fine.

A five-to-four decision by the Supreme Court in a Section 1983 suit against the police held that Atwater's arrest and custody were constitutional. The majority maintained a **bright-line rule**—officers do not have to guess whether an offense is or is not jailable or whether the arrested person is a flight risk. Guessing wrong could subject officers to lawsuits. Justice Sandra Day O'Connor, dissenting, noted that a full-custody arrest imposes severe limitations on liberty. Atwater could have been detained for up to forty-eight hours before seeing a magistrate, could have been jailed with potentially violent offenders, and could have received a permanent arrest record. Justice O'Connor argued that a flat ban on arrests for nonjailable misdemeanors created no problem because an officer who decides that an exception applies and detains the person has immunity from civil liability for making erroneous judgment calls. She concluded that the decision, allowing the detention of nonjailable misdemeanants, violated basic Fourth Amendment principles and that the balance between liberty and security should have been struck in favor of liberty.

There is a distinction between a **mistaken arrest** and an **illegal arrest,** and each has different consequences. An illegal arrest occurs if a person is taken into custody by a government officer without probable cause. Cases of illegal arrests usually occur without any malicious intent on the part of the law enforcement officers. Nevertheless, having violated the Constitution, the arrest is illegal because the probable cause standard for arrest is objective, not subjective. The most important consequence of an illegal arrest is that any evidence seized as a result of the arrest is inadmissible under the exclusionary rule. This gives arrested defendants found with contraband an incentive to challenge the legality of the arrest. An officer can also be held civilly liable for an illegal arrest.

Another way in which an arrest can be illegal is if the arresting officer had no jurisdiction to make the arrest. This occurred in *Frisbie v. Collins* (1952), when police officers from southwest Michigan traveled to Chicago to arrest Collins for a murder rather than seeking extradition or requesting that the arrest be made by an Illinois law enforcement agency. Collins argued that this illegal arrest, possibly a violation of the Federal Kidnapping Act, deprived the trial court of jurisdiction to try him and that his conviction was a nullity. The Supreme Court upheld the common law rule that a court does not lose jurisdiction to try a defendant who is brought to the court by illegal means. Once a court has *in personam* **jurisdiction,** or physical custody over a criminal defendant, it does not inquire into the means by which the person was brought into court. The Supreme Court stood by this rule in a much criticized case, *United States v. Alvarez-Machain* (1992), in which American agents had the defendant abducted in Mexico and transferred to the United States for trial.[11]

A mistaken arrest occurs when an officer makes an arrest with probable cause but it turns out that in fact the wrong person was arrested. The only consequence is that the person arrested must be released if no evidence of criminality is discovered. An innocent person has no civil cause of action against the police because the officer acted in a reasonable manner. However, a search conducted pursuant to the mistaken arrest is valid insofar as it discovered any contraband. The rule reflects the idea that probable cause does not require certainty but only an assessment of facts that would lead a prudent person to believe that the suspect was involved in a crime. In *Hill v. California* (1971), the Supreme Court ruled that police had probable cause to arrest Hill. Two men, using Hill's car, were arrested for narcotics possession. A search of the car produced evidence of a robbery. The two men admitted to the robbery and implicated Hill. The police verified Hill's ownership of the car, his description, and his association with one of the men. Armed with this probable cause, the police went to Hill's motel room to arrest him. They knocked, and the door was opened by Miller, who fit Hill's description. Miller was arrested despite the fact that he produced identification indicating he was Miller. Articles seized in plain view and incident to the search were used to convict Hill of robbery.

Miller's arrest was supported by probable cause; he could not satisfactorily explain why he was in Hill's room, and his personal identification could have been fabricated. This probable cause was based on reasonable facts and circumstances and not on the subjective good faith of the police. As a result, contraband seized during the arrest was admissible. Because it can be difficult to ascertain the true motives of police officers, the distinction between an illegal and a mistaken arrest turns on the objective reasonableness of the officers' behavior, not on subjective motives.

Defining a Fourth Amendment Seizure and Arrest

The Supreme Court has offered two definitions for an arrest: the *Mendenhall* definition and the *Hodari D.* definition.

In *United States v. Mendenhall* (1980), the Court said: "[A] person has been 'seized' within the meaning of the Fourth Amendment only if, in view of all of the circumstances surrounding the incident, a reasonable person would have believed that he was not free to leave." A person, therefore, can be arrested even though not physically held or even touched by an officer. Also, there are no specific words that have to be spoken to effect an arrest: Neither an announcement that a person is under arrest, nor a description of a crime for which a person is arrested, nor a reading of *Miranda* warnings (a popular misconception) is required. Examples of personal seizure offered by the Court in *Mendenhall* include: "the threatening presence of several officers, the display of a weapon by an officer, some physical touching of the person of the citizen, or the use of language or tone of voice indicating that compliance with the officer's request might be compelled."

The *Mendenhall* definition, however, does not encompass every situation. The Court amended the *Mendenhall* definition in *California v. Hodari D.* (1991) to rule that a seizure (and hence an arrest) occurs *only* when an assertion and intent to arrest, on the part of an officer, are followed by submission of the arrested party. The rationale for the *Hodari D.* definition and the issues raised by the case are explored later in this chapter.

A Fourth Amendment seizure can occur in a variety of ways. In *Tennessee v. Garner* (1985), the Court ruled that a person who is shot by the police is arrested: "there can be no question that apprehension by the use of deadly force is a seizure subject to the reasonableness requirement of the Fourth Amendment." A **roadblock** set up intentionally to intercept a driver fleeing from the police becomes the instrument of an arrest if the driver plows into it (*Brower v. Inyo County,* 1989). This is an arrest because there has been an "intentional acquisition of physical control" over the person by the use of the roadblock. "[A] roadblock is not just a significant show of authority to induce a voluntary stop, but is designed to produce a stop by physical impact if voluntary compliance does not occur." Finally, a person, after hearing that a warrant has been issued for his or her arrest and voluntarily surrendering to the police, is seized for purposes of the Fourth Amendment (*Albright v. Oliver,* 1994, Ginsburg, J., concurring).

In each of these cases, there was an intent on the part of the police to gain custody of the suspect and actual custody. If either element is absent, there is no seizure. The intent element was clarified in *County of Sacramento v. Lewis* (1998), a civil lawsuit against an officer whose car hit and killed a motorcycle passenger. The officer was engaged in a high-speed pursuit of a speeding motorcycle. The passenger was thrown from the motorcycle and killed by the oncoming patrol car. To resolve the legal issue, the Court found that the Fourteenth Amendment Due Process Clause applied to the case, and not the more specific

Fourth Amendment. On the basis of *Brower v. Inyo County,* the Court reasoned that a Fourth Amendment seizure does not result every time an officer terminates an individual's freedom of movement, but only where freedom of movement is terminated "through means intentionally applied." The officer's almost instinctive chase of a motorcyclist who sped away after an order to stop displayed no deliberate or reckless indifference to life. The officer's acts therefore did not shock the conscience and did not violate the substantive due process rights of the deceased passenger.

Probable Cause to Arrest

Probable cause to arrest can be determined by a magistrate issuing an arrest warrant. Most arrests, however, are made without warrants, and in such cases the officer must make a probable cause determination.

> Whether that arrest was constitutionally valid depends in turn upon whether, at the moment the arrest was made, the officers had probable cause to make it—whether at that moment the facts and circumstances within their knowledge and of which they had reasonably trustworthy information were sufficient to warrant a prudent man in believing that the petitioner had committed or was committing an offense. (*Beck v. Ohio,* 1964, p. 91)

In *Beck v. Ohio* (1964), police officers in a squad car saw William Beck driving his car and stopped and arrested him without a warrant. One officer testified that he knew what Beck looked like and had heard only general reports that Beck had a criminal record and was involved in gambling. A search of Beck's person at the police station disclosed betting slips in his shoe. The Supreme Court ruled this arrest illegal. At the time the police stopped the car, the officers did not have a level of evidence that would have satisfied a magistrate that Beck was then transporting betting slips. Beck's appearance and prior record were not "inadmissible or entirely irrelevant upon the issue of probable cause. But to hold that knowledge of either or both of these facts constituted probable cause would be to hold that anyone with a previous criminal record could be arrested at will." Thus hearsay can be lawfully used to support probable cause, but it must be more reliable than simple rumors.

Ultimately, a court will review whether probable cause existed to make a warrantless arrest, and courts must be given facts to make the decision; they cannot rely on the officer's good faith:

> We may assume that the officers acted in good faith in arresting the petitioner. But "good faith on the part of the arresting officers is not enough." If subjective good faith alone were the test, the protections of the Fourth Amendment would evaporate, and the people would be "secure in their persons, houses, papers, and effects," only in the discretion of the police. (*Beck v. Ohio,* 1964, p. 97)

Thus the probable cause standard for arrest is objective, not subjective.

In a typical case, probable cause is established by the officer's observation of a crime in progress or by the report of an eyewitness. In *Peters v. New York* (1968), a companion case to *Terry v. Ohio* (1968), a police officer observed two men in his apartment building tiptoeing in the hallway. In the twelve years he had been living there, Officer Lasky had never seen these men. The men were still there when the officer had completed a phone call. When he approached them, they fled. He apprehended Peters, who gave no satisfactory reason for his actions. Lasky searched him and found burglar's tools. The Supreme Court ruled that "[i]t is difficult to conceive of stronger grounds for an arrest, short of actual eyewitness observation of criminal activity." While Lasky did not actually see Peters trying to jimmy a lock, the other evidence supplied probable cause: facts that would lead a prudent person to believe that Peters was engaged in an attempt to break and enter.

In *Chambers v. Maroney* (1970), a light blue compact station wagon carrying four men was stopped by police on a spring evening in North Braddock, Pennsylvania, about one hour after the robbery of a Gulf service station and about two miles from the station. Chambers, one of the men in the car, was wearing a green sweater, and there was a trench coat in the car:

> Two teen-agers, who had earlier noticed a blue compact station wagon circling the block in the vicinity of the Gulf station, then saw the station wagon speed away from a parking lot close to the Gulf station. About the same time, they learned that the Gulf station had been robbed. They reported to police, who arrived immediately, that four men were in the station wagon and one was wearing a green sweater. [The station attendant] told the police that one of the men who robbed him was wearing a green sweater and the other was wearing a trench coat. A description of the car and the two robbers was broadcast over the police radio.

This is a typical example of police obtaining probable cause from a reliable (and nonsecret) informant. Although hearsay, it is fully reliable. Of course, such information should never be taken for absolute proof of a crime. In rare cases, the initial information may be given as a misguided prank or out of malice. In many cases, facts are garbled and eyewitness identification of key facts may be wrong, especially about the identity of an offender. (See Chapter 8.)

Probable cause must focus on a specific individual. In *Johnson v. United States* (1948), an officer standing outside an apartment smelled burning opium in the hallway but was not sure who occupied the apartment. The officer knocked and announced his presence. Anne Johnson opened the door, and the officer told her, "Consider yourself under arrest." The Supreme Court held that the entry into the home without a warrant was a Fourth Amendment violation. Further, the arrest itself was illegal because "the arresting officer did not have probable cause to arrest [Johnson] until he had entered her room and found her to be the sole occupant."

Another common problem confronting police is whether probable cause exists to arrest a person who is in close proximity to another person who is lawfully arrested. Mere proximity to a person committing a crime does not create probable cause. For example, in *United States v. Di Re* (1948), an informer, Reed, told investigators that he was going to buy counterfeit ration coupons from one "Buttitta at a named place in the City of Buffalo, New York." Agents followed a car driven by Buttitta. Michael Di Re was the front seat passenger, and Reed sat in the back. Di Re was not known to the agents. The car was stopped, and Buttitta and Di Re were arrested. Di Re was searched at the station house after the arrest, and counterfeit ration coupons were found in an envelope concealed between his shirt and underwear. The Supreme Court ruled that this evidence was seized illegally because the agents did not have probable cause to believe that Di Re was involved in the crime, invalidating the arrest. Reed had not named Di Re as a suspect. The police suspicion against Buttitta was based on the word of their informant, Reed. "But the officer had no such information as to Di Re. All they had was his presence, and if his presence was not enough to make a case for arrest for a misdemeanor, it is hard to see how it was enough for the felony" of possessing illegal coupons with knowledge that they were counterfeit. The Court also dismissed the argument that there was a conspiracy simply because Di Re was in the car.

In contrast to *Di Re* is *Ker v. California* (1963). (See Chapter 3.) By their own observations and the word of an informer, police had probable cause to believe that George Ker was dealing marijuana from his house. The Court held that the police entered lawfully without a warrant. After entering, an agent saw George Ker sitting in the living room and Diane Ker emerging from the kitchen. The officer observed "through the open doorway a small scale atop the kitchen sink, upon which lay a "brick-like—brick-shaped package containing the green leafy substance which he recognized as marijuana." The Court conceded that the police did not have probable cause to arrest Diane Ker when they entered the apartment. But it ruled that viewing the marijuana in plain view established probable cause to believe that she was involved in the illicit business with her husband. This was not simply guilt by association, but a rational inference. In *Di Re,* the police could not infer, to the level of probable cause, that Di Re possessed counterfeit ration coupons. But Diane Ker had to know that there was marijuana in the kitchen, which she had just left, and given the probable cause that police had that George Ker was illegally dealing, it was a rational inference that she was "in joint possession with her husband." This amounted to probable cause to believe that she was "committing the offense of possession of marijuana in the presence of the officers."

In *Maryland v. Pringle* (2003), police officers stopped a car at 3:16 A.M. for speeding. Partlow was driving, Pringle sat in the front seat, and Smith was in the backseat. When Partlow opened the glove compartment to retrieve the vehicle registration, the officer observed a large roll of cash. A consent search of the vehicle uncovered five plastic glassine baggies containing cocaine behind the upright rear seat armrest. None of the three men admitted to owning the drugs, and all three were arrested. Pringle later confessed to owning the drugs. The issue in the case was whether finding drugs in the rear seat gave police probable cause to arrest Pringle. This is not a case of guilt by association. Unlike the tavern patrons in *Ybarra v. Illinois* (1979), Pringle was in a small car with two men he knew, and car passengers are often involved in a "common enterprise with the driver." Unlike *United States v. Di Re* (1948), this was not a case where the police had previous probable cause to suspect only the driver. The Supreme Court held that under the facts of the case, there was probable cause to arrest Pringle. It was objectively reasonable for the officer on the scene to believe "that any or all three of the occupants had knowledge of, and exercised dominion and control over, the cocaine. Thus a reasonable officer could conclude that there was probable cause to believe Pringle committed the crime of possession of cocaine, either solely or jointly" (*Maryland v. Pringle,* 2003).

Judicial Determination of Probable Cause.

If police arrest without a warrant, their probable cause determination must be reviewed by a judge or magistrate as soon as possible. A Florida law allowed a person to be arrested on a prosecutor's bill of information and held for a month before being brought before a magistrate. This law was struck down as a Fourth Amendment violation in *Gerstein v. Pugh* (1975):

> [A] policeman's on-the-scene assessment of probable cause provides legal justification for arresting a person suspected of crime, and for a brief period of detention to take the administrative steps incident to arrest. Once the suspect is in custody, however, the reasons that justify dispensing with the magistrate's neutral judgment evaporate. There no longer is any danger that the suspect will escape or commit further crimes while the police submit their evidence to a magistrate. And, while the State's reasons for taking summary action subside, the suspect's need for a neutral determination of probable cause increases significantly. The consequences of prolonged detention may be more serious than the interference occasioned by arrest. Pretrial confinement may imperil the suspect's job, interrupt his source of income, and impair his family relationships. Even pretrial release may be accompanied by burdensome conditions that effect a significant restraint on liberty. When the stakes are this high, the detached judgment of a neutral magistrate is essential if the Fourth Amendment is to furnish meaningful protection from unfounded interference with liberty. Accordingly, we hold that the Fourth Amendment requires a judicial determination of probable cause as a prerequisite to extended restraint on liberty following arrest. (*Gerstein v. Pugh,* 1975)

The law in every state and for the federal government, based on common law practice, has long required police to bring arrested persons promptly before a magistrate for initial processing. The Florida rule was quite unusual. The Court in *Gerstein* did not define what constituted a prompt arraignment.

The Supreme Court clarified the time period for which a person can be held after arrest before being brought before a magistrate in *County of Riverside v. McLaughlin* (1991). The majority, in an opinion by Justice O'Connor, ruled that a jurisdiction must bring an arrested person before a magistrate for a probable cause hearing as soon as is reasonably feasible, but in no event later than forty-eight hours after arrest. Where an arrested person does not receive a probable cause determination within forty-eight hours, the burden of proof shifts to the government to demonstrate the existence of a bona fide emergency or other extraordinary circumstance, which cannot include intervening weekends. Under the county's rule, which excluded weekends, a "person arrested on Thursday may have to wait until the following Monday before they receive a probable cause determination" or up to seven days over a Thanksgiving holiday. The Court also suggested that holding off bringing a person before a magistrate in order to gather additional evidence was not a bona fide emergency.

There were two dissents—by liberal and by conservative/originalist justices. The liberal position (per Justice Thurgood Marshall) was that the proper constitutional rule is that a person must be brought before a magistrate immediately upon completion of the administrative steps incident to arrest. Justice Scalia opted for a twenty-four-hour time period based on his "originalist" research, which found that such a time period was common in the late eighteenth and early nineteenth centuries. In the past, lengthy postarrest detention without recourse to a magistrate was used to force confessions out of suspects. Such a practice tempts police to abuse their control over a suspect. The rules of *Gerstein* and *Riverside County* rightfully make constitutional what is now standard practice.

Use of Secondary Information.

A police officer may depend on a reliable informant to establish probable cause to arrest. An informant could be an impartial witness, a victim, or an "undercover" informant who works for the police or receives lenient treatment in return for information about crimes such as drug sales (*Draper v. United States*, 1959; *McCray v. Illinois*, 1967).

In this era of high mobility and instantaneous communications, police often rely on the radio bulletins or computer notifications from other police departments as a basis for probable cause to arrest. In **Whiteley v. Warden** (1971), the Court ruled that police may rely on a radio bulletin from another police department informing them that an arrest warrant was issued. In *Whiteley*, the original arrest warrant was defective; the magistrate erred in finding probable cause. As a result, the arrest was illegal, and the evidence seized in a search incident to the arrest was not admissible. The clear implication of *Whiteley*, however, was that the officers who made the arrest reasonably relied on the radio bulletin and should not be held civilly liable for the arrest. They acted reasonably even if there was no probable cause for the original arrest warrant.

In **Arizona v. Evans** (1995) (see Chapter 2), Evans was stopped for driving the wrong way on a one-way street. The police computer indicated, erroneously, that Evans had an outstanding warrant. He was arrested on that basis. Because the error was based on mistakes in the court clerk's office, the Supreme Court refused to suppress a marijuana cigarette discovered in the search, on the grounds that the exclusionary rule applied only to police errors. The merits of *Arizona v. Evans* (1995) aside, the case points to the need for accuracy in police records to prevent unconstitutional searches. Justice O'Connor, concurring, expressed some concerns that widespread computer errors might undermine individual rights.

The Felony/Misdemeanor Rule.

The traditional common law rules for felony and misdemeanor arrests by law enforcement officers differ. A police officer may arrest a person for a felony when he or she has probable cause to believe that a crime has been committed and that the arrestee is the perpetrator.[12] For a misdemeanor arrest to be lawful, however, the misdemeanor must have been committed in the officer's presence. The reason for this distinction is that the public safety requires swift arrests for more serious crimes. Because petty crimes are often the result of squabbles between individuals, an arrest based on a complainant's say-so may result in instances of false arrest and legally sanctioned harassment. The victim of a misdemeanor had to obtain an arrest warrant from a judge via a formal complaint in order to initiate the criminal process. In recent years, the

in-presence rule has come under severe criticism because it has prevented police from making arrests in cases of domestic violence. State legislatures have rethought the rule, and virtually all have modified it to allow or require an officer to arrest in cases of domestic violence. (See the "Law in Society" section in this chapter.) Statutes have also modified the misdemeanor arrest rule for traffic-related misdemeanors not observed directly by a police officer.[13]

Citizen's Arrests.

Private individuals have the right to arrest a felon. However, the personal consequences for a sworn law enforcement officer and a private person making a mistaken arrest differ. A police officer who makes a mistaken arrest (e.g., arrests the wrong person) that is based on probable cause cannot be held civilly liable for the tort of false arrest because the officer acted reasonably. A private person who effects a **citizen's arrest** is held strictly accountable to the arrested person for any errors made during the arrest. No matter how reasonable the citizen's arrest, if a mistake was made, the person making the arrest may be successfully sued for the tort of **false arrest.** The rule places a high premium on individual liberty to be free from unwarranted interference. The relaxation of the common law rule of strict liability for law enforcement officers is evidence of a policy that encourages officers to be less fearful of the consequences of their acts so that they will not shirk their duty. This recognizes the difficulties that confront law enforcement officers when hard decisions must be made with little time for reflection and under circumstances of heightened stress.

This common law rule has great effect on security guards; they cannot arrest a person for theft, for example, without the threat of liability unless they are actually correct. "Unless the owner has given consent, a security guard's search of private property will generally constitute a trespass. And arrests or detentions not authorized by state law generally will expose a security guard to civil and criminal liability for false imprisonment and, if force is involved, for assault."[14] On the other hand, "most states have codified a **'merchant's privilege'** that allows store investigators, and in some instances other categories of private security personnel, to conduct brief investigatory detentions that would be tortious or criminal if carried out by ordinary citizens."[15]

The Use of Force

"The criminal justice process rests basically on force, the authority of the state to use raw power, properly and appropriately applied, to apprehend, detain, try, and imprison. The basis of force pervades and colors the whole criminal justice system."[16] The system's force may be mute, as in prison walls or symbolized by the judge's robe and the patrol officer's uniform, or it may be mostly held in reserve; but when consent and compliance fail, the system, and especially the police, are required to use physical power to carry out its functions. The use of force is problematic because liberty is primary in the American constitutional scheme, but it is justified by the goal of enforcing public law.

The application of force, however, must be appropriate and lawful. The common law of arrest provides a simple, but ambiguous, rule: The force used to effect an arrest must be reasonable; it must not be excessive. What is **reasonable force**? Few guidelines exist. One guideline is that the force must be commensurate with the resistance offered by a person whom the police try to arrest. If a person resists with nonlethal force, then the police may use nonlethal force to subdue him. If a person resists with deadly force, then the police can reply in kind.

The "Fleeing Felon" Rule.

Under the common law, a police officer could use deadly force to subdue and arrest a "fleeing felon" even though the felon had not used deadly force. Presumably because most common law felonies were punishable by death, their seriousness tended to increase the likelihood that felons were dangerous to the life of others. The "fleeing felon" rule served as a substitute for the executioner! In America, the **"fleeing felon" rule** had been controversial and seriously criticized in the decades since 1960, as the use of the death penalty decreased and many felonies were no longer dangerous to life. By 1980, most states had modified the "fleeing felon" rule by statute, and many police departments altered their policies so that deadly force could be used only when a suspect presented clear evidence of violent intentions. These states felt that a blanket rule allowing police to shoot at any fleeing felon was excessive.

The issue came before the Supreme Court, giving it a rare opportunity to discuss the police use of force from a constitutional perspective, in *Tennessee v. Garner* (1985). The Court modified the "fleeing felon" rule as a matter of Fourth Amendment law and held, in an opinion by Justice Byron White, that

> [t]he use of deadly force to prevent the escape of all felony suspects, whatever the circumstances, is constitutionally unreasonable. It is not better that all felony suspects die than that they escape. Where the suspect poses no immediate threat to the officer and no threat to others, the harm resulting from failing to apprehend him does not justify the use of deadly force to do so. (*Tennessee v. Garner,* 1985)

The "fleeing felon" rule violated the Fourth Amendment rather than the Due Process Clause of the Fourteenth Amendment. *Garner* created a flat rule: A statute that allows police to shoot to kill *any* fleeing felon is void. A due process rule would have subjected the issue to painstaking case-by-case analysis. Deadly force against a fleeing felon is still allowed where reasonable: "Where the officer has probable cause to believe that the suspect poses a threat of serious physical harm, either to the officer or to others, it is not constitutionally unreasonable to prevent escape by using deadly force." Thus the Court in *Garner* upheld the common law framework: The legality of the use of force by police is based on what was reasonable under all the facts and circumstances of a case; all the Court did was to announce that as a matter of the Constitution, a flat use-of-deadly-force rule in all fleeing felon circumstances was unreasonable.

Justice O'Connor dissented, joined by Chief Justice Warren Burger and Justice Rehnquist. A teenager of average height was shot and killed by a police officer while trying to get over a fence after running from a nonviolent house burglary. "[T]he officer fired at the upper part of the body, using a 38-calibre pistol loaded with hollow point bullets, as he was trained to do by his superiors at the Memphis Police Department. He shot because he believed the boy would elude capture in the dark once he was over the fence. The officer was taught that it was proper under Tennessee law to kill a fleeing felon rather than run the risk of allowing him to escape."[17] The youth died of the gunshot wound. On his person was ten dollars and jewelry he had taken from the house. Justice O'Connor pointed out that no matter how regrettable were the consequences of this case, it was not unreasonable for an officer to shoot at a fleeing burglar at night since it was not known whether the burglar was armed or what had happened in the burglarized house. "With respect to a particular burglary, subsequent investigation simply cannot represent a substitute for immediate apprehension of the criminal suspect at the scene." The dissent is more willing to grant unreviewed discretion to the police than the majority.

The "real-world" effects of legal rules are often unknown. *Tennessee v. Garner,* however, has had a positive effect, stimulating police departments to modify policies and practices that have had lifesaving effects, not only for suspects but also for police. Jerome Skolnick and the late James Fyfe, leading police scholars, write:

> When police have started their attempts to develop policy with the principle that good policing in any situation consists of the actions that best meet the primary police responsibility to protect life, the results have been remarkably successful. Deadly force policies that, in both philosophy and substance, emphasize the sanctity of life over the need to apprehend suspects have reduced killings by police—and the backlash that often follows—without negative effects on the safety of citizens or the safety and effectiveness of officers.[18]

Section 1983 cases dealing with excessive use of force by police offer some guidance on the legal meaning of excessive force. In ***Graham v. Connor*** (1989), Officer Connor stopped Dethorne Graham a half mile from a crowded convenience store in Charlotte, North Carolina, after seeing him hastily enter and then leave. Connor did not know that Graham, a diabetic, was driven to the store by a friend so he could buy orange juice to counteract an insulin reaction. Graham left the store because of a long line to go to a friend's house to get sugar. When stopped, Graham told Connor about the insulin reaction. Connor told him to wait until he returned to the store to discover what happened and to call for backup forces. Graham was handcuffed, his pleas for sugar were ignored by one officer who said, "I've seen a lot of people with sugar diabetes that never acted like this. Ain't nothing wrong with the M. F. but drunk. Lock the S. B. up." Graham passed out twice. He asked an officer to look into his wallet for a diabetic decal and was told to "shut up." A friend brought some orange juice to the patrol car for Graham, but the officers refused to let him have it. After discovering that nothing criminal occurred at the convenience store, the police drove Graham home and released him. Graham sustained a broken foot, cuts on the wrist, a bruised forehead, and an injured shoulder. The lower federal courts held that Officer Connor did not violate Graham's rights.

Did the police violate Graham's Fourth Amendment rights? Did they act reasonably? The Supreme Court ruled that a case in which an officer seizes a person, as occurred here, must be decided under the Fourth Amendment rather than the more general rules of substantive due process under the Fourteenth Amendment. Therefore the question of whether excessive force was used is to be decided by objective factors—the officer's motive is irrelevant. "An officer's evil intentions will not make a Fourth Amendment violation out of an objectively reasonable use of force; nor will an officer's good intentions make an objectively unreasonable use of force constitutional" (*Graham v. Connor,* 1989, p. 397). Next, the

> reasonableness of a particular use of force must be judged from the perspective of a *reasonable officer on the scene,* rather than with the 20/20 vision of hindsight. . . . The calculus of reasonableness must embody allowance for the fact that police officers are often forced to make split-second judgments—in circumstances that are tense, uncertain, and rapidly evolving—about the amount of force that is necessary in a particular situation. (*Graham v. Connor,* 1989, emphasis added)

Under the more open-ended substantive due process analysis that most courts had used prior to *Graham,* looking at the amount of force used under the circumstances, the extent of injuries, and the motive of the officer, plaintiffs may have had greater leeway to prevail in Section 1983 action. Nevertheless, the Court's decision was unanimous. The case was remanded for reconsideration by lower courts.

Brower v. Inyo County (1989) established that a roadblock can be an instrument of force that effects an arrest. Brower stole a car and eluded the police in a high-speed twenty-mile chase. A police roadblock was set up consisting of an unilluminated eighteen-wheel tractor-trailer blocking both lanes of a road behind a curve, with a police car's headlights pointing at the oncoming traffic. Brower was killed when his car hit the roadblock. This constituted an arrest. The remaining question is whether excessive force was used. The Supreme Court, indicating that this was a factual issue depending on the circumstances of the roadblock, remanded the case for further proceedings.

THE ARREST WARRANT REQUIREMENT

The need to obtain an **arrest warrant,** and the form the warrant takes, is determined by the circumstances and settings under which the suspect is to be taken into custody. This section reviews the law that pertains to arresting suspects (1) in public, (2) in their own homes, and (3) in the homes of third parties. It also reviews the question of detaining and searching people while executing a search warrant.

Arrest in Public

United States v. Watson (1976) upheld the authority of the police to arrest felons in public places without a warrant.

> Read Case and Comments: *United States v. Watson.*

Watson left several questions unresolved, the most important of which was whether an arrest warrant is necessary to enter a home in order to make an arrest. This question was answered four years later in *Payton v. New York* (1980).

Arrest in the Home

Payton v. New York (1980) held that, absent an exigency, police are required to have an arrest warrant to enter a person's home to make an arrest. In this case, police had probable cause to believe that Payton had committed a murder and robbery. Around 7:30 A.M., six officers went to Payton's apartment without an arrest warrant, intending to arrest him. Lights were on and music was heard in the apartment, but there was no response to their knock on the metal door. About thirty minutes later, the police used crowbars to break open the door and enter the apartment. No one was there, but a .30-caliber shell casing in plain view was seized and admitted into evidence at Payton's murder trial. Payton moved to suppress the shell casing as the product of an illegal arrest.

The majority (per Justice Stevens) held that entering the home to make a routine felony arrest without a warrant violated the Fourth Amendment. The government argued that the Fourth Amendment was designed only to prevent "general warrants" and not to require warrants when the police had probable cause to arrest. The Court replied, "[T]he evil the Amendment was designed to prevent was broader than the abuse of a general warrant. Unreasonable searches or seizures conducted without any warrant at all are condemned by the plain language of the first clause of the Amendment."

Was this ruling consistent with *Watson,* which overlooked the literal words of the Fourth Amendment? The Court did not disturb the *Watson* rule but instead distinguished arrests made in the home from arrests made in public places: "[H]owever, . . . [a] greater burden is placed . . . on officials who enter a home or dwelling without consent. Freedom from intrusion into the home or dwelling is the archetype of the privacy protection secured by the Fourth Amendment." The "right of a man to retreat into his own home and there be free from unreasonable governmental intrusion" stands at the very core of the Fourth Amendment. *Payton* is one of several post-*Katz* cases that place a special emphasis on the privacy of the home rather than treating all "expectations of privacy" the same. The majority supported its position with common law history and trends among the states: A "long-standing, widespread practice is not immune from constitutional scrutiny. But neither is it to be lightly brushed aside." As for the concern by law enforcement that the rule would undermine public safety, the Court made it clear that the police may enter a home without a warrant when there is an exigency.

Justice White dissented, joined by Chief Justice Burger and Justice Rehnquist, giving four reasons to uphold the rule that had allowed police to enter a house without a warrant to make an arrest: (1) The rule was limited to felonies and did not apply to misdemeanors, (2) the privacy of the resident was protected by the "knock and announce" rule, (3) the arrest had to be made in the daytime, and (4) such arrest was lawful only if supported by "stringent probable cause." These are rather weak arguments since the dissent restates conditions that would exist in any event. If pushed to the extreme, such arguments could totally eliminate the requirement for arrest warrants for home arrests, just as *Watson* had, in effect, destroyed any constitutional underpinning for arrest warrants in public places.

The difference between the *Watson* and *Payton* decisions is, at one level, explained by the factual difference between an arrest in public and an arrest in one's home. Yet there is enough similarity in these cases to illustrate how "middle-of-the-road" or "swing" justices influence Supreme Court decision making. In these cases, two consistently liberal justices, William Brennan and Thurgood Marshall, voted for a warrant in both *Watson* and

CASE AND COMMENTS

United States v. Watson

423 U.S. 411, 96 S.Ct. 820, 46 L.Ed.2d 598 (1976)

MR. JUSTICE WHITE delivered the opinion of the Court.

This case presents questions under the Fourth Amendment as to the legality of a warrantless arrest. * * *

I

[A reliable informant, Khoury, informed postal inspectors that Watson would furnish stolen credit cards. Acting under their instructions, Khoury arranged a meeting with Watson five days later in a restaurant.] Khoury had been instructed that if Watson had additional stolen credit cards, Khoury was to give a designated signal. The signal was given, the officers closed in, and Watson was forthwith arrested. [No stolen credit cards were found on Watson, but some were found in his automobile. The court of appeals ruled that the arrest was a violation of the Fourth Amendment because there was no arrest warrant and no exigency; consequently, evidence obtained from the search of Watson's automobile and seizure of the credit cards had to be excluded as the fruits of an illegal arrest.]

II

* * *

Contrary to the Court of Appeals' view, Watson's arrest was not invalid because executed without a warrant. **[a]** Title 18 U.S.C. sec. 3061(a)(3) expressly empowers the * * * Postal Service to authorize Postal Service officers and employees "performing duties related to the inspection of postal matters" to

> "make arrests without warrant for felonies * * * if they have reasonable grounds to believe that the person to be arrested has committed or is committing such a felony."

* * * Because there was probable cause in this case to believe that Watson had violated [the law], the inspector and his subordinates, in arresting Watson, were acting strictly in accordance with the governing statute and regulations. **[b]** The effect of the judgment of the Court of Appeals was to invalidate the statute as applied in this case and as applied to all the situations where a court fails to find exigent circumstances justifying a warrantless arrest. We reverse that judgment.

Under the Fourth Amendment, the people are to be "secure in their persons, houses, papers, and effects, against unreasonable searches and seizures, * * * and no Warrants shall issue, but upon probable cause. * * * " **[c]** Section 3061 represents a judgment by Congress that it is not unreasonable under the Fourth Amendment for postal inspectors to arrest without a warrant provided they have probable cause to do so. This was not an isolated or quixotic judgment of the legislative branch. Other federal law enforcement officers have been expressly authorized by statute for many years to make felony arrests on probable cause but without a warrant. * * * **[d]**

* * * [T]here is nothing in the Court's prior cases indicating that under the Fourth Amendment a warrant is required to make a valid arrest for a felony. Indeed, the relevant prior decisions are uniformly to the contrary.

"The usual rule is that a police officer may arrest without warrant one believed by the officer upon reasonable cause to have been guilty of a felony. . . ." * * * **[e]** Just last Term, while recognizing that maximum protection of individual rights could be assured by

[a] The Court states its decision at the outset. What follows are the reasons for this decision. The court of appeals invalidated the statute under its reading of the Fourth Amendment. Does the statute's authorization of warrantless arrests end the constitutional reasoning process?

[b] Would *you* nevertheless require the police to get a judicial arrest warrant in investigations where they have plenty of time to get one?

[c] Does the judgment of Congress violate the Fourth Amendment's plain words?

[d] *Entick v. Carrington* (1765) said that an illegal practice does not become legal simply because it has been practiced for a long time. Does this point weaken Justice White's argument?

[e] Is the need for law enforcement efficiency a constitutional reason? Could this reasoning lead to the total elimination of arrest warrants?

requiring a magistrate's review of the factual justification prior to any arrest, we stated that "such a requirement would constitute an intolerable handicap for legitimate law enforcement" and noted that the Court "has never invalidated an arrest supported by probable cause solely because the officers failed to secure a warrant." *Gerstein v. Pugh.* * * *

The cases construing the Fourth Amendment thus reflect the ancient common-law rule that a peace officer was permitted to arrest without a warrant for a misdemeanor or felony committed in his presence as well as for a felony not committed in his presence if there was reasonable ground for making the arrest. * * * This has also been the prevailing rule under state constitutions and statutes. * * * **[f]**

The balance struck by the common law in generally authorizing felony arrests on probable cause, but without a warrant, has survived substantially intact. It appears in almost all of the States in the form of express statutory authorization. * * * [The American Law Institute's *Model Code of Pre-arraignment Procedure* in 1975 adopted] "the traditional and almost universal standard for arrest without a warrant."

* * * Congress has plainly decided against conditioning warrantless arrest power on proof of exigent circumstances. Law enforcement officers may find it wise to seek arrest warrants where practicable to do so, and their judgments about probable cause may be more readily accepted where backed by a warrant issued by a magistrate. * * * **[g]** But we decline to transform this judicial preference into a constitutional rule when the judgment of the Nation and Congress has for so long been to authorize warrantless public arrests on probable cause rather than to encumber criminal prosecutions with endless litigation with respect to the existence of exigent circumstances, whether it was practicable to get a warrant, whether the suspect was about to flee, and the like.

Watson's arrest did not violate the Fourth Amendment, and the Court of Appeals erred in holding to the contrary.

* * *

MR. JUSTICE POWELL, concurring.

* * * Today's decision is the first square holding that the Fourth Amendment permits a duly authorized law enforcement officer to make a warrantless arrest in a public place even though he had adequate opportunity to procure a warrant after developing probable cause for arrest. **[h]**

On its face, our decision today creates a certain anomaly. There is no more basic constitutional rule in the Fourth Amendment area than that which makes a warrantless search unreasonable except in a few "jealously and carefully drawn" exceptional circumstances. * * * On more than one occasion this Court has rejected an argument that a law enforcement officer's own probable cause to search a private place for contraband or evidence of crime should excuse his otherwise unexplained failure to procure a warrant beforehand. * * * **[i]**

Since the Fourth Amendment speaks equally to both searches and seizures, and since an arrest, the taking hold of one's person, is quintessentially a seizure, it would seem that the constitutional provision should impose the same limitations upon arrests that it does upon searches. Indeed, as an abstract matter an argument can be made that the restrictions upon arrest perhaps should be greater. **[j]** A search may cause only annoyance and temporary inconvenience to the law-abiding citizen, assuming more serious dimension only when it turns up evidence of criminality. An arrest, however, is a serious personal intrusion regardless of whether the person seized is guilty or innocent. Although an arrestee cannot be held for a significant period without some neutral determination that there are grounds to do so, * * * no decision that he should go free can come quickly enough to erase the invasion of his privacy that already will have occurred. * * * Logic therefore would seem to dictate that arrests be subject to the warrant requirement at least to the same extent as searches.

[f] This assumes that the Fourth Amendment absorbed common law practice. Another perspective is that the amendment changed common law practices to expand the protection of individual liberty.

[g] If this makes arrest warrants totally discretionary, of what use is the Fourth Amendment?

[h] It is interesting that a practice could exist for centuries before being challenged legally. There was greater acceptance of the legal status quo in the past.

[i] Justice Powell politely says that the majority opinion has skirted the main question.

[j] Does this argument undermine the Court's decision? How can the Court avoid the "logic" of the Fourth Amendment?

(continued)

[k] Is this too easy an out? Does this mean that the Court need not follow the Constitution just because it has not been followed for a long time?

But logic sometimes must defer to history and experience. **[k]** [Justice Powell then goes on to argue that historical practice shows that the Fourth Amendment was not intended to require arrest warrants and that to adopt such a rule would severely hamper law enforcement.]

* * *

MR. JUSTICE MARSHALL, with whom MR. JUSTICE BRENNAN joins, dissenting.

* * *

There is no doubt that by the reference to the seizure of persons, the Fourth Amendment was intended to apply to arrests. * * *

The Court next turns to history. It relies on the English common-law rule of arrest and the many state and federal statutes following it. There are two serious flaws in this approach. First, as a matter of factual analysis, the substance of the ancient common-law rule provides no support for the far-reaching modern rule that the Court fashions on its model. Second, as a matter of doctrine, the longstanding existence of a Government practice does not immunize the practice from scrutiny under the mandate of our Constitution.

The common-law rule was indeed as the Court states it. * * * To apply the rule blindly today, however, makes [little] sense * * * without understanding the meaning of * * * words in the context of their age. For the fact is that a felony at common law and a felony today bear only slight resemblance, with the result that the relevance of the common-law rule of arrest to the modern interpretation of our Constitution is minimal.

* * * Only the most serious crimes were felonies at common law, and many crimes now classified as felonies under federal or state law were treated as misdemeanors. * * * **[l]**

[l] Does Justice Marshall's analysis (requiring arrest warrants for non-life-threatening crimes) make more sense than the majority's? Would such a rule undermine effective law enforcement?

* * * To make an arrest for any of these crimes [misdemeanors] at common law, the police officer was required to obtain a warrant, unless the crime was committed in his presence. Since many of these same crimes are commonly classified as felonies today, however, under the Court's holding a warrant is no longer needed to make such arrests, a result in contravention of the common law.

Thus the lesson of the common law, and those courts in this country that have accepted its rule, is an ambiguous one. Applied in its original context, the common-law rule would allow the warrantless arrest of some, but not all, of those we call felons today. Accordingly, the Court is simply historically wrong when it tells us that "[t]he balance struck by the common law in generally authorizing felony arrests on probable cause, but without a warrant, has survived substantially intact." As a matter of substance, the balance struck by the common law in accommodating the public need for the most certain and immediate arrest of criminal suspects with the requirement of magisterial oversight to protect against mistaken insults to privacy decreed that only in the most serious of cases could the warrant be dispensed with. This balance is not recognized when the common-law rule is unthinkingly transposed to our present classifications of criminal offenses. Indeed, the only clear lesson of history is contrary to the one the Court draws: the common law considered the arrest warrant far more important than today's decision leaves it.

[m] Does Justice Marshall's analysis better comport with the "originalist" idea of adhering to the "intent of the Framers"?

* * * [T]he Court's unblinking literalism cannot replace analysis of the constitutional interests involved. **[m]** While we can learn from the common law, the ancient rule does not provide a simple answer directly transferable to our system. Thus, in considering the applicability of the common-law rule to our present constitutional scheme, we must consider *both* of the rule's two opposing constructs: the presumption favoring warrants, as well as the exception allowing immediate arrests of the most dangerous criminals. The Court's failure to do so, indeed its failure to recognize any tension in the common-law rule at all, drains all validity from its historical analysis.

* * *

Payton. Similarly, three more conservative justices—Byron White, William Rehnquist, and Warren Burger—voted against the warrant in both cases. The different outcomes in the two cases may be explained by the thinking of the three swing justices—Potter Stewart, Harry Blackmun, and Lewis Powell—who voted against a warrant in *Watson* (1976) but in favor of a warrant in *Payton* (1980). The swing justices were joined by Justice John Paul Stevens, who was appointed to the Court between the two cases. Thus the facts alone did not explain the different holding in *Watson* and *Payton.* Rather, the attitudes of the justices who evaluated those facts were decisive. The pre-existing leanings in favor of or against law enforcement of the "conservative" and "liberal" justices made their votes unresponsive to the differing facts of *Watson* and *Payton.* The justices with less ideological leanings concerning this issue were able to evaluate the cases differently. This "political" evaluation of the Supreme Court does not explain every case, but it does show that justices' personalities, temperaments, life experiences, and belief systems come into play in fashioning the rules and doctrines of constitutional law.

Exigent Circumstances.   *Payton* held that police may enter the suspect's home to make an arrest without a warrant when exigent circumstances exist. The Supreme Court has been highly protective of the expectation of privacy in one's home and has narrowly viewed police claims that they have entered under an "exigency." For example, in *Welsh v. Wisconsin* (1984) (see Chapter 5), police entered a suspect's home without a warrant or consent in "hot pursuit" of a person suspected in a nonjailable, first-time civil driving under the influence traffic offense. The police tried to justify the entry on an exigency basis: that the blood alcohol level of a suspected drunk driver was decreasing over time. The Court found that this "exigency" simply did not outweigh the sanctity of the home.

In **Minnesota v. Olson** (1990), police made a warrantless entry into an apartment in which Olson was a guest and discovered incriminating evidence. The Court first held that under *Rakas v. Illinois,* Olson had a legitimate expectation of privacy. (See Chapter 2.) Did the police breach that privacy by entering without a warrant? In this case, the crime—a robbery and murder—was far more serious than in *Welsh.* The Minnesota Supreme Court applied a "totality of the circumstances approach" to find there was no exigency compelling the police to enter the home without a warrant. That court looked at the gravity of the crime, whether the suspect was reasonably believed to be armed, the strength of the probable cause against the defendant, and the likelihood of escape.[19] In this case, Olson was not clearly identified as the driver of a car involved in a robbery and murder. The only link was a few papers found in the car and identified by an unverifiable, anonymous tip. The police did not rush to arrest him when they learned of his identity and knew that he was in the apartment with women who called the police. They had sufficient time to obtain a warrant. There was no hot pursuit of a dangerous felon. The destruction of incriminating evidence was not imminent. The apparent danger of violence or escape was low in light of the police actions. The Minnesota courts found that no exigency existed and suppressed the incriminating evidence. The U.S. Supreme Court upheld this fact-based application of the lower court's suppression of the evidence and agreed that there was no exigency to override the *Payton* rule.

Arrests and Searches in Third-Party Homes

Is a search warrant needed to arrest a person who is in the home of a third party, or is an arrest warrant for the suspect sufficient? In **Steagald v. United States** (1981), police obtained an arrest warrant for Ricky Lyons. Two days later, they proceeded to Steagald's home, where they believed Lyons was hiding. Outside the premises, they stopped and frisked Gary Steagald and an acquaintance and then entered the home to look for Lyons. Lyons was not present, but the police observed cocaine in plain sight. Based on that observation, a search warrant was obtained, and large quantities of cocaine were seized. The Supreme Court held that the initial intrusion into the home was unconstitutional.

There was neither an exigency nor a search warrant nor consent to authorize or allow entry into the home of a third party to look for Lyons: An arrest warrant does not give officers the right to enter the home of a third party who knows the person named in the arrest warrant. Even if the officers had a reasonable belief that the suspect was in the house, that belief was not "subjected to the detached scrutiny of a judicial officer." The privacy interests of the homeowner superseded the authority of the police to enter under these circumstances.

SEARCH INCIDENT TO ARREST

The police have the authority to conduct a warrantless search of a person for weapons and evidence whenever a person is lawfully arrested upon probable cause for any crime. An arrest always creates an exigency—the risk of injury to the officer and the likelihood of destruction of evidence. Under the warrant-preference construction of the Fourth Amendment, the **search incident to arrest** is one of three well-accepted warrant exceptions; the other two are entry into a home in hot pursuit and automobile searches. Waiting for a magistrate's warrant to search a person just arrested would indeed undermine legitimate law enforcement interests.

The Scope of a Search Incident to Arrest

The question of the **scope of a search incident to arrest** proceeds in two directions—toward and away from the arrested person, that is, how intrusive a search of the body and clothing of the arrested person is allowed? And how far away from the suspect can a search incident to arrest go to areas under the arrestee's control?

The first part of the "scope" rule was clarified in **United States v. Robinson** (1973). Officer Jenks of the Washington, D.C., Police Department saw Robinson driving an automobile and knew that Robinson's driver's license had been revoked four days earlier. Having reason to believe that Robinson was driving without a license, Jenks stopped Robinson and cited him for driving without a license. Under Washington, D.C., law, driving without a license was a crime for which a person could be brought into custody at a police station. According to police department procedures, Officer Jenks patted down Robinson's clothing. "He felt an object in the left breast pocket of the heavy coat" Robinson was wearing, could not tell what it was, and reached into the pocket and pulled out a "crumpled up cigarette package." The officer opened it and found fourteen gelatin capsules of heroin.

Writing for the Court, Justice Rehnquist distinguished between the search that may be made of the person and a search of the area under his control following a lawful arrest, the issue decided four years earlier in *Chimel v. California* (1969). Unlike the area of control rule, which had varied over time, courts have consistently upheld the right of the police to thoroughly search a person incident to arrest in order to secure and preserve evidence of crime and "to disarm the suspect in order to take him into custody." These reasons are in force when a police officer has probable cause and makes a **custodial arrest.** When a person is taken into custody, a *Terry* pat-down does not afford the officer sufficient protection against weapons that may be concealed and could be used during the transport to a police station. The arrest was considered proper, and the search was allowed under the Fourth Amendment, making the evidence admissible.

Four dissenting judges argued that an arrest for a traffic violation does not raise suspicion of drug possession and that the extent of the search must be limited by the nature of the crime. The majority, however, refused to limit the authority of the police in such a manner. "A police officer's determination as to how and where to search the person of a suspect whom he has arrested is necessarily a quick *ad hoc* judgment which the Fourth Amendment does not require to be broken down in each instance into an analysis of each step in the search. The authority to search the person incident to a lawful custodial arrest, while based upon the need to disarm and to discover evidence, does not depend on what a court may later decide was the probability in a particular arrest situation that weapons or evidence would in fact be found upon the person of the suspect." The Court thus created a bright-line rule: Police do not have to weigh each arrest situation on the street to guess whether this particular crime justifies a particular level of search. The constitutional rule is that the police may conduct a thorough search of the person upon arrest, without having to account for whether the search was related to the crime or the circumstances of the arrest.

The rule of *Atwater v. City of Lago Vista* (2001), discussed earlier in this chapter, authorizing an officer to take a person into custody for a fine-only offense, means that there is no longer such a thing as a noncustodial arrest. There are two situations in which a personal search is not authorized after a person is seized by police. The first is a temporary investigative stop made under the authority of *Terry v. Ohio* (1967), which authorized only a brief pat-down of the outer clothing for weapons. The second situation came into play in **Knowles v. Iowa** (1998). A police officer stopped an automobile driver for speeding, issued the driver a citation rather than arresting him, and, with neither the driver's consent nor probable cause, conducted a full automobile search, yielding a bag of marijuana and a "pot pipe." Iowa statutes allow either an officer to arrest a person for a traffic offense and bring the person before a magistrate or "the far more usual practice of issuing a citation in lieu of arrest or in lieu of continued custody after an initial arrest." The statutes also authorize officers to make a full-custody search of a stopped car, even though a citation has been issued. The Supreme Court held that the search in this case violated the Fourth Amendment, even though authorized by state law. The two rationales for the *Robinson* search incident to arrest rule are not strongly supported here. "The threat to officer safety from issuing a traffic citation . . . is a good deal less than in the case of a custodial arrest." As for the second rationale: "Nor has Iowa shown the second justification for the authority to search incident to arrest—the need to discover and preserve evidence. Once Knowles was stopped for speeding and issued a citation, all the evidence necessary to prosecute that offense had been obtained. No further evidence of excessive speed was going to be found either on the person of the offender or in the passenger compartment of the car." The Court also rejected Iowa's contention that a full-blown search of the car might turn up evidence of another, undetected crime.

Chimel v. California (1969) deals with the other "direction" of the scope of a search incident to arrest: How far *away* from the arrested individual may the search be conducted? Although the right to conduct a warrantless search incident to arrest has never been questioned, the Supreme Court had, over a half-century period from 1914 to 1969, issued an inconsistent string of rulings on the scope question. In *Chimel,* the Supreme Court sought to finally resolve the issue by handing down a clear statement concerning the proper extent of boundaries of warrantless searches around the person following an arrest.

Read Case and Comments: *Chimel v. California.*

In **New York v. Belton** (1981), the Supreme Court conflated the automobile search exception to the search warrant (see Chapter 5) and the search incident to arrest rationale in upholding a search. A lone New York State trooper stopped a speeding car on the New York Thruway, discovered that none of the four men in the car owned it, smelled burnt marijuana, and saw an envelope on the floor of the car characteristic of those containing marijuana. The trooper ordered the men out of the car, separated them, searched each, and then searched the passenger compartment of the car. He found that the envelope contained marijuana and placed the four men under arrest. The trooper then found a leather jacket belonging to Roger Belton, one of the occupants, unzipped one of the pockets, and discovered cocaine. The issue is whether the opening of the zippered jacket pocket was a constitutional search.

The Court relied on the automobile search rule and the search incident to arrest rule to hold the search valid under the Fourth Amendment. "[W]e hold that when a policeman has made a lawful custodial arrest of the occupant of an automobile, he may, as a contemporaneous incident of that arrest, search the passenger compartment of that automobile."

Chimel v. California

395 U.S. 752, 89 S.Ct. 2034, 23 L.Ed.2d 685 (1969)

[a] Why did the officers wait for Chimel to return home before searching the home? If Chimel's wife had refused them entry and they arrested Chimel outside his house, would a search of his house be just as reasonable? Justified? Could they have demanded entry under the arrest warrant?

[b] A magistrate specifies the things to be searched for in a search warrant. By searching without a warrant or under an arrest warrant, does an officer potentially have a greater scope for the search than if a search warrant had been obtained?

[c] The words "in his control" and "search the place" could logically apply to the actions of the police in Chimel's house.

[d] Does the *Marron* decision appear to authorize the search of an entire house where an arrest is made?

MR. JUSTICE STEWART delivered the opinion of the Court.

This case raises basic questions concerning the permissible scope under the Fourth Amendment of a search incident to a lawful arrest.

* * * Late [one] afternoon * * * three police officers arrived at the * * * home of the petitioner with a warrant authorizing his arrest for [a] burglary. * * * The officers knocked on the door, identified themselves to the petitioner's wife, and asked if they might come inside. She ushered them into the house, where they waited 10 or 15 minutes until the petitioner returned home from work. **[a]** When the petitioner entered the house, one of the officers handed him the arrest warrant and asked for permission to "look around." The petitioner objected, but was advised that "on the basis of the lawful arrest," the officers would nonetheless conduct a search. No search warrant had been issued.

Accompanied by the petitioner's wife, the officers then looked through the entire three-bedroom house, including the attic, the garage, and a small workshop. In some rooms the search was relatively cursory. In the master bedroom and sewing room, however, the officers directed the petitioner's wife to open drawers and "to physically move contents of the drawers from side to side so that [they] might view any items that would have come from [the] burglary." **[b]** After completing the search, they seized numerous items— primarily coins, but also several medals, tokens, and a few other objects. The entire search took between 45 minutes and an hour.

[Items seized during the search were admitted in evidence against Chimel at a criminal trial.] * * *

[The Court assumed that the arrest was valid.] This brings us directly to the question whether the warrantless search of the petitioner's entire house can be constitutionally justified as incident to that arrest. The decisions of this Court bearing upon that question have been far from consistent, as even the most cursory review makes evident.

[Dictum in *Weeks v. United States* (1914) referred in passing to a well-known exception to the warrant requirement: "to search the person of the accused when legally arrested."] That statement made no reference to any right to search the *place* where an arrest occurs. * * * Eleven years later the case of *Carroll v. United States* (1925) brought the following embellishment of the *Weeks* statement:

"When a man is legally arrested for an offense, whatever is found upon his person *or in his control* which it is unlawful for him to have and which may be used to prove the offense may be seized and held as evidence in the prosecution." * * * (Emphasis added.)

[Another 1925 case, *Agnello v. United States,* "still by way of dictum" said:] **[c]**

"The right without a search warrant contemporaneously to search persons lawfully arrested while committing crime and to search the place where the arrest is made in order to find and seize things connected with the crime as its fruits or as the means by which it was committed, as well as weapons and other things to effect an escape from custody, is not to be doubted." * * *

And in *Marron v. United States* (1927), two years later, the dictum of *Agnello* appeared to be the foundation of the Court's decision, [where agents with a search warrant to seize liquor and a still also seized a ledger. **[d]** The ledger was seized as incident to the arrest of the illicit producers at the still.] The Court upheld the seizure of the ledger by holding that since the agents had made a lawful arrest, "[t]hey had a right without a warrant contemporaneously to search the place in order to find and seize the things used to carry on the criminal enterprise." * * *

That the *Marron* opinion did not mean all that it seemed to say became evident, however, a few years later in *Go-Bart Importing Co. v. United States* (1931), and *United States v. Lefkowitz* (1932). * * * [In these cases, the Supreme Court limited the *Marron* ruling to situations where the things seized incident to arrest "were visible and accessible and in the offender's immediate custody."] * * * [I]n *Lefkowitz,* * * * the Court held unlawful a search of desk drawers and a cabinet despite the fact that the search had accompanied a lawful arrest. * * * **[e]**

[e] If *Lefkowitz* or *Go-Bart* did not explicitly overrule *Marron,* does this inject uncertainty into the law? Or does the most recent case control?

The limiting views expressed in *Go-Bart* and *Lefkowitz* were thrown to the winds, however, in *Harris v. United States,* decided in 1947. * * * [Harris] was arrested [on an arrest warrant] in the living room of his four-room apartment, and in an attempt to recover two canceled checks thought to have been used in effecting the forgery, the officers undertook a thorough search of the entire apartment. Inside a desk drawer they found a sealed envelope marked "George Harris, personal papers." The envelope, which was then torn open, was found to contain altered Selective Service documents, and those documents were used to secure Harris' conviction for violating the Selective Training and Service Act of 1940. The Court rejected Harris' Fourth Amendment claim, sustaining the search as "incident to arrest." * * *

Only a year after *Harris,* however, the pendulum swung again. In *Trupiano v. United States,* [1948], [the Court invalidated the seizure of evidence at an illegal distillery made without a search warrant but pursuant to arrests.] The opinion stated:

* * *

"A search or seizure without a warrant as an incident to a lawful arrest has always been considered to be a strictly limited right. It grows out of the inherent necessities of the situation at the time of the arrest. But there must be something more in the way of necessity than merely a lawful arrest." * * *

In 1950, two years after *Trupiano,* came *United States v. Rabinowitz,* the decision upon which California primarily relies in the case now before us. **[f]** In *Rabinowitz,* federal authorities * * * [armed with an arrest warrant, arrested the defendant] at his one-room business office. At the time of the arrest, the officers "searched the desk, safe, and file cabinets in the office for about an hour and a half," * * * and seized 573 stamps with forged overprints. * * * The Court held that the search in its entirety fell within the principle giving law enforcement authorities "[t]he right to search the place where the arrest is made in order to find and seize things connected with the crime." * * * The test, said the Court, "is not whether it is reasonable to procure a search warrant, but whether the search was reasonable." * * * **[g]**

[f] Two of the most liberal justices, Frank Murphy and Wiley Rutledge, died in 1949 and were replaced by more conservative justices, Tom Clark and Sherman Minton.

[g] On a sheet of paper, trace the zigzag of the Court's rulings on the scope of the search incident to arrest.

* * * [The *Rabinowitz*] doctrine, however, at least in the broad sense in which it was applied by the California courts in this case, can withstand neither historical nor rational analysis.

* * *

[The Court then noted that the line of cases supporting the *Rabinowitz* rule was quite wavering. Furthermore, the historic background of the Fourth Amendment was the strongly felt abuses of general warrants, hated by the American colonists, implying that] * * * the general requirement that a search warrant be obtained is not lightly to be dispensed with, and "the burden is on those seeking [an] exemption [from the requirement] to show the need for it." * * *

Only last Term in *Terry v. Ohio* (1968), we emphasized that "the police must, whenever practicable, obtain advance judicial approval of searches and seizures through the warrant procedure," * * * and that "[t]he scope of [a] search must be 'strictly tied to and justified by' the circumstances which rendered its initiation permissible." * * *

A similar analysis underlies the "search incident to arrest" principle, and marks its proper extent. When an arrest is made, it is reasonable for the arresting officer to search the

(*continued*)

[h] The dual purposes of the search incident to arrest of the person are extended to the search of the immediate area around the arrest. The Court here states the operative rule of *Chimel*.

[i] The search of a closed drawer is consistent with *Lefkowitz* (1932).

person arrested in order to remove any weapons that the latter might seek to use in order to resist arrest or effect his escape. **[h]** Otherwise, the officer's safety might well be endangered, and the arrest itself frustrated. In addition, it is entirely reasonable for the arresting officer to search for and seize any evidence on the arrestee's person in order to prevent its concealment or destruction. And the area into which an arrestee might reach in order to grab a weapon or evidentiary items must, of course, be governed by a like rule. A gun on a table or in a drawer in front of one who is arrested can be as dangerous to the arresting officer as one concealed in the clothing of the person arrested. **[i]** There is ample justification, therefore, for a search of the arrestee's person and the area "within his immediate control"—construing that phrase to mean the area from within which he might gain possession of a weapon or destructible evidence.

There is no comparable justification, however, for routinely searching any room other than that in which an arrest occurs—or, for that matter, for searching through all the desk drawers or other closed or concealed areas in that room itself. Such searches, in the absence of well-recognized exceptions, may be made only under the authority of a search warrant. The "adherence to judicial processes" mandated by the Fourth Amendment requires no less.

* * *

[j] The *Chimel* case is evaluated through the lens of the warrant-preference construction of the Fourth Amendment rather than the general-reasonableness construction.

It is argued in the present case that it is "reasonable" to search a man's house when he is arrested in it. But that argument is founded on little more than a subjective view regarding the acceptability of certain sorts of police conduct, and not on considerations relevant to Fourth Amendment interests. **[j]** Under such an unconfined analysis, Fourth Amendment protection in this area would approach the evaporation point. It is not easy to explain why, for instance, it is less subjectively "reasonable" to search a man's house when he is arrested on his front lawn—or just down the street—than it is when he happens to be in the house at the time of arrest. * * * Thus, although "[t]he recurring questions of the reasonableness of searches" depend upon "the facts and circumstances—the total atmosphere of the case," * * * those facts and circumstances must be viewed in the light of established Fourth Amendment principles.

* * *

[k] The Court here explicitly overrules cases that allowed a broad interpretation of the scope of a search incident to arrest. This clarifies the wavering line of prior cases and seeks to put a definite end to the Court's "pendulum swings."

[The Court noted that the *Rabinowitz* rule creates the possibility for "pretext" arrests, where the police deliberately attempt to arrest a suspect at home so as to avoid the necessity to obtain a search warrant, especially where probable cause does not exist. Thus, in effect, police could operate as if they had general warrants.]

Rabinowitz and *Harris* have been the subject of critical commentary for many years and have been relied upon less and less in our own decisions. **[k]** It is time, for the reasons we have stated, to hold that on their own facts, and insofar as the principles they stand for are inconsistent with those that we have endorsed today, they are no longer to be followed.

Application of sound Fourth Amendment principles to the facts of this case produces a clear result. The search here went far beyond the petitioner's person and the area from within which he might have obtained either a weapon or something that could have been used as evidence against him. There was no constitutional justification, in the absence of a search warrant, for extending the search beyond that area. The scope of the search was, therefore, "unreasonable" under the Fourth and Fourteenth Amendments, and the petitioner's conviction cannot stand.

Reversed.

[Justice White dissented, joined by Justice Black. He argued that the broad "search incident to arrest" rule of *Rabinowitz* was correct because the searches must adhere to a general rule of reasonableness. In this case, the search was reasonable because the arrest alerted Mrs. Chimel, and she would have been in a position to get rid of incriminating evidence after the police had left the house.]

The rationale for the holding was that police needed a bright-line rule to guide them in postarrest searches of persons arrested in automobiles. Was *Chimel* stretched too far? The suspects were not near the interior of the car when the search was actually made. *Belton* was not an unjustifiable extension of *Chimel* because the officer was outnumbered by four arrestees, and even though he had secured them outside the car, he could not be certain that one of them would not bolt for the car and find a concealed weapon. *Belton*'s bright-line holding, however, precludes the argument that under some circumstances a search incident to arrest at a vehicle is unreasonable, as, for example, when two police officers arrest a sole driver.

The Protective Sweep Exception

Maryland v. Buie (1990) established the **protective sweep** warrant exception under the Fourth Amendment. Justice White's majority opinion defined a protective sweep as "a quick and limited search of a premises, incident to an arrest and conducted to protect the safety of police officers or others. It is narrowly confined to a cursory visual inspection of those places in which a person might be hiding." It can be thought of as a "frisk" of a house to search for persons other than the arrested person who might endanger the officers.

In *Buie,* two robbers, one wearing a red running suit, held up a pizza parlor and fled. An arrest warrant was obtained against Jerome Buie and his alleged accomplice, Lloyd Allen. Buie's house was placed under surveillance. Two days later, the arrest warrant was executed by seven officers who entered the house after verifying that Buie was home. They knew that the robbery had been committed by a pair of men and could not be sure that Buie was alone in the house. Upon entering, the officers "fanned out through the first and second floors." A corporal shouted down to the basement, and Buie, hiding there, surrendered and "emerged from the basement." He was arrested and handcuffed. A detective then entered the basement "in case there was someone else down there." He spotted a red running suit lying on a stack of clothes in plain view and seized it as evidence. If the detective's entry into the basement was an improper intrusion on Buie's expectation of privacy, the running suit would be inadmissible as the fruit of an illegal search.

The Court held the running suit admissible under the plain view doctrine: The officer was legitimately in the basement, although Buie had already been arrested. The majority justified the officer's going into another part of the house on the basis of police officer *safety.* When police enter a house under an arrest warrant, in hot pursuit, or under a valid exigency (as in *Arizona v. Hicks,* 1987), they can go throughout the house looking for the suspect in any likely places where the suspect might reasonably hide. It is true that once the person has been seized, the arrest warrant is executed or the exigency is at an end. At that point, the underlying expectation of privacy in the home comes into play.

However, Buie's expectation of privacy in his home, once he was arrested, did not immunize other rooms from entry after his arrest. The balancing approach of Fourth Amendment analysis of *Terry v. Ohio* shows a basic concern for officers' safety by allowing them to frisk potentially armed suspects. The protective sweep, similarly, is designed to protect the arresting officers by allowing them "to take steps to assure themselves that the house in which a suspect is being or had just been arrested is not harboring other persons who are dangerous and who could unexpectedly launch an attack" (*Maryland v. Buie,* 1990). The risk of danger in a home arrest is as great as, if not greater than, an on-the-street or roadside investigatory encounter:

> A frisk occurs before a police-citizen confrontation has escalated to the point of arrest. A protective sweep, in contrast, occurs as an adjunct to the serious step of taking a person into custody for the purpose of prosecuting him for a crime. Moreover, unlike an encounter on the street or along a highway, an in-home arrest puts the officer at the disadvantage of being on his adversary's "turf." An ambush in a confined setting of unknown configuration is more to be feared than it is in open, more familiar surroundings. (*Maryland v. Buie,* 1990)

Once holding that a protective sweep was reasonable, the Court had to determine the standard of evidence needed by police to go beyond the room in which the person sought was arrested: (1) probable cause, (2) reasonable suspicion, or (3) no evidence at all? In *Buie,* the prosecution argued for position 3—that the police should be permitted to conduct a protective sweep whenever they make an in-home arrest for a violent crime. The Maryland courts and the U.S. Supreme Court disagreed. The Maryland courts had ruled that for officers to go beyond the place of arrest in a home, they were required to have probable cause (position 1) to believe that other people were present.

The Supreme Court instead created a two-part rule. First, "there must be articulable facts which, taken together with the rational inferences from those facts, would warrant a reasonably prudent officer in believing that the area to be swept harbors an individual posing a danger to those on the arrest scene." A protective sweep of the entire house must be based on reasonable suspicion. Second, however, the Court also held "that as an incident to the arrest the officers could, as a precautionary matter and without probable cause or reasonable suspicion, look in closets and other spaces *immediately adjoining* the place of arrest from which an attack could be immediately launched." Thus the "sweep" of the entire house is differentiated from a search of the "adjoining space."

Justice White emphasized that the protective sweep of an entire house is *limited* only to protecting the safety of arresting officers if justified by the circumstances, may extend only to a cursory inspection of those spaces where a person may be found, and is limited to that period necessary to dispel the reasonable suspicion of danger "and in any event no longer than it takes to complete the arrest and depart the premises."

Justice Brennan, joined by Justice Marshall, dissented. He said that the narrow *Terry* exception swallowed the general rule that searches are reasonable only if based on proba- ble cause. He argued that the majority's characterization of a protective sweep as a "minimally intrusive" search akin to a *Terry* frisk "markedly undervalues the nature and scope of the privacy interests involved." As he saw it, a protective sweep was not far removed from the full-blown search that was disallowed in *Chimel v. California:*

> A protective sweep would bring within police purview virtually all personal possessions within the house not hidden from view in a small enclosed space. Police officers searching for potential ambushers might enter every room including basements and attics; open up closets, lockers, chests, wardrobes, and cars; and peer under beds and behind furniture. The officers will view letters, documents and personal effects that are on tables or desks or are visible inside open drawers; books, records, tapes, and pictures on shelves; and clothing, medicines, toiletries and other paraphernalia not carefully stored in dresser drawers or bathroom cupboards. While perhaps not a "full-blown" or "top-to-bottom" search, a protective sweep is much closer to it than to a "limited patdown for weapons."

Searching at the Station House

Inventory Search.   When an arrested person is brought to a police lockup or a jail for booking, it is standard practice for officers to inventory every item of property that the arrestee has on his or her person. In **Illinois v. Lafayette** (1983), Ralph Lafayette was arrested for disturbing the peace. He was taken to the Kankakee police station where, in the process of booking him, a warrantless search of his shoulder bag, made for the purpose of inventorying his possessions, turned up amphetamine pills. The Illinois Appellate Court, ruling that the privacy interest in an item of personal luggage like a shoulder bag during an **inventory search** is greater than that in an automobile inventory search, suppressed the evidence of the drugs. The U.S. Supreme Court reversed.

In the Court's opinion, Chief Justice Burger ruled that because an inventory search does not rest on probable cause, the lack of a warrant is immaterial. The inventory search constitutes a well-defined exception to the warrant requirement: It "is not an independent legal concept but rather an incidental *administrative* step following arrest and preceding incarceration" (emphasis added). An inventory search of a jailed person's backpack or similar items is justified by balancing privacy interests in the bag versus the government's interests. The Court found that the state's interests outweighed those of the individual—the routine inventorying of all items in a person's possession is therefore reasonable under the Fourth Amendment. The Illinois Supreme Court's ruling was reversed, and the plain view seizure of the amphetamines was upheld.

The governmental and individual interests that support the conclusion that a station house inventory search is reasonable include

- Protecting the arrestee's property from theft by police officers.
- Protecting police from false claims of theft by the arrestee. ("A standardized procedure for making a list or inventory as soon as reasonable after reaching the station house not only deters false claims but also inhibits theft or careless handling of articles taken from the arrested person.")
- Accurately determining the identity of the arrested person.
- Ensuring the safety of everyone in jail. ("Dangerous instrumentalities—such as razor blades, bombs, or weapons—can be concealed in innocent-looking articles taken from the arrestee's possession.")

Chief Justice Burger stated that "[t[he governmental interests underlying a stationhouse search of the arrestee's person and possessions may in some circumstances be even greater than those supporting a search immediately following arrest." He dismissed the suggestion of the Illinois court that it was feasible in such situations to secure the property of arrestees in secure lockers and thus preserve their individual rights of privacy.

In dictum, the chief justice referred to whether or not a person can be ordered to undress at the station house: "Police conduct that would be impractical or unreasonable—or embarrassingly intrusive—on the street can more readily—and privately—be performed at the station. For example, the interests supporting a search incident to arrest would hardly justify disrobing an arrestee on the street, but the practical necessities of routine jail administration may even justify taking a prisoner's clothes before confining him, although that step would be rare."

Warrantless Station House Search for Evidence.
A locked footlocker that police take into custody following an arrest, with probable cause to believe it contains drugs, cannot be opened by the police without having obtained a search warrant (*United States v. Chadwick,* 1977). It constitutes an "effect" protected by the Warrant Clause of the Fourth Amendment.

To the contrary, station house investigative seizures are allowed where an exigency exists that the suspect can destroy evidence. In **United States v. Edwards** (1974), police had probable cause to believe that the clothing worn by Edwards, who was arrested and in a police lockup, contains evidence of a crime—paint chips from the scene of a burglary. The Court held that the police could, without a warrant, require him to exchange his clothing for other clothing, even ten hours after his jailing. The time delay was reasonable because the police waited until morning, when a substitute set of clothing could be purchased. *Edwards* fell within the search incident to arrest exception and made clear that when a person is in a police lockup or jail, the exigency that supports the search incident to arrest (i.e., the destruction of evidence) may continue for considerable periods of time. The exchange of clothing could also be allowed at the time of an inventory.

A warrantless search was also upheld in **Cupp v. Murphy** (1973). The search and seizure consisted of police at a police station taking dry blood scrapings from the finger of a man who voluntarily appeared at a police station after the strangulation death of his wife. When the police noticed the stain and the man held his hands behind his back, an exigency arose because he might have destroyed evidence. *Cupp* is problematic because at the time the blood was scraped from the individual's finger, there was no formal custodial arrest. In that case, the police had only reasonable suspicion that the man murdered his wife, but their action was a very limited intrusion and the evidence was the kind that could be readily destroyed. Under these circumstances, the search and seizure were held to be constitutional.

Strip Searches.   The Supreme Court has not dealt with the issue of whether the **strip search** of a person held in jail on a minor offense is reasonable. In ***Bell v. Wolfish*** (1979), the Court ruled on the conditions of confinement of pretrial detainees in facilities that also housed convicted prisoners awaiting transportation or serving short sentences. Detainees who were held in a federal jail on serious federal charges were required to expose their body cavities for visual inspection as a part of a strip search conducted after every contact visit with a person from outside the institution. The practice was justified by correctional authorities "not only to discover but also to deter the smuggling of weapons, drugs, and other contraband into the institution." The Supreme Court applied the general reasonableness construction of the Fourth Amendment in upholding this practice as reasonable. "A detention facility is a unique place fraught with serious security dangers. Smuggling of money, drugs, weapons, and other contraband is all too common an occurrence."

On the other hand, lower federal and state courts have held blanket strip searches, or **body cavity searches,** regulations and practices to be unreasonable for minor crimes. The Seventh Circuit Court of Appeals, in *Mary Beth G. v. City of Chicago* (1983),[20] described strip searches as "demeaning, dehumanizing, undignified, humiliating, terrifying, unpleasant, embarrassing, repulsive, signifying degradation and submission." A City of Chicago policy in force from 1952 to 1980 required all female detainees to be subjected to a strip search, regardless of the charges, while all male detainees were patted down. In four consolidated cases, women had been subjected to strip searches after arrests for having outstanding parking tickets, failing to produce a driver's license, and disorderly conduct. The Court of Appeals for the Seventh Circuit found these searches to be within the search incident to arrest exception to the warrant requirement and relied on the *Bell v. Wolfish* balancing test to determine whether these strip searches were reasonable. The government's primary justification for the strip searches was to prevent the women from bringing weapons or contraband into the jail. The specific holding of *Wolfish* did not apply to the Chicago cases because the essential facts differed: In *Mary Beth G.,* the plaintiffs "are minor offenders who were not inherently dangerous and who were being detained only briefly while awaiting bond." Further, *Wolfish* "does not validate strip searches in detention settings *per se.*" After carefully weighing the competing interests, the Seventh Circuit held that the strip searches in Chicago bore an insubstantial relationship to security needs and, when balanced against the plaintiff's privacy interests, could not be considered reasonable.[21] Despite such rulings, municipal police departments in many places have continued to use strip and body cavity searches in inappropriate situations and have lost substantial lawsuits as a result. Some departments have instituted regulations to utilize these searches when reasonable. "Two states, New Jersey and Tennessee, have passed statutes requiring a search warrant or consent in order to perform a visual body cavity search." In neither state have police departments complained that these laws made their lockups unsafe.[22]

STOP AND FRISK

This section explores the second major category of personal seizure: the investigative stop.

Establishing the Constitutional Authority to Stop

Arrest law is rooted in common law cases going back hundreds of years. Virtually no law existed regarding the temporary stopping of individuals by the police in order to obtain information. Organized police forces, however, exercised this power as a matter of custom since their inception in the nineteenth century. In the 1960s, state statutes and cases began to define the so-called **stop and frisk** power. These laws generated constitutional challenges that soon landed on the Supreme Court's doorstep. The basic rules were formulated in *Terry v. Ohio* (1968).

Terry was handed down during an explosive moment in American history—an extended period of intense racial conflict that boiled over into hundreds of inner-city riots between 1964 and 1972, reaching its highest pitch in the summers of 1967 and 1968. The immediate catalysts of these riots often were episodes between largely all-white police forces and mostly young male African Americans who felt that the promises of the civil rights movement were not being fulfilled.[23] Given the overheated political climate of 1968, some commentators suggest that the liberal Warren Court justices voted to extend the powers of the police in part as a way of mollifying the bitter attacks on the Court by the police establishment and by many conservatives in Congress following the 1966 decision in *Miranda v. Arizona*.[24] Journalist Fred Graham, in this skeptical vein, noted that "[t]he Supreme Court has never conceded that it intentionally compensates for a tough decision on one point by handing down a soft ruling on another, but its actions occasionally give that impression."[25] Thus, within two years after *Miranda,* the Court upheld the use of informers and electronic eavesdropping, dropped the mere evidence restriction on searches, and authorized stop and frisk on less than probable cause. This does not prove that the Court acted from narrow political motives, but it does fuel speculation that the Supreme Court's decisions are not entirely divorced from major national events.

Read Case and Comments: *Terry v. Ohio.*

Terry *and Vagrancy Laws: Closing a Legal Loophole.*

While *Terry* can be viewed as a conservative turn for the decidedly liberal Warren Court, several years later, in **Papachristou v. City of Jacksonville** (1972), the more conservative Burger Court took a "liberal" stance in restricting the use of overly broad or vague **vagrancy statutes.** These laws had for centuries given police in England and the United States a "cover" to stop and question individuals who merely appeared suspicious but against whom no probable cause to arrest existed.[26] Vagrancy laws were used not only to question those suspected of a crime but also to control and harass social deviants and the poor. A destructive aspect of these laws was their use as "cover" charges: A police officer ensured against a lawsuit for false arrest by charging a person stopped with "vagrancy." The Supreme Court, by openly recognizing the field-interrogation power of the police in *Terry,* and by shutting down the abusive extremes of overly broad vagrancy laws in *Papachristou,* eliminated a source of hypocrisy in police work and in theory brought this area of police activity under judicial scrutiny.

After *Papachristou,* the states could continue to rely on loitering laws but tended to narrowly tailor them to specifically target disruptive behavior, such as prowling around homes, streetwalking prostitution, and conducting on-the-street drug sales. These laws provided very detailed definitions of loitering. The change worked by *Papachristou* was that now citizens could turn to the courts to determine if such specifically targeted laws met due process criteria.

The Supreme Court has applied the stop and frisk doctrine in a variety of cases in the years following *Terry.* While some cases have limited the power of police officers to stop, most have expanded the investigative stop doctrine beyond a strict reading of *Terry.* Most commentators believe that a rough balance between police rights and individual rights established during the Burger Court years has given way to a legal regime that decidedly favors police in the Rehnquist Court. The mostly Republican-appointed Court has been charged with creating a "drug exception" to the Fourth Amendment linked to the nation's "war on drugs."[27]

In the cases that follow, the Court often has had to determine whether police action constituted an arrest, a *Terry* stop, or a consensual encounter, and if a seizure occurred, whether the seizure was justified by probable cause or reasonable suspicion. Instead of

CASE AND COMMENTS

Terry v. Ohio

392 U.S. 1, 88 S.Ct. 1868, 20 L.Ed.2d 889 (1968)

MR. CHIEF JUSTICE WARREN delivered the opinion of the Court.

This case presents serious questions concerning the role of the Fourth Amendment in the confrontation on the street between the citizen and the policeman investigating suspicious circumstances.

Petitioner Terry was convicted of carrying a concealed weapon. * * * Officer McFadden testified that while he was patrolling in plain clothes in downtown Cleveland [one] afternoon * * * his attention was attracted by two men, Chilton and Terry, standing on the corner of Huron Road and Euclid Avenue. * * * [H]e was unable to say precisely what first drew his eye to them. However, he testified that he had been a policeman for thirty-nine years. * * * [H]e had developed routine habits of observation over the years[;] * * * he would "stand and watch people or walk and watch people at many intervals of the day." **[a]** He added: "Now, in this case when I looked over they didn't look right to me at the time."

* * * [Officer McFadden saw them pace up and down the block five or six times each, pausing frequently to look into the window of a jewelry store and to confer.] After this had gone on for 10 to 12 minutes, the two men walked off together [following a third]. * * *

* * * He testified that * * * he suspected the two men of "casing a job, a stick-up," and that he considered it his duty as a police officer to investigate further. He added that he feared "they may have a gun." **[b]** * * * Deciding that the situation was ripe for direct action, Officer McFadden approached the three men, identified himself as a police officer and asked for their names. At this point his knowledge was confined to what he had observed. * * * When the men "mumbled something" in response to his inquiries, Officer McFadden grabbed petitioner Terry, spun him around * * * and patted down the outside of his clothing. In the left breast pocket of Terry's overcoat Officer McFadden felt a pistol. * * * At this point, * * * the officer ordered all three men to enter Zucker's store. As they went in, he removed Terry's overcoat completely [and] removed a .38-caliber revolver from the pocket. * * * [Pat-downs of Chilton and Katz produced a gun on Chilton but not on Katz.] The officer testified that he only patted the men down to see whether they had weapons, and that he did not put his hands beneath the outer garments of either Terry or Chilton until he felt their guns.

* * *

I

* * * Unquestionably petitioner was entitled to the protection of the Fourth Amendment as he walked down the street in Cleveland. * * * The question is whether in all the circumstances of this on-the-street encounter, his right to personal security was violated by an unreasonable search and seizure.

* * * [T]his question thrusts to the fore difficult and troublesome issues regarding a sensitive area of police activity[:] * * * the power of the police to "stop and frisk"—as it is sometimes euphemistically termed—suspicious persons.

* * *

[The police claim that they need authority to deal with street encounters and that the brief detention of a "stop and frisk" not amounting to arrest should not be governed by the Fourth Amendment. It is a petty indignity. **[c]** The defendant argues that unless the police have probable cause to arrest, they have no power under the Fourth Amendment to forcibly detain a person temporarily or to **frisk** him or her.]

---

[a] The case does not indicate that Terry and Chilton were African Americans and the third who joined them, Katz, was a white male. Should this be suspicious?

[b] Is Officer McFadden's suspicion based on facts? Are they reasonable? Does probable cause exist to arrest these men on the basis of what he saw? For what crime?

[c] The police are asking that their forcible stops of persons *never* be subject to court review unless they make an arrest. Terry argues that the police should have *no* right to stop him without probable cause.

In this context we approach the issues in this case mindful of the limitations of the judicial function in controlling the myriad daily situations in which policemen and citizens confront each other on the street. * * *

* * * [I]n some contexts the [exclusionary] rule is ineffective as a deterrent [to police misconduct]. Street encounters between citizens and police officers are incredibly rich in diversity. They range from wholly friendly exchanges of pleasantries or mutually useful information to hostile confrontations of armed men involving arrests, or injuries, or loss of life. Moreover, hostile confrontations are not all of a piece. Some of them begin in a friendly enough manner, only to take a different turn upon the injection of some unexpected element into the conversation. Encounters are initiated by the police for a wide variety of purposes, some of which are wholly unrelated to a desire to prosecute for crime. **[d]** Doubtless some police "**field interrogation**" conduct violates the Fourth Amendment. But a stern refusal by this Court to condone such activity does not necessarily render it responsive to the exclusionary rule. Regardless of how effective the rule may be where obtaining convictions is an important objective of the police, it is powerless to deter invasions of constitutionally guaranteed rights where the police either have no interest in prosecuting or are willing to forgo successful prosecution in the interest of serving some other goal.

* * * The wholesale harassment by certain elements of the police community, of which minority groups, particularly Negroes, frequently complain, will not be stopped by the exclusion of any evidence from any criminal trial. * * * **[e]** Nothing we say today is to be taken as indicating approval of police conduct outside the legitimate investigative sphere. Under our decision, courts still retain their traditional responsibility to guard against police conduct which is overbearing or harassing, or which trenches upon personal security without the objective evidentiary justification which the Constitution requires. When such conduct is identified, it must be condemned by the judiciary and its fruits must be excluded from evidence in criminal trials. * * *

* * * [W]e turn our attention to the quite narrow question posed by the facts before us: whether it is always unreasonable for a policeman to seize a person and subject him to a limited search for weapons unless there is probable cause for an arrest. * * *

II

Our first task is to establish at what point in this encounter the Fourth Amendment becomes relevant. That is, we must decide whether and when Officer McFadden "seized" Terry and whether and when he conducted a "search." * * * It must be recognized that whenever a police officer accosts an individual and restrains his freedom to walk away, he has "seized" that person. And it is nothing less than sheer torture of the English language to suggest that a careful exploration of the outer surfaces of a person's clothing all over his or her body in an attempt to find weapons is not a "search." * * * It is a serious intrusion upon the sanctity of the person. * * * **[f]**

* * * This Court has held in the past that a search which is reasonable at its inception may violate the Fourth Amendment by virtue of its intolerable intensity and scope. * * * The scope of the search must be "strictly tied to and justified by" the circumstances which render its initiation permissible. * * *

* * * We therefore reject the notions that the Fourth Amendment does not come into play at all as a limitation upon police conduct if the officers stop short of something called a "technical arrest" or a "full-blown search."

[The next question is whether this seizure and search were unreasonable—that is, whether the officer's action was justified at its inception and whether it was reasonably related in scope to the circumstances that justified the interference in the first place.]

(continued)

[d] The Court admits that bringing the stop and frisk power within the Constitution will not enable courts to supervise instances of police misconduct where the stop does not result in an arrest and the person is simply let go.

[e] The Court signals its awareness and condemnation of widespread police misconduct and racism, which were rampant in that era.

[f] Thus by stopping and frisking Terry, Officer McFadden seized and searched him. Note that the frisk is defined as a limited search for one purpose only.

III

[g] *Terry* here solidifies the general-reasonableness construction of the Fourth Amendment.

[h] What is an "articulable fact"? It seems to be any reason other than a hunch. This suggests a lower standard than probable cause, which is defined as facts that would lead a prudent person to conclude that a crime is occurring or has occurred.

[i] Here the Court provides a standard closer to traditional probable cause. Note that this paragraph does not use the words "reasonable suspicion," although later cases concluded that this lower standard is the rule.

[j] The Court turns its attention to the frisk and devotes more attention to this subject than to the stop.

[k] In this case, Officer McFadden placed his hands on Terry's coat (the frisk) simultaneously with the stop. He did not have probable cause to believe Terry was armed. Terry was arrested *after* the frisk disclosed a gun. Thus the case facts do not fit the rules of a search incident to arrest.

* * * [W]e deal here with an entire rubric of police conduct—necessarily swift action predicated upon the on-the-spot observations of the officer on the beat—which historically has not been, and as a practical matter could not be, subjected to the warrant procedure. [g] Instead, the conduct involved in this case must be tested by the Fourth Amendment's general proscription against unreasonable searches and seizures.

Nonetheless, the notions which underlie both the warrant procedure and the requirement of probable cause remain fully relevant in this context. * * * [h] [I]n justifying the particular intrusion the police officer must be able to point to specific and articulable facts which, taken together with rational inferences from those facts, reasonably warrant that intrusion. The scheme of the Fourth Amendment becomes meaningful only when it is assured that at some point the conduct of those charged with enforcing the laws can be subjected to the more detached, neutral scrutiny of a judge who must evaluate the reasonableness of a particular search or seizure in light of the particular circumstances. [i] And in making that assessment it is imperative that the facts be judged against an objective standard: would the facts available to the officer at the moment of the seizure or the search "warrant a man of reasonable caution in the belief" that the action taken was appropriate? * * * Anything less would invite intrusions upon constitutionally guaranteed rights based on nothing more substantial than inarticulate hunches, a result this Court has consistently refused to sanction. * * * And simple "'good faith on the part of the arresting officer is not enough.' * * * If subjective good faith alone were the test, the protections of the Fourth Amendment would evaporate, and the people would be 'secure in their persons, houses, papers, and effects,' only in the discretion of the police." * * *

[The Court noted that the police have an interest to prevent and detect crime that necessitates temporary stops of individuals to inquire into suspicious circumstances.]

The crux of this case, however, is not the propriety of Officer McFadden's taking steps to investigate petitioner's suspicious behavior, but rather, whether there was justification for McFadden's invasion of Terry's personal security by searching him for weapons in the course of that investigation. [j] * * * Certainly it would be unreasonable to require that police officers take unnecessary risks in the performance of their duties. American criminals have a long tradition of armed violence, and every year in this country many law enforcement officers are killed in the line of duty. * * *

In view of these facts, we cannot blind ourselves to the need for law enforcement officers to protect themselves and other prospective victims of violence in situations where they may lack probable cause for an arrest. * * *

We must still consider, however, the nature and quality of the intrusion on individual rights which must be accepted if police officers are to be conceded the right to search for weapons in situations where probable cause to arrest for crime is lacking. Even a limited search of the outer clothing for weapons constitutes a severe, though brief, intrusion upon cherished personal security, and it must surely be an annoying, frightening, and perhaps humiliating experience. [k] Petitioner contends that such an intrusion is permissible only incident to a lawful arrest, either for a crime involving the possession of weapons or for a crime the commission of which led the officer to investigate in the first place. However, this argument must be closely examined.

* * * [Terry] says it is unreasonable for the policeman to [disarm a suspect] until such time as the situation evolves to a point where there is probable cause to make an arrest. When that point has been reached, petitioner would concede the officer's right to conduct a search of the suspect for weapons, fruits or instrumentalities of the crime, or "mere" evidence, incident to the arrest.

There are two weaknesses in this line of reasoning, however. First, it fails to take account of traditional limitations upon the scope of searches, and thus recognizes no distinction in purpose, character, and extent between a search incident to an arrest and a limited search for weapons. **[l]** The former, although justified in part by the acknowledged necessity to protect the arresting officer from assault with a concealed weapon, * * * is also justified on other grounds, and can therefore involve a relatively extensive exploration of the person. A search for weapons in the absence of probable cause to arrest, however, must, like any other search, be strictly circumscribed by the exigencies which justify its initiation. * * * Thus it must be limited to that which is necessary for the discovery of weapons which might be used to harm the officer or others nearby, and may realistically be characterized as something less than a "full" search. * * *

* * * [Second,] [a]n arrest is a wholly different kind of intrusion upon individual freedom from a limited search for weapons, and the interests each is designed to serve are likewise quite different. An arrest is the initial stage of a criminal prosecution. It is intended to vindicate society's interest in having its laws obeyed, and it is inevitably accompanied by future interference with the individual's freedom of movement, whether or not trial or conviction ultimately follows. **[m]** The protective search for weapons, on the other hand, constitutes a brief, though far from inconsiderable, intrusion upon the sanctity of the person. It does not follow that because an officer may lawfully arrest a person only when he is apprised of facts sufficient to warrant a belief that the person has committed or is committing a crime, the officer is equally unjustified, absent that kind of evidence, in making any intrusions short of an arrest. Moreover, a perfectly reasonable apprehension of danger may arise long before the officer is possessed of adequate information to justify taking a person into custody for the purpose of prosecuting him for a crime. * * *

IV

* * * We think * * * a reasonably prudent man would have been warranted in believing petitioner was armed and thus presented a threat to the officer's safety while he was investigating his suspicious behavior. * * * **[n]** We cannot say [Officer McFadden's] decision at that point to seize Terry and pat his clothing for weapons was the product of a volatile or inventive imagination, or was undertaken simply as an act of harassment; the record evidences the tempered act of a policeman who in the course of an investigation had to make a quick decision as to how to protect himself and others from possible danger, and took limited steps to do so.

*** * ***

* * * **[o]** The sole justification of the search in the present situation is the protection of the police officer and others nearby, and it must therefore be confined in scope to an intrusion reasonably designed to discover guns, knives, clubs, or other hidden instruments for the assault of the police officer.

*** * ***

V

* * * We merely hold today **[p]** that where a police officer observes unusual conduct which leads him reasonably to conclude in light of his experience that criminal activity may be afoot and that the persons with whom he is dealing may be armed and presently dangerous, where in the course of investigating this behavior he identifies himself as a policeman and makes reasonable inquiries, and where nothing in the initial stages of the encounter serves to dispel his reasonable fear for his own or others' safety, he is entitled for the protection of himself and others in the area to conduct a carefully limited search of the outer clothing of

(continued)

[l] The Court draws a fairly clear distinction between a full search after arrest and a limited frisk (pat-down) after or accompanying a stop.

[m] The Court slips back to explaining and justifying a stop and compares it to a full custody arrest. This analysis of the stop is interleaved with that of the frisk, making it difficult to untangle the two issues.

[n] The general rules laid down in the case are applied to the specific facts. The Court concludes that Terry's seizure was based on more than a hunch.

[o] The Court reemphasizes the limited scope of the frisk.

[p] This paragraph summarizes the case.

such persons in an attempt to discover weapons which might be used to assault him. Such a search is a reasonable search under the Fourth Amendment, and any weapons seized may properly be introduced in evidence against the person from whom they were taken.

Affirmed.

MR. JUSTICE HARLAN, concurring.

* * *

* * * [I]f the frisk is justified in order to protect the officer during an encounter with a citizen, the officer must first have constitutional grounds to insist on an encounter, to make a *forcible* stop. * * * I would make it perfectly clear that the right to frisk in this case depends upon the reasonableness of a forcible stop to investigate a suspected crime. **[q]**

[q] Justice Harlan's point is that officers need have no additional reasonable suspicion to believe that the person stopped is armed; a legal frisk is justified solely by the legality of the stop. As with his concurrence in *Katz,* Justice Harlan's point came to be accepted as part of the *Terry* rule.

Where such a stop is reasonable, however, the right to frisk must be immediate and automatic if the reason for the stop is, as here, an articulable suspicion of a crime of violence. Just as a full search incident to a lawful arrest requires no additional justification, a limited frisk incident to a lawful stop must often be rapid and routine. There is no reason why an officer, rightfully but forcibly confronting a person suspected of a serious crime, should have to ask one question and take the risk that the answer might be a bullet. * * *

* * *

MR. JUSTICE DOUGLAS, dissenting.

I agree that petitioner was "seized" within the meaning of the Fourth Amendment. I also agree that frisking petitioner and his companions for guns was a "search." But it is a mystery how that "search" and that "seizure" can be constitutional by Fourth Amendment standards, unless there was "probable cause" to believe that (1) a crime had been committed or (2) a crime was in the process of being committed or (3) a crime was about to be committed. **[r]**

[r] Justice Douglas, perhaps the most liberal member of the Warren Court, here combines a liberal policy result with a nonactivist position of adhering to established rules of law.

* * * If loitering were in issue and that was the offense charged, there would be "probable cause" shown. But the crime here is carrying concealed weapons; and there is no basis for concluding that the officer had "probable cause" for believing that that crime was being committed. * * * [A] magistrate would, therefore, have been unauthorized to issue [a warrant], for he can act only if there is a showing of "probable cause." We hold today that the police have greater authority to make a "seizure" and conduct a "search" than a judge has to authorize such action. We have said precisely the opposite over and over again. **[s]**

[s] By putting his point this way, Justice Douglas created a startling and appalling conclusion—that the Court gave police greater power than judges over the liberty of citizens. Was this the first step toward a police state?

* * *

To give the police greater power than a magistrate is to take a long step down the totalitarian path. Perhaps such a step is desirable to cope with modern forms of lawlessness. But if it is taken, it should be the deliberate choice of the people through a constitutional amendment. * * *

* * *

organizing the cases in a purely chronological fashion, they are presented, somewhat artificially, by the source of reasonable suspicion and the place in which the stop occurs.

The Sources of Reasonable Suspicion

Hearsay.   At first, it seemed that the novel *Terry* rule, allowing a Fourth Amendment seizure on less than probable cause (on "reasonable suspicion"), had to be based on the personal observations of an experienced police officer. *Terry* stated: "[I]n determining whether the officer acted reasonably in such circumstances, due weight must be given, not to his inchoate and unparticularized suspicion or 'hunch,' but to the specific reasonable inferences which he is entitled to draw from the facts in light of his experience." Nevertheless, the Court soon established that reasonable suspicion can be based upon reliable hearsay.

In *Adams v. Williams* (1972), a person known to Police Sergeant Connolly approached him at 2:15 A.M. in a high-crime area and told him that an individual in a nearby car was carrying narcotics and had a gun at his waist. Sergeant Connolly approached the car, tapped on the driver's window, and asked the occupant to open the door. Williams, who was alone in the car, rolled down the window instead, and the officer reached in and seized a loaded gun from Williams's waistband. Based on the discovery of the gun, Connolly arrested Williams for illegal possession of a weapon, searched him, and discovered drugs that were admitted into evidence. Unlike Officer McFadden in *Terry,* who personally saw suspicious behavior, Sergeant Connolly did not personally see the gun or corroborate this fact before simultaneously stopping and frisking (i.e., searching and seizing) Williams. The Court expressly ruled that reliable hearsay may be the basis of an officer's investigative stop, which occurred when Sergeant Connolly tapped on the window and demanded that the occupant step out.

Adams v. Williams also extended the *Terry* ruling in several other ways. It extended the stop and frisk authority to crimes of possession. Some felt *Terry* should be limited to violent crimes or thefts. This extension has made stop and frisk a potent tool in the "war on drugs" and has also been at the center of the bitter controversy over racial profiling. (See the "Law in Society" section in Chapter 5.) *Adams* is not a perfect precedent for the proposition that a frisk does not need to be supported by independent reasonable suspicion, but if an officer has reasonable suspicion that a person stopped is armed, the officer may frisk before asking any questions.

Anonymous Tips.   The Court in *Adams* noted that "[t]his is a stronger case than obtains in the case of an anonymous telephone tip." Such a situation was resolved by the Court in *Alabama v. White* (1990). At 3 P.M., Montgomery police received "a telephone call from an anonymous person, stating that Vanessa White would be leaving 235-C Lynwood Terrace Apartments at a particular time in a brown Plymouth station wagon with the right taillight lens broken and that she would be going to Dobey's Motel and would be in possession of about an ounce of cocaine inside a brown attaché case." The police did not know Vanessa White or what she looked like, but they corroborated most of the facts (White was not carrying an attaché case) and stopped White in her car shortly before she reached Dobey's Motel. The officers told her she was stopped because she was suspected of carrying cocaine; they obtained consent to look into a locked, brown attaché case that was in the car. They found drugs in the attaché case.

The Supreme Court held (6–3) that "the tip, as corroborated by independent police work, exhibited sufficient indicia of reliability to provide reasonable suspicion to make the investigatory stop." The decision was assisted to some extent by the ruling of *Illinois v. Gates* (see Chapter 3) in which the Court approved a "totality of circumstances" approach to determining whether an anonymous informant who supplied probable cause for a search warrant was reliable and truthful and had a basis of knowledge. In *White,* the Court applied this approach to find that the totality of circumstances apparently indicated that the informant was so familiar with Vanessa White's movements as to be reliable and truthful and have a basis of knowledge. In the course of its opinion, the Court made an important distinction between probable cause and reasonable suspicion. Reasonable suspicion not only is a lesser quantum of proof, but it is also less reliable. "[R]easonable suspicion can arise from information that is less reliable than that required to show probable cause." This language gives police greater leeway to stop individuals, without great concern that the information supplied is unreliable, than to search.

Justice Stevens, dissenting, saw these facts differently. "An anonymous neighbor's prediction about somebody's time of departure and probable destination is anything but a reliable basis for assuming that the commuter is in possession of an illegal substance." He suggested that White may have been a room clerk at the motel and offered a much more troubling suggestion—that in cases like this, the tipster could be another police officer who has a "hunch" about a person. This is not mere surmise, but it is a technique used by corrupt police, as noted in a book on the subject:

> There happened to be money missing on a job they went on, and the guy who lost the money came into the precinct bitching. It was a set-up job. It wasn't a real radio run. They [the police] had dropped a dime on the guy. They had called 911 themselves and then responded to the bogus call to get inside the building.[28]

The Supreme Court has limited the acceptability of anonymous information that presented only general information. In *Florida v. J. L.* (2000), an anonymous caller reported to the Miami-Dade police that a young black male standing at a particular bus stop and wearing a plaid shirt was carrying a gun. Officers went to the bus stop and saw three black males, one of whom, respondent J. L., was wearing a plaid shirt. Apart from the tip, the officers had no reason to suspect any of the three of illegal conduct. The officers did not see a firearm or observe any unusual movements. One of the officers frisked J. L. and seized a gun from his pocket. J. L., who was then almost sixteen years of age, was charged under state law with carrying a concealed firearm without a license and possessing a firearm while under the age of eighteen. In its unanimous opinion, the Court distinguished *Alabama v. White* by noting that although the tip itself in *White* did not amount to reasonable suspicion, once "police observation showed that the informant had accurately predicted the woman's movements, . . . it become reasonable to think the tipster had inside knowledge about the suspect and therefore to credit his assertion about the cocaine" (*Florida v. J. L.,* 2000). Justice Ginsburg, in her opinion, called *White* a "borderline" decision:

> The tip in the instant case lacked the moderate indicia of reliability present in *White* and essential to the Court's decision in that case. The anonymous call concerning J. L. provided no predictive information and therefore left the police without means to test the informant's knowledge or credibility. That the allegation about the gun turned out to be correct does not suggest that the officers, prior to the frisks, had a reasonable basis for suspecting J. L. of engaging in unlawful conduct. The reasonableness of official suspicion must be measured by what the officers knew before they conducted their search. All the police had to go on in this case was the bare report of an unknown, unaccountable informant who neither explained how he knew about the gun nor supplied any basis for believing he had inside information about J. L. If *White* was a close case on the reliability of anonymous tips, this one surely falls on the other side of the line. (*Florida v. J. L.,* 2000)

Police Bulletin. The *Terry* basis of reasonable suspicion was also expanded in ***United States v. Hensley*** (1985). *Hensley* ruled that police may stop a suspect based on information contained in a flyer or bulletin they receive from another law enforcement department. If the flyer has been issued on the basis of articulable facts supporting a reasonable suspicion that the wanted person has committed an offense (rather than probable cause), then it justifies a stop to check identification, to pose questions to the person, or to detain the person briefly while attempting to obtain further information. *Hensley* therefore held that stops not only may be made to prevent a future crime or to stop ongoing offenses, as was the case in *Terry*, but also may be used to inquire about past criminal acts. Justice O'Connor maintained that although the crime prevention rationale and the exigency present in *Terry* did not exist in *Hensley*, the ability to stop a suspect for questions based on reasonable suspicion promotes the government interest of solving crime and prevents the chance that a suspect might flee.

Terry on the Streets

Several post-*Terry* cases held that police stopped individuals without reasonable suspicion, violating their liberty rights. ***Sibron v. New York*** (1968) was a **companion case** to *Terry*. An NYPD patrol officer saw Sibron "hanging around" a street corner for many hours in the late afternoon and evening in a place where drug sales were believed to occur, talking to known drug addicts. Sibron went into a diner and, as he was eating pie and drinking coffee, was ordered outside by the officer. The officer had seen no evidence of a drug sale, but he approached Sibron, said "You know what I'm after," reached into Sibron's pocket, and found a packet of heroin. The Court held that this seizure was not based on reasonable suspicion and therefore was an unreasonable and unconstitutional stop. There were no articulable objective facts to establish drug dealing or possession. The officer clearly was not "frisking" Sibron for a weapon but simply searching for drugs. The drugs were suppressed as the product of an illegal search and seizure. *Sibron* illustrates the line between legal and illegal stops.

Identification and Loitering Laws.   General loitering statutes must adhere to *Terry* boundaries. The Supreme Court has held that statutes giving police the power to obtain the identification of people walking in public are not valid in the absence of reasonable suspicion to effect a stop. In ***Brown v. Texas*** (1979), an officer in a high-crime area in El Paso saw Brown and a man in an alley around noon. The officer testified that the situation "looked suspicious," but he was unable to point to any facts supporting that conclusion. There is no indication in the record that it was unusual for people to be in the alley." Brown angrily refused to give identification when asked. He was arrested, jailed, convicted, and fined $20 for violating a Texas statute making it a crime for a person to intentionally refuse to report his name and address to a police officer who has lawfully stopped the person and requested such information. The Court ruled that the application of the statute violated the Fourth Amendment because the police had no grounds for stopping Brown in the first place. The mere fact that the area was frequented by drug users was not reasonable suspicion to stop him.

The Court went a step beyond *Brown v. Texas* in favoring individual liberty in ***Kolender v. Lawson*** (1983), holding that a California statute violated due process. The statute required those who "loiter or wander on the streets" to identify themselves and account for their presence when asked to do so by a peace officer. Edward Lawson was detained or arrested under this statute, while walking, on approximately fifteen occasions between March 1975 and January 1977. He was prosecuted twice and convicted once and brought a civil suit to have the law declared unconstitutional. California courts limited the application of the statute only to instances where a police officer "has reasonable suspicion of criminal activity sufficient to justify a *Terry* detention." The Supreme Court ruled that even as so construed, the statute still violated the Fourteenth Amendment in that it was "void for vagueness."

This doctrine states that a law violates due process if it is not sufficiently definite, so that ordinary people are unable to understand what conduct is prohibited. The essential fault with a vague law is that it gives police open-ended and standardless authority, so as to encourage arbitrary and discriminatory law enforcement. The California statute left police with virtually complete discretion to determine whether the suspect offered "credible and reliable" identification. It violated the due process of law as applied. This may be discerned from the facts: An African American man, a business consultant in his mid-thirties who wore his hair in dreadlocks, was arrested fifteen times within two years for simply walking about. (See the "Law in Society" section in Chapter 5.) Justice O'Connor wrote for the majority about the values that underpin these rules: "Our Constitution is designed to maximize individual freedoms within a framework of ordered liberty."

Justice Brennan, concurring, argued that the statute was facially unconstitutional under the Fourth Amendment—that is, it was unconstitutional however applied. Justices White and Rehnquist dissented on the ground that people given actual notice of the application of the statute cannot challenge it on vagueness grounds because they are apprised of the law's impact.

A distinguishing hallmark of American life is the lack of a general requirement that citizens carry official identification at all times. Many democratic nations require their citizens to carry **internal passports.** But even if reasonable, internal passports are opposed because of the powerful cultural norms of individuality and freedom that mark the American character, norms that help to explain the *Kolender v. Lawson* ruling. However, after 9/11 some have called for a national identification card or a system that links driver's licenses to a national registry.[29]

The Court reconsidered a loitering statute in **City of Chicago v. Morales** (1999). A Chicago "gang congregation" ordinance prohibited loitering together in any public place by two or more people if at least one individual was a "criminal street gang member." It defined *loitering* as remaining in any one place with no apparent purpose. A police officer observing what was reasonably believed to be loitering was required to order the group to disperse on threat of criminal penalties. The Chicago Police Department promulgated guidelines to prevent arbitrary or discriminatory enforcement of the ordinance. These allowed only designated gang squad officers to use the ordinance, established detailed criteria for determining street gangs and membership, and limited enforcement to areas with high gang activity (not disclosed to the public). The Court struck down the ordinance on the grounds of due process vagueness.

The ordinance had been vigorously enforced: Forty-two thousand people were arrested for loitering in three years. Justice Stevens, a Chicago native, wrote for the majority. There was no dispute that gang violence imperils safety and disrupts normal street life, he wrote. As *Papachristou v. City of Jacksonville* (1972) made clear, however, a person has a right to "loiter"—that is, "to remove from one place to another according to inclination." Such "loitering" is "an attribute of personal liberty" protected by the Constitution. The Court held that the ordinance specifically violated the Due Process Clause by not clearly defining terms like *disperse* and leaving the *locality.* What exactly would purported gang members have to do to "disperse"? How quickly did they have to move? How far would they have to go? Also, the ordinance did not adequately define "loitering" with the specificity seen in loitering ordinances that targeted drug dealing or prostitution. It therefore "necessarily entrusts lawmaking to the moment-to-moment judgment of the policeman on his beat." Finally, the ordinance could apply to essentially peaceful activity and not to underlying activities that are dangerous. In sum, the ordinance violated the Due Process Clause.

Stop and Identify Statutes.

In *Hiibel v. Sixth Judicial District Court* (2004), the Supreme Court answered a question left open in *Brown v. Texas* (1979) and upheld a law requiring a person who was lawfully stopped by police to give his or her name. "Stop and identify statutes often combine elements of traditional vagrancy laws with provisions intended to regulate police behavior in the course of investigatory stops. The statutes vary from State to State, but all permit an officer to ask or require a suspect to disclose his identity. . . . In some States, a suspect's refusal to identify himself is a misdemeanor offense or civil violation; in others, it is a factor to be considered in whether the suspect has violated loitering laws. In other States, a suspect may decline to identify himself without penalty" (*Hiibel,* 2004).

In the *Hiibel* case, a Nevada sheriff's department received a call about a man assaulting a woman in a red and silver GMC truck on Grass Valley Road. The deputy sheriff who was dispatched to investigate found the truck parked on the side of the road, Hiibel standing outside the truck, and a young woman sitting inside it. Skid marks in the gravel behind the vehicle indicated that the truck had come to a sudden stop. Hiibel was arrested after being asked for his name eleven times and refusing to give it. He was convicted and fined for obstructing a public officer in discharging his duty. Under Nevada's stop and identify statute, the officer had a right to ask only for the name of a stopped person and no right to ask for a driver's license or any other document.

The issue in this case was not whether an officer could properly ask a suspect to identify himself in the course of a *Terry* stop. This practice was recognized in many cases. The issue was whether a lawfully detained suspect could be arrested and prosecuted for failing to give his or her name. The source of Hiibel's obligation to answer the officer was a state law, not the Fourth Amendment. The Supreme Court found that the statutory obligation is consistent with *Terry*'s principles of reasonably balancing police officers' needs with suspects' expectation of privacy. This conclusion was linked to the majority's positive view of identification:

> Obtaining a suspect's name in the course of a *Terry* stop serves important government interests. Knowledge of identity may inform an officer that a suspect is wanted for another offense, or has a record of violence or mental disorder. On the other hand, knowing identity may help clear a suspect and allow the police to concentrate their efforts elsewhere. Identity may prove particularly important in cases such as this, where the police are investigating what appears to be a domestic assault. Officers called to investigate domestic disputes need to know whom they are dealing with, in order to assess the situation, the threat to their own safety, and possible danger to the potential victim. (*Hiibel v. Sixth Judicial District Court,* 2004)

Four justices dissented. Justice Stevens believed that the Fifth Amendment privilege against self-incrimination was violated because a person forced to give his or her name provides a *testimonial* communication. The person's name can be used to incriminate him or her:

> A person's identity obviously bears informational and incriminating worth, even if the [name] itself is not inculpatory. A name can provide the key to a broad array of information about the person, particularly in the hands of a police officer with access to a range of law enforcement databases. And that information, in turn, can be tremendously useful in a criminal prosecution. It is therefore quite wrong to suggest that a person's identity provides a link in the chain to incriminating evidence only in unusual circumstances. (*Hiibel v. Sixth Judicial District Court,* 2004, Stevens, J., dissenting, internal quote marks and citations omitted)

Justices Stephen Breyer, David Souter, and Ruth Bader Ginsburg based their dissent on the Fourth Amendment, arguing that the rule against requiring identification during a stop was well established.

Fleeing from the Police.

Among the most hotly contested post-*Terry* cases have been those concerning scenarios in which a police officer follows or chases a person. *Michigan v. Chesternut* (1988) held that police "intrusion" did not amount to an illegal detention and search. Chesternut, standing on a Detroit street corner, began to run when he saw a police car drive near. The patrol car turned the corner and followed to see where he was going. The car quickly caught up with him and drove alongside for a short distance. The officers saw Chesternut discard packets from his right-hand pocket; when they retrieved the packets, they found pills that one officer, who was trained as a paramedic, identified as codeine. Chesternut was arrested and searched, and more drugs were found on his person. The Michigan courts held that the police were engaged in an "investigatory pursuit" that amounted to a seizure under *Terry*.

A unanimous Supreme Court reversed, holding that the police conduct of driving alongside the defendant did not constitute a stop or a Fourth Amendment seizure. The police used no flashers or siren, drew no weapons, and did not order the defendant to stop. The car was not operated in an aggressive way to block Chesternut's course or otherwise control his speed or movement. "While the very presence of a police car driving parallel to a running pedestrian could be somewhat intimidating, this kind of police presence does not, standing alone, constitute a seizure. . . . The police therefore were not required to have 'a particularized and objective basis for suspecting [Chesternut] of criminal activity,' in order to pursue him" (*Michigan v. Chesternut*, 1988). *Chesternut* is an example of the rule that police need no evidentiary basis for observing on-the-street behavior, even if the observation becomes obvious.

In *California v. Hodari D.*, the police did not simply follow, but clearly chased, a person on foot.

Read Case and Comments: *California v. Hodari D.*

One commentator sees *Hodari D.* as the "culmination of a struggle between two factions of the Supreme Court," and a victory by the group led by conservative Justices Kennedy and Scalia. If the *Mendenhall* Court meant what it said when it proposed that a seizure is to be measured by the reasonable understanding of the individual, then the majority in *Hodari D.* created a new rule when it added a "physical restraint" element to Fourth Amendment seizures.[30] A year before *Hodari D.*, a leading scholar accepted as an established rule that "[w]hen a cop accosts a citizen on the street, the constitutional standard for measuring whether a seizure occurs is whether—in light of the totality of the circumstances—a reasonable person would feel free to leave the scene."[31] Professor Tracey Maclin saw this as a matter of commonsense reality: "In the typical street encounter, few persons, if any, feel free to ignore or leave the presence of a police officer who has approached and questioned them. . . . [T]he average individual who is approached by a police officer does not feel free to leave."[32] The implication of a pure *Mendenhall* rule plus "what everyone knows about being approached by the police" was that a police officer who "rushes" an individual without reasonable suspicion has seized that person; and if the person flees and tosses away contraband, its seizure is the product of an illegal search and seizure. The *Hodari D.* modification allows the tossed contraband to be taken and used as "abandoned" property.

The unresolved issue in *Hodari D.*—whether mere flight from the sight of a police officer established reasonable suspicion for an officer to give chase—was settled in favor of the police in **Illinois v. Wardlow** (2000). A four-car police caravan was cruising through a high-crime neighborhood, looking for on-the-street drug deals. Sam Wardlow was standing alone and holding an opaque bag; he made eye contact with an officer in the last car and "fled." Two officers in the car watched Wardlow run through a passageway and an alley and eventually cornered him on the street. One officer exited his car, stopped Wardlow, "and immediately conducted a protective pat-down search for weapons because in his experience it was common for there to be weapons in the near vicinity of narcotics transactions. During the frisk, Officer Nolan squeezed the bag respondent was carrying and felt a heavy, hard object similar to the shape of a gun. The officer then opened the bag and discovered a .38-caliber handgun with five live rounds of ammunition. The officers arrested Wardlow."

The Court emphasized the rule of *Brown v. Texas* (1979)—the simple presence of a person in a high-crime area does not give officers reasonable suspicion to stop a person. On the other hand, the Court ruled that unprovoked flight from the police, coupled with "commonsense judgment . . . and inferences about human behavior," constitutes reasonable suspicion. The Court did not say that flight is a per se factor that always established reasonable suspicion. While simple unprovoked flight tends to be a basis of reasonable suspicion, under this view, the officer may also take into account other factors, such as the belief that a neighborhood is a high-crime area. Four justices in *Wardlow*—Stevens, Souter, Ginsburg, and Breyer—concurred in part and dissented in part. The concurring opinion kept alive the idea that under some conditions flight will not be viewed as reasonable suspicion for a stop.

The ruling creates some tension with another rule of *Terry:* that a person against whom the police do not have reasonable suspicion may refuse to talk to the officer and, citing *Bostick,* that "any 'refusal to cooperate, without more, does not furnish the minimal level of objective justification needed for a detention or seizure.'" If a police officer, with no reasonable suspicion, approaches a person on the street to ask if the person will consent to talk to the officer and the person "flees," this could invoke reasonable suspicion. Much would depend on the facts of such a scenario. *Wardlow* does not fully define what is meant by flight. Thus, under the facts of *Wardlow,* it is unclear whether flight occurs if a person, after looking at an officer, gets on a bicycle and rides away, hails a taxi and drives off, or enters the building he was standing in front of.[33] Such issues will be resolved in future cases. *Wardlow* clearly expands the actual authority of police to control the streets.

Terry on the Road

Many *Terry* cases have developed auxiliary rules for interpreting the stop and frisk authority in automobile stop situations. The scope of a warrantless automobile search based on probable cause is dealt with in Chapter 5.

Scope of a Terry *Stop and Frisk.*

Most *Terry* cases involve a frisk of a person. *Michigan v. Long* (1983) held that when police stop a driver without arresting him, they may make a quick and cursory examination of the car's interior—a frisk of the car, so to speak. In *Long,* sheriff's deputies stopped a speeding and erratically driven car. The driver pulled into a ditch and exited the car. The door was left open. The driver, David Long, did not produce identification when asked to do so. Long began to walk back to the car but was stopped and frisked. No weapons were found. The deputies saw a hunting knife on the floorboard of the driver's side of the car. One deputy peered into the car with a flashlight and saw something protruding from under the armrest on the front seat. He knelt in the vehicle and lifted the armrest, saw an open pouch on the front seat, and, upon flashing his light on the pouch, determined that it contained what appeared to be marijuana. Long was arrested, and a search of the car's trunk revealed seventy-five pounds of marijuana.

The Court held the search constitutional under the principles of *Terry.* One reason is that "investigative detentions involving suspects in vehicles are especially fraught with danger to police officers." Thus, to protect their safety, police officers who stop cars may engage in a cursory examination of the passenger areas of the vehicle to look for weapons in those areas in which a weapon may be placed or hidden when they have a reasonable belief based on articulable facts that the suspect poses a danger and may gain immediate control of the weapons.

Inferential Reasoning and Reasonable Suspicion.

Terry defines reasonable suspicion, which justifies a stop, as "specific and articulable facts which, taken together with *rational inferences from those facts,* reasonably warrant that intrusion" (*Terry v. Ohio,* 1968; emphasis added). This important part of the *Terry* doctrine was clarified and extended in **United States v. Cortez** (1981). U.S. Border Patrol officers, alerted by distinctive footprints and tire tracks in a sparsely settled area of desert thirty miles north of the Mexican border, deduced that a truck capable of holding eight to twenty people would approach from the east and stop between 2 A.M. and 6 A.M. near milepost 122 on Highway 86. As the officers surveyed the road on a particularly bright moonlit night, a camper passed traveling west and then returned approaching from the east at about the time it would take to return from milepost 122. Agents stopped the camper, and illegal aliens were found inside. The Court unanimously held that this stop

CASE AND COMMENTS

California v. Hodari D.

499 U.S. 621, 111 S.Ct. 1547, 113 L.Ed.2d 690 (1991)

[a] Does a group of huddled teenagers provide grounds to arrest them? To forcibly stop them under *Terry?*

[b] Do you think that a teen who runs from the sight of a cop should be chased? If caught, should he be arrested or subjected to field interrogation?

[c] California conceded that the flight of the youths upon seeing the police was not in itself reasonable suspicion for a *Terry* stop. Although Justice Scalia thought the point was arguable, he was bound by this concession. The issue was left open for a later case.

[d] Is the chase of a sailing ship on the high seas a good analogy for a police officer chasing a youth through a city neighborhood?

JUSTICE SCALIA delivered the opinion of the Court.

Late one evening in April 1988, Officers Brian McColgin and Jerry Pertoso were on patrol in a high-crime area of Oakland, California. They were dressed in street clothes but wearing jackets with "Police" embossed on both front and back. Their unmarked car proceeded west on Foothill Boulevard, and turned south onto 63rd Avenue. [a] As they rounded the corner, they saw four or five youths huddled around a small red car parked at the curb. When the youths, [including Hodari D.], saw the officers' car approaching they apparently panicked, and took flight. * * *

The officers were suspicious and gave chase. [b] McColgin remained in the car * * *; Pertoso left the car [and chased on foot]. Hodari [emerged from an alley and did not see] Pertoso until the officer was almost upon him, whereupon he tossed away what appeared to be a small rock. A moment later, Pertoso tackled Hodari, handcuffed him, and radioed for assistance. Hodari was found to be carrying $130 in cash and a pager; and the rock he had discarded was found to be crack cocaine.

In the juvenile proceeding brought against him, Hodari moved to suppress the evidence relating to the cocaine. The court denied the motion without opinion. The California Court of Appeal reversed, holding that Hodari had been "seized" when he saw Officer Pertoso running towards him, that this seizure was unreasonable under the Fourth Amendment, and that the evidence of cocaine had to be suppressed as the fruit of that illegal seizure. The California Supreme Court denied the State's application for review. We granted certiorari. * * *

As this case comes to us, the only issue presented is whether, at the time he dropped the drugs, Hodari had been "seized" within the meaning of the Fourth Amendment. [c] If so, respondent argues, the drugs were the fruit of that seizure and the evidence concerning them was properly excluded. If not, the drugs were abandoned by Hodari and lawfully recovered by the police, and the evidence should have been admitted. (In addition, of course, Pertoso's seeing the rock of cocaine, at least if he recognized it as such, would provide reasonable suspicion for the unquestioned seizure that occurred when he tackled Hodari. * * *).

We have long understood that the Fourth Amendment's protection against "unreasonable . . . seizures" includes seizure of the person. * * * From the time of the founding to the present, the word "seizure" has meant a "taking possession." * * * For most purposes at common law, the word connoted not merely grasping, or applying physical force to, the animate or inanimate object in question, but actually bringing it within physical control. [d] A ship still fleeing, even though under attack, would not be considered to have been seized as a war prize. * * * To constitute an arrest, however—the quintessential **seizure of the person** under our Fourth Amendment jurisprudence— the mere grasping or application of physical force with lawful authority, whether or not it succeeded in subduing the arrestee, was sufficient. * * *

To say that an arrest is effected by the slightest application of physical force, despite the arrestee's escape, is not to say that for Fourth Amendment purposes there is a *continuing* arrest during the period of fugitivity. If, for example, Pertoso had laid his hands upon Hodari to arrest him, but Hodari had broken away and had *then* cast away the cocaine, it would hardly be realistic to say that that disclosure had been made during the course of an arrest. * * * The present case, however, is even one step further removed. It does not involve the application of any physical force; Hodari was untouched by Officer Pertoso at the time he discarded the cocaine. His defense relies instead upon the proposition that a seizure occurs "when the officer, by means of physical force *or show of authority,* has in some way restrained the liberty of a citizen." *Terry v. Ohio* (emphasis added). Hodari contends (and we accept as true for purposes of this decision) that Pertoso's pursuit qualified as a "show of authority" calling upon Hodari to halt. The narrow question before us is whether, with respect to a show of authority as with respect to application of physical force, a seizure occurs even though the subject does not yield. We hold that it does not.

The language of the Fourth Amendment, of course, cannot sustain respondent's contention. The word "seizure" readily bears the meaning of a laying on of hands or application of physical force to restrain movement, even when it is ultimately unsuccessful. ("She seized the purse-snatcher, but he broke out of her grasp.") It does not remotely apply, however, to the prospect of a policeman yelling "Stop, in the name of the law!" at a fleeing form that continues to flee. That is no seizure. **[e]** Nor can the result respondent wishes to achieve be produced—indirectly, as it were—by suggesting that Pertoso's uncomplied-with show of authority was a common-law arrest, and then appealing to the principle that all common-law arrests are seizures. An arrest requires *either* physical force (as described above) *or,* where that is absent, *submission* to the assertion of authority. * * *

We do not think it desirable, even as a policy matter, to stretch the Fourth Amendment beyond its words and beyond the meaning of arrest, as respondent urges. Street pursuits always place the public at some risk, and compliance with police orders to stop should therefore be encouraged. * * *

Respondent contends that his position is sustained by the so-called *Mendenhall* test, . . . "A person has been 'seized' within the meaning of the Fourth Amendment only if, in view of all the circumstances surrounding the incident, a reasonable person would have believed that he was not free to leave." * * * **[f]** In seeking to rely upon that test here, respondent fails to read it carefully. It says that a person has been seized "only if," not that he has been seized "whenever"; it states a *necessary,* but not a *sufficient* condition for seizure—or, more precisely, for seizure effected through a "show of authority." *Mendenhall* establishes that the test for existence of a "show of authority" is an objective one: not whether the citizen perceived that he was being ordered to restrict his movement, but whether the officer's words and actions would have conveyed that to a reasonable person. * * *

[This case is like the chase in *Brower v. Inyo County* (1989): there was no arrest until Brower crashed into the roadblock.]

In sum, assuming that Pertoso's pursuit in the present case constituted a "show of authority" enjoining Hodari to halt, since Hodari did not comply with that injunction he was not seized until he was tackled. The cocaine abandoned while he was running was in this case not the fruit of a seizure, and his motion to exclude evidence of it was properly denied. We reverse the decision of the California Court of Appeal, and remand for further proceedings not inconsistent with this opinion.

JUSTICE STEVENS, with whom JUSTICE MARSHALL joins, dissenting.

The Court's narrow construction of the word "seizure" represents a significant, and in my view, unfortunate, departure from prior case law construing the Fourth Amendment. * * * [T]he Court now adopts a definition of "seizure" that is unfaithful to a long line of Fourth Amendment cases. Even if the Court were defining seizure for the first time, which it is not, the definition that it chooses today is profoundly unwise. **[g]** In its decision, the Court assumes, without acknowledging, that a police officer may now fire his weapon at an innocent citizen and not implicate the Fourth Amendment—as long as he misses his target.

For the purposes of decision, the following propositions are not in dispute. First, when Officer Pertoso began his pursuit of respondent, the officer did not have a lawful basis for

(continued)

[e] As *Watson* demonstrated, a strict reading of the language of the Constitution does not always bind the Court. Is it reasonable to view a chase as a seizure if the police officer is close to the person running and is likely to capture him?

[f] Would it not seem to a reasonable person, from the officer's actions, that Hodari D. believed he was not free to leave? Does this conclusion help Hodari D.'s argument?

[g] If a police officer, without probable cause or reasonable suspicion, fired a gun at you and missed, should you be able to claim a violation of your Fourth Amendment rights in a civil suit against the officer? If so, this example undermines Justice Scalia's argument.

either stopping or arresting respondent. * * * Second, the officer's chase amounted to a "show of force" as soon as respondent saw the officer nearly upon him. * * * Third, the act of discarding the rock of cocaine was the direct consequence of the show of force. * * * Fourth, as the Court correctly demonstrates, no common-law arrest occurred until the officer tackled respondent. * * * Thus, the Court is quite right in concluding that the abandonment of the rock was not the fruit of a common-law arrest.

[h] A touching would manifest the officer's intent to arrest and would make the person liable for resisting arrest. Should constitutional rights turn on whether the officer "tagged" the fleeing youth?

It is equally clear, however, that if the officer had succeeded in touching respondent before he dropped the rock—even if he did not subdue him—an arrest would have occurred. **[h]** * * * In that event (assuming the touching precipitated the abandonment), the evidence would have been the fruit of an unlawful common-law arrest. The distinction between the actual case and the hypothetical case is the same as the distinction between the common-law torts of assault and battery—a touching converts the former into the latter. Although the distinction between assault and battery was important for pleading purposes, * * * the distinction should not take on constitutional dimensions. The Court mistakenly allows this common-law distinction to define its interpretation of the Fourth Amendment.

[i] This challenges the accuracy and completeness of Justice Scalia's common law analysis—an especially sharp attack because Justice Scalia, as an originalist, relies heavily on the common law.

At the same time, the Court fails to recognize the existence of another, more telling, common-law distinction—the distinction between an arrest and an attempted arrest. As the Court teaches us, the distinction between battery and assault was critical to a correct understanding of the common law of arrest. * * * ("An arrest requires either physical force . . . *or,* where that is absent, *submission* to the assertion of authority"). However, the facts of this case do not describe an actual arrest, but rather, an unlawful *attempt* to take a presumptively innocent person into custody. Such an attempt was unlawful at common law. **[i]** Thus, if the Court wants to define the scope of the Fourth Amendment based on the common law, it should look, not to the common law of arrest, but to the common law of attempted arrest, according to the facts of this case.

* * *

[The dissent goes on to criticize the majority for taking a narrow view of seizure that goes against the policy purposes of *Katz* that broadened the range of behaviors that came within the scope of Fourth Amendment seizures, such as the stop and frisk in *Terry v. Ohio*. *Terry* said that a Fourth Amendment seizure occurs when an officer, by means of physical force or show of authority, has in some way restrained a citizen's liberty. Such an interference with liberty occurred in this case, and so the majority's common law reasoning fails to comport with the constitutional dimensions of Fourth Amendment law after *Terry.*]

Even though momentary, a seizure occurs whenever an objective evaluation of a police officer's show of force conveys the message that the citizen is not entirely free to leave—in other words, that his or her liberty is being restrained in a significant way. * * *

* * *

was based on reasonable suspicion. Chief Justice Burger established a structure for reasonable suspicion analysis:

> Courts have used a variety of terms to capture the elusive concept of what cause is sufficient to authorize police to stop a person. Terms like "articulable reasons" and "founded suspicion" are not self-defining; they fall short of providing clear guidance dispositive of the myriad factual situations that arise. But the essence of all that has been written is that the totality of the circumstances—the whole picture—must be taken into account. . . .
>
> The idea that an assessment of the whole picture must yield a particularized suspicion contains two elements, each of which must be present before a stop is permissible. First, the assessment must be based upon all the circumstances. The analysis proceeds with various objective observations, information from police reports, if such are available, and consideration of the modes or patterns of operation of certain kinds of lawbreakers. From these data, a trained officer draws inferences and makes deductions—inferences and deductions that might well elude an untrained person.
>
> The process does not deal with hard certainties, but with probabilities. . . .
>
> The second element contained in the idea that an assessment of the whole picture must yield a particularized suspicion is the concept that the process just described must raise a suspicion that the particular individual being stopped is engaged in wrongdoing. (*United States v. Cortez,* 1981)

Cortez continues to support the concept of **police officer expertise,** which was a basis of finding reasonable suspicion in the *Terry* case.

Inferences were key to the decision in ***United States v. Arvizu*** (2002). Arvizu was driving a minivan with his wife and children on an unpaved road in a remote area in the Coronado National Forest of southeastern Arizona known for drug trafficking. Border patrol checkpoints are staffed intermittently, and roving patrols are used to apprehend smugglers trying to circumvent the checkpoints. Magnetic sensors facilitate agents' efforts in patrolling these areas. A sensor was triggered around 2:15 P.M. This timing coincided with the point when agents begin heading back to the checkpoint for a shift change, leaving the area unpatrolled. Alien smugglers do extensive scouting and seem to be most active when agents are returning to the checkpoint. An agent told Agent Stoddard that the same sensor had gone off several weeks before, leading to the apprehension of a drug-carrying minivan using the same route.

Stoddard proceeded to the area and observed the minivan passing. As it approached, it slowed dramatically, from about 50 miles per hour to 25 or 30 miles per hour. He saw five occupants inside: two adults in the front seat and three children in the back. The driver appeared stiff and his posture very rigid. He did not look at Stoddard and seemed to be trying to pretend that Stoddard was not there. Stoddard thought this suspicious because in his experience on patrol most people look over and see what is going on, and in that area most drivers give border patrol agents a friendly wave. Stoddard noticed that the knees of the two children sitting in the very back seat were unusually high, as if their feet were propped up on some cargo on the floor. As Stoddard followed the minivan, all of the children, still facing forward, put their hands up at the same time and began to wave at Stoddard in an abnormal way. It looked to Stoddard as if the children were being instructed. Their odd waving continued on and off for about four to five minutes. A registration check disclosed that the minivan was registered to an address in Douglas, Arizona, four blocks north of the border in an area notorious for alien and narcotics smuggling. Stoddard stopped the van, asked if he could search, and Arvizu agreed. A duffel bag containing 128.85 pounds of marijuana was found.

The U.S. Court of Appeals struck down the stop, by isolating the factors and noting that each was innocent. For example, that court noted that slowing down after seeing an officer is common. It dismissed entirely the children's waving, saying, "If every odd act engaged in by one's children . . . could contribute to a finding of reasonable suspicion, the vast majority of American parents might be stopped regularly within a block of their homes."

The Supreme Court reversed the decision and unanimously upheld the stop. It emphasized that the totality of the circumstances must be considered. "This process allows officers to draw on their own experience and specialized training to make inferences from and deductions about the cumulative information available to them that 'might well elude an untrained person.'" The Court noted that it has deliberately avoided reducing reasonable suspicion to "a neat set of legal rules." Giving due weight to the factual inferences drawn by Stoddard and the district court judge, the Court ruled that the agent had reasonable suspicion to believe that Arvizu was engaged in illegal activity.

Brevity Requirement.

Another automobile stop and frisk case clarified an important *Terry* rule: A legal detention must be reasonably brief. In ***United States v. Sharpe*** (1985), a Drug Enforcement Agency (DEA) agent patrolling a road under surveillance for suspected drug trafficking noticed an overloaded pickup truck with an attached trailer being followed closely by a Pontiac. After following the two vehicles for twenty miles, the officer decided to make an investigatory stop and radioed the South Carolina Highway Patrol for assistance. When the DEA agent and the state police officer indicated that the two vehicles were to pull over, the Pontiac did so, but the truck continued along the road in an attempt to evade the state police. The driver of the Pontiac was detained for twenty minutes while the DEA agent followed the truck, approached it after it was stopped, smelled marijuana in it, and returned to the detained Pontiac. While the Court found that the officer had reasonable suspicion to make the initial stop, at issue was whether a twenty-minute detention was too long under the *Terry* doctrine because it violated the **brevity requirement** for stops. The Supreme Court held that whether a stop is too long (and thus becomes an arrest) depends not only on the length of time of the stop but also on the surrounding circumstances. The question is whether the length of time employed was reasonable. In *Sharpe*, the delay occurred because of the evasive action of the driver of the truck. The Court found that because the police acted diligently to ascertain the facts without creating unnecessary delays, *Terry* was not violated. Note that a twenty-minute stop was sufficiently long so that a special reason had to be supplied to justify it. *Terry* stops are supposed to be just long enough for an officer to ask questions to determine, based on objective factors, whether there is probable cause to arrest or no basis for further detention.

Authority to Stop an Automobile.

In ***Delaware v. Prouse*** (1979), a patrol officer made a "routine" stop of a car, explaining, "I saw the car in the area and wasn't answering any complaints, so I decided to pull them off." Prior to the vehicle stop, he did not observe any traffic or equipment violations or any suspicious activity. He made the stop merely to check the driver's license and registration. The officer did not act pursuant to any standards, guidelines, or procedures pertaining to document spot checks as defined by his department or the state attorney general. During the stop, the officer smelled marijuana and made an arrest and seizure.

Lower courts had split on whether this kind of vehicle stop, without reasonable suspicion or probable cause, violated the Fourth Amendment. The Supreme Court, holding this kind of stop and seizure unconstitutional, was not writing on a blank slate. Four years earlier, it had decided in ***United States v. Brignoni-Ponce*** (1975) that Border Patrol agents conducting roving patrols near the international border violated the Fourth Amendment by stopping vehicles at random. Although intercepting illegal aliens was important, the Court felt that it was unconstitutional to stop cars—not at the border or at fixed checkpoints—but on roads within one hundred miles of the Mexican border, without establishing reasonable suspicion. The reasons are that such stops (1) interfere with freedom of movement, (2) are inconvenient and time consuming, and (3) may create substantial anxiety for a driver who is pulled over for no apparent reason. In contrast, a motorist does not feel the same anxiety at a roadblock or fixed checkpoint where other motorists are observed going through the same drill. The Court dismissed the arguments that an automobile stop is an administrative search or that people have a lesser expectation of privacy in a car than in a home:

> An individual operating or traveling in an automobile does not lose all reasonable expectation of privacy simply because the automobile and its use are subject to government regulation. Automobile travel is a basic, pervasive, and often necessary mode of transportation to and from one's home, workplace, and leisure activities. Many people spend more hours each day traveling in cars than walking on the streets. Undoubtedly, many find a greater sense of security and privacy in traveling in an automobile than they do in exposing themselves by pedestrian or other modes of travel. Were the individual subject to unfettered governmental intrusion every time he entered an automobile, the security guaranteed by the Fourth Amendment would be seriously circumscribed. (*Delaware v. Prouse,* 1979)

The stop in *Prouse* was unconstitutional, and the evidence had to be suppressed.

An important related issue is whether a police officer can stop a car based on reasonable suspicion of a traffic offense when the *true motive* of the officer is to search for drugs—the **pretext search** issue. This question is highly contentious because police departments, especially those astride busy highways, "earn" billions of dollars in drug asset forfeitures of cars and cash and so have an incentive to stringently enforce traffic laws. The question has become politically explosive because it has been shown that this practice has been accompanied with "racial profiling" that disproportionately targets minorities. (See the "Law in Society" section in Chapter 5.)

A unanimous Supreme Court resolved the pretext search issue in favor of the police in **Whren v. United States** (1996) by making it clear that an automobile stop and arrest are valid whenever the police have objective evidence of probable cause of a traffic violation. On a June evening,

> plainclothes vice-squad officers of the District of Columbia Metropolitan Police Department were patrolling a "high drug area" of the city in an unmarked car. Their suspicions were aroused when they passed a dark Pathfinder truck with temporary license plates and youthful occupants waiting at a stop sign, the driver looking down into the lap of the passenger at his right. The truck remained stopped at the intersection for what seemed an unusually long time—more than 20 seconds. When the police car executed a U-turn in order to head back toward the truck, the Pathfinder turned suddenly to its right, without signalling, and sped off at an "unreasonable" speed. The policemen followed, and in a short while overtook the Pathfinder when it stopped behind other traffic at a red light. They pulled up alongside, and Officer Ephraim Soto stepped out and approached the driver's door, identifying himself as a police officer and directing the driver, petitioner Brown, to put the vehicle in park. When Soto drew up to the driver's window, he immediately observed two large plastic bags of what appeared to be crack cocaine in petitioner Whren's hands. Petitioners were arrested, and quantities of several types of illegal drugs were retrieved from the vehicle. (*Whren v. United States,* 1996)

Whren argued that the stop was not "really" for the traffic infractions—that the traffic stop was a pretext for searching for drugs. The Supreme Court, however, ruled that the Fourth Amendment review standard is objective, rather than subjective, placing examination of the officer's motives off limits. Whren then argued that D.C. police regulations "permit plainclothes officers in unmarked vehicles to enforce traffic laws 'only in the case of a violation that is so grave as to pose an immediate threat to the safety of others.'" In light of these regulations, he suggested that for an auto stop for a traffic violation to be valid, in addition to having probable cause of the traffic infraction, the stop must be one that would typically be made for a traffic infraction.

The Court refused to establish such a rule. The motives of officers are irrelevant in inventory searches, administrative searches, maritime searches, and searches incident to arrest as long as there is an objective legal standard—probable cause—to support the intrusion. The only cases in which the Court has balanced the interests of a defendant against the state to find that probable cause is not a sufficient standard are cases involving

> searches or seizures conducted in an extraordinary manner, unusually harmful to an individual's privacy or even physical interests—such as, for example, seizure by means of deadly force, [*Tennessee v. Garner* (1985)], unannounced entry into a home, [*Wilson v. Arkansas* (1995)], entry into a home without a warrant, [*Welsh v. Wisconsin* (1984)], or physical penetration of the body, [*Winston v. Lee* (1985)]. The making of a traffic stop out-of-uniform does not remotely qualify as such an extreme practice, and so is governed by the usual rule that probable cause to believe the law has been broken "outbalances" private interest in avoiding police contact. (*Whren v. United States*, 1996)

Field interrogation following an automobile search was an issue in ***Ornelas v. United States*** (1996). On an early December morning in Milwaukee, an experienced detective spotted a 1981 two-door Oldsmobile with California license plates in a motel parking lot. The car was registered to Ornelas, who with no reservations had checked into the motel with another man at 4 A.M. "The car attracted [the detective's] attention for two reasons: because older model, two-door General Motors cars are a favorite with drug couriers because it is easy to hide things in them; and because California is a 'source State' for drugs." To confirm this "profile" information, a check of the DEA's "Narcotics and Dangerous Drugs Information System (NADDIS), a federal database of known and suspected drug traffickers" revealed that both names of the motel guests appeared as known or suspected drug dealers.

The two men were subjected to a *Terry* stop when entering the car later that morning. The officers, who had searched two thousand cars for drugs over a period of nine years, looked into the car. One "noticed that a panel above the right rear passenger armrest felt somewhat loose and suspected that the panel might have been removed and contraband hidden inside. . . . [He] dismantled the panel and discovered two kilograms of cocaine." Was there reasonable suspicion to stop the men and probable cause to remove the panel? The district court ultimately answered each question in the affirmative.

The trial judge found that reasonable suspicion existed because "the model, age, and source-State origin of the car, and the fact that two men traveling together checked into a motel at 4 o'clock in the morning without reservations, formed a *drug-courier profile*. This profile, together with the NADDIS reports, gave rise to reasonable suspicion of drug-trafficking activity. . . . [R]easonable suspicion became probable cause when [the officer] found the loose panel." Although the Supreme Court remanded the case to the Court of Appeals to review the District Court's decision, Chief Justice Rehnquist, a Milwaukee native who had moved to the warmer climate of Arizona, recited specific local facts to guide that court. "For example, what may not amount to reasonable suspicion at a motel located alongside a transcontinental highway at the height of the summer tourist season may rise to that level in December in Milwaukee." Given Milwaukee's cold temperatures in December, it is "a reasonable inference that a Californian stopping in Milwaukee in December is either there to transact business or to visit family or friends." *Ornelas* also indicates that the use of drug courier profiles is now pervasive in American policing.

Controlling People in the Stopped Automobile.
The Supreme Court has given police almost complete control either to order the driver and passengers to remain in the automobile when it is stopped or to order the driver and passengers out. The primary rationale in these case is the safety of the officer.

In ***Pennsylvania v. Mimms*** (1977), an automobile was stopped for an expired license plate. On ordering the driver out, the officer noticed a bulge under the driver's sports jacket. A frisk produced a loaded revolver in Mimms's waistband. Balancing the interests of individual privacy against the safety of law enforcement officers, the Court unanimously upheld the officer's frisk and noted that many police officers are killed during routine traffic stops. Against this, the added intrusion of requiring that a driver exit the car momentarily is so minimal that it hardly rises to the level of a "petty indignity"; at most, it is a mere inconvenience that cannot prevail against legitimate concerns for the officer's safety.

The rule of *Mimms* was extended to passengers in **Maryland v. Wilson** (1997). Police stopped a speeding automobile—a rental car with no regular license plate. The officer ordered the driver and the passengers to exit the car. There was no legal suspicion that the passengers were engaged in any illegal activity. As Wilson, a passenger, got out of the car, an amount of crack cocaine fell to the ground. Maryland's highest court suppressed the evidence on the ground that the police had no authority to order passengers out of the car without some level of individualized suspicion. The court viewed the order to exit as a Fourth Amendment personal seizure. The Supreme Court, in an opinion by Chief Justice Rehnquist, reversed. The *Mimms* rationale—the officer's safety—applied equally to passengers. Indeed, the presence of additional people in the car increases the danger to the police. Despite the lack of probable cause or reasonable suspicion against the passenger, and the fact that a passenger has a greater liberty interest than the driver, as a practical matter the passenger is already stopped by the police detaining the vehicle. This case is analogous to *Michigan v. Summers* (1981), which states that police may temporarily detain a person whose home is being searched under a search warrant.

Justice Stevens dissented, arguing that statistics show no greater danger to police from passengers in stopped cars; the decision intrudes on personal liberty without solid reason. Justice Kennedy dissented, saying, "Traffic stops, even for minor violations, can take upwards of 30 minutes. When an officer commands passengers innocent of any violation to leave the vehicle and stand by the side of the road in full view of the public, the seizure is serious, not trivial." This decision, plus *Whren* (pretextual stops), "puts tens of millions of passengers at risk of arbitrary control by the police." When the *Wilson* rule is combined with the decision of *Wyoming v. Houghton* (1999) (see Chapter 5), which allows the police to search the handbag of a passenger when there is probable cause to search the automobile, and with the *Atwood* rule, which authorizes the custodial seizure for any arrest, an officer's control over a stopped automobile is complete.[34]

Terry in Tight Places

The nature of a stop was explored in **Immigration and Naturalization Service v. Delgado** (1984). In that case, INS officers looking for illegal immigrants walked through a factory with the owner's consent. They briefly questioned workers at their workstations and, if reasonable, asked to see immigration papers. Agents were posted at the factory exits. The Supreme Court held that the illegal workers were not seized within the meaning of the Fourth Amendment, reasoning that "police questioning, by itself, is unlikely to result in a Fourth Amendment violation." The factory workers were not free to leave, but the "detention" was caused not by the police but by the workers' normal employment requirements. The Court held that the agents were simply questioning people and that these encounters were consensual. Justices Brennan and Marshall dissented, arguing that the show of authority by the immigration officials was sufficiently substantial to "overbear the will of any reasonable person." Based on this show of authority, reasoned the dissenters, the factory workers were forcibly stopped within the meaning of *Terry*.

The use of drug courier profiles at airports (discussed later in this chapter) spawned similar practices at bus and train stations. In **Florida v. Bostick** (1991), decided shortly after *Hodari D.*, the Supreme Court confirmed its sharp swing toward supporting the police in investigatory stops.

> Two [Broward County sheriff's] officers, complete with badges, insignia and one of them holding a recognizable zipper pouch, containing a pistol, boarded a bus bound from Miami to Atlanta during a stopover in Fort Lauderdale. Eyeing the passengers, the officers admittedly without articulable suspicion, picked out the defendant passenger and asked to inspect his ticket and identification. The ticket, from Miami to Atlanta, matched the defendant's identification and both were immediately returned to him as unremarkable. However, the two police

officers persisted and explained their presence as narcotics agents on the lookout for illegal drugs. In pursuit of that aim, they then requested the defendant's consent to search his luggage. (*Florida v. Bostick,* 1991)

Cocaine was found in the bag. Before they began this encounter, the officers had no reasonable suspicion or probable cause to believe that Terrance Bostick was carrying drugs.

The issue was whether Bostick consented to the search or whether he was seized. Justice O'Connor's majority opinion held that Bostick consented: "Our cases make it clear that a seizure does not occur simply because a police officer approaches an individual and asks a few questions. So long as a reasonable person would feel free to disregard the police and go about his business, . . . the encounter is consensual and no reasonable suspicion is required" (*Florida v. Bostick,* 1991, internal quotation marks modified). It is curious that the Court cited *Hodari D.* for this proposition rather than relying exclusively on *Mendenhall.* The Court's majority in these cases appears to have selected a different theory in each case to ensure the decision would favor law enforcement: Under *Hodari D.,* one who flees is not seized; under *Mendenhall-Bostick,* one who relents, consents. This seems to create a "heads I win, tails you lose" rule, with the police holding the coin.

Justice Marshall dissented, joined by Justices Blackmun and Stevens. He harshly castigated this form of investigation: "These sweeps are conducted in 'dragnet' style," noting that this high-volume practice (sweeps of three thousand buses in a nine-month period) inconveniences a large number of innocent people (one case found that sweeps of a hundred buses resulted in seven arrests). The heart of the dissent was that the police questioning is inherently coercive, undermining consent:

> To put it mildly, these sweeps "are inconvenient, intrusive, and intimidating." They occur within cramped confines, with officers typically placing themselves in between the passenger selected for an interview and the exit of the bus. Because the bus is only temporarily stationed at a point short of its destination, the passengers are in no position to leave as a means of evading the officers' questioning. (*Florida v. Bostick,* 1991, Marshall, J. dissenting)

The majority pointed out, to the contrary, that

> [t]he present case is analytically indistinguishable from *Delgado.* Like the workers in that case, Bostick's freedom of movement was restricted by a factor independent of police conduct—i.e., by his being a passenger on a bus. Accordingly, the "free to leave" analysis on which Bostick relies is inapplicable. In such a situation, the appropriate inquiry is whether a reasonable person would feel free to decline the officers' requests or otherwise terminate the encounter. (*Florida v. Bostick,* 1991)

Indeed, Bostick was told he had a right to refuse; the pouched gun was never removed, nor did the officers ever point it at Bostick or use it in a threatening manner; and Bostick agreed to open his bag. These factors, according to the majority, negated coercion and supported the conclusion that Bostick volunteered to open his bag.

In **United States v. Drayton** (2002), a bus sweep case with facts very similar to *Bostick,* the Supreme Court held that the police need not inform a bus rider that he has a right to refuse to consent to a search of his baggage, relying on *Ohio v. Robinette* (1996) and *Schneckloth v. Bustamonte* (1973). Justice Souter dissented, joined by Justices Stevens and Ginsburg. He argued that if three officers approached a person on the street, hemmed him in very closely, and asked if they could search any luggage, this would be intimidation that undermines consent. The same is the case in the close quarters of a bus with an aisle fifteen inches wide, cramped seats, the police in apparent control of the bus, and officers saying that they were "conducting a bus interdiction" and "wanted cooperation."

Most scholarly commentators agree with the dissent in *Bostick* and refer to the decisions in this case and *Hodari D.* as the "no seizure" rule. Professor Gerald Ashdown, for example, writes, "Hardly anyone who is confronted and questioned by armed officers, asked for identification and permission to search, believes he is free to do much of anything, certainly not to refuse to answer or to walk away. Anyone with a lick of sense knows that doing these things will only aggravate the situation and cause him more trouble."[35]

Automobile Checklanes.   In *Delaware v. Prouse* (1979), discussed earlier in this chapter, the Court held that a car cannot be stopped while proceeding in traffic unless an officer has specific suspicion to believe that it was engaged in a traffic violation or a criminal act. *Prouse* distinguished on-the-road stops from stops at roadblocks or fixed checkpoints, contending that motorists do not feel the same anxiety in the latter situations because they observe other motorists going through the same drill. The Supreme Court specifically upheld sobriety checklanes in ***Michigan Department of State Police v. Sitz*** (1990). These stops are not Fourth Amendment seizures.

In deciding that **sobriety checklanes** are not a violation of a person's reasonable expectation of privacy, the Court relied on border search fixed checkpoint cases: *United States v. Ortiz* (1975) and *United States v. Martinez-Fuerte* (1976). Those cases compared the subjective and psychological level of intrusion of fixed checkpoints on the highway as compared to stops made by roving patrols. Since at the fixed checkpoint the motorist sees other vehicles being briefly detained and sees the visible indicia of the police officers' authority, "he is much less likely to be frightened or annoyed by the intrusion" (*United States v. Ortiz,* quoted in *United States v. Martinez-Fuerte*). These findings were applied to the Michigan sobriety checklane situation: "Here, checkpoints are selected pursuant to the guidelines, and uniformed police officers stop every approaching vehicle. The intrusion resulting from the brief stop at the sobriety checkpoint is for constitutional purposes indistinguishable from the checkpoint stops we upheld in *Martinez-Fuerte*" (*Michigan Department. of State Police v. Sitz*). Chief Justice Rehnquist's majority opinion also pointed out that drunk driving is a serious national problem resulting in approximately twenty-five thousand deaths annually. The idea of the checklane as a regulatory device played some role in the decision.

In *Sitz,* the Court also considered whether the *effectiveness* of checklanes in combating drunk driving was a factor of Fourth Amendment balancing. Sitz argued that other methods were more effective. The Court ruled that the choice of enforcement modalities was up to the legislature and the executive branches—politically accountable officials—rather than allowing the courts to determine which law enforcement techniques to employ to deal with a serious public danger.

Justice Stevens, dissenting, disagreed with the Court's finding that sobriety checklanes are essentially the same as border checklanes. Sobriety checklanes, for example, occur at night, are not at fixed checkpoints but are set up quickly to effect the element of surprise, and are less standardized than a review of registration papers, for the officer must visually assess the sobriety of the driver.

An important ruling, ***City of Indianapolis v. Edmond*** (2000), limited the *Sitz* ruling to sobriety checklanes. The Court decided (6–3) that a roadblock whose primary purpose was general law enforcement and the detection of ordinary criminal wrongdoing, and not traffic safety, violated the Fourth Amendment. Indianapolis police set up roadblocks identified as "narcotics checkpoints," detained drivers for about two to three minutes each, examined each driver's license and registration, and had a narcotics-detection dog walk around the vehicle. In finding this practice unconstitutional, the Court distinguished the reasoning of pretext stops (*Whren*), of brief checkpoint stops for purposes of detecting alcohol-impaired drivers or illegal aliens (*Sitz* and *Martinez-Fuerte*), and special needs (*National Treasury Employees Union v. Von Raab,* 1989). The city argued that all other checkpoint stops upheld by the Court employed arrests and criminal prosecutions in pursuit of other goals that were essentially not the enforcement of the criminal law. In a statement that captured the deep policy concerns of the Court, Justice O'Connor, in her majority opinion, replied:

> If we were to rest the case at this high level of generality, there would be little check on the ability of the authorities to construct roadblocks for almost any conceivable law enforcement purpose. Without drawing the line at roadblocks designed primarily to serve

the general interest in crime control, the Fourth Amendment would do little to prevent such intrusions from becoming a routine part of American life. (*City of Indianapolis v. Edmond*, 2000)

After a raft of cases that expanded the ability of police to stop virtually any car, control the passengers, and examine all containers, the Court was faced with a line, which if crossed might have made the total surveillance of anyone walking abroad subject to inspection. The Court was informed by a brief by the National League of Cities that many cities were prepared to initiate narcotics checkpoints depending on the outcome of *Edmond*. What was left unsaid was that a ruling favorable to the government in *Edmond* could have opened the door to virtually unrestricted on-the-street surveillance with drug-sniffing dogs and with highly intrusive electronic and thermal-sensing devices that penetrated the clothing of individuals. It is noteworthy that the three most conservative justices—Rehnquist, Scalia, and Thomas—dissented but that swing justices—O'Connor and Kennedy—voted to declare such practices unconstitutional.

Edmond was held not to prevent informational roadblocks. In **Illinois v. Lidster** (2004), police in Lombard, Illinois, partially blocked a highway to force cars into a single lane. At the checkpoint, an officer asked the occupants whether they had seen anything happen there the previous weekend. Each driver was handed a flyer that said "ALERT . . . FATAL HIT & RUN ACCIDENT." It requested "assistance in identifying the vehicle and driver in this accident which killed a 70 year old bicyclist." Each stop lasted about ten to fifteen seconds. As Lidster approached the roadblock, he swerved, nearly hit an officer, and was arrested and convicted for driving under the influence of alcohol. He challenged the constitutionality of the roadblock stop. The Supreme Court held that a roadblock of this type is constitutional as long as it is reasonably tailored to the particular circumstances of the case and to a legitimate law enforcement function. The stop in this case was constitutional for a variety of reasons. The primary purpose of the stop was not to investigate the occupants for criminal activity but to obtain information about an unsolved fatal hit-and-run that had occurred in the same area a few days before. Such stops are brief and not likely to produce anxiety. Police are not likely to ask incriminating questions, any more than would police questioning pedestrians in the vicinity of a crime as to whether they have seen anything suspicious. Voluntary requests for information "play a vital role in police investigatory work." The traffic delays that result "should prove no more onerous than many that typically accompany normal traffic congestion." The crime being investigated was serious, and the informational checkpoint in this case was narrowly tailored to getting specific information about it. The law enforcement needs and the reasonableness of the intrusion outweighed the minimal interference with liberty in this case.

Terry at the Airport: Drug Stops and Drug Courier Profiles

The typical scenario of the cases in this section, previously described in **United States v. Mendenhall** (1980) (see Chapter 3), is for narcotics agents to ask to speak with a person at an airport. The officers regularly scan airports and other transportation hubs for people who may be transporting illegal drugs. These cases differ from those in which agents have been tipped off by informants that a specific courier is arriving at an airport. Instead, the officers approach a person on a hunch that he or she (often young people of college age) may be carrying drugs or based on a person fitting a "profile" of variables that seem to be characteristic of drug couriers. The cases in this section ask whether the facts amount to a voluntary consent encounter, a *Terry* stop and search, or an arrest. They also describe the path of the Court's cases that eventually accepted the drug courier profile as a constitutional basis for an investigative stop.

The **drug courier profile** was developed in the early 1970s by DEA agent Paul Markonni, who was working out of the Detroit Metropolitan Airport. He borrowed the idea from an airplane hijacker profile developed in the late 1960s. The use of drug profiles spread to airports throughout the nation.[36] "Because even local police officers now receive high quality training by the DEA, street level drug interdiction programs have resulted in surprisingly few complaints of individual police officer misconduct, such as unjustified, armed threats or arbitrary harassment."[37] Stephen Hall briefly describes how drug courier profiles are used:

> One or more DEA agents (or other law enforcement officers) observe individuals at an airport for characteristics that match the profile. Agents single out an individual as a match, approach the suspect, and identify themselves as law enforcement officers. They then ask the suspect's name and destination. If the Agents are still suspicious, they usually ask the suspect to accompany them to another location for further questioning. At this point, agents ask the suspect to consent to a search of his person, luggage or both.[38]

In *Mendenhall* (1980), a young woman who deplaned at Detroit Metropolitan Airport was politely approached by DEA agents and asked to accompany them to a room. (See "Consent Searches" in Chapter 3.) After some discussion, Mendenhall agreed to be searched by a female officer in private, and drugs were found on her person. *Mendenhall* can be read for three purposes. First, given the numerous opinions of the justices, it demonstrates the difficulty of sorting out the facts to determine whether they amounted to a consent encounter or a personal seizure. Second, it shows a concern with drug courier profiles. Third, it established the test for a seizure: Did the person reasonably believe that he or she was not free to leave in view of all of the circumstances surrounding the incident? Although the *Mendenhall* test was modified to fit the contours of the chase in *Hodari D.*, it was, and still is, the standard that is applied in airport scenarios.

The stop of Mendenhall at the airport was triggered by her supposedly fitting the characteristics of a drug courier profile. Justice Powell spoke favorably of this device. He referred to "highly skilled agents" carrying out a "highly specialized law enforcement operation" being assigned to the Detroit airport "as part of a nationwide program to intercept drug couriers transporting narcotics between major drug sources and distribution centers in the United States." He noted, "During the first 18 months of the program, agents watching the Detroit Airport searched 141 persons in 96 encounters. They found controlled substances in 77 of the encounters and arrested 122 persons" (*United States v. Mendenhall*, 1980, Powell, J., concurring). Despite this endorsement, neither the lead opinion nor the concurrence in *Mendenhall* was based on a blanket acceptance of the profile. The tone of Justice White's dissent was less enthusiastic: "[T]he Government sought to justify the stop by arguing that Ms. Mendenhall's behavior had given rise to reasonable suspicion because it was consistent with portions of the so-called 'drug courier profile,' an informal amalgam of characteristics thought to be associated with persons carrying illegal drugs" (*United States v. Mendenhall*, 1980, pp. 567–68, White, J., dissenting). Although the majority in *Mendenhall* held that the encounter did not violate the Fourth Amendment, it did so on the basis of consent. *Mendenhall* did not constitutionalize the drug courier profile.

The Supreme Court expressed skepticism of profiles and found no basis of reasonable suspicion in **Reid v. Georgia** (1980, *per curiam*). The mere fact that a man who got off a plane in Atlanta from Fort Lauderdale, Florida (a "principal place of origin of cocaine sold elsewhere in the country"), and, exiting in a single file line, occasionally looked back in the direction of another man carrying a similar shoulder bag, who caught up with Reid and exchanged a few words with him is hardly the kind of fact that creates a drug courier profile or establishes reasonable suspicion to support an investigative stop.

In **Florida v. Royer** (1983), the Supreme Court held that a seizure at the airport violated Mark Royer's Fourth Amendment rights, but the justices could not agree on a reason. Royer was approached by two county narcotics officers at the Miami International Airport because he purportedly fit a drug courier profile: He had purchased a one-way ticket to New York City, was carrying two American Tourister suitcases that appeared to be heavy, was casually dressed, appeared pale and nervous, paid for his ticket in cash with a large number of bills, and wrote only a name on the airline identification tag. The officers identified themselves and asked Royer if he had a "moment" to speak with them. He said yes. Without oral consent, he produced his ticket and a driver's license upon request. He explained a discrepancy between his name and the name "Holt" written on the baggage tag by saying that a friend named Holt had made the reservations. The officers did not return the ticket or license but asked Royer to accompany them to a room forty feet away. In the small office, Royer was told that he was suspected of transporting narcotics and was asked if he would consent to a search of the suitcases. Without orally responding, Royer produced a key, opened the baggage, and marijuana was found. These events took about fifteen minutes.

The Court's five-judge majority found that, by holding onto Royer's ticket and driver's license, the officers had in effect arrested him without probable cause. When police officers retain these important documents, a reasonable person could not believe that he is free to leave. Thus when Royer went along with the police to the room, he did not consent but had to follow or give up his ticket and license! Holding these documents was the equivalent of a show of force.

Four of the majority justices (White, Powell, Marshall, and Stevens) also believed, however, that facts in *Royer* established reasonable suspicion that would have supported a temporary stop and questioning of Royer to confirm or dispel the suspicion. Because a majority did not share this view, the *Royer* case did not establish the constitutionality of drug courier profiles. It did indicate that a number of justices were leaning in that direction. Nevertheless, the majority felt that the police actions of obtaining the key to Royer's luggage went beyond that justified by a *Terry* stop. This was not a frisk for weapons, but a search for evidence.

Justice Brennan, concurring, thought the majority was wrong to comment on its belief that reasonable suspicion existed. Four dissenting justices (Burger, Blackmun, Rehnquist, and O'Connor) believed that the acts of the police officers were reasonable and would have upheld the encounter as based on consent.

The next airport search case, **United States v. Place** (1983), held the stop unconstitutional because the brevity requirement of *Terry* was violated. Raymond Place aroused the suspicions of DEA agents at the Miami International Airport. They briefly detained him for questioning. He agreed to a search of his luggage, but because his airplane was departing, the search was postponed. The agents called ahead to LaGuardia Airport in New York City, where another team of DEA agents observed Place when he arrived. Their suspicions also aroused, they detained him and told Place that they believed he was carrying narcotics. Place did not consent to a search of his luggage. The agents seized the bags, giving Place information as to where they could be retrieved. The bags were then sent to Kennedy Airport, unopened, where a trained narcotics detection dog indicated the presence of drugs. This process took ninety minutes. After the positive identification, as it was Friday afternoon, the bags were held until Monday, when a search warrant was obtained and drugs were found in the bags.

Because Place was detained, not on probable cause but at best on reasonable suspicion, the extent of the detention must be "minimally intrusive of the individual's Fourth Amendment interests." By holding a person's luggage, the person is detained by the police although the person is technically free to go. "[S]uch a seizure can effectively restrain the person since he is subjected to the possible disruption of his travel plans in order to remain with his luggage or to arrange for its return." Thus the seizure of luggage at the airport effectively "seizes" a person. Indeed, the *Terry* brevity principle was violated simply by the length of the detention of Place's luggage. Justice O'Connor noted:

> Although the 90-minute detention of respondent's luggage is sufficient to render the seizure unreasonable, the violation was exacerbated by the failure of the agents to accurately inform respondent of the place to which they were transporting his luggage, of the length of time he might be dispossessed, and of what arrangements would be made for return of the luggage if

the investigation dispelled the suspicion. In short, we hold that the detention of respondent's luggage in this case went beyond the narrow authority possessed by police to detain briefly luggage reasonably suspected to contain narcotics. (*United States v. Place*, 1983)

The constitutionality of drug courier profiles was finally upheld in **United States v. Sokolow** (1989). Andrew Sokolow was forcibly stopped by DEA agents at the Honolulu airport because he fit the following profile elements: He paid $2,100 for two airplane tickets from a roll of $20 bills; he traveled under a name that did not match the name under which his telephone number was listed; his original destination was Miami, a **source city** for illicit drugs; he stayed in Miami for only forty-eight hours even though a round-trip flight from Honolulu to Miami takes twenty hours; he appeared nervous during his trip; and he checked none of his luggage. He wore the same black jumpsuit with gold jewelry on both his outgoing and returning trips. In Honolulu, Sokolow and a traveling companion were forcibly stopped. They were taken to a DEA office at the airport, where a canine sniff indicated the presence of drugs. Sokolow was arrested, warrants were obtained to search his luggage, and over a thousand grams of cocaine were found.

The Supreme Court held that a suspect fitting a drug courier profile raises the mere suspicion of the agent to the level of reasonable suspicion that allows a *Terry* stop. The majority held that the profile elements in this case amounted to reasonable suspicion. Although each of the facts separately is not indicative of criminality, taken together they were out of the ordinary and amounted to reasonable suspicion. Justice Rehnquist wrote, "While a trip from Honolulu to Miami, standing alone, is not a cause for any sort of suspicion, here there was more: surely few residents of Honolulu travel from that city for 20 hours to spend 48 hours in Miami during the month of July." Second, the Court ruled explicitly that reasonable suspicion may be established even though each articulable element of suspicion is innocent. It is not necessary that there also be evidence of ongoing criminal activity to establish reasonable suspicion, as the lower court had held. Finally, the majority also ruled that it was not necessary for the officers to use the "**least intrusive means** available to verify or dispel their suspicions that he was smuggling narcotics," for example, by approaching the suspect and speaking with him, rather than forcibly detaining him. The least intrusive rule "would unduly hamper the police's ability to make swift on-the-spot decisions—here, respondent was about to get into a taxicab—and it would require courts to 'indulge in "unrealistic second-guessing" ' " (*United States v. Sokolow,* 1989).

Justice Marshall offered a spirited attack on the drug courier profiles in *Sokolow* but failed to convince a majority that profiles are flawed. He noted that many cases applying *Terry* required evidence of ongoing criminality—such as taking evasive action, "casing" a store, using an alibi, or being pinpointed by an informant—to trigger the reasonable suspicion standard. No such indicator of criminality existed in this case. Next, he warned that the mechanistic application of a profile would "dull the officer's ability and determination to make sensitive and fact-specific inferences 'in light of his experience.'" Most telling, he observed that what constituted profile factors seemed to shift from case to case. Citing specific cases, previously decided by lower courts, he pointed out that the profile has been held to be established by

- The fact that the suspect was the first to deplane, or was the last to deplane, or got off in the middle.
- That the suspect purchased a one-way ticket or a round-trip ticket.
- That the suspect took a nonstop flight or that the suspect changed planes.
- That the suspect had one shoulder bag or that the suspect had a new suitcase.
- That the suspect was traveling alone or that the suspect was traveling with a companion.
- That the suspect acted too nervously or that he acted too calmly.

Justice Marshall thus demonstrated that the majority's belief that drug courier profiles are sufficiently stable and reliable to authorize investigatory stops is belied by the cases that show that the elements of the profile may shift from case to case.

There is little research on the effectiveness of these profiles, but a reporter's sampling of records at the New York, Miami, and Houston airports indicates "a success rate of about fifty–fifty." A DEA spokesperson conceded that innocent persons are stopped as often as guilty ones, adding, "It's not a science, . . . [i]t's a technique." The story noted that those stopped under a profile are often handcuffed and held for several hours, including being taken to a hospital for x-rays, before being released. The story also suggested that African Americans and Hispanics are stopped more frequently than whites, although the DEA does not keep records of airport stops that can confirm these observations. Finally, the reporter also noted that drug courier profiles are used on highways, in train stations, and on interstate buses, although less frequently than in airports.[39]

Most scholarly commentators are skeptical or critical of these profiles. A primary reason is given by Justice Marshall: "[N]o uniform drug courier profile exists throughout the nation. Instead, agents create their own individual profiles based on their own professional experiences and observations."[40] A trial court noted that the profile consists of "anything that arouses the agent's suspicion."[41] Professors W. R. Janikowski and D. J. Giacopassi point out that unlike the Federal Aviation Administration's "skyjacker profile," which was formulated by psychologists and tested on half a million passengers yielding 1,406 stops and sixteen arrests, "there is some concern as to whether a profile truly exists or whether the profile is, in reality, a loose and malleable compilation of characteristics based on experiential knowledge of the drug trade and the exigencies of the situation."[42] A highly detailed analysis of the use of the profiles by Morgan Cloud, predating *Sokolow,* confirms Justice Marshall's analysis that the profiles are not predictive. By relying on the profiles, the courts are abdicating their constitutional responsibilities.[43]

Terry and Canine Detection Cases

The Court in *United States v. Place* (1983) commented favorably on the canine sniff as an important investigative technique because a "'canine sniff' by a well-trained narcotics detection dog . . . does not require opening the luggage. It does not expose noncontraband items that otherwise would remain hidden from public view, as does, for example, an officer's rummaging through the contents of the luggage. Thus, the manner in which information is obtained through this investigative technique is much less intrusive than a typical search." This premise depended on a second, that the sniff or alerting of trained dogs "discloses only the presence or absence of narcotics, a contraband item." If this is true, then the dog sniff reveals information that is limited to contraband, to which the possessor has no constitutionally protected right. The Court created a special niche for the dog sniff technique: "In these respects, the canine sniff is **sui generis.** We are aware of no other investigative procedure that is so limited both in the manner in which the information is obtained and in the content of the information revealed by the procedure." As a result, *Place* held that where police have reasonable suspicion that a person possesses drugs, a trained drug-sniffing canine can properly be used to confirm its presence.

The Supreme Court extended the scope of the dog-sniffing technique in **Illinois v. Caballes** (2005), which upheld the use of a trained dog to sniff the car of a motorist stopped for a traffic offense, where the stop did not exceed the time needed to process the traffic matter and was not accompanied by any suspicion against the driver. Caballes was stopped for speeding (6 miles per hour over the speed limit) on an interstate highway. A member of the State Police Drug Interdiction Team overheard the radio report and immediately headed for the scene with his narcotics-detection dog. The dog was walked around the stopped vehicle and alerted at the trunk. "Based on that alert, the officers searched the trunk, found marijuana, and arrested respondent. The entire incident lasted less than 10 minutes." Caballes was convicted of a narcotics offense. The Illinois Supreme

Court ruled the marijuana inadmissible because the dog sniff was made without articulable facts to suspect drug activity: It "unjustifiably enlarged the scope of a routine traffic stop into a drug investigation."

The Supreme Court (6–2) reversed. Justice Stevens's brief majority opinion essentially reiterated the logic of *Place*. The traffic stop was lawful, and the dog sniff did not extend the time of that stop. The sniff of the exterior of the car does not compromise any legitimate interest in privacy and so is not a search subject to the Fourth Amendment.

Justice Souter's dissent threw cold water on the use of trained dogs: "The infallible dog, however, is a creature of legal fiction." He cited numerous cases that indicated error rates in the use of dogs from 7 to 38 percent. If a dog sniff is erroneous, then "the dog does not smell the disclosed contraband; it smells a closed container" (*Illinois v. Caballes*, 2005, Souter, J., dissenting). Since the dog sniff is a police action used to find incriminating evidence, it should be treated as a search, limited by *Terry*, and allowed only when police have reasonable suspicion that contraband is present.

In her dissent, Justice Ginsburg argued that the fact that the procedure in *Caballes* did not extend the length of time of the stop did not mean that the scope of the search was not extended. Caballes was stopped only for speeding, and his car was sniffed only after he refused to give consent to search, although it does not appear that the officer who stopped his vehicle called for the dog unit. In this view, "A drug-detection dog is an intimidating animal" (*Illinois v. Caballes*, 2005, Ginsburg, J., dissenting). Even if trained dogs are effective, "The Court has never removed police action from Fourth Amendment control on the ground that the action is well calculated to apprehend the guilty." Justice Ginsburg raised the concern that "[t]oday's decision, in contrast, clears the way for suspicionless, dog-accompanied drug sweeps of parked cars along sidewalks and in parking lots." Both dissenting justices made it clear that their opinions were contextually related to drug detection and did not apply to dogs trained to sniff out explosives, dangerous chemicals, or biological weapons. A dog sniff for such purposes "would be an entirely different matter" because in its Fourth Amendment cases, the "Court has distinguished between the general interest in crime control and more immediate threats to public safety" (*Illinois v. Caballes*, 2005, Ginsburg, J., dissenting).[44] *Caballes* is not likely to be the last case on the use of drug-detection dogs.

LAW IN SOCIETY

Domestic Violence and Arrest

Domestic violence is a serious problem. "Approximately 20% of emergency department visits for trauma and 25% of homicides of women involve intimate partner violence (IPV)."[45] In 2001, there were 588,000 nonfatal violent crimes against female intimate partners and 103,000 against male intimate partners, according to national victimization surveys. This was a decline of 50 percent in nonfatal IPV since 1994, mirroring the general decline in crime in the late 1990s, but still a very large number.[46] It is estimated that only half of IPV incidents are reported to police.[47]

Before police forces existed, arrests were executed by court-appointed constables or citizens acting on their own or organized into posses. Arrests for traditional felonies like burglary and felony assault were purely reactive. For the most part, wife beating was condoned in English and American society, and perpetrators were not subject to arrest or prosecution, with the short-lived exception of the Puritan communities in the Massachusetts Bay Colony, where family violence was viewed as sinful and "threatened the individual's and the community's standing before God."[48] When nosy neighbors and pastoral intervention failed to end family violence, the courts intervened with criminal punishment.[49] The Puritan example faded from history, and domestic violence was forgotten as a social problem and was ignored by organized police forces until the mid-1970s.[50]

However, "[d]uring the last 25 years, social definitions of domestic violence have evolved from private wrongs to acts meriting an aggressive response from the criminal justice system. The change reflects the impact of the women's movement, civil liability lawsuits, changing criminal justice system ideology and academic research."[51] Feminist demands for gender equality empowered women and "forced society at large to shake off the selective social vision that formerly took little notice of the physical abuse of spouses."[52] The arrest of suspected batterers became a central issue in this major shift in social attitudes.

Prior to the 1970s, police called to the scene of a domestic disturbance were prevented from making arrests in some cases because the common law misdemeanor arrest doctrine did not allow arrests unless the crime took place in the officer's presence. Arrests might be made for violent felonies where a spouse was severely injured, but much depended on the officer's discretion. Officers who absorbed cultural norms that condoned spousal abuse were disinclined to arrest.

Feminist arguments of the 1970s concerning violence against women coincided with conservative "tough on crime" political agendas and were broadly accepted. The common law misdemeanor arrest rule was quickly changed by every state legislature to allow police officers to arrest if they had probable cause to believe that a suspect had committed a misdemeanor involving domestic violence.[53] This change was important because two-thirds of domestic violence cases are classified as misdemeanors,[54] and half of female victims of IPV reported a physical injury.[55]

In the 1970s, the New York Police Department (NYPD) pioneered a proactive approach to domestic violence that emphasized counseling the alleged batterer but leaving him (most perpetrators were male) in the premises. This approach was almost immediately criticized by feminists who understood male violence not simply as a private problem but as a public problem. Those concerned with women's safety lobbied for the passage of mandatory arrest laws.[56] Changing norms were having an effect on police practices.

Changing Norms and Domestic Violence Laws

By the mid-1980s, in addition to eliminating the misdemeanor arrest rule in domestic violence cases, all state legislatures provided legal and material assistance to domestic violence victims, including judicial protection orders, shelters for battered women, and diversion programs for offenders subjected to prosecution.[57] Without legislation, some police departments began to adopt a law enforcement approach to domestic violence by

the mid-1970s.[58] Police resistance to arresting batterers was partly overcome by experience with enforcing protection orders and by several successful civil lawsuits against police departments based on cases where police virtually abandoned abused wives to vicious spouses.[59]

A national shift in mood was signaled by the U.S. Attorney General's Task Force on Family Violence, which in 1984 declared, "Family violence should be recognized and responded to as a criminal activity."[60] Women's and victim's rights groups "were particularly vocal in their support of a more punitive approach."[61]

Impediments to Change: Police Discretion and Domestic Violence

Legal rules regarding arrest define probable cause, the use of force, the scope of a search incident, and when a warrant is required. Yet no common law or constitutional doctrine guides the vital question of discretion: When is it proper for a police officer to arrest or not arrest a suspect? Total enforcement of criminal law is impossible. Police discretion to arrest is inevitable for several reasons:[62] Some laws (e.g., disorderly conduct) are vague or open-ended;[63] police departments are understaffed; and enforcing every minor offense to the maximum extent is excessively rigid and unfair. Police discretion typically is exercised by the lowest-ranking officers with minimal guidance from supervisors—a "low-visibility" practice that often undermines the equal application of the law. Ideally, police use discretion to arrest all serious offenders and to mitigate the harshness of the crime according to "common sense," but it does not always work that way.

Discretion can also breed unfairness if it is shaped by warped "commonsense" values that support widespread racist or sexist discrimination.[64] Thus a response to a domestic call—whether by arrest, avoidance, lecturing, or clinical-type counseling—was not a matter of departmental policy but depended on the individual police officer's beliefs about the acceptability of spousal abuse.[65] The police reflected the larger society that traditionally condoned spousal abuse to such an extent that it was not considered a criminal act by many.[66] Yet the crimes committed by a batterer "include assault and/or battery, aggravated assault, intent to assault or to commit murder, and, in cases where the woman is coerced sexually, rape."[67] The combination of traditional views and police discretion thus discouraged the arrest of batterers before 1970.

Into this volatile mix of social and ideological change bearing down on police practices came one of the most influential social science studies ever published: the Minneapolis experiment.[68]

The Minneapolis Experiment and the Replication Experiments

A 1984 report described a small-sample experiment in the Minneapolis Police Department that randomly assigned the type of police intervention to misdemeanor domestic violence cases before the police entered the house. Professors Lawrence Sherman and Richard Berk showed that arresting batterers reduced the number of domestic violence reports for six months, when compared to giving the parties on-the-spot mediation or simply separating the couple.[69]

The report, suggesting that arrest alone deterred spousal abuse, caused a sensation. Criminologists were skeptical because the results contradicted substantial research evidence that specific programs generally do not measurably deter crime. Nevertheless, the report had a tremendous impact and accelerated police policies in favor of arresting domestic violence perpetrators. Sherman publicized the research in the news media and to the general public and police chiefs.[70] The study was published at a time when a trend toward arresting batterers was already under way and likely accelerated and legitimized the trend.[71]

Because the findings were controversial and the issue was important, in the 1980s the National Institute of Justice funded replications of the Minneapolis experiment in Charlotte, Colorado Springs, Miami, Milwaukee, and Omaha. The results of these experiments unleashed a new barrage of controversy: Most found no evidence of an unambiguous deterrent effect of arrest on domestic violence recidivism. In a book summarizing the Minneapolis experiment and the Spouse Assault Replication Project (SARP), Sherman, who conducted one of the replications, summarized the paradoxical and contradictory findings. First, the studies, viewed individually, showed that arrest reduces domestic violence in some cities but increases it in others. One study suggested that arrest may reduce domestic violence only among employed people. Another indicated that arrest might increase domestic violence in the long run. Sherman argued that police can predict which couples are most likely to suffer future violence, but our society values privacy too highly to encourage preventive action.[72]

It would clearly be incoherent and unconstitutional to fine-tune an arrest policy that mandates arrests of employed batterers but not those without a job! Ultimately, Sherman favored repealing mandatory arrest laws, allowing warrantless misdemeanor arrests, and encouraging police departments to develop local policies. He also favored special units and policies to focus on chronically violent couples.[73]

Mandatory Arrest: Policies, Polemics, and Findings

Despite the Minneapolis experiment and the adoption of pro-arrest policies by many police departments, as of 1992 only seven states mandated arrest. The criminal trial of O. J. Simpson for the killing of his wife, Nicole Brown, whom he had allegedly abused, galvanized the majority of states to pass mandatory or preferred arrest laws. As of 2005, thirty states had passed laws mandating arrest when probable cause exists to believe that a protection order was violated, and another twenty-six plus the District of Columbia had laws with either a mandatory or a pro-arrest policy for domestic violence whether or not a protection order was violated.[74]

The SARP findings created controversy within feminist ranks. Joan Zorza, a senior attorney with the National Center on Women and Family Law, continued to support the mandatory arrest of batterers in an article critical of the replication studies. She correctly pointed to the need for broader coordinated efforts to deal effectively with domestic violence, but her conclusion about mandatory arrest did not entirely come to grips with the SARP findings.[75]

A number of legal writers support mandatory arrest.[76] Even mandatory arrest policies and laws, however, may not result in more arrests—a point borne out in a study by Professor Kathleen Ferraro, who observed arrest patterns by Phoenix police officers in domestic cases under a mandatory arrest law. Police discretion shaped how officers assessed the existence of probable cause, leading to questionable no-probable-cause decisions.[77] Mandatory arrest laws, therefore, are needed to counteract police bias and send a message that arrest is the appropriate response to battering. The point of heated controversy among feminists concerns the argument that mandatory arrest removes the decision to arrest from the victim's control, where her fear and powerlessness in an abusive relationship are likely to prevent her from demanding the arrest of her batterer. Proponents argue that mandatory arrest laws may thus empower victims by giving them the courage to call the police in the first place. Also, a lax criminal justice system strengthens cultural norms that tolerate domestic assaults, which in turn perpetuate the social and political subjugation of women.[78]

Other legal writers oppose mandatory arrest laws and their prosecutorial "no-drop" counterparts. They are skeptical of the lasting deterrent effect of mandatory arrest and worry that mandatory arrest and prosecution will lead to retaliation by the abusing spouse and the loss of economic support, putting the victim in a worse situation.

But the most heated point of contention that raises ideological differences is the concern that mandatory arrest laws will disempower women who have been battered by their spouses or boyfriends, undermine their autonomy, and fail to consider the unique circumstances of each case.[79]

Mandatory Arrest: Empirical Studies

More recent empirical studies shed light on this issue but do not provide unambiguous policy direction. One study by Christopher D. Maxwell and colleagues combined all of the SARP data and examined the reduction of assaults using two measures: official arrest records and interviews with female victims six months after the initial police call. Official records indicated increases in assault in the follow-up period, while victim interviews indicated a reduction in assault. Unfortunately, 30 percent of the victims could not be interviewed six months after the initial assault. Not knowing whether the missing were victims of retaliatory assaults casts some doubt on the deterrent findings of those who were interviewed. Further, even where arrest was shown to have a deterrent effect, the strength of the arrest factor was weak and overshadowed by factors like the offender's prior criminal record.[80]

A national study by Richard B. Felson and colleagues, using victimization data that were more representative of the nation than the SARP data, found that the effect of arrest on reoffending was not statistically significant; it tended toward deterrence, but it was small. On the other hand, the reporting of abuse by victims had a strong, statistically significant deterrent effect. This supports the women's empowerment argument.[81]

An analysis of the interviews of victims in the Dade County SARP study indicated that arrest did have a short-term deterrent effect; 14 percent of the victims of assault where batterers were arrested experienced an episode of violence within six months, compared to 21 percent overall. The arrest of suspects was not related to the victim's perception of personal power, was negatively related to the victim's sense of legal power, and was positively related to the victim's sense of safety. The latter finding, however, varied considerably among the victims, and the best predictor of recurrent violence was the level of stress in the relationship. On the whole, Miller concluded that Dade County victims "were unlikely to have experienced long-term benefits as a consequence of suspect arrest."[82]

Rodney F. Kingsnorth and Randall C. MacIntosh's study of more than five thousand domestic violence cases processed through the Sacramento County prosecutor's office examined victim support for arrest and prosecution. The researchers found that support varied depending on the victim's race or ethnicity, sex, and age; marital, cohabitation, and parental status; the severity of the attack and injury; whether there was medical treatment; prior incidents; and whether there was a protective order. The study suggested that "victims are engaged in a complex decision making process in which they seek to weigh the costs and benefits of involving criminal justice system officials in their lives."[83] The study strongly suggested that a victim's wishes usually ought to be taken into account.

Laura Dugan examined domestic victimization using national data and comparing states with strong versus weak protection order laws and mandatory arrest provisions. She concluded that "those households residing in states with aggressive legislation have a lower probability of domestic violence."[84]

Conclusion

Overall, the studies tend to show that mandatory arrest alone has at best a weak deterrent effect on the reoccurrence of domestic violence; some studies have found no effect. Further, the effect of mandatory arrest differs by population, and victims usually make rational decisions about the overall effects that the arrest and prosecution of their abusers will have on their lives. This in turn suggests that policies that allow and even encourage arrest and prosecution are preferable to strict mandatory arrest policies. Unfortunately, the rational weighing and discussion of policies with great effects on people's lives tend to be nonexistent in the political arena. Having "found" mandatory arrest and prosecutorial no-drop policies, politicians can be expected to vigorously endorse these policies.[85]

Even proponents of mandatory arrest laws support the need for additional services.[86] Within law enforcement, coordinated domestic violence teams and prosecutors' victim support units increase victim support for these services, and an unusual experiment with intensive bail supervision found a deterrent effect on repeat victimization.[87] Recently, police have formed partnerships with communities, and many communities have established coordinated responses to domestic violence.[88]

The police continue to play a critical role as gatekeeper in domestic violence cases. The arrest experiments have shed light on the exercise of police discretion and are a part of the larger arenas of study and action concerning domestic violence and violence against women. Much needs to be done in these areas, but this exploration demonstrates the value of scientific inquiry into legal and police processes.

SUMMARY

In the aftermath of the September 11, 2001, attacks, federal agents rounded up twelve hundred people, mostly aliens. The government has not released all the information about this initial wave of detainees, but it appears that few were in any way involved in terrorism. This overreaction in the aftermath of the horrific attacks of 9/11, though understandable, is evidence of unpreparedness and unprofessionalism. It reflects the awesome power that federal and local law enforcement agencies can amass when called for and adds a caution for the need for legal restraints.

The detention of a person by a police officer may be legal or illegal. Legal detentions or seizures under the Fourth Amendment fall into two categories: arrests supported by probable cause and investigative stops supported by reasonable suspicion. In addition, a person may consent to engage in an encounter with a law enforcement agent, for which the officer requires no level of evidence. Police have no right to detain people at will to investigate without a level of suspicion. A lawful arrest authorizes an officer to take a person into custody to begin the process of prosecution. An officer who has only reasonable suspicion may temporarily detain a person for brief questioning to confirm or dispel the suspicion. A person in a premises may be detained during the time a search warrant is executed and may be handcuffed for the duration of the search if it is reasonable. An arrestee may be subjected to a thorough search for evidence of crime or weapons. A person briefly detained for an investigatory stop may only be subjected to a "frisk": a brief pat-down of outer clothing to detect the presence of a weapon. The police have a general duty to the public to arrest criminal perpetrators. They do not have a specific duty to crime victims that is enforceable by civil lawsuits—except in rare instances where they establish a protective relationship that a person relies on for protection.

The Supreme Court has issued two definitions of *arrest:* (1) An arrest occurs when a person believes he or she is not free to leave (*Mendenhall*), and (2) an arrest occurs when a person is physically stopped (*Hodari D.*). A person who is fleeing from a police officer intent on stopping him or her is not seized until the instant the person is physically stopped. An arrested person loses his or her right to privacy and may be kept in view of police at all times. An officer must have probable cause *before* making an arrest. Probable cause is an objective standard supported by facts, not on the good faith of an officer. Proximity to a crime alone does not establish probable cause. Every warrantless arrest is subjected to a probable cause determination by a judicial officer soon after an arrest—and typically within forty-eight hours. Probable cause can also be based on direct observation of an officer, hearsay, or reports from other police departments. Misdemeanor arrests can be made only for offenses committed in the officer's presence, except that in most states, by statute, misdemeanor arrests can be made on probable cause in domestic violence cases. A court does not lose jurisdiction of a case if an officer makes an illegal arrest. Evidence seized during an illegal arrest is inadmissible, but evidence obtained during an arrest based on probable cause that was in fact mistaken is admissible. A citizen's arrest may be made on probable cause, but if mistaken, the person making the arrest is strictly liable for the tort of false arrest. Police may use reasonable force to effect an arrest, and they may use deadly force where it is reasonable. The common law rule allowing an officer to shoot to kill a fleeing felon even without evidence that the felon is armed and dangerous violates the Fourth Amendment because it is excessive and unreasonable.

The Fourth Amendment does not require an arrest warrant for a lawful arrest that is made in a public place, even if the police had time to obtain a warrant. On the other hand, police must have an arrest warrant to enter a person's home to arrest that person unless the entry is justified by an exigency. An exigency is not created merely because the crime for which the arrest is made was a serious crime. Police cannot rely on an arrest warrant to enter the home of a third party to arrest a person—such an entry has to be justified with a search warrant.

A person arrested for a crime that authorizes the officer to take the person into custody may be thoroughly searched for weapons and for evidence. The evidence from a search incident to arrest need not pertain to the crime for which a person was arrested. A police officer who stops a speeding car and issues a citation rather than making an arrest has no justification to search the car. When a person is arrested, the police may search the area within the person's immediate control for weapons or evidence but may not go beyond to search a house or other premises. When police enter a premises and arrest a person, they may look into the adjoining room, without any evidentiary basis, to look for another person who could injure the officers. However, for them to conduct a protective sweep of the entire premises to look for a confederate of the arrested person, they must have reasonable suspicion to believe that another person is in the house. Police may conduct an inventory of all of an arrested person's belongings at a police lockup or jail; this is not a Fourth Amendment search for evidence but an administrative procedure designed to promote safety and to deter theft and false claims of theft of the prisoner's goods. A search incident to arrest may be made at the police station. Pretrial detainees held in a jail may be subjected to strip and body cavity searches when reasonable.

The Court has recognized the law enforcement power to briefly detain suspects who are reasonably believed to be involved in criminal activity in order to question them about their suspicious activity and to frisk them for weapons. The standard of evidence for such a stop and frisk is reasonable suspicion, a lesser standard than probable cause to believe that a crime has been committed and that the suspect committed it. Reasonable suspicion can be based on an officer's expertise in drawing inferences from observed facts, on an informant's hearsay, from a verified and reliable anonymous call, or from a police bulletin. Reasonable suspicion is based on a totality of the circumstances, including inferences from facts. An investigatory stop must be brief and nonintrusive.

A person cannot be stopped on the street simply for identification under an indefinite vagrancy statute or because he or she is standing in a high-crime neighborhood. A gang loitering ordinance that makes it a crime for a gang member to simply "loiter" and not disperse when so ordered violates the "void for vagueness" doctrine of the Fourteenth Amendment. A person who is chased by a police officer is not seized until the person is physically caught, and any property that the person throws away before being caught has been abandoned and is not protected by the Fourth Amendment expectation of privacy. A person who flees from a police officer without provocation establishes reasonable suspicion for an investigatory stop.

Automobile drivers cannot be stopped at random on the highway by police for a registration and license check without probable cause or reasonable suspicion of a crime or a motor vehicle violation. When a person is stopped in a car for an investigatory stop, officers may visually scan the interior of the car for weapons. There is no Fourth Amendment violation if an officer who stops a car for an existing traffic offense did so for the purpose of searching for drugs—a pretext search is constitutional. A drug courier profile can be the basis for making a stop of a person in an automobile. Once a car is stopped, the officer may, for his or her own safety, order the driver and passengers to exit the automobile.

When police officers accost a person in a nonthreatening manner in a space where the person would not ordinarily be free to move about, such as at a factory workstation or in an intercity bus, that fact alone does not turn a consensual encounter into a seizure. A motorist stopped in an open sobriety checklane is not seized for Fourth Amendment purposes. Police who accost a person at an airport and ask to speak to him or her about drug transportation do not seize that person unless they retain the passenger's ticket or luggage for more than a few moments. A sniff of luggage or the exterior of a car (that has been lawfully stopped) by a trained narcotics dog is not a Fourth Amendment search. A person who gets off an airplane from Florida on an early morning flight and looks behind him for a companion does not fit a drug courier profile. A drug courier profile may be based on a series of innocent facts that, when taken together, allows an officer to draw a reasonable conclusion that the person is a drug courier. Police have reasonable suspicion to stop a person who fits a drug courier profile.

LEGAL PUZZLES

How Have Courts Decided These Cases?

"Clothing Exception"

4–1. A criminal complaint was sworn against Walter Jackson and another person for distributing crack cocaine. The next day, police executed an arrest warrant against Jackson at his apartment. After knocking, police heard shuffling inside. Jackson opened the door after two minutes and was arrested and handcuffed. Officers made a protective sweep of the apartment and found no one else there. Jackson was barefoot. He asked Officer Powell to get his shoes from his bedroom. Powell found Jackson's shoes on the floor between the bed and an open closet. As he walked into the room toward the shoes, he observed in plain view "what appeared to be the handle of a handgun" protruding from between the two mattresses of the bed. He lifted the mattress and retrieved a loaded .38-caliber semiautomatic handgun with its serial numbers filed off.

Was Officer Powell's entry into Jackson's bedroom justified? Is there a general "clothing exception" to the Fourth Amendment?

HELD: Yes, the officer's entry into the bedroom was justified. Federal appellate courts split on the existence of a "clothing exception." In *Washington v. Chrisman* (1982), the arresting officer accompanied a student into his dorm room; in this case, Jackson was left in the custody of other officers while his shoes were retrieved. This distinction does not require a different outcome because it was objectively reasonable for the officers to not bring Jackson "awkwardly" into the bedroom to retrieve his shoes. Officer Powell was given reasonable and voluntary consent to enter the bedroom, providing the constitutional foundation for a lawful plain view seizure.

Some federal circuits have found a "clothing exception" allowing officers to go into an arrested person's room without a warrant as a plain view justification. Others have explicitly rejected such an exception. The judge in this case suggested that "the clothing exception appears to expand the scope of the Supreme Court's exigent circumstances precedents beyond their plain meaning. In crafting the exigent circumstances exception, the Court conditioned its application on the existence of a dangerous or emergency situation."

United States v. Walter Jackson, 414 F.Supp.2d 495 (D. N.J. 2006)

Arrest and Detention

4–2.   Officers lunching at a McDonald's saw Jose Ortiz-Hernandez and Selmo Valenzuela there. Valenzuela was later seen walking northbound on Eighty-second Avenue. Officer Anderson testified that he thought he saw Ortiz and Valenzuela drive away from the McDonald's in a Toyota Four Runner. He testified that he had seen the Toyota earlier circling in an area where people congregated to deal drugs. After lunch, the officers drove past a Safeway parking lot, where they spotted the Toyota. Officer Anderson then saw Ortiz and Valenzuela using a public telephone outside the Safeway; he testified that another Hispanic male, later identified as Wilfredo Alvarez, got into the Toyota. A gray Jeep occupied by a man and a woman then drove up, and Ortiz and Valenzuela entered the Jeep. Anderson told his fellow officers that Ortiz and Valenzuela were the ones originally driving the Toyota and that the "dope was rolling" in the Toyota, which was now being driven by a different "two Hispanics." Plainclothes undercover officers watched the Jeep while Officer Anderson followed and stopped the Toyota.

Anderson was mistaken on all counts. Ortiz and Valenzuela were never inside the Toyota and were not acquainted with Alvarez and his nephew, who were in Portland on routine business. They had driven around because they were lost, and no contraband was found in a consent search of their car.

The Jeep was then driven from the Safeway parking lot, and the driver, Marie Lewis, failed to use a turn signal. Using this as a pretext, the undercover officers called for a uniformed officer to stop the Jeep twenty blocks away.

A check of documents showed that Lewis's license had been suspended, and she admitted to being a recovering heroin addict. Officer Anderson joined the group. He brought Ortiz, who gave his name as Luis Perez-Cota, into a coffee shop restroom and "conducted an invasive strip search." No contraband was found, only a Safeway card and a piece of paper with "Marie" and a phone number written on it. Ortiz was arrested for delivery of drugs. After the arrest, "a syringe with residue" was found near Lewis's purse under the front seat. At the police station, Ortiz was fingerprinted.

Was there probable cause to arrest Ortiz? Was Ortiz's fingerprinting constitutional?

Holding available from instructor.

Detention and Warrant Execution

4–3.   Twenty-five SWAT team officers executed a search warrant against the home of Don Antonio Jones, Calvin Edgar Bolden (his grandfather), and Calvileen Bolden (his mother), who were operating an open-air drug market from and around their home. A four-year investigation established that (1) significant quantities of drugs were brought into the house; (2) the drugs were being sold not only in the house but around it as well, from the front porch, and within what we would regard as the curtilage; (3) many of the individuals observed in the trafficking had extensive drug and violent criminal records; and (4) Jones associated with individuals with extensive criminal records, had established an elaborate countersurveillance network around the house, and had threatened a member of the police department. The warrant empowered the police to search Jones, the Boldens, and "any other persons found in [the] premises who may be participating in violations of [those statutes] and who may be concealing evidence, paraphernalia, and Controlled Dangerous Substances."

Steven Cotton, not named in the warrant, was standing outside the house next to Jones when the warrant was executed. He and others were handcuffed, allowed to sit, and made to wait fifteen minutes while the house was secured. One person was investigated and released. Cotton was read the *Miranda* rights and asked if he had anything on him. He admitted to possessing a "bag of weed" and was then searched and arrested.

Was Cotton constitutionally detained during the search?

Holding available from instructor.

Pedestrian Stop: *Terry* and *Wardlow*

4–4.   Kansas City Police Officers Vernon Huth and Randy Evans observed Sylvester Cornelius walking down a street at approximately 10 A.M. in a high-crime area. One officer recognized Cornelius from previous arrests and recalled seeing two outstanding felony drug-distribution warrants for him on the police computer the day before. As the officers approached Cornelius in their patrol car, they observed him change direction and place his left hand in his pocket. Officer Huth got out of the car and directed Cornelius to remove his hand from his pocket. When Cornelius failed to comply, Officer Huth grabbed him and compelled him to lean over the hood of the patrol car.

Was there reasonable suspicion to stop Cornelius?

Holding available from instructor.

FURTHER READING

Human Rights Watch, *Shielded from Justice: Police Brutality and Accountability in the United States* (New York: Human Rights Watch, 1998).

William Ker Muir Jr., *Police: Streetcorner Politicians* (Chicago: University of Chicago Press, 1977).

Lawrence P. Tiffany, Donald M. McIntyre Jr., and Daniel L. Rotenberg, *Detection of Crime* (Boston: Little, Brown, 1967).

USEFUL WEB SITES

National District Attorneys Association and American Prosecutors Research Institute

http://www.ndaa-apri.org/

Provides information about prosecutors. The American Prosecutors Research Institute lists many relevant publications and offers downloadable reports.

Domestic Violence and Sexual Assault Data Resource Center

http://www.jrsa.org/dvsa-drc/index.html

Provides information on data collection and use in the states. Identifies types of information currently obtained by state and local agencies and includes all aspects of domestic violence.

ENDNOTES

1. Stephen J. Schulhofer, *The Enemy Within: Intelligence Gathering, Law Enforcement, and Civil Liberties in the Wake of September 11* (New York: Century Foundation Press, 2000), 11.

2. Press release, "The September 11 Detainees: A Review of the Treatment of Aliens Held on Immigration Charges in Connection with the Investigation of the September 11 Attacks" (Office of the Inspector General, U.S. Department of Justice, June 2003), http://www.usdoj.gov/oig/special/03-06/press.htm (accessed January 15, 2007).

3. Eric Lichtblau, "U.S. Report Faults the Roundup of Illegal Immigrants after 9/11," *New York Times*, June 3, 2003.

4. Lichtblau, "U.S. Report."

5. Lichtblau, "U.S. Report."

6. Schulhofer, *The Enemy Within*, 12 (emphasis in original).

7. Deborah Sontag, "Who Is This Kafka That People Keep Mentioning?" *New York Times Magazine*, October 21, 2001.

8. Nate Blakeslee, *Tulia: Race, Cocaine, and Corruption in a Small Texas Town* (New York: Public Affairs, 2005).

9. Kenneth Adams et al., *Use of Force by Police: Overview of National and Local Data* (Washington, D.C.: National Institute of Justice and Bureau of Justice Statistics, October 1999).

10. Robert A. Shapiro, "Annotation: Personal Liability of Policeman, Sheriff, or Similar Peace Officer or His Bond, for Injury Suffered as a Result of Failure to Enforce Law or Arrest Lawbreaker," *American Law Reports*, 3rd series, 41 (1972, updated weekly): 700; and Licia A. Esposito Eaton, "Annotation: Liability of Municipality or Other Governmental Unit for Failure to Provide Police Protection from Crime," *American Law Reports*, 5th series, 90 (2001, updated weekly): 273.

11. Michael J. Glennon, "International Kidnapping: State-Sponsored Abduction: A Comment on *United States v. Alvarez-Machain*," *American Society of International Law Newsletter* 86 (October 1992): 746.

12. These rules may have originated in the late eighteenth and nineteenth centuries. See Thomas Y. Davies, "Recovering the Original Fourth Amendment,"

Michigan Law Review 98, no. 3 (1999): 547–750, 634–42, 724–26.

13. See J. Bradley Ortins, "District of Columbia Survey: Warrantless Misdemeanor Arrest for Drunk Driving Found Invalid in *Schram v. District of Columbia*," *Catholic University Law Review* 34 (1985): 1241–54.

14. David A. Sklansky, "The Private Police," *UCLA Law Review* 46 (1999): 1165–1287, 1183.

15. Sklansky, "Private Police," 1184.

16. F. J. Remington et al., *Criminal Justice Administration: Materials and Cases,* 1st ed. (Indianapolis: Bobbs–Merrill, 1969), 20.

17. *Garner v. Memphis Police Department,* 710 F.2d 240 (6th Cir. 1983).

18. Jerome H. Skolnick and James J. Fyfe, *Above the Law: Police and the Excessive Use of Force* (New York: Free Press, 1993), 246.

19. *Dorman v. United States,* 435 F.2d 385, 392–93 (D.C. Cir. 1970).

20. *Mary Beth G. v. City of Chicago,* 723 F.2d 1263 (7th Cir. 1983).

21. Robin Lee Fenton, "Comment: The Constitutionality of Policies Requiring Strip Searches of All Misdemeanants and Minor Traffic Offenders," *University of Cincinnati Law Review* 54 (1985): 175–89, 180–81.

22. William J. Simonitsch, "Comment: Visual Body Cavity Searches Incident to Arrest: Validity under the Fourth Amendment," *University of Miami Law Review* 54 (2000): 665–88, 681–82.

23. D. Caute, *The Year of the Barricades: A Journey through 1968* (New York: Harper and Row, 1988).

24. However, one biographer read *Terry* at face value as a balancing of law enforcement needs against privacy rights: G. Edward White, *Earl Warren: A Public Life* (New York: Oxford University Press, 1982), 276–78.

25. F. Graham, *The Due Process Revolution: The Warren Court's Impact on Criminal Law* (New York: Hayden, 1970), 22–23.

26. P. Chevigny, *Police Power: Police Abuses in New York City* (New York: Pantheon, 1969).

27. M. Lippman, "The Drug War and the Vanishing Fourth Amendment," *Criminal Justice Journal* 14 (1992): 229–308.

28. M. McAlary, *Buddy Boys: When Good Cops Turn Bad* (New York: Putnam's, 1987), 87.

29. Daniel J. Steinbock, "National Identity Cards: Fourth and Fifth Amendment Issues," *Florida Law Review* 56 (2004): 697–760.

30. T. J. Devetski, "Fourth Amendment Protection against Unreasonable Seizure of the Person: The New (?) Common Law Arrest Test for Seizure," *Journal of Criminal Law and Criminology* 82 (1992): 747–72.

31. Tracey Maclin, "Book Review: Seeing the Constitution from the Backseat of a Police Squad Car," *Boston University Law Review* 70 (1990): 543–91, 550 (emphasis added).

32. Maclin, "Book Review," 550.

33. Marvin Zalman, "Fleeing from the Fourth Amendment," *Criminal Law Bulletin* 36, no. 2 (2000): 129–47.

34. David Moran, "The New Fourth Amendment Vehicle Doctrine: Stop and Search Any Car at Any Time," *Villanova Law Review* 47 (2002): 815–38.

35. G. G. Ashdown, "Drugs, Ideology, and the Deconstitutionalization of Criminal Procedure," *West Virginia Law Review* 95 (1992): 1–54, 22 (paragraph breaks omitted).

36. M. Cloud, "Search and Seizures by the Numbers: The Drug Courier Profile and Judicial Review of Investigative Formulas," *Boston University Law Review* 65 (1985): 843–921, 844–45, 847–48; and S. E. Hall, "A Balancing Approach to the Constitutionality of Drug Courier Profiles," *University of Illinois Law Review* 1993 (1993): 1007–36, 1009–10.

37. S. Guerra, "Domestic Drug Interdiction Operations: Finding the Balance," *Journal of Criminal Law and Criminology* 82 (1992): 1109–61, 1114.

38. Hall, "A Balancing Approach," 1010.

39. Lisa Belkin, "Airport Anti-Drug Nets Snare Many People Fitting 'Profiles,'" *New York Times,* March 20, 1990, 1.

40. Hall, "A Balancing Approach," 1010–11.

41. Cases cited in Hall, "A Balancing Approach," 1011, n. 35.

42. W. R. Janikowski and D. J. Giacopassi, "Pyrrhic Images, Dancing Shadows, and Flights of Fancy: The Drug Courier Profile as Legal Fiction," *Journal of Contemporary Criminal Justice* 9 (1993): 60–69.

43. Cloud, "Search and Seizures by the Numbers," n. 32.

44. Justice Ginsberg cited *Michigan Department of State Police v. Sitz* (1990) and *City of Indianapolis v. Edmond* (2000) in support.

45. L. Bensley, et al., "Prevalence of Intimate Partner Violence and Injuries—Washington, 1998," *Journal of the American Medical Association* 284, no. 5 (August 2, 2000): 559–60 (from the Centers for Disease Control and Prevention: Morbidity and Mortality Weekly Report).

46. Callie Marie Rennison, *Crime Data in Brief: Intimate Partner Violence, 1993–2001* (Washington, D.C.: Bureau of Justice Statistics, NCJ 197838, February 2003).

47. Callie Marie Rennison and Sarah Welchans, *Special Report: Intimate Partner Violence* (Washington, D.C.: Bureau of Justice Statistics, NCJ 178247, May 2000).

48. Elizabeth Pleck, *Domestic Tyranny* (New York: Oxford University Press, 1987), 17.

49. Pleck, 18.

50. Pleck, 182.

51. Rodney F. Kingsnorth and Randall C. MacIntosh, "Domestic Violence: Predictors of Victim Support for Official Action," *Justice Quarterly* 21, no. 2 (2004): 301–28, 301–2.

52. M. Zalman, "The Courts' Response to Police Intervention in Domestic Violence," in E. S. Buzawa and C. G. Buzawa, eds., *Domestic Violence: The Changing Criminal Justice Response* (Westport, Conn.: Auburn House, 1992), 79–110, 82.

53. Lisa G. Lerman, "Statute: A Model State Act: Remedies for Domestic Abuse," *Harvard Journal on Legislation* 21 (1984): 61–143, 126–27.

54. Patrick A. Langan and Christopher A. Innes, *Special Report: Preventing Domestic Violence against Women* (Washington, D.C.: Bureau of Justice Statistics, 1986).

55. Rennison and Welchans, *Special Report: Intimate Partner Violence.*

56. Marion Wanless, "Note: Mandatory Arrest: A Step Toward Eradicating Domestic Violence, But Is It Enough?" *University of Illinois Law Review* 1996 (1996): 533–75, 539–40.

57. Lerman, "Statute."

58. International Association of Chiefs of Police, *Training Key 245: Wife Beating* (Gaithersburg, Md.: International Association of Chiefs of Police, 1976): "The officer who starts legal action may give the wife the courage she needs to realistically face and correct her situation."

59. Ruth Gundle, "Civil Liability for Police Failure to Arrest: *Nearing v. Weaver,*" *Women's Rights Law Reporter* 9, no. 3–4 (1986): 259–65, 259–60, 262. Injunction suits were brought: *Bruno v. Codd,* 90 Misc.2d 1047, 396 N.Y.S.2d 974 (Sup Ct. Special Term 1977), rev'd in part, appeal dismissed in part, 64 A.D.2d 582, 407 N.Y.S.2d 165 (1978), aff'd, 47 N.Y.2d 582, 393 N.E.2d 976 (1979) (class action; consent decree entered to enforce protection orders); *Scott v. Hart,* No. C–76–2395 (N.D., Cal., filed Nov. 24, 1976); and *Raguz v. Chandler,* No. C–74–1064 (N.D., Ohio, filed Nov. 20, 1974).

60. U.S. Attorney General's Task Force on Family Violence, *Report* (Washington, D.C.: U.S. Department of Justice, 1984).

61. A. Binder and J. Meeker, "The Development of Social Attitudes toward Spousal Abuse," in Buzawa and Buzawa, eds., *Domestic Violence,* 3–19, 12.

62. American Bar Association, *Standards Relating to the Urban Police Function* (1972), 116; J. Goldstein, "Police Discretion Not to Invoke the Criminal Process: Low-Visibility Decisions in the Administration of Justice," *Yale Law Journal* 69 (1960): 543–94; and William Ker Muir Jr., *Police: Streetcorner Politicians* (Chicago: University of Chicago Press, 1977).

63. Indeed, legislatures at times assume that laws they pass will not be strictly enforced by the police. See M. Zalman, "Mandatory Sentencing Legislation: Myth and Reality," in M. Morash, ed., *Implementing Criminal Justice Policies* (Beverly Hills, Calif.: Sage, 1982), 61–69.

64. K. C. Davis, *Discretionary Justice: A Preliminary Inquiry* (Baton Rouge: Louisiana State University Press, 1969), 3, 5.

65. Muir, *Police,* 57, 82–100.

66. Lloyd Ohlin and Michael Tonry, "Family Violence in Perspective," in Ohlin and Tonry, eds., *Family Violence* (Chicago: University of Chicago Press, 1989), 1–18.

67. A 1970 survey found that 25 percent of the male respondents and 17 percent of the females approved of a husband's slapping his wife under certain circumstances. Irene H. Frieze and Angela Browne, "Violence in Marriage," in Ohlin and Tonry, eds., *Family Violence,* 165.

67. Del Martin, *Battered Wives,* rev. ed. (San Francisco: Volcano Press, 1981), 87–88.

68. R. B. Felson, J. M. Ackerman, and C. A. Gallagher, "Police Intervention and the Repeat of Domestic Assault," *Criminology* 43, no. 3 (2005): 563–88, 564.

69. The report was published in the *Police Foundation Reports* (1984) and was based on a scholarly article: L. Sherman and R. Berk, "The Specific Deterrent Effects of Arrest for Domestic Violence," *American Sociological Review* 49, no. 2 (1984): 261–72. The article was cautious in drawing policy conclusions.

70. R. Lempert, "Humility Is a Virtue: On the Publicization of Policy-Relevant Research," *Law and Society Review* 23 (1989): 146–61.

71. J. Zorza, "Must We Stop Arresting Batterers? Analysis and Policy Implications of New Police Domestic Violence Studies," *New England Law Review* 28 (1994): 929–90, 935–36.

72. The Minneapolis report, L. Sherman's replication report, and a general analysis of these issues are found in L. Sherman, *Policing Domestic Violence: Experiments and Dilemmas* (New York: Free Press, 1992).

73. Sherman, *Policing Domestic Violence,* 22–24.

74. G. Kristian Miccio, "A House Divided: Mandatory Arrest, Domestic Violence, and the Conservatization of the Battered Women's Movement," *Houston Law Review* 42 (2005): 237–323, n. 2.

75. Zorza, "Must We Stop Arresting Batterers?" 985.

76. Wanless, "Note: Mandatory Arrest," 533–75; and Catherine Popham Durant, "Note: When to Arrest: What Influences Police Determination to Arrest When There Is a Report of Domestic Violence?" *Southern California Review of Law and Women's Studies* 12 (2003): 301–35.

77. K. J. Ferraro, "Policing Women Battering," *Social Problems* 36, no. 1 (1989): 61–74.

78. E. S. Buzawa and C. G. Buzawa, "Domestic Violence," in Buzawa and Buzawa, *Domestic Violence,* 20.

79. Miccio, "A House Divided"; Jessica Dayton, "Student Essay: The Silencing of a Woman's Choice: Mandatory Arrest and No Drop Prosecution Policies in Domestic Violence Cases," *Cardozo Women's Law Journal* 9 (2003): 281–97; and Erin L. Han, "Note: Mandatory Arrest and No-Drop Policies: Victim Empowerment in Domestic Violence Cases," *Boston College Third World Law Journal* 23 (2003): 159–91.

80. C. D. Maxwell, J. H. Garner, and J. A. Fagan, "The Effects of Arrest in Intimate Partner Violence: New Evidence from the Spouse Assault Replication Program," National Institute of Justice Research in Brief (NCJ 188199, July 2001).

81. Felson, Ackerman, and Gallagher, "Police Intervention," 581–82.

82. Joann Miller, "An Arresting Experiment: Domestic Violence Victim Experiences and Perceptions," *Journal of Interpersonal Violence* 18, no. 7 (2003): 695–716, 708.

83. Kingsnorth and MacIntosh, "Domestic Violence," 301–28, 321–22.

84. Laura Dugan, "Domestic Violence Legislation: Exploring Its Impact on the Likelihood of Domestic Violence, Police Involvement, and Arrest," *Criminology and Public Policy* 2, no. 2 (2003): 283–312, 303.

85. See press release of Governor George Pataki of New York, "Governor: Keep Mandatory Arrest in Domestic Violence Law" (March 9, 2001), http://www.ny.gov/governor/press/01/march9_01.htm (accessed July 24, 2006).

86. Wanless, "Note: Mandatory Arrest," 562.

87. Thomas S. Whetstone, "Measuring the Impact of a Domestic Violence Coordinated Response Team," *Policing* 24, no. 3 (2001): 371–98; and James Lasley, "The Effect of Intensive Bail Supervision on Repeat Domestic Violence Offenders," *Policy Studies Journal,* 31, no. 2 (2003): 187–207.

88. M. Reuland et al., *Police-Community Partnerships to Address Domestic Violence* (PERF, COPS, Department of Justice, n.d.); and Alissa P. Worden, Models of Community Coordination in Partner Violence Cases (NCJ 187351, 2001).

JUSTICES OF THE SUPREME COURT

Stalwart Conservatives, 1938–1962: Reed, Vinson, Burton, Minton, and Whittaker

These five justices, appointees of Presidents Franklin D. Roosevelt, Harry S. Truman, and Dwight D. Eisenhower, were instrumental in delaying the implementation of the due process "incorporation" revolution of the 1960s. They were largely conservative in their criminal procedure rulings, both in denying the validity of the incorporation argument and in construing the Due Process Clause narrowly. For the most part, legal commentators rank these justices as not especially distinguished: Their vision of the Court's role tended to be cramped, and they failed to explain their positions with intellectual force. They typically followed the lead of justices with more manifest abilities, especially Justices Felix Frankfurter and John Marshall Harlan II. They displayed basic legal competence but little independence in their decisions, and their opinions were not written with the high craft that is critical to shaping the law.

This group of justices, with Justice Tom Clark, formed a majority of the Court from 1949 to 1953 (excluding Justice Whittaker, who sat from 1957 to 1962). From 1953 to 1962, a combination of centrist and less dyed-in-the-wool conservatives kept the Court from breaching the *Palko* doctrine until Justice Clark's decision in *Mapp*. With Justice Frankfurter's retirement and replacement by Justice Arthur Goldberg in 1962, the Court took a decidedly liberal turn that marked the Warren Court of the 1960s.

Collection of the Supreme Court of the United States. Photographer: Harris and Ewing.

Stanley F. Reed

Kentucky, 1884–1980

Democrat

Appointed by Franklin Delano Roosevelt

Years of Service: 1938–1957

Life and Career. Reed held B.A. degrees from Kentucky Wesleyan College and Yale University and studied law at the Sorbonne, Columbia University, and the University of Virginia without graduating. He completed his legal studies by reading law in a Kentucky lawyer's office, and he practiced from 1910 to the 1920s. He entered government service under President Herbert Hoover but remained in the attorney general's office as a faithful New Dealer under President Roosevelt. As solicitor general from 1935, he argued some of the key New Deal cases before the Supreme Court and developed a good reputation for legal craftsmanship. He was President Roosevelt's second appointment to the Supreme Court.

Contribution to Criminal Procedure. He was a stalwart supporter of Justice Frankfurter and helped to block the movement toward incorporation, applying the criminal provisions of the Bill of Rights to the states.

Signature Opinion. *Adamson v. California* (1947). Justice Reed's majority opinion in *Adamson* kept the Court's anti-incorporation position intact. Adamson was tried for murder; he did not take the stand in his own defense, knowing that if he did so, prior convictions for burglary, larceny, and robbery would have been introduced into evidence to impeach him. California law allowed the judge to comment to the jury on the defendant's silence. Writing for the majority, Reed relied on a long train of cases, including *Twining v. New Jersey* (1908), for the proposition that the Self-Incrimination Clause was not a fundamental right incorporated into the Due Process Clause of the Fourteenth Amendment. He relied on the *Palko* case, noting that this ruling allowed the states to pursue their own criminal procedure policies unfettered by rules under the Bill of Rights that had limited the federal government. "It accords with the constitutional doctrine of federalism by leaving to the states the responsibility of dealing with the privileges and immunities of their citizens except those inherent in national citizenship."

In addition, Justice Reed made it clear that he did not entirely disapprove of the practical impact of a judge's telling a jury that they could take the defendant's refusal to testify into account in weighing the evidence, even though by 1947 a majority of the states had abolished the practice by statute or state constitutional rule. Adamson argued that this placed a penalty on his right to silence under the California constitution and shifted the burden of proof from the government to him. Justice Reed, to the contrary, noted: "[W]e see no reason why comment should not be made upon his silence. It seems quite natural that when a defendant has opportunity to deny or explain facts and determines not to do so, the prosecution should bring out the strength of the evidence by commenting upon defendant's failure to explain or deny it. The prosecution evidence may be of facts that may be beyond the knowledge of the accused. If so, his failure to testify would have little if any weight. But the facts may be such as are necessarily in the knowledge of the accused. In that case a failure to explain would point to an inability to explain."

Assessment.   Justice Reed's record was "liberal" in regard to New Deal economic issues. He was a strong believer in judicial restraint and feared what he called "krytocracy," or government by judges. He was a judicial conservative in many civil liberties areas, and he voted consistently with Justice Frankfurter's bloc. On the question of school desegregation, he had consistently voted against segregated facilities under the "separate but equal" doctrine but was at first reluctant to overturn the doctrine in *Brown v. Board of Education* (1954). After Chief Justice Vinson died during deliberations, Chief Justice Earl Warren persuaded Reed to join a unanimous Court in overruling *Plessy v. Ferguson* (1896).

Further Reading.

John D. Fassett, *New Deal Justice: The Life of Stanley Reed of Kentucky* (New York: Vantage, 1994).

Collection of the Supreme Court of the United States. Photographer: Harris and Ewing.

Fred M. Vinson

Kentucky, 1890–1953

Democrat

Appointed Chief Justice by Harry Truman

Years of Service: 1946–1953

Life and Career.   Vinson, born in Kentucky, was educated at Kentucky Normal School and Centre College, where he excelled in athletics and received a law degree. Vinson practiced law from 1911 to 1931. Elected to the House of Representatives in 1924, he rose to a position of power on the Ways and Means Committee and, as a loyal ally to Roosevelt, was instrumental in developing New Deal tax and coal programs. He was appointed to the U.S. Circuit Court for the District of Columbia in 1938 but resigned during World War II to become director of economic stabilization and later director of war mobilization. He developed a strong friendship with President Truman, who appointed him secretary of the treasury.

Vinson's public philosophy, including his theory of the Supreme Court's role, was shaped by these momentous events. He believed the federal government needed the power to solve the enormous problems threatening the nation. He was pragmatic and, while serving in all three branches, had participated in the process through which big government won the greatest war in history and tamed the worst political-economic crisis in the life of the United States. He had faith born of experience that American political institutions and the American public had the judgment to successfully resolve competing interests for the public good.

Contribution to Criminal Procedure. In 1946, a liberal bloc of four justices (Hugo Black, William O. Douglas, Frank Murphy, and Wiley Blount Rutledge) came close to inaugurating the incorporation of the Bill of Rights. Justice Vinson opposed this action, and during his tenure, the number of justices opposed to incorporation increased as Murphy and Rutledge were replaced by Clark and Minton. Justices Felix Frankfurter and Robert H. Jackson, while of a more liberal temperament and more willing to find for defendants under the Due Process Clause, were also opposed to the incorporation doctrine.

Signature Opinion. *Stack v. Boyle* (1951). Although Justice Vinson voted in favor of the federal government in its heavy-handed repression of American Communists in loyalty cases during the cold war, he drew the line at the use of the courts to stifle traditional rights. The right to bail came up in *Stack v. Boyle* (1951). Pretrial bail was set at $50,000 each for leaders of the American Communist Party on trial for the theoretical advocacy of the violent overthrow of the government. Writing for the Court, Justice Vinson held that the bail was excessive because it was set at a figure higher than reasonably calculated to ensure that the defendants would return to stand trial and submit to sentence. He wrote: "This traditional right to freedom before conviction permits the unhampered preparation of a defense, and serves to prevent the infliction of punishment prior to conviction. Unless this right to bail before trial is preserved, the presumption of innocence, secured only after centuries of struggle, would lose its meaning."

Assessment. Justice Vinson believed in judicial restraint. Having seen a conservative Supreme Court subvert the political will at the beginning of the New Deal, Vinson consistently voted to uphold the power of government in civil liberties (in loyalty oath and Communist conspiracy cases), in economic affairs, and in criminal law. He was appointed chief justice in part to calm several personal antagonisms that had developed among more brilliant justices, but his lack of constitutional vision and craft made him an ineffective chief justice.

Further Reading.

Melvin I. Urofsky, *Division and Discord: The Supreme Court under Stone and Vinson, 1941–1953* (Columbia: University of South Carolina Press, 1997).

Collection of the Supreme Court of the United States. Photographer: Harris and Ewing.

Harold Burton

Ohio, 1888–1964

Republican

Appointed by Harry S. Truman

Years of Service: 1945–1958

Life and Career. Burton was born in Jamaica Plain, Massachusetts; was educated at Bowdoin College and Harvard Law School; and practiced law in the west before settling in Cleveland. His political career included service in the Ohio House of Representatives from 1929, election to mayor of Cleveland in 1935—serving two terms—and election to the U.S. Senate in 1941. Although a Republican mayor, he cooperated with the national government, a position taken by few midwestern Republicans. Although sometimes critical of the Democratic administration, Burton supported the economic and social policies of the New Deal and the entry of the United States into the United Nations. These positions made Burton an acceptable Republican nominee by a Democratic president. As with all of Truman's nominees, the president and Senator Burton were friends; Burton had been a member of Truman's committee to investigate wartime fraud.

Contribution to Criminal Procedure. Justice Burton was a stalwart conservative in opposing the incorporation doctrine. In confessions cases, he was unwilling to use the Due Process Clause to exclude confessions that the Court's majority found coercive. On the other hand, he was in the minority in a case that held that a person who was electrocuted and lived could be executed a second time without violating any constitutional provision, including the fundamental fairness aspect of due process.

Signature Opinion. *Rovario v. United States* (1957). Writing for a six-to-one majority, Justice Burton held that the identity of a secret undercover informant must be made known to the defendant, Rovario, during a trial for heroin possession where the informer had taken a material part in bringing about Rovario's possession of the drugs, had been present with him while the crime occurred, and might have been a material witness as to whether he knowingly transported the drugs. Justice Burton ruled that the so-called informer's privilege is in reality the government's privilege to withhold from disclosure the identity of those who furnish information of violations of law to officers charged with enforcing that law. This "privilege" assists effective law enforcement by encouraging people to inform about crime, but where it conflicts with fundamental fairness, it must give way to the defendant's right to a fair trial. In effect, where a conviction depends on the disclosure of the identity of a secret informant, the government must either divulge the informant's identity or dismiss the prosecution. *Rovario* indicates that the stalwart conservatives in criminal procedure, while tending to favor the prosecution, adhered to fundamental standards of a fair trial.

Assessment. On the Court, Justice Burton's conservative positions on civil liberties were close to those of Justice Reed. As Chief Justice Vinson and Justices Minton and Clark were appointed, they joined to form what seemed to be a voting bloc that upheld the government's loyalty oath programs.

Further Reading.

Mary Frances Berry, *Stability, Security, and Continuity: Mr. Justice Burton and Decision-Making in the Supreme Court, 1945–1958* (Westport, Conn.: Greenwood Press, 1978).

Sherman Minton

Indiana, 1890–1965
Democrat
Appointed by Harry S. Truman
Years of Service: 1949–1956

Collection of the Supreme Court of the United States. Photographer: Harris and Ewing.

Life and Career. Minton was born in Indiana, graduated at the head of his class at Indiana University, studied law at Yale University, and returned home to practice law while engaging in local politics. In 1933, he was appointed counselor to Indiana's Public Service Commission. He played a significant role in developing a state version of the New Deal and was elected in 1934 to the U.S. Senate, where he was a staunch supporter of the Roosevelt administration. His legal knowledge and militant manner in debate led to his rise to a Senate leadership role in which he supported Roosevelt's "court-packing" plan. Minton was an internationalist, a position that was not too popular in the Midwest, and he lost his Senate seat in 1940. He worked as a presidential assistant for the next year and was appointed to the U.S. Court of Appeals for the Seventh Circuit (Indiana, Illinois, and Wisconsin) in 1941. It was Minton's good fortune to be seated next to another freshman senator, Harry S. Truman, in 1934. They became and remained good friends, which was a key element in each of Truman's appointments to the Supreme Court.

Contribution to Criminal Procedure.   As a stalwart conservative on criminal matters, Justice Minton joined the Frankfurter-led bloc to halt any advance toward incorporation.

Signature Opinion.   *United States v. Rabinowitz* (1950). He wrote the majority opinion in *Rabinowitz,* which established the rule that a search incident to arrest could justify the search of the entire premises. This rule stood until overturned by the *Chimel* decision in 1969. Justice Minton wrote: "What is a reasonable search is not to be determined by any fixed formula. The Constitution does not define what are 'unreasonable' searches and, regrettably, in our discipline we have no ready litmus-paper test. The recurring questions of the reasonableness of searches must find resolution in the facts and circumstances of each case." In *Rabinowitz,* Justice Minton viewed the search as reasonable because the search and seizure were incident to a valid arrest; the place of the search was a business room to which the public was invited; the room was small and under the immediate and complete control of the respondent; the search did not extend beyond the room used for unlawful purposes; and the possession of the forged stamps was a crime. The Court was clearly influenced by the crime control model of criminal justice: "A rule of thumb requiring that a search warrant always be procured whenever practicable may be appealing from the vantage point of easy administration. But we cannot agree that this requirement should be crystallized into a *sine qua non* to the reasonableness of a search. . . . The judgment of the officers as to when to close the trap on a criminal committing a crime in their presence or who they have reasonable cause to believe is committing a felony is not determined solely upon whether there was time to procure a search warrant. Some flexibility will be accorded law officers engaged in daily battle with criminals for whose restraint criminal laws are essential."

Assessment.   Justice Minton replaced liberal Justice Rutledge and was thought by most observers at the time to be in the liberal mold. However, he fit very closely into the Vinson-Reed-Burton camp; as a New Dealer, he acquiesced to Congress in economic matters, but in civil rights issues, he had the most conservative record, voting for the government even more than Chief Justice Vinson. As a judicial conservative, he strongly maintained that the Court had no special obligation to support civil rights and that the Court had no power to legislate.

Further Reading.

Harry L. Wallace, "Mr. Justice Minton: Hoosier Justice on the Supreme Court," *Indiana Law Journal* 34 (1959): 145–205.

Collection of the Supreme Court of the United States. Photographer: Abdon Daoud Ackad.

Charles E. Whittaker

Missouri, 1901–1973

Republican

Appointed by Dwight D. Eisenhower

Years of Service: 1957–1962

Life and Career.   Whittaker was born and raised on a modest Kansas farm, where he trapped small animals and tracked game to supplement his family's income. He attended the University of Kansas City Law School at night while working as a clerk in a law firm, graduating in 1924. From then until 1954 (as partner from 1930), he practiced law in the same firm, which represented many large corporations doing business in Missouri. He was first a litigator and later an adviser to the firm's large business clients. He was active in bar association activities and became president of the Missouri State Bar Association. In 1954, he was appointed by President Eisenhower as a federal district judge and, in 1956, as a judge to the U.S. Court of Appeals for the Eighth Circuit.

Known for his hard work and efficiency as a judge, he established conservative credentials in ruling that a tenured professor in a private university could be dismissed for refusing to answer questions asked by a congressional committee and the university's board of trustees about possible Communist Party affiliations. He was selected by President Eisenhower as a conservative Republican judge to replace Justice Reed.

Contribution to Criminal Procedure.   Justice Whittaker strove to put aside ideological considerations and decide cases on their merits alone. This led to a somewhat inconsistent position. While he voted for the defendant in a number of cases, he also opposed the incorporation of the Fourth Amendment exclusionary rule in *Mapp v. Ohio* (1961).

Signature Opinion.   *Draper v. United States* (1959). Writing for a six-to-one majority, Whittaker ruled that probable cause existed to arrest Draper based on evidence given by a known reliable informant. An officer was told that Draper, a known drug peddler in Denver, would return by train from Chicago with a supply of heroin. The informant described the clothing that Draper would be wearing (a light-colored raincoat, brown slacks, and black shoes). The Court held that probable cause existed because the officer, having corroborated every factual element about Draper, except the possession of drugs when he detrained, "had 'reasonable grounds' to believe that the remaining unverified bit of [the informant's] information—that Draper would have the heroin with him—was likewise true."

Assessment.   On the Court, Justice Whittaker aligned himself with such conservatives as Justices Frankfurter, Harlan, Clark, Burton, and Potter Stewart to maintain a slim majority in several civil liberties and criminal procedure cases. Unlike these conservative justices, he never was able to articulate a coherent philosophy of judging by which to guide his opinions. Thus, when he did rule in favor of defendants, his votes appeared to be based more on emotional factors of sympathy than on a firm understanding of the role of the federal judiciary. It would appear that he did not outgrow his position as a district court judge who could achieve success in applying the law; as a Supreme Court justice, it is necessary to expound the contours of the Constitution in novel and difficult cases. It is possible that Justice Whittaker's abilities were overtaxed, for he apparently put in an enormous number of hours and worried substantially about the cases. He fell ill in March 1962, apparently exhausted from his work. He resigned from the Court that year and accepted a position as a legal adviser to the General Motors Corporation.

Further Reading

Barbara B. Christensen, "Mister Justice Whittaker: The Man on the Right," *Santa Clara Law Review* 19 (1979): 1039–62.

5 Warrantless Searches

CHAPTER OUTLINE

KEY TERMS

administrative search

automobile search

border

border search

crime scene investigation exception

exigency exception

extraterritorial

fixed checkpoint

hot pursuit

impound

in loco parentis

inventory search

pervasively regulated industry

roving patrol

special needs doctrine

warrantless search

[T]he most basic constitutional rule in this area is that "searches conducted outside the judicial process, without prior approval by judge or magistrate, are per se unreasonable under the Fourth Amendment— subject only to a few specifically established and well-delineated exceptions." . . . In times of unrest, whether caused by crime or racial conflict or fear of internal subversion, this basic law and the values that it represents may appear unrealistic or "extravagant" to some. But the values were those of the authors of our fundamental constitutional concepts.

—Justice Potter Stewart, *Coolidge v. New Hampshire,*
403 U.S. 443, 455 (1971)

Warrantless searches are of enormous practical importance to police work. Despite the Supreme Court's preference for a search warrant, warrantless searches are far more common. Every warrantless search is conducted without prior judicial review but is subject to judicial review after the fact. Nevertheless, a search based on an officer's assessment of probable cause is more likely to be arbitrary than one subjected to the warrant process.

This text has already discussed several kinds of warrantless searches: plain view, consent, search incident to arrest, and the *Terry* stop and frisk. Each is based on a different rationale and is held to different legal standards. An item seized in plain view, for example, involves no Fourth Amendment interest or expectation of privacy because the officer is in a public or other lawful place when the "plain view" occurs. The Fourth Amendment is not burdened by a consent search because the person has voluntarily given up the right of privacy. An officer can seek consent without having probable cause or reasonable suspicion to believe that a person is carrying contraband, and he or she can even exploit the person's ignorance of the right to refuse. The Fourth Amendment, however, imposes one absolute standard on all warrantless searches—they must be reasonable. Thus, for example, consent must be truly voluntary, and an item in plain view must be immediately apparent as contraband.

In contrast to consent searches, which do not directly interfere with Fourth Amendment rights, a group of warrantless searches are valid even though they directly interfere with a person's rights under the search and seizure amendment. These warrantless searches impinge on a person's expectation of privacy but are deemed reasonable because each occurs under emergency conditions. These **exigency exceptions** include (1) home entries under a condition of hot pursuit, (2) the "automobile exception," and (3) search incident to arrest (see Chapter 4). The Supreme Court has also allowed forcible warrantless searches for evidence in a few miscellaneous cases that Professors Whitebread and Slobogin have labeled "evanescent evidence." That is, when evidence may be destroyed or may disappear, police can forcibly restrain a suspect and take the evidence, as long as the methods are not brutal.[1] This includes taking blood from a vehicular homicide suspect (*Schmerber v. California*, 1966; see Chapter 3) or scrapings of dried blood from the finger of a homicide suspect (*Cupp v. Murphy*, 1973; see Chapter 4). In addition, warrantless entries into premises are allowed for exigencies, as in police officers entering a home in *Arizona v. Hicks* (1987) (see Chapter 3) and firefighters entering a burning building (this chapter).

For an exigency search to be lawful, an officer must have probable cause to believe that contraband is in the place or vehicle being entered or probable cause to arrest the person being searched incident to arrest. These exigency exceptions are compatible with the warrant-preference construction of the Fourth Amendment (see "The Fourth Amendment's Structure" in Chapter 2):

> Thus the most basic constitutional rule in this area is that "searches conducted outside the judicial process, without prior approval by judge or magistrate, are *per se* unreasonable under the Fourth Amendment—subject only to a few specifically established and well-delineated exceptions." The exceptions are "jealously and carefully drawn," and there must be "a showing by those who seek exemption . . . that the exigencies of the situation made that course imperative." (*Coolidge v. New Hampshire*, 1971)

The exigency exceptions existed under common law and, because of their obvious necessity, do not undermine the warrant requirement. The warrant-preference construction warns against creating new categories of exceptions. Recently, however, the Court has indeed weakened the warrant-preference policy of the Fourth Amendment by extending the scope of automobile searches and by creating a class of warrantless searches justified by "special needs beyond the normal need for law enforcement." This chapter also reviews other kinds of non-exigency warrantless searches: inventory searches, administrative searches, and border searches.

To reiterate, the basic rule that justifies all warrantless searches under the Fourth Amendment is reasonableness. Beyond this basic requirement, the exigency exceptions require the prior existence of probable cause. Some warrantless searches dispense with probable cause and rely on reasonable suspicion (e.g., *Terry* stops and searches of public school students' bags by teachers). Other warrantless searches require no probable cause or reasonable suspicion (e.g., automobile inventory searches). And still others dispense with particularized suspicion against a specific person (e.g., automobile sobriety checklanes).

HOT PURSUIT AND OTHER EXIGENCY SEARCHES

Hot Pursuit

Hot pursuit occurs when a dangerous criminal suspect is being chased by police and enters a place that is protected by the Fourth Amendment expectation of privacy, such as the suspect's home. The suspect presents a danger to society: He or she may flee or harm someone or may destroy evidence. Police officers need to enter the premises immediately to make an arrest and to search for weapons and contraband. The immediacy of a hot pursuit makes it absurd to "stop the action" to obtain a search warrant to enter. A greater danger to the public and to the police might develop if police cordoned off a house; it gives the suspect an opportunity to destroy evidence and to fortify the residence. As a result, the hot pursuit exception allows the police to enter immediately, without an arrest or search warrant, to make an arrest. If evidence of a crime is observed in plain view during the hot pursuit entry for purposes of arrest, it may be seized and is admissible in a criminal trial.

In *Warden v. Hayden* (1967), cab drivers followed Hayden to a house after he had robbed the taxi company office. They transmitted the information to the taxi dispatcher, who in turn relayed the information to the police. Police officers arrived at Hayden's home "within minutes" of receiving the call, knocked on his door, and entered when the door was opened by his wife. They searched through the house looking for the suspect and found incriminating evidence (clothing similar to that worn by the robber). This evidence would be admissible only if the initial entry was lawful. The Supreme Court, holding the entry and search constitutional, explained the basis of the hot pursuit exception to the warrant requirement:

> The Fourth Amendment does not require police officers to delay in the course of an investigation if to do so would gravely endanger their lives or the lives of others. Speed here was essential, and only a thorough search of the house for persons and weapons could have ensured that Hayden was the only man present and that the police had control of all weapons which could be used against them or to effect an escape. (*Warden v. Hayden,* 1967)

Several legal principles of the hot pursuit exception can be derived from this case. First, the hot pursuit warrant exception, as an exigency exception, must be based on probable cause to believe that the person who has just entered the premises has committed a felony or is dangerous to the safety of others. Second, hot pursuit may be based either on the officer's personal observations or on reliable hearsay. Third, the pursuit need not be immediate; there may be a short time lapse between the suspect's entry into the house and the arrival of the police. The fourth rule concerns the scope of the search pursuant to the hot pursuit entry. "The permissible scope of search must, . . . at the least, be as broad as may reasonably be necessary to prevent the dangers that the suspect at large in the house may resist or escape" (*Warden v. Hayden,* 1967). In other words, until the offender is found, the police may search the entire premises for suspects, weapons, and evidence of the crime. However, once the offender has been apprehended, the police may not search beyond the limits of a search incident to an arrest.

Most hot pursuits proceed from public property onto private property. ***United States v. Santana*** (1976) established a fifth rule: The pursuit may begin on private property.

Officers had reliable information that the suspect was in possession of marked money from a heroin buy. As the police approached her house, Santana was standing in the doorway holding a paper bag. She retreated to a vestibule, where the police seized her. In a brief struggle, heroin packets fell from the bag and were lawfully seized by the police. Here, although the pursuit technically began on private property, the Court held that for Fourth Amendment purposes, it was a public place. The *Santana* ruling, however, does not allow the police to enter a house where there is no exigency and thereby "create" one.

The sixth rule, established by **Welsh v. Wisconsin** (1984), concerns the gravity of the offense: Police may enter a premises without a warrant in hot pursuit only for serious crimes. A minor offense does not create an exigency that overrides the Fourth Amendment rule that police must obtain an arrest warrant in order to arrest a suspect in his or her home (*Payton v. New York,* 1980). The offense in *Welsh* was a civil infraction of driving while intoxicated (DWI). Welsh's erratic driving resulted in his car's careening off a road and into a ditch on a rainy night. A witness saw the apparently intoxicated driver walk off into the night and called the police, who arrived at Welsh's nearby home within the hour. They entered the house without a warrant or the consent of Welsh's stepdaughter, found Welsh in bed, arrested him, and took him to the police station, where he refused to submit to a breath analysis test. His refusal could result in a license revocation only if the arrest was legal, and this, in turn, depended on the legality of the forcible, warrantless home entry. The state's only rationale for a constitutional entry was hot pursuit.

The Wisconsin Supreme Court upheld the warrantless entry because of the need to prevent harm to the offender and the public resulting from drunk driving and to prevent the "destruction" of the blood alcohol evidence by its dissipation before testing could be completed. The U.S. Supreme Court reversed. It discounted the weak public safety reasoning because the offender was in bed and thus no longer a threat to anyone. Preservation of evidence is a basis of the hot pursuit exigency, but the Court held "that an important factor to be considered when determining whether any exigency exists is the gravity of the underlying offense for which the arrest is being made." Under Wisconsin law, the underlying offense in this case—first offense DWI—was a noncriminal violation subject to a $200 fine. Justice Brennan, writing for the majority, noted that a warrantless entry into a home is presumptively unreasonable and that the burden of proof is on the government to show that an exigency makes a warrantless entry reasonable. The Court felt that a hot pursuit entry for a minor crime is presumptively unreasonable and difficult for the government to rebut.

The entry and search in this case violated the Fourth Amendment because (1) "there was no immediate or continuous pursuit of the petitioner from the scene of a crime," (2) Welsh had arrived home and abandoned his car so there was little remaining threat to the public safety, and (3) the exigency of ascertaining Welsh's blood-alcohol level was outweighed by the fact that first-offense DWI was classified as a civil offense. The majority believed that this would be "unreasonable police behavior that the principles of the Fourth Amendment will not sanction."

Justice Byron White's dissent noted that a warrantless entry into a home is as serious a Fourth Amendment intrusion for a person wanted for a serious felony as for a minor crime. He disagreed with the majority's assessment of gravity because of the danger to highway safety by drunk drivers. The warrantless intrusion into Welsh's bedroom promoted the "valid and substantial state interests" of prosecuting drunk driving. He also suggested that police are better served by bright-line rules so that what constitutes a serious offense—justifying hot pursuit—is not open to interpretation. The dissent also urged the Court to defer to the state's judgment as to the seriousness of the offense.

Welsh does not indicate what constitutes a nonserious crime, beyond the civil offense of first-time DWI punishable by a fine. Justice William Brennan implied that a simple bright-line division between felonies and misdemeanors is not the proper line between serious and nonserious offenses. Even if the *Welsh* rule does not apply only to civil offenses punishable by a fine, the case itself does not establish the serious-nonserious criterion. Perhaps, then, it is the penalty, such as imprisonment for thirty days or six months. Possibly, hot pursuit is not proper for some nonviolent felonies but is for some violent misdemeanors. Another uncertainty left by *Welsh* is whether the hot pursuit exception for minor crimes applies in premises other than the home.

The Supreme Court held in ***Minnesota v. Olson*** (1990) that being wanted for a serious felony does not in itself create an exigency. Police suspected that Olson, a murder suspect, was in a house, and they entered without a warrant. Their attempt to justify the warrantless entry on the basis of hot pursuit was undercut by several factors:

- The suspect was thought to be the driver of a get-away car and not the shooter.
- The police had already recovered the murder weapon.
- There was no suggestion of danger to other people from the suspect.
- The entry occurred a day after the murder-robbery.
- Three or four police squads surrounded the house, which was secured.

Minnesota v. Olson demonstrates that the finding of an exigency is a factual determination made by a court assessing all of the circumstances of the case.

Other Exigencies

The hot pursuit warrant exception is an example of a general rule that police may enter a premises or conduct a search without a warrant when exigent circumstances justify the search or intrusion. The exigent circumstance may be an imminent threat to the life or safety of people that no police officer should ignore. In *Arizona v. Hicks* (1987) (see Chapter 3), the officer properly entered an apartment to search for a man who had shot a bullet through the floor into another apartment, injuring an occupant and creating an obvious and continuing threat to life and safety. In *Hicks,* there was probable cause to believe that a person had committed a felony. There was no hot pursuit as such, but the entry met the reasonableness criterion of an exigency exception.

Warrantless entry into homes by government agents who are not police officers enforcing the criminal law must also be supported by a real exigency: firefighting is a prime example (*Michigan v. Tyler,* 1978; *Michigan v. Clifford,* 1984). Where probable cause exists to believe that a suspect committed a crime and that an immediate search is essential to prevent the destruction of evidence of the crime, the search is constitutional if it is reasonable and the intrusion on privacy interests is minimal. An example is *Schmerber v. California* (1966), in which a driver was arrested at a hospital while being treated for injuries suffered in an automobile accident. The police directed a physician to draw a blood sample, and a blood alcohol test was admitted in evidence to convict Schmerber of driving while intoxicated. The critical evidence would quickly be lost if the blood were not drawn promptly. The Court upheld this warrantless search for blood alcohol, noting that the collection of blood by medical workers in this case was not dangerous, was routine, was not very invasive or humiliating, and was likely to produce highly accurate evidence.

Other cases have upheld warrantless searches as reasonable because of the exigency that evidence might be destroyed. In these cases, privacy rights were minimal, and the cases did not precisely fit the search incident to arrest warrant exception. *United States v. Edwards* (1974) involved taking potentially incriminating paint chips from the clothing of a police lockup inmate who was ordered to exchange his clothing for jail issue. *Cupp v. Murphy* (1973), discussed in Chapter 4, upheld the removal of what was apparently dried blood from the finger of a potential murder suspect, who had not been arrested, at a police station.

The police warrantless entry in *Arizona v. Hicks* (1987) (see Chapter 3) was made under the so-called emergency aid doctrine (***Brigham City v. Stuart,*** 2006). The duty of police to come to the aid of those who are in danger of losing life or limb is so apparent that it gives rise to little litigation. In *Stuart,* police were called to a loud house party at

3 A.M., heard loud shouting, walked down a driveway, and saw two teenagers drinking beer in the yard. Through a screen door and windows, they saw an altercation in the kitchen between four adults and a juvenile, who punched the face of one of the adults, causing him to spit blood in the sink. The other adults pushed the juvenile up against a refrigerator to restrain him. "At this point, an officer opened the screen door and announced the officers' presence. Amid the tumult, nobody noticed. The officer entered the kitchen and again cried out, and as the occupants slowly became aware that the police were on the scene, the altercation ceased." Under these circumstances, the officer's warrantless entry was justified. As a matter of Fourth Amendment law, the test of the entry's reasonableness is objective. The circumstances made it objectively reasonable for an officer to believe that the injured adult needed medical aid and that the violence in the kitchen might continue. "Nothing in the Fourth Amendment required [the officers] to wait until another blow rendered someone 'unconscious' or 'semi-conscious' or worse before entering. The role of a peace officer includes preventing violence and restoring order, not simply rendering first aid to casualties; an officer is not like a boxing (or hockey) referee, poised to stop a bout only if it becomes too one-sided" (*Brigham City v. Stuart*, 2006).

Rejecting the Crime Scene Investigation Exception. The Supreme Court rejected a **crime scene investigation exception** to the warrant requirement in *Mincey v. Arizona* (1978). A police officer was killed in a drug raid in the Tucson, Arizona, apartment of Rufus Mincey, who was apparently shot by the slain officer. Backup officers entered the apartment, located other people, called for emergency assistance, and refrained from further investigation. Ten minutes later, homicide investigators arrived, arranged for the removal of the fatally injured officer and the suspects, and then secured the apartment. They then proceeded to gather evidence.

> Their search lasted four days, during which period the entire apartment was searched, photographed, and diagrammed. The officers opened drawers, closets, and cupboards, and inspected their contents; they emptied clothing pockets; they dug bullet fragments out of the walls and floors; they pulled up sections of the carpet and removed them for examination. Every item in the apartment was closely examined and inventoried, and 200 to 300 objects were seized. In short, Mincey's apartment was subjected to an exhaustive and intrusive search. No warrant was ever obtained. (*Mincey v. Arizona*, 1978)

The evidence obtained in the search was introduced at trial to convict Mincey of homicide and drug possession. The Arizona Supreme Court upheld the warrantless search as reasonable when conducted to investigate "the scene of a homicide—or of a serious personal injury with likelihood of death where there is reason to suspect foul play" as long as "the purpose [is] limited to determining the circumstances of death and the scope [does] not exceed that purpose. The search must also begin within a reasonable period following the time when the officials first learn of the murder (or potential murder)."

The Supreme Court unanimously reversed, holding that this warrantless search violated the Fourth Amendment. Although Mincey was a suspect, he retained some reasonable expectation of privacy in his home. To strip a suspect of all rights of privacy in the home "would impermissibly convict the suspect even before the evidence against him was gathered." The fact that Mincey was arrested and was in custody does not lessen "his right to privacy in his entire house" (*Mincey v. Arizona*, 1978). An exigency after the violent crime authorized the initial entry into Mincey's apartment, the protective sweep, the securing of the apartment, and the seizure of contraband items in plain view. But "a four-day search that included opening dresser drawers and ripping up carpets can hardly be rationalized in terms of the legitimate concerns that justify an emergency search" (*Mincey v. Arizona*, 1978). The Court also rejected the idea that special promptness was required to search the scene of a homicide, suggesting that an exception for that crime would lead to a blanket crime scene warrant exception and the argument that dispensing with a warrant would be more efficient. There was no suggestion that a search warrant could not have been easily and conveniently obtained. The Supreme Court later held that a warrantless, thorough, sixteen-hour homicide investigation of a cabin violated the *Mincey* ruling (*Flippo v. West Virginia,* 1999).

THE AUTOMOBILE EXCEPTION

An Overview of Vehicle Search Rules

The stop and search of mobile vehicles by police raises a variety of constitutional issues, some of which are discussed in Chapters 3, 4, and 7.

1. *Stopping I:* Probable cause or reasonable suspicion is required to stop a mobile vehicle (*Delaware v. Prouse,* 1979; see Chapter 4).

2. *Stopping II:* Innocent behavior can be the basis for stopping an automobile (*United States v. Arvizu,* 2002; see Chapter 4).

3. *Pretext stops:* An officer may stop a car with objective reasonable suspicion or probable cause of a traffic violation even though the real (subjective) reason for the stop is to search for drugs and there is no legal basis to stop the car for drugs (*Whren v. United States,* 1996; see Chapter 4).

4. *Stop and frisk:* An officer may enter an automobile to frisk a suspect or to inspect the interior (*Adams v. Williams,* 1972; *Michigan v. Long,* 1983; see Chapter 4).

5. *Control of driver and passengers:* An officer may order the driver and passengers to remain in or exit the vehicle (*Pennsylvania v. Mimms,* 1977; *Maryland v. Wilson,* 1997; see Chapter 4).

6. *Knowledge and consent:* An officer need not inform a driver that he or she is free to go before obtaining consent to search a vehicle (*Schneckloth v. Bustamonte,* 1973; *Ohio v. Robinette,* 1996; see Chapter 3).

7. *Scope of consent:* Consent to search a car includes consent to search a container in the car (*Florida v. Jimeno,* 1991; see Chapter 3).

8. *Questioning:* An officer need not read *Miranda* warnings for a routine stop or for most aspects of a stop for drunk driving (*Berkemer v. McCarty,* 1984; *Pennsylvania v. Muniz,* 1990; see Chapter 7).

9. *Checklanes:* Mobile vehicles may be stopped at checklanes to examine drivers for sobriety but not for illegal drug possession (*Michigan Department of State Police v. Sitz,* 1990; *City of Indianapolis v. Edmond,* 2000; see Chapter 4).

10. *Automobile exception: search of vehicle:* What is the scope of an officer's authority to search a stopped mobile vehicle without a warrant? (See *United States v. Ross,* 1982, in this chapter.)

11. *Automobile exception: search of containers:* What is the scope of an officer's authority to look into or to search closed areas or closed containers in a stopped mobile vehicle without a warrant? (See *California v. Acevedo,* 1991, in this chapter.)

12. *Impounded vehicles:* What rules guide the inventory search of impounded vehicles? (See *Florida v. Wells,* 1990, in this chapter.)

Clearly, an **automobile search** is a complex legal area. The development of various auto search rules over the last three decades has been one of the most confusing and contentious areas of criminal procedure. Most legal scholars have criticized the Supreme Court automobile search rulings that cut into the Fourth Amendment, accusing the Court of twisting principles to ensure that police officers can search automobiles almost at will. One scholar states, "Although the Court has described warrantless searches as presumptively invalid, more than twenty seemingly haphazard exceptions to the warrant clause in fact have swallowed the warrant requirement."[2] The relentless pressure by police to search cars is driven by the "war on drugs" and by the fact that police departments can augment their budgets by the forfeiture of automobiles found to be transporting illegal drugs.[3] The constitutional debate has recently become an explosive law enforcement and political issue as the practice of racial profiling has been exposed. (See the "Law in Society" section in this chapter.)

Professor David Steinberg has classified the constitutional law of automobile searches into three broad categories: (1) the automobile, or mobile vehicle, exception to the Warrant Clause; (2) cases concerning whether a warrant is required before police can open a closed container found in an automobile, and (3) groups of cases in which the police "do not rely on the automobile exception at all." This third category includes search incident to arrest (see *New York v. Belton,* 1981, later in this chapter), inventory search, plain view search (see *Texas v. Brown,* 1983, in Chapter 3), consent, and fixed checkpoint searches. The discussion of the automobile exception, narrowly defined, usually focuses on the first two categories. However, in the "real world" of policing, all of the rules and exceptions come together to produce a powerful regime of rules that makes it possible for a police officer to search virtually any car that he or she has a mind to stop. Driving is a pervasive activity in America, and it is nearly impossible for anyone to drive without violating some motor vehicle law, including speeding, driving over a line, changing lanes without signaling, inoperative taillight, headlights not on one-half hour after sunset to one-half hour before sunrise "and at such other times as atmospheric conditions render visibility as low as or lower than is ordinarily the case during that period," and an excessively loud muffler.[4] Therefore a police officer following a vehicle is likely to spot a violation at some point and, upon stopping that car, can utilize one of the various automobile search rules to engage in some level of lawful search. The potential—and the reality—of the pervasive stopping of black and Hispanic drivers in large numbers on pretextual grounds has led Professor David Harris to claim that "[i]ndeed, it is no exaggeration to say that in cases involving cars, the Fourth Amendment is all but dead."[5] Professor David Moran indicates that this trend culminated in *United States v. Arvizu* (2002), which found reasonable suspicion based on a family driving in a camper and "scrupulously obeying all traffic laws. . . . The Court's new vehicle doctrine is now complete: The police may lawfully stop any car at any time and virtually always search the car."[6] The following section demonstrates how a major component of the Court's automobile search doctrine was fashioned.

The Automobile Exception

The Supreme Court has upheld warrantless searches of automobiles for two reasons:

> Our first cases establishing the automobile exception to the Fourth Amendment's warrant requirement were based on the automobile's "ready mobility," an exigency sufficient to excuse failure to obtain a search warrant once probable cause to conduct the search is clear. . . . *Carroll v. United States* (1925). More recent cases provide a further justification: the individual's reduced expectation of privacy in an automobile, owing to its pervasive regulation. (*Pennsylvania v. Labron,* 1996)

Early on, the Supreme Court applied the "automobile" exception to a boat, and lower courts have applied the rule to searches of such mobile vehicles as trains, airplanes, ferries, and houseboats (*United States v. Lee,* 1927).[7]

Carroll v. United States (1925) is the foundation case for the automobile exigency exception. Chief Justice William Howard Taft wrote:

> The guaranty of freedom from unreasonable searches and seizures by the Fourth Amendment has been construed, practically since the beginning of the government, as recognizing a difference between a search of a store, dwelling house or other structure in respect of which a proper official search warrant readily may be obtained, and a search of a ship, motor boat, wagon or automobile for contraband goods, where it is not practicable to secure a warrant, because the vehicle can be quickly moved out of the locality or jurisdiction in which the warrant must be sought. (**Carroll v. United States,** 1925)

The *Carroll* rule requires that (1) police have probable cause to believe that the vehicle contains contraband, and (2) there is a "mobility exigency"—the vehicle will be driven off if it is not immediately seized. It is absurd for the police to leave a suspected vehicle to obtain a warrant. In *Carroll,* the officers had probable cause to believe that bootleggers were transporting illegally imported liquor in violation of the Prohibition laws when they spotted the "Carroll boys" driving toward Grand Rapids, Michigan. The officers stopped the car, felt the backseat, noticed that it was hard, and proceeded to rip and destroy the seat in order to get to the bottles of whiskey. The Court did not comment on this, indicating that the authority to search for contraband may reasonably include the destruction of some property necessary to get to the evidence.

The second rationale for a warrantless automobile search, a lesser expectation of privacy than exists in homes or in luggage, was explained in *California v. Carney* (1985):

> Even in cases where an automobile was not immediately mobile, the lesser expectation of privacy resulting from its use as a readily mobile vehicle justified application of the vehicular exception. In some cases, the configuration of the vehicle contributed to the lower expectation of privacy; for example we held in *Cardwell v. Lewis* (1974) that, because the passenger compartment of a standard automobile is relatively open to plain view, there are lesser expectations of privacy. But even when enclosed "repository" areas have been involved, we have concluded that the lesser expectations of privacy warrant application of the exception. We have applied the exception in the context of a locked car trunk, a sealed package in a car trunk, a closed compartment under the dashboard, the interior of a vehicle's upholstery, or sealed packages inside a covered pickup truck.
>
> These reduced expectations of privacy derive not from the fact that the area to be searched is in plain view, but from the pervasive regulation of vehicles capable of traveling on the public highways. (*California v. Carney,* 1985)

The pervasive regulation includes periodic inspection and licensing requirements, and ticketing for driving with expired license plates or inspection stickers or for such violations as exhaust fumes or excessive noise. Furthermore, all members of the public are fully aware of these regulations and know that they can be stopped while driving for such errors.

The mobility rationale—a traditional, common-law exigency exception to the warrant requirement—easily fits into the warrant-preference construction of the Fourth Amendment. It is a commonsense explanation for dispensing with a warrant. Professor Steinberg states that the lesser-expectation of privacy rationale, however, "makes no sense. Under this line of reasoning, a state could eviscerate Fourth Amendment protections simply by heavy regulation of an activity or location." Also, although houses are "regulated extensively by building codes," police cannot search them without a warrant.[8] It suggests a policy preference on the part of the Supreme Court's majority to simply give police a free hand when searching in and around an automobile. This conclusion is drawn by Harris, who believes the Court is motivated by "the desire that the police have wide latitude to investigate and the safety of the officers while they carry out these duties."[9]

The Mobility Factor.

In *Coolidge v. New Hampshire* (1971), a plurality of the Court ruled that the exception does not apply to immobilized vehicles. The defendant was arrested and detained for murder. Two days later, his car was impounded by police and searched pursuant to a search warrant that was later found to be defective. The state argued that the search was nevertheless constitutional under the automobile search exception. The Court rejected this argument, holding that the exception does not apply simply because an automobile was searched:

> The word "automobile" is not a talisman in whose presence the Fourth Amendment fades away and disappears. And surely there is nothing in this case to invoke the meaning and purpose of the rule of *Carroll v. United States*—no alerted criminal bent on flight, no fleeting opportunity on an open highway after a hazardous chase, no contraband or stolen goods or weapons, no confederates waiting to move the evidence, not even the inconvenience of a special police detail to guard the immobilized automobile. In short, by no possible stretch of

the legal imagination can this be made into a case where "it is not practicable to secure a warrant," . . . and the "automobile exception," despite its label, is simply irrelevant. (*Coolidge v. New Hampshire,* 1971)

The Court, unfortunately, has not strictly held to this aspect of *Coolidge*. It has in numerous cases invoked the automobile exception to uphold the search of a parked automobile where mobility was not a factor. *Coolidge* appeared to say that the mobility exigency was based on actual mobility—the immediate, or almost immediate, possibility that the car would be driven away by the suspect. More recently, the Court has diluted this rationale by leaning toward the potential mobility of the vehicle. Thus, in ***Pennsylvania v. Labron*** (1996), the Court upheld the search of a car belonging to a suspect who had been arrested for a drug transaction. There was no confederate to take the car away, and a warrant could have been obtained. The Pennsylvania Supreme Court ruled that a warrant was required. The U.S. Supreme Court reversed, stating: "If a car is *readily* mobile and probable cause exists to believe it contains contraband, the Fourth Amendment thus permits police to search the vehicle without more" (*Pennsylvania v. Labron,* 1996, emphasis added).

Time Frame of the Exigency.

The rights of drivers have also been weakened in cases dealing with the time frame of the exigency, both before and after the search. In *Coolidge,* the automobile was searched two and a half weeks after the police obtained probable cause, far after the time that any real exigency might have existed. The Court, however, has expanded the time frame within which an exigency is said to exist in ways that do not seem reasonable. The foundation for this approach was laid in a Prohibition Era case of the same vintage as *Carroll:* ***Husty v. United States*** (1931). A reliable informant told a Prohibition officer that Husty, a previously convicted bootlegger, "had two loads of liquor in automobiles of a particular make and description, parked in particular places on named streets." The agent proceeded to one of the cars, although he had sufficient time to obtain a warrant. He saw Husty and two other men get into the car. At that point, the agent approached, and the two other men fled. The car was searched, and contraband was found. In response to the argument that the agents had sufficient time to obtain a warrant, Justice Harlan Fiske Stone reasoned that the agent "could not know when Husty would come to the car or how soon it would be removed. In such circumstances we do not think the officers should be required to speculate upon the chances of successfully carrying out the search, after the delay and withdrawal from the scene of one or more officers which would have been necessary to procure a warrant" (*Husty v. United States,* 1931). Under these circumstances, an actual exigency existed.

Four decades later, the Supreme Court moved the time frame from the actual to the potential exigency and beyond. When an automobile is stopped by police with probable cause to believe that it contains contraband, the police can search on the spot or perhaps uphold a strict reading of the Fourth Amendment by securing the vehicle until a warrant has been obtained. The Supreme Court properly rejected the argument that a warrant had to be obtained in ***Chambers v. Maroney*** (1970): "For constitutional purposes, we see no difference between on the one hand seizing and holding a car before presenting the probable cause issue to a magistrate and on the other hand carrying out an immediate search without a warrant. Given probable cause to search, either course is reasonable under the Fourth Amendment." Although the Court has stated a preference for a search warrant, holding a person at the roadside until a warrant can be obtained is a severe intrusion of liberty. Justice John M. Harlan II, dissenting, preferred the latter course; he thought that the warrantless search was more intrusive because it could lead to a criminal conviction. He believed that a person with nothing to hide would give police consent to search the car. Despite this reasoning, requiring police to obtain a warrant to search a stopped vehicle can create unnecessary risks and burdens on law enforcement.

In *Chambers,* the police stopped a car at night because the car and its four passengers fit the description of a car recently involved in a gas station robbery. Under these circumstances, it was neither practical nor safe for the officers to conduct the search on the roadside; consequently, the car was searched at the police station after the suspects were detained. No warrant was obtained to search the car. The Supreme Court held the search to be constitutional as an automobile search. This is a difficult decision because the time of the exigency had ended. Perhaps it was possible for a confederate or a stranger to enter the automobile and destroy evidence, but this reasoning stretches belief. The *Chambers* decision demonstrates that the Court ignored the mobility rationale of *Carroll,* even before establishing the lesser expectation of privacy rationale for automobile searches. In more recent years, as a practical matter, the ad hoc custody of the automobile practiced in *Chambers* has been replaced by the more routine police practice of impounding all seized vehicles and subjecting them to a detailed inventory search.

Chambers may be explained in part by the Court's desire to protect police officers' safety. This made it reasonable for the officer to take the car to the station house instead of searching it on the road at night; there was a real exigency when the car was first seized. But in **Texas v. White** (1975), the Court allowed the search of a vehicle at the station house, although there was, at best, a potential exigency when the car was seized. White was arrested at 1:30 P.M. while attempting to pass fraudulent checks at a drive-in window of a bank, after police had a report of a similar incident at another bank earlier that day by a person matching White's description. He was ordered to park his car, and a bank employee and an officer observed him attempting to stuff something between the seats of his car. White was driven to the station house while another officer drove his car there. After thirty to forty-five minutes of questioning, White refused to consent to a search of his car, but the officers proceeded to search it anyway. During the search, four wrinkled checks corresponding to those White had attempted to pass at the first bank were discovered. The Court, in a brief *per curiam* opinion, upheld the search on this reading of *Chambers:* "[P]olice officers with probable cause to search an automobile on the scene where it was stopped could constitutionally do so later at the station house without first obtaining a warrant." Justice Thurgood Marshall, joined by Justice Brennan, dissented. He took the majority to task for misreading the holding of *Chambers.* The facts in *Chambers* included a nighttime stop of a car with four suspected armed robbers, a clearly perilous scenario. "*Chambers* simply held [the station house search] to be the rule when it is *reasonable* to take the car to the station house in the first place" (*Texas v. White,* 1975, emphasis added). By ignoring these facts, the Court created a per se rule that allows a car seized with probable cause to be searched, even if the car's mobility was at an end.

The decisions in *Chambers* and *White* stretch the time frame of an "exigency" to mythic proportions. A commonsense understanding of an exigency indicates that no true exigency was present when the police searched the cars in these two cases. It is useful to note that these cases occurred before the Supreme Court validated the routine inventory search (discussed later in this chapter). A routine inventory search is not an exigency search and serves other constitutional interests than those of a probable cause search. Nevertheless, as a functional matter, if not as a matter of constitutional law, routine inventory searches in effect allow the seizure of all contraband found in a car that is searched well after an arrested person has been taken into custody. In any event, the creation of the lesser expectation of privacy rationale and the "stretching" of the time frame for an exigency were vital elements in the Court's expansion of the power of police to search cars. The next step was the Court's willingness to authorize warrantless automobile searches of parked cars.

What Is an Automobile?   *California v. Carney* (1985) gave a precise definition of an automobile for Fourth Amendment purposes. Carney lived in a fully mobile motor home. Police, suspicious that he was trading drugs for sex, had his motor home under surveillance while it was parked in a downtown San Diego public parking lot not far from the courthouse. They observed a youth enter the vehicle and stay there for an hour and a quarter. When the youth emerged, he was stopped by the police and told them that he received marijuana in return for allowing Carney sexual contact. The police and the youth went to the motor home, knocked, and after Carney stepped out, entered it without a warrant and seized illegal drugs.

Carney argued that because this vehicle was also his home, it had to be given the same Fourth Amendment protection as a stationary home—that is, the police could not search it without obtaining a warrant. The Supreme Court disagreed, holding that such a motor home is a mobile vehicle, subject to similar licensing and regulation requirements as an automobile; therefore, the reasonable (i.e., objective) expectation of privacy in a motor home is equivalent to what one expects in an automobile, not a home. These factors brought the vehicle under the exigency exception to the warrant requirement: "Our application of the vehicle exception has never turned on the other uses to which a vehicle might be put."

Justice John Paul Stevens dissented in *Carney* on the grounds that there was no exigency. He urged the Court to rule that the automobile exception should not apply to a parked vehicle where there is time to obtain a warrant, but only to vehicles in motion along the highway. The majority refused to adopt this restriction. However, in *Coolidge v. New Hampshire* (1971), there was time to obtain a warrant, and the search was held to violate the Fourth Amendment. The Court in *Carney* distinguished *Coolidge* on its facts. The seizure in *Coolidge* was preceded by a two-week investigation, and the vehicle was in full police control, while in *Carney* the surveillance of the van lasted for a little over an hour. The police had ample time to plan their action in *Coolidge,* while the police in *Carney* acted with less preparation or planning, although they apparently had the ability to obtain a warrant. In *Coolidge,* the car was taken to the police station, while in *Carney,* the mobile home was in a public parking lot. In *Coolidge,* neither the defendant nor anyone associated with him had access to the car, while Carney was in his vehicle and could have driven it away if he was not arrested. The Court stated in *Carney,* "[T]he respondent's motor home was readily mobile. Absent the prompt search and seizure, it could readily have been moved beyond the reach of the police."

The Supreme Court is clearly reluctant to add any qualification or addition to the automobile exigency rule that benefits defendants. In **Maryland v. Dyson** (1999), police had advance warning, amounting to probable cause, that a specific vehicle would come into the jurisdiction with illegal drugs. An intermediate Maryland appellate court ruled that because the police had time to obtain a warrant, there was no exigency, and a search warrant was required. The Court, in a *per curiam* opinion, reversed. "[U]nder our established precedent, the 'automobile exception' has no separate exigency requirement." Nevertheless, the *Dyson* decision does not seem consistent with the principle, if not the precise facts, of *Coolidge v. New Hampshire* (1971).

The VIN Rule.   The Supreme Court demonstrated its creativity in upholding the legality of a warrantless police entry into a vehicle in **New York v. Class** (1986) by fabricating a limited right of intrusion into a car without probable cause in order to view a vehicle identification number (VIN) not viewable from outside the car. Police stopped a car for speeding. The driver produced a registration certificate and proof of insurance but no driver's license. The officer could not see the VIN on the dashboard so he "reached into the interior of the car to move some papers obscuring the area of the dashboard where the VIN is located in all post–1969 models. In doing so, the officer saw the handle of a gun, and respondent was promptly arrested." With a valid entry, the gun was in plain view and thus admissible. The Court reasoned that the VIN is needed to protect safety and property and is required by federal regulations to be in a place that can be easily read by someone standing outside the automobile. Combining the special requirements of the VIN with the lesser expectation of privacy in an automobile, the Court felt justified in creating a warrant exception authorizing such an entry without probable cause to believe there was contraband in the car. *Class* created a limited police power, because police cannot enter a vehicle if the VIN is observable from the car's exterior, and newer model cars are designed to make it impossible to cover the VIN.

Seizure of a Car Subject to Forfeiture.   In *Florida v. White* (1999), officers observed Tyvessel Tyvorus White make cocaine deliveries in his car in July and August 1993 but did not arrest him. Under the Florida Contraband Forfeiture Act, his car was subject to forfeiture. Several months later, White was arrested at his workplace on charges unrelated to the cocaine delivery. Police officers went to the employee parking lot, where White's car was parked, and seized it without a warrant. A subsequent inventory search disclosed cocaine. The Florida Supreme Court ruled the warrantless seizure to be unconstitutional. The U.S. Supreme Court reversed and offered two reasons for upholding the warrantless seizure: (1) Although the police had no probable cause to believe that the car contained contraband, "they certainly had probable cause to believe that the vehicle *itself* was contraband under Florida law," and the mobility rationale applies to the warrantless seizure of contraband in a mobile vehicle and the mobile vehicle itself; and (2) "our Fourth Amendment jurisprudence has consistently accorded law enforcement officials greater latitude in exercising their duties in public places." The Court treated the owner's private property as a public place for Fourth Amendment purposes and concluded that "the Fourth Amendment did not require a warrant to seize respondent's automobile" (*Florida v. White*, 1999).

Justice Stevens dissented in *White*, joined by Justice Ruth Bader Ginsburg. Under *Soldal v. Cook County* (1992), the Fourth Amendment protects property as well as privacy interests. There was no exigency here. White had been arrested, and there was sufficient time to obtain a search warrant. The car is not inherent contraband, such as drugs or firearms, so its seizure is not required to preserve public safety. A "warrant application interjects the judgment of a neutral decisionmaker, one with no pecuniary interest in the matter." Justice Stevens found it "particularly troubling . . . not that the State provides a weak excuse for failing to obtain a warrant either before or after White's arrest, but that it offers us no reason at all" and concluded that "the officers who seized White's car simply preferred to avoid the hassle of seeking approval from a judicial officer." The simple convenience of officers was thought too feeble a reason to override Fourth Amendment rights. Although the majority paid lip service to the warrant requirement, "its decision suggests that the exceptions have all but swallowed the general rule."

Searches of Containers in Mobile Vehicles

In the 1970s and 1980s, the most hotly contested issue in automobile search cases was the scope of a search of closed areas and containers found in mobile vehicles. The "container" cases demonstrate that visions of constitutional interpretation are shaped by judges' ideologies. On the one side stood liberal-moderate justices Brennan, Marshall, and Stevens. They urged the Court to require warrants to search mobile containers that had been secured by police. This position supported the warrant-preference construction of the Fourth Amendment and reflected the Due Process Model of criminal justice. On the other side stood a growing conservative majority on the Court. They found the Crime Control Model of criminal justice more congenial. Despite some doctrinal difficulties, they ultimately ruled that under the general-reasonableness construction of the Fourth Amendment, warrants are not needed to open closed areas and containers in automobiles if there is probable cause to believe that the containers contain contraband.

Searches of Containers Not in Automobiles.   In *Carroll v. United States* (1925), the Supreme Court held that when the automobile exception comes into play, officers could search any part of the car in which the contraband could reasonably be found. The officer's determination of what to search was coextensive with that of a magistrate. In

Carroll, an agent determined that the back seat of the roadster was hard and began to tear up the seat cushion. Thus the destruction of parts of the car within which contraband was stored was allowed if reasonably necessary to find the contraband.

In contrast to this aspect of the *Carroll* case, **United States v. Chadwick** (1977) held that a person's "effects" are given full constitutional protection. A container, out of the context of the automobile exception, cannot lawfully be opened by an officer unless the officer has a warrant, even if the officer has probable cause to believe that the container holds contraband. *Chadwick* involved a controlled delivery of the kind upheld in *United States v. Van Leeuwen* (1970), where police temporarily seized a suspicious package without a warrant in order to give them time to continue investigating, to corroborate their suspicion, and to obtain a warrant to search the package. In *Chadwick,* Amtrak officials in San Diego became suspicious when two people, one of whom fit the profile of a drug trafficker, loaded a footlocker that was unusually heavy for its size and leaking talcum powder (used to mask the odor of marijuana) on a Boston-bound train. Federal narcotics agents in Boston were on hand two days later when the footlocker arrived. They had no arrest or search warrant, but a trained dog signaled the presence of a controlled substance inside the trunk. Three people took possession of the footlocker and loaded it into the trunk of a car. At that moment, the agents arrested the three men and seized the footlocker, which was taken to the federal building. An hour and a half later, the agents obtained the key to the footlocker, opened it, and found large amounts of marijuana.

The Supreme Court, in a seven-to-two opinion authored by Chief Justice Warren Burger, held that this warrantless search violated the Fourth Amendment. Although the agents had probable cause to believe that the footlocker contained illicit drugs, it was protected by the Warrant Clause, which "makes a significant contribution to [the] protection" against unreasonable searches and seizures. As early as 1878, the Supreme Court had said that "[l]etters and sealed packages . . . are as fully guarded from examination and inspection, except as to their outward form and weight, as if they were retained by the parties forwarding them in their own domiciles" (*Ex Parte Jackson,* 1878). Important privacy interests are at stake when a person sends a locked trunk to another place, both subjective and reasonable (socially objective). There is a constitutional expectation of privacy in such a container. The Court ruled that brief contact of the footlocker with a car did not turn this into an automobile search case. The Court also found that under the facts of the case, a warrantless search of the footlocker could not be justified as a search incident to arrest. The *Chadwick* Court distinguished a footlocker (an "effect") from an automobile. Although a footlocker is mobile, it is afforded greater Fourth Amendment protection because it is not subjected to the pervasive government regulation of an automobile. Furthermore, once the footlocker's general mobility was ended and it was secured in the Boston federal building under the exclusive control of the police, there was no exigency that required an on-the-spot search without a warrant. "With the footlocker safely immobilized, it was unreasonable to undertake the additional and greater intrusion of a search without a warrant" (*United States v. Chadwick,* 1977).

Searches of Mobile Containers in Automobiles. If *Chadwick* is to be
logically followed, when police search an automobile under the automobile exigency exception and they discover a container that does not immediately indicate that it holds contraband (e.g., the hardness of the backseat of the roadster in *Carroll* indicated bottles of whiskey), they should seize the container and apply to a magistrate for a search warrant. The court followed this mode of analysis in **Arkansas v. Sanders** (1979). The police had probable cause, supplied by a reliable informant's tip, that Sanders would arrive at an airport with drugs. They followed Sanders, who carried a suitcase and entered a taxicab. The police followed the cab for several blocks and pulled it over. Without asking permission, they took the suitcase from the cab, opened it, and found over nine pounds of marijuana. The Supreme Court held that although the police had probable cause to believe that the suitcase contained drugs, and although they were justified in stopping the taxi and

seizing the suitcase, the suitcase could not be opened and searched without a search warrant because the mobility exigency regarding the suitcase had ended. The *Sanders* decision was a straightforward application of *Chadwick:*

> [W]e hold that the warrant requirement of the Fourth Amendment applies to personal luggage taken from an automobile to the same degree it applies to such luggage in other locations. Thus, insofar as the police are entitled to search such luggage without a warrant, their actions must be justified under some exception to the warrant requirement other than that applicable to automobiles stopped on the highway. (*Arkansas v. Sanders*, 1979)

The *Sanders* rule, however, proved to be unstable and short-lived. The five justices in the majority included liberal and moderate justices (Justice Lewis Powell authored the opinion, joined by Justices Brennan, Stewart, White, and Marshall). Justices Harry Blackmun and William Rehnquist dissented on the grounds that *Chadwick* was not correctly decided and that even if it were, a container that police had probable cause to believe held contraband in a mobile vehicle should be subject to the rules of *Carroll* (1925) and *Chambers v. Maroney* (1970); that is, the police should be able to open it on the spot without a warrant. The dissent stressed the "untoward costs on the criminal justice system of this country in terms of added delay and uncertainty" caused by the *Chadwick-Sanders* rule. Quite significantly, two concurring justices (Chief Justice Burger and Justice Stevens) argued that the situation in *Sanders* was not an automobile exigency search, thus clouding an understanding of the scope of a search of containers found in a mobile vehicle.

Sanders was followed by **New York v. Belton** (1981), which held that a police officer who had probable cause to arrest a suspect after stopping his automobile acquired the right to search the interior compartment of the automobile. In *Belton,* a New York State Trooper stopped a speeding car on the New York Thruway, ordered the driver and three passengers to exit, found that none had a vehicle registration, and smelled marijuana in the vehicle. He arrested all four occupants, secured them with handcuffs, searched them individually, and returned to the car to pick up an envelope marked "Supergold." He unzipped a pocket of a black leather jacket that was lying on the backseat of the car and found that it contained cocaine. The admissibility of the cocaine into evidence was contested. The Supreme Court held that "when a policeman has made a lawful custodial arrest of the occupant of an automobile, he may, as a contemporaneous incident of that arrest, search the passenger compartment of that automobile." And as an extension of that rule, the Court stated that "the police may also examine the *contents of any containers* found within the passenger compartment, for if the passenger compartment is within reach of the arrestee, so also will containers be within his reach" (emphasis added). This language was inconsistent with the *Chadwick-Sanders* rule.

The apparent inconsistency between *Belton* and *Chadwick-Sanders* can be explained by *Belton*'s specific facts and the *search incident to arrest* rationale for the search. One police officer arresting four men at the side of a limited-access highway could reasonably be in danger that one of them would run to the car to seize a weapon or evidence in the passenger compartment. This is factually distinguishable from several officers arresting individuals in possession of a locked footlocker, where there is no ready chance that they could overwhelm the officers and flee. The Supreme Court, however, preferred not to establish a rule that tracked the precise extent of the exigency, but rather established a bright-line rule to give better guidance to police officers in fast-moving street situations. As a result, *Belton* proved to be a confusing precedent because its absolute language in support of a container search in a car was undercut by its facts. While it did not clarify the authority of officers to search closed containers in a motor vehicle, it seemed to be at odds with *Chadwick-Sanders*.

The issue was further confused by the Court's fractured decision in **Robbins v. California** (1981). Police stopped a station wagon traveling erratically. An officer smelled marijuana smoke when Robbins emerged, searched him, and found a vial of liquid. The officer searched the interior of the car and found marijuana. Police officers then opened the tailgate of the station wagon and raised the cover of a recessed luggage compartment, in which they found two packages wrapped in green opaque plastic. The police unwrapped the packages and discovered a large amount of marijuana in each. The issue was whether the opening of the two packages violated the Fourth Amendment. The Supreme Court, in a plurality opinion by Justice Stewart, held this an unreasonable search and seizure on the authority of *Chadwick* and *Sanders:* (1) the outward appearance of the package did not undermine Robbins's expectation of privacy; and (2) there was no constitutional difference between a footlocker (a "worthy" container) and a plastic bag or package (an "unworthy" container). Concurring Justice Powell and Chief Justice Burger, however, expressed reservations about the decision and suggested a line of reasoning that would soon undermine the *Chadwick-Sanders* rule, namely that "when the police have probable cause to search an automobile, rather than only to search a particular container that fortuitously is located in it, the exigencies that allow the police to search the entire automobile without a warrant support the warrantless search of every container found therein."

Bright-Line Rules for the Scope of Automobile Exception
Searches.   The reasoning of *Robbins* undermined its strength as a precedent. In the following year, Justice Stewart retired and was replaced by the more conservative Justice Sandra Day O'Connor. This allowed reconsideration of the doubts raised in *Robbins.* Indeed, the Court overturned *Robbins* the next year in **United States v. Ross** (1982). In *Ross* and *California v. Acevedo* (1991), a conservative tide on the Court swept away the *Chadwick-Sanders* rule in two waves, finally establishing the bright-line rule that allowed police to search automobiles and *any* closed compartments or containers in them without a search warrant whenever probable cause existed to believe that contraband was in the car generally or in a specific container. Their rules are simple. *Ross* holds that when police have probable cause to believe that contraband is located in an automobile, they may, under the automobile exception, open any closed container in the car that may logically hold the contraband; this overrules *Robbins*. *Acevedo* holds that when an officer has probable cause to believe that a specific container located in a car contains contraband, the officer may, upon lawfully stopping the car and gaining access to its interior, open the container. This overrules *Sanders* but not *Chadwick,* because *Chadwick* was not treated as an automobile exception case.

In *Ross,* a known reliable informant telephoned a police detective and told him that an individual known as "Bandit" was selling narcotics that he kept in the trunk of a "purplish maroon" Chevrolet Malibu parked at a specific street location. The informant had just observed "Bandit" complete a sale and said that "Bandit" told him that additional narcotics were in the trunk. Police officers drove to the street address and saw a maroon Malibu parked there. The officers completed a computer check and discovered that the car was registered to Albert Ross, who fit the informant's description and who used the alias "Bandit." The officers drove through the neighborhood twice but did not observe anyone matching Ross's description. They returned five minutes later and saw the maroon Malibu being driven off by a man matching the informant's description. The officers stopped the car and ordered Ross out of the car. Officers observed a bullet on the front seat so they searched the interior of the car and found a pistol in the glove compartment, whereupon they arrested and handcuffed Ross. A detective took Ross's keys, opened the trunk, and found a closed brown paper bag that was found to contain a number of glassine bags filled with a white powder that was later determined to be heroin. At the station house, the car trunk was searched without a warrant, and a zippered red leather pouch was found and opened. It contained $3,200 in cash. Did the officers have constitutional authority to open the paper bag in the trunk of Ross's automobile?

Ross squarely presented the issue of the scope of an automobile search wherein police had probable cause to believe that contraband was located somewhere in the car or the trunk, but not in a specific bag or container. On the one hand, the *Carroll* case allowed police, without a warrant, to rip open the upholstery of a car stopped at the side of the road to get at the contraband. On the other hand, *Chadwick* ruled that the container can be seized and held (but not opened) until a search warrant was obtained. The Court opted for the *Carroll* approach. The details of *Ross* were not the same as the facts of *Sanders,* where police had probable cause to believe that there was contraband in a specific container located in a moving car, but no probable cause to believe that there was contraband elsewhere in the car. For the time being, *Chadwick* controlled *Sanders*-type situations.

The Court advanced several reasons for its decision in *Ross*. It noted that from the *Carroll* case in 1925 up to *Chadwick* in 1977, decisions of lower courts and the Supreme Court never questioned the right of police to open bags of suspected contraband found in lawfully stopped cars. The practical benefits of the *Carroll* rule would be largely nullified by not allowing police to open closed containers reasonably suspected of housing contraband because illegal materials are usually secured to be kept out of sight. Also, *Carroll* did not increase the scope of a lawful search, but instead "merely relaxed the requirements for a warrant on grounds of practicability" (*Henry v. United States,* 1959). Thus a search warrant allowing a search for contraband implies that officers may open containers in the premises that could logically hold the kind of contraband sought.

> When a legitimate search is under way, and when its purpose and its limits have been precisely defined, nice distinctions between closets, drawers, and containers, in the case of a home, or between glove compartments, upholstered seats, trunks, and wrapped packages, in the case of a vehicle, must give way to the interest in the prompt and efficient completion of the task at hand. (*United States v. Ross,* 1982)

This rule applies to all containers; the Court upheld the concept of *Robbins* that a constitutional distinction between "worthy" and "unworthy" containers was improper, as long as the container shielded its contents from plain view. Finally, because a search under the automobile exception was as valid as a search incident to arrest or a search under a warrant, the suspect loses the expectation of privacy to the same extent as in these cases, which allow the opening of "some containers." In conclusion, the "scope of a warrantless search of an automobile . . . is not defined by the nature of the container in which the contraband is secreted [but] by the object of the search and the places in which there is probable cause to believe that it may be found" (*United States v. Ross,* 1982). Significantly, the majority rejected the holding of *Robbins* but upheld the specific holding in *Sanders,* although it rejected some of its reasoning, thus allowing police to seize but not search containers where they have probable cause to believe that the specific container holds contraband.

Justice Marshall dissented, joined by Justices Brennan and White, harshly accusing the Court of "repeal[ing] the Fourth Amendment warrant requirement itself" and "utterly disregard[ing] the value of a neutral and detached magistrate." He reiterated the value of a search warrant and the positive effect of the warrant process on officers who had to write affidavits to justify searches. He noted that in many automobile warrant exception cases there was an actual exigency that justified the police in searching without a warrant. To the contrary, however, Fourth Amendment principles are undermined when the automobile exigency exception is applied to every search of an automobile, even when the suspect is arrested and there is no likelihood that another person will get to the car. Ignoring this difference is a sleight of hand on the part of the majority. A decision based on Fourth Amendment principles must apply the *Chadwick* rule to a search of an automobile when the exigency is over. Finally, the majority's ruling in *Ross* is inconsistent with the rule of *Sanders*. Prophetically, Justice Marshall stated, "This case will have profound implications for the privacy of citizens traveling in automobiles."

A decade later, the Court dropped the other shoe and, in **California v. Acevedo** (1991), overruled *Arkansas v. Sanders* (1979). Between 1982 and 1991, the composition of the Court had become considerably more conservative, with Justice Rehnquist becoming Chief Justice upon the retirement of Chief Justice Burger, the addition of Justices Antonin Scalia, Anthony Kennedy, and David Souter to the Court, and the retirement of Justices Powell and Brennan. Justice Blackmun, who had dissented in *Sanders,* now had the opportunity to bury that decision in his majority opinion, and he was joined by Chief

Justice Rehnquist and Justices O'Connor, Kennedy, and Souter. Justice Scalia concurred with the majority. Justices White, Stevens, and Marshall dissented.

In *Acevedo,* marijuana lawfully seized by the Drug Enforcement Administration (DEA) in Hawaii was shipped to Officer Coleman of the Santa Ana, California, Police Department. He set up a controlled delivery to one Jamie Daza, who picked up the package from a Federal Express office at 10:30 A.M. Daza, package in hand, was followed to his apartment. At 11:45 A.M., Daza left the apartment and dropped the marijuana container's wrapping into a trash bin. Officer Coleman left the scene to get a search warrant. At 12:30 P.M., respondent Charles Steven Acevedo arrived. He entered Daza's apartment, stayed for about ten minutes, and emerged carrying a brown paper bag that appeared to be full. Other officers observing the scene noticed that the bag was the size of one of the wrapped marijuana packages sent from Hawaii. Acevedo walked to a silver Honda in the parking lot, placed the bag in the trunk of the car, and started to drive away. Fearing the loss of evidence, officers in a marked police car stopped him. They opened the trunk and the bag and found marijuana. The California Court of Appeals suppressed the marijuana on the basis of *Chadwick* (instead of *Ross*) because the officers had probable cause to believe that the paper bag contained drugs but lacked probable cause to suspect that Acevedo's car itself otherwise contained contraband.

The reasons given for allowing a warrantless search of a closed container in an operative vehicle, which had become immobilized and the driver taken into custody, began with an observation on *Ross:* Where police have probable cause to believe that contraband is located in a car but have not pinpointed a specific container, "the time and expense of the warrant process would be misdirected if the police could search every cubic inch of an automobile until they discovered a paper sack, at which point the Fourth Amendment required them to take the sack to a magistrate for permission to look inside." The majority forthrightly noted

> that a container found after a general search of the automobile and a container found in a car after a limited search for the container are equally easy for the police to store and for the suspect to hide or destroy. In fact, we see no principled distinction in terms of either the privacy expectation or the exigent circumstances between the paper bag found by the police in *Ross* and the paper bag found by the police here. Furthermore, by attempting to distinguish between a container for which the police are specifically searching and a container which they come across in a car, we have provided only minimal protection for privacy and have impeded effective law enforcement. (*California v. Acevedo,* 1991)

Put this way, it seems clear that the fine line between *Chadwick-Sanders* (specific probable cause) cases and *Carroll-Ross* (general probable cause) cases is a thin one and that it would be better for the cases to be decided consistently: Either all containers can be opened by the police, or all containers should be held until a magistrate has ruled on the police officer's assessment of probable cause.

Which way is best? The path chosen by the majority was based, first, on its stated assumption that the *Ross* rule provided "minimal protection for privacy" because in the *Chadwick-Sanders* situation, the suspicious package is seized and held for a warrant in any event. Next, the Court noted that the clear theoretical distinction is not always clear to a police officer in the field searching a car. If some doubt exists about the locus of probable cause in an automobile search case, a defendant would inevitably argue that the probable cause applied to the container and not the entire vehicle to get the protection of *Chadwick-Sanders,* causing unneeded litigation. Also, police might try to circumvent the *Chadwick-Sanders* rule by needlessly searching an entire car to make it seem as if the *Ross* rule operates when they really had probable cause to believe that the contraband is located in a specific container. Further, the opening of a container is less physically intrusive than a full search of an automobile: "If destroying the interior of an automobile is not unreasonable, we cannot conclude that looking inside a closed container is." Justice Blackmun's majority opinion argued that the dichotomy between the two automobile search rules has created confusion in the lower courts and impeded effective law enforcement. "The *Chadwick-Sanders* rule is the antithesis of a 'clear and unequivocal' guideline." The Supreme Court thus overruled *Arkansas v. Sanders* (1979) and stated that it had returned all automobile search cases to the basic rule of *Carroll.*

Justice Stevens's dissent was unusually blunt and specifically referred to the Court's relying "on arguments that *conservative judges* have repeatedly rejected in past cases" (emphasis added). Justices are aware of their and their colleagues' ideological leanings, but they rarely state this so forthrightly in an opinion. Because a dissent is the justice's personal statement, it is often more freewheeling or idiosyncratic than a majority opinion, which reflects the judgment of each justice who joins the opinion. By stating that conservative justices in the past supported the *Sanders* rule, Justice Stevens suggested that the justices of the *Acevedo* majority are extremists. His opinion began with an exposition on constitutional policy favoring the use of warrants and reminding that "[t]he Fourth Amendment is a restraint on Executive power." The burdens of obtaining warrants "are outweighed by the individual interest in privacy that is protected by advance judicial approval." He then argued that *Ross* and *Chadwick-Sanders* were not inconsistent; *Ross* applied to the scope of an automobile search, whereas *Sanders* applied to the search of all closed containers, whether found in automobiles or not. He also noted, as did Justice Marshall dissenting in *Ross,* that the *Chadwick-Sanders* rule allows for exigency exceptions.

Justice Stevens challenged three specific points made in Justice Blackmun's majority opinion. First, the majority claimed that the existence of the *Chadwick-Sanders* rule and the *Ross* rule was confusing and anomalous. Justice Stevens recited cases that seemed to have no difficulty in distinguishing between the two and so disagreed as to the confusion. If there was an anomaly in the law, it was created by the majority, "[f]or, surely it is anomalous to prohibit a search of a briefcase while the owner is carrying it exposed on a public street yet to permit a search once the owner has placed the briefcase in the locked trunk of his car" (*California v. Acevedo*, 1991). Justice Stevens thought that making the automobile search rules the same by eliminating the warrant requirement in both was the worse solution because the person had the same expectation of privacy in the container, whether found in or out of a car.

Second, he disagreed that the *Chadwick-Sanders* rule does not protect any significant interest in privacy. "Every citizen clearly has an interest in the privacy of the contents of his or her luggage, briefcase, handbag or any other container that conceals private papers and effects from public scrutiny. . . . Under the Court's holding today, the privacy interest that protects the contents of a suitcase or a briefcase from a warrantless search when it is in public view simply vanishes when its owner climbs into a taxicab. Unquestionably the rejection of the *Sanders* line of cases by today's decision will result in a significant loss of individual privacy."

The majority's third argument was that the older rules impede effective law enforcement. Justice Stevens noted that the Court cited no authority for this contention. Even if true, it was, "in any event, an insufficient reason for creating a new exception to the warrant requirement." This last point, of course, is an expected statement for one who leans toward the Due Process Model; a proponent of the Crime Control Model of criminal justice would disagree.

Ross and *Acevedo* are significant cases because, by creating bright-line rules, they resolved the tangled legal threads on the scope of automobile and sealed container searches. To the dissenting justices, these cases seriously undermine Fourth Amendment rights and give the police carte blanche to search cars. Each majority opinion, however, mandates that there must be a clear connection between probable cause and the scope of a search. Doctrinally, *Ross* and *Acevedo* do not grant police unbridled searching power; for example, police cannot search the locked trunk of a car if its driver is arrested for driving under the influence of alcohol or a controlled substance. However, the real fear is that lenient rules will be applied by the police as license to use their discretion to search, guided only by their common sense and innate sense of decency, and that when police step over the legal line, lower court judges will excuse such behavior. Indeed, as suggested at the beginning of this section, it appears that the totality of automobile search rules provide very little restraint on auto searches.

The *Ross* rule was extended to automobile passengers in *Wyoming v. Houghton.*

Read Case and Comments: *Wyoming v. Houghton.*

Wyoming v. Houghton

526 U.S. 295, 119 S.Ct. 1297, 143 L.Ed.2d 408 (1999)

JUSTICE SCALIA delivered the opinion of the Court.

This case presents the question whether police officers violate the Fourth Amendment when they search a passenger's personal belongings inside an automobile that they have probable cause to believe contains contraband.

In the early morning hours * * * a Wyoming Highway Patrol officer stopped an automobile for speeding and driving with a faulty brake light. There were three passengers in the front seat of the car: David Young (the driver), his girlfriend, and respondent. While questioning Young, the officer noticed a hypodermic syringe in Young's shirt pocket. He left the occupants under the supervision of two backup officers as he went to get gloves from his patrol car. Upon his return, he instructed Young to step out of the car and place the syringe on the hood. The officer then asked Young why he had a syringe; with refreshing candor, Young replied that he used it to take drugs. **[a]**

[The two female passengers were ordered out of the car. Asked for identification, Houghton falsely identified herself as "Sandra James." In light of Young's admission, the officer searched the passenger compartment of the car for contraband, and found a purse on the backseat that Houghton claimed as hers. He removed her wallet containing her driver's license. When the officer asked her why she had lied about her name, she replied: "In case things went bad." The officer then removed a brown pouch and a black wallet-type container. Houghton denied that the pouch was hers and claimed ignorance of how it came to be there. It contained drug paraphernalia and a syringe with 60 cc of methamphetamine. The officer also found fresh needle-track marks on Houghton's arms. He placed her under arrest. The trial court denied Houghton's motion to suppress evidence obtained from the purse as the fruit of a Fourth Amendment violation. She was convicted of felony possession of methamphetamine. The trial court held that the officer had probable cause to search the car for contraband and, by extension, any containers therein that could hold such contraband.

[The Wyoming Supreme Court, reversing the conviction, ruled that where an officer has probable cause to believe that contraband is somewhere in a lawfully stopped car, the officer may search all containers in the car *except* containers that the officer knows or should know is a personal effect of a passenger who is not suspected of criminal activity, "*unless* someone had the opportunity to conceal the contraband within the personal effect to avoid detection."]

II

* * *

* * * [I]n the present case [] the police officers had probable cause to believe there were illegal drugs in the car. **[b]** *Carroll v. United States* (1925) * * * held that "contraband goods concealed and illegally transported in an automobile or other vehicle may be searched for without a warrant" where probable cause exists.

We have furthermore read the historical evidence to show that the Framers would have regarded as reasonable (if there was probable cause) the warrantless search of containers *within* an automobile. **[c]** In *Ross* we upheld as reasonable the warrantless search of a paper bag and leather pouch found in the trunk of the defendant's car by officers who had probable cause to believe that the trunk contained drugs. * * *

Ross summarized its holding as follows: "If probable cause justifies the search of a lawfully stopped vehicle, it justifies the search of *every part of the vehicle and its contents*

[a] Suppose you are driven to classes by a friend and the car is stopped for speeding. The officer orders your friend out of the car and notices a single marijuana cigarette on the floor. Should the officer be able to search your backpack, which is sitting on the backseat? Should it matter if you claim the backpack as your property?

[b] Notice that the exigency reasoning of *Carroll* is not mentioned.

[c] As an "originalist," Justice Scalia justifies Fourth Amendment rulings by "finding" what he thinks the Framers would have ruled in 1791.

that may conceal the object of the search." (emphasis added). **[d]** And our later cases describing *Ross* have characterized it as applying broadly to *all* containers within a car, without qualification as to ownership. * * *

[d] This logically includes Houghton's purse.

* * *

In sum, neither *Ross* itself nor the historical evidence it relied upon admits of a distinction among packages or containers based on ownership. When there is probable cause to search for contraband in a car, it is reasonable for police officers—like customs officials in the Founding era—to examine packages and containers without a showing of individualized probable cause for each one. **[e]** A passenger's personal belongings, just like the driver's belongings or containers attached to the car like a glove compartment, are "in" the car, and the officer has probable cause to search for contraband *in* the car.

[e] *Ross* did not involve passengers and so does not establish direct precedent for a rule that allows an officer to open a passenger's purse.

　　Even if the historical evidence, as described by *Ross,* were thought to be equivocal, we would find that the balancing of the relative interests weighs decidedly in favor of allowing searches of a passenger's belongings. Passengers, no less than drivers, possess a reduced expectation of privacy with regard to the property that they transport in cars, which "travel public thoroughfares." * * *

　　In this regard—the degree of intrusiveness upon personal privacy and indeed even personal dignity—the two cases the Wyoming Supreme Court found dispositive differ substantially from the package search at issue here. **[f]** *United States v. Di Re* (1948), held that probable cause to search a car did not justify a body search of a passenger. And *Ybarra v. Illinois,* (1979), held that a search warrant for a tavern and its bartender did not permit body searches of all the bar's patrons. These cases turned on the unique, significantly heightened protection afforded against searches of one's person. * * *

[f] *Di Re* is central to Justice Steven's dissent. The majority does not overrule *Di Re* but instead distinguishes it, so that the rule of *Di Re* still exists, but so too does the rule of *Houghton.*

　　Whereas the passenger's privacy expectations are, as we have described, considerably diminished, the governmental interests at stake are substantial. **[g]** Effective law enforcement would be appreciably impaired without the ability to search a passenger's personal belongings when there is reason to believe contraband or evidence of criminal wrongdoing is hidden in the car. As in all car-search cases, the "ready mobility" of an automobile creates a risk that the evidence or contraband will be permanently lost while a warrant is obtained. In addition, a car passenger—unlike the unwitting tavern patron in *Ybarra*—will often be engaged in a common enterprise with the driver, and have the same interest in concealing the fruits or the evidence of their wrongdoing. **[h]** A criminal might be able to hide contraband in a passenger's belongings as readily as in other containers in the car,—perhaps even surreptitiously, without the passenger's knowledge or permission. * * *

[g] Given the control that the police had over the car in this case (the driver arrested, the car subject to impoundment), do references to "ready mobility" become a smoke screen that allows police to search a car and all its contents simply because it is a car?

[h] The real difference between the majority and the dissenters is that the majority imposes a per se, bright-line rule allowing no *Ross* exception for the belongings of a passenger. The dissent allows a search of a passenger's bag if an officer has probable cause to believe that it holds contraband. Justice Scalia suggests that such a rule would lessen the number of seizures from automobiles and enmesh police in fine-tuned adjudications of probable cause.

　　To be sure, these factors favoring a search will not always be present, but the balancing of interests must be conducted with an eye to the generality of cases. To require that the investigating officer have positive reason to believe that the passenger and driver were engaged in a common enterprise, or positive reason to believe that the driver had time and occasion to conceal the item in the passenger's belongings, surreptitiously or with friendly permission, is to impose requirements so seldom met that a "passenger's property" rule would dramatically reduce the ability to find and seize contraband and evidence of crime. [Litigation would increase over the issue of whether the police officer should have believed a passenger's claim of ownership.] We think they militate in favor of the needs of law enforcement, and against a personal-privacy interest that is ordinarily weak.

* * *

(continued)

We hold that police officers with probable cause to search a car may inspect passengers' belongings found in the car that are capable of concealing the object of the search. The judgment of the Wyoming Supreme Court is reversed.

[Justice Breyer concurred.]

JUSTICE STEVENS, with whom JUSTICE SOUTER and JUSTICE GINSBURG join, dissenting.

* * *

[i] See *Di Re* in Chapter 4. In that case, an informer was riding in the car and would have seen the driver pass contraband to Di Re.

[j] If *Di Re* is still good law and the search of Houghton's purse is constitutional, could an officer lawfully open a "fanny pack" worn by a passenger on a belt?

[k] Although *Ross* is not direct precedent for the search of a passenger's bag, the "object" of the search in *Ross* was drugs located somewhere in the car, not in a specific container, making the extension of *Ross* to a passenger's belongings logical. Justice Stevens, the author of the *Ross* opinion, did not mention a pocket or pocketbook in that opinion. The *Ross* case made no reference to *Di Re*. Does Justice Stevens regret the Ross decision or simply believe that the majority is going too far?

* * * In the only automobile case confronting the search of a passenger defendant—*United States v. Di Re,* (1948)—**[i]** the Court held that the exception to the warrant requirement did not apply (addressing searches of the passenger's pockets and the space between his shirt and underwear, both of which uncovered counterfeit fuel rations). In *Di Re,* as here, the information prompting the search directly implicated the driver, not the passenger. Today, instead of adhering to the settled distinction between drivers and passengers, the Court fashions a new rule that is based on a distinction between property contained in clothing worn by a passenger and property contained in a passenger's briefcase or purse. **[j]** In cases on both sides of the Court's newly minted test, the property is in a "container" (whether a pocket or a pouch) located in the vehicle. Moreover, unlike the Court, I think it quite plain that the search of a passenger's purse or briefcase involves an intrusion on privacy that may be just as serious as was the intrusion in *Di Re.*

Even apart from *Di Re,* the Court's rights-restrictive approach is not dictated by precedent. **[k]** For example, in *United States v. Ross* (1982), we were concerned with the interest of the driver in the integrity of "his automobile," and we categorically rejected the notion that the scope of a warrantless search of a vehicle might be "defined by the nature of the container in which the contraband is secreted," . . . "Rather, it is defined by the object of the search and the places in which there is probable cause to believe that it may be found." We thus disapproved of a possible container-based distinction between a man's pocket and a woman's pocketbook. * * *

Nor am I persuaded that the mere spatial association between a passenger and a driver provides an acceptable basis for presuming that they are partners in crime or for ignoring privacy interests in a purse. Whether or not the Fourth Amendment required a warrant to search Houghton's purse, at the very least the trooper in this case had to have probable cause to believe that her purse contained contraband. The Wyoming Supreme Court concluded that he did not.

Finally, in my view, the State's legitimate interest in effective law enforcement does not outweigh the privacy concerns at issue. I am as confident in a police officer's ability to apply a rule requiring a warrant or individualized probable cause to search belongings that are—as in this case—obviously owned by and in the custody of a passenger as is the Court in a "passenger-confederate[']s" ability to circumvent the rule. Certainly the ostensible clarity of the Court's rule is attractive. But that virtue is insufficient justification for its adoption. Moreover, a rule requiring a warrant or individualized probable cause to search passenger belongings is every bit as simple as the Court's rule; it simply protects more privacy.

* * *

AUTOMOBILE INVENTORY SEARCHES

Statutes and local ordinances provide several reasons to **impound** vehicles:

- To remove vehicles involved in accidents to permit the flow of traffic and preserve evidence.
- To remove damaged vehicles from the highways.
- To tow away automobiles that violate parking ordinances.
- To remove cars after the driver has been arrested.
- To impound automobiles subject to forfeiture.

Of course, a vehicle seized after the driver's felony arrest may also be impounded and subjected to an **inventory search.** Unlike these numerous administrative reasons for vehicle impoundment, an inventory of an arrested person's property at a police lockup or a jail is legal only if the underlying arrest is legal. (See Chapter 4.) Impounded vehicles have been placed in the unsecured private lot of a local garage (*Cady v. Dombrowski,* 1973) (rural area; lot seven miles from the police station) or in an impoundment lot operated by a municipality (*South Dakota v. Opperman,* 1976).

An inventory search of an impounded motor vehicle by law enforcement officers is an **administrative search,** deemed reasonable under the Fourth Amendment and designed to perform a caretaking function. An inventory is a list of all items found in an impounded car. A vehicle inventory search is not a search for evidence that requires a warrant and probable cause. Any contraband disclosed in an inventory is in plain view and hence is admissible in a criminal prosecution.

Consequently, inventory searches do not come under the automobile exigency warrant exception of *Carroll v. United States* (1925). Neither a judicial warrant, probable cause, nor reasonable suspicion is needed to justify an inventory search. Indeed, an inventory search is the opposite of an exigency search—it must be conducted under standardized rules and regulations so that each inventory search is as much like another as possible. The Supreme Court has ruled that the inventory's administrative "interests outweighed the individual's Fourth Amendment interests" (*Colorado v. Bertine,* 1987). In *Cady v. Dombrowski* (1973), Justice Rehnquist explained that "[l]ocal police officers . . . frequently investigate vehicle accidents in which there is no claim of criminal liability and engage in what, for want of a better term, may be described as community caretaking functions, totally divorced from the detection, investigation, or acquisition of evidence relating to the violation of a criminal statute."

Reasons for the Inventory Search.   The purposes of the inventory of an automobile and the inventory of a person taken into custody are similar. First, the routine listing of the contents of the vehicle protects the owner's property against theft or careless handling by the police while it remains in police custody. Second, the inventory protects the police against false claims or disputes over lost or stolen property by the owner. Third, it protects the police from potential danger. Additionally, the inventory helps determine whether a vehicle has been stolen (*South Dakota v. Opperman,* 1976). A prime reason to inventory people taken into custody in police lockups—to prevent them from injuring themselves or others with weapons or dangerous instruments—is rarely the case in vehicle inventories. In unusual cases, however, explosives or weapons may be present, which if stolen from an impounded vehicle, can pose a threat to the public. Also, opening a vehicle containing explosives endangers the lives of officers.[10]

Scope of an Inventory Search.   The cases show that an inventory search can be extremely thorough. In *South Dakota v. Opperman* (1976), the Supreme Court upheld the inventory of items in the unlocked glove compartment of an automobile. In *Michigan v. Thomas* (1982), the Court upheld the inventory search of a car's locked trunk, the space under the front seat and under the dashboard, and the opening of air vents under the dashboard, where a loaded revolver was found. The Court rejected the argument that the search of the air vents was improper because that is not a place where personal items are normally stored. In a *per curiam* opinion in *Florida v. Meyers* (1984), the Court upheld, without explanation, a second inventory search of an automobile made eight hours after the car was first searched and impounded. In *Illinois v. Lafayette* (1983), a police lockup inventory case (see Chapter 4), the police searched a purse-type shoulder bag belonging to a person taken into custody; the Supreme Court held that the police were under no obligation to place it in a secure box or locker, even if this was less intrusive than the inventory search. "The reasonableness of any particular governmental activity does not necessarily or invariably turn on the existence of alternative 'less intrusive' means" (*Illinois v. Lafayette,* 1983).

The issue of the scope of an inventory was revisited in **Colorado v. Bertine** (1987) to determine whether *United States v. Chadwick* (1977)—holding warrantless searches of closed trunks and suitcases to violate the Fourth Amendment—modified the rule for vehicle inventory searches. *Bertine* reaffirmed the *Opperman* decision. A van was impounded after the driver was arrested for driving under the influence of alcohol. The van's contents were subjected to a detailed inspection and inventory in accordance with local police procedures. An officer then opened a closed backpack and found drugs. The Supreme Court found that the search was legal and the drugs admissible in evidence. Chief Justice Rehnquist, for the majority, said that an inventory search is made for regulatory reasons and is not a search for criminal evidence. There was no proof that the police had acted in bad faith for the sole purpose of investigation, and the police department's regulations mandated the opening of closed containers and the listing of their contents. Justice Marshall, dissenting, argued that, in fact, the procedures were not standardized, thereby making the action a criminal search rather than an inventory. He wrote that the search was conducted in a "slipshod" manner that undermined the purposes of an inventory procedure and that the rule of *Chadwick* should apply to a backpack.

The Necessity of Standardized Rules.

The Supreme Court's motor vehicle inventory doctrine has evolved from allowing an *ad hoc* inventory when made for inventory purposes (*Cady v. Dombrowski,* 1973) to a rule that requires that a police department have in place standardized inventory rules and procedures in order for an inventory search to be constitutional (*Florida v. Wells,* 1990).

In *Colorado v. Bertine* (1987), the Court emphasized the importance of written, standardized procedures to guide the inventory search. No such procedures apparently existed in **Cady v. Dombrowski** (1973), which involved the warrantless search of a car for the express purpose of finding the weapon in the private vehicle of a drunk driver who was a police officer. The inventory search was upheld because it was clearly performed for administrative purposes and not as a search for criminal evidence. A driver involved in a serious single-car accident was taken into custody one evening for drunk driving in a rural Wisconsin town. He stated that he was a Chicago police officer. The Wisconsin officers believed that Chicago police officers were required by regulation to carry their service revolvers at all times. They were concerned that someone would steal the weapon from the car, which was placed in an unsecured lot. As a result, they looked into the passenger compartment and glove box but found no service revolver. A tow truck arrived and removed the disabled car to a garage seven miles from the police station, where it was left unguarded. Dombrowski, the driver, was hospitalized after lapsing into a coma. Hours later, after midnight, an officer went to the car to search for Dombrowski's police weapon. The officer testified that the effort to find the revolver was "standard procedure in our department." He opened the trunk of Dombrowski's car and did not find a gun but did find his police uniforms, a Chicago police baton with his name imprinted on it, and fresh blood that was introduced into evidence to convict Dombrowski of first-degree murder. Under these circumstances, the Court treated this search as a valid administrative search and not as a search for criminal evidence. "Where, as here, the trunk of an automobile, which the officer reasonably believed to contain a gun, was vulnerable to intrusion by vandals, we hold that the search was not 'unreasonable' within the meaning of the Fourth and Fourteenth Amendments" (*Cady v. Dombrowski,* 1973).

From the somewhat loose procedure upheld in *Dombrowski,* the Court has moved to a position that, for an inventory search to be constitutionally reasonable, it must be authorized by (1) departmental policy and regulations that establish standard procedures, or (2) established routine. The rationale is that one inventory search should be conducted like another and that the procedure should actually produce an inventory—a list. The goal is to limit the discretion of the officer as to the manner in which the inventory is to be conducted. "The individual police officer must not be allowed so much latitude that inventory searches are turned into 'a purposeful and general means of discovering evidence of crime'" (*Florida v. Wells,* 1990, citing *Colorado v. Bertine,* 1987).

Florida v. Wells (1990) is an example of an officer turning a routine inventory into a search for evidence because he overstepped administrative regulations. Wells was stopped for speeding and was arrested for DWI after an officer smelled alcohol on his breath. An inventory search of the car revealed two marijuana cigarette butts in an ashtray and a locked suitcase in the trunk. There was no departmental inventory policy. The officer used his discretion to order the suitcase forced open. Large quantities of marijuana were found. The U.S. Supreme Court agreed with the Florida Supreme Court that the evidence should be suppressed as a Fourth Amendment violation because the police department had no inventory policy at all. In the course of his majority opinion, Chief Justice Rehnquist said:

> A police officer may be allowed sufficient latitude to determine whether a particular container should or should not be opened in light of the nature of the search and characteristics of the container itself. Thus, while policies of opening all containers or of opening no containers are unquestionably permissible, it would be equally permissible, for example, to allow the opening of closed containers whose contents officers determine they are unable to ascertain from examining the containers' exteriors. The allowance of the exercise of judgment based on concerns related to the purposes of an inventory search does not violate the Fourth Amendment. (*Florida v. Wells,* 1990)

This quote was treated as dictum by four justices who disagreed with it. Thus the question of whether an officer has discretion to open some containers has not been finally resolved. The concurring justices felt that the officer should not have such discretion—that is, that an inventory policy should order an officer to open all containers or none. Justice Brennan expressed concern that "police may use the excuse of an 'inventory search' as a pretext for broad searches of vehicles and their contents."

BORDER SEARCHES

Every sovereign nation has a right to control its **borders** to determine who or what shall come into or exit the country, to collect customs, and to control smuggling. To enforce this plenary power, a country may search entering persons and luggage. As a general rule, the Fourth Amendment does not apply to searches and seizures at the border of the United States. As Justice Rehnquist noted:

> Since the founding of our Republic, Congress has granted the Executive plenary authority to conduct routine searches and seizures at the border, without probable cause or a warrant, in order to regulate the collection of duties and to prevent the introduction of contraband into this country. . . . This Court has long recognized Congress' power to police entrants at the border. (*United States v. Montoya de Hernandez,* 1985)[11]

United States v. Ramsey (1977) described **border searches** as "reasonable" simply because a person or item enters into the country from outside, without any regard to the existence of probable cause or recourse to a judicial warrant. In practice, any automobile or passenger entering the United States at the Canadian or Mexican border, or any international traveler entering at an international seaport or airport, may be searched at random by customs officers. Such a practice, of course, would be intolerable and blatantly unconstitutional if it were conducted by law enforcement officers within the United States.

In recent decades, as the United States has dealt with mounting problems of drug importation, illegal aliens, and foreign terrorists, issues concerning border searches have proliferated. Along with thorny political and law enforcement issues, the constitutional law of border searches has become complex because the Supreme Court has had to resolve issues arising from variations on the location of the "border" search and specific kinds of intrusions. The cases deal with five types of border searches:

1. At the actual border.
2. At a **fixed checkpoint** miles from the border.
3. **Roving patrols** by the Border Patrol up to a hundred miles from the border.
4. Search of international mail.
5. Boarding ships in open waters.

Searches at the Actual Border.

For routine searches by customs officers, the general rule is alive and well—any person seeking entry may be stopped and searched without probable cause or reasonable suspicion. In 1999, acting on a hunch, a customs officer stopped an Algerian national at the small Port Angeles, Washington, checkpoint on the U.S.-Canadian border. She discovered explosives in the wheel well of the Algerian's car. As it turned out, the suspect, Ahmed Ressam, was then thought to have ties to Osama bin Laden.[12] After the 9/11 attacks, Ressam, who was awaiting sentencing for plotting to bomb the Los Angeles International Airport during the 2000 millennium celebrations, provided federal authorities with new information about people involved in al Qaeda–related terrorist cells.[13]

For nonroutine border searches, the Fourth Amendment requires that officials have reasonable suspicion of a crime to justify search and detention. In **United States v. Montoya de Hernandez** (1985), Rosa Elvira Montoya de Hernandez arrived in Los Angeles on a flight from Bogotá, Colombia. An experienced customs agent thought she was smuggling drugs by having swallowed drug-filled balloons. An airline refused to return her to Colombia because she did not have a proper visa. As a result, she was held without a warrant in a locked room for sixteen hours, during which she "refused all offers of food and drink, and refused to use the toilet facilities." She "exhibited symptoms of discomfort consistent with 'heroic efforts to resist the usual calls of nature.'" Ultimately, a court order was obtained and a medical examination determined the existence of a foreign substance in her rectal canal. Subsequently, she "passed 88 balloons containing a total of 528 grams of 80 percent pure cocaine hydrochloride."

The Supreme Court found that the customs officer had reasonable suspicion to believe she was smuggling drugs, and this was sufficient grounds for the court order and the body cavity search. She said she came to Los Angeles to purchase merchandise for her husband's store. However, because she arrived from a "source city" for drugs, could not speak English, and did not have family or friends in the United States, her explanation was questionable. She had not scheduled appointments with merchandise vendors nor made hotel reservations. Even though she carried $5,000 in cash (mostly $50 bills), she did not have a billfold, nor did she possess checks, waybills, credit cards, or letters of credit, and she did not recall how her ticket was purchased. She told an implausible story that she "planned to ride around Los Angeles in taxicabs visiting retail stores such as J.C. Penney and K-Mart in order to buy goods for her husband's store with the $5,000." These articulable facts "clearly supported a reasonable suspicion that respondent was an alimentary canal smuggler."

Was the sixteen-hour detention without a warrant and the delay in summoning medical personnel "reasonably related in scope to the circumstances which justified it initially"? The Court rejected a hard-and-fast time limit as to what is reasonable. In this case, Montoya refused to be X-rayed, falsely claiming to be pregnant. The alternatives were to hold her for observation or allow her into the interior of the country.

Justice Brennan dissented, joined by Justice Marshall. He felt that more intrusive border detentions and searches are constitutionally reasonable only if authorized by a judicial officer upon probable cause of criminality. There was no exigency in this case, and a warrant could have been obtained at the outset. The majority replied that "not only is the expectation of privacy less at the border than in the interior, . . . [but] the Fourth Amendment balance between the interests of the Government and the privacy right of the individual is also struck much more favorably to the Government at the border."

Stops and Searches at Fixed Checkpoints.

Permanent or fixed checkpoints may be located up to one hundred miles from the U.S. boundary. The Supreme Court has applied standard Fourth Amendment reasoning to fixed checkpoint searches, employing the concepts of administrative searches, stop and frisk, and arrest. The rule is that no level of evidence sufficiency is needed to stop a vehicle at a fixed checkpoint, but that probable cause is required to search a car that has been stopped.

A well-marked checkpoint at San Clemente, California, warned motorists a mile in advance that they would have to slow down or stop. At the checkpoint, a "point" agent visually screened all northbound traffic. Standing between two lanes of traffic, the agent directed some cars to a secondary inspection area where the driver and passengers were questioned for three to five minutes. If the stop produced proof that the passengers were illegal aliens, they were arrested and returned to Mexico. In *United States v. Martinez-Fuerte* (1976), a detected illegal alien challenged his conviction on the basis that the stop at the San Clemente checkpoint was without reasonable suspicion, probable cause, or a warrant and therefore violated the Fourth Amendment.

The Court agreed "that checkpoint stops are 'seizures' within the meaning of the Fourth Amendment," but held that they are a reasonable and valid governmental response to a serious problem. A requirement that the stops be based on reasonable suspicion "would be too impractical because the flow of traffic tends to be too heavy to allow the particularized study of a given car that would enable it to be identified as a possible carrier of illegal aliens." The intrusion of these stops "is quite limited" and involves only a brief detention during which a few questions must be answered. "Neither the vehicle nor its occupants are searched, and visual inspection of the vehicle is limited to what can be seen without a search." Unlike a roving patrol, checkpoint stops involve less discretion, and notice of the checkpoint is clearly given to those approaching it; checkpoints do not create the same concern or fear that may be generated during a stop along a road by a patrol car. As a result, no evidentiary requirement is necessary for a fixed checkpoint stop.

The Supreme Court held unanimously in *United States v. Ortiz* (1975) that the trunk of a car cannot be opened (i.e., searched) during a checkpoint stop unless the officers have probable cause to believe that contraband or illegal aliens are present in the closed area. The Court reasoned that Fourth Amendment considerations come to the fore when a brief stop at a checkpoint, miles from the border, moves beyond a brief visual inspection and the asking of a few questions, which is a seizure, to a more intrusive search by customs officials. The Court noted that many factors could be taken into account by the Border Patrol officers to determine probable cause, including "the number of persons in a vehicle, the appearance and behavior of the driver and passengers, their inability to speak English, the responses they give to officers' questions, the nature of the vehicle, and indications that it may be heavily loaded." No such factors were apparent in *Ortiz,* and the Court found the search to be unconstitutional.

Stops and Searches by Roving Customs Patrols.

Because of the difficulties involved in enforcing customs and immigration rules along our extensive borders, Congress authorized the Border Patrol to conduct roving patrols along the roads and in off-road areas within one hundred air miles of the border. Roving patrol stops by the Border Patrol are more intrusive than checkpoint stops and, therefore, **United States v. Brignoni-Ponce** (1975) held that they must be justified with reasonable suspicion. An officer must be "aware of specific articulable facts, together with rational inferences from those facts, that reasonably warrant suspicion" that a vehicle contains illegal aliens. Four years later, the reasoning in *Brignoni-Ponce* led the Court to extend the same right to drivers throughout the United States in *Delaware v. Prouse* (1979). Earlier, **Almeida-Sanchez v. United States** (1973) held that the search of an automobile stopped by Border Patrol officers is a great intrusion on personal privacy mandating the need for probable cause for the search to be constitutional. The majority was concerned that allowing roving patrol searches up to one hundred miles from the border would destroy the Fourth Amendment rights of local residents.

Inspections and Investigation of International Mail.   *United States v. Ramsey* (1977) held that customs officials may inspect incoming mail from outside the United States if they have reasonable suspicion to believe that the mail contains contraband. While examining a sack of international mail from Thailand, a customs inspector noticed eight bulky envelopes bound for four different locations in the Washington, D.C., area. The addresses had apparently been typed on the same typewriter. He felt and weighed the envelopes and determined that they contained items other than paper. He opened the envelopes and in each found plastic bags containing heroin placed between cardboard. A warrant was then obtained, and the presence of heroin reconfirmed. The packages were resealed and delivered, which ultimately led to the arrest of the defendant.

The Supreme Court held that the more exacting probable cause standard was not required to justify opening the mail under the Fourth Amendment because (1) the federal statute that guided this action imposes a less stringent requirement than that of probable cause required for the issuance of warrants, and (2) mail inspection is justified by the greater authority that the government has to make stops at the border. Justice Stevens dissented in *Ramsey,* joined by Justices Brennan and Marshall. He argued that the 1866 statute that authorized mail stops was intended to apply to large packages and that until 1971, the post office opened mail only in the presence of the addressee or under the authority of a court order supported by probable cause.

Controlled Deliveries.   In *Illinois v. Andreas* (1983), the Supreme Court ruled that an initial inspection of international shipments that discloses contraband may lead to a "controlled delivery" to suspects in the interior of the country. Those to whom contraband-laden packages are delivered may be arrested and the packages searched without a warrant when they take possession of the delivered contraband. In *Andreas,* customs agents found marijuana in a table shipped from India, repackaged it, and had police officers posing as deliverymen convey it. The defendant accepted the package and was arrested less than an hour later as he exited his house. The warrantless arrest and search were justified by the initial customs inspection that found contraband, thus creating a lesser expectation of privacy for Andreas. Resealing the package does not function to revive or restore the lawfully invaded privacy rights. After the first inspection, the contraband was, in effect, in plain view. The lapse of time during which the police could not see the defendant did not reinstate his privacy rights. The Court noted that perfectly controlled deliveries are not always possible, and the arrest and search were not unreasonable because there was a "substantial likelihood" that the illegal contents of the container were not changed.

Boarding and Searching Seagoing Vessels.   Under federal law in force continuously since 1790, Coast Guard and customs officers may, without a warrant or reasonable articulable suspicion of criminal activity, hail, stop, and board any vessel located in waters that provide ready access to the open sea. The purpose is to inspect the ship's

manifest and other documents. In contrast, automobiles may not be stopped without probable cause or reasonable suspicion of a traffic violation or crime (*United States v. Brignoni-Ponce,* 1975; *Delaware v. Prouse,* 1979). This rule for ships was held to be reasonable in **United States v. Villamonte-Marquez** (1983) because at sea it is impossible to establish the equivalent of border checkpoints or roadblocks. Although checkpoints could be established in ports, smugglers could easily avoid ports by anchoring at obscure points along the shore or by transferring cargo to other vessels. Also, the documentation requirements for vessels are different and more complex than automobile licensure, and information about the ship's registry and travel manifests cannot be known without boarding to inspect the documents, as the identity of ships involved in smuggling may be falsified.[14] The intrusion on a ship's Fourth Amendment interests by the Coast Guard boarding is limited, constituting "a brief detention while officials come on board, visit public areas of the vessel, and inspect documents." In *Villamonte-Marquez,* a forty-foot sailboat named the *Henry Morgan II* was packed with tons of marijuana, and the odor gave customs officials plain view authority to search. Justice Brennan, joined by Justice Marshall, dissented in *Villamonte-Marquez,* arguing that as a practical matter, ships in a channel can be funneled into a checkpoint area that allows the uniform checking of documents of all ships.

EXTRATERRITORIAL LAW ENFORCEMENT IN A TIME OF TERROR

After 9/11, noted an FBI senior legal adviser, "as a result of the globalization of crime and the emergence of international terrorism, the apprehension of those who violate American criminal laws will often have to take place abroad."[15] Even before 9/11, the FBI established permanent offices in dozens of cities overseas to fight organized crime and terrorism.[16] The Supreme Court had to decide whether the Constitution "follows the flag"— that is, whether the constitutional limitations on government power apply to the activities of U.S. civilian law enforcement personnel in other countries.

This section examines the **extraterritorial** reach of the Constitution: whether an illegal arrest deprives a court of jurisdiction to try a defendant, whether the Fourth Amendment exclusionary rule applies to searches conducted overseas, whether officers are liable for their actions in other countries, whether the Fifth Amendment and the *Miranda* rule apply to overseas interrogation by U.S. personnel, and whether "extraordinary rendition" is a practice that ought to be permitted.

Kidnapping and Illegal Arrests

The Supreme Court has ruled that the illegal arrest or even kidnapping of a defendant does not divest a court of the jurisdiction to try the defendant (*Frisbie v. Collins,* 1952; see Chapter 4). The Supreme Court extended this rule to cases where a defendant was seized in another country (**United States v. Alvarez-Machain**, 1992). The *Alvarez-Machain* case began in 1985 when a Drug Enforcement Administration (DEA) agent, Enrique Camarena Salazar, was kidnapped, tortured, and killed by Mexican drug dealers, an event that strained relations between the United States and Mexico. The United States indicted nineteen Mexicans, including high-level government officials, for Camarena's torture-killing. Among those indicted was Dr. Humberto Alvarez-Machain, a gynecologist practicing in Guadalajara, Mexico.[17] In 1990, the DEA hired Mexican bounty hunters to kidnap Dr. Alvarez-Machain and bring him to the United States, where he was arrested and put on trial for Camarena's murder. "The arrest of Alvarez took place without an extradition request by the United States, without the involvement of the Mexican judiciary or law enforcement, and under protest by Mexico."[18]

Did the United States have jurisdiction to try Alvarez-Machain? In a six-to-three decision before the trial, the Supreme Court held that it did. Although an extradition treaty existed between Mexico and the United States, the treaty did not specifically address the question of forcible abductions. Therefore, according to Chief Justice Rehnquist's majority opinion, the treaty and its procedural history did not prohibit forcible abductions. The treaty, in this view, did not specify the *only* way that one country could gain custody over a citizen of the other country. The Supreme Court refused to interpret the treaty beyond its terms, even if the actions of the DEA agents were "shocking" and "in violation of general international law principles." Justice Stevens, dissenting for himself and Justices Blackmun and O'Connor, argued that the majority's interpretation in effect nullified the extradition treaty, breaking faith with Mexico. Justice Stevens showed that the trial of Dr. Alvarez-Machain violated the rules of customary international law concerning jurisdiction. The world would view the majority's decision as "monstrous" and the ruling would weaken America's quest to strengthen the rule of law in the international arena by demonstrating that the United States did not live up to international law.

The case ended badly for the United States. Dr. Alvarez-Machain was acquitted of murder and torture in the Los Angeles Federal District Court in December 1992. The trial judge threw out the case, calling the prosecution's case the "wildest speculation" after discovering that the wrong doctor was kidnapped. Others were convicted for the murder. The incident caused much resentment of the United States in Mexico, and as a result, the Clinton administration promised Mexico that the United States will not engage in any cross-border kidnapping of Mexican citizens pending a revised extradition treaty. International opinion and international law scholars roundly criticized the United States.

Dr. Alvarez-Machain sued federal law enforcement officials for $20 million in damages for kidnapping, torture, and false imprisonment. After lengthy litigation, the Ninth Circuit ruled en banc that the doctor had a right to sue the United States under the Alien Tort Claims (ATC) Act and the Federal Tort Claims Act (FTCA).[19] The Supreme Court, however, reversed, finding that the FTCA's exception for acts committed in foreign countries precluded the liability of the government and its agents and employees. The Court also held that the ATC Act, which was enacted as a jurisdictional statute in 1789, did not support Alvarez-Machain's claim, although it would support some claims under international law. The Court cautiously ruled that "federal courts should not recognize private claims under federal common law for violations of any international law norm with less definite content and acceptance among civilized nations than the historical paradigms familiar when [the ATC] was enacted." It further found that no act of Congress or treaty of international law clearly established a substantive right claimed by Alvarez-Machain (***Sosa v. Alvarez-Machain***, 2004).

In contemporary terms, the *Alvarez-Machain* cases have legitimated "rendition to justice," or "the covert transfer of a suspected criminal from one state to another for the purpose of an investigation or trial"[20]—in other words, the kidnapping of suspects from foreign countries.

Extraterritorial Application of the Fourth Amendment

The Supreme Court held in ***United States v. Verdugo-Urquidez*** (1990) that the Fourth Amendment does not apply when U.S. officers search the premises of an alien in a foreign country. This is true even if the alien is lawfully in federal custody on American soil at the time of the search and the purpose of the search is to obtain evidence for his or her conviction of a federal crime in a U.S. court. Verdugo-Urquidez, a reputed drug dealer, was arrested in Mexico by Mexican officers at the request of American authorities and was charged in federal court for the kidnapping and murder of DEA special agent Enrique Camarena Salazar. A joint Mexican Police–DEA task force carried out a raid of Verdugo-Urquidez's home in Mexico, and the evidence obtained was used by the DEA to prosecute him. No approval or warrant was sought from U.S. attorneys or magistrates for the raid. The Ninth Circuit Court of Appeals held that a warrant was required for such a search. Although the warrant would have no legal validity in Mexico, it would "define the scope of the search" for American authorities. In rejecting this argument, Chief Justice Rehnquist, writing for the majority, noted that the Fourth Amendment had never been extended to protect aliens on foreign soil. The fact that Verdugo-Urquidez was in custody on American soil at the time of the raid is a "fortuitous circumstance" that should not dictate the outcome of the case.

Foreign relations activities may have influenced the *Verdugo-Urquidez* decision. While the case was being considered, the United States invaded Panama to rid that country of its military dictator, Manuel Noriega, who was under federal indictment for drug dealing. Noriega surrendered to U.S. forces and was transported to the United States for trial.[21] Chief Justice Rehnquist noted that the United States had employed its armed forces over two hundred times on foreign soil. "Application of the Fourth Amendment to those circumstances could significantly disrupt the ability of the political branches to respond to foreign situations involving our national interest." The Court clearly thought it would be bad policy to impose the burden or concern on the president and members of Congress "as to what might be reasonable in the way of searches and seizures conducted abroad" before authorizing such military actions.

Justice Brennan, dissenting, noted that in recent years the extraterritorial reach of American criminal law against foreign nationals has been increasing under U.S. drug, antitrust, securities, antiterrorist, and piracy statutes. If the United States can extend its criminal law overseas, then the Fourth Amendment should "travel with" American agents who go abroad to exercise criminal jurisdiction. It is unlikely that the Supreme Court will adopt such a rule in the context of what will probably be a very long war on terrorism worldwide.[22]

Extraterritorial Application of the Fifth Amendment and *Miranda*

As will be discussed in Chapter 7, the Fifth Amendment privilege against self-incrimination requires that *Miranda* warnings be given where confessions are taken in foreign countries by American agents; otherwise, the confessions are not admissible in trials in the United States. This is not based on the Fifth Amendment's extraterritorial reach, but on the theory that unlike the Fourth Amendment, which applies at the time and place where a search occurs, the Fifth Amendment rule against self-incrimination is an exclusionary rule that applies in court. It is interesting that U.S. agents in the bin Laden embassy-bombing investigations and prosecutions acted as if the defendants were protected by various Fifth Amendment provisions.[23]

Extraordinary Rendition

The irregular and controversial practice of "rendition to justice," which avoided the legal extradition process and was upheld by the Supreme Court in *United States v. Alvarez-Machain* (1992), was first used by the U.S. Marshals Service in the 1970s. "Today, rendition to justice stands juxtaposed to a newer form of rendition developed with the advent of the U.S. war on terrorism: rendition to torture."[24]

The first major popular account of rendition to justice was provided by *Washington Post* journalists in December 2002.[25] Administration officials acknowledge renditions but publicly deny that torture is involved. The rationale for sending suspected terrorists to countries like Egypt, Jordan, Morocco, Saudi Arabia, and Syria for interrogation is that the linguistic and cultural affinities of the interrogators will produce better results. President Bush defended renditions as vital to the nation's defense.[26] Nevertheless, unnamed officials in the 2002 news story bluntly stated that suspects were sent to countries with poor human rights records specifically because those countries tortured suspects, and they supported violence against captives as just and necessary. Officials from the United States monitored cases of interrogation under torture.[27] By 2005, a former FBI agent who was involved in renditions stated that there was "no doubt that Egypt engaged in torture" and that torture "has become bureaucratized," but the agent felt that the method was not productive of useful intelligence.[28]

A thorough definition of the newer term *extraordinary rendition* has been provided:

> Extraordinary rendition is a hybrid human rights violation, combining elements of arbitrary arrest, enforced disappearance, forcible transfer, torture, denial of access to consular officials, and denial of impartial tribunals. It involves the state-sponsored abduction of a person in one country, with or without the cooperation of the government of that country, and the subsequent transfer of that person to another country for detention and interrogation. As is the case with state-sponsored disappearances, extraordinary rendition appears to be a practice in which perpetrators attempt to avoid legal and moral constraints by denying their involvement in the abuses.[29]

Among several notorious extraordinary rendition cases, that of Maher Arar is arguably the worst. Based on faulty Canadian intelligence, Arar, a Syrian-born Canadian software engineer and successful entrepreneur, was taken into custody by American authorities as a suspected terrorist while in a New York airport in 2002. He was in transit from a family vacation in Tunisia, waiting for a plane to Montreal. He was questioned, and his requests to see a lawyer were denied. American authorities assured Canada that Arar would not be tortured. Although Arar pleaded that he would be tortured, he was transferred to Syria through Jordan. For almost a year, Arar was subjected to incessant and brutal torture while held in a foul, tiny, subterranean cell. He was forced to sign a false confession but was finally released. The outcry generated by Arar's case led Canada to initiate a Commission of Inquiry, headed by the Associate Chief Justice of Ontario. In September 2006, after several years of investigation, the commission issued a three-volume report that completely exonerated Arar of any involvement in terrorism and made extensive recommendations for improving Canada's security procedures.[30]

One analyst notes that "rendition to torture in its explicit form is not directly prohibited by international and U.S. domestic law," although the concept conflicts with the U.N. Convention against Torture (CAT), to which the United States is a signatory, with some reservations.[31] "The CAT not only requires signatory states to abolish the practice of government-sponsored torture within their own borders, but Article 3 provides, 'no State Party shall expel, return or extradite a person to another State where there are substantial grounds for believing that he would be in danger of being subjected to torture.'"[32] The United States publicly condemns rendition to torture while surreptitiously engaging in the practice. Federal laws against torture seem to exclude the specific act of rendition to torture, and *Sosa v. Alvarez-Machain* (2004) appears to preclude civil liability for agents who engage in the act even though extraordinary rendition seems to violate section 3 of the CAT.[33]

THE SPECIAL NEEDS DOCTRINE AND REGULATORY SEARCHES

Origins of the Doctrine and Administrative Searches

In *New Jersey v. T.L.O.* (1985), the Supreme Court ruled that a public high school student has a Fourth Amendment expectation of privacy in her purse. Nevertheless, the Court ruled that when the circumstances make it reasonable, a public school official can inspect the content of the student's purse, looking for materials that could subject the student to criminal prosecution, without first obtaining a warrant and even without probable cause to believe that the purse contains illegal contraband. This case set off a chain of rulings that have collectively come under a rule known as the **special needs doctrine.** It is not clear that the Court intended to create a doctrine, for the cases that have relied on the reasoning of "special needs *beyond the need for normal law enforcement*" involve different factual settings and even allow searches with different evidentiary foundations. In some cases, a government official must have reasonable suspicion of wrongdoing before searching without a warrant, whereas under other factual circumstances there need be no individualized suspicion for a search to take place. What the cases have in common is that in each case the search is conducted by a government officer who is *not* a police officer engaged in the enforcement of criminal law.

The special needs cases are closely related to administrative searches—a type of search that the Supreme Court brought under the aegis of the Fourth Amendment in 1967. The section in Chapter 3 on "Revolutionizing the Fourth Amendment" notes that in the 1960s, the *Katz* "expectation of privacy" doctrine, which replaced the idea that privacy protection depended on property rights, expanded Fourth Amendment protection. In addition, the Supreme Court modified search and seizure jurisprudence by making it more *flexible*. *Terry v. Ohio* (1968) thus allowed police, for the first time in common law history, to stop a person on less than probable cause, and *Warden v. Hayden* (1967) held that police could seize and possess a defendant's "mere property" for the duration of a prosecution if it could be used to prove guilt.

The fourth "revolutionary" case, *Camara v. Municipal Court* (1967), ruled that the Fourth Amendment applied even to home entry by administrative officers enforcing municipal safety, health, or occupancy ordinances, and not investigating crimes. *Camara* overruled an earlier case that held that the Fourth Amendment did not apply at all to these kinds of essentially noncriminal searches.[34] The Court in *Camara* recognized that the Fourth Amendment protected against all official intrusions into the privacy of a home, whether by police officers or by government regulatory inspectors looking for unsanitary conditions and the like. The *Camara* decision to extend the Fourth Amendment to administrative searches created a dilemma because it allowed a householder to refuse entry to an inspector without a warrant. But it was close to impossible for an inspector to obtain probable cause to believe that *this* particular householder, for example, kept oily rags next to her furnace. The warrant requirement threatened to undermine the effectiveness of inspection programs, which relied on the inspections of *all* the houses in a neighborhood to be effective. The Supreme Court got around this sticking point by holding that administrative search warrants could be obtained by proving to a court that the conditions in an area made inspections necessary. Without quite saying so, the Supreme Court indicated that the particularity requirement in the amendment's Warrant Clause could be modified as long as the warrant was reasonable. In effect, the Supreme Court authorized general warrants, so hated by the Framers of the Constitution.

The Supreme Court applied the administrative search doctrine, with its "area warrants," to inspections of commercial establishments in *See v. City of Seattle* (1967). Indeed, the Court soon held that even area warrants could be dispensed with when inspectors entered a **pervasively regulated industry,** such as liquor stores or gun dealerships, as long as they did so during normal business hours and did not use force. Dealers who refused inspections could lose their licenses (*Colonnade Catering v. United States,* 1970; *United States v. Biswell,* 1972). Under the administrative search rules, unannounced safety inspections of mines without a warrant was permissible under the Mine Safety and Health Act because the law was known to all mine owners and provides a constitutionally adequate substitute for a warrant (*Donovan v. Dewey,* 1981). The Supreme Court did require area warrants for worker safety inspections under the Occupational Safety and Health Administration (OSHA). It ruled that simply requiring safety and health regulations does not transform monitored industries into "pervasively regulated industries" (*Marshall v. Barlow's, Inc.,* 1978).

The flexible interpretation of the Fourth Amendment established by the administrative search cases, then, made the Court receptive to relying on the Reasonableness Clause of the Fourth Amendment to uphold a variety of warrantless searches under the special needs rubric.

Early Special Needs Cases: Creating a Doctrine

The special needs doctrine originated in **New Jersey v. T.L.O.** (1985). Keep in mind that no special needs doctrine existed prior to this case. In the course of deciding a case that did not fit easily into a preexisting category, the Court laid a conceptual foundation that later cases recognized as a basis for decisions applied to dissimilar facts.

In *T.L.O.,* a teacher discovered a fourteen-year-old public high school freshman smoking in a lavatory in violation of a school rule. She was brought to the principal's office and questioned by an assistant vice principal. The girl, T.L.O., denied that she had been smoking and claimed that she did not smoke at all. The assistant vice principal then demanded to see her purse, opened the purse, found a pack of cigarettes, and, upon removing the cigarettes, noticed a pack of cigarette rolling papers. Rolling papers are closely associated with the use of marijuana. The assistant vice principal proceeded to search the purse thoroughly and found a small amount of marijuana, a pipe, a number of empty plastic bags, a substantial quantity of money in one-dollar bills, an index card containing a list of students who owed T.L.O. money, and two letters that implicated the student in marijuana dealing. This discovery led to T.L.O.'s adjudication as a delinquent and a one-year probation sentence.

Was the assistant vice principal's search of T.L.O.'s purse a constitutional violation? State action existed in this search and seizure case because a public school is established by a local government. Its administrators and teachers exercise legitimate control over students by virtue of their positions. Justice White's majority opinion explored the question of whether T.L.O. had a Fourth Amendment privacy interest in her purse. The Court's unanimous decision on this point rested on a close analysis of the actualities of school life in the 1980s:

> Students at a minimum must bring to school not only the supplies needed for their studies, but also keys, money, and the necessaries of personal hygiene and grooming. In addition, students may carry on their persons or in purses or wallets such nondisruptive yet highly personal items as photographs, letters, and diaries. Finally, students may have perfectly legitimate reasons to carry with them articles of property needed in connection with extracurricular or recreational activities. In short, school children may find it necessary to carry with them a variety of legitimate, noncontraband items, and there is no reason to conclude that they have necessarily waived all rights to privacy in such items merely by bringing them onto school grounds. (*New Jersey v. T.L.O.,* 1985)

The state argued that public school students had *no* reasonable expectation of privacy in school. If this were the rule, school authorities could search the belongings of high school students at will. The Court rejected the idea that teachers stood ***in loco parentis***—in the place of parents. The old-fashioned idea that a parent transfers personal authority to teachers does not fit the reality that modern schools are in many ways large bureaucracies.

Having decided that public school students, at least those in high school, enjoy an expectation of privacy, the next issue was whether the assistant vice principal's search violated this right. This involved two further issues: Was a warrant necessary? And if not, what was the proper standard of evidence for a lawful warrantless search in a school setting? The Court stated that schools have an interest in maintaining order by enforcing such school rules as the ban on smoking. To further this goal, all the justices agreed that the "warrant requirement, in particular, is unsuited to the school environment: requiring a teacher to obtain a warrant before searching a child suspected of an infraction of school rules (or of the criminal law) would unduly interfere with the maintenance of the swift and informal disciplinary procedures needed in the schools."

The final question was whether the balance between the student's expectation of privacy in her purse and the school's need to enforce rules was properly met by the search in this case. Since T.L.O. denied smoking after being caught, it was reasonable for the assistant vice principal to determine whether T.L.O. carried cigarettes, as that would help to resolve a dispute between the teacher and the student. When the assistant vice principal saw the rolling papers, he had some suspicion that T.L.O. might be in possession of marijuana. On the other hand, some students might use the paper to roll tobacco. It was also possible that she was carrying the rolling paper for another student or for another person. In short, the observation of the papers did not establish probable cause but did provide the assistant vice principal with reasonable suspicion that T.L.O. had marijuana in her purse.

The Court rejected the probable cause standard, saying that it is not an irreducible requirement of a valid search. The decision to uphold the constitutionality of the search based on reasonable suspicion of marijuana possession was based on application of the general-reasonableness construction of the Fourth Amendment to the specific facts of this school search.

Justice Brennan, dissenting, noted that an exception to Fourth Amendment requirements had been allowed in past cases only where there was some pressing emergency. He and Justices Marshall and Stevens did not find that the facts in this case rose to such a level of seriousness as to cause the constitutional balance to tip in favor of the school's interests when measured against the student's right to privacy. The suspected infraction, smoking, was not a crime. "Considerations of the deepest significance for the freedom of our citizens counsel strict adherence to the principle that no search may be conducted where the official is not in possession of probable cause" (*New Jersey v. T.L.O.,* 1985, Brennan, J., dissenting). Justice Stevens, also dissenting, stated that the kind of search involved in this case would have been justified if there had been an allegation involving in-school violence.

This case is an example of how legal doctrines evolve. In a footnote, Justice White wrote that "the special needs of the school environment require assessment of the legality of such searches against a standard less exacting than that of probable cause." Justice Blackmun, in a concurring opinion, wrote that "[o]nly in those exceptional circumstances in which special needs, beyond the normal need for law enforcement, make the warrant and probable-cause requirement impracticable, is a court entitled to substitute its balancing of interests for that of the Framers" (*New Jersey v. T.L.O.* 1985). The use of the term *special needs* was probably not meant to define a new doctrine but simply to explain the basis of the Court's ruling.

Two years after *T.L.O.,* however, the Supreme Court decided three cases that relied on *T.L.O.* as precedent and used the "special needs" language as justification for the decisions. These cases established the idea that the ruling of *New Jersey v. T.L.O.* established a new doctrine. None of the cases involved public school searches.

The first, **O'Connor v. Ortega** (1987), was a civil suit in which a supervisor thoroughly searched the office, desk, and filing cabinet of a psychiatrist, Dr. Ortega, employed by a state hospital. The psychiatrist was suspected of improprieties in the acquisition of a computer, and charges were brought against him for sexual harassment of female hospital employees and inappropriate disciplinary action against a resident. Because the search was ordered by the executive director of a state hospital, it constituted state action. The Supreme Court found that Dr. Ortega had a reasonable expectation of privacy in his office but also stated that an expectation of privacy can be overcome if a governmental interest outweighs an individual's privacy interests. In her majority opinion justifying the search, Justice O'Connor relied heavily on the incipient rule in Justice Blackmun's *T.L.O.* concurrence and quoted his special needs formulation (i.e., "special needs, beyond the normal need for law enforcement") as a reason for upholding the search of a public employee's office on less than probable cause. Both Justice O'Connor and Justice Scalia referred to these words, but both omitted the opening words in Justice Blackmun's sentence in *T.L.O.,* recognizing a "special needs" exception only in "exceptional circumstances." If *T.L.O.* had been known as the "exceptional circumstances" doctrine, perhaps it would have been less frequently employed.

In the next special needs case, the Court combined that doctrine with the pervasively regulated industry exception to administrative search warrants. *New York v. Burger* (1987) held that evidence found in plain view during a police inspection of automobile junk shops could be admitted in a criminal case. A state statute required vehicle dismantlers to maintain records of cars in their junkyards and to allow police or motor vehicle inspectors to examine the records during working hours. Failure to produce records was a misdemeanor. NYPD officers, who were part of a team that conducted five to ten junk shop inspections daily, identified stolen vehicles by their VINs during such an inspection.

The Court upheld this search and seizure even though the police had no warrant or any suspicion of wrongdoing. The Court relied on three reasons: (1) junkyards are a pervasively regulated industry providing a reduced expectation of privacy; (2) warrantless inspections are necessary to make the inspection system work and are of limited scope; and (3) the statute is not a pretext for criminal searches without a warrant. As to the last point, the Court said that a state can address a major social problem through both the administrative system and penal sanctions. In this regard, the police officers were treated simply as regulatory agents. This last point is rather weak, as the major "social problem" targeted by the New York law was the dismantling of stolen cars. If this logic were pushed to its extreme, every crime could be declared a social problem, and constitutional protections would be eliminated.

The third special needs case of 1987, *Griffin v. Wisconsin,* ruled that a probationer's home could be entered and searched without a warrant by probation officers as long as there were reasonable grounds to believe contraband was present, as was required by state law. Justice Scalia offered this justification: "The search of Griffin's home satisfied the demands of the Fourth Amendment because it was carried out pursuant to a regulation that itself satisfies the Fourth Amendment's reasonableness requirement under well-established principles."

> A probationer's home, like anyone else's, is protected by the Fourth Amendment's requirement that searches be "reasonable." Although we usually require that a search be undertaken only pursuant to a warrant (and thus supported by probable cause, as the Constitution says warrants must be), . . . we have permitted exceptions when "special needs, beyond the normal need for law enforcement, make the warrant and probable-cause requirement impracticable."

In support, Justice Scalia cited *New Jersey v. T.L.O., O'Connor v. Ortega,* and the administrative search cases. The creation of a new doctrine requires a certain amount of maneuvering. Strictly speaking, neither *T.L.O.* nor *O'Connor v. Ortega* applied to a home. Justice Scalia also cited *Payton v. New York* (1980), which held that an arrest warrant is necessary for entry into a home to make a felony arrest. But instead of characterizing the search of a probationer's home as a home search, the Court instead lumped the search in with a part of operating a probation system "like [the] operation of a school, government office or prison, or . . . supervision of a regulated industry." As a form of punishment, the probationer is under correctional supervision and enjoys only conditional liberty. This diminishes his or her expectation of privacy, even in the home.

These initial special needs cases demonstrate how new legal doctrines are formed. First, a case is decided that does not precisely fit earlier precedent. In its opinion, the Court provides a phrase that helps to explain the decision. Subsequent cases apply the phrase as a basis for decisions to cases that are not precisely the same as the first. The phrase is now becoming a doctrine—a legal category that can be used as a framework to decide future cases. This produces the appearance that the system of common law reasoning is more inductive than deductive.[35] By organizing the cases under a doctrine, the Court attempts to offer a consistent and satisfactory explanation to lower court judges and police officers who must decide novel cases.

The creation of a doctrine is not simply a neutral process of logic. In the example of the special needs doctrine, the new category allowed a conservative Court to advance a theory that relied on the Reasonableness Clause and the general-reasonableness construction of the Fourth Amendment. (See "The Fourth Amendment's Structure" in Chapter 2.) This made it feasible to get around the obstacles of the Warrant Clause and the probable cause requirement to uphold action by government officers that intruded on the Fourth Amendment privacy in different situations. Liberal justices saw the special needs cases as an assault on fundamental rights. As Justice Thurgood Marshall wrote, "In the four years since this Court, in *T.L.O.,* first began recognizing "special needs" exceptions to the Fourth Amendment, the clarity of Fourth Amendment doctrine has been badly distorted, as the Court has eclipsed the probable-cause requirement in a patchwork quilt of settings" (*Skinner v. Railway Labor Executives' Association,* 1989).

Before returning to the expansion of the special needs doctrine in the area of drug testing, we examine the rules regarding the search of premises for inspecting the causes of fires under the Fourth Amendment. These rules combine the basic law of criminal searches with those of administrative searches.

Fire Inspections

Determining the cause of a blaze involves an inspection, which is conducted for both administrative and criminal investigation purposes, after the fire. Rules for these kinds of searches were established in *Michigan v. Tyler* (1978) and *Michigan v. Clifford* (1984) and provide a mix of administrative search and criminal search rules:

Rule 1. "A burning building creates an exigency that justifies a warrantless entry by fire officials to fight the blaze."

Rule 2. "Moreover, . . . once in the building, officials need no warrant to remain for 'a reasonable time to investigate the cause of a blaze after it has been extinguished.'"

Rule 3. "Where, however, reasonable expectations of privacy remain in the fire-damaged property, additional investigations begun after the fire has been extinguished and fire and police officials have left the scene, generally must be made pursuant to a warrant or the identification of some new exigency."

Rule 4. "If the primary object [of a renewed search] is to determine the cause and origin of a recent fire, an administrative warrant will suffice. To obtain such a warrant, fire officials need show only that a fire of undetermined origin has occurred on the premises, that the scope of the proposed search is reasonable and will not intrude unnecessarily on the fire victim's privacy, and that the search will be executed at a reasonable and convenient time."

Rule 5. "If the primary object of the [renewed] search is to gather evidence of criminal activity, a criminal search warrant may be obtained only on a showing of probable cause to believe that relevant evidence will be found in the place to be searched."

Rule 6. "If evidence of criminal activity is discovered during the course of a valid administrative search [or during the initial firefighting], it may be seized under the 'plain view' doctrine. . . . This evidence then may be used to establish probable cause to obtain a criminal search warrant."

In ***Michigan v. Tyler*** (1978), a fire broke out in a furniture store at midnight. At 2 A.M., just as the firefighters were "watering down smoldering embers," fire inspectors arrived to determine the cause, and they seized two plastic containers of flammable liquid. A police detective arrived at 3:30 A.M. and took photographs of the suspected arson. Shortly thereafter, the police investigator abandoned the investigation because the smoke and darkness made careful observation of the crime scene impossible. The fire inspectors returned briefly at 8 A.M. after the fire had been fully extinguished and the building was empty. They left and returned with the police investigator at 9:30 A.M. During this search, they discovered more evidence of arson: pieces of tape on a stairway with burn marks and pieces of carpet suggesting a fuse trail. The investigators left to obtain tools, returned, and seized the incriminating evidence. Three weeks later, an investigator with the state police arson section returned to take pictures. All the entries were made without consent or warrants.

The Court held that the Fourth Amendment applied to searches following a fire, noting that a magistrate must not be a "rubber stamp" when issuing an administrative search warrant. Instead, the magistrate must ensure that the investigation does not stray beyond reasonable limits. The magistrate's role is to prevent undue harassment of property owners and to keep the inspection to a minimum.

Applying the search rules to the facts of *Tyler,* the Court held that the warrantless entry and search immediately after the fire was proper (Rules 1 and 2). The search at 9:30 the next morning was construed by the Court as a continuation of the search begun a few hours before: that search was cut off owing to the smoke and darkness, and "[l]ittle purpose would have been served by their remaining in the building, except to remove any doubt about the legality of the warrantless search and seizure later that same morning." The photographs taken by the state police investigator, however, were not admissible without a warrant: Too much time had elapsed, and suspicion had accrued.

Michigan v. Clifford involved an early-morning house fire. Firefighters arrived on the scene at 5:40 A.M., extinguished the blaze, and left the scene shortly after 7 A.M. One hour later, a police fire investigator received an order to investigate. Because he was working on other cases, he did not arrive on the scene until 1 P.M. When he arrived, a work crew hired by the owner was boarding up the house and pumping water out of the basement. Clifford was out of town on a vacation and was communicating about the situation through his insurance agent and a neighbor. After the work crew departed, the investigators entered the basement of the house without obtaining consent or an administrative warrant and quickly found evidence of arson (a strong odor of fuel and a crock pot attached to a timer set for 3:45 A.M. that stopped at 4 A.M.). This evidence was seized and marked. The officer proceeded through the remainder of the house, much of which was still intact, and seized other suspicious evidence.

The Supreme Court held this seizure to be a Fourth Amendment violation. The owner, by hiring a crew to board up and pump out his house, clearly maintained an expectation of privacy in his home. Therefore, before entry, the officer should have obtained an administrative search warrant. The time lapse meant that there was no longer an exigent circumstance. Once the officer found incriminating items in the basement, it was necessary to halt the search and take the evidence to a magistrate to seek a criminal search warrant. Thus all the evidence was inadmissible.

In sum, fire officials have the right to enter burned premises immediately after a fire in an attempt to determine the cause of the fire. Owners or residents, however, do not lose their right to privacy; more extensive, long-term investigations and searches must be accompanied by a warrant.

Drug Testing

Increased awareness of the personal and social costs of alcohol and illicit-drug abuse has made them prime domestic issues. Government agencies and private employers, including major league sports franchises, have turned to random or mandatory drug testing as a way to deter drug use and to identify users. The pervasiveness and visibility of drug testing has assured court challenges. Drug testing by private businesses is not a Fourth Amendment concern, just as searches in private schools do not infringe on a constitutional right of privacy; drug testing by government agencies, on the other hand, comes under the Fourth Amendment. The Supreme Court has decided six special needs cases arising from drug testing by government authorities. In two of the cases, the Court found that there were no special needs justifying intrusions on privacy and held the testing programs to be unconstitutional.

Early Cases. The first two cases were decided in favor of the government-mandated testing programs in 1989. One upheld the mandatory testing of every crew member after any major rail accident (*Skinner v. Railway Labor Executives' Association,* 1989). The other allowed the U.S. Customs Service to test virtually all of its agents for drugs at some point in their careers (*National Treasury Employees Union v. Von Raab* (1989).

An initial issue in both cases was whether taking and testing blood and urine samples intruded on reasonable expectations of privacy. As noted in Chapter 3, under the doctrine of *Katz v. United States* (1967) the Court held in *Skinner* that urine collection and testing to ascertain the presence of drugs in a person's body intrudes upon expectations of privacy that society has long recognized as reasonable. "There are few activities in our society more personal or private than the passing of urine. Most people describe it by euphemisms if they talk about it at all. It is a function traditionally performed without public observation; indeed, its performance in public is generally prohibited by law as well as social custom." The Court noted that the expectation of privacy is not only rooted in the traditional dictates of modesty, but also in the fact that the chemical analysis of urine, like that of blood, can reveal a host of medical facts about a person. Although urine testing by state agencies in order to detect drugs or alcohol is protected by the Fourth Amendment, the collection is allowed under certain conditions (*Skinner v. Railway Labor Executives' Association,* 1989).

The second issue in both cases concerned the standards needed to ascertain the constitutionality of drug testing. In each case, the Court applied the special needs doctrine to find these drug-testing programs reasonable under the Fourth Amendment, even though no warrant was required and no level of individualized suspicion was needed to trigger drug testing. Each case was decided on the particular facts of the respective testing program. The linchpin of the holdings in *Skinner* and *Von Raab* was that the purposes of these laws were essentially administrative, although the discovery of the presence of drugs could lead to criminal prosecution.

In *Skinner v. Railway Labor Executives' Association* (1989), the Court upheld a federal law that mandated drug testing of all on-site employees after a major train accident, whether the employees worked for a private railroad company or a line run by the government. State action was based on the fact that the program was mandated by law for the public safety. The Court's decision that mandatory testing was reasonable and constitutional was based on several points: (1) preserving the life and safety of train passengers is of great importance; (2) the employees subjected to the testing program are involved in safety-sensitive tasks; (3) the absolute prohibition of alcohol and drug use while on the job is a reasonable requirement; and (4) the usual sanction for on-the-job intoxication is dismissal and not criminal prosecution. The warrant requirement would add little to further the aims of the drug-testing program because the tests were standardized. The fact that blood alcohol levels drop at a constant rate requires swift testing and creates an exigency. Waiting to get a warrant before testing would effectively undermine the usefulness of the testing.

The railway union argued in *Skinner* that there must be a particularized suspicion against specific railroad employees after an accident before they could be tested. The Court disagreed and concluded that mandatory and comprehensive testing was constitutional for the following reasons:

- Although blood and urine testing are Fourth Amendment searches, they are relatively limited encroachments on the expectations of privacy of the railway employees because they are job- and safety-related requirements in a pervasively regulated industry.
- The testing is relatively limited in time, intrusiveness, and ancillary risk.
- The government's interest in testing without individualized suspicion is compelling because it is not easy for supervisors to spot individuals who have used a drug and are still under its influence.
- A mandatory testing and dismissal rule has a greater deterrent effect than a weaker mandatory testing policy.
- An accident scene is chaotic, and it may be extremely difficult for supervisors to sort out who is to be tested and who is not to be tested on the basis of individualized suspicion.
- The fact that drug tests are not, in themselves, conclusive proof of impairment does not solely render the program unconstitutional because the statistical evidence obtained from mandatory, across-the-board testing is very useful to the railway industry in assessing the causes of accidents.

The balance of interests in *National Treasury Employees Union v. Von Raab* (1989) differed in several respects. The challenged rule of the U.S. Customs Service required the automatic drug testing of all officers who (1) are directly involved in drug interdiction or the enforcement of drug laws, (2) are required to carry firearms, or (3) handle classified material that would be useful to drug smugglers and could be relinquished through the bribery or blackmail of drug-dependent employees. This testing program was not triggered by a particular negative incident but was required for hiring or promotion into sensitive posts. The government interest was not proposed to prevent on-the-job impairment as a direct result of alcohol or drug use. Instead, the interest was to ensure that customs officers in drug enforcement positions who carried firearms would lead drug-free lives. The government argued that drug-addicted customs agents are targets for bribery and cannot carry out their functions in a positive way (i.e., they may be sympathetic to the goals of drug traffickers). Furthermore, government employees in sensitive jobs (i.e., employees of the U.S. Mint, military or intelligence officers, and customs officers) "have a diminished expectation of privacy in respect to the intrusions occasioned by" their positions.

Justice Anthony Kennedy, writing for the majority, held as he did in *Skinner* that neither a warrant nor individualized suspicion would serve a useful purpose in such a program. The majority agreed with the first two rationales presented by the Customs Service, upholding the program of drug testing for those agents directly involved in drug law enforcement and for those who carried firearms. It could not agree on the reasonableness of the third rationale, preventing the compromise of agents handling classified information, and remanded the case for further fact finding.

Justice Marshall, joined by Justice Brennan, dissented in both *Skinner* and *Von Raab* on the grounds that their special needs analyses were flawed. They did not find that the goals and methods of the two programs provided a reasonable basis to dispense with the Fourth Amendment's requirement that individualized suspicion is the basis of interfering with a person's constitutional rights. Justice Marshall did not believe that the need for individualized suspicion would undermine these programs. He accused the majority of submitting to popular pressure generated by public hysteria over the drug problem and giving away precious rights.

Justices Scalia and Stevens concurred in *Skinner* but dissented in *Von Raab*. Justice Scalia's dissent noted that the factual predicate for the two cases differed. In *Skinner,* the government gave evidence to show that a substantial number of train accidents were caused by intoxicated railroad employees. In *Von Raab,* on the other hand, "neither the frequency of use nor connection to harm is demonstrated or even likely. In my view the Customs Service rules are a kind of immolation of privacy and human dignity in symbolic opposition to drug use." Justice Scalia noted that the government did not supply even one example in which the purported state interest of preventing bribe taking, poor intentions, unsympathetic law enforcement, or the compromise of classified information was endangered by drug use. Some of the government's arguments were weak. For example, the fact that an agent used drugs does not necessarily mean the officer would be hostile or indifferent to drug enforcement. Calling the Customs Service's reasons "feeble," Justice Scalia noted that its commissioner said that the drug-testing program would "set an important example in our country's struggle with this most serious threat to our national health and security." In effect, Justice Scalia agreed with Justice Marshall's point, that the testing of customs officers was an unnecessary sacrifice of constitutional freedoms as a result of public and political pressure.

Drug Testing of Political Candidates.   The Supreme Court finally drew the

line at mandatory drug testing in ***Chandler v. Miller*** (1997). A Georgia law required every candidate for state office to be tested for drugs. Two libertarian candidates for statewide offices challenged the law as an infringement of their Fourth Amendment rights. The Supreme Court, in an eight-to-one opinion authored by Justice Ginsburg, agreed. Drug testing under the law was not based on individualized suspicion against the candidate. Indeed, the program was "relatively noninvasive" because it permitted a candidate to provide a urine specimen in the office of his or her private physician. The results are given to the candidate, who controls further dissemination of the report. The core issue was whether the certification of drug testing required before a person's name could be placed on a ballot is a special need that overrides the basic requirements of the Fourth Amendment.

> Nothing in the record hints that the hazards respondents broadly describe [i.e., drug-addicted candidates] are real and not simply hypothetical for Georgia's polity. The statute was not enacted, as counsel for respondents readily acknowledged at oral argument, in response to any fear or suspicion of drug use by state officials. (*Chandler v. Miller,* 1997)

The testing program was simply too weak to identify or to deter candidates who violate antidrug laws. In contrast to other drug-testing programs designed to deal with the real dangers of illicit drug use, Justice Ginsburg wrote that the real purpose of the Georgia law was simply to project an "image" of being tough on drugs. "By requiring candidates for public office to submit to drug testing, Georgia displays its commitment to the struggle against drug abuse. The suspicionless tests, according to respondents, signify that candidates, if elected, will be fit to serve their constituents free from the influence of illegal drugs" (*Chandler v. Miller,* 1997). A law that is merely symbolic does not create the special need that allows an individual's right to privacy to be overridden without a warrant and individualized suspicion.

Chief Justice Rehnquist, the lone dissenter, found no infringement on a personal right and, displaying his pro-state philosophy, wrote, "Nothing in the Fourth Amendment or in any other part of the Constitution prevents a State from enacting a statute whose principal vice is that it may seem misguided or even silly to the members of this Court" (*Chandler v. Miller,* 1997).

Drug Testing of Pregnant Women.

The Supreme Court drew a line against the special needs justification for drug testing pregnant women enrolled in a public prenatal care program in *Ferguson v. City of Charleston* (2001). Staff members at a Charleston, South Carolina, public hospital in 1988 were concerned that patients who were receiving prenatal treatment were using cocaine. A policy was established to identify and test pregnant patients suspected of drug use. Women who tested positive were referred to the county substance abuse commission for counseling and treatment. The program did not reduce the incidence of cocaine use among patients.

A task force then developed a policy, in conjunction with the local prosecutor and police, to perform drug screens on all women in the program who met one of nine criteria, including "late prenatal care after 24 weeks gestation," " incomplete prenatal care," "abruptio placentae," "IUGR [intrauterine growth retardation] 'of no obvious cause,'" "previously known drug or alcohol abuse," or "unexplained congenital anomalies." The new policy had a treatment component but also required that information about drug use be forwarded to police authorities for prosecution. The policy also prescribed in detail the precise offenses with which a woman could be charged, depending on the stage of her pregnancy, from simple possession to possession and distribution to a person under the age of eighteen, and unlawful neglect of a child. Although women in the prenatal care program signed consent forms, it was not clear that they were informed of the possibility of prosecution for receiving health care. The Court assumed that the women did not know they were being tested for drugs and that the results were forwarded to law enforcement officials for prosecution.

The Supreme Court decided the case on the issue of whether there were special needs beyond the normal need for law enforcement that justified the drug testing of these women without a search warrant or any individualized suspicion. In reaching its conclusion that the testing program was unconstitutional, the Court concluded that the nine criteria used to initiate testing did not amount to probable cause or even reasonable suspicion that a woman had ingested cocaine. Justice Stevens's majority opinion noted that there was no "evidence in the record indicating that any of the nine search criteria was more apt to be caused by cocaine use than by some other factor, such as malnutrition, illness, or indigency." The Circuit Court's decision upholding the testing program rested "on the premise that the policy would be valid even if the tests were conducted randomly" (*Ferguson v. City of Charleston,* 2001).

The key factor that distinguished *Ferguson* from the earlier drug-testing special needs cases is that in the earlier cases there was some administrative rationale, and the consequences involved such action as dismissal from a position or discipline for substance use. In *Ferguson,* on the other hand, although a goal of the program was to prevent cocaine use by pregnant women, "the central and indispensable feature of the policy from its inception was the use of law enforcement to coerce the patients into substance abuse treatment." However beneficent the ultimate goal of the policy, as in *City of Indianapolis v. Edmond* (2000), "the purpose actually served by the [hospital's] searches 'is ultimately indistinguishable from the general interest in crime control'" (*Ferguson v. City of Charleston,* 2001). The fact is that Charleston police and prosecutors "were extensively involved in the day-to-day administration of the policy." This close involvement had the effect of making the hospital staff so closely involved in law enforcement that they had "a special obligation to make sure that the patients are fully informed about their constitutional rights, as standards of knowing waiver require" (*Ferguson v. City of Charleston,* 2001).

Justice Scalia dissented, joined by Chief Justice Rehnquist and Justice Clarence Thomas. He argued that drug testing is not a search, but at most "a 'derivative use of the product of a past unlawful search,' which, of course, 'works no new Fourth Amendment wrong' and 'presents a question, not of rights, but of remedies.'" (*Ferguson v. City of Charleston,* 2001, Scalia, J., dissenting). Thus the dissenters were attempting to have the case decided as a matter of the applicability of the exclusionary rule.

Writing in 1999, Lynn Paltrow, program director of the National Advocates for Pregnant Women (NAPW), noted that "[i]n the name of fetal rights, over 200 pregnant women or new mothers in approximately twenty states have been arrested. Most of the women arrested have been low-income women of color with untreated drug addictions. Thus, the arrests focus on those people and issues that are hardest to defend in the court of public opinion. Wrongly prejudged as irresponsible and uncaring, the public has expressed little support for them."[36] She viewed these prosecution programs as an assault on the reproductive rights of women. Some justification for this is that "[m]any more children are harmed every year from prenatal alcohol use than by cocaine or marijuana. Yet fetal alcohol syndrome, which is characterized by retardation, is not prosecuted under such laws, because alcohol, like other possible detriments to a healthy baby, is legal."[37] Recent studies have shown that the impairment of fetuses from alcohol use is far worse than that resulting from cocaine, and that impairment previously attributed to cocaine use was the result of alcohol ingestion.[38]

Drug Testing of High School Students.

In two cases, the Supreme Court has upheld the mandatory testing of all high school students who are involved in athletics and extracurricular activities. In the first case, **Vernonia School District 47J v. Acton** (1995), the Court upheld a policy of mandatory drug testing of all students involved in interscholastic athletic programs. As in *Skinner* (1989) and *Von Raab* (1989), the Court upheld intrusions on Fourth Amendment privacy by searches conducted without a warrant or any level of individualized suspicion. *Vernonia* went beyond *T.L.O.,* in which the search of a student's belongings was based on individualized suspicion of wrongdoing and a violation of a school rule.

Justice Scalia's majority opinion gave several reasons for finding that the blanket searches, not based on individual suspicion, were reasonable:

- Drug use had become evident in the school system and was believed to be widespread. The school district was concerned, among other things, that student athletes using drugs were prone to injury.
- Urine testing constitutes a Fourth Amendment search.
- The actual privacy interests of student athletes, however, are "negligible." Public schools have "custodial and tutelary responsibility for children"; students are subject to physical examinations and vaccinations for health purposes; and "school sports are not for the bashful," as the athletes bathe in communal showers.
- The intrusion is limited. The school personnel who collect the urine samples do not directly observe the function; all student athletes are subject to testing; laboratories reveal only the presence of illicit drugs and not other health information; the results are known only by a limited group of school personnel; and results are not turned over to police.
- The state's interest is very important because drug use is especially harmful to youngsters.

As a result, the district need not base its testing on individualized suspicion. The state is not required to select the "least intrusive" method of search; it can balance the practicalities and select this method. The Court noted that focusing on "troublesome" students for testing could lead to arbitrary testing decisions.

Justice Ginsburg, concurring, noted that the decision does not determine whether routine testing of all public school students in a school or a district, not just those enrolled in interscholastic athletics, is allowable.

A spirited dissent in *Vernonia* was written by Justice O'Connor, joined by Justices Stevens and Souter. She focused on the lack of individualized suspicion. The Court's decision means that millions of student athletes, the "overwhelming majority" who have given school officials "no reason whatsoever to suspect they use drugs at school, are open to an intrusive bodily search." The Framers of the Constitution were concerned with general searches as well as with general warrants. "[M]ass, suspicionless searches" are unreasonable in the criminal law enforcement context, and each "special needs" case that dispenses with individualized suspicion has to advance a "sound reason[] why such a regime would likely be ineffectual under the usual circumstances." Furthermore, her careful review of the facts discounted the costs of not drug testing. The failure to test school athletes simply did not put the lives and safety of many people at risk. Therefore, the district cannot simply decide to discard individualized suspicion. Without specific and compelling reasons to show that eliminating individualized suspicion is reasonable, the requirement is constitutionally necessary.

We cannot know the deeper reasons why two conservative justices split in this case. I speculate that the *Vernonia* opinions offer glimpses into the justices' constitutional norms, their views of political theory, and even their personal backgrounds. Justice O'Connor gave the following reason for her dissent:

> Searches based on individualized suspicion also afford potential targets considerable control over whether they will, in fact, be searched because a person can avoid such a search by not acting in an objectively suspicious way. And given that the surest way to avoid acting suspiciously is to avoid the underlying wrongdoing, the costs of such a regime, one would think, are minimal. (*Vernonia School District 47J v. Acton,* 1995)

This logical, deterrence-based argument connects the Fourth Amendment's individualized suspicion requirement to a political philosophy of individualism. The Constitution balances public safety against individual liberty. The Framers have commanded later generations of Americans to take risks in regard to public safety by trusting its citizens to make their own personal decisions to obey the law. Perhaps this strong leaning toward individualism can be explained, in part, by Justice O'Connor's upbringing. She "spent her early years on the Lazy B ranch doing the chores expected of a child growing up on a ranch—driving tractors, fixing fences, branding cattle. Sandra learned to be independent at an early age."[39]

In contrast, Justice Scalia's majority opinion can be seen as statist. The Vernonia District formulated a school policy that emphasizes public control of all students, under the pain of penalty, rather than individual self-control. Justice Scalia's opinion refers positively to the fact that teachers in private schools "stand *in loco parentis* over the children entrusted to them." This had no direct bearing on a case involving public schools, but it offers insight into his authority-based reasoning in this and later cases. We can speculate that Justice Scalia's comfort with an authoritarian regime of drug testing is not entirely unrelated to the fact that he attended high school at a Catholic military academy.[40] Finally, to return to Justice O'Connor's dissent, she writes: "Blanket searches, because they can involve 'thousands or millions' of searches, 'pose a greater threat to liberty' than do suspicion-based ones, which 'affect one person at a time,'" citing her dissent in *Illinois v. Krull* (1987). As suggested in Chapter 2, this concern by a conservative justice may have been generated by her experience as a state legislator.

In ***Board of Education of Independent School District No. 92 of Pottawatomie County v. Earls*** (2002), the Court, in a five-to-four decision, extended the rule of *Vernonia v. Acton* to high school students engaged in extracurricular activities. The basis for the majority ruling in *Earls* was much weaker than in *Vernonia*. For example, there was no evidence of a widespread drug problem in the Tecumseh, Oklahoma, schools. Justice Thomas's majority opinion suggests that the national problem of teen drug use had grown worse since 1995. As for Tecumseh, the rural school district's basis for concern was the testimony of two teachers that a student once appeared to be under the influence of drugs and another was overheard talking about drugs, marijuana cigarettes detected by a drug dog near the school's parking lot, and that "[p]olice officers once found drugs or drug paraphernalia in a car driven by a Future Farmers of America member" (*Earles*, 2002).

In *Vernonia,* as Justice Ginsburg's dissent (joined by Justices Stevens, O'Connor, and Souter) pointed out, there were two good reasons for the decision—that drug use could be physically harmful for athletes and that athletes were leaders of an aggressive drug cult. Neither reason applies to all extracurricular activities. It borders on the comical to be concerned about potential injury to band members lifting heavy instruments, Future Farmers guiding livestock, and Future Homemakers of America using sharp cutlery. It appears, then, that the majority based the special needs determination allowing drug testing of all students engaged in extracurricular activity on a generalized concern about drug use among teens. In support of the decision, Justice Thomas noted that "the test results are not turned over to any law enforcement authority" (*Earls,* 2002). The majority characterized the urine collection and testing as "minimally intrusive" and concluded that "the invasion of students' privacy is not significant" (*Earls,* 2002).

The dissent noted that although extracurricular activities are nominally voluntary, a large proportion of students engage in them. "Participation in such activities is a key component of school life, essential in reality for students applying to college, and, for all participants, a significant contributor to the breadth and quality of the educational experience" (*Earls,* 2002, Ginsburg, J., dissenting). Ironically, a cited study indicated that students enrolled in extracurricular activities are less likely to develop substance abuse problems than their peers. It seems, then, that the majority decision is close to allowing schools to require mandatory drug testing for all students. The dissent viewed the school policy as closer to the symbolic program adopted in *Chandler v. Miller* (1997).

Although *Earls* allows school districts to adopt drug-testing programs, a recent study of school administrators in one suburban district found that the level of support for drug testing was mixed and that the *Earls* case itself did not lead to the adoption of random testing in schools without such policies.[41] Thus the case may have limited practical effect. In this vein, a large study of 76,000 high school students nationwide found that drug use was no different in schools with or without random drug-testing programs. A newspaper article reporting the study noted that "[m]ost schools have shied away from drug testing." and that "only 18 percent of the nation's schools did any kind of screening from 1998 to 2001."[42]

The special needs doctrine has garnered scholarly criticism. Robert Dodson, citing eight critical law review articles, notes that "[c]onsiderable doubt exists over whether the Court should have ever adopted the special needs doctrine."[43] As Justice Marshall noted, there is no textual support for this doctrine, which weakens civil liberties, in the Fourth Amendment. Dodson notes that the "Court has never adequately defined what it means by special need."[44] He proposes that the special needs doctrine be modified to ensure that warrantless searches be allowed only if the program affects the safety of large numbers of people and only if the courts can identify factors that make the policy truly special. He notes that evidence obtained under the special needs doctrine has indeed led to a large number of prosecutions, and he recommends that an exclusionary rule apply to these instances to prevent the perversion of the doctrine into another tool of law enforcement.

LAW IN SOCIETY

RACIAL PROFILING AND CONSTITUTIONAL RIGHTS

Confronting the continuing roles played by race and racism is essential to understanding law enforcement and constitutional rights. The brutal subjugation of blacks during slavery and the legal segregation and lynching of the Jim Crow Era no longer exist. The blatant racism common in America until the 1970s has faded. Nevertheless, more subtle forms of racism continue to influence criminal justice.[45] The use of racial profiling in highway stops in an effort to interdict drugs shows these lingering effects. "The essence of racial profiling is a judgment that the targeted group . . . —usually African

Americans or Hispanics— . . . is more prone to crime in general, or to a particular type of crime, than other racial or ethnic groups"[46] At worst, this stereotyping attributes criminality to all minority group members.

Racial profiling is not primarily a problem of racist white cops harassing minorities for the purposes of social and political repression, although this does happen.[47] Indeed, a 1999 national study of police vehicle stops and searches found "that officers' race does not have a statistically significant influence on the use of coercive actions toward drivers."[48] This suggests that "historic discrimination" has been replaced not by color-free attitudes, but by the complex reality of "contemporary discrimination."[49] Policing now occurs in a social matrix with a substantial black middle class and a substantial black underclass.[50] Increased political participation of African Americans has "not led to equality with whites commensurate to that achieved in civil status."[51] Residential segregation remains high.[52] And closer to our inquiry, "there has been a steady increase in support among white Americans for *principles* of racial equality, but substantially less support for *policies* intended to implement principles of racial equality."[53] These themes mark race relations in all aspects of American life and are reflected in racial profiling.

Racial Profiling and the "War on Drugs"

Racial and ethnic profiling exists in different contexts and at different places. Profiling for terrorists at airports may involve different considerations than profiling drivers on interstate highways. Profiles of drug couriers may differ from profiles of tax cheaters. And profiling differs from the use of race to identify a suspect in a particular crime.

The profiling of minorities by police can take place in a number of venues—on the streets, in airports and bus stations, while shopping, and even at home.[54] There is good reason, however, to focus on highway stops of minorities by police searching for drugs. For one thing, "traffic stops were the most common reason cited for contact between citizens and police."[55] A national study estimated that 16.8 million drivers were stopped by the police in 2002, and of those, 838,000 resulted in vehicle or driver searches. Studies show that while the proportion of minorities who are stopped only slightly exceeds that of white drivers, the search rates are clearly disproportionate: 3.5 percent of white drivers are searched, compared to 10.2 percent of black drivers and 11.4 percent of Hispanic drivers.[56] This disproportion alone does not indicate that racial profiling has occurred, however.

The aggressive stopping and searching of drivers are, however, a result of the so-called "war on drugs." In the 1980s, the Drug Enforcement Administration "initiated a program named Operation Pipeline, a nationwide highway interdiction program that focuses on private motor vehicles." The DEA trained local officers around the country to look

for telltale factors that might identify a car carrying drugs. Operation Pipeline was "an 'intensified enforcement' program to find illegal drugs by generating a very high volume of legal traffic enforcement stops to screen for criminal activity, which may include drug trafficking."[57] It created the impetus for more aggressive highway stops and searches in an apparently failed attempt to end the problem of drug use and addiction.

A 1999 national statistical study of drivers confirmed the disparities that occur as a consequence of these traffic stops. "[C]ontrolling for other relevant extralegal and legal factors, the odds of *citation*, *search*, *arrest*, and *use of force* for black drivers are 1.5, 1.5, 1.8, and 2.1 times higher, respectively, than for white drivers."[58]

An argument can be made that African Americans and Hispanics are stopped and searched at higher rates not because of race but because of other factors not listed in the data. This is countered, first, by the virtually complete police discretion to stop cars:

> [T]he police may, if they want, stop just about any car that is driving down the highway. The laws regulating driving are so elaborate, so detailed, and so unrealistic that virtually every driver violates one or another almost all the time—or at least there is probable cause to believe she might be, which is all that's required to justify a stop. [Studies] confirm what everybody knows: almost all cars on interstate highways speed. But even the rare driver who doesn't speed may be stopped if an officer has probable cause to believe that he has a burned-out license-plate light, an obscured tag or rear-view mirror, a cracked windshield, misaligned headlights, or is not wearing a seat belt. As one California Highway Patrol Officer put it: "The vehicle code gives me fifteen hundred reasons to pull you over." [59]

Next, the Supreme Court has "enabled" the use of racial profiling through its automobile rulings. A narcotics officer is authorized to stop a car for any traffic violation, no matter how trivial, when the real reason is to search for drugs, even if the police used race as the only reason or one of several reasons for the stop.[60] Once a motor vehicle is stopped, the police have complete control over whether the driver and passengers should exit, allowing further inspection for drugs.[61] Although police are authorized to stop a car only on probable cause or reasonable suspicion of a crime or traffic violation, reasonable suspicion can be based on entirely innocent factors.[62] Even if an officer has no right to search a stopped automobile, the officer can ask for consent without informing the driver of his or her right to refuse.[63] Professor Tracey Maclin concludes that a "huge gap exists between the law as theory and the law that gets applied to black males on the street,"[64] but it may be the case that the Supreme Court justices who created the permissive automobile search rules when the "war on drugs" was a major domestic policy understood how the rules would be applied.

The data support the link among lenient Supreme Court rulings, the proactive highway stops for drugs, and open-ended police discretion to create a foundation for suspecting racial profiling. Thus the national study of police stops found that

> [o]f the drivers who were stopped by police, officers asked 2.9% if they could search their person and/or their vehicle. Of these 2.9% of drivers, nearly all (97.7%) gave consent to be searched. Officers' requests to search, however, differed significantly by drivers' race-ethnicity. Officers asked for consent to search 2.5% of white drivers, compared to 3.9% of black drivers, 4.1% of Hispanic drivers, and 3.9% of drivers of other races. . . . Contraband was discovered on 12.5% of those who gave consent to be searched.[65]

Further, whites were more likely than minorities to be stopped for speeding (52 percent compared to 41 percent), while minorities (40 percent) were more likely than whites (31 percent) to be stopped for other traffic offenses or for vehicle defects. Yet drivers who were stopped for reasons other than speeding "were significantly more likely to be searched, arrested, and have force used against them. . . . Note, however, that it is unknown if police are inappropriately stopping minorities for minor offenses. It is possible that racial and ethnic minorities, who are overrepresented in low-income groups, may be more likely to drive vehicles with equipment violations."[66] The data, to this point, only suggest that minority drivers stopped on the highway are targeted because of their race or ethnicity. This point will be pursued below.

The Discovery of Racial Profiling

In the 1990s, racial profiling was well known to minorities and was half-jokingly referred to as DWB—driving while black—in the African American community.[67] Racial profiling became a major political issue only after 1998, and the DWB "joke," along with general knowledge of racial profiling, has since become mainstream.[68] Up to that time, the evidence for racial profiling was largely anecdotal. It is indicative of the socioeconomic divide among African Americans that many, if not most, of the anecdotes related to upper- and middle-class blacks being stopped and even harassed.

"It has happened to actors Wesley Snipes, Will Smith, Blair Underwood, and LeVar Burton. It has also happened to football player Marcus Allen, and Olympic athletes Al Joyner and Edwin Moses."[69] The late Johnnie Cochran, lead attorney in the O. J. Simpson murder trial, was stopped by police while driving with his children when he was a Los Angeles assistant district attorney;

police released him quickly when they realized that "they had made what could be a career-ending mistake."[70] Similar stories are documented about African American and Hispanic judges and lawyers in New Jersey, Michigan, and Texas.[71] Prominent black writers experienced racial profiling.[72] A black, Los Angeles psychologist took to leaving his work identification badge on during his drive home from work to show police that he was a professional and not a criminal.[73] A former police officer, an African American, was stopped by Long Beach, California, police officers while driving, and during questioning he was pushed through a plate glass window. He was documenting police discrimination, and the incident was filmed by NBC News.[74] The stories can be multiplied.[75]

Professor R. Richard Banks has noted the middle-class slant of the anecdotal evidence of racial profiling:

> The media and civil rights groups have featured those victims of racial profiling and police mistreatment who are not only innocent, but also respectable and middle class: the Harvard-educated lawyer driving home from a relative's funeral who was detained on the highway in the freezing rain, the military officer made to sit handcuffed in the police car while his young son watched, the four young men on their way to a college basketball tryout who were stopped by police officers and nearly fatally wounded, without any evidence of wrongdoing. Commentators have highlighted these sorts of sympathetic plaintiffs.[76]

These class-based anecdotes may reflect an underlying reality of the "increasing polarization of the black population into middle-class and disadvantaged segments."[77] A national survey by Ronald Weitzer and Steven Tuch based on a Gallup poll found that "better educated African Americans are more likely than the less educated to disapprove of profiling, to view it as a pervasive practice, and to say that they have personally experienced it."[78] This may reflect a greater media awareness of these respondents, the greater likelihood that middle-class minorities would be driving in mixed or "white" neighborhoods, and the stereotyping of police who appraise the symbols of success differently for whites and for minorities.[79]

The anecdotes provided moving evidence of the harm and resentments inflicted by racial profiling but did not prove that the traffic stops were statistically disproportionate, because other innocent minority drivers had never been stopped in pretextual drug searches.[80] In the late 1990s, at least three empirical studies found such evidence (which has since been confirmed by the national surveys referred to earlier). Studies of stops on the New Jersey Turnpike and I–95 in Maryland by state troopers were conducted by Dr. John Lamberth of Temple University, who was given access to official data as a result of lawsuits brought by stopped drivers against the state police agencies. Also, a study of four Ohio cities by law professor David Harris provided statistical evidence to show that blacks and Hispanics were stopped in far greater numbers than whites in comparable situations.[81]

Lamberth and colleagues developed a baseline of the proportion of drivers by race by direct observation of forty-two thousand cars on the New Jersey Turnpike and compared these figures to police records of stops, tickets, and arrests on the same stretch of road. They found that the speeding rates of black and white drivers were similar and that while blacks were 13.5 percent of all drivers, they were 35 percent of all drivers stopped and 73.2 percent of all drivers arrested. Lamberth concluded that the odds of these results occurring by chance was "substantially less than one in one billion" and that "it would appear that the race of the occupants and/or drivers of the cars is a decisive factor" for stops and arrests.[82]

Similar findings surfaced in the Maryland I–95 study, where blacks constituted 17.5 percent of the population violating the traffic code but more than 72 percent of those stopped and searched. "The disparity between 17.5 percent black and 72 percent stopped includes 34.6 standard deviations. Such statistical significance, Lamberth said, 'is literally off the charts.'" He concluded that "[w]hile no one can know the motivation of each individual trooper in conducting a traffic stop, the statistics presented herein, . . . show without question a racially discriminatory impact on blacks . . . from state police behavior along I–95. The disparities are sufficiently great that taken as a whole, they are consistent and strongly support the assertion that the state police targeted the community of black motorists for stop, detention, and investigation."[83]

The Political Reaction to Racial Profiling

In a formal sense, the political campaign against racial profiling has been a success. In 2000, a rally in Washington, D.C., drew tens of thousands of demonstrators, and national news coverage focused on the issue of racial profiling.[84] A federal anti-racial profiling bill passed the House of Representatives but died in the Senate due to law enforcement opposition.[85] Despite this setback, by 2004, twenty-nine states had passed laws against racial profiling, although some statutes are limited.[86] "As a result of the campaign against racial profiling, law enforcement agencies and government officials now publicly disavow the practice. Numerous jurisdictions have prohibited it, as has the Bush administration for federal law enforcement agencies."[87] By 2004, "[n]ew reporting requirements and data collection efforts by over four hundred law enforcement agencies across the country—including entire states such as Maryland, Missouri, and Washington—are producing a continuous flow of new evidence on highway police searches"[88]

Public opinion supports these laws and monitoring efforts. Weitzer and Tuch's national survey found widespread disapproval of racial profiling, although the results indicated the different experiences of white and black respondents: 94 percent of African American respondents disapproved, compared to 84 percent of white respondents. While 82 percent of black respondents thought that racial profiling was widespread, 60 percent of white respondents thought so. And as for personal experience, 40 percent of black respondents felt they had been stopped by police because of their race, while only 5 percent of white respondents felt that way.[89]

Despite the laws, the monitoring requirements, and the broad disapproval of racial profiling, the evidence is that minorities continue to be stopped and searched at disproportionate rates as drug enforcement continues.[90] What is going on? A major intellectual debate is now under way. Empirical studies and legal analyses by "[e]conomists, civil liberties advocates, legal and constitutional scholars, political scientists, lawyers, and judges . . . [are] reaching, in many cases, quite opposite conclusions about racial profiling."[91]

Is Racial Profiling a Rational Policy?

An influential 2001 study of racial profiling data by economists concluded that the racial disproportions in stops and searches in the Maryland I–95 study did not reflect discrimination against blacks but rather "a bias against white motorists."[92] They came to this conclusion by subjecting "hit rates"—the percentage of searches resulting in drug confiscations—to econometric analysis. The raw data indicated that the rates of finding any drugs on stopped drivers, by their race or ethnicity, was 34 percent for African Americans, 32 percent for whites, and 11 percent for Hispanic drivers. Furthermore, when looking not at any amount, but at large ("felony") quantities of drugs, the hit rates are 13 percent for African Americans, 3 percent for whites, and 6 percent for Hispanic drivers.[93] The study concluded that "the probabilities of being found with drugs in any amount are equal across African Americans and whites which is consistent with maximizing behavior by police who are not racially prejudiced." This shows that police "are trying to maximize the number of successful searches." On the other hand, the smaller percentage of drug finds among Hispanics "suggests that police may be biased against Hispanics."[94] Other hit rates produce different conclusions. Thus a study of Missouri drivers in which hit rates for drugs were higher for whites than for African Americans or Hispanics concluded that "the data are consistent with racial prejudice rather than statistical discrimination."[95]

The economists have challenged the idea that the strong racial disproportion of searches of stopped drivers is automatically unconstitutional or improper racial profiling. This challenge has generated an interesting debate that widens our thinking about the purposes and context of racial profiling on the highways. The most complete response has been published by University of Chicago law professor Bernard Harcourt.[96]

Harcourt moves the debate beyond racial profiling to challenge the value of criminal profiling as an effective crime-fighting tool. He argues that several factors must be considered before concluding that racial (or criminal) profiling is worthwhile. First, we must go beyond hit rates as a measure of success and ask whether the profiling reduces the amount of profiled crime. Next, we must consider whether profiling has a ratchet effect, by which the more police focus on minorities the greater the conviction rates of minorities above that of a comparable group of whites. Others call this effect a "racial tax."[97] An additional factor to consider is whether police resources are allocated efficiently. Finally, the costs of racial profiling on innocent motorists and on the minority community has to be taken into account.

Underlying much of Harcourt's analysis is his use of the economics term *elasticities* to indicate that neither offending rates nor law enforcement practices remain static. Over time, the proportion of drivers who carry drugs may change. If it becomes known, for example, that state troopers disproportionately stop and search minorities, over time fewer minorities and more whites will carry drugs on that stretch of road. These elasticities result from the deterrent and incapacitation effects of law enforcement on the highway. If troopers continue to target minorities because they continue to get "hits," this will ratchet up the proportion of guilty blacks subjected to stops compared to guilty whites who carry drugs but are not stopped and searched. Not only is this an inefficient enforcement strategy, but it inflicts real harm on the vast majority of innocent minority drivers who are stopped.

If this scenario is the case, the "narrow efficiency" of police officers in targeting minority drivers, who may have higher rates of carrying felony quantities of drugs, may have the ironic effect of increasing the overall amount of drugs being transported on the highway because there are more white drivers. Harcourt establishes this effect by employing econometric analysis. The narrow efficiency of officers (who do not necessarily harbor any malice toward minorities but still believe that racial profiling is good police work) does not answer "the key question of racial profiling, namely whether it is racist. If targeting minority motorists increases long-term offending on the highways or the overall costs to society, then it is in effect racially prejudiced. It may be inadvertent and mistaken, but it is effectively racist because it uses a racial category without any benefit to society."[98]

Harcourt notes that the data are inadequate to make firm statements about the comparative offending elasticities of white and minority populations. National self-report survey data suggest that drug use is about the same among Hispanics, whites, and African Americans, although medical data imply higher use among minorities.[99] Nevertheless, summarizing all

of his analysis, he concludes that making conservative assumptions about a lower relative elasticity of offending among minorities and "slightly higher natural total offending rates among minority motorists—it is fair to infer that racial profiling on the highways may *increase* the total number of persons transporting drug contraband on the roads."[100] Also, given the fact that 85 percent of the hits were for trace or personal amounts of drugs, it is fanciful to think that highway interdiction seriously impedes the flow of drugs.

Next, given that police are disproportionately searching minority motorists, it is likely that police are more likely to base stops and searches of whites on neutral and crime-related factors (e.g., luxury vehicle, third-party vehicle, late-model cars with tinted windows, bumper stickers). This in turn produces equal or lower hit rates for minority drivers that may mask higher offending by "comparably situated minority motorists," undermining "any reliable conclusion as to the narrow efficiency of highway searches."[101] This means that police resources are inefficiently allocated.

Finally, Harcourt concludes that "[r]acial profiling on the highways likely has a significant ratchet effect on the profiled population . . . that has a significant cost to minority families and communities."[102] In addition, racial profiling imposes real costs on innocent minority drivers who are stopped and has a negative effect on the general public (white and minority) vis-à-vis law enforcement.

What are the implications of Harcourt's analysis for the law? Under current Fourth Amendment doctrines, as shown above, the tactics used by police are constitutional. Of course, simply because a policy is constitutional does not mean that it is wise. Harcourt suggests that the kind of economic analysis he undertakes could be used to challenge (and to defend) racial profiling under the Equal Protection Clause, where the use of race is a suspect category that can be overcome if the government can show a compelling state interest, such as reducing crime. No court has yet received such a challenge, but "in the jurisdictions where the new [racial profiling] data reveal disparities, a reviewing court should find the statistical evidence of racial profiling on the highways to be sufficient evidence of unconstitutional police practices."[103]

The Costs of Racial Profiling

As noted earlier, the African American community has become increasing polarized into middle-class and disadvantaged segments. Disadvantaged minorities commit a disproportionate number of serious "street felonies," resulting in much higher rates of conviction and imprisonment by race. There is a good case to be made that these rates are in part a result of social inequities that are maintained and exacerbated by the continuation of subtle racism. Nevertheless, careful studies of the modern criminal justice system, from the point of investigation and arrest, do not find that racism plays a significant role in enforcing laws against murder, robbery, and the like.[104]

To the contrary, there is strong evidence that since the mid-1980s, the expanded and intensive use of discretionary police power in enforcing ever more harsh drug laws has selectively targeted minorities, increasing their proportion in the U.S. penal population. One major consequence has been to severely depress the voting power of minorities in their home communities while increasing the electoral base in rural and predominantly white electoral districts where prisons are located but where prisoners do not vote.[105]

One lesson is that the issue of racial profiling cannot be rationally discussed or dealt with without addressing the larger issue of the "war on drugs" and the overpenalization that characterizes American culture. The other lesson is that the way in which police overgeneralize and see most African Americans as criminals has a real negative effect on the "roughly 97.9 percent of the national population of blacks [who] in any given year will not be arrested for committing a crime"[106] Studies by social psychologists Tom Tyler and Cheryl Wakslak show that people believe that racial profiling exists, whether or not they believe they have personally been profiled, and the stronger the belief that racial profiling exists, the lower the support for and belief in the legitimacy of the police, especially for minorities.[107]

This coincides with the conclusions of Weitzer and Tuch that "[s]tops by police officers can have lasting, adverse effects on citizens, especially when the stop appears to be motivated by race."[108]

In conclusion, racial profiling was a byproduct of a misguided national law enforcement strategy that had no impact on illicit drug use or sales. It is supported by lingering racial stereotypes rather than the racial prejudice of individual officers. On its face it seems to be rational to the police, but on closer examination it promotes inefficient and counterproductive law enforcement policies. Even so, police may continue to support profiling because occasional large drug busts are seen as good police work and may result in the forfeiture of the cars carrying the drugs. The ratcheting effect imposes extra costs on black and Hispanic underclass communities, while racial profiling alienates middle-class minorities from the police. Racial profiling makes a substantial proportion of the citizenry suspicious of police and acts counter to the community policing ethic. The Supreme Court has helped to encourage racial profiling in its rulings. Current statutes are not likely to stop the disproportionate stops of minorities on the highways, but data-collection efforts, along with better analysis, may convince police and policymakers that the costs of the policy outweigh any benefits.

SUMMARY

Warrantless searches are routine and of enormous practical importance to police work, despite the Supreme Court's preference for a search warrant. Each type of warrantless search is based on a unique rationale. Every warrantless search must meet the minimum constitutional requirement for reasonableness. Exigency exceptions to the warrant requirement are lawful only if police have probable cause to believe that contraband is present; they include hot pursuit home entries, the automobile exception, search incident to arrest, and miscellaneous exigencies that impinge on Fourth Amendment interests. They are compatible with the warrant-preference construction of the Fourth Amendment.

Hot pursuit occurs when a dangerous criminal suspect is being chased by police and is seen entering a premises that is cloaked with Fourth Amendment protection. An exigency exists that allows the police to enter without a warrant. A constitutional hot pursuit entry must be accompanied by probable cause, may be based on hearsay, may occur a few minutes after the suspect has entered the premises, may begin on private property outside the premises, authorizes the police to search the entire premises to find the suspect, and is limited to chases involving suspects of serious crimes.

Automobile searches constitute another exception to the search warrant requirement based on the exigency of

mobility and on the lesser expectation of privacy accorded to people in cars. In addition to the automobile exigency exception, an automobile search involves several other warrantless search rules, including consent, plain view, stop and frisk, and pretext searches. The Supreme Court appears to allow warrantless automobile searches even when cars are immobilized and the suspect is in custody, as long as the car is potentially mobile. Any operative motor vehicle is an automobile for purposes of the exception, even if it is also a person's home. The automobile exception applies even if police have time to obtain a warrant. A car subject to forfeiture may be seized from a public area without warrant.

A "container"—whether a footlocker or a closed paper bag—is an effect and is thus protected by Fourth Amendment privacy rights. If police arrest a person and have probable cause to believe there is contraband in a closed container, a warrant must be obtained to open the container (unless it is subject to a search incident to arrest). However, after some case development, the Supreme Court has held that when police have probable cause to believe that contraband is located in a automobile, they may, under the automobile exception, open any closed container located in the car that could logically hold the contraband

(*United States v. Ross,* 1982). When an officer has probable cause to believe that a specific container located in a car contains contraband, the officer may, upon lawfully stopping the car and gaining access to its interior, open the container (*California v. Acevedo,* 1991). In a later case, *Ross* was extended to passengers: Police officers with probable cause to search a car may inspect passengers' belongings found in the car if they are capable of concealing the object of the search (*Wyoming v. Houghton,* 1999).

An automobile inventory search is a regulatory search based on a routine policy to make an inventory of items contained in all cars that are impounded by police for traffic or other violations. No probable cause is required. The main purposes for making an inventory are to protect the owner's property against theft or careless handling by the police, to protect the police against false claims or disputes over lost or stolen property, and to protect the police from potential danger. Inventory searches must be made routinely and under proper standards and procedures that limit the discretion of the officer. Officers conducting inventory searches may look into an unlocked glove compartment, a locked trunk, the space under the front seat and under the dashboard, and the opening of air vents under the dashboard as well as the passenger compartment. Any contraband found in the course of an inventory search is seized in plain view and is admissible in evidence.

A border search is based on a nation's sovereign power to control entry and egress of people and goods; it requires no warrant or probable cause. In addition to a search at the actual border, this area of law covers roving patrols and fixed checkpoints. In general, there is a lesser expectation of privacy at the border, but both aliens and citizens retain some Fourth Amendment protections. At the border, or its functional equivalent, a person may be detained and searched at random, but the search must be reasonable. Reasonable suspicion must exist before border agents may subject a person to a body-cavity search. Border agents operating fixed checkpoints or roving patrols must have probable cause to search parties who have been stopped under reasonable suspicion by roving patrols or under no suspicion at fixed checkpoints. Reasonable suspicion of contraband

is required before international mail can be searched. Because of the well-established rules for ships, the complex nature of ships' documents, and the special difficulties of stopping seagoing vessels, government agents may stop and board vessels for document inspections without warrants or reasonable suspicion.

Searches by government employees infringe on Fourth Amendment interests but may be allowed without a warrant or probable cause if they are conducted for "special needs beyond the normal need for law enforcement." This has been applied to a public school administrator searching the bag of a student who is reasonably suspected of violating a school no-smoking rule; the search of the office of a psychiatrist hired by a state hospital and suspected of violating rules; the warrantless search of the home of a probationer for violating a condition of probation (no reasonable suspicion required); and a police inspection of automobile junk shops without a warrant under a regulatory law.

An administrative search warrant may be forgone for searches of pervasively regulated industries (such as gun and liquor dealers) or safety inspections of mines. OSHA safety inspections require warrants.

Firefighters who enter a premises to extinguish a fire intrude on an expectation of privacy but may do so because the fire creates an exigency. They may stay after the fire is extinguished to investigate the cause of the blaze. If the firefighters leave the site of a fire and the owner retains an expectation of privacy, they must obtain an administrative warrant before returning to determine the cause and origin of a recent fire and must obtain a criminal search warrant if they are suspicious of arson.

Drug testing by government agencies intrudes on a reasonable expectation of privacy but may be upheld if special needs beyond the normal need for law enforcement make it reasonable. The Supreme Court has upheld the drug testing of railway workers after a crash without individualized suspicion, the drug testing of Customs Service officers who are in drug enforcement positions or who carry firearms, and the testing of high school varsity athletes. The Court found that the required testing of candidates for state office without particularized suspicion did not meet the criteria of special needs.

LEGAL PUZZLES

How Have Courts Decided These Cases?

Hot Pursuit; Gravity of the Offense

5–1. A witness at the scene of an overturned car told police that the driver was a woman, that her breath smelled of alcohol, and that she was driven away by a man in another vehicle. An open bottle of beer, containing a small amount of

alcohol, was found outside the overturned vehicle, and five empty bottles of beer were inside the vehicle. More than two hours later, after 11 P.M., police came to the apartment of Tanya Hopkins, a cousin of Sheila Lovig, the driver. Lovig stayed there overnight an average of three nights a week. The police heard two women talking inside the apartment. Hopkins at first refused to let the police enter and said Lovig was not there. After a lengthy series of talks at the apartment door, officers were allowed to enter after threatening to charge Hopkins with interfering with an investigation. Lovig was in a locked bedroom and refused to exit until police threatened to force the door down. Lovig was charged with operating a motor vehicle while intoxicated (OWI), second offense, an aggravated misdemeanor punishable by at least seven days of incarceration and a fine of at least $1,500.

Was the warrantless and nonconsensual entry of the police into Hopkins's apartment constitutionally justified by exigent circumstances?

Held. No. The police had probable cause to believe that Lovig operated a vehicle while intoxicated and that she was in the apartment, but Lovig had a reasonable expectation of privacy in the apartment. Unlike the civil offense in *Welsh v. Wisconsin* (1984), first offense OWI is classified as a serious misdemeanor in Iowa; additional OWI convictions can rise to a felony level. A serious misdemeanor OWI offense carries a jail sentence of two days to one year, as well as a substantial fine. Based on this legislative judgment, and the other serious consequences that can be associated with the offense, OWI is a relatively serious crime that can support a warrantless home entry if probable cause and exigent circumstances exist.

The collection of alcohol evidence can be altered or destroyed by a delay in making an arrest. A suspect could ingest more alcohol, skewing the alcohol content higher and corrupting any evidence of prior consumption. Second, the blood alcohol level naturally dissipates over time. The state claimed that, considering the seriousness of the offense, the destruction of evidence resulting from a delay in obtaining a warrant justified the warrantless entry into the apartment.

In this case, however, there was no hot pursuit. In the absence of hot pursuit, the claim of destruction of evidence must be carefully examined. A defendant is permitted to refuse a chemical test, making the claim of evidence destruction illusory. Lovig had been in the apartment for a period of time before police arrived, providing her with several means of destruction of evidence that would still exist even if a warrantless entry was made once police arrived. There was no indication that the police sought a warrant or tried to determine the amount of time it would take to secure a warrant. The circumstances do not support the warrantless entry.

State v. Lovig, 675 N.W.2d 557 (Iowa 2004)

Crime Scene Search

5–2. At 11:48 P.M., a police dispatcher received a 911 call from a home, and a call from a neighbor, indicating that Sharon Phillips had been stabbed and that her estranged husband was seen running away. Officers arrived at the residence about six minutes later. Phillips's body was lying in the doorway. Her throat had been cut. The officers conducted a protective sweep of the house in two minutes and observed blood throughout. No evidence was removed. By that time, emergency personnel had arrived; they pronounced Phillips dead at 12:03 A.M. The police officers secured the crime scene by placing yellow tape around the residence and covering the door so no one could "see in or get in."

A crime scene technician arrived between 12:20 A.M. and 12:31 A.M. to photograph and videotape the scene and to collect evidence. The lead detective arrived at the scene at approximately 1:01 A.M. He, the officers, and the technician again conducted a walk-through, and the technician was instructed to collect blood samples.

An officer arrived at the emergency room at approximately 12:40 A.M. and talked to the defendant, Edwin Phillips, about the incident. The officer did not obtain Phillips's consent to search the house. A warrant was obtained the following day. After the investigation, the defendant was charged with and convicted of first-degree murder.

Did the presence of the police and the crime scene investigator in the house violate Edwin Phillips's Fourth Amendment rights?

Holding available from instructor.

Warrantless Search of a Car

5–3. Sergeant Castleberry, alone on patrol at 11:45 P.M., came upon a sedan and a truck stopped in a pullout in a desolate and frequent crime area, next to each other with their engines running. He approached the sedan's driver's side window. A fifteen-year-old female occupied the driver's seat. She said the car's owner was in the backseat. Through fogged-up windows, Castleberry saw two people in the backseat. He opened the rear driver's side door. The car's owner and driver, Angie Brake, identified herself. Castleberry told Brake that he was concerned for the well-being of a young girl far away from home late at night in a high-crime area.

Castleberry asked Brake for identification. She replied that her identification was in her purse in the front seat of the car. She offered to retrieve it, but the sergeant instructed her not to. Instead, he walked around the rear of the vehicle and opened the front passenger's side door. While reaching for a purse on the front passenger's seat, he noticed next to it a small white bundle that contained cocaine. Up to that point, Castleberry had paid no attention to the truck. He then investigated the occupants of the truck and ultimately arrested Brake.

Did Castleberry violate Brake's Fourth Amendment rights by opening the front car door without consent? Is opening the front door to get identification information about the driver the same as reaching into a car for the limited purpose of viewing the VIN (*New York v. Class*, 1986)?

Holding available from instructor.

Border Search

5–4.   In 1983, Stefan Irving, a school pediatrician, was convicted of attempted sexual abuse of a seven-year-old boy. He was imprisoned and lost his license to practice medicine. In 1996, the federal government initiated a nationwide investigation of individuals suspected of traveling to Mexico for the purpose of engaging in sexual acts with children. Two years later, Irving traveled to Acapulco, Mexico, to visit a guesthouse serving as a place where men from the United States could have sexual relations with Mexican boys. Upon returning to the United States from Mexico through the Dallas-Fort Worth Airport, Irving was stopped, searched, and interviewed by U.S. Customs inspectors at the request of a special agent who was investigating him.

The initial search of Irving's luggage in the "sterile area" of the Dallas-Fort Worth Airport revealed children's books and drawings apparently made by children but nothing incriminating. Nonetheless, the customs agents questioned Irving further. He admitted he was a convicted pedophile but denied having visited the guesthouse, saying he had visited a friend. A second search of Irving's luggage, in a Customs Service office forty yards from the initial inspection, revealed a disposable camera and two 3.5-inch computer diskettes, which the agents said they would need to examine. Irving denied having any child pornography on either the diskettes or the camera and refused to sign a customs form consenting to their seizure. The film Irving was carrying turned out to have pictures of boys taken at the guesthouse. Images of child erotica were found on the diskettes.

Several years later, the information obtained at the border search was used to get a warrant to search Irving's home for evidence of child pornography and violations of traveling outside the United States for the purpose of engaging in sexual acts with children under the age of eighteen.

Was the initial search of Irving's luggage at the airport constitutional? Was the second search of the film and diskettes constitutional?

Holding available from instructor.

Special Needs; Drug Testing

5–5.   A union challenged drug-testing provisions in a collective-bargaining agreement. The program required testing of 15 percent of covered employees, meaning that an individual employee could expect to be tested only once every seven years on average. The urine specimen collector was outside the bathroom in near proximity, and the employee could close and lock the door and have full privacy while urinating. Covered employees included probation or parole officers who had regular unsupervised access to and direct contact with probationers or parolees; noncustodial prison employees who had regular unsupervised access to and direct contact with prisoners (including athletic and program coordinators, chaplains, counselors, therapists, special education teachers, dietitians/nutritionists, and general office assistants); and medical workers in prisons and mental health facilities (including nurses, occupational therapists, psychologists, social workers, psychiatrists, physicians, and dentists). There was no preexisting drug problem among these employees.

Was the drug-testing program justifiable under the special needs doctrine?

Holding available from instructor.

FURTHER READING

Randall Kennedy, *Race, Crime, and the Law* (New York: Pantheon, 1997).

Leonard W. Levy, *A License to Steal: The Forfeiture of Property* (Chapel Hill: University of North Carolina Press, 1996).

James F. Simon, *The Center Holds: The Power Struggle inside the Rehnquist Court* (New York: Simon and Schuster, 1995).

USEFUL WEB SITE

Northeastern University Racial Profiling Data Collection Resource Center

http://www.racialprofilinganalysis.neu.edu

Funded by the U.S. Department of Justice, Bureau of Justice Assistance. Designed as a central clearinghouse for information about current data collection efforts, legislation and model policies, police-community initiatives, and methodological tools to collect and analyze data.

ENDNOTES

1. Charles Whitebread and Christopher Slobogin, *Criminal Procedure: An Analysis of Cases and Concepts,* 4th ed. (New York: Foundation Press, 2000), 216–23.

2. David E. Steinberg, "The Drive toward Warrantless Auto Searches: Suggestions from a Back Seat Driver," *Boston University Law Review* 80, no. 2 (2000): 545–75.

3. Marvin Zalman, "Judges in Their Own Case: A Lockean Analysis of Drug Asset Forfeiture," *Criminal Justice Review* 21, no. 2 (1996): 197–230; and Eric Blumenson and Eva Nilsen, "Policing for Profit: The Drug War's Hidden Economic Agenda," *University of Chicago Law Review* 65 (1998): 35–114.

4. David Harris, "Car Wars: The Fourth Amendment's Death on the Highway," *George Washington Law Review* 66 (1998): 556–91, 560–61.

5. Harris, "Car Wars," 556.

6. David Moran, "The New Fourth Amendment Vehicle Doctrine: Stop and Search Any Car at Any Time," *Villanova Law Review* 47 (2002): 815–38, 835, 837.

7. *United States v. Whitehead,* 849 F.2d 849 (4th Cir. 1988); *United States v. Nigro,* 727 F.2d 100 (6th Cir. 1984); *United States v. Boynes,* 149 F.3d 208 (3rd Cir. 1998); and *United States v. Albers,* 136 F.3d 670 (9th Cir. 1998).

8. Steinberg, "The Drive toward Warrantless Auto Searches," 549.

9. Harris, "Car Wars," 566–67.

10. Whitebread and Slobogin, *Criminal Procedure,* 309.

11. See *Carroll v. United States* (1925); and *United States v. 12 200–Foot Reels of Film* (1973).

12. Robin Wright, "Bin Laden Tie Seen in Border Arrest," *Los Angeles Times,* December 19, 1999.

13. Timothy Egan, "A Nation Challenged: The Convicted Terrorist; Man Caught in 2000 Plot Is Helping Investigators," *New York Times,* September 27, 2001.

14. See William Langewiesche, "Anarchy at Sea," *The Atlantic,* September 2003.

15. Roberto Iraola, "A Primer on Legal Issues Surrounding the Extraterritorial Apprehension of Criminals," *American Journal of Criminal Law* 29 (2001): 1–27, 4.

16. "F.B.I. Plans to Open an Office in Poland," *New York Times,* July 2, 1994; and David Johnston, "Fighting the Mob; The F.B.I. Makes Friends in (of All Places) Moscow," *New York Times,* July 10, 1994, sec. 4; and David Johnston, "Strength Is Seen in a U.S. Export: Law Enforcement," *New York Times,* April 17, 1995.

17. Richard L. Berke, "2 Ex-Mexican Aides Charged in Slaying of U.S. Drug Agent," *New York Times,* February 1, 1990.

18. *Alvarez-Machain v. United States,* 331 F.3d 604 (9th Cir. 2003).

19. *Alvarez-Machain v. United States,* 331 F.3d 604 (9th Cir. 2003). See Michael J. Glennon, "International

Kidnapping: State-Sponsored Abduction: A Comment on *United States v. Alvarez-Machain,*" *American Society of International Law Newsletter* 86 (October 1992): 746.

20. Beth Henderson, "Note and Comment: From Justice to Torture: The Dramatic Evolution of U.S.-Sponsored Renditions," *Temple International and Comparative Law Journal* 20 (2006): 189–218, 189.

21. Andrew Rosenthal, "Noriega Gives Himself up to U.S. Military; Is Flown to Florida to Face Drug Charges," *New York Times,* January 4, 1990.

22. See Robert A. Pape, "Dying to Kill Us," *New York Times,* September 22, 2003 (arguing on the basis of research that the number of suicide bombings is increasing and is due not to religion but to a secular and specific goal to compel liberal democracies to withdraw from territory that terrorists consider their homelands).

23. *United States v. Usama Bin Laden,* 132 F.Supp.2d 168, 184 (grand jury indictment, no multiplicitous charges, privilege against compelled self-incrimination).

24. Henderson, "From Justice to Torture," 189.

25. Dana Priest and Barton Gellman, "U.S. Decries Abuse but Defends Interrogations: 'Stress and Duress' Tactics Used on Terrorism Suspects Held in Secret Overseas Facilities," *Washington Post,* December 26, 2002. See also Jane Mayer, "Outsourcing Torture: The Secret History of America's Extraordinary Rendition Program," *New Yorker,* February 14, 2005.

26. Dana Priest, "CIA's Assurances on Transferred Suspects Doubted; Prisoners Say Countries Break No-Torture Pledges," *Washington Post,* March 17, 2005.

27. Priest and Gellman, "U.S. Decries Abuse."

28. Mayer, "Outsourcing Torture."

29. David Weissbrodt and Amy Bergquist, "Extraordinary Rendition: A Human Rights Analysis," *Harvard Human Rights Journal* 19 (2006): 123–60, 127 (footnotes omitted).

30. Commission of Inquiry into the Actions of Canadian Officials in Relation to Maher Arar, *Report of the Events Relating to Maher Arar* (September 18, 2006), http://www.ararcommission.ca/eng/06.htm (accessed January 16, 2007); and Ian Austen, "Canadians Fault U.S. for Its Role in Torture Case," *New York Times,* September 19, 2006.

31. Henderson, "From Justice to Torture," 198.

32. Henderson, "From Justice to Torture," 201 (footnotes omitted).

33. Henderson, "From Justice to Torture," 217.

34. *Frank v. Maryland* (1959).

35. See Edward Levi, *An Introduction to Legal Reasoning* (Chicago: University of Chicago Press, 1949, 1961).

36. Lynn M. Paltrow, "Pregnant Drug Users, Fetal Persons, and the Threat to *Roe v. Wade,*" *Albany Law Review* 62 (1999): 999–1055, 1002–3.

37. Editorial, "Policing of Pregnancies Won't Protect Children," *New York Times,* August 4, 1996, sec. 4.

38. Linda Carroll, "Alcohol's Toll on Fetuses: Even Worse Than Thought," *New York Times,* November 4, 2002, sec. F.

39. Nancy Maveety, *Justice Sandra Day O'Connor: Strategist on the Supreme Court* (Lanham, Md.: Rowman and Littlefield, 1996), 12–13. See Sandra Day O'Connor and H. Alan Day, *Lazy B: Growing up on a Cattle Ranch in the American Southwest* (New York: Random House, 2002).

40. David A. Schultz and Christopher E. Smith, *The Jurisprudential Vision of Justice Antonin Scalia* (London: Rowman and Littlefield, 1996), xiii.

41. Cynthia Kelly Conlon, "Urineschool: A Study of the Impact of the *Earls* Decisions on High School Random Drug Testing Policies," *Journal of Law and Education* 32 (2003): 297–319.

42. Greg Winter, "Study Finds No Sign That Testing Deters Students' Drug Use," *New York Times,* May 17, 2003.

43. Robert D. Dodson, "Ten Years of Randomized Jurisprudence: Amending the Special Needs Doctrine," *South Carolina Law Review* 51 (2000): 258–89, 278.

44. Dodson, "Ten Years of Randomized Jurisprudence," 284.

45. Randall Kennedy, *Race, Crime, and the Law* (New York: Pantheon, 1997); Michael Tonry, *Malign Neglect-Race, Crime, and Punishment in America* (New York: Oxford University Press, 1995); and David C. Anderson, *Crime and the Politics of Hysteria: How the Willie Horton Story Changed American Justice* (New York: Times Books/Random House, 1995).

46. Samuel R. Gross and Katherine Y. Barnes, "Road Work: Racial Profiling and Drug Interdiction on the Highway," *Michigan Law Review* 101 (2002): 651–754, 654–55.

47. An Ohio lawsuit uncovered a group of Reynoldsburg, Ohio, police officers who identified themselves as a "SNAT" ("special nigger arrest team"). The courts found that this was, at best, "a crude and offensive joke" but, at worst, that these officers "intentionally discriminated against blacks" (*Murphy v. Reynoldsburg,* 1991 WL 150938 [Ohio Court App. 10th App. Dist. Franklin Co. (1991)]) "in an attempt to keep blacks out of the city" (*Murphy v. Reynoldsburg,* 65 Ohio St. 3d 356, 604 N.E.2d 138 [1992]).

48. Robin Shepard Engel and Jennifer M. Calnon, "Examining the Influence of Drivers' Characteristics during Traffic Stops with Police: Results from a National Survey," *Justice Quarterly* 21, no. 1 (2004): 49–90, 78–79.

49. W. J. Wilson, *The Truly Disadvantaged* (Chicago: University of Chicago Press, 1987).

50. G. J. Jaynes and R. M. Williams Jr., *A Common Destiny: Blacks and American Society* (Washington, D.C.: National Academy Press, 1989), 6, 274.

51. Jaynes and Williams, *A Common Destiny,* 258.

52. Jaynes and Williams, *A Common Destiny,* 88–91.

53. Jaynes and Williams, *A Common Destiny,* 117 (emphasis added).

54. Amnesty International, *Threat and Humiliation: Racial Profiling, Domestic Security, and Human Rights in the United States* (New York: Amnesty International, 2004), 3–12.

55. Michael R. Smith and Geoffrey P. Alpert, "Searching for Direction: Courts, Social Science, and the Adjudication of Racial Profiling Claims," *Justice Quarterly* 19, no. 4 (2002): 673–703, 674, n. 1 (quotations omitted).

56. Erica L. Smith and Matthew R. Durose, *Special Report: Characteristics of Drivers Stopped by Police, 2002* (Washington, D.C.: Bureau of Justice Statistics, NCJ 211471, June 2006).

57. Gross and Barnes, "Road Work," 671 (internal quotations omitted); and Engel and Calnon, "Drivers' Characteristics," 50–53.

58. Engel and Calnon, "Drivers' Characteristics," 77 (emphasis added).

59. Gross and Barnes, "Road Work," 670–71 (footnotes omitted).

60. *Whren v. United States* (1996).

61. *Pennsylvania v. Mimms* (1977); and *Maryland v. Wilson* (1997).

62. *Delaware v. Prouse* (1979); *United States v. Arvizu* (2002).

63. *Schneckloth v. Bustamonte* (1973); and *Ohio v. Robinette* (1996).

64. T. Maclin, "'Black and Blue Encounters'—Some Preliminary Thoughts about Fourth Amendment Seizures: Should Race Matter?" *Valparaiso University Law Review* 26 (1991): 243–79, 252.

65. Engel and Calnon, "Drivers' Characteristics," 76.

66. Engel and Calnon, "Drivers' Characteristics," 70, 80.

67. Henry Louis Gates Jr., "Thirteen Ways of Looking at a Black Man," *New Yorker,* October 23, 1995, cited in Kennedy, *Race, Crime, and the Law,* 151–52.

68. John L. Burris (with Catherine Whitney), *Blue vs. Black: Let's End the Conflict between Cops and Minorities* (New York: St. Martin's Press, 1999); and Kenneth Meeks, *Driving While Black: Highways, Shopping Malls, Taxicabs, Sidewalks* (New York: Broadway, 2000).

69. David A. Harris, "The Stories, the Statistics, and the Law: Why 'Driving while Black' Matters," *Minnesota Law Review* 84 (1999): 265–326.

70. K. B. Noble, "A Showman in the Courtroom, for Whom Race Is a Defining Issue," *New York Times,* January 20, 1995.

71. Judge Claude Coleman, cited in Tonry, *Malign Neglect,* 50–51; Judge Dennis Archer, who later became a Michigan Supreme Court justice, mayor of Detroit, and president of both the Michigan and the American Bar Associations, and his son, attorney Dennis Archer Jr.: Robyn Meredith, "Near Detroit, a Familiar Sting in Being a Black Driver," *New York Times,* July 16, 1999; and federal judge Filemon B. Vela: Jim Yardley, "Some Texans Say Border Patrol Singles Out Too Many Blameless Hispanics," *New York Times,* January 26, 2000.

72. Tonry, *Malign Neglect,* 51, describing the experiences of Brent Staples, a *New York Times* editorial board writer, and philosopher Cornel West.

73. A. Wallace and S. Chavez, "Understanding the Riots Six Months Later: Separate Lives/Dealing with Race in L.A.; Can We All Get Along?" *Los Angeles Times,* November 16, 1992.

74. Maclin, "'Black and Blue Encounters,'" 243–79, 254.

75. Amnesty International, *Threat and Humiliation;* and David Rudovsky, "Law Enforcement by Stereotypes and Serendipity: Racial Profiling and Stops and Searches without Cause," *University of Pennsylvania Journal of Constitutional Law* 3 (2001): 296–366, 296–98.

76. R. Richard Banks, "Beyond Profiling: Race, Policing, and the Drug War," *Stanford Law Review* 56 (2003): 571–603, 576–7 (footnotes omitted).

77. Ronald Weitzer and Steven A. Tuch, "Perceptions of Racial Profiling: Race, Class, and Personal Experience," *Criminology* 40, no. 2 (2002): 435–56, 437.

78. Weitzer and Tuch, "Perceptions of Racial Profiling," 450.

79. Weitzer and Tuch, "Perceptions of Racial Profiling," 450–51.

80. Bill Johnson, "The Answer to Driving while Black Is Not More Racial Profiling," *Detroit News,* July 30, 1999.

81. Information about the three studies is taken from Harris, "The Stories."

82. Harris, "The Stories," 279.

83. Harris, "The Stories," 281.

84. Cindy Loose and Chris L. Jenkins, "Rallying to 'Redeem the Dream': Rights' Leaders Target Racial Profiling," *Washington Post,* August 27, 2000.

85. Harris, "The Stories," 319–21.

86. Amnesty International, *Threat and Humiliation,* vii, 28–29.

87. R. Richard Banks, "Beyond Profiling: Race, Policing, and the Drug War," *Stanford Law Review* 56 (2003): 571–603, 574–5 (footnotes omitted).

88. Bernard E. Harcourt, "Rethinking Racial Profiling: A Critique of the Economics, Civil Liberties, and Constitutional Literature, and of Criminal Profiling More Generally," *University of Chicago Law Review* 71 (2004): 1275–1381, 1275 (footnote omitted).

89. Weitzer and Tuch, "Perceptions of Racial Profiling," 441–42.

90. Gross and Barnes, "Road Work," 661.

91. Harcourt, "Rethinking Racial Profiling," 1276.

92. John Knowles, Nicola Persico, and Petra Todd, "Racial Bias in Motor Vehicle Searches: Theory and Evidence," *Journal of Political Economy* 109 (2001): 203–29, 2007.

93. Knowles, Persico, and Todd, "Racial Bias in Motor Vehicle Searches," 222.

94. Knowles, Persico, and Todd, "Racial Bias in Motor Vehicle Searches," 228.

95. Harcourt, "Rethinking Racial Profiling," 1293, citing Rubén Hernández-Murillo and John Knowles, "Racial Profiling or Racist Policing? Testing in Aggregated Data" (working paper, April 18, 2003).

96. Other responses include Gross and Barnes, "Road Work"; Banks, "Beyond Racial Profiling"; and William J. Stuntz, "Local Policing after the Terror," *Yale Law Journal* 111 (2002): 2137–94. Stuntz would allow the limited use of group profiling and seek to control it. Gross and Barnes and Banks conclude that racial profiling, even if the product of police who are not racially prejudiced and who seek to interdict drugs, has virtually no effect on stopping the flow of drugs and inflicts harm on innocent drivers. Gross and Barnes, while not claiming that the data in the Maryland I–95 study are entirely flawed, show that police have manipulated highway stop data to "improve" their success rates.

97. Kennedy, *Race, Crime, and the Law,* 159; and Banks, "Beyond Racial Profiling," 589.

98. Harcourt, "Rethinking Racial Profiling," 1306–07.

99. Harcourt, "Rethinking Racial Profiling," 1361–71.

100. Harcourt, "Rethinking Racial Profiling," 1371 (emphasis added).

101. Harcourt, "Rethinking Racial Profiling," 1372.

102. Harcourt, "Rethinking Racial Profiling," 1372–73.

103. Harcourt, "Rethinking Racial Profiling," 1354.

104. Tonry, *Malign Neglect,* 65–68; and Alfred Blumstein, "On the Racial Disproportionality of United States' Prison Populations," *Journal of Criminal Law and Criminology* 73 (1982): 1259–81.

105. Tonry, *Malign Neglect,* 10–12; Anderson, *Crime and the Politics of Hysteria;* and Jason Belmont Conn, "Note: Felon Disenfranchisement Laws: Partisan Politics in the Legislatures," *Michigan Journal of Race and Law* 10 (2005): 495–539.

106. "Developments in the Law: Race and the Criminal Process," *Harvard Law Review* 101 (1988): 1472–1641, 1508.

107. Tom R. Tyler and Cheryl J. Wakslak, "Profiling and Police Legitimacy: Procedural Justice, Attributions of Motive, and Acceptance of Police Authority," *Criminology* 42, no. 2 (2004): 253–81.

108. Weitzer and Tuch, "Perceptions of Racial Profiling," 452.

JUSTICES OF THE SUPREME COURT

Thoughtful Conservatives: Clark, Harlan II, Stewart, and White

Justices Tom Clark, John Marshall Harlan II, Potter Stewart, and Byron White were appointed by presidents with differing political philosophies (Harry S. Truman, Dwight D. Eisenhower, and John F. Kennedy). Nevertheless, these four justices exhibited several similarities. On criminal procedure issues, all were conservative in that they generally opposed incorporation and tended to find for the prosecution. On the other hand, all were receptive to the civil rights claims of African Americans. Clark, as a key architect of President Truman's anticommunist loyalty oath program, was fiercely opposed to easing the application of these rules. All of these justices were thorough and thoughtful in their review of cases, and each had at times ruled in support of criminal defendants in significant cases.

Among these justices, John Harlan ranks as the most acute legal thinker. Known as a lawyer's justice, he carefully crafted opinions without ambiguity to be applied by practicing lawyers and trial judges. Potter Stewart was the most centrist in criminal procedure matters. He dissented in *Miranda v. Arizona* (1966), but his opinions in such cases as *Chimel v. California* (1969) (reach-and-lunge rule) and *Coolidge v. New Hampshire* (1971) (warrant preference interpretation) were quite liberal. His opinion in *Katz v. United States* (1967) was the keystone in modernizing Fourth Amendment law.

Justice White may have been a surprise; nominated by a liberal president, he quickly joined the conservative wing of the Court on many issues, especially criminal procedure. In this regard, he stands in sharp contrast to Kennedy's other appointee, Arthur Goldberg. Justice White's influence on the Court was enhanced by his lengthy tenure and his practice of at times shifting to the center of the Court so as to occupy the pivotal middle ground.

Collection of the Supreme Court of the United States. Photographer: Harris and Ewing.

Tom C. Clark

Texas, 1899–1977

Democrat

Appointed by Harry S. Truman

Years of Service: 1949–1967

Life and Career.   The son of a Dallas lawyer, Clark served in the U.S. Army during World War I, graduated from the University of Texas Law School, and practiced in his father's law firm from 1922 to 1927. Thereafter, he held appointed posts as civil district attorney and assistant (criminal) district attorney for Dallas. His involvement in politics led to his appointment to the U.S. Justice Department in 1937, where he worked on a variety of issues, including war claims, antitrust, the evacuation of Japanese Americans from the West Coast to camps during World War II, and war frauds. In 1943, he was appointed assistant attorney general and headed the antitrust and the criminal divisions.

He supported Truman for the vice presidential nomination in 1944 and was appointed by Truman as attorney general in 1945. Clark was a vigorous attorney general, instituting 160 antitrust cases, supporting civil rights actions designed to end racial segregation, and playing a key role in developing President Truman's anticommunist loyalty oath program, generated by cold war fears of internal subversion.

In 1967, Justice Clark resigned from the Court as a gesture of paternal love when his son, Ramsey Clark, was appointed by President Lyndon Johnson as attorney general. If he had continued to serve, a conflict of interest would have arisen in every Supreme Court case involving the U.S. government. For the next decade of his life, he actively participated as a judge in the various federal circuits and contributed to numerous programs designed to enhance the quality of the American judiciary.

Contribution to Criminal Procedure.   Justice Clark more often than not voted in favor of the state in cases involving criminal procedure issues. For example, he dissented in *Miranda v. Arizona* (1966). He dissented in a case that held that probable cause could not be based on a person's general reputation (*Beck v. Ohio,* 1964); he dissented in a case that excluded evidence seized from one person pursuant to an illegal arrest of another person (*Wong Sun v. United States,* 1963); and he joined Justice Sherman Minton's decision in *United States v. Rabinowitz* (1950). Nevertheless, he wrote the majority opinion in the breakthrough incorporation decision of *Mapp v. Ohio* (1961), and he was a staunch supporter of fair trials, as seen in his opinions finding constitutional error because of excessive pretrial publicity.

Signature Opinion.   *Mapp v. Ohio* (1961). Why did a justice who was generally conservative on criminal matters support the incorporation of the exclusionary rule? In a revealing interview after retirement, Justice Clark told seminar students that as a young lawyer, he defended his cook's son against a Prohibition charge (possessing liquor) after Dallas police simply entered the accused's room, ripped open a mattress, and gave the bottle of liquor they found to federal agents. Clark was shocked that police could do this. Thus, although as a justice he was loath to curb the legitimate power of police officers, the facts of *Mapp* were excessive. To Justice Clark, the exclusionary rule, applied to the states as well as the federal government, simply made sense, and as he wrote in *Mapp,* "there is no war between the Constitution and common sense."

Assessment.   Clark replaced the staunch liberal Justice Frank Murphy in 1949, tilting the Vinson Court in a more conservative direction. Clark generally joined Justices Stanley Reed, Felix Frankfurter, Robert Jackson, and Harold Burton, although he was somewhat more liberal than Chief Justice Fred Vinson. During the 1950s, he supported the government in antitrust and loyalty cases, where his experiences as attorney general shaped his approaches, thus taking a liberal stance in the first area and a conservative stance in the latter. His positions on First Amendment issues, voting district reapportionment, and racial segregation were in sync with the liberal Warren Court.

Further Reading

Richard Kirkendall, "Tom C. Clark," in Leon Friedman and Fred L. Israel, eds., *The Justices of the United States Supreme Court, 1789–1969*, vol. 4 (New York: Chelsea House, 1969), 2665–95.

John M. Harlan II

New York, 1899–1971
Republican
Appointed by Dwight D. Eisenhower
Years of Service: 1955–1971

Collection of the Supreme Court of the United States. Photographer: Harris and Ewing.

Life and Career.   The grandson of a Supreme Court justice by the same name, Harlan was viewed as a "progressive Republican" when appointed. He was born in Chicago, was educated at private schools, and served briefly in World War I. He received his bachelor's degree from Princeton in 1920, was a Rhodes Scholar at Oxford, and completed his legal studies at New York Law School in 1924. He practiced law in New York with a prestigious Wall Street law firm up until his appointment to the Second Circuit Court of Appeals in early 1954. However, his background also included years of public service. He prosecuted a former U.S. attorney general for corruption when he was an assistant U.S. attorney in the 1920s, acted as a special prosecutor for New York State in a major investigation of municipal graft in the 1930s, directed a critical unit of experts advising the commanding general of the Eighth Air Force on bombing operations in Europe during World War II, and was chief counsel of an organized crime investigation for the state of New York in the early 1950s. After less than a year on the Second Circuit Court of Appeals, he was nominated by President Eisenhower to the Supreme Court.

Contribution to Criminal Procedure.   Justice Harlan opposed incorporation and dissented in *Mapp v. Ohio* (1961) and *Miranda v. Arizona* (1966); he believed the federal government should be held to higher standards of procedural regularity under the Bill of Rights than states under the Fourteenth Amendment. He was generally conservative and voted for the state, but not slavishly so. Thus he concurred on extending the right to counsel to all felony defendants (*Gideon v. Wainwright,* 1963); he concurred in extending the right to counsel to juveniles (*In re Gault,* 1967; *Katz v. United States,* 1967). He dissented in *United States v. White* (1971), arguing that police agents should not be able to wear body mikes without a prior judicial warrant.

Signature Opinion.   *Spinelli v. United States* (1969). Justice Harlan's opinion upheld the two-prong test for determining when the hearsay evidence of a confidential informant can amount to probable cause for a search warrant. He closely examined the facts put forth by the FBI and penetrated the affidavit's veneer of certainty to show that the agency was, in effect, asking for a blank check on its decision. The opinion highlights the vital importance of judicial scrutiny of police affidavit requests to the preservation of Fourth Amendment privacy and liberty.

Assessment.   Justice Harlan developed a close intellectual friendship with Justice Frankfurter; with the latter's resignation in 1962, Harlan took on the mantle of the chief spokesperson for judicial restraint and traditional judicial conservatism. During the entire period of the due process revolution, Justice Harlan wrote the most exhaustive and penetrating dissents against the incorporation doctrine.

Justice Harlan was "a lawyer's judge"—he closely examined cases and often based decisions on fine factual distinctions rather than upon broad generalizations, and his opinions reflected his desire to give lawyers and judges clear guidance in applying the rules of the case. He had a profound respect for judicial precedent and felt that the Court should interfere as little as possible into the political workings of both state and federal governments. His incorporation dissents noted that "the American federal system is itself constitutionally ordained, that it embodies values profoundly making for lasting liberties in this country" (*Pomtar v. Texas,* 1965). He was skeptical about the ability of courts to ensure true liberty by their rulings, believing that liberty "can rise no higher or be made more secure than the spirit of a people to achieve and maintain it." (*Pomtar v. Texas,* 1965) He also believed that federalism encouraged differences between the states and that it was not the role of the Supreme Court to eradicate these differences by applying the Bill of Rights as a steamroller over variations of state procedure.

Further Reading

Tinsley E. Yarbrough, *John Marshall Harlan: Great Dissenter of the Warren Court* (New York: Oxford University Press, 1992).

Collection of the Supreme Court of the United States. Photographer: Harris and Ewing.

Potter Stewart

Ohio, 1915–1985

Republican

Appointed by Dwight D. Eisenhower

Years of Service: 1958–1981

Life and Career.   Born into a politically active Republican family with "a strong tradition of public service," Stewart was educated at the Hotchkiss School, Yale University (where he was a Phi Beta Kappa), and Yale Law School, where he generally supported the New Deal. He served as a deck officer on an oil tanker during World War II, which put him in contact with men of a different background than he would meet at Yale or in corporate law practice. He practiced law in his hometown of Cincinnati from 1946 to 1954. His political activity (he was twice elected to the Cincinnati City Council) and his support of Eisenhower's bid for the Republican presidential nomination in 1952 against Ohio senator Robert Taft led President Eisenhower to name him to the Sixth Circuit Court of Appeals in 1954 at the young age of thirty-nine. His reputation as an excellent judge led to his nomination to the Supreme Court in 1958.

Contribution to Criminal Procedure.   Although known as a middle-of-the-road justice who did not automatically side with either the liberals or the conservatives, Justice Stewart wrote a large number of Fourth Amendment opinions for the Supreme Court that tended to expand defendants' rights. On the liberal, or pro-defendant, side were *Vale v. Louisiana* (1970) (a doorstep arrest does not authorize a general search of a premises) and *Coolidge v. New Hampshire* (1971) (supporting the warrant preference construction of the Fourth Amendment). On the conservative, or pro-prosecution, side, Justice Stewart opposed incorporation, dissented in *Miranda v. Arizona* (1966), and wrote the majority opinion in *Schneckloth v. Bustamonte* (1973), holding that the police need not warn suspects of their Fourth Amendment rights before requesting consent to search.

Justice Stewart had a talent for turning a pithy phrase that encapsulates a rule, and he wrote logical, well-organized opinions. This was seen in his most important Fourth Amendment opinion, *Katz v. United States* (1967), where his emblematic statement—"For the Fourth Amendment protects people, not places"—nicely summed up the major shift in Fourth Amendment jurisprudence from its foundations in property law to its new basis on an expectation of privacy.

Signature Opinion.   *Chimel v. California* (1969). His majority opinion in *Chimel* ended the long zigzag course of opinions on the scope of a search incident to arrest. It confirmed that while officers may reasonably search the area within the immediate control of an arrested suspect to seize weapons and contraband, they may not use the arrest as an excuse to search a premises without a warrant.

Assessment.   Justice Stewart's approach to constitutional law was cautious and restrained. His middle-of-the-road votes made him a "swing justice" in many areas. His judicial philosophy appeared to be that a judge should first defer to legislative and executive branch authority but not hesitate to exercise judicial review in order to maintain essential procedural safeguards and to prevent abuses of power. Justice Stewart favored narrow rulings and preferred that cases be resolved on the specific facts when necessary. He was a lone dissenter in the case that held school prayer to violate the First Amendment, but he voted for free speech in censorship cases. On the death penalty, he held it to be unconstitutional as applied in 1972, but he voted to uphold revised death penalty laws in 1976 that incorporated the element of guided discretion. He decided a very large number of criminal procedure cases. Ultimately, it is not possible to classify Justice Stewart simply as a liberal or conservative or as an activist or passivist judge.

Further Reading

Tinsley E. Yarbrough, "Justice Potter Stewart: Decisional Patterns in Search of Doctrinal Moorings," in Charles M. Lamb and Stephen C. Halpern, eds., *The Burger Court: Political and Judicial Profiles* (Urbana: University of Illinois Press, 1991), 375–406.

Collection of the Supreme Court of the United States. Photographer: Joseph Bailey.

Byron R. White

Colorado, 1917–2002

Democrat

Appointed by John F. Kennedy

Years of Service: 1962–1993

Life and Career.   White's youth was filled with hard work in the beet fields of rural Colorado and on railroad section crews. He was an excellent student and an outstanding athlete in high school and at the University of Colorado, where he was elected to Phi Beta Kappa, graduated first in his class in 1938, and attracted national attention as a star tailback (nicknamed "Whizzer") on Colorado's unbeaten football team. He also won varsity letters in basketball and baseball. Between 1938 and 1942, White spent a year at Oxford University as a Rhodes Scholar (where he met Ambassador Joseph Kennedy's son, John), was the highest paid professional football player in America, and began law school. While serving as a naval intelligence officer in the South Pacific during World War II, White again met John F. Kennedy. He completed his law degree at Yale after the war, clerked for Chief Justice Fred Vinson (1946–1947), and while in Washington, had numerous opportunities to meet with John Kennedy, then a freshman congressman from Massachusetts. In 1947, he returned to Colorado and the private practice of law.

In 1959, White led the Colorado organization on behalf of Kennedy's efforts to gain the Democratic presidential nomination. He was appointed deputy U.S. attorney general in 1961 and won recognition as an able administrator, effectively acting as "chief of staff" of the Justice Department. During the tense days in May 1961, when Attorney General Robert Kennedy dispatched four hundred federal marshals to Alabama to protect the Freedom Riders, White calmly and competently supervised the marshals and deputies. As deputy attorney general, he ably screened candidates for federal judgeships.

Contribution to Criminal Procedure.   Justice White was generally conservative on criminal procedure issues; he dissented strongly in *Escobedo v. Illinois* (1964) and *Miranda v. Arizona* (1966) and was clearly opposed to the incorporation of the Fourth Amendment exclusionary rule. On occasion, he decided in favor of the defendant. In *Duncan v. Louisiana* (1968), however, he effectively ended the *Palko* (1937) approach to fundamental rights, arguing that if a Bill of Rights procedure is fundamental to the American system of justice, it ought to be incorporated.

His pro-government rulings include the late 1980s ruling that a helicopter overflight of a backyard at four hundred feet is not a search; there is no expectation of privacy in abandoned trash; an indicted defendant may waive his right to counsel and be interrogated without his attorney present; and government forfeiture of funds to prevent paying an attorney does not violate the right to counsel. On the other hand, in *Arizona v. Fulminante* (1991), he led a liberal coalition in holding that a confession was coerced and dissenting against a new rule that a coerced confession can be harmless error.

Signature Opinion.   *United States v. Leon* (1984). Justice White's most significant Fourth Amendment opinion held that evidence obtained without probable cause by a police officer relying in good faith on a faulty judicial warrant was admissible. *Leon* was the first clear exception to the *Mapp v. Ohio* (1961) exclusionary rule and a significant victory for conservative justices opposed to the expansion of the rights of criminal suspects. *Leon*'s reasoning relied heavily on a balancing analysis and to some extent on shaky empirical research.

Assessment.   Justice White was generally a middle-of-the-road or swing justice. In the 1960s, he supported governmental authority over individual liberty in cases involving the investigation of communists and other groups. On the other hand, his votes on the civil rights of minorities usually favored integration, school busing, and affirmative action. Justice White has puzzled commentators because of his apparent lack of a clear judicial philosophy. Thus, despite his generally strong support for civil rights and "one man one vote," he ruled inconsistently on occasion. Some inconsistent decisions can be explained by his concern with the specific factual and procedural contours of each case.

Further Reading

Dennis J. Hutchinson, *The Man Who Once Was Whizzer White: A Portrait of Byron R. White* (New York: Free Press, 1998).

CHAPTER OUTLINE

KEY TERMS

actual imprisonment rule
appointed counsel
asset forfeiture
assigned counsel
authorized imprisonment rule
conflict of interest
continuance
counsel

critical stage
deficient performance
formal charge rule
indigent
multiple representation
parallel right
prejudice the case
pro bono publico

pro se defense
public defender
recoupment
retained counsel
self-representation
special circumstances rule
standby counsel
waiver of counsel

It is a fundamental principle of our constitutional scheme that government, like the individual, is bound by the law. We do not subscribe to the totalitarian principle that the Government is the law, or that it may disregard the law even in pursuit of the lawbreaker.

—Justice Abe Fortas, dissenting,
Alderman v. United States, 394 U.S. 165, 202 (1969)

It is during our most challenging and uncertain moments that our Nation's commitment to due process is most severely tested; and it is in those times that we must preserve our commitment at home to the principles for which we fight abroad.

—Justice Sandra Day O'Connor,
Hamdi v. Rumsfeld, 542 U.S. 507, 532 (2004)

A defense lawyer stands next to her criminal client in court. Both face judge and jury while awaiting verdict. The defendant will suffer the penalty for a guilty verdict, but their standing together is a powerful reminder that the attorney is the defendant's surrogate—the lawyer "stands in the defendant's shoes." The attorney owes the client an undivided duty of representation, within the law, marked by "warm zeal." The attorney is cloaked with the attorney-client privilege, which preserves a criminal client's right against self-incrimination. Without adequate representation, a fair trial is impossible.

The link between a fair trial and a competent lawyer was not always so. Attorneys were not permitted in the English common law jury trial from its origins in the Middle Ages until the nineteenth century—criminal defendants defended themselves. Also, except in major treason trials, public prosecutors did not exist. An English criminal trial was a "long argument" between the defendant and a private accuser.[1] English law first allowed a defendant the right to legal representation in treason trials only in 1695. Lawyers began to advise ordinary felony defendants shortly after that date, but by law they were barred from speaking in the trial. This rule was seen as unjust and was at times breached in practice.[2] Nevertheless, it was not until 1836 that English defendants gained the ability to be represented by a paid lawyer in a felony trial.

In contrast to England, colonial America embraced the use of attorneys in criminal trials. John Adams, later the second president of the United States, was hired as a defense lawyer in many criminal cases. In the celebrated Boston Massacre case, Adams, although a member of the pro-liberty party, vigorously defended and won acquittals for the British soldiers who fired in self-defense on a large stone-throwing mob of zealous patriots.[3] Many early state constitutions guaranteed **counsel** in criminal cases.[4] Despite the guarantee of counsel in the federal Bill of Rights and states' bill of rights, most **indigent** defendants represented themselves in those days. Judges ideally took special care to advise such indigent defendants, to ensure that they did not completely ruin their defenses. The right to counsel existed only for those who could afford a lawyer. In death penalty cases, however, judges often ordered lawyers to donate their services free of charge as a professional obligation.

The Constitution's Framers viewed the right to counsel favorably, even if not intending to provide free lawyers for indigent defendants. The Sixth Amendment is the primary source of the right to counsel: "In all criminal prosecutions, the accused shall enjoy the right . . . to have the Assistance of Counsel for his defence."[5] The Sixth Amendment right is limited to criminal prosecutions. In other proceedings, counsel may be guaranteed on the basis of other rights. The due process (Fifth and Fourteenth amendments) fairness concept is the basis for providing counsel in probation revocation hearings, depending on facts and circumstances. The Fourteenth Amendment Equal Protection Clause has been applied by the Supreme Court to guarantee equitable treatment in the trial process by relieving indigent defendants of paying filing fees or the costs of transcripts if they are important for the defense. The Due Process and Equal Protection clauses, combined, guarantee a lawyer for a convicted defendant's first appeal as of right. The right to counsel at a custodial interrogation, a right made famous by the *Miranda* warnings, is based on the Fifth Amendment privilege against self-incrimination. Also, prior to the incorporation of the Sixth Amendment right to counsel into the Due Process Clause in 1963 by *Gideon v. Wainwright,* the Due Process Clause of the Fourteenth Amendment was an important vehicle for guaranteeing the provision of counsel in certain state proceedings.

Before the mid-twentieth century, the Sixth Amendment right to counsel meant that a court or statute could not abolish a defendant's right to be represented in court by a paid, licensed lawyer of his or her choosing. At first, the right did not mean that the state had to pay for a defense lawyer. Until the early twentieth century, it was constitutionally acceptable for a poor person to defend him- or herself without a lawyer in a felony trial, with whatever help the judge was disposed to grant. In complex or death penalty cases, judges might order local lawyers to represent indigent defendants for no charge, ***pro bono publico,*** but the practice was not uniform. The development of the right to counsel in the twentieth century has centered on the practical issue of whether the state has to pay for lawyers for persons who are themselves too poor to pay.

Lawyers play a key role in ensuring fair criminal trials. In the common law trial by jury, the truth is seen to emerge from the clash of evidence provided by prosecution and defense. The trial is a technical and intimidating process. Criminal attorneys are trained in the rapidly changing and intricate substantive criminal law, have to know all the rules of local criminal procedure, must have the rules of evidence at their fingertips, and must have developed the practical skills to bring these rules to life in the conduct of trials. In addition to trial advocacy, an attorney directs pretrial investigations (for evidence of innocence and for such defenses as insanity) and protects the defendant's rights in legally complex pretrial hearings. Motions for bail, discovery, suppression of illegally obtained evidence, change of venue in notorious cases, and the conduct of plea negotiations require experienced attorneys. Plea bargaining, contrary to common belief, is quite adversarial. Attorneys who prepare negotiated cases as if they were going to trial learn strengths and weaknesses of the case and are in a position to back up their negotiating position with a resort to trial if needed. The adversarial nature of American trials pervades the entire adjudication process and makes even routine cases dependent on the abilities of trained, professional advocates. A defendant without a lawyer is at a severe disadvantage.

The benefits of a defense attorney were once available only to those who could afford one. The critical issue that ran through all of the cases that came before the Supreme Court was whether the state had to provide counsel for indigents—those who were too poor to pay for a lawyer.

THE DEVELOPMENT OF THE RIGHT TO COUNSEL TO 1961

The twentieth-century growth of urban populations and bureaucratic, multi-judge courts required that *ad hoc* methods of providing lawyers for indigents be replaced with more formal legal aid and defender systems. Some cities and states began to do this in the early twentieth century. But under the U.S. Constitution, there was no obligation in federal or state criminal trials that the government, which was prosecuting the defendant, had any obligation to ensure a fair trial by providing defense counsel. In 1932, the Supreme Court began to define the right to counsel. Thirty years later, it applied the Sixth Amendment right to the states by incorporating that right into the Fourteenth Amendment Due Process Clause. The constitutional journey began with one of the most celebrated trials in American history, the infamous Scottsboro case. In *Powell v. Alabama* (1932), the Court found that under certain circumstances state courts had to provide criminal defendants with free counsel.

Powell v. Alabama: The Scottsboro Case

Nine African American teens, arrested after a fistfight with several white boys on a freight train rolling through Alabama in 1931, were falsely accused of rape by two white female passengers. The teens were tried for a capital crime in Scottsboro, Alabama. Thus began one of the great trial sagas in American history. It did not end until the last of the defendants was released from prison decades later.[6] The "Scottsboro boys" were tried three times in a climate dripping with racism; they were sentenced to death, gained national notoriety, grew to maturity in prison, and were saved by appeals, stays of execution, and commutations. Twice they saw their cases go before the U.S. Supreme Court.[7]

The first trials were one-day affairs held on successive days. Eight of the teens were sentenced to death. The Alabama Supreme Court affirmed seven of the capital sentences. The U.S. Supreme Court accepted the case and reversed the convictions in November 1932. Justice George Sutherland's majority opinion in *Powell v. Alabama* (1932) held that the defendants' due process rights had been violated.

The issue in *Powell* was whether the defendants' due process rights were violated by the denial of the right to counsel, "with the accustomed incidents of consultation and opportunity of preparation for trial." Prior to 1932, the Supreme Court had not incorporated any of the criminal procedure rights in the Bill of Rights, which included the guarantee of the assistance of counsel. The Supreme Court, however, had ruled less than a decade before that a state prosecution obtained through the pressure of a lynch mob infringed a state defendant's constitutional rights under the Fourteenth Amendment Due Process Clause (*Moore v. Dempsey,* 1923; see Chapter 1). "Mob justice" was not the precise basis of the *Powell* decision, although Justice Sutherland did note that the atmosphere surrounding the trials was one of "tense, hostile and excited public sentiment."

How were the defendants represented in the Scottsboro case? The transcript indicated that lawyers for the defendants examined and cross-examined witnesses and made arguments. On this basis, the Alabama Supreme Court ruled that Ozie Powell and the other youths had been represented by counsel and not denied due process. Why did the U.S. Supreme Court conclude otherwise? Justice Sutherland noted that the defendants, who were young and poor strangers in Scottsboro, were not asked if they had access to lawyers. They were not given much time to contact their families in other states to arrange for counsel:

> It is hardly necessary to say that, the right to counsel being conceded, a defendant should be afforded a fair opportunity to secure counsel of his own choice. Not only was that not done here, but such designation of counsel as was attempted was either so indefinite or so close upon the trial as to amount to a denial of effective and substantial aid in that regard. (*Powell v. Alabama,* 1932)

Indeed, the trial transcript disclosed that in fact none of the lawyers was willing to definitely be a lawyer for a specific defendant. Steven Roddy, a Tennessee lawyer, was asked by the court whether he intended to appear for the defendants. Roddy replied that he was not really hired although he "would like to appear along with counsel that the court might appoint."[8] Ultimately, no single lawyer was appointed for all the defendants, nor was each defendant appointed individual counsel. Instead, the trial judge "appointed all the members of the bar for the purpose of arraigning the defendants" and continued that arrangement for the trial when neither Roddy nor any of the local lawyers would stand up to be *the* attorney of record.[9] The white lawyers were obviously unwilling to vigorously defend poor African American teens and drifters accused of the rape of two white women in the segregated South. In the critical time period before trial, when a lawyer could have organized an investigation into the facts and marshaled legal arguments, no one focused on this task. This lack of resolution and focus clearly offended Justice Sutherland:[10]

> It is not enough to assume that counsel thus precipitated into the case thought there was no defense, and exercised their best judgment in proceeding to trial without preparation. Neither they nor the court could say what a prompt and thoroughgoing investigation might disclose as to the facts. No attempt was made to investigate. No opportunity to do so was given. Defendants were immediately hurried to trial. . . . Under the circumstances disclosed, we hold that defendants were not accorded the right of counsel in any substantial sense. To decide otherwise, would simply be to ignore actualities. (*Powell v. Alabama,* 1932)

Did Justice Sutherland's holding—that the defendants were not accorded the right to counsel in any substantial sense—incorporate the Sixth Amendment? That is, did it directly apply the Sixth Amendment's assistance of counsel right to the state courts in all felony trials? Although his bare words can give that impression, Justice Sutherland based his decision on the Due Process Clause alone. A review of history showed that twelve of the original states established the right to counsel when no such right existed in England, showing its importance. In death penalty cases, some colonies required the appointment of defense counsel, as did Alabama by statute in 1931.

Addressing the incorporation issue, Justice Sutherland noted that *Hurtado v. California* (1884), standing alone, held that the federal courts could not incorporate a Bill of Rights provision into the Fourteenth Amendment Due Process Clause, making it a state requirement. But *Hurtado* did not stand alone. *Chicago, Burlington and Quincy Railroad Co. v. Chicago* (1897) held that the states, as a matter of Fourteenth Amendment due process, had to grant just compensation when the state took private property for public use, even though a Just Compensation Clause existed in the Fifth Amendment. Furthermore, "freedom of speech and of the press are rights protected by the Due Process Clause of the Fourteenth Amendment, although in the First Amendment, Congress is prohibited in specific terms from abridging the right."[11] Therefore, a right found in the Bill of Rights as a proscription on the federal government could also exist as a **parallel right,** within the scope of due process. This "parallel right" approach is clearly not the "total incorporation" under the Privileges or Immunities Clause (desired by Justices John Harlan I and Hugo Black), nor is it the modern approach of "selective incorporation." Yet it seems clear that Justice Sutherland was influenced by the "fundamental rights" reasoning of *Twining v. New Jersey* (1908). (See Chapter 1.)

Although Justice Sutherland and the Court did not cleanly incorporate the Sixth Amendment right to counsel, his opinion came rather close to calling it a fundamental right. The philosopher Hadley Arkes suggests that Justice Sutherland was concerned with basic principles: "To begin at the root, the purpose of a trial was to do justice, to punish the guilty and vindicate the innocent. The central task was to make reasoned discriminations between the innocent and the guilty and arrive at verdicts that were substantially just."[12] At minimum, due process requires notice, a fair hearing, and a competent tribunal. Justice Sutherland's classic passage explains the vital importance of a fully committed defense attorney to fulfilling the ideal of a fair trial:

> What, then, does a hearing include? Historically and in practice, in our own country at least, it has always included the right to the aid of counsel when desired and provided by the party asserting the right. The right to be heard would be, in many cases, of little avail if it did not comprehend the right to be heard by counsel. Even the intelligent and educated layman has small and sometimes no skill in the science of law. If charged with crime, he is incapable, generally, of determining for himself whether the indictment is good or bad. He is unfamiliar with the rules of evidence. Left without the aid of counsel he may be put on trial without a proper charge, and convicted upon incompetent evidence, or evidence irrelevant to the issue or otherwise inadmissible. He lacks both the skill and knowledge adequately to prepare his defense, even though he had a perfect one. He requires the guiding hand of counsel at every step in the proceedings against him. Without it, though he be not guilty, he faces the danger of conviction because he does not know how to establish his innocence. If that be true of men of intelligence, how much more true is it of the ignorant and illiterate, or those of feeble intellect. If in any case, civil or criminal, a state or federal court were arbitrarily to refuse to hear a party by counsel, employed by and appearing for him, it reasonably may not be doubted that such a refusal would be a denial of a hearing, and, therefore, of due process in the constitutional sense. (*Powell v. Alabama,* 1932)

With this, the Court easily ruled that the Fourteenth Amendment due process rights of the Scottsboro defendants were violated, and a new trial was required.

Note, however, that *Powell v. Alabama* did not rule that the states had to provide a lawyer for every indigent defendant in every felony trial. The scope of its application was narrower. The decision was based on the facts and circumstances of the case.

> All that it is necessary now to decide, as we do decide, is that in a capital case, where the defendant is unable to employ counsel, and is incapable adequately of making his own defense because of ignorance, feeble mindedness, illiteracy, or the like, it is the duty of the court, whether requested or not, to assign counsel for him as a necessary requisite of due process of law. (*Powell v. Alabama,* 1932)

As a Due Process Clause precedent, *Powell* became known as the **special circumstances rule:** That is, due process requires counsel in cases where "special circumstances" exist.

After *Powell:* Toward Incorporation

Six years after *Powell,* Justice Hugo Black's majority opinion in ***Johnson v. Zerbst*** (1938) forcefully made the assistance of counsel in a federal case—directly applying the Sixth Amendment, uncluttered by states' rights or special circumstances considerations—an absolute right. Two soldiers on leave in South Carolina, convicted in a federal prosecution of passing counterfeit currency, were tried without the assistance of counsel. The case shows why a lawyer is necessary. The defendants presented a defense that was not artful at best and one that a jury could read as an evasion of guilt. Johnson misused his time by attempting to answer minor, possibly prejudicial, statements by the prosecutor (e.g., that he was a "hoodlum from New York"). Johnson also failed to challenge the evidence and neglected to raise legal challenges that could have mitigated the crime or won an acquittal.

Justice Black's majority opinion secured two important constitutional rules. First, it held for the first time that a federal felony trial conducted without a defense lawyer, unless properly waived, is a jurisdictional violation. It is not a mere technical mistake but an infringement of the Sixth Amendment that deprives the court of "the power and authority to deprive an accused of his life or liberty" (*Johnson v. Zerbst,* 1938).

> This is [a] safeguard[] . . . deemed necessary to ensure fundamental human rights of life and liberty. [It is an] essential barrier[] against arbitrary or unjust deprivation of human rights. The Sixth Amendment stands as a constant admonition that if the constitutional safeguards it provides be lost, justice will not "still be done." (*Johnson v. Zerbst,* 1938, p. 462)

Second, the case specified the rules for **waiver of counsel.** There is a presumption against the waiver of such a fundamental right. Even if the defendant silently goes along with the conduct of a trial without complaining about the lack of counsel, his or her silence does not amount to a waiver. A waiver is defined as "an intelligent relinquishment or abandonment of a known right or privilege." For a waiver to be constitutional, the defendant must know that he or she has a right to counsel and must voluntarily give it up knowing that the right to claim it exists. The Supreme Court later required trial judges to carefully investigate waivers of counsel and make a written record of any waivers (*Von Moltke v. Gillies,* 1948). "Presuming waiver from a silent record is impermissible. The record must show . . . that an accused was offered counsel but intelligently and understandably rejected the offer" (*Carnley v. Cochran,* 1962). These rules became the standard for all Fifth and Sixth amendment waivers, including waivers of the right to remain silent after having been read the *Miranda* warnings.

Betts v. Brady (1942), decided a decade after *Powell,* was a setback to the incorporation of the Sixth Amendment. *Betts* confirmed the special circumstances rule of *Powell.* Betts, a farmhand, was indicted for noncapital robbery. Not having the money to hire a lawyer, he asked the judge for **appointed counsel** at his arraignment. The judge refused, saying that the Carroll County Court appointed counsel for indigent defendants only in prosecutions for murder and rape. Betts pleaded not guilty and defended himself in a non-jury trial before the judge.

> At his request witnesses were summoned in his behalf. He cross-examined the State's witnesses and examined his own. The latter gave testimony tending to establish an alibi. Although afforded the opportunity, he did not take the witness stand. The judge found him guilty and imposed a sentence of eight years. (*Betts v. Brady,* 1942)

The issue before the Supreme Court, sharpened by Betts's explicit request for a lawyer, was (as in *Powell*) whether a state felony trial conducted without defense counsel was a deprivation of Fourteenth Amendment due process liberty. The majority, in an opinion by Justice Owen Roberts, clearly rejected incorporation: "[T]he Sixth Amendment of the national Constitution applies only to trials in federal courts." Relying on *Palko v. Connecticut* (1937), it refused to apply the rule of *Johnson* to state cases. The Court found that the Sixth Amendment right to counsel is not in the Due Process Clause. Instead, the contours of the Due Process Clause, insofar as the clause required the appointment of a lawyer for an indigent in a state case, were set out in *Powell*. The Court dealt with Betts's petition as a "pure" due process issue, which must decide, on an "appraisal of the totality of facts in a given case," whether a trial without defense counsel is "a denial of fundamental fairness, shocking to the universal sense of justice" (*Betts v. Brady,* 1942).

Applying *Powell*, Justice Roberts concluded that special circumstances did not exist in Betts's case. Therefore, due process did not require the state to appoint counsel. The case was not complicated: Did Betts commit a robbery? He put alibi witnesses on the stand, and the issue for the judge was a simple matter of witness credibility. Unlike the Scottsboro defendants, Betts was "not helpless, but was a man forty-three years old, of ordinary intelligence, and [able] to take care of his own interests on the trial of that narrow issue. He had once before been in a criminal court, pleaded guilty to larceny and served a sentence and was not wholly unfamiliar with criminal procedure" (*Betts v. Brady,* 1942). None of the racism and lynch-mob atmosphere of *Powell* surrounded this run-of-the-mill case. In affirming Betts's uncounseled conviction of a noncapital felony, the majority was satisfied that its conclusion did not violate "natural, inherent, and fundamental principles of fairness." First, uncounseled defense was a common practice to "those who have lived under the Anglo-American system of law." Most states then provided an attorney at no charge to the defendant in noncapital cases only at the discretion of the court and not as a mandatory right. At that time, the provision of counsel was seen as a legislative or political issue, not as a fundamental right. Furthermore, Maryland law required the appointment of counsel if special circumstances existed. The Supreme Court worried that a flat rule would burden states with the cost of providing counsel even in "small crimes tried before justices of the peace" and in "trials in the Traffic Court."

Justice Black's spirited dissent, joined by Justices Douglas and Murphy, urged incorporation of the Sixth Amendment right to counsel into the Fourteenth Amendment. Failing that, he argued that Justice Sutherland's logic in *Powell*—that it is difficult for any layperson to adequately defend him- or herself in a criminal trial—means that a felony trial conducted without defense counsel is always unfair and a due process violation. Justice Black sought to extend *Johnson v. Zerbst* to state cases. The former populist senator emphasized the greater risks of unjust conviction to poor people. "A practice cannot be reconciled with 'common and fundamental ideas of fairness and right,' which subjects innocent men to increased dangers of conviction merely because of their poverty. . . . Denial to the poor of the request for counsel in proceedings based on charges of serious crime has long been regarded as shocking to the 'universal sense of justice' throughout this country" (*Betts v. Brady,* 1942, 476, paragraph break disregarded).

Justice Black was later vindicated in *Gideon v. Wainwright* (1963). In the two decades following *Betts,* the Court undermined the special circumstances test by finding that special circumstances existed in many instances. The Court held that counsel was required by due process in all death penalty trials (*Bute v. Illinois,* 1948), in all capital case arraignments (*Hamilton v. Alabama,* 1961), and in cases involving an unsworn defendant who wishes to make a statement (*Ferguson v. Georgia,* 1961). Justice Stanley Reed revealed that the Court was divided as to noncapital cases but that several justices felt that "the Due Process Clause . . . requires counsel for all persons charged with serious crimes" (*Uveges v. Pennsylvania,* 1948). These cases paved the way to *Gideon.*

The Equal Protection Approach

Griffin v. Illinois (1956) opened the door to a new theory on which to base rights connected to the right to counsel. The Court held that under the Fourteenth Amendment Equal

Protection Clause indigent defendants are entitled to a trial transcript in order to facilitate appeals. Under Illinois procedure then in effect, to obtain a full appeal of a criminal conviction, a defendant had to furnish the appellate court with a bill of exceptions specifying the legal grounds for the appeal, certified by the trial judge. The state agreed that "it is sometimes impossible to prepare such bills of exceptions . . . without a stenographic transcript of the trial proceedings." Stenographic transcripts are quite expensive, and free transcripts were provided at county expense only to indigent defendants sentenced to death. "In all other criminal cases defendants needing a transcript, whether indigent or not, must themselves buy it." In this case, the Court held that a free transcript must be provided. Justice Black's opinion did not rule that trial transcripts had to be provided to indigent defendants in every case: only where the effect of not having a transcript effectively denied indigents a right to appeal because of their poverty. The opinion noted that although the Constitution did not mandate appellate courts, once a state established them, appellate review could not be administered in a manner that discriminated against the poor.

Justice Harold Burton's dissent (joined by Justices Sherman Minton, Stanley Reed, and John Marshall Harlan II) expressed a concern for federalism. A free transcript was a fine thing, but it should be provided by the states as they saw fit and not required by federal constitutional law. They expressed concern that an equal protection ruling saying that rich and poor had to be treated equally would lead to "leveling," by abolishing all laws that had any disparate economic impact on the rich and the poor (e.g., disallowing fixed taxes like a sales tax).

Justice Black's opinion in *Griffin* was probably designed to undermine the *Betts* special circumstances rule, replacing it with a flat requirement that the state had to provide counsel to indigents. He wrote: "There can be no equal justice where the kind of *trial* a man gets depends on the amount of money he has" (emphasis added). This seems to be a logical derivation from *Griffin*'s principle: that the state should eliminate the differences between the rich and the poor so as to ensure equal justice. If people with the means had an absolute right to counsel, and if counsel is essential to a fair trial, should not a lawyer be provided for indigents? As it turned out, however, the Equal Protection Clause was not the platform for the rule requiring trial counsel.

Cases under the *Griffin* equality principle did benefit the indigent by eliminating filing fees in criminal appeals and state postconviction/habeas corpus hearings[13] and ensuring the right on appeal to free transcripts of preliminary hearing records, lower court habeas corpus hearings, and local ordinance violation trials.[14] By 1970, it appeared to be an absolute rule requiring that an indigent who was involved in the criminal process be given any benefit that a wealthier person could afford. Still, the more conservative Burger Court limited the expansion of the equal justice doctrine when it came to providing counsel on discretionary appeals, as discussed below.

GIDEON V. WAINWRIGHT AND ITS AFTERMATH

In *Gideon v. Wainwright,* the Supreme Court guaranteed the right to counsel to all state felony defendants by incorporating the Sixth Amendment into Fourteenth Amendment due process.

Read Case and Comments: *Gideon v. Wainwright.*

Does *Gideon* Apply to Misdemeanor Trials?

In *Argersinger v. Hamlin* (1972), the Supreme Court found no constitutional basis for distinguishing between a misdemeanor and a felony for purposes of **assigned counsel** for indigents. It held that counsel was required by the Sixth Amendment in misdemeanor cases where a defendant is actually sentenced to imprisonment. The Court reserved the issue of whether counsel is constitutionally required in cases involving imprisonment as an authorized punishment, but the defendant does not actually lose liberty.

CASE AND COMMENTS

Gideon v. Wainwright

372 U.S. 335, 83 S.Ct. 792, 9 L.Ed.2d 799 (1963)

MR. JUSTICE BLACK delivered the opinion of the Court. **[a]**

[Gideon, charged with breaking into a pool hall, a felony, demanded (because of his indigence) and was refused appointed counsel. He conducted his own defense.] He made an opening statement to the jury, cross-examined the State's witnesses, presented witnesses in his own defense, declined to testify himself, and made a short argument "emphasizing his innocence to the charge contained in the Information filed in this case." The jury returned a verdict of guilty, and petitioner was sentenced to serve five years in the state prison. [The Court characterized the facts as similar to *Betts v. Brady* (this text) and set the case for review to reconsider the *Betts* rule because of the "continuing source of controversy and litigation in both state and federal courts" that the *Betts* rule presented.]

* * * Upon full reconsideration we conclude that *Betts v. Brady* should be overruled.

We have construed [the Sixth Amendment] to mean that in federal courts counsel must be provided for defendants unable to employ counsel unless the right is competently and intelligently waived. [Justice Black reviewed *Betts v. Brady,* noting that it held the Sixth Amendment right of counsel not to be fundamental and thus not incorporated into the Due Process Clause of the Fourteenth Amendment.] **[b]**

We accept *Betts v. Brady*'s assumption, based as it was on our prior cases, that a provision of the Bill of Rights which is "fundamental and essential to a fair trial" is made obligatory upon the States by the Fourteenth Amendment. We think the Court in *Betts* was wrong, however, in concluding that the Sixth Amendment's guarantee of counsel is not one of these fundamental rights. Ten years before *Betts v. Brady,* this Court, after full consideration of all the historical data examined in *Betts,* had unequivocally declared that "the right to the aid of counsel is of this fundamental character." *Powell v. Alabama.* * * * While the Court at the close of its *Powell* opinion did by its language, as this Court frequently does, limit its holding to the particular facts and circumstances of that case, its conclusions about the fundamental nature of the right to counsel are unmistakable. * * *

* * * The fact is that in deciding as it did—that "appointment of counsel is not a fundamental right, essential to a fair trial"—the Court in *Betts v. Brady* made an abrupt break with its own well-considered precedents. In returning to these old precedents, sounder we believe than the new, we but restore constitutional principles established to achieve a fair system of justice. **[c]** Not only these precedents but also reason and reflection require us to recognize that in our adversary system of criminal justice, any person haled into court, who is too poor to hire a lawyer, cannot be assured a fair trial unless counsel is provided for him. This seems to us to be an obvious truth. Governments, both state and federal, quite properly spend vast sums of money to establish machinery to try defendants accused of crime. Lawyers to prosecute are everywhere deemed essential to protect the public's interest in an orderly society. Similarly, there are few defendants charged with crime, few indeed, who fail to hire the best lawyers they can get to prepare and present their defenses. That government hires lawyers to prosecute and defendants who have the money hire lawyers to defend are the strongest indications of the widespread belief that lawyers in criminal courts are necessities, not luxuries. The right of one charged with crime to counsel may not be deemed fundamental and essential to fair trials in some countries, but it is in ours. From the very beginning, our state and national constitutions and laws have laid great emphasis on procedural and substantive safeguards designed to assure fair trials before impartial tribunals in which every defendant stands equal before the law. This noble ideal cannot be realized if the poor man charged with crime has to face his accusers without a lawyer to assist him. * * *

[a] Justice Black had the pleasure of writing the opinion in a landmark decision overruling a case in which he had strenuously dissented two decades before.

[b] This was the Supreme Court's third criminal procedure incorporation case of the 1960s. As in other incorporation cases, the federal rule interpreting a Bill of Rights provision was more favorable to the defendant's rights than the state rule.

[c] Justice Black seems to be stretching a fair reading of the "older precedent" of *Powell v. Alabama* by viewing it as having guaranteed the right of counsel to indigents in *all* felony cases. Compare this reading of precedent to that made in the concurrence by Justice Harlan.

(continued)

[d] The case was remanded, and Earl Clarence Gideon was tried again in Panama City, Florida, this time represented by counsel. Anthony Lewis's celebrated book, *Gideon's Trumpet,* recounts the second trial. Gideon's lawyer, Fred Turner, prepared the case carefully by thoroughly reviewing the facts and observing the pool hall. His skillful cross-examination of the lead prosecution witness raised the real possibility that the teen who had identified Gideon as the criminal was himself the burglar. Gideon was acquitted.

[e] Justice Harlan correctly points out that in the twenty years between *Betts* and *Gideon,* many narrow decisions began to shift toward granting the right to counsel in more and more cases. He posits a less absolutist view of constitutional rights and constitutional change than does Justice Black. In Justice Harlan's view, the meaning of constitutional provisions can change gradually over time to take into account new social realities. This was anathema to Justice Black, who strenuously rejected what he saw as judicial lawmaking.

The judgment is reversed. * * * **[d]**

[Justices Douglas and Clark concurred in separate opinions.]

MR. JUSTICE HARLAN, concurring.

I agree that *Betts v. Brady* should be overruled, but consider it entitled to a more respectful burial than has been accorded, at least on the part of those of us who were not on the Court when that case was decided.

I cannot subscribe to the view that *Betts v. Brady* represented "an abrupt break with its own well-considered precedents." * * * In 1932, in *Powell v. Alabama,* * * * a capital case, this Court declared that under the particular facts there presented—"the ignorance and illiteracy of the defendants, their youth, the circumstances of public hostility * * * and above all that they stood in deadly peril of their lives" * * *—the state court had a duty to assign counsel for the trial as a necessary requisite of due process of law. It is evident that these limiting facts were not added to the opinion as an afterthought; they were repeatedly emphasized, * * * and were clearly regarded as important to the result.

Thus when this Court, a decade later, decided *Betts v. Brady,* it did no more than to admit of the possible existence of special circumstances in noncapital as well as capital trials, while at the same time insisting that such circumstances be shown in order to establish a denial of due process. The right to appointed counsel had been recognized as being considerably broader in federal prosecutions [*Johnson v. Zerbst*], but to have imposed these requirements on the States would indeed have been "an abrupt break" with the almost immediate past. The declaration that the right to appointed counsel in state prosecutions, as established in *Powell v. Alabama,* was not limited to capital cases was in truth not a departure from, but an extension of, existing precedent.

The principles declared in *Powell* and in *Betts,* however, have had a troubled journey throughout the years. * * * **[e]**

[More and more capital and noncapital cases found "special circumstances," even in doubtful instances.] The Court has come to recognize, in other words, that the mere existence of a serious criminal charge constituted in itself special circumstances requiring the services of counsel at trial. In truth the *Betts v. Brady* rule is no longer a reality.

This evolution, however, appears not to have been fully recognized by many state courts, in this instance charged with the front-line responsibility for the enforcement of constitutional rights. To continue a rule which is honored by this Court only with lip service is not a healthy thing and in the long run will do disservice to the federal system.

The special circumstances rule has been formally abandoned in capital cases, and the time has now come when it should be similarly abandoned in noncapital cases, at least as to offenses which, as the one involved here, carry the possibility of a substantial prison sentence. (Whether the rule should extend to *all* criminal cases need not now be decided.) This indeed does no more than to make explicit something that has long since been foreshadowed in our decisions.

[Justice Harlan then stated his disagreement with the majority over the incorporation question, stating that in his opinion, the *Gideon* decision falls under the Fourteenth Amendment only and not the Sixth.]

On these premises I join in the judgment of the Court.

Justice Lewis Powell, dissenting in *Argersinger,* urged the Court to choose a due process special circumstances rule rather than the majority's approach of requiring counsel if a defendant was to spend even one day in jail. An example of special circumstances would be whether there were complex legal issues; in such case, the trial court could appoint an attorney in its discretion. Justice Powell was concerned with requiring the states to shoulder the costs of providing counsel in each and every case, no matter how straightforward and simple the issues.

The issue reserved in *Argersinger* was decided in a case concerning a shoplifter who was convicted without the assistance of a lawyer and fined $50, although the law authorized a jail term. In *Scott v. Illinois* (1979), the Court ruled that *Argersinger* meant that actual imprisonment differs from a penalty of a fine or a threat of jailing. Therefore, "the Sixth and Fourteenth Amendments to the United States Constitution require only that no indigent criminal defendant be sentenced to a term of imprisonment unless the State has afforded him the right to assistance of appointed counsel in his defense." The mere fact that one is being tried under a statute that authorizes incarceration does not automatically guarantee counsel. Justice William Brennan, dissenting, argued that *Argersinger* required appointment of counsel if there is actual incarceration *or* if the crime charged is punishable by more than six months in prison. He thus urged the Court to adopt an **authorized imprisonment rule** rather than an **actual imprisonment rule**.

Scott injects an illogical element into the Sixth Amendment: A person charged with a felony must have a lawyer, even if not sentenced to prison, but this is not so for a misdemeanor defendant in the same circumstance. Justice Powell, concurring, expressed some concern that the actual imprisonment rule would lead judges to guess in advance of the trial what the likely outcome would be and thus distort the judicial process. He concurred because he thought the Court should substitute the flexible due process rule rather than the rigid Sixth Amendment requirement to misdemeanor trials.

When Does the Right to Counsel Attach? Pretrial: The Critical Stage and Formal Charge Rules

Gideon did not resolve all issues concerning the right to counsel. The Sixth Amendment, now applicable to state as well as federal felony trials, applies to "all criminal prosecutions." What proceedings are included in a Sixth Amendment criminal prosecution? The answer is found in the **critical stage** doctrine developed by the Court. Counsel is required at a pretrial proceeding if it is one in which factual determinations can be made that could determine the outcome of the case and in which a lawyer plays a significant role.

Arraignment.
The critical stage doctrine was developed prior to *Gideon.* A unanimous Court in **Hamilton v. Alabama** (1961) ruled that, under Alabama law, an arraignment in a capital *case* was a critical stage because it was the only point in the criminal process at which a defendant could raise an insanity defense without the approval of the trial judge. Other important motions, such as a challenge to the systematic exclusion of one race from the grand jury, had to be made at arraignment. "Available defenses may be as irretrievably lost, if not then and there asserted, as they are when an accused represented by counsel waives a right for strategic purposes" (*Hamilton v. Alabama,* 1961). If an arraignment is a simple formality where no important decision is made (such as arranging for bail), then the lack of counsel is not a due process or Sixth Amendment violation. Otherwise, a defendant must be represented by an attorney.

Preliminary Examination.
In **Coleman v. Alabama** (1970), the Supreme Court ruled that a preliminary examination is a critical stage requiring assistance of counsel. Under Alabama law, the defendant was not required to raise a defense, but if he was without counsel to cross-examine prosecution witnesses, any testimony taken was inadmissible at trial. The Alabama courts saw this as a fair rule that prevented the lack of counsel from caus-

ing prejudice to the defendant's case. Yet Justice Brennan's majority opinion noted that (1) a lawyer's skilled cross-examination of witnesses can expose fatal weaknesses in the prosecution case that will lead a magistrate to dismiss; (2) cross-examination of witnesses may establish a basis for impeaching witnesses at the trial; (3) trained counsel can use the hearing as a way of discovering prosecution information that can prove helpful in devising a defense strategy; and (4) counsel can be influential in making arguments for bail or for a psychiatric examination. "The inability of the indigent accused on his own to realize these advantages of a lawyer's assistance compels the conclusion that the Alabama preliminary hearing is a 'critical stage' of the State's criminal process at which the accused is 'as much entitled to such aid [of counsel] . . . as at the trial itself'" (*Coleman v. Alabama,* 1970).

Plea Bargaining.

The Supreme Court has made it clear that the assistance of counsel is as important in plea bargaining as it is in the felony trial. A decision rendered a month after *Gideon* held that an arraignment conducted without counsel was unconstitutional because "petitioner entered a plea before the magistrate and that plea was taken at a time when he had no counsel" (*White v. Maryland,* 1963). When a lawyer is not present at a critical stage, the Court does "not stop to determine whether prejudice resulted: 'Only the presence of counsel could have enabled this accused to know all the defenses available to him and to plead intelligently'" (*White v. Maryland*). "Since an intelligent assessment of the relative advantages of pleading guilty is frequently impossible without the assistance of an attorney, this Court has scrutinized with special care pleas of guilty entered by defendants without the assistance of counsel and without a valid waiver of the right to counsel. . . . Since *Gideon v. Wainwright* it has been clear that a guilty plea to a felony charge entered without counsel and without a waiver of counsel is invalid" (*Brady v. United States,* 1970).

Police Investigation.

No court has ever held that a lawyer must accompany police in conducting interviews or in gathering physical evidence of a crime. A lawyer has no traditional role to play during investigation, and any problems with the evidence may be derived from discovery or cross-examination. Counsel is not required in investigative hearings, such as grand jury and legislative hearings,[15] or when taking fingerprints, handwriting samples, or voice exemplars.[16]

Custodial Interrogation.

In *Miranda v. Arizona* (1966), the Supreme Court ruled that police interrogation conducted while a suspect is in custody raises a sufficient level of compulsion to become a potential violation of the suspect's right against self-incrimination under the Fifth Amendment, requiring warnings that include a right to counsel. This right is included under the Fifth Amendment and is *not* part of Sixth Amendment critical stage analysis. (See Chapter 7.)

Lineup Identification.

The Supreme Court has held that a Sixth Amendment right to counsel applies to postindictment lineup identifications (*United States v. Wade,* 1967) but *not* to preindictment showups (**Kirby v. Illinois,** 1972). The basis for this distinction was that the laying of a formal charge, by indictment or information, brought the Sixth Amendment into play. The Court in *Kirby* said that the initiation of a prosecution is not a "mere formalism," for it is "then that a defendant finds himself faced with the prosecutorial forces of organized society, and immersed in the intricacies of substantive and procedural criminal law." Nevertheless, in *United States v. Ash* (1973), the Court held that counsel was not required under the Sixth Amendment during a postindictment photographic display because, since the defendant was not present, there is not the kind of confrontation that was contemplated in *Wade.* The dissent in *Ash* reasoned that the same suggestibility that can taint a lineup can taint a photographic identification, and an attorney can play the same role of preventing or observing the suggestive acts. (See Chapter 8.)

Prison Administrative Detention.   Four prison inmates were suspected of murdering another prisoner. They were held in administrative detention for ninety days without counsel during the investigation and were indicted for the murder nineteen months after the crime. The federal court of appeals held that they were entitled to counsel during the period of detention. The Supreme Court reversed in **United States v. Gouveia** (1984), holding that the **formal charge rule** of *Kirby* applied to prison as well as to nonprison settings: There is no right to counsel until the accused has been formally charged.

The formal charge rule of *Kirby v. Illinois* and the cases and the critical stage rule of *Coleman v. Alabama* seem to conflict. *Kirby* involves formal line drawing. *Coleman* provides a functional analysis as to whether in fact the lack of counsel could result in the conviction of an innocent person or could deprive a defendant of a legitimate defense. *Kirby* can be explained in part by the effort of an ideologically conservative Court attempting to limit the right of counsel. It seems logical, for example, that if counsel plays an important role in preventing or observing suggestive behaviors during a postindictment lineup, the same role is played during a preindictment lineup or a photographic identification.

When Does the Right to Counsel Attach? Postconviction and Other Processes

Important criminal justice processes occur after conviction in the correctional system and in other proceedings that affect the rights of convicted persons. If a procedure is part of the Sixth Amendment criminal prosecution, *Gideon* applies, and counsel is absolutely required. Otherwise, if counsel is required at all, it must be through the more flexible "facts and circumstances" approach of due process.

Sentencing and Deferred Sentencing.   **Mempa v. Rhay** (1967) involved a sentencing hearing following a deferred sentence with probation. The Court held that counsel was required under the Sixth Amendment. Justice Thurgood Marshall, for the majority, stated that the Sixth Amendment right to counsel applied to sentencing because it was part of the "criminal prosecution." Sentencing was held to include deferred sentencing that involved the revocation of conditional liberty. The Court announced a broad principle: "appointment of counsel for an indigent is required at every stage of a criminal proceeding where substantial rights of a criminal accused may be affected." But in subsequent years, the Court has refused to extend this logic to probation and parole revocations and prison disciplinary hearings, which apply to convicted persons.

Probation and Parole Revocation.   The Supreme Court ruled in **Gagnon v. Scarpelli** (1973) (probation) and **Morrissey v. Brewer** (1972) (parole) that "[p]robation revocation, like parole revocation, is not a stage of a criminal prosecution, but does result in a loss of liberty" (*Gagnon v. Scarpelli,* 1973). As a result, neither probation nor parole can be revoked without a formal due process hearing that requires notice, disclosure of evidence, an opportunity to be heard, a neutral hearing body, and written statements of the fact finders. In neither case, however, was counsel required by the Sixth Amendment. Instead of holding that counsel be required as a matter of due process fundamental fairness, the Court established more flexible due process rules. The Court offered guidelines in *Gagnon:*

> Presumptively, . . . counsel should be provided in cases where, after being informed of his right to request counsel, the probationer or parolee makes such a request, based on a timely and colorable claim (i) that he has not committed the alleged violation of the conditions upon which he is at liberty; or (ii) that, even if the violation is a matter of public record or is uncontested, there are substantial reasons which justified or mitigated the violation and make revocation inappropriate, and that the reasons are complex or otherwise difficult to develop or present. In passing on a request for the appointment of counsel, the responsible agency also should consider, especially in doubtful cases, whether the probationer appears to be capable of speaking effectively for himself. (*Gagnon v. Scarpelli,* 1973)

Gagnon in effect resurrected the *Betts v. Brady* special circumstances test for the requirement of counsel for indigent defendants at probation revocation hearings.

Prison Disciplinary Hearings.

Prisoners have even fewer procedural rights in disciplinary hearings than do probationers or parolees facing revocation, since they have much less freedom to lose than probationers or parolees. In *Wolff v. McDonnell* (1974), the Court required a due process hearing before an inmate could be subjected to major institutional forms of discipline involving losses of liberty, such as placement in solitary confinement or a loss of good time. But the dangerous reality of prisons, when combined with the lesser liberty interest of prisoners, led the Court to conclude that inmates had no absolute right to confront and cross-examine witnesses and were, therefore, at the mercy of the prison hearing officer's discretion. As for counsel, the Court, after reviewing its ruling in *Gagnon,* said, "At this stage of the development of these procedures we are not prepared to hold that inmates have a right to either retained or appointed counsel in disciplinary proceedings." Thus, whereas a probationer facing revocation has a right to the assistance of **retained counsel,** a prisoner has no Fourteenth Amendment right to a paid lawyer's presence in an administrative prison disciplinary hearing. In the interests of inmate safety and prison security, a prison may legitimately bar all attorneys from disciplinary hearings.

Psychiatric Expert Witness.

The case-by-case approach was applied in *Ake v. Oklahoma* (1985), where the Court held that a psychiatrist must be provided for an indigent defendant whenever insanity is reasonably raised as an issue. The holding was based on a combination of equal protection and due process reasoning. According to Justice Marshall, "Meaningful access to justice has been the consistent theme of these cases. . . . [A] criminal trial is fundamentally unfair if the State proceeds against an individual defendant without making certain that he has access to the raw materials integral to the building of an effective defense."

Summary Court-Martial.

Middendorf v. Henry (1976) held that a summary court-martial was not a criminal prosecution within the meaning of the Sixth Amendment. Under due process, a defendant is not constitutionally entitled to counsel in a summary court-martial where the maximum penalty could not exceed thirty days' confinement. In addition, analysis of the summary court-martial's function demonstrated that, unlike special and general courts-martial where counsel was provided, in summary proceedings the goal is to exercise justice promptly for purposes of discipline. The proceeding, informal and conducted by one officer, has none of the trappings of a courtroom. Justice William Rehnquist noted that the potential of confinement was not a controlling factor in not labeling the proceeding a criminal prosecution because it occurred within the special context of the military community.

Juvenile Delinquency Trials.

The Court held in *In re Gault* (1967) that a juvenile delinquency adjudication is not a criminal trial within the contemplation of the Sixth Amendment. Yet, under the Due Process Clause, the Court held that an adjudication of juvenile delinquency, which may result in commitment to an institution, is so much like an adult criminal trial that the provision of counsel was essential. If the child or parents could not afford counsel, the state was required to appoint a lawyer to represent the child.

Limitations on the Right to Counsel

Right to Choose Retained Counsel.

The right to retain one's own counsel for a criminal defense is not absolute. "Regardless of his persuasive powers, an advocate who is not a member of the bar may not represent clients (other than himself) in court. Similarly, a defendant may not insist on representation by an attorney he cannot afford or who for other reasons declines to represent the defendant. Nor may a defendant insist on the counsel of an attorney who has a previous or ongoing relationship with an opposing party, even when the opposing party is the government" (***Wheat v. United States***, 1988). In *Wheat,* the Court held that a trial court could deny a defendant the counsel of his choice if, according to the district court's opinion, the representation carried a substantial possibility of a **conflict of interest.** This ruling subordinates the right to counsel to that of a fair adversary trial. In *Wheat,* the Court was concerned that **multiple representation** of three drug-sale defendants in separate trials by the same lawyer would undermine the lawyer's ability to cross-examine his clients. Thus, even though the defendants were willing to waive their right to a trial free of conflict of interest, the Court refused to accept their waivers. Four dissenting justices agreed that the right to select a lawyer is not absolute, but they would recognize a presumption in favor of a defendant's counsel of choice. In a stinging dissent, Justice John Paul Stevens characterized the Court's rule in *Wheat* as paternalistic and said, "This is not the first case in which the Court has demonstrated 'its apparent unawareness of the function of the independent lawyer as a guardian of our freedom.'"

Payment and Asset Forfeiture.

Two 1989 decisions upheld congressional acts that allow prosecutors to freeze assets of suspected organized crime members and drug dealers "before trial [and] without regard to whether the person will have enough money left to hire a lawyer."[17] The **asset forfeiture** law, used aggressively by federal prosecutors, was thought by many to undermine the Sixth Amendment right to adequate representation. ***Caplin & Drysdale v. United States*** (1989) was a suit by a law firm for its legal fees, which had been placed in escrow before trial and which the government tried to seize after the client's conviction. In ***United States v. Monsanto*** (1989), pretrial freezing of assets forced the defendant to rely on a **public defender.** The Supreme Court (5–4) found both practices to be constitutional.

The forfeiture law made assets that were proceeds of crime government property from the time of the commission of the crime. Since illegal assets were declared government property, a defendant's payment to his or her lawyer was, in effect, spending someone else's (i.e., the government's) money. Relying on *Wheat v. United States,* the Court said that "a defendant may not insist on representation by an attorney he cannot afford." The law created some exemptions to this rule (for owners of stolen property and some innocent retailers), but none for attorneys' fees.

Four dissenting justices felt that the constitutional requirement of adequate representation required the Court to create an exemption for legal fees so that the alleged proceeds of a crime could be used for lawyers. They argued that pretrial asset freezing would "undermine the adversary system as we know it" because it gives the government "an intolerable degree of power over any private attorney who takes on the task of representing a defendant in a forfeiture case." It allows prosecutors to

> use the forfeiture weapon against a defense attorney who is particularly talented or aggressive on the client's behalf—the attorney who is better than what, in the Government's view, the defendant deserves. The spectre of the Government's selectively excluding only the most talented defense counsel is a serious threat to the equality of forces necessary for the adversarial system to perform at its best. (*Caplin & Drysdale v. United States,* 1989)

Meaningful Attorney-Client Relationship.

Morris v. Slappy (1983) held that the Sixth Amendment does not guarantee a meaningful relationship between defendant and appointed counsel. A deputy public defender represented Slappy at a preliminary hearing and supervised an extensive investigation in his rape prosecution. Shortly before trial, the deputy public defender was hospitalized for emergency surgery and a senior trial attorney from the public defender's office was assigned to the case. Slappy claimed that the attorney did not have enough time to prepare the case and moved for a **continuance.** The newly assigned attorney stated that he was prepared and that a further delay would not benefit him in presenting the case. The trial court denied Slappy's motion, the trial continued, and Slappy was found guilty by a jury on three counts. During a second trial of counts left unresolved in the first trial, Slappy refused to cooperate with or even speak to his attorney. The jury returned a guilty verdict on the other counts. The federal appeals court, in a federal habeas corpus action, held that the Sixth Amendment includes the right to a meaningful attorney-client relationship.

The Supreme Court reversed and held that, under the circumstances of this case, there was no Sixth Amendment violation by the trial court's refusing to grant a continuance when the attorney himself did not want one. The Court rejected the novel idea that an indigent defendant is guaranteed a "meaningful" relationship with assigned counsel; furthermore, an indigent defendant does not have an unqualified right to the appointment of counsel of his or her own choosing. Justice Brennan, while concurring in the decision, noted that lower federal courts have recognized the importance of a defendant's relationship with his attorney so that a defendant with retained counsel was seen to have "a qualified right to continue that relationship." The qualified right is not the guarantee of "rapport" between client and attorney. Rather, according to Justice Brennan, where an attorney has put sufficient work into a case so that he or she has become knowledgeable of its intricacies, a court should take into account the length of delay before allowing another attorney to try the case.

Recoupment of Costs.

The governmental unit that pays for indigents' assigned counsel may constitutionally seek to recoup the costs of the defense whenever the defendant has the means to pay. According to *Fuller v. Oregon* (1974), a **recoupment** law does not violate the Equal Protection Clause, provided that it allows the indigent person to claim all the exemptions granted to other judgment debtors in the state's civil code and does not require payment if the defendant remains or again becomes indigent. The exemption of indigents who are acquitted was deemed a rational distinction in the law. Dissenting justices felt that recoupment would have a "chilling effect" on the right to counsel; an indigent defendant would decline to accept free counsel knowing that he or she may have to repay the costs of the defense. However, Justice Potter Stewart thought this unlikely because of the protections in the statute ensuring that an indigent cannot be compelled to pay. The Court also noted that defendants whose financial status places them just above the poverty line may have to go into debt in order to pay the costs of a criminal defense. "We cannot say that the Constitution requires that those only slightly poorer must remain forever immune from any obligation to shoulder the expenses of their legal defense, even when they are able to pay without hardship."

The Right to Counsel on Appeal

"[E]very state and the federal system provide some means of review to defendants in criminal cases. However, according to a long line of Supreme Court opinions, there is no constitutional mandate that states provide any type of review process for defendants convicted in their criminal courts."[18] If so, does this mean that there is no right to counsel on appeal? The appellate process is not included within the wording of the Sixth Amendment's "criminal prosecution." The Supreme Court analyzed the question of the right to counsel on appeal in state courts under the Fourteenth Amendment and has applied a functional analysis. It has concluded that counsel is required on first appeals as of right but is not required for subsequent, discretionary appeals.

Right to Counsel on First, Mandatory Appeal.

Douglas v. California (1963) held that the Fourteenth Amendment guarantees a defendant the right to representation of counsel on a first, mandatory appeal. By 1963, every state granted a convicted criminal defendant the right to one mandatory appeal, but not every state guaranteed counsel for these appeals. In California, the rule allowed a court after reviewing part of the trial record to appoint counsel for an indigent convicted person if in the court's discretion an attorney would serve any useful purpose. In contrast, counsel was always appointed for indigents on mandatory first appeals from convictions in federal court, whether or not the federal court thought that a lawyer was needed.

The U.S. Supreme Court held that the California procedure was invidious discrimination against those who were too poor to hire a lawyer to assist them on appeal. It relied on *Griffin v. Illinois* and its "equality principle" in its opinion. The majority thought it unfair that a person with means will present his or her case to the appellate court with "the full benefit of written briefs and oral argument by counsel," while a person who cannot afford a lawyer has to rely on a judge to review the record without the benefit of partisan legal analysis and argument. A case often has hidden merit, and a neutral reviewer, rather than a partisan attorney, can miss it. Justice William O. Douglas's majority opinion was not a model of doctrinal clarity, and his writing mixed up Due Process Clause fairness concerns with Equal Protection Clause equality concerns, a point that was challenged by the dissent. This decision did not apply to second, discretionary appeals, such as writs of habeas corpus or petitions for certiorari. The decision also acknowledged that some differences based on wealth can stand as long as the state does not draw pernicious lines between the rich and the poor. For example, an indigent granted counsel cannot insist on the most highly paid lawyer available.

Justice Harlan's dissenting opinion concluded that the Equal Protection Clause is not the proper basis for a holding. Rather, the issue should be whether California's procedure violated the fair trial rule of the Due Process Clause. He felt that it did not. In his view, there was no equal protection violation because the state does not deny appeals to indigents and because the state cannot lift all disabilities flowing from economic differences. As for the due process issue, he noted that appellate review is not required by the Fourteenth Amendment, and therefore issues of fairness had to be decided in the context of the state's providing a discretionary benefit. He felt that issues that arise on appeal are not as complex as factual issues at a trial, and so it was fair to allow state judges to review a case to see whether a lawyer was needed in a particular appeal.

Halbert v. Michigan (2005) held, under the precedent of *Douglas,* that counsel must be appointed for an indigent defendant who pleaded guilty and was first appealing to an intermediate court of appeals, whose role was to correct errors in defendants' convictions. Michigan amended its constitution to make first appeals discretionary where defendants waived trials and pleaded guilty. The Supreme Court noted that complicated issues could confront defendants who pleaded guilty, including constitutional defects irrelevant to factual guilt, jurisdictional defects, preserved entrapment claims, mental competency claims, and the like. Furthermore, at least two-thirds of inmates, most of whom pleaded guilty, suffer from illiteracy or very low reading skills, failure to complete high school, learning disabilities (like Antonio Halbert), or mental illness, making it unlikely that they could properly prepare the papers required to file leaves to appeal.

Right to Counsel on Second, Discretionary Appeals.

A decade later, a more conservative Supreme Court refused to extend the guarantee of counsel to second, discretionary appeals. *Ross v. Moffitt* (1974) involved two convictions against Claude Moffitt for uttering forged instruments in two different North Carolina counties. In both cases, Moffitt appealed as of right, represented by assigned counsel, and lost both appeals. He then sought the appointment of counsel to pursue a discretionary habeas corpus writ to the state supreme court. After a failure in the state appeal, he sought appointment of counsel to prepare petitions for a writ of certiorari to the U.S. Supreme Court. North Carolina opposed the granting of counsel as a matter of constitutional right. The U.S. Court of Appeals for the Fourth Circuit ruled that the principle of *Douglas v. California* applied even when a convicted person was taking a second appeal to a court that had discretion to deny the appeal. Many state supreme courts, like the U.S. Supreme Court, will decide to hear cases primarily because the issue raised is of significant public importance. They may deny appeals even if a particular case might have been wrongly decided against a petitioner's interest. Nevertheless, according to the Court of Appeals,

[a] defendant with adequate resources to engage counsel has a meaningful right to seek access to the state's highest court. An indigent should be afforded counsel to give him a comparably meaningful right. . . . Denied the assistance of a competent lawyer, the quality of justice for the indigent has been substantially impaired in comparison with the quality of justice afforded his more affluent brothers. (*Moffitt v. Ross,* 483 F.2d 650, 653, 4th Cir. 1973)

The Supreme Court reversed in an opinion by Justice Rehnquist, borrowing somewhat from Justice Harlan's dissent in *Douglas.* Justice Rehnquist first ruled that the Due Process Clause does not require a state to provide a convicted person—who has been represented by counsel at trial and by counsel at the one appeal as of right—with counsel on his discretionary appeal to the state supreme court. Relying on the fact that the Constitution does not mandate appeals and that a defendant in Moffitt's position is seeking to overturn a conviction, he reasoned that there would be unfairness "only if indigents are singled out by the State and denied meaningful access to the appellate system because of their poverty." Viewing the issue as one better analyzed under equal protection, he turned to that clause.

The "Fourteenth Amendment 'does not require absolute equality or precisely equal advantages.' . . . It does require that the state appellate system be 'free of unreasoned distinctions.'" The majority noted that because the indigent person had already "received the benefit of counsel in examining the record of his trial" in the appeal as of right, there was no "unreasoned distinction" in allowing a wealthier person with a lawyer to pursue a writ while not providing counsel for an indigent petitioner. The high court will have the transcript and appellate papers prepared by counsel for the earlier appeal. This is especially so because the purpose of discretionary appeals "is not whether there has been 'a correct adjudication of guilt' in every individual case, . . . but rather whether 'the subject matter of the appeal has significant public interest,' [or] whether 'the cause involves legal principles of major significance to the jurisprudence of the State.'"

Justice William Douglas, at the twilight of his career, dissented in *Ross* on the equality and fairness grounds specified in *Douglas.* He quoted from *Douglas v. California* that the "same concepts of fairness and equality, which require counsel in a first appeal of right, require counsel in other and subsequent discretionary appeals." But that belief, so resonant to an older generation, failed to convince a newer generation of justices that the Constitution required state and local governments to pay for counsel in the context of discretionary appeals.

Right to Counsel for Discretionary Appeal by Indigent Death-Row Inmates.

Murray v. Giarratano (1989) held that, under *Ross,* indigent death-row inmates seeking postconviction review of their death sentences, after their first appeals, had no Fourteenth Amendment right to counsel at the expense of the state. The majority was unmoved by the petitioner's three arguments, which four dissenting justices saw as valid: (1) Death-row inmates are under greater emotional stress than other inmates and thus less able to write adequate legal briefs; (2) Virginia's law postponed some issues normally heard at first appeal to the postconviction proceedings, thus making these second appeals more like first appeals for death-row inmates; and (3) "a grim deadline imposes a finite [time] limit on the condemned person's capacity for useful research." In rejecting these arguments, the Court emphatically limited the right to counsel on Fourteenth Amendment equal protection and due process grounds in procedures other than the trial. While indigents retain the same basic rights as wealthier persons, there are limits to what the state must do to remedy the infirmities in the justice system caused by economic inequality.

THE RIGHT TO SELF-REPRESENTATION

The Sixth Amendment right to the assistance of counsel coexists with a defendant's seemingly contradictory right of self-representation. Before the Supreme Court constitutionalized the right of a defendant to proceed *pro se*—in one's own behalf—federal statutes and the laws of thirty-six states upheld such a right.[19] Data are not kept on the prevalence of ***pro se* defense;** one expert estimates that approximately fifty such trials occurred in 1997. A survey in one jurisdiction indicates that civil litigants are more likely to represent themselves than are criminal defendants and that the number of *pro se* defendants is rising.[20]

Self-Representation and the Waiver of Counsel

Self-representation reflects the American value of self-reliance and a distrust of lawyers. It also may conflict with the right to a fair trial. Some defend themselves in notorious political trials in order to publicize their point of view. Angela Davis, an African American communist and philosophy instructor, was tried in California for abetting the murder of a judge in the Soledad Brothers case. She won an acquittal in 1972. She represented herself but had substantial assistance. Jack Kevorkian, the well-known proponent and practitioner of physician-assisted suicide, was acquitted three times when ably defended by counsel but was convicted of murder when he sought to defend himself.[21] *Pro se* defense is more likely to occur when a defendant becomes frustrated with the actual or perceived incompetence of assigned counsel or a public defender, or when a defendant sharply disagrees with counsel's legal strategy. A defendant may also request self-representation with the underhanded intention of causing delay or a mistrial by asking for a lawyer once the trial has begun.

Several problems can result from self-representation. One is that a *pro se* defendant may cause a mockery of justice. A prime example is Colin Ferguson, who shot and killed six and wounded nineteen commuters on a Long Island Rail Road car in 1993. He claimed to have acted out of a sense of "black rage." The Supreme Court had ruled in ***Godinez v. Moran*** (1993) that the standard of competency to waive counsel is the same as the standard to stand trial—a rational and factual understanding of the proceedings. Under this standard, Ferguson was allowed to dismiss his well-known "radical" lawyers, Ronald Kuby and the late William Kunstler, who wanted him to plead insanity and who correctly predicted that the trial would become a circus.[22] Against overwhelming evidence, Ferguson, speaking clearly but saying bizarre and fanciful things, claimed that an unknown white man did the shooting; asked to subpoena President Clinton; without any evidence claimed that the jury he helped pick was biased;[23] and blandly cross-examined surviving shooting victims who then testified that Ferguson shot them.[24] He told jurors, "There were 93 counts to that indictment, 93 counts only because it matches the year 1993. If it had it been 1925, it would have been a 25-count indictment."[25] His standby counsel, Alton Rose, sitting silently by while Ferguson made it impossible for an insanity defense to succeed, could "only watch in silence from the defense table, where he often slumps, clasping his head as if trying to prevent it from splitting apart in frustration."[26] A person who avidly watched the televised trial said, "I know it's the way the legal system works, but the way we let this guy carry on [made] buffoons out of all of us."[27]

A more recent example arose in the pretrial process of Zacarias Moussaoui, the alleged conspirator in the September 11, 2001, terrorist attack. Federal Judge Leonie M. Brinkema allowed him to represent himself in mid-2002, "a decision that his court-appointed lawyers warned could turn the courtroom into a circus."[28] By November 2003, that prediction proved to have been accurate, and the judge revoked Moussaoui's right of self-representation. In the seventeen months he had been in charge of his case, the judge said, "he had repeatedly violated her orders by filing court papers that were 'frivolous, scandalous, disrespectful or repetitive.'" He flooded the docket with "rambling, sometimes incoherent and often anti-Semitic and racist filings that insulted Judge Brinkema and the court-appointed defense team he tried to fire." The judge noted that he had used "contemptuous language that would never be tolerated from an attorney and will no longer be tolerated from this defendant." Moussaoui, who has acknowledged that he is loyal to Osama bin Laden, accused his attorneys "of conspiring with the government to ensure his execution, calling them the 'death team.'" In handwritten court filings, he said he wanted "anthrax for

Jew sympathisers only" and referred to Judge Brinkema as "Leonie you Despotically Judge." In an earlier filing, he requested that Attorney General John Ashcroft "be sent to Alexandria jail so I can torture him. After all," he added, "torture is now part of the American way of life." Judge Brinkema said the court-appointed lawyers, who had continued to file motions on Moussaoui's behalf even without his cooperation, would now formally resume control of the case.[29]

Another problem with *pro se* defense is that it may require a judge to intervene and tell the defendant that he has made an error and instruct him as to how to proceed. This creates the appearance of bias to the jury and may make it difficult for the judge to be completely impartial in ruling on trial motions. In these instances, it falls to the trial judge, while inquiring into a waiver of the right to counsel, to discover whether the defendant has the legal knowledge to conduct a trial and whether his or her actions are likely to cause costly delays, a mistrial, or a subsequent appeal.

Faretta v. California

In *Faretta v. California* (1975), the Supreme Court decided (6–3) that the Sixth Amendment established a right to self-representation and set down guidelines for *pro se* defense. Justice Stewart, writing for the majority, said that the issue "is whether a State may constitutionally hale a person into its criminal courts and there force a lawyer upon him, even when he insists that he wants to conduct his own defense" (*Faretta v. California,* 1975). Faretta, charged with grand theft, had previously defended himself in court. He believed his assigned counsel in the Los Angeles Superior Court was too burdened with a large caseload to adequately assist him. The trial judge questioned Faretta about the hearsay rule and the law regarding challenges to potential jurors and ruled that he had no constitutional right to self-representation. The trial was conducted with appointed counsel.

The core of the Supreme Court's decision was the basic significance of the Sixth Amendment's text:

> The Sixth Amendment does not provide merely that a defense shall be made for the accused; it grants to the accused personally the right to make his defense. It is the accused, not counsel, who must be "informed of the nature and cause of the accusation," who must be "confronted with the witnesses against him," and who must be accorded "compulsory process for obtaining witnesses in his favor." Although not stated in the Amendment in so many words, the right to self-representation—to make one's own defense personally—is thus necessarily implied by the structure of the Amendment. The right to defend is given directly to the accused; for it is he who suffers the consequences if the defense fails.
>
> . . .
>
> The counsel provision supplements this design. It speaks of the "assistance" of counsel, and an assistant, however expert, is still an assistant. The language and spirit of the Sixth Amendment contemplate that counsel, like the other defense tools guaranteed by the Amendment, shall be an aid to a willing defendant—not an organ of the State interposed between an unwilling defendant and his right to defend himself personally. To thrust counsel upon the accused, against his considered wish, thus violates the logic of the Amendment. In such a case, counsel is not an assistant, but a master; and the right to make a defense is stripped of the personal character upon which the Amendment insists. It is true that when a defendant chooses to have a lawyer manage and present his case, law and tradition may allocate to the counsel the power to make binding decisions of trial strategy in many areas. . . . This allocation can only be justified, however, by the defendant's consent, at the outset, to accept counsel as his representative. An unwanted counsel "represents" the defendant only through a tenuous and unacceptable legal fiction. Unless the accused has acquiesced in such representation, the defense presented is not the defense guaranteed him by the Constitution, for, in a very real sense, it is not his defense. (*Faretta v. California,* 1975)

Therefore, the right to counsel announced in *Gideon v. Wainwright* was not inconsistent with the right to self-representation: "Personal liberties are not rooted in the law of averages. The right to defend is personal" (*Faretta v. California,* 1975).

On the other hand, self-representation is not a license. To accept a waiver of counsel, a judge has to be convinced that a defendant has the minimal ability to conduct the trial. "A defendant need not himself have the skill and experience of a lawyer in order competently and intelligently to choose self-representation" (*Faretta v. California*, 1975). A judge cannot deny self-representation to a defendant simply because the defendant does not have expert knowledge of criminal law and procedure. The record in the case showed "that Faretta was literate, competent, and understanding, and that he was voluntarily exercising his informed free will." The trial judge was in error in denying him the right to represent himself, even if he did not have expert knowledge of hearsay rules (*Faretta v. California*, 1975).

Chief Justice Burger dissented in *Faretta*. He saw the basic right as the Sixth Amendment right to a fair trial. The entire justice system and the people at large have a stake in a fair and competent trial system. "That goal is ill-served, and the integrity of and public confidence in the system are undermined, when an easy conviction is obtained due to the defendant's ill-advised decision to waive counsel." Furthermore, the dissent saw the majority opinion as undermining the authority of the trial judge, who should retain final discretion on this question, because the judge "is in the best position to determine whether the accused is capable of conducting his defense."

In sum, the waiver of counsel is an unusual and extreme step. When requested, a judge should personally inform the defendant who wishes to defend *pro se* "of the many procedural complications of representing oneself, that he will be given no special treatment, and that waiving counsel is generally unwise."[30] In the colloquy with the defendant, the judge takes pains to ensure that the waiver is voluntary, that it is unequivocal and expressed, that it is knowing and intelligent, and that the defendant is mentally able to make the waiver. The verbal exchange between the judge and the defendant is placed on the record. If, after all this, the defendant meets the minimum standard of competency and continues to insist on self-representation, the judge has no right to deny self-representation.

Standby Counsel

The practice of the judge appointing **standby counsel** to assist a *pro se* defendant was upheld by the Supreme Court in ***McKaskle v. Wiggins*** (1984). Justice Sandra Day O'Connor ruled that a defendant's Sixth Amendment rights are not violated when standby counsel is appointed, even over the defendant's objection. To ensure that standby counsel does not overwhelm the defendant's personal right to make a defense, two rules guide the conduct of such counsel and determine when the attorney might have undermined the defendant's rights:

> First, the *pro se* defendant is entitled to preserve actual control over the case he chooses to present to the jury. . . . If standby counsel's participation over the defendant's objection effectively allows counsel to make or substantially interfere with any significant tactical decisions, or to control the questioning of witnesses, or to speak instead of the defendant on any matter of importance, the *Faretta* right is eroded.
>
> Second, participation by standby counsel without the defendant's consent should not be allowed to destroy the jury's perception that the defendant is representing himself. The defendant's appearance in the status of one conducting his own defense . . . exists to affirm the accused's individual dignity and autonomy. (*McKaskle v. Wiggins*, 1984)

Dissenting justices suggested that this two-pronged rule actually gives trial judges little guidance on how to restrain standby counsel from taking over the case from the self-represented defendant. Also, the dissenters sharply differed with the majority about whether the activity of standby counsel in this case (including over fifty interventions in a three-day trial precipitating some disagreements that were observed by the jury) amounted to a violation of the *Faretta* self-representation right.

Four reasons support the regular appointment of standby counsel. First, if a *pro se* defendant, purposely or out of confusion, decides during trial to ask for a lawyer, there will be no delay—standby counsel will be able to immediately continue the case. Second, by providing expert advice, standby counsel helps the *pro se* defendant "exercise his right of self-representation more effectively and begins to level the playing field in the courtroom."[31] Third, standby counsel can assist "a defendant of questionable mental or emotional fortitude" who still meets the low appointment standard of *Godinez v. Moran* (1993) in making a meaningful defense and thus maintain the fairness of the judicial process.[32] Finally, standby counsel eliminates the appearance of bias created when the judge gives the defendant practice pointers during the trial.

Some problems may occur from the use of standby counsel, however. As *McKaskle v. Wiggins* noted, when standby counsel interferes too much, the defendant may feel that his or her right to self-representation is infringed. Also, it is unwise for a court to appoint as standby counsel the lawyer whom the defendant dismissed. Finally, "hybrid representation," where both the defendant and standby counsel appear before the jury, should be disallowed. It causes confusion in the jury's mind and may **prejudice the case.** To correct this, Marie Williams suggests that (1) standby counsel be appointed in every *pro se* defense, (2) the jury be instructed as to the constitutionality and nature of standby counsel, and (3) that hybrid representation not be allowed except when the defendant is cross-examining the victim and when the defendant takes the stand to testify.[33]

THE EFFECTIVE ASSISTANCE OF COUNSEL

In 1970, the Supreme Court ruled that the Sixth Amendment assistance of counsel guarantee in criminal cases means the *effective* assistance of retained and appointed counsel (*McMann v. Richardson,* 1970). The Court clarified the meaning of effective assistance in *Strickland v. Washington* (1984) and established rules for interpreting this standard in practice.

Read Case and Comments: *Strickland v. Washington.*

Applying the *Strickland* Test

Strickland's rules apply not only to felony trials and death penalty sentencing proceedings, but also at plea bargaining (*Hill v. Lockhart,* 1985). **Glover v. United States** (2001) held that an attorney's failure to argue a point under the federal sentencing guidelines, possibly resulting in an increase in the defendant's sentence of six months' imprisonment, was a sufficiently large loss to raise an effective assistance of counsel argument. Under *Strickland v. Washington,* a defendant established prejudice when a trial court made a sentencing guidelines error, the attorney failed to argue against the error, and as a result the defendant's sentence was increased. It is not clear whether *Glover* applies to state sentencing processes that are entirely indeterminate, discretionary, and unstructured. These proceedings may be informal and involve standardless discretion. As such, it may be impossible to establish criteria of effective assistance. Capital sentencing and guideline sentencing, however, have elements of an adversary trial so that the standards of the *Strickland* two-pronged test can be applied.

Proof of Ineffective Assistance.   **United States v. Cronic** (1984) ruled that ineffective assistance of counsel must be affirmatively proven and is not to be inferred. A defendant convicted of mail fraud claimed ineffective assistance of counsel because (1) his lawyer was inexperienced; (2) the charge was serious; (3) the case facts were complex; (4) the time to investigate was limited to thirty days; and (5) some witnesses were inaccessible. The *Strickland* standard puts the burden of proof on the convicted

Strickland v. Washington

466 U.S. 668, 104 S.Ct. 2052, 80 L.Ed.2d 674 (1984)

JUSTICE O'CONNOR delivered the opinion of the Court.

* * *

I

A

[Respondent, David Leroy Washington, was found guilty and sentenced to death in Florida for a crime spree that included three murders, torture, kidnapping, and theft. He confessed to the police. Against the advice of his experienced, assigned defense lawyer, Washington waived a jury trial and pleaded guilty, telling the judge that he accepted responsibility for his acts. Against counsel's advice, once again, Washington also waived an advisory jury on the death penalty issue.] **[a]**

[After his trial, conviction, and death sentence, Washington appealed as of right to the Florida Supreme Court, which upheld his conviction and sentence. A collateral state appeal on the grounds of ineffective assistance of counsel resulted in a ruling, upheld by the Florida Supreme Court, that Washington's lawyer was competent. Washington then filed a petition for a writ of habeas corpus in federal district court; an evidentiary hearing resulted in finding the lawyer competent. An en banc decision of the federal circuit court ultimately reversed and remanded. Florida petitioned the federal decision to the U.S. Supreme Court, which reversed the court of appeals, finding that the federal district court was correct in denying the writ of habeas corpus.]

* * *

In preparing for the sentencing hearing, counsel spoke with respondent about his background. He also spoke on the telephone with respondent's wife and mother, though he did not follow up on the one unsuccessful effort to meet with them. He did not otherwise seek out character witnesses for respondent. **[b]** * * * Nor did he request a psychiatric examination, since his conversations with his client gave no indication that respondent had psychological problems. * * *

Counsel decided not to present and hence not to look further for evidence concerning respondent's character and emotional state. That decision reflected trial counsel's sense of hopelessness about overcoming the evidentiary effect of respondent's confessions to the gruesome crimes. * * * It also reflected the judgment that it was advisable to rely on the plea colloquy for evidence about respondent's background and about his claim of emotional stress: the plea colloquy communicated sufficient information about these subjects, and by foregoing the opportunity to present new evidence on these subjects, counsel prevented the State from cross-examining respondent on his claim and from putting on psychiatric evidence of its own.

Counsel also excluded from the sentencing hearing other evidence he thought was potentially damaging. He successfully moved to exclude respondent's "rap sheet." **[c]** * * * Because he judged that a presentence report might prove more detrimental than helpful, as it would have included respondent's criminal history and thereby undermined the claim of no significant history of criminal activity, he did not request that one be prepared. * * *

At the sentencing hearing, counsel's strategy [stressed Washington's remorse, his acceptance of responsibility, the stress that he claimed he was under at the time of the crime spree, and his apparently clean prior criminal record]. The State put on evidence and witnesses largely for the purpose of describing the details of the crimes. Counsel did not cross-examine the medical experts who testified about the manner of death of respondent's victims.

[a] For purposes of effective assistance of counsel, the guilt phase and the death penalty phase of a capital trial are treated the same; the jury's binary decision of one of two sentences, death or life, parallels the guilty/not guilty verdict.

[b] Character witnesses testify only about a defendant's general reputation and rarely make negative statements. Judges are less likely to be impressed by character witnesses than are jurors.

[c] Washington's lawyer seems to be doing little to present mitigating factors and present some positive and human side of his client, but he also keeps damaging information out of consideration by this strategy.

(continued)

[The trial judge found that the aggravating circumstances outweighed the mitigating circumstances and sentenced Washington to death.]

* * *

B

[d] This information was gathered by Washington's appellate lawyers, who sought to reverse the death penalty by showing that it resulted from the ineffectiveness of his trial attorney.

* * * Respondent challenged counsel's assistance in six respects. He asserted that counsel was ineffective because he failed to move for a continuance to prepare for sentencing, to request a psychiatric report, to investigate and present character witnesses, to seek a pre-sentence investigation report, to present meaningful arguments to the sentencing judge, and to investigate the medical examiner's reports or cross-examine the medical experts. **[d]** In support of the claim, respondent submitted 14 affidavits from friends, neighbors, and relatives stating that they would have testified if asked to do so. He also submitted one psychiatric report and one psychological report stating that respondent, though not under the influence of extreme mental or emotional disturbance, was "chronically frustrated and depressed because of his economic dilemma" at the time of his crimes.

[Florida courts found Washington's six claims to be groundless: (1) there was no legal basis for seeking a continuance; (2) state psychiatric examinations of Washington disclosed no mental abnormalities; (3) character witnesses would not have rebutted aggravating circumstances and would have added no mitigating circumstances; (4) a presentence report would have brought out the respondent's prior criminal record, which was otherwise kept out of the proceedings; (5) counsel presented an "admirable" argument for the respondent in light of the overwhelming nature of the aggravating circumstances; and (6) cross-examination of the state's medical witnesses could have led the prosecution, on rebuttal, to undermine Washington's claim that he was under stress when he went on his crime spree.]

* * * [T]he trial court concluded * * * "there is not even the remotest chance that the outcome would have been any different. The plain fact is that the aggravating circumstances proved in this case were completely *overwhelming.* * * * "

II

[e] The right to counsel is placed in the context of the right to a fair trial; thus it serves the interests of society while benefiting the individual defendant.

* * * The right to counsel plays a crucial role in the adversarial system embodied in the Sixth Amendment, since access to counsel's skill and knowledge is necessary to accord defendants the "ample opportunity to meet the case of the prosecution" to which they are entitled. * * * **[e]**

* * * That a person who happens to be a lawyer is present at trial alongside the accused, however, is not enough to satisfy the constitutional command. The Sixth Amendment recognizes the right to the assistance of counsel because it envisions counsel's playing a role that is critical to the ability of the adversarial system to produce just results. An accused is entitled to be assisted by an attorney, whether retained or appointed, who plays the role necessary to ensure that the trial is fair.

[f] Justice O'Connor's "benchmark" means that some errors by counsel can be overlooked *if* the overall result of the trial was just.

For that reason, the Court has recognized that "the right to counsel is the right to the effective assistance of counsel." * * *

* * * The benchmark for judging any claim of ineffectiveness must be whether counsel's conduct so undermined the proper functioning of the adversarial process that the trial cannot be relied on as having produced a just result. **[f]**

III

[g] The Court establishes a two-prong test for the effective assistance of counsel. The "performance" prong is discussed in III.A. and the "prejudice" prong in III.B.

A convicted defendant's claim that counsel's assistance was so defective as to require reversal of a conviction or death sentence has two components. **[g]** First, the defendant must show that counsel's performance was deficient. This requires showing that counsel made errors so serious that counsel was not functioning as the "counsel" guaranteed the defendant by the Sixth Amendment. Second, the defendant must show that the **deficient performance** prejudiced the defense.

This requires showing that counsel's errors were so serious as to deprive the defendant of a fair trial, a trial whose result is reliable. Unless a defendant makes both showings, it cannot be said that the conviction or death sentence resulted from a breakdown in the adversary process that renders the result unreliable.

A

[T]he proper standard for attorney performance is that of reasonably effective assistance. * * * When a convicted defendant complains of the ineffectiveness of counsel's assistance, the defendant must show that counsel's representation fell below an objective standard of reasonableness. **[h]**

More specific guidelines are not appropriate. The Sixth Amendment * * * relies instead on the legal profession's maintenance of standards sufficient to justify the law's presumption that counsel will fulfill the role in the adversary process that the Amendment envisions. * * * The proper measure of attorney performance remains simply reasonableness under prevailing professional norms. **[i]**

* * * Counsel's function is to assist the defendant, and hence counsel owes the client a duty of loyalty, a duty to avoid conflicts of interest. * * * From counsel's function as assistant to the defendant derive the overarching duty to advocate the defendant's cause and the more particular duties to consult with the defendant on important decisions and to keep the defendant informed of important developments in the course of the prosecution. Counsel also has a duty to bring to bear such skill and knowledge as will render the trial a reliable adversarial testing process. * * *

These basic duties neither exhaustively define the obligations of counsel nor form a checklist for judicial evaluation of attorney performance. In any case presenting an ineffectiveness claim, the performance inquiry must be whether counsel's assistance was reasonable considering all the circumstances. Prevailing norms of practice as reflected in American Bar Association standards and the like * * * are guides to determining what is reasonable, but they are only guides. No particular set of detailed rules for counsel's conduct can satisfactorily take account of the variety of circumstances faced by defense counsel or the range of legitimate decisions regarding how best to represent a criminal defendant. Any such set of rules would interfere with the constitutionally protected independence of counsel and restrict the wide latitude counsel must have in making tactical decisions. * * *

Judicial scrutiny of counsel's performance must be highly deferential. **[j]** It is all too tempting for a defendant to second-guess counsel's assistance after conviction or adverse sentence, and it is all too easy for a court, examining counsel's defense after it has proved unsuccessful, to conclude that a particular act or omission of counsel was unreasonable. * * * [A] court must indulge a strong presumption that counsel's conduct falls within the wide range of reasonable professional assistance. * * * There are countless ways to provide effective assistance in any given case. Even the best criminal defense attorneys would not defend a particular client in the same way. * * *

[Intense scrutiny of attorneys' performances by appellate courts would produce a flood of ineffectiveness challenges that would make lawyers less willing to represent criminal defendants and would undermine trust between attorney and client.]

* * * A convicted defendant making a claim of ineffective assistance must identify the acts or omissions of counsel that are alleged not to have been the result of reasonable professional judgment. The court must then determine whether, in light of all the circumstances, the identified acts or omissions were outside the wide range of professionally competent assistance.

* * *

(continued)

[h] "Reasonableness" is not a precise standard; what standard of reasonableness does the Court rely on? Note that the burden of proof is on the convicted defendant to prove that his or her lawyer was ineffective.

[i] The "objective" measure is the performance of other lawyers. Only general guidelines of effective (or deficient) performance by a criminal defense lawyer are provided here. Thus deficient performance must be determined from case-by-case decisions of the courts.

[j] "Deferential" review means that the benefit of doubt is resolved in favor of finding a lawyer's performance competent.

B

[k] The "prejudice" prong asks whether counsel's performance substantially contributed to the guilty verdict or sentence of death. It does not mean "discrimination" in this context.

An error by counsel, even if professionally unreasonable, does not warrant setting aside the judgment of a criminal proceeding if the error had no effect on the judgment. * * * The purpose of the Sixth Amendment guarantee of counsel is to ensure that a defendant has the assistance necessary to justify reliance on the outcome of the proceeding. **[k]** Accordingly, any deficiencies in counsel's performance must be prejudicial to the defense in order to constitute ineffective assistance under the Constitution.

In certain Sixth Amendment contexts, prejudice is presumed. Actual or constructive denial of the assistance of counsel altogether is legally presumed to result in prejudice. * * * Prejudice in these circumstances is so likely that case-by-case inquiry into prejudice is not worth the cost. * * *

One type of actual ineffectiveness claim warrants a similar, though more limited, presumption of prejudice. In *Cuyler v. Sullivan* (1980), the Court held that prejudice is presumed when counsel is burdened by an actual conflict of interest. In those circumstances, counsel breaches the duty of loyalty, perhaps the most basic of counsel's duties. * * * Prejudice is presumed only if the defendant demonstrates that counsel "actively represented conflicting interests" and that "an actual conflict of interest adversely affected his lawyer's performance." * * * **[l]**

[l] Two kinds of "automatic prejudice" eliminate the defendant's need to prove prejudice: (1) no assistance of counsel and (2) conflict of interest. In other cases, prejudice must be proven beyond a reasonable doubt on the facts.

Conflict of interest claims aside, actual ineffectiveness claims alleging a deficiency in attorney performance are subject to a general requirement that the defendant affirmatively prove prejudice. * * * Attorney errors come in an infinite variety and are as likely to be utterly harmless in a particular case as they are to be prejudicial. They cannot be classified according to likelihood of causing prejudice. Nor can they be defined with sufficient precision to inform defense attorneys correctly just what conduct to avoid. Representation is an art, and an act or omission that is unprofessional in one case may be sound or even brilliant in another. Even if a defendant shows that particular errors of counsel were unreasonable, therefore, the defendant must show that they actually had an adverse effect on the defense.

* * *

[The defendant cannot argue that his or her conviction would likely not have occurred because the jury would have nullified the law. The prejudice prong must be assessed on the basis of assuming that a conscientious jury would have applied legal standards impartially.]

[m] The appellate court must decide whether the outcome would likely have differed if the attorney had not made the errors that established deficient performance under the first prong.

* * * When a defendant challenges a conviction, the question is whether there is a reasonable probability that, absent the errors, the fact-finder would have had a reasonable doubt respecting guilt. **[m]** When a defendant challenges a death sentence such as the one at issue in this case, the question is whether there is a reasonable probability that, absent the errors, the sentencer * * * would have concluded that the balance of aggravating and mitigating circumstances did not warrant death.

[n] A "facts and circumstances" or "totality of the evidence" standard is open-ended; it is the antithesis of a bright-line rule. As with the "deficient-performance" prong, standards will develop incrementally as the courts decide specific cases.

In making this determination, a court hearing an ineffectiveness claim must consider the totality of the evidence before the judge or jury. Some of the factual findings will have been unaffected by the errors, and factual findings that were affected will have been affected in different ways. Some errors will have had a pervasive effect on the inferences to be drawn from the evidence, altering the entire evidentiary picture, and some will have had an isolated, trivial effect. Moreover, a verdict or conclusion only weakly supported by the record is more likely to have been affected by errors than one with overwhelming record support. **[n]** Taking the unaffected findings as a given, and taking due account of the effect of the errors on the remaining findings, a court making the prejudice inquiry must ask if the defendant has met the burden of showing that the decision reached would reasonably likely have been different absent the errors.

[In Part V, the Court applied the standards announced in Parts II and III to the facts of the case. The majority concluded that the conduct of Washington's lawyer was adequate and was not the cause of the death penalty sentence.]

JUSTICE MARSHALL, dissenting.

* * *

I

A

My objection to the performance standard adopted by the Court is that it is so malleable that, in practice, it will either have no grip at all or will yield excessive variation in the manner in which the Sixth Amendment is interpreted and applied by different courts. To tell lawyers and the lower courts that counsel for a criminal defendant must behave "reasonably" and must act like "a reasonably competent attorney," is to tell them almost nothing. In essence, the majority has instructed judges called upon to assess claims of ineffective assistance of counsel to advert to their own intuitions regarding what constitutes "professional" representation, and has discouraged them from trying to develop more detailed standards governing the performance of defense counsel. **[o]** In my view, the Court has thereby not only abdicated its own responsibility to interpret the Constitution, but also impaired the ability of the lower courts to exercise theirs.

[o] If Justice Marshall is correct, is it possible to specify good lawyering? Should Washington's lawyer have performed each of the six acts not done?

* * *

B

I object to the prejudice standard adopted by the Court for two independent reasons. First, it is often very difficult to tell whether a defendant convicted after a trial in which he was ineffectively represented would have fared better if his lawyer had been competent. Seemingly impregnable cases can sometimes be dismantled by good defense counsel. On the basis of a cold record, it may be impossible for a reviewing court confidently to ascertain how the government's evidence and arguments would have stood up against rebuttal and cross-examination by a shrewd, well-prepared lawyer. The difficulties of estimating prejudice after the fact are exacerbated by the possibility that evidence of injury to the defendant may be missing from the record precisely because of the incompetence of defense counsel. **[p]** In view of all these impediments to a fair evaluation of the probability that the outcome of a trial was affected by ineffectiveness of counsel, it seems to me senseless to impose on a defendant whose lawyer has been shown to have been incompetent the burden of demonstrating prejudice.

[p] Justice Marshall would eliminate the "prejudice" prong entirely. Would this make it very difficult to uphold convictions on appeal?

Second and more fundamentally, the assumption on which the Court's holding rests is that the only purpose of the constitutional guarantee of effective assistance of counsel is to reduce the chance that innocent persons will be convicted. In my view, the guarantee also functions to ensure that convictions are obtained only through fundamentally fair procedures. The majority contends that the Sixth Amendment is not violated when a manifestly guilty defendant is convicted after a trial in which he was represented by a manifestly ineffective attorney. **[q]** I cannot agree. Every defendant is entitled to a trial in which his interests are vigorously and conscientiously advocated by an able lawyer. A proceeding in which the defendant does not receive meaningful assistance in meeting the forces of the State does not, in my opinion, constitute due process.

[q] Justice Marshall was the most experienced trial attorney sitting on the Court. As an African American lawyer challenging racial segregation in Southern courts in the 1930s, 1940s, and 1950s, he often worked under extremely hostile circumstances. Should his experience give his views special weight?

* * *

complainant to prove that his or her lawyer's assistance was ineffective. Cronic raised a set of relevant factors but could not point to any specific action by his lawyer that showed deficient performance. If Cronic's position were accepted, the Court could find ineffective assistance even though the lawyer's performance was flawless. None of the factors in the case, alone or in combination, deprived Cronic of a fair trial: Relevant evidence was supplied, and the government's evidence was cross-examined. The Court also noted in *Cronic* that the test of adequate performance did not require that the lawyer perform flawlessly in a trial. "When a true adversarial criminal trial has been conducted—even if defense counsel may have made demonstrable errors—the kind of testing envisioned by the Sixth Amendment has occurred."

A death penalty was appealed on the grounds of ineffective assistance of counsel in *Bell v. Cone* (2002). Gary Cone was convicted for a brutal murder; his insanity defense was rejected. At the death penalty phase, the prosecutor established aggravating factors warranting the death penalty. After the junior prosecutor gave a low-key closing, defense counsel waived final argument in order to prevent the lead prosecutor, by all accounts an extremely effective advocate, from arguing in rebuttal. The defense counsel cross-examined prosecution witnesses but called no other witnesses. He directed the jury's attention to the mitigating evidence presented at trial, relating to Gary Cone's substance abuse and posttraumatic stress disorders resulting from his Vietnam military service; the jury was reminded that his mother testified that Cone had returned from Vietnam a changed person. The jury found four aggravating factors and no mitigating circumstances, which required the imposition of the death penalty.

The Supreme Court upheld the state appellate court's finding that the performance of Cone's counsel was within the permissible range of competency under the attorney-performance standard of *Strickland v. Washington*. The Supreme Court agreed that the state court's application of *Strickland* was reasonable, especially in light of the guideline that "judicial scrutiny of a counsel's performance must be highly deferential" and that "every effort [must] be made to eliminate the distorting effects of hindsight, to reconstruct the circumstances of counsel's challenged conduct, and to evaluate the conduct from counsel's perspective at the time" (*Bell v. Cone*, 2002, citing *Strickland*). In this light, the defense attorney's decision to not make a closing statement so as to preclude an effective close by an experienced prosecutor, plus his cross-examination and bringing out mitigating factors, can reasonably be considered sound trial strategy.

Examples of Ineffective Assistance.
An example of deficient performance is found in *Kimmelman v. Morrison* (1986). The defense lawyer in a rape prosecution failed to object to the introduction of illegally seized evidence, filed a late motion for the suppression of evidence, and did not ask for discovery of police reports that would have indicated that the seizure of evidence was arguably unconstitutional. The attorney's excuse was that he believed it was the state's responsibility to turn over all relevant evidence. Since there is no such general obligation, the Supreme Court ruled that the lawyer's failure to take normal and routine steps before trial to obtain relevant evidence was inexcusable negligence, amounting to deficient performance. The Court remanded to determine if the deficient performance prejudiced the outcome of the case.

In *Williams v. Taylor* (2000), the Supreme Court reinstated a trial court's finding that counsel was ineffective at the death penalty phase of a trial, after the Virginia Supreme Court ruled that the performance was reasonable. In this robbery and capital murder case, the trial judge found that defense counsel had not presented and explained the significance of all the available mitigating factors. If they had, the cumulative mitigation evidence would have raised a reasonable probability that the result of the sentencing proceeding would have been different. Defense counsel began to prepare for the capital sentencing only a week before the trial and failed to conduct an investigation that would have uncovered extensive records of mitigation—not because of any strategic calculation, but because the attorneys incorrectly thought that state law barred access to such records. The mitigating factors would have included Terry William's borderline mental retardation; his parents' conviction for neglect; his severe and repeated beatings by his father; his stay in an abusive foster home; his return to his abusive parents after their release from prison; prison records indicating that Williams received commendations for helping to crack a prison drug ring and for returning a guard's missing wallet; and testimony of prison officials who described Williams as among the inmates least likely to act in a violent, dangerous, or provocative way.

In **Rompilla v. Beard** (2005), two public defenders were held to be deficient in failing to examine the court file on Ronald Rompilla's prior conviction for the death penalty phase of a Pennsylvania murder trial. The attorneys interviewed Rompilla, who was recalcitrant and unhelpful, and family members and medical experts who were equally unhelpful in uncovering mitigating factors. Prior to the trial, the prosecutor notified defense counsel and the court that it would use Rompilla's court file containing his prior criminal conviction as a basis for finding aggravating factors. The prosecutor introduced Rompilla's prior felony conviction as an aggravating factor; the mitigating factors consisted of family members pleading for mercy. Rompilla was sentenced to death. When appellate lawyers looked at the prior conviction file, they "found a range of mitigation leads that no other source had opened up." The information showed that Rompilla had a horrendous upbringing by a violent father and an alcoholic mother who drank during her pregnancy with Ronald. His father severely beat his mother and beat young Ronald with his hands, fists, leather straps, belts, and sticks. His mother once stabbed his father. Rompilla had run-ins with juvenile authorities, a drinking problem, and a third-grade level of cognition after nine years of schooling. He was diagnosed as bordering on schizophrenia. The Rompilla children lived in terror and in isolation from other children; there were no expressions of parental love, affection, or approval; Rompilla and his brother Richard were locked in a small wire mesh dog pen that was filthy and filled with excrement. The Rompilla house had no indoor plumbing; Ronald slept in the attic with no heat, and the children attended school in rags.

These were clearly mitigating factors. The Court's majority held that the public defenders' defense was deficient in failing to adhere to the "norms of adequate investigation in preparing for the sentencing phase of a capital case." Further, the evidence found in the sentencing file "has shown beyond any doubt that counsel's lapse was prejudicial." Justice O'Connor concurred, noting that the defense counsel did not fail to look at the prior conviction file as a matter of trial strategy but claimed that they were overworked. Four dissenting justices, in an opinion by Justice Anthony Kennedy, were concerned that a "*per se* rule requiring counsel in every case to review the records of prior convictions used by the State as aggravation evidence is a radical departure from *Strickland*" and would impose impossible burdens in future cases.

Effective Assistance and Truth.
The attorney's obligation to maintain the integrity of the trial process and to elicit the truth can appear to conflict with the specific obligation to provide the best defense. It is fundamental to the adjudication process that evidence cannot be fabricated. A lawyer has no obligation to support a defendant with false testimony. In **Nix v. Whiteside** (1986), a defendant charged with murder claimed self-defense. He told his lawyer that he did not actually see a gun in his assailant's hand but believed it was there. He wanted to testify that he saw "something metallic" because a jury would be more likely to believe the assailant had a gun. Counsel told Whiteside that as a matter of law, it was not necessary for the defendant to see a gun to prove self-defense and made it clear that if Whiteside perjured himself, the

lawyer would indicate this to the judge. Whiteside was convicted and argued that the lawyer's advice was ineffective assistance. The Supreme Court ruled that because there is no right, constitutional or otherwise, to testify falsely, the lawyer's assistance was not deficient.

Conflict of Interest

Multiple representation occurs when a retained or assigned attorney represents two or more co-defendants. In *Cuyler v. Sullivan* (1980), attorneys DiBona and Peruto represented three defendants. DiBona was primarily responsible for Sullivan's trial, while Peruto, responsible for the trial of Sullivan's co-defendants, advised DiBona in the Sullivan trial. The Supreme Court held that this constituted multiple representation, but the multiple representation did not, in itself, violate an attorney's obligations to adequately defend and to give full and complete attention to the client's defense. Multiple representation, therefore, is not automatically a conflict of interest. This rule takes economic realities of providing counsel into consideration. As Justice Stevens said in *Burger v. Kemp* (1987), "Particularly in smaller communities where the supply of qualified lawyers willing to accept the demanding and unrewarding work of representing capital prisoners is extremely limited, the defendants may actually benefit from the joint efforts of two partners who supplement one another in their preparation. Moreover, we generally presume that the lawyer is fully conscious of the overarching duty of complete loyalty to his or her client."

A conflict of interest arises when, in the circumstance of multiple representation, an attorney renders less effective assistance to one client out of consideration for the interests of the other client. The long-standing rule is that where a conflict of interest exists, the defendant establishes ineffective assistance of counsel per se and need not show that the conflict of interest prejudiced the case (*Glasser v. United States,* 1942). A trial judge is not obligated to hold a hearing into the possibility of a conflict of interest in every case of multiple representation (*Cuyler v. Sullivan,* 1980). However, should an assigned attorney raise a timely objection to multiple representation on the grounds that it constitutes a conflict of interest, the trial judge is required to hold a hearing to make certain that there is no genuine conflict before the trial can proceed (*Holloway v. Arkansas,* 1978).

A conflict of interest can be difficult to prove, as the defendant "must demonstrate that an actual conflict of interest adversely affected his lawyer's performance" (*Cuyler v. Sullivan,* 1980). *Burger v. Kemp* (1987) is an example where the mere possibility of a conflict of interest does not amount to ineffective assistance of counsel under *Strickland.* Burger first argued that his lawyer failed in an appellate brief to raise, as a death penalty mitigation, the argument that Burger was less culpable for the killing than a co-defendant. The Supreme Court rejected this contention because (1) the lesser culpability defense was raised and rejected at trial; (2) Burger actually killed the victim; (3) the Georgia Supreme Court found his acts to be "inhuman"; and (4) lower courts found that it was not deficient performance by the attorney to forgo this avenue on appeal.

Burger next claimed that the lawyer failed to obtain a plea bargain resulting in a life sentence. However, the facts indicated that the defense lawyer attempted to obtain a plea, but the prosecutor simply refused to agree to a plea bargain. Finally, Burger claimed that the lawyer failed to bring out mitigating circumstances at the death penalty sentencing hearing. The omission of some mitigating information was deemed a tactical decision by the lawyer, designed to keep the defendant off the stand and thereby keep aggravating information from the court. Over the vigorous dissent of four justices, the Supreme Court held in this case that there was no deficient performance or conflict of interest.

COUNSEL IN A TIME OF TERROR

In 1770, a thirty-four-year-old Boston lawyer, a warm partisan of the growing movement for independence from Great Britain, nevertheless took on the unpopular defense of an English officer and soldiers charged with murder for killing five members of a rock-throwing mob. The incident, known as the Boston Massacre in the iconography of American history, is well known as one of the sparks that led to the Revolutionary War, but it is less well remembered for the role played by the young lawyer, John Adams, who would be a legislative leader during the war for independence and second president of the United States. Adams's skillful defense won acquittals for the captain and six of the eight soldiers who fired into the mob. Adams was severely criticized in the press for his "zealous defense of the Redcoats," and his practice suffered. Yet he was later praised for his "fierce integrity" to the law. In defending his action, Adams said that "no man in a free country should be denied the right to counsel and a fair trial."[34]

It is easy to praise principled and courageous defenses of liberty that occurred during half-forgotten past crises and put out of mind how difficult it is to uphold rights during the pressure of present crises. On the day the USA PATRIOT Act was signed into law, less than two months after the 9/11 attacks gripped the nation with fears of terrorism, Attorney General Ashcroft quietly implemented a new prison regulation that allowed the Department of Justice (DOJ) to listen in on and tape confidential attorney-client conversations of people in custody.[35] Previously, federal prison authorities were allowed to impose special administrative measures (SAMs) on *convicted* inmates where probable cause existed to believe they had ordered killings.[36]

The new regulations applied not only to convicted inmates but to witnesses, detainees, pretrial defendants, and anyone in federal custody. The new monitoring could be triggered just by reasonable suspicion to believe "that an inmate may use communications with attorneys or their agents to facilitate acts of terrorism." Unlike an ordinary criminal case in which prosecutors believe that an attorney is acting corruptly, the decision to monitor conversations is not made by a judge but by DOJ officers in their unreviewable discretion. As a safeguard, the regulations stipulate that the conversations will be heard only by "privilege teams" or "taint teams" who will listen only for statements that appear to further or support terrorism. Nevertheless, "it will be impossible for inmates and their counsel to know in advance what parts of their intercepted communications will be deemed to be 'properly privileged materials'" and which will be flagged as assistance to terrorism. Prior to the Ashcroft regulations, SAMs were limited to 120-day periods; they now last for renewable one-year terms. The attorney and the detainee, who is supposedly protected by an attorney-client privilege, are told that conversations will be monitored.[37]

What was the purpose of the Ashcroft regulations? The government's stated intention was to prevent an inmate from passing "messages through the lawyer in order to further terrorist activity."[38] Given the fact that SAMs had already been imposed on lawyers defending terrorism suspects in earlier trials, it is impossible to avoid the conclusion that an additional, covert reason for the even more restrictive monitoring was to intimidate defense attorneys from either agreeing to represent terror suspects or to deter them from effectively representing clients. This may be the case as the attorney general "provided no factual basis for his assertion that this extraordinary procedure is necessary to prevent violent crime or terrorism."[39] Needless to say, "stunned defense lawyers and civil libertarians . . . assailed [the regulations] as an unconstitutional attack on the right to counsel and, in the words of American Civil Liberties Union official Laura W. Murphy, 'a terrifying precedent.'"[40]

Joshua Dratel, a leading defense attorney, was appointed to defend a terrorism suspect in the case that arose from the bombing of U.S. embassies in Kenya and Tanzania in 1998. He worked under the SAMs that preceded the Ashcroft regulations and explained the many ways in which they made the already difficult task of defending terrorism defendants even tougher. Unlike most pretrial detainees who have access to family and others in order to prepare a defense and to maintain some level of morale, a SAM detainee is kept in solitary confinement and can communicate only with his attorney. The "complete isolation, lack of exercise and emotional and mental stimulation" result in the client having "difficulty concentrating" and becoming "irritable, listless, demanding, and uncooperative." This distracts the client from concentrating on the substance of the case. The attorney's time and energies are also taken up in dealing with the "petty and capricious aspects of the SAMs." The client, who is likely to be either a naturalized citizen or an alien and unfamiliar with American legal norms, takes out his frustrations on the attorney and may come to see the lawyer as just a part of the prosecution. The lack of candid disclosure by the client may lead the lawyer to be blindsided at trial by evidence and information that the client did not reveal.[41]

An interesting and self-defeating problem with the SAMs and the Ashcroft regulations, noted by attorney Joshua Dratel and Professor Stephen Schulhofer, is that because the detainee knows the prosecutors are listening in, he will not divulge potentially incriminating information to his defense attorney. In a truly confidential attorney-client relationship, the client's admission may become the basis of plea negotiations. A terrorism client who provides useful information about actual or suspected terrorist networks in return for a lesser sentence would clearly benefit the government, especially as the government should be interested in gaining as much actionable and timely intelligence on at-large terrorists as possible.[42]

Dratel also called the "taint team," which was supposed to raise a "firewall" between the suspect and his lawyer, on the one hand, and prosecutors, on the other, a sham. "The 'firewall' Assistant U.S. Attorney [prosecutor] for the first stage of the Embassy Bombings case—from indictment through the trial of four of the six defendants in custody—became the prosecutor at the next stage, handling the prosecution of the same defendants for whom he had acted as the 'firewall' AUSA for the previous three years."[43]

The prosecution and conviction of attorney Lynne Stewart for violating SAMs strongly suggest that the Ashcroft regulations were designed to intimidate defense attorneys. Described as "matronly looking, plump, and somewhat unkempt . . . Lynne Stewart does not fit the stereotype of a radical attorney."[44] In her mid-sixties, the former school librarian has spent her legal career "mostly representing poor African-American and Latino men accused of street crime," but as an avowed leftist has also defended high-profile radicals.[45] In the 1990s, she was persuaded by Ramsey Clark, former U.S. attorney general turned radical lawyer, to represent the "blind sheik" Omar Abdel Rahman in a trial for instigating the plot to bomb the World Trade Center in 1993 and for other terrorist plots. He was found guilty and sentenced to life plus sixty-five years in 1995.[46]

To visit Sheik Abdel Rahman in prison, as his appellate attorney, Stewart signed SAMs in which she agreed to communicate with Rahman only concerning legal matters, to employ an interpreter, and not to "use my meetings, correspondence, or phone calls with Abdel Rahman to pass messages between third parties (including, but not limited to, the media) and Abdel Rahman." The blind cleric was a leading figure in the Islamic Group (IG), founded in Egypt and designated as a terrorist organization by the U.S. government.[47]

Stewart was indicted in April 2002, and in February 2005 she was "convicted on two counts of conspiring to provide material aid to terrorists, by making the views and instructions of Mr. Abdel Rahman available to his followers in the Islamic Group, . . . [and] of three counts of perjury and defrauding the government for flouting [the SAMs] that barred [the] blind Islamic cleric from communicating with anyone outside his federal prison in Minnesota except his lawyers and his wife."[48] Commentators favorable to Stewart agreed that she stepped over the line of advocacy and flouted the SAMs when she spoke "gibberish" to distract prison officials trying to record the sheikh's conversation with his interpreter.[49] She also let the news media know that Abdel Rahman, who wished to make his voice and influence heard to his followers in Egypt, had withdrawn his support for a cease-fire in Egypt. At trial, Stewart claimed it was part of a defense strategy to ultimately have Abdel Rahman transferred to prison in Egypt.[50] Her sentencing was delayed while she underwent treatment for breast cancer. Federal prosecutors recommended that the grandmother of thirteen receive a sentence of thirty years for "blatantly and repeatedly violating the law."[51]

Former Attorney General Ashcroft flew to New York to announce Stewart's prosecution. There has been no showing that the leaking of Abdel Rahman's statement to his followers has had any real effect on political stability in Egypt or has further stimulated terrorism. Stewart did violate the SAMs, and one experienced advocate, writing before Stewart's conviction, saw her acts as a result of the "excessive zeal" that even experienced defense attorneys can succumb to. Abbe Smith's level-headed analysis notes that "zealous lawyers contemplate getting in a *little* trouble from time to time, though they do not expect to be criminally prosecuted. . . . [W]hat zealous, devoted defender refrains from speaking for clients simply because they are told not to?"[52] There was nothing in Stewart's background to show that she was interested in promoting terrorism, and "there is no indication that Stewart knew anything about, much less passionately believed in the sheik's cause."[53] In this light, a thirty-year sentence recommendation for a prosecution that included counts of promoting terrorism as well as violating the SAMs easily seems like a move on the part of the DOJ and federal prosecutors to intimidate defense lawyers. The federal judge sentenced Ms. Stewart to prison for twenty-eight months, citing her years as a "government-appointed lawyer for unsavory criminal and penniless outcasts" and allowed her to remain free on bail pending appeal.[54] Although this ended Ms. Stewart's legal career, it was not the virtual life sentence demanded by the government. The judge "broadly rejected the prosecutors' portrayal of her as a serial liar and terrorist conspirator who would be a danger to society if she remained free."[55] As for Ms. Stewart's co-defendants, the translator also received a light sentence, but the man who had arranged to send a message to terrorists and to the sheik's followers in Egypt sreceived a twenty-four year sentence.

The vigorous prosecution of persons suspected of having committed acts of terrorism, conspiring to commit acts of terrorism, and providing material support for terrorist organizations is a far preferable way to respond to terror threats than to expand the administration's use of military commissions to civilian cases. (See Chapter 11.) Prosecutors, however, have great powers that, if used unfairly, can undermine the effective and reasonable legal representation of those charged with terrorism. When Lynne Stewart was arrested, for example, her "office was searched, and confidential records and computer files were seized."[56] A similar fate befell the clients of Oregon lawyer, former army lieutenant, and convert to Islam Brandon Mayfield, whose fingerprints were erroneously linked to the Madrid train bombing by bumbling FBI agents who disregarded the objections of Spanish investigators. Mayfield, who had defended a terrorism suspect, discovered that agents had surreptitiously entered his office while he was jailed as a material witness for two weeks and had taken information from his computer files.[57]

This kind of intrusiveness, reminiscent of the tactics of totalitarian states, is bound to have a chilling effect on some lawyers, and the Ashcroft regulations clearly weaken if not completely undermine attorney-client confidentiality, which is the foundation of effective representation. This confidentiality can be breached by government prosecutors when they have probable cause to believe that a lawyer is participating in a criminal conspiracy with a client. In such cases, they can obtain a judge-ordered electronic eavesdropping warrant.[58] Joshua Dratel writes of the extraordinary pressures faced by a lawyer defending accused terrorists. The defense lawyer's "sole obligation and loyalty" to the defendant in ordinary cases become tested in the extreme when the defendant is an accused terrorist who may, if guilty, place the attorney in the class of victims (i.e., "all Americans around the world"). As a result, the defense lawyer is "placed squarely in the middle, tugged in opposite directions by his polar obligations as advocate and citizen. The presence of all these factors results in a sharper appreciation of the essence of a defense lawyer's responsibility, as well as of the panoply of protections and threshold level of treatment and accommodation that criminal defendants enjoy in the average case, but which are denied even to counsel in terrorism cases."[59] Lawyers who defend terrorists "already pay an enormous price. Hate mail, death threats, bomb scares and ostracism by other potential clients are routine costs of representing social pariahs."[60] Under these circumstances, it is necessary to keep steadily in mind the service John Adams rendered to his yet-unborn nation in the Boston Massacre case. Terrorists seek to eliminate the rights that Americans have taken for granted for more than two centuries. Criminal procedure rights will quickly dissolve if the government crushes the ability of defense attorneys to play their assigned constitutional role, which ultimately is to keep the adversary system true.

LAW IN SOCIETY

THE UNMET PROMISE OF EQUAL JUSTICE

Gideon v. Wainwright (1963), *Argersinger v. Hamlin* (1972), and *Strickland v. Washington* (1984) guarantee a competent attorney for every defendant facing a serious criminal charge—even if the defendant is too poor to pay for legal services. A legal guarantee "on the books" is only as good as its enforcement, however. The promise of equal justice is meaningless if the lawyers, courts, county commissions, state legislators, and governors—and ultimately the American people—fail to implement it substantially. Have the legal community and responsible government units responded to the guarantee of equal justice?

It is true that the nation established several methods for providing lawyers for indigent defendants in criminal cases.[61] Different cities, counties, and states either assign lawyers, fund legal aid and public defenders' agencies, or establish contract systems by which bar associations of private firms agree to provide indigent defense for a set fee. As a result, a lawyer always represents an indigent client at public expense. Nevertheless, fees are usually capped and quite low for assigned counsel, and public defenders often have unrealistically large caseloads. It is a struggle to obtain adequate investigators or expert witnesses. The lack of funding for indigent defense undermines the ability even of competent attorneys to provide adequate defense. Proper criminal defense work is an expensive, labor-intensive, expert undertaking. Sadly, America's people and its governmental servants have grown increasingly insensitive in the last few decades to the promise of equal justice.

The Expense of Private Criminal Defense

The cost of retaining a private defense lawyer can be enormous. A 1996 survey by journalists of indigent cases in Houston found that retained lawyers "often can earn $25,000 to $75,000 to defend a felony case, depending on the complexity of the case and the probability that it will go to trial. Several top criminal defense attorneys acknowledged that fees for complex, high-profile cases can run into the hundreds of thousands of dollars."[62] As the following examples show, effective assistance of counsel is a major professional undertaking that is very expensive.

- A car service dispatcher in Queens, New York, who was charged with felonious assault in 1995, claimed self-defense. A seasoned attorney charged $15,000 and hired an investigator at $50 an hour to find witnesses. The dispatcher was found guilty of a lesser charge "and probably avoided prison time." His father mistakenly believed that the money would be returned if his son was found not guilty.[63]

- In the notorious Wenatchee, Washington, "witch hunt," police officer Robert Perez accused Pentecostal Minister Robert Roberson, his wife, Connie, and more than forty parishioners of conducting orgies with children. The case ultimately collapsed after several poor and mentally retarded parishioners were imprisoned. Attorney Robert Van Siclen, who volunteered to defend Mr. Roberson, estimated that the case cost his firm $100,000. He planned to sue the county in an effort to recoup the cost of defending his client during the six-week trial.[64]

- Karen and Jeffrey Wilson, a paralegal and a high school teacher, respectively, were charged with child abuse when their seven-month-old son, Brock, was treated for a head injury. They spent $60,000 in legal fees to regain custody of Brock, who was taken from them by the social services department. Charges were dismissed by the family court.[65]

- Between January and March 2000, Representative Earl Hilliard spent $37,500 in legal fees, out of the $40,000 that he raised for his reelection campaign, to defend himself against an ethics investigation involving his previous race.[66]

- An injured trucker, accused of perpetrating criminal workers' compensation fraud, spent more than $100,000 in attorneys' fees fighting criminal allegations. The trucker was vindicated.[67]

- In late 1999, seven big vitamin companies pleaded guilty to price fixing and agreed to pay more than $1 billion in damages. Their attorneys' fees were estimated at $122 million.[68]

- Linda Tripp, whose Maryland charges for wiretapping in the Whitewater and Lewinsky scandals were ultimately dismissed, ran up legal bills of about $750,000. A defense fund was set up to help her pay her debt.[69]

- Monica Lewinsky, a central figure in the scandal that led to the impeachment of President Bill Clinton, was represented by top lawyers Plato Cacheris and Jacob Stein, who charge about $400 per hour. At the time she hired this team, it was predicted that "she'll likely owe more than $300,000 to her first legal team," which was led by William Ginsburg, whom she dismissed.[70]

- President Clinton's bill for legal services in his impeachment trial exceeded $10 million. To pay these bills, President Clinton created a legal defense fund to receive private donations.[71]

- Murder cases are in a special league. "'In a murder case, practically every defendant is indigent,' says Larry Hammond, a criminal lawyer in Phoenix, Arizona. 'They may not have started that way, but for anyone other than the super-rich, they will be indigent before the case is over.'" Dr. Dale Bertsch, an anesthesiologist accused of murdering his ex-wife in a case with no physical evidence against him, was quoted fees in the $250,000 range. Hammond took the case for the sum total of Bertsch's liquidated assets, which came to about $160,000. He could not pay for an evidentiary hearing, which would have required $50,000, or a mock jury for $30,000. Dr. Bertsch was convicted.[72]

- As for the "super-rich," O. J. Simpson, whose net worth before his trial was said to be $10 million, took out a $3 million credit line on his Brentwood home. He spent $100,000 for a jury consultant, paid a fee of $100,000 a month for twelve months to Robert Shapiro, and paid Johnnie Cochran Jr. "a large flat fee," to mention only the lead attorneys.[73]

- Multimillionaire Robert Durst, acquitted of murdering a neighbor and dismembering the corpse while living in obscurity in a run-down Galveston, Texas, neighborhood, was taped in a jail conversation with his wife mentioning $1.2 million as the cost of his defense, but defense attorneys declined to say what Durst paid for their successful representation.[74]

Funding for Indigent Defense

The underfunding of indigent criminal defense makes a mockery of the constitutional ideal of equal justice. The "largely hospitable funding environment" for indigent defense of the 1960s has given way to "public outcry over the neglect of . . . crime victims" and a steering of "resources toward law enforcement and away from indigent defense."[75] The late David Bazelon, chief judge of the Washington, D.C., U.S. Court of Appeals, wrote in 1984 that the "battle for equal justice is being lost in the trenches of the criminal courts," as the poor, uneducated, and unemployed are being represented all too often by "walking violations of the sixth amendment."[76]

In all jurisdictions, the amounts paid to assigned counsel are significantly below what retained counsel charge. As of May 2000, New York State had not raised fees for assigned attorneys in fourteen years.[77] In 1999, the federal Criminal Justice Act, which since 1964 has provided funding for assigned counsel in federal cases, set a maximum fee of $60 per hour for in-court time and $40 per hour for out-of-court time, far below going rates for retained lawyers.[78] Virginia placed a cap of $845 on the amount an attorney can receive for representing a defendant on a murder charge, but its general assembly approved a 24 percent increase in fees, effective July 1, 2001. "That level of funding will keep Virginia at or near the bottom of the rankings for payment of court-appointed attorneys' fees."[79]

As for public defenders' offices, in most places, the caseloads of public defenders are so high, because of underfunding, the ability of defenders to perform at the best of their abilities is diminished. There is no survey that assesses the total picture in the United States, but there is substantial evidence of real underfunding of indigent defense.

> . . . Across the nation, the bulk of criminal justice funds go to the police, prosecutors, and jails. Only 2.3% of the seventy-four billion dollars spent on the justice system in 1990 went to pay for attorneys for indigent defendants while 7.4% went to the prosecution. However, the number of defendants unable to afford an attorney had risen dramatically, from forty-eight percent in 1982 to eighty percent today. Public defenders handle over 11 million of the 13 million cases which are tried annually. Yet, as of 1990, the United States Department of Justice found that nationally, public defenders are receiving less than one-third of the resources provided to the prosecution. Prosecutors' offices received $5.5 billion from federal, state, local, county, and municipal governments, as opposed to the $1.7 billion provided for public defense by the same government sources. Moreover, defense lawyers are

further overwhelmed by additional resources provided to prosecutors, including a great deal of investigatory work by law enforcement which are officially classified as "police expenditures."[80]

The following examples provide a glimpse of the conditions and pressures that cause ineffective assistance of counsel.

- An assistant public defender in the western United States admitted in open court to doing an inadequate job. She testified that she had collapsed in court and that her health was seriously threatened by a caseload of two thousand cases per year. She resigned from the public defenders' office, saying that she was "actually doing the defendants more harm by just presenting a live body than if they had no representation at all."[81]

- A New Orleans public defender, representing 418 clients in the first seven months of 1991 and with seventy cases pending trial, obtained a court ruling that his excessive caseload precluded effective representation to the clients. "Not even a lawyer with an 'S' on his chest," the judge ruled, "could handle this docket."[82]

- In 1992, New Jersey eliminated $2.9 million budgeted to the Department of the Public Advocate to pay for counsel in cases where a conflict of interest barred the public defender. This left some indigent defendants jailed without an attorney to represent them. The public advocate resigned "in disgust" to protest the budget reductions.[83]

- A survey in the late 1980s showed an annual starting salary of $24,259 for public defenders and an average salary of $34,787 for a defender with five years' experience. This may not have improved by the late 1990s, as the legal profession became "saturated."[84]

The Crisis in Death Penalty Cases

The most serious cases, involving capital punishment, are among the most severely affected by underfunding and incompetent attorneys. Here are some examples:

- George Alec Robinson, charged with capital murder in Virginia, was vigorously defended by two appointed attorneys who worked a combined total of six hundred hours. Robinson was found guilty but was spared death by the electric chair. The attorneys submitted a bill of approximately $55,000 at prevailing rates for private clients. During this trial, the attorneys neglected their private practices and even their personal lives under the pressure of having responsibility for a man's life. The state of Virginia paid them $573 each. "The two lawyers subsequently removed their names from the list of attorneys willing to accept appointments. They joined an increasing number of experienced attorneys nationwide who are no longer willing to provide

their services at such great personal and financial sacrifice."[85]

- Calvin Jerold Burdine was released by a federal court from a Texas prison after spending sixteen years on death row. His lawyer had no co-counsel and had slept through substantial portions of his trial. The Texas Court of Criminal Appeals did not think that this constituted ineffective assistance of counsel. Burdine's case was one of several of Texas prisoners on death row whose lawyers slept during their trials. In 1999, George W. Bush, then the governor of Texas, vetoed a bill to improve the quality of legal representation of poor defendants, expressing satisfaction with the Texas justice system.[86]

- Frederico Martinez-Macias, a common laborer convicted of a double murder, was defended by a court-appointed attorney who was paid $11.84 an hour. His attorney did no legal research to correct his erroneous view about key evidence and failed to call an alibi witness who would have placed the defendant miles away from the crime. After Martinez-Macias was sentenced to death, a Washington firm took his case *pro bono*. Full investigation established his innocence.[87] The *pro bono* lawyers invested about $1 million of billable hours, spent $11,599 for psychological testimony, and found eyewitnesses who did not identify Martinez-Macias at the murder scene.[88] Other cases like this exist.[89]

- Attorney Mike Williams, a small-town Alabama lawyer, was assigned the capital murder case of James Wyman Smith. Williams was given no money for an investigator and estimated that he received $4.98 per hour to prepare for the defense. Another Alabama solo practitioner in Birmingham, Wilson Meyers, submitted an itemized bill for $13,399 to the trial court for representing an indigent in a capital murder trial. The judge reduced the amount of payment to $4,128. The court agreed that Meyers had put in the time but called the fees too excessive. After paying his investigator and paralegal, Meyers netted $5.05 an hour on this case. As a result, earnest lawyers like Mike Williams and Wilson Myers drop out of defending indigents in capital cases because of the financial burden, leaving inexperienced or incompetent lawyers to take such cases.[90]

- Some lawyers are forced to take assigned capital cases or face contempt of court. They may put in about fifty hours on death penalty cases when, according to experts, adequate preparation requires five hundred to one thousand hours.[91]

Causes of Ineffective Counsel

What causes the diminished funding for indigent defense?

- *Tough on crime attitudes.* "Providing free attorneys to accused criminals is probably one of the government's least popular functions. In recent years, 'victim's rights' movements have become increasingly popular. Many politicians, being sensitive to public opinion, are concerned with appearing to be 'tough on crime.' Citizens and politicians alike often have little understanding of or sympathy for the needs of the adversary system, at least insofar as it requires a strong defense advocate. Defense attorneys are often seen as obstacles to justice."[92]

- *Rising caseloads.* From 1982 to 1984, there was a 40 percent increase in caseloads for the nation's indigent defense systems. A 1990 study, commissioned by Chief Justice Rehnquist, concluded that the most pressing problem for federal courts was the unprecedented number of federal drug prosecutions. In 1964, federal courts made sixteen thousand compensated appointments of counsel under the Criminal Justice Act of that year. By 1993, that number rose to eighty-nine thousand indigent appointments in federal courts.[93]

- *Diminishing government resources.* "Recently, many local governments, the primary locus of funding of defense services, have seen their resources dwindle, as tax-cutting measures are passed by the electorate and federal funds for local programs are cut."[94]

- *Greater demands on defense attorneys.* Prosecutors have either limited or eliminated plea bargaining for certain crimes, have increased the number of charges filed against defendants, and have charged more serious crimes. All of this requires greater defense efforts. New crimes and harsher penalties passed by legislatures require defense attorneys to spend time learning the law, developing appellate challenges to the new provisions, and offering a more dogged defense against higher penalties.[95]

Solving the Problem of Ineffective Counsel

Several steps can be taken to solve the problem of the ineffective assistance of counsel, including these suggestions:

- Modify the rule of *Strickland v. Washington* (1984) to make it easier for courts to find ineffective assistance of counsel.
- Improve the efficiency of public defenders' offices through the widespread use of advanced technology for managing information in complex cases, in case tracking, and for information exchange.[96]
- Reengineer the role of chief public defenders from that of narrow and defensive managers to spokespeople for the need for adequate funding for indigent defense. This may include developing better relations with legislators, prosecutors, police, corrections, the media, and community groups in an effort to advocate the need for indigent defense and to sponsor community crime-prevention programs.[97]
- Tie the expenditure of indigent defense (all systems) to a percentage of funding of public prosecution, at a suggested rate of 75 percent.[98]
- Allow public defenders' offices to negotiate reasonable caseload limits with courts and funding agencies.
- Require a minimum level of experience before assigning major cases to counsel.[99]
- Eliminate the practice of judges' compelling attorneys to take major cases on a *pro bono* basis.[100]
- Finance indigent defense in part with a portion of court fees.
- Reduce the enforcement component of the "war on drugs," with its draconian punishments for low-level crimes, and replace this with more treatment options.

Until such practical solutions are implemented, the promise of the Constitution—equal justice under the law—will go unfulfilled.

SUMMARY

The right to the assistance of counsel in a criminal prosecution is guaranteed by the Sixth Amendment. It is fundamental to the proper conduct of criminal trials and the adversary system of justice. In other proceedings, a right to counsel has been guaranteed by the Due Process and Equal Protection Clauses of the Fourteenth Amendment as well as the Fifth Amendment right against self-incrimination. Defense counsel is more important in common law trials than in trials under the European civil law system. The actual use of lawyers in trials was a late common law development.

Prior to its incorporation into the Fourteenth Amendment in *Gideon v. Wainwright* (1963), the Sixth Amendment right applied only to federal prosecutions. Under federal law, a defendant had to be represented and could waive counsel only if it specifically appeared on

the record that the defendant did so knowingly and voluntarily (*Johnson v. Zerbst*, 1938). In state cases, lack of counsel violated a defendant's Fourteenth Amendment due process right to a fair trial only when special circumstances existed—for example, the death penalty, the defendant's immaturity or ignorance, complex issues, or an atmosphere of prejudice (*Powell v. Alabama*, 1932). *Griffin v. Illinois* (1956) held that under the Fourteenth Amendment Equal Protection Clause, in which the state allows certain legal benefits to those who can afford them, the state must provide indigent defendants with free benefits, such as transcripts for appeals.

Gideon v. Wainwright (1963) incorporated the Sixth Amendment right to counsel into the Fourteenth Amendment Due Process Clause. The right to counsel was later applied to all misdemeanor cases in which the defendant was actually imprisoned. The Sixth Amendment right to counsel extends to all critical stages (preliminary examination, capital arraignment, and sentencing) but not to postconviction correctional processes (probation revocation, parole revocation, or prison disciplinary hearings). The Sixth Amendment requires appointment of a psychiatric expert when necessary to decide an insanity issue.

In proceedings that are not Sixth Amendment prosecutions, counsel is authorized by the Due Process Clause in some proceedings (probation and parole revocations, juvenile delinquency adjudication) but not in others (prison discipline, summary court martial). In probation revocation hearings, courts have discretion to appoint counsel to indigents when special circumstances exist, but in juvenile adjudication, counsel must be provided.

Courts can prevent those who are not licensed in the practice of law from serving as counsel and can bar an attorney from representing a person if the court believes there will be a conflict of interest. A federal forfeiture statute that allows the confiscation of attorneys' fees before trial does not violate the Sixth Amendment right to counsel. The Sixth Amendment does not guarantee a meaningful relationship between a defendant and assigned counsel. When counsel is provided without cost to an indigent defendant, the state has a right to seek compensation at a later time when the defendant has obtained the money to repay the costs.

Counsel is guaranteed on a first appeal under the Due Process and Equal Protection Clauses (*Douglas v. California,* 1963). The Court limited the extension of this rule in *Ross v. Moffitt* (1974) so that counsel is not constitutionally required for indigent litigants pursuing discretionary, second appeals or habeas corpus proceedings, as long as the state allows indigent prisoners to pursue such appeals.

The right to representation at a criminal trial is personal, and a defendant has a right to waive the assistance of counsel and to conduct a defense *pro se* (*Faretta v. California,* 1975). A waiver requires the trial judge to closely examine the defendant to be sure he or she understands the benefits of counsel and waives appointed counsel voluntarily and to be sure that the defendant has the minimum skills needed to conduct a reasonable defense. The court cannot disqualify a *pro se* defense because the defendant does not have expert knowledge of the law or of the trial process. In instances of *pro se* defense, the court may appoint standby counsel over the defendant's objection.

A federal regulation allowed a judge to authorize eavesdropping on conversations between lawyers and clients in federal jail or prison where there was cause to believe the attorney was involved in furthering criminal activity. In the aftermath of 9/11, the federal government quietly replaced the judicial warrant requirement, allowing agents to listen in on attorney-client conversations with the approval of the attorney general based only on reasonable suspicion that a prisoner *might* use communications with attorneys to further terrorism. This rule, plus the partially failed attack on defense attorney Lynne Stewart, suggests that, in the name of fighting terrorism, the government has used measures that are unduly broad and actually ineffective, perhaps for political advantage, imperiling basic liberties.

The Sixth Amendment requires that the assistance afforded to a defendant be effective. The basic rules of effective assistance are, first, that the attorney's conduct must be reasonable, or not deficient, according to the prevailing standards of practicing attorneys in the locality and, second, that if the attorney's performance was deficient, this must have prejudiced the defendant's case so that the conviction was a result of the deficient performance. The complaining defendant has the burden of proving ineffective assistance. Ineffective assistance will not be presumed. It is not deficient performance to refuse to assist a client in committing perjury. In cases involving a real conflict of interest, ineffective assistance is presumed, but the mere fact that an attorney represented two clients is not in itself a conflict of interest. If an attorney raises a reasonable possibility of a conflict of interest, a trial judge must hold a hearing to inquire into the matter.

LEGAL PUZZLES

How Have Courts Decided These Cases?

Right to Counsel versus Self-Representation

6–1.   Cooks was charged with two robberies with very similar fact patterns that occurred within fifteen days of one another. In one case Cooks was represented by counsel, and in the other he chose to represent himself. The prosecution moved to consolidate the cases into one trial. The court granted the motion and required Cooks to choose between being represented by counsel or representing himself. Cooks initially chose the public defender but later decided to represent himself, which he did throughout the trial. A jury convicted Cooks of both robberies.

Did the consolidation of the trials unconstitutionally force Cooks to choose between his right under *Gideon v. Wainwright* (1963) and his right under *Faretta v. California* (1975)?

Held: No. *Faretta* held that a criminal defendant has a Sixth Amendment right to represent himself. *Gideon* held that the Sixth Amendment requires the state to appoint counsel for indigent criminal defendants. The right to self-representation, however, is not absolute; it cannot be a license to not comply with relevant rules of procedural and substantive law, and a trial court may terminate self-representation if the defendant deliberately engages in serious and obstructionist misconduct. The trial court may also, even over objection by the accused, appoint a standby counsel to aid the accused. Therefore, the government's interest in ensuring the integrity and efficiency of the trial, as by properly joining two cases under state laws, at times outweighs the defendant's interest in acting as his own lawyer.

Cooks v. Newland, 395 F.3d 1077 (9th Cir. 2005)

Counsel or Empty Suit?

6–2.   Heath, who had four driving under the influence (DUI) convictions prior to 1990, pleaded guilty to drunk driving charges in 2000 stemming from an incident that injured three teenagers. Represented by Public Defender Jason Shwiller, Heath entered a plea with a sentence recommendation of thirty years, to serve between four and fifteen years. Shwiller advised Heath that he could expect to be sentenced "at the lower end" of the range. After hearing victim-impact evidence, the court sentenced him to fifteen years in confinement plus fifteen years on probation. A motion to withdraw the plea failed.

Heath had no memory of the collision and informed Shwiller that his coworker may have been driving the truck that caused the accident. Shwiller was given the witness's name but did not try to find him, telling Heath's niece that his workload was so large that he could get nothing done if he "looked into every nook and cranny." Shwiller told the court before sentencing that Heath was the driver and said, "There's nothing I can say to excuse what Mr. Heath has done. There's no good spin that I can put on it. He consumed a great deal of alcohol, he drove on Georgia's road and caused a terrible tragedy." He did not review victim-impact evidence. On cross-examination during a hearing to withdraw the plea, Shwiller admitted that he could not recall the elements of the offense of serious injury by vehicle and that he conducted no research to determine whether the victims' injuries fit within the statutory definition of "serious." Shwiller admitted that he never consulted with Heath in person during the thirteen months between arraignment and the entry of the plea.

Heath appealed from the denial of his petition to withdraw his plea, claiming ineffective assistance of counsel.

Was counsel so deficient in this case that it was not necessary to prove prejudice (i.e., that prejudice was presumed)?

Holding available from instructor.

Probation Revocation

6–3.   In 1995, Smith pleaded guilty to second-degree burglary and third-degree sexual assault in one case and to a violation of probation in a second case, based on the underlying offenses of being in possession of narcotics with intent to sell and interfering with an officer. He was sentenced to a minimum term of four years' imprisonment, followed by five years' probation. The original conditions of the defendant's probation included no contact with the victim, compliance with a standing criminal restraining order, substance abuse evaluation, and "treatment as deemed appropriate." While Smith was incarcerated, his probation officer modified his probation to include participation in a sex-offender treatment program, and Smith signed a copy of the amended condition. After release, Smith's probation was revoked, and he was reincarcerated for twice showing up late for his sex-offender therapy sessions.

Were Smith's due process rights violated when his probation officer added a condition of probation without a hearing and counsel?

Holding available from instructor.

Effective Assistance

6–4.   A search warrant was issued based on a bare-bones affidavit. A detective's affidavit stated that three months earlier, an informant had bought "a quantity of crack" from Owens at a house believed to be Owens's residence. A search of the premises turned up cocaine, marijuana, and guns, and this evidence was used against Owens at his trial. There was no indication in the affidavit either of the actual quantity of crack or of the reliability of the informant. Owens's trial lawyer moved to suppress the evidence, arguing that the sale of an unknown quantity of an illegal drug three months before a search warrant was sought does not, by itself, establish probable cause to believe that the search of the premises on which the sale took place would turn up contraband or evidence of crime. This is a good argument because if the amount sold was very small, it does not support the belief that the house was a crack house where police could expect to find drugs and other evidence.

Owens's lawyer was unable to get the fruits of the search suppressed because he failed to argue that it was

Owens's house in which the crack was found. This omission enabled the government to argue successfully that if it wasn't Owens's house, no right of his had been violated by the search. Thus the motion to suppress failed.

Was the lawyer's failure to argue that the warrant was issued against Owens's house ineffective assistance of counsel?

Holding available from instructor.

FURTHER READING

David J. Bodenhamer, *Fair Trial: Rights of the Accused in American History* (New York: Oxford University Press, 1992).

James Goodman, *Stories of Scottsboro* (New York: Pantheon, 1994).

Anthony Lewis, *Gideon's Trumpet* (New York: Vintage, 1964).

USEFUL WEB SITES

National Association of Criminal Defense Lawyers

http://www.nacdl.org/public.nsf/freeform/WhoWeAre?OpenDocument

Site of membership organization. Offers informative press releases, *amicus curiae* briefs, and articles in *Champion Magazine,* as well as data on indigent defense, the death penalty, and more.

National Legal Aid and Defenders Association

http://www.nlada.org/

Site of organization representing public defenders; materials on the right to counsel; timely news items.

ENDNOTES

1. *Faretta v. California* (1975), quoting Holdsworth, *History of English Law;* C. Rembar, *The Law of the Land* (New York: Simon and Schuster, 1980), 181; and L. Levy, *Origins of the Fifth Amendment* (New York: Oxford University Press, 1968), 19.

2. William Blackstone, *Commentaries on the Laws of England, Volume 4—Of Public Wrongs* (Chicago: University of Chicago Press, 1979, facsimile of 1st ed., 1769), 349–50.

3. Hiller B. Zobel, *The Boston Massacre* (New York: W. W. Norton, 1970).

4. *Powell v. Alabama* (1932), citing the right to counsel in the first constitutions of Maryland, Massachusetts, New Hampshire, New York, Pennsylvania, Delaware, New Jersey, and Connecticut (not adopted until 1818), the statutes of North Carolina and South Carolina, and the later constitutions of Georgia and Rhode Island.

5. In England and Canada and in the colonies and early republican United States, the word was spelled *defence.* The modern American spelling is *defense.*

6. Two excellent histories of the Scottsboro case are D. T. Carter, *Scottsboro: A Tragedy of the American South,* rev. ed. (Baton Rouge: Louisiana State University Press, 1979), and J. Goodman, *Stories of Scottsboro* (New York: Pantheon, 1994). The case narrative is taken from these sources.

7. The second appeal to the U.S. Supreme Court, *Norris v. Alabama* (1934), held that the exclusion of African Americans from juries violated the defendants' right to equal protection under the Fourteenth Amendment.

8. H. Arkes, *The Return of George Sutherland: Restoring a Jurisprudence of Natural Rights* (Princeton, N.J.: Princeton University Press, 1994).

9. Arkes, *The Return of George Sutherland.*

10. Arkes, *The Return of George Sutherland,* 265.

11. Justice Sutherland cited *Gitlow v. New York* (1925), *Stromberg v. California* (1931), and *Near v. Minnesota* (1931).

12. Arkes, *The Return of George Sutherland,* 268.

13. *Smith v. Bennett* (1961); and *Burns v. Ohio* (1959).

14. *Roberts v. Lavallee* (1967); *Gardner v. California* (1969); and *Mayer v. Chicago* (1971).

15. *In re Groban* (1957) (dictum).

16. *Davis v. Mississippi* (1969); *Gilbert v. California* (1967); and *United States v. Dionisio* (1973).

17. Linda Greenhouse, "High Court Backs Seizure of Assets in Criminal Cases," *New York Times,* June 22, 1989.

18. David Rossman, "'Were There No Appeal': The History of Review in American Criminal Courts," *Journal of Criminal Law and Criminology* 81, no. 3 (1990): 518–66, 519.

19. Marie Higgins Williams, "Comment: The Pro Se Criminal Defendant, Standby Counsel, and the Judge: A Proposal for Better Defined Roles," *University of Colorado Law Review* 71 (2000): 789–818, 795–97.

20. Williams, "The Pro Se Criminal Defendant," 793, n. 28, citing a former president of the National Association of Criminal Defense Lawyers.

21. Ron Christenson, ed., *Political Trials in History* (New Brunswick, N.J.: Transaction, 1991), 91–93; and Williams, "The Pro Se Criminal Defendant," 789–90.

22. J. T. McQuiston, "Suspect in L.I.R.R. Killings Ruled Competent for Trial," *New York Times,* December 10, 1994, sec. 1, p. 28. They became standby counsel but later resigned when Ferguson's antics became intolerably bizarre: J. T. McQuiston, "Adviser to L.I.R.R. Suspect Threatens to Quit," *New York Times,* February 7, 1995.

23. J. T. McQuiston, "L.I.R.R. Defendant Helps Pick Jury, Then Says It Is Biased," *New York Times,* January 24, 1995.

24. J. T. McQuiston, "In the Bizarre L.I.R.R. Trial, Equally Bizarre Confrontations," *New York Times,* February 5, 1995.

25. D. Van Biema, "A Fool for a Client; Accused L.I.R.R. Killer Colin Ferguson Is Defending Himself, and That May Be Something of a Crime," *Time,* February 6, 1995.

26. J. Hoffman, "Hapless Lawyer, Thankless Job; Colin Ferguson's Adviser Sees Reputation and Practice Suffer," *New York Times,* February 14, 1995.

27. P. Marks, "Relief That the Book Is Closed on a Looking-Glass Trial," *New York Times,* February 19, 1995.

28. Philip Shenon, "Judge Lets Man Accused in September. 11 Plot Defend Himself," *New York Times,* June 14, 2002.

29. Philip Shenon, "Judge Bars 9/11 Suspect from Being Own Lawyer," *New York Times,* November 15, 2003.

30. Williams, "The Pro Se Criminal Defendant," 801.

31. Williams, "The Pro Se Criminal Defendant," 805.

32. Williams, "The Pro Se Criminal Defendant," 805.

33. Williams, "The Pro Se Criminal Defendant," 809–15.

34. Abbe Smith, "The Bounds of Zeal in Criminal Defense: Some Thoughts on Lynne Stewart," *South Texas Law Review* 44 (2002): 31–52, 38–40. Smith relied on David McCullough, *John Adams* (New York: Simon and Schuster, 2001). For a more detailed and nuanced account, see Hiller B. Zobel, *The Boston Massacre* (New York: Norton, 1970).

35. Rules and Regulations, Bureau of Prisons, U.S. Department of Justice, 28 C.F.R. §§ 500, 501 (2002); Prevention of Acts of Violence and Terrorism, 66 *Fed. Reg.* 55062 (October. 31, 2001).

36. Rules and Regulations, Bureau of Prisons, U.S. Department of Justice, 28 C.F.R. §§ 540.18, 540.19, 540.48; and Joshua Dratel, "Ethical Issues in Defending a Terrorism Case: How Secrecy and Security Impair the Defense of a Terrorism Case," *Cardozo Public Law, Policy and Ethics Journal* 2 (2003): 81–105, 83–85.

37. George Lardner Jr., "U.S. Will Monitor Calls to Lawyers; Rule on Detainees Called 'Terrifying,'" *Washington Post,* November 9, 2001; and Marjorie Cohn, "Looking Backward: The Evisceration of the Attorney-Client Privilege in the Wake of September 11, 2001," *Fordham Law Review* 71 (2003): 1233–55, 1241–47.

38. Stephen J. Schulhofer, *The Enemy Within: Intelligence Gathering, Law Enforcement, and Civil Liberties in the Wake of September 11* (New York: Century Foundation Press, 2002), 23.

39. Cohn, "Looking Backward," 1244.

40. Lardner, "U.S. Will Monitor Calls to Lawyers."

41. Dratel, "Ethical Issues in Defending a Terrorism Case," 83–87.

42. Schulhofer, *The Enemy Within,* 25–26; Dratel, "Ethical Issues in Defending a Terrorism Case," 91.

43. Dratel, "Ethical Issues in Defending a Terrorism Case," 88.

44. Smith, "The Bounds of Zeal," 35–36.

45. Smith, "The Bounds of Zeal," 32.

46. Alissa Clare, "We Should Have Gone to Med School: In the Wake of Lynne Stewart, Lawyers Face Hard Time for Defending Terrorists," *Georgetown Journal of Legal Ethics* 18 (2005): 651–68, 653.

47. Benjamin Weiser and Robert F. Worth, "Indictment Says Lawyer Helped a Terror Group," *New York Times,* April 10, 2002.

48. Weiser and Worth, "Indictment Says Lawyer Helped a Terror Group"; and Julia Preston, "Lawyer Is Guilty of Aiding Terror," *New York Times,* February 11, 2005.

49. Smith, "The Bounds of Zeal," 44–51; Clare, "We Should Have Gone to Med School," 665; and Andrew P. Napolitano, "No Defense," *New York Times,* February 17, 2005.

50. Preston, "Lawyer Is Guilty of Aiding Terror."

51. Barbara Ross, "Terror Lawyer Could Get Life behind Bars," *New York Daily News,* September 5, 2006.

52. Smith, "The Bounds of Zeal," 51.

53. Smith, "The Bounds of Zeal," 52.

54. Julia Preston, "Sheik's Lawyer, Facing 30 Years, Gets 28 Months, to Dismay of U.S.," *New York Times,* October 17, 2006.

55. Preston, "Sheik's Lawyer."

56. Deborah L. Rhode, "Terrorists and Their Lawyers," *New York Times,* April 16, 2002.

57. Sarah Kershaw and Eric Lichtblau, "Bomb Case against Lawyer Is Rejected," *New York Times,* May 25, 2004; and

Noelle Crombie, "Mayfield Home Was Searched in Secret," *Portland Oregonian,* March 30, 2005. See Bryan Denson, "Lawyer Thinks Office Was Searched in Secret," *Portland Oregonian,* March 21, 2006.

58. Charles W. Wolfram, "Lecture: Lawyer Crimes: Beyond the Law?" *Valparaiso University Law Review* 36 (2001): 73–117.

59. Dratel, "Ethical Issues in Defending a Terrorism Case," 81–82 (emphasis in original).

60. Rhode, "Terrorists and Their Lawyers."

61. See the Spangenberg Group, *Indigent Defense and Technology: A Progress Report* (Bureau of Justice Assistance, NCJ 179003 November 1999).

62. Bob Sablatura, "Study Confirms Money Counts in County's Courts: Those Using Appointed Lawyers Are Twice as Likely to Serve Time," *Houston Chronicle,* October 17, 1999.

63. "I Think You Get All the Justice You Can Afford," *Time,* June 19, 1995, 46–47.

64. Gregg Herrington, "Sex Ring Attorney Looks to Civil Trial," *Columbian,* December 15, 1995; T. Egan, "Pastor and Wife Are Acquitted on All Charges in Sex-Abuse Case," *New York Times,* December 12, 1995; and D. Nathan, "Justice in Wenatchee," *New York Times,* December 19, 1995. See Dorothy Rabinowitz, *No Crueler Tyrannies* (New York: Wall Street Journal Book Publishing, 2003).

65. D. West, "Cleared of Child Abuse, but the Anguish Lingers," *New York Times,* October 19, 1995.

66. Bulletin Broadfaxing Network, The Bulletin's Frontrunner, April 26, 2000: "Legal Fees Reduce Hilliard's Warchest to $149; Blames Racism for His Problem."

67. "CHSWC Okays New Study on Drug Costs," *Workers' Comp Executive* 9, no. 22 (December 1, 1999).

68. David Lawsky, "$1 Billion Settlement Reported in Vitamin Suit," *Toronto Star,* November 4, 1999, business sec.

69. Del Quentin Wilber, "Tripp Seeks Help Paying Lawyers," *Des Moines Register,* November 18, 1999.

70. Jill Abramson, "The Nation: The Price of Being Lewinsky; Dream Team, Nightmare Tab," *New York Times,* June 7, 1998, sec. 4.

71. Don Van Natta Jr., "Fewer Donations Coming in for Clinton Defense Fund," *New York Times,* August 13, 1999.

72. "I Think You Get All the Justice You Can Afford," *Time,* June 19, 1995.

73. E. Gleick, "Rich Justice, Poor Justice," *Time,* June 19, 1995.

74. Kevin Moran, "Durst Told Wife He Would Be Acquitted," *Houston Chronicle,* November 13, 2003.

75. Kim Taylor-Thompson, "Effective Assistance: Reconceiving the Role of the Chief Public Defender," *Journal of the Institute for the Study of Legal Ethics* 2 (1999): 199–200.

76. David Bazelon, quoted in R. Klein, "The Emperor *Gideon* Has No Clothes: The Empty Promise of the Constitutional Right to Effective Assistance of Counsel," *Hastings Constitutional Law Quarterly* 13 (1986): 625–93, 656.

77. Editorial, "Judicial Reforms in Albany," *New York Times,* May 26, 2000.

78. Martha K. Harrison, "Note: Claims for Compensation: The Implications of Getting Paid When Appointed under the Criminal Justice Act," *Boston University Law Review* 79 (1999): 553–76, 555, n. 15.

79. Alan Cooper, "Appointed Lawyer's Low Fee Ruled No Bar to Fair Trial," *Richmond Times Dispatch,* May 5, 2000.

80. R. Marcus, "Racism in Our Courts: The Underfunding of Public Defenders and Its Disproportionate Impact upon Racial Minorities," *Hastings Constitutional Law Quarterly* 22 (1994): 219–67, 228–29 (footnotes omitted, emphasis added).

81. S. Mounts, "The Right to Counsel and the Indigent Defense System," *New York University Review of Law and Social Change* 14 (1986): 221–41, 221, citing *Cooper v. Fitzharris,* 551 F.2d 1162, 163 n. 1 (9th Cir. 1977).

82. R. L. Spangenberg and T. J. Schwartz, "The Indigent Defense Crisis Is Chronic," *Criminal Justice* (Summer 1994): 13, citing *State v. Peart,* 621 So.2d 780 (La. 1993).

83. Spangenberg and Schwartz, "The Indigent Defense Crisis," citing *National Law Journal,* August 20, 1992.

84. R. L. Spangenberg, "We Are Still Not Defending the Poor Properly," *Criminal Justice* (Fall 1989): 11–131, 12.

85. S. E. Mounts and R. J. Wilson, "Systems for Providing Indigent Defense: An Introduction," *New York University Review of Law and Social Change* 14 (1986): 193–201, 194, citing *Washington Post,* June 25, 1984.

86. Ross E. Milloy, "Judge Frees Texas Inmate Whose Lawyer Slept at Trial," *New York Times,* March 2, 2000; and Paul Duggan, "George W. Bush: The Record in Texas; Attorneys' Ineptitude Doesn't Halt Executions," *Washington Post,* May 12, 2000.

87. S. Bright, "Counsel for the Poor: The Death Sentence Not for the Worst Crime but for the Worst Lawyer," *Yale Law Journal* 103 (1994): 1835–83, 1838–39.

88. A. Cohen, "The Difference a Million Makes," *Time,* June 19, 1993.

89. "Another Wrongly Convicted Man," *Indianpolis Star,* February 10, 2000; and Bright, "Counsel for the Poor."

90. Sara Rimer, "Questions of Death Row Justice for Poor People in Alabama," *New York Times,* March 1, 2000.

91. Rimer, "Questions of Death Row Justice."

92. Mounts and Wilson, "Systems for Providing Indigent Defense," 200–201.

93. Spangenberg and Schwartz, "The Indigent Defense Crisis," 14; and J. J. Cleary, "Federal Defender Services: Serving the System or the Client?" *Law and Contemporary Problems* 58 (1995): 65–80, 65.

94. Mounts and Wilson, "Systems for Providing Indigent Defense," 200–201.

95. Spangenberg and Schwartz, "The Indigent Defense Crisis."

96. Spangenberg Group, *Indigent Defense and Technology,* 1999.

97. Taylor-Thompson, "Effective Assistance."

98. Taylor-Thompson, "Effective Assistance," 207–8.

99. Jo Becker, "Rules Set for Death Row Lawyers," *St. Petersburg* (Fla.) *Times,* October 30, 1999.

100. Stafford Henderson Byers, "Delivering Indigents' Right to Counsel While Respecting Lawyers' Right to Their Profession: A System 'between a Rock and a Hard Place,'" *St. John's Journal of Legal Commentary* 13 (1999): 491–526.

JUSTICES OF THE SUPREME COURT

Warren Court Liberals: Warren, Goldberg, and Fortas

The liberal reputation of the Warren Court (1953–1969) rests primarily on its work in four major areas: destroying legalized racial segregation, mandating equal voting power through the apportionment of voting districts so that each voter's vote was of approximately equal weight, expanding First Amendment rights, and incorporating most of the criminal procedure provisions of the Bill of Rights. The last achievement, in fact, began in 1961 with *Mapp v. Ohio* and gathered momentum only with the appointment of Justice Arthur Goldberg upon the retirement of Justice Felix Frankfurter. The incorporation cases often, but not invariably, hinged on the votes of a slim majority—Chief Justice Earl Warren and Justices Hugo Black, William Douglas, William Brennan, and Arthur Goldberg (and Justice Abe Fortas after him). This is not surprising to constitutional scholars because important constitutional innovations often embody one side of a large conflict of ideals of the society. The competing ideals of liberty and security are both essential, so the law of criminal procedure is bound to exhibit some tension and shift. The adoption of a competing ideal in a particular case is less a matter of "right and wrong" in a factual sense than a value choice between the approaches and a response to differing perceived needs of the nation at a given time. This may explain why American electoral politics, policy choices, and constitutional doctrines are subject to broad swings over the decades; there may be no other way to maintain peaceful continuity in a nation so vast and so varied.

Collection of the Supreme Court of the United States. Photographer: Abdon Daoud Ackad.

Earl Warren

California, 1891–1974

Republican

Appointed Chief Justice by Dwight D. Eisenhower

Years of Service: 1953–1969

Life and Career.   The son of a Norwegian immigrant railroad car inspector, Warren received his undergraduate and law degrees from the University of California, Berkeley. After army service in World War I, he entered public service and became the district attorney of Alameda County, California, in 1925. His vigorous prosecution of corrupt politicians and organized crime helped to elevate him to California's attorney general in 1938. In that role, he backed the relocation of Japanese Americans from their homes to internment camps for the duration of World War II. He was elected governor of California in 1943, and he ran for vice president of the United States in 1948 on the losing Republican ticket with Thomas Dewey of New York. His support of a rule that allowed Dwight Eisenhower to win the nomination of the Republican Party led to his appointment as chief justice in 1953.

Contribution to Criminal Procedure.   After his first two terms on the Court, Chief Justice Warren became a critical liberal vote, and with the appointment of Justice Goldberg to replace Justice Frankfurter in 1962, the way was clear to accomplish the due process revolution by which most of the criminal provisions of the Bill of Rights were incorporated. His important majority opinions include *Terry v. Ohio* (1968) (stop and frisk); *Sherman v. United States* (1958) (entrapment); and *Klopfer v. North Carolina* (1967) (incorporating the Sixth Amendment right to a speedy trial). Chief Justice Warren, who had been a tough prosecutor, knew well how such public servants could abuse their great powers of office to overwhelm the will of the individual.

Signature Opinion.   *Miranda v. Arizona* (1966). *Miranda* is the case that revolutionized the law of confessions. In his majority opinion, Chief Justice Warren characteristically devoted relatively little space to a discussion of precedents, which would ordinarily be critical to justify a decision, and instead devoted the lion's share of the opinion to documenting the numerous ways that law enforcement officers "subjugated the individual to the will of his examiner." The decision in *Miranda* spelled out practical rules and their application for police and prosecutors, an approach that has been derided by critics as judicial legislation. *Miranda* was characteristic of Chief Justice Warren's activism and liberalism and of his willingness to ignite controversy if he believed his position was the fair course to take.

Assessment.   Earl Warren is ranked as a great chief justice, not because he had a brilliant legal mind or because of his judicial craft in writing opinions, but for his leadership. He was a progressive with strong streaks of moralism and populism, as well as a superb administrator who knew how to motivate people and get things done. He is remembered for his masterful ability to take a Court divided on the monumental issue of school segregation and steer it to a unanimous opinion in *Brown v. Board of Education* (1954), a feat considered to be the hallmark of judicial statesmanship. During an oral argument, he often cut through technical presentations to ask lawyers if the position they were supporting was fair, a question some saw as unsophisticated. However, this approach provided the framework for rulings that transformed American politics, law enforcement, and society. Under Chief Justice Warren, the Supreme Court was marked by activism, liberalism, and populism. It outlawed racial segregation, ended unrepresentative voting districts in the states, extended First Amendment rights, and vigorously upheld antitrust laws.

Further Reading

Bernard Schwartz, *Super Chief: Earl Warren and His Supreme Court—A Judicial Biography* (New York: New York University Press, 1983).

Collection of the Supreme Court of the United States. Photographer: Abdon Daoud Ackad.

Arthur J. Goldberg

Illinois 1908–1990

Democrat

Appointed by John F. Kennedy

Years of Service: 1962–1965

Life and Career.   The youngest of eleven children of Russian immigrants, Goldberg was educated in Chicago public schools and received his bachelor's and law degrees from Northwestern University, graduating first in his law school class. He practiced law in Chicago until World War II and, in 1938, began to practice labor law. During the war, he served in the Office of Strategic Services in charge of labor espionage behind enemy lines.

After the war, he became a leading labor lawyer and, in 1948, became general counsel for the United Steelworkers Union. He played a central role in the merger of the American Federation of Labor and the Congress of Industrial Organizations (AFL-CIO) and became the group's general counsel. In 1957, he led the fight to expel the crime-ridden Teamsters Union from the labor body. Through this work and his excellent reputation as a negotiator, Goldberg gained national prominence. He became an adviser to Senator John F. Kennedy in his 1960 bid for the presidency and was selected by President Kennedy to be secretary of labor, where he played an active role in settling several major strikes. In 1962, he was nominated by Kennedy to replace Justice Frankfurter.

In 1965, President Lyndon Johnson persuaded Justice Goldberg to resign his seat on the Court to become ambassador to the United Nations in the hope that his negotiating skills would help in bringing a speedy end to the Vietnam War.

Contribution to Criminal Procedure.   Despite his short period of service, Justice Goldberg's appointment created a liberal majority on the Court and inaugurated the due process revolution of applying the Bill of Rights to the states in criminal procedure.

Signature Opinion.   *Escobedo v. Illinois* (1964). In *Escobedo,* the Court held that police refusal of a lawyer's request to see a client violated the right to counsel and that a confession obtained under those conditions was inadmissible in court. This breakthrough case paved the way for *Miranda v. Arizona* (1966).

Assessment.   Justice Goldberg was a liberal who believed that the Court has a legitimate problem-solving role and an important role in democracy by imposing constitutional majoritarian restraints to protect minority rights. He was a creative justice and established himself as the leading liberal spokesperson on a wide variety of explosive civil rights issues. In *Griswold v. Connecticut* (1965), the contraceptive case that established a framework for abortion rights, Goldberg concurred on the intellectually daring position that the rarely used Ninth Amendment should be the basis for removing criminal penalties against physicians who dispense, and married people who seek, contraception advice. He argued that the Court should look to the "traditions and [collective] conscience of our people" to discover which rights are fundamental and beyond the reach of the legislature. He also opposed the death penalty, arguing in 1963 that the Court should decide its constitutionality, an issue that the Court did not confront until the 1970s. He took a bold approach to civil rights, urging the Court to go beyond declaring discriminatory laws unconstitutional and instead require the states to act affirmatively to guarantee civil rights, a position shared by only two other justices.

Further Reading

Stephen J. Friedman, "Arthur Goldberg," in Leon Friedman and Fred L. Israel, eds., *The Justices of the United States Supreme Court, 1789–1969,* vol. 4 (New York: Chelsea House, 1969), 2977–90.

Collection of the Supreme Court of the United States. Photographer: Harris and Ewing.

Abe Fortas

Tennessee, 1910–1982

Democrat

Appointed by Lyndon Johnson

Years of Service: 1965–1969

Life and Career.   A native of Memphis and the son of a poor tailor, Fortas graduated from Southwest College and Yale Law School. At Yale, he came to the attention of Professor William O. Douglas, who brought Fortas to Washington, D.C., during the New Deal. Fortas was a tough and brilliant government lawyer. At age thirty-two, as undersecretary of the interior, he argued unsuccessfully against the removal of Japanese Americans from the West Coast.

After World War II, he went into private law practice in Washington, D.C. The firm of Arnold, Porter, and Fortas developed a reputation for effectively representing large corporations and for courageously defending the civil liberties of people hounded by the government during the anticommunist hysteria of the late 1940s and early 1950s. Fortas skillfully represented Texas Congressman Lyndon Johnson, under charges of election fraud, in a notorious 1948 Senate primary election vote recount that secured Johnson a Senate seat. Fortas then became a close adviser to Johnson.

As a private lawyer, Fortas took several *pro bono* cases that significantly changed criminal law and procedure. *Durham v. United States* (District of Columbia Court of Appeals, 1954, later reversed) made a major change in the insanity defense in Washington, D.C. He argued for the defendant in *Gideon v. Wainwright* (1963), playing an important role in advancing the incorporation doctrine and expanding the right to counsel.

Fortas was appointed to the Supreme Court by President Johnson in 1965, and after Earl Warren announced his *prospective* retirement in 1968, Johnson nominated him to be chief justice. Johnson did not seek a new term because of the intense politics surrounding the Vietnam War. As a result, Republicans in the Senate blocked Justice Fortas's appointment, and he eventually withdrew it. During the nomination process, the press discovered that he was a major presidential adviser while sitting on the bench and that he was receiving an annual payment of $20,000 from the family foundation of a businessman who had gone to prison for stock manipulation. In 1969, under intense public scrutiny and abetted by inside pressure from President Nixon's attorney general, John Mitchell, Justice Fortas resigned, although he had done nothing illegal.

Contribution to Criminal Procedure.   As a Warren Court liberal, Justice Fortas voted for the incorporation doctrine and for the expansion of suspects' and defendants' procedural rights in several important cases, providing the crucial fifth majority vote in *Miranda v. Arizona* (1966). He had a special interest in the rights of juvenile delinquents, a novel area for the Court, and his majority opinion in *Kent v. United States* (1966) held that a juvenile is entitled to a hearing under the Due Process Clause before a delinquency case can be transferred from juvenile court into the adult criminal system.

Signature Opinion.   *In re Gault* (1967). This case resulted in major changes in the way that juvenile court proceedings would be conducted. Before being adjudged delinquent, juveniles were entitled to many of the same procedural guarantees afforded to adults, including counsel, notice, the confrontation of witnesses, cross-examination, a written transcript, and appellate review. Justice Fortas's opinion was powerful because it recognized that a benevolent governmental purpose can mask oppression in practice. It emphasized that the procedural rights of the Constitution are critical to the legitimacy of American courts, even special courts designed to help juveniles and not merely to punish. No matter how noble the goal of the state, the Due Process Clause applies whenever any person, including a minor, is stripped of life, liberty, or property.

Assessment.   Justice Fortas was a solid liberal in all civil rights areas, but unlike most liberal justices, in antitrust matters he was not opposed to big business and usually did not vote against corporate mergers. His resignation allowed an additional appointment by President Nixon, thus shifting the Court from a liberal to a moderate-conservative stance in the area of criminal procedure.

Further Reading

Laura Kalman, *Abe Fortas: A Biography* (New Haven: Yale University Press, 1990).

7 Interrogation and the Law of Confessions

CHAPTER OUTLINE

KEY TERMS

admission

compulsion

confession

cruel trilemma

dying declaration

exculpatory

immunity

inculpatory

interrogation

involuntary confession

material witness

privilege

real evidence

self-incrimination rule

supervisory authority

testimonial evidence

third degree

voluntariness test

The Constitution of the United States stands as a bar against the conviction of any individual in an American court by means of a coerced confession. There have been, and are now, certain foreign nations with governments dedicated to an opposite policy: governments which convict individuals with testimony obtained by police organizations possessed of an unrestrained power to seize persons suspected of crimes against the state, hold them in secret custody, and wring from them confessions by physical or mental torture. So long as the Constitution remains the basic law of our Republic, America will not have that kind of government.

—Justice Hugo Black, *Ashcraft v. Tennessee,*
322 U.S. 143, 155 (1944)

INTRODUCTION

Interviewing witnesses and interrogating suspects are essential police investigation techniques.[1] Interviewing witnesses helps police understand what occurred at a crime scene. Police will interrogate an arrested suspect to obtain **admissions** or **confessions** of guilt that can be used in court to convict the suspect. Abusive interrogation, including torture, was common in American policing until the 1940s. Instances of excessive force still occur, and the potential for brutality must constantly be guarded against.[2] Furthermore, recent research shows that contemporary practices of "psychological interrogation" produce many false confessions by the innocent.[3] (See the "Law in Society" section in this chapter.)

Courts apply three constitutional rights to check abusive **interrogation:** (1) due process to prevent torture and abuse of suspects, (2) the privilege against self-incrimination to preserve a suspect's right to silence, and (3) the right to counsel for post-indictment questioning of defendants. Since 1966, *Miranda v. Arizona* (1966) and other cases interpreting the Self-Incrimination Clause have been the major focus of interrogation law. Although *Miranda* includes a Fifth Amendment right to counsel that applies only during custodial interrogation, the Sixth Amendment Right to Counsel Clause requires a lawyer for all questioning of a person who has been formally charged with a crime (*Massiah v. United States*, 1964).

In a nutshell, (1) the due process clauses (Fifth and Fourteenth Amendments) prohibit the introduction of **involuntary confessions;** (2) the *Miranda* doctrine holds that police interrogation of a suspect in custody is inherently coercive and any confession or admission is presumed to be the product of **compulsion** unless a suspect is informed of his or her rights and voluntarily waives the right of silence under the privilege against self-incrimination; and (3) the right to counsel prohibits questioning a criminal defendant to elicit incriminating statements without the defendant's lawyer being present.

The Privilege against Self-Incrimination

The Self-Incrimination Clause appears to focus on testimony in a criminal trial: "No person . . . shall be compelled in any criminal case to be a witness against himself." The meaning of this famous rule, regarding confessions, is even now not fully settled. The state of confessions law has been in flux since *Miranda v. Arizona* (1966) was decided. Despite a decision in 2000 declaring the *Miranda* rule to be constitutional (*Dickerson v. United States*), a civil case that followed added confusion concerning the effect of the **privilege** against self-incrimination and *Miranda* (*Chavez v. Martinez,* 2003). More recent cases have only partially determined that *Miranda* is enforceable, and conservative justices seem ready to neuter the *Miranda* rule. These cases, discussed below, require a basic understanding of contemporary self-incrimination law.

The privilege against self-incrimination clearly allows a defendant to remain silent in a criminal trial and have a defense conducted by counsel entirely by cross-examination. Defendants cannot be forced to testify, no matter how relevant their testimony. A prosecutor or judge who mentions a defendant's silence, except at the behest of the defendant or under limited circumstances, violates the defendant's right against self-incrimination (*Griffin v. California*, 1965; *Lakeside v. Oregon*, 1978). Jurors may believe that a defendant who does not take the stand has something to hide, but a hint by a judge or prosecutor so unbalances the scales of justice in the state's favor as to undermine a fair adversary trial. Prosecutorial or judicial comment also puts pressure (compulsion) on the defendant to give up the right to silence.

Claiming the Privilege.   To ensure that the right is not destroyed before a criminal prosecution begins, a person may refuse to testify under the Fifth Amendment in a variety of proceedings where he or she is called as a witness. These include criminal and civil cases (*McCarthy v. Arndstein*, 1924; *United States v. Monia,* 1943); administrative proceedings (*Malloy v. Hogan,* 1964); congressional investigations (*Watkins v. United States,* 1957); and grand juries (*Counselman v. Hitchcock,* 1892). If witnesses testify in these proceedings, their preserved testimony, if incriminating, can later be introduced against them in a criminal trial.

The privilege has to be actively invoked in these proceedings because it is an exception to the general rule that individuals have an obligation to testify (either voluntarily or under subpoena) to assist the state in prosecuting crimes and gathering information for legitimate purposes. Before formal proceedings, state officers may request information, as when a police officer asks residents for information about a criminal incident. At this stage, the officer cannot compel a person to provide information. Given Americans' well-honed sense of privacy, many may refuse to "get involved." Nevertheless, as Chief Justice Earl Warren stated, "It is an act of responsible citizenship for individuals to give whatever information they may have to aid in law enforcement" (*Miranda v. Arizona,* 1966). A person not in custody who does respond to questions of a federal police officer has an obligation to answer questions truthfully and may face criminal charges for lying (*Brogan v. United States,* 1998). If the prosecution believes that a person has information material to the prosecution of a pending criminal charge or grand jury investigation, the person may be arrested and confined as a **material witness** if a judge believes the person will flee.[4]

In sum, persons formally subpoenaed by judicial, executive, or legislative bodies or by grand juries or held as material witnesses must give testimony *unless* they have a legal privilege or right to refuse to testify. Failure to testify will lead to a finding of contempt, which can be punished with fines or even jail. The law recognizes several privileges that exempt a person from providing information to lawful authority. These include the privileges of religious, medical, or legal practitioners not to divulge information given in professional confidence; the marital privilege that protects the natural privacy of spouses[5]; and the privilege against self-incrimination.

Values Protected by the Privilege.

The privilege against self-incrimination "is widely regarded as both fundamental to human liberty and venerable in the history of the development of civil rights."[6] It is related to modern notions of privacy and is a mainstay of the adversary system. It supports the rule that the burden of proof of guilt rests on the prosecution and that guilt must be proven beyond a reasonable doubt.

The privilege against self-incrimination stands in contrast to brutal legal measures in ancient Rome and medieval continental Europe that allowed the use of torture to obtain evidence of serious crime.[7] It also contrasts with far more civilized European criminal justice systems today that many view as more effective in getting at the truth.[8] As the Supreme Court has stated, the privilege

> reflects many of our fundamental values and most noble aspirations: our unwillingness to subject those suspected of crime to the **cruel trilemma** of self-accusation, perjury or contempt; our preference for an accusatorial rather than an inquisitorial system of criminal justice; our fear that self-incriminating statements will be elicited by inhumane treatment and abuses; our sense of fair play which dictates a fair state-individual balance by requiring the government to leave the individual alone until good cause is shown for disturbing him and by requiring the government in its contest with the individual to shoulder the entire load; our respect for the inviolability of the human personality and of the right of each individual to a private enclave where he may lead a private life; our distrust of self-deprecatory statements; and our realization that the privilege, while sometimes a shelter to the guilty, is often a protection to the innocent. (*Murphy v. Waterfront Commission of New York Harbor,* 1964, internal references and quotation marks omitted)

Truth values underlie the Fifth Amendment privilege, which as a trial right was said by the Court to be closely related to the "correct ascertainment of guilt." As such, the privilege itself and the *Miranda* rule that followed serve to "guard against the use of unreliable statements at trial" (*Withrow v. Williams,* 1993, citing similar cases).

Prior to 1964, the privilege applied only to the federal government. In *Malloy v. Hogan* (1964), it was incorporated into the Fourteenth Amendment Due Process Clause and held to "secure . . . against state invasion the same privilege that the Fifth Amendment guarantees against federal infringement—the right of a person to remain silent unless he chooses to speak in the unfettered exercise of his own will, and to suffer no penalty . . . for such silence."

Application of the Privilege.

The privilege applies only to "natural persons." It cannot be claimed on behalf of corporations or other business entities by their officers, even sole proprietorships; they are deemed to be "artificial persons" for self-incrimination purposes (*Wilson v. United States,* 1911; *Bellis v. United States,* 1974; *United States v. Doe,* 1984). Tax records created by an individual and delivered to her attorney are not immune from subpoena power (*Fisher v. United States,* 1976). The privilege applies only to **testimonial evidence**—evidence given by a live witness (or in personal writings like a diary) that is of a "communicative nature." Testimony conveys information based on what the witness knows or believes he or she knows. A testimonial communication "must itself, explicitly or implicitly, relate a factual assertion, or disclose information" that expresses "the contents of an individual's mind" (*Doe v. United States,* 1988). This is important because even if testimony is not directly self-incriminating, a witness who speaks reveals something about his or her mental process to the listener. This opens up the witness's mind and psychological process to the listener's scrutiny. A witness who testifies raises the possibility that her statements will lead the listener to infer that the witness has admitted to an incriminating fact, even if no explicit confession is made.

The privilege against self-incrimination does not apply to physical evidence, also called **real evidence,** no matter how incriminating, because it is not testimonial. Justice Oliver Wendell Holmes Jr. ruled that a suspect has no right to prevent the court, jury, or witnesses from viewing the suspect's face and person (***Holt v. United States***, 1910). The government can "compel a person to reenact a crime; shave his beard or mustache; try on clothing; dye her hair; demonstrate speech or other physical characteristics; furnish handwriting samples, hair samples, or fingerprints; have her gums examined; or take a blood-alcohol, breathalyser [*sic*], or urine test."[9] A suspect can be photographed or measured, have tattoos and scars examined, and be required to stand in a lineup. Police can require a person to provide blood samples taken by medical personnel where blood alcohol levels are relevant evidence (***Schmerber v. California***, 1966). A driver stopped for driving under the influence (DUI) who refuses to take a Breathalyzer test may have his driving license revoked, and the fact of refusal can be used against him at a subsequent criminal trial, even if the police did not inform the driver of that fact (*South Dakota v. Neville,* 1983). Blood taking is distinguished from a "lie detector" session, which not only gathers physiological attributes, but also may elicit testimonial responses. Police departments uniformly give *Miranda* warnings before administering polygraph examinations.

Compulsion.

Compulsion is an element of the right against self-incrimination. A purely voluntary admission of guilt to a friend or to an undercover agent is not made under compulsion; therefore the listener can later testify to what was said. An ordinary witness in a trial or grand jury hearing need not be warned of his or her privilege because the witness is not deemed to be under such compulsion, although subpoenaed and sworn to testify (***United States v. Monia***, 1943). In other words, the privilege against self-incrimination is not self-executing and must be claimed by the witness or it will be lost.

Although the Fifth Amendment appears to absolutely prohibit prosecutorial compulsion against a suspect or against a witness who claims the privilege, this is not so. The state can lawfully compel a witness to testify by granting **immunity** from prosecution, and in this way the state can achieve its legitimate goal of gathering information in an inquiry or furthering a prosecution. Immunity is granted when the prosecutor believes that an individual who claims the privilege has relevant information. If immunity from prosecution is granted and the witness continues to refuse to testify, the courts have power "to compel testimony . . . by use of civil contempt and coerced imprisonment" (*Lefkowitz v. Turley,* 1973, citing *Shillitani v. United States,* 1966).

An important consequence of granting immunity—for understanding the most recent controversy regarding confessions law—is that once immunity is granted, the statement made cannot be used against the witness in *any* way. "Testimony given in response to a grant of legislative immunity is the *essence of coerced testimony*. In such cases there is no question whether physical or psychological pressures overrode the defendant's will; the witness is told to talk or face the government's coercive sanctions, notably, a conviction for contempt" (*New Jersey v. Portash*, 1979, emphasis added). Therefore, grand jury testimony compelled by a grant of immunity cannot be used later in a trial to impeach the witness's credibility. The rule is different under *Miranda* law.

The government can also compel testimony, for purposes other than criminal prosecution, in the so-called penalty cases. Police officers were required to testify to an administrative body about corruption or forfeit their jobs, as long as their testimony was not later admitted in a criminal case (*Garrity v. New Jersey,* 1967). Also, an officer who refused to testify or to waive immunity could not be fired because it was based on his "refusal to waive a constitutional right" (*Gardner v. Broderick,* 1968). In *Spevak v. Klein* (1967), an attorney under judicial investigation for misconduct "asserted the privilege and refused to comply with a subpoena duces tecum demanding testimony and documents, despite facing disciplinary action for his refusal. When he appealed his resulting disbarment, a plurality of the Court determined that the threat of disbarment constituted compulsion under the Fifth Amendment and held that the state could not impose the penalty for an assertion of the privilege."[10]

These early cases implied that the state could not compel the officers to testify, but as the Court later made clear, the state can require officers to testify on pain of losing their jobs and can require contractors to testify on pain of losing contracts, as long as they were granted immunity from criminal prosecution (*Lefkowitz v. Turley,* 1973). The result of these cases is to treat penalties (e.g., loss of jobs or contracts, disbarment) as compulsion, but to allow the compulsion as long as the witnesses are immunized from the use of their testimony in later criminal prosecutions.

The act of a police officer simply asking questions of a person is not Fifth Amendment compulsion. *Miranda v. Arizona* (1966), however, held that when questions are asked of a suspect during *custodial interrogation,* Fifth Amendment compulsion exists. In this case, the privilege is not self-executing, and the police must inform the suspect of his or her rights by reading several warnings. (Cases that distinguish between police interviewing and interrogation are reviewed later in this chapter.)

Incrimination.   Under the privilege, a person cannot lawfully refuse to testify to protect another, to avoid trouble with private parties, or for any reason *except* to avoid being prosecuted for a crime or for juvenile delinquency, as the penalties for a delinquency adjudication are essentially penal in nature (*In re Gault,* 1967). Similarly, any incriminating statements obtained from a defendant who spoke with a state psychiatrist in a pretrial hearing to determine competence to stand trial cannot be introduced in the defendant's sentencing hearing unless the defendant waived his right against self-incrimination at the hearing following *Miranda* warnings (*Estelle v. Smith*, 1981).

On the other hand, the Court has not extended self-incrimination protection to proceedings under sexual offender statutes that lead to incarceration or additional penalties. These programs are declared civil, and not penal, in nature. In *Allen v. Illinois* (1986), sexual assault charges were dropped against the defendant, and the state proceeded against him under the Sexually Dangerous Persons Act. Examining psychiatrists for the state testified at the bench trial on the state's commitment petition. The trial court found that the state proved Allen had a mental disorder and a propensity to commit sexual assaults. Based on the psychiatrists' testimony, and that of the sexual assault victim, the court found Allen to be a sexually dangerous person. The act authorized potentially indefinite commitment to the "sex deviate facility" located in the Wisconsin State Prison. Allen claimed that information elicited from him violated his right against self-incrimination. The Supreme Court held (5–4) that the program was one of civil commitment, despite the fact that the act provides safeguards applicable in criminal trials (counsel, jury trial, confrontation and cross-examination of witnesses), that the state had to prove dangerousness beyond a reasonable doubt, and that a person adjudged sexually dangerous is committed to a maximum-security institution that also houses convicts needing psychiatric care.

In **McKune v. Lile** (2002), a prison inmate convicted of rape was ordered into a treatment program a few years before his scheduled release. To participate, Robert Lile had to answer questions that would disclose criminal activity. No immunity was granted for any incriminating disclosures. Lile refused to participate. As a result, his prison privileges were reduced. He lost visitation rights, earnings, work opportunities, the ability to send money to family, canteen expenditures, access to a personal television, and other privileges. He also was transferred to a potentially more dangerous maximum-security unit. The Supreme Court held (5–4) that the requirement to disclose criminal information did not violate the Self-Incrimination Clause. In a plurality opinion, Justice Anthony Kennedy reasoned that although prisoners have Fifth Amendment rights, the program does not compel prisoners to testify because the lost privileges and transfer to a maximum-security unit "are not [consequences] that compel a prisoner to speak about his past crimes despite a desire to remain silent." The loss of privileges that Lile suffered was, furthermore, related to the objectives of a program that had legitimate penological goals. There was no self-incrimination violation as long as the program objectives did not constitute atypical and significant hardships. Justice John Paul Stevens, dissenting, felt that the penalties imposed for not participating were severe. More fundamentally, Lile was punished for exercising his rights under the Self-Incrimination Clause.

Allen was criticized because it "is insensitive to the reality of the commitment system" that makes it very much like an indefinite prison sentence.[11] The kinds of programs upheld in *Allen* and *McKune* are politically popular attempts to deal with highly predatory criminals. Nevertheless, there is evidence that some offenders placed in these programs do not fit the profiles of mentally aberrant patients and that the programs may be covert ways of imposing virtual life sentences. The evidence used to place prisoners in programs may consist more of their prior record than any medical information.[12]

The privilege protects only against incrimination in American courts. A former Nazi camp guard, unprosecutable in the United States because the statute of limitations had run out, was subpoenaed to testify in deportation hearings. He claimed self-incrimination protection because his testimony could be used to prosecute him in other countries, including Lithuania or Germany. The Supreme Court held that the Self-Incrimination Clause refers to American procedures, as do the other clauses of the Fifth Amendment (Grand Jury, Double Jeopardy, Due Process, and Just Compensation) (*United States v. Balsys*, 1998).

The Act of Producing Evidence.

Federal appellate courts have held that although "the *contents* of voluntarily produced papers are not protected by the Fifth Amendment, the *act of producing* such documents is protected . . . if the act itself is both testimonial and incriminating."[13] Production of subpoenaed evidence exposes the producer to four potentially incriminating facts in regard to the evidence: (1) its existence, (2) its authenticity, (3) its possession, and (4) the belief that the documents match the terms of a subpoena (*Fisher v. United States*, 1976). The Supreme Court has not established a bright-line rule that immunizes compelled production of records from prosecution. Each case must be resolved on its own facts. Where a court determines that production itself is incriminating, the individual may still have to produce the records but may be granted immunity, although this is not automatic (*United States v. Doe*, 1984).

Certainly, the oddest and most dramatic act-of-production case is ***Baltimore Department of Social Services v. Bouknight*** (1990). The Baltimore City Department of Social Services (BCDSS), fearing child abuse, removed an infant, Maurice, from his mother, Jacqueline Bouknight. He was returned to her a few months later, under various conditions. Eight months later, fearing for Maurice's safety, the juvenile court ordered his return to BCDSS custody. Bouknight refused to turn over the boy. A diligent search by police and relatives failed to produce him. Bouknight was held in contempt of court for failing to produce Maurice and was jailed. She challenged this in the U.S. Supreme Court on the ground that the compelled production of Maurice might tend to incriminate her.

The Supreme Court held that Bouknight had no Fifth Amendment claim because Maurice's physical condition was not testimonial evidence. She argued that "her implicit communication of control over Maurice at the moment of production might aid the State in prosecuting [her]." The Court ruled that even if the boy's production were testimonial, it still did not give her the right to refuse the order "because she has assumed *custodial duties* related to production [of Maurice] and production is required as a part of a *noncriminal regulatory scheme*" (emphasis added). The Court did not answer the question of whether the Fifth Amendment would protect Bouknight against prosecution if she complied with the order, produced Maurice, and was prosecuted for child abuse because of evidence obtained from her act of production.

Having lost her case, Bouknight remained in jail for contempt of court for seven and a half years, one of the longest terms for contempt in U.S. history. She was released in October 1995. The judge who ordered the release said that continued imprisonment was no longer an effective tool to force the information from her. Her lawyers called Bouknight a hero of civil disobedience, but the judge who had held her in contempt expressed fears that the child might be dead.[14]

Confessions Law before *Miranda*

English and American courts developed a common law exclusionary rule for coerced confessions in the years around 1800. Police could question suspects, and incriminating statements could be used in evidence against them, as long as the statements were not "induced by force, threat of force, or promise of leniency from a person in authority, for if it has been so obtained, it is considered 'involuntary' and excluded."[15] In 1912, the English courts advanced the protection offered to a suspect from coercive interrogation by establishing the so-called Judges' Rules for the guidance of police officers. The Judges' Rules stated that before asking a person about to be charged with a crime if he or she wished to say anything in answer to the charges, that person should be told, "You are not obliged to say anything unless you wish to do so, but whatever you say will be taken down in writing and may be given in evidence."[16] A failure to give the warning rendered a statement improper, and it could be excluded from consideration at trial. The English Judges' Rules were well known to American jurists and established the idea that it is proper to inform suspects of their basic right against self-incrimination.

The **voluntariness test** was established in each American state by the late nineteenth century. The Supreme Court, in ***Bram v. United States*** (1897), held that coerced confessions in federal cases were guided by the Fifth Amendment right against self-incrimination. The test of admissibility under *Bram,* however, was essentially the voluntariness test. In both state and federal law, therefore, coerced or involuntary confessions were excluded from evidence, although no warning requirement was yet established. Before the 1960s, the criminal justice amendments of the Bill of Rights had not yet been incorporated, and so *Bram*'s **self-incrimination rule** did not apply to the states.

In practice, state courts were often reluctant to exclude confessions even when there was compelling evidence of coercion. As a result, defendants whose confessions were the product of coercion turned to the federal courts, claiming that coerced confessions violated the Fourteenth Amendment Due Process Clause. From 1936 until 1966, the Supreme

Court decided more than thirty confessions cases from the states under the Due Process Clause. In 1964, the Fifth Amendment self-incrimination rule was incorporated, paving the way to *Miranda v. Arizona* (1966). A brief review of the due process voluntariness test helps us appreciate the significance of the "*Miranda* revolution."

In **Brown v. Mississippi** (1936), the first Supreme Court case to review a confession obtained by state or local officers, three African American men confessed to committing a murder after being subjected to torture during their interrogation by the local sheriff and others. Their treatment included being hung by a rope from a tree, being let down, and being hung again, and whipping "with a leather strap with buckles on it" that cut their backs to pieces. After resisting these tortures over three days, they were told that it would continue until they signed a confession dictated by a deputy. The Supreme Court held that confessions obtained by such physical torture were "not consistent" with Fourteenth Amendment due process of law, rendering the trial and conviction void because they were "a mere pretense where the state authorities have contrived a conviction resting solely upon confessions obtained by violence" (*Brown v. Mississippi*, 1936). The legal foundation of *Brown* was not a specific Bill of Rights provision but the "fair trial" idea of the Fourteenth Amendment Due Process Clause, first adopted by the Court in *Moore v. Dempsey* (1923). (See Chapter 1.)

The due process approach toward involuntary confessions initiated by *Brown* was not limited to physical torture. The Court soon applied the voluntariness test to lesser forms of coercion. The basic question was whether, under the facts and circumstances of the case, a particular confession was voluntary. Was it made of the defendant's free will? Was it obtained by police interrogation tactics that overcame the defendant's will? In case after case, the Supreme Court moved inexorably toward more refined standards. In **Ashcraft v. Tennessee** (1944), for example, the police did not beat the defendant but questioned him "in relays" for thirty-six hours with no interruption until he confessed to murdering his wife. The Supreme Court held that the long period of straight questioning was itself sufficient coercion so that his statements were not voluntary but compelled. Justice Hugo Black cited the Wickersham Commission's report of 1930 that condemned this kind of police behavior, known as the **third degree,** "as a secret and illegal practice."[17] The third degree, common in that era, ranged from severe questioning to police beatings of suspects to force confessions out of them. The Court's stream of state confessions cases, enforcing the involuntary confessions rule, was aimed at pressuring police departments to adopt more civilized interrogation methods. *Chambers v. Florida* (1940), a coerced confessions case, "clearly acknowledged that the federal government had a duty to guarantee fair trials in state as well as federal courts."[18]

Other practices held to undermine the defendant's will and induce involuntary confessions in violation of the Fourteenth Amendment included

- Defendant moved to secret places so that family, lawyers, or friends could not contact him (*Chambers v. Florida,* 1940; *Ward v. Texas,* 1942).
- Defendant kept naked for several hours (*Malinski v. New York,* 1945).
- Defendant told by a state-employed psychiatrist that the doctor was there to help him and would provide medical assistance, thus gaining the defendant's confidence and incriminating information (*Leyra v. Denno,* 1954).
- Suspect, a young African American, told that he would be handed over to a lynch mob (*Payne v. Arkansas,* 1958).
- Defendant, in his cell, told by a police officer, who had been a childhood friend, over a period of days that the officer would lose his job if he did not get a statement (*Spano v. New York,* 1959).
- Vigorous interrogation of a mentally defective or insane suspect (*Blackburn v. Alabama,* 1960; *Culombe v. Connecticut,* 1961).
- Use of "truth serum" (*Townsend v. Sain,* 1963).
- Defendant told that her children's welfare assistance would be cut off and her children taken from her if she failed to cooperate with police (*Lynumn v. Illinois,* 1963).

The justices were clearly appalled by these excessive and coercive methods. Indeed, the Supreme Court held that where police action in forcing a confession was so egregious as to clearly violate due process, the police could be subject to prosecution under the federal criminal laws (*Williams v. United States,* 1951). As a court of law, however, the Supreme Court could not directly require police to follow more civilized procedures. Through its due process jurisdiction, the Court could only indirectly influence police practices by reversing convictions when police went too far. By progressively refining the standard of what constituted an involuntary confession, the Court signaled the police community to eliminate coercive methods of interrogation. On the positive side, the due process approach balanced the operating realities of policing with an expression of society's highest values. The negative side was that the Court's piecemeal approach seemed to hardly make a dent in the problem of police coercion.

Problems with the Voluntariness Rule.

The due process approach was highly subjective; it provided no clear guidance for lower courts and police and was unsatisfactory to many judges and lawyers. This piecemeal method gave the police examples of what to avoid, but no clear-cut or bright-line rule explaining how constitutional interrogation should be conducted. This growing dissatisfaction was a reason why the Court adopted the seemingly clear, rulelike guidelines in *Miranda.* Professor Richard Cortner comments:

> Adhering to the fair trial approach to the Due Process Clause, the Court followed a meandering and ofttimes puzzling course in state criminal cases during the 1950s. . . . [T]he Court's performance under the Due Process Clause was such as to involve it in unpredictable intrusions into the state criminal process on the basis of standards nowhere satisfactorily articulated—with the result that serious federal-state strains developed.[19]

The "totality of the circumstances" approach to coerced confessions was *ad hoc* case-by-case decision making that seemed the opposite of firm constitutional policy.

More fundamentally, the Court based the due process voluntariness test on different constitutional reasons: "(1) ensuring that convictions are based on reliable evidence; (2) deterring improper police conduct; or (3) assuring that a defendant's confession is the product of his free and rational choice."[20] The Court shuttled between these rationales, leaving lawyers and trial judges in confusion. In early cases like *Brown* and *Ashcraft,* all three elements coincided: Excessive police conduct overpowered the suspect's will and raised real doubts about the accuracy of the confession. In some later cases, the Court seemed to focus primarily on the reliability or accuracy of confessions. *Lyons v. Oklahoma* (1944) ruled that a confession would be upheld if the state "employed a fair standard in adjudicating common law in voluntariness claims" as long as it appeared that the confession was true, a rationale that would have narrowed the scope of the voluntariness rule. But in other cases, the Court set aside convictions even where the confession's truthfulness was substantially corroborated, because the police misconduct was too great to ignore (*Watts v. Indiana*, 1949). A police misconduct rationale would broaden the Court's control over police behavior. Indeed, without signaling a clear intention to do so, the Court in the 1950s seemed to be shifting toward a police conduct test, concerned less with the accuracy of the confession or its actual voluntariness and more with controlling egregious police conduct. In *Rogers v. Richmond* (1961), for example, the Court struck down a seemingly accurate and voluntary confession because the police tricked the suspect into thinking that they were going to arrest his ailing wife for questioning. The Court, nevertheless, did not rely on *Rogers* as a vehicle to sharply limit police interrogation practices. It thus produced inconsistent results by emphasizing different purposes in different cases. The lack of clarity of the rules and the underlying purposes of its due process cases led the Court to search for bright-line confessions rules to give police firmer guidance.

The Federal "Time Test." One attempt to create a bright-line exclusionary rule was established only for federal officers in ***McNabb v. United States*** (1943) and applied later in ***Mallory v. United States*** (1957). The rule excluded confessions if an arrested suspect was not brought before a magistrate without "unnecessary delay," as required by the Federal Rules of Criminal Procedure. *McNabb* stated that a goal of this rule was to reduce opportunities for police coercion and third-degree practices. *Mallory* repeated this rationale, noting that an important function of the judge at the initial appearance is to inform a suspect of his or her right to remain silent.

The dangers inherent in the police holding suspects in custody without bringing them to a judge were highlighted shortly before *Miranda* in ***Davis v. North Carolina*** (1966). Elmer Davis Jr., an African American with low mental functioning who had escaped from a prison camp, was held as a suspect in a rape-murder for sixteen days in a police lockup cell measuring six by ten feet and was questioned every day in order to obtain a confession. A written station house order instructed police not to allow anyone to have contact with Davis. Only after confessing was he taken before a magistrate, despite the state rule requiring that an arrested person be brought before a magistrate within a reasonable period of time. The Supreme Court ruled Davis's confession to be involuntary.

The *McNabb-Mallory* rule applied only to federal law enforcement officers and agencies because it was not based on the Fourteenth Amendment due process doctrine of "fundamental fairness." It was instead based on the Supreme Court's inherent **supervisory authority** over lower federal courts and federal law enforcement. The "time test," although not applicable to the states, showed that the justices were displeased with heavy-handed police actions in obtaining confessions, a concern that would animate the *Miranda* decision.

Right to Counsel. The secrecy of police interrogation was a major concern. Without representation by counsel, the defendant is alone and vulnerable to improper police tactics. In two late 1950s cases, ***Crooker v. California*** (1958) and ***Cicenia v. LaGay*** (1958), dissenting justices argued that voluntary confessions should be excluded on the grounds that defendants' requests for attorneys were denied. The majority, however, held that a mere denial to see one's attorney was not in itself a due process violation. This position began to erode in ***Spano v. New York*** (1959), which held that overbearing police tactics led to an involuntary confession. Four concurring justices in *Spano* argued that the defendant had a right of access to counsel, noting that he had been formally indicted before confessing. *Gideon v. Wainwright* (1963), decided four years later, incorporated the right to counsel at trial and increased the pressure to view police interrogation as a critical stage in the prosecution. Furthermore, in 1964 the Court in *Massiah v. United States* (this chapter) held that indicted defendants who had already obtained counsel could not be secretly taped or questioned by the police without the consent of the defendant's lawyer.

The turning point in the move to replace the voluntariness test with a clearer rule came in ***Escobedo v. Illinois*** (1964). It held that a preindictment suspect had a Sixth Amendment right to counsel during police interrogation, but only if the lawyer had been hired before the interrogation began. The *Escobedo* case was, according to Fred Graham, "enigmatic" because its holding was based on a complicated set of facts, and it was not clear which of these facts would be crucial in extending the right to counsel during interrogation in later cases.[21] In *Escobedo*, a lawyer was hired by the family of a murder suspect. The lawyer made repeated attempts over a period of three or four hours to see his client at the police station. At one point, Escobedo and his lawyer made eye contact, but the police refused to allow them to meet. The Court held that although Escobedo's confession was made voluntarily, it was unconstitutional because his Sixth Amendment right to counsel had been violated. Was *Escobedo* another "special circumstances" case (like *Powell v. Alabama* and *Betts v. Brady* regarding the right to counsel), or was it a first step toward requiring attorneys during every police interrogation?

The Court's opinion muddied the Sixth Amendment basis for its holding by injecting Fifth Amendment concerns: "Without informing him of his absolute right to remain silent in the face of this accusation, the police urged him to make a statement." *Escobedo* was an important case, but it was clearly not the final word or a firm rule for the guidance of police interrogation. First, the holding was fact-specific, limiting its future application to other scenarios. Also, it was problematic to base a right to counsel at police interrogation on the Sixth Amendment because the amendment applies to the "criminal prosecution," which does not commence until formal charges have been issued against a defendant. *Escobedo* left many questions unanswered. The Supreme Court expected a trickle of appeals designed to clarify the case's ambiguities but instead received a flood. Within two years it startled the legal community with its monumental *Miranda* decision. *Miranda* took a new turn and, "decid[ing] to answer all of the questions at once" placed state confessions law firmly on a Fifth Amendment foundation.[22]

THE *MIRANDA* DECISION

Miranda was not an incorporation case. The recently incorporated rights to counsel and against self-incrimination gave the Supreme Court the impetus to forge a new approach to establish a definitive confessions rule after three decades of due process cases. The *Miranda* majority chose the Fifth Amendment, not the Sixth Amendment, as the constitutional foundation of confessions law. *Miranda* was, for a time, one of the most severely criticized cases in the Court's history, referred to by some as a "self-inflicted wound." Many lawyers were offended by the unprecedented and legislative-like style of the ruling, while police officials and conservative politicians denounced the Court for its pro-defendant ruling.[23]

After the Supreme Court decision excluding Ernesto Miranda's confession, he was retried for rape and convicted in 1967 on the testimony of his common law wife. He was later paroled but continued to get into trouble. Miranda was stabbed to death on January 31, 1976, in the restroom of a cheap bar in Phoenix, Arizona, after a fistfight. Police caught the man who had assailed Ernesto and read him his *Miranda* warnings.[24]

Read Case and Comments: *Miranda v. Arizona.*

An Interpretation of *Miranda*

Although critics saw *Miranda* as a revolutionary break with the due process voluntariness rule, it can also be seen as an extension of that test for the constitutionality of confessions. The underlying rationale of the Self-Incrimination Clause and the Due Process Clause is the same: forbidding compelled testimony. The voluntariness test had itself evolved over time from outlawing torture to finding that certain psychological pressure tactics were unconstitutional. In this light, *Miranda* has continued the progressive civilizing approach of the confessions exclusionary rule by attacking the source of undue compulsion.

If the Court, therefore, correctly assessed modern police interrogation as so highly manipulative as to amount to compulsion, *Miranda* can be seen as a conservative ruling in that it preserved police interrogation. A logical extension of the voluntariness test could have led the Court to rule that all secret interrogation is unconstitutional. The effect of such a rule would have been like the *Massiah* rule (discussed at the end of this chapter), forbidding all questioning of a suspect in the absence of a lawyer.

Miranda can also be seen as a logical and not very extreme extension of the privilege against self-incrimination. As seen above, a witness can invoke the privilege in any official venue when subpoenaed to testify, whether at a criminal trial, civil trial, administrative hearing, grand jury proceeding, or legislative inquiry. It makes sense to extend the privilege to a suspect in the station house. A court cannot order a witness claiming the privilege to talk on the witness stand under a threat of a contempt citation and then use what is said against the witness in a criminal trial. Likewise, not protecting a suspect's ability to remain silent in the station house would entirely nullify the defendant's absolute right to silence at the trial.

CASE AND COMMENTS

Miranda v. Arizona

384 U.S. 436, 86 S.Ct. 1602, 16 L.Ed.2d 694 (1966)

[a] The Supreme Court stated that these facts did not make the confessions unconstitutional under the due process voluntariness test. In Part V of the majority opinion, it applied the general rules of the decision and found that in each case the self-incrimination rights of the defendants had been violated.

[b] The Court clearly specifies the factual predicate of these cases (custodial police interrogation) and the decision's constitutional basis (the privilege against self-incrimination).

[c] This is disingenuous. As the dissenters state, this case was clearly a constitutional innovation.

[In four consolidated cases none of the defendants were fully informed of their constitutional rights, although some were informed of their right to remain silent. **[a]** In *Miranda v. Arizona,* Miranda confessed to a rape after being interrogated for only two hours at a police station. In *Vignera v. New York,* a robbery suspect questioned by police made an oral admission in the afternoon and a written confession to a prosecutor that evening. In *Westover v. United States,* local police arrested Westover for a robbery and interrogated him that evening. The next day, FBI agents began to interrogate the defendant at 9 A.M. He was read warnings at noon and confessed at 2:00 P.M. In *Stewart v. California,* the defendant was interrogated nine times over five days by the police and was held incommunicado until he confessed. He was then taken before an examining magistrate. There was no evidence of threats or violence in any of these cases. The majority opinion discussed the facts of the cases after fifty pages of constitutional analysis.]

MR. CHIEF JUSTICE WARREN delivered the opinion of the Court.

The cases before us raise questions which go to the roots of our concepts of American criminal jurisprudence: the restraints society must observe consistent with the Federal Constitution in prosecuting individuals for crime. **[b]** More specifically, we deal with the admissibility of statements obtained from an individual who is subjected to custodial police interrogation and the necessity for procedures which assure that the individual is accorded his privilege under the Fifth Amendment to the Constitution not to be compelled to incriminate himself.

* * *

We start here, as we did in *Escobedo,* with the premise that our holding is not an innovation in our jurisprudence, but is an application of principles long recognized and applied in other settings. **[c]** * * *

* * *

Our holding * * * briefly stated is this: the prosecution may not use statements, whether **exculpatory** or **inculpatory,** stemming from custodial interrogation of the defendant unless it demonstrates the use of procedural safeguards effective to secure the privilege against self-incrimination. By custodial interrogation, we mean questioning initiated by law enforcement officers after a person has been taken into custody or otherwise deprived of his freedom of action in any significant way.

I

[d] The case is decided not on the specific facts in each of the four consolidated cases, but merely on the fact that in each there was police custodial interrogation and rights were not explained to the defendants. There was no physical or psychological coercion in these cases. A review of interrogation techniques found in police manuals substituted for finding specific case facts.

* * * [All the cases here] share salient features—incommunicado interrogation of individuals in a police-dominated atmosphere, resulting in self-incriminating statements without full warning of constitutional rights. **[d]**

An understanding of the nature and setting of this in-custody interrogation is essential to our decisions today. The difficulty in depicting what transpires at such interrogations stems from the fact that in this country they have largely taken place incommunicado. From extensive factual studies undertaken in the early 1930s, including the famous Wickersham Report to Congress by a Presidential Commission, it is clear that police violence and the "third degree" flourished at that time. In a series of cases decided by this Court long after these studies, the police resorted to physical brutality—beatings, hanging, whipping—and to sustained and protracted questioning incommunicado in order to extort confessions. * * *

* * *

Again we stress that the modern practice of in-custody interrogation is psychologically rather than physically oriented. * * * ["T]his Court has recognized that coercion can be mental as well as physical, and that the blood of the accused is not the only hallmark of an unconstitutional inquisition." * * * [e] Interrogation still takes place in privacy. Privacy results in secrecy and this in turn results in a gap in our knowledge as to what in fact goes on in the interrogation rooms. A valuable source of information about present police practices, however, may be found in various police manuals and texts which document procedures employed with success in the past, and which recommend various other effective tactics. * * *

The officers are told by the manuals that the "principal psychological factor contributing to a successful interrogation is privacy—being alone with the person under interrogation." * * *

To highlight the isolation and unfamiliar surroundings, the manuals instruct the police to display an air of confidence in the suspect's guilt and from outward appearance to maintain only an interest in confirming certain details. [f] The guilt of the subject is to be posited as a fact. The interrogator should direct his comments toward the reasons why the subject committed the act, rather than court failure by asking the subject whether he did it. Like other men, perhaps the subject has had a bad family life, had an unhappy childhood, had too much to drink, had an unrequited desire for women. The officers are instructed to minimize the moral seriousness of the offense, to cast blame on the victim or on society. These tactics are designed to put the subject in a psychological state where his story is but an elaboration of what the police purport to know already—that he is guilty. Explanations to the contrary are dismissed and discouraged. * * *

* * *

When the techniques described above prove unavailing, the texts recommend they be alternated with a show of some hostility. One ploy often used has been termed the "friendly-unfriendly" or the "Mutt and Jeff" act. * * *

The interrogators sometimes are instructed to induce a confession out of trickery. [g] The technique here is quite effective in crimes which require identification or which run in series. In the identification situation, the interrogator may take a break in his questioning to place the subject among a group of men in a line-up [and to coach a witness to identify the suspect]. * * * A variation on this technique is called the "reverse line-up":

> "The accused is placed in a line-up, but this time he is identified by several fictitious witnesses or victims who associated him with different offenses. It is expected that the subject will become desperate and confess to the offense under investigation in order to escape from the false accusations."

* * *

From these representative samples of interrogation techniques, the setting prescribed by the manuals and observed in practice becomes clear. [h] In essence, it is this: To be alone with the subject is essential to prevent distraction and to deprive him of any outside support. The aura of confidence in his guilt undermines his will to resist. He merely confirms the preconceived story the police seek to have him describe. Patience and persistence, at times relentless questioning, are employed. To obtain a confession, the interrogator must "patiently maneuver himself or his quarry into a position from which the desired objective may be attained." When normal procedures fail to produce the needed result, the police may resort to deceptive stratagems such as giving false legal advice. It is important to keep the subject off balance, for example, by trading on his insecurity about himself or his surroundings. The police then persuade, trick, or cajole him out of exercising his constitutional rights.

(*continued*)

[e] Notice the negative attitude toward interrogation. Early findings of brutality or extreme psychological pressure are taken to be a risk in any police interrogation. Thus every custodial interrogation, conducted in secrecy, establishes compulsion under the privilege against self-incrimination.

[f] Are these practices outrageous or simply like high-pressure sales tactics used to get the suspect to admit to the crime?

[g] Is using tricks and lies ethical if it is the only way to get a "guilty" person to confess? What if the suspect is in fact not guilty? Should there be a limit to trickery?

[h] These examples from police manuals are not scientifically drawn random samples of police activity; nevertheless, there is no reason to believe that they are uncommon. In your opinion, are they inherently coercive?

* * *

[i] The Court puts the finishing touch on its argument: (1) The self-incrimination clause forbids compelled testimony; (2) secret police interrogation is inherently compelling; therefore (3) safeguards are required in order to "dispel" compulsion.

In the cases before us today, given this background, we concern ourselves primarily with this interrogation atmosphere and the evils it can bring. * * *

In these cases, we might not find the defendants' statements to have been involuntary in traditional terms. [i] Our concern for adequate safeguards to protect precious Fifth Amendment rights is, of course, not lessened in the slightest. * * * The fact remains that in none of these cases did the officers undertake to afford appropriate safeguards at the outset of the interrogation to insure that the statements were truly the product of free choice.

It is obvious that such an interrogation environment is created for no purpose other than to subjugate the individual to the will of his examiner. This atmosphere carries its own badge of intimidation. To be sure, this is not physical intimidation, but it is equally destructive of human dignity. * * * Unless adequate protective devices are employed to dispel the compulsion inherent in custodial surroundings, no statement obtained from the defendant can truly be the product of his free choice.

* * *

[Part II of the opinion reviewed the history of the right against self-incrimination in English and American law and its incorporation into the Fourteenth Amendment in *Malloy v. Hogan* (1964), which established the constitutional jurisdiction for the Court to apply the Fifth Amendment's privilege against self-incrimination to the states.]

III

Today, then, there can be no doubt that the Fifth Amendment privilege is available outside of criminal court proceedings and serves to protect persons in all settings in which their freedom of action is curtailed in any significant way from being compelled to incriminate themselves. We have concluded that without proper safeguards the process of in-custody interrogation of persons suspected or accused of crime contains inherently compelling pressures which work to undermine the individual's will to resist and to compel him to speak where he would not otherwise do so freely. In order to combat these pressures and to permit a full opportunity to exercise the privilege against self-incrimination, the accused must be adequately and effectively apprised of his rights and the exercise of those rights must be fully honored.

[j] The suggestion that other protective techniques could replace the warnings became an extremely controversial point. A more conservative Court used this statement to argue that *Miranda* warnings are not rules required by the Constitution.

It is impossible for us to foresee the potential alternatives for protecting the privilege which might be devised by Congress or the States in the exercise of their creative rule-making capacities. [j] Therefore we cannot say that the Constitution necessarily requires adherence to any particular solution for the inherent compulsions of the interrogation process as it is presently conducted. Our decision in no way creates a constitutional strait-jacket which will handicap sound efforts at reform, nor is it intended to have this effect. We encourage Congress and the States to continue their laudable search for increasingly effective ways of protecting the rights of the individual while promoting efficient enforcement of our criminal laws. However, unless we are shown other procedures which are at least as effective in apprising accused persons of their right of silence and in assuring a continuous opportunity to exercise it, the following safeguards must be observed.

At the outset, if a person in custody is to be subjected to interrogation, he must first be informed in clear and unequivocal terms that he has the right to remain silent. [k] For those unaware of the privilege, the warning is needed simply to make them aware of it—the threshold requirement for an intelligent decision as to its exercise. More important, such a warning is an absolute prerequisite in overcoming the inherent pressures of the interrogation atmosphere. * * *

[k] The first warning. Are the reasons for it convincing?

The Fifth Amendment privilege is so fundamental to our system of constitutional rule and the expedient of giving an adequate warning as to the availability of the privilege so simple, we will not pause to inquire in individual cases whether the defendant was aware of his rights without a warning being given. * * *

The warning of the right to remain silent must be accompanied by the explanation that anything said can and will be used against the individual in court. **[l]** This warning is needed in order to make him aware not only of the privilege, but also of the consequences of foregoing it. It is only through an awareness of these consequences that there can be any assurance of real understanding and intelligent exercise of the privilege. Moreover, this warning may serve to make the individual more acutely aware that he is faced with a phase of the adversary system—that he is not in the presence of persons acting solely in his interest.

[l] The second warning.

The circumstances surrounding in-custody interrogation can operate very quickly to overbear the will of one merely made aware of his privilege by his interrogators. **[m]** Therefore, the right to have counsel present at the interrogation is indispensable to the protection of the Fifth Amendment privilege. * * *

[m] The third warning. It is *not* based on the Sixth Amendment; it is required to protect Fifth Amendment rights.

* * *

In order fully to apprise a person interrogated of the extent of his rights under this system then, it is necessary to warn him not only that he has the right to consult with an attorney, but also that if he is indigent a lawyer will be appointed to represent him. **[n]** Without this additional warning, the admonition of the right to consult with counsel would often be understood as meaning only that he can consult with a lawyer if he has one or has the funds to obtain one. * * *

[n] The fourth warning.

Once warnings have been given, the subsequent procedure is clear. If the individual indicates in any manner, at any time prior to or during questioning, that he wishes to remain silent, the interrogation must cease. **[o]** At this point he has shown that he intends to exercise his Fifth Amendment privilege; any statement taken after the person invokes his privilege cannot be other than the product of compulsion, subtle or otherwise. Without the right to cut off questioning, the setting of in-custody interrogation operates on the individual to overcome free choice in producing a statement after the privilege has been once invoked. If the individual states that he wants an attorney, the interrogation must cease until an attorney is present. At that time, the individual must have an opportunity to confer with the attorney and to have him present during any subsequent questioning. If the individual cannot obtain an attorney and he indicates that he wants one before speaking to police, they must respect his decision to remain silent.

[o] Consequences of the warnings. The suspect can "invoke" the privilege and lawfully refuse to answer by "just saying no" when asked to talk by the police, even after answering some questions.

This does not mean, as some have suggested, that each police station must have a "station house lawyer" present at all times to advise prisoners. * * *

If the interrogation continues without the presence of an attorney and a statement is taken, a heavy burden rests on the government to demonstrate that the defendant knowingly and intelligently waived his privilege against self-incrimination and his right to retained or appointed counsel. **[p]** * * * Since the State is responsible for establishing the isolated circumstances under which the interrogation takes place and has the only means of making available corroborated evidence of warnings given during incommunicado interrogation, the burden is rightly on its shoulders.

[p] The burden of proof of a voluntary waiver is on the state; the state must produce some proof of a waiver.

An express statement that the individual is willing to make a statement and does not want an attorney followed closely by a statement could constitute a waiver. But a valid waiver will not be presumed simply from the silence of the accused after warnings are given or simply from the fact that a confession was in fact eventually obtained. * * *

* * *

The warnings required and the waiver necessary in accordance with our opinion today are, in the absence of a fully effective equivalent, prerequisites to the admissibility of any statement made by a defendant. No distinction can be drawn between statements which are direct confessions and statements which amount to "admissions" of part or all of an

(continued)

[q] This paragraph closes potential loopholes in the *Miranda* rules. A suspect might be led to say things he *thinks* will clear him (*exculpatory* statements) but that instead lead to independent evidence of guilt. These too are covered by the *Miranda* warnings.

[r] This is a critical point. The Fifth Amendment privilege applies prior to formal charges during custodial police interrogation, and not only at judicial-like hearings as the dissenters argued.

[s] Some critics feared that the Supreme Court would make all extra-judicial confessions illegal. The Court tries to allay these fears.

[t] Recent scholarship casts some doubt on Justice White's historical argument.[25]

offense. **[q]** The privilege against self-incrimination protects the individual from being compelled to incriminate himself in any manner; it does not distinguish degrees of incrimination. Similarly, for precisely the same reason, no distinction may be drawn between inculpatory statements and statements alleged to be merely "exculpatory." If a statement made were in fact truly exculpatory it would, of course, never be used by the prosecution. In fact, statements merely intended to be exculpatory by the defendant are often used to impeach his testimony at trial or to demonstrate untruths in the statement given under interrogation and thus to prove guilt by implication. These statements are incriminating in any meaningful sense of the word and may not be used without the full warnings and effective waiver required for any other statement. In *Escobedo* itself, the defendant fully intended his accusation of another as the slayer to be exculpatory as to himself.

The principles announced today deal with the protection which must be given to the privilege against self-incrimination when the individual is first subjected to police interrogation while in custody at the station or otherwise deprived of his freedom of action in any significant way. **[r]** It is at this point that our adversary system of criminal proceedings commences, distinguishing itself at the outset from the inquisitorial system recognized in some countries. * * *

Our decision is not intended to hamper the traditional function of police officers in investigating crime. * * *

* * *

In dealing with statements obtained through interrogation, we do not purport to find all confessions inadmissible. Confessions remain a proper element in law enforcement. Any statement given freely and voluntarily without any compelling influences is, of course, admissible in evidence. * * * There is no requirement that police stop a person who enters a police station and states that he wishes to confess to a crime, or a person who calls the police to offer a confession or any other statement he desires to make. **[s]** Volunteered statements of any kind are not barred by the Fifth Amendment and their admissibility is not affected by our holding today.

* * *

[Part IV presented policy arguments in favor of the warnings requirement, noting that warnings were required in England and many Commonwealth nations and were routinely given by FBI agents and military police without any loss of effective law enforcement.]

[Justices Clark (concurring in *Stewart v. California*), Harlan, and White each wrote dissenting opinions.]

MR. JUSTICE WHITE, with whom MR. JUSTICE HARLAN and MR. JUSTICE STEWART join, dissenting. * * *

I

The proposition that the privilege against self-incrimination forbids in-custody interrogation without the warnings specified in the majority opinion * * * has no significant support in the history of the privilege or in the language of the Fifth Amendment. * * * The rule excluding coerced confessions matured about 100 years [after the privilege against self-incrimination did,] "but there is nothing in the reports to suggest that the theory has its roots in the privilege against self-incrimination. . . ." * * * **[t]**

* * *

* * * [T]he Fifth Amendment privilege was . . . extended to encompass the then well-established rule against coerced confessions * * * [in] *Bram v. United States.* * * *

***

Bram, however, itself rejected the proposition which the Court now espouses. The question in *Bram* was whether a confession, obtained during custodial interrogation, had been compelled. * * * [T]he Court declared that:

> "* * * the mere fact that the confession is made to a police officer, while the accused was under arrest in or out of prison, or was drawn out by his questions, does not necessarily render the confession involuntary; but, as one of the circumstances, such imprisonment or interrogation may be taken into account in determining whether or not the statements of the prisoner were voluntary" * * *

***

III

* * * Rather than asserting new knowledge, the Court concedes that it cannot truly know what occurs during custodial questioning, because of the innate secrecy of such proceedings. **[u]** It extrapolates a picture of what it conceives to be the norm from police investigatorial manuals, published in 1959 and 1962 or earlier, without any attempt to allow for adjustments in police practices that may have occurred in the wake of more recent decisions of state appellate tribunals or this Court. But even if the relentless application of the described procedures could lead to involuntary confessions, it most assuredly does not follow that each and every case will disclose this kind of interrogation or this kind of consequence. Insofar as appears from the Court's opinion, it has not examined a single transcript of any police interrogation, let alone the interrogation that took place in any one of these cases which it decides today. * * * [T]he factual basis for the Court's premise is patently inadequate.

[u] Justice White accuses the majority of fabricating the constitutional element of coercion by assuming that the police manuals describe the reality of every interrogation, without proof of coercion in each specific case.

***

* * * [E]ven if one assumed that there was an adequate factual basis for the conclusion that all confessions obtained during in-custody interrogation are the product of compulsion, the rule propounded by the Court would still be irrational, for, apparently, it is only if the accused is also warned of his right to counsel and waives both that right and the right against self-incrimination that the inherent compulsiveness of interrogation disappears. **[v]** But if the defendant may not answer without a warning a question such as "Where were you last night?" without having his answer be a compelled one, how can the Court ever accept his negative answer to the question of whether he wants to consult his retained counsel or counsel whom the court will appoint? * * * The Court apparently realizes its dilemma of foreclosing questioning without the necessary warnings but at the same time permitting the accused, sitting in the same chair in front of the same policemen, to waive his right to consult an attorney. * * *

    * * * By considering any answers to any interrogation to be compelled regardless of the content and course of examination and by escalating the requirements to prove waiver, the Court not only prevents the use of compelled confessions but for all practical purposes forbids interrogation except in the presence of counsel. That is, instead of confining itself to protection of the right against compelled self-incrimination the Court has created a limited Fifth Amendment right to counsel—or, as the Court expresses it, a "need for counsel to protect the Fifth Amendment privilege." * * * The focus then is not on the will of the accused but on the will of counsel and how much influence he can have on the accused. Obviously there is no warrant in the Fifth Amendment for thus installing counsel as the arbiter of the privilege.

    In sum, for all the Court's expounding on the menacing atmosphere of police interrogation procedures, it has failed to supply any foundation for the conclusions it draws or the measures it adopts.

[v] Justice White sees a logical flaw in the opinion. If the station house atmosphere is inherently coercive, is it logically impossible for suspects to voluntarily waive their rights in that atmosphere, after being informed of their rights? He assumes that in the future all interrogation will occur with defense counsel present. This has not been the case.

(continued)

IV
* * *

[w] There is always a trade-off between security and liberty in criminal procedure; Justice White sees little gain in civil liberties by limiting the power of the police in this area.

In some unknown number of cases the Court's rule will return a killer, a rapist or other criminal to the streets and to the environment which produced him, to repeat his crime whenever it pleases him. [w] As a consequence, there will not be a gain, but a loss, in human dignity. The real concern is not the unfortunate consequences of this new decision on the criminal law as an abstract, disembodied series of authoritative proscriptions, but the impact on those who rely on the public authority for protection and who without it can only engage in violent self-help with guns, knives and the help of their neighbors similarly inclined. * * *

Nor can this decision do other than have a corrosive effect on the criminal law as an effective device to prevent crime. A major component in its effectiveness in this regard is its swift and sure enforcement. The easier it is to get away with rape and murder, the less the deterrent effect on those who are inclined to attempt it. This is still good common sense. * * *

* * *

There is an irony about *Miranda*. The Court's desire—to replace numerous case-specific decisions under the "facts and circumstances" approach of the voluntariness test with one bright-line rule for determining the constitutionality of confessions—was not to be. After *Miranda*, the Court had to deal with a cascade of cases litigating its meaning. These cases are reviewed in subsequent sections.

Voluntariness after *Miranda*

Miranda v. Arizona did not eliminate the due process voluntariness test. A suspect can obviously be coerced into confessing after being read *Miranda* warnings. Such a confession is inadmissible under the Fifth or Fourteenth Amendment due process clauses. Additionally, a coerced confession cannot be used to impeach a defendant who chooses to testify at trial.

Mincey v. Arizona (1978) is a blatant example of involuntariness. Rufus Mincey, who was shot and left semiconscious after a shoot-out with a police officer, was brought to a hospital intensive care unit in critical condition and was treated. That evening, Detective Hust went to the intensive care unit, told Mincey he was under arrest for the murder of a police officer, gave him *Miranda* warnings, and proceeded to ask questions about the shoot-out. Mincey asked repeatedly that the interrogation stop until he could get a lawyer, but Hust continued to question him until almost midnight. Throughout, Mincey was heavily medicated by an intravenous device; tubes were inserted into his throat to help him breathe and through his nose into his stomach to keep him from vomiting; and a catheter was inserted into his bladder. Mincey could not talk, so answers were written on pieces of paper.

When asked by Detective Hust, "Did you shoot anyone?" it seemed clear to the Court that Mincey's reply, "I can't say. I have to see a lawyer," was evidence of a clear desire not to speak. Yet he was pressed by the detective and made an incriminating statement. Justice Potter Stewart wrote:

It is hard to imagine a situation less conducive to the exercise of "a rational intellect and a free will" than Mincey's. He had been seriously wounded just a few hours earlier, and had arrived at the hospital "depressed almost to the point of coma," according to his attending physician. Although he had received some treatment, his condition at the time of [Detective] Hust's interrogation was still sufficiently serious that he was in the intensive care unit. He complained to Hust that the pain in his leg was "unbearable." He was evidently confused and unable to think clearly about either the events of that afternoon or the circumstances of his interrogation, since some of his written answers were on their face not entirely coherent. Finally, while Mincey was being questioned he was lying on his back on a hospital bed, encumbered by tubes, needles, and breathing apparatus. He was, in short, "at the complete mercy" of Detective Hust, unable to escape or resist the thrust of Hust's interrogation. (*Mincey v. Arizona,* 1978)

Despite the fact that Mincey had made some coherent statements, the Court concluded:

It is apparent from the record in this case that Mincey's statements were not "the product of his free and rational choice." . . . To the contrary, the undisputed evidence makes clear that Mincey wanted *not* to answer Detective Hust. But Mincey was weakened by pain and shock, isolated from family, friends, and legal counsel, and barely conscious, and his will was simply overborne. Due process of law requires that statements obtained as these were cannot be used in any way against a defendant at his trial. (*Mincey v. Arizona,* 1978)

Thus, the state could not use Mincey's statements for impeachment purposes.

In a five-to-four decision, the Supreme Court held a confession to be involuntary in **Arizona v. Fulminante** (1991). Fulminante, in federal prison for a weapons offense, was suspected of having murdered his stepdaughter. He was befriended by another inmate, Anthony Sarivola, a former police officer who became a paid informant for the FBI. Masquerading as an organized crime figure, Sarivola promised to protect Fulminante against violence from other inmates if they discovered he had killed his daughter, but only if he told Sarivola whether he committed the crime. Fulminante admitted the crime to Sarivola, who later testified at Fulminante's murder trial. The Supreme Court affirmed the Arizona Supreme Court's decision that "the confession was obtained as a direct result of extreme coercion and was tendered in the belief that the defendant's life was in jeopardy if he did not confess. This is a true coerced confession in every sense of the word." Both courts drew on common knowledge of the fact that prisoners are known to assault and even murder child abusers and, thus, could conclude that Fulminante had spoken out of fear for his life.

Crane v. Kentucky (1986) held that when a defendant raises the issue of a coerced confession under the Due Process Clause at trial, he must be allowed to introduce evidence of "the physical and psychological environment in which the confession was obtained." Even if a judge finds a confession to be voluntary in a pretrial hearing, a jury may disagree and find that the confession was involuntary or decide not to give it great weight. Innocent suspects have made voluntary confessions that they later regret. It would be impossible for a defendant alleging a coerced confession to prove it if evidence about the environment in which the confession was taken was excluded.

It is worth keeping in mind that *Miranda* violations and due process voluntariness rule violations are not entirely distinct. In **Withrow v. Williams** (1993), a defendant claimed that his *Miranda* rights were violated when at a police station during an "interview" (i.e., supposedly not an interrogation), police told Williams to "give us the truth" or else "we're simply gonna charge you and lock you up and you can tell it to a defense attorney and let him try and prove differently." In deciding that federal courts could hear *Miranda* claims under habeas corpus jurisdiction, the Court noted that if it decided otherwise, state prisoners could simply convert *Miranda* claims into due process claims that their convictions were based on involuntary confessions.

MIRANDA AS A CONSTITUTIONAL RULE

Attacking the Constitutional Basis of *Miranda*

***Theories of* Miranda.**   A theoretical debate with real-world consequences about the nature of *Miranda* warnings has divided the Court for decades. President Nixon's conservative appointees, generally hostile to Warren Court rulings, seemed poised to overrule *Miranda*[26] but instead reinterpreted it in several 1970s cases to say that *Miranda* warnings were not themselves constitutional rules. As a result, statements taken during custodial interrogation with defective or no warnings, although inadmissible at trial, could be used for collateral purposes. These peripheral purposes included impeaching a defendant who testified at trial or using the statements as a lead to other incriminating evidence. In contrast, as noted above, statements obtained by "pure" compulsion to testify under a grant of immunity (Fifth Amendment violations), or involuntary confessions produced by egregious police behavior (due process violations), cannot be used for collateral purposes.

If *Miranda* was not a constitutional ruling, as implied by the collateral use cases, then it would appear that the Court had no jurisdiction to impose a supervisory rule on the states, an issue that the Court simply ignored.[27] Instead of overruling *Miranda*, the Court continued to narrow its application in decisions favoring the state and allowing the use of confessions. Having "defanged" the rule, the Court became somewhat supportive of the case, as noted by Chief Justice Warren Burger's dictum: "The meaning of *Miranda* has become reasonably clear and law enforcement practices have adjusted to its strictures; I would neither overrule *Miranda*, disparage it, nor extend it at this late date" (*Rhode Island v. Innis,* 1980, concurring). Reasons for this position included (1) a concern that overruling *Miranda* might be misread by the police as tacitly condoning abusive police tactics, (2) a desire to maintain the symbol of the Court as a guarantor of individual liberties, and, most important, (3) a realization by 1980 that *Miranda* did not stop police from obtaining confessions. Under this attenuated *Miranda* regime, a public safety exception was carved out of the rule (*New York v. Quarles,* 1984).

The Court seemed to shift direction in *Dickerson v. United States* (2000), holding that a statute purporting to overrule *Miranda* was void because *Miranda* was in fact a constitutional rule. This, however, did not change the Court's collateral use position. *Chavez v. Martinez* (2003) held that the mere failure to read *Miranda* warnings to a suspect is not a violation of the right against self-incrimination. The use of leads was continued in *United States v. Patane* (2004), and a "cured statement" use was only qualified in *Missouri v. Seibert* (2004). These cases are discussed in greater detail later in this chapter.

Collateral Use of Miranda-*Violated Statements.*   *Harris v. New York*

(1971) held that a confession obtained without complete *Miranda* warnings—that is, in violation of *Miranda*—could still be used at trial, not to prove guilt but to impeach the credibility of the defendant whose testimony contradicted his earlier confession. This suggested that *Miranda* was not based on the privilege against self-incrimination. Justice William Brennan Jr., dissenting, quoted a passage from *Miranda* that explicitly stated that incriminating statements taken without the full warnings being given *cannot* be used to impeach the defendant's testimony at trial. Chief Justice Burger's majority opinion, however, got around this by declaring the statement in *Miranda* to be mere dictum that "was not at all necessary to the Court's holding and cannot be regarded as controlling." Recall that *New Jersey v. Portash* (1979) held that grand jury testimony compelled by a grant of immunity could not be used to impeach the witness at a later trial because such use was a violation of the Self-Incrimination Clause. The Court in *Harris* began to chip away at the theory that *Miranda* warnings are constitutional rules.

The *Harris* ruling was confirmed by ***Oregon v. Hass*** (1975). Hass, arrested for theft and burglary, was read *Miranda* warnings. On the way to the police station, Hass said he wanted to call his attorney. Instead of ceasing to question him, the officer said that Hass could do so when they reached the station. Hass then made incriminating statements in the police car. At the trial, the defendant claimed that he was innocent, testifying that a friend impulsively stole a bicycle and threw it into Hass's truck and that Hass was arrested after the police traced the truck to him. In rebuttal, the officer testified that Hass made incriminating statements in the patrol car after asking for his attorney. The trial court allowed the officer's testimony to evaluate Hass's credibility as a witness (i.e., to impeach him) but not as proof of guilt.

The Supreme Court applied the *Harris* rule and upheld the trial court even though the officer's continuing interrogation after Hass asked for a lawyer was a *Miranda* violation. Justice Harry Blackmun, for the majority, wrote that "the shield provided by *Miranda* is not to be perverted to a license to testify inconsistently, or even perjuriously, free from the risk of confrontation with prior inconsistent utterances" (*Oregon v. Hass,* 1975). Justice Brennan, dissenting, repeated his point in *Harris* that "[a]n incriminating statement is as incriminating when used to impeach credibility as it is when used as direct proof of guilt and no constitutional distinction can legitimately be drawn." He noted that once *Miranda* warnings were given, the state has no incentive to obey the rule, for by continuing to question, the "police may obtain a statement which can be used for impeachment if the accused has the temerity to testify in his own defense."

Michigan v. Tucker (1974) continued to undermine *Miranda* by providing the conceptual framework that has limited the *Miranda* ruling. Deficient *Miranda* warnings were given to Tucker before interrogation (he was not informed of the right to appointed counsel). Tucker gave police the name of a supposedly favorable witness whose statements nevertheless incriminated him. Nothing that Tucker said was used against him, but evidence derived from his statement (i.e., the witness's statement) was used against him to prove his guilt of a rape.[28]

Tucker was important because of Justice William Rehnquist's reasoning that *Miranda* warnings are prophylactic rules designed to protect the underlying Fifth Amendment right of silence, but not constitutional rules in their own right. The police failure to give warnings therefore did not violate Tucker's privilege against self-incrimination but only the *Miranda* protective rules. Justice Rehnquist, however, based this on a selective reading of *Miranda* by quoting the following passage: "We cannot say that the Constitution necessarily requires adherence to any particular solution for the inherent compulsions of the interrogation process as it is presently conducted" (*Miranda v. Arizona,* 1966). However, he failed to quote a passage that appeared three sentences later: "However, unless we are shown other procedures which are at least as effective in apprising accused persons of their right of silence and in assuring a continuous opportunity to exercise it, the following safeguards must be observed" (*Miranda v. Arizona,* 1966). It seems that the Warren Court majority intended that *Miranda*'s mandatory warnings were based on the Fifth Amendment privilege and that the *Tucker* Court changed the meaning of *Miranda*.

Nevertheless, the *Tucker* majority interpreted these words as dictum, and not as a rule. The majority in *Tucker* concluded that the police did not violate Tucker's right against compulsory self-incrimination "but rather failed to make available to him the full measure of procedural safeguards associated with that right since *Miranda*." Since a violation of the *Miranda* warnings was not a violation of the right against self-incrimination, it did not require the exclusion of derivative evidence. The majority added that no additional deterrence to police misconduct could be expected by the use of evidence derived from a good faith failure to follow the *Miranda* rules.

Oregon v. Elstad (1985) provides another way in which a violation of *Miranda* rules did not prevent the use of the defendant's statements. Police arrested eighteen-year-old Michael Elstad in his home. He was suspected of stealing $150,000 worth of art objects and furnishings from the home of his friend. Just after his arrest, Elstad made incriminating statements to the police upon being questioned about the burglary. He was not warned of his rights. At the sheriff's offices later in the day, Elstad was again questioned, but this time *Miranda* warnings were read and he initialed a waiver form. He again made incriminating statements, and these statements were admitted into evidence. The Court ruled that the "fruits of the poisonous tree" doctrine did not bar the second confession: It was not "tainted" as a result of the prior, unwarned, admission. Justice Sandra Day O'Connor believed that the police action did not in itself violate the self-incrimination privilege. She noted that "[t]he *Miranda* exclusionary rule, however, serves the Fifth Amendment and sweeps more broadly than the Fifth Amendment itself. It may be triggered even in the absence of a Fifth Amendment violation" (*Oregon v. Elstad,* 1985). A *Miranda* default, however, does not preclude other constitutional challenges. The *Elstad* majority felt that if the first admission had been coerced under the voluntariness test, a later confession might have been invalid.

Justice Brennan dissented strongly. He argued that the *Elstad* example was a classic ploy designed to break a suspect's will. The first question might have been asked of eighteen-year-old Michael Elstad to "soften him up" into a confessing mood. This made him more willing to waive his rights and talk at the police station, since the "cat was out of the bag." The majority and the dissenters clearly differed as to whether *Miranda* is a constitutional rule. Justice Brennan believed that "*Miranda* clearly emphasized that warnings and an informed waiver are essential to the Fifth Amendment privilege itself."

The Public Safety Exception

The doctrinal foundation laid in *Harris, Hass,* and *Tucker* bore full fruit in **New York v. Quarles** (1984), a case that created a public safety exception to *Miranda.* By creating an explicit exception to *Miranda* based on a balancing test, the Court seemed to confirm its view that the *Miranda* warnings were not themselves constitutional requirements.

At 12:30 A.M., two police officers were approached by a woman who told them that she had just been raped by a black male. She described his jacket with the name "Big Ben" printed in yellow letters on the back and told the officers that the man had just entered a nearby supermarket carrying a gun. The officers spotted the man in the supermarket and arrested him after a brief chase through the aisles. When frisked, the man, Benjamin Quarles, was found to be wearing an empty shoulder holster. After handcuffing him, Officer Kraft asked him where the gun was. Quarles nodded in the direction of some empty cartons and responded, "The gun is over there." Officer Kraft then retrieved a loaded .38-caliber revolver from a carton, formally placed Quarles under arrest, and read him his *Miranda* rights from a printed card. Quarles said that he would be willing to answer questions. When Officer Kraft asked him if he owned the gun and where he had purchased it, Quarles answered that he did own it and that he had purchased it in Miami.

The New York courts, at every level, excluded Quarles's initial statement and the gun from evidence in the trial because he had not been read *Miranda* warnings before the question was asked, and they also excluded the statement about the ownership and purchase of the gun as being derived from an illegal interrogation. The Supreme Court agreed that the brief scenario in *Quarles* constituted custodial interrogation by police, a situation that calls for warning a suspect of his rights under *Miranda* for any statement to be admissible in evidence. Nevertheless, the Court (6–3) reversed the New York Court of Appeals, that state's highest court.

The basis of the Court's holding was that "this case presents a situation where concern for public safety must be paramount to adherence to the literal language of the prophylactic rules enunciated in *Miranda.*" The Court thus injected something like the Fourth Amendment balancing test and an exigent circumstances exception into a Fifth Amendment area. Were *Miranda* a constitutional rule, this would not be permissible because "the Fifth Amendment's strictures, unlike the Fourth's, are not removed by showing reasonableness" (*New York v. Quarles,* 1984), that is, the Fifth Amendment privilege is absolute. Since *Quarles* creates an exception to the *Miranda* warnings requirement, the warnings cannot be the same as the privilege because, in theory, an exception cannot be made for the privilege. The Court characterized the warnings as "'practical reinforcement' for the Fifth Amendment right" (*New York v. Quarles,* 1984, citing *Michigan v. Tucker,* 1974). The likelihood of police committing "constitutionally impermissible practices" during interrogation is lessened by the administration of the warnings.

Justice Rehnquist, writing for the majority, held that

> on these facts there is a "public safety" exception to the requirement that *Miranda* warnings be given before a suspect's answers may be admitted into evidence, and that the availability of that exception does not depend upon the motivation of the individual officers involved. In a kaleidoscopic situation such as the one confronting these officers, where spontaneity rather than adherence to a police manual is necessarily the order of the day, the application of the exception which we recognize today should not be made to depend on . . . the subjective motivation of the arresting officer. Undoubtedly most police officers, if placed in Officer Kraft's position, would act out of a host of different, instinctive, and largely unverifiable motives— their own safety, the safety of others, and perhaps as well the desire to obtain incriminating evidence from the suspect. (*New York v. Quarles,* 1984)

The holding was criticized by three dissenting justices. Justice Marshall wrote that because the "Court in *Miranda* determined that custodial interrogations are inherently coercive . . . [it] therefore created a *constitutional presumption* that statements made during custodial interrogations are compelled in violation of the Fifth Amendment and are thus inadmissible in criminal prosecutions" (*New York v. Quarles,* 1984, Marshall, J., dissenting, emphasis added). He chided the majority for substituting its view that a threat to public safety existed, when the New York courts unanimously found no threat to public safety: The store was deserted in the middle of the night; there was no indication that Quarles had a confederate who might use the gun; the police were certain that the gun was in the immediate area of the arrest; Quarles was handcuffed; and "the arresting officers were sufficiently confident of their safety to put away their guns." Justice Marshall noted that if there was a genuine threat of violence, the officers could violate *Miranda* to get the weapon, but the statement should not be admissible.

The dissent noted that conservative justices often defer to state court evaluations of the facts in a case. Consequently, the majority's analysis of the facts seemed wrong and hypocritical. It is as if the majority wanted to create an exception and manipulated the facts of the case to ensure the "proper" outcome. Justice O'Connor concurred, raising a concern that the exception blurred *Miranda*'s bright-line rule.

Rehabilitating *Miranda*?

In *Dickerson v. United States* (2000), the Supreme Court finally confronted the issue of whether *Miranda* was a constitutional ruling. To the surprise of many, the Court held that it is. Charles Dickerson was indicted by a federal grand jury for bank robbery and related crimes. He moved to suppress a statement he had made to FBI agents during an interrogation on the ground that he had not received *Miranda* warnings. The district court granted the motion to suppress because of technical errors in warning Dickerson and specifically ruled that the confession was otherwise voluntary. Federal prosecutors appealed this ruling to the Court of Appeals for the Fourth Circuit, reputed to be the most conservative federal court of appeals in the nation.[29] That court found that although the *Miranda* warnings were defective, the confession was admissible under 18 U.S.C. § 3501, which says that in any federal prosecution a confession "shall be admissible in evidence if it is voluntarily given."

This federal statute was passed in 1968, shortly after the *Miranda* decision, expressing political outrage against the decision. Under the law, being advised of one's right to remain silent is not required for a confession to be admissible but is only one factor to be taken into account to determine if the confession is voluntary. The law sought, in effect, to overrule *Miranda*. One commentator called it "the most sweeping attack on the Supreme Court since Franklin Roosevelt tried to expand its membership in 1937."[30] The law had not been used by federal prosecutors or the Justice Department prior to the *Dickerson* case because they did not want to create a constitutional clash between the Court and Congress. At this point, the Clinton administration, through a letter from Attorney General Janet Reno to Congress, asserted that insofar as Section 3501 sought to overrule *Miranda,* it was unconstitutional.

The court of appeals nevertheless held (2–1) that "Congress, pursuant to its power to establish the rules of evidence and procedure in the federal courts, acted well within its authority in enacting § 3501, [and] § 3501, rather than *Miranda,* governs the admissibility of confessions in federal court." The stage was set for a showdown between the Supreme Court and Congress over *Miranda.* It is fundamental to American constitutionalism that Congress can by legislation modify or void a Court-made rule but cannot overrule a Court-made doctrine of constitutional law. When the Supreme Court establishes a constitutional doctrine through its interpretation of a constitutional provision, the only way in which that can properly be modified is by the Court itself overruling its own rulings (e.g., *Gideon v. Wainwright* overruled *Betts v. Brady*) or by constitutional amendment (e.g., the first sentence of the Fourteenth Amendment "overruled" the *Dred Scott* case).

In a 7–2 opinion for the Court, Chief Justice Rehnquist, acknowledging that Congress had intended to overrule *Miranda,* wrote:

> We hold that *Miranda,* being a constitutional decision of this Court, may not be in effect overruled by an Act of Congress, and we decline to overrule *Miranda* ourselves. We therefore hold that *Miranda* and its progeny in this Court govern the admissibility of statements made during custodial interrogation in both state and federal courts. (*Dickerson v. United States,* 2000)

The majority opinion in *Dickerson* declared the federal statute unconstitutional for a number of reasons:

- Chief Justice Rehnquist simply brushed away decades of calling *Miranda* a prophylactic rule: "[W]e concede that there is language in some of our opinions that supports the view" that *Miranda* is not a constitutional rule.
- He reasoned, tautologically, that *Miranda* was not based on the Court's supervisory power (which applies only to federal courts and agents) because it had applied the *Miranda* rule to the states from the very beginning.
- Further, the justices in the *Miranda* case, both the majority and the dissenters, understood the Court's ruling as a constitutional rule; the *Miranda* case itself stated that it was giving "concrete *constitutional* guidelines" to law enforcement officers, a point that was trounced by a later Court in *Tucker.*
- Another reason adopted the argument of the dissenters in *Tucker:* The warnings required by *Miranda* have not been superseded by other methods of securing a suspect's right to remain silent in the coercive atmosphere of a police station.
- As for cases like *Quarles* and *Harris* that created exceptions to *Miranda* or that allowed collateral use of *Miranda,* the answer was (1) that the Court had also broadened the scope of *Miranda* in a few cases and (2) that a constitutional rule can have exceptions.
- Chief Justice Rehnquist relied heavily on the concept of stare decisis, or precedent:

  > Whether or not we would agree with *Miranda*'s reasoning and its resulting rule, were we addressing the issue in the first instance, the principles of *stare decisis* weigh heavily against overruling it now. * * * While *stare decisis* is not an inexorable command, particularly when we are interpreting the Constitution, even in constitutional cases, the doctrine carries such persuasive force that we have always required a departure from precedent to be supported by some special justification.
  >
  > We do not think there is such justification for overruling *Miranda. Miranda* has become embedded in routine police practice to the point where the warnings have become part of our national culture. (*Dickerson v. United States,* 2000, internal citations and quotations omitted)

- A final reason was that the due process voluntariness test "is more difficult than *Miranda* for law enforcement officers to conform to, and for courts to apply in a consistent manner."

Ultraconservative justices Antonin Scalia and Clarence Thomas, dissenting, accurately accused some majority justices of having reversed their prior decisions. Justice Scalia's dissent also suggests that the majority did not fully establish the constitutionality of *Miranda* warnings by using phrases like "*Miranda* is a constitutional decision," "*Miranda* is constitutionally based," and *Miranda* has "constitutional underpinnings," without saying "that custodial interrogation that is not preceded by *Miranda* warnings or their equivalent violates the Constitution of the United States" (*Dickerson v. United States*, 2000, Scalia, J., dissenting). The dissent viewed the *Dickerson* decision as constitutionally unprincipled. Chief Justice Rehnquist's adroit opinion, on the other hand, can be seen as a mature reflection of the fact that constitutional government can be based on understandings—constitutional norms—that develop over time. The decision also signals to Congress that it cannot tread on an area within the preserve of the Supreme Court's authority.

Dickerson was silent on whether the collateral uses of statements taken in violation of *Miranda* (e.g., impeachment, derivative use) had to be eliminated now that *Miranda* was declared to be a constitutional rule, to be consistent with *New Jersey v. Portash* (1979) and *Mincey v. Arizona* (1978). **Chavez v. Martinez** (2003) provided mixed signals. Two police officers were questioning a person about drug dealing in an open area when Oliverio Martinez, a field worker, rode by on his bicycle. Martinez, who had no drugs, was detained and severely injured when a frisk and scuffle led to an officer shooting Martinez five times, leaving him blind and paralyzed. Sergeant Chavez arrived with paramedics and interrogated Martinez for about ten minutes during a forty-five-minute drive in the ambulance, suspecting that Martinez attempted to murder the officers. Concerned that Martinez might die before providing information or an admission, *Miranda* warnings were never administered. Martinez intermittently cried out in pain, begged for treatment, and expressed fear of dying. He answered Chavez's questions inconsistently, at one point admitting to pointing Officer Salinas's gun at him, after having denied it.

Martinez, never charged with a crime, sued Chavez and the municipality under Section 1983 for violating his rights under the Self-Incrimination and Due Process clauses by interrogating him without reading *Miranda* warnings and for abusive interrogation. Five justices remanded the case to decide the due process issue. Justice Kennedy recognized that police interrogation can occur under difficult situations that might involve taking a **dying declaration** from a suspect, and he noted that there "is no rule against interrogating suspects who are in anguish and pain" in exigency situations (*Chavez v. Martinez*, 2003). A due process violation would occur if Chavez gave the impression that Martinez would be treated only if he answered the questions. This was the equivalent of the police creating the injuries to Martinez in order to get him to talk and was akin to torture.

As for the self-incrimination issue, all nine justices agreed that the simple failure of a police officer to read *Miranda* warnings to a suspect prior to custodial interrogation does not violate the suspect's privilege against self-incrimination. Beyond this agreement, the justices offered sharply different views of the Self-Incrimination Clause. A plurality of four justices (Thomas, Rehnquist, O'Connor, and Scalia), viewing the clause as an exclusionary rule, posited that what happens during interrogation, even torture, could never be a violation of the Fifth Amendment privilege because it can only be violated by the introduction of tainted evidence into a criminal trial.[31]

Justice Kennedy (joined by Justices Stevens and Ruth Bader Ginsburg), dissenting, suggested that "the Self-Incrimination Clause is applicable at the time and place police use compulsion to extract a statement from a suspect." This position views the Self-Incrimination Clause as more than an exclusionary rule. Although a simple failure to read *Miranda* warnings is not a violation of the suspect's privilege against self-incrimination, "an actionable violation arose at once under the Self-Incrimination Clause (applicable to the States through the Fourteenth Amendment) when the police, after failing to warn, used severe compulsion or extraordinary pressure in an attempt to elicit a statement or confession" (*Chavez v. Martinez*, 2003).

If *Dickerson* held that *Miranda* is a constitutional decision, *Chavez v. Martinez* left open the specific nature and the effectiveness of the *Miranda* warnings. Were the warnings in and of themselves constitutional rights? Justice Thomas's plurality opinion in *Chavez* continued to describe the warnings as "judicially crafted prophylactic rules" and did not once cite *Dickerson*. If the failure to warn a suspect cannot lead to civil liability, it means either that the warnings themselves are *not* constitutional requirements or that only very serious violations of *Miranda* rise to the level of constitutional violations, which seems to be Justice Kennedy's minority view.

The most important post-*Chavez* question was whether the collateral use approach to *Miranda* law still existed. This has tremendous practical effect because in the 1990s some police departments began to deliberately violate *Miranda* in order to obtain a statement for impeachment use or to get leads against a suspect.[32] When done deliberately, this was known as "interrogation outside *Miranda*." For example, if a suspect invokes the right to silence or asks for an attorney, according to *Miranda,* interrogation must cease. The interrogator may believe that it is worth it to violate the suspect's *Miranda* rights to obtain statements that can be used for collateral purposes. This is especially so after the ruling in *Chavez v. Martinez* that the simple failure to give warnings does not impose any civil liability on police officers. The practical effect of wide-open police flouting of *Miranda*'s rules would be to severely limit the practical effectiveness of the case.

In 2004, the Court decided two cases, one involving the derivative evidence exception to *Miranda* and the other involving the cured statement exception. The Court continued to uphold the derivative evidence exception of *Michigan v. Tucker* (1974) in **United States v. Patane** (2004), where the violation of *Miranda* was inadvertent. To the contrary, in *Missouri v. Seibert* (2004), the Supreme Court held that the cured statement exception of *Oregon v. Elstad* (1985) did not extend to *Miranda* violations that are deliberate. Samuel Patane was arrested by Officer Fox just outside his house for violating a domestic violence restraining order. Fox was accompanied by Detective Benner, who was investigating Patane's alleged illegal gun possession (he was a convicted felon). Immediately after the arrest, Benner began advising Patane of his *Miranda* rights but only got as far as the right to silence when Patane said that he knew his rights. No further *Miranda* warnings were given. Benner continued to question Patane about guns, and Patane said that a Glock pistol was in his bedroom. Benner obtained permission to enter the house and seized the gun where Patane said it was. The government conceded that Patane's *Miranda* rights had been violated and that the statements made to Benner were inadmissible.

The Supreme Court held in *United States v. Patane* (2004) that the gun was admissible. Justice Thomas's plurality opinion (joined by Justices Rehnquist and Scalia) held that the "fruits of the poisonous tree" doctrine does not exclude physical evidence taken on the basis of information obtained as a result of incomplete *Miranda* warnings because "police do not violate a suspect's constitutional rights (or the *Miranda* rule) by negligent or even deliberate failures to provide the suspect with the full panoply of warnings prescribed by *Miranda*" (*United States v. Patane,* 2004). Justice Kennedy (joined by Justice O'Connor) agreed but felt it was unnecessary for the plurality to suggest that a failure to give warnings might not be a *Miranda* violation or that as long as an incriminating statement was not admitted into evidence, there were no deterrence concerns. Justice David Souter's dissent, joined by Justices Stevens and Ginsburg, was based squarely on the need to deter deliberate police violations of *Miranda*. "There is no way to read this case except as an unjustifiable invitation to law enforcement officers to flout *Miranda* when there may be physical evidence to be gained" (*United States v. Patane,* 2004). Justice Stephen Breyer, dissenting, would apply the "fruits of the poisonous tree" doctrine to evidence derived from a *Miranda* violation unless the violation occurred in good faith. *Patane* leaves open the question of whether a deliberate *Miranda* violation can be the basis for the introduction of a lead derived from the statement.

In ***Missouri v. Seibert*** (2004), a woman suspected of involvement in a homicide resulting from an arson was awakened at 3 A.M. in a hospital where her son was being treated for burns incurred during the arson. She was taken to a police station, deliberately not read *Miranda* warnings, and questioned for forty minutes in a suggestive manner designed to elicit an admission of guilt. After she confessed, Seibert was given a twenty-minute coffee break, advised of her *Miranda* rights, and interrogated after waiving her rights. She made another confession. The issue was whether this deliberate two-step process came under the cured statement rule of *Oregon v. Elstad* (1985), allowing the use of the second confession. Justice Souter's plurality opinion (joined by Justices Stevens, Ginsburg, and Breyer) argued that *Miranda* warnings are designed to provide a suspect with a real choice between talking and not talking. The question-first technique employed in the two-step procedure is designed to render *Miranda* warnings ineffective by waiting to give them until after the suspect has already confessed. The method effectively disabled Seibert from freely choosing whether to speak and thus undermined a basic purpose of *Miranda*. This practice is not protected by the *Elstad* ruling, which does not authorize admission of a confession repeated under the question-first strategy. Unlike the brief and tentative unwarned question in *Elstad,* here the questioning was systematic, exhaustive, and managed with psychological skill.

Justice Breyer concurred on the ground that "[c]ourts should exclude the 'fruit' of the initial unwarned questioning unless the failure to warn was in good faith." This made clear the distinction between inadvertent and deliberate failures to administer warnings to suspects. Justice Kennedy also concurred in the judgment of the Court. He wrote that not every *Miranda* violation leads to the exclusion of evidence, and so he supported the existing exceptions, including *Elstad*. He agreed with Justice Souter's conclusion and wrote that the two-step procedure "relies on an intentional misrepresentation of the protection that *Miranda* offers and does not serve any legitimate objectives that might otherwise justify its use." However, he appeared inclined to give police more leeway in the future in how interrogations and warnings can be structured: "The admissibility of postwarning statements should continue to be governed by the principles of *Elstad* unless the deliberate two-step strategy was employed." Thus he suggested that a two-step procedure may be allowable where there is "a substantial break in time and circumstances" between the two interrogation sessions.

Justice O'Connor (joined by Justices Rehnquist, Scalia, and Thomas) dissented in a formalistic opinion that, while recognizing the psychological impact of a two-step interrogation, noted that the Court in *Elstad* refused "to 'endow' those 'psychological effects' with 'constitutional implications.'" Further, the dissent would shift confessions law back to the voluntariness standard: "I would analyze the two-step interrogation procedure under the voluntariness standards central to the Fifth Amendment." This would harken back to *Bram v. United States* (1897), which ruled that involuntary confessions violated the privilege and would be a way for the Court to sidestep *Miranda* in many circumstances.

The decisions in *Patane* and *Seibert* are not the last word on the collateral use exceptions under *Miranda*. An open question following *Seibert* involves the length of the break between the first, non-*Mirandized,* and the second, *Mirandized,* interrogation sessions. Given the Court's focus on the specific policies underlying different exceptions, it seems likely that the impeachment collateral use will continue, as it is designed to prevent a defendant from taking advantage of a misrepresentation of what was said before taking the stand.

INTERPRETING *MIRANDA*

Miranda v. Arizona (1966) spawned scores of cases that interpreted each particular rule that is part of the decision. For the most part, the rulings have provided sufficient flexibility to the police to ensure that the rules do not unduly hamper interrogations. In some areas, however, the Court has strengthened protections for suspects being interrogated.

Adequacy of Warnings

Police officers need not use the precise words found in *Miranda,* or any rigid formula, when reciting the four warnings to a suspect prior to interrogation. They must, however, adequately convey the substance of each warning (***California v. Prysock***, 1981). Randall Prysock, a minor, was arrested for murder and declined to talk to his interrogator, Sergeant Byrd. His parents spoke with Randall at the sheriff's office, and he agreed to talk. In a taped interrogation, Byrd informed Randall and his parents of Randall's right to silence, of the fact that incriminating evidence would be used against him, of his right to have a lawyer present before and during questioning, and of his right, as a juvenile, to have his parents present. Byrd stated the right to have counsel provided for an indigent person with these words: "You all, uh—if—you have the right to have a lawyer appointed to represent you at no cost to yourself." The Supreme Court majority found that "[i]t is clear that the police in this case fully conveyed to respondent his rights as required by *Miranda.*" Justice Stevens dissented because, as the California courts found, the warning failed to inform Prysock "that the services of a free attorney were available *prior* to the impending questioning." It was more likely that Prysock would have decided not to talk until he had a lawyer had the warning been clearer.

In ***Duckworth v. Eagan*** (1989), the Court again refused (5–4) to find somewhat "nonstandard" language in the warnings given to a defendant to be inadequate. Eagan was told, as part of otherwise complete *Miranda* warnings:

> You have a right to talk to a lawyer for advice before we ask you any questions, and to have him with you during questioning. You have this right to the advice and presence of a lawyer even if you cannot afford to hire one. *We have no way of giving you a lawyer, but one will be appointed for you, if you wish, if and when you go to court.* If you wish to answer questions now without a lawyer present, you have the right to stop answering questions at any time. You also have the right to stop answering at any time until you've talked to a lawyer. (*Duckworth v. Eagan,* 1989, emphasis added)

Chief Justice Rehnquist, for the majority, noted that the warnings as a whole "touched all of the bases required by *Miranda.*" The additional phrase that a lawyer will be appointed "if and when you go to court" merely informs the suspect of the normal routine of how lawyers are appointed. He also noted that under *Miranda,* lawyers need not be producible on call, nor do police stations need to have attorneys on the premises at all times to advise suspects.

Justice Marshall, for the dissenters, thought the warnings given here would mislead the average suspect into believing that only suspects who could afford lawyers could have one immediately; others "not so fortunate" must wait. Also, "a warning qualified by an 'if and when' caveat still fails to give a suspect any indication of when he will be taken to court. Upon hearing the warnings given in this case, a suspect would likely conclude that no lawyer would be provided until trial" (*Duckworth v. Eagan,* 1989, Marshall, J., dissenting). The dissents in *Prysock* and *Eagan* aimed at making *Miranda* protections clear and unambiguous to defendants, even to the point of expanding the content of the required warnings. The majority opinions adhere more closely to the contours of *Miranda* on this issue.

The Supreme Court has not added new warnings or additional information to the four basic warnings (***Colorado v. Spring***, 1987). Spring was questioned twice while in jail, about three months apart, first by federal agents and a second time by Colorado officers. Complete *Miranda* warnings were administered both times, and Spring signed waiver forms. The federal agents questioned Spring about a firearms violation. They knew he was a homicide suspect and asked him, during the questioning, if he had ever shot anyone. "Spring admitted that he had 'shot [a] guy once.'" This statement was later used in evidence against him in his Colorado murder trial. The Supreme Court held that it was not necessary, under *Miranda,* for the federal officers to tell Spring that they knew he was a murder suspect or that he would later be approached by Colorado officers about that crime. "The Constitution does not require that a criminal suspect know and understand every possible consequence of a waiver of the Fifth Amendment privilege. . . . Here, the additional information could affect only the wisdom of a *Miranda* waiver, not its essential voluntary and knowing nature." Justice Marshall, dissenting, saw this as a psychological ploy designed to undermine Spring's will to remain silent. Under these circumstances, he argued, a failure to give the suspect additional information nullified the voluntary, knowing, and intelligent nature of the waiver of rights, making the confession unconstitutional.

Waiver of Rights

Miranda v. Arizona (1966) held that if a confession is obtained, "a *heavy burden* rests on the Government to demonstrate that the defendant *knowingly* and *intelligently* waived his privilege against self incrimination and his right to retained or appointed counsel." The Court allowed an oral waiver but stated that "a valid waiver will not be presumed simply from the silence of the accused after warnings are given or simply from the fact that a confession was in fact eventually obtained."

The "heavy burden" of proving a voluntary waiver was met in **North Carolina v. Butler** (1979). Butler was read his rights and refused to sign a waiver form. The officer told him that he did not have to speak or sign the form but that he wanted to talk to Butler. Butler replied, "I will talk to you, but I am not signing any form." Justice Stewart ruled this a valid waiver:

> An express written or oral statement of waiver of the right to remain silent or of the right to counsel is usually strong proof of the validity of that waiver, but is not inevitably either necessary or sufficient to establish waiver. The question is not one of form, but rather whether the defendant in fact knowingly and voluntarily waived the rights delineated in the *Miranda* case. As was unequivocally said in *Miranda* mere silence is not enough. That does not mean that the defendant's silence, coupled with an understanding of his rights and a course of conduct indicating waiver, may never support a conclusion that a defendant has waived his rights. (*North Carolina v. Butler*, 1979)

The majority found, after examining the facts and circumstances, that the defendant had knowingly and voluntarily waived his rights. The minority view, expressed by Justice Brennan for three dissenting justices, interpreted *Miranda* to require an affirmative waiver. They therefore considered Butler's confession invalid. While an affirmative waiver, such as signing a *Miranda* form, is the normal practice today, *Butler* indicates that where the state meets its heavy burden of proving a voluntary waiver, a verbal agreement to speak can constitute a waiver of rights. *Butler* is an example of the Court's reluctance to strictly enforce the rules of *Miranda*.

The "heavy burden" was not met in **Tague v. Louisiana** (1980), where the state produced no evidence to show that the defendant knowingly or voluntarily waived his rights. In *Butler,* the record indicated that the full complement of warnings was read and that the defendant understood them. In *Tague,* the arresting officer who testified at the hearing to suppress the confession could not recall whether the defendant understood his rights. Without a record, it was an error to presume that the suspect understood the warnings.

Connecticut v. Barrett (1987) held that a suspect can partially waive *Miranda* rights. After warnings were read to him, Barrett said he was willing to talk to the police but would not sign a statement without a lawyer present. As a general rule, questioning should have ceased. In this case, however, Barrett was very clear that he was willing to talk about the crime but wanted a lawyer's advice as to whether he should sign a statement. He repeated this at his trial. The Supreme Court held his incriminating statements to be admissible. Here, his "affirmative announcements of his willingness to speak with the authorities" overrode his limited request for a lawyer. This is an exceptional case, and the general rule is that a request for a lawyer ends a confession session.

Termination and Resumption of Questioning

> Once warnings have been given, the subsequent procedure is clear. If the individual indicates in any manner, at any time prior to or during questioning, that he wishes to remain silent, the interrogation must cease. At this point he has shown that he intends to exercise his Fifth Amendment privilege; any statement taken after the person invokes his privilege cannot be other than the product of compulsion, subtle or otherwise. Without the right to cut off questioning, the setting of in-custody interrogation operates on the individual to overcome free choice in producing a statement after the privilege has been once invoked. (*Miranda v. Arizona,* 1966)

Chief Justice Warren, an experienced former prosecutor, knew it was quite common for interrogating officers to badger suspects—that is, to continue questioning them even after they invoke their right to remain silent. Although the passage may seem clear on its face, the Supreme Court later thought that it was ambiguous:

> This passage . . . does not state under what circumstances, if any, a resumption of questioning is permissible. The passage could be literally read to mean that a person who has invoked his "right to silence" can never again be subjected to custodial interrogation by any police officer at any time or place on any subject. Another possible construction of the passage would characterize "any statement taken after the person has invoked his privilege" as "the product of compulsion" and would therefore mandate its exclusion from evidence, even if it were volunteered by the person in custody without any further interrogation whatever. Or the passage could be interpreted to require only the immediate cessation of questioning, and to permit a resumption of interrogation after a momentary respite. (***Michigan v. Mosley***, 1975)

Richard Mosley was arrested for a robbery. During questioning at Detroit police headquarters, after having been read his rights, Mosley said he did not want to talk about the case, whereupon questioning ceased. A few hours later, Mosley was taken from his fourth-floor cell to the homicide division on the fifth floor of the same building. He was read his rights, agreed to talk, and made an incriminating statement that led to evidence that was used to convict him of a homicide. The Supreme Court ruled that Mosley's second statement was admissible at trial. Justice Stewart fashioned a "facts and circumstances" rule that allows the police to question a defendant who has invoked his rights about an entirely different crime after a lapse of time. Mosley's statement was admissible in evidence because he was properly warned and never requested a lawyer. Also, when he had asked earlier that questioning cease, his request was immediately honored. The mere fact that he once terminated the interrogation, however, did not bar questioning for a different criminal act.

The *Mosley* test is treated as a "totality of the circumstances" test. Lower courts have identified five *Mosley* factors that support the use of a statement after a suspect has invoked his or her right of silence: (1) Initial *Miranda* warnings were given; (2) police immediately ceased interrogation when the suspect invoked the right to silence; (3) a significant time period elapsed between the two interrogations; (4) a fresh *Miranda* warning was given before the second interrogation; and (5) the second interrogation was for a different crime than that investigated in the first interrogation or was triggered by new circumstances (e.g., a confession by a confederate).[33]

Invoking the Right to Counsel

> [A]n individual held for interrogation must be clearly informed that he has the right to consult with a lawyer and to have the lawyer with him during interrogation. . . . This warning is an absolute prerequisite to interrogation. No amount of circumstantial evidence that the person may have been aware of this right will suffice to stand in its stead. (*Miranda v. Arizona,* 1966)

Once a defendant claims a desire to see an attorney, questioning must stop. The Supreme Court has, with a few exceptions, interpreted this requirement favorably for suspects.

For example, in **Smith v. Illinois** (1984), an eighteen-year-old robbery suspect, while in custody, was read the required *Miranda* warnings. Told that he had a right to consult with a lawyer and have a lawyer present while being questioned, he replied, "Uh, yeah. I'd like to do that." The officer continued to advise Smith of his rights and asked, "Do you wish to talk to me at this time without a lawyer being present?" Smith replied, "Yeah and no, uh, I don't know what's what really." To this, the officer said, "Well. You either have [to agree] to talk to me this time without a lawyer being present and if you do agree . . . you can stop at any time you want to." Smith replied, "All right. I'll talk to you then." He subsequently confessed.

The Court found that Smith invoked his right to counsel by his first statement in a clear and unambiguous way. While the statements made after the first request for counsel may have been ambiguous, the Court held that "[w]here nothing about the request for counsel or the circumstances leading up to the request would render it ambiguous, all questioning must cease" (*Smith v. Illinois,* 1984). The Court also ruled that "an accused's postrequest responses to further interrogation may not be used to cast retrospective doubt on the clarity of the initial request itself. Such subsequent statements are relevant only to the distinct question of waiver." Justice Rehnquist, writing for three dissenters, believed that the interrogation had not yet begun but that police were still in the process of giving Smith his warnings. He noted that Smith had not been badgered. Justice Rehnquist felt that the *Miranda* warning process should be examined in its totality. The holding of *Smith v. Illinois,* however, demonstrates that invocation of the right to counsel is defined strictly by the Supreme Court.

Nonlegal Advisers.
The Court's strict posture regarding requests for counsel is not extended to requests for help from other individuals or officials. In **Fare v. Michael C.** (1979), a juvenile in custody asked to see his probation officer during a murder interrogation. Justice Blackmun held that a request for a probation officer was not equivalent to a *Miranda* request for an attorney. "The *per se* aspect of *Miranda* [was] based on the unique role the lawyer plays in the adversarial system of criminal justice." A probation officer is a state employee who is a peace officer and does not act unequivocally on behalf of the suspect. Justice Marshall dissented (joined by Justices Brennan and Stevens), reinterpreting *Miranda* to say that questioning should stop whenever a juvenile requests an adult who is obligated to represent his or her interests. He suggested that it is unrealistic to expect a juvenile to call for a lawyer; it is more likely for a youth to turn to parents or another adult, such as a welfare worker, as the only means of securing legal counsel. However reasonable this point is, the Court was not willing to expand *Miranda* rights.

Third-Party Involvement.
What happens if third parties—such as parents, friends, or relatives—request an attorney for suspects being held by the police, even though the accused themselves have not invoked their *Miranda* rights? The Court has ruled that this is not an invocation of Fifth Amendment rights by the suspect personally, and any confession made while an attorney is trying to contact the suspect does not violate the *Miranda* rule.

In **Moran v. Burbine** (1986), Brian Burbine was arrested for breaking and entering and was suspected of an earlier murder. After his arrest, his sister called the public defender's office to obtain an attorney's assistance. Allegra Munson, a staff attorney, called the police department. Advised that Burbine was in custody, she told the police, over the telephone, that she was representing him in the event he was questioned or placed in a lineup. The unidentified officer told Munson that Burbine would not be questioned that night. An hour later, however, police did *Mirandize* and question Burbine, who waived his rights and ultimately made incriminating statements.

Burbine raised issues of waiver and the right to counsel. Regarding waiver, Justice O'Connor, for the majority, held that "[e]vents occurring outside of the presence of the suspect and entirely unknown to him surely can have no bearing on the capacity to comprehend and knowingly relinquish a constitutional right." Even the officer's deception of attorney Munson, whether inadvertent or not, unethical or not, does not change the fact that Burbine knowingly and intelligently waived his rights. The Court refused to add a requirement to *Miranda* that the police must inform a defendant of an attorney's attempts to reach him or her, citing practical problems that such a requirement would raise.

That someone had procured counsel for Burbine before he was questioned did not change the complexion of his rights. Justice O'Connor stated:

> [T]he suggestion that the existence of an attorney-client relationship itself triggers the protections of the Sixth Amendment misconceives the underlying purposes of the right to counsel. The Sixth Amendment's intended function is not to wrap a protective cloak around the attorney-client relationship for its own sake any more than it is to protect a suspect from the consequences of his own candor. Its purpose, rather, is to assure that in any "criminal prosecutio[n]" the accused shall not be left to his own devices in facing the "prosecutorial forces of organized society." (*Moran v. Burbine,* 1986)

Also, since Burbine had not yet been charged by a grand jury or by information, the Sixth Amendment right to an attorney did not yet apply. The majority refused to apply *Escobedo v. Illinois,* which had come to be reinterpreted as a case concerned more with the right against self-incrimination than the right to counsel. In effect, the *Escobedo* ruling became a dead letter.

Justice Stevens wrote a scathing dissent. "Until today, incommunicado questioning has been viewed with the strictest scrutiny by this Court; today, incommunicado questioning is embraced as a societal goal of the highest order that justifies police deception of the shabbiest kind" (*Moran v. Burbine,* 1986). He noted that the rulings of many state courts and the standards of the American Bar Association find that statements taken after the deception of a client's attorney should be excluded from evidence. He noted that police "interference with communications between an attorney and his client is a recurrent problem" and was concerned that the ruling in *Moran* would do nothing to curb this kind of improper behavior.

Termination and Resumption of Questioning.

The Supreme Court protects the rights of suspects who invoke the right to counsel more strictly than those who terminate questioning without asking for the assistance of counsel. In ***Edwards v. Arizona*** (1981), Robert Edwards was arrested for robbery, burglary, and murder. Questioned at the police station after being given proper *Miranda* warnings, he told the officers that he wanted to "make a deal," but the police terminated the discussion when he said, "I want an attorney before making a deal." The next day, detectives came to the lockup and reinterrogated him. After playing him the taped statement of an alleged accomplice, Edwards agreed to talk as long as it was not tape-recorded, and he implicated himself in the crime. The Supreme Court reversed his conviction. Although a person may validly waive rights, Justice Byron White, for the majority, held that

> when an accused has invoked his right to have counsel present during custodial interrogation, a valid waiver of that right cannot be established by showing only that he responded to further police-initiated custodial interrogation even if he has been advised of his rights. We further hold that an accused, such as Edwards, having expressed his desire to deal with the police only through counsel, is not subject to further interrogation by the authorities until counsel has been made available to him, *unless the accused himself initiates* further communication, exchanges, or conversations with the police. (*Edwards v. Arizona,* 1981, emphasis added)

Oregon v. Bradshaw (1983) dealt with the issue of the suspect's initiating further questioning. In this case, interrogation ceased after Bradshaw requested counsel. The Court held that further questioning was properly initiated by Bradshaw's question during the trip between the police station and jail: "Well, what is going to happen to me now?" Bradshaw was again read his rights, and in a "general conversation," he agreed to take a lie detector test. The next day, Bradshaw took a lie detector test, preceded by *Miranda* warnings, that resulted in an incriminating admission. A four-justice plurality said that Bradshaw's question, although ambiguous, "evinced a willingness and a desire for a generalized discussion about the investigation." A four-justice dissent, written by Justice Marshall, found this interpretation placed on Bradshaw's words by the plurality to be preposterous:

> If respondent's question had been posed by Jean-Paul Sartre before a class of philosophy students, it might well have evinced a desire for a "generalized" discussion. But under the circumstances of this case, it is plain that respondent's only "desire" was to find out where the police were going to take him. (*Oregon v. Bradshaw,* 1983)

The Supreme Court, in **Davis v. United States** (1994), held that in order to invoke the protection of *Edwards,* the request for counsel must be made *clearly.* Naval investigators suspected that Robert L. Davis beat another sailor to death with a pool cue. Davis was arrested, was advised of his rights under military law, and waived his rights to remain silent. An hour and a half into the interview, Davis said, "Maybe I should talk to a lawyer." A Navy investigator testified:

> We made it very clear that we're not here to violate his rights, that if he wants a lawyer, then we will stop any kind of questioning with him, that we weren't going to pursue the matter unless we have it clarified is he asking for a lawyer or is he just making a comment about a lawyer, and he said, "No, I'm not asking for a lawyer," and then he continued on, and said, "No, I don't want a lawyer." (*Davis v. United States,* 1995)

The investigators took a short break and then reminded Davis of his rights to remain silent and to counsel. They continued the interview for another hour, and at that point Davis said, "I think I want a lawyer before I say anything else." Questioning then ceased. Davis made an incriminating statement after saying, "Maybe I should talk to a lawyer." The Court held that the statement was admissible and that Davis's rights under *Edwards* were not violated.

Analytically, there are three possible options to determine if a suspect's mention of a lawyer invoked the right to counsel: (1) Any mention of counsel, however ambiguous, invokes counsel; (2) the *Edwards* protection is invoked if the suspect's request meets a "threshold" standard of clarity; or (3) whenever a suspect mentions a lawyer, questioning must cease, but interrogators may ask "narrow questions designed to clarify the earlier statement and the [suspect's] desires respecting counsel." The Court selected the second option.

Noting that *Edwards*'s prohibition on questioning is not itself a constitutional right but, like the *Miranda* rule, a protection for the Fifth Amendment, Justice O'Connor, writing for the Court, held that "after a knowing and voluntary waiver of the *Miranda* rights, law enforcement officers may continue questioning until and unless the suspect clearly requests an attorney." Justice O'Connor said that asking "clarifying questions" (option number three), while good police practice, is not required. *Davis* upholds the bright-line rule of *Edwards* by not forcing interrogating officers "to make difficult judgment calls about whether the suspect in fact wants a lawyer even though he hasn't said so, with the threat of suppression if they guess wrong."

Although the *Bradshaw* plurality strained in order to rule in favor of the state, and *Davis* burdens a suspect's rights under *Edwards,* the following cases show that, for the most part, the Supreme Court has interpreted the *Edwards* "bright-line rule" in favor of suspects.

For example, **Michigan v. Jackson** (1986) held that a suspect invokes the right to counsel for interrogation purposes when, at a formal arraignment, the suspect tells a judge that he or she wants a lawyer. Police officers present at Jackson's arraignment were bound by the *Edwards* rule and could not lawfully interrogate him simply by reading him his *Miranda* warnings. And in **Arizona v. Roberson** (1988), the Court held that once a suspect asks to see a lawyer before speaking, this knowledge applies not only to the officer who first *Mirandized* the suspect but to every officer in the same agency. This is a necessary corollary to the *Edwards* rule since it would be too easy for police officers to sidestep the *Edwards* rule by claiming ignorance of an invocation of rights by the suspect. Justice Stewart noted that "custodial interrogation must be conducted pursuant to established procedures, and those procedures in turn must enable an officer who proposes to initiate an interrogation to determine whether the suspect has previously requested counsel." In a well-run police department, an officer who questions a suspect should know which other officers have previously questioned him and should be apprised of any request for counsel.

Support for the *Edwards* rule continued in **Minnick v. Mississippi** (1990). A suspect invoked the right to counsel during an interrogation, was allowed to consult with a lawyer, and was thereafter interrogated without counsel present. He made an admission during the second interrogation. The Court held, in an opinion by Justice Kennedy, that simply allowing the suspect to confer with counsel does not satisfy *Edwards*. A suspect who asks to speak to a lawyer is demanding a right to have a lawyer present during interrogation. Unless a subsequent uncounseled conversation is initiated by the suspect, as required by *Edwards,* the police cannot reinterrogate. The Court emphasized that a different standard would dilute the clarity of *Edwards*'s bright-line rule; it could create confusion whereby a suspect would gain *Edwards* protection at several points during custody by invoking the right to counsel and then lose it after conferring with an attorney.

Justice Kennedy listed several benefits of maintaining the *Edwards* rule. It prevents the police from badgering suspects; it conserves judicial resources that would be expended in making factually complex voluntariness determinations; it avoids the burden on officials to determine when a prior consultation with counsel is sufficient to create a waiver; and it prevents counsel from delaying meetings with clients so as to preserve their *Edwards*'s protections.

Justice Scalia dissented, joined by Chief Justice Rehnquist. He stressed that both *Miranda* and *Edwards* were prophylactic and not constitutional rules and that *Edwards* sets a higher standard for waiver of rights than that of *Johnson v. Zerbst* (1938). He believed that the Court in *Minnick* established an irrebuttable presumption (i.e., virtually a firm rule) against waiving the right to counsel. Instead, he would allow the state to prove—after an invocation of the right to counsel and after counsel has been provided—that a confession was made knowingly and voluntarily.

Defining Custody

> By custodial interrogation, we mean questioning initiated by law enforcement officers after a person has been taken into custody or deprived of his freedom of action in any significant way. (*Miranda v. Arizona,* 1966)

The Supreme Court expanded *Miranda*'s definition of *police custody* beyond the station house. The basic question is this: Does the setting in which a confession is given create the compulsion contemplated by the Fifth Amendment privilege that brings the *Miranda* requirement and its exclusionary rule into play? Is the interrogation setting coercive? This eliminates the Sixth Amendment "focus" or "target" test of *Escobedo* and of grand jury procedure that forbids questioning the *target* of the investigation. This is appropriate because the Fifth Amendment does not forbid interrogation but looks instead to see whether the questioning is accompanied by compulsion.

Home. Being questioned in one's own home may be custodial depending upon the facts. There was custody in **Orozco v. Texas** (1969) when police entered the defendant's house at 4 A.M. and questioned him while he was under arrest, not free to leave, and surrounded by police officers. There was no custody in *Beckwith v. United States* (1975). Beckwith was the target of a criminal tax investigation. Internal Revenue Service (IRS) agents came to his home during the day, politely requested admittance, and gave him time to finish dressing. The interview was conducted in a friendly and relaxed manner at Beckwith's dining room table. He was not pressed to answer questions and was told at the beginning of the interview that he had a right to refuse to answer questions. On these facts, the interview was not conducted in custody; therefore, *Miranda* warnings did not have to be given even though Beckwith, as an investigation target, could have legally refused to answer questions had he been subpoenaed.

Prison.   *Mathis v. United States* (1968) seems to hold that all interrogations of inmates that occur in prison must be preceded by *Miranda* warnings. IRS agents interviewed Mathis in prison, without issuing *Miranda* warnings, about tax issues unrelated to his prison conviction. Based on his custody status, the Supreme Court found a *Miranda* violation and overturned the conviction. Justice White, dissenting, believed that the underlying rationale of *Miranda* "rested not on the mere fact of physical restriction but on a conclusion that coercion—pressure to answer questions—usually flows from a certain type of custody, police station interrogation," of a suspect. Since Mathis was in familiar surroundings when questioned, even though confined, Justice White felt he was under no pressure to talk.

Police Station.   Interrogation in a police station does not become custodial merely because of the location; it depends instead on the circumstances of the interrogation atmosphere. The majority in *Oregon v. Mathiason* (1977) found no custody or significant curtailment of freedom of action when a suspect voluntarily complied with a police request that he come to the station house for an interview. Carl Mathiason, a parolee, was identified as a probable burglar. A police officer left a card at Mathiason's residence asking him to call. A meeting was held at the police station at Mathiason's convenience. The officer shook Mathiason's hand when he came to the station, and they met in a closed office with the officer sitting across a desk. The officer falsely told Mathiason that his fingerprints were found, whereupon he confessed. *Miranda* warnings were then read, and another confession was taken.

The Court concluded that Mathiason was not in custody before he confessed, and so no *Miranda* warnings had to be read. The Court said that "[a]ny interview of one suspected of a crime by a police officer will have coercive aspects to it, simply by virtue of the fact that the police officer is part of a law enforcement system which may ultimately cause the suspect to be charged with a crime." This kind of pressure can be thought of as "background radiation" that attaches to police officers and is different from the heightened compulsion that occurs when a person is taken into custody. Justice Marshall dissented. He felt that Mathiason's freedom of movement was curtailed in a true sense and that he was in custody even though not formally placed under arrest. The Court reached the same result in *California v. Behler* (1983) on similar facts, except that the defendant was not a parolee and he went voluntarily to the police station to tell the police that he was at the scene of a homicide.

The test of custody is an objective determination of whether the suspect was deprived of freedom in any significant way. In *Stansbury v. California* (1994), a police detective investigating the abduction and rape-murder of a ten-year-old girl questioned Robert Stansbury, one of two ice cream truck drivers whom the girl had spoken to on the day she was killed. Stansbury was not read *Miranda* warnings because the detective thought the other driver was the likely suspect. During the interview, Stansbury described a borrowed car he drove on the night of the murder that was similar to a description of the car given by a witness. This aroused the officer's suspicion, and in his mind he focused on Stansbury as a suspect. Stansbury had no way of reading the officer's mind. The officer did not, by word or deed, convey to Stansbury that he was not free to leave. Under the objective standard, therefore, Stansbury was not yet in custody, and his incriminating statement about the car was admissible. As the questioning continued, Stansbury said that he had prior convictions for rape, kidnapping, and child molestation. At this point, the officer terminated the interview and another officer read Stansbury his *Miranda* warnings. The Court ruled that "an officer's subjective and undisclosed view concerning whether the person being interrogated is a suspect is irrelevant to the assessment whether the person is in custody."

In *Yarborough v. Alvarado* (2004), the Supreme Court considered whether youth and inexperience would turn a station house interview into a custodial interrogation but failed to issue a definitive ruling on this point. Reasons for believing that the seventeen-year-old suspected of being an accessory to a murder was not in custody included these facts: The police did not bring him to the station, he was not threatened, his parents were told the interview "was not going to be too long," the detective focused on the acts of the shooter, she appealed to Alvarado's interest in telling the truth, and at the end of the interview, Alvarado went home. Other factors pointed to custody: The interview took place at the police station and lasted two hours; Alvarado was not told he was free to leave; he was brought to the station by his parents, making control over his movement questionable; and his parents were not allowed to be present at the interview. Justice Kennedy's five-to-four majority opinion allowed that reasonable jurists could differ as to whether Alvarado was in custody, and because of the general nature of the issue of custody and the structure of federal habeas corpus law, it was not unreasonable for the state courts to decide that Alvarado was not in custody. Justice O'Connor concurred, noting that Alvarado's age was a factor and that it might be unreasonable to find that a younger suspect questioned under similar circumstances was not in custody.

Probation Interview. The Supreme Court held in ***Minnesota v. Murphy*** (1984) that a probation interview is not custody for *Miranda* purposes, even though a probationer is legally required to attend probation interviews and a condition of probation is that he or she answer all questions truthfully. The probationer, Marshall Murphy, was not under arrest, nor was his freedom of movement seriously restrained. In this case, Murphy's probation officer planned in advance to ask him about previous crimes in an effort to elicit incriminating information. She gave Murphy no prior warning of such questions. He admitted to previously committing a rape and murder, and the statement to the probation officer was admissible in his first-degree murder trial.

The reason Murphy's statement was not compelled is that, except for the *Miranda* situation, the Fifth Amendment privilege against self-incrimination is not self-executing. Incriminating statements are not automatically excluded simply because a person makes them to a listener. With the exception of a police custodial interrogation, in which a person must be informed of his rights, a person must claim the privilege in order to rely on it. Once a person utters an incriminating statement, it is presumed voluntary, and the listener can tell what he or she heard to prosecutorial authorities (or anyone else) and may testify in court as to what was heard.

Murphy claimed that the probation condition that required truthful answers to the probation officer's questions amounted to compulsion. The Court disagreed. The probationer is in a similar situation as a witness subpoenaed before a grand jury. Both are legally compelled to attend and to answer truthfully, and they are not granted immunity. The probation conditions did not deprive Murphy of his Fifth Amendment rights. He could have refused to answer the questions that could have incriminated him. Murphy claimed that he feared revocation of probation if he did not answer. There was no proof, however, that Minnesota law or practice punished a probationer who claimed the protection of the Fifth Amendment.

Traffic Stops.
A motorist stopped for a moving violation, whether a misdemeanor or a felony, such as speeding or operating under the influence of drugs or alcohol, is detained for the time it takes to write a ticket or to proceed to an arrest. Writing for a nearly unanimous Court in **Berkemer v. McCarty** (1984), Justice Marshall held that "persons temporarily detained pursuant to" police roadside stops of vehicles for traffic violations "are not 'in custody' for the purposes of *Miranda*." Such stops do not significantly restrain the freedom of movement to such an extent as to deprive them of their will, as contemplated by *Miranda*, for two simple reasons. First, "detention of a motorist pursuant to a traffic stop is presumptively temporary and brief." Second, the stop occurs in public so that the motorist does not feel completely at the mercy of the police. Thus, although the motorist is detained, these factors "mitigate the danger that a person questioned will be induced 'to speak where he would not otherwise do so freely'" (*Berkemer v. McCarty*, 1984, quoting *Miranda*). The stopped motorist is far less likely, under this reasoning, to be coerced into giving up Fifth Amendment rights.

McCarty was stopped by a trooper who saw his car weaving in traffic. After he failed a field sobriety test, he was told he would be taken into custody. Asked if he had taken any intoxicants, McCarty said that "he had consumed two beers and had smoked several joints of marijuana a short time before." At the jail, McCarty was again asked questions and gave incriminating answers. At no time were *Miranda* warnings read. McCarty's roadside statements were admitted into evidence.

Berkemer v. McCarty, however, did hold that once a motorist has been arrested or taken into custody on traffic felony or misdemeanor charges, *Miranda* warnings must be read prior to interrogation. The Court equated traffic misdemeanors with felonies in order to uphold the "simplicity and clarity of the holding of *Miranda*." An exception from warnings for traffic misdemeanors would create confusion and the potential for endless litigation. For example, some crimes escalate from misdemeanors to felonies depending on the number of prior convictions, and it is not clear at the time of the vehicle stop whether a driving offense is a misdemeanor or felony. Thus admissions made by McCarty on the roadside were admissible, but those made at the police station were inadmissible.

Pennsylvania v. Muniz (1990) further clarified the application of *Miranda* when a driver is stopped for driving under the influence (DUI) and is ordered to undergo a field sobriety test. The Supreme Court held that *Miranda* warnings were not required simply for stopping a driver for DUI. The fact that the driver's speech is slurred, however incriminating, does not come under *Miranda* because physical inability to articulate words is not testimonial evidence. Similarly, ordering a driver to perform and videotaping standard physical sobriety tests—the horizontal gaze nystagmus test, the walk-and-turn test, and the one-leg stand test—are not testimonial. The officer ordered the DUI suspect to perform the tests in "carefully scripted instructions as to how the tests were to be performed. These instructions were not likely to be perceived as calling for any verbal response and therefore were not 'words or actions' constituting custodial interrogation." As a result, *Miranda* warnings are not required. Furthermore, an officer can ask a driver's name, address, height, weight, eye color, date of birth, and current age. The Court held that answers to these questions are admissible under a "routine booking question" exception to *Miranda*. Biographical data needed to complete booking or pretrial services and requested for record-keeping purposes only are reasonably related to police administrative concerns. In this case, Muniz made unsolicited, incriminating statements that he had been drinking while the officer read him another carefully prepared script concerning the nature of Pennsylvania's implied consent law and a request to submit to a Breathalyzer test. The only questions asked of Muniz were whether he understood the instructions and whether he wished to submit to the test. "These limited and focused" questions were a part of legitimate police procedure and were not designed or likely to be perceived as calling for an incriminating response. Therefore Muniz's statements that he had been drinking were admissible.

The Court held that *Miranda* warnings were required only as to one question posed by the officer: "Do you know what the date was of your sixth birthday?" This was held to be testimonial interrogation; Muniz's incoherent response implied that he was intoxicated. This was not admissible because the question was asked before *Miranda* warnings were administered. Justice Brennan, for the majority, reasoned that the *content* of the answer allowed the police officer to infer that the driver's mental state was confused. Because the incriminating inference was drawn from a testimonial act rather than a physical fact, the question confronted the suspect with the classic "trilemma" of self-incrimination, perjury, or contempt. Chief Justice Rehnquist disagreed on this point, claiming that Justice Brennan's assumption about human behavior was wrong. Given the nature of the question to Muniz, which was basically to check how well he could add the number six to his date of birth, there was no real incentive for Muniz to lie and commit perjury. In this view, the question was closer to the physical tests and the "booking questions" that did not violate the Fifth Amendment in this case.

The Nature of Interrogation

Miranda v. Arizona (1966) applies to custodial interrogation. **Rhode Island v. Innis** (1980) ruled that

> *Miranda* safeguards come into play whenever a person in custody is subjected to either *express questioning* or its *functional equivalent.* That is to say, the term "interrogation" under *Miranda* refers not only to express questioning, but also to any words or actions on the part of the police (other than normally attendant to arrest and custody) that the police should know are reasonably likely to elicit an incriminating response from the suspect. (*Rhode Island v. Innis,* 1980, emphasis added)

The functional equivalent of express interrogation can be discovered from the facts and circumstances of cases.

Police arrested Innis at 4:30 A.M. on suspicion of murdering a taxicab driver with a shotgun. They advised him of his rights. He said he wanted to speak with a lawyer, terminating any interrogation. Innis was placed in the back of a patrol car and driven to the station. On the way to the station, Officer Gleckman spoke to Officer McKenna about the shotgun, saying there was a school for handicapped children in the area "and God forbid one of them might find a weapon with shells and they might hurt themselves." McKenna agreed and suggested that they should continue to search for the shotgun. At that point, Innis interrupted the conversation, stating that he could lead the officers to the gun, which he did. This incriminating statement and the shotgun were admitted into evidence to convict him.

Was this exchange the functional equivalent of interrogation? Justice Stewart, writing for the majority, said "no." He characterized the comments as only a few offhand remarks that the police could not have known would suddenly move Innis to make a self-incriminating response. A lengthy and more pointed "harangue" might become interrogation, but not the conversation here. The Court suggested that an example of a functional equivalent of interrogation is a "reverse lineup" where the police plant a "witness" in the lineup room to vocally accuse the suspect of a fictitious crime to induce him to confess to the actual crime. The Court added an important embellishment to its "functional equivalent" rule:

> But, since the police surely cannot be held accountable for the unforeseeable results of their words or actions, the definition of interrogation can extend only to words or actions on the part of police officers that they *should have known* were reasonably likely to elicit an incriminating response. (*Rhode Island v. Innis,* 1980)

To go further, police knowledge includes not only the likely effect of words on a hypothetical person, but also on a suspect with known weaknesses or susceptibilities.

Justice Marshall concurred with the definition of *interrogation* but dissented from its application to the facts in this case. He noted that appeals to the decency and the honor of the suspect are classic interrogation ploys and that "[o]ne can scarcely imagine a stronger appeal to the conscience of a suspect." Justice Stevens, also dissenting, suggested a different definition of *interrogation:* "[A]ny statement that would normally be understood by the average listener as calling for a response is the functional equivalent of a direct question, whether or not it is punctuated by a question mark." This definition focuses on the intention of the officers to some degree. The majority's rule, however, "focuses primarily upon the perceptions of the suspect, rather than the intent of the police."

The *Innis* definition was applied in **Arizona v. Mauro** (1987). William Mauro was arrested for the murder of his son after turning himself in at a local K-Mart store. He refused to make statements without a lawyer present, and he was not questioned. Police interviewed Mrs. Mauro at the station house. She insisted on speaking with her husband and was allowed to after some resistance on the part of the police. She was told that an officer would be present, and a tape recorder was placed prominently on the table. William Mauro told his wife not to answer questions until a lawyer was present. At trial, the taped conversation was admitted into evidence to refute Mauro's insanity defense.

The Court held (5–4), in an opinion by Justice Powell, that the recording of the conversation was not the functional equivalent of interrogation under *Miranda* or *Innis.* The police did not send Mrs. Mauro in to speak with her husband, and the presence of the officer during their conversation was not improper. The mere possibility that a suspect in custody will incriminate himself under these circumstances does not amount to interrogation. "[T]he actions in this case were far less questionable than the 'subtle compulsion' that we held *not* to be interrogation in *Innis.* . . . Officers do not interrogate a suspect simply by hoping that he will incriminate himself."

Justice Stevens, for the dissenters, reasoned that the police used a "powerful psychological ploy" when they allowed Mrs. Mauro to speak to her husband; it was bound to generate some discussion after he had manifested a clear desire to remain silent. The legitimacy of the police presence is irrelevant to this finding, for on the witness stand, the police captain admitted that one reason for allowing the meeting was to obtain statements that could "shed light on our case." Also, a police detective testified that a standard police technique used to get juveniles to talk is to bring their parents into the police station. It is noteworthy that in both the *Innis* and *Mauro* cases, the state supreme courts believed that interrogation, or its functional equivalent under *Miranda,* had occurred.

Colorado v. Connelly (1986) is an example of noninterrogation. Francis Connelly, a chronic schizophrenic, traveled from Boston to Denver because the "voice of God" commanded him to do so. He approached a police officer on a downtown Denver street "and, without any prompting, stated that he had murdered someone and wanted to talk about it." Connelly was immediately informed of his rights, but he insisted he wanted to speak. He gave a confession on the street, after two additional *Miranda* warnings, and appeared at that point to be mentally normal. Connelly's confession was held to be valid because it was a purely voluntary statement not barred by the Fifth Amendment. Justice Brennan dissented, joined by Justice Marshall, finding the admission of a statement by a person diagnosed with chronic paranoid schizophrenia to be a due process violation. "Today the Court denies Mr. Connelly his fundamental right to make a vital choice with a sane mind, involving a determination that could allow the State to deprive him of liberty or even life. This holding is unprecedented" (*Colorado v. Connelly,* 1986, Brennan, J., dissenting).

The Use of Deception

The defendant in *Frazier v. Cupp* (1969) was arrested for a murder and interrogated by the police. After a time, an officer told the defendant that his cousin, who was also a suspect, had confessed. This was a lie. "Petitioner [Frazier] still was reluctant to talk, but after the officer sympathetically suggested that the victim had started a fight by making homosexual advances, petitioner began to spill out his story." The fact that the police officer told a flat lie in order to induce Frazier to confess was not even raised as an issue in the case. This is taken as precedent for the proposition that oral lies told by the police during interrogation do not violate the suspect's due process or self-incrimination rights.

Police are allowed to employ deception during interrogation, and the literature reports frequent instances of police deceitfully telling suspects that a confederate lied or that a fingerprint or blood test put them at the crime scene when that is not the case. The idea is that a truly guilty party may at that point confess, while a truly innocent person will deny such charges. A risk is that police deception, combined with forceful and prolonged interrogation, has also led innocent people to confess.[34] (See the "Law in Society" box in this chapter.) Deception should not extend to express lies about the law.

Illinois v. Perkins (1990) upheld the use of a jail "plant"—an undercover agent—to obtain an incriminating statement from a suspect. Charlton, a state prisoner, told the police that Perkins admitted to committing a murder. Shortly after this, Perkins was transferred to a jail on an unrelated aggravated battery charge. An undercover agent, posing as an escaped convict, was admitted to the jail and placed in the same cell as Charlton and Perkins. The undercover officer won Perkins's confidence by suggesting that they escape from the jail together, and he initiated Perkins's narration of the crime by asking him whether he had ever "done someone." Perkins then recounted the events of the murder in detail. Perkins was later charged with the murder, and the agent testified at his murder trial to what Perkins had said while in the jail cell. As Justice Kennedy dryly noted, the officer did not give Perkins *Miranda* warnings before the conversation in the jail cell. The Illinois courts held that because Perkins was in correctional custody and the agent's statement was indirect interrogation under *Rhode Island v. Innis,* the rule of *Mathis v. United States* (1968) required that *Miranda* warnings be given.

The Supreme Court disagreed (8–1). It held that the conversation was *not* interrogation because the essential *Miranda* ingredients of a "police-dominated atmosphere" and compulsion were missing. Perkins had no idea he was speaking to a police officer, and "[c]oercion is determined from the perspective of the suspect." The Court reasoned that for the purposes of *Miranda,* Perkins was not in custody. "We reject the argument that *Miranda* warnings are required whenever a suspect is in custody in a technical sense and converses with someone who happens to be a government agent. . . . [W]here a suspect does not know that he is conversing with a government agent, [mutually reinforcing psychological pressures that weaken a suspect's will] are not present."

Finally, Justice Kennedy noted that a certain amount of deception by law enforcement officers is allowed under *Miranda* as long as the deception does not become coercive. "Ploys to mislead a suspect or lull him into a false sense of security that do not rise to the level of compulsion or coercion to speak are not within *Miranda's* concerns." The Court distinguished *Mathis* by noting that in that case, the defendant knew he was questioned by law enforcement officers. The majority opinion distinguished *Perkins* from *United States v. Henry* (1980) and *Maine v. Moulton* (1985), discussed later, which were decided under the *Massiah* Sixth Amendment right to counsel rule. Those cases involved interactions between undercover agents and suspects *after* the suspects had been formally charged and had attorneys. In *Perkins,* no charges had been filed on the subject of the interrogation, so the Sixth Amendment did not come into play. *Perkins* allows the use of a valuable investigation tool, although law enforcement should be vigilant about abuses that can occur in using inmates as snitches.

QUESTIONING AFTER FORMAL CHARGING: THE SIXTH AMENDMENT

Interrogation of a suspect in police custody is limited by rules developed under the Due Process and Self-Incrimination clauses. Once the suspect is formally charged, whether by grand jury indictment, a prosecutor's information, or a magistrate's bind-over after a preliminary examination, the legal picture changes. At this point, the criminal prosecution has begun, and the Sixth Amendment right to counsel "attaches." Once a defendant is charged, different and more stringent constraints on police questioning and eavesdropping apply. Postindictment statements obtained by the police surreptitiously, or in disregard of the defendant's right to counsel, are excluded from the trial.

This rule was established in *Massiah v. United States* (1964). Winston Massiah, a crew member on a ship from South America, was charged in New York with transporting cocaine into the United States, indicted, and released on bail. While on bail, Massiah's codefendant, Colson, agreed to cooperate with the government. A listening device placed in Colson's car transmitted Massiah's incriminating statements. A government agent testified to the incriminating statements at Massiah's trial. The Supreme Court held that introducing the testimony violated Massiah's Sixth Amendment right to counsel. The Court said that counsel has long been considered essential during the pretrial stages and held that secretly obtaining incriminating statements from an indicted defendant interfered with his right to legal representation.

Justice Stewart's majority opinion repeated his views in *Spano v. New York* (1959), a pre-*Miranda* confession case decided under the voluntariness test. He noted that obtaining a confession from an indicted defendant without notifying an attorney "might deny a defendant 'effective assistance of counsel at the only stage when legal aid and advice would help him'" (*Massiah v. United States,* 1964, quoting *Spano*), that is, secretly taping incriminating statements virtually convicts the defendant, in effect creating a critical stage where counsel has to be present. The same goes for open interviews between police or prosecutors and the defendant. If a plea arrangement is desired, the defendant's lawyer must be present.

Justice White, dissenting, believed that there was no interference with Massiah's right to counsel. Unlike the Canon of Professional Ethics that prevents an attorney from interviewing an opposing party, he argued that there is no ethical restriction on investigators' contacting a defendant. "Law enforcement may have the elements of a contest about it, but it is not a game" (*Massiah v. United States,* 1964, p. 213, White, J., dissenting). Justice White's view failed to acknowledge that once the investigator speaks to or overhears a suspect and gets incriminating statements, the value of a lawyer's advice is nullified.

The *Massiah* area of law deals with similar functional issues to those that arise under *Miranda,* including the definition of *interrogation* and the validity of a waiver. Such questions arose in the notorious Christian burial speech case of *Brewer v. Williams* (1977). Williams, incidentally, was retried and found guilty. The Supreme Court upheld the second conviction under the doctrine of inevitable discovery in *Nix v. Williams* (1984), also referred to as *Williams II*; see Chapter 2.

Read Case and Comments: *Brewer v. Williams.*

The *Massiah* Right after *Brewer v. Williams*

The Supreme Court found in favor of defendants in *Michigan v. Jackson* (1986). A defendant who requests a lawyer at arraignment has invoked his right to counsel, and police may not initiate interrogation until counsel has been made available to the suspect. This seemed to extend the rule of *Edwards v. Arizona* (1981) to the Sixth Amendment (a questioned suspect who asks for a lawyer under *Miranda* cannot be interrogated without counsel present). However, the Court shrank this extension of a defendant's Sixth Amendment rights in the following cases.

Brewer v. Williams

430 U.S. 387, 97 S.Ct. 1232, 51 L.Ed.2d 424 (1977)

MR. JUSTICE STEWART delivered the opinion of the Court.

I

* * * [Robert Williams, a mental hospital escapee, turned himself in to Davenport, Iowa, police for the murder of a ten-year-old girl at a Des Moines YMCA on December 26, 1968. **[a]** He was arrested, formally arraigned (charged) for the crime, and advised of his rights by the judge, who noted that Williams was represented by attorney McKnight in Des Moines and attorney Kelly in Davenport. McKnight spoke to Williams on the phone in the presence of Des Moines police detective Leaming. He informed Williams that Des Moines officers would drive to Davenport, pick him up, and would not interrogate him or mistreat him. He warned Williams not to talk to the officers about the crime. When Detective Leaming picked up Williams, Kelly, the Davenport lawyer, was denied a request to ride back to Des Moines with them. Kelly repeated to Detective Leaming that Williams was not to be questioned on the ride back.]

[On the 160-mile ride to Des Moines, Williams expressed no desire to be interrogated without his lawyer present; he said he would tell the whole story at the end of the trip. Leaming knew Williams was a deeply religious man and engaged him in a general discussion. Soon after the trip began, Leaming delivered the so-called] "Christian burial speech." Addressing Williams as "Reverend," the detective said: **[b]**

> "I want to give you something to think about while we're traveling down the road. . . . Number one, I want you to observe the weather conditions, it's raining, it's sleeting, it's freezing, driving is very treacherous, visibility is poor, it's going to be dark early this evening. They are predicting several inches of snow for tonight, and I feel that you yourself are the only person that knows where this little girl's body is, that you yourself have only been there once, and if you get a snow on top of it you yourself may be unable to find it. And, since we will be going right past the area on the way into Des Moines, I feel that we could stop and locate the body, that the parents of this little girl should be entitled to a Christian burial for the little girl who was snatched away from them on Christmas [E]ve and murdered. And I feel we should stop and locate it on the way in rather than waiting until morning and trying to come back out after a snow storm and possibly not being able to find it at all."

Williams asked Detective Leaming why he thought their route to Des Moines would be taking them past the girl's body, and Leaming responded that he knew the body was in the area of Mitchellville—a town they would be passing on the way to Des Moines. **[c]** Leaming then stated: "I do not want you to answer me. I don't want to discuss it any further. Just think about it as we're riding down the road."

As the car approached Grinnell, a town approximately 100 miles west of Davenport, Williams asked whether the police had found the victim's shoes. When Detective Leaming replied that he was unsure, Williams directed the officers to a service station where he said he had left the shoes; a search for them proved unsuccessful. As they continued towards Des Moines, Williams asked whether the police had found the blanket, and directed the officers to a rest area where he said he had disposed of the blanket. Nothing was found. The car continued towards Des Moines, and as it approached Mitchellville, Williams said that he would show the officers where the body was. He then directed the police to the body of Pamela Powers.

* * *

[This evidence was introduced and used to convict Williams of murder. The Iowa courts ruled that Williams waived his right to counsel, but the lower federal courts, on a writ of

[a] Numerous facts are stated. Which are essential to the holding of the case?

[b] Do you think Detective Leaming made the speech to deliberately elicit incriminating evidence or just to pass the time?

[c] The call for silence at this point allowed Leaming's speech to work on Williams's mind.

habeas corpus, ruled the evidence inadmissible on the alternative grounds of denial of assistance of counsel, a *Miranda* violation, and that his statements were involuntary.]

II

B

* * * [*Miranda v. Arizona* does not apply to this case.] For it is clear that the judgment before us must in any event be affirmed upon the ground that Williams was deprived of a different constitutional right—the right to the assistance of counsel. **[d]**

This right, guaranteed by the Sixth and Fourteenth Amendments, is indispensable to the fair administration of our adversary system of criminal justice. [It is a] vital need at the pretrial stage. * * *

* * * Whatever else it may mean, the right to counsel granted by the Sixth and Fourteenth Amendments means at least that a person is entitled to the help of a lawyer at or after the time that judicial proceedings have been initiated against him—"whether by way of formal charge, preliminary hearing, indictment, information, or arraignment." * * *

There can be no doubt in the present case that judicial proceedings [by arraignment] had been initiated against Williams before the start of the automobile ride from Davenport to Des Moines. * * * **[e]**

There can be no serious doubt, either, that Detective Leaming deliberately and designedly set out to elicit information from Williams just as surely as—and perhaps more effectively than—if he had formally interrogated him. Detective Leaming was fully aware before departing for Des Moines that Williams was being represented in Davenport by Kelly and in Des Moines by McKnight. Yet he purposely sought during Williams' isolation from his lawyers to obtain as much incriminating information as possible. Indeed, Detective Leaming conceded as much when he testified at Williams' trial. * * *

The circumstances of this case are thus constitutionally indistinguishable from those presented in *Massiah v. United States*. * * * **[f]**

That the incriminating statements were elicited surreptitiously in the *Massiah* case, and otherwise here, is constitutionally irrelevant. * * * Rather, the clear rule of *Massiah* is that once adversary proceedings have commenced against an individual, he has a right to legal representation when the government interrogates him. * * *

III

The Iowa courts recognized that Williams had been denied the constitutional right to the assistance of counsel. **[g]** They held, however, that he had waived that right during the course of the automobile trip from Davenport to Des Moines. * * *

[The Iowa courts applied a totality of circumstances test to ascertain whether Williams waived his right to counsel. The federal courts held that this was the wrong standard under the constitutional guarantee to counsel: There must be an affirmative waiver.]

* * *

The [lower federal courts] were also correct in their understanding of the proper standard to be applied in determining the question of waiver as a matter of federal constitutional law— that it was incumbent upon the State to prove "an intentional relinquishment or abandonment of a known right or privilege." * * * **[h]** We have said that the right to counsel does not depend upon a request by the defendant, * * * and that courts indulge in every reasonable presumption against waiver. * * * This strict standard applies equally to an alleged waiver of the right to counsel whether at trial or at a critical stage of pretrial proceedings. * * *

[d] As noted in Chapter 6, the right to counsel attaches pretrial at critical stages. *Hamilton v. Alabama* (1961) required counsel at arraignment.

[e] Is this obvious? If so, is there any logic in Justice Blackmun's dissent? Should the Supreme Court allow blatant violations of rights if the crime is horrible?

[f] This clarifies the *Massiah* ruling. It is, essentially, a right-to-counsel case and is not limited to cases where government agents eavesdrop.

[g] Part III deals with whether Williams properly waived his right to counsel.

[h] This is the test of *Johnson v. Zerbst* (1938), which is the test for waiver of counsel at trial.

(continued)

[i] The state had the burden of proof that Williams voluntarily waived his right to counsel. The majority thinks the burden was not met. Compare this to Justice White's dissent. Should Detective Leaming have informed Williams of his right to counsel and given him the chance to waive that right?

We conclude, finally, that the Court of Appeals was correct in holding that, judged by these standards, the record in this case falls far short of sustaining petitioner's burden. It is true that Williams had been informed of and appeared to understand his right to counsel. **[i]** But waiver requires not merely comprehension but relinquishment, and Williams' consistent reliance upon the advice of counsel in dealing with the authorities refutes any suggestion that he waived that right. [He spoke to both the Des Moines and Davenport attorneys numerous times before the trip.] Throughout, Williams was advised not to make any statements before seeing McKnight in Des Moines, and was assured that the police had agreed not to question him. His statements while in the car that he would tell the whole story *after* seeing McKnight in Des Moines were the clearest expressions by Williams himself that he desired the presence of an attorney before any interrogation took place. But even before making these statements, Williams had effectively asserted his right to counsel by having secured attorneys at both ends of the automobile trip, both of whom, acting as his agents, had made clear to the police that no interrogation was to occur during the journey. Williams knew of that agreement and, particularly in view of his consistent reliance on counsel, there is no basis for concluding that he disavowed it.

Detective Leaming proceeded to elicit incriminating statements from Williams. Leaming did not preface this effort by telling Williams that he had a right to the presence of a lawyer, and made no effort at all to ascertain whether Williams wished to relinquish that right. The circumstances of record in this case thus provide no reasonable basis for finding that Williams waived his right to the assistance of counsel.

The Court of Appeals did not hold, nor do we, that under the circumstances of this case Williams *could not,* without notice to counsel, have waived his rights under the Sixth and Fourteenth Amendments. It only held, as do we, that he did not.

IV

[j] The majority refuses to "bend the rules" of constitutional rights to gain a conviction in a terrible crime. Compare the remarks of Chief Justice Burger.

The crime of which Williams was convicted was senseless and brutal, calling for swift and energetic action by the police to apprehend the perpetrator and gather evidence with which he could be convicted. **[j]** No mission of law enforcement officials is more important. Yet, "[d]isinterested zeal for the public good does not assure either wisdom or right in the methods it pursues." * * * Although we do not lightly affirm the issuance of a writ of habeas corpus in this case, so clear a violation of the Sixth and Fourteenth Amendments as here occurred cannot be condoned. The pressures on state executive and judicial officers charged with the administration of the criminal law are great, especially when the crime is murder and the victim a small child. But it is precisely the predictability of those pressures that makes imperative a resolute loyalty to the guarantees that the Constitution extends to us all.

The judgment of the Court of Appeals is affirmed.

It is so ordered.

[Justices Marshall, Powell, and Stevens concurred in separate opinions.]

MR. CHIEF JUSTICE BURGER, dissenting. **[k]**

[k] This is political "tough on crime" rhetoric. Does it belong in a Supreme Court opinion? Do suspects have too many rights? Can this rhetoric lead to the permanent loss of rights?

The result in this case ought to be intolerable in any society which purports to call itself an organized society. It continues the Court—by the narrowest margin—on the much-criticized course of punishing the public for the mistakes and misdeeds of law enforcement officers, instead of punishing the officer directly, if in fact he is guilty of wrongdoing. It mechanically and blindly keeps reliable evidence from juries whether the claimed constitutional violation involves gross police misconduct or honest human error.

* * *

[Further in his opinion, the CHIEF JUSTICE argued that the exclusionary rule should not apply to nonegregious police conduct.]

MR. JUSTICE WHITE, with whom MR. JUSTICE BLACKMUN and MR. JUSTICE REHNQUIST join, dissenting.

* * *

Respondent relinquished his right not to talk to the police about his crime when the car approached the place where he had hidden the victim's clothes. [l] Men usually intend to do what they do, and there is nothing in the record to support the proposition that respondent's decision to talk was anything but an exercise of his own free will. Apparently, without any prodding from the officers, respondent—who had earlier said that he would tell the whole story when he arrived in Des Moines—spontaneously changed his mind about the timing of his disclosures when the car approached the places where he had hidden the evidence. However, even if his statements were influenced by Detective Leaming's above-quoted statement, respondent's decision to talk in the absence of counsel can hardly be viewed as the product of an overborne will. The statement by Leaming was not coercive; it was accompanied by a request that respondent not respond to it; and it was delivered hours before respondent decided to make any statement.

Respondent's waiver was thus knowing and intentional.

* * *

MR. JUSTICE BLACKMUN, with whom MR. JUSTICE WHITE and MR. JUSTICE REHNQUIST join, dissenting.

* * *

What the Court chooses to do here, and with which I disagree, is to hold that respondent Williams' situation was in the mold of *Massiah v. United States,* [m] that is, that it was dominated by a denial to Williams of his Sixth Amendment right to counsel after criminal proceedings had been instituted against him. The Court rules that the Sixth Amendment was violated because Detective Leaming "purposely sought during Williams' isolation from his lawyers to obtain as much incriminating information as possible." I cannot regard that as unconstitutional *per se.*

First, the police did not deliberately seek to isolate [n] Williams from his lawyers so as to deprive him of the assistance of counsel. * * * The isolation in this case was a necessary incident of transporting Williams to the county where the crime was committed.

Second, Leaming's purpose was not solely to obtain incriminating evidence. The victim had been missing for only two days, and the police could not be certain that she was dead. Leaming, of course, and in accord with his duty, was "hoping to find out where that little girl was," * * * but such motivation does not equate with an intention to evade the Sixth Amendment. * * *

Third, not every attempt to elicit information should be regarded as "tantamount to interrogation." * * * [o] I am not persuaded that Leaming's observations and comments, made as the police car traversed the snowy and slippery miles between Davenport and Des Moines that winter afternoon, were an interrogation, direct or subtle, of Williams. * * * In summary, it seems to me that the Court is holding that *Massiah* is violated whenever police engage in any conduct, in the absence of counsel, with the subjective desire to obtain information from a suspect after arraignment. Such a rule is far too broad. Persons in custody frequently volunteer statements in response to stimuli other than interrogation. * * * When there is no interrogation, such statements should be admissible as long as they are truly voluntary. * * *

* * *

[l] What is Justice White's logic? Can this logic make legal any incriminating statement except those obtained by torture? Was Williams's admission spontaneous?

[m] A question not settled by this case is whether it is ever possible for police to interview a suspect without his or her lawyer present after formal charges.

[n] Do the first two points made by Justice Blackmun pass the "giggle test"?

[o] Like *Rhode Island v. Innis* and *Arizona v. Mauro,* the case is also about the functional equivalent of interrogation. If Detective Leaming's speech is not the functional equivalent, what is?

Patterson v. Illinois (1988) resolved an issue not completely answered in *Brewer v. Williams*. It held that an indicted defendant who is read *Miranda* warnings may validly waive his right to counsel. Under some circumstances, then, a charged defendant can speak to police without an attorney present, as long as there is an express waiver of the right to counsel. Dissenters in *Patterson* wanted the Court to impose additional warnings to the four required by *Miranda* for suspects who have been formally charged, but the majority refused to do so. Justice Stevens, dissenting in *Patterson,* raised a different point: that it is unethical for investigators or prosecutors during trial preparation to go behind the backs of their adversaries and communicate with a defendant. In his view, since it is a breach of professional ethics for an attorney to communicate with an opposing party without the knowledge of opposing counsel, the *Massiah* rule also "suggest[s] that law enforcement personnel may not bypass counsel in favor of direct communications with an accused." The majority did not accede to this view.

The Court further limited *Massiah* rights in **McNeil v. Wisconsin** (1991). A defendant who invokes the right to counsel for one crime (and cannot be questioned about it) is not automatically protected against police questioning for another crime. The Court held that the Sixth Amendment right to counsel is offense-specific, unlike the right to counsel created by the Supreme Court in *Miranda* to protect Fifth Amendment rights. The reason for this distinction is that the purpose of the Sixth Amendment right to counsel is to protect the unaided layperson at a critical confrontation. The purpose of the *Miranda-Edwards* rule is to protect a suspect's desire to deal with police only through counsel.

A strong example of the Rehnquist Court's activist, conservative reasoning is found in **Michigan v. Harvey** (1990), which held that a statement taken in violation of one's *Massiah* rights under *Michigan v. Jackson* (1986) can be used at a trial to impeach the defendant should he or she choose to testify. Since a violation of *Jackson* seems to be a direct violation of a suspect's Sixth Amendment rights, it is difficult to see how a statement obtained by a blatant violation of *Massiah* and *Jackson* could be used in any proceeding. Chief Justice Rehnquist, writing for the majority, achieved this goal by muddying the clear distinction between Fifth and Sixth Amendment rights that Justice Stewart had worked to achieve in cases like *Spano, Massiah,* and *Brewer v. Williams*. Rehnquist's opinion minimized the difference between *Miranda* and *Massiah,* arguing that although *Michigan v. Jackson* "is based on the Sixth Amendment . . . its roots lie in this Court's decisions in *Miranda v. Arizona* and succeeding cases." It is difficult to comprehend the cause and effect since *Massiah* (1964) preceded *Miranda* (1966) by two years. The Court reasoned that *Michigan v. Jackson* borrowed its bright-line rule from *Edwards v. Arizona,* a *Miranda* case. By this reasoning, the Court held that the rights announced in *Michigan v. Jackson* were mere prophylactic rules and so could be used to impeach the defendant.

Justice Stevens dissented (joined by Justices Brennan, Marshall, and Blackmun). He stated that the right to counsel is much more pervasive than other rights "because it affects the ability of the accused to assert any other rights he may have." Because of this, rules for waiving counsel are extremely stringent. Further, he said that the majority argument was a ploy to confuse the true basis of a *Massiah* right. In this case, Harvey's right to see his lawyer was violated by a police officer who told a confused Harvey that he didn't have to see his lawyer. Stevens virtually accused the majority's recharacterization of the facts of this case as one "involving nothing more than the violation of a 'prophylactic' rule" as a smoke screen that undermined the rule of *Massiah* and a suspect's primary right to counsel.

Justice Stevens added a practical reason for excluding all use of evidence obtained in violation of *Massiah* rights:

> The police would have everything to gain and nothing to lose by repeatedly visiting with the defendant and seeking to elicit as many comments as possible about the pending trial.

Knowledge that such conversations could not be used affirmatively would not detract from the State's interest in obtaining them for their value as impeachment evidence.

Michigan v. Harvey is an example of judicial decision making that reflects the crime control and due process models of criminal justice discussed in Chapter 1.

Undercover Policing and the Right to Counsel

In *Illinois v. Perkins* (1990), discussed earlier, the Court allowed undercover policing to proceed without warning individuals that they were suspects, because incriminating statements made to false friends are not compelled. This kind of deception is not a substitute for coercion. *Massiah,* on the other hand, seems to rule out this kind of deception once a person has been formally charged and is clothed with the right to counsel. The Court has maintained, but softened, the *Massiah* rule to some degree when agents or informants are planted in a suspect's jail cell to listen for incriminating statements.

Jail Cell Cases.

An incriminating statement made by a suspect in a jail cell to an informant in **United States v. Henry** (1980) was thrown out as a *Massiah* violation because the informant "deliberately elicited" the statement from Henry by engaging in conversations that resulted in the incriminating statement. On the other hand, in **Kuhlman v. Wilson** (1986), a jail informant placed in a cell with Wilson did not deliberately elicit the incriminating evidence. The informant did not initiate any conversations about the crime but "only listened" to Wilson and took notes later. The rule, then, is that the police can place in a cell a passive listener who acts like a listening device, which is allowed in a jail setting, as long as the cellmate does not start conversations that are likely to lead the suspect to incriminate himself. This ruling, favorable to the prosecution, does not take into account the human tendency of an inmate to talk to a cellmate, increasing the likelihood of making incriminating statements.

Undercover Informant.

Maine v. Moulton (1985) is factually similar to *Massiah* and restates the jail case rules in the context of undercover policing. Colson, a codefendant of Moulton, agreed to obtain information for the police in return for the state's dropping charges against him.[35] Both Moulton and Colson, out on bail, got together to plan trial strategy, during which Moulton made incriminating statements. The Supreme Court held that the statements were barred by the *Massiah* rule:

> The Sixth Amendment guarantees the accused, at least after the initiation of formal charges, the right to rely on counsel as a "medium" between him and the State. . . . [T]his guarantee includes the State's affirmative obligation not to act in a manner that circumvents the protections accorded the accused by invoking this right. . . . Thus, the Sixth Amendment is not violated whenever—by luck or happenstance—the State obtains incriminating statements from the accused after the right to counsel has attached. . . . However, *knowing exploitation* by the State of an opportunity to confront the accused without counsel being present is as much a breach of the State's obligation not to circumvent the right to the assistance of counsel as the intentional creation of such an opportunity. (*Maine v. Moulton,* 1985, emphasis added)

The majority agreed that handing up an indictment does not prevent the police from continuing to investigate a case or from investigating the defendant for other crimes. However, they must not obtain evidence surreptitiously from an indicted defendant in a way that cuts the defendant off from the defense lawyer. Therefore, the majority made it clear that if the police are investigating a suspect for Crime B and the suspect has already been indicted for Crime A, an undercover agent may investigate the suspect for Crime B for which the suspect has not been charged. Evidence obtained by the undercover agent pertaining to Crime A may not be admitted. Only evidence for the new crime (Crime B) is admissible.

TORTURE AND INTERROGATION IN A TIME OF TERROR

Torture

After the terrorist attacks on September 11, 2001, whether to use torture to elicit information from would-be terrorists became a lively topic. Professor Alan Dershowitz of Harvard Law School suggested that "torture warrants" would be appropriate in some cases, provoking a torrent of criticism.[36] The question is no longer theoretical. Although the Bush administration has denied it, the authorization and use of techniques like "waterboarding," hypothermia, and sleep deprivation to obtain confessions from suspected terrorists are forms of torture categorically forbidden by international and American law.[37]

In international law, both torture and "other cruel, inhuman or degrading treatment or punishment" are forbidden.[38] The European Court of Human Rights stated that the "difference between torture and inhuman treatment 'derives principally from a difference in the intensity of the suffering inflicted.'"[39] Torture is absolutely prohibited for all reasons. The international Convention against Torture (CAT) states: "No exceptional circumstances whatsoever, whether a state of war or threat of war, internal political instability or any other public emergency, may be invoked as a justification of torture." Signatories to CAT, like the United States, must "undertake to prevent" inhuman treatment, but the "no exceptional circumstances" statement that applies to torture is omitted.[40] The exception, however, does not condone cruel, inhuman, or degrading treatment. Planning, authorizing, or carrying out torture is a war crime.[41]

The United States is a CAT signatory. The Senate ratification softened the international definition by providing that torture includes the *intent* to inflict severe physical or mental pain and by narrowing the definition of mental pain. Commenting on the news reports of treatment of al Qaeda prisoners at Bagram Air Base, Professor John Parry concludes that if true, they "reveal that the United States is involved or implicated in a range of interrogation practices that are illegal under domestic and international law."[42]

Is torture effective? Dershowitz, who is morally opposed to torture, writes that he believes that law enforcement officials will employ torture in "ticking bomb" cases.[43] Philosophical supporters of torture emphasize this scenario, and even opponents allow that illegal torture should be used to save lives in such situations.[44] The problem is that the "ticking bomb" scenario is a myth. The English commentator Christopher Hitchens makes the wise point that the "favourite experimental scenario—the man knows where the bomb is, put the hooks into him swiftly—is actually a contingency almost impossible to visualise. I certainly know of no such real-life case."[45] A very careful analysis of the literature on the effectiveness of torture allows that in rare instances threats of the use of physical force might have worked.[46] Against this is the evidence that many anecdotes of successful torture, including three used by Dershowitz, may be less clear on careful examination and that security agencies have not provided careful documentation of success.

More important, the historical accounts, psychological studies, and case analyses of the failures and problems with coercive interrogation are legion.[47] CIA and FBI reports point out the problems of inaccurate recollection and false confessions. The use of torture in Algeria, Northern Ireland, and Israel have not produced the desired political results. The slippery slope problem cannot be dismissed as a fantasy after the indelible stain that the photographs of the abuse of Iraqi detainees at Abu Ghraib prison have left on America in the Arab and Islamic worlds. Consider the case of captured Iraqi Major General Abed Hamed Mowhoush. He initially cooperated with his captors without the use of coercion. It was then decided that further information could be gained by physical coercion. A "secret CIA-sponsored group of Iraqi paramilitaries, working with Army interrogators, [beat] Mowhoush nearly senseless, using fists, a club and a rubber hose."[48] He died in U.S. military custody without divulging further information.[49]

Torture is hideous and degrading both to the victims and to the torturers; it has always deeply scarred societies that allow it.[50] There is a certain irony in the fact that the administration-Senate compromise bill on detainees in late September 2006 could still allow some "wiggle room" for CIA coercive measures,[51] while at the same time the U.S. Army, which fields the largest number of terrorist interrogators, has promulgated a single standard of noncoercive interrogation. As Lieutenant General John Kimmons, the army's deputy chief of staff for intelligence, explained in a news conference: "I am absolutely convinced [that] no good intelligence is going to come from abusive practices. I think history tells us that. I think the empirical evidence of the last five years, hard years, tell[s] us that," said the general. "Moreover, any piece of intelligence which is obtained under duress, through the use of abusive techniques, would be of questionable credibility, and additionally it would do more harm than good when it inevitably became known that abusive practices were used. And we can't afford to go there."[52]

Interrogation of terror suspects, of course, is a necessary and effective intelligence tool in counterterrorism and has yielded successes. Indeed, in most European countries, "an anti-terrorism apparatus based on aggressive domestic spying and extensive judicial power" has dismantled most extremist cells "well before the attack stage."[53] The use of torture and inhuman treatment may (or may not) assist the short-term goals of interrogation, but in the long run they may prove self-defeating.

Extraterritoriality and *Miranda*

As noted in Chapter 5, extraterritorial interrogations must adhere to at least a modified version of the *Miranda* warnings. Mohamed Rashed Daoud Al-'Owhali, a member of al Qaeda, was prosecuted in 2001 in a New York federal court for the 1998 bombing of the U.S. embassy in Nairobi, Kenya. He claimed that his statements, made during his interrogation in Kenya by an FBI special agent and an Assistant U.S. Attorney, violated his right against self-incrimination. Federal Judge Leonard Sand ruled, in a case of first impression, that U.S. law enforcement personnel interrogating suspects abroad with the consent of the host country for purposes of prosecuting the suspects in U.S. courts must abide by *Miranda*:

> [A] principled, but realistic application of *Miranda*'s familiar warning/waiver framework, in the absence of a constitutionally-adequate alternative, is both necessary and appropriate under the Fifth Amendment. Only by doing so can courts meaningfully safeguard from governmental incursion the privilege against self-incrimination afforded to all criminal defendants in this country—wherever in the world they might initially be apprehended—while at the same time imposing manageable costs on the transnational investigatory capabilities of America's law enforcement personnel. . . .
>
> . . . We therefore hold that a defendant's statements, if extracted by U.S. agents acting abroad, should be admitted as evidence at trial only if the Government demonstrates that the defendant was first advised of his rights and that he validly waived those rights.[54]

Judge Sand noted that prior case law required warnings when U.S. agents were involved in questioning by foreign police personnel. He specifically held that a suspect questioned on foreign soil must be warned of the right to silence. "He must also be told that anything he does say may be used against him in a court in the United States or elsewhere. This much is uncontroversial."[55] However, the need to warn a suspect that he has a right to the presence of counsel depends on whether that is a right that exists under the law of the host country:

> *Miranda* does not require law enforcement to promise that which they cannot guarantee or that which is in fact impossible to fulfill. No constitutional purpose is served by compelling law enforcement personnel to lie or mislead subjects of interrogation. Nor does *Miranda* mandate that U.S. agents compel a foreign sovereign to accept blind allegiance to American

criminal procedure, at least when U.S. involvement in the foreign investigation is limited to mutual cooperation.[56]

Judge Sand rejected the prosecution argument that giving the warnings, with modifications as necessary, would impose intolerable costs on international investigations with cooperating nations or on America's ability to deter transnational crime. Indeed, the federal agents did read extensive warnings to Al-'Owhali, relying on an "Overseas FBI Advice of Rights Form." Judge Sand held that the form was facially deficient because it only informed the suspect that he would have a right to counsel if he was in the United States, creating the impression that no such right was available in the country in which the interrogation occurred. Indeed, Kenyan law raised the possibility that counsel might be available at interrogation. As a result, five days of Al-'Owhali's interrogation were suppressed.

Al-'Owhali later indicated that he wished to inculpate himself in exchange for a guarantee that he be tried in the United States; statements taken on that day were admissible because they were preceded by an oral statement by a U.S. attorney that he could have an attorney present. Al-'Owhali got his wish. He and three others were found guilty of the embassy bombing in the U.S. federal court in Manhattan, just weeks after the 9/11 attacks. They were sentenced to life in prison without any chance of release.[57]

It is worth noting that the decision in the Al-'Owhali case accords with the theory put forth in *Chavez v. Martinez* (2003)—that *Miranda* rights and the right against self-incrimination are essentially exclusionary rules, violations of which occur at the time and place of introducing compelled statements. Therefore the requirement of *Miranda* rights in Kenya is designed to protect a suspect's privilege against self-incrimination in New York.

LAW IN SOCIETY

THE SOCIAL REALITY OF CONFESSIONS

The Acceptance of *Miranda*

Despite its bitter reception by police and others in 1966, the *Miranda* ruling has since been accepted by the legal and law enforcement communities. Chief Justice Warren Burger stated in 1980, "The meaning of *Miranda* has become reasonably clear and law enforcement practices have adjusted to its strictures; I would neither overrule *Miranda,* disparage it, nor extend it at this late date" (*Rhode Island v. Innis*). This signaled that *Miranda*'s opponents could now live with it, in part because the case did not undermine effective policing. Chief Justice Burger also wanted to avoid another round of appeals designed to clarify a major legal revolution in established and well-known confessions rules.

Many police see *Miranda,* and the study of constitutional law in general, as enhancing the professional status of policing. Some officers accept that without legal strictures, their crime-fighting behavior could turn to lawlessness. Others have internalized the *Miranda* rules and are happy to apply them to the extent that they accord with what they believe is "fair and decent" behavior.[58] In

this light, it is important to be clear that "*Miranda* has not failed to achieve its limited goals"[59]—which were *not* to eliminate interrogation and confessions or to completely equalize the power relationship between a suspect and the police or to lower confession rates. *Miranda* was designed to reduce the compulsion of the interrogation process. Understanding this, police officers are happy to follow the letter of the *Miranda* decision if the goals of law enforcement can be generally realized.[60] This has resulted in police adaptation to the *Miranda* requirements.

Police Interrogation Today: Adapting to *Miranda*

What do we know about how custodial interrogation is conducted? "During the first few years after *Miranda,* empirical studies suggested that *Miranda*'s impact was minimal."[61] Few studies of *Miranda*'s effect appeared for some time, but since 1996 several have enlarged our understanding of *Miranda,* and some have generated a lively debate over the "costs" to law enforcement of the need to warn interrogated suspects of their rights.

How Are Interrogations Conducted? As a routine practice, third-degree tactics—the use and threats of beatings—have disappeared as police interrogation techniques. Police today use sophisticated psychological techniques to "persuade" recalcitrant defendants to admit their guilt. A study by Professor Richard Leo of 182 interrogations observed in three California police departments in 1992 and 1993 provided a picture of contemporary interrogation. Most of the suspects were young working-class African American males. Seventy percent of the primary detectives conducting the questioning were white, and 90 percent were males. In 69 percent of the cases, interrogation was conducted by one officer, and in 31 percent, two officers interrogated. Forty-three percent of the cases were for robberies, 24 percent were for assault, 12 percent were for homicide, and the other 21 percent were for burglaries, thefts, and other crimes.

Only 22 percent of the suspects invoked their *Miranda* rights after they were read. Suspects with prior felony records invoked their rights more often (30 percent) than those with no record (8 percent) or with prior misdemeanor involvement (11 percent) in the criminal justice system. Thirty-six percent of the suspects made no incriminating statement, 22 percent made an incriminating statement, 18 percent made a partial admission, and 24 percent made a full confession. Thirty-five percent of the interrogations lasted less than thirty minutes, 36 percent lasted thirty to sixty minutes, 21 percent lasted for one to two hours, and 8 percent lasted more than two hours.[62] Leo concluded that under legal criteria, only four out of 182 cases, or 2 percent, "rose to the level of 'coercion.'"[63]

Leo provides six in-depth vignettes from the cases he observed. In each, the officers used a variety of psychological ploys to get confessions. A suspect accused of smashing in a car's window and stealing its contents was told that several witnesses saw him do this. "The detective was, of course, fabricating evidence against the suspect, but the suspect did not know this."[64] The interrogation lasted more than an hour; the suspect admitted breaking into the car and, on a plea bargain, received a one-year sentence. Another suspect, a twenty-one-year-old Hispanic male, was accused of kidnapping a fourteen-year-old girl from a party and brutally raping and anally and orally sodomizing her before returning the girl to the party with a warning that he would shoot her if she spoke. The victim immediately told a friend, who called the police. A swift medical examination confirmed severe physical injury. During the interrogation, the detective, a Hispanic female, "went from somewhat formal language (which it appeared he didn't understand) to slang, crude, and even profane language to ask him questions about the sexual acts." He appeared nervous, but "she quickly put her hand on his in a friendly

gesture, smiled, and told him to trust her, that she wouldn't be embarrassed by anything he told her." The suspect invoked counsel, ending the interrogation after thirty-four minutes. He pleaded guilty to statutory rape and received a one-month sentence plus four years of "formal probation."[65] This indicates that failure to obtain confessions in some cases may allow guilty parties to go free or receive less than adequate punishment.

Why Do Suspects Waive Their *Miranda* Rights? Observations of police interrogation practices show that a variety of psychological methods are used to get suspects to talk. If the police follow the spirit of *Miranda*, they at least deliver the warnings in a neutral way at the beginning of an interrogation session. Some do. But many others deemphasize the importance of *Miranda* waivers in several ways. They may indicate that the waiver is an unimportant bureaucratic detail (a mere formality) or may build rapport and engage in small talk before mentioning *Miranda*. Another "selling" technique is to stress the importance of the suspect's "telling his side of the story."[66] A more insidious technique is to weave the warnings into questions and answers over a long period of time so that the suspect waives rights and after this is read the warnings in a block—a method dubbed "participating *Miranda*" by Professors Peter Lewis and Harry Allen.[67]

Leo describes the process by characterizing police interrogation as a "confidence game." Like a "con man," or perhaps any good salesperson, the police interrogator must psychologically "size up" and figure out how to manipulate the suspect. This requires knowledge of the crime, the victim, and the suspect. Unlike a true confidence man, a police interrogator cannot select or "qualify" the "mark." The officer "cultivates" the suspect by projecting a friendly and sincere image, offering coffee, and engaging in light banter. Simultaneously, the barren interrogation room, the thick case folder with the suspect's name prominently attached, and various interrogation techniques, such as pitting the suspect against a shadowy but fearsome prosecutor or judge and jury, are designed to raise the suspect's anxiety. The police frame their questions with admonitions about telling the truth; telling the truth will "make it go better" for the suspect and make him or her feel better. To elicit a confession, the police draw on various techniques of persuasion, deception, and neutralization: contradicting false statements, minimizing the immoral nature of what was done, posing false statements, and many more. Finally, the officers, knowing that the confessions will be attacked once defense lawyers come into the case, "cool the mark" by complimenting the suspect for his or her honesty and cooperation and maintaining a neutral tone and a positive reaction to the defendant to the end.[68]

Interrogation "Outside" *Miranda*. As noted in the body of this chapter, a troubling interrogation practice known as "interrogation outside *Miranda*" has become prevalent in some places. In this practice, police deliberately violate a suspect's *Miranda* rights in order to gain the collateral use of evidence. The Supreme Court is examining the practice, the existence of which reveals the need for vigilance in protecting individual rights.[69]

The Benefits of *Miranda*. Leo asserts that *Miranda* has had four positive long-range social effects. In his view, conservative critics of the 1980s were wrong to contend that *Miranda* has undermined effective law enforcement, and liberals have been shortsighted in saying that *Miranda*'s effects have been more symbolic than real.[70] First, Leo says, "*Miranda* has exercised a civilizing influence on police behavior inside the interrogation room" by accelerating a process that was in place in 1966. This has helped to make the police more professional by establishing objective and written standards of police behavior. As a result, "American police in the last thirty years have, by necessity, become more solicitous of suspects' rights, more respectful of their dignity, and more concerned with their welfare inside the interrogation room."[71] Second, *Miranda* "has transformed the culture—the shared norms, values and attitudes—of police . . . by fundamentally re-framing how police talk and think about the process of custodial interrogation."[72] Third, *Miranda* has increased public awareness of constitutional rights. Finally, "*Miranda* has inspired police to develop more specialized, more sophisticated and seemingly more effective interrogation techniques with which to elicit inculpatory statements from custodial suspects."[73] Thus *Miranda* is part of a larger and longer term trend in Western society in which government power is "more controlling of its subjects" but at the same time "more subject to control itself [in the areas of] legal institutions, professional standards, and social norms."[74]

Improving *Miranda*: Videotaping. This does not mean that police interrogation is without its problems. As will be explored later, numerous false confessions raise concerns about how interrogation is conducted. To ensure that interrogation becomes more professional and effective, Leo, borrowing from a 1993 Department of Justice study, has urged that courts mandate the videotaping of interrogations as a matter of due process.[75] There are many good reasons for videotaping interrogations: (1) It creates an "objective, reviewable record of custodial questioning that protects [police] against false accusations—accusations such as 'softening up' a suspect prior to *Miranda*, failing to correctly read the *Miranda* warnings, or eliciting a confession through improper inducements." (2) It is "likely to improve the quality of police work and thus contribute to more professional and more effective interrogation practices. Officers and detectives who know they will be videotaped are more likely to prepare their strategies beforehand and to be more self-conscious about their conduct during questioning." (3) Tapes can be used for training. (4) Videotaping can increase law enforcement effectiveness because it "facilitates the identification, prosecution, and conviction of guilty offenders." For example, it "preserves the details of a suspect's statement that may not have been initially recorded in a detective's notes but may subsequently become important." (5) Videotapes are believed to have helped prosecutors negotiate a higher percentage of guilty pleas and obtain longer sentences because they provide "a more complete record with which to better assess the state's case against the accused," including "the demeanor and sophistication of the suspect." As a result, some defense attorneys oppose videotaping confessions because it makes it more difficult to challenge the stories of detectives, although public defenders with high caseloads appreciate videotapes because it helps them to more quickly cut through clients' lies and produce accurate guilty pleas.

Why Do Innocent People Confess?

The English common law harbors a traditional distrust of confessions (found in the rule that uncorroborated confessions are inadmissible in court) out of fear that psychological manipulation would induce innocent people to confess. This problem still exists, despite *Miranda*, and requires precautions in how interrogation is conducted. As improbable as it may seem, when police use modern "psychological interrogation" rather than torture (e.g., *Brown v. Mississippi*, 1936), they still get innocent people to confess.

How Innocent People Confess. Recent scholarship by Professors Richard Leo and Richard Ofshe, drawing on prior scholarship regarding false confessions and on their own inquiry, has explored many cases of false confessions. In one article, they review sixty cases of allegedly false confessions and, after examining available court and news media records, classify them into three groups: thirty-four confessions that were proven false, eighteen highly probable false confessions, and eight probable false confessions.[76] In other writings, Ofshe and Leo acknowledge that the actual number of false confessions cannot be known because (1) police do not keep complete records of interrogations, making it difficult to evaluate the reliability of the interrogation or whether there was any undue pressure; (2) no criminal justice agency keeps records or collects statistics on the number or frequency of interrogations; and (3) many cases of false confession are not reported.[77] Nevertheless, there are so many documented cases just in the past decade that false confessions must be seen as an important policy area to be addressed.[78]

Leo and Ofshe have intensively explored false confessions in a lengthy article that relies heavily on field data—transcripts of both true and false confessions—to display how certain processes lead to false confessions by the innocent.[79] They identify four types of false confessions: [80]

- *Stress-compliant false confessions.* The modern psychological interrogation is stressful by design, and for some individuals—especially those with an abnormal reactivity to stress, who may be phobic, or with intellectual limitations who cope by becoming submissive—the pressure requires alleviation by saying, "I did it."

- *Coerced-compliant false confessions.* These false confessions often result from the familiar "accident scenario technique" or "maximization/minimization." This is a subtle promise and threat (traditionally outlawed in England) by which the police convince the suspect that what he did was not all that serious because there is a legal excuse or mitigation and that by confessing, he will receive lenient treatment.

- *Voluntary and involuntary persuaded false confessions.* These are instances where, after a good deal of interviewing and subtle or not-so-subtle badgering, the innocent person becomes so confused that confidence in his own memory is shattered. He reports that despite no overt memory of committing the crime, he agrees that the interrogators' recitation of events and (fabricated) "facts" must mean he is guilty.

Ofshe and Leo do not suggest that confessions be abolished. They recommend safeguards because the process by which the innocent confess is very close to the process by which investigators obtain confessions from the guilty. The steps by which confessions are obtained in the era of psychological interrogation show why this is so. Detectives have two categories of suspects: "likely suspects, for whom there exists solid evidence suggesting their guilt; and possible suspects, which includes everyone whose name comes up during an investigation." Interrogation is superficially the same for both types. The detective may begin with an interview rather than interrogation format, especially for a possible suspect, to gain rapport and lull the interviewee into forgetting the adversarial nature of the encounter. Once *Miranda* warnings are read, neither "an innocent nor a guilty party is likely to appreciate the full significance of the . . . warnings." The innocent person thinks that he or she has nothing to hide. At that point, the tone and content of the interaction become confrontational and demanding. To get the suspect to say, "I did it," an investigator must strongly reject denials and insist that objective evidence points to guilt. At this point, a truly innocent person "is likely to experience considerable shock and disorientation . . . because he is wholly unprepared for the confrontation and accusations that are the core of the process, and will not understand how an investigator could possibly suspect him." The tragedy of wrongful confessions occurs because the responses to questioning by the guilty and the innocent "are often indistinguishable to an investigator." The investigator must now convince the suspect that arrest is imminent and get the suspect to make an admission. Once this watershed is crossed, the investigator then moves the process toward obtaining a full confession.[81]

An Example of a False Confession.   In 1986, Thomas F. Sawyer, a thirty-six-year-old groundskeeper, was charged with the murder of his next-door neighbor, a single twenty-five-year-old woman, in Clearwater, Florida, on the basis of a confession. Janet Staschak was found strangled, nude, face down on her bed with wire and tape marks on her ankles. Sawyer, a recovering alcoholic, was extremely shy, suffered from bouts of anxiety, and often turned red and sweated profusely in ordinary social situations. When Sawyer was initially questioned by police officers, they noted his odd mannerisms and targeted him as a suspect. However, hair and blood samples obtained from Sawyer before his interrogation did not match samples found on the dead woman.

Although there was no corroborating evidence, two Clearwater detectives, John Dean and Peter Fire, obtained a confession from Sawyer. Before, during, and after the interrogation, Sawyer maintained his innocence. Then how or why would an innocent person confess?[82]

Understanding Sawyer's confession in this case is aided by the transcript of what occurred during the entire taped sixteen-hour interrogation session, which stretched from 4:00 P.M. to 8:00 A.M., with time out for a ninety-minute nap. After several hours of questioning, the detectives asked Sawyer to pretend he was a police officer and to suggest methods and motives for the crime. Later during the questioning, they would take his statements and say that he knew too much about the crime to have guessed about the state of the room and the way in which the crime was carried out. Yet police officers had for some time before the questioning been back and forth between Sawyer's and Staschak's apartment, and he may have heard a good deal about the crime; furthermore, the transcript, at this point, included a good deal of prompting by the detectives.

At about 8:00 P.M., four hours after the questioning began in a small room at the police station, the officers warned Sawyer of his rights, an example of "participating *Miranda*":

> DEAN: All right. We got this squared away. Now Tom, because this is a criminal investigation, obviously, what

we've been doing—There's a new phase we have to enter into now. And before I do that, I have to read you your rights. You watch television. You know. So just let me read you these. You have the right to remain silent. Do you understand that?

SAWYER: Uh-huh.

DEAN: Anything you say can and will be used against you in a court of law. Do you understand that? *[Sawyer nods.]*

FIRE: You got to go "yes."

SAWYER: Yes.

FIRE: Okay.

DEAN: You have the right to talk to a lawyer—

FIRE: No, wait a minute. You don't *have* to say yes. You answer the way you want to answer, but we have to hear you. I know you're saying yes with your nod, okay? You nodded yes, but—Okay?

SAWYER: Yeah. Okay.

DEAN: You have the right to talk to a lawyer. Have him present with you while you are being questioned. Do you understand that?

SAWYER: Yes.

DEAN: If you can't afford to hire a lawyer, one will be appointed to represent you before any questioning if you wish. Do you understand that?

SAWYER: Say it again. I wasn't—

DEAN: Okay. If you cannot afford to hire a lawyer, one will be appointed to represent you before any questioning if you wish. Do you understand that?

SAWYER: Yes.

DEAN: Okay. You can decide at any time to exercise your rights and not answer any questions or make any statements. Do you understand that?

SAWYER: Yes.

DEAN: Okay.

FIRE: Okay. So you understand everything. Okay. Listen, Tom. John and I—we've been talking to you all evening about this. Right? Okay? So why don't you tell us what happened. Tell us what happened.

This was followed by continuous denials by Sawyer and insistent statements by Dean and Fire that Sawyer was guilty.

SAWYER: I didn't do it.

FIRE: Tommy, it's not the truth.

SAWYER: Yes, it is.

FIRE: No it's not. Tom. Tell me the truth. Tell me what happened. It was an accident, Tom. I know it was. I know it was an accident. I need for you to tell me what happened.

SAWYER: I was never there. I never did it.

FIRE: Tom.

SAWYER: I'll look you in the eye and say that all night.

FIRE: I know, we got all night.

Throughout the session, Sawyer believed that his hair samples matched those found on Janet Staschak and that a polygraph test indicated he was lying.[83] Playing on this, the detectives suggested to Sawyer that he had "blacked out" during the crime and committed it, although he did not remember anything. Throughout the session, Dean and Fire told Sawyer that he was an intelligent and good person, that the crime was not premeditated, that he would feel a great sense of relief if he confessed. Worn down, Sawyer finally confessed not only to a murder, but also to having raped Janet Staschak when in fact there was no physical evidence of sexual penetration. Many of the facts he admitted to were stated only after several false starts with persistent prompting by Fire and Dean. He made his confession conditional on the physical evidence: "The only reason I believe I did it is if my hairs were in her car and on her body and in her apartment."

At the preliminary examination, the trial court, lacking corroborating physical evidence, threw out the confession in a detailed decision. By fastening onto the closest possible suspect, the police apparently did not diligently follow up possible leads. Staschak had taken in roommates to help pay her rent; at first a heterosexual couple who were dealing drugs and later a homosexual couple. She had evicted both couples, and both had left her in some fear. It seems likely that by fastening on Sawyer, the Clearwater officers let the real culprits escape. The trial judge described the interrogation session as an intellectual wrestling match. The Florida Court of Appeals agreed and upheld the suppression of the confession.

Preventing False Confessions. As noted above, Ofshe and Leo do not recommend abolishing police interrogation, but they do have recommendations to lessen the possibility of false confessions. One recommendation, discussed earlier, is that custodial interrogations be videotaped. A lengthy interrogation contains so many subtle, forward-moving points of persuasion-threat-coercion, such as maximization-minimization techniques, that "it is beyond human ability to remember just what happened." Since interrogators are zealous in achieving their goal of obtaining confession, they are naturally biased and simply will not see that they did anything that might induce a false confession.

Ofshe and Leo's central point is that false confessions come about when commonplace interrogation methods (including the verbal fabrication of "evidence") are used improperly, inappropriately, or ineptly.[84] Therefore, police training is critical to avoiding false confessions. Police need to be educated in the facts of false confessions and to understand that they do occur. Since there is a subtle difference between the proper and improper use of the psychological interrogation, the most important factor is for police to be aware that when they have a possible suspect, as opposed to a likely suspect, they should seek corroborating evidence. "If police and prosecutors recognized that the mere admission 'I did it' is not necessarily a true statement, they would be far less likely to arrest and prosecute suspects who give false confessions."[85]

The last recommendation is that trial judges "should evaluate the reliability of confession statements," as they do hearsay statements, to determine whether they should be allowed into evidence. "Oddly, the constitutional law of criminal procedure has no substantive safeguards in place to specifically prevent the admission of even demonstrably false confessions." The constitutional rules for confessions under the Fifth and Sixth amendments are designed to ensure procedural regularity but not reliability, and the same has become true under the due process voluntariness test. Given this constitutional vacuum, it is critically important for judges to perform this task. The stakes for fairness are high: "It has been shown that placing a confession before a jury is tantamount to an instruction to convict, even when the confession fails to accurately describe the crime, fails to produce corroboration, and is contradicted by considerable evidence pointing to a suspect's innocence." Therefore, judges should demand that confessions display a minimal level of reliability. This can be done without any change in statutes or court rules. Judges routinely rule on admissibility and would, for example, not allow a jury to see a photograph that had been doctored. "A false confession is analogous to a doctored photograph. The mechanism for creating it is the ancient technology of human influence carried forward into the interrogation room."

A short decade ago, there was at best a vague awareness that false confessions were a rare and tragic human failing. Recent scholarship has brought the problem to the forefront. Judges, prosecutors, leaders of the bar, and police officials have no reason to claim ignorance. It remains to be seen if the legal world will respond to this challenge.

SUMMARY

The Constitution protects against abusive interrogation by the due process exclusionary rule of involuntary confessions, the Fifth Amendment privilege against self-incrimination for suspects who have not yet been indicted, and the Sixth Amendment right to counsel for those who have been formally charged. The privilege against self-incrimination allows "natural persons" who are sworn to testify in formal proceedings to claim the privilege if their testimony would tend to incriminate them. The privilege does not bar the taking and use of physical evidence, including a person's appearance and evidence from his body (e.g., hair, blood, DNA), to convict that person. The privilege prevents a person from having to face the "cruel trilemma" of self-accusation, perjury, or contempt. When applicable, the privilege against self-incrimination is an absolute bar against the use of compelled testimony taken from natural persons. The privilege may not be claimed to protect against civil commitment, as under Sexually Dangerous Person Acts.

Under the Due Process Clause, state or federal confessions or admissions are inadmissible if they are not made voluntarily. Statements obtained by threats, promises, the use of force, or undue psychological pressure are involuntary and inadmissible as due process violations. The Court gave various purposes of the voluntariness rule: to ensure accurate confessions, to prevent egregious police behavior, and to ensure that a confession is the product of a free and rational choice. Judicial displeasure with the subjectivity of the voluntariness test led the Supreme Court to seek a more concrete rule. In 1963 and 1964, the Supreme Court incorporated the Sixth Amendment right to the assistance of counsel and the privilege against self-incrimination.

Miranda v. Arizona (1966) held that custodial interrogation by police is inherently coercive, requiring that police inform suspects of their rights in order to dispel the coercive atmosphere of police custody. Four warnings must be given: that the suspect has a right to remain silent; that any statement may be used as evidence against him; that he has a right to the presence of an attorney; and that if he cannot afford an attorney, one will be appointed. A defendant may waive these rights if the waiver is made voluntarily, knowingly, and intelligently.

Following the *Miranda* decision, a more conservative Supreme Court declared that *Miranda* warnings were not themselves constitutional rights but prophylactic rules designed to protect the underlying Fifth Amendment right against self-incrimination. As a result, statements taken in violation of *Miranda* could be used to impeach the defendant and to lead to other evidence. The Court also allowed the use of warned confessions taken after a violation of the *Miranda* rule. A public safety exception was created under this theory, allowing the admission into evidence of unwarned statements made in answers to questions designed to protect the safety of arresting officers and others in the immediate area (*New York v. Quarles,* 1984).

Despite this, *Dickerson v. United States* (2000) held that the *Miranda* warnings were constitutional rules that could not be overridden by a congressional statute purporting to reinstate the voluntariness test as the sole measure of the constitutionality of confessions in federal cases. The Supreme Court recognized that *Miranda* had become so widely accepted that the concerns of precedent (stare decisis) compelled a recognition of the rule as being constitutional. But the effect of *Dickerson* has been put into question by *Chavez v. Martinez* (2003), which held that a simple failure to read *Miranda* warnings is not a violation of any right. A plurality of the Court held that the privilege and the *Miranda* warnings operate only as exclusionary rules, so that violations occur only when compelled evidence is sought to be introduced.

More recently, the Supreme Court has continued to interpret *Miranda* as a rule with exceptions, even though it is deemed a constitutional ruling. Therefore, physical evidence obtained in violation of *Miranda* is admissible (*U.S. v. Patane,* 2004). On the other hand, police cannot rely on the rule of *Oregon v. Elstad* (1985) to "cure" a statement taken in violation of *Miranda* by administering warnings and reinterrogating a suspect where the "second" interrogation is part of a single interrogation session (*Missouri v. Seibert,* 2004). The Fourteenth Amendment due process voluntariness test exists as a backstop to, and not a replacement for, the *Miranda* rule.

Numerous cases clarify the meaning of *Miranda*. Warnings need not be given in the precise language found in *Miranda* as long as the correct understanding of the warnings is conveyed. Police do not have to add anything to the warnings, such as the consequences of confessing or their knowledge that the suspect may have committed crimes that are not the immediate subject of the questioning. The prosecution has the burden of proving that a waiver is made voluntarily. A waiver is not presumed from silence, and an oral waiver is allowable as long as it was made expressly and is shown on the record. Written waivers are the common form of proving that the rights to silence and counsel were waived voluntarily.

Police must cease questioning a suspect who has waived his or her rights but indicates during interrogation the wish to terminate the interrogation. However, police may resume questioning at a later time if the resumption is reasonable. Police must cease questioning a suspect who personally and clearly invokes a desire to see an attorney but not another kind of counselor. The police may not thereafter resume questioning unless it is initiated by the suspect. This rule is violated if an officer in a department reinterrogates a suspect who invoked counsel in ignorance of his or her prior request for an attorney. Simple consultation with a lawyer does not dispel *Edwards* protection; a defendant has a right, after invoking counsel, to be questioned by police or prosecutors only with counsel present.

A person is in *Miranda* custody if the circumstances or surroundings are objectively coercive. Depending on the circumstances, interviews in one's home, at a police station, or by a probation officer may not be coercive. Interrogation in prison, even for a crime unrelated to the original crime, requires *Miranda* warnings. Questioning by a patrol officer after a routine traffic stop is generally not custodial because this kind of common detention is in public and lacks the coercive atmosphere of the police station. Questions designed to produce an incriminating answer or questions asked after a person has been arrested at the roadside constitute custodial interrogation.

Interrogation consists of express questioning or its functional equivalent: words or actions on the part of the police (other than normally attendant to arrest and custody) that the police should know are reasonably likely to elicit an incriminating response from the suspect. Deception by police interrogators is allowed. Undercover agents, in or out of jail, are not required to give *Miranda* warnings when they ask incriminating questions because the interrogation is not conducted in a coercive atmosphere.

The war on terrorism has raised concerns about the use of excessive force by American agents seeking background information from suspects. A federal court has ruled that U.S. agents must read *Miranda* warnings to suspects interrogated overseas in order for their statements to be admissible in U.S. courts.

Once a person is formally arraigned, the police may not question or eavesdrop on him or her without a lawyer present. A defendant may waive this Sixth Amendment right after being read *Miranda* warnings. This rule was violated in *Brewer v. Williams* (1977) when an officer made the functional equivalent of an interrogation designed to elicit a response by delivering a Christian burial speech to an isolated mental patient. Undercover agents who investigate a person who has been formally charged must not ask any questions or initiate conversations likely to generate incriminating statements. They may, however, listen for such statements, which are then admissible.

LEGAL PUZZLES

How Have Courts Decided These Cases?

Interrogation

7–1. A high school liaison officer approached two males walking back and forth in front of the school, asked them to identify themselves, and asked them what they were doing in the area. One identified himself as Pha Vue. The officer recognized Vue's name because the county sheriff's department had issued a warrant for Vue for attempted murder. The officer arrested Vue. While being transported to the county jail, Vue refused to answer any questions posed by investigator Ronald Smith. Two weeks later, Vue was transported from the county jail to the Green Bay Police Department to be fingerprinted and photographed. While waiting for the pictures to be developed, Smith told Vue that he did not want to ask him any questions. Vue was there only for the photo and ID processing. Vue then asked Smith about the length of time he was facing if convicted. Smith stated that it was "something like 90 to 100 years." Vue then stated, "That's if you have any witnesses, right?" Vue had not been given his *Miranda* warning.

Was Vue's statement admissible?

Held. Yes. Vue had clearly invoked his right to remain silent during transport to the jail. Vue's statement, however, was spontaneous and volunteered. The statement was not given as an answer to a question by the police. Smith had specifically told Vue that he did not want to ask him any questions and that he was there only for the photo and ID processing. Vue asked Smith about the length of time he was facing, and Smith told him. Vue's statement was in response to Smith's answer. This statement is admissible under *Miranda* for two reasons. First, as *Miranda* points out, "volunteered statements of any kind are not barred by the Fifth Amendment." Second, *Miranda* does not apply to all statements resulting from police contact, but only those statements resulting from a custodial interrogation of a defendant. Here, the defendant was in custody when he made the statement at issue, but there was no interrogation by the police. Nor were there "any words or actions on the part of the police (other than those normally attendant to arrest and custody) that the police should know are reasonably likely to elicit an incriminating response from the suspect" (*Rhode Island v. Innis,* 1980).

State v. Vue, 246 Wis. 2d 990, 632 N.W.2d 125 (2001)

Custody

7–2. Asif Mahmood, a recent immigrant from Pakistan, was charged with engaging in marriage fraud to evade the immigration laws. One morning at about 11:30 A.M., three Immigration and Customs Enforcement (ICE) agents arrived at his residence to investigate a report by a woman purporting to be Mahmood's ex-girlfriend who claimed that he had paid her money to marry him. In an application to change his immigration status, Mahmood claimed to be married. The agents wanted to know whether this marriage to Miriam Santos was legitimate.

Mahmood let the agents in voluntarily. Two agents, without asking permission, conducted a "protective sweep" of the premises, ordering Mahmood to remain in the living room, within view at all times of at least one agent. Satisfied that they were alone, the agents asked Mahmood a series of questions without informing him that he was free to decline to answer or that he could terminate the interrogation at his discretion. Despite his obvious foreign accent and tentative grasp of English, the agents did not ask if he would prefer to speak with them through an interpreter. Whenever Mahmood asked the agents to slow down or repeat themselves, they became visibly annoyed and harsh in their tone. He was unaware that he had the right to remain silent, to seek the advice of an attorney, or to ask the agents to leave. The questioning lasted an hour, and the agents' behavior during the session, including preventing Mahmood from answering a ringing telephone, left him with the reasonable conclusion that he was not free to leave or to ask the agents to leave. At the end of the hour, he admitted that Miriam Santos did not live with him at his residence and that he had paid her to marry him. He provided a written statement to that effect. During the ninety-five-minute interrogation, the agents did not ask Mahmood if he cared to use the bathroom, and he did not feel he was entitled to do so. He was anxious and concluded that he was obliged to be compliant. One agent described Mahmood as meek, mild, and very soft-spoken.

Was Mahmood in custody for purposes of *Miranda* during this interrogation?

Holding available from instructor.

Voluntariness; Voluntary Waiver

7–3. Mayhew killed his ex-girlfriend and her fiancé and then abducted his daughter and took her across state lines. He shot an officer who stopped him for a minor traffic offense and then killed his daughter and shot himself.

On the way to the hospital in an ambulance, Mayhew was administered *Miranda* warnings, waived his rights, and made incriminating statements to the police. The entire conversation in the ambulance was videotaped.

Mayhew was in moderate pain during the interrogation, as evidenced by grimaces and moans, but he never complained of "unbearable" discomfort. He complained of blood in the back of his throat. His eyes were closed when he was loaded into the ambulance, prompting the paramedics to instruct him to open his eyes. The paramedics used a blood pressure cuff and an intravenous drip to treat him. He did not lose consciousness at any point during the ambulance ride, but he claims that he was generally confused at the time because of the days' traumatic events, as supported by the EMT report, which noted that Mayhew was "confused to time/place/surroundings." During interrogation, he made a number of inquiries to the officers. A police lieutenant occasionally pulled Mayhew's oxygen mask down toward his lower lip and chin in an apparent effort to hear his words clearly. Each time the mask was removed, the paramedics returned the mask over Mayhew's mouth and nose. On two separate occasions, the lieutenant, who was a trained emergency medical first responder, aided the paramedics. Mayhew was not intoxicated and had taken no prescription or illicit drugs. Many of his statements were couched in voluntary language, he coherently answered almost all of the questions posed, and he answered those questions with absolute accuracy.

Did Mayhew voluntarily waive his *Miranda* rights, and were his statements voluntary?

Holding available from instructor.

Two-Step Interrogation

7–4. Gonzalez-Lauzan was serving a ten-month sentence for violating supervised release on a previous conviction. Officers took him to a federal courthouse to question him about his involvement in a murder. The officers, who agreed among themselves in advance not to administer *Miranda* warnings, instructed Gonzalez-Lauzan several times just to listen and told him that they did not have any questions. "The officers hoped that the strength of this evidence would persuade Gonzalez-Lauzan to talk about his participation in the killing." Approximately two and a half hours into the meeting, Gonzalez-Lauzan stated suddenly, "Okay, you got me." He was then immediately read his *Miranda* rights, signed a waiver form, and subsequently made multiple incriminating statements during the interrogation.

Were the statements Gonzalez-Lauzan made after *Miranda* warnings were read admissible?

Holding available from instructor.

Jail Plant: Eliciting Evidence or Listening Post

7–5. Manning was arrested and jailed in 1990 in the Cook County (Illinois) jail on kidnapping charges relating to a crime committed in Missouri. Manning was also a suspect in an Illinois murder, and the FBI planted a government informant in his cell to try to collect evidence about the Illinois crimes. The informant's agreement specified that he was not to elicit any information about Manning's pending Missouri charges. The informant disobeyed these orders and did talk about the Missouri charges; he agreed to help Manning fabricate an alibi defense using the informant's girlfriend, Sylvia Herrera. The FBI then met with Herrera to go over what information she should attempt to elicit from Manning. Pursuant to her agreement with the FBI, Herrera began to record her conversations with Manning. She testified extensively about her work as a government informant and the plan to fabricate an alibi defense. Manning was charged by complaint rather than indictment, was convicted of kidnapping, and received two life sentences.

Did the introduction of Herrera's testimony violate Manning's right to counsel?

Holding available from instructor.

FURTHER READING

Liva Baker, *Miranda: Crime, Law and Politics* (New York: Atheneum, 1985).

R. H. Helmholz et al., *The Privilege against Self-Incrimination: Its Origins and Development* (Chicago: University of Chicago Press, 1997).

Richard A. Leo and George C. Thomas III, *The Miranda Debate: Law, Justice and Policing* (Boston: Northeastern University Press, 1998).

USEFUL WEB SITES

American Civil Liberties Union

http://www.aclu.org/

Information on criminal justice, the death penalty, and other topics from a liberal/individual rights–oriented perspective.

Cato Institute

http://www.cato.org/index.html

Publications and reports on criminal justice topics from a conservative/libertarian perspective.

ENDNOTES

1. See, e.g., George Seibel, *Enlightened Police Questioning: Interviewing, Interrogation and Investigation* (Mesilla, N.M.: Prairie Avenue Press, 2003); and Charles E. O'Hara and Gregory O'Hara, *Fundamentals of Criminal Investigation,* 5th ed. (Springfield, Ill.: Charles C. Thomas, 1988).

2. Human Rights Watch, *Shielded from Justice: Police Brutality and Accountability in the United States* (New York: Human Rights Watch, 1998); and Malcolm Holmes, "Minority Threat and Police Brutality: Determinants of Civil Rights Criminal Complaints in U.S. Municipalities," *Criminology* 38, no. 2 (2000): 343–67.

3. See Steven A. Drizin and Richard A. Leo, "The Problem of False Confessions in the Post-DNA World," *North Carolina Law Review* 82 (2004): 891.

4. Stacey M. Studnicki and John P. Apol, "Witness Detention and Intimidation: The History and Future of Material Witness Law," *St. John's Law Review* 76 (2002): 483–533.

5. Amanda H. Frost, "Updating the Marital Privileges: A Witness-Centered Rationale," *Wisconsin Women's Law Journal* 14 (1999): 1–44.

6. R. H. Helmholz, "Introduction," in R. H. Helmholz et al., *The Privilege against Self-Incrimination: Its Origins and Development* (Chicago: University of Chicago Press, 1997), 1.

7. John H. Langbein, *Torture and the Law of Proof: Europe and England in the Ancien Régime* (Chicago: University of Chicago Press, 1977); and Edward Peters, *Torture* (Oxford: Basil Blackwell, 1985).

8. Richard S. Frase, "Review Essay: The Search for the Whole Truth about American and European Criminal Justice" (review of William T. Pizzi, *Trials without Truth* [New York: New York University Press, 1999]), *Buffalo Criminal Law Review* 3 (2000): 785–849.

9. "Project: Twenty-fifth Annual Review of Criminal Procedure," *Georgetown Law Journal* 84 (1996): 641, 1212–13 (footnotes omitted).

10. Steven D. Clymer, "Are Police Free to Disregard *Miranda?*" *Yale Law Journal* 112 (2002): 447–552, 468–69 (footnotes omitted).

11. Charles H. Whitebread and Christopher Slobogin, *Criminal Procedure: An Analysis of Cases and Concepts,* 4th ed. (New York: Foundation Press, 2000), 379.

12. Laura Mansnerus, "Questions Rise Over Imprisoning Sex Offenders Past Their Terms," *New York Times,* November 17, 2003.

13. "Project: Twenty-ninth Annual Review of Criminal Procedure," *Georgetown Law Journal* 88 (2000), 879, 1431–32 (footnotes omitted, emphasis added).

14. P. W. Valentine, "Woman, Jailed for Contempt, Freed After 7 Years; Md. Mother Failed to Reveal Son's Location," *Washington Post,* November 1, 1995; and "Mother Ends 7-Year Jail Stay, Still Silent about Missing Child," *New York Times,* November 2, 1995.

15. Delmar Karlen, *Anglo-American Criminal Justice* (New York: Oxford University Press, 1967), 121; and David J. Bodenhamer, *Fair Trial: Rights of the Accused in American History* (New York: Oxford University Press, 1992), 53–4. Some scholars suggest that the rule excluding the admission of coerced confessions at trial may have had an organic connection with the privilege against self-incrimination; see Lawrence Herman, "The Unexplored Relationship between the Privilege against Compulsory Self-Incrimination and the Involuntary Confession Rule," *Ohio State Law Journal* 53 (1992): 101–209, 497–553.

16. Karlen, *Anglo-American Criminal Justice,* 122.

17. See Samuel Walker, *Popular Justice: A History of American Criminal Justice* (New York: Oxford University Press, 1980), 173–75, 189, 231. Richard Leo, *Police Interrogation in America: A Study of Violence, Civility, and Social Change* (unpublished Ph.D. diss., University of California at Berkeley, 1995), 12–66, examined the third degree and suggested that the practice declined because of

increasing police professionalism, changing attitudes, and changes in legal doctrine.

18. Bodenhamer, *Fair Trial,* 101.

19. Richard C. Cortner, *The Supreme Court and the Second Bill of Rights* (Madison: University of Wisconsin Press, 1981), 150.

20. "Note: Developments in the Law of Confessions," *Harvard Law Review* 79 (1966): 935, 963–83.

21. Fred P. Graham, *The Due Process Revolution: The Warren Court's Impact on Criminal Law* (New York: Hayden, 1970), 154.

22. Graham, *The Due Process Revolution,* 155.

23. Graham, *The Due Process Revolution,* 153–93; Liva Baker, *Miranda: Crime, Law and Politics* (New York: Atheneum, 1985).

24. Baker, *Miranda,* 191–94, 408–9.

25. Herman, "The Unexplored Relationship," 101–209, 497–553.

26. Politicians and police officials sharply criticized the liberal majority that decided *Miranda.* Richard Nixon denounced *Miranda* and the liberal Warren Court in his 1968 presidential campaign, and as president he appointed four conservatives to the Court (Chief Justice Burger and Justices Blackmun, Powell, and Rehnquist) after three liberals and one conservative retired (Chief Justice Warren and Justices Black, Harlan, and Fortas), creating a pro-prosecution, centrist-to-conservative Court. See Baker, *Miranda,* 221–324, 346; and C. M. Lamb and S. C. Halpern, eds., *The Burger Court: Political and Judicial Profiles* (Urbana: University of Illinois Press, 1991).

27. The issue was raised by a leading conservative scholar, Joseph D. Grano, *Confessions, Truth and the Law* (Ann Arbor: University of Michigan Press, 1993), 173–222, who felt that *Miranda* should be overruled. See Yale Kamisar, *Police Interrogation and Confessions: Essays in Law and Policy* (Ann Arbor: University of Michigan Press, 1980). Both sides are presented in Richard A. Leo and George C. Thomas III, eds., *The Miranda Debate: Law, Justice and Policing* (Boston: Northeastern University Press, 1998).

28. The interrogation occurred before *Miranda* was decided, but the trial took place after the *Miranda* decision. Therefore, the *Miranda* ruling applied to this case.

29. The moving force behind the appeal invoking Section 3501, which federal prosecutors had studiously avoided for three decades, was the passionate advocacy of Paul Cassell, then a law professor, who mounted a crusade to overturn *Miranda.* See George C. Thomas and Richard Leo, "The Effects of *Miranda v. Arizona:* 'Embedded' in Our National Culture?" *Crime and Justice: A Review of Research* 29 (2002): 203–71, 264; and Roger Parloff, "*Miranda* on the Hot Seat," *New York Times Magazine,* September 26, 1999, who describes Professor Cassell as "an indefatigable, ideologically driven young law professor at the University of Utah" who has made a career of trying to get the courts to use Section 3501 to overrule *Miranda.* "For seven years, Cassell filed such briefs in one or two cases a year, primarily in the District of Utah or in the Fourth Circuit. These were his current and former stomping grounds and two of the most inviting venues legally, based on controlling Federal precedents in those regions."

30. Richard Harris, *The Fear of Crime* (New York: Praeger, 1969), 58.

31. Arnold H. Loewy, "Police-Obtained Evidence and the Constitution: Distinguishing Unconstitutionally Obtained Evidence from Unconstitutionally Used Evidence," *Michigan Law Review* 87 (1989): 907–39, 926: "[T]he fifth amendment does not contain an exclusionary rule; it is itself an exclusionary rule."

32. Charles D. Weisselberg, "Saving Miranda," *Cornell Law Review* 84 (1998): 109–92, citing Devallis Rutledge, *Questioning "Outside Miranda," Did You Know . . .* (Sacramento: California District Attorneys Association, June 1995), 133; M. Zalman, "The Coming Paradigm Shift on *Miranda:* The Impact of *Chavez v. Martinez,*" *Criminal Law Bulletin* 39 (2003): 334–52; and M. Zalman, "Reading the Tea Leaves of *Chavez v. Martinez:* The Future of *Miranda,*" *Criminal Law Bulletin* 40, no. 4 (2004): 299–368.

33. *Weeks v. Angelone,* 176 F.3d 249 (4th Cir. 1999).

34. See *Gauger v. Hendle,* 2002 U.S. Dist. LEXIS 18002 (U.S. Dist. Ct. N.D. Ill. 2002).

35. It was not the same Colson in the *Massiah* case.

36. Alan M. Dershowitz, "Is There a Torturous Road to Justice?" *Los Angeles Times,* November 8, 2001; Barry Gewin, "Thinking the Unthinkable," *New York Times Book Review,* September 15, 2002 (reviewing Alan M. Dershowitz, *Terrorism Works* [New Haven: Yale University Press, 2002]); and Seth Kreimer, "Too Close to the Rack and the Screw: Constitutional Constraints on Torture in the War on Terror," *University of Pennsylvania Journal of Constitutional Law* 6 (2003): 278–325.

37. Dana Priest and Barton Gellman, "U.S. Decries Abuse but Defends Interrogations; 'Stress and Duress' Tactics Used on Terrorism Suspects Held in Secret Overseas Facilities," *Washington Post,* December 26, 2002; and Michael Hirsh and Mark Hosenball, "The White House: The Politics of Torture," *Newsweek,* September 25, 2006.

38. John T. Parry, "What Is Torture, Are We Doing It, and What If We Are?" *University of Pittsburgh Law Review* 64 (2003): 237–62.

39. Parry, "What Is Torture?" 2, n. 25, citing *Ireland v. United Kingdom,* App. No. 5310/71, 2 Eur. H.R. Rep. 25 (1980) (Eur. Court of H.R.).

40. See Parry, "What Is Torture?" 243 No. 10, Convention against Torture and Other Cruel, Inhuman or Degrading Treatment or Punishment (1984), available at http://www.un.org/documents/ga/res/39/a39r046.htm (accessed January 24, 2007).

41. Jordan J. Paust, "Executive Plans and Authorizations to Violate International Law Concerning Treatment and Interrogation of Detainees," *Columbia Journal of Transnational Law* 43 (2005): 811–63, 823.

42. Parry, "What Is Torture?" 249–50.

43. Alan M. Dershowitz, "Reply: Torture without Visibility and Accountability Is Worse Than with It," *University of Pennsylvania Journal of Constitutional Law* 6 (2003): 326.

44. Mirko Bagaric and Julie Clarke, "Not Enough Official Torture in the World? The Circumstances in Which Torture Is Morally Justifiable," *University of San Francisco Law Review* 39 (2005): 581–616; and Parry, "What Is Torture?" 258–60.

45. Christopher Hitchens, "In Case Anyone's Forgotten: Torture Doesn't Work," *The Guardian* (London), November 14, 2001.

46. Philip N. S. Rumney, "Is Coercive Interrogation of Terrorist Suspects Effective? A Response to Bagaric and Clarke," *University of San Francisco Law Review* 40 (2006): 479–513, 512.

47. Rumney, "Coercive Interrogation."

48. Josh White, "Documents Tell of Brutal Improvisation by GIs," *Washington Post,* August 3, 2005.

49. Rumney, "Coercive Interrogation," 493.

50. Parry, "What Is Torture?" 26–62.

51. R. Jeffrey Smith, "McCain Names Practices Detainee Bill Would Bar; Senator Says 3 Interrogation Methods Are among the 'Extreme Measures' the Plan Would Outlaw," *Washington Post,* September 25, 2006.

52. Joe Conason, "Opponents of Torture Are True Patriots," *New York Observer,* September 25, 2006. The full text of the press conference can be found at http://www.globalsecurity.org/security/library/news/2006/09/sec-060906-dod02.htm (accessed January 24, 2007).

53. Sebastian Rotella, "The Enemies in Their Midst; Europe Confronts Suspected Terrorists Home-Grown and Inspired Abroad," *Los Angeles Times,* September 5, 2006.

54. *United States v. Usama Bin Laden,* 132 F.Supp.2d 168, 185–86, 187 (S.D.N.Y. 2001).

55. *United States v. Usama Bin Laden,* 132 F.Supp.2d 168, 188 (S.D.N.Y. 2001).

56. *United States v. Usama Bin Laden,* 132 F.Supp.2d 168, 188 (S.D.N.Y. 2001).

57. Benjamin Weiser, "Four Are Sentenced to Life in Prison in 1998 U.S. Embassy Bombing," *New York Times,* October 19, 2001. The jury had voted nine to three for the death sentence; execution required a unanimous verdict of death.

58. T. Jacoby, "Fighting Crime by the Rules," *Newsweek,* July 18, 1988, reviewing R. Uviller, *Tempered Zeal.*

59. Leo, *Police Interrogation in America,* 335.

60. Leo, *Police Interrogation in America,* 336–42.

61. Richard A. Leo and Welsh S. White, "Adapting to *Miranda:* Modern Interrogators' Strategies for Dealing with the Obstacles Posed by *Miranda,*" *Minnesota Law Review* 84 (1999): 397–472, 402, n. 18 lists some of the early studies.

62. Leo, *Police Interrogation in America,* 258–68, 276–77. Leo's dissertation has been published in several articles: "Inside the Interrogation Room," *Journal of Criminal Law and Criminology* 86 (1996): 266–303; and "Miranda's Revenge: Police Interrogation as a Confidence Game," *Law and Society Review* 30 (1996): 259–88.

63. Leo, *Police Interrogation in America,* 271.

64. Leo, *Police Interrogation in America,* 191.

65. Leo, *Police Interrogation in America,* 212–20.

66. Leo and White, "Adapting to *Miranda,*" 431–47.

67. P. W. Lewis and H. E. Allen, "'Participating *Miranda*': An Attempt to Subvert Certain Constitutional Safeguards," *Crime and Delinquency* 23, no. 2 (1977): 75–80.

68. See Leo, *Police Interrogation in America,* 230–51; and D. Simon, *Homicide: A Year on the Killing Streets* (Boston: Houghton Mifflin, 1991).

69. Weisselberg, "Saving *Miranda,*"; and Leo and White, "Adapting to *Miranda,*" 447–50.

70. Leo, *Police Interrogation in America,* 354.

71. Leo, *Police Interrogation in America,* 357–59.

72. Leo, *Police Interrogation in America,* 359–60.

73. Leo, *Police Interrogation in America,* 361–63.

74. Leo, *Police Interrogation in America,* 416.

75. Richard Leo, "The Impact of *Miranda* Revisited," *Journal of Criminal Law and Criminology* 86 (1996): 621–92, 683–84, relying on William A. Geller, *Videotaping Interrogations and Confessions* (U.S. Department of Justice, March 1993).

76. Richard A. Leo and Richard J. Ofshe, "The Consequences of False Confessions: Deprivations of Liberty and Miscarriages of Justice in the Age of Psychological Interrogation," *Journal of Criminal Law and Criminology* 88 (1998): 429–96.

77. Richard A. Leo and Richard J. Ofshe, "Missing the Forest for the Trees: A Response to Paul Cassell's 'Balanced Approach' to the False Confession Problem," *Denver University Law Review* 74 (1997): 1135.

78. In Jim Dwyer, Peter Neufeld, and Barry Scheck, *Actual Innocence* (New York: Doubleday, 2000), 78–106. The law professors who operate the "innocence project" list false confessions as one of several problems that contribute to what DNA testing has disclosed is a major problem of convicting the innocent.

79. Richard J. Ofshe and Richard A. Leo, "The Decision to Confess Falsely: Rational Choice and Irrational Action," *Denver University Law Review* 74 (1997): 979–1122.

80. Ofshe and Leo, "The Decision to Confess Falsely," 997–1000.

81. Ofshe and Leo, "The Decision to Confess Falsely," 986–94.

82. The information on the Sawyer case is derived from a 292-page transcript of the police interrogation. The secondary sources used that reprinted parts of the transcript are found in "Readings: [Transcript] True Confession?"

Harper's, October 1989, 17–201; and Philip Weiss, "Untrue Confessions," *Mother Jones,* September 1989, 18–24+.

83. The lie detector examination was given during the evening when he was under great stress. A later polygraph examination indicated that Sawyer's denial of the murder was truthful.

84. Leo and Ofshe, "Missing the Forest," n. 49.

85. Ofshe and Leo, "The Decision to Confess Falsely," 1119–20, n. 51.

JUSTICES OF THE SUPREME COURT

Enduring Liberals: Brennan and Marshall

When William Brennan was appointed by President Dwight Eisenhower and Thurgood Marshall by President Lyndon Johnson, the Supreme Court was representative of the ascendant liberal ideology of the day. Their backgrounds, experiences, and beliefs about the Court's role well suited them to play a part in expanding the rights of society's outcasts. As justices with long tenures, their careers coincided with the long swing of the political pendulum, from liberal to conservative, that has marked American politics since the 1960s. The careers of Justices Brennan and Marshall exemplify an important institutional aspect of the Supreme Court: Presidents nominate individuals who represent the political aspirations of the day, but with life tenure, justices who sit for several decades can extend their philosophies over time. This places the Court somewhat above the political passions of the period and offers a form of stability. The disadvantage is that at times it makes the Court unresponsive to the needs and demands of the polity.

The resignation of Justices Arthur Goldberg and Abe Fortas and Chief Justice Earl Warren between 1965 and 1969 led to a change in the Court's composition that reflected and possibly accelerated a shift toward conservatism on some issues. This has persisted since 1970, as the ten nominees of Republican Presidents Richard Nixon, Gerald Ford, Ronald Reagan, and George H. W. Bush moved the Court progressively to the right. Democratic President Jimmy Carter had no opportunity to nominate a justice, and President Clinton carefully selected moderate rather than liberal justices.

Thus for two decades, Justices Brennan and Marshall, the enduring liberals, penned more than a normal share of dissents in many criminal procedure cases. At times, their dissents expressed outrage and dire warnings that the conservative justices were subverting constitutional rights. Less frequently, they joined with at least three moderate justices to rule in favor of the defendant. For the most part, their dissents after 1970 were written not so much for the present but for the future, in the hope that a new generation of justices would be more open to defendants' claims.

Collection of the Supreme Court of the United States. Photographer: Robert Oakes.

William J. Brennan Jr.

New Jersey, 1906–1997

Democrat

Appointed by Dwight Eisenhower

Years of Service: 1956–1990

Life and Career.   The son of an Irish immigrant who became a political leader in Newark, New Jersey, noted for integrity and efficiency, William Brennan grew up in comfortable circumstances. He graduated from the Wharton School of the University of Pennsylvania with honors and was in the top 10 percent of his class at Harvard Law School in 1931. He practiced law with a prestigious Newark firm that specialized in labor issues for corporate clients. During World War II, he was a labor productivity troubleshooter for the undersecretary of war, rising to the rank of colonel. After the war, he became associated with the judicial reform efforts of New Jersey's renowned Chief Justice Arthur Vanderbilt and, as a result, was appointed a trial judge. As an associate justice of the New Jersey Supreme Court, Brennan came to the attention of U.S. Attorney General Brownell at a conference on judicial administration, where he sat in for Vanderbilt. The next year, when a vacancy appeared on the Court, Brennan fit the political requirements for the job: He was a Catholic, an easterner, and a nominal Democrat acceptable to Republicans. The only senator to vote against his confirmation to the Supreme Court was Joseph McCarthy, the demagogic Communist hunter who may have been angered by Brennan's earlier public criticism of "McCarthyism."

Contribution to Criminal Procedure.   Justice Brennan wrote few criminal procedure majority opinions in the 1960s, although he consistently voted for incorporation and defendants' rights. Under a more conservative Court, he authored many criminal procedure dissents, including *United States v. Leon* (1984) (good faith exception to exclusionary rule), *Illinois v. Gates* (1983) (abolishing the *Spinelli* two-pronged test for reliability of informant), *United States v. Calandra* (1974) (use of illegally obtained evidence in grand jury is constitutional), *Florida v. Riley* (1989) (helicopter overflights not a search subject to Fourth Amendment warrant requirement), *Hampton v. United States* (1976) (no entrapment if government agent supplies illegal drug), *Michigan v. Mosley* (1975) (reinterrogation allowed after a suspect claims right to silence), *United States v. Ash* (1973) (*Wade* lineup rule does not apply to photographic identification), and *Kuhlman v. Wilson* (1986) (passive jail informant does not violate a suspect's right to counsel under the *Massiah* doctrine).

In many dissents, he was outspokenly critical of the majority, often accusing it of ignoring facts or twisting precedent simply to arrive at a desired outcome—the same charge of result-oriented jurisprudence that was hurled at the activist Warren Court during the 1960s. In reaction to the curtailment of defendants' rights, Justice Brennan called on state court judges to apply their own state constitutions to afford more rights to suspects than were granted under the current reading of the Bill of Rights. This indeed has been a growing trend and is an ironic twist for a justice who championed federal rights in the 1960s.

Signature Opinion.   Dissenting opinion in *Illinois v. Gates* (1983). In this tour de force, Justice Brennan directly attacked the ideological basis of the conservative Court's criminal procedure rulings as "code words for an overly permissive attitude toward police practices in derogation of the rights secured by the Fourth Amendment."

Assessment.   Justice Brennan was called "a towering figure in modern law who embodied the liberal vision of the Constitution as an engine of social and political change," and many commentators referred to the Warren Court as the "Brennan Court," so great was the influence of his prolific opinions and his ability to gain majorities for his opinions. He strongly influenced all the major areas of the Warren Court's liberal agenda, including free speech, free press, separation of church and state, voting apportionment, school busing, and criminal procedure.

Further Reading

Kim Isaac Eisler, *Justice for All: William J. Brennan, Jr., and the Decisions That Transformed America* (New York: Simon and Schuster, 1993).

Collection of the Supreme Court of the United States. Photographer: Joseph Lavenburg.

Thurgood Marshall

New York, 1908–1993

Democrat

Appointed by Lyndon Johnson

Years of Service: 1967–1991

Life and Career.   Marshall had one of the most distinguished and significant legal careers in American constitutional history. Born in Baltimore into a middle-class family, this great-grandson of a slave graduated from Lincoln University (Chester, Pennsylvania) and was first in his class at Howard University Law School. From 1933 to 1938, he was the counsel for the National Association for the Advancement of Colored People (NAACP) in Baltimore, and from 1938 to 1960, he was the chief counsel of the Legal Defense Fund, the legal organization spun off from the NAACP to defend the civil rights of African Americans in a then legally segregated society. He led the legal battle to overturn segregation laws and thus played a central role in the civil rights movement. He appeared before the Supreme Court thirty-two times and won thirteen of the sixteen cases in which he was the principal attorney. His most significant victories were *Shelly v. Kramer* (1948), which declared restrictive covenants on real estate deeds unenforceable in the courts, and *Brown v. Board of Education* (1954), the most important case of the twentieth century, which overturned the "separate but equal doctrine" and outlawed school segregation. In 1961, President John F. Kennedy named Marshall to the Court of Appeals for the Second Circuit, and in 1965, President Johnson named him as the solicitor general, the chief federal attorney to argue cases before the Supreme Court. Two years later, Marshall was appointed to the Court.

Contribution to Criminal Procedure.　As the Court moved steadily to the right after 1970, Justice Marshall, along with Justice Brennan and on occasion Justices Harry Blackmun and John Paul Stevens, dissented in most criminal procedure cases. His opinions were often trenchant and eloquent denunciations of what he saw as the conservative majority's oppressive misreading of the Bill of Rights and its attempt to dismantle constitutional protections. In *Schneckloth v. Bustamonte* (1973) (knowledge of rights not required to give valid consent to search), for example, he stated, "I have difficulty in comprehending how a decision made without knowledge of available alternatives can be treated as a choice at all."

　　Along with Justice Brennan, he held that the death penalty is a flat violation of the cruel and unusual punishment clause of the Eighth Amendment and voted to overturn each capital punishment case, a position adopted by Justice Blackmun a few months before his retirement. On occasion, he wrote a majority opinion for a unanimous Court, as in the ruling that a brief roadside stop of a motorist for a traffic violation does not constitute the kind of custodial interrogation that triggers the need for *Miranda* warnings (*Berkemer v. McCarty,* 1984).

Signature Opinion.　Concurring opinion in *Batson v. Kentucky* (1986). Although the Court's majority issued a "liberal" decision, that the exclusion of a juror on account of race in a single trial could be challenged, Marshall moved beyond the frontiers of the decision and argued that the use of peremptory challenges during voir dire perpetuates the potential for discrimination and should be eliminated altogether.

Assessment.　Marshall was a staunch supporter of civil rights. He consistently voted throughout the Burger Court era and into the Rehnquist Court era to uphold liberal positions that were staked out during the 1960s. He dissented powerfully in cases that limited the scope of school integration orders to districts that had practiced deliberate discrimination. Marshall was often an engaging, blunt, and humorous speaker, but he issued critical dissents and was sharply critical of his successor on the bench, Clarence Thomas. Nevertheless, Thurgood Marshall exuded great warmth and, when he retired, was praised by his colleagues. Even those who did not agree with him respected his convictions, accomplishments, and fierce candor.

Further Reading

Michael E. Davis and Hunter R. Clark, *Thurgood Marshall: Warrior at the Bar, Rebel on the Bench*, rev. ed. (New York: Citadel Press, 1994).

Glossary

Absolute immunity   Rule that a party need not answer in law to civil claim or wrongdoing, based on the function the party has performed; applies to witnesses in regard to their testimony, judges performing judicial duties, and prosecutors performing essential prosecutorial duties. Immunity is claimed before trial in a motion for summary judgment.

Abuse of discretion   A high standard for an appellate court to reverse the decision of a lower court where the trial court was lawfully invested with discretion. It does not imply an intentional wrong or act of bad faith, just that the exercise of discretion was clearly against logic.

Accusatorial trial   The type of trial that is at the heart of the Anglo-American or common-law system of adjudication. Key elements: the judge is an impartial referee; lawyers control the presentation of evidence; witnesses are cross-examined; innocence is presumed; the prosecutor must prove guilt beyond a reasonable doubt; the privilege against self-incrimination protects the defendant from testifying; facts are conclusively determined by a citizen jury.

Actual border   For purposes of border search cases, stops that are made at or very near to the actual border between the United States and a neighboring nation. Border searches may also take place further inland, either at fixed checkpoints or by roving patrols.

Actual imprisonment   Counsel is an absolute Sixth Amendment requirement for the trial of a misdemeanor only if the defendant has been actually imprisoned after conviction.

Actual mobility   The automobile exception to the search warrant requirement applies to vehicles that are actually capable of being driven.

Ad hoc   Literally, "for this." For a special purpose without application to a general purpose. For example, an *ad hoc* rule is intended to apply to only the particular circumstances at hand and is not intended to be a general rule.

Adequate and independent state grounds   A state court ruling concerning the rights of a suspect that is based exclusively on state constitutional grounds cannot be disturbed by a federal court as long as the state constitutional ruling does not fall below the minimum standards of the Fourteenth Amendment Due Process Clause. To determine whether a state ruling is based on state or federal grounds, where the ruling discussed both federal and state law, the Supreme Court examines it to determine if the holding is based on adequate and independent state grounds. See also *judicial federalism.*

Adjudicate   To judge a case; to resolve an issue in the exercise of judicial authority.

Administrative search   The entry and search of a premises by a government officer who is enforcing a government regulation regarding public health or safety rather than a police search for people or items in relation to the enforcement of the criminal law.

Admission   Statements made by a party that acknowledge the existence of certain facts. Compare *confession.*

Adversarial trial   See *accusatorial trial.*

Adverse comment   A comment by the judge or prosecutor to a jury in a criminal case, pointing out that the defendant did not take the witness stand.

Advisory opinion   An opinion issued by a court at the request of the government or a party indicating how it would rule on an issue were it to arise in litigation. Some state supreme courts issue advisory opinions. The U.S. Supreme Court does not issue such opinions because its jurisdiction is limited by Article III, Section 2, of the Constitution to "cases and controversies."

Affiant   The person who makes and subscribes an affidavit.

Affidavit   A written declaration or statement of facts made voluntarily and confirmed by oath before a person with the authority to take such an oath.

Affirm   To uphold the ruling of a lower court.

Agent provocateur   Police undercover agent who infiltrates a criminal or a legitimate organization with the intention of stimulating members of the organization to commit illegal or violent acts.

Anticipatory warrant   A search warrant authorized by the Federal Rules of Criminal Procedure that may be issued on probable cause that evidence will be located in a particular place on the date of execution. See *controlled delivery.*

Antifederalists   Those opposed to the ratification of the Constitution in 1788 on the grounds that it created too much central power.

Appearance bond   See *bail bond.*

Appellate decision   The outcome of an appellate court trial; an appellate court may affirm, modify, reverse, and remand the decisions of a lower court.

Appellate opinion   See *opinion.*

Appointed counsel   A lawyer for an indigent defendant, appointed by the court on an informal basis through organized lists established by a local bar association or by the court. The lawyer is paid by the county according to a fee schedule for work performed. Also called "assigned counsel."

Arraignment   The procedure whereby a defendant is brought before a court to plead to a criminal charge.

Arrest   To deprive a person of liberty by legal authority; an arrest occurs in law when a person is taken into custody by government officers, even if the purpose is for investigation or harassment. It is not necessary for a booking to occur for an arrest to be made. An arrest may be made with or without a warrant.

Arrest warrant Judicial warrant concluding that probable cause exists supporting the belief that a crime has been committed, and that the named person has committed it, and authorizing law enforcement to take the suspect into custody. An arrest warrant is required, except for an exigency, if officers must enter the home of the person to be arrested.

Asset forfeiture Laws that authorize the forfeiture of noncontraband assets used in and money derived from the commission of certain crimes. The assets may be seized as of the time the crime was committed and thus be denied to lawyers representing defendants whose assets are forfeited.

Assigned counsel See *appointed counsel.*

Assizes General trial courts in England and France.

Attenuation An exception to the "fruits of the poisonous tree" doctrine. It comes into play when the link between the initial illegality and the evidence sought to be introduced has become so weak or tenuous that the "fruits" have become "untainted."

Authorized imprisonment A position that counsel should be absolutely guaranteed by the Sixth Amendment in all misdemeanor trials where the statutory penalty allows for imprisonment. This rule was rejected by the Supreme Court.

Automobile search An exception to the requirement that a search of an effect be authorized in advance by a judicial search warrant, based on the exigency of a mobile vehicle and on the lower expectation of privacy accorded to automobiles. The officer must have probable cause to believe there is contraband in the automobile. Also called the "vehicle exception."

Bail To procure the release of a person charged with a crime by ensuring his or her further attendance in court; this is done by having the person pledge or deposit something of value that will be returned when he or she appears in court and/or by having a third party agree to be responsible for the return of the person.

Bail bond A bond (an "instrument" or written promise to pay money) that is executed by a third party promising to forfeit money to the court if the defendant who is released on bail does not appear for further criminal proceedings. Also called an "appearance bond."

Bail bondsman A businessperson who receives a portion of the bail amount from a defendant, usually 10 percent, and posts a bail bond with the court promising to pay the full bail amount if the defendant does not return to court as required. The bail bondsman is responsible for ensuring the appearance of the defendant in court.

Balancing of interests See *balancing test.*

Balancing test A widely used phrase in criminal procedure, especially in Fourth Amendment adjudication, referring to the attempt of appellate courts to balance the needs of effective law enforcement against the privacy rights of individuals.

Beeper An electronic device that emits a signal indicating its location. It may be used by agents to track the movement of a vehicle or object.

Bench In law, a term for the court or the judge. For an appellate court, the bench consists of all the judges on the court or who are sitting on a panel of the court.

Bench trial A trial without a jury. The judge (who sits on the "bench") is the trier of both the facts and the law. In a jury trial, on the other hand, the judge is the finder only of legal issues, and the jury is the finder of the facts. Also called "waiver trial."

Bill of attainder A special act of a legislature passing the death penalty or other penalty on a person without recourse to standard judicial proceedings. In England, attainder led to the entire estate of a person convicted of a felony or treason being forfeited to the Crown. The U.S. Constitution (Art. I, §§ 9 and 10) forbids the federal government and the states from passing bills of attainder.

Bill of particulars A form of discovery in which the prosecution sets forth the time, place, manner, and means of the commission of the crime as alleged in the complaint or indictment.

Bill of Rights A designation for the first ten amendments to the U.S. Constitution.

Bind-over decision The decision of the judge, at the conclusion of the preliminary examination, as to whether there is sufficient evidence to establish probable cause that the defendant committed the crime and to "bind the defendant over,"—that is, to require him or her to go to trial.

Bivens suit A federal tort suit by a person against federal officers alleged to have violated the person's Fourth Amendment rights; created in *Bivens v. Six Unknown Named Agents* (1971).

Body cavity search Procedure whereby authorized law enforcement or correctional personnel conduct a visual inspection of oral, genital, or anal areas for contraband. Also called "strip search."

Booking An administrative process conducted by police officials that typically follows an arrest and includes recording the suspect's name and identifying information; photographing, fingerprinting, and searching the suspect; and inventorying the suspect's personal property.

Border The international boundary of a nation. For purposes of law, immigration, and customs searches, the border includes international airports, inland ports, and fixed checkpoints remote from the actual boundary.

Border search A search at the national border by immigration officers for illegal immigrants and by customs officers for contraband, criminals, fugitives, and terrorists.

Brevity requirement A rule under *Terry v. Ohio* (1968) that a "stop and frisk" be concluded quickly, or in just enough time for an officer to confirm or dispel whether the officer's reasonable suspicion constitutes probable cause. The brevity requirement has been strictly interpreted by the Supreme Court.

Brief A written argument presented to a trial or appellate court by a lawyer to support the attorney's position on legal issues. Briefs can be as long as fifty to one hundred pages. Appellate briefs are accompanied with the record on appeal and may include the trial transcript.

Briefing a case Taking notes that abstract the essential points of an opinion, especially the facts, legal issues, holding, and reasons for the holding.

Bright-line rule A clear-cut and easy-to-apply standard established by a court to distinguish legal categories.

Bug An electronic listening device that is placed surreptitiously to overhear conversations.

Burger Court The Supreme Court during the period that Warren Burger was Chief Justice of the United States (1969 to 1986); a moderately conservative period in criminal procedure.

Capital crime In common law, a crime punishable with death. Today, in some states, it includes crimes punishable with life imprisonment. Under the laws of some states, bail may be denied to defendants charged with capital crimes.

Case law See *common law.*

Case of first impression A law case in which the issue to be decided has never been resolved by an appellate court.

Caveat A warning to be careful.

Certiorari, writ of A writ used by the U.S. Supreme Court to determine in its discretion which filed cases it will hear and decide.

Challenge for cause In the voir dire, the ability of one of the sides to request the judge to dismiss a prospective juror because the juror has indicated a bias. The number of challenges for cause are unlimited.

Chancery English court established under the king's chancellor to do equity or to decide cases according to rules of justice rather than under formal writs of common law courts of Common Pleas and King's Bench. Over time, chancery courts became part of the common law court system. Common law courts render money judgments as legal remedies, whereas equity or chancery courts grant "equitable relief,"—i.e., orders requiring that a party perform or cease some activity. Most American states merged courts of law and equity; a few still have separate chancery or equity courts. Also called "equity."

Charging The process by which the prosecutor decides which offenses to formally prefer, or "charge," against a suspect in either a prosecutor's information or an indictment.

Checks and balances A political and constitutional doctrine for maintaining balanced government by giving different branches of government the power to limit the authority of other branches in specified ways. This doctrine is closely related to the separation of powers doctrine.

Citizen's arrest An arrest made by a person who is not a law enforcement officer. If the arrest is in error (i.e., no crime was committed or the wrong person was arrested), the citizen who made the arrest is subject to a civil suit for false arrest, even if probable cause existed.

Civil law system The legal system of the nations of Europe, Latin America, Africa, and Asia (except for England and former British colonies). The civil law system is found primarily in codes, and trials follow the inquisitorial model. It is contrasted to the common law system.

Civil rights function One of two broad functions of criminal procedure law: to protect the civil rights of suspects and defendants. Compare *facilitating function.*

Civil War amendments The Thirteenth, Fourteenth, and Fifteenth amendments to the Constitution, ratified in 1866, 1868, and 1870, respectively. Also called the "Reconstruction amendments."

Collateral proceeding Not a direct appeal from a conviction on a point of law, but instead a second "appeal," not of right. Habeas corpus proceedings are collateral proceedings.

Common law In England, America, and other common law countries (e.g., Australia, Canada, and India), law is created by judges through appellate court opinions. Also called "case law" or "precedent" because the rule established in one case becomes a binding precedent on later courts. The term arose because the law created by royal judges was common to all of England. Common law is subordinate to legislation.

Common law trial system See *accusatorial trial.*

Companion case A case decided along with another case. Companion cases may be consolidated into one case.

Compulsion A person is protected by the Fifth Amendment against being "compelled in any criminal case to be a witness against himself." The Fifth Amendment applies only if evidence is obtained by compulsion, as by a court order or a grand jury subpoena. Fifth Amendment compulsion in the law of confessions, under *Miranda,* is supplied by in-custody police interrogation, which is inherently compelling. See also *self-incrimination rule.*

Compulsory process A subpoena to produce witnesses or real evidence. The compulsory process is a right guaranteed to defendants by the Sixth Amendment.

Confession A statement made by one person to another, admitting guilt of an offense and disclosing facts about the crime and the person's role in it. A confession may include inculpatory or exculpatory statements. Compare *admission.*

Conflict of interest In regard to the right to counsel, a conflict of interest most typically arises when, as a result of multiple representation, an attorney must sacrifice a defense strategy for one defendant to better defend another defendant. See also *multiple representation.*

Confrontation Clause The provision of the Sixth Amendment that, in all criminal prosecutions, "the accused shall enjoy the right . . . to be confronted with the witnesses against him."

Consent The voluntary agreement of one person who has the capacity to make an agreement of free will to do an act proposed by another. In the administration of criminal justice, a suspect or defendant can consent to cooperate with police or prosecutors. More specifically, a person can consent to a search or seizure of an area over which the person has an expectation of privacy. See also *waiver.*

Consent search A search made by a police officer after a person has given consent to the search. Consent to search validates a warrantless search or a search made without probable cause.

Constitutionalism A political theory of balanced government. Modern constitutionalism includes the concepts of civil rights and the rule of law.

Constitutionally protected area Obsolete test to determine if the Fourth Amendment applies to protect a person whose privacy has been invaded by government officers; replaced by the "expectation of privacy" doctrine announced in *Katz v. United States* (1968).

Contempt of court An act calculated to embarrass, hinder, or obstruct a court in the administration of justice. A judge may punish contempt of court with a fine or imprisonment.

Continuance A delay in legal proceedings granted by the judge.

Contraband Any property that is illegal either to produce or to possess, such as controlled substances or untaxed, smuggled goods.

Controlled delivery A law enforcement technique by which contraband is intercepted and then delivered to the suspected criminal party under police surveillance. "Anticipatory warrants" may be issued in cases where controlled deliveries are set up.

Counsel   Lawyer. The term is used interchangeably with *lawyer, attorney,* and *attorney-at-law.*

Court of general jurisdiction   A trial court with jurisdiction to try all matters, including felonies; typically called a "superior" or "circuit court."

Court of limited jurisdiction   A trial court whose jurisdiction is limited by statute to certain matters— usually to civil cases where the amount in dispute is below a certain amount (e.g., $10,000), to the dispositions of misdemeanors, and to conducting the preliminary phases of a felony case before binding over the case to a court of general jurisdiction for trial.

Covert facilitation   See *encouragement.*

Crime control model   A theory developed by Herbert Packer that suggests that within a constitutional system of criminal justice, there are two general attitudes. The crime control model stresses crime control, efficiency, a presumption of guilt, and finality. Compare *due process model.*

Crime scene investigation exception   A Fourth Amendment exception, which the Supreme Court has refused to create, to allow police, without warrant, to remain beyond the time of the exigency, on the premises where a crime has been committed, for purposes of conducting an investigation of the premises.

Criminal law approach   In the law of entrapment, the majority rule, known also as the "subjective test." It is based on the legal fiction that the legislature did not intend the statute to apply to those who were not predisposed to commit the crime but were induced to do so by the police.

Criminal procedure approach   In regard to the law of entrapment, another term for the objective test, which is the minority rule of entrapment.

Critical stage   The point in criminal proceedings when counsel is constitutionally required because, at that point, rights may be lost, defenses waived, or privileges claimed or waived that can affect the outcome of the case.

Cross-examination   The examination of a witness at a trial or hearing by the party opposed to the side that produced the witness. Cross-examination occurs after direct examination and is used to test the truth of the witness, to further develop the evidence, or for other purposes.

Cruel trilemma   Three negative consequences faced by a witness who is asked a question that may prove to be incriminating: self-accusation, perjury, or the risk of being held in contempt of court for refusing to testify.

Curtilage   The area around a house protected by the Fourth Amendment. The curtilage includes the area under the eaves of the main house; within the fenced-in area around the house; and various small structures that are near the main house, such as a garage, shed, or smokehouse. Compare *open fields.*

Custodial arrest   When a police officer arrests a person for a crime that authorizes the officer to take the suspect into custody, the officer may perform a complete search incident to arrest

Custody   The keeping, guarding, care, watch, inspection, preservation, or security of a thing or person. The custody of a

person is a prerequisite for a Fourth Amendment seizure under *California v. Hodari D.* (1991).

Damages   Monetary compensation awarded by a court in a civil case to compensate a party for losses.

Decoy   In entrapment law, an officer who poses as a potential victim (usually of a crime of violence such as a street robbery) and waits to be attacked in order to arrest the perpetrator.

Deficient performance   The first prong of the rule that the ineffective assistance of counsel in a criminal trial violates the Sixth Amendment rights of the defendant. The deficient performance of an attorney is an objective standard determined by what constitutes reasonably effective assistance according to prevailing norms of legal practice.

De minimis   Shorthand for *de minimis non curat lex:* The law does not take notice of very small or trifling matters. In other words, a technical violation of a law that results in trifling or purely theoretical injury may not be recognized by a court.

Democracy   A political philosophy that emphasizes the participation of all citizens in government decisions on an equal basis, either directly or by representation. It is a value that underlies constitutional criminal procedure.

De novo **review**   A rehearing of an issue that does not take into consideration findings made at an earlier hearing.

De novo **trial**   See *trial de novo.*

Deposit bond   A bail bond that is executed by the defendant. Under the laws of several states, the defendant puts up 10 percent of the bail amount, which is returned, except for a 1 percent fee, when the defendant returns to court for the trial.

Derivative evidence   In the Fourth and Fifth amendment context, evidence that police obtain on the basis of illegally seized evidence. Under the "fruits of the poisonous tree" doctrine, derivative evidence must be excluded from trial and cannot be used to prove the guilt of the defendant.

Dictum   An abbreviated form of *obiter dictum:* a "remark by the way"—that is, a remark by a judge in an opinion, commenting on the legal rule of the case, that is not essential to the determination of the holding or decision and therefore does not have weight as precedent.

Discovery   A set of practices in both civil and criminal trial procedure that allows both sides to obtain factual evidence in the possession of the other side. Discovery is designed to encourage settlements or to prevent surprises at the trial so as to avoid delays.

Disgorgement   A theory of jurisprudence stating that a person who has wrongfully obtained goods should be made to give them up.

Disseised   In English and medieval land law, to be dispossessed of one's land. See also *novel disseisin.*

Diversity of citizenship jurisdiction   Article III of the Constitution allows federal courts to hear cases between "citizens" of different states.

Domestic tranquillity   A phrase in the Preamble to the Constitution of the United States. It recognizes that maintaining public safety is a fundamental purpose of government.

Dossier   French for "a bundle of papers"; a report on an individual.

Drug courier profile A set of behavioral characteristics developed by the Drug Enforcement Agency to identify people who are likely to be surreptitiously transporting illegal drugs. The profile itself, even if it consists entirely of innocent actions, constitutes a basis for finding that reasonable suspicion exists.

Due process approach In constitutional criminal procedure, a philosophy on the part of Supreme Court justices that errors in state criminal procedure that constitute grossly unfair and unjust proceedings can be reviewed by the federal courts under the Due Process Clause of the Fourteenth Amendment. The term also conveys the idea that a decision made under this approach does not necessarily produce bright-line rules because every case is decided on the totality of its facts and circumstances.

Due Process Clause A clause found in the Fifth and Fourteenth amendments saying that no person shall be deprived of life, liberty, or property without due process of law. The Fifth Amendment clause applies against the federal government, and the Fourteenth Amendment clause against state governments.

Due process defense In entrapment law, the theory that entrapment may be established by police conduct that was so outrageous as to violate the Due Process Clause.

Due process model One of two general attitudes within a constitutional system of criminal justice, as identified in a theory by Herbert Packer. The due process model stresses formal, adjudicative, adversary fact-finding, the prevention and elimination of mistakes, legal (as opposed to actual) guilt, and viewing the presumption of innocence to mean that every suspect must be treated as if he were innocent. Compare *crime control model.*

Due process revolution The period from 1961 to 1969 when most of the criminal provisions of the Bill of Rights were incorporated. See also *incorporation doctrine.*

Dying declaration In the law of evidence, an exception to the hearsay rule that allows a witness to testify to the statement of a dying person on the theory that a person who believes that he or she is about to die will not lie.

Egalitarianism A political theory that supports the eradication of legal and social distinctions between citizens. Egalitarianism is an ideal of American republicanism and has been a force behind the expansion of rights, such as the right of all citizens to serve on juries; it is a value that underlies constitutional criminal procedure. Also called "equality."

En banc An appellate case heard and decided by the entire appellate bench rather than by a panel of judges drawn from the entire bench.

Encouragement A police investigatory activity designed to create a criminal opportunity for offenders who commit crimes that are difficult to detect, but without inducing them to commit the crime. Compare *entrapment.*

Enhancement device A mechanism that is used to enhance the natural senses of a law enforcement officer to detect contraband. Enhancement devices may include flashlights, binoculars, and sophisticated electronic listening and thermal detection devices.

Entrapment An act of police officers or government agents inducing a person to commit a crime for the purpose of arresting and prosecuting the person. Also, a criminal defense. Compare *encouragement.*

Equality See *egalitarianism.*

Equal Protection Clause The guarantee in Section 1 of the Fourteenth Amendment that "[n]o state shall . . . deny to any person within its jurisdiction the equal protection of the laws." This right can be enforced by federal courts and by congressional legislation.

Equity See *chancery.*

Exclusionary rule A legal rule stating that illegally obtained evidence may not be used in legal proceedings. The exclusionary rule may be created by common law (e.g., to the exclusionary rule for coerced confessions), constitutional adjudication (e.g., the Fourth Amendment exclusionary rule established in *Weeks v. United States* [1914]), or by statute (e.g., the exclusionary rule for illegal electronic eavesdropping).

Exculpatory Tending to justify, excuse, or clear the defendant from alleged fault or guilt. Compare *inculpatory.*

Exigency Generally, an emergency requiring immediate action; something that is pressing or urgent. In Fourth Amendment law, an exigency is an emergency that gives rise to an exception to the warrant requirement.

Exigency exception In search and seizure law, police can intrude on areas and things normally protected by the expectation of privacy without a warrant when an emergency exists and the police intrusion or action is a reasonable response to the emergency.

Ex parte On one side only. A judicial hearing is *ex parte* when it occurs at the request of one party in the absence of the other party.

Expectation of privacy The basis for determining the existence of Fourth Amendment rights under *Katz v. United States* (1967).

Expert witness A witness who, by reason of specialized education or experience, possesses superior knowledge regarding a subject about which people having no particular training are incapable of forming an accurate opinion. A witness who is qualified as an expert is allowed to assist the jury in understanding complicated or technical subjects and may be allowed to answer hypothetical questions.

Ex post facto law A criminal law passed after the occurrence of an act that retrospectively changes the legal consequences by making an innocent act criminal, by increasing the penalty for the act, or by changing rules of evidence, making it easier to obtain a conviction. Article I, §§ 9 and 10, of the U.S. Constitution prohibits the federal and state governments from creating such laws.

Extraterritorial Beyond the physical and juridical boundaries of a particular state or nation. Laws may have extraterritorial effect.

Eyewitness A person who saw the act, fact, or transaction to which he or she testifies. An eyewitness may be distinguished from an ear-witness (*auritus*), but for purposes of the law of identification, similar rules apply.

Facial attack A legal challenge to the constitutionality of a statute "on its face," or in every way in which the statute may be applied. Statutes may also be challenged "as applied," a narrower attack claiming that the statute is unconstitutional only if applied in a certain way.

Facilitating function One of two broad functions of criminal procedure law: to facilitate prosecution. Compare *civil rights function.*

Fair cross section See *representative cross section.*

False arrest An arrest that is not based upon probable cause. Evidence seized as the result of a false arrest is inadmissible. A false arrest is a basis for a civil action against a peace officer who made the arrest.

Federalism The division and relationship of power between the state and federal governments.

Federalists Those favoring the ratification of the Constitution in 1788; those favoring a strong federal government. This group emerged as the political party of Presidents George Washington and John Adams; Chief Justice John Marshall was a prominent Federalist.

Field interrogation The police practice of ordering people to briefly stop and answer questions in regard to suspicious behavior.

Fixed checkpoint In border search law, a search of vehicles for illegal aliens at a fixed checkpoint on a road within one hundred air miles of the U.S. border. An investigative stop of a car slowed at such a point must be based on reasonable suspicion.

"Fleeing felon" rule A common law rule that allows a police officer to shoot to kill any fleeing felon, whether or not the felon had used deadly force. The rule was brought under the Fourth Amendment by *Tennessee v. Garner* (1985): An officer may now lawfully shoot at a fleeing felon only if the suspect is reasonably believed to be armed and dangerous.

Formal charge rule A rule stating that the right to counsel at a lineup or showup attaches only after the defendant has been formally charged with a crime. In these procedures, the Supreme Court has not applied the critical stage rule.

Formal charges The charges upon which the state intends to prosecute the defendant. A suspect is informally charged with an offense by a police officer's report or arrest warrant or other initial charging document issued by the magistrate after an initial appearance. Formal charges typically are found in a prosecutor's information that has been found by a magistrate to establish probable cause in a bind-over proceeding or in an indictment that has been voted on by a grand jury. Formal charges can only be amended with the approval of a court.

Formal rights In the history of the incorporation doctrine, prior to 1961 the designation of rights located in the Bill of Rights as "formal" (as opposed to "fundamental") meant that they were not incorporated into the Fourteenth Amendment Due Process Clause.

Framers The men involved in the drafting of the U.S. Constitution and the Bill of Rights. It is a narrower term than *founders,* which refers to the individuals who led the rebellion from England and helped to found the federal republic of the United States.

Frisk A colloquial term used to describe a police search of a person who is stopped. A frisk consists of a pat-down of the outer clothing to determine whether the person stopped has a weapon.

"Fruits of the poisonous tree" doctrine A Fourth Amendment doctrine stating that evidence derived from illegally seized evidence cannot be used by the prosecution. The doctrine applies to confessions if an otherwise valid confession is obtained from a suspect who is illegally detained.

Fundamental fairness A meaning attached to due process—i.e., a procedure violates due process if the procedure is deemed by a court to be fundamentally unfair. It is another way of stating the "due process approach," so that for a court to decide if a procedure is fundamentally unfair, it must examine the totality of the circumstances.

Fundamental rights test The test by which it is decided whether a right located in the Bill of Rights is to be incorporated into the Due Process Clause of the Fourteenth Amendment by a process of selective incorporation and made applicable to the states. A right that is "fundamental" must be incorporated, but one deemed "formal" need not.

General-reasonableness construction In Fourth Amendment jurisprudence, a conservative doctrine that emphasized the idea that the constitutionality of a search and seizure is to be decided by whether it is reasonable.

General warrant A search warrant without a limit. A general warrant violates the particularity requirement of the Fourth Amendment. The term was used at the time of the Revolution by Americans to describe the writs of assistance issued by colonial governors.

Grand jury A jury summoned to hear charges against those accused of crime to determine whether there is enough evidence for the accused to stand trial. The common law grand jury (i.e., the "large" jury) consists of twenty-three people and decides whether to indict by a majority vote.

Habeas corpus, writ of A judicial writ requiring that a person claiming illegal detention be brought to court forthwith to determine the legality of the detention.

Hearsay evidence A statement, other than one made by the declarant while testifying at the trial or hearing, offered in evidence to prove the truth of the matter asserted. In ordinary affairs, hearsay evidence may be reliable, but a hearsay statement cannot be subject to cross-examination. The general rule of evidence is that hearsay statements are not admissible, but there are numerous exceptions to the hearsay evidence rule.

Hierarchy of constitutional rights The Burger Court's rulings in criminal procedure have tended to be more supportive of Fifth and Sixth amendment rights in comparison to the Fourth Amendment, especially the Fourth Amendment exclusionary rule, which is treated as a right of lesser status.

Hierarchy of courts Courts may be ranked by their authority to declare precedent, with a supreme court establishing common law rules that must be followed by all courts "below" it, and an intermediate appellate court having such authority over trial courts.

Hierarchy of law The relative authority of law derives from the body that creates it; thus constitutional law is superior to legislation, which may in turn abolish or modify court-made common law.

Holding The legal principle to be drawn from the opinion or decision. In an appellate case, the holding includes the rule and the facts on which the decision rests.

Hot pursuit A common law right of a police officer to follow a felon across jurisdictional lines or to enter a house or other area protected by a Fourth Amendment expectation of privacy to make an arrest if the officer is in hot pursuit—that is, closely following the felon.

Human rights A special class of rights held by a person simply by virtue of being human; moral rights grounded in the equal moral dignity of each person that can and should be made legally binding in national, regional, or international law.

Hypothetical person test In entrapment law, an element of the "objective test," where the inducement offered by the government agent is so great as to persuade people other than those who are ready and willing to commit the crime.

Identification parade British term for a lineup.

Illegal arrest An arrest that is made by an officer who has no legal authority or jurisdiction to make such an arrest—e.g., where an officer arrests a person in a foreign state. Where a suspect is brought into the jurisdiction of a court on the basis of an illegal arrest, the court does not thereby lose jurisdiction to try the case.

Immunity In criminal law, a binding promise by the government, allowed by statute, to not prosecute a person in return for the person's testimony in another prosecution. Immunity is granted to override the person's privilege against self-incrimination. See also *transactional immunity* and *use immunity*.

Impaneling a jury A process whereby the clerk of court makes up a list of the jurors selected for a particular trial.

Impeach To challenge the truthfulness of a witness by presenting evidence that tends to contradict the testimony or to show that for some other reason the witness might have lied.

Impound To seize and take an item, such as an automobile, into the lawful custody of a court or law enforcement agency. An impoundment is a prelude to an inventory search, and the rules of many police departments require an inventory search following an impoundment.

In camera Hearings held in the judge's chamber, away from the public and the jury.

Incompetent evidence Evidence that is relevant to prove an issue but is not allowed to be used in the trial because of other policy considerations; generally, inadmissible evidence. Examples are hearsay or unconstitutionally seized evidence.

Incorporation by reference The method of making one document of any kind become a part of a separate document by referring to the former in the latter.

Incorporation doctrine The constitutional doctrine by which provisions of the Bill of Rights become "incorporated" (in a rough analogy to the legal concept of incorporation by reference) into the Fourteenth Amendment and thus made applicable to the states.

Incorporation plus The incorporation doctrine plus the ability of courts to apply the due process approach where a specific right in the Bill of Rights does not apply.

Inculpatory Tending to establish guilt or to incriminate. Compare *exculpatory*.

Independent source An exception to the "fruits of the poisonous tree" doctrine. It comes into play when the evidence in question also was obtained in a lawful manner via an independent source.

Index crime One of eight felonies counted by the FBI to construct a "crime index." The index crimes are murder or nonnegligent manslaughter, rape, robbery, aggravated assault, burglary, automobile theft, larceny, and arson.

Indictment A formal, written criminal accusation voted on by a grand jury, setting out the charges (crimes) for which the defendant must stand trial.

Indigent Needy; poor. An indigent defendant is a person without funds to hire a lawyer for his or her defense and is entitled to appointed counsel by operation of the Sixth and Fourteenth amendments.

Inducement In entrapment law, the benefits offered by an undercover agent to commit a crime.

Industrial curtilage The privacy protection of the curtilage rule under search and seizure law applies not only to private homes but also to commercial property.

Inevitable discovery A Fourth Amendment doctrine that overlooks unconstitutional police acts so as not to exclude evidence if the evidence would have been discovered in any event.

Inferior courts Lower courts; for example, trial courts, which are "below" appellate courts in the judicial hierarchy.

Information A formal, written, criminal accusation drawn up by a prosecutor, setting out the charges (crimes) for which the defendant must stand trial. An information replaces the indictment in many states and often follows the bind-over decision.

Initial appearance The hearing before a magistrate that occurs typically within twenty-four hours after a defendant's arrest. The purposes of the hearing are to inform the defendant of the charges, take an initial plea, set bail, and determine whether a defendant has an attorney. The initial appearance is known as the "arraignment on the [arrest] warrant" in some states.

Injunction A court order requiring that a party perform some act or refrain from some act; a remedy in an action in a court of equity or in a court with equitable powers.

In loco parentis The doctrine that a schoolteacher stands in the place of a parent and may exercise parental authority. The Supreme Court has ruled that this is *not* a basis for a search of a public school student under the Fourth Amendment.

In personam **jurisdiction** The jurisdiction a court has over a person in its custody. A court does not lose *in personam* jurisdiction if a defendant was brought into the court's custody as the result of an illegal arrest.

In-presence rule In the law of arrest, the general common law rule is that a police officer can arrest a person for a misdemeanor only if the crime was committed in the officer's presence. Exceptions for traffic violations and domestic violence have been created by statute.

Inquisitorial trial The mode of trial in Europe and most countries, except England and former English colonies, based on Roman law in civil law countries. Distinguishing features include cases are developed by civil service prosecutors operating under judicial instruction; defendants are under a general obligation to answer some questions in the preliminary stages but need not answer at trial; defendants' silence may be used against them; the judge plays an active role in the trial by questioning witnesses; there is no independent jury, although jurors may advise the professional judges.

Internal passport Official personal identification. In some countries, residents must carry personal identification at all times; in the United States, under the Fourth Amendment, there can be no general obligation to carry an internal passport or to provide identification without an arrest or stop.

Interrogation   Generally, to question. In criminal procedure, the term refers more specifically to the series of questions posed by the police to a suspect or a witness in an effort to solve a crime. Interrogation may also include the functional equivalent of questioning whereby actions by the police are designed to elicit incriminating statements from a suspect.

Inventory and return   A sworn document prepared by law enforcement officers who have been issued and have executed a search warrant, indicating the execution of the warrant and itemizing the items seized.

Inventory search   A search made for the purpose of making an inventory—that is, a detailed list of articles of property.

Investigative stop   The forceful stopping of a person for field questioning when reasonable suspicion exists to believe that the person is involved in criminal activity. Also called a "*Terry* stop."

Invidious discrimination   The kind of distinction based on race, gender, or other irrational factor that allows a court to determine that a distinction caused by law violates the rights of a person to the "equal protection of the laws" under the Fourteenth Amendment. Not every legal distinction between people is invidious.

Involuntary confession   A confession is involuntary if it was induced by interrogation that included coercion, threats of coercion, or promises of lenient treatment. An involuntary confession is not admissible in court.

Ipse dixit   "He himself said it"; a bare assertion resting on the authority of the individual.

Irrelevant evidence   Evidence that does not logically pertain to the issue to be decided.

Judicial craftsmanship   The quality of a judge's opinions, based on the intensity of the judge's legal scholarship, the judge's understanding of issues, and the caliber of the judge's writing style.

Judicial federalism   In constitutional criminal procedure, the interaction between federal and state constitutional rights. The Fourteenth Amendment establishes a "constitutional floor" of minimum standards of rights that cannot be violated by a state; above this "floor" a state may grant additional rights under its own constitution or statutes. See also *adequate and independent state grounds*.

Judicial independence   The right and the actual ability of a court to decide cases on the basis of the facts and its interpretation of law without interference from other branches of the government; a vital aspect of the rule of law. Judicial independence is made more certain by the appointment of judges for good behavior and by the provision of Article III that the compensation of federal judges shall not be diminished.

Judicial philosophy   An aspect of judicial statesmanship—whether a judge favors judicial restraint or judicial activism.

Judicial policy   An aspect of judicial statesmanship—what particular policy views a judge may hold on any issue. For example, in criminal procedure, some justices are identified by their voting patterns as being "pro-prosecution," others as "pro-defense," and others as "middle of the road."

Judicial restraint   A philosophy of the judicial function holding that judges should not make broad rulings that have legislative effect.

Judicial review   The authority of a court to review a statute and declare it null and void if the statute is in conflict with a provision of the state or federal constitution.

Judicial statesmanship   The ability of Supreme Court justices to write opinions that properly guide the nation.

Jurisdiction   Legal power or authority.

Jurisprudence   The philosophy of law; also, a body of rules in a subfield of law—e.g., "criminal jurisprudence."

Jury deliberation   In deciding on a verdict, a jury is supposed to discuss the evidence, and not simply take a vote.

Jury independence   The right of a jury to determine the facts of a case independently without judicial interference. This right was held to be a part of the common law jury process in *Bushell's* case (1670).

Jury nullification   The idea that a jury may disregard the legal instruction of the judge and render a verdict purely on the basis of conscience or feelings. Although this happens, it is not usually authorized by legal doctrine.

Jury pool   The group of prospective jurors called to the courthouse from which juries are chosen.

Jury trial   The trial of a matter before a jury. Jury trials are guaranteed by the U.S. Constitution (Art. III, § 2) and by the Sixth and Seventh amendments. Compare *bench trial*.

Jury wheel   A physical device or electronic system for the storage and random selection of the names or identifying numbers of prospective jurors.

Just Compensation Clause   A clause in the Fifth Amendment stating that "private property [shall not] be taken for public use without just compensation." This provision was in effect incorporated as a due process right that federal courts applied against state takings (*Chicago, Burlington and Quincy Railroad Co. v. Chicago*, 1897) in an era when personal rights were not incorporated, thus creating a double standard.

Justice   A judge of the Supreme Court.

"Key man" method   A method of selecting members of petit or grand juries whereby a judge picks a small number of jury commissioners known to him personally, and the commissioners in turn select people known to them for the grand jury. This method, which dates back to the nineteenth century and tends to perpetuate established power relationships in county government while keeping minorities or new residents from jury service, is no longer used.

"Knock and announce" rule   The common law rule that before an officer may open or break in the door to a premises to execute a search warrant, the officer must announce the presence of police and demand entry. It was declared to be a constitutional rule in *Wilson v. Arkansas* (1995). Compare *no-knock warrant*.

Law   A body of written rules issued by legitimate sources of order in a state (e.g., the legislature or the appellate courts) and designed to guide and control the actions of citizens. Law also derives from the text of a written constitution and, in common law jurisdictions, from the opinions of appellate judges.

Law of the land   A phrase in Magna Carta, indicating that no peer could be punished except by "the law of the land," believed to express the concept of due process.

Least intrusive means When a constitutional liberty collides with a state action required to maintain order, courts at times require that the state's intrusion be done in a manner that intrudes the least on individual privacy. Such a rule has not been applied to arrest or stop under the Fourth Amendment.

Legal doctrine The common law process of case interpretation results in the development of rules that arise from the decisions of numerous similar, but not identical, cases. The rules in a related body of law are formed into legal doctrines. Over time, the rationales for such doctrines often change or erode. Thus many legal doctrines of the common law often have a life cycle of birth, a period of growth and utility, change, and decline.

Legal fiction A legal doctrine or assumption that may not be true but that is adopted in order to achieve a beneficial end. For example, the idea that entrapment is a criminal defense that is inferred by the legislature is a legal fiction adopted by judges who first announced the doctrine.

Legal reasoning The mental process of ratiocination by a judge, by which the rules of an earlier case are discerned and applied to a case at hand. Legal reasoning is not a mechanical process and is considered a branch of jurisprudence or legal philosophy. See also *precedent.*

Legislative history The background and events, including committee reports, hearings, and floor debates, leading up to the enactment of a law (including constitutional provisions). Such history is important to courts when they are required to determine the legislative intent of a particular statute.

Liberty A political theory that undergirds criminal procedure. It connotes that the purpose of government is to allow individuals maximum freedom to pursue their individual and collective goals within the rule of law.

Lineup A police identification procedure by which the suspect in a crime is exhibited before the victim or witness to determine if the suspect committed the offense. In a lineup, the suspect is lined up with other individuals for purposes of identification.

Magistrate An inferior (i.e., lower) judicial officer; any judge; or any public civil officer with executive or judicial authority.

Magna Carta (1215) A charter of liberties sworn by King John of England to his barons. Its "law of the land" clause is believed to be the forerunner of due process.

Mandamus, writ of A judicial writ ordering a government officer to perform some "ministerial act,"—that is, an act required by law over which the officer has no discretion to not carry out.

Master jury list The master list compiled by a county or district jury commission from the most widely available lists of eligible voters, including voting registration lists, driver's license and state identification lists, and city directories. Jury venires are drawn from the master jury list. Also called a "jury wheel."

Material witness A person who can give testimony that no one else, or very few other people, can give. A material witness may be held by the state against his or her will to ensure testimony.

Media ride-along A practice of some police departments to invite news reporters, photographers, and broadcast journalists to accompany officers during the execution of warrants. Media ride-alongs were held to violate the Fourth Amendment rights of householders in *Wilson v. Layne* (1999).

Merchant's privilege A statutory right enacted in most states that allows security personnel to conduct brief investigatory detentions of suspected shoppers—an act that would be tortious or criminal if carried out by ordinary citizens.

Missouri Compromise A compromise measure adopted by Congress in 1820 declaring that slavery could not be introduced into new states north of the southern boundary of Missouri. The compromise paired the admission of new free and slave states into the union as a way of maintaining parity between the North and the South. It was designed to preserve the Union and to prevent sectional conflicts from erupting into disunion or civil war. An 1850 extension was declared unconstitutional in *Scott v. Sandford* (1857), hastening the Civil War.

Mistaken arrest An arrest that is based on probable cause but results in the arrest of a person who is not, in fact, the suspect. A police officer who makes such an arrest is protected against civil liability; a private person who makes a mistaken citizen's arrest is subject to a tort action for false imprisonment. A statutory exception exists; see *merchant's privilege.*

Mixed question of law and fact A question depending for solution on questions of both law and fact, but really a question of either law or fact to be decided by either judge or jury.

Motion An application made to a court to obtain an order requiring some act to be done in the favor of the applicant.

Multiple-district prosecution A practice of federal prosecutors whereby an enterprise is simultaneously prosecuted in several districts in which the enterprise does business. This is generally viewed as an unfair prosecution tactic.

Multiple representation A situation in which one attorney represents two or more defendants in the same matter. The defendants may be tried in the same or in different (severed) trials. See also *conflict of interest.*

Neutral and detached magistrate A phrase from *Johnson v. United States* (1948) explaining the rationale for Fourth Amendment search warrants: that a judicial officer is less partisan than a police officer in deciding whether probable cause exists on the basis of the institutional role and traditions of the judicial officer.

No-knock warrant A warrant that explicitly authorizes police officers to enter a premises without knocking and announcing their presence, based on probable cause to believe that the occupants are likely to immediately destroy contraband or pose a threat of deadly violence to officers executing the warrant. Compare *"knock and announce" rule.*

Nonincorporation era A period designated in this text as falling between the ratification of the Bill of Rights in 1791 and the ratification of the Civil War amendments in 1870, when it was clear doctrine that the Bill of Rights was not intended to be applied to the states. Thereafter, the issue became contested.

Notice The due process requirement that a defendant be informed in writing of the precise crimes charged and the facts on which those charges are based. The defendant can be tried only on those charges.

Novel disseisin A medieval English writ that set up an efficient procedure to determine the rightful possession of land taken by force. It utilized a precursor to the modern jury to determine facts.

Nulla poena sine lege   "No punishment without law."

Nullum crimen sine lege   "No crime without law."

Objective test   In entrapment law, the view held by a minority of Supreme Court justices and a minority of the states that entrapment should be based on whether the conduct of the police reached such a level as would induce a hypothetical person to engage in the criminal behavior.

Open fields   Private land not protected against police trespass under the Fourth Amendment. Compare *curtilage.*

Opinion   The essay written by the majority in an appellate court trial, expounding the law that applies to the case and giving the reasons for its decision. A signed majority opinion is primarily written by the named judge, but the judges in the majority may have suggested that certain points be included or excluded. Individual judges may write concurring or dissenting opinions. Compare *per curiam opinion.*

Order   The lawful limits placed on the freedom of individuals to maintain the "domestic tranquillity" that is a necessary function of government. The contrast to liberty cannot be absolute because public order is necessary for individuals and groups to enjoy their liberty.

Ordered liberty   A resonant phrase found in *Palko v. Connecticut* (1937) and other cases that encapsulates the tension between two fundamental aspects of American governance: liberty and order.

Originalism   A theory of constitutional interpretation that holds that judges must apply the Constitution in accordance with the true intent of the Framers. The theory is based on the principle of separation of powers and the idea that judges should not "make" law. Opponents argue that the true intent of the Framers cannot be known with certainty in regard to broad constitutional rights (e.g., due process) and that changing conditions require justices to interpret provisions to meet contemporary needs.

Outrageous conduct test   See *due process defense.*

Overrule   To replace with a different ruling. When an appellate court finds that one of its prior decisions was incorrect or unsound, it may overrule the prior case and replace it with a different ruling. Thus, strictly speaking, an appellate court is not bound by its own precedent. See also *reverse.*

Parallel right   Prior to the incorporation of the Bill of Rights, the Supreme Court established certain rights under the Due Process Clause that were parallel to rights found in the Bill of Rights but were not applied with the same level of certainty. An example is the Sixth Amendment rule stating that counsel was automatically required in every federal felony trial, unless waived, whereas due process required states to provide counsel for indigents only if special circumstances existed.

Parliamentary supremacy   The English system in which the statute (a declaration of the legislature) is superior to any written or unwritten constitutional provision or custom.

Particularity requirement   The requirement, drawn from the Fourth Amendment, that search warrants "particularly describ[e] the place to be searched, and the persons or things to be seized." The opposite is a general warrant, which the Fourth Amendment was designed to abolish.

Pattern and practice suit   A review of a local police department by the U.S. Justice Department for discriminatory patterns and practices. Under the law passed in 1994, a special master can be appointed to oversee modifications in the training and supervision provided by the local police department.

Peer   In England, a member of the nobility. Originally, "jury of peers" meant that non-nobles could not sit on juries to judge the guilt of peers. In modern usage, the term refers to equals. A "jury of peers" in America is composed of fellow citizens, without regard to class, gender, race or ethnicity, economic status, or other irrelevant attributes.

Pen register   A device that electronically registers the telephone numbers with which a particular telephone connects, without recording the contents of the conversations.

Per curiam **opinion**   An unsigned opinion written by the entire appellate court.

Peremptory challenge   In the voir dire, each side has a limited number of challenges that may be used to excuse a prospective juror even though the person has not exhibited any clear bias. Recently, the Supreme Court has limited the ability of parties to exercise peremptory challenges in ways that are based primarily on race or gender. See also voir dire.

Persuasive authority   When an appellate court follows the reasoning of another court, even though the other court has no power to set binding precedent for the appellate court, the opinion followed is called "persuasive authority."

Pervasively regulated industry   In the law of administrative searches, an administrative warrant is not required to search the place of a "pervasively regulated" industry.

Petit jury   The common law, twelve-person trial jury that has the authority to determine the facts and to render a verdict in criminal trials. *Petit* is the French word for "small" and refers to the size of the jury in contrast to the twenty-three-person grand jury.

Petty crime   A crime that may be tried without a jury.

Plain feel rule   The concept that evidence seized in plain view includes evidence lawfully felt by police and that is immediately apparent as contraband.

Plain statement   The U.S. Supreme Court will not disturb a state court criminal procedure ruling if the state opinion includes a plain statement that the ruling is based on adequate and independent state grounds.

Plain view   Contraband that is located in a public place or in a private place where an officer has a right to be present may be seized "in plain view" without a search warrant.

Plurality opinion   A decision of the Supreme Court (or any appellate court) that is based on a vote of less than a majority. A plurality opinion occurs when there are concurring opinions but fewer than five justices (if nine justices participate) agree on the reason for a rule. Plurality opinions represent the law but do not have the same authority as majority opinions, and they are more easily subject to being overruled.

Police officer expertise   In *Terry v. Ohio* (1968), the traditional rule that a Fourth Amendment seizure of a person may be based only on probable cause was eased to allow a temporary stop on the basis of reasonable suspicion based in part on the fact that the on-the-street situation was evaluated by a police officer applying his or her special expertise. This element of *Terry* was dropped when the Court decided that reasonable suspicion could be based on the hearsay statement of an informant.

Police power   A concept of constitutional law that state governments have plenary or general authority to pass laws for the health, safety, morals, general welfare, and good ordering of the people.

Precedent   In law, an adjudged case or decision of a court that furnishes authority for an identical or similar case that arises afterward on a similar question of law. See also *legal reasoning*.

Predisposition   In entrapment law, a defendant's state of mind that is inclined toward the commission of the crime in question prior to the police "encouragement" activity.

Prejudice   In appellate procedure, an error that occurred at the trial or pretrial stage that was the likely cause of the guilty verdict. In some instances, a conviction will not be overturned unless the appellate court finds prejudice in this sense.

Prejudice the case   The second prong of the rule stating that the ineffective assistance of counsel in a criminal trial violates the Sixth Amendment rights of the defendant. Prejudice in this sense is made out by a reasonable probability that, absent the errors, the fact finder would have had a reasonable doubt respecting guilt.

Preliminary examination   A hearing before a magistrate to determine whether the prosecution can present sufficient evidence to establish probable cause to show that the defendant committed a crime. If so, the judge binds the defendant over for trial.

Presentment   Instead of an indictment, a formal accusation based on the personal knowledge of the grand jurors themselves. This is rare or nonexistent today. Also, an accusation initiated by the grand jury; an instruction to the prosecutor to prepare an indictment.

Presumption of innocence   A feature of the common law trial that is guaranteed by the Due Process Clause. It requires that the burden of proof of guilt of every element of a crime be placed on the prosecution and that the burden be proof beyond a reasonable doubt.

Pretext search   A search of an automobile made by an officer who stops the car on the objectively correct basis of a traffic violation even though the traffic stop is made for the real purpose of searching the automobile for drugs. Pretext searches were found to be valid in *Whren v. United States* (1996).

Preventive detention   The confinement of a defendant before trial; the formal denial of bail on the grounds that the defendant is likely to commit a crime while awaiting trial.

Prima facie case   Sufficient evidence to require a criminal defendant to proceed with his case; evidence to sustain an indictment; if uncontradicted, evidence sufficient to establish a guilty verdict.

Private law   Law involving the rights and disputes of private individuals, groups, and corporations. Subject matter areas include contracts, property, torts (the law of injuries), commercial law, and civil procedure. Compare *public law*.

Privilege   In law, a particular benefit or a right or immunity against or beyond the course of law. Thus the privilege against self-incrimination allows a person to refuse to testify despite the general legal obligation that a person has to testify when summoned to a court.

Privileges or Immunities Clause   A clause in Section 1 of the Fourteenth Amendment stating that "[n]o state shall make or enforce any law which shall abridge the privileges or immunities of citizens of the United States." This clause was thought to be the basis of the idea of "total incorporation." The clause was interpreted in such a manner as to render it a virtual nullity by the *Slaughterhouse Cases* (1873).

Probable cause   A standard to determine whether sufficient evidence exists that allows a prudent person to conclude that other facts exist; also, the standard for the validity of an arrest, a lawful search, and the holding of a person for trial.

Pro bono publico   For the good of the public. Attorneys take a certain number of cases without fee to represent indigents *pro bono*.

Procedural law   Law that prescribes the methods of enforcing rights that are breached and includes rules of jurisdiction and the serving of legal process (e.g., a summons) and rules that guide the conduct of a trial.

Pro forma   "As a matter of form." A decision made *pro forma* is made not because it is right, but merely to facilitate further proceedings.

Property theory   The concept that Fourth Amendment rights are based on an individual's legal claims over private property. This theory has been superseded by the "expectation of privacy" concept.

Prosecutor's information   A formal document charging a defendant with crimes on which the defendant must stand trial. The prosecutor's information replaces the grand jury indictment in some states; it is used in jurisdictions with grand juries in cases in which the defendant waives the right to a grand jury.

***Pro se* defense**   Latin for "for himself"; self-representation.

Protective sweep   "A quick and limited search of a premises, incident to an arrest and conducted to protect the safety of police officers or others. It is narrowly confined to a cursory visual inspection of those places in which a person might be hiding" (*Maryland v. Buie,* 1990).

Public defender   A full-time paid position as a defense attorney for indigent defendants. Caseloads of public defenders tend to be high.

Public duty doctrine   The idea that, under ordinary circumstances, a municipality or other government unit is not liable to an individual for tortious failure to provide adequate police protection because the duty to provide such protection is owed to the public generally rather than to specific individuals.

Public law   Law that concerns the powers of government bodies and involves disputes between government departments or between private individuals and government. Public law includes such subjects as constitutional law, administrative law, tax law, substantive criminal law, and criminal procedure. Compare *private law*.

Qualified immunity   Rule that government agents need not answer in law to civil claims for wrongful conduct when their conduct does not violate clearly established statutory or constitutional rights of which a reasonable person would have known. Immunity is claimed before trial in a motion for summary judgment.

Quash   To annul or make void—e.g., to quash an indictment.

Radio bulletin   Information transmitted by radio from one police department to others, notifying them that a specified individual is wanted for a crime. Evidence seized in a search incident to an arrest made on the basis of such a report is admissible, even if there was no probable cause for the initial report; it has the effect of a mistaken arrest.

Real evidence   Physical evidence.

Reasonable doubt   The standard of evidence sufficiency for a verdict of guilt in a criminal case; a doubt that would cause a prudent person to hesitate before acting in a matter of personal importance; not a fanciful doubt.

Reasonable force   Police may use reasonable force to make an arrest, as determined by all the facts and circumstances.

Reasonableness Clause   The first part of the Fourth Amendment, which prohibits "unreasonable searches and seizures." It is the basis of the *general-reasonableness construction.*

Reasonable suspicion   The standard of evidence sufficiency that allows a police officer to temporarily stop a person in order to ask questions to either dispel the suspicion or gather probable cause to arrest; defined as articulable facts that would lead an experienced police officer to believe that a crime has been, is, or is about to be committed.

Reconstruction amendments   See *Civil War amendments.*

Recoupment   The process by which the state or unit of local government later recovers the cost of providing assistance of counsel to a formerly indigent defendant.

Rehnquist Court   The Supreme Court during the period that William Rehnquist was chief justice of the United States (1986–2005); a conservative period in criminal procedure.

Release on recognizance   Pretrial release of a defendant without the posting of a bail bond or other security, but only on the promise of the defendant to return to court for trial or further proceedings.

Remand   An action of an appellate court sending all or part of a case back to the lower court without overturning the lower court's ruling but with instructions for further proceedings that may range from conducting a new trial to entering a proper judgment.

Remedial law   Law that determines the actual benefits or remedies that a successful party to a lawsuit will receive. In criminal law, the "remedy" is the punishment meted out. In constitutional criminal procedure, the exclusion of evidence after a court has decided that evidence has been seized in violation of a person's constitutional protections is deemed a "remedy."

Reparation   Repayment; a remedy designed to restore the injured party to his or her position before the injury occurred.

Representative cross section   In jury selection, the larger groups of prospective jurors on the jury master list or jury wheel, or the venire, must be selected in a manner to be most likely to statistically represent the larger community under federal law and constitutional standards of equal protection. The particular jury panel (or venire) from which the petit jury is selected, and the jury itself, need not be a representative sample. Also called "fair cross section."

Republicanism   The political theory that government is instituted for the benefit of all the people. Formal classes, nobility, and monarchy are inconsistent with republicanism. As a result, for example, "jury of peers" means a jury of citizens.

Retained counsel   A lawyer hired by and paid for by the defendant.

Reverse   To disagree with the decision of a lower court and order it to change the decision to conform to the appellate court ruling. See also *overrule.*

Roadblock   An automobile that crashes into a police roadblock effectively arrests the driver; injuries that result from such a crash may be the basis of police liability for effecting the arrest with excessive force if the placement of the roadblock was unreasonable.

Roving patrol   The stop of a vehicle being driven on the highway by border patrol agents within one hundred air miles of the U.S. border. Compare *fixed checkpoint stop.*

Rule application   A major function of trial courts: to decide cases in accordance with the law. Compare *rule making.*

Rule making   A process of interpretation of prior cases, statutes, or constitutional provisions by appellate courts by which rules of common law are developed. See also *legal reasoning* and *precedent.*

Rule of law   The political and legal principle that the government must act in accordance with established law and that government officers must not exceed their authority. Also known as the "principle of legality."

Scope of a search incident to arrest   The area that the police may search within an arrested person's immediate control to ensure officer safety and to secure evidence from destruction. The scope may include an area to which the arrested person may reach, but does not authorize the search of an entire premises.

Screening   The preliminary hearing and grand jury are pretrial screening devices. They screen out cases where probable cause cannot be established in order to prevent hasty or oppressive prosecutions.

Search incident to arrest   The search of an individual and the person's immediate surroundings that takes place immediately upon or after the person's arrest. The search, a part of the arrest process, is for weapons (to protect the arresting officer and others) and for incriminating evidence.

Secret informant   A person who supplies evidence of probable cause to obtain a search warrant but whose identity is not divulged to the magistrate in order to maintain the security of an investigation; may be an undercover police agent or a paid "snitch."

Section 1983 suit   A civil lawsuit in federal court against a state officer, or a municipality, who has violated the federal or constitutional rights of an individual; established under 42 U.S.C. § 1983 and enacted in 1871 as a civil rights act designed to curb the terrorism of the Ku Klux Klan. Also called a "constitutional tort suit."

Sectional conflict   Political, economic, or social friction between different sections of the nation; specifically, the conflict between the North and the South before the Civil War.

Seditious libel   A writing intended to incite the people to overthrow the government by force. Seditious libel was long a political crime in Great Britain.

Seizure of the person   Under the Fourth Amendment, an arrest or stop.

Selective incorporation   The concept that individual provisions of the Bill of Rights may become incorporated into the Fourteenth Amendment due process doctrine if the Supreme Court finds that such provisions are fundamental to our system of ordered liberty. Compare *total incorporation.*

Selective prosecution   The prosecution of a defendant singled out for charging on impermissible grounds, such as race, religion, or political beliefs or for exercising constitutional rights.

Self-incrimination rule   The constitutional doctrine that a criminal defendant is privileged to remain silent in the face of an accusation, whether made in court or before. The right extends to all people questioned in official hearings where what they say may "incriminate" them. The right is based on the constitutional provision in the Fifth Amendment that "[n]o person. . . shall be compelled in any criminal case to be a witness against himself." See also *compulsion*.

Self-representation   A situation in which the defendant waives the right to appointed counsel and conducts his or her own defense.

Separation of powers   A political and constitutional doctrine that states that the essential functions of one branch of government are not to be exercised by another.

Sequester a jury   To require a jury to be removed from the community during the period of a trial to avoid the contaminating influences of news accounts or discussions with friends, relatives, and strangers about a crime. Sequestered juries were required in the early common law but are now rare.

"Shocks the conscience" test   A formula for the due process test to determine when police action is so egregious during arrest and/or search activity so as to violate the Due Process Clause. The test excludes the notions of the application of the Fourth Amendment and its exclusionary rule.

Showup   A one-to-one confrontation between the suspect and a witness to the crime. It is a form of pretrial identification procedure in which the suspect is confronted by or exposed to the victim or witness to a crime.

"Silver platter" doctrine   Rules established by the U.S. Supreme Court under its supervisory power prior to *Mapp v. Ohio* (1961) that forbade federal officers from supplying state officers with illegally seized evidence and then testifying as to the evidence in state court, and from receiving illegally seized evidence from state officers.

"Sneak and peak" warrant   Under the USA PATRIOT Act, a judge issuing a search warrant may allow a delay in notifying the owner of a premises that a warrant was executed if the court finds that immediate notification may endanger a person's life or safety, or cause a suspect to flee from prosecution, tamper with evidence, or intimidate witnesses. Such warrant may be issued in any kind of case, not just terrorism investigations.

Sobriety checklane   A roadblock set up by police to determine whether drivers are under the influence of intoxicants. A detention at a sobriety checklane is not considered a stop for criminal investigation, and therefore such temporary detentions without individualized suspicion do not violate the Fourth Amendment.

Source city   An element of the drug courier profile is that the place from which the stopped person has traveled from is a "source city" for drugs.

Source of law   The specific institution that created the law: Courts develop rules of common law; legislatures and governors fashion legislation, and constitutions are made by "the people" in special constitutional conventions or by special rules for amending constitutions.

Sovereign immunity   The legal doctrine that prevents a party from suing a government unless the government by law allows itself to be sued.

Special circumstances rule   The rule of *Powell v. Alabama* (1932) that due process requires a state to pay for a lawyer for an indigent defendant only if special circumstances exist.

Special needs doctrine   A doctrine developed by Supreme Court constitutional adjudication that allows government agents to search without a warrant, and possibly without individualized suspicion, when searches are conducted for "special needs beyond the normal need for law enforcement," such as the search of the bags of public school students suspected of carrying items banned under school rules.

Standby counsel   Counsel appointed at the discretion of the trial judge to advise a *pro se* defendant and to ensure that the defendant's rights are not undermined.

Standing   The ability to sue in court. A plaintiff has standing to sue in a court when there is an actual case or controversy between the plaintiff and a defendant that a court may hear and decide; the party must have a real stake in the outcome of the case. In Fourth Amendment cases, a defendant's standing is based on the violation of his or her reasonable expectation of privacy.

Stare decisis   The doctrine of precedent.

Status quo ante   The existing state of things before a given time.

Stop   The temporary restraint of a person's mobility by a police officer where the officer has reasonable suspicion to believe that the person stopped has just committed, is committing, or is about to commit a crime. The practice was declared constitutional in *Terry v. Ohio* (1968).

Stop and frisk   The colloquial term for a *Terry* stop. See *investigative stop*.

Strip search   See *body cavity search*.

Sub rosa   Confidential, secret.

Subjective test   The majority rule of entrapment law; the theory that entrapment occurs when police activity plants the idea of the crime in a person who is otherwise not predisposed to commit it.

Subpoena   The command of a court to a witness to appear at a certain time and place to give testimony. A grand jury also has subpoena power. If the subpoena is not obeyed, the person refusing to appear may be held in contempt of court and fined or jailed until he or she agrees to cooperate with the legal process. The word derives from the Latin, meaning under (*sub*) the penalty (*poena*) of law.

Subpoena *ad testificandum*   A subpoena to testify.

Subpoena *duces tecum*   A subpoena to produce documents, books, papers, and other materials for inspection.

Subpoena power   The power of a court, or the authority granted by statute to a grand jury or other body, to compel a person or organization to testify or to produce documents or things under a threat of being cited for contempt of court.

Substantive due process   The concept that the Due Process Clause includes substantive rights that limit the power of government to legislate. The concept was applied to property rights by the Supreme Court before the New Deal. The right to privacy that supports the abortion rights case, *Roe v. Wade* (1973), is a substantive due process concept.

Substantive law   Establishes, defines, and governs rights, powers, obligations, and freedoms. Rules of substantive law, for example, establish contractual obligations, property rights, or the right to recovery for personal injuries (torts). Substantive criminal law defines crimes like homicide and theft and defenses like insanity.

Suggestibility   The human process by which the subtle reactions of one person can influence the thinking of another. In *U.S. v. Wade* (1967), suggestibility was the legal basis for the Supreme Court to determine that state action existed as the basis for its holding.

Sui generis   Of its own kind or class; unique; the only one of its kind.

Supervisory authority   The power of higher courts to require lower courts to act within their jurisdiction. The power is sometimes used by the U.S. Supreme Court as a way of enforcing appropriate standards on federal law enforcement agencies.

Supremacy Clause   Article VI, paragraph 2, of the U.S. Constitution, which declares that the Constitution, laws, and treaties of the federal government are the "Supreme Law of the Land"—that is, that they supersede state laws when there is a conflict between state and federal law.

Target theory   The idea that when the prosecution seeks to introduce evidence against a defendant, the defendant has an automatic right to challenge the legality of the seizure. The target theory would eliminate the need for "standing" in Fourth Amendment cases.

Telephonic warrant   A search warrant, allowed by the Federal Rules of Criminal Procedure and the laws of some states, that allows a magistrate to receive an affidavit from an officer by telephonic means.

Terry stop   See *stop* and *stop and frisk.*

Testimonial evidence   Evidence elicited from a witness to prove a fact, as opposed to documentary evidence or real (i.e., tangible) evidence.

Thermal imaging   An advanced technology used by law enforcement to detect whether an unusually high amount of heat is emanating from a premises, suggesting the commercial cultivation of marijuana indoors.

Third degree   The process of securing a confession or information from a suspect or a prisoner by prolonged questioning, the use of threats, or actual violence.

Tort   A private or civil wrong or injury, other than a breach of contract, for which the court will provide a remedy in the form of an action for damages.

Total incorporation   The concept that the Privileges and Immunities Clause or the Due Process Clause of the Fourteenth Amendment was intended to make the first eight amendments of the Bill of Rights applicable to the states upon ratification in 1868. Compare *selective incorporation.*

Totality of circumstances   See *due process approach.*

Transactional immunity   A blanket immunity against prosecution for the crimes about which the immunized witness is testifying. Transactional immunity offers broader protection than use immunity.

Treason Clause   Provisions of U.S. Constitution (Art. 3, § 3) that limit the definition and punishment of treason against the United States. Such limitation implies that the republican government intended to be liberal and restrained and to operate within the rule of law.

Trespass   A common law tort; the wrongful interference with property rights.

Trial *de novo*   A second or new trial that is held as if no decision had been previously rendered. A trial *de novo* is not an appeal because the facts are relitigated. Also called "*de novo* trial."

True bill   An indictment that has not yet been signed by the prosecuting attorney. When the grand jury votes to indict an accused person, it issues a "true bill"; when it votes against indicting an accused, it votes a "no bill."

Two-pronged test   In Fourth Amendment law, a test to be applied by a magistrate on whether or not to issue a warrant where information has been supplied by a secret informant. The test requires that the affidavit indicate the basis of the informant's knowledge and a basis for accepting the informant's veracity. The test has been supplanted by a "totality of the circumstances" test.

Undercover agent   A police officer who lies about his or her identity in order to pose as a victim or criminal for the purposes of law enforcement investigation.

Unenumerated Rights Clause   The Ninth Amendment to the constitution: "The enumeration in the Constitution, of certain rights, shall not be construed to deny or disparage others retained by the people." The Supreme Court has yet to decide a case that declares an unenumerated right to be protected by the Court.

Unindicted co-conspirator   A person, named by a grand jury, against whom there may be a prima facie case of guilt but who for some reason is not indicted.

Universal Declaration of Human Rights   A formal document promulgated by the United Nations in 1948 that attempts to codify all human rights. Many provisions are borrowed from or parallel to provisions of the Bill of Rights.

Use immunity   A form of immunity that prohibits the witness's compelled testimony or its fruits from being used in any way to prosecute the witness. However, the witness may be prosecuted on the basis of independently obtained evidence. Use immunity offers a narrower protection than transactional immunity.

Vagrancy statute   A law making it a crime to loiter. Older vagrancy statutes prior to *Papachristou v. City of Jacksonville* (1972) were quite vague and gave police discretion to arrest whom they would; modern vagrancy statutes are closely tailored to describe particular types of vagrancy, such as house prowling or streetwalking prostitution.

Venire   In jury practice, the list of jurors summoned to serve during a particular court term; from the Latin word meaning "to come"; to appear in court.

Venue   The locality or place where a trial is to be held. The usual rule is that it is to be held in the locality (often the county) in which the crime was committed. The venue may be changed if there is so much publicity in the locality that it becomes impossible to select an unbiased jury.

Verdict   The decision of a jury or judge as finder of fact in a criminal case; guilty or not guilty of the charges.

Vindictive prosecution   The bringing of new and more serious charges against the defendant simply because he or she has exercised statutory or constitutional rights.

Voir dire   The process of jury selection involving the questioning of prospective jurors in order to determine biases. After questioning, the juror is either selected or dismissed for cause or for no reason under the peremptory challenge. See also *challenge for cause* and *peremptory challenge.*

Voluntariness test   A common law rule developed in the eighteenth and nineteenth centuries claiming that any confession obtained by violence, threats, or promises is involuntary and is excluded from evidence. The rule was adopted as a due process rule that the Supreme Court applied to state cases. The rule still exists as a backup to the *Miranda* rule.

Waiver   The waiver of a Fifth or Sixth amendment right must be an "intelligent relinquishment or abandonment of a known right or privilege." See also *consent.*

Waiver of counsel   A defendant can waive the right to the assistance of counsel if the decision is made with full knowledge of the right. A trial judge cannot require that a defendant be represented by counsel if the defendant can do a minimally competent job of defending himself or herself.

Waiver trial   A trial that occurs when the defendant waives the right to a jury and opts to be tried by a sole judge. Also called "bench trial."

Warrant   Generally, the command of an authority; in criminal procedure, a written order issued by a judge or magistrate. A search warrant authorizes police officers to search a premises where there is probable cause to believe that contraband is hidden. An arrest warrant authorizes officers to arrest a named person where there is probable cause to believe that the person committed a crime.

Warrant Clause   The second clause of the Fourth Amendment specifying rules concerning a search warrant.

Warrantless search   A search conducted by an officer without having obtained a search or arrest warrant.

Warrant-preference construction   A liberal construction of Fourth Amendment rights that holds that a search is presumptively unreasonable if it is not accompanied by a search warrant unless there exists a narrowly drawn exception to the warrant requirement.

Warren Court   The Supreme Court during the period that Earl Warren was chief justice of the United States (1953–1969); a liberal period in criminal procedure.

Whig party   A political party in the United States in the first half of the nineteenth century. It was absorbed by the Republican Party in the 1850s.

Wiretap   A means of listening in on telephone conversations by electronically intercepting the conversations at some point outside the place where the telephone is located. Also called a "tap."

Writ of assistance   General search warrants issued by British colonial governors in America to enforce the hated Stamp Act. These writs and their enforcement became political issues that helped to ignite the American Revolution.

Index